China

郜

Robert Storey
Nicko Goncharoff
Damian Harper
Marie Cambon
Thomas Huhti
Caroline Liou
Alexander English

郜 郜 郜 郜 郜 郜 郜 郜 郜

China

6th edition

Published by

Lonely Planet Publications

Head Office:	PO Box 617, Hawthorn, Vic 3122, Australia
Branches:	150 Linden St, Oakland, CA 94607, USA
	10a Spring Place, London NW5 3BH, UK
	1 rue du Dahomey, 75011 Paris, France

Printed by

SNP Printing Pte Ltd, Singapore

Photographs by

Glenn Beanland	Thomas Huhti	Martin Moos
Sonia Berto	Richard I'Anson	Damian Simonis
Marie Cambon	Clem Lindenmayer	Robert Storey
Juliet Coombe/La Belle Aurore	Caroline Liou	Dallas Stribley
Steve Davey/La Bella Aurore	Diana Mayfield	Chris Taylor
Alexander English	Shaun McVicar	Merrilee Zellner
Nicko Goncharoff		

Front cover: Ming Pagoda, Guilin (Grant V Faint, The Image Bank)

First Published

October 1984

This Edition

July 1998

Although the authors and publisher have tried to make the information as accurate as possible, they accept no responsibility for any loss, injury or inconvenience sustained by any person using this book.

National Library of Australia Cataloguing in Publication Data

China.

6th ed.
Includes index.
ISBN 0 86442 524 4

1. China - Guidebooks. I. Storey, Robert.

915.10459

Robert Storey

Robert has had a colourful past, starting with his first job as a monkey-keeper at a zoo and continuing with a stint as 'taco-flipper' at Jack-In-The-Box. He received a liberal arts degree from the University of Nevada, working evenings as a slot machine repairman in a Las Vegas casino. After graduation, he travelled to Asia and finally got his first respectable job (English teacher). Somewhere along the way it was discovered that Robert could write, and he has written and/or updated 13 Lonely Planet guides.

Nicko Goncharoff

Escaping from New York at age 17, Nicko headed for the mountains (and university) in Colorado. After graduating he moved to Taiwan for a brief stint that ended up lasting eight years, including four years covering financial news in Hong Kong. In 1995 Nicko joined LP to work on the 5th edition of *China*. He has since contributed to four other guides in Asia and the USA. At the time of writing he was living out of his backpack, still in search of a home.

Damian Harper

Damian spent six years in the book-selling world of London, Paris and Dublin before returning to university in London to gain a degree in modern and classical Chinese. After graduating he fled, with his Chinese wife Dai Min, to Hong Kong. After a stint in the ceramics department at Sotheby's, he applied himself to this edition of *China*, his first book for LP. Damian has lived for a year in Beijing and regularly returns to China to visit his parents-in-law.

Marie Cambon

Marie was born and raised in Vancouver. Two trips to Asia convinced her to live and work in Shanghai, and she has been there for the better part of the last decade. Marie gained a Masters degree in 1993, her research focusing on the history of the Shanghai film industry. She has also held various jobs as a freelance writer, production assistant and translator. Prior to joining LP, Marie finished her first documentary for broadcast; she is now working on another. This is her first book for LP.

Thomas Huhti

Thomas Huhti hails from Wisconsin in the US and still calls it home when not barrelling around the world with a backpack. After studying in East Asia, he eventually returned to the University of Wisconsin, which agreed to award him a degree in Linguistics, English and (almost) Chinese. He would always rather be playing ice hockey, although this is balanced by epic bouts of loafing, watching movies, and reading. He has contributed to books on Thailand, Myanmar, French Polynesia, Northern Mexico, Canada and the USA. This is his first book for Lonely Planet.

Caroline Liou

Caroline grew up in Michigan, Holland and Louisiana. After attending university in Hong Kong and Louisiana, she escaped from the Louisiana suburbs to New York. There she embarked upon a career in book publishing, working for Cambridge University Press and Random House, before moving to San Francisco to work as the guidebook publisher at Lonely Planet's US office. She recently left LP to pursue studies in Chinese language in Beijing.

Alexander English

Brought up in Melbourne, Alex got his first job at the ripe old age of 10, selling newspapers and working in a butcher shop. He then spent four years eating the profits in a chocolate deli at Melbourne's Victoria Market. Alex has travelled throughout Asia, Europe and the Indian subcontinent, and hopes to complete a Chinese BA in the near future. He and his Korean wife, Eunkyong, will soon discover the true meaning of family. This is Alex's first book for LP.

From the Authors

Robert Storey Robert would like to extend his special thanks to Chiu Miaoling, Jiang Fang, Han Jin, Brian Vick, Laura Pokorny, David Douglas, Sara Gossens, Chris Stanley, Katrien Costenoble, Lodewijk Kleijn and Josh Green. I'm also deeply grateful to a number of Chinese people I met along the way who provided helpful advice, companionship, hospitality and some terrific dumplings.

Nicko Goncharoff From Tashkurgan to Taiyuan I was fortunate to meet many fine people who helped lighten the load. Lisa Colvin was an excellent travel companion, Uighur linguist and steady source of good humour and perspective. Douglas, serving time as a student in Chengdu, proved a fine drinking partner in the heat of Turpan.

To our man in the straw hat who served as Uighur/Mandarin translator on that 40 hour bus odyssey, a thousand thanks. In Kashgar Cui Xiuying, Xiao Cui, Hu Jianmei and Hu Jianjun were excellent hosts, as were the endlessly patient desk staff at the Seman Hotel.

Matthew Russell, Kate Longden and Damian Roche helped make the trip to Karakuri Lake even more enjoyable, and Bruces Barnes was a good friend in Ürümqi, as were Edward Yan, Akbar, Winny Chen and Jessica Zhai.

Derrick, Chris and William gave me great info on the ride from Golmud to Dunhuang: thanks gentlemen. Also a nod to Garth, Erica and Jayne for their recollections of the journey from Ruoqiang to Golmud. And here, special mention must go to Herbert Anholts, the mad Dutch cyclist who gave me a big hand in exploring the less-than-glamorous Golmud.

In Lanzhou, Lu Zhiqiang, Yang Shifu and the staff at Western travel were both very helpful and fun to hang out with, as was Eoin Langan, who furnished info on the Gansu-Sichuan route. Also special thanks to Tsering Dolma in Xiahe, who fed and took care of me when I needed it most. In Xining, Wang Jin and Yang Wenhu gra- ciously took me into their home. To Guan Shifu in Yinchuan a special debt of thanks.

In Datong, and later Xi'an, Arik Knobel provided an invaluable service by giving me someone to try out all the restaurants with. Sarah Ball provided great info on the Xi'an bar and restaurant scene. Ren Ming at Golden Bridge Travel offered hospitality I some day hope to repay. Also thanks to Ron Low and Zeng Mingzhong at the Hyatt.

Mike Laris and Katherina Hesse not only made Yan'an fun, they helped get me the hell out of there when I needed to: I would have been one near-frantic bus passenger without you two. And, deep thanks and appreciation to all my friends at the Old Gun Bar in Xi'an: Ah Sun, Li Dong, Lao San, Zhong (Eric Clapton) Wei and everyone else. Finally, a bow, as always to Byron, Chris, Neal, Murray and Rieko: good friends who have helped me during my Asian sojourns in countless ways.

Damian Harper Special thanks to my wife, Dai Min, who accompanied me on this trip and helped me in all aspects of research for this edition. Enormous thanks also to my Chinese parents-in-law in Shandong for their patience and good humour while I stayed with them.

Many travellers along the way helped with hints and tips, making the going easier. The fast evolving metropolis of Shanghai was brought to heel by Ju Weihong, thank you. Xie Zhaoyou gave us an eventful guided tour of Hainan island which was greatly appreciated. Chen Yong, to whom we owe a great debt of gratitude, opened the doors to Dalian and warmly entertained us.

Thanks also to Dai Lu for looking after us both in Beijing and to Liu Ji who gave us a splendid tour of Qingdao. A slap on the back to John Silver in Hong Kong for the use of his PCMCIA card and his unflagging good humour.

Thanks also to Anna Porteus (USA) and Kay McCluskey (USA) for help on Guangzhou and Shanghai and to Brian Hicks (UK) for last minute information.

We would have been stuck more than once without Zhang Bingjian and his dazzling computer know-how – much appreciated. Thanks also to Robert Storey for his help and encouragement.

Marie Cambon I would like to thank Jolanda Jonkhart and Ron Gluckman for pointing me in the direction of Lonely Planet. I would also like to thank Maria Barbieri, OJ Tang, Mary Cao, Jenny Wang, Robert Storey, Chris Taylor, Tess Johnston, Michael Liu, Rocky at Phoenix, Paul Chu at CTS Vancouver, Karla Loveall, Ann Watterson and Randy Law in Wuhan, Karen Jordan for her amusing stories about the grassland tours, Tanis Wilkie for her care packages and all the taxi drivers in China who took pity on me, especially Mr. Su who let me drive his car on the grasslands around Manzhouli. And my parents.

Thomas Huhti Thanks to the following people, either for being outstanding travel companions, or simply for tolerating a professional pest rooting out information: Matt Matthewson, Brendan Howe, Assaf Iannar, Tim Lanigan and John Forde (who knew not what I was getting them into but kept a stiff upper lip nonetheless), Frederic Dubois and Valerie Nicolas, the three British lads who made the tail end of the trip as entertaining as could be, Lizzie and Nia, the fountain of information and good cheer Sun Zhi Gang, Richard Yang (would that all travellers could have him as a waystation), Barclay and Fiona, Lincoln from Brazil, Jerome Daljuria, Anthony Yeung (who made the wilds of western Sichuan so much clearer and more enjoyable), and especially Pascal Guillaume and Alex Limkin, whose keen eye for humour and the philosophy in everything made even the madness enjoyable. To all those local Chinese who go way, way above and beyond the call to assist us clueless foreigners for no other reason than simply wanting to make friends; and they get zero thanks – may karma smile upon them. Priceless support has come from my family, as always. An appreciative nod to colleague and good friend 'Khun' Joe Cummings; the circle is now complete. For help with those migraine and psychosis-inducing epic bus rides, I acknowledge the modern technology of personal stereos and the artistry of Uncle Tupelo, DJ Shadow, the Blue Nile and Cui Jian.

Caroline Liou Thanks to all who helped along the way: Dr Veeck and Dr Henderson for sharing their knowledge of the region; Howard (thanks for the good conversation), Xiao Hong Shen, He Hui,

---

Warning & Request

Things change – prices go up, schedules change, good places go bad and bad places go bankrupt – nothing stays the same. So, if you find things better or worse, recently opened or long since closed, please tell us and help make the next edition even more accurate and useful.

We value all of the feedback we receive from travellers. Julie Young coordinates a small team who read and acknowledge every letter, postcard and email, and ensure that every morsel of information finds its way to the appropriate authors, editors and publishers.

Everyone who writes to us will find their name in the next edition of the appropriate guide and will also receive a free subscription to our quarterly newsletter, *Planet Talk*. The very best contributions will be rewarded with a free Lonely Planet guide.

Excerpts from your correspondence may appear in new editions of this guide; in our newsletter, *Planet Talk*; or in updates on our Web site – so please let us know if you don't want your letter published or your name acknowledged. ∎

Shannon, John and Brian (where will we run into each other next?) in Nanjing; Hilaire and Gabriel in Wuxi; Josh Parr for his Yixing research; Theresa Tse Bartholemew; my teacher Fang Ming; Amy and Billy; Joyce Lupack for taking my photo for this book; my travelling companion and sister Jeanne; and Dad and Katherine.

Alexander English I would like to thank my travelling partner and wife, Eunkyong, and Tashi from Lhasa.

From the Publisher
This sixth edition of China was produced in LP's Melbourne office. Pete Cruttenden co-ordinated the editorial side of things, with the sterling assistance of Emma Miller, Anne Mulvaney, Miriam Cannell, Greg Alford, Mic Looby and Carolyn Papworth. Thanks, too, to Linda Suttie for initially banging the manuscript into shape.

Janet Watson was responsible for mapping and design groundwork, but on her return to the academic world it was left to Glenn Beanland (design and layout) and Rachael Scott (mapping and colour map) to drag the book over the line. Mapping assistance was provided by Leanne Peake, Sally Gerdan, Chris Love, Paul Piaia, Maree Styles and Lyndell Taylor. Particular thanks go to Kristin Odijk for her unflagging support, and to the team of LP seniors who dropped everything to do the final manuscript checks.

Mick Weldon produced the spiffing new illustrations, Quentin Frayne scrutinised the various language sections, and Simon Bracken was responsible for the front cover. Thanks also to special contributors Linda Jaivin and William Lindesay, to Charles Qin for his language skills, Andrew Tudor for Quark know-how, Dan Levin for computer script stuff, and Sue Galley, Russ Kerr and Tim Fitzgerald for their contributions to the Great Wall section.

This Book
The first edition of this book appeared after Michael Buckley and Alan Samagalski spent many months on the road in China in 1983. Alan Samagalski and Robert Strauss wrote the second edition, preparing the way for Joe Cummings and Robert Storey for the third edition. The fourth edition was researched by Robert Storey, Chris Taylor and Clem Lindenmayer. The fifth rendition was done by Chris Taylor, Robert Storey and Nicko Goncharoff.

The book you're holding was updated by Robert Storey, Nicko Goncharoff, Damian Harper, Marie Cambon, Thomas Huhti, Caroline Liou and Alexander English.

Thanks
All those involved in producing this book greatly appreciate the contributions of travellers who put so much effort into writing and telling us of their experiences. Your names appear on page 1110.

Contents

Map Legend

BOUNDARIES

▬ ▬ ▪ ▬ ▬ ▪ ▬	................International Boundary
▬ ▪ ▪ ▬ ▪ ▪ ▬	..................Provincial Boundary
▬ ▬ ▬ ▬ ▬	...................Disputed Boundary

ROUTES

▬▬▬ A25 ▬▬▬	....Freeway, with Route Number
▬▬▬▬▬	............................Major Road
▬▬▬▬▬	............................Minor Road
▬ ▬ ▬ ▬ ▬	............Minor Road - Unsealed
▬▬▬▬▬	...............................City Road
▬▬▬▬▬	.............................City Street
▬▬▬▬▬	...............................City Lane
├─┼─●─┼─┤	...........Train Route, with Station
├─┼─Ⓜ─┼─┤	..........Metro Route, with Station
╫╫╫╫╫╫	...............Cable Car or Chairlift
▬ ▬ ▬ ▬	................................Ferry Route
▬ ▬ ▬ ▬	...............................Walking Track

AREA FEATURES

▓▓▓▓▓	..................................Building
+++++++	...................................Cemetery
××××××	...........Non-Christian Cemetery
▓▓▓▓▓	.....................................Market
▓▓ ✿	...........................Park, Gardens
▓▓▓▓▓	........................Pedestrian Mall
▓▓▓▓▓	....Reef
▓▓▓▓▓	...............................Urban Area

HYDROGRAPHIC FEATURES

‒ ‒ ‒ ‒	......................................Canal
～～～	...................................Coastline
～～～	..............................Creek, River
⬭ ⬭	.................Lake, Intermittent Lake
»» »» ▓	.......................Rapids, Waterfalls
⬭	....................................Salt Lake
⸜ ⸜ ⸜ ⸜	...................................Swamp

SYMBOLS

❂	**CAPITAL**	.........National Capital	✈	..........................Airport	⚑	...................Pagoda
◉	**CAPITAL**	......Provincial Capital	⌒	....Ancient or City Wall	Ⓟ	...................Parking
●	**CITY**	..............................City	∴	.......Archaeological Site	)(	.......................Pass
●	**Town**	................................Town	⚐	.........................Beach	⛽	.............Petrol Station
●	Village	.....................Village	⛫	...........Castle or Fort	★	..........Police Station
			⌒	..............................Cave	✉	...............Post Office
■		.............Place to Stay	⛪	.....Cathedral/Church	◆	......Shopping Centre
⚑		.......Camping Ground	⌒⌒	....Cliff or Escarpment	🏠	...........Stately Home
⌂		.............Caravan Park	◤	.................Dive Site	▭	.........Swimming Pool
⌂		...............Hut or Chalet	◌	.................Embassy	▨	...........Taoist Temple
			▥	...........Hindu Temple	☎	................Telephone
▼		.............Place to Eat	✛	...................Hospital	▣	....Temple, Monastery
⛾		...............Pub or Bar	※	...................Lookout	▣	.........................Tomb
			◙	...................Mosque	❶	....Tourist Information
			▲	.........Mountain or Hill	◉	.................Transport
			🏛	...................Museum	🐘	...........................Zoo

Note: not all symbols displayed above appear in this book

Province Map Index

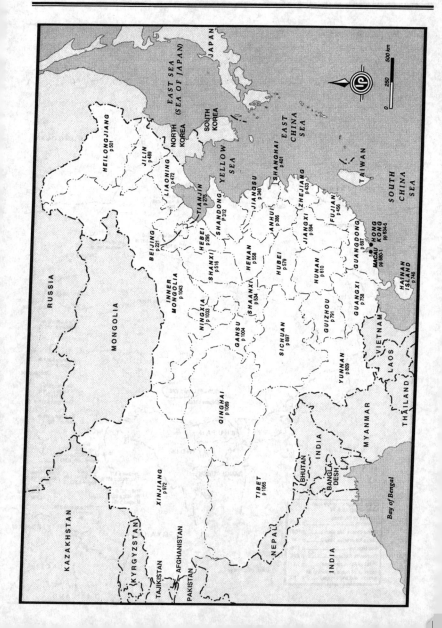

City Map Index

Province Map Index

RUSSIA

KAZAKHSTAN

MONGOLIA

KYRGYZSTAN

Yining p 1000

Ürümqi p 976

Turpan p 984
Around Turpan
p 986

Kuqa p 990

Kashgar p 994

Dunhuang p 1026
Around Dunhuang
p 1029

Jiayuguan p 1021
Jiayuguan Fort
p 1022

Zhangye p 1019

Xining p 1090

Lanzhou p 1006

Golmud p 1096

Xiahe & Labrang
Monastery p 1015

Jiuzhaigou p 967
Songpan p 963

Chengdu p 904

Lhasa p 1076

Shigatse p 1085

Qingcheng Shan
& Qingcheng Hou
Shan p 915
Dujiangyan p 917

NEPAL

BHUTAN

Emeishan p 921
Leshan p 928

INDIA

Lijang p 846
Lijang Old Town p 848
Around Lijang p 853

INDIA

BANGLADESH

Baoshan p 878
Tengchong p 881

Dali p 838
Dali & Erhai Lake
Region p 843

Kunming p 816
Around Kunming
(Lake Dian) p 826

Ruili p 887
Wanding p 892
Mangshi p 894

Stone Forest
p 830

Xishuangbanna p 863
Jinghong p 866

VIETNAM

China Colour Country Map
between pp 16 & 17
Extents of Chinese
Influence.............................. p 21
China Itineraries Map .... p 103
China Itineraries Map 2 .... p 104
Sea Routes .... p 198
Domestic Airfares .... p 203
Index of Province Maps .... p 13
Index of all maps (including all
provincial & town maps) .... p 1100

MYANMAR

Bay of Bengal

LAOS

THAILAND

Relve =

Eikel.

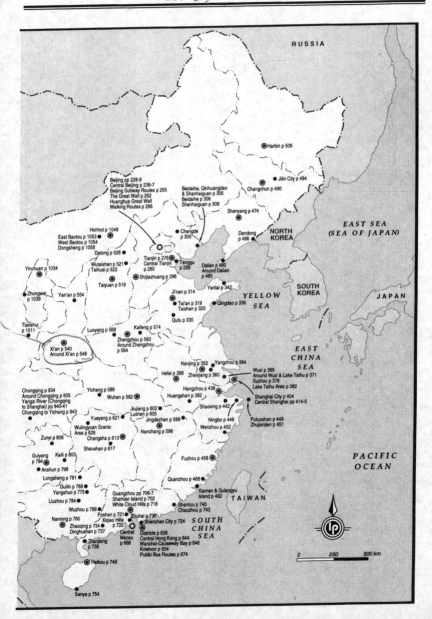

Introduction

China is a sleeping giant. Let her lie and sleep, for when she awakens she will astonish the world.

Napoleon

Western economists and military analysts have always been fond of saying that 'China is a country that cannot be ignored'. However, from 1949 until 1979, it was China that was ignoring the rest of humanity – the country had virtually sealed itself off from the 'contaminating influence' of the outside world.

After almost 30 years of being closed for repairs, the Middle Kingdom finally creaked open its big red doors in the late 1970s. Tour groups trickled in, but the prospects for individual travel looked extremely dim. Individuals were welcome to the People's Republic of China (PRC) only by invitation. The first hint that things might be changing was the arrival of solo visitors from Sweden and France (nations favoured by China), who stepped off the Trans-Siberian Railway in 1979.

In 1981, with little fanfare, the Chinese began issuing visas to solo and uninvited travellers through some of their embassies overseas, but mainly through various agencies in Hong Kong. News spread slowly by word of mouth, until by 1983 it seemed that just about everyone who landed in Hong Kong was going to China. After all, the world had been waiting over 30 years to travel in the country unfettered by tour guides.

Fifteen years later, the Chinese world has changed immensely. Gone is the socialist paradise of hardy peasants and sturdy workers, uniformly clothed in blue, fashioning a brave new world to the beat of the hammer and anvil. Today a growing middle class shops for Chanel perfume and Lacoste polo shirts. Chinese cinematic productions sweep up awards in the film festivals of Europe. Chinese rockers perform on

17

Asian MTV. China's first sex shop opened recently in Beijing. McDonald's and KFC have spawned a fast-food revolution in Chinese eating habits. And karaoke has invaded the East and set the whole of China singing.

As many commentators like to remark (perhaps a little hopefully) China is slowly becoming more and more like other nations. To be sure, the problems of travel permits, dual currencies, poor transport connections, poor sanitation and lackadaisical service standards have all been vastly improved. Travellers of the 1980s are stunned when they return to China today and see how much better things are.

But problems remain. China is not always an easy country to travel in. Inflation and a booming local tourist industry have pushed hotel and transport prices through the roof in many provinces; the increased mobility of local Chinese has put a squeeze on the availability of train and plane tickets; and the authorities are still bent on enforcing double-pricing systems on airlines and keeping foreigners out of certain hotels. To top it all off, many foreigners complain that the need to be constantly alert for rip-offs is exhausting.

Nevertheless, somewhere between the push and shove of railway station crowds, the overcharging and the clangour of jackhammers, China is an experience that stays with you for years after you leave. From the deserts of Xinjiang to the mountains of Tibet, from the Forbidden City of Beijing to the Army of Terracotta Warriors of Xi'an, from relaxing getaways like Yangshuo and Dali to Shanghai's juggernaut assault on the future, China packs more punch than almost anywhere else in the world.

What's more, whether we like it or not, something miraculous is happening in China – the latest of many revolutions. The country is reinventing itself and, whatever you feel about the place, China is a country that cannot be ignored.

Facts about the Country

HISTORY
Mythological Beginnings

The Chinese claim a history of 5000 years, but early 'records' are of a mythological and legendary nature. The very existence of the Xia Dynasty, documented in early Chinese histories as the first Chinese dynasty, still awaits archaeological verification.

According to legend, the Xia Dynasty was preceded by three sovereigns and five emperors. The first of the three sovereigns, Fuxi, is usually depicted alongside his wife and sister, the goddess Nügua. The two are human from the waist up, but have the tails of dragons. Nügua is credited with having fashioned human beings from clay and having created the institution of marriage, while Fuxi bestowed the gifts of hunting, fishing and animal husbandry.

The ox-headed Shennong, another of the three sovereigns, bestowed agriculture and knowledge of the medicinal properties of plants on the Chinese.

The five emperors (like the three sovereigns) are also credited with having founded certain key elements of the Chinese cultural tradition. For example, the first of them, Huang Di, is said to have brought the agricultural calendar, boats, armour and pottery to the Chinese people. A later emperor, Shun, devised the writing brush. Dynastic rule commenced when the same Shun abdicated in favour of Yu, the first emperor of the Xia.

Xia & Shang Dynasties

Many historians believe that the Xia Dynasty actually may have existed, although not in the terms depicted in Chinese mythology. The dynasty is claimed to have held power for nearly five centuries from 2200 to 1700 BC, before becoming corrupt and being overthrown by the Shang.

There is more evidence of the existence of the Shang than of the Xia. Archaeological finds have shown for certain that a state existed in the Yellow River plain in the present provinces of Shandong, Shanxi and Shaanxi, and that it held power from 1554 to 1045 BC. It was an agricultural society that practised a form of ancestor worship. It was also marked by the presence of what seems to be a caste of high priests who practised divination using so-called oracle bones. Associated with ancestor worship and divination are the Shang bronze vessels, the surfaces of which are covered with extraordinarily detailed linear designs. Like the Xia before it, the Shang Dynasty fell prey to corruption and degeneracy, and was toppled by the Zhou.

Zhou Dynasty

Like the Shang before it, little is known with any great certainty about the Zhou Dynasty (1100-221 BC). It is thought that they were a nomadic tribe who came under the influence of the Shang and later displaced it. The Zhou capital was known as Hao and was near Chang'an (present-day Xi'an), the site that was to become the imperial seat of power for many subsequent Chinese dynasties. The Zhou also established another power centre close to present-day Luoyang in Henan, from where they governed the subjugated Shang. The Zhou social structure seems to have been heavily influenced by the Shang, from whom they inherited the practices of divination and ancestor worship.

Historians generally divide the Zhou period into the Western Zhou (1100-771 BC) and the Eastern Zhou (770-221 BC). The demarcation point is the sacking of the traditional Zhou capital of Hao by barbarian tribes, the transfer of power to Luoyang and a loss of effective control by the Zhou over its feudatory states. Nevertheless, Zhou nobles remained symbolic heads of state over a land of warring kingdoms until 221 BC, when they were displaced by the Qin.

The Eastern Zhou, though riven by strife,

CHINESE DYNASTIES & REPUBLICS

Xia Dynasty	2200 – 1700 BC		**Northern**	**386 – 581**
Shang	1700 – 1100		Northern Wei	386 – 534
Zhou	1100 – 221		Eastern Wei	534 – 577
Western Zhou	1100 – 771		Western Wei	535 – 556
Eastern Zhou	770 – 221		Northern Qi	550 – 577
Spring & Autumn Period	722 – 481		Northern Zhou	557 – 581
Warring States Period	453 – 221		**Sui**	**589 – 618**
Qin	221 – 207		**Tang**	**618 – 907**
Han	206 BC – 220 AD		**Five Dynasties**	**907 – 960**
Former Han	206 BC – 24 AD		Later Liang	907 – 923
Later Han	25 – 220		Later Tang	923 – 936
Three Kingdoms Period	220 – 280		Later Jin	936 – 946
Wei	220 – 265		Later Han	947 – 950
Shu Han	221 – 263		Later Zhou	951 – 960
Wu	222 – 280		**Liao**	**916 – 1125**
Jin	265 – 420		**Song**	**960 – 1279**
Western Jin	265 – 316		Northern Song	960 – 1126
Eastern Jin	317 – 420		Southern Song	1127 – 1279
Southern & Northern			**Western Xia**	**1038 – 1227**
Dynasties	386 – 581		**Jin**	**1115 – 1234**
Southern	420 – 589		**Yuan (Mongol)**	**1271 – 1368**
Song	420 – 479		**Ming**	**1368 – 1644**
Qi	479 – 502		**Qing (Manchu) Dynasty**	**1644 – 1911**
Liang	502 – 557		**Republic of China**	**1911 – 1949**
Chen	557 – 589		**People's Republic of China**	**1949 –**

is thought of as the crucible of Chinese culture. The traditional Chinese division of the period into the Spring and Autumn period (722-481 BC) and the Warring States period (453-221 BC) doesn't follow any historical logic, but rather refers to the periods covered by two historical books of the same names, written during the period, which were to become cornerstones of the classical education system until the Qing collapsed in 1911.

The *Spring & Autumn Annals* is traditionally ascribed to Confucius (551-479 BC), a scholar who wandered from state to state during these troubled times in search of a ruler who would put his ideas for the perfect state into practice.

Mandate of Heaven The Zhou period is important for the establishment of some of the most enduring Chinese political concepts. Foremost is the 'mandate of heaven', in which heaven gives wise and virtuous leaders a mandate to rule and removes it from those who are evil and corrupt. It was a concept that was later extended to incorporate the Taoist theory that heaven expresses disapproval of bad rulers through natural disasters such as earthquakes, floods and plagues of locusts.

In keeping with this was the idea that heaven also expressed its displeasure with corrupt rulers through rebellion and withdrawal of support by the ruled. This has been referred to as the 'right to rebellion'. It is a slippery concept, because the right to rebellion could only be confirmed by success.

Nevertheless, rebellious expressions of heaven's will were an essential ingredient in China's dynastic cycle, and mark an essential difference with, say, Japan, where the authority of the imperial family derives from a single lineage that, according to legend, can be traced back to the Sun goddess.

Qin Dynasty

The tenuous authority of the Zhou ended in the 3rd century BC, when the state of Qin united the Chinese, for the first time, into a single empire. The First Exalted Emperor Qin Shihuang ruled only from 221 to 207 BC, and is remembered above all for his tyranny and cruelty. At the same time, the Qin Dynasty developed administrative institutions that were to remain features of the Chinese state for the following 2000 years.

The state of Qin grew in power during the 5th and 4th centuries BC. In 246 BC the state conquered present-day Sichuan and proceeded to do likewise with the remaining kingdoms that stood in its way. By 221 BC the Qin was victorious, and Qin Shihuang fashioned his conquests into an empire, giving himself the newly coined title *huángdì*, or emperor.

The Qin Dynasty's chief historical legacy was its strong centralised control. It divided its territory into provincial units administered by centrally appointed scholars. Weights and measures and the writing system were standardised. All books inimical to the laws of the state were burnt in accordance with imperial edict. Construction of what much later was to become the Great Wall was undertaken largely by conscripts, of whom countless numbers perished.

Qin Shihuang's heir to the imperial throne proved ineffectual and, shaken by rebellion, the Qin capital near Chang'an fell to an army led by the commoner Liu Bang in 207 BC. Liu lost no time in taking the title of emperor and establishing the Han Dynasty.

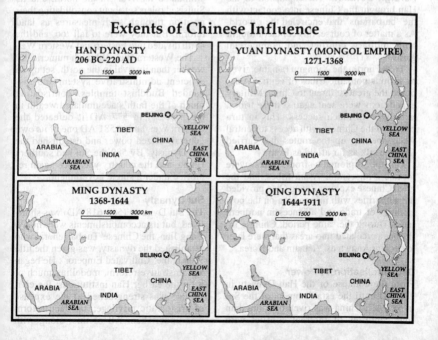

Extents of Chinese Influence

HAN DYNASTY
206 BC-220 AD

0   1500   3000 km

BEIJING ✪
TIBET   YELLOW
        CHINA   SEA
ARABIA   EAST
        INDIA   CHINA
ARABIAN   SEA
SEA

YUAN DYNASTY (MONGOL EMPIRE)
1271-1368

0   1500   3000 km

BEIJING ✪
TIBET   YELLOW
        CHINA   SEA
ARABIA   EAST
        INDIA   CHINA
ARABIAN   SEA
SEA

MING DYNASTY
1368-1644

0   1500   3000 km

BEIJING ✪
TIBET   YELLOW
        CHINA   SEA
ARABIA   EAST
        INDIA   CHINA
ARABIAN   SEA
SEA

QING DYNASTY
1644-1911

0   1500   3000 km

BEIJING ✪
TIBET   YELLOW
        CHINA   SEA
ARABIA   EAST
        INDIA   CHINA
ARABIAN   SEA
SEA

Han Dynasty

The Han Dynasty ruled China from 206 BC to 220 AD. While it held the reins of power less tightly than the preceding Qin, it nevertheless maintained many of the institutions of the dynasty that it followed. Its history is complicated by the fact that it is often divided into a Western Han and an Eastern Han, with an interregnum of 14 years (9-23 AD), during which the country was governed by the Xin.

The Western Han was a period of consolidation, notable for the true establishment of the Chinese state and the military extension of the empire's borders. The Eastern Han, after a brief period of stability, fell prey to a process of a weakening and decentralisation of power that in 220 AD saw the abdication of the last of the Han emperors and the beginning of some 400 years of turmoil.

Foreign Contacts The expansion of the Han brought the Chinese into contact with the 'barbarians' that encircled their world. As a matter of course, this contact brought both military conflict and commercial gains.

To the north, the Xiongnu (a name given to various nomadic tribes of central Asia) posed the greatest threat to China. Military expeditions were sent against these tribes, initially with much success. This in turn provided the Chinese with access to central Asia, opening up the routes that carried Chinese silk as far afield as Rome.

On the diplomatic front, links were formed with central Asian tribes, and the great Chinese explorer Zhang Qian provided the authorities with information on the possibilities of trade and alliances in northern India. During the same period, Chinese influence percolated into areas that were later to become known as Vietnam and Korea.

Decentralisation of Power

From the collapse of the Han Dynasty in 220 AD until the establishment of the Sui in 581 AD, China was riven by more than four centuries of internal conflict with some of the most terrible wars in the nation's history. Curiously, however, the turmoil still allowed for a widespread flowering of Buddhism and the arts.

Chinese historians refer to this period as the Wei, Jin and Southern & Northern dynasties. This is a simplification. Altogether 19 kingdoms and fiefdoms competed for power in the period of 316-439 AD alone. Initially the country divided into three large kingdoms; the Wei governing the area roughly north of the Yangzi River while the south was represented by the Wu to the east and the Shu to the west (Sichuan Province is still often referred to as Shu).

The Wei lasted little more than 40 years. Its successor, the Western Jin, fared not much better. By 306 AD its capital, Luoyang, had fallen to Xiongnu horsemen, issuing in 150 years of bloodshed as non-Han tribes fought together for absolute power. In the 5th century the Tuoba tribe eliminated its rivals in the north, and its Sinisised rulers set about consolidating their position through such measures as land reform. But they were to fall too, and the north divided into Eastern and Western Wei.

The Western Wei, although numerically weaker than its rival in the north, set up an efficient administrative system and disbanded Buddhist temples, confiscating much of the faith's accumulated wealth in the process. In 577 AD it defeated the Eastern Wei, and in 581 AD one of its own generals seized power and established the Sui Dynasty. By 589 the Sui had southern China, and the country was once again reunified under a single government.

Sui Dynasty

The Sui Dynasty (589-618 AD) was short-lived, but its accomplishments were many. Yang Jian, the Chinese-Tuoba general who established the dynasty, was given the title Wendi, the 'Cultivated Emperor'. He began administrative reform, modelling much of it on the earlier Han institutions; the civil service was strengthened at the expense of aristocratic privilege; and land reform was undertaken. All of this, along with revisions of the law code, was to serve as the basis for the institutions of the Tang Dynasty that followed fast on the heels of the Sui's collapse.

The Sui went into rapid decline under the rule of Wendi's son, Yangdi. His massive public works in restoring strategically important sections of the Great Wall and establishing the Grand Canal (which did much to achieve the economic cohesion of China) were clearly aimed at strengthening the empire. However, his three unsuccessful incursions onto Korean soil put an enormous burden on the national coffers and fanned the flames of revolt.

Tang Dynasty

Faced with disastrous military setbacks in Korea and revolt on the streets, Yangdi was assassinated by one of his high officials. Meanwhile, another Sui official, posted in the border garrison of Taiyuan, turned his troops back on the capital. His name was Li Yuan (known posthumously as Gaozu) and he was to establish the Tang Dynasty (618-907), commonly regarded by the Chinese as the most glorious period in their history.

Gaozu's grab at dynastic succession was not without contest, and it was to take 10 years before the last of his rivals was defeated. Once this was achieved, however, the Tang set about putting the house in order. A pyramidical administration was established, with the emperor at its head, two policy-formulating ministries and a Department of State Affairs below this, followed in turn by nine courts and six boards dealing with specific administrative areas. In a move to discourage the development of regional power bases, the empire was divided into 300 prefectures (*zhōu*) and 1500 counties (*xiàn*), a regional breakdown that persists to this day.

The accession of Gaozu's son, Taizong (600-49), to the imperial throne saw a continuation of the early Tang successes. Military conquests re-established Chinese control of the silk routes and contributed to an influx of traders, producing an unprecedented 'internationalisation' of Chinese society.

The major cities of Chang'an, Luoyang and Guangzhou (formerly Canton), as well as many other trading centres, were all home to foreign communities. Mainly from central Asia, these communities brought with them new religions, food, music and artistic traditions. Later in the Tang Dynasty, foreign contact was extended to Persia, India, Malaysia, Indonesia and Japan. By the 9th century the city of Guangzhou was estimated to have a foreign population of 100,000.

Buddhism also flourished under the Tang. Chinese pilgrims, notably the famous wanderer Xuan Zang, made their way to India, bringing back with them Buddhist scriptures that in their turn brought about a Buddhist renewal. Translation, which until this time had extensively Sinisised difficult Buddhist concepts, was undertaken with a new rigour, and Chinese Buddhist texts increased vastly in number. One of the consequences of this, however, was a schism in the Buddhist faith.

In reaction to the complexity of many Buddhist texts being translated from Sanskrit, the Chan school (more famously known by its Japanese name, Zen) arose. Chan looked to bypass the complexities of scriptural study through discipline and meditation, while another Buddhist phenomenon, the Pure Land school (later to become the most important form of Chinese Buddhism), concerned itself with attaining the 'Western Paradise'.

For the Chinese, the apex of Tang dynastic glory was the reign of Xuanzong (685-761), known also by the title Minghuang, or the 'Radiant Emperor'. His capital of Chang'an was one of the greatest cities in the world, with a population of over one million. His court was a magnet to scholars and artists throughout the country, and home for a time to poets such as Du Fu and Li Bai, perhaps China's two most famous rhymers. His reign similarly saw a flourishing of the arts, dance and music, as well as a remarkable religious diversity.

Some might say that all this artistic activity was a indication that the empire was beginning to go a bit soft at the core. Xu-anzong's increasing preoccupation with the arts, Tantric Buddhism, Taoism, one of his consorts Yang Guifei and whatever else captured his fancy, meant that the affairs of state were largely left to his administrators.

An Lushun, a general in the north-east, took this opportunity to build up a huge power base in the region, and before long (755) he made his move on the rest of China. The fighting, which dragged on for nearly 10 years, overran the capital and caused massive dislocations of people and millions of deaths. Although Tang forces regained control of the empire, it was the beginning of the end for the Tang.

Anarchy & Discord
Tang power gradually weakened during the 8th and 9th centuries. In the north-west, Tibetan warriors overran Tang garrisons, while to the south the Nanzhao kingdom centred in Dali, Yunnan, posed a serious threat to Sichuan. Meanwhile, in the Chinese heartland of the Yangzi region and Zhejiang, heavy taxes and a series of calamities engendered wide-ranging discontent that culminated in Huang Zhao, the head of a loose grouping of bandit groups, ransacking the capital.

From 907 to 959, until the establishment of the Song Dynasty, China was once again racked by wars between contenders for the mandate of heaven. It is a period often referred to as the Five Dynasties and Ten Kingdoms period.

Song Dynasty
In 959 Zhao Kuangyin, the leader of the palace corps of one of the so-called Five Dynasties (the Later Zhou), usurped power from a seven-year-old head of state. By 976 he had conquered the dozen or so other kingdoms that stood in the way to reunifying China and established yet another dynasty: the Song (960-1279).

The Song is generally divided into the Northern Song (960-1126) and the Southern Song (1127-1279). The reason behind this division lies with the Jurchen Jin

Dynasty, which took control of the north from 1126 and drove the Song from its capital of Kaifeng to the southern capital of Hangzhou.

Despite the continual threat of powerful forces on its borders (the Tibetan/Tangut Xixia kingdom, the Mongol Liao Dynasty and the Jurchen Jin Dynasty), the Song is memorable for its strong centralised government, a renewal of Confucian learning, a restoration of the examination system that fostered a civilian-dominated bureaucracy, and what has been referred to as a commercial revolution.

The economic progress of the Song period can be attributed in large part to dramatically increased agricultural production. Land reclamation, new rice strains and improved agricultural techniques and tools all played a role in this development. At the same time improvements in the transport infrastructure, the rise of a merchant class and the introduction of paper money facilitated the growth of wider markets. This commercial revolution allowed for the growth of more urban centres nourished by the influx of goods from around the country.

When Marco Polo arrived in China in the 13th century he found prosperous cities on a grander scale than those he was used to at home in Europe. Historians point to the Song Dynasty as the turning point in China's development of an urban culture.

Mongol Reign (Yuan Dynasty)
Beyond the Great Wall lay the Gobi Desert. Beyond that lay only slightly more hospitable grassland stretching all the way from Manchuria to Hungary and inhabited by nomadic Turkic and Mongol tribes who endured a harsh life as shepherds and horse breeders. The Mongols, despised for what was considered their ignorance and poverty, occasionally went to war with the Chinese, but had always been defeated.

In 1206, after about 20 years of internal war, Genghis Khan united the roaming Mongol tribes into a new national entity: the 'Blue Mongols', under the protection

Did Marco Polo go to China?

Beijing has its 'Marco Polo Bridge' and Cathay Pacific Airlines offers a 'Marco Polo Club' Westerners might be forgiven for thinking that Marco Polo 'discovered' China. Towering over everyone who went before and after him, the Italian merchant occupies a special place in the western imagination.

The stuff of fairy tales – the man who brought spaghetti to Italy (or was it noodles to China?) and invented ice cream. An early pioneer of the travelogue, diligently cataloguing the bizarre wonders of the Far East, Polo has inspired travellers for centuries. Even Christopher Columbus travelled with (and jotted notes in) a copy of *Description of the World*, Polo's account of his wanderings.

It is hardly surprising then that virtually no one has ever thought to ask the question that Frances Wood asks in her book, *Did Marco Polo Go to China?* Ms Wood herself admits to having quoted Marco Polo in her university essays and having drawn on his descriptions of Beijing in her PhD dissertation on the domestic architecture of that city, but this was before her attention was drawn to research into Polo's case by German Mongolists. German Mongolists, she admits, may not 'form a large lobby, but their research is not to be lightly dismissed'. The German Mongolists argue that Polo's travels and observations are of dubious authenticity. For a start his book – written in 1298 – was 'ghosted' by a popular romance writer of the time with whom Polo shared a Genoese prison cell. The original has not survived and the more than 150 early versions of the book that have are the work of copyists who often 'improved' the tale – there are major discrepancies between them. Moreover, no mention of a Marco Polo can be found in Chinese records, a curious fact when Polo claims variously to have governed Yangzhou, ended a major siege and enjoyed a 17 year special relationship with Kublai Khan as his special emissary to China.

But it is less his extravagant claims than his omissions that go hardest against Polo. Among the many things that Polo fails to have noticed during 17 years wandering around China are Chinese women's bound feet, the popularity of tea, the unique Chinese writing system and, perhaps most damning of all, the Great Wall. No matter how they arrive in China, asserts Frances Wood, 'only someone who is severely visually challenged could fail to notice the Great Wall'. She has a point.

Frances Wood cautiously takes the view that 'Marco Polo himself probably never travelled much further than his family's trading posts on the Black Sea and in Constantinople'. Nevertheless, she concedes, there is much in his account of China that concurs with other contemporary accounts – some of them Persian and Arabic. His book remains a fascinating compendium of medieval knowledge about China – tantalisingly sketchy, wide-eyed and fabulous. For many centuries it was one of the few references available for travellers setting out to China, even if it was compiled from hearsay and unreliable secondary sources.

Besides, we at Lonely Planet have a grudging respect for Marco, whether he went to China or not. With prices rising by the day and new roads and railway lines springing up everywhere, our guide has barely hit the shelves before travellers are speculating as to whether *we* went to China. It took 700 years for anyone to ask the same question of Marco Polo. ∎

of the 'heavenly sky'. In 1211 he turned his attention on China, penetrated the Great Wall two years later and then took Beijing in 1215. Stubborn resistance from the Chinese rulers, conflict within the Mongo-

lian camp and campaigns in Russia delayed the conquest of Song China for many years. Not until 1279 did the grandson of Genghis, Kublai Khan, bring southern China under his sway and establish the

Yuan Dynasty (1271-1368). The China ruled by Kublai was the vastest empire the world has ever seen.

The Mongols established two capitals: a summer capital of Shangdu in Inner Mongolia and a winter capital of Dadu, or, as it's now known, Beijing. They made many administrative changes to the Chinese court; the major difference from the Song being the militarisation of administrative organs. Another major feature of the Yuan Dynasty was that the Chinese became 3rd and 4th class citizens in their own country. Society was split into four categories, with the Mongols first, their central Asian allies next, northern Chinese third and southern Chinese last.

The Mongols were harsh in administering their rule, but on the economic front at least they were less interfering than the Chinese dynasties that had preceded them. More work was carried out on China's canal system and roads, offering a further stimulus to trade. The commercial revolution that had gathered pace in the Song continued unabated in the Yuan, with inter-regional and even international trade flourishing. Taxes were heavy, however, except for those of Mongol descent who were exempt.

Despite internal intrigues and widespread Chinese disaffection with their Mongol rulers, the grip of the Yuan Dynasty over its vast empire remained strong almost until the very end. By the middle of the 14th century, however, the country had become convulsed by rebellion. Chief among the rebel groups were the Red Turbans, who were guided in their mission by a belief structure of diverse religious sources, ranging from Buddhism to Manichaeism, Taoism and Confucianism. By 1367 Zhu Yuanzhang, originally an orphan and Buddhist novice, had climbed to the top of the rebel leadership, and in 1368 he established the Ming Dynasty and restored Chinese rule.

Ming Dynasty

Upon founding the Ming Dynasty (1368-1644), Zhu Yuanzhang took the name of Hongwu. He established his capital in Nanjing, but in 1402 Yongle (strictly speaking the third, but effectively the second, Ming emperor) set about building a new seat of imperial power on the site of the old Yuan capital in Beijing.

In 1420 Beijing was designated the first capital and Nanjing designated the second (their names mean 'Northern Capital' and 'Southern Capital' respectively).

Hongwu is remembered for his despotism (he had some 10,000 scholars and their families put to death in two paranoid purges of his administration), but he was also a strong leader who did much to set China back on its feet in the aftermath of the Yuan collapse. This consolidation was continued by Yongle. He ruled less autocratically, running the court bureaucracy with a steadier hand than Hongwu, and he carried out effective campaigns in protection of the Great Wall against the Mongols.

During Yongle's reign, China developed into a strong maritime nation. Zheng He, a eunuch general of Muslim descent, undertook seven great expeditions to South-East Asia, Persia, Arabia and even eastern Africa.

In the final years of Ming rule, official corruption, excessive eunuch power, intellectual conservatism and costly wars in defence of Korea (and ultimately China itself) against Japan's Toyotomi Hideyoshi brought the nation to virtual bankruptcy. A famine in Shaanxi Province, coupled with governmental neglect, was the spark for a massive peasant rebellion that brought the Ming to a close.

Qing Dynasty

The Manchus to the north had long been growing in power, and looked with keen interest to the convulsions of rebellion in their huge neighbour. Taking advantage of the turmoil in China, they launched an invasion. Initially held back by the Great Wall, they were allowed to pass by a Ming general, who saw an alliance with the Manchus as the only hope for defeating the peasant rebel armies that now threatened Beijing itself.

The Manchus lost no time in inflicting a

decisive defeat on the peasant forces, and in June 1644 they marched into the Ming capital and made it their own. They proclaimed their new dynasty the Qing (1644-1911), although it was to be four decades before they finally cleared the south of Ming loyalist forces and pacified the whole country. Today's 'triads' in China (the modern secret societies generally thought to be involved in criminal activity, especially drug trafficking) are actually the descendants of secret societies originally set up to resist the Manchus.

Although the Manchus concentrated power in their own hands and alienated the Han Chinese, the reign of the early Qing emperors from 1663 to 1796 was a period of great prosperity. The throne was occupied by three of the most able rulers China has known: Kangxi, Yongcheng and Qianlong. The Qing expanded the empire to its greatest limits since the Han Dynasty, bringing Mongolia and Tibet under Qing suzerainty. Reduced taxation and massive flood control and irrigation projects benefited the peasants.

One problem was that the first three emperors' exceptional competence led to a concentration of power in their hands that none of their successors was a match for. Like the Mongols, the Manchu rulers succumbed to the ways of the Chinese and soon became culturally indistinguishable from them, modelling their government on the Ming Dynasty. Thus the isolationism and intellectual conservatism of the Ming was passed on to the Qing.

China continued to be an inward-looking nation, oblivious to the technological and scientific revolutions taking place in Europe. The coming of Europeans to China hastened the fall of the Qing and helped mould the China we know today.

Coming of the West

The first European ships to anchor off the shores of China, in 1516, were Portuguese. Although by 1557 they had set up a trade mission in Macau, it was not until 1760 that other European powers – the British, Dutch and Spanish – gained secure access to Chinese markets via a base in Guangzhou. All trade was carried out via a monopolistic guild known as the Cohong; the same guild mediated all non-commercial dealings with the Chinese empire, effectively keeping foreigners at a long arm's length from the political centre in Beijing.

Trade flourished under the auspices of the Cohong – in China's favour. British purchases of tea, silk and porcelain far outweighed Chinese purchases of wool and spices. In 1773, the British decided to balance the books with sales of opium. Despite imperial declarations of wars against drugs, opium addiction in China skyrocketed and with it so did sales.

After much imperial vacillation and hand-wringing, in March 1839 Lin Zexiu, an official of great personal integrity, was dispatched to Guangzhou to put a stop to the illegal traffic once and for all. He acted promptly, demanding and eventually getting some 20,000 chests of opium stored by the British in Guangzhou. This, along with several other minor incidents, was just the pretext that hawkish elements in the British government needed to win support for military action against China. In 1840 a British naval force assembled in Macau and moved up the coast to Beihe, not far from Beijing. The Opium War was on.

For the Chinese, the conflicts centred on the opium trade were a fiasco from start to finish. While the Qing court managed to fob the first British force off with a treaty that neither side ended up recognising, increasing British frustration soon led to an attack on Chinese positions close to Guangzhou.

The resulting treaty ceded Hong Kong to the British and called for indemnities of six million yuan and the full resumption of trade. The furious Qing emperor refused to recognise the treaty, and in 1841 British forces once again headed up the coast, taking Fujian and eastern Zhejiang. They settled in for the winter, and in the spring of 1842, their numbers swollen with reinforcements, they moved up the Yangzi duly dispatching all comers. With British guns trained on Nanjing, the Qing fighting spirit evaporated, and they reluctantly signed the humiliating Treaty of Nanjing.

Decline of the Qing

The Qing was simply the latest inheritor of power in many centuries of dynastic rule. It was administered by Confucian-trained scholars and was headed by Empress Dowager Cixi (1834-1908), a former concubine who saw all attempts to reform the ancient institutions of the empire as a threat to the conservative power base of her government. In short, it was poorly equipped to adapt to the demands of dynamic western powers who refused to enter into relations with China as mere vassals. Reforming elements within the Qing were perpetually thwarted; rural poverty and western influence were factors in promoting civil unrest that emerged in four major rebellions in the mid-19th century.

The western powers went on a land-grabbing spree that carved China up into 'spheres of influence'. The first to go was China's colonial 'possessions'. A war with France from 1883 to 1885 ended Chinese suzerainty in Indo-China and allowed the French to maintain control of Vietnam and eventually gain control of Laos and Cambodia. The British occupied Myanmar (Burma). In 1895 Japan forced the Chinese out of Korea and made them cede Taiwan. By 1898 the European powers were on the verge of carving up China and having her for dinner – a feast that was thwarted only by a US proposal for an 'open-door' policy that would leave China open to trade with any foreign power.

In the face of so much national humiliation it was inevitable that rebellions aiming to overthrow the Qing would emerge. The first major rebellion was the Taiping. Led by Hong Xiuquan, a native of Guangdong and a failed scholar whose encounters with western missionaries had led him to believe he was the younger brother of Jesus, the rebellion commanded forces of 600,000 men and 500,000 women.

The Taipings owed much of their ideology to Christianity. They forbade gambling, opium, tobacco and alcohol; advocated agricultural reform; and outlawed foot-binding for women, prostitution and slavery. Ironically, they were defeated by a coalition of Qing and western forces – the Europeans preferring to deal with a corrupt and weak Qing government than a powerful, united China governed by the Taipings.

The second major rebellion to rock China was that of the Boxers United in Righteousness, or more simply the Boxer Rebellion. It emerged in Shandong in 1898 out of secret societies who trained in martial arts. The Boxers were fanatically anti-foreign, saw 1900 as the dawn of the new age and believed themselves invincible to the bullets of the foreign forces. Poorly organised, the Boxers roamed in bands attacking Chinese Christians and foreigners. The Empress Dowager attempted to ride the tide of anti-foreign feeling by declaring war on the foreign powers in 1900. In the event, a combined British, US, French, Japanese and Russian force of 20,000 troops defeated the Boxers, the empress fled to Xi'an and the foreign forces levied yet another massive indemnity on the Qing government.

Fall of the Qing

With the defeat of the Boxers, even the Empress Dowager realised that China was too weak to survive without reform. But, while the civil service examinations based on irrelevant 1000-year-old Confucian doctrines were abolished, other court-sponsored reforms proved to be a sham. Furthermore, by now secret societies aimed at bringing down the Qing Dynasty were legion, even overseas where they were set up by disaffected Chinese who had left their homeland.

To make matters worse for the Qing, in 1908 the Empress Dowager died and the two-year-old Emperor Puyi ascended to the throne. The Qing was now rudderless, and quickly collapsed in two events: the Railway Protection Movement and the Wuchang Uprising of 1911.

The railway incident began with the public Chinese sentiment that newly constructed railways should be in Chinese control, not in the hands of the foreigners who had financed and built them. Plans to construct lines to provincial centres using local funds soon collapsed, and the despairing Qing government adopted a policy of nationalisation and foreign loans to do the work. Opposition by vested interests and provincial leaders soon fanned violence that spread and took on an anti-Qing nature. The violence was worst in Sichuan, and troops were taken from the Wuchang garrison in Wuhan to quell the disturbances.

As it happened, revolutionaries in Wuhan, coordinated by Sun Yatsen's Tokyo-based Alliance Society, were already planning an uprising in concert with disaffected Chinese troops. With the garrisons virtually empty, the revolutionaries were quickly able to take control of Wuhan and ride on the back of the large-scale Railway Protection uprisings to victory over all China.

Two months later representatives from 17 provinces throughout China gathered in Nanjing to establish the Provisional Republican Government of China. China's long dynastic cycle had come to an end.

Early Days of the Republic

The Provisional Republican Government was set up on 10 October 1911 (a date that is still celebrated in Taiwan as 'Double Tenth') by Sun Yatsen and Li Yuanhong, a military commander in Wuchang. Lacking the power to force a Manchu abdication, they had no choice but to call on the assistance of Yuan Shikai, head of the imperial army and the same man the Manchus had called on to put down the Republican uprisings. The favour cost the Republicans dearly. Yuan Shikai placed himself at the head of the Republican movement and forced Sun Yatsen's resignation.

Yuan lost no time in dissolving the Republican government and amending the constitution to make himself president for life.

When this met with regional opposition, he took the natural next step in 1915 of declaring an imperial restoration and pronouncing himself China's latest emperor. Yunnan seceded, taking Guangxi, Guizhou and much of the rest of the south with it, forces were sent to bring the breakaway provinces back into the imperial ambit, and in the confusion Yuan himself passed away. What followed was a virtual warlord era, with no single power strong enough to hold the country together until the Communists established the People's Republic of China (PRC) in 1949.

Intellectual Revolution

Chinese intellectuals had been probing the inadequacies of the old Confucian order and looking for a path to steer China into the 20th century ever since early contact with the west, but a sense of lost possibilities with the collapse of the Republican government and the start of a new period of social decay lent an urgency to their worries in the early years of the 1900s. Intellectuals and students were also supported by a sense of nationalism that had been slowly growing in force since the late years of the Qing.

Beijing University became a hotbed of intellectual dissent, attracting scholars from all over China (even Mao Zedong was present in his capacity as library assistant). They were merciless in their criticisms of orthodox Chinese society. Some explored ideas of social Darwinism, the Communist Manifesto was translated into Chinese and became the basis for countless discussion groups, others favoured anarchism, and all looked keenly to events unfolding in Russia, where revolutionaries had taken power.

The catalyst for the demonstrations that became known as the May Fourth Movement was the decision of the Allies in Versailles to pass defeated Germany's rights in Shandong over to the Japanese. A huge public outcry ensued and on 4 May 1919 students took to the streets in a protest that combined a sense of nationalist outrage with demands for modernisation. Mass strike action in support of the students took place throughout China. Although the disturbances were quelled and many of the ringleaders temporarily imprisoned, the May Fourth incident is considered a watershed in contemporary Chinese history.

Perhaps most interesting today is the way in which the student protests at Tiananmen in 1989 echoed the slogans and catchcries of the 1919 protests. Students bearing placards marked with 'Mr Science' and 'Mr Democracy' in 1989 were harking back to 1919, when the same slogans were used – perhaps, in fine Chinese tradition, seeking the authority of historical precedent.

Kuomintang & Communists

After initial setbacks, Sun Yatsen and the Kuomintang (also known as the Guomindang, KMT or Nationalist Party), which had emerged as the dominant political force after the fall of the Qing Dynasty, managed to establish a secure base in southern China, and began training a National Revolutionary Army (NRA) with which to challenge the northern warlords.

Meanwhile, talks between representatives of the Soviet Communist International (Comintern) – the international body dedicated to world revolution – and prominent Chinese Marxists eventually resulted in several Chinese Marxist groups banding together to form a Chinese Communist Party (which became the CCP) at a meeting in Shanghai in 1921.

The Comintern, from 1922, pushed the CCP to ally with the Kuomintang, probably motivated more by the hope of forming a buttress against Japanese expansionism than by the promise of a Soviet-style revolution in China. The union was short lived. After Sun Yatsen's death in 1925 a power struggle emerged in the Kuomintang between those sympathetic to the Communists and those who – headed by Chiang Kaishek – favoured a capitalist state dominated by a wealthy elite and supported by a military dictatorship.

Chiang Kaishek – the intractable enemy of the Communist movement, his extermination campaigns led to the Long March in 1933.

Shanghai Coup

Chiang Kaishek attempted to put an end to growing Communist influence during the 1926 Northern Expedition, which set out to wrest power from the remaining warlords. With Chiang as commander in chief, NRA forces took the cities of Wuhan and Nanchang, and prepared to move on Shanghai.

As NRA troops advanced on the city, Shanghai workers were called upon to strike and take over key installations. Having lured the Communists out of the woodwork, Chiang let loose a reign of terror against the Communists and their sympathisers.

With the help of Shanghai's underworld leaders and with financial backing from Shanghai bankers and foreigners, Chiang armed hundreds of gangsters, dressed them in Kuomintang uniforms and launched a surprise attack overnight on the workers' militia. About 5000 Shanghai Communists were killed. Massacres of Communists and various anti-Chiang factions followed in other Chinese cities. Zhou Enlai managed to escape by a hair's breadth. Another prominent CCP leader, Li Dazhao, was executed by slow strangulation.

Kuomintang Government

By the middle of 1928 the Northern Expedition had reached Beijing and a national government was established, with Chiang holding both military and political leadership. Nevertheless, only about half of the country was under the direct control of the Kuomintang; the rest was ruled by local warlords.

China's social problems were legion: children were used as slave labour in factories; domestic slavery and prostitution were rife; the destitute and starving died on the streets; and strikes were ruthlessly suppressed by foreign and Chinese factory owners. In the face of such endemic social malaise, Chiang became obsessed with countering the influence of the Communists.

Civil War

After the massacre of 1927, the Communists were divided between an insurrectionary policy of targeting large urban centres and one of basing its rebellion in the countryside. After costly defeats in Nanchang and Changsha, the tide of opinion started to shift towards Mao Zedong, who, along with Zhu De, had established his forces in the Jinggangshan mountains on the border between Jiangxi and Hunan and who advocated rural-based revolt.

Communist-led uprisings in other parts of the country met with some success. However, the Communist armies were still small and hampered by limited resources. They adopted a strategy of guerrilla warfare, emphasising mobility and deployment of forces for short attacks on the enemy, followed by swift separation once the attack was over. Pitched battles were avoided except where their force was overwhelmingly superior. The strategy was summed up in a four line slogan:

The enemy advances, we retreat;
The enemy camps, we harass;
The enemy tires, we attack;
The enemy retreats, we pursue.

By 1930, the ragged Communist forces had been turned into an army of perhaps 40,000 which presented such a serious challenge to the Kuomintang that Chiang had to wage a number of extermination campaigns against them. He was defeated each time, and the Communist army continued to expand its territory.

The Long March

Chiang's fifth extermination campaign began in October 1933, when the Communists suddenly changed their strategy. Mao and Zhu's authority was being undermined by other members of the Party who advocated meeting Chiang's troops in pitched battles, but this strategy proved disastrous. By October 1934 the Communists had suffered heavy losses and were hemmed into a small area in Jiangxi.

On the brink of defeat, the Communists decided to retreat from Jiangxi and march north to Shaanxi. In China's northern mountains the Communists controlled an area which spread across Shaanxi, Gansu and Ningxia, held by troops commanded by an ex-Kuomintang officer who had sided with the Communists after the 1927 massacre.

There was not one 'Long March' but several, as various Communist armies in the south made their way to Shaanxi. The most famous was the march from Jiangxi Province which began in October 1934, took a year to complete and covered 8000km over some of the world's most inhospitable terrain. On the way the Communists confiscated the property of officials, landlords and tax-collectors, redistributed the land to the peasants, armed thousands of peasants with weapons captured from the Kuomintang and left soldiers behind to organise guerrilla groups to harass the enemy.

Of the 90,000 people who started out in Jiangxi only 20,000 made it to Shaanxi.

Mao Zedong, the Great Helmsman and paramount leader of the Chinese Communist Party. A brilliant military strategist, his radical tactics once in power led variously to famine, economic catastrophy and the liquidation of the cream of China's artistic and intellectual communities.

Fatigue, sickness, exposure, enemy attacks and desertion all took their toll.

The march proved, however, that the Chinese peasants could fight if they were given a method, an organisation, leadership, hope and weapons. It brought together many people who later held top positions after 1949, including Mao Zedong, Zhou Enlai, Zhu De, Lin Biao, Deng Xiaoping and Liu Shaoqi. It also established Mao as the paramount leader of the Chinese Communist movement; during the march a meeting of the CCP hierarchy recognised Mao's overall leadership, and he assumed supreme responsibility for strategy.

Japanese Invasion
In September 1931 the Japanese took advantage of the confusion in China to invade and occupy Manchuria, setting up a puppet state with the last Chinese emperor, Puyi, as the symbolic head. Chiang, still obsessed with the threat of the Communists, went ahead with his fifth extermination drive: 'pacification first, resistance later' was his slogan.

The Communists had other plans. In late 1936 in Xi'an they convinced Chiang's own generals to take him hostage, and an anti-Japanese alliance was formed after negotiations with Zhou Enlai. But it did little to halt the advance of the Japanese, who in 1937 launched an all-out invasion; by 1939 they had overrun most of eastern China, forcing the Kuomintang to retreat west to Chongqing.

In 1941 the Japanese assault on Pearl Harbor brought the Americans into the conflict. Hoping to use Chiang's troops to tie down as many Japanese as possible, the Americans instead found Chiang actively avoiding conflict, saving his troops for renewed attacks on the Communists once the Americans had defeated the Japanese. The US general Joseph Stilwell, who was sent to China in 1942 by President Roosevelt to improve the combat effectiveness of the Chinese army, concluded that 'the Chinese government was a structure based on fear and favour in the hands of an ignorant, arbitrary and stubborn man ...' and that its military effort since 1938 was 'practically zero'.

Defeat of the Kuomintang
The Kuomintang-Communist alliance had collapsed by 1941 and by the end of WWII China was in the grip of an all-out civil war. The 900,000-strong Communist army was backed by the militia and several million active supporters. With the surrender of Japan in 1945, a dramatic power struggle began as the Kuomintang and Communist forces gathered in Manchuria for the final showdown.

By 1948 the Communists had captured so much US-supplied Kuomintang equipment and had recruited so many Kuomintang soldiers that they equalled the Kuomintang in both numbers and supplies.

Highlights in China
Top: Jinshanling, one of the less tourist-developed Great Wall sites around Beijing.
Middle Left: The remarkable Yungang Caves in Shanxi Province contain more than 50,000 statues.
Middle Right: The architecture of the Bund in Shanghai – one of China's most recognisable skylines.
Bottom: Huangshan range (Anhui Province) offers sublime scenery, but beware the tourist hordes.

RUSSIA

Karaganda

KAZAKHSTAN

TURPAN
A desert oasis
dotted with abandoned
ancient cities

DUNHUANG
Mogao Caves, the best
preserved Buddhist
grottoes in China

XIAHE
A restful and
beautiful Tibetan
monastery town

MONGOLIA

ALMATY

BISHKEK

Ürümqi
Turpan

KYRGYZSTAN

XI'AN
The Army of
Terracotta Warriors

Kashgar

QINGHAI LAKE
China's largest lake, with
breathtaking scenery and
abundant wildlife

XINJIANG

Dunhuang
Jiayuguan

Zhangye

Wuwei
Tianzhu

Lanzho

Qinghai Lake
Golmud
Chaka

Xining

*Under
administration
of China*

QINGHAI

Linxia
Xiahe

GANSU

Huashixia

TIBET

Xiwu

Songpan

SICHUAN

Chengdu

DELHI

Shigatse
Tingri   Sakya   **Lhasa**
Zhangmu   Gyantse
KATHMANDU   Mt Everest
(8848 m)

Emeishan
Lesh

Zigong

Agra

Ganges

Lucknow

NEPAL   **THIMPHU**
BHUTAN

Liupanshui

Varanasi

Patna

River

INDIA

Xiaguan
(Dali City)

LHASA
Home of the Potala
Palace, Jokhang Temple
and Tibetan culture

BANGLADESH

DHAKA

Kunming

YUNNAN

Jabalpur

Calcutta

Gejiu

Ha Gia

INDIA

DALI
A relaxing, lakeside
walled town, home to
the Dai people

VIETNA

EMEISHAN
Hiking, temples,
pavillions and pilgrims
on this sacred mountain

MYANMAR

CHONGQING
Cruise the Yangzi
River through the
Three Gorges

THAILAND

LAOS

BAY OF
BENGAL

YANGON

VIENTIANE

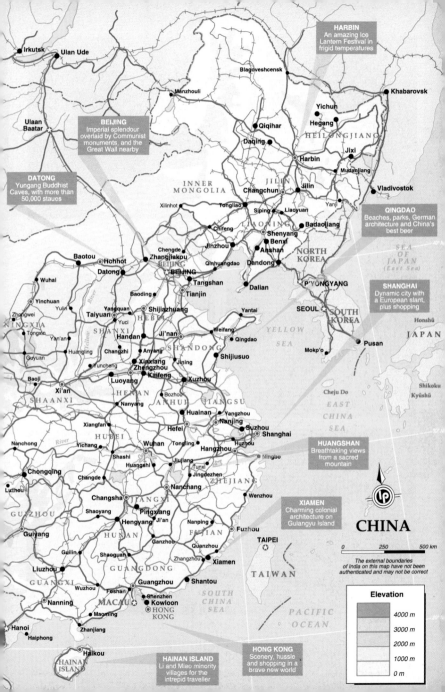

HARBIN
An amazing Ice Lantern Festival in frigid temperatures

BEIJING
Imperial splendour overlaid by Communist monuments, and the Great Wall nearby

DATONG
Yungang Buddhist Caves, with more than 50,000 staues

QINGDAO
Beaches, parks, German architecture and China's best beer

SHANGHAI
Dynamic city with a European slant, plus shopping

HUANGSHAN
Breathtaking views from a sacred mountain

XIAMEN
Charming colonial architecture on Gulangyu Island

CHINA

0   250   500 km

The external boundaries of India on this map have not been authenticated and may not be correct

HAINAN ISLAND
Li and Miao minority villages for the intrepid traveller

HONG KONG
Scenery, hussle and shopping in a brave new world

Elevation

4000 m
3000 m
2000 m
1000 m
0 m

Irkutsk
Ulan Ude
Ulaan Baatar
Blagoveshcensk
Manzhouli
Khabarovsk
Yichun
Hegang
Qiqihar
Daqing
HEILONGJIANG
Jixi
Harbin
Mudanjiang
Vladivostok
JILIN
Changchun
Jilin
Tongliao
Siping
Liaoyuan
Yanji
Xilinhot
Badaojiang
Chifeng
LIAONING
Shenyang
Jinzhou
Benxi
Anshan
NORTH KOREA
Chengde
Zhangjiakou
Qinhuangdao
Dandong
Baotou
Hohhot
BEIJING
Datong
Wuhai
Tangshan
Baoding
Tianjin
P'YONGYANG
Yinchuan
Yulin
Yangquan
Shijiazhuang
Yantai
SEOUL
SOUTH KOREA
Dalian
Zhongwei
Taiyuan
Yuci
HEBEI
Ji'nan
Weifang
Pusan
NINGXIA
Tongxin
SHANXI
Handan
Qingdao
YELLOW SEA
Yan'an
Huangling
Changzhi
Anyang
SHANDONG
Shijiusuo
Guyuan
Yuncheng
Xinxiang
Jining
Zhengzhou
Baoji
Xi'an
Luoyang
Kaifeng
Xuzhou
Mokp'o
JAPAN
Honshū
SHAANXI
HENAN
Nanyang
Bozhou
ANHUI
JIANGSU
Cheju Do
Shikoku
Kyūshū
Nanchong
Xiangfan
HUBEI
Huainan
Yangzhou
EAST CHINA SEA
Yichang
Wuhan
Hefei
Nanjing
Suzhou
Shashi
Tongling
Hangzhou
Huzhou
Shanghai
Chongqing
Changde
Huangshi
Jiujiang
Ningbo
Luzhou
Tunxi
Jingdezhen
ZHEJIANG
Changsha
Nanchang
Wenzhou
JIANGXI
GUIZHOU
Shaoyang
Pingxiang
Ji'an
Nanping
Hengyang
HUNAN
FUJIAN
TAIPEI
Guiyang
Ganzhob
Quanzhou
Fuzhou
Guilin
Shaoguan
Zhangzhou
Xiamen
TAIWAN
Liuzhou
GUANGDONG
GUANGXI
Wuzhou
Foshan
Guangzhou
Shantou
Nanning
Shenzhen
Kowloon
MACAU
HONG KONG
SOUTH CHINA SEA
Maoming
PACIFIC OCEAN
Hanoi
Zhanjiang
Haiphong
Haikou
HAINAN ISLAND

MARTIN MOOS

CHRIS TAYLOR

GLENN BEANLAND

MERRILEE ZELLNER

Highlights in China
Top: A riverweed collector balances on a bamboo boat at Yangshou (Guangxi Province).
Middle Left: A Buddhist monk plays a traditional trumpet at a Lhasa temple (Tibet).
Middle Right: The sun sets over Hong Kong Island and Victoria Harbour.
Bottom: Xiahe's Labrang Monastery (Gansu Province) has a 3km pilgrims' way with 274 prayer wheels.

massive social discontent. On 22 April 1989, a week after Hu's death, China's leaders gathered in the Hall of the People for an official mourning service. Outside, approximately 150,000 students and other activists held an unofficial service that soon became a massive pro-democracy protest.

All through April, crowds continued to fill Tiananmen Square, and by the middle of May protesters in and around the square had swelled to nearly one million. Workers and even members of the police force joined in. Protests erupted in at least 20 other cities. Approximately 3000 students staged a hunger strike for democracy in the square. Railway workers assisted students travelling to Beijing by allowing them free rides on the trains.

Students enrolled at Beijing's Art Institute constructed the 'Goddess of Democracy' in Tiananmen Square – a statue which bore a striking resemblance to America's Statue of Liberty. The students made speeches demanding a free press and an end to corruption and nepotism. Huge pro-democracy demonstrations in Hong Kong, Macau and Taiwan lent support. The arrival of the foreign press corps turned the 'Beijing Spring' into the media event of 1989.

Throughout much of May, the CCP was unable to quell the protests, and the imminent arrival of Mikhail Gorbachev for the first Sino-Soviet summit since 1959 precluded the use of arms to dispel the crowds. On 20 May, however, immediately after Gorbachev's departure, martial law was declared, and by 2 June, 350,000 troops had been deployed around Beijing. In the early hours of the morning on 4 June the 27th Army division attacked. Other units loyal to Deng were also employed. Heavy tanks and armoured vehicles made short work of the barricades, crushing anyone who got in their way, while troops with automatic weapons strafed the crowds on the streets.

The number of deaths that resulted from the action is widely disputed. Eyewitness accounts have indicated that hundreds died in the square alone, and it's likely that fighting in the streets around the square and in the suburbs of Beijing may have led to several thousand casualties. Hospitals were filled to overflowing, PLA troops are said to have refused to allow doctors to treat their patients, and rumours circulated of mass graves.

The truth will probably never be known. What is certain is that the Party lost whatever remaining moral authority it had in the action, and will no doubt one day have to deal with widespread recriminations. Indeed, much of China's current political repression may indeed be motivated by fear among the leadership that they could, in the future, be put on trial for the massacre at Tiananmen Square.

Hong Kong

In 1984 a Sino-British agreement allowed for the reversion of Hong Kong to China in 1997. The original 'unequal' Treaty of Nanjing (1840) foisted on China by Britain in the Opium War had ceded Hong Kong to the British 'in perpetuity', but the New Territories adjoining Kowloon were 'leased' to the British for 99 years in 1898. In the event, Britain agreed to hand the entire colony lock, stock and skyscrapers back to China when the New Territories' lease expired.

The transition of power has not been entirely smooth. According to the terms of the 1984 agreement, Hong Kong's transfer to Chinese rule was to take place under the concept of 'one country, two systems'. The implementation of this system was laid out in the Basic Law, which promised the former colony a 'high degree of autonomy'.

However, Hong Kong's much ballyhooed 'high degree of autonomy' is largely a slogan. The 'autonomy' basically consists of the freedom to make money. Most telling was the fact that the Chinese government scrapped the entire democratically elected Legislative Council (LEGCO) and replaced it with a puppet legislature appointed by Beijing. Elections are being promised for 1998, but only under a system that will disenfranchise 95% of the voters. Beijing has also prevented the establishment of a Court of Final Appeal, an institution that Hong Kong politicians claim is essential to guaranteeing an independent legal system. Starting from 1 July 1997, thousands of PLA troops have moved into Hong Kong.

Taiwan

The people of Taiwan have been watching the Chinese takeover of Hong Kong with trepidation. The Kuomintang government of Chiang Kaishek fled to Taiwan in 1949 following the Communist takeover and has been there ever since, getting steadily richer and, in recent years, increasingly democratic.

Its foreign currency reserves are among the world's largest; it is arguably the most democratic of the 'Four Little Tigers', or 'Dragons' as the Chinese refer to them (the others are South Korea, Singapore and Hong Kong).

Taiwan has a lively, uncensored press; and it has lifted all travel restrictions for its nationals. However, over this remarkable success story lies the shadow of Communist-Kuomintang politics.

The problem is a simple one. The Nationalists (Kuomintang) occupied Taiwan while still maintaining the fiction that they were the legitimate government of all China (the Republic of China, or ROC). The Communists, for their part, maintain that Taiwan is a province of China (the People's Republic of China, or PRC). The only thing that both sides could agree on was that China should be reunited 'very soon'.

Reunification was once a burning issue for the Kuomintang, but no longer. Many Taiwanese have now had the opportunity to visit mainland China and see for themselves the kind of system they might have to live under if the two countries came together again. Not surprisingly, most Taiwanese would prefer the status quo, if not outright independence.

The Taiwanese are extremely sceptical of the sincerity of China's 'one country,

two systems' promises. They have seen how China seems obsessed with crushing the limited democratic rights that the British installed in Hong Kong before the colony was handed over to China. Not surprisingly, enthusiasm for reunification (at least on China's terms) is minuscule.

China, on the other hand, is unwavering in its claims on Taiwan and is not averse to using the threat of invasion to bring the Taiwanese to the table. With Taiwan pushing hard for international recognition (attempts to enter the UN have been vetoed by China), the reality is that invasion is probably the only way China could convince the Taiwanese that it was in their interests to unite.

In 1996, Taiwan conducted its first direct presidential election (previous Taiwanese presidents had been chosen by the National Assembly). China was displeased by this exercise in democracy, widely billed as 'the first presidential election in Chinese history'. Even more disturbing to China was that the incumbent Kuomintang candidate, Lee Tenghui, has pushed hard for Taiwan's entry into the UN and the World Trade Organisation. China went berserk when Lee made a visit to the USA, denouncing the Americans as 'declaring war' on China by issuing Lee a visitor's visa. China denounced Lee as a 'splitist' (one who wants to break up the Chinese 'Motherland') – a charge that Lee denied.

China was further infuriated by the appearance on the ballot of candidate Peng Mingmin of the Democratic Progressive Party (DPP), an avowed 'splitist' who made it clear that he already considered Taiwan an independent nation. Two other candidates in the four way race took a strong pro-reunification stance, and it was clear that China favoured them.

In an attempt to scare voters away from Lee and Peng, China conducted a series of intimidating 'missile tests' just 40km off the coast of Taiwan. Taiwan sent out an international plea for help, and the US government responded by parking two American aircraft carriers just off the coast of Taiwan to ensure that China would not attempt any further military adventures. There were threats from China to 'nuke Los Angeles' if Taiwan declared independence.

Relations between the USA and China plummeted, but most of the world kept silent – only Japan spoke up and condemned China's bullying tactics. Despite China's attempt at missile diplomacy, the presidential election went off smoothly and Lee Tenghui won another term with 54% of the vote. Peng Mingmin came in second with 21% of the vote, and the remaining 25% was split between the two pro-China candidates.

Rhetoric has cooled since the election, but China's invasion threats and crushing of democratic institutions in Hong Kong has made the Taiwanese even more independence minded. The next presidential and National Assembly elections could very well give victory to the pro-independence DPP. Relations between China and Taiwan have been frosty since 1996, and the situation could yet lead to war.

Holding It Together
Overall, the Deng years brought political stability and rising living standards, but Deng died in early 1997. Jiang Zemin heads both the government and the Party as state president and Communist Party general secretary. But Jiang's power is held in place by a fragile web of alliances and compromises. The reality is that China has never had a system for orderly succession.

Faced with a looming inner-Party power struggle and an overall situation of increasingly uneven economic development, both Chinese and foreign experts have begun to voice concerns that China might break up. It has become fashionable to quote the first paragraph of *Romance of the Three Kingdoms*, a classic novel that describes the struggles to reunify the empire during the Three Kingdoms period: 'The empire, long united, must divide; long divided, must unite. Thus it has always been'.

China's empires do indeed have a long tradition of breaking up, and the problems facing the current regime make it ripe for radical change, if not total collapse. Despite spectacular economic growth rates on paper, many of the masses are no better off than they were 20 years ago. Rural incomes have stagnated in recent years, leading to widespread social unrest. Official corruption permeates the entire system despite occasional widely publicised drives to stamp it out. The central government meanwhile complains of increasing regional power – in particular the affluent coastal cities of Shanghai and Guangzhou – and has difficulties collecting the taxes.

Ironically, however, if the western press is not announcing the coming collapse of China (with its attendant consequences for the world economy), it is warning of the dangers of an ascending and newly empowered China. Defence spending has been steadily on the rise in recent years and foreign sources currently place figures at anywhere between US$10 and US$75 billion annually. Both the USA and China's Asian neighbours are watching the situation with intense interest.

The next few years will be critical for China. If China's hardline policies bring down Hong Kong's economy, the whole country could plunge into chaos. Ongoing disputes with the USA over trade issues and human rights threatens China's export industries. A war with Taiwan could be a disaster.

Slowly dismantling the bankrupt state sector is a delicate process that must continue if the government wants to deliver the affluent lifestyle that more and more Chinese are demanding as their right. And the central government will probably find itself under increasing pressure to provide greater freedoms and to undertake a degree of democratic reform. All in all, these are interesting times to be in the Middle Kingdom.

GEOGRAPHY
China is bounded to the north by deserts and to the west by the inhospitable Tibet-Qinghai Plateau. The Han Chinese, who

first built their civilisation around the Yellow River, moved south and east towards the sea. The Han did not develop as a maritime people so expansion was halted at the coast; they found themselves in control of a vast plain cut off from the rest of the world by oceans, mountains and deserts.

China is the third largest country in the world, after Russia and Canada, and has an area of 9.5 million square kilometres. Only half of China is occupied by Han Chinese; the rest is inhabited by Mongols, Tibetans, Uighurs and a host of other 'national minorities' who occupy the periphery of China. The existence of numerous minority languages is why maps of China often have two spellings for the same place – one spelling being the minority language, the other being Chinese. For example, Kashgar is the same place as Kashi.

From the capital, Beijing, the government rules 21 provinces and the five 'autonomous regions' of Inner Mongolia, Ningxia, Xinjiang, Guangxi and Tibet. The 'special municipalities' of Beijing, Tianjin and Shanghai are administered directly by the central government.

Taiwan, Hong Kong and Macau are all firmly regarded by the PRC as Chinese territory. Hong Kong has already returned to Chinese sovereignty and Macau will be handed over in 1999. There is conflict with Vietnam concerning sovereignty over the Nansha and Xisha island groups in the South China Sea; Vietnam claims both and has occupied some of the Nansha Islands. In 1989 the Chinese took some of these islands from Vietnam by force. Other disputed islands in the Nansha group are also claimed by the Philippines, Taiwan and Malaysia.

China's topography varies from mountainous regions with towering peaks to flat, featureless plains. The land surface is a bit like a staircase descending from west to east. At the top of the staircase are the plateaus of Tibet and Qinghai in the southwest, averaging 4500m above sea level. Tibet is referred to as the 'Roof of the World'. At the southern rim of the plateau is the Himalayan mountain range, with peaks averaging 6000m high; 40 peaks rise 7000m or more. Mt Everest, known to the Chinese as Qomolangma Feng, lies on the China-Nepal border.

Melting snow and ice from the mountains of western China and the Tibet-Qinghai Plateau provides the headwaters for many of the country's largest rivers: the Yangzi (Chang Jiang), Yellow (Huang He), Mekong (Lancang Jiang) and Salween (Nu Jiang) rivers. The latter runs from eastern Tibet into Yunnan Province and on into Myanmar.

The Tarim Basin is the largest inland basin in the world and is the site of the Xinjiang Autonomous Region. Here you'll find the Taklamakan Desert (the largest in China) as well as China's largest shifting salt lake, Lop Nur (luóbù pō), where nuclear bombs are tested. The Tarim Basin is bordered to the north by the Tianshan mountains.

To the east of this range is the low-lying Turpan Depression, known as the 'Oasis of Fire' and the hottest place in China. The Junggar Basin lies in the far north of Xinjiang Province, beyond the Tianshan range.

As you cross the mountains on the eastern edge of this second step of the topographical staircase, the altitude drops to less than 1000m above sea level. Here, forming the third step, are the plains of the Yangzi River valley and northern and eastern China. These plains – the homeland of the Han Chinese, their 'Middle Kingdom' – are the most important agricultural areas of the country and the most heavily populated. It should be remembered that two-thirds of China is mountain, desert or otherwise unfit for cultivation. If you exclude the largely barren regions of Inner Mongolia, Xinjiang and the Tibet-Qinghai Plateau from the remaining third, all that remains for cultivation is a meagre 15% or 20% of land area. Only this to feed more than a billion people!

In such a vast country, the waterways have taken on a central role as communication and trading links. Most of China's rivers flow east. At 6300km long, the Yangzi is the longest river in China and the third longest in the world after the Nile and the Amazon.

The Yellow River, about 5460km long and the second longest river in China, is the birthplace of Chinese civilisation. The third great waterway of China, the Grand Canal, is the longest artificial canal in the world. It originally stretched for 1800km from Hangzhou in south China to Beijing in the north, although most of it is now silted over and no longer navigable.

CLIMATE

China has a lot of it. Spread over such a vast area, the country is subject to the worst extremes in weather, from the bitterly cold to the unbearably hot. There isn't really an 'ideal' time to visit the country, so use the following information as a rough guide to avoid temperature extremes. The warmest regions in winter are found in the south and south-west in areas such as Xishuangbanna in Yunnan, the southern coast and Hainan Island. In summer, high spots like Emeishan are a welcome relief from the heat.

North

Winters in the north fall between December and March and are incredibly cold. Beijing's temperature doesn't rise above 0°C (32°F), although it will generally be dry and sunny. North of the Great Wall, into Inner Mongolia or Heilongjiang, it's much colder with temperatures dropping to -40°C (-40°F) – you'll see the curious sight of sand dunes covered in snow.

Summer in the north is around May to August. Beijing temperatures can rise to 38°C (100°F) or more. July and August are also the rainy months in this city. In both the north and south most of the rain falls during summer.

Spring and autumn are the best times for visiting the north. Daytime temperatures range from 20°C to 30°C (68°F to 86°F) and there is less rain. Although it can be

quite hot during the day, nights can be bitterly cold and bring frost.

Central

In the Yangzi River valley area (including Shanghai) summers are long, hot and humid. Wuhan, Chongqing and Nanjing have been dubbed 'the three furnaces' by the Chinese. You can expect very high temperatures any time between April and October.

Winters are short and cold, with temperatures dipping well below freezing – almost as cold as Beijing. It can also be wet and miserable at any time apart from summer. While it is impossible to pinpoint an ideal time to visit, spring and autumn are probably best.

South

In the far south, around Guangzhou, the hot, humid periods last from around April to September, and temperatures can rise to 38°C (100°F). This is also the rainy season. Typhoons are liable to hit the south-east coast between July and September.

There is a short winter from January to March. It's nowhere near as cold as in the north, but temperature statistics don't really indicate just how cold it can get, so bring warm clothes.

Autumn and spring can be good times to visit, with day temperatures in the 20°C to 25°C (68°F to 75°F) range. However, it can be miserably wet and cold, with perpetual rain or drizzle, so be prepared.

North-West

It gets hot in summer, but at least it's dry. The desert regions can be scorching in the daytime. Turpan, which sits in a depression 150m below sea level, more than deserves the title of the 'hottest place in China' with maximums of around 47°C (117°F).

In winter this region is as formidably cold as the rest of northern China. In Ürümqi the average temperature in January is around -10°C (14°F), with minimums down to almost -30°C (-22°F). Temperatures in Turpan are only slightly more favourable to human existence.

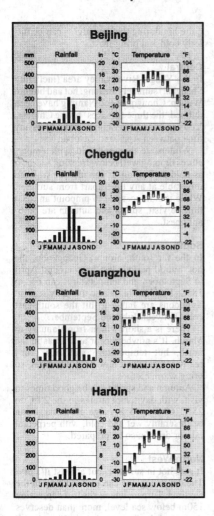

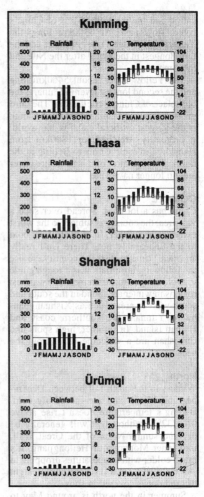

Tibet

In Tibet it's easy to get the impression that all four seasons have been compressed into one day. Temperatures can vary from below zero during the evening and early morning to a sizzling 38°C (100°F) at midday, but it always feels remarkably cool in the shade.

Winter brings intense cold and fierce winds. Snowfall is far less common in Tibet than the name 'Land of Snows' implies – it's an arid place and the sun is quick to melt off snowfalls. Rainfall is scarcest in the north and west of Tibet. Northern monsoons can sweep across the plains for days on end, often whipping up dust storms, sandstorms, snowstorms, or (rarely) rainstorms.

ECOLOGY & ENVIRONMENT

If you think that travelling abroad is like getting a breath of fresh air, you'd better not look at the facts and figures on China's environment. China's current economic boom has come at the expense of controls on air pollution, land clearing, deforestation, endangered species, rural and industrial waste ... the list goes on.

China has a very long history of development and exploitation of its natural resources and it is only more recently that China has acknowledged the fact that it has an environment to protect. Prior to the reforms that began in 1978, environmental concerns were more likely to be dismissed as a bourgeois conspiracy. For a country that has constantly been going through an enormity of social change and development, it is surprising that there is much of an environment left to be concerned about. Despite this, there is a large body of concerned scientists and economists who have been lobbying for the current reforms and a 'spirit of learning' from abroad.

Energy Use & Air Pollution

Five out of ten of the world's most polluted cities are found in China, and it is estimated that by 2005 China may have the not-so-prestigious status of being the world's largest source of air pollution. The land of the bicycle is facing stiff competition with an increase of cars and trucks on the road, which is exacerbating the already poor air quality of most Chinese cities.

Most of the major cities lie smothered under great canopies of smog. Tests conducted by the World Health Organisation (WHO) and China's National Environmental Protection Agency showed levels of airborne suspended particles average 526 micrograms per square metre in northern China (WHO recommends a safe limit of 60 to 90 micrograms per square metre). The first problem is coal. It provides for some 70% of China's energy needs and around 900 million tonnes of it go up in smoke every year. Some of it comes back to earth in the form of acid rain. This heavy reliance on coal has lead to an estimated 40 per cent of the country being affected by acid rain. Even Korea and Japan have been airing their concerns about damage to their forests from acid rain that is believed to have come from China.

Along with China's ongoing building boom comes increased air and noise pollution, as well as the increased pressure on the country's infrastructure. While the government continues to echo the need to fulfil the people's basic needs, it is depriving most of them of a clean environment to enjoy their new-found wealth in.

China is believed to be the least efficient consumer of energy on the planet and the future looks bleak with the current growth of the economy fuelling an incredible appetite for new energy resources. Renewable energy use is still in its infant stages in China, with most of the resources going into hydro power. The main problem is that renewable energy is uncompetitive against an unsustainable and heavily subsidised coal power industry.

Desertification & Land Use

China has been combating the spread of its deserts for more than 40 years via aggressive afforestation programmes. They have met with mixed success, as they're continually hampered by the ongoing stress placed on the land by overgrazing and irrigation. Nevertheless, forest coverage has doubled since 1949.

Every year large dust storms blow across Korea and Japan from China's loess plateau. The main cause of these storms is the desertification of large parts of northern and western China due to a lack of sustainable land management. China has been trying to avoid future drought and soil erosion through afforestation. Unfortunately this has been hampered by the expansion of cash crops, particularly rubber, into old-growth forests by cash-strapped villages.

Water & Wetlands

China's rivers and wetlands face a great deal

of pressure from draining and reclamation, as well as pollution from untreated industrial liquids, domestic sewerage, human waste and chemicals. It is estimated that China annually dumps three billion tonnes of untreated water into the ocean via its rivers. Some reports indicate that half the population is supplied with polluted water. This poor quality water, coupled with often acute water shortages, is creating significant environmental health hazards.

Environment versus Development

International expertise is slowly convincing reserve managers to better implement conservation policies. However, the economic necessity of resource exploitation usually prevails over badly managed conservation policies.

The good news is that the Chinese are acutely aware of both the short and long term effects of continuing degradation of grassland, forest, cropland, aquatic and coastal ecosystems. The problem lies in the low priority given to environmental and conservation issues in the light of the emphasis on the rapid expansion and development of the agricultural, industrial and energy resource base. Two dramatic examples of this are the construction of the Three Gorges Dam (Sanxiamen) on the Yangzi River and the Xiaolangdi Dam on the Yellow River. Both dams promise much, but the realities of such grand schemes may be harder to fulfil.

Culture

China is faced with the pressing problem of protecting its dwindling cultural heritage from the pressures of economic advancement. Traditionally, the communist authorities have viewed most cultural relics as memories of the tyranny and oppression of the past and therefore destroyed or let them go to waste. However, Beijing has recently switched to a policy of attempting to salvage remaining structures of historical and cultural importance in a nationalistic bid to embody the country's grand history. With an increase in cultural tourism, there will be more incentive to preserve important sites due to the resulting cash flow.

Global Implications

The impact of China's environmental problems doesn't stop at the country's borders – acid rain, desert sand storms, and silted and polluted rivers are all too familiar to China's neighbours. Across the north of China, rampaging natural fires are believed to consume more than 200 million tonnes of coal a year, further exacerbating China's contribution to global warming.

Education

None of these environmental hazards is good for anyone's health, and the government has made noises about taking action.

The problem is not that China lacks legislation designed to curb the worst excesses of industry (the central government recently established 230 new environmental standards), but that these laws are rarely enforced. It's not unusual to see huge billboards proclaiming the need to 'Preserve the Environment for Future Generations' plonked right next to huge industrial complexes belching out plumes of viscous-looking smoke and oozing untreated waste into a nearby river.

The countryside is feeling the pressure too, with pesticide poisoning becoming more prevalent. There has also been a move away from traditional farming methods towards the increased reliance on costly and hazardous fertilisers and pesticides.

The compelling economic pressure to exploit nature is exacerbated by a lack of awareness and education on the part of the masses. This translates into a lack of concern, although recent surveys suggest that a large proportion of the urban population is unhappy with the current state of the environment. The government is tackling the issue with radio and television campaigns which include publicising the names of companies and industries responsible for polluting the environment. There has also been an increase in the severity of penalties for violating China's conservation laws, with the death penalty and life sentences not uncommon. However, it must be said that there is still very little room for debating the issues in the media.

For the most part, the Chinese people seem to be taking the attitude that China can get rich and dirty, and then spend some of the proceeds on cleaning up. It's a time-honoured tradition, but then China (the world's most populous nation) is unique in the grand scale it's abusing the environment. If the environment continues to be a secondary concern, then China's economic development may be severely retarded in the new millennium.

FLORA & FAUNA

Although China has an incredible diversity of plant and animal life, the closest encounters most travellers to China will have with them is at the dinner table. Don't be surprised if you spot the domestic dog and cat roasted on a spit, or even a marinated rat on a stick. More exotic dishes might include snake, monkey, pangolin, bear, giant salamander and racoon. The Chinese don't stop with their animals, but take delight in the fact that almost anything that grows in China can be used for cooking.

Stir-fries aside, China is endowed with an extremely diverse range of natural vegetation and animal life. There are about 30,000 species of seed plants and 2,500 species of forest trees, representing a large variety of genera, many of which are indigenous to China. Unfortunately, human beings have had a considerable impact and much of China's rich natural heritage is rare, endangered or extinct. Many animals are officially protected, though illegal hunting and trapping continues. A bigger challenge is habitat destruction, caused by encroaching agriculture, urbanisation and industrial pollution. To the government's credit, more than 700 nature reserves have been established protecting about 7% of China's land area.

Flora

One of China's most famous plants must be bamboo. There are actually more than 300 species of bamboo plant covering about 3% of the total forest area in China. Most of this bamboo is located in the sub-tropical zones south of the Yangzi River. The plant is not only valued by the giant panda, but cultivated for use as a building material and food.

Many other well known plants are indigenous to China, including the azalea, rhododendron, lotus flower, magnolia, ginkgo, maple, birch, poplar and spruce. The variety and intermixture of temperate and tropical plants in China is best understood by comparing the vegetation of Jilin Province in the semifrigid north and Hainan Province in the tropical south. It would be difficult to find one common plant species shared by the two provinces with the exception of a few weeds.

China's diversity of ecosystems supports an equivalent range of flora: the tropical forests of South China; the desert and steppe vegetation of north-western China; the taiga coniferous forests of the border areas adjoining Russia; and the mangrove swamps along the shores of the South China Sea. Tropical and temperate coniferous forests with broad-leaved evergreen and deciduous plants prevail in the southern provinces of Hainan, Yunnan and Guangxi, whereas vast areas of desolate and very sparse salt-tolerant and drought-resistant vegetation prevails in the arid north-west. Along the borders of the Gobi desert are wide plains of grasslands and just across to the north-east are the last great tracts of forests in China.

Fauna

Animals are animals – in the wild they wisely avoid humans. Other than some pathetic specimens in zoos, it's unlikely that you will get to see many exotic animals in China. However, China's wealth of vegetation and variety of landscapes has fostered the development of a great diversity of fauna.

In spite of the odds against them, a number of rare animals continue to survive

Despite a number of international conservation and breeding programmes, the Giant Panda remains very much on the endangered list.

in small and remote areas of China. Notable among such survivors are the small species of alligator in central and eastern China, the giant salamander in western China, and the Yangzi River dolphin. The diversity of fauna is perhaps greatest in the valleys and ranges of Sichuan and Tibet and it is here that the giant panda is confined.

Perhaps no animal better represents both the beauty and the struggle of wildlife in China than the panda. These splendid animals are endangered by a combination of hunting, habitat encroachment and natural disasters. Through a number of joint programmes run by Chinese and overseas agencies, animals like the giant panda and the Yangzi River dolphin are receiving more attention and protection, which will hopefully guarantee their survival.

Throughout the Chinese mountains, takin (or goat antelope), wild yaks, argali sheep, numerous species of pheasants, and a variety of laughing thrushes may be found. The extreme north-eastern part of China is inhabited by some interesting mammals, such as reindeer, moose, musk deer, bears, sables and tigers.

This region also features considerable birdlife, such as cranes, ducks, bustards, swans and herons. Good bird-watching possibilities exist, especially in the spring. Some good places for this activity include the Zhalong Nature Reserve in Heilongjiang Province; Qinghai Lake in Qinghai Province; and Poyang Lake in northern Jiangxi Province, China's largest freshwater lake.

For sheer diversity of flora and fauna, the tropical south of Yunnan Province, particularly the area around Xishuangbanna, is one of the richest in China. This region provides habitats for the parrot, hornbill, slender loris, gibbon, snub-nosed monkey, and herds of wild Indian elephants. Sadly, China's variety of fauna is nowhere more obvious than the array of tasty dishes available on most menus throughout the country.

If you're interested in delving further into China's flora and fauna, two good books on the subject are *Living Treasures* by Tang Xiyang and *The Natural History of China* by Zhao Ji, et al.

Cruelty to Animals
While China's treatment of animals is not the best, it's not the worst either. Travellers most frequently come up against hard reality when they visit some of the markets, many of which resemble take-away zoos. The southern provinces of Guangdong and Guangxi are particularly notable for the wide selection of unusual still-living delicacies on offer – dogs, cats, rats, snakes, monkeys, scorpions, lizards, turtles and other exotica.

In western countries, shoppers are usually shielded from the messy business of slaughtering animals, but in China it's often done right in front of the customer – for larger animals, a swift blow on the head with a club is the usual means of execution.

Things can get nasty down on the farm – the way in which deer are confined in dark hovels is not very humane. The notorious bear-bile extraction industry has come in for particularly virulent condemnation by animal rights activists.

You Are What You Eat

The Chinese notion of 'health food' (*yàoshàn*) differs somewhat from that of the west. While western health food emphasises low-fat, high-fibre and a lack of chemical additives, the Chinese version puts its main emphasis on the use of traditional ingredients and herbs.

It is a widely held belief in China that overwork and sex wears down the body and that such 'exercise' will result in a short life. To counter the wear and tear, some Chinese practice *jinbu* (the consumption of tonic food and herbs). This can include, for example, drinking raw snake's blood or bear's bile, or eating deer antlers, all of which are claimed to improve vision, strength and sexual potency.

In a literal interpretation of 'you are what you eat', it's widely believed that consuming tiger meat will produce a miraculous increase in one's vigour and virility. Rhinoceros horn has long been touted as a tonic for whatever ails you. Eating monkey's brain is said to increase intelligence, and may also explain the behaviour of Beijing's taxi drivers.

Environmentalists are not too happy about the consumption of products such as tiger meat and rhinoceros horn, given that both tigers and rhinos are endangered species. To be fair, the Chinese government has cracked down on the practice, and much of what gets passed off nowadays as ultra-expensive tiger meat and rhino horn is in fact fake.

Animal rights activists have sharply criticised the way that bear's bile is obtained – by strapping a living bear into a metal vest and running a tube into the creature's liver. However, China has reacted to such criticism the same way the country reacts to reports of human rights violations – by telling everyone that this is one of China's 'internal affairs'.

If the animal rights activists happen to be British, the Chinese remind them of Britain's rude behaviour in the Opium War of 1841; if the critics are Americans, they get reminded of 19th century slavery in southern USA; the Aussies get reminded about mistreatment of the Aborigines. No word yet on just what the bears get told. ∎

However, for westerners ready to take to the streets to demonstrate against such abuses, it might be worth recalling China's record on human rights too.

Endangered species

China's endangered plants and animal list is depressingly long. Animals on the list include the giant panda, snow leopard, Yangzi River dolphin, South China tiger, crested ibis, Asian elephant, golden monkey, red-crowned crane and black-crowned crane, to name just a few.

Unprotected forest areas are diminishing due to intensive farmland cultivation, the reclaiming of wetlands, damming of rivers, industrial and rural waste, and desertification, putting more pressure on isolated populations.

Most of China's endangered species are found in and adjoining the 500 or so protected nature reserves. The problems of monitoring and managing the reserves, as well as adjacent areas, are complicated by a complex network of government departments that are supposedly responsible.

National Parks

China has some outstanding areas of natural beauty, but the country has only recently made a belated effort to establish national parks. Some notable ones include Jiuzhaigou in Sichuan Province, Zhangjiajie in Hunan Province and Changbaishan in Jilin Province. Most of China's sacred mountains (including Putuoshan, Wutaishan, Emeishan, Huashan and Jiuhuashan) have also been converted into national parks.

The prospect for increasing the total number of national parks looks good, however, environmentalists shouldn't cheer too loudly since most of China's parklands are under heavy pressure from commercial development.

GOVERNMENT & POLITICS

Precious little is known about the inner workings of the Chinese government, but what is known is that the entire monolithic structure, from grassroots work units to the upper echelons of political power, is controlled by the Communist Party.

Power in China is by no means visible in the form of appointed leaders and designated institutions, as could be seen in the case of Deng Xiaoping, who long before his death remained the most powerful man in China even when he was officially retired and held no official titles whatsoever.

The highest authority rests with the Standing Committee of the CCP Politburo. The Politburo comprises 25 members and below it is the 210 member Central Committee, made up of younger Party members and provincial Party leaders. At grassroots level the Party forms a parallel system to the administrations in the army, universities, government and industries. Real authority is exercised by the Party representatives at each level in these organisations. They, in turn, are responsible to the Party officials in the hierarchy above them, thus ensuring strict central control.

The day-to-day running of the country lies with the State Council, which is directly under the control of the CCP. The State Council is headed by the premier and beneath the premier are four vice-premiers, 10 state councillors, a secretary-general, 45 ministers and various other agencies. The State Council implements the decisions made by the Politburo: it draws up quotas, assesses planning, establishes priorities and organises finances. The ministries include Public Security, Education, Defence, Culture, Forestry, Railways, Tourism, Minority Affairs, Radio & TV, the Bank of China and Family Planning.

Rubber-stamping the decisions of the CCP leadership is the National People's Congress (NPC). It comprises a 'democratic alliance' of both Party members and non-Party members who include intellectuals, technicians and industrial managers. In theory they are empowered to amend the constitution and to choose the premier and members of the State Council. The catch is that all these office-holders must first be recommended by the Central Committee, and thus the NPC is only an approving body.

The Chinese government is also equipped with a massive bureaucracy. The term 'cadre' is usually applied to bureaucrats, and their monopoly on power means that wide-ranging perks are a privilege of rank for all and sundry – from the lowliest clerks to the shadowy puppet masters of Zhongnanhai. China's bureaucratic tradition is a long one. It's chief purpose seems to be to make the life of ordinary Chinese as miserable as possible.

At grassroots level, the basic unit of social organisation outside the family is the work unit (dānwèi). Every Chinese person is theoretically a member of one, whether he or she works in a hospital, school, office, factory or village, although many Chinese nowadays slip through the net by being self-employed or working in a private operation. For those who are members, tight controls are exercised by the leaders of the unit they belong to.

The work unit is a perfect organ of social control and little proceeds without it. It approves marriages and divorces and even childbirth. It assigns housing, sets salaries, handles mail, recruits Party members, keeps files on each unit member, arranges transfers to other jobs or other parts of the country, and gives permission to travel abroad. The work unit's control extends into every part of the individual's life.

The wild card in the system is the army. Comprising land forces, the navy and the air force, it has a total of around 2.9 million members. China is divided into seven military regions, each with its own military leadership – in some cases with strong regional affiliations.

A breakdown of central power might result in a return to the warlordism of the early 20th century or a unified putsch by the PLA. In any event, the PLA is a force to be reckoned with.

Political Dissidence & Repression

The brutal massacre in Tiananmen Square in 1989 focused world attention on China's political repression, but it was not the end of the story. In the mid-1990s there were a few cases of high-profile, relatively organised dissent. In mid-1995, 12 petitions had been signed by prominent intellectuals, largely calling for greater freedom of speech and, specifically, a re-evaluation of the Tiananmen Square protests.

The petitions resulted predictably in a round of arrests, and at the time of writing the hardliners seemed to be reasserting themselves and China was cracking down once again. Wang Dan, a leader in the Tiananmen Square protests, was re-arrested in 1996 and sentenced to 11 years in prison. Wei Jingsheng received another 14 year sentence. In 1997, two dissidents in Shenzhen (Li Wenming and Guo Baosheng) were each sentenced to 3½ years in prison. Many other dissidents are being held under house arrest.

One of the great problems of Chinese dissenters is that they rarely find much to agree on. The ringleaders of the Tiananmen protests, most of whom fled the country in the wake of the massacre, have failed to organise as a group outside China, and some of them have given up politics entirely; Chen Kaige, famously captured on TV arguing it out with Li Peng, was last seen running a Sizzler-style steak bar in California.

Other prominent foreign-based dissidents such as Fang Lizhi and Liu Binyan are considered too old and too removed from current events in China to really matter to many young dissidents. It's fair to say that, for the moment, China has successfully crushed any organised resistance to the government.

Democracy?

While the previous description of China's government makes it appear anything but democratic, there is one curious anomaly – local governments for villages with a population under 10,000. In the 1990s, a little-noticed reform permitted small villages to elect their own leaders.

Optimists have pointed to this reform, suggesting it's the beginning of a major movement towards democracy throughout China. Believers in this scenario predict that China will continue to democratise as the wheelchair leadership dies off and is replaced by the younger generation. The fact that more and more young Chinese have had the chance to travel, live, work and study in the west should encourage this trend.

Pessimists note that the central government has swiftly squashed all attempts to extend democratic elections to larger towns and cities. Certainly, the case of Hong Kong is not encouraging. Hong Kong's democratically elected Legislative Council was dismissed on the day the British handed over the colony to China. The world will no doubt be watching with bated breath to see if the dragon can be tamed by a foreign notion called democracy.

ECONOMY

Under Mao, China's economy was a prisoner to ideology and incompetence. The reign of Deng Xiaoping (essentially 1977 to 1997) has been a period of reforms. The moribund Maoist economy has been dramatically reinvigorated. In short, Deng chose a pragmatic approach to achieving the so-called 'Four Modernisations': namely, modernisation of China's industry, agriculture, defence and science and technology. The aim is to transform China into a modern state by the year 2000.

Many observers now say that China has transformed itself from a left-wing dictatorship into a right-wing dictatorship. The transition, however, from the centrally controlled, ideologically motivated economy of the Mao years to Deng's vast free-enterprise experiment has not been an entirely smooth one. The hurdle has been the sponsor of change itself: the Party. The transition has had one overwhelming consequence – guaranteed far-reaching control of the Party's subjects. But economic freedoms have eroded Party power and will continue to do so. Thus the Party has written a catch-22 clause into its mandate to rule: without continued economic freedoms, the Party's days are numbered; with continued economic freedoms Party influence will continue to diminish. The result has been bursts of economic growth followed by panicky austerity drives.

Rural China was the birthplace of Deng's pioneering economic reforms. Having been forcibly collectivised during the Mao era, the 'household responsibility system' of the late 1970s allowed farmers to sell whatever they wanted on the free market after government quotas had been filled. Productivity rose and a new era of plenty was heralded for rural China.

Unfortunately, rural earnings lag far behind urban incomes. Increased mechanisation and fertiliser use has increased productivity, but has also led to a scarcity of work – there are perhaps as many as 100 million farm labourers without regular employment. Rural industries (factories in the countryside) have absorbed some of the surplus agricultural workers, but one of the costs has been serious rural pollution, which threatens China's delicate agricultural land and fisheries. As many as 15 million peasants a year flock to the coastal cities every year in hopes of finding employment – often they end up working long hours in poorly paid factory jobs.

The state is also saddled with some 100,000 state-owned firms, of which at least half are thought to be losing money. Together they employ over 100 million workers; restructuring would result in massive lay-offs and social dislocation.

China also faces a banking crisis. The state-run banks continue to pour money into near-bankrupt state companies that will never be able to repay the loans. Technically, China's banks are already insolvent – disaster has been staved off by the high savings rate. As long as the masses do not try to withdraw their savings from the banks, the system can stay afloat. However, the day may come when Chinese workers will want their cash back (perhaps to buy a house), and the banks simply won't have the money. It's this thought that keeps China's financiers awake at night.

POPULATION & PEOPLE

The official figures for 1996 show mainland China (excluding Taiwan, Hong Kong and Macau) with a population of 1.2 billion people. Officially, only 30% of the total population is classified as urban, which is low by any standards (Australia's population is 86% urban). The figures are changing though, as the countryside urbanises and farmers abandon the land and migrate into the cities in search of work.

The huge population has to be fed with the produce of around 15% to 20% of the land they live on – the sum total of China's arable land. The rest is barren wasteland or can only be lightly grazed. Much of the productive land is also vulnerable to flood and drought caused by the vagaries of China's summer monsoons or unruly rivers.

Worse still, China's arable land is shrinking at an alarming rate. Industrialisation, urbanisation and erosion are robbing the country of valuable farmland while the population continues to grow. The Malthusian prospect of an ever-growing population, with an ever-shrinking capacity to feed itself, led the government to promote a limited birth control programme in the 1950s, but this was abandoned during the Cultural Revolution. The responsibility lies with Mao Zedong, whose decision was probably his greatest mistake. He believed that birth control was a capitalist plot to make China weak and that the country would find strength in a large population. His ideas very much reflected his background of the peasant farmer for whom many hands make light work in the fields. It wasn't until 1973 that a nationwide birth-control programme was instituted, with each couple permitted to have just one child.

The current plan is to limit growth to 1.25 billion people by the year 2000, hold that figure steady somehow, and allow birth control and natural mortality to reduce the population to 700 million, which China's leaders estimate would be ideal. Current projections, however, indicate that China's population will be close on 1.5 billion by the year 2010, and that the present population could double within 50 years.

In recent years the main thrust of the campaign in the cities has been to encourage couples to sign a one child pledge by offering them an extra month's salary per year until the child is 14, plus housing normally reserved for a family of four (a promise sometimes not kept because of the housing shortage). If the couple have a second child then the privileges are rescinded, and penalties such as demotion at work or even loss of job are imposed. If a woman has an abortion it entitles her to a vacation with pay.

Birth-control measures appear to be working in the cities, but it's difficult to say what's happening in the villages or if the target of zero growth can ever be reached. The catch is that Chinese agriculture still relies on human muscle and farmers still find it desirable to have many children.

On the other hand, families who do abide by the one child policy will often go to great lengths to make sure their child is male. This is particularly true in rural China, where the ancient custom of female infanticide continues to this day. In parts of China, this is creating a serious imbalance of the sexes. One survey in Shaanxi Province, for example, determined that 145 male infants were being born for every 100 females. The overall average for China is 114 males for every 100 females. Spread over such a huge population, this amounts to a lot of unmarriageable men liable to become very frustrated and potentially dangerous.

If China's one child policy does succeed, one soon-to-be-felt consequence will be a rapidly ageing population. The baby boom generated by Mao's policies has created a population that is today overwhelmingly young. The baby bust of the one child policy will create the opposite. The consequence of having to support a large number of retired geriatrics in the next century is yet another challenge that China will be soon facing. Only when the birth and death rates are in balance (and China is able to re-adopt a two child policy) will the population be reasonably middle-aged.

Han Chinese make up about 93% of the population; the rest is composed of China's 55 officially recognised ethnic minorities. China actually claims that there are 56 by creating the somewhat bogus 'Gaoshan' minority in Taiwan. It's 'somewhat bogus' because the nine aboriginal tribes in Taiwan all reject the label 'Gaoshan' which Beijing has assigned to them, and because many Taiwanese do not agree that Taiwan is part of China.

Although minorities account for about 7% of the population, they are distributed over some 50% of Chinese-controlled territory, mostly in the sensitive border regions. Minority separatism has always been a threat to the stability of China, particularly among the Uighurs and the Tibetans, who have poor and often volatile relations with the Han Chinese. The minority regions provide China with the greater part of its livestock and hold vast untapped deposits of minerals.

Keeping the minorities under control has been a continuous problem for the Han Chinese. Tibet and Xinjiang are heavily garrisoned by Chinese troops, partly to protect China's borders and partly to prevent rebellion among the local population. Han Chinese migration to minority areas has been encouraged as a means of controlling the minorities by the sheer weight of numbers.

The Chinese government has also set up special training centres, like the National Minorities Institute in Beijing, to train loyal minority cadres for these regions. Since 1976 the government has tried to diffuse discontent by relaxing some of its grasp on

Fengshui

Fengshui, literally meaning 'wind and water', is a collection of ancient geomantic principles that supports the existence of bodies of water and configurations of land forms which direct the flow of universal *qi* (vital energy or cosmic currents). With the help of a fengshui master this qi can be successfully courted to maximise a person's wealth, happiness, longevity and procreation, however, at the same time, a negative flow of qi may bring on disaster.

One reason for fengshui's success may be that wealth *(cai)*, happiness *(fu)*, long life *(shou)* and healthy offspring *(zi)* are the four major concerns of fengshui and parallel the general concerns of the Chinese population.

Pagodas, temples, houses and even whole cities and villages have been located and built so as to be in harmony with the surrounding landscape. Even a household will try and maximise its own benefits by placing the family's house, tomb, business or furniture in an appropriate location so as to receive the optimum qi. The positioning of such a structure will determine the lasting wellbeing of the inhabitants; good placement should result in good fortune.

Fengshui cosmology has been used to select the most auspicious site of cities as far back as the 3rd or 4th century. Yet, Fengshui as a tradition has been constantly attacked throughout Chinese history – by imperialists, nationalists and Communists alike. Despite the aggressive actions of this century, it has survived and prospered among the people. While Chinese geomancy is inherently conservative, especially in architecture, accusations of disturbances to the natural balance of fengshui have been often vented by peasants against the state. Even during the early stages of European and Japanese expansion into China, many Chinese were incensed at the disturbances caused by the construction of train lines and over-shadowing churches to their happy balance of seemingly hidden powers in the surrounding geography. The Chinese called for the removal of the offending steeples and the redirecting of train lines so as to be more in harmony with the local fengshui.

Fengshui has its origins on the mainland of China, but during the last century it has been more closely associated with Singapore, Hong Kong, Taiwan and the Overseas Chinese communities. This is mainly due to the way the Communist regime has exploited fengshui as a means of securing power for some, while breaking the fengshui of

the day-to-day life of the minority peoples, in particular allowing temples and mosques closed during the Cultural Revolution to reopen.

EDUCATION

China records an official literacy rate of 80%, which is above average for a third world country, but still far short of developed country standards. Many minority people cannot read Chinese characters, but may be literate in their own native scripts.

In theory, China still upholds the Confucian system in which one gains entrance to the best schools through competitive examinations rather than connections. In practice, money and political connections definitely help. Getting one's child into an elite school is the dream of every Chinese parent, but only about 1% of applicants are so lucky.

Until very recently, all education right through to university level was 100% state-funded. In return, university graduates must accept whatever job the state wishes to assign them to. However, the past couple of years has seen a radical new experiment – students can pay their own way through others. During the Cultural Revolution the authorities set about the systematic destruction of graves, ancestral halls, shrines and tablets to destroy the peasants' links with their ancestors and clans. The authorities classified the practice of fengshui as illegal and yet at the same time used fengshui to punish those of a 'bad-class' background, by destroying their ancestors' tombs and cremating the bones to truncate the family lines.

A fengshui master or geomancer is normally trained by his father and passes his skills down through the generations. When called upon to inspect a prospective housing or grave site, the master usually brings along his compass *(loupan)* and calendar *(nongli)* and after a little scrutiny, involving the consultation of his tools of trade and an inspection of the nearby landscape to locate the Green Dragon and White Tiger, decides the most favourable location. Then a combination of dates including, say the birth of the owner, is included in the analysis to decide upon the starting date for construction.

This is a simplistic summary of a trade that draws on more intuition and practical experience than books of learning, however, if a geomancer is in possession of a fengshui manual or calendar then he would have an advantage over many others who rely purely on oral and practical training.

The geomancer is also often called upon to aid in the determination of appropriate marriage and funeral dates, as well as to write 'prayers' to protect and bring good fortune upon a household.

During the past two decades rural China has seen a building boom that has not only increased the demand for optimal qi sites, but also put the pressure on possible disturbances to the fengshui of the neighbours. The demand for the fengshui master has seen a recent increase in areas outside the placement of a house or grave. Today, households are more likely to call on the mysterious powers of the geomancer for advice on how to realign the fengshui of households that have been afflicted by premature death, sickness, poor business performance and mental disease.

So what do you do if you require the services of a fengshui master? The current situation in mainland China is a lot more tolerant of geomancers and a cash payment would be generally appreciated for services rendered, but don't bargain too hard as it may disturb the fragile qi. ■

school and are then free to take a job of their own choosing. Of course, most Chinese cannot afford this, although some manage by borrowing money from their relatives.

China has belatedly recognised the economic value of having an educated population at least semi-fluent in various foreign languages. English is by far the most popular foreign language, and there's many young Chinese who will be anxious to practice with you.

If you want to meet English-speaking Chinese then go to the 'English corners' which have developed in many large Chinese cities. Usually held on a Sunday morning in a convenient park, Chinese people who speak, or are learning, English gather to practise the language. Also seek out the 'English Salons' – evening get-togethers at which the Chinese practise English, listen to lectures or hold debates in English.

Don't expect to remain a member of the audience for very long – you may soon find yourself giving the evening lecture and struggling to answer difficult questions about the outside world.

SOCIETY & CONDUCT
Traditional Culture

Chinese culture literally took a beating during the Cultural Revolution – the country has yet to recover completely. It should be noted that there is a cultural gap between Hong Kong, Macau and the rest of China. Hong Kong and Macau, while outwardly more modern, are also more traditionally Chinese because the Cultural Revolution didn't have such a big effect there.

Some of the more notable aspects of traditional Chinese culture are mentioned below.

Face

'Face' could be loosely defined as 'status', 'ego' or 'self-respect' and is by no means alien to foreigners. Essentially it's about avoiding being made to look stupid or being forced to back down in front of others. In the west it's somewhat important – in China, it's critically important.

A negotiated settlement of differences that provides benefits to both parties is always preferable to confrontation. Outright confrontation should be reserved as a last resort (Chinese are not shy of using it) and problems should first be tackled with smiling persistence – if one tack fails, try another.

Handling Paper

If you want to impress your Chinese hosts, always use both hands when presenting them with a piece of paper. This gesture shows respect, but only use it if the person you're dealing with is somebody important (like a government official or a business associate).

This tradition has been frowned upon by the Communists as being yet another throwback to feudal times, but using two hands still goes down well.

Fortune Telling

Being a fortune teller was not the safest of occupations during the Cultural Revolution. Most of them either quickly changed their profession or spent 20 years breaking rocks at a labour camp in Qinghai.

It's a different case in Hong Kong and Macau. The lucrative business of fortune telling is how many temples in Hong Kong and Macau pay their bills. Palmists (who also read your face) set up in some of the night markets.

Dos & Don'ts
Speaking Frankly

People often don't say what they think, but rather what they think you want to hear or what will save face for them. Thus, the staff at the CAAC office may tell you that your flight will be here 'very soon' even if they know it will be delayed for two days.

Smiling

A smile doesn't always mean happiness. Some Chinese people smile when they are embarrassed or worried. This explains the situation where the foreign tourist is ranting and raving at the staff in the hotel lobby, while the person behind the desk stands there grinning from ear to ear.

Guanxi

In their daily life, Chinese often have to compete for goods or services in short supply and many have been assigned jobs for which they have zero interest and often no training. Those who have *guānxì* (connections) usually get what they want because the connections network is, of course, reciprocal.

Obtaining goods or services through connections is informally referred to as 'going through the back door' (*zǒu hòu mén*). Cadres are well placed for this activity; foreigners will have to resort to some sort of gift giving (bribery?) to achieve the same result.

Negotiate Over Dinner

If you're planning to cut any business deals in China, you'd best invite the relevant officials or business partners to dinner. Proposals which were 'impossible' a few hours earlier can suddenly become very possible when discussed over a plate of Beijing duck and a bottle of Johnny Walker.

Gift Giving

This is a complicated issue with the Chinese. It's good manners when visiting people at their homes to bring

---

Up in Smoke

Both Mao Zedong and Deng Xiaoping were chain smokers, and both lived to a ripe old age. Nevertheless, awareness of tobacco's harmful effects are sinking in. The Chinese government is beginning to make good on a long-held promise to do something about public smoking, banning cigarettes in airports and many railway stations. Overall, however, the authorities have a real battle on their hands.

In rural China smokers are very cavalier towards non-smokers, and buses and trains are generally thick with wafting cigarette smoke. Smokers in buses often toss their burning butts into the aisles where they continue to smoulder and occasionally start fires. Tossing lit cigarette butts out of bus windows is also common, with little regard about where they might land. Hotel rooms are often covered in cigarette burns – many Chinese guests grind their cigarettes into the carpet.

As with drinking hard liquor, smoking in public has traditionally been a male activity, though more women are starting to smoke. If you cannot tolerate smoking in crowded public places like buses and restaurants, you will either have to leave the country or buy a gas mask – the Chinese will be positively offended if you tell them not to smoke.

For smokers, on the other hand, the good news is that cigarettes are cheap (around US$1 per pack for foreign brands) and you can smoke almost anywhere. Chinese cigarettes are a mixed bag. The cheapest brands can cost less than Y2, while the best brands (such as Red Pagoda Mountain – *hongtashan)* cost double the most expensive foreign cigarettes. Curiously, regardless of the price, they all taste very much the same. ∎

---

some sort of gift, especially if you've been invited for a meal. Flowers are OK, or a box of chocolates. Money is not generally appropriate (and indeed would be an insult). Imported goods have much prestige value and will help you win points in the face game.

One of the reasons to give gifts is to build some connections (see 'guanxi' previously).

Tobacco Diplomacy At least in the case of male-to-male relationships, it is always polite to offer a cigarette when meeting somebody. You are under no obligation to smoke, but if refusing always remember to do so politely with a smile and a wave of the hand.

When offering a cigarette to someone, you must extend the open pack with a cigarette protruding from it – it would be impolite to remove a single cigarette from the pack and hand it over.

When dealing with officialdom, ciga-

rettes make an excellent subtle bribe. To really curry favour, you could then perhaps tell the official to 'just keep the pack, I'm trying to quit smoking'.

If you want to engage in this sort of tobacco diplomacy, prestigious foreign brands like Marlboro and 555 are almost mandatory.

Greater China The official party line is that Taiwan is a part of China, even if the Taiwanese don't happen to agree. Ditto for Tibet, the Spratly Islands and perhaps even Chinatown in San Francisco. The educational system also pounds this into everyone's head. The authorities are constantly warning of plots by foreign imperialists and 'splitists' who want to divide and weaken China.

In short, if you have any pro-independence sentiments about Tibet and Taiwan (or Xinjiang for that matter), you'd best keep them to yourself.

Chinese Arts

Many of China's ancient art treasures were ransacked or razed to the ground during the Cultural Revolution. Precious pottery, calligraphy and embroidery was defaced or destroyed.

Fortunately, since the early 1970s a great deal of work has been done to restore what was destroyed in the Cultural Revolution. Initially, restoration was carried out only on major attractions with foreign tourism in mind, but with local tourism emerging as a major money-spinner in the 1990s tourist attractions all over China are having cash pumped into them. On a less positive note, China's cultural and artistic tourist attractions have often been tackily restored and are swarming with pushy souvenir entrepreneurs advertising with loud speakers.

Music

Traditional Chinese musical instruments include the two stringed fiddle (*èrhú*), three stringed flute (*sānxián*), four stringed banjo (*yuèqín*), two stringed viola (*húqín*), vertical flute (*dòngxiāo*), horizontal flute (*dízi*), piccolo (*bāngdí*), four stringed lute (*pípa*), zither (*gǔzhēng*), ceremonial trumpet (*suǒnà*) and ceremonial gongs (*dàluó*).

Popular Music

China is beginning to develop a thriving music industry. Much of it is heavily influenced by the already well established music industries in Taiwan and Hong Kong, but these are in turn influenced by western musical trends, as the recent popularity of Cantonese rap and Taiwanese-language rock experiments have shown.

China has generally been slow in developing a market for western music (much of what is available in the shops is of The Carpenters ilk), but the advent of satellite TV (now widely available) and the popularity of MTV and Channel V, broadcast via Hong Kong's Star TV network, is set to change all that.

China's first concert featuring a foreign rock group was in April 1985, when the British group Wham! performed. The audience remained sedate – music fans who dared to get up and dance in the aisles were hauled off by the PSB. Since then, things have become more liberal and China has produced some notable local bands.

Beijing seems to be the hard rock and heavy metal capital of China. Cui Jian was a pioneer in bringing real rock and roll to China in the late 1980s, and he is still active – in 1997 he even did a concert in Taiwan. More recently popular is Li Jie. Cobra (*yǎnjìngshé*) is an all-woman rock band from Beijing. Recent years have even spawned a number of heavy metal bands, better known ones being Tang Dynasty (*táng cháo*), Black Panther (*hēi bào*) and Reincarnation (*lúnhui*).

Ceramics

Earthenware production has a long history in China. As many as 8000 years ago Chinese tribes were making artefacts with clay. The primitive 'Yangshao' culture (which existed along the Yellow River) is noted for its distinctive pottery painted with flowers, fish, animals, human faces and geometric designs. Around 3500 BC the 'Lungshanoid' culture (first found near the village of Lungshan in Shandong Province) was making white pottery and eggshell-thin black pottery.

Pottery making was well advanced by the Shang period; the most important development occurred around the middle of the dynasty with the manufacture of a greenish glaze applied to stoneware artefacts. During the Han Dynasty the custom of glazing pottery became fairly common. However, the production of terracotta items – made from a mixture of sand and clay, fired to produce a reddish-brown colour and left unglazed – continued.

During the Southern and Northern dynasties, a type of pottery halfway between Han glazed pottery and true porcelain was produced. The proto-porcelain was made by mixing clay with quartz and the mineral feldspar to make a hard, smooth-surfaced vessel. Feldspar was mixed with traces of iron to produce an olive-green glaze.

Chinese pottery reached its artistic peak under the Song rulers. During this time true porcelain was developed. It was made of fine kaolin clay and was white, thin and translucent. Porcelain was produced under the Yuan, but gradually lost the delicacy and near-perfection of the Song products. However, it was probably during the Yuan Dynasty that 'blue-and-white' porcelain made its first appearance. Another noted invention was mono-coloured porcelain in ferrous red, black or dark blue. A new range of mono-coloured vessels was developed under the Qing.

During the Qing period the production of coloured porcelain continued with the addition of new colours and glazes and more complex decorations. This was the age of true painted porcelain, decorated with delicate landscapes, birds and flowers. Elaborate designs and brilliant colouring became the fashion. Porcelain imitations of other materials, such as gold and silver, mother of pearl, jade, bronze, wood and bamboo, also became popular.

Bronze Vessels

Bronze is an alloy whose chief elements are copper, tin and lead. Tradition ascribes the first casting of bronze to the legendary Xia Dynasty of 5000 years ago.

The Shang Dynasty ruler and the aristocracy are believed to have used a large number of bronze vessels for sacrificial offerings of food and wine. Zhou Dynasty bronze

CHINESE ARTS

vessels tend to have long messages in ideographic characters; they describe wars, rewards, ceremonial events and the appointment of officials.

Bronze mirrors were used as early as the Shang Dynasty and had already developed into an artistic form by the Warring States period. Ceramics gradually replaced bronze utensils by Han times, but bronze mirrors were not displaced by glass mirrors until the Qing Dynasty. The backs of bronze mirrors were inscribed with wishes for good fortune and protection from evil influence. Post-Han writings are full of fantastic stories of the supernatural powers of mirrors. One of them relates the tale of Yin Zhongwen, who held a mirror to look at himself, but found that his face was not reflected – soon after, he was executed.

Jade

 The jade stone has been revered in China since Neolithic times. While the pure white form is the most highly valued, the stone varies in translucency and colour, including many shades of green, brown and black.

Jade is also thought to be empowered with magical and life-giving properties, and was considered a guardian against disease and evil spirits. Perhaps it still is – even now you can purchase pillow cases in Chinese department stores with jade squares attached (sleeping with your head on such a pillow may prevent brain tumours and boost your IQ).

Taoist alchemists, hoping to become immortal, ate an elixir of powdered jade, a 'high-fibre' diet if there ever was one. Plugs of jade were placed over the orifices of corpses to prevent the life force from escaping. Opulent jade suits, meant to prevent decomposition, have been found in Han tombs.

Funerary Objects

 As early as Neolithic times (9000-6000 BC), offerings of pottery vessels and stone tools or weapons were placed in graves to accompany the departed.

During the Shang Dynasty, precious objects such as bronze ritual vessels, weapons and jade were buried with the dead. Dogs, horses and even human beings were sacrificed for burial in the tombs of great rulers. When this practice was abandoned, replicas (usually in pottery) were made of human beings, animals and precious objects. A whole repertoire of objects was produced especially for burial, making symbolic provision for the dead without wasting wealth or making human sacrifice.

Burial objects made of earthenware were very popular from the 1st to the 8th centuries AD. During the Han Dynasty, pottery figures were cast in moulds and painted in bright colours after firing. Statues of attendants, entertainers, musicians, acrobats and jugglers were made, as well as models of granaries, watchtowers, pigpens, stoves and various other things.

Close trade links with the west were illustrated among these models by the appearance among funerary objects of the two humped Bactrian camel, which carried merchandise along the Silk Road. Warriors with west Asian faces and heavy beards appeared as funerary objects during the Northern Wei Dynasty.

The cosmopolitan life of Tang China was illustrated by its funerary wares; western and central Asians flocked to the capital at Chang'an and were portrayed in figurines of merchants, attendants, warriors, grooms, musicians and dancers. Tall western horses with long legs, introduced to China from central Asia at the beginning of the 1st century BC, were also popular subjects for tomb figurines.

Other funerary objects commonly seen in Chinese museums are fearsome military figures dressed in full armour, often trampling oxen underfoot. The figures may have served as tomb guardians and may represent the four heavenly kings. These kings guard the four quarters of the universe and protect the state; they have been assimilated into Buddhism and you see statues of them in Buddhist temples.

Guardian spirits are some of the strangest funerary objects. A common one has bird wings, elephant ears, a human face, the body of a lion and the legs and hooves of a deer or horse, all rolled into one.

Literature

China has a rich literary tradition. Unfortunately – barring many years of intensive study – much of it is inaccessible to western readers. Many of the most important Chinese classics are available in translation, but much of the Chinese literary heritage (particularly its poetry) is untranslatable, although scholars persevere.

The essential point to bear in mind when discussing Chinese literature is that prior to the 20th century there were two literary traditions: the classical and the vernacular. The classical tradition was the Chinese equivalent of a literary canon. The classical canon, largely Confucian in nature, consisted of a core of texts written in ancient Chinese that had to be mastered thoroughly by all aspirants to the Chinese civil service, and was the backbone of the Chinese education system – it was nearly indecipherable to the masses. The vernacular tradition arose in the Ming Dynasty and consisted largely of prose epics written for entertainment.

For western readers it is the vernacular texts, precursors of the contemporary Chinese novel and short story, that are probably of more interest. Most of them are available in translation and provide a fascinating insight into life in China centuries past.

Perhaps the three most famous early 'novels' are: *The Water Margin (shuǐhǔ zhuàn)*, also translated as *Rebels of the Marsh*;

The Dream of the Red Chamber (hónglóu mèng), also translated as *The Dream of Red Mansions* and *The Story of the Stone*; and *Journey to the West (xīyóu jì)*.

Another classic is the *Jin Ping Mei*, a racy story about a wealthy Chinese man and his six wives – it's banned in China, but available elsewhere in English. The *I Ching (jìjìng)*, or *Book of Changes*, is used to predict the future, but is regarded by the Chinese (and New Agers) as an ancient source of wisdom. *The Art of War (bīngfǎ)* by Sun Tzu (*sūnzǐ*) was studied by Mao and is still required reading for modern military strategists in the west.

By the early 19th century, western novels had begun to appear in Chinese translations in increasing numbers. Chinese intellectuals began to look at their own literary traditions more critically, in particular the classical one, which was markedly different in form from the Chinese that was spoken by modern Chinese. Calls for a national literature based on vernacular Chinese rather than the stultifying classical language grew in intensity.

The first of the major Chinese writers to write in colloquial Chinese as understood by the masses was Lu Xun (1881-1936), and for this reason he is regarded by many as the father of modern Chinese literature. Most of his works were short stories that looked critically at the Chinese inability to drag its nation into the 20th century. His first set of short stories was entitled *Call to Arms* (*nàhǎn*) and included his most famous tale *The True Story of Ah Q*. His second collection was entitled *Wandering*, and his last collection was called *Old Tales Retold*.

Lao She (1899-1966), another important early novelist, also produced an allegorical work in *Cat City*, but is famous most of all for *The Rickshaw Boy*, a book that has been translated many times into English. It is a social critique of the living conditions of rickshaw drivers in Beijing. Lao She died from wounds inflicted by zealous Red Guards during the Cultural Revolution.

Literary creativity in post-1949 China was greatly hampered by ideological controls. Mao's 'Yan'an Talks on Art & Literature' edict basically reduced literature to the status of a revolutionary tool, and writers were extolled to seek out ideal forms and to find the 'typical in the individual'. Works that did not show peasants triumphing over huge odds were considered not inspirational enough and condemned as bourgeois.

There has been increased creative freedom in the Chinese literary scene in the years following the Cultural Revolution, but it remains an area in which the government maintains careful vigilance. Most writers belong to state-sponsored literary guilds and many write on salary. Naturally they are careful not to bite the hand that feeds them.

Wang Meng was born in Beijing in 1934 and his writings have touched on all sorts of sensitive topics including reform, elections, family, politics and technology. He was labelled a 'rightest' in 1957 because one of his short stories, *The Young Newcomer in the Organisation Department*, mildly criticised bureaucracy. In 1963 he was forced to move to a labour camp in rural Xinjiang where he spent the next 16 years. His 'rightest' label was officially removed in 1979 and he was allowed to take up writing again. He was given the prestigious job of Minister of Culture in 1986, but was forced to step down in the wake of the 1989 democracy protests in Tiananmen Square. However, he was later appointed vice chairmen of the Chinese Writers' Association. Wang Meng has authored a number of excellent stories including *The Stubborn Porridge*, *A Winter's Topic*, *The Butterfly* and *Kitty*.

Ba Jin is the pen name of Li Feigan who was born in 1904 and is reportedly still alive. He studied in Paris and translated some French works into Chinese, but become well known for his own novels which he produced in the 1930s and 1940s. He was brutally persecuted during the Cultural Revolution, but managed to survive. His best-known works include *Family*, *Autumn*, *Spring*, *Garden of Repose* and *Bitter Cold Nights*.

Shen Congwen (1902-88) lived in Hunan Province and his fiction reflects the lifestyle in that region. More than 20 of his best stories have been gathered into the book *Imperfect Paradise*, published in English by the University of Hawaii Press.

One of the most interesting writers in contemporary China is Zhang Xianliang, whose book *Half of Man Is Woman* was extremely controversial for its sexual content. Most western readers find Zhang's sexual politics highly suspect, but his book, now published by Penguin, is worth reading all the same.

The work of another writer, Wang Shuo, still awaits translation into English, but this must only be a matter of time. Much of his work has been adapted for film and he is popular with the younger generation. For the authorities, however, his stories about disaffected urban youth, gambling, prostitution and confidence tricksters are considered a bad influence.

Blood Red Dusk by Lao Gui (literally 'old devil') is available in English by Panda (the Chinese publisher). It's a fascinatingly cynical account of the Cultural Revolution years.

Feng Jicai is a writer who has enjoyed great success in China with stories like *The Magic Ponytail* and *A Short Man & His Tall Wife*, which have a satirical magic realist touch to them. His often horrific account of the Cultural Revolution, *Voices from the Whirlwind*, is a collection of anonymous personal accounts of those turbulent years and has recently been published in English by Pantheon Books.

For a recap of some of the latest trends in Chinese literature, look out for a copy of *The Lost Boat: Avant Garde Fiction From China*, edited by Henry YH Zhao (Wellsweep Press, 1994). It has samples from what Zhao identifies as the three main strands in Chinese literature since 1986.

Bookshops

Finding any of the above books in non-Chinese editions takes perseverance. The Foreign Languages Bookstores and Friendship

Stores in Beijing and Shanghai are the cheapest places to find western-language editions of Chinese literature. Some bookstores in Hong Kong also have excellent collections, although prices are higher than elsewhere in China. For information on the exact location of bookstores in China, see the relevant chapters of this book.

Taiwan is another good source, although you won't find much there from mainland China.

Some made-in-China books are exported to western countries and sold at vastly inflated prices. You can search in the various Chinatowns around the world, although mostly what you'll find are titles printed in Chinese.

The USA seems to have the most complete collections of English-language books about China, probably because of the large number of ethnic Chinese living there. Some of the US-based bookshops can be accessed online and will do mail orders to other countries.

If you wish to search for Chinese literature, you can check out the following:

China

China National Publishing Industry Trading Corporation (☎ (10) 6421-5031, 6421-5793; fax 6421-4540 – for journal subscriptions only), 504 Anhuali, Andingmenwai (PO Box 782), Beijing, 100011, China

France

L'Harmattan (☎ 1 46 34 13 71), 21 Rue des Écoles, in the Latin Quarter

Le Tiers Mythe (☎ 1 43 26 72 70), 21 Rue Cujas

Taiwan

Eslite (☎ (02) 2773-0095), 2nd floor, 245 Tunhua South Rd, Section 1 (near Jenai Rd), Taipei. This is Taiwan's largest book shop.

Caves Books (☎ (02) 2537-1666), 103 Chungshan North Rd, Section 2, Taipei

UK

Stanford's Bookshop (☎ (0171) 836 1915), 12-14 Long Acre, London WC2E 9LP. It's one of the best shops of its kind in the UK.

The Travel Bookshop (☎ (0171) 229 5260), 13 Blenheim Cres, London W11 2EE. This is another good source of travel literature.

USA

China Books & Periodicals Inc (☎ (415) 282-2994; fax 282-0994; www.chinabooks.com), 2929 24th St, San Francisco, CA 94110

The Asia Society's Bookstore, 725 Park Ave (at 70th St), New York City, NY

CHRIS TAYLOR

CHRIS TAYLOR

Chinese opera is a highly stylised form of theatre involving singing, dancing, speaking, mime, acrobatics and dancing. The face painted roles are called 'jing' and represent warriors, heroes, statesmen, adventurers and demons.

CHINESE ARTS

GLENN BEANLAND

Top: This ornate facade from a Forbidden City hall is typical of the architectural style for official buildings constructed during the Ming Dynasty.

Bottom: This famille verte jar with lid was produced in Jingdezhen (Jiangxi Province) during the reign of Emperor Wanli (1573-1620 AD). It's on display in the Zande Lou ceramics gallery at the Shanghai Museum.

Top Left: This blue vase with gold and silver floral design dates from the reign of Emperor Qianlong (1736-95 AD). Made in the noted pocelain town of Jingdezhen (Jiangxi Province), it's on display in the Zande Lou ceramics gallery at the Shanghai Museum.

Top Right: Also from this collection is this ceramic pillow with incised peony design. It was made in the town of Dengfeng (Henan Province) during the Northern Song Dynasty (960-1127 AD).

Bottom: Initially developed in about 2000 BC, China's pictogram-based style of writing demands a high degree of skill by the calligrapher. Each of the several thousand characters in common use today can be produced from 20 basic strokes.

SONIA BERTO

DIANA MAYFIELD

Top: The Naxi Orchestra in Lijiang (Yunnan Province) is the only group in China still playing music drawn from Taoist scriptures (dating from the Song Dynasty, 960-1279 AD) on original instruments.

Right: China's acrobatic tradition goes back centuries and is incorporated into formal opera as well as being performed by travelling troupes and circuses. More than 80 troupes are active in China today and remain a popular form of entertainment.

STEVE DAVEY/LA BELLE AURORE

Architecture

Modern China is not exactly an architectural treasure-trove, and since 1949 this situation has been exacerbated by the widespread construction of brick and concrete housing blocks, unimaginative office buildings and outright ugly factories. Nevertheless, between the imperial structures of Beijing, the lingering colonial buildings of Shanghai, the temples being restored across the country and the occasional rural village that has somehow escaped the ravages of the 20th century, there's still plenty to see.

Traditionally, Chinese architecture – from the lowliest village homestead to imperial palace – follows certain principles. A north-south-oriented walled compound (with the main entrance to the south) that houses one or more structures was the basic form. As Chinese lived together in extended-family groups, a walled home would generally house the living quarters for the head of the family in the north, with housing for children and their families on the side.

Chinese Temples

Temple architecture in China also tends to follow a certain uniformity. There is little external difference between Buddhist, Confucian and Taoist temples, which again are housed in compounds with a north-south orientation.

Architecturally, the roof is the dominant feature of a Chinese temple. It is usually green or yellow and is decorated with figures of divinities and lucky symbols such as dragons and carp. Stone lions often guard the temple entrance.

Inside is a small courtyard with a large bowl where incense and paper offerings are burnt. Beyond is the main hall with an altar table, often with an intricately carved front. Depending on the size and wealth of the temple there are gongs, drums, side altars and adjoining rooms with shrines to different gods, chapels for prayers to the dead and displays of funerary plaques. There are also living quarters for the temple keepers. There is no set time for prayer and no communal service except for funerals. Worshippers enter the temple whenever they want to make offerings, pray for help or give thanks.

The dominant colours in a Chinese temple are red, gold or yellow, and green. The orange-red colour range represents joy, green signifies harmony while yellow and gold herald heavenly glory. White stands for purity and is also the colour of death. Grey and black are the colours of disaster and grief.

The most striking feature of the Buddhist temple is the pagoda. It was probably introduced from India along with Buddhism in the 1st century AD. They were often built to house religious artefacts and documents, to commemorate important events, or to store the ashes of the deceased. It was during the Northern Wei period that the construction of Buddhist cave temples began and was continued during later dynasties. The caves at Longmen near Luoyang, at Mogao near Dunhuang and at Yungang near Datong are some of the finest examples.

Film

While most travellers in China manage to get to at least one opera or acrobatics performance, few get around to seeing any Chinese films. Part of the problem of course is purely linguistic – films are usually dull when you can't follow the dialogue. Still, a number of Chinese releases have enjoyed success at western film festivals and art house cinemas, and these are always subtitled into English.

You should make an effort to track down at least a few Chinese videos to see what it's all about. Video rental shops in Hong Kong are your best bet (at least until China cracks down on them). Another source is Taiwan or video shops in the various Chinatowns around the world. Some of the major video rental chains in the west carry a few of the trendier Chinese films.

Sadly, the best Chinese films cannot be produced in China. The government prefers film-makers to deal with non-controversial topics such as comedies, musicals, love stories and nature photography. Any film dealing with the more seedy side of life is almost certain to be clipped by the censors or banned outright. Directors who run afoul of the censors have often been denied passports to go abroad to work or attend foreign film festivals. Hong Kong's film festival used to be the place to go for a sneak preview of China's best, but the festival seems doomed now that Hong Kong has been reunified with the mainland. Taipei's annual Golden Horse Film Festival (late November to late December) is now the only truly uncensored Chinese film festival (assuming, of course, that you consider Taiwan to be part of China).

Much of the early post-1949 film work was ideologically motivated – heroic workers and peasants battling (and emerging victorious) against evil foreigners and Kuomintang devils. As can be expected, the years of the Cultural Revolution did nothing to improve this state of affairs.

The major turning point took place with the graduation of the first intake of students since the end of the Cultural Revolution from the Beijing Film Academy in 1982. This group of adventurous directors, the most well known of whom are Zhang Yimou, Chen Kaige, Wu Ziniu and Tian Zhuangzhuang, became known collectively as the 'Fifth Generation'. The new directors of the 1990s have been dubbed the 'sixth generation' and include such people as He Jianjun, Jiang Wen, Ning Ying, Wu Wenguang and Zhang Yuan.

Both the fifth and sixth generation directors have constantly run into problems with the authorities, and the most controversial works get clipped by censors or banned outright. The government has even retaliated against 'troublesome' directors by denying them film to work with, or revoking their passports so they cannot attend foreign film festivals.

Tragedy is a central element of Chinese art films, and plots tend to move slowly. Many westerners have a hard time keeping awake, but it's all a matter of taste. Ge You is arguably China's most popular actor and Gong Li the most popular actress.

The first film by the fifth generation directors to come to the attention of film buffs in the west was *Yellow Earth* (1984; *huáng tǔdì*) by Chen Kaige. Chen's most notable work was *Farewell My Concubine* (1993), a rather long 157 minutes. Other movies by Chen include *Life on a String* and *The Big Parade*.

Zhang Yimou made *Red Sorghum* (1987; *hóng gāoliang*), a film that was adventurous by Chinese standards in portraying an illicit love affair against the backdrop of the Sino-Japanese War. Zhang has emerged as China's foremost director (and sometimes cameraman) with award-winning releases such as *The One & the Eight* (1984), *The Story of Qiu Ju* (1991), *The Old Well* (1987), *To Live* (1994; *huózhe*), *Ju Dou* (1990), *Raise the Red Lantern* (1991) and *Shanghai Triad* (1995). Young actress Gong Li has appeared in most of Zhang's films.

Huang Jianxin directed *Stand Up, Don't Bend Over* and *The Black Cannon Incident* (1986; *hēipào shìjiàn*). The latter is without a doubt the sharpest satire released by any of the Fifth Generation directors.

Tian Zhuangzhuang directed *The Blue Kite* (1993; *lán fēngzheng*), a Cultural Revolution tragedy which is banned in China. Other notable films include: *Swan Song*, the tragic story of a Cantonese opera composer who dies neglected after his best work is stolen and made famous by a music student; *The Horse Thief*, a haunting story set in Tibet; and *The Women from the Lake of Scented Souls*, which portrays the unhappiness of a woman who runs a sesame-oil mill. For information on the Hong Kong film industry, see that chapter.

Theatre

 Chinese theatre draws on very different traditions from western theatre. The crucial difference is the importance of music to Chinese theatre, and thus it is usually referred to as opera. Contemporary Chinese theatre, of which the most famous is Beijing opera, has a continuous history of some 900 years, having evolved from a convergence of comic and balladic traditions in the Northern Song period. From this beginning, Chinese opera has been the meeting ground for a disparate range of forms: acrobatics, martial arts, poetic arias and stylised dance.

Operas were usually performed by travelling troupes whose social status was very low in traditional Chinese society. In fact, their status was on a par with prostitutes and slaves and their children barred from social advancement by a government decree that made them ineligible to participate in public-service examinations. Chinese law also forbade mixed-sex performances, forcing actors to act out roles of the opposite sex. Opera troupes were frequently associated with homosexuality in the public imagination, contributing further to their 'untouchable' social status.

Despite this, opera remained a popular form of entertainment, although it was considered unworthy of the attention of the scholar class. Performances were considered an obligatory adjunct to New Year celebrations and marriages, and sometimes to funerals and ancestral ceremonies.

Opera performances usually take place on a bare stage, with the actors taking on stylised roles that are instantly recognisable to the audience. The four major roles are the female role, the male role, the 'painted-face' role (for gods and warriors) and the clown.

Calligraphy

Calligraphy has traditionally been regarded in China as the highest form of visual art. In the past, children were trained at a very early age to write beautifully, and good calligraphy was a social asset. A scholar, for example, could not pass his examination to become an official if he was a poor calligrapher. A person's character was judged by their handwriting; if it was elegant it revealed great refinement.

The basic tools of calligraphy are paper, ink, ink-stone (on which the ink is mixed) and brush. These are commonly referred to as the 'four treasures of the scholar's study'.

All over China, decorative calligraphy can be found in temples, adorning the walls of caves and on the sides of mountains and monuments.

Painting

Chinese painting is the art of brush and ink. The basic tools are those of calligraphy, which influenced painting in both technique and theory. The brush line, which varies in thickness and tone, is the important feature of a Chinese painting. Shading is regarded as a foreign technique (introduced to China via Buddhist art from central Asia between the 3rd and 6th centuries) and colour plays only a minor symbolic and decorative role.

From the Han Dynasty until the end of the Tang Dynasty, the human figure occupied the dominant position in Chinese painting, as it did in pre-modern European art. Figure painting flourished against a Confucian background, illustrating moral themes. Landscape painting for its own sake started in the 4th and 5th centuries. The practice of seeking out places of natural beauty and communing with nature first became popular among Taoist poets and painters. By the 9th century the interest of artists began to shift away from figures and, from the 11th century onwards, landscape dominated Chinese painting.

When the Communists came to power, much of the country's artistic talent was turned to glorifying the revolution and bombarding the masses with political slogans. Colourful billboards of Mao waving to cheering crowds holding up the 'little red book' were once popular, as were giant Mao statues standing above smaller statues of enthusiastic workers and soldiers. Music and opera were also co-opted for political purposes.

Since the late 1970s, the Chinese art scene has gradually recovered. The work of traditionally influenced painters can be seen for sale in shops and galleries all over China, while in the major cities (particularly Beijing) a flourishing avant-garde scene has emerged. The work of Chinese painters has been arguably more innovative and dissident than that of writers, possibly because the political implications are harder to interpret by the authorities. Art collecting has become a fashionable hobby among China's new rich, and many of China's young artists have exhibited work overseas to critical acclaim.

RELIGION

Chinese religion has been influenced by three great streams of human thought: Taoism, Confucianism and Buddhism. Although each has separate origins, all three have been inextricably entwined in popular Chinese religion along with ancient animist beliefs. The founders of Taoism, Confucianism and Buddhism have been deified. The Chinese worship them and their disciples as fervently as they worship their own ancestors and a pantheon of gods and spirits.

Taoism

(dào jiào)

It is said that Taoism is the only true 'home-grown' Chinese religion – Buddhism was imported from India and Confucianism is mainly a philosophy. According to tradition, the founder of Taoism was a man known as Laotzu (lǎozǐ in Pinyin), whose name has been variously misspelled in western literature as 'Laotse' and 'Laotze'. He is said to have been born around the year 604 BC, but there is some doubt that he ever lived at all. Almost nothing is known about him, not even his real name. Laotzu translates as the 'Old One' or the 'Grand Old Master'. It's widely believed that Laotzu was the keeper of the government archives in a western state of China, and that Confucius consulted with him.

At the end of his life, Laotzu is said to have climbed on a water buffalo and ridden west towards what is now Tibet, in search of solitude for his last few years. On the way, he was asked to leave behind a record of his beliefs. The product was a slim volume of only 5000 characters, the *Tao Te Ching* (*Dao De Jing*) or *The Way & Its Power*. He then rode off on his buffalo.

It's doubtful that Laotzu ever intended his philosophy to become a religion. Chuangtzu (zhuāngzǐ), who lived between 399 and 295 BC, picked up where Laotzu left off. Chuangtzu is regarded as the greatest of all Taoist writers and *The Book of Chuangtzu* is still required reading for anyone trying to make sense of Taoism.

However, like Laotzu, Chuangtzu was a philosopher and was not actually trying to establish a religion.

Credit for turning Taoism into a religion is generally given to Zhang Daoling, who formally established his Celestial Masters movement in 143 BC.

At the centre of Taoism is the concept of *Dao*. Dao cannot be perceived because it exceeds senses, thoughts and imagination; it can be known only through mystical insight which cannot be expressed with words. Dao is the way of the universe, the driving power in nature, the order behind all life, the spirit which cannot be exhausted. Dao is the way people should order their lives to keep in harmony with the natural order of the universe.

Just as there have been different interpretations of the 'way', there have also been different interpretations of *De* – the power of the universe. This has led to the development of three distinct forms of Taoism in China.

Taoism later split into two divisions, the 'Cult of the Immortals' and 'The Way of the Heavenly Teacher'. The Cult of the Immortals offered immortality through meditation, exercise, alchemy and various other techniques. The Way of the Heavenly Teacher had many gods, ceremonies, saints, special diets to prolong life and offerings to the ghosts. As time passed, Taoism increasingly became wrapped up in the supernatural, self-mutilation, witchcraft, exorcism, fortune telling, magic and ritualism. Taoists eventually produced a collection of over 1400 baffling scriptures known as the *Daozang*.

Taoism today has been much embraced in the west by New Agers, parapsychologists and others who offer their own various interpretations of what Laotzu and Chuangtzu were really trying to tell us.

Confucianism

(rújiā sīxiǎng)

More a philosophy than a religion, Confucianism has nevertheless become intertwined with Chinese religious beliefs.

Chinese Zodiac

Astrology has a long history in China and is integrated with religious beliefs. As in the western system of astrology, there are 12 zodiac signs; however, unlike the western system, your sign is based on the year rather than the month in which you were born. Still, this is a simplification. The exact day and time of birth is also carefully considered in charting an astrological path.

If you want to know your sign in the Chinese zodiac, look up your year of birth in the chart, though it's a little more complicated than this because Chinese astrology goes by the lunar calendar. The Chinese Lunar New Year usually falls in late January or early February, so the first month will be included in the year before. Future years are included here so you'll know what's coming:

Rat	1924	1936	1948	1960	1972	1984	1996
Ox/Cow	1925	1937	1949	1961	1973	1985	1997
Tiger	1926	1938	1950	1962	1974	1986	1998
Rabbit	1927	1939	1951	1963	1975	1987	1999
Dragon	1928	1940	1952	1964	1976	1988	2000
Snake	1929	1941	1953	1965	1977	1989	2001
Horse	1930	1942	1954	1966	1978	1990	2002
Goat	1931	1943	1955	1967	1979	1991	2003
Monkey	1932	1944	1956	1968	1980	1992	2004
Rooster	1933	1945	1957	1969	1981	1993	2005
Dog	1934	1946	1958	1970	1982	1994	2006
Pig	1935	1947	1959	1971	1983	1995	2007

With the exception of Mao, the one name which has become synonymous with China is Confucius (*kǒngzǐ*). He was born of a poor family around the year 551 BC, in what is now Shandong Province. His ambition was to hold a high government office and to reorder society through the administrative apparatus. At most he seems to have had several insignificant government posts, a few followers and a permanently blocked career.

At the age of 50 he perceived his divine mission, and for the next 13 years tramped from state to state offering unsolicited advice to rulers on how to improve their governing, while looking for an opportunity to put his own ideas into practice. That opportunity never came, and he returned to his own state to spend the last five years of his life teaching and editing classical literature. He died in 479 BC, aged 72.

The glorification of Confucius began after his death. Mencius (372-289 BC), or Mengzi, helped raise Confucian ideals into the national consciousness with the publication of The Book of Mencius.

Eventually, Confucian philosophy permeated every level of Chinese society. To hold government office presupposed a knowledge of the Confucian classics, and spoken proverbs trickled down to the illiterate masses.

During the Han Dynasty, Confucianism effectively became the state religion – the teachings were made the basic discipline for training government officials and remained so until almost the end of the Qing Dynasty in 1911.

In the 7th and 8th centuries, temples and shrines were built in memory of Confucius and his original disciples. During the Song Dynasty, the Confucian bible, the *Analects*, became the basis of all education.

It is not hard to see why Confucianism

took hold in China. Confucianism defines codes of conduct and patterns of obedience. Women obey and defer to men, younger brothers to elder brothers, and sons to fathers. Respect flows upwards, from young to old, from subject to ruler. Certainly, any reigning Chinese emperor would quickly see the merits of encouraging such a system.

All people paid homage to the emperor, who was regarded as the embodiment of Confucian wisdom and virtue – the head of the great family-nation. For centuries administration under the emperor lay in the hands of a small Confucian scholar class. In theory anyone who passed the examinations qualified, but in practice the monopoly of power was held by the educated upper classes.

There has never been a rigid code of law, because Confucianism rejected the idea that conduct could be enforced by some organisation; taking legal action implied an incapacity to work things out by negotiation. The result, however, was arbitrary justice and oppression by those who held power. Dynasties rose and fell, but the Confucian pattern never changed. Indeed, it still holds true in today's China.

The family retains its central place as the basic unit of society; Confucianism reinforced this idea, but did not invent it. The key to family order is filial piety – children's respect for and duty towards their parents. Teaming up with traditional superstition, Confucianism reinforced the practice of ancestor worship. Confucius himself is worshipped and temples are built for him. The strict codes of obedience were held together by these concepts of filial piety and ancestor worship, as well as by the concept of 'face' – to let down the family or group is a great shame for Chinese.

In its early years, Confucianism was regarded as a radical philosophy, but over the centuries it has come to be seen as conservative and reactionary. Confucius was strongly denounced by the Communists as yet another incorrigible link to the bourgeois past. During the Cultural

Revolution, Confucian temples, statues and Confucianists themselves took quite a beating at the hands of rampaging Red Guards. However, in recent years the Chinese government has softened its stance, perhaps recognising that Confucianism can still be an effective instrument of social control. Confucian temples (particularly the ones at Qufu in Shandong Province) are now being restored.

Buddhism

(fó jiào)

Buddhism was founded in India by Siddhartha Gautama (563-483 BC) of the Sakyas. Siddhartha was his given name, Gautama his surname and Sakya the name of the clan to which his family belonged.

The story goes that although he was a prince brought up in luxury, Siddhartha became discontented with the world when he was confronted with the sights of old age, sickness and death. He despaired of finding fulfilment on the physical level, since the body was inescapably subject to these weaknesses.

Around the age of 30 Siddhartha broke from the material world and sought 'enlightenment' by following various yogic disciplines. After several failed attempts he devoted the final phase of his search to intensive contemplation. One evening as he sat beneath a bo (banyan) tree, he slipped into a deep meditation and emerged having achieved enlightenment. His title 'Buddha' means 'the awakened' or 'the enlightened one'.

Buddha founded an order of monks and preached his ideas for the next four decades until his death. To his followers he was known as Sakyamuni, the 'silent sage of the Sakya clan', because of the unfathomable mystery that surrounded him. It is said that Gautama Buddha was not the first buddha, but the fourth, and is not expected to be the last.

The cornerstone of Buddhist philosophy is the view that all life is suffering. Everyone is subject to the traumas of birth, sickness, decrepitude and death; to what they most dread (an incurable disease or an ineradicable personal weakness); and to separation from what they love.

The cause of suffering is desire – specifically the desires of the body and the desire for personal fulfilment. Happiness can only be achieved if these desires are overcome, and this requires following the 'eightfold path'. By following this path the Buddhist aims to attain nirvana. Volumes have been written in attempts to define nirvana; the *suttas* (discourses of the Buddha) simply say that it's a state of complete freedom from greed, anger, ignorance and the various other 'fetters' of existence.

The first branch of the eightfold path is 'right understanding': the recognition that life is suffering, that suffering is caused by desire for personal gratification and that suffering can be overcome. The second branch is 'right-mindedness': cultivating a mind free from sensuous desire, ill will and cruelty. The remaining branches of the path require that one refrain from abuse and deceit; that one show kindness and avoid self-seeking in all actions; that one develop virtues and curb passions; and that one practise meditation.

Buddhism developed in China from the 3rd to 6th centuries AD. In the middle of the 1st century AD the religion gained the interest of the Han emperor Ming. He sent a mission to the west, which returned in 67 AD with Buddhist scriptures, two Indian monks and images of the Buddha.

Centuries later, other Chinese monks like Xuan Zang journeyed to India and returned with Buddhist scriptures which were then translated from the original Sanskrit. Buddhist monasteries and temples sprang up everywhere in China, and played a similar role to the churches and monasteries of medieval Europe – functioning as guesthouses, hospitals and orphanages for travellers and refugees. Gifts from the faithful allowed them to amass considerable wealth and set up money-lending enterprises and pawnshops. These pawnshops functioned as unofficial banks for the poor right up to the mid-20th century.

The Buddha wrote nothing; the Buddhist writings that have come down to us date from about 150 years after his death. By the time these texts came out, divisions had already appeared within Buddhism. Some writers tried to emphasise the Buddha's break with Hinduism, while others tried to minimise it. At some stage Buddhism split into two major schools: Theravada and Mahayana.

The Theravada, or 'doctrine of the elders', school (also called Hinayana or 'little vehicle' by non-Theravadins) holds that the path to nirvana is an individual pursuit. It centres on monks and nuns who make the search for nirvana a full-time profession. This school maintains that people are alone in the world and must tread the path to nirvana on their own; buddhas can only show the way. The Theravada school is the Buddhism of Sri Lanka, Myanmar, Thailand, Laos and Cambodia.

The Mahayana, or 'big vehicle', school holds that since all existence is one, the fate of the individual is linked to the fate of others. The Buddha did not just point the way and float off into his own nirvana, but continues to offer spiritual help to others seeking nirvana. The Mahayana school is the Buddhism of Vietnam, Japan, Tibet, Korea, Mongolia and China.

Mahayana Buddhism is replete with innumerable heavens, hells and descriptions of nirvana. Prayers are addressed to the Buddha and combined with elaborate ritual. There are deities and bodhisattvas – a rank of supernatural beings in their last incarnation before nirvana. Temples are filled with images such as the future buddha, Maitreya (often portrayed as fat and happy over his coming promotion) and Amitabha (a saviour who rewards the faithful with admission to a Christian-like paradise). The ritual, tradition and superstition that Buddha rejected came tumbling back in with a vengeance.

In Tibet and areas of Gansu, Sichuan and Yunnan, a unique form of the Mahayana school is practised: Tantric or Lamaist Buddhism (*lǎmā jiào*). Tantric Buddhism, often called *Vajrayana* or 'thunderbolt vehicle' by its followers, has been practised since the early 7th century AD and is heavily influenced by Tibet's pre-Buddhist Bon religion, which relied on priests or shamans to placate spirits, gods and demons.

Generally speaking, it is much more mystical than other forms of Buddhism, relying heavily on *mudras* (ritual postures), *mantras* (sacred speech), *yantras* (sacred art) and secret initiation rites. Priests called *lamas* are believed to be reincarnations of highly evolved beings; the Dalai Lama is the supreme patriarch of Tibetan Buddhism.

Islam

(*yīsīlán jiào*)

The founder of Islam was the Arab prophet Mohammed. Strictly speaking, Muslims believe it was not Mohammed who shaped the religion but God, and Mohammed merely transmitted it from God to his people. To call the religion 'Mohammedanism' is also incorrect, since it implies that the religion centres around Mohammed and not around God. The proper name of the religion is Islam, derived from the word *salam*, which primarily means 'peace', and in a secondary sense 'surrender' or 'submission'. The full connotation is something like 'the peace which comes by surrendering to God'. The corresponding adjective is 'Muslim'.

The prophet was born around 570 AD and came to be called Mohammed, which means 'highly praised'. His ancestry is traditionally traced back to Abraham, who had two wives, Hagar and Sarah. Hagar gave birth to Ishmael, and Sarah had a son named Isaac. Sarah demanded that Hagar and Ishmael be banished from the tribe. According to Islam's holy book, the Koran, Ishmael went to Mecca, where his line of descendants can be traced down to Mohammed. There have been other true prophets before Mohammed, but he is regarded as the culmination of them and the last.

Mohammed said that there is only one God, Allah. The name derives from joining *al*, which means 'the', with *Illah*, which means 'God'. His uncompromising monotheism conflicted with the pantheism and idolatry of the Arabs. Also, his moral teachings and vision of a universal brotherhood conflicted with what he believed was a corrupt and decadent social order based on class divisions.

The initial reaction to his teachings was hostile. He and his followers were forced to flee from Mecca to Medina in 622, where Mohammed built up a political base and an army which eventually defeated Mecca and brought all of Arabia under his control. He died in 632, two years after taking Mecca. By the time a century had passed the Arab Muslims had built a huge empire which stretched all the way from Persia to Spain. Although the Arabs were eventually supplanted by the Turks, the strength of Islam has continued to the present day.

Islam was brought to China peacefully. Arab traders who landed on the southern coast of China established their mosques in great maritime cities like Guangzhou and Quanzhou, and Muslim merchants travelling the Silk Road through central Asia to China won converts among the Han Chinese in the north of the country. There are also large populations of Muslim Uighur people (of Turkic descent), whose ancestors first moved into China's Xinjiang region during the Tang Dynasty.

Christianity

(*jīdū jiào*)

The earliest record of Christianity in China dates back to the Nestorians, a Syrian Christian sect. They first appeared in China in the 7th century when a Syrian named Raban presented Christian scriptures to the imperial court at Chang'an. This event and the construction of a Nestorian monastery in Chang'an are recorded on a large stone stele made in 781 AD, now displayed in the Shaanxi Provincial Museum in Xi'an.

The next major Christian group to arrive in China were the Jesuits. The priests

Matteo Ricci and Michael Ruggieri were permitted to set up base at Zhaoqing in Guangdong Province in the 1580s, and eventually made it to the imperial court in Beijing. Large numbers of Catholic and Protestant missionaries established themselves in China following the invasion of China by the western powers in the 19th century. Christians are estimated to comprise about 1% of China's population.

Judaism
(*yóutài jiào*)
Kaifeng in Henan Province has been the home of the largest community of Chinese Jews. Their religious beliefs and almost all the customs associated with them have died out, yet the descendants of the original Jews still consider themselves Jewish. Just how the Jews got to China is unknown. They may have come as traders and merchants along the Silk Road when Kaifeng was the capital of China, or they may have emigrated from India. For more details, see the Kaifeng section in the Henan chapter.

Religion & Communism
Today the Chinese Communist government professes atheism. It considers religion to be base superstition, a remnant of old China used by the ruling classes to keep power. This is in line with the Marxist belief that religion is the 'opiate of the people'.

Nevertheless, in an effort to improve relations with the Muslim, Buddhist and Lamaist minorities, the Chinese government is once again permitting open religious activity. However, only atheists are permitted to be members of the CCP. Since almost all of China's 55 minority groups adhere to one religion or another, this rule precludes most of them from becoming Party members.

Traditional Chinese religious beliefs took a battering during the Cultural Revolution when monasteries were disbanded, temples were destroyed and the monks were sometimes killed or sent to the fields to labour. Traditional Chinese religion is

strong in places like Macau, Hong Kong and Taiwan, but in mainland China the temples and monasteries are pale shadows of their former selves.

Since the death of Mao, the Chinese government has allowed many temples (sometimes with their own contingent of monks and novices) to reopen as active places of worship. All religious activity is firmly under state control and many of the monks are caretakers within renovated shells of monasteries which serve principally as tourist attractions.

Confucius has often been used as a political symbol, his role 'redefined' to suit the needs of the time. At the end of the 19th century he was upheld as a symbol of reform because he had worked for reform in his own day. After the fall of the Qing Dynasty, Chinese intellectuals vehemently opposed him as a symbol of a conservative and backward China. In the 1930s he was used by Chiang Kaishek and the Kuomintang as a guide to proper, traditional values. Today Confucius is back in favour, with the Chinese government seeing much to be admired in the neo-Confucianist authoritarianism espoused by Lee Kuan Yew of Singapore.

Christianity is still officially frowned upon by the government as a form of spiritual pollution, but nevertheless you can see new churches being built. What the Chinese government does, however, is make it difficult for Chinese Christians to affiliate with fellow Christians in the west. Churches are placed under the control of the government: the Three-Self Patriotic Movement was set up as an umbrella organisation for the Protestant churches, and the Catholic Patriotic Association was set up to replace Rome as the leader of the Catholic churches.

Proselytising is forbidden and western missionaries are routinely denied visas to enter China – those who enter on tourist visas but are caught proselytising on the sly are unceremoniously booted out.

There is much friction between the government and the Chinese Catholic church because the church refuses to disown the Pope as its leader. For this reason, the Vatican maintains diplomatic relations with Taiwan, much to China's consternation.

Muslims are believed to be the largest identifiable religious group still active in China today, numbering perhaps 2% to 3% of the nation's population. The government has not published official figures of the number of Buddhists, but they must be substantial since most Tibetans, Mongolians and Dai people follow Buddhism. There are around three million Catholics and four million Protestants. It's impossible to de-

termine the number of Taoists, but the number of Taoist priests is very small.

Of all people in China, the Tibetan Buddhists most felt the brunt of Mao's Cultural Revolution. The Dalai Lama and his entourage fled to India in 1959 when the Tibetan rebellion was put down by Chinese troops. During the Cultural Revolution the monasteries were disbanded (some were levelled to the ground) and the theocracy which had governed Tibet for centuries was wiped out overnight. Some Tibetan temples and monasteries have been re-opened and the Tibetan religion is still a very powerful force among the people.

Language

The official language of the PRC is the dialect spoken in Beijing. It is usually referred to in the west as 'Mandarin', but the Chinese call it Putonghua – common speech. Putonghua is variously referred to as the 'Han language' *(hànyǔ)*, the 'national language' *(guóyǔ)* or simply 'Chinese' *(zhōngwén or zhōngguóhuà)*.

Spoken

Dialects Discounting ethnic minority languages, China has eight major dialect groups: *Putonghua* (Mandarin), *Yue* (Cantonese), *Wu* (Shanghainese), *Minbei* (Fuzhou), *Minnan* (Hokkien-Taiwanese), *Xiang*, *Gan* and *Hakka*.

All of these are mutually unintelligible. These dialects also divide into many more sub-dialects.

Almost the entire population speaks Mandarin, although this doesn't mean that it's their first language or that they can read it.

Grammar Chinese grammar is much simpler than that of European languages. There are no articles ('a'/'the'), no tenses and no plurals. The basic point to bear in mind is that, like English, Chinese word order is subject-verb-object. In other words, a basic English sentence like 'I *(subject)* love *(verb)* you *(object)*' is constructed in exactly the

---

Chinglish

Initially you might be puzzled by a sign in the bathroom that reads 'Please don't take the odds and ends put into the nightstool'. In fact this is a warning to resist sudden impulses to empty the contents of your pockets or backpack into the toilet. An apparently ambiguous sign with anarchic implications like the one in the Lhasa Bank of China that reads 'Question Authority' is really just an economical way of saying 'Please address your questions to one of the clerks'.

On the other hand, just to confuse things, a company name like the 'Risky Investment Co' means just what it says. An English-Chinese dictionary proudly proclaims in the preface that it is 'very useful for the using'. And a beloved sign in the Liangmao Hotel in Tai'an proclaims:

Safety Needing Attention!
Be care of depending fire
Sweep away six injurious insect
Pay attention to civilisation

If this all sounds confusing, don't worry. It won't be long before you have a small armoury of Chinglish phrases of your own. Before you know it, you'll know without even thinking that 'Be careful not to be stolen' is a warning against thieves; that 'Shoplifters will be fined 10 times' means that shoplifting is not a good idea in China; that 'Do not stroke the works' (generally found in museums) means 'No touching'; and that you 'very like' something means that you 'like it very much'.

The best advice for travellers in China grappling with the complexities of a new language is not to set your sights too high. Bear in mind that it takes a minimum of 15 years of schooling in the Chinese language and a crash course in English to be able to write Chinglish with any fluency. ■

LANGUAGE

Mandarin & Cantonese

The character below means 'to go', and is displayed with its pronunciation in Mandarin (on the left) and Cantonese (on the right).

去   去
qu   hui

Chinese dialects display a whole host of differences, yet share close affinities as well – Cantonese (the dialect spoken in Guangdong, including Hong Kong, and parts of Guangxi) is probably as different from Mandarin (a northern dialect that has become the common language of China) as French is from Italian. This means that mutual intelligibility is not possible unless a lot of guesswork and patience (or alcohol) is called into play. However, many southern Chinese speakers of Cantonese are at least familiar with Mandarin and have little problem with it, while many Mandarin speakers just switch off when they hear Cantonese. In the balance, Mandarin is a useful dialect, while Cantonese is not.

Mandarin speakers who turn to the colossal task of learning Cantonese have to contend with seven tones (seven if you're keen, six if you're not), different pronunciation and a bus-load of slang that Mandarin doesn't have. The tones of Cantonese are in a far wider range than those of Mandarin, and that's what gives the dialect its sing-song quality; Mandarin only has four tones which are tightly bunched together.

The sounds of Cantonese are sometimes similar to those of Mandarin, and sometimes wildly different, so guessing doesn't always work, although guessing is done wholesale leading to much puzzlement and laughter all round.

Cantonese slang is a rich part of the dialect, and is constantly evolving, especially in Hong Kong. In its pure form, and because it has to act as the lowest common denominator of communication, Mandarin finds itself almost devoid of an evolving slang vocabulary.

On the plus side, most of the grammar is the same (apart from a few anomalies) so cross-dialect learners can at least hit the ground running on that front. Many of the proverbs, idioms and phrases are the same, even though some basic expressions differ (the differences are easily learned) And the written form is the same. Cantonese does insist on a few of its own non-standard characters, but for the most part it is the same language. Written Chinese in Hong Kong is composed of traditional characters, while simplified characters are used on the mainland, but problems of intelligibility are not huge. There are also strong indications that a war is being waged between simplified characters and traditional characters on the mainland.

Last but not least, a tonal relationship amazingly exists between Mandarin and Cantonese which can lead to reasonably accurate guesswork as to how the tone will translate. For example, the rising tone of Mandarin almost exclusively becomes its opposite, the low falling tone of Cantonese. With a little study, the relationship between the tones of the two dialects can be learned.

Damian Harper

same way in Chinese. The catch is mastering the tones.

Tones Chinese is a language with a large number of words with the same pronunciation but a different meaning; what distinguishes these 'homophones' is their 'tonal' quality – the raising and lowering of pitch on certain syllables. Mandarin has four tones – high, rising, falling-rising and falling, plus a fifth 'neutral' tone which you can all but ignore. To illustrate, look at the word *ma* which has four different meanings according to tone:

high	*mā*	'mother'
rising	*má*	'hemp' or 'numb'
falling-rising	*mǎ*	'horse'
falling	*mà*	'to scold' or 'swear'

As intimidating as this all sounds, spoken Chinese isn't a particularly difficult language to master. On the other hand, learning to read and write Chinese characters takes considerable time and effort.

Writing System
Chinese is often referred to as a language of pictographs. Many of the basic Chinese characters are in fact highly stylised pictures of what they represent, but most Chinese characters (around 90%) are compounds of a 'meaning' element and a 'sound' element.

So just how many Chinese characters are there? It's possible to verify the existence of some 56,000 characters, but the vast majority of these are archaic. It is commonly felt that a well educated, contemporary Chinese might know and use between 6000 and 8000 characters. To read a Chinese newspaper you will need to know 2000 to 3000, but 1200 to 1500 would be enough to get the gist.

Writing systems usually alter people's perception of a language, and this is certainly true of Chinese. Each Chinese character represents a spoken syllable, leading many people to declare that Chinese is a 'monosyllabic language.' Actually, it's more a case of having a monosyllabic writing system. While the building block of the Chinese language is indeed the monosyllabic Chinese character, Chinese words are usually a combination of two or more characters. You could think of Chinese words as being compounds. The Chinese word for

Name Chops
(yìnzhāng)

The traditional Chinese name chop or seal has been used for thousands of years. It is quite likely that people began using name chops because Chinese characters are so complex and few people in ancient times were able to read and write. In addition, chops date back to a time when there was no other form of identification such as fingerprinting, picture ID cards and computer files.

A chop served both as a form of identification and as a valid signature. All official documents in China needed a chop to be valid. Naturally, this made a chop quite valuable, for with another person's chop it was possible to sign contracts and other legal documents in their name.

Today, most Chinese are literate, but the tradition is still kept alive in China. In fact, without a chop it is difficult or impossible to enter into legally binding contracts in China. It might occur to you that obtaining a fake or forged chop would be very easy. Indeed, it is. It's also a very serious crime in China.

If you spend any length of time in China, you will almost certainly need to have a chop made. If you're staying a short time, a chop makes a great souvenir. A chop can be made quickly, but first you will need to have your name translated into Chinese characters.

There are many different sizes and styles of chops. Inexpensive small chops can be carved from wood or plastic – upmarket chops are made from ivory, jade, marble or steel. Only a special type of slow-drying red ink is used for a name chop, so if you buy a chop in China then get an inkpad too. ■

LANGUAGE

Divination

Divination, as practised by Shang priests, was a procedure that involved applying heat to the bones of cattle or to the shells of turtles. Grooves were carved on one side of the bones and shells, and heated rods were inserted into them. The resulting cracks that appeared on the other side could be 'read' for clues to everything from the outcome of crops to whether it was wise to put a down payment on that new plough.

For scholars of ancient Chinese, the Shang practice of writing the topic of divination and often the outcome on the bones provide the only surviving record of early Chinese ideographs. Some 50,000 oracle bones and fragments have been unearthed, mainly from storage pits in Xiaotun in Henan. From these, 3000 early Chinese characters have been identified. ■

'east' is composed of a single character (*dōng*), but must be combined with the character for 'west' (*xī*) to form the word for 'thing' (*dōngxī*). English has some compound words too (although not nearly as many as Chinese), examples being 'whitewash' and 'backslide'.

Theoretically, all Chinese dialects share the same written system. In practice, Cantonese adds about 3000 specialised characters of its own and many of the dialects don't have a written form at all.

Simplification In the interests of promoting universal literacy, the Committee for Reforming the Chinese Language was set up by the Beijing government in 1954. Around 2200 Chinese characters were simplified. Chinese communities outside China (notably Taiwan and Hong Kong), however, continue to use the traditional, full-form characters.

Over the past few years – probably as a result of large-scale investment by Overseas Chinese and tourism – full-form characters have returned to China. These are mainly seen in advertising (where the traditional characters are considered more attractive) and on restaurant, hotel and shop signs. While the government is adamant that the simplified characters are the only officially recognised system, there are indications that the two systems are coming into competition in China.

Pinyin The Chinese in 1958 adopted a system of writing their language using the Roman alphabet. It's known as *pīnyīn*. The original idea was to eventually do away with characters. However, tradition dies hard, and the idea has been abandoned.

Pinyin is often used on shop fronts, street signs and advertising billboards. Don't expect Chinese people to be able to use Pinyin, however. There are indications that the use of the Pinyin system is diminishing.

In the countryside and the smaller towns you may not see a single Pinyin sign anywhere, so unless you speak Chinese you'll need a phrasebook with Chinese characters.

Since 1979 all translated texts of Chinese diplomatic documents, as well as Chinese magazines published in foreign languages, have used the Pinyin system for spelling names and places. Pinyin replaces the old Wade-Giles and Lessing systems of romanising Chinese script. Thus under Pinyin, 'Mao Tse-tung' becomes Mao Zedong; 'Chou En-lai' becomes Zhou Enlai; and 'Peking' becomes Beijing. The name of the country remains as it has been written most often: 'China' in English and German, and 'Chine' in French – in Pinyin it's Zhongguo.

Now that Hong Kong (a romanisation of Cantonese for 'fragrant harbour') has gone over to China, many think it will only be a matter of time before it gets renamed Xianggang.

Pronunciation

Most letters are pronounced as in English, with the exception of the following:

Vowels

a	as in 'father'
ai	as in 'high'
ao	as the 'ow' in 'cow'
e	as the 'u' in 'fur'
ei	as the 'ei' in 'weigh'
i	as the 'ee' in 'meet' (or like the 'oo' in 'book' after **c, ch, r, s, sh, z** or **zh**)
ian	as in 'yen'
ie	as the English word 'yeah'
o	as in 'or'
ou	as the 'oa' in 'boat'
u	as in 'flute'
ui	as in the word 'way'
uo	like a 'w' followed by 'o'
yu	as in the German 'ü' – pucker your lips and try saying 'ee'
ü	as the German 'ü'

Consonants

c	as the 'ts' in 'bits'
ch	as in 'chop', but with the tongue curled back
h	as in 'hay', but articulated from farther back in the throat
q	as the 'ch' in 'cheese'
r	as the 's' in 'pleasure'
sh	as in 'ship', but with the tongue curled back
x	as in 'ship'
z	as the 'dz' in 'suds'
zh	as the 'j' in 'judge' but with the tongue curled back

The only consonants that occur at the end of a syllable are **n, ng** and **r.**

In Pinyin, apostrophes are occasionally used to separate syllables in order to prevent ambiguity, eg the word *píng'ān* can be written with an apostrohe after the 'g' to prevent it being pronounced as *pín'gān.*

Gestures

Hand signs are frequently used in China. The 'thumbs-up' sign has a long tradition as an indication of excellence. An alternative way to indicate excellence is to gently pull your earlobe between your thumb and index finger.

Finger counting is widely used in China, but usually as a confirmation of a spoken number. One of the disadvantages of finger counting is that there are regional differences. The sign for No 10, for instance, can also be made with a single fist in many parts of China.

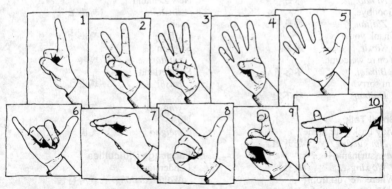

The Chinese system of finger counting.

LANGUAGE

Phrasebooks

Phrasebooks are invaluable, but it's a better idea to copy out the appropriate phrases in Chinese rather than show someone the book – otherwise they may take it and read every page! Reading place names or street signs isn't difficult since the Chinese name is usually accompanied by the Pinyin form; if not you'll soon learn lots of characters just by repeated exposure. A small dictionary with English, Pinyin and Chinese characters is also useful for learning a few words.

Lonely Planet publishes a *Mandarin phrasebook*, a *Cantonese phrasebook* and a *Tibetan phrasebook*.

Pronouns

I
wǒ 我
you
nǐ 你
he, she, it
tā 他/她/它
we, us
wǒmen 我们
you (plural)
nǐmen 你们
they, them
tāmen 他们

Greetings & Civilities

Hello.
Nǐ hǎo. 你好
Goodbye.
Zàijiàn. 再见
Thank you.
Xièxie. 谢谢
You're welcome.
Búkèqi. 不客气
I'm sorry.
Duìbùqǐ. 对不起

Small Talk

May I ask your name?
Nín guìxìng? 您贵姓?
My (sur)name is ...
Wǒ xìng ... 我姓...
Where are you from?
Nǐ shì cōng nǎr láide? 你是从哪儿来的?

I'm from ...
Wǒ shì cōng ... láide. 我是从 ... 来的
No. (don't have)
Méi yǒu. 没有
No. (not so)
Búshì. 不是
I'm a foreign student.
Wǒ shì liúxuéshēng. 我是留学生
What's to be done now?
Zěnme bàn? 怎么办?
It doesn't matter.
Méishì. 没事
I want ...
Wǒ yào ... 我要
No, I don't want it.
Búyào. 不要

Countries

Australia
àodàlìyà 澳大利亚
Canada
jiānádà 加拿大
Denmark
dānmài 丹麦
France
fǎguó 法国
Germany
déguó 德国
Netherlands
hélán 荷兰
New Zealand
xīnxīlán 新西兰
Spain
xībānyá 西班牙
Sweden
ruìdiǎn 瑞典
Switzerland
ruìshì 瑞士
UK
yīngguó 英国
USA
měiguó 美国

Language Difficulties

I understand.
Wǒ tīngdedǒng. 我听得懂
I don't understand.
Wǒ tīngbudǒng. 我听不懂

Do you understand?
Dǒng ma?　　　懂吗?
Could you speak more slowly please?
Qīng nǐ shuō màn yīdiǎn, hǎo ma?
　　　请你说慢一点, 好吗?

Visas & Documents
passport
hùzhào　　　护照
visa
qiānzhèng　　　签证
visa extension
yáncháng qiānzhèng 延长签证
Public Security Bureau (PSB)
gōng'ān jú　　　公安局
Foreign Affairs Branch
wài shì kē　　　外事科

Toilets
toilet (restroom)
cèsuǒ　　　厕所
toilet paper
wèishēng zhǐ　　　卫生纸
bathroom (washroom)
xǐshǒu jiān　　　洗手间

Money
How much is it?
Dūoshǎo qián?　　　多少钱?
Is there anything cheaper?
Yǒu piányi yìdiǎn de ma?
　　　有便宜一点的吗?
That's too expensive.
Tài guìle.　　　太贵了
Bank of China
zhōngguó yínháng 中国银行
change money
huàn qián　　　换钱

Accommodation
hotel
lǚguǎn　　　旅馆
tourist hotel
bīnguǎn/fàndiàn/jiǔdiàn
　　　宾馆/饭店/酒店
reception desk
zǒng fúwù tái　　　总服务台
dormitory
duōrénfáng　　　多人房

single room
dānrénfáng　　　单人房
twin room
shuāngrénfáng　　　双人房
bed
chuángwèi　　　床位
economy room (no bath)
pǔtōngfáng　　　普通房
standard room
biāozhǔn fángjiān 标准房间
studio suite
tàofáng　　　套房
deluxe suite
háohuá tàofáng　　　豪华套房
book a whole room
bāofáng　　　包房
Is there a room vacant?
Yǒu méiyǒu kōng fángjiān?
　　　有没有空房间?
Yes, there is.
Yǒu.　　　有
No, there isn't.
Méiyǒu.　　　没有
Can I see the room?
Wǒ néng kànkan fángjiān ma?
　　　我能看看房间吗?
I don't like this room.
Wǒ bù xǐhuan zhèijiān fángjiān.
　　　我不喜欢这间房
Are there any messages for me?
yǒu méiyǒu liú huà?
　　　有没有留话?
May I have a hotel namecard?
yǒu méiyǒu lǚguǎn de míngpiàn?
　　　有没有旅馆的名片?
Could I have these clothes washed, please?
qīng bǎ zhè xiē yīfú xǐ gānjìng, hǎo ma?
　　　请把这些衣服洗干净, 好吗?

Post
post office
yóujú　　　邮局
letter
xìn　　　信
envelope
xìnfēng　　　信封
package
bāoguǒ　　　包裹

LANGUAGE

air mail
  hángkōng xìn   航空信
surface mail
  píngyóu   平邮
stamps
  yóupiào   邮票
postcard
  míngxìnpiàn   明信片
aerogramme
  hángkōng xìnjiàn   航空信件
poste restante
  cúnjú hòulǐnglán   存局候领栏
express mail (EMS)
  yóuzhèng tèkuài
  zhuāndì   邮政特快专递
registered mail
  guà hào   挂号

Telecommunications

telephone
  diànhuà   电话
telephone office
  diànxùn dàlóu   电讯大楼
telephone card
  diànhuà kǎ   电话卡
international call
  guójì diànhuà   国际电话
collect call
  duìfāng fùqián diànhuà
     对方付钱电话
direct-dial call
  zhíbō diànhuà   直拨电话
fax
  chuánzhēn   传真

Directions

map
  dìtú   地图
Where is the ...?
  ... zài nǎlǐ?   ... 在哪里?
I'm lost.
  Wǒ mílùle.   我迷路了
Turn right.
  Yòu zhuǎn.   右转
Turn left.
  Zuǒ zhuǎn.   左转
Go straight ahead.
  Yìzhí zǒu.   一直走
Turn around.
  Wàng huí zǒu.   往回走

alley
  nòng   弄
lane
  xiàng, hútóng   巷\胡同
road
  lù   路
boulevard
  dàdào   大道
section
  duàn   段
street
  jiē, dàjiē   街，大街
No 21
  21 hào   21号

Bicycle

bicycle
  zìxíngchē   自行车
I want to hire a bicycle.
  Wǒ yào zū yíliàng
  zìxíngchē.
     我要租一辆自行车
How much is it per day?
  Yìtiān duōshǎo qián?   一天多少钱?
How much is it per hour?
  Yíge xiǎoshí
  duōshǎo qián?   一个小时多少钱?
How much is the
deposit?
  Yājīn dūoshǎo qián?   押金多少钱?

Time

What's the time?
  Jǐ diǎn?   几点?
... hour ... minute
  ... diǎn ... fēn   ... 点 ...分
3.05
  sān diǎn wǔ fēn   3点5分
now
  xiànzài   现在
today
  jīntiān   今天
tomorrow
  míngtiān   明天
day after tomorrow
  hòutiān   后天
three days from now
  dàhòutiān   大后天
yesterday
  zuótiān   昨天

Wait a moment.
  Děng yī xià. 等一下

Transport
I want to go to ...
  Wǒ yào qù ... 我要去 ...
I want to get off.
  Wǒ yào xiàchē. 我要下车
luggage
  xíngli 行李
left-luggage room
  jìcún chù 寄存处
one ticket
  yìzhāng piào 一张票
two tickets
  liǎngzhāng piào 两张票
What time does it
  depart?
  Jǐdiǎn kāi? 几点开?
What time does it arrive?
  Jǐdiǎn dào? 几点到?
How long does the trip take?
  Zhècì lǚxíng yào huā duōcháng
  shíjiān?
  这次旅行要花多长时间?
buy a ticket
  mǎi piào 买票
refund a ticket
  tuì piào 退票
taxi
  chūzū chē 出租车
microbus ('bread') taxi
  miànbāo chē, miàndī 面包车，面的
Please use the meter.
  Dǎ biǎo. 打表

Air
airport
  fēijīchǎng 飞机场
CAAC ticket office
  zhōngguó mínháng shòupiào chù
  中国民航售票处
charter flight
  bāojī 包机
one way ticket
  dānchéng piào 单程票
round-trip ticket
  láihuí piào 来回票
boarding pass
  dēngjì kǎ 登机卡

reconfirm
  quèrèn 确认
cancel
  qǔxiāo 取消
bonded baggage
  cúnzhàn xínglǐ 存栈行李

Bus
bus
  gōnggòng qìchē 公共汽车
minibus
  xiǎo gōnggòng qìchē 小公共汽车
long-distance bus
  station
  chángtú qìchē zhàn 长途汽车站
When is the first bus?
  Tóubān qìchē jǐdiǎn kāi?
  头班汽车几点开?
When is the last bus?
  Mòbān qìchē jǐdiǎn kāi?
  末班汽车几点开?
When is the next bus?
  Xià yìbān qìchē jǐdiǎn kāi?
  下一班汽车几点开?

Train
train
  huǒchē 火车
ticket office
  shòupiào chù 售票处
railway station
  huǒchē zhàn 火车站
hard-seat
  yìngxí, yìngzuò 硬席, 硬座
soft-seat
  ruǎnxí, ruǎnzuò 软席, 软座
hard-sleeper
  yìngwò 硬卧
soft-sleeper
  ruǎnwò 软卧
platform ticket
  zhàntái piào 站台票
Which platform?
  Dìjǐhào zhàntái? 第几号站台?
upgrade ticket (after boarding)
  bǔpiào 补票
subway (underground)
  dìxiàtiě 地下铁
subway station
  dìtiě zhàn 地铁站

LANGUAGE

Emergency

emergency
  jǐnjí qíngkuàng   紧急情况
hospital emergency
room
  jízhěn shì   急诊室
police
  jǐngchá   警察
Fire!
  Zháohuǒ le!   着火了!
Help!
  Jiùmìng a!   救命啊!
Thief!
  Xiǎotōu!   小偷!

Health

I'm sick.
  Wǒ shēngbìngle.   我生病了
I'm injured.
  Wǒ shòushāngle.   我受伤了
hospital
  yīyuàn   医院
laxative
  xièyào   泻药
anti-diarrhoea
medicine
  zhǐxièyào   止泻药
rehydration salts
  *shūwéizhí dīnàfā
pàodìng*
      舒维质低钠发泡锭
aspirin
  āsīpǐlín   阿斯匹林
antibiotics
  kàngjùnsù   抗菌素
condom
  bìyùn tào   避孕套
tampon
  wèishēng mián tiáo 卫生棉条
sanitary napkin
(Kotex)
  wèishēng mián   卫生棉
sunscreen (UV)
lotion
  fáng shài yóu   防晒油
mosquito coils
  wénxiāng   蚊香
mosquito pads
  diàn wénxiāng   电蚊香

Numbers

0	*líng*	零
1	*yī, yāo*	一，么
2	*èr, liǎng*	二，两
3	*sān*	三
4	*sì*	四
5	*wǔ*	五
6	*liù*	六
7	*qī*	七
8	*bā*	八
9	*jiǔ*	九
10	*shí*	十
11	*shíyī*	十一
12	*shí'èr*	十二
20	*èrshí*	二十
21	*èrshíyī*	二十一
100	*yìbǎi*	一百
200	*liǎngbǎi*	两百
1000	*yìqiān*	一千
2000	*liǎngqiān*	两千
10,000	*yíwàn*	一万
20,000	*liǎngwàn*	两万
100,000	*shíwàn*	十万
200,000	*èrshíwàn*	二十万

Studying Chinese

China and Taiwan are the two best places to study Mandarin Chinese. Logically, one would expect Taiwan to be more expensive, but in fact mainland China is at least as expensive because foreigners are charged very highly for tuition. However, if you want to study only the simplified characters and the Pinyin romanisation scheme, then mainland China is the logical place to go.

Foreigners are usually assigned to a separate dormitory and aren't permitted to live with Chinese locals, although it is possible to request a Chinese roommate (who most likely will use the opportunity to practice English with you). Some schools (Beijing University is one) try to coerce foreigners into 'volunteer teaching' at special summer camps – basically, you're being used as unpaid labour.

Most foreign students prefer Beijing Language Institute (BLI) (*yǔyán xuéyuàn*) over Beijing University. There are several other schools in Beijing that accept foreign

Learning Chinese

More and more people are developing an interest in learning the Chinese language, and this is not surprising. Never has interest in China been more widespread. If you can speak English, and you learn Chinese, the result of all that effort is that you will be able to communicate with approximately one out of every two people in the world, because they will speak either Chinese or English. Of course, no other two languages share such a large slice of the pie.

As a consequence of this fresh interest in Chinese and its dialects, schools, universities and colleges around the world are gearing up for serious over-subscription of Chinese courses. But before taking the plunge, a lot of people want an answer to the question, how hard is Chinese?

Learning Chinese is, quite simply, a major headache. But it all depends on whether you tackle the written form or just concentrate on the spoken form of Chinese. The spoken form can be tackled reasonably quickly, and depends on personal aptitude for spoken language and other variables such as confidence and sociability, but the written form is just a case of sitting down and slogging it out with a dictionary and vast amounts of patience.

The student of French or German, or any language that uses an alphabet, can quite quickly fall into step with similar written forms, because as a child, years of work have already been invested in speed-reading the very same alphabet. Just a glance at a French or German newspaper will reveal recognisable words and patterns of meaning that require little effort. Learning Chinese, however, introduces the learner to a novel system of writing that takes roughly as long to learn as it takes the Chinese child to learn.

The Chinese written language uses pictures, rather than sounds, to represent ideas. Unfortunately, we are dealing with an archaic script and most of the characters only obliquely suggest the image in question. Each character has to be learned, not only with its meaning, but with its pronunciation because the pronunciation is at best only suggested by the character. Learning is a very slow process and decent fluency only comes with a knowledge in excess of 5000 characters; an ability to read a newspaper fluently will come after at least six years full time exposure to the language.

To be able to read with the same ease that English-speaking students of French can glance over a French newspaper will take even longer. Writing the language is another matter entirely, as memorising the script for the purposes of writing is much harder than reading, and learning how to write harmonious Chinese characters is harder still.

Sticking with the spoken language is easier and, of course, more useful. Reasonable fluency can be achieved much more quickly; however, Chinese is linguistically and culturally very different from English, and again, perseverance and patience are essential for success. The main challenge are the tones, which must be learned if you want people to understand, rather than guess what you are saying. Tones are very hard to learn, but they differentiate the meaning of words, so they are an essential part of the language. Once you have learned one dialect of Chinese, you have broken the back of the language and learning other dialects is not hard.

For those who take to it, learning Chinese is a joy that surprises and fascinates. The language has a wonderful balance that gives it an attractive symmetry and logic. And for those who struggle with the written form, they learn to unravel a mysterious and beautiful script that is both intriguing and unique. These rewards can only be obtained through hard work and patience, which makes the goal even more rewarding. Those who succeed will also be part of a small community of foreigners who speak the language; for quite a few years now, a Canadian by the name of Dashan (literally 'big mountain') has been known to all Chinese in China because he speaks flawless Mandarin, so find your place on the bandwagon and start learning!

Damian Harper

students, and tuition fees vary considerably. Other well known schools with Chinese language programs include Nankai University in Tianjin, Nanjing University in Nanjing and Fudan University in Shanghai. Fees for full-time study can run as high as US$7000 per semester, but this usually includes tuition, room and board. The summer semester is normally half price (US$3500).

In Taiwan, the best place to study Chinese is probably Taiwan Normal University (☎ (02) 2363-9123), Mandarin Training Centre (*táiwān shīfàn dàxué*), 129-1 Hoping E Rd, Section 1, Taipei. Gaining admission is fairly easy – you can pretty much show up a few weeks before the semester begins and enrol without making any prior arrangements. Tuition only is US$800 per semester, but room and board has to be arranged separately and living costs in Taipei aren't cheap.

A more formal course (with academic credit) is offered at Chengchi University (☎ (02) 2939-3091) (*zhèngzhì dàxué*) 64 Chihnan Rd, Section 2, Wenshan District, Taipei. Application has to be made well in advance.

Hong Kong is a good place for studying Cantonese. Although about half the population of Hong Kong speaks Mandarin, the local accent is so radically different from what you hear in Beijing that comprehension can be very difficult. The New Asia Yale in China Language School, at the Chinese University in the New Territories, offers courses in both Mandarin and Cantonese. Another option is the Hong Kong Baptist University.

While studying in China, Hong Kong or Taiwan, it's possible to receive academic credit towards a degree in your home country. However, this is only possible if your university has a foreign exchange programme and arrangements are made in advance. Student organisations have some information on these programs – in the USA try the Council for International Educational Exchange (☎ (888) 268-6245; www.ciee.org).

FOOD VOCABULARY

For a full discussion of Chinese cuisine see the Food section in the Facts for the Visitor chapter.

Useful Terms

restaurant
   cāntīng   餐厅
I'm vegetarian.
   wǒ chī sù   我吃素
menu
   cài dān   菜单
bill (cheque)
   mǎi dān/jiézhàng
               买单/结帐
set meal (no menu)
   tàocān   套餐
to eat/let's eat
   chī fàn   吃饭
chopsticks
   kuàizi   筷子
knife
   dàozi   刀子
fork
   chāzi   叉子
spoon
   tiáogēng/tāngchí
               调羹/汤匙

Rice   饭
steamed white rice
   mǐfàn   米饭
watery rice porridge
   xīfàn   稀饭
rice noodles
   mǐfěn   米粉

Bread, Buns & Dumplings 麦类
western-style bread
   miànbāo   面包
fried roll
   yínsī juǎn   银丝卷
steamed bun
   mántóu   馒头
steamed meat bun
   bāozi   包子
fried bread stick
   yóutiáo   油条
dumplings
   jiǎozi   饺子
prawn cracker
   lóngxiā piàn   龙虾片

Vegetable Dishes 菜类

fried rice with vegetables
  shūcài chǎofàn 蔬菜炒饭
fried noodles with
vegetables
  shūcài chǎomiàn 蔬菜炒面
spicy peanuts
  wǔxiāng huāshēng mǐ
             五香花生米
fried peanuts
  yóuzhà huāshēng mǐ
             油炸花生米
spiced cold vegetables
  liángbàn shíjǐn 凉拌什锦
Chinese salad
  jiācháng liángcài 家常凉菜
fried rape in oyster sauce
  háoyóu pácài dǎn
             蚝油扒菜胆
fried rape with
mushrooms
  dōnggū pácài dǎn
             冬菇扒菜胆
fried bean curd in
  oyster sauce
  háoyóu dòufǔ 蚝油豆腐
spicy hot bean curd
  mápó dòufǔ 麻婆豆腐
bean curd casserole
  shāguō dòufǔ 沙锅豆腐
bean curd and mushrooms
  mógū dòufǔ 磨菇豆腐
garlic and morning
  glory
  dàsuàn kōngxīn cài
             大蒜空心菜
fried garlic
  sù chǎo dàsuàn 素炒大蒜
fried eggplant
  sùshāo qiézi 素烧茄子
fried beansprouts
  sù chǎo dòuyá 素炒豆芽
fried green vegetables
  sù chǎo qīngcài 素炒青菜
fried green beans
  sù chǎo biǎndòu 素炒扁豆
fried cauliflower
  and tomato
  chǎo fānqié càihuā
             炒蕃茄菜花

broiled mushroom
  sù chǎo mógū 素炒磨菇
black fungus and mushroom
  mù'ěr huákǒu mó 木耳滑口磨
fried white radish patty
  luóbo gāo 萝卜糕
assorted hors d'oeuvre
  shíjǐn pīnpán 什锦拼盘
assorted vegetarian food
  sù shíjǐn 素什锦

Egg Dishes 蛋类

preserved egg
  sōnghuā dàn 松花蛋
fried rice with egg
  jīdàn chǎofàn 鸡蛋炒饭
fried tomatoes and eggs
  xīhóngshì chǎo jīdàn
             西红柿炒鸡蛋
egg and flour omelette
  jiān bǐng 煎饼

Beef Dishes 牛肉类

fried rice with beef
  niúròusī chǎofàn 牛肉丝炒饭
noodles with beef
  (soupy)
  niúròu tāng miàn 牛肉汤面
spiced noodles with beef
  niúròu gān miàn 牛肉干面
fried noodles with beef
  niúròu chǎomiàn 牛肉炒面
beef with white rice
  niúròu fàn 牛肉饭
beef platter
  niúròu tiěbǎn 牛肉铁板
beef with oyster sauce
  háoyóu niúròu 蚝油牛肉
beef braised in soy sauce
  hóngshāo niúròu 红烧牛肉
beef with tomatoes
  fānqié niúròu
  piàn 番茄牛肉片
beef with green peppers
  qīngjiāo niúròu piàn
             青椒牛肉片
beef curry and rice
  gālí niúròu fàn 咖喱牛肉饭
beef curry and noodles
  gālí niúròu miàn 咖喱牛肉面

Chicken Dishes　鸡肉类

fried rice with chicken
　jīsī chǎofàn　鸡丝炒饭
noodles with chicken (soupy)
　jīsī tāng miàn　鸡丝汤面
fried noodles with chicken
　jīsī chǎomiàn　鸡丝炒面
chicken leg with white rice
　jītuǐ fàn　鸡腿饭
spicy hot chicken and peanuts
　gōngbào jīdīng　宫爆鸡丁
fruit kernal with chicken
　guǒwèi jīdīng　果味鸡丁
sweet and sour chicken
　tángcù jīdīng　糖醋鸡丁
sauteed spicy chicken pieces
　làzi jīdīng　辣子鸡丁
sauteed chicken with green peppers
　jiàngbào jīdīng　酱爆鸡丁
chicken slices and
　tomato sauce
　fānqié jīdīng　蕃茄鸡丁
mushrooms and chicken
　cǎomó jīdīng　草蘑鸡丁
chicken pieces in oyster sauce
　háoyóu jīdīng　蚝油鸡丁
chicken braised in soy sauce
　hóngshāo jīkuài　红烧鸡块
sauteed chicken
　with water chestnuts
　nánjiè jīpiàn　南芥鸡片
sliced chicken with
　crispy rice
　jīpiàn guōbā　鸡片锅巴
chicken curry
　gālí jīròu　咖喱鸡肉
chicken curry and rice
　gālí jīròu fàn　咖喱鸡肉饭
chicken curry and noodles
　gālí jīròu miàn　咖喱鸡肉面

Duck Dishes　鸭肉类

Beijing Duck
　běijīng kǎoyā　北京烤鸭
duck with white rice
　yāròu fàn　鸭肉饭
duck with noodles
　yāròu miàn　鸭肉面
duck with fried noodles
　yāròu chǎomiàn　鸭肉炒面

Pork Dishes　猪肉类

pork chop with white rice
　páigǔ fàn　排骨饭
fried rice with pork
　ròusī chǎofàn　肉丝炒饭
fried noodles with pork
　ròusī chǎomiàn　肉丝炒面
pork and mustard greens
　zhàcài ròusī　榨菜肉丝
noodles, pork and mustard greens
　zhàcài ròusī miàn　榨菜肉丝面
pork with crispy rice
　ròupiàn guōbā　肉片锅巴
sweet and sour pork fillet
　tángcù zhūròu piàn
　　　　　糖醋猪肉片
sweet and sour pork fillet
　tángcù lǐjī　糖醋里脊
pork fillet with white sauce
　huáliū lǐjī　滑溜里脊
shredded pork fillet
　chǎo lǐjī sī　炒里脊丝
soft pork fillet
　ruǎnzhá lǐjī　软炸里脊
spicy hot pork pieces
　gōngbào ròudīng　宫爆肉丁
fried black pork pieces
　yuánbào lǐjī　芫爆里脊
sauteed diced pork and soy sauce
　jiàngbào ròudīng　酱爆肉丁
spicy pork cubelets
　làzi ròudīng　辣子肉丁
pork cubelets and cucumber
　huángguā ròudīng　黄瓜肉丁
golden pork slices
　jīnyín ròusī　金银肉丝
sauteed shredded pork
　qīngchǎo ròusī　清炒肉丝
shredded pork and hot sauce
　yúxiāng ròusī　鱼香肉丝
shredded pork and green peppers
　qīngjiāo ròusī　青椒肉丝
shredded pork and bamboo shoots
　dōngsǔn ròusī　冬笋肉丝
shredded pork and green beans
　biǎndòu ròusī　扁豆肉丝
pork with oyster sauce
　háoyóu ròusī　蚝油肉丝
boiled pork slices
　shuǐzhǔ ròupiàn　水煮肉片

pork, eggs and black fungus
   mùxū ròu   木须肉
pork and fried onions
   yángcōng chǎo ròupiàn
                 洋葱炒肉片
fried rice (assorted)
   shíjǐn chǎofàn   什锦炒饭
fried rice Cantonese-style
   guǎngzhōu chǎofàn
                 广州炒饭

Seafood Dishes   海鲜类
fried rice with shrimp
   xiārén chǎofàn   虾仁炒饭
fried noodles with shrimp
   xiārén chǎomiàn 虾仁炒面
diced shrimp with peanuts
   gōngbào xiārén   宫爆虾仁
sauteed shrimp
   qīngchǎo xiārén 清炒虾仁
deep-fried shrimp
   zhà xiārén   炸虾仁
fried shrimp with
  mushroom
   xiānmó xiārén   鲜蘑虾仁
squid with crispy rice
   yóuyú guōbā   鱿鱼锅巴
sweet and sour squid roll
   suānlà yóuyú juàn 酸辣鱿鱼卷
fish braised in soy sauce
   hóngshāo yú   红烧鱼
braised sea cucumber
   hóngshāo hǎishēn 红烧海参
clams
   gé   蛤
crab
   pángxiè   螃蟹
lobster
   lóngxiā   龙虾

Soup   汤类
three kinds seafood soup
   sān xiān tāng   三鲜汤
squid soup
   yóuyú tāng   鱿鱼汤
hot and sour soup
   suānlà tāng   酸辣汤
tomato and egg soup
   xīhóngshì dàn tāng
               西红柿蛋汤

corn and egg thick soup
   fènghuáng lìmǐ gēng
               凤凰栗米羹
egg and vegetable soup
   dànhuā tāng   蛋花汤
mushroom and egg soup
   mógu dànhuā tāng 蘑菇蛋花汤
fresh fish soup
   shēng yú tāng   生鱼汤
vegetable soup
   shūcài tāng   蔬菜汤
cream of tomato soup
   nǎiyóu fānqié tāng
               奶油蕃茄汤
cream of mushroom soup
   nǎiyóu xiānmó tāng
               奶油鲜蘑汤
pickled mustard green soup
   zhàcài tāng   榨菜汤
bean curd and vegetable
  soup
   dòufǔ cài tāng   豆腐菜汤
wanton soup
   húndùn tāng   馄钝汤
clear soup
   qīng tāng   清汤

Miscellanea & Exotica 其它
kebab
   ròu chuàn   肉串
goat, mutton
   yáng ròu   羊肉
dogmeat
   gǒu ròu   狗肉
deermeat (venison)
   lùròu   鹿肉
snake
   shé ròu   蛇肉
ratmeat
   lǎoshǔ ròu   老鼠肉
pangolin
   chuānshānjiǎ   穿山甲
frog
   qīngwā   青蛙
eel
   shàn yú   鳝鱼
turtle
   hǎiguī   海龟
Mongolian hotpot
   huǒguō   火锅

LANGUAGE

Condiments 佐料

garlic
  dàsuàn   大蒜

black pepper
  hújiāo   胡椒

hot pepper
  làjiāo   辣椒

hot sauce
  làjiāo jiàng   辣椒酱

ketchup
  fānqié jiàng   蕃茄酱

salt
  yán   盐

MSG
  wèijīng   味精

soy sauce
  jiàng yóu   酱油

vinegar
  cù   醋

sesame seed oil
  zhīmá yóu   芝麻油

butter
  huáng yóu   黄油

sugar
  táng   糖

jam
  guǒ jiàng   果酱

honey
  fēngmì   蜂蜜

DRINKS VOCABULARY

For more information about Chinese beverages, see the Drinks section in the Facts for the Visitor chapter.

beer
  píjiǔ   啤酒

whiskey
  wēishìjì jiǔ   威士忌酒

vodka
  fútèjiā jiǔ   伏特加酒

fizzy drink (soda)
  qìshuǐ   汽水

Coca-Cola
  kěkǒu kělè   可口可乐

tea
  chá   茶

coffee
  kāfēi   咖啡

coffee creamer
  nǎijīng   奶精

water
  kāi shuǐ   开水

mineral water
  kuàng quán shuǐ   矿泉水

red grape wine
  hóng pútáo jiǔ   红葡萄酒

white grape wine
  bái pútáo jiǔ   白葡萄酒

rice wine
  mǐ jiǔ   米酒

milk
  niúnǎi   牛奶

soybean milk
  dòujiāng   豆浆

yoghurt
  suānnǎi   酸奶

fruit juice
  guǒzhī   果汁

orange juice
  liǔchéng zhī   柳橙汁

coconut juice
  yézi zhī   椰子汁

pineapple juice
  bōluó zhī   波萝汁

mango juice
  mángguǒ zhī   芒果汁

hot
  rède   热的

ice cold
  bīngde   冰的

ice cube
  bīng kuài   冰块

CHINA GAZETTEER

Place names with Chinese pinyin and characters (provinces in **bold**).

Altai
ā'lètài 阿勒泰

Anhui
ānhuī 安徽

Anshun
ānshùn 安顺

Anyang
ānyáng 安阳

Badaling Great Wall
bādálǐng chángchéng 八达岭长城

Baisha
báishā 白沙

Baiyanggou
báiyánggōu 白洋沟

Baoding
bǎodǐng shān 宝顶山

Baoshan
bǎoshān 保山

Baotou
bāotóu 包头

Batang
bātáng 八塘

Beidaihe
běidàihé 北戴河

Beihai
běihǎi 北海

Beijing
běijīng 北京

Beishan
běi shān 北山

Bozhou
bózhōu 亳州

Cangyanshan
cāngyánshān 苍岩山

Changchun
chángchūn 长春

Changsha
chángshā 长沙

Changshu
chángshú 常熟

Chaozhou
cháozhōu 潮州

Chengde
chéngdé 承德

Chengdu
chéngdū 成都

Chenggong County
chénggòng xiàn 呈贡县

Chong'an
chóng'ān 重安

Chongqing
chóngqìng 重庆

Chongwu
chóngwǔ 崇武

Chun'an County
chún'ān xiàn 淳安县

Crescent Moon Lake
yuèyáquán 月牙泉

Daheyan
dàhéyàn 大河沿

Dali
dàlǐ 大理

Dalian
dàlián 大连

Damenglong
dà měnglóng 大勐龙

Dandong
dāndōng 丹东

Datong
dàtóng 大同

Dazu
dàzú 大足

Dêgê
dégé 德格

Dongshan
dōngshān 东山

Dongsheng
dōngshèng 东胜

Drepung
zhébàng sì 哲蚌寺

Dujiangyan
dūjiāngyàn 都江堰

Dunhuang
dūnhuáng 敦煌

Emeishan
éméishān 峨眉山

Erhai Lake
érhǎi hú 俳海湖

Fengdu			Hailar	
fēngdū	峰都		*hǎilāěr*	海拉尔
Flaming Mountains			**Hainan Island**	
huǒyànshān	火焰山		*hǎinán dǎo*	海南岛
Foshan			Hangzhou	
fóshān	佛山		*hángzhōu*	杭州
Fujian			Harbin	
fújiàn	福建		*hāěrbīn*	哈尔滨
Fuzhou			**Hebei**	
fúzhōu	福州		*héběi*	河北
			Hefei	
Ganden			*héféi*	合肥
gāndān sì	甘丹寺		Heihe	
Ganlanba			*hēihé*	黑河
gǎnlǎnbà	橄榄坝		**Heilongjiang**	
Gansu			*hēilóngjiāng*	黑龙江
gānsù	甘肃		Helanshan	
Ganzi			*hèlánshān*	贺兰山
garzê	甘孜		**Henan**	
Gaochang Ruins			*hénán*	河南
gāochāng gùchéng	高昌故城		Hengyang	
Golmud			*héngyáng*	衡阳
géěrmù	格尔木		Heqing	
Grand Canal			*hèqìng*	鹤庆
dà yùnhé	大运河		Heshun Village	
Guangdong			*héshùn xiāng*	和顺乡
guǎngdōng	广东		Hezuo	
Guangfu			*hézuò*	合作
guāngfú	光福		Hohhot	
Guangxi			*hūhéhàotè*	呼和浩特
guǎngxī	广西		**Hong Kong**	
Guangzhou			*xiāng gǎng*	香港
guǎngzhōu	广州		Hotan	
Guichi			*hétián*	和田
guìchí	贵池		Huaihua	
Guilin			*huáihuà*	怀化
guìlín	贵林		Huangguoshu Falls	
Guiping			*huángguǒshù*	
guìpíng	桂平		*dàpùbù*	黄果树瀑布
Guiyang			Huanglong	
guìyáng	贵阳		*huánglóng*	黄龙
Guizhou			Huangshan	
guìzhōu	贵州		*huángshān*	黄山
Guyuan			Huangyaguan Great Wall	
gùyuán	固原		*huángyáguān*	
Gyantse			*chángchéng*	黄崖关长城
gyangzê	江孜		Huashan	
			huáshān	华山
Haikou			**Hubei**	
hǎikǒu	海口		*húběi*	湖北

Humen		Kaifeng		
hŭmén	虎门	*kāifēng*	开封	
Hunan		Kaili		
Húnán	湖南	*kăilĭ*	凯里	
		Kangding		
Ili Valley		*kāngdìng*	康定	
yīlí gŭ	伊犁谷	Karakoram		
Inner Mongolia		Highway		
nèi ménggŭ	内蒙古	*zhōngbā gōnglù*	中巴公路	
		Kashgar		
Ji'nan		*kāshí*	喀什	
jĭ'nán	济南	Korla		
Jianchuan		*kùěrlè*	库尔勒	
jiànchuān	剑川	Kowloon		
Jiangsu		*jiŭlóng*	九龙	
jiāngsū	江苏	Kunming		
Jiangxi		*kūnmíng*	昆明	
jiāngxī	江西	Kuqa		
Jiayuguan		*kùchē*	库车	
jiāyùguān	嘉峪关			
Jigongshan		Lake Taihu		
jīgōngshān	鸡公山	*tàihú*	太湖	
Jigongshan		Langmusi		
jīgōngshān	鸡公山	*lăngmùsì*	朗木寺	
Jilin		Lanzhou		
jílín	吉林	*lánzhōu*	兰州	
Jingdezhen		Leshan		
jĭngdézhèn	景德镇	*lèshān*	乐山	
Jinggangshan (Ciping)		Lhasa		
jĭnggāng shān	井冈山	*lāsà*	拉萨	
Jinghong		Li River		
jĭnghóng	景洪	*lí jiāng*	漓江	
Jingzhen		Lianyungang		
jĭngzhēn	景真	*liányúngăng*	连云港	
Jinjiang		**Liaoning**		
jīnjiāng	金江	*liáoníng*	辽宁	
Jinning County		Lijiang		
jìnníng xiàn	晋宁县	*lìjiāng*	丽江	
Jintiancun		Lingyanshan		
jīntiáncūn	金田村	*língyán shān*	灵岩山	
Jiuhuashan		Linxia		
jiŭhuá shān	九华山	*línxià*	临夏	
Jiujiang		Litang		
jiŭjiāng	九江	*lĭtáng*	理塘	
Jiuzhaigou		Liuyuan		
jiŭzhàigōu	九寨沟	*liŭyuán*	柳园	
Jixian		Liuzhou		
jìxiàn	蓟县	*liŭzhōu*	柳州	
Jizushan		Longsheng		
jīzú shān	鸡足山	*lóngshèng*	龙胜	

LANGUAGE

Luding			Nanluoshan	
lúdìng	泸定		*nánlúoshān*	南罗山
Lunan			Nanning	
lùnán	路南		*nánníng*	南宁
Luomen			New Territories	
luòmén	洛门		*xīnjiè*	新界
Luoyang			Ningbo	
luòyáng	洛阳		*níngbō*	宁波
Lushan			Ningxia	
lúshān	庐山		*níngxià*	宁夏
			Nongdao	
Macau			*nóngdǎo*	弄岛
àomén	澳门			
Maijishan			Panshan	
màijīshān	麦积山		*pánshān*	盘山
Mangshi			Penglai	
mángshì	芒市		*pénglái*	蓬莱
Manzhouli			Pingxiang	
mǎnzhōulǐ	满洲里		*píngxiáng*	凭祥
Meishan			Putuoshan	
méishān	眉山		*pǔtuóshān*	普陀山
Meizhou				
méizhōu	湄州		Qianshan	
Menghai			*qiānshān*	千山
ménghǎI	勐海		Qingcheng Shan	
Menghun			*qīngchéng shān*	青城山
mēnghùn	勐混		Qingdao	
Menglun			*qīngdǎo*	青岛
mēnglún	勐伦		Qinghai	
Mengyang			*qīnghǎi*	青海
mēngyáng	勐养		Qingyuanshan	
Mogao Caves			*qīngyuánshān*	青原山
mògāo kū	莫高窟		Qinhuangdao	
Mohe			*qínhuángdǎo*	秦皇岛
mòhé	漠河		Qiongzhong	
Monkey Island			*qióngzhōng*	琼中
nánwān hóudǎo	南湾猴岛		Qiqihar	
Moxi			*qíqíhā'ěr*	齐齐哈尔
móxī	磨西		Qiuci Ancient City	
Mudanjiang			Ruins	
mǔdānjiāng	牡丹江		*qiūcī gǔchéng*	龟兹古城
Mutianyu Great Wall			Quanzhou	
mùtiányù chángchéng	慕田峪		*quánzhōu*	泉州
			Qufu	
Nam-tso Lake			*qūfù*	曲阜
nàmùcuò	纳木错		Qutang Gorge	
Nanchang			*qútáng xiá*	瞿塘峡
nánchāng	南昌			
Nanjing			Resonant Sand Gorge	
nánjīng	南京		*xiǎng shāwān*	响沙湾

Ruicheng			Shijiazhuang		
ruìchéng	芮城		*shíjiāzhuāng*	石家庄	
Ruili			Shiwan		
ruìlì	瑞丽		*shíwān*	石湾	
			Sichuan		
			sìchuān	四川	
Sakya			Simao		
sàjiā	萨迦		*sīmáo*	思茅	
Sanjiang			Simatai Great Wall		
sānjiāng	三江		*sīmǎtái chángchéng*	司马台长城	
Sanya			Songhuahu Qingshan		
sānyà	三亚		*sōnghuā*		
Sayram Lake			*hú qīngshān*	松花湖青山	
sàilǐmù hú	赛里木湖		Songpan		
Sera			*sōngpān*	松潘	
sèlā sì	色拉寺		Stone Forest		
Shaanxi			*shílín*	石林	
shǎnxī	陕西		Suifenhe		
Shandong			*suífēnhé*	绥芬河	
shāndōng	山东		Suzhou		
Shanghai			*sūzhōu*	苏州	
shànghǎi	上海				
Shanhaiguan			Tai'an		
shānhǎiguān	山海关		*tài'ān*	泰安	
Shantou			Taishan		
shàntóu	汕头		*tàishān*	泰山	
Shanxi			Taiyuan		
shānxī	山西		*tàiyuán*	太原	
Shaoshan			Tanggu		
sháoshān	韶山		*tánggū*	塘沽	
Shaoxing			Tangshan		
shàoxīng	绍兴		*tángshān*	唐山	
Shapotou			Tashkurgan		
shāpōtóu	沙坡头		*tǎshíkù ěrgān*	塔什库尔干	
Shennongjia			Tengchong		
shénnóngjià	神农架		*téngchōng*	腾冲	
Shenyang			Tianchi		
shěnyáng	沈阳		*tiānchí*	天池	
Shenzhen			**Tianjin**		
shēnzhèn	深圳		*tiānjīn*	天津	
Shexian			Tianpingshan		
shèxiàn	歙县/涉县		*tiānpíng shān*	天平山	
Shibing			Tianshui		
shībǐng	施秉		*tiānshuǐ*	天水	
Shidu			Tiantaishan		
shídù	十渡		*tiāntái shān*	天台山	
Shigatse			**Tibet**		
rìkāzé	日喀则		*xīzàng*	西藏	
Shigu			Tiger Leaping Gorge		
shígǔ	石鼓		*hǔtiào xiá*	虎跳峡	

Tingri *dìngrì*	定日	Xanadu *yuánshàngdū*	元上都
Tongjiang *tóngjiāng*	同江	Xiaguan *xiàguān*	下关
Tsetang *zédang*	泽当	Xiahe *xiàhé*	夏河
Tunxi *túnxī*	屯溪	Xiamen *xiàmén*	厦门
Turpan *tǔlǔfān*	吐鲁番	Xi'an *xī'ān*	西安
Ürümqi *wūlǔmùqí*	乌鲁木齐	Xianyang *xiányáng*	湘潭
Wanding *wǎndīng*	畹町	Xibaipo *xībǎipō*	西柏坡
Weihai *wēihǎi*	威海	Xidongtingshan Island *xīdòngtíng shān*	西洞庭山
Weishan *wēishān*	巍山	Xikou *xīkǒu*	西口
Wenchang *wénchāng*	文昌	Xiling Gorge *xīlíng xiá*	西陵峡
Wenzhou *wēnzhōu*	温州	Xincun *xīncūn*	新村
Wolong Nature Reserve *wòlóng zìrán bǎohùqū*	卧龙自然保护区	Xinglong *xīnglóng*	兴隆
Wudalianchi *wǔdàliánchí*	五大连池	Xinglongshan *xīnglóngshān*	兴隆山
Wudangshan *wǔdāng shān*	武当山	Xingyi *xīngyì*	兴义
Wu Gorge *wū xiá*	巫峡	Xining *xīníng*	西宁
Wuhan *wǔhàn*	武汉	**Xinjiang** *xīnjiāng*	新疆
Wuhu *wúhú*	芜湖	Xiqiao Hills *xīqiáo shān*	西樵山
Wulingyuan *wǔlíngyuán*	武陵源	Xishuangbanna *xīshuāngbǎnnà*	西双版纳
Wuqing *wǔqīng*	武清	Xizhou *xǐzhōu*	喜洲
Wutaishan *wǔtáishān*	五台山	Xuzhou *xúzhōu*	徐州
Wuxi *wúxī*	无锡	Yan'an *yán'ān*	延安
Wuyishan *wǔyíshān*	武夷山	Yangshuo *yángshuò*	阳朔
Wuzhou *wúzhōu*	梧州	Yantai *yāntái*	烟台
		Yarlung Valley *yǎlǔ liúyù*	雅鲁流域

LANGUAGE

Yichang
yíchāng 宜昌

Yinchuan
yínchuān 银川

Yingjiang
yíngjiāng 盈江

Yingtan
yīngtán 鹰潭

Yining
yíníng 伊宁

Yixian
yīxiàn 黟县

Yongding
yǒngdìng 永定

Yongping
yǒngpíng 永平

Yueyang
yuèyáng 岳阳

Yulin
yúlín 榆林

Yuncheng
yùnchéng 运城

Yungang Caves
yúngāng shíkū 云岗石窟

Yunfengshan
yúnfēng shān 云蜂山

Yunnan
yúnnán 云南

Zhalong Nature Reserve
zhālóng zìrán bǎohùqū 扎龙自然保护区

Zhangmu
zhāngmù 樟木

Zhanjiang
zhànjiāng 湛江

Zhaoqing
zhàoqìng 肇庆

Zhejiang
zhèjiāng 浙江

Zheng He Park
zhènghé gōngyuán 郑和公园

Zhengding
zhèngdìng 正定

Zhengzhou
zhèngzhōu 郑州

Zhenjiang
zhènjiāng 镇江

Zhenyuan
zhènyuán 镇远

Zhongdian
zhōngdiàn 中甸

Zhongshan City
zhōngshān shì 中山市

Zhongwei
zhōngwèi 中卫

Zhuhai
zhūhǎi 珠海

Zhujiajian
zhūjiājiān 朱家尖

Zhuzhou
zhūzhōu 株州

Zibo
zībó 淄博

Zöigê
ruòěrgài 若尔盖

Zouxian
zōuxiàn 邹县

Zunyi
zūnyì 遵义

Facts for the Visitor

PLANNING
When to Go
Local tourism has taken off in a big way in China, and in the summer months, when it hits its peak, getting around and finding accommodation can become quite a headache.

Winter is obviously the quietest time of year to get about and there are good discounts on hotels, but the weather can be frigid and many travellers succumb to killer flus that lay them out for days and leave them with a hacking cough for weeks afterwards. Spring and autumn are the best months to be on the road.

See the Climate section in the Facts about the Country chapter for information on seasonal weather variations throughout China.

Major public holidays are to be avoided if possible. Chinese New Year is a terrible time of year to be travelling.

For information on buying your airline ticket, see the following Getting There & Away chapter.

Maps
One of the big changes to occur in China over the past decade has been the increase in availability of good quality maps. In the early 1980s, maps were treated as military secrets. The few that were available were great works of fiction – doctored to trick the foreign spies and saboteurs. As China opened up, it slowly dawned on the Chinese leadership that the satellite-based maps published in the west were much better quality than those available in China.

Now the situation has reversed: top quality maps of almost every Chinese city – even many small towns – are readily available. Some of these show incredible detail – bus routes (including names of bus stops), the locations of hotels, shops and so on. City maps normally only cost Y2 to Y4 – the cost may be partly subsidised by the advertisements.

Maps are most easily purchased from bookstalls or street vendors around railway and bus stations, from branches of the Xinhua Bookstore or from hotel front desks (even cheap Chinese hotels where foreigners can't stay). Unfortunately maps are almost always in Chinese characters. It is only in tourist centres that you will find English-language maps.

The places to look for English-language editions are the hotel giftshops, Friendship Stores and sometimes the foreign-language bookshops. There are also a few atlases – these cover only major cities and tourist sites, and most are in Chinese characters although there are a few English editions around. English-language editions invariably cost more than the Chinese equivalents.

There seems to be no central place in China where you can go to purchase maps for the entire country. The selection at the Xinhua Bookstore on Wangfujing Dajie in Beijing is decent, but hardly comprehensive.

Some of the most detailed maps of China available in the west are the aerial survey 'Operational Navigation Charts' (Series ONC). These are prepared and published by the Defence Mapping Agency Aerospace Center, St Louis Air Force Station, Missouri 63118, USA. Cyclists and mountaineers have recommended these highly because of their extraordinary detail. In the UK you can obtain these maps from Stanfords Map Centre (☎ (0171) 836-1321), 12-14 Long Acre, London WC2E 9LP, or from The Map Shop (☎ (06) 846-3146), AT Atkinson & Partner, 15 High St, Upton-on-Severn, Worcestershire, WR8 OHJ.

Australians can contact Mapland (☎ (03) 9670 4383) at 372 Little Bourke St in Melbourne, or The Travel Bookshop (☎ (02) 9241 3554) at 20 Bridge St in Sydney.

In France see Ulysse (☎ 1 43 25 17 35) at 26 rue Saint Louis en l'Île, or IGN (☎ 01 43 98 80 00) at 107 rue de la Boetie in Paris.

What to Bring

As little as possible. It's much better to buy things as you need them than to throw things away because you've got too much to carry. Lightweight and compact are two words that should be etched in your mind when you're deciding what to bring. Drill holes in the handle of your toothbrush if you have to – anything to keep the weight down!

That advice having been given, there are some things you will want to bring from home.

Backpacks Chinese-made backpacks are generally terrible – some won't last a day! Investing in a good backpack is one outlay you will never regret. Look into buying a frameless or internal-frame pack – these are generally easier to store on buses and trains and also more comfortable to walk with. Also consider buying a pack that converts into a carry bag by way of a flap that zips over the shoulder and waist straps – it is less likely to be damaged on airport carousels and is more presentable if you ever need to discard the backpacker image.

A day pack is essential for carrying things around after you've dumped your backpack at the hotel or railway station. A belt pack is OK for maps, extra film and other miscellanea, but don't use it for valuables such as your travellers cheques and passport – it's an easy target for pickpockets.

If you don't want to use a backpack, a shoulder bag is much easier to carry than a suitcase. Some cleverly designed shoulder bags double as backpacks by re-arranging a few straps. Bring suitcases only if you know you won't be carrying your luggage on buses and trains.

Clothes In theory, you need only two sets of clothes – one to wear and one to wash. Dark coloured clothing is preferable because it doesn't show the dirt – white clothes will force you to do laundry daily. Clothing is one of the best cheap buys in China, so don't feel compelled to bring everything from home.

China is pretty informal, although fashionable clothing is in vogue in Hong Kong, Beijing and Shanghai. Shorts and T-shirts are respectable summer wear, but try to look clean. Flip-flops (thongs) are *not* acceptable for outdoor wear, but sandals (with a mandatory strap across the back of your ankle) are OK.

If you're travelling in the north of China at the height of winter, prepare yourself for incredible cold. Good down jackets are available in China, but it's hard to find good quality hats, mittens and boots (at least in western sizes). Western long johns are more comfortable and warmer than the Chinese variety.

Sleeping Bag Should you, shouldn't you? A sleeping bag is required in China only if you are planning to go camping. Hotels provide copious bedding during the winter months, as do the sleeper carriages on trains. Even in Tibet, you can do without a sleeping bag if you are going to be staying in hotels.

Necessities Absolutely essential is a good pair of sunglasses, particularly in the Xinjiang desert or the high altitudes of Tibet. Ditto for sunscreen (UV) lotion. A water bottle can be a lifesaver in the western deserts.

Outside the major cities, some pharmaceutical items are hard to find, such as shaving cream, decent razor blades, mosquito repellent, deodorant, dental floss, tampons and contact lens solution. Chinese nail clippers are of poor quality. An alarm clock is essential for getting up on time – make sure it is lightweight and bring extra batteries. Size AA rechargeable batteries can be bought in China, but the rechargers are bulky – bring a portable one and plug adaptors if you can't live without your Walkman. The following is a checklist of things you might want to consider packing:

Passport, visa, documents (vaccination certificate, diplomas, marriage licence photocopy, student ID card), money belt or vest, address book, reading matter, pen, note-pad, gluestick, name cards, visa photos (about 20), Swiss army knife, camera and accessories, extra camera battery, colour slide film, video camera and blank tapes, radio, Walkman and rechargeable batteries, small battery recharger (220V), padlock, cable lock (to secure luggage on trains), sunglasses, contact lens solution, leakproof water bottle, torch (flashlight) with batteries and bulbs, comb, compass, day pack, long pants, short pants, long shirt, T-shirt, nylon jacket, sweater, raincover for backpack, umbrella or rain poncho, razor, shaving cream, sewing kit, spoon, sunhat, sunscreen (UV lotion), toilet paper, tampons, laundry detergent, underwear, socks, thongs, nail clippers, tweezers, mosquito repellent, vitamins, laxatives, Lomotil, condoms, contraceptives, special medications you use and a medical kit (see the Health section later in this chapter).

Gifts

Many Chinese people study English and appreciate old English books and magazines. Stamps make good gifts; the Chinese are avid collectors, congregating outside the philatelic sections of the post offices and dealing on the footpath. Odd-looking foreign coins and currency are appreciated. Foreign postcards are sought after, and pictures of you and your family make popular gifts.

SUGGESTED ITINERARIES

Unless you have a couple of years up your sleeve, oodles of patience and inexhaustible funds, you are only going to be able to see a small part of China on any one trip. It's a good idea to have a loose itinerary to follow. The following suggestions assume you have at least four weeks in China.

Beijing to Tibet via Xi'an

Beijing – Xi'an – Xining – Golmud – Lhasa
This route has emerged as a very popular one with many travellers, particularly those overlanding from Europe by train and heading for Nepal and India via Tibet. The great thing about this route is that it gives you the best of China's historical sights (Beijing and Xi'an) and at the same time gives you an opportunity to travel out into China's remote and sparsely populated western regions.

Beijing, Xi'an and Lhasa are the main attractions on this route. En route to Xi'an, you can also visit Datong and Taiyuan, although they are not particularly pleasant cities. Xining is worth a day or so, mainly for the nearby lamasery of Ta'ersi. The less time spent in Golmud, the better. From Lhasa, it is possible to travel on to Nepal via the Tibetan temple towns of Gyantse, Shigatse and Sakya – some travellers make a detour to the Everest base camp. The journey from Lhasa to Kathmandu is a once-in-a-lifetime trip.

Beijing to Hong Kong via the South-West

Beijing – Xi'an – Kunming – Guilin (Yangshuo) – Guangzhou – Hong Kong
There are many variations on this route, depending on how much time you have and how much you enjoy travelling on Chinese trains (or, more to the point, trying to get tickets for the trains).

A stopover in Kunming allows travellers to explore Yunnan, which is arguably the most exotic of China's provinces – rich in ethnic colour and some of the best scenery in all China. From Kunming, many travellers also opt to travel on to Chengdu (via Dali and Lijiang).

From Chengdu there are many options: onwards to Chongqing and from here to Shanghai or Wuhan down the Yangzi River, or onwards to Guizhou and Guilin and on to Hong Kong. You can speed things up on this route with a flight or two.

Coastal Routes

If you look at a map of China, an obvious route is one that takes you up (or down) the east of China between Guangzhou and Beijing. It is possible to do this. From Beijing, you might travel to Shandong and from here make a beeline southward via Shanghai and Zhejiang and Fujian provinces to Guangzhou.

The only problem with this route is that you are passing through some of the most densely populated regions in the world's most populous nation. There is intense competi-

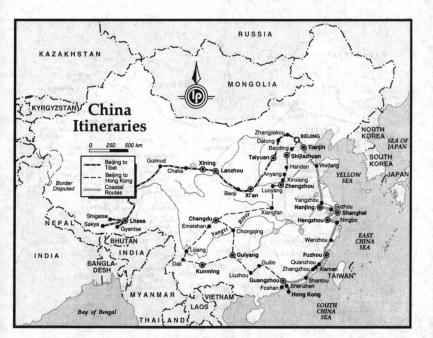

tion for train tickets (where trains are available), and as a result if you don't fly you will inevitably spend days and days bouncing around in crowded buses. To make matters worse, China's coastal cities are little more than a blur of smog and chimneys, grey housing estates and factories. Think of it as an industrial-wastelands tour.

Hong Kong to Kunming via Guilin
Hong Kong – Guangzhou – Guilin (Yangshuo) – Kunming – Xishuangbanna – Dali – Lijiang
This has long been China's most favoured backpacker trail. The standard routine is a brief stay in Guangzhou (one or two nights), followed by a ferry to Wuzhou, and from there a direct bus to Yangshuo (very few travellers bother with Guilin itself). Many travellers end up seduced by Yangshuo and spending much longer there than they planned.

Onward travel to Kunming can be undertaken by train or by plane. From Kunming, there is a wide range of choices – south to the regional areas of Xishuangbanna and Dehong or north-west to Dali and Lijiang (or both). Other possibilities include flights from Kunming to Chiang Mai or Bangkok in Thailand, or taking a train to Hanoi in Vietnam.

Yangzi River Routes
Cruises on the Yangzi River have long been touted as one of China's premier attractions. In reality they get mixed reports. Some travellers have even found the famed Three Gorges (the whole reason for cruising the river) quite overrated, and in any event the area will soon be submerged by the Three Gorges Dam project.

The most interesting part of the Yangzi is the section between Chongqing (Sichuan) and Wuhan; the section east of here between

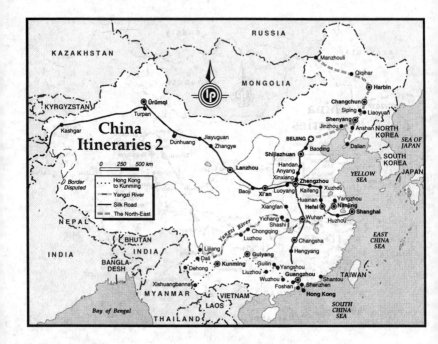

Wuhan and Shanghai is of little interest (the Yangzi gets so wide you cannot even see its shores and most of the cities have little to recommend them).

Silk Road Route

Beijing/Guangzhou/Shanghai – Kaifeng – Zhengzhou – Xi'an – Dunhuang – Ürümqi – Turpan – Kashgar

Kashgar and the Karakoram Highway (to Pakistan) can be approached directly from Beijing, but a fascinating trip is the overland route once used for transporting silk to Europe. It includes little-travelled parts of central China (Kaifeng) and passes through the archaeological treasure houses of Xi'an and Dunhuang, before heading into the deserts of Xinjiang.

From Ürümqi you will have to travel by bus to Turpan and Kashgar. Onward travel to Pakistan and India via the Karakoram Highway is also an option.

North-East Route

Beijing – Dalian – Shenyang – Changchun – Harbin – Qiqihar – Manzhouli – Russia (via the Trans-Siberian Railway)

Visit the former treaty port of Dalian that is an up and coming metropolis then head north to what used to be Manchuria and the cities of Shenyang, Changchun and Harbin. It's a region that feels less Chinese than a combination of Canadian prairies, rust belt heavy industry, leftover traces of Japanese colonialism and undeniably Russian influences from both the past and present. Apart from the cities, it's also possible to try and commune with nature (always an elusive prospect in China) in the Changbaishan and Zhalong Nature Reserves. The north-east also offers a true winter experience, including skiing and -30° C (-22° F) weather, and during the summer is a good place to go and escape the heat while the rest of China bakes. You could keep heading north to the grasslands of Inner Mongolia at Manzhouli and on to Siberia or Europe along the Trans-Siberian Railway.

TOURIST OFFICES
Local Tourist Offices

CITS The China International Travel Service (CITS) deals with China's foreign tourist hordes, and mainly concerns itself with organising and making travel arrangements for group tours. CITS existed as far back as 1954, when there were few customers; now they're inundated with a couple of hundred thousand foreign tourists a year. Unfortunately, after 40 years of being in business, CITS has still not gotten its act totally together.

Nowadays, many solo travellers make their way around China without ever having to deal with CITS. In many remote regions, CITS does not offer much in the way of services. In other places, CITS may sell hard-to-get-hold-of train tickets or tickets for the opera or acrobatics or perhaps provide tours of rural villages or factories. It really all depends on where you are.

There will usually be a small service charge added on to the price of any train, boat or plane tickets purchased through CITS.

CITS is a frequent target of ire for all kinds of reasons: rudeness, inefficiency, laziness and even fraud. Bear in mind, however, that service varies enormously from office to office. Expect the worst, but be prepared to be pleasantly surprised.

CTS The China Travel Service (CTS) was originally set up to handle tourists from Hong Kong, Macau and Taiwan and foreign nationals of Chinese descent (Overseas Chinese). These days your gene pool and nationality make little difference – CTS has now become a keen competitor with CITS. CITS is trying to cash in on the lucrative Taiwan and Hong Kong markets, while CTS is targeting the western market, which was previously the exclusive domain of CITS.

Many foreigners use the CTS offices in Hong Kong and Macau to obtain visas and book trains, planes, hovercraft and other transport to China.

CTS can sometimes get you a better deal on hotels booked through their office than you could obtain on your own (of course, this doesn't apply to backpackers' dormitories).

CYTS The name China Youth Travel Service (CYTS) implies that this is some sort of student organisation, but these days CYTS performs essentially the same services as CITS and CTS. Being a smaller organisation, CYTS seems to try harder to compete against the big league. This could result in better service, but not necessarily lower prices.

CYTS is mostly interested in tour groups, but individual travellers could find it useful for booking air tickets or sleepers on the trains.

Chinese Tourist Offices Abroad

Although Hong Kong is now part of China and Macau will soon be, for the purposes of doing visas and making other travel arrangements we'll list the Hong Kong and Macau offices of CITS/CTS as if they were in foreign countries.

CITS Outside China and Hong Kong, CITS is usually known as the China National Tourist Office (CNTO). CITS (or CNTO) representatives include:

Australia
  CNTO (☎ (02) 9299-4057; fax 9290-1958), 19th floor, 44 Market St, Sydney NSW 2000
France
  Office du Tourisme de Chine (☎ 1 44 21 82 82; fax 44 21 81 00), 116 Avenue des Champs Elysees, 75008, Paris
Germany
  CNTO (☎ (069) 520-135; fax 528-490), Ilkenhansstr 6, D-60433 Frankfurt am Main
Hong Kong
  CITS (☎ 2732-5888; fax 2721-7154), New Mandarin Plaza, Tower A, 12th floor, 14 Science Museum Rd, Tsimshatsui East

Israel
  CNTO (☎ (03) 522-6272; fax 522-6281), 19 Frishman St, PO Box 3281, Tel-Aviv 61030
Japan
  China National Tourist Administration (☎ (03) 3433-1461; fax 3433-8653), 6th floor, Hamamatsu-cho Building, 1-27-13 Hamamatsu-cho, Minato-ku, Tokyo
Singapore
  CNTO (☎ 221-8681; fax 221-9267), 1 Shenton Way, No 17-05 Robina House, Singapore 0106
Spain
  CNTO (☎ (01) 548-0011; fax 548-0597), Gran Via 88, Grupo 2, Planta 16, 28013 Madrid
UK
  CNTO (☎ (0171) 935-9787; fax 487-5842), 4 Glenworth St, London NW1
USA
  CNTO Los Angeles Branch (☎ (818) 545-7504; fax 545-7506), Suite 201, 333 West Broadway, Glendale CA 91204; New York Branch (☎ (212) 760-9700; fax 760-8809), Suite 6413, Empire State Building, 350 Fifth Ave, New York, NY 10118

CTS Overseas representatives include the following:

Australia
  (☎ (02) 9211-2633; fax 9281-3595), ground floor, 757-9 George St, Sydney, NSW 2000
Canada
  (☎ (800) 663-1126, (604) 872-8787; fax 873-2823), 556 West Broadway, Vancouver, BC V5Z 1E9;
  (☎ (800) 387-6622, (416) 979-8993; fax 979-8220), Suite 306, 438 University Ave, Box 28, Toronto, Ontario M5G 2K8
France
  (☎ 1 44 51 55 66; fax 44 51 55 60), 32 Rue Vignon, 75009, Paris
Germany
  (☎ (69) 223-8522; fax 223-2324), Düsseldorfer Strasse 14, D-60329, Frankfurt am Main; (☎ (30) 393-4068; fax 391-8085), Beusselstrasse 5, D-10553, Berlin
Hong Kong
  Head Office (☎ 2853-3888; fax 2854-1383), 4th floor, CTS House, 78-83 Connaught Rd (GPO Box 6016)
  Central Kowloon Branch, (☎ 2315-7188; fax 2721-7757), 1st floor, Alpha House, 27-33 Nathan Rd, Tsimshatsui

Indonesia
  (☎ (21) 629-4452; fax 629-4836), PT Cempaka Travelindo, Jalan Hayam Wuruk 97, Jakarta-Barat
Japan
  (☎ (03) 3273-5512; fax 3273-2667), 103 Buyoo Building, 3-8-16, Nihombashi, Chuo-Ku, Tokyo
Macau
  (☎ 705-506; fax 706-611), Xinhua Building, Rua de Nagasaki
Malaysia
  (☎ (03) 201-8888; fax 201-3268), ground floor, 112-4 Jalan Pudu, 55100, Kuala Lumpur
Philippines
  (☎ (02) 733-1274; fax 733-1431), 801-3 Gandara St (corner Espeleta St), Santa Cruz, Manila
Singapore
  (☎ 532-9988; fax 535-4912), 1 Park Rd, No 03-49 to 52, People's Park Complex, Singapore, 059108
South Korea
  (☎ (02) 566-9361; fax 557-0021), 8th floor, Chung Oh Building, 164-3 Samsung-dong, Kangnam-gu, Seoul
Thailand
  (☎ (02) 226-0041; fax 226-4701), 559 Yaowaraj Rd, Sampuntawang, Bangkok 10100
UK
  (☎ (0171) 836-9911; fax 836-3121), CTS House, 7 Upper St, Martins Lane, London WC2H 9DL
USA
  Main Office (☎ (800) 332-2831, (415) 398-6627; fax 398-6669), L/F, 575 Sutter St, San Francisco, CA 94102;
  Los Angeles Branch (☎ (818) 457-8668; fax 457-8955), Suite 303, US CTS Building, 119 South Atlantic Blvd, Monterey Park, CA 91754

VISAS & DOCUMENTS
Passport
The Chinese government requires that your passport must be valid for at least six months after the expiry date of your visa.

  You'll need at least one entire blank page in your passport for the visa. Your country's embassy or consulate can usually add additional pages to your passport if need be.

  Losing your passport is very bad news indeed. Getting a new one takes time and money. However, if you will be staying in

China or any foreign country for a long time, it helps tremendously to register your passport with your embassy. This will eliminate the need to send telexes back to your home country to confirm that you really exist.

If you lose your passport, you should certainly have some ID card with your photo – many embassies require this before issuing a new passport. Some embassies will accept a driver's licence, but others will not – an expired passport will often save the day.

Visas

At the time of writing, visas were not required for most western nationals to visit Hong Kong or Macau. However, now that Hong Kong has been reunified with China, be aware that new visa regulations could be issued at any time. Macau will remain a Portuguese colony until 1999, so there should be no problem at least until then.

For the rest of China, a visa is required, but these are normally very easy to get. The Chinese will even issue visas to individuals from countries which do not have diplomatic relations with the People's Republic of China (PRC).

There are seven types of visas, as follows:

L   Travel (lǚxíng)
F   Business (fǎngwèn)
D   Resident (dìngjū)
G   Transit (guòjìng)
X   Student (liúxué)
Z   Working (rènzhí)
C   Stewardess (chéngwù)

For most travellers, the type of visa is 'L', from the Chinese word for travel (lǚxíng). This letter is stamped right on the visa.

Visas are readily available from Chinese embassies and consulates in most western and many other countries. A standard 30 day, single-entry visa from most Chinese embassies abroad can be issued in three to five working days. Get an application form in person at the embassy or consulate. A visa mailed to you will take up to three weeks. Rather than going through an embassy or consulate, you can also make arrangements at some travel agencies, especially Chinese government-owned agencies (such as CITS and CTS) which have overseas representatives. Visa applications require one photo.

You can easily get a visa in Hong Kong. The standard 30 day visa can be obtained from almost any travel agency. The cheapest visas are available from the Visa Office (☎ 2585-1794, 2585-1700) at the Ministry of Foreign Affairs of the PRC, 5th floor, Low Block, China Resources Building, 26 Harbour Rd, Wanchai. It charges HK$100 for next-day service and HK$250 for same-day service. The office is open Monday to Friday from 9 am to 12.30 pm and from 2 to 5 pm, and on Saturday from 9 am to 12.30 pm.

If you need more than 30 days or a multiple-entry visa, head to one of the branches of CTS in Hong Kong or Macau (see the Tourist Offices section earlier in this chapter). Prices range from HK$160 for a single-entry, 90 day visa issued in 2½ days to HK$1500 for a six month, multiple-entry visa issued in four hours. Some Hong Kong travel agencies can also get you 60 and 90 day multiple-entry visas.

A 30 day visa is activated on the date you enter China, and must be used within three months of the date of issue. The 60 day and 90 day visas are activated on the date they are issued.

Visas valid for more than 30 days are usually difficult to obtain anywhere other than in Hong Kong.

Multiple-entry visas allow you to enter and leave the country an unlimited number of times and are available through CTS and some travel agencies in Hong Kong and Macau. The cheapest multiple-entry visas cost HK$650 and are valid for 90 days; six month multiple-entry visas cost HK$900, but allow stays of only 30 days at a time and extensions are close to impossible. The latter are business visas and normally will be issued only if you've been to China at least once before and have a stamp in your passport to prove it.

It is possible to obtain single-entry visas at the border at Shenzhen (next to Hong Kong) and Zhuhai (next to Macau). Unfortunately, they are valid for travel only within the Shenzhen Special Economic Zone or the Zhuhai Special Economic Zone respectively, and the price of HK$360 is hardly worth it. Furthermore, you might not get the full 30 days. See the Land section in the Getting There & Away chapter for information on visas for travelling on the Trans-Siberian Railway.

Visa Extensions Visa extensions are handled by the Foreign Affairs Branch of the local Public Security Bureau (PSB) – the police force. Government travel organisations – like CITS – have nothing to do with extensions, so don't bother asking. Extensions can cost nothing for some, but Y110 for most nationalities.

The situation with visa extensions seems to change frequently. Extensions of 15 days to one month seem fairly easy to get if you entered China with a 30 day visa.

At an agreeable PSB you may be able to wangle more, especially with cogent reasons like illness (except for AIDS) or transport delays, but don't count on it. Second extensions are rarely granted.

The penalty of overstaying your visa in China is at least Y300 *per day!*

Photocopies
Considering the Chinese bureaucracy's obsession with impressive bits of paper, originals are usually preferred to photocopies. However, copies are certainly better than nothing and will often do in a pinch.

If you're thinking about working or studying in China or anywhere else along the way, photocopies of university diplomas, transcripts and letters of recommendation could prove helpful.

Married couples should have a copy of their marriage certificate with them, especially if either husband or wife is ethnic Chinese (or looks Chinese). The PSB has made it their mission to be sure that foreigners do not have sex with Chinese

people, although enforcement tends to be slack in big cities. So in the case of a foreigner married to a local, you need both certificates (husband's and wife's) to check into a hotel room together. Chinese marriage certificates are little red books which resemble passports (which in a sense they are).

Travel Permits
In the early 1980s only 130 places in China were officially open to foreign tourists. Then the number swept to 244, and nowadays most of the country is open except for certain remote border areas, especially those inhabited by ethnic minorities.

Most of the places described in this book are open to foreigners, but one incident (like an ethnic riot in Xinjiang or Tibet) can cause new permit regulations to be issued overnight. Even worse is the fact that some small towns in China require these permits for the sole reason to extract fines from any foreigners who show up without one (Kaili in Hunan Province is one such example). To find out about latest restrictions, it's best to check with the police in provincial capitals, but don't be surprised if even they can't tell you.

To travel to closed places you officially require an Alien Travel Permit (*tōngxíng zhèng*). The police have wide discretion in issuing a permit to a closed place. However, the choice of open places is now so extensive that most travellers won't need to apply. Foreign academics and researchers wanting to poke around remote areas usually need the right credentials or letter of introduction (*jièshào xìn*) before being given a free hand to pursue their lizards, steam trains, yellow-bellied sapsuckers or whatever in remote places.

Travel permits can be demanded from you at hotel registration desks, boat or bus ticket offices and unusual areas during spot checks by police. If you're off the track, but heading towards a destination for which you have a permit, the police will either stop you and cancel the destination or let you continue on your way.

The permit also lists the modes of transport you're allowed to take: plane, train, ship or car – and if a particular mode is crossed out then you can't use it. If a mode is cancelled it can be reinstated at the next police station, but that may be for only a single trip from point A to point B. You could try and carry on regardless – or you could lose the permit in the next open city and have to start again.

If you manage to get a permit for an unusual destination, the best strategy is to get to that destination as fast as you can (by plane if possible). Local police do not have to honour the permit and can cancel it and send you back. Take your time getting back – you're less likely to be hassled if you're returning to civilisation. Transit points usually don't require a permit, and you can stay the night.

Travel Insurance

Although you may have medical insurance in your own country, it is probably not valid in China. But ask your insurance company anyway – you *might* already be covered. You also *might* be automatically covered if you hold a valid International Student Identity Card (ISIC), GO 25 International Youth Travel Card or International Teachers' Identity Card (ISTC) – ask at the place where you purchased the card.

A travel insurance policy is a very good idea – the best ones protect you against cancellation penalties on advance-purchase flights, against medical costs through illness or injury, against theft or loss of possessions and against the cost of additional air tickets if you get really sick and have to fly home. Cover depends on the insurance and your type of ticket, so ask both your insurer and the ticket-issuing agency to explain where you stand. Ticket loss is also covered by travel insurance.

Some policies offer lower and higher medical expense options; the higher ones are chiefly for countries such as the USA which have extremely high medical costs. There is a wide variety of policies available so check the small print.

Some policies specifically exclude 'dangerous activities', which can include scuba diving, motorcycling, and even trekking. A locally acquired motorcycle licence is not valid under some policies. Check that the policy covers ambulances or an emergency flight home.

You may prefer a policy which pays doctors or hospitals directly rather than you having to pay on the spot and claim later. If you have to claim later make sure you keep all documentation. Some policies ask you to call back (reverse charges) to a centre in your home country where an immediate assessment of your problem is made.

Buy travel insurance as early as possible. If you buy it the week before you fly, you may find, for instance, that you're not covered for delays to your flight caused by strikes or other industrial action that may have started or been threatened before you took out the insurance. Paying for your airline ticket with a credit card often provides limited travel accident insurance and you may be able to reclaim the payment if the operator doesn't deliver. Ask your credit-card company what it's prepared to cover.

Student travel offices are one place to inquire about relatively inexpensive insurance policies. Better travel agencies also sell travel insurance policies – do a little checking around before you buy. Again, read the fine print – the coverage may be cheap, but very limited.

Driving Licence

An International Driving Permit is not recognised by the Chinese authorities. Nor will you get any use out of your home country's licence unless you have a Chinese residence permit.

Foreign residents (as opposed to tourists) are governed by a different set of regulations. A Chinese driver's licence is required, and getting it will be much easier if you bring along a valid licence from your home country. If you do not have a licence from home, you'll have to take a driving course in China, as well as the driving test itself – two hassles best avoided.

Before you can obtain your Chinese licence, you must first secure a residence permit (see the entry on Resident Permits further on). Then you must hand in your native country's driver's licence – the police keep this licence and issue you with a Chinese one. When you leave China, you must turn in your Chinese licence and your native country's licence will then be returned to you. Just to complicate things, you need to prove you have a car before the Chinese licence can be issued! Foreign residents may face restrictions on where they can drive – ask the local police how far you are permitted to drive from your place of residence.

Hostel Card

You won't find much use for an International Youth Hostel Federation (IYHF) card in China. If you already have a valid card, you can bring it along on the odd chance you might actually get to use it, but it certainly would *not* be advisable to buy one just for China. You can purchase an IYHF card in Hong Kong if you need one. See the Accommodation section later in this chapter for more information on hostels in China.

Student & Youth Cards

If you are studying in China, you'll be issued a student card by your school. These are occasionally useful to get a discount on admission fees – at least you should be charged the local price rather than the foreigner price.

International student cards and youth cards can sometimes get you a discount on international flights to China. However, these cards are unlikely to get you any discounts in China itself. The cost to buy one of these cards varies according to country, but is typically between US$10 and US$20.

As mentioned earlier, you may be automatically covered with a travellers' health insurance policy if you hold one of these cards (be sure to ask). Another supposed benefit is access to a 24 hour toll-free help line which can provide emergency medical, legal and financial services (ie finding a doctor or lawyer, replacing lost or stolen documents and arranging an emergency flight home).

International Student Identity Cards (ISIC) and International Teacher Identity Cards are issued through representative offices of the International Student Travel Confederation (ISTC). To qualify for an ISIC, you need to be a full-time student, but there are no age limits. Full-time teachers and faculty can apply for an ITIC. You can apply for these cards through various student travel organisations in your home country. To get the ISIC, you need an official letter from your school confirming that you are indeed a student (or teacher, as the case may be).

If are *not* a student or teacher, but are aged 25 or under, then you can qualify for a GO 25 International Youth Travel Card (just call it a 'GO 25 Card'). These are issued by representative offices of the Federation of International Youth Travel Organisations (FIYTO). These cards offer essentially the same benefits as the ISIC and ISTC.

Student travel offices in various cities and university campuses can provide you with application forms for these cards.

International Health Card

Useful, although not essential, is a yellow International Health Certificate to record your vaccinations. It's unlikely you'll ever be asked to show it, unless you've been in an epidemic area.

Resident Permits

The 'green card' is a residence permit, issued to English teachers, foreign experts and students who live in the PRC. It's such a valuable document that you'd better not lose it or the police will be all over you. Foreigners living in China say that if you lose your green card, you might want to leave the country rather than face the music.

A green card will permit you to pay

Chinese prices in hotels, on flights, on trains and elsewhere. In addition, many hotels offer major discounts to green-card holders (even five star hotels!).

The green card is not really a card, but resembles a small passport – it would be very difficult to forge without modern printing equipment and special paper. Green cards are issued for one year and must be renewed annually.

EMBASSIES
Chinese Embassies
Some of the addresses of China's embassies and consulates in major cities overseas include:

Australia
 (☎ (02) 6273-4780, 6273-4781) 15 Coronation Drive, Yarralumla, ACT 2600
 Consulates: Melbourne, Perth and Sydney
Austria
 (☎ (06) 713-6706) Metternichgasse 4, 1030 Vienna
Belgium
 (☎ (02) 640-4006) Boulevare General Jacques 19, 1050 Bruxelles
Canada
 (☎ (613) 789-3509) 515 St Patrick St, Ottawa, Ontario K1N 5H3
 Consulates: Toronto and Vancouver
Denmark
 (☎ (039) 625-806) Oregards Alle 25, 2900 Hellerup, Copenhagen
France
 (☎ 1 47 23 36 77) 11 Avenue George V, 75008, Paris
Germany
 (☎ (0228) 361-095) Kurfislrstenallee 125-300 Bonn 2
 Consulate: Hamburg
Hungary
 (☎ 122-4872) Budapest VI-1068
Italy
 (☎ (06) 3630-8534, 3630-3856) 00135 Roma Via Della Camilluccia 613
 Consulate: Milan
Japan
 (☎ (03) 3403-3380, 3403-3065) 3-4-33 Moto-Azabu, Minato-ku, Tokyo 106
 Consulates: Fukuoka, Osaka and Sapporo
Netherlands
 (☎ (070) 355-1515) Adriaan Goekooplaan 7, 2517 JX, The Hague

New Zealand
 (☎ (04) 587-0407) 104A Korokoro Rd, Petone, Wellington
 Consulate: Auckland
Poland
 (☎ 313836) 200-203 Warsaw St, Bonifraterska 1
Singapore
 (☎ 734-3361) 70 Dalvey Rd
South Korea
 (☎ 319-5101) 83 Myŏng-dong 2-ga, Chunggu
Spain
 (☎ (341) 519-4242) Arturo Soria 111, 28043 Madrid
 Consulate: Barcelona
Sweden
 (☎ (08) 767 87 40, 767 40 83) Ringvagen 56 18134 Lidings
Switzerland
 (☎ (031) 951 14 01, 951 14 02) 7 JV Widmannstrasse, 3074, Muri, Bern
UK
 (☎ (0171) 636-9756) 31 Portland Place, W1N 5AG, London
USA
 (☎ (202) 328-2517) 2300 Connecticut Ave NW, Washington, DC 20008
 Consulates: Chicago, Houston, Los Angeles, New York and San Francisco

Foreign Embassies in China
In Beijing there are two main embassy compounds – Jianguomenwai and Sanlitun.

The following embassies are situated in Jianguomenwai, east of the Forbidden City:

Austria
 (☎ 6532-2061; fax 6532-1505) 5 Xiushui Nanjie
Bangladesh
 (☎ 6532-2521; fax 6532-4346) 42 Guanghua Lu
Czech Republic
 (☎ 6532-1531; fax 6532-5653) Ritan Lu
India
 (☎ 6532-1908; fax 6532-4684) 1 Ritan Donglu
Ireland
 (☎ 6532-2691; fax 6532-2168) 3 Ritan Donglu

Foreign Embassies in China section continued on page 116

Highlights in China

With the exception of good beaches, China has something of everything: deserts, grasslands, forests, sacred mountains, imperial remains, crumbling city walls and temples galore. Listed here are some tips for getting started.

Backpacker Getaways

Unlike the South-East Asian trail, which seems to harbour some little getaway with travellers' breakfasts, walks, waterfalls and fabulous beaches at every turn, in China such rest-up retreats are few and far between. In fact, there are only two places that have achieved a legendary status on the travel circuit: Yangshuo (Guangxi Province) and Dali (Yunnan Province).

Yangshuo is a village set amid the famous karst scenery of Guilin. The surrounding countryside alone, which can be explored by bicycle, makes Yangshuo worth a stay of a few days, but there are also river trips, nearby rural markets, caves to explore, cheap accommodation and banana pancakes for breakfast. What more could you ask for?

Dali is arguably more exotic, but is essentially a similar deal to Yangshuo. The old walled town, home to the Bai minority, nestles beside the Erhai Lake close to the Cangshan mountains. It is a superb place to rest up for a few days.

There are other parts of Yunnan which have the potential to become legendary backpacker destinations. **Lijiang**, home to the matriarchal Naxi minority and around six hours by bus from Dali, has already become very popular. **Xishuangbanna**, on the border of Laos and Myanmar, is also favoured for its minority colours and subtropical weather.

Imperial Splendour

Dynasties have risen and fallen for at least a few millennia in China. Nevertheless, there's not as much imperial debris about as you might expect. Dynasties rarely fell gracefully, with imperial decline generally marked by rampaging peasant uprisings and pillaging armies led by turncoat generals. More often than not a new dynasty was built on the ashes of the last.

Add to this the turmoil of China in the 20th century, the assault on the past led by the Cultural Revolution and finally the rapid modernisation and urbanisation of the nation over the past 15 years and it's a wonder there's anything left to see. Fortunately there is.

China's imperial jewel in the crown is of course **Beijing**. It has been the capital of China for around 500 years (most of the time) and is home to sights such as the **Forbidden City**, the off-limits palace of Ming and Qing emperors, their eunuch servants, princesses and harems. The **Summer Palace** in Beijing was established in the late Qing period, but is also a major attraction. Beijing is the jumping off point for China's most famous imperial legacy – the **Great Wall**. The wall can actually be viewed from many places, but most visitors approach it from Beijing.

Scattered around China are many other cities that have served as the imperial seat of power at one time or another. Many of them are now heavily industrialised and yield little clues as to what they must have been in the past. One notable exception is **Nanjing** (the name means 'Southern Capital'; Beijing is the 'Northern Capital'). Nanjing was briefly capital of China in the early days of the Ming Dynasty. Its city walls survive in some places, and near-by at Zijinshan Park is the tomb of the first Ming emperor and other imperial relics.

China's other major imperial drawcard is also its most ancient: **Xi'an**. The Qin Dynasty (221-207 BC) was headquartered here, and Xi'an was later the capital of the Tang Dynasty, when it was known as Chang'an. Today it is the most impressive of China's few remaining walled cities, and the nearby entombed warriors of the Qin Dynasty is one of China's major tourist sights.

Minority Regions

China is around 93% Han Chinese. The remainder of the population belongs to one of China's approximately 55 minorities. Some of these minorities, such as the Hui (Muslim Chinese) and the Man (natives of Manchuria), are ethnically indistinguishable from the Han Chinese and speak only Chinese. Other minorities, such as the Uighurs and the Tibetans, are ethnically distinct and speak languages that have little relation to Chinese.

China's minorities are scattered around the edges of the Chinese empire, and many travellers make a beeline directly to these regions. The provinces richest in minorities are all in the south-west of China, notably in **Yunnan** and **Guizhou**. Yunnan alone, which is bordered by Myanmar, Laos and Vietnam, is home to around 20 different minority groups. In large urban areas these minorities are difficult to distinguish from the Chinese, but in the country many still dress in traditional costumes and regularly hold colourful festivals and markets. Notable minority areas in south-west China include Yunnan's **Xishuangbanna** (mainly Dai), **Dali** (Bai), **Lijiang** (Naxi) and **Dehong** (Burmese, Dai and Jingpo); and in Guizhou, **Kaili** and further south-east (Dong and Miao).

With a population of close to five million, Tibetans make up one of China's largest minorities. Naturally the place to go is **Tibet** itself, but there are also large Tibetan communities in parts of China that once belonged to Tibet. In south-western Gansu Province, the Labrang Monastery in **Xiahe** is one of the six major monasteries of the Gelugpa sect of Tibetan Buddhism and is very much a little Tibet. Ta'er Monastery near **Xining** in Qinghai Province is another of the six major Gelugpa monasteries.

Sacred Mountains

Eulogised through the centuries in countless paintings and poems, the sacred mountains of China were once places of pilgrimage, towering peaks whose vastness inspired the climber with a sense of the frailty of human existence. Nowadays most of them are being turned into major tourist attractions complete with swift-footed armies of souvenir sellers, cable cars and extortionate entry fees. This does not mean that they are not worth the effort; simply that the climber gets few solitary contemplative moments.

Strictly speaking there are a total of nine sacred mountains: five Taoist peaks and four Buddhist peaks. Added to this list, however, are peaks that got onto the pilgrimage trail due to a reputation for superlative beauty. These include Huangshan (Anhui Province) and Lushan (Jiangxi Province).

China's Taoist peaks are **Huashan** (Shanxi Province), **Hengshan** (Hunan Province), **Hengshan** (Hebei Province – yes, there are two of them), **Taishan** (Shandong Province) and **Songshan** (Henan Province). The Buddhist mountains are **Emeishan** (Sichuan Province), **Wutaishan** (Shanxi Province), **Putuoshan** (Zhejiang Province) and **Jiuhuashan** (Anhui Province).

China's sacred mountains have been pilgrimage destinations for centuries and all have well marked trails to the summits. Usually there are stairways carved into rock faces, and sights en route include poems and inscriptions and numerous temples, many of which have accommodation (unfortunately often off limits to foreigners). The chief attraction is, inevitably, sunrise at the summit, where camera-toting crowds gather to gaze on the 'sea of clouds'. The most popular with foreign visitors are Huangshan, Taishan and Emeishan.

Cave Art

The **Mogao Caves** are the most impressive and best preserved examples of Buddhist cave art anywhere in China. They are set into desert cliffs above a river valley about 25km south-east of Dunhuang in Gansu Province. Some 492 grottoes are still standing.

The **Yungang Buddhist Caves** (Shanxi Province) are cut into the southern cliffs of Wuzhoushan, near Datong, next to the pass leading to Inner Mongolia. The caves contain over 50,000 statues and stretch for about 1km east to west. On top of the mountain ridge are the remains of a 17th century Qing Dynasty fortress.

The **Grand Buddha** at Leshan (Sichuan Province) is the largest buddha in the world. At 71m high, it is carved into a cliff face overlooking the confluence of the Dadu and Min rivers. You can go to the top, opposite the head, and then descend a short stairway to the feet for a Lilliputian perspective. Tour boats pass by for a frontal view.

Foreign Concessions

The European powers never managed to colonise China, but by the end of the 19th century the weakness of the Qing government allowed them to grab a large number of 'foreign concessions'. Much of the old architecture is still standing, nowadays often functioning as schools and government offices. In some cities, such buildings are being torn down and replaced with hastily thrown together high-rises. In other cities, such as Guangzhou and Shanghai, some of the concession buildings are being gentrified.

China's most famous collection of European architecture is lined up facing the sea on the Bund in **Shanghai**. The city's French Concession, mostly derelict and falling in swathes to modern building projects, also turns up some delightful architectural surprises. **Guangzhou**, home to China's earliest foreign concession, has an unexpectedly peaceful enclave of European buildings on Shamian Island. Some of the buildings are falling into disrepair, others are being renovated.

Xiamen (Fujian Province) has one of China's most charming collections of colonial architecture, on Gulangyu Island. The fact that there are no motorised vehicles on the small island makes this one of the only places in the country where it is possible to take peaceful walks and appreciate the buildings at leisure.

Qingdao (Shandong Province) was ceded to the Germans in 1898, and by 1904 the inevitable brewery was in place, along with countless villas and administrative buildings. Qingdao's architectural attractions are scattered (modern construction has taken its toll on the city's charms), but there is enough left to make a visit worthwhile.

Tianjin became a treaty port for the British in 1858. By the turn of the century they had been joined by the French, Germans, Italians, Belgians and Japanese. The result is a remarkable potpourri of architectural styles divided up into concessions, but modern intrusions are also taking their toll.

Foreign Embassies in China section continued from page 111

Israel
 (☎ 6505-0328) Room 405, West Wing, China World Trade Centre, 1 Jianguomenwai Dajie

Japan
 (☎ 6532-2361; fax 6532-4625) 7 Ritan Lu

Mongolia
 (☎ 6532-1203; fax 6532-5045) 2 Xiushui Beijie

New Zealand
 (☎ 6532-2731; fax 6532-4317) 1 Ritan Dong 2-Jie

North Korea
 (☎ 6532-1186; fax 6532-6056) Ritan Beilu

Philippines
 (☎ 6532-1872; fax 6532-3761) 23 Xiushui Beijie

Poland
 (☎ 6532-1235; fax 6532-5364) 1 Ritan Lu

Romania
 (☎ 6532-3315) Ritan Lu Dong 2-Jie

Singapore
 (☎ 6532-3926; fax 6532-2215) 1 Xiushui Beijie

South Korea
 (☎ 6505-2608; fax 6505-3458), China World Trade Centre, 1 Jianguomenwai Dajie

Sri Lanka
 (☎ 6532-1861; fax 6532-5426) 3 Jianhua Lu

Thailand
 (☎ 6532-1903; fax 6532-1748) 40 Guanghua Lu

UK
 (☎ 6532-1961; fax 6532-1937) 11 Guanghua Lu

USA
 (☎ 6532-3831; fax 6532-6057) 3 Xiushui Beijie

Vietnam
 (☎ 6532-1155; fax 6532-5720) 32 Guanghua Lu

The Sanlitun Compound, north-east of the Forbidden City, is home to the following embassies:

Australia
 (☎ 6532-2331; fax 6532-6957) 21 Dongzhimenwai Dajie

Belgium
 (☎ 6532-1736; fax 6532-5097) 6 Sanlitun Lu

Cambodia
 (☎ 6532-1889; fax 6532-3507) 9 Dongzhimenwai Dajie

Canada
 (☎ 6532-3536; fax 6532-4072) 19 Dongzhimenwai Dajie

Denmark
 (☎ 6532-2431; fax 6532-2439) 1 Sanlitun Dong 5-Jie

Finland
 (☎ 6532-1817; fax 6532-1884) 1-10-1 Tayuan Diplomatic Building, 14 Liangmahe Nanlu

France
 (☎ 6532-1331; fax 6532-4841) 3 Sanlitun Dong 3-Jie

Germany
 (☎ 6532-2161; fax 6532-5336) 5 Dongzhimenwai Dajie

Hungary
 (☎ 6532-1431; fax 6532-5053) 10 Dongzhimenwai Dajie

Italy
 (☎ 6532-2131; fax 6532-4676) 2 Sanlitun Dong 2-Jie

Kazakhstan
 (☎ 6532-6182; fax 6532-6183) 9 Sanlitun Dong 6-Jie

Malaysia
 (☎ 6532-2531; fax 6532-5032) 13 Dongzhimenwai Dajie

Myanmar (Burma)
 (☎ 6532-1584; fax 6532-1344) 6 Dongzhimenwai Dajie

Nepal
 (☎ 6532-1795; fax 6532-3251) 1 Sanlitun Xi 6-Jie

Netherlands
 (☎ 6532-1131; fax 6532-4689) 4 Liangmahe Nanlu

Norway
 (☎ 6532-2261; fax 6532-2392) 1 Sanlitun Dong 1-Jie

Pakistan
 (☎ 6532-2504) 1 Dongzhimenwai Dajie

Portugal
 (☎ 6532-3497; fax 6532-4637) 2-15-1 Tayuan Diplomatic Building, 14 Liangmahe Nanlu

Russia
 (☎ 6532-1267; fax 6532-4853) 4 Dongzhimen Beizhongjie, west of the Sanlitun Compound in a separate compound

Spain
 (☎ 6532-1986; fax 6532-3401) 9 Sanlitun Lu

Sweden
 (☎ 6532-3331; fax 6532-5008) 3 Dongzhimenwai Dajie

Switzerland
 (☎ 6532-2736; fax 6532-4353) 3 Sanlitun Dong 5-Jie

Ukraine
 (☎ 6532-6359; fax 6532-6765) 11 Sanlitun Dong 6-Jie

Consulates In Shanghai there are consulates for Australia, Austria, Brazil, Canada, Cuba, Denmark, France, Germany, India, Iran, Italy, Japan, New Zealand, Poland, Russia, Singapore, Sweden, the Netherlands, the UK and the USA.

In Guangzhou, there are consulates for Australia, France, Poland, Thailand, the USA and Vietnam. Oddly, there is a US consulate in Shenyang in Liaoning Province. See the relevant chapters on those cities for details.

CUSTOMS

Chinese border crossings have gone from being severely traumatic to exceedingly easy. Although there may seem to be lots of uniformed police around, the third degree at Customs seems to be reserved for local pornography smugglers rather than western travellers.

Note that there are clearly marked 'green channels' and 'red channels'; take the red channel only if you have something to declare.

You're allowed to import 400 cigarettes (or the equivalent in tobacco products), 2L of alcoholic drink and 50g of gold or silver. Importation of fresh fruit is prohibited. You can legally bring in or take out only Y6000 in Chinese currency. There are no restrictions on foreign currency except that you should declare any cash that exceeds US$5000 (or its equivalent in another currency).

A very peculiar restriction is the Y300 limit (Y150 if going to Hong Kong or Macau) on taking herbal medicines out of the country. One would think that China would like to encourage the export of Chinese medicine, a profitable (and mostly state-run) industry.

Cultural relics, handicrafts, gold and silver ornaments and jewellery purchased in China have to be shown to Customs on leaving. If these items are deemed to be 'cultural treasures', they will be confiscated. All bags are x-rayed, and foreigners have indeed had nearly worthless pottery and paintings (on sale in any tourist shop) seized by overzealous Customs agents.

It's illegal to import any printed material, film, tapes etc 'detrimental to China's politics, economy, culture and ethics'. But don't be too concerned about what you take to read.

As you leave China, any tapes, manuscripts, books etc 'which contain state secrets or are otherwise prohibited for export' can be seized.

MONEY

Costs

How much will a trip to China cost? That's largely up to the degree of comfort you need. It also depends on how much travelling you do, and what parts of China you visit. Eastern China, for example, is much more expensive than the west.

Eastern China (basically everywhere between Heilongjiang and Hainan Island) has become very difficult to do on a shoestring. Outside the major cities of Beijing, Guangzhou and Shanghai, it is very unusual to come across dorm accommodation, and in many cities accommodation rates start at US$25 to US$35 for a double (singles are rarely available).

Food costs remain reasonable throughout China, and if you are careful they can be as little as US$5 per day. Transport costs can be kept to a minimum by travelling by bus wherever possible or by travelling hard-seat on the train. In other words, travelling through the booming coastal cities of China for less than US$35 per day is quite a challenge.

Western China, however, remains relatively inexpensive (but for how long is anyone's guess). Popular backpacker destinations such as Yunnan, Sichuan, Guangxi, Gansu, Xinjiang, Qinghai and Tibet abound in budget accommodation and cheap eats. Generally, keeping costs down to US$25 per day is not too difficult. The main drain on the savings will be the long train journeys, on which generally only the hardiest of travellers can face hard-seat.

On average, mid-range hotels will cost around US$35 to US$50 for a double with air-con, bathroom, TV etc. It is usually

Attitude Problem

Foreigners are overcharged for many things in China, though the situation is not as ridiculous as it was just a few years ago. True, foreigners get ripped off in many parts of the world, but the big difference in China is that it's official policy. The state-owned Chinese airlines, for example, add a 50% surcharge onto foreigners' air tickets. Not long ago the railways and buses did the same, but this has changed. Some hotels still have a 'foreigner's surcharge', and cheaper hotels tend to be off limits to foreigners anyway. Many parks, museums and other sites force you to buy a special 'foreigner's ticket' costing two to 10 times the Chinese rate. Not long ago, there was even a special currency called 'Foreign Exchange Certificates' (FEC), which all foreigners were forced to use – the skewed exchange rate for FECs effectively amounted to an extra 50% surcharge on foreigners.

It's important to realise that in many parks, museums and other tourist sites (Beijing's Forbidden City being a good example) there are numerous halls and pavilions within the compound, each with its own admission gate charging separate fees. The locals have the option of buying a cheap general admission ticket for the compound and then buying separate tickets for each pavilion or just one high-priced all-inclusive ticket which grants admission to every pavilion. Most Chinese ticket vendors will sell you the all-inclusive ticket, whether you want it or not. Making your wishes known to the ticket booth staff might save you some cash – all-inclusive tickets are *tàopiào* in Chinese while general admission tickets are called 'door tickets' (*ménpiào*) or 'common tickets' (*pǔtōngpiào*).

The good news is that the damage to both the tourist industry and China's image is finally being recognised by the authorities. Observing plunging tourist revenues and loud retaliatory threats from China's trading partners, there is now an official policy to overturn the previous official policy. However, it's happening in fits and starts – it will still be some years before 'foreigners' prices' are completely eliminated.

Out on the street it's another problem entirely. After so many years of official support for overcharging, it's not surprising that many ordinary Chinese view cheating foreigners as their patriotic duty. Far from considering it a crime, everyone from taxi drivers to street vendors feels that ripping off foreigners is fully justified. Be prepared for some arguments. ■

possible to eat well in hotel restaurants for around US$5 to US$10.

Transport costs are rising rapidly for those who want to move around in a degree of comfort – an eight hour soft-sleeper train journey, for example, will cost around US$70. It is worth comparing the cost of a flight versus soft-sleeper train travel – often the flights are cheaper or only marginally more expensive.

Top-end travel in China? It's possible to hit the major attractions of the country staying in five star hotels (US$100 upwards for a double), flying long distances, taking taxis to and from airports, dining on Chinese haute cuisine and enjoying a few drinks in the lobby bar in the evenings for between US$200 and US$250 per day.

Carrying Money

A money belt or pockets sewn inside your clothes is the safest way to carry money. Velcro tabs sewn to seal your pockets shut will also help thwart roving hands. During the cooler weather, it's more comfortable to wear a vest (waistcoat) with numerous pockets, but you should wear this under a light jacket or coat since visible pockets invite sticky fingers even if they're sealed with zippers.

Keeping all your eggs in one basket is not advised – guard against possible loss by leaving a small stash of money (say US$100) in your hotel room or buried in your backpack, with a record of the travellers cheque serial numbers and your passport number.

Cash

A lot of Chinese vendors and taxi drivers cannot make change for even a Y50 note, so stock up on Y10 bills at the nearest bank.

Counterfeit bills are a problem in China. Very few Chinese will accept a Y50 or Y100 bill without first checking to see whether or not it's a fake. Notes that are old and tattered are also sometimes hard to spend. If you are having problems with a note, exchange it for a new one or small change at the Bank of China – counterfeits, however, will be confiscated.

Local Chinese have a variety of methods for checking bills. First of all, they look for the watermark – obviously, if it doesn't have one it's a fake. Many locals maintain that colours tend to be more pronounced in counterfeit notes and the drawn lines less distinct. The texture of a note is also a telltale sign – counterfeits tend to be smoother than authentic bills.

Travellers Cheques

Besides the advantage of safety, travellers cheques are useful to carry in China because the exchange rate is actually more favourable than what you get for cash.

Cheques from most of the world's leading banks and issuing agencies are now acceptable in China – stick to the major companies such as Thomas Cook, American Express and Citibank and you'll be OK.

ATMs

At the present time, ATMs in most Chinese cities only work with the Chinese banking system and foreign cards will be rejected. An exception, of course, is Hong Kong, where you'll find ATMs advertising international bank settlement systems such as GlobalAccess, Cirrus, Interlink, Plus, Star, Accel, The Exchange and Explore. The rear side of your ATM card should tell you which systems will work with your card. Visa, MasterCard and American Express will work in many Hong Kong machines as well.

Shanghai is trying hard to catch up with Hong Kong, so don't be surprised if that city soon becomes more hospitable to foreign ATM cards.

Credit Cards

Plastic is gaining more acceptance in China for use by foreign visitors in major tourist cities. Useful cards include Visa, MasterCard, American Express, JCB and Diners Club. They can be used in most mid-range to top-end hotels (three star and up), Friendship Stores and some department stores. Note that it is still impossible to use credit cards to finance your transportation costs; even flights have to be paid for in cash.

Credit card cash advances have become fairly routine at head branches of the Bank of China, even in places as remote as Lhasa. Bear in mind, however, that a 4% commission is generally deducted and usually the minimum advance is Y1200.

International Transfers

Except in Hong Kong and Macau, having money sent to you in China is a time-consuming and frustrating task that is best avoided. If dealing with the Bank of China, the process can take weeks, although it can be much faster at CITIC Bank.

China Courier Service Corporation (a joint-venture with Western Union Financial Services in the USA) is very fast and efficient. In Beijing, there is a branch (☎ 6318-4285) at 173 Yong'an St.

Bank Accounts

Foreigners can indeed open bank accounts in China – both RMB and US dollar accounts (the latter only at special foreign-exchange banks). You do not need to have resident status – a tourist visa is sufficient. Virtually every foreigner working in China will tell you that CITIC is far better to do business with than the Bank of China.

Currency

The Chinese currency is known as Renminbi (RMB), or 'People's Money'. Formally the basic unit of RMB is the *yuan*, which is divided into ten *jiao*, which is again divided into ten *fen*. Colloquially, the yuan is referred to as *kuai* and jiao as *mao*. The fen has so little value these days that it is rarely used.

The Bank of China issues RMB bills in denominations of two, five, 10, 50 and 100 yuan. Coins are in denominations of one yuan, five jiao and one, two and five fen. There are still a lot of paper versions of the coins floating around, but it is likely that these will gradually disappear in favour of the coins.

Hong Kong's currency the Hong Kong dollar and Macau's is the Pataca. Both currencies are worth about 7% more than Renminbi.

Currency Exchange

Exchange rates for Chinese RMB are as follows:

Australia	A$1	=	Y5.56
Canada	C$1	=	Y5.88
France	FF1	=	Y1.36
Germany	DM1	=	Y4.54
Hong Kong	HK$1	=	Y1.07
Japan	¥1	=	Y0.064
New Zealand	NZ$1	=	Y4.82
Switzerland	SFr1	=	Y5.59
UK	UK£1	=	Y13.76
USA	US$1	=	Y8.31

Changing Money

Foreign currency and travellers cheques can be changed at border crossings, international airports, the main centres of the Bank of China, the tourist hotels, some Friendship Stores and some of the big department stores. Top-end hotels will generally change money for hotel guests only. The official rate is given almost everywhere, so there is little need to shop around looking for the best deal.

Australian, Canadian, US, UK, Hong Kong, Japanese and most Western European currencies are acceptable in China. In some of the backwaters, it may be hard to change lesser known currencies – US dollars are still the easiest to change.

Keep at least a few of your exchange receipts. You will need them if you want to exchange any remaining RMB you have at the end of your trip. Those travelling to Hong Kong can change RMB for Hong Kong dollars there.

Black Market

The abolition of Foreign Exchange Certificates (FEC) in 1994 basically knocked China's flourishing black market on its head. Black market moneychangers still attempt to eke out a meagre living in some major cities, but the rates they offer are often less than those offered by the banks – given the *very likely* risk of short-changing and rip-offs and the abundance of counterfeit currency floating about, it would be wise to avoid changing money on the streets.

Tipping & Bargaining

As some compensation for constantly being the target for rip offs, China is at least one of those wonderful countries where tipping is not practised and almost no-one asks for tips. When tips are offered in China, they are offered *before* you get the service, not after – that will ensure (hopefully) that you get better service. All things considered, tip-ping isn't a good idea because it will make it rough for foreigners who follow you.

Since foreigners are so frequently overcharged in China, bargaining becomes essential. You can bargain in shops, hotels, with taxi drivers, with most people – but not everywhere. In large shops where prices are clearly marked, there is usually no latitude for bargaining. In small shops and street stalls, bargaining is expected, but there is one important rule to follow – be polite.

There is nothing wrong with asking for a discount, if you do so with a smile. Some foreigners seem to think that bargaining should be an exercise in intimidation. This is not only unpleasant for all concerned, it seldom results in a lower price – indeed, in 'face-conscious' China, intimidation is likely to make the vendor more recalcitrant and you'll be overcharged.

You should keep in mind that entrepreneurs are in business to make money – they aren't going to sell anything to you at a loss. Your goal should be to pay the Chinese price, as opposed to the foreigners' price – if you can do that, you've done well.

Taxes

Although big hotels and top-end restaurants may add a tax or 'service charge' of 10% or more, all other consumer taxes are included in the price tag.

POST & COMMUNICATIONS
Postal Rates

Postage for domestic letters up to 20g is Y0.50, and domestic postcards are Y0.30. International air mail postal rates are as follows:

Letters (weight)	International	HK, Macau & Taiwan	Asia-Pacific
0-20g	Y5.40	Y2.50	Y4.70
21-100g	Y11.40	Y5.00	Y9.80
101-250g	Y21.80	Y9.50	Y18.60
251-500g	Y40.80	Y17.70	Y34.80
501-1kg	Y76.70	Y32.70	Y65.30
1kg-2kg	Y124.00	Y56.80	Y105.00
Postcards	Y4.20	Y2.00	Y3.70
Aerograms	Y5.20	Y1.80	Y4.50

There are discounts for printed matter and small packets.

Post offices are very picky about how you pack things; don't finalise your packing until the thing has got its last Customs clearance. Most countries impose a maximum weight limit (10kg is typical) on packages received – this rate varies from country to country, but the Chinese post office should be able to tell you what the limit is.

If you have a receipt for the goods, put it in the box when you're mailing it, since it may be opened again by Customs further down the line.

EMS Domestic Express Mail Service (EMS) parcels up to 200g cost Y15; each additional 200g costs Y5. For international EMS, the charges vary according to country. Some sample minimal rates (up to 500g parcels) are as follows:

Australia	Y195
Eastern Europe	Y382
Hong Kong & Macau	Y105
Japan & Korea	Y135
Middle East	Y375
North America	Y217
South America	Y262
South Asia	Y255
South-East Asia	Y150
Western Europe	Y232

Registration Fees The registration fee for letters, printed matter and packets is Y1. Acknowledgement of receipt is Y1 per article.

Sending Mail

The international postal service seems efficient, and air mail letters and postcards will probably take around five to 10 days to reach their destinations. If possible, write the country of destination in Chinese, as this should speed up the delivery. Domestic post is amazingly fast – perhaps one or two days from Guangzhou to Beijing. Within a city it may be delivered the same day it's sent.

As well as the local post offices, there are branch post offices in just about all the major tourist hotels where you can send letters, packets and parcels (the contents of packets and parcels are checked by the post office staff before mailing). Even at cheap hotels you can usually post letters from the front desk – reliability varies, but in general it's OK. In some places, you may only be able to post printed matter from these branch offices. Other parcels may require a Customs form attached at the town's main post office, where their contents will be checked.

The post office requires that you use an envelope of an approved size. If you bring envelopes from abroad, these might not meet the standard. They will still be delivered, but given low priority and will take a long time to arrive at the intended destination.

Large envelopes are a bit hard to come by; try the department stores. If you expect to be sending quite a few packets, stock up when you come across such envelopes. A roll of strong, sticky tape is a useful item to bring along and serves many purposes. String, glue and sometimes cloth bags are supplied at the post offices, but don't count on it. The Friendship Stores will sometimes package and mail purchases for you, but only goods bought at the store.

Private Carriers There are a number of foreign private couriers in China (mostly joint-venture operations) which offer international express posting of documents and parcels. None of these private carriers are cheap, but they're fast and secure. In major cities these companies have pick-up service as well as drop-off centres, so call their offices for the latest details.

The major players in this market are United Parcel Service, DHL, Federal Express and TNT Skypak. See the relevant city entries in this book to find the courier office nearest you.

Receiving Mail
There are poste restante services in just about every city and town, and they seem to work. The collection system differs from place to place, but one thing all post offices seem to agree on is the Y1 to Y2 charge for each item of poste restante mail you collect. Remember, you will need your passport to be able to retrieve your letters or parcels.

Some major tourist hotels will hold mail for their guests, but this is a less reliable option. Receiving a parcel from abroad is a bit complicated. The mail carrier will not deliver the parcel to your address – what you get is a slip of paper (in Chinese only). Bring this to the post office (indicated on the paper) along with your passport – the parcel will be opened and inspected in front of you. Along as it contains nothing nasty you will then be allowed to take it. One good thing about this system is that it mostly eliminates the possibility of your goods being pinched by corrupt Customs officials.

Officially, the PRC forbids certain items from being mailed to it – the regulations specifically prohibit 'reactionary books, magazines and propaganda materials, obscene or immoral articles'. You also cannot mail Chinese currency abroad or receive it by post. As elsewhere, mail-order hashish and other recreational chemicals will not amuse the authorities.

Telephone
China's phone system is undergoing a major overhaul and, given the size of the task, it has so far been reasonably successful. Both international and domestic calls can be made with a minimum of fuss from your hotel room. Even card phones are increasingly widespread.

Most hotel rooms are equipped with phones from which local calls are free. Alternatively, local calls can be made from public pay phones or from privately run phone booths (there's one of these on every corner nowadays). Long-distance domestic calls can also be made from the phone booths, but not usually international calls. In the lobbies of many hotels, the reception desks have a similar system – free calls for guests, Y1 for non-guests, and long-distance calls are charged by the minute.

You can place both domestic and international long-distance phone calls from main telecommunications offices. Generally you pay a deposit of Y200 and are given a card with the number of the phone booth you call from. The call is timed by computer, charged by the minute and a receipt will be provided.

Domestic long-distance rates in China vary according to distance, but are cheap. International calls are expensive. Rates for station-to-station calls to most countries in the world are around Y20 per minute. There is a minimum charge of three minutes. Reverse-charge calls are often cheaper than calls paid for in China. Time the call yourself – the operator will not break in to tell you that your minimum period of three minutes is approaching. After you hang up, the operator will ring back to tell you how much it cost. There is no call cancellation fee.

If you are expecting a call – either international or domestic – try to advise the caller beforehand of your hotel room number. The operators frequently have difficulty understanding western names and the hotel receptionist may not be able to locate you. If this can't be done, then try to inform the operator that you are expecting the call and write down your name and room number – this should increase your chances of success.

Card Phones Card phones can be found in hotel lobbies and in most telecommunications buildings. Calls made on card phones are charged by the minute, so you avoid the expense of making a minimum three-minute call. The cards come in two flavours – magnetic phone cards and 'Smartcards'.

The magnetic cards are an older design. The phone company has a problem with these – they can be magnetically recharged using a simple device readily available on the black market. The cards do eventually wear out, but it is possible to recharge it over 100 times – thus, a Y100 phone card can be used to make over Y10,000 worth of phone calls! This situation is not unique to China.

The phone company's response has been to introduce the so-called Smartcards. The cards aren't really smart, but they are resistant to tampering and – as far as is known – nobody has yet built a device to recharge them.

At the present time you'll find both kinds of card phones, but the phone company will definitely phase out the magnetic cards over the next couple of years. Note that magnetic cards can only be used in the province where you buy them. Smartcards can be used throughout China, provided you can find a Smartcard phone.

Direct Dialling Card phones are the cheapest way to make calls in China, but telecommunications centres, hotel business centres and mid-range to top-end hotel rooms also provide Domestic Direct Dialling (DDD) and International Direct Dialling (IDD). Bear in mind that hotels generally levy a 30% surcharge on long-distance calls.

The international access code in China is ☎ 00. Add the country code, then the local area code (omitting the 0 before it) and the number you want to reach. Another option is to dial the home country direct dial number (☎ 108), which puts you straight through to a local operator there. You can then make a reverse-charge (collect) call or a credit card call with a telephone credit card valid in the destination country.

Dialling codes include:

Country	Direct Dial	Home Country Direct
Australia	☎ 00-61	☎ 108-61
Canada	☎ 00-1	☎ 108-1
Hong Kong	☎ 00-852	☎ 108-852
Japan	☎ 00-81	☎ 108-81
Netherlands	☎ 00-31	☎ 108-31
New Zealand	☎ 00-64	☎ 108-64
UK	☎ 00-44	☎ 108-44
USA	☎ 00-1	☎ 108-1*

*For the USA you can dial ☎ 108-11 (AT&T), ☎ 108-12 (MCI) or ☎ 108-13 (Sprint)

The domestic codes for China's major cities appear on the following page.

Essential Numbers There are several telephone numbers which are the same for all major cities. Only international directory assistance is likely to have English speaking operators:

Local directory assistance	☎ 114
Long-distance assistance	☎ 113, ☎ 173
International assistance	☎ 115
Police hotline	☎ 110
Fire hotline	☎ 119

If you will be staying in China for more than a few months and make frequent overseas calls, it's worthwhile to sign up with a callback service. Virtually all such services

Telephone Codes for Major Cities

Anhui
Guichi (0566)
Hefei (0551)
Jiuhua (0566)
Wuhu (0553)

Beijing (010)

Fujian
Fuzhou (0591)
Meizhou (0753)
Quanzhou (0595)
Xiamen (0592)

Gansu
Dunhuang (0937)
Jianyuguan (0947)
Lanzhou (0931)
Maijishan (0938)
Xiahe (0941)
Zhangye (0936)

Guangdong
Foshan (0757)
Guangzhou (020)
Shantou (0754)
Shenzhen (0755)
Zhanjiang (0759)
Zhaoqing (0758)
Zhongshan (07654)
Zhuhai (0756)

Guangxi
Beihai (0779)
Guilin (0773)
Liuzhou (0772)
Nanning (0771)

Guizhou
Guiyang (0851)
Zunyi (0852)

Hainan
Haikou (0898)
Sanya (0899)

Hebei
Chengde (0314)
Shijiazhuang (0311)
Qinhuangdao (0335)

Heilongjiang
Harbin (0451)
Mudanjiang (0453)

Henan
Kaifeng (0378)
Luoyang (0379)
Zhengzhou (0371)

Hubei
Wudangshan (0719)
Wuhan (027)
Yichang (0717)

Hunan
Changsha (0731)
Yueyang (0730)
Wulingyuan (0744)

Inner Mongolia
Baotou (0472)
Dongsheng (0477)
Hailar (0470)
Hohhot (0471)
Manzhouli (0470)
Xanadu (0479)
Xilinhot (0479)

Jiangsu
Nanjing (025)
Suzhou (0512)
Wuxi (0510)
Xuzhou (0516)
Yangzhou (0514)
Zhenjiang (0511)

Jiangxi
Jingdezhen (0798)
Jiujiang (0792)
Lushan (0792)
Nanchang (0791)

Jilin
Changchun (0431)
Jilin (0432)

Liaoning
Dalian (0411)
Dandong (0415)
Shenyang (024)

Ningxia
Guyuan (0954)
Yinchuan (0951)
Zhongwei (0953)

Qinghai
Golmud (0979)

Huangzhong (0972)
Ta'er (0972)
Xining (0971)

Shaanxi
Xi'an (029)
Yan'an (0911)
Yulin (0912)

Shandong
Ji'nan (0531)
Qingdao (0532)
Qufu (05473)
Weihai (05451)
Yantai (0535)
Zibo (0533)

Shanghai (021)

Shanxi
Datong (0352)
Ruicheng (0359)
Taiyuan (0351)

Sichuan
Baoding (0312)
Chengdu (028)
Chongqing (0811)
Leshan (0833)

Tianjin (022)

Tibet
Lhasa (0891)

Xinjiang
Altai (0906)
Hotan (0903)
Kashgar (0998)
Kuqa (0997)
Turpan (0995)
Ürümqi (0991)
Yining (0999)

Yunnan
Kunming (0871)
Simao (0879)

Zhejiang
Hangzhou (0571)
Ningbo (0574)
Shaoxing (0575)
Wenzhou (0577)
Xikou (0574)

are based in the USA (to take advantage of the USA's cheap phone rates). Some of the choices available include:

Justice Technology (☎ (310) 526-2000; fax 526-2100; www.justicecorp.com)
Kallback (☎ (206) 599-1992; fax 599-1982; email info@kallback.com; ww.kallback.com)
Kallmart (☎ (407) 676-1717; fax 676-5289; mail sales@kallmart.com; www.kallmart.com)
New World (☎ (201) 488-5811; email economist @newworldtele.com; www.newworldtele.com)

The cheapest (if not the most convenient) way to make overseas calls is through the Internet. Getting this to work requires making prior arrangements with the person you wish to call, having the proper software, a fast modem connection and a bit of luck. There are various publications which explain how to do it, but it's beyond the scope of this travel guide.

Fax, Telegraph & Email

Major hotels usually operate a business centre complete with telephone and fax service, not to mention photocopying and perhaps the use of typewriters and computers.

Telegraph services are offered at the phone company main offices.

Email is still in its infancy in China. A major stumbling block is that the government monopolises all telecommunications, so only state-run companies can offer email services. Foreign companies such as CompuServe have tried to come into China and set up local nodes, but the government gives them so little band-width that their systems soon overload. As a result, you'll have much difficulty getting online in China if you want to use a foreign-based Internet Service Provider (ISP). If you're travelling with a portable computer and want to access your email, your only alternative may be to make an expensive call to Hong Kong or abroad.

If you're travelling with a portable computer and modem, all you need is an IDD line with an RJ-11 phone jack to call to your favourite email service abroad.

However, it's risky to attach your modem to the phone in your hotel room and dial out through the switchboard – if the switchboard is digital (as opposed to analog) you risk frying your modem. Ironically, this is a bigger problem at newer hotels – old hotels usually have analog equipment. One of the few companies to market a solution to this problem is Konexx (www.konexx. com) – they sell a device called a 'mobile konnector' which not only protects the modem, but also allows you to hook up to the phone's handset cord.

There are a small but growing number of cybercafes in China. Probably the cheapest way to keep in touch while on the road is to sign up for a free account with Hotmail (www.hotmail.com/), Rocketmail (www. rocketmail.com/) or NetAddress (netaddress.usa.net) and access your account from a cybercafe. These services are free because you have to put up with advertising. If you're willing to spend US$15 per year, you can get all your email forwarded to any address of your choice by signing up with Pobox (www.pobox.com) – this service can also be used to block advertising and mail bombs.

Things are a lot easier if you're a legal foreign resident of China and wish to set up a local Internet account. Chinese ISPs are all government run, but the service is gradually improving and costs have come down. You do have to put up with some censorship – the Chinese government has blocked access to sites that peddle pornography or contain political content deemed unsuitable for the masses. Nevertheless, you can get quite a lot of useful work done on the Internet. Some Chinese companies offering Internet service are as follows:

3CNET
(☎ (010) 6496-1814; www.netchina.co.cn)
Eastnet
(☎ (010) 6529-2268; www.home.eastnet.co.cn)
International United Online
(☎ (010) 6492-3076; www.iuol.cn.net)

China's packet-switching network, CHINAPAC, should be avoided as the charges are nothing short of outrageous (even more than an IDD call).

BOOKS

Fathoming the enigma of China is such a monumental task that the need for 'China-watchers' and their publications will probably never dry up. Indeed, just keeping up with the never-ending flood of conjecture on the Middle Kingdom would be a full-time job in itself. Be aware that a book might be a hardcover rarity in one country while it's readily available in paperback in another. The following is just an abbreviated tour of the highlights.

Lonely Planet

Other Lonely Planet guides to the region include the *Beijing City Guide* and *Hong Kong City Guide* and regional guides for *Tibet, South-West China* (upcoming) and *Hong Kong, Macau & Guangzhou*. There are also phrasebooks covering Mandarin, Cantonese, Tibetan and Arabic.

Guidebooks

The Hong Kong publisher Odyssey is gradually producing a series of illustrated provincial guides to China. To date there are guides to Yunnan, Guizhou, Sichuan, Shanghai, Xi'an and Beijing. There is less emphasis on the kind of practical travel information you find in Lonely Planet guides, but they are attractively packaged and provide good background reading.

It is worth keeping an eye out for reprints of old guidebooks to China. Oxford has re-released *In Search of Old Peking* by LC Arlington and William Lewisohn, which is a wonderfully detailed guide to a world that is now long gone.

Travel Tales

Iron and Silk by Mark Salzman recounts the adventures of a young Chinese-speaking kungfu student in China (filmed as a telemovie). Another good travel book, *From Heaven Lake* by Vikram Seth of *A Suitable Boy* fame, follows Seth's journey from Xinjiang to Tibet and on to Delhi, in the days when it was a difficult undertaking. Another possibility is *Danziger's Travels* by Nick Danziger – a good 'Silk Road' book that takes quite a long time to get to China.

China by Bike: Taiwan, Hong Kong, China's East Coast, by Roger Grigsby, is just what the title implies.

The greatest backpacker of all time was, of course, Marco Polo. Author Ronald Latham published *Marco Polo, The Travels* in 1958, and it's still available as a Penguin reprint.

History & Politics

The most comprehensive history of China available is the *Cambridge History of China*. The series runs to 15 volumes (so far) and traces Chinese history from its earliest beginnings to 1982. The two big problems are that it's very expensive and won't fit in your backpack.

A far more practical overview for travellers is *The Walled Kingdom: A History of China from 2000 BC to the Present* by Witold Rodzinsky. It should be available in a handy paperback edition of around 450 pages.

The best recent history of modern China is Jonathan Spence's *The Search for Modern China*. It fully covers China's history from the late Ming through to the Tiananmen Massacre in lively prose that is a pleasure to read. Spence's *The Gate of Heavenly Peace: The Chinese and Their Revolution, 1895-1980* is also recommended – it is a history of ideas and personalities.

The Great Chinese Revolution 1800-1985 by John King Fairbank is another highly rated modern history.

A polemical overview of what Chinese history has been about and where it is all heading is provided in *The Tyranny of History: The Roots of China's Crisis* by WJF Jenner. The essential argument that China's history has been one of tyranny, and that China's attachment to history continues to tyrannise it, is a fascinating one, if perhaps a little too clever for its own good.

A political history of the Deng years has

already appeared in *Burying Mao* by Richard Baum. For anyone seriously interested in China's stop-go reforms of the last 20 years, this is the book to read. Merle Goldman also looks at the tortuous course of democratic reform over recent years in *Sowing the Seeds of Democracy in China: Political Reform in the Deng Xiaoping Era*.

Hungry Ghosts: Mao's Secret Famine by Jasper Becker is perhaps the best book on the disastrous Great Leap Forward. The book focuses on the 1958-62 famine that killed up to 30 million people. China's leaders still try to hide this disaster because it was largely they who caused it.

It is worth picking up a copy of *The Soong Dynasty* by Sterling Seagrave for a racy account of the bad old days under the Kuomintang.

Finally, all of Peter Hopkirk's books are worth reading. None of them deal with China specifically, but in *The Great Game*, *Foreign Devils on the Silk Road* and *Trespassers on the Roof of the World* Hopkirk writes breezily of 19th century international espionage, exploration, pilfering of lost art treasures and the struggle for territorial domination at the far-flung edges of the Chinese empire in Xinjiang (Chinese Turkestan, as it was then known) and Tibet.

China's takeover of Hong Kong continues to stir up strong feelings. Mark Roberti contributes his thoughts in *The Fall of Hong Kong – China's Triumph and Britain's Betrayal*.

General

Insights *Wild Swans* by Jung Chang is one of the more ambitious of the long line of I-survived-China (but only just) books. *Life and Death in Shanghai* by Nien Cheng focuses largely on the Cultural Revolution and is also recommended.

Son of the Revolution by Liang Heng and Judith Shapiro, an early inside-China book, is still well worth reading.

Red Azalea by Anchee Min is a strange and racy account of what it was like to grow up in the Cultural Revolution.

Less riveting, perhaps, is a fine account

of life in rural China in *Mr China's Son: A Villager's Life* by He Liuyi.

State of the nation accounts of contemporary Chinese politics and society by western scholars and journalists are thick on the ground and tend to become repetitive if you read too many of them.

One of the best recent works is *China Wakes* by Nicholas D Kristof and Sheryl Wudunn. Orville Schell has also been diligently tracking China's awakening in several books, the latest being *Mandate of Heaven*.

For an insight into Chinese society, check out Perry Link's *Evening Chats in Beijing*. It is everything you could wish of a book about China: intelligent, well written and packed with illuminating insights and observations culled from a long career of writing and thinking about China.

Real China: From Cannibalism to Karaoke by John Gittings is informative and entertaining, even if the title is unfortunate.

Human Rights *Eighteen Layers of Hell: Stories from the Chinese Gulag* by Kate Saunders blows the lid off China's human rights violations.

Harry Wu, imprisoned by Chinese authorities for 19 years, exposes China's *laogai* (forced labour camps) in his eloquently written *Bitter Winds: A Memoir of My Years in China's Gulag*. Wu returned to China again in 1995 and was immediately arrested and tried for espionage, but was expelled after intervention by the US congress and President Clinton. He wrote about that experience in his sequel, *Troublemaker: One Man's Crusade Against China's Cruelty*.

The smuggled prison letters of dissident Wei Jingsheng have been collected and published in *The Courage to Stand Alone: Letters from Prison and Other Writings*, edited by Kristina Torgeson.

Some earlier works, not out of print, can be tracked down in libraries. Two such examples are *Prisoner of Mao* by Bao Ruo-Wang (1976) and *Seeds of Fire – Chinese*

Voices of Conscience (1989), edited by Geremie Barmé and John Minford.

You can also check out Amnesty International's Web site (www.amnesty.org) or get its China report in print. Perhaps a more immediate Web site is run by Support Democracy in China (www.christusrex.org/www1/sdc/sdchome.html).

Biography Biographical appraisals of China's shadowy leaders are immensely popular. Mao, of course, has been the subject of countless biographies (the classic is *Red Star over China* by Edgar Snow, but it was his personal physician, Zhisui Li, who finally blew the lid on the world's most famous dictator cum pop icon. Li's *The Private Life of Chairman Mao* is absolutely compelling in its account of Mao as a domineering manipulator who hypocritically flouted the authoritarian and puritanical rules he foisted on his people – fascinating stuff.

Mao gets similar treatment in *The New Emperors* by Harrison E Salisbury. The book covers the lives of Mao and Deng, but it is Mao who gets the bulk of the book. Deng Xiaoping himself remains quite elusive.

Richard Evans has written an excellent book in *Deng Xiaoping and the Making of Modern China*, which has a particularly good synopsis of the events leading up to the killings in Beijing's Tiananmen Square in 1989.

Fiction *The Good Earth,* by Pearl S Buck, has become a classic. Ms Buck lived most of her life in 19th century China, and was a prolific writer. Some of her lesser known books are still in print, including *Sons – Good Earth Trilogy Volume 2, The Big Wave, The Child Who Never Grew, Dragon Seed, East Wind: West Wind, A House Divided, Imperial Woman, Kinfolk, The House of Earth Volume 9, The Living Reed, The Mother, Pavilion of Women, Peony, The Three Daughters of Madame Liang, Little Red* and *The Promise*.

Manchu Palaces: A Novel, by Jeanne Larsen, is the story of Lotus, a woman struggling to secure a job for herself in Beijing's Forbidden City during the 18th century Manchu dynasty.

Unfortunately a lot of fiction written by westerners involving China tends to be of the potboiler variety, involving dashing western heroes going about their daredevil business in a romanticised and stereotyped oriental world. If that's your thing, James Clavell probably claims the biggest market share with *Tai-Pan* and *Noble House*.

The work of Jonathan Spence occupies an unusual space somewhere between biography, fiction and history. *The Memory Palace of Matteo Ricci* is a study of the most famous Jesuit to take up residence in China. *The Question of Hu* and *Emperor of China: Self-Portrait of K'ang Hsi* are also highly recommended.

Rose Crossing by Nicholas Jose is a quirky account of a chance encounter of a 17th century English naturalist and a eunuch of the deposed Ming court on a deserted island.

The Chinese-American writers Maxine Hong Kingston and Amy Tan have both written books about the experiences of immigrant Chinese in the USA. Although their novels are not directly about China, they tell a great deal about Chinese relationships and customs. Look out for Kingston's *The Woman Warrior* and *China Men,* or Tan's *The Kitchen God's Wife* and *The Joy Luck Club*.

Language A good dictionary is an essential learning tool for anyone who is even considering tackling the Chinese language. A list of the best dictionaries follows, and these should be available in most western countries, as well as China, Hong Kong and Taiwan. Alternatively, you could try ordering through the Internet (http://www.amazon.com).

The *Concise English-Chinese Chinese-English Dictionary* by AP Cowie and A Evison is one of the best for beginners right through to advanced students. This is one of the classics, with pinyin pronunciation throughout. It's available in several versions with varying degrees of quality (some versions have poor bindings).

Chinese Character Genealogy – A Chinese-English Dictionary by Rick Harbaugh is very recently published and particularly good if you want to understand the etymology of Chinese characters.

The *ABC Chinese-English Dictionary: Alphabetically Based Computerized* by John Defrancis is unique in that it is arranged by word pronunciation, rather than by character pronunciation. It's most useful for students who don't wish to learn written Chinese, but just want to learn how to speak.

The *Far East Chinese-English Dictionary* is published in Taiwan and uses the traditional characters only, not the simplified ones found in mainland China. It's arranged by radicals (stroke order), but includes a pinyin index, as well as Taiwan's own *bopomofo* phonetic system. This title is a particularly good dictionary for intermediate to advanced students of Chinese language.

There is also a companion *Far East English-Chinese Dictionary*, but this one is harder for foreigners to use because it doesn't show the pronunciation of Chinese characters. Both dictionaries are available in pocket-size and desktop-size editions.

Religion Being able to make sense out of Chinese religion will require considerable patience and perseverance.

Aside from the Taoist classics, you can check out *The Butterfly as Companion* by Wu Kuang-Ming; *365 Tao: Daily Meditations* by Deng Ming-Dao; *Awaken Healing Energy Through Tao* by Mantak Chyi; *Couples and the Tao of Congruence* by Barbara Jo Brothers, and too many others to list.

The definition of the Tao is so loosely applied these days that almost any topic can be related to it. Even the late kungfu expert Bruce Lee chips in with *The Tao of the Dragon Warrior* – what, one wonders, would Laotzu make of that?

Confucian enthusiasts may wish to dig through some of the following titles:

Confucius: The Secular As Sacred by Herbert Fingarette

Confucius: The Wisdom, Volume 1, edited by Claudia Karabaic

Confucius As a Teacher by Chen Jingpan

Confucius Speaks: Words to Live By by Chih-Chung Tsai

Confucius, Lao Tzu and Chinese Philosophy by Crispin Sartwell (also available on audio cassette)

Dream of Confucius by Jean Levi and Barbara Bray

The Essential Confucius: The Heart of Confucius' Teachings in Authentic I Ching Order by Thomas Cleary

Genesis and the Mystery Confucius Couldn't Solve by Ethel Nelson and Richard Broadberry

The Heart of Confucius: Interpretations of 'Genuine Living' and 'Great Wisdom' by Archie J Bahm

In the Path of the Masters: Understanding the Spirituality of Buddha, Confucius, Jesus, and Muhammad by Denise Lardner Carmody and John Tully Carmody

Sayings of Confucius by Shih Ching.

Fengshui (Geomancy) Books about fengshui are easy to come by. Currently in-print titles include: *The Feng Shui Companion: A User-Friendly Guide to the Ancient Art of Placement* by George Birdsall; *Feng Shui for the Home* by Evelyn Lip; *The Feng Shui Handbook: A Practical Guide to Chinese Geomancy* by Derek Waltersand; and *Handbook of Geomancy* by Aleister Crowley.

CD ROM
There are plenty of CD ROMs about China, but finding ones published in English will take some effort. However, there are a few sources.

In the USA, check out HyperDrive.Com (☎ (800) 901-8622; www.hyperdrive.com), PO Box 4242, Sunland, CA; or the China Guide Company (☎ (718) 389-4876, (888) 242-8805; www.china-guide.com), 642 Leonard St, 2R, Brooklyn, NY.

In Canada, there's BIS Information Systems (☎ (604) 688-8916; email: orders @voyagerco.com), No 203-124 East Pender St, Vancouver, BC V6A 1T3.

Hong Kong is a good place to shop for CD ROMs, but you'll have to look hard to find titles in English.

Taiwan – if you happen to be there – is also a rich source of multimedia products. Summit Computer Technology of Taiwan (www.sinanet.com/mkt/sum/index.html) puts out a good range of CD-ROMs (mostly in Chinese language) which can be ordered by post.

For better or worse, Microsoft Windows is the dominant operating system. Macintosh users who want to buy Chinese CD ROMs are left twisting in the wind. Except when otherwise noted, the following CD ROMs are for Windows.

Entertainment

Monkey King, China Guide Company (www. china-guide.com); US$30; in English, French and German

Qin, Time Warner Electronic Publishing (available from HyperDrive.Com); a game to explore the subterranean tomb of China's first emperor, Qin Shihuang

The Complete Stamp Collection of China, Beijing Golden Disc (available from Hyper-Drive.Com); US$35

Touring

The Great Wall, Beijing Golden Disc (available from HyperDrive.Com); US$35

The Imperial Palace of Beijing, Beijing Golden Disc (also available from HyperDrive.Com); US$35

The National Palace Museum, available in Taiwan at the museum's gift shop or from Lambert Publishing Co (lambert@lambert. com.tw), 6th floor, 201-24 Tunhwa N Rd, Taipei; US$60 (Most of the original art treasures of China's emperors are in fact in Taiwan's National Palace Museum in Taipei, *not* in Beijing.)

The Silk Road, DNA Multimedia (available from HyperDrive.Com); US$42; available for both Windows and Macintosh

The Yangtze River and the Three Gorges of China, Beijing Golden Disc (available from HyperDrive.Com); US$35

Language

There are several good interactive CD ROMs on the market which are useful for learning to speak and read Chinese:

The Far East Illustrated English-Chinese Dictionary, China Guide Company (www.china-guide.com); US$50

Super Lexicomp Multiple Function Dictionary, China Guide Company (www.china-guide. com); US$60

Professional Interactive Chinese for Windows, VentureTech USA (www.venturetech.com/ educate.html), but cheaper from the China Guide Company (www.china-guide.com); US$199; a good all-around package that can teach you up to 2000 characters

Shang Mao Putonghua, City University of Hong Kong & Digital Vision Multimedia (available from Take 5, Unit 10 & 11, Room 701, Level 7, Dragon Centre, 37K Yen Chow St, Shamshuipo, Kowloon, Hong Kong); US$60 for three CD ROMs; geared towards business Chinese for advanced speakers

Step Into China, English Version, Superlan Technology, Taiwan (available from CDMate, Shop 1014-1015, 10th floor, The In Square, Windsor House, 311 Gloucester Rd, Causeway Bay, Hong Kong); US$63; it has a very user-friendly interface, which is good for beginners

Teach Yourself Chinese – The Sinophile, Version 2.0, Comsun, China (available from CD-ROM Gallery, Unit 1-2, 13th floor, Kenning Industrial Building, 19 Wang Hoi Rd, Kowloon Bay, Kowloon, Hong Kong); US$18; it has a boring interface, but the content is good at a very low price

ONLINE SERVICES

The Internet changes so fast that almost anything we can recommend about it is liable to be out of date tomorrow. You could try going online and searching on the words 'China' or 'Chinese', but this will likely turn up many thousands of hits, most of them worthless.

Lonely Planet has China information on its Internet site (www.lonelyplanet.com.au).

We've done some exploring ourselves, and have found some pretty good Web sites. One word of warning: many Chinese Web sites require that you have a Chinese-enabled Web browser to see the Chinese characters, but look for an icon which you can click on to change the display to English.

The most interesting sites are not in China itself – that should come as no surprise, seeing how most Chinese cannot afford a computer (plus the fact that the Chinese government censors the Internet).

Some sites which are *not* in China include:

China News Digest (www.cnd.org), an ancient (by online standards) Ezine

Asia, Inc (www.asia-inc.com) for online business reports

Australian National University (coombs.anu.edu.au/wwwvl.AsianStudies.html) for general information on Asian studies

www.sinanet.com, if you want to tackle a fully Chinese language site, but do not have the Chinese fonts

Rick Harbaugh (zhongwen.com/) present a superb etymological dictionary of the Chinese language

Army Area Handbook for China (gopher://umslvma.umsl.edu/11/library/stacks/books/armyahbs/aahb9), an online edition of this rather out-of-date US government publication

Carlos McEvilly (www.webcom.com/bamboo/chinese) for one of the best Chinese linguistic sites around

philo.ucdavis.edu/CHINESE/online.htm, for some basic Chinese online

Shanghai-ed (www.shanghai-ed.com), an online city guide to Shanghai

There are a few Web sites in China that you might want to take a look at. The selection includes:

Asia Online
   www.asia1.com.sg
Beijing Online
   www.bol.co.cn
Beijing University
   www.pku.edu.cn
China Economic Windows
   www.cei.go.cn
China Education & Research Network
   www.net.edu.cn
China News Services
   www.chinanews.com
China Sciences & Technology Network
   www.cnc.ac.cn

ChinaNet
   www.bta.net.cn
People's Daily
   www.snweb.com
Qinghua University
   www.tsinghua.edu.cn

Hong Kong has a lot of interesting Web sites, but we suspect that some of these will get censored or axed now that China has taken over. Nevertheless, some of the following may still exist:

Larry Feign, the artist whose political cartoons got him blacklisted from the Hong Kong newspapers, has fought back by going online. For a good laugh, browse Lily Wong's home page (www.asiaonline.net/lilywong).

BC Magazine has the inside scoop on Hong Kong's entertainment and nightlife scene. Check out its home page (ourworld.compuserve.com/homepages/puregoodness/bconline.htm).

Some other Hong Kong Web sites are:

Asian Sources Online, the centre of Asian trade on the World Wide Web
   www.asiansources.com
Hong Kong government information
   www.info.gov.hk
Hong Kong information page
   www-geog.hkbu.edu.hk/hkwww.html
Hong Kong jobs
   www-geog.hkbu.edu.hk/career.html£hk
Hong Kong Tourist Association
   www.hkta.org

FILMS

Movies produced by westerners and filmed in China are thin on the ground, largely because the Chinese government has a habit of demanding huge fees for the privilege. Still, there are a few that have become well known classics.

The definitive classic has to be *The Last Emperor*, released in 1988 by Columbia Pictures and directed by Bernardo Bertolucci.

American-Chinese author Amy Tan has seen some of her books made into films – *The Joy Luck Club* gives some some useful insights into Chinese culture, however, most of the action takes place in California.

Another well-known book turned into a motion picture is *Wild Swans* by Jung Chang.

On the other hand, documentaries about China are numerous, although tracking down a video tape to rent or buy might take some effort.

The Gate of Heavenly Peace by Carma Hinton and Richard Gordon is a well-balanced video about the democracy protests and bloodshed at Tiananmen Square in 1989. Another serious video is *The Dying Rooms* by Kate Blewett and Britain's Channel Four.

If nature documentaries are your style, you could try *The Amazing Panda Adventure* (1995, Warner Brothers). The National Geographic Society has produced a number of excellent videos on China.

Lonely Planet also has a video available entitled *South-West China*.

NEWSPAPERS & MAGAZINES
Chinese-Language Publications
Newspapers in China contain little hard news. Mostly, they are devoted to sloganeering and editorialising.

It's hard to say how many Chinese believe what they read, but certainly most Chinese are familiar with the official line: 'the Dalai Lama is worse than Hitler', 'Taiwan is a horrible dictatorship', 'foreign imperialists are always plotting against China', and so on.

When Hong Kongers held a candlelight vigil for the students who were massacred by Communist troops in Tiananmen Square, the Chinese press showed the photo with the caption, 'Hong Kong people are expressing their joy and happy feelings at being reunited with the motherland'.

There are more than 2000 national and provincial newspapers in China. The main one is *Renmin Ribao* (*People's Daily*), with nationwide circulation. Every city worth its salt in China will have its own local version of the *People's Daily* and, like the banner publication, they tend to serve chiefly as a propaganda vehicle. The sports page usually attracts the most interest.

At the other end of the scale is China's version of the gutter press – several hundred 'unhealthy papers' and magazines hawked on street corners and bus stations in major cities with nude or violent photos and stories about sex, crime, witchcraft, miracle cures and UFOs. These have been severely criticised by the government for their obscene and racy content. They are also extremely popular. There are also about 40 newspapers for the minority nationalities.

The Letters to the Editor section in the *People's Daily* provides something of a measure of public opinion, and complaints are sometimes followed up by reporters.

Foreign-Language Publications
China publishes various newspapers, books and magazines in a number of European and Asian languages. The *China Daily* is China's official English-language newspaper and is available in most major cities – it even makes its way as far as Lhasa, usually a couple of weeks out of date. The *Shanghai Star* is available in Shanghai only (sadly, since it's better than the *China Daily*).

China also publishes a large number of very dull magazines in English and other languages. They are seldom seen in China itself, but often clutter up periodical racks in university libraries around the world. They have titles like *China Philately* (for stamp collectors), *China's Patents & Trademarks*, *China's Tibet* (the name says it all) and *Women in China*. An old classic is *China Reconstructs*, renamed *China Today* after 30 years because – as one official put it – '30 years is a hell of a long time to be reconstructing your country'. It's difficult to imagine who reads any of these magazines.

Imported Publications
In large cities like Beijing, Shanghai and Guangzhou, it's fairly easy to score copies of popular imported English-language magazines like *Time, Newsweek, Far Eastern Economic Review* and *The Economist*.

It is also usually possible to find European magazines such as *Le Point* and *Der Spiegel*.

Foreign newspapers like the *Asian Wall Street Journal*, *International Herald-Tribune* and Hong Kong's now-muzzled *South China Morning Post* are also available. Imported periodicals are most readily available from the big tourist hotels, though a few Friendship Stores also stock copies.

To China's credit, foreign-language magazines and newspapers are seldom, if ever, censored, even when they contain stories critical of the PRC. Of course, a different set of rules applies to Chinese-language publications from Taiwan and overseas Chinese communities – essentially, these cannot be brought into China without special permission.

RADIO & TV

Domestic radio broadcasting is controlled by the Central People's Broadcasting Station (CPBS). Broadcasts are made in *pǔtōnghuà*, the standard Chinese speech, as well as in local Chinese dialects and minority languages.

There are also broadcasts to Taiwan in putonghua and Fujianese, and Cantonese broadcasts aimed at residents of Guangdong Province, Hong Kong and Macau.

Radio Beijing is China's overseas radio service and broadcasts in about 40 foreign languages, as well as in putonghua and several local dialects.

If you want to keep up with the world news, a short-wave radio receiver would be worth bringing with you. You can buy these in China, but the ones from Hong Kong are usually more compact and better quality.

Chinese Central Television (CCTV) began broadcasting in 1958, and colour transmission began in 1973. Major cities may have a second local channel, like Beijing Television (BTV). There is little of interest here for foreigners.

Hong Kong's STAR TV does satellite broadcasts to China. There are both Chinese and English-language shows, and a few are actually worth watching. In order to get the right to broadcast in China, STAR TV had to agree to remove the BBC World News.

VIDEO SYSTEMS

In a nutshell, the problem is that the various countries of the world cannot agree on a single TV broadcasting standard. China subscribes to the PAL broadcasting

Paper Propaganda

Apart from the mass media, the public notice board retains its place as an important means of educating the people or influencing public opinion. Other people who want to get a message across glue up big wall posters (*dàzìbào*, or 'big character posters') in public places.

This is a traditional form of communicating ideas in China. If the content catches the attention of even a few people then word-of-mouth can spread it very quickly. Deng Xiaoping personally removed from China's constitution the right to put up wall posters.

Public notice boards abound in China. Two of the most common subjects are crime and accidents. In China it's no-holds-barred – before-and-after photos of executed criminals are plugged up on these boards along with a description of their heinous offences. Other memorable photos include people squashed by trucks, blown up by fireworks or fried after smoking cigarettes near open petrol tanks. Other popular themes include industrial safety and family planning. Inspiring slogans such as 'The PLA Protects the People' or 'Follow the Socialist Road to Happiness' are also common. ■

standard, the same as Australia, New Zealand, the UK and most of Europe.

Competing systems not used in China include SECAM (France, Germany, Luxembourg) and NTSC (Canada, Japan, Taiwan, Korea, Latin America and the USA).

PHOTOGRAPHY & VIDEO
Film & Equipment
Imported film and cameras are expensive, but major Japanese companies like Fuji and Konica now have factories in China – this has brought film prices down to what you'd pay in the west. Cameras are still mostly pricey; although there are some made-in-China models.

While colour print film is available almost everywhere, it's almost always 100 ASA (21 DIN). Slide film can be found in big cities only (look for it in Friendship Stores and major camera shops). Black & white film is virtually unobtainable nowadays.

Finding the special lithium batteries used by many cameras is generally not a problem, but it would be wise to bring a couple of spares. Some cameras have a manual mode which allows you to continue shooting with a dead battery, although the light meter won't work. Fully automatic cameras totally drop dead when the battery goes.

You're allowed to bring in 8mm movie cameras; 16mm or professional equipment may raise eyebrows with Customs. Motion picture film is hard enough to find in the west these days, and next to impossible in China.

Photography
China is a mixed bag when it comes to photography. The deserts of Xinjiang and the high plateau of Tibet are among the most photogenic places in the world, as are the minority, subtropical regions of south-west China such as Yunnan Province. The coastal cities and towns of east China, on the other hand, are almost uniformly grey and bleak.

Video
Video cameras were once subject to shaky regulations, but there seems to be no problem now, at least with the cheap camcorders that tourists carry. A large professional video camera might raise eyebrows – the Chinese government is especially paranoid about foreign TV crews filming unauthorised documentaries.

For the average video hobbyist, the biggest problem is recharging your batteries off the strange mutations of plugs in China – bring all the adaptors you can, and remember that it's 220V.

Restrictions
Photography from planes and photographs of airports, military installations, harbour facilities and railroad terminals are prohibited; bridges may also be a touchy subject. With the possible exception of military installations, these rules are rarely enforced.

Photography most definitely is prohibited, however, in many museums, at archaeological sites and in some temples, mainly to protect the postcard and colour slide industry. It also prevents valuable works of art from being damaged by countless flash photos, but in most cases you're not allowed to take even harmless natural light photos or time exposures. There should be a sign in English advising of such restrictions, but ask if you're not sure.

If you're caught taking photos where you shouldn't, generally the film is ripped out of your camera. Make sure you start with a new roll if you don't want to lose any previous shots.

Photographing People
There are three basic approaches to photographing people. One is the polite 'ask for permission and pose it' shot, which is sometimes rejected. The second is the 'no-holds barred and upset everyone' approach. The third is surreptitious, standing half a kilometre away with a metre-long telephoto lens.

If you have befriended a Chinese, he or she is generally more than happy for you to be a model. Candid shots of people, however, are viewed with suspicion by many Chinese – why is that foreigner taking my picture? The idea of using photography as a creative outlet is alien to most Chinese, for whom cameras are used to snap friends and family at get-togethers or posed in front of tourist sights. Make contact with people you want to photograph – often a smile and a wave will do the trick.

Airport Security

Most x-ray machines in China's airports are marked 'film safe', and this seems to be the case. However, films with a very high ASA rating could be fogged by repeated exposures to x-rays – you may wish to hand carry such film rather than zip it with rays.

As elsewhere in the world, airport security personnel don't want you taking photographs and they're especially protective about the area around the x-ray machines. You can get away with taking pictures in the airport gift shop, but otherwise keep the camera closed.

TIME

Time throughout China is set to Beijing time, which is eight hours ahead of GMT/UTC. When it's noon in Beijing it's also noon in far-off Lhasa, Ürümqi and all other parts of the country. Since the sun doesn't cooperate with Beijing's whims, people in China's far west follow a later work schedule so they don't have to commute two hours before dawn.

When it's noon in Beijing the time in other cities around the world is:

Hong Kong	noon
Melbourne	2 pm
Wellington	4 pm
Los Angeles	8 pm
Montreal	11 pm
New York	11 pm
London	4 am
Frankfurt	5 am
Paris	5 am
Rome	5 am

ELECTRICITY

Electricity is 220V, 50 cycles AC. Plugs come in at least five designs – three pronged angled pins (like in Australia), three pronged round pins (Singapore style), two flat pins (American style, but without the ground wire), two narrow round pins (European style) and three rectangular pins (British style). For the most part, however, you can safely travel with two plugs – American style and Australian style.

Conversion plugs are easily purchased in Hong Kong, but are more difficult to find in China. Battery chargers are widely available, but these are generally the bulky style which are not suitable for travelling – buy a small one in Hong Kong.

Many Chinese cities experience sudden blackouts, especially in summer due to the increasing use of air-conditioning. It is very helpful to have a torch (flashlight) for such occasions.

WEIGHTS & MEASURES

The metric system is widely used in China. However, the traditional Chinese measures are often used for domestic transactions and you may come across them. The following equations will help:

Metric	Chinese	Imperial
1m (mǐ)	3 chi	3.28 feet
1km (gōnglǐ)	2 li	0.62 miles
1L (gōngshēng)	1 gongsheng	0.22 gallons
1kg (gōngjīn)	2 jin	2.2 pounds

LAUNDRY

Each floor of just about every hotel in China has a service desk, usually near the elevators. The attendant's job is to clean the rooms, make the beds and collect and deliver laundry. Almost all tourist hotels have a laundry service, and if you hand in clothes one day you should get them back a day or two later. If the hotel doesn't have a laundry, they can usually direct you to one. Hotel laundry service tends to be expensive and you might wind up doing what many travellers do – hand-washing your own clothes.

Herbal Medicine

Many foreigners visiting China never try Chinese herbal medicine *(zhōng yào)* because they either know nothing about it or simply don't believe in it. Prominent medical authorities in the west often dismiss herbalists as no better than witch doctors. The ingredients, which may include such marvellous things as snake gall bladder or powdered deer antlers, will further discourage potential non-Chinese customers. Many of the herbs are bitter powders (you may want to load these into empty gelatine capsules if you can't stand the taste). And finally, even true believers are baffled by the wide assortment of herbs available on the shelves of any Chinese pharmacy – it's hard to know where to begin.

Having experimented with Chinese herbs ourselves, we've found several of them to be remarkably effective, but some warnings are in order. Chinese herbalists have all sorts of treatments for stomach aches, headaches, colds, flu and sore throats. They also have herbs to treat long-term problems like asthma. While many of these herbs seem to work, remember that herbs are not miracle drugs.

Chinese medicine seems to work best for the relief of unpleasant symptoms (pain, sore throat etc) and for some long-term conditions which resist western medicines, such as migraine headaches, asthma and chronic backache. But for acute life-threatening conditions, such as a heart attack, it would be foolish to trust your life to herbs.

When reading about the theory behind Chinese medicine, the word 'holistic' appears often. Basically, this means that Chinese medicine seeks to treat the whole body rather than focusing on a particular organ or disease.

Using appendicitis as an example, a Chinese doctor may try to fight the infection using all the body's defences, whereas a western doctor would simply cut out the appendix. In this instance the western technique works better, since removing the appendix surgically is 100% effective, though there is always some risk from the surgical procedure itself. In the case of migraine headaches, on the other hand, Chinese herbs may actually prove more effective than western medical treatments.

Another point to be wary of when taking herbal medicine is the tendency of some manufacturers to falsely claim that their product contains numerous potent and expensive ingredients. For example, some herbal formulas may list rhinoceros horn as an ingredient. Rhinoceros horn, widely acclaimed by herbalists as a cure for fever, is practically impossible to buy. Any formula listing rhinoceros horn may, at best, contain water buffalo horn. In any case, the rhino is a rare and endangered species, and you would not wish to hasten its extinction by demanding rhino-horn products.

Another benefit of Chinese medicine is that there are relatively few side effects. Nevertheless, herbs are still medicines, not candy, and there is no need to take them if you're feeling fine to begin with. In fact, some herbs are mildly toxic and if taken over a long period of time can actually damage the liver and other organs.

Before shopping for herbs, keep in mind that although a broad-spectrum remedy such as snake gall bladder may be good for treating colds, there are many different types of colds. The best way to treat a cold with herbal medicine is to see a Chinese doctor

Bags of medicinal herbs as displayed for sale in Chinese marketplaces.

and get a specific prescription. Otherwise, the herbs you take may not be the most appropriate for your condition. However, if you can't get to a doctor, you can just try your luck at the pharmacy.

If you visit a Chinese doctor, you might be surprised by what he or she discovers about your body. For example, the doctor will almost certainly take your pulse and then may tell you that you have a slippery pulse or perhaps a thready pulse. Chinese doctors have identified more than 30 different kinds of pulses. The doctor may then examine your tongue to see if it is slippery, dry, pale or greasy, or has a thick coating or maybe no coating at all. The doctor, having discovered that you have wet heat, as evidenced by a slippery pulse and a red greasy tongue, will prescribe the herbs for your condition.

Beware of quackery – there is one Chinese herbal medicine, for instance, which pregnant women take to ensure that their foetus will develop into a boy. Other herbal tonics promise to boost your IQ, sexual prowess and cure baldness. All sorts of overblown claims have been made for herbal medicines, especially by those who make and sell them. Most of these miracle herbs are expensive, and the promised results have never been confirmed by any scientific studies. Yet some gullible westerners have persuaded themselves that Chinese herbs can cure any disease. A visit to any of China's hospitals will quickly shatter this myth.

Counterfeiting is another problem. Everything gets copied in China, and the problem extends even to medications. If the herbs you take seem to be totally ineffective, it may be because you've bought sugar pills rather than medicine.

If you spend a good deal of time on buses and boats, you'll get to see how the Chinese deal with motion sickness, nausea and headaches – usually by smearing liniments on their stomach or head. Look for White Flower Oil *(bái huā yóu)*, probably the most popular brand. A variation on the theme are salves, the most famous being Tiger Balm, which originated in Hong Kong. And should you strain yourself carrying that heavy backpack around, try applying 'sticky dog skin plaster'*(gǒupí gāoyào)* to your sore muscles. You might be relieved to know that these days it's no longer made from real dog skin.

Robert Storey

HERBAL MEDICINE

HEALTH

Although China presents a few particular health hazards that require your attention, overall it's a healthier place to travel than many other parts of the world. Large cities like Beijing and Shanghai have decent medical facilities – the problem is out in the backwaters like Inner Mongolia, Tibet or Xinjiang.

Medical services are generally very cheap in China, although random foreigner surcharges may be exacted. At least foreigners get better service – Chinese patients usually have to wait for hours in long queues.

In case of accident or illness, it's best just to get a taxi and go to the hospital directly – try to avoid dealing with the authorities (police and military) if possible. One traveller who broke his leg near Dali made the mistake of calling on the police for help. They took him to the military hospital, where a cast was put on his leg – he was then charged Y20,000 for this service! A civilian hospital would have charged him about Y100. This particular foreigner didn't have that much money, so the police took his passport away and basically held him for ransom until his family could come up with the cash.

The Chinese do not have Rh-negative blood and their blood banks don't store it.

Predeparture Planning

Immunisations For some countries no immunisations are necessary, but the further off the beaten track you go the more necessary it is to take precautions.

Plan ahead for getting your vaccinations: some of them require an initial shot followed by a booster, while some vaccinations should not be given together. It is recommended you seek medical advice at least six weeks before travel.

The only vaccination requirement for travellers to China is yellow fever if coming from an infected area (parts of Africa and South America). There is no risk of yellow fever in China.

In some countries immunisations are available from airport or government health centres – ask travel agents or airline offices.

Record all vaccinations on an International Health Certificate, available from your doctor or government health department.

Discuss your requirements with your doctor, but vaccinations you should consider for this trip include:

Cholera This vaccine is not recommended: protection is poor, immunisation lasts only six months and it's contraindicated during pregnancy. Furthermore, China doesn't have a big problem with cholera anyway.

Diphtheria & Tetanus Everyone should make sure they are up-to-date with these vaccinations. After an initial course of three injections, boosters are necessary every 10 years.

Hepatitis A This is the most common travel-acquired illness which can be prevented by vaccination. Havrix 1440 is the vaccine of choice – it provides long term immunity (possibly more than 10 years) after an initial injection and a booster at six to 12 months. It takes about three weeks to provide protection.

Gamma globulin is ready-made antibody collected from blood donations. It should be given close to departure because, depending on the dose, it only protects for two to six months.

A combined hepatitis A and hepatitis B vaccination, Twinrix, is also available. This combined vaccination is recommended for people wanting protection against both these types of viral hepatitis. Three injections over a six month period are required.

Hepatitis B China is one of the world's great reservoirs of hepatitis B infection. The vaccination involves three injections, the quickest course being over three weeks and a booster at 12 months.

Japanese B Encephalitis This mosquito borne disease is a risk for travellers to rural areas of China. Consider the vaccination if spending a month or longer in a high risk area, making repeated trips to a risk area or visiting during an epidemic (usually associated with the rainy season). It involves three injections over 30 days.

The vaccine is expensive and has been associated with serious allergic reactions so the decision to have it should be balanced against the risk of contracting the illness.

Polio Polio is a very serious, easily transmitted disease, still prevalent in many developing countries. Everyone should keep up-to-date with this vaccination. A booster every 10 years maintains immunity.

Rabies Pre-travel rabies vaccination involves having three injections over 21 to 28 days and should be considered if you're visiting any ethnic Tibetan areas (packs of wild dogs are a feature of any Tibetan village). Cyclists are prone to attacks by dogs anywhere in the world.

If someone who has already been vaccinated is bitten or scratched by an animal they will require two booster injections of vaccine. Those not vaccinated will require more.

Tuberculosis TB risk to travellers is usually very low. For those who will be living with or closely associated with local people in high risk areas such as China, there may be some risk.

As most healthy adults do not develop symptoms, a skin test before and after travel to determine whether exposure has occurred may be considered. A vaccination is recommended for children living in these areas for three months or more.

Typhoid Travellers to China are at risk for this disease, especially if travelling to smaller cities, villages or rural areas. The vaccine is available either as an injection or as capsules to be taken orally.

Malaria Medication Antimalarial drugs do not prevent you from being infected but kill the malaria parasites during a stage in their development and significantly reduce the risk of becoming very ill or dying.

Expert advice on medication should be sought, as there are many factors to consider including the area to be visited, the risk of exposure to malaria-carrying mosquitoes, the side effects of medication, your medical history and whether you are a child or adult or pregnant.

Travellers to isolated areas in high risk countries may like to carry a treatment dose of medication for use if symptoms occur.

Health Insurance Make sure that you have adequate health insurance. See the Travel Insurance entry under Visas & Documents earlier in this chapter.

Travel Health Guides If you have the time and inclination, the classic medical reference to read is the *Merck Manual*, a weighty volume which covers virtually every illness known to humanity. *Where There Is No Doctor* by David Werner is useful, though intended for people going to work in an underdeveloped country rather than for the average traveller. Lonely Planet's *Travel with Children* by Maureen Wheeler gives a rundown on health precautions to be taken with kids, or if you're pregnant and travelling.

There are also a number of excellent travel health sites on the Internet. From the Lonely Planet home page there are links at www.lonelyplanet.com/weblinks/wlprep. htm to the World Health Organisation and the US Center for Diseases Control & Prevention.

Other Preparations Make sure you're healthy before you start travelling. If you are going on a long trip make sure your teeth are OK. If you wear glasses take a spare pair and your prescription.

If you require a particular medication take an adequate supply, as it may not be available locally. Take part of the packag-

Medical Kit Check List

You certainly don't need all the medications listed below; it depends on how much time you'll be spending hiking the backwaters of Tibet, Xinjiang or wherever. Look over the following list and consider what's worth carrying:

Aspirin or **paracetamol** (acetaminophen in the USA) – for pain or fever.

Antihistamine (such as Benadryl) – useful as a decongestant for colds and allergies, to ease the itch from insect bites or stings, and to help prevent motion sickness. Antihistamines may cause sedation and interact with alcohol so care should be taken when using them; take one you know and have used before, if possible.

Antibiotics – useful if you're travelling well off the beaten track, but they must be prescribed; don't take them unless you understand exactly what they are for, and carry the prescription with you.

Loperamide (eg Imodium) or **Lomotil** – for diarrhoea; **prochlorperazine** (eg Stemetil) or **metaclopramide** (eg Maxalon) for nausea and vomiting.

Rehydration mixture – for treatment of severe diarrhoea; particularly important for travelling with children.

Antiseptic such as povidone-iodine (eg Betadine) – for cuts and grazes.

Multivitamins – especially useful in backwaters like Tibet, or during the winter when fresh fruit and vegetables are a rarity, and dietary vitamin intake may be inadequate.

Calamine lotion or **aluminium sulphate spray** (eg Stingose) – to ease irritation from bites or stings.

Cold & flu tablets and **throat lozenges**. Pseudoephedrine hydrochloride (Sudafed) may be useful if flying with a cold to avoid ear damage.

Bandages and **Band-Aids**.

Scissors, **tweezers** and a **thermometer** (note that mercury thermometers are prohibited by airlines).

Insect repellent, **sunscreen**, **chap stick** and **water purification tablets**.

A couple of syringes – in case you need injections in an area with medical hygiene problems. Ask your doctor for a note explaining why they have been prescribed. ■

ing showing the generic name, rather than the brand, which will make getting replacements easier. It's a good idea to have a legible prescription or letter from your doctor to show that you legally use the medication to avoid any problems.

Basic Rules

Food Salads and fruit should be washed with purified water or peeled where possible. Ice cream is usually OK if it is a reputable brand name, but beware of ice cream which is sold on the street or has melted and refrozen. Shellfish such as mussels, oysters and clams should be avoided as well as undercooked meat, particularly in the form of mince. Steaming does not make shellfish safe for eating.

Water Tap water is not considered safe to drink anywhere in China except Hong Kong. On the other hand, in most cities it's chlorinated and probably won't kill you. You need to be really careful in remote areas like Tibet, especially when drinking surface water.

If you don't know for certain that the water is safe, then assume the worst. Milk should be treated with suspicion as it is often unpasteurised, though boiled milk is fine if it is kept hygienically. Drinking tea should be OK – after all, it's boiled.

Bottled water or soft drinks are fine – the main problem is that the exterior of the bottle may be encrusted in dust (or worse) as Chinese vendors don't give a damn about where they store the stuff. Try to find a place to wash off the bottle or can before opening it.

Water Purification You've got to pay attention to water purification if you're going to be camping or hiking upcountry. The simplest way of purifying water is to boil it thoroughly. Vigorous boiling should be satisfactory; however, at high altitude water boils at a lower temperature, so germs are less likely to be killed. Boil it longer in these environments.

Consider purchasing a water filter for a long trip. There are two main kinds of filter. Total filters take out all parasites, bacteria and viruses, and make water safe to drink. They are often expensive, but they can be more cost effective than buying bottled water.

Simple filters (which can even be a nylon mesh bag) take out dirt and larger foreign bodies from the water so that chemical solutions work much more effectively; if water is dirty, chemical solutions may not work at all.

It's very important when buying a filter to read the specifications, so that you know exactly what it removes from the water and what it doesn't.

Simple filtering will not remove all dangerous organisms, so if you cannot boil water it should be treated chemically. Chlorine tablets (Puritabs, Steritabs or other brand names) will kill many pathogens, but not those causing giardiasis and amoebic dysentery.

Iodine is very effective in purifying water and is available in tablet form (such as Potable Aqua), but follow the directions carefully and remember that too much iodine can be harmful. Iodine tastes as bad as it sounds.

Medical Problems & Treatment
Self-diagnosis and treatment can be risky, so wherever possible seek qualified help. Although we do give drug dosages in this section, they are for emergency use only.

A five star hotel can usually recommend a good place to go for medical advice. In some places standards of medical attention are so low that for some ailments the best advice is to get on a plane and go to Beijing, Shanghai or Hong Kong.

Antibiotics should ideally be administered only under medical supervision. Take only the recommended dose at the prescribed intervals and use the whole course, even if the illness seems to be cured earlier. Stop immediately if there are any serious reactions and don't use the antibiotic at all if you are unsure that you have the correct one.

Everyday Health

Normal body temperature is 37°C or 98.6°F; more than 2°C (4°F) higher indicates a high fever. The normal adult pulse rate is 60 to 100 beats per minute (children 80 to 100, babies 100 to 140). As a general rule, the pulse increases about 20 beats per minute for each °C (2°F) rise in fever.

Respiration (breathing) rate is also an indicator of illness. Count the number of breaths per minute: between 12 and 20 is normal for adults and older children (up to 30 for younger children, 40 for babies). People with a high fever or serious respiratory illness breathe more quickly than normal. More than 40 shallow breaths a minute may indicate pneumonia. ∎

Nutrition

If your food is poor (Tibet travellers take note), if you're travelling hard and fast and therefore missing meals, or if you simply lose your appetite, you can soon start to lose weight and place your health at risk.

Make sure your diet is well balanced. Cooked eggs, tofu, beans, lentils and nuts are all safe ways to get protein. Fruit you can peel (bananas, oranges or mandarins for example) is usually safe (melons can harbour bacteria in their flesh and are best avoided) and a good source of vitamins.

Try to eat plenty of grains (including rice) and bread. With all the rice in China, you should be able to get your daily ration of grains. Remember that although food is generally safer if it is cooked well, overcooked food loses much of its nutritional value. If your diet isn't well balanced or if your food intake is insufficient, it's a good idea to take vitamin and iron pills.

In the hot, high altitude deserts of western China, make sure you drink enough – don't rely on feeling thirsty to indicate when you should drink. Not needing to urinate or small amounts of very dark yellow urine is a danger sign. Always carry a water bottle with you on long trips. Excessive sweating can lead to loss of salt and therefore muscle cramping. Salt tablets are not a good idea as a preventative, but in places where salt is not used much adding salt to food can help. Add a few squirts of soy sauce to your rice to make sure you're getting some salt every day. ■

Some people are allergic to commonly prescribed antibiotics such as penicillin or sulpha drugs; carry this information when travelling (eg on a bracelet).

Environmental Hazards

Altitude Sickness Lack of oxygen at high altitudes (over 2500m) affects most people to some extent. There are bus journeys in Tibet, Qinghai and Xinjiang where the road goes over 5000m. Acclimatising to such extreme elevations takes several weeks at least, but most travellers come up from sea level very fast – a bad move! If you ever have a chance to experience Acute Mountain Sickness (AMS), you won't forget it.

Symptoms of AMS usually develop during the first 24 hours at altitude, but may be delayed up to three weeks. Mild symptoms include headache, lethargy, dizziness, difficulty sleeping and loss of appetite. AMS may become more severe without warning and can be fatal.

These mild symptoms are unpleasant, but a far more serious complication is high-altitude pulmonary oedema. This is usually seen only at elevations above 3000m about 24 to 72 hours after ascent.

Symptoms include coughing up frothy sputum, which usually progresses from white to pink to bloody. A rattling sound in the chest can be heard, often without a stethoscope. The symptoms might be mistaken for pneumonia, but the suddenness of their appearance in a rapidly ascending climber should make you suspect pulmonary oedema. *This is a medical emergency!* Coma and death can follow rapidly – the only effective treatment is to get the victim to a lower elevation as soon as possible.

Treat mild symptoms by resting at the same altitude until recovery, usually a day or two. Paracetamol or aspirin can be taken for headaches. If symptoms persist or become worse, however, *immediate descent is necessary*; even 500m can help. Drug treatments should never be used to avoid descent or to enable further ascent.

The drugs acetazolamide (Diamox) and dexamethasone have been recommended for prevention of AMS. They can reduce the symptoms, but they also mask warning signs; severe and fatal AMS has occurred in people taking these drugs. In general they are not recommended for travellers.

To prevent acute mountain sickness:

- Ascend slowly – have frequent rest days, spending two to three nights at each rise of 1000m. If you reach a high altitude by trekking, acclimatisation takes place gradually and you are less likely to be affected than if you fly directly to a higher altitude.
- It is always wise to sleep at a lower altitude than the greatest height reached during the day. Also, once above 3000m, care should be taken not to increase the sleeping altitude by more than 300m per day.
- Drink extra fluids. The mountain air is dry and cold and moisture is lost as you breathe.
- Eat light, high-carbohydrate meals for more energy.
- Avoid alcohol as it may increase the risk of dehydration.
- Avoid sedatives.

Fungal Infections Fungal infections such as ringworm occur more commonly in hot weather and are usually found on the scalp, between the toes (athlete's foot) or fingers, in the groin (jock itch or crotch rot) and on the body. You get ringworm (which is a fungal infection, not a worm) from infected animals or by walking on damp areas, like shower floors.

To prevent fungal infections wear loose, comfortable clothes, avoid artificial fibres, wash frequently and dry carefully. If you do get an infection, wash the infected area daily with a disinfectant or medicated soap and water, and rinse and dry well. Apply an antifungal cream or powder like Tinaderm (tolnaftate). If you don't have that, then try plain old talcum powder – it's better than nothing. Try to expose the infected area to air or sunlight as much as possible and wash all towels and underwear in hot water, changing them often.

Heat Exhaustion Dehydration or salt deficiency can cause heat exhaustion. Take time to acclimatise to high temperatures, drink sufficient liquids and do not do anything too physically demanding.

Salt deficiency is characterised by fatigue, lethargy, headaches, giddiness and muscle cramps; salt tablets may help.

Anhydrotic heat exhaustion, caused by an inability to sweat, is quite rare. It is likely to strike people who have been in a hot climate for some time, rather than newcomers.

Heatstroke This serious, occasionally fatal, condition can occur if the body's heat-regulating mechanism breaks down and the body temperature rises to dangerous levels. Long, continuous periods of exposure to high temperatures can leave you vulnerable to heat stroke.

The symptoms are feeling unwell, not sweating very much or at all and a high body temperature (39°C to 41°C or 102°F to 106°F). Where sweating has ceased the skin becomes flushed and red. Severe, throbbing headaches and lack of coordination will also occur, and the sufferer may be confused or aggressive. Eventually the victim will become delirious or convulse. Hospitalisation is essential, but in the interim get victims out of the sun, remove their clothing, cover them with a wet sheet or towel and then fan continually. Give fluids if they are conscious.

Hypothermia Too much cold can be even more dangerous than too much heat. If you are trekking at high altitudes or simply taking a long bus trip over mountains, particularly at night, be prepared. In Tibet it can go from being mildly warm to blisteringly cold in a manner of minutes – blizzards have a way of just coming out of nowhere. If you're out walking, cycling or hitching, this can be more than inconvenient.

Hypothermia occurs when the body loses heat faster than it can produce it and the core temperature of the body falls. It is surprisingly easy to progress from very cold to dangerously cold due to a combination of wind, wet clothing, fatigue and hunger, even if the air temperature is above freezing. It is best to dress in layers; silk, wool and some of the new artificial fibres are all good insulating materials. A hat is important, as a lot of heat is lost through the head. A strong, waterproof outer layer and a space blanket are essential. Carry basic supplies, including food (along with some chocolate to generate heat quickly) and fluid to drink.

Symptoms of hypothermia are exhaustion, numb skin (particularly the toes and fingers), shivering, slurred speech, irrational or violent behaviour, lethargy, stumbling, dizzy spells, muscle cramps and violent bursts of energy. Irrationality may take the form of sufferers claiming they are warm and trying to take off their clothes.

To treat mild hypothermia, first get the person out of the wind and/or rain, remove their clothing if it's wet and replace it with dry, warm clothing. Give them hot liquids – not alcohol – and some high-kilojoule, easily digestible food. Do not rub victims, instead allow them to slowly warm themselves. This should be enough to treat the early stages of hypothermia. The early recognition and treatment of mild hypothermia is the only way to prevent severe hypothermia, which is a critical condition.

Frostbite This is a severe condition that can cause loss of limbs and (on the face) disfigurement for life. Although you'll feel little or no pain when the tissue is frozen, it becomes excruciating when the wound thaws out. Ironically, the condition is not unlike a third-degree burn. Prevention is by far the best cure – if you must travel in intense cold, protect your limbs with fur-lined boots and mittens, and wear a parka and a ski mask.

Motion Sickness Eating lightly before and during a trip will reduce the chances of motion sickness. The Chinese believe the opposite – they think the cure for motion sickness is to keep eating. As you'll notice, the Chinese seem to be very susceptible to motion sickness – it's probably due to their eating habits.

If you are prone to motion sickness try to find a place that minimises disturbance –

near the wing on aircraft, close to midships on boats, near the centre on buses. Fresh air usually helps; reading and cigarette smoke don't. Commercial motion-sickness preparations, which can cause drowsiness, have to be taken before the trip commences. Ginger (available in capsule form) and peppermint (including mint-flavoured sweets) are natural preventatives.

Prickly Heat Prickly heat is an itchy rash caused by excessive perspiration trapped under the skin. The pores of the skin get clogged, causing painful swelling. It usually strikes people who have just arrived in a hot climate. Keeping cool, bathing often, using a mild talcum powder or resorting to air-conditioning may help until you acclimatise.

Sunburn It's very easy to get sunburnt at high elevations (Tibet), in the deserts (Xinjiang) or the tropics (Hainan Island). Use a sunscreen, hat, and barrier cream for your nose and lips. Calamine lotion is good for mild sunburn. Protect your eyes with good quality sunglasses, particularly if you will be near water, sand or snow.

Infectious Diseases
The China Syndrome Upper respiratory tract infections (URTIs), or the common cold, are the most common ailment to afflict visitors to China. The Chinese call it *gǎnmào* and it is a particular problem here – transmission rates are high because of the crowding and the cold.

China also has a special relationship with the influenza virus. You may not remember the notorious 'Hong Kong flu' of 1968, but you may have heard of the more recent 'Shanghai flu'(1989) and 'bird flu' (1997-8) epidemics. There have been various other influenza strains named after Chinese cities. This is because China is the production house for new strains of influenza virus. The reason for this is thought to be the proximity in which people live to ducks and pigs, which are reservoirs for the two other main populations of the virus. This

Acupuncture

Chinese acupuncture *(zhēnjiū)* has received enthusiastic reviews from its many satisfied patients. Of course, one should be wary of overblown claims. Acupuncture is not likely to cure terminal cancer or heart disease, but it is of genuine therapeutic value in the treatment of chronic back pain, migraine headaches, arthritis and other ailments.

Acupuncture is a technique employing needles which are inserted into various points of the body. In former times, needles were probably made from bamboo, gold, silver, copper or tin. These days, only stainless steel needles of hairlike thinness are used, causing very little pain when inserted. Dirty acupuncture needles can spread disease rather than cure, so good acupuncturists sterilise their needles or use disposable ones. As many as 2000 points for needle insertion have been identified, but only about 150 are commonly used.

One of the most amazing demonstrations of acupuncture's power is that major surgery can be performed using acupuncture alone as the anaesthetic. The acupuncture needle is inserted into the patient and a small electric current is passed through the needle. The current is supplied by an ordinary torch battery.

The exact mechanism by which acupuncture works is not fully understood by modern medical science. The Chinese have their own theories, but it is by no means certain they really know either. Needles are inserted into various points of the body, each point believed by the acupuncturist to correspond to a particular organ, joint, gland or other part of the body. These points are believed to be connected to the particular area being treated by an 'energy channel', also translated as a 'meridian', but more likely it has something to do with the nerves. By means not fully understood, it seems the needle can block pain transmission along the meridian. No matter how it works, many report satisfactory results.

Acupuncture is practised in hospitals of traditional Chinese medicine, which can be found all over China. Some hospitals in major cities like Guangzhou, Beijing and Shanghai also train westerners in the technique. And if you need some emergency acupuncture, even hotels (upmarket ones, at least) provide such services at their in-house clinics.

If you're (justifiably) concerned about catching diseases from contaminated acupuncture needles, you might consider buying your own before undergoing treatment. Good quality needles are available in major cities in China. Needles come in a bewildering variety of gauges – try to determine from your acupuncturist which type to buy. ∎

provides the opportunity for the viruses to chop and change, reappearing in different forms or strains.

During winter, practically the entire population of 1.2 billion is stricken with *gǎnmào*. URTIs are aggravated by cold weather, poor nutrition and China's notorious air pollution. Smoking makes it worse, and half the population of China smokes. Overcrowded conditions increase the opportunity for infection. Another reason is that Chinese people spit a lot, which helps spread the disease. It's a vicious circle: they're sick because they spit and they spit because they're sick.

Winter visitors to China should bring a few favourite cold remedies. These can easily be purchased from any good pharmacy in Hong Kong or Macau. Such items can be found elsewhere in China, but with considerably more difficulty.

Symptoms of influenza include fever, weakness, sore throat and a feeling of malaise. Any URTI, including influenza, can lead to complications such as bronchitis and pneumonia, which may need to be treated with antibiotics. Seek medical help in this situation. Finally, if you can't get well in China, leave the country and take a nice holiday on a warm beach in Thailand.

Diarrhoea Travellers' diarrhoea (*lā dùzi*) has been around a long time – even Marco Polo had it. A change of water, food or climate can all cause the runs; diarrhoea caused by contaminated food or water is more serious. Despite all your precautions you may still get a mild bout of travellers' diarrhoea, but a few rushed toilet trips with no other symptoms is not indicative of a serious problem.

Dehydration is the main danger with any diarrhoea, particularly in children or the elderly as dehydration can occur quite quickly. Under all circumstances *fluid replacement* (at least equal to the volume being lost) is the most important thing to remember. Soda water or soft drinks allowed to go flat and diluted 50% with clean water are good. With severe diarrhoea a rehydrating solution is preferable to replace minerals and salts lost.

Commercially available oral rehydration salts (ORS) are very useful; add them to boiled or bottled water. In an emergency you can make up a solution of six teaspoons of sugar and a half teaspoon of salt to a litre of boiled or bottled water.

You need to drink at least the same volume of fluid that you are losing in bowel movements and vomiting. Urine is the best guide to the adequacy of replacement – if you have small amounts of concentrated urine, you need to drink more. Keep drinking small amounts often. Stick to a bland diet as you recover.

Gut paralysing drugs like Lomotil or Imodium can be used to bring relief from the symptoms, although they do not actually cure the problem. Only use these drugs if you do not have access to toilets eg if you *must* travel. For children under 12 years Lomotil and Imodium are not recommended. Do not use these drugs if the person has a high fever or is severely dehydrated.

In certain situations antibiotics may be required: diarrhoea with blood or mucus (dysentery), any diarrhoea with fever, watery diarrhoea with fever and lethargy, persistent diarrhoea not improving after 48 hours and severe diarrhoea. In these situations Imodium or Lomotil should be avoided.

A stool test is necessary to diagnose which kind of dysentery you have, so you should seek medical help urgently in this situation. Where this is not possible the recommended drugs for dysentery are norfloxacin 400mg twice daily for three days or ciprofloxacin 500mg twice daily for five days. These are not recommended for children or pregnant women. The drug of choice for children would be co-trimoxazole (Bactrim, Septrin, Resprim) with dosage dependent on weight. A five day course is given. Ampicillin or amoxycillin may be given in pregnancy, but medical care is necessary.

Amoebic dysentery is characterised by a gradual onset of symptoms; fever may not be present. It will persist until treated and can recur and cause other health problems.

Giardiasis is another type of diarrhoea. The parasite causing this intestinal disorder is present in contaminated water. The symptoms are stomach cramps; nausea; a bloated stomach; watery, foul-smelling diarrhoea; and frequent gas.

Giardiasis can appear several weeks after you have been exposed to the parasite. The symptoms may disappear for a few days and then return; this can go on for several weeks. Tinidazole, known as Fasigyn, or metronidazole (Flagyl) are the recommended drugs. Treatment is a 2g single dose of Fasigyn or 250mg of Flagyl three times daily for five to 10 days.

Hepatitis Hepatitis is a general term for inflammation of the liver. It is a common disease worldwide. The symptoms are fever, chills, headache, fatigue, feelings of weakness and aches and pains, followed by loss of appetite, nausea, vomiting, abdominal pain, dark urine, light-coloured faeces, jaundiced (yellow) skin and the whites of the eyes may turn yellow.

Hepatitis A is transmitted by contaminated food and drinking water. The disease poses a real threat to the western traveller.

You should seek medical advice, but there is not much you can do apart from resting, drinking lots of fluids, eating lightly and avoiding fatty foods. People who have had hepatitis should avoid alcohol for some time after the illness, as the liver needs time to recover.

Hepatitis E is transmitted in the same way and can be very serious in pregnant women.

There are almost 300 million chronic carriers of **hepatitis B** in the world. It is spread through contact with infected blood, blood products or body fluids, for example through sexual contact, unsterilised needles and blood transfusions, or contact with blood via small breaks in the skin. Other risk situations include having a shave, tattoo, or having your body pierced with contaminated equipment.

The symptoms of type B may be more severe and may lead to long term problems. **Hepatitis D** is spread in the same way, but the risk is mainly in shared needles.

Hepatitis C can lead to chronic liver disease. The virus is spread by contact with blood – usually via contaminated transfusions or shared needles. Avoiding these is the only means of prevention.

HIV/AIDS HIV, the Human Immunodeficiency Virus, may develop into AIDS – Acquired Immune Deficiency Syndrome. HIV is a major problem worldwide. Any exposure to blood, blood products or bodily fluids may put the individual at risk.

The disease is often transmitted sexually, but it can be passed through infected blood transfusions; China is notorious for *not* screening blood donors! It can also be spread by dirty needles – vaccinations, acupuncture, tattooing and body piercing can be potentially as dangerous as intravenous drug use. If you do need an injection, ask to see the syringe unwrapped in front of you, or take a needle and syringe pack with you.

Fear of HIV infection should never preclude treatment for serious medical conditions.

Intestinal Worms These parasites are most common in rural, tropical areas. The different worms have different ways of infecting people. Some may be ingested on food including undercooked meat and some enter through your skin.

Infestations may not show up for some time, and although they are generally not serious, if left untreated some can cause severe health problems later.

Consider having a stool test when you return home to check for these and determine the appropriate treatment.

Schistosomiasis Also known as bilharzia, this disease is found in the central Yangtze River basin. It is carried in water by minute worms which infect certain varieties of freshwater snails found in rivers, streams, lakes and particularly behind dams. The worms multiply and are eventually discharged into the water.

The worm enters through the skin and attaches itself to your intestines or bladder. The first symptom may be a tingling and sometimes a light rash around the area where it entered. Weeks later a high fever may develop. A general feeling of being unwell may be the first symptom, or there may be no symptoms.

Once the disease is established, abdominal pain and blood in the urine are other signs. The infection often causes no symptoms until the disease is well established (several months to years after exposure) and damage to internal organs irreversible.

Avoiding swimming or bathing in fresh water where bilharzia is present – this is the main method of preventing the disease. Even deep water can be infected. If you do get wet, dry off quickly and dry your clothes as well.

A blood test is the most reliable test, but the test will not show positive in results until a number of weeks after exposure.

Sexually Transmitted Diseases Gonorrhoea, herpes and syphilis are among these diseases; sores, blisters or rashes around the genitals, discharges or pain when urinating are common symptoms.

In some STDs, such as wart virus or chlamydia, symptoms may be less marked or not observed at all, especially in women. Syphilis symptoms eventually disappear completely, but the disease continues and can cause severe problems in later years. While abstinence from sexual contact is the only 100% effective prevention, using condoms is also effective. The treatment of gonorrhoea and syphilis is with antibiotics.

The different sexually transmitted diseases all require specific antibiotics. There is no cure for herpes or AIDS.

Tuberculosis China has traditionally had a high rate of TB infection, and there is now a world-wide resurgence of this severe disease.

It is a bacterial infection which is usually transmitted from person to person through coughing, but may be transmitted via the consumption of unpasteurised milk. Milk that has been boiled is safe to drink, and the souring of milk to make yoghurt or cheese also kills the bacilli.

Travellers are usually not at great risk as close household contact with the infected person is usually required before the disease is passed on.

Typhoid Typhoid fever is a dangerous gut infection caused by contaminated water and food. As with cholera, it tends to occur in summer in areas that have had severe flooding. Medical help must be sought.

In its early stages sufferers may feel they have a bad cold or flu on the way, as early symptoms are a headache, body aches and a fever which rises a little each day until it is around 40°C (104°F) or more. The victim's pulse is often slow relative to the degree of fever present – unlike a normal fever where the pulse increases. There may also be vomiting, abdominal pain, diarrhoea or constipation.

In the second week the high fever and slow pulse continue and a few pink spots may appear on the body; trembling, weight loss, delirium, weakness and dehydration may occur.

Complications such as pneumonia, perforated bowel or meningitis also may occur.

The fever should be treated by keeping the victim cool and giving them fluids as dehydration should be watched for. Ciprofloxacin 750mg twice a day for 10 days is good for adults.

Chloramphenicol is recommended in many countries. The adult dosage is two 250mg capsules, four times a day. Children aged between eight and 12 years should have half the adult dose; and younger children one-third the adult dose.

Insect-Borne Diseases
Filariasis, Dengue fever, Japanese B encephalitis, leishmaniasis and typhus are all insect-borne diseases, but they do not pose a great risk to travellers. For more information on them, see the Less Common Diseases entry later in this section.

Malaria Malaria has been nearly eradicated in China and is not generally a risk for travellers visiting the cities. It is found predominately in rural areas in the southwestern region – principally Guangdong, Guizhou, Yunnan, Hainan, Sichuan and Fujian.

Transmission occurs mainly during summer in most risk areas, but occurs year-round in Hainan and Yunnan. If you are travelling to rural Hainan or peripheral Yunnan it is important to take anti-malarial tablets and to take steps to avoid mosquito bites.

The symptoms of this serious and potentially fatal disease range from fever, chills and sweating, headache, diarrhoea and abdominal pains to a vague feeling of ill-health.

Seek medical help immediately if malaria is suspected. Without treatment malaria can rapidly become more serious and can be fatal.

If medical care is not available, malaria tablets can be used for treatment. You need to use a malaria tablet which is different to the one you were taking when you contracted malaria.

The treatment dosages are mefloquine (three 250mg tablets and a further two six hours later) or fansidar (single dose of three tablets). If you were previously taking mefloquine and cannot obtain fansidar, then alternatives are halofantrine (three doses of two 250mg tablets every six hours) or quinine sulphate (600mg every six hours). There is a greater risk of side effects with these dosages than in normal use if used with mefloquine, so medical advice is preferable. Travellers are advised to prevent mosquito bites at all times. The main messages are:

- wear light coloured clothing
- wear long pants and long sleeved shirts
- use mosquito repellents containing the compound DEET on exposed areas (overuse of DEET may be harmful, especially to children, but it's considered preferable to being bitten by disease-transmitting mosquitoes)
- avoid wearing perfumes or aftershave
- use a mosquito net impregnated with mosquito repellent (permethrin) – it may be worth taking your own
- impregnating clothes with permethrin effectively deters mosquitoes and other insects

Cuts, Bites & Stings

Bedbugs & Lice Bedbugs live in various places, but particularly in dirty mattresses and bedding. Spots of blood on bedclothes or on the wall could be an indication that perhaps you ought to find another hotel. Alternatively, you can fight the little buggers with insecticide. Bedbugs leave itchy bites in neat rows. Calamine lotion or Stingose spray may help.

All lice cause itching and discomfort. They make themselves at home in your hair (head lice), your clothing (body lice) or in your pubic hair (crabs). You catch lice through direct contact with infected people or by sharing combs, clothing and the like. Chemical powder or shampoo treatment will kill the lice and infected clothing should then be washed in very hot water.

Insect Bites & Stings Ant bites, bee and wasp stings are usually painful rather than dangerous, but it's another story if you're

allergic. People who are allergic to them may develop severe breathing difficulties and require urgent medical attention.

People who have this allergy usually are aware of it, and should carry a kit containing an antihistamine and epinephrine.

Cuts & Scratches Wash well and treat any cut with an antiseptic such as povidone-iodine. Where possible avoid bandages and Band-Aids, which can keep wounds wet.

Ticks You should always check all over your body if you have been walking through a potentially tick-infested area as ticks can cause skin infections and other more serious diseases.

If a tick is found attached, press down around the tick's head with tweezers, grab the head and gently pull upwards. Avoid pulling the rear of the body as this may squeeze the tick's gut contents through the attached mouth parts into the skin, increasing the risk of infection and disease.

Smearing chemicals on the tick will not make it let go and is not recommended.

Snakes China has a variety of poisonous snakes, the most famous being cobras. *All* sea snakes are poisonous and are readily identified by their flat tails, but opportunities for ocean swimming in China are few and far between.

Thanks to American cowboy movies, people often associate snakes with the desert, but they are in fact most common in forested areas, where they have far more to eat.

Snakes are not generally aggressive with creatures larger than themselves – they won't chase after you, but they can get nasty if you corner or step on them. To minimise your chances of being bitten always wear boots, socks and long trousers when walking through undergrowth where snakes may be present. Don't put your hands into holes and crevices, and be careful when collecting firewood.

Snake bites do not cause instantaneous

death and antivenenes are usually available. Keep the victim calm and still, wrap the bitten limb tightly, as you would for a sprained ankle, and then attach a splint to immobilise it. Then seek medical help, if possible bringing the dead snake for identification. Don't attempt to catch the snake if there is a possibility of being bitten again. Tourniquets and sucking out the poison are now comprehensively discredited.

Less Common Diseases

Cholera The bacteria responsible for this disease are carried in contaminated food or water. This is the worst of the watery diarrhoeas and medical help should be sought.

China does not have a serious problem with this, but there can be outbreaks during floods (the Yellow River basin is notorious). Floods and corresponding cholera outbreaks are generally widely reported, so you can avoid such problem areas.

Fluid replacement is the most vital treatment – the risk of dehydration is severe as you may lose up to 20L a day. If there is a delay in getting to hospital then begin taking tetracycline. The adult dose is 250mg four times daily. It is not recommended for children under nine years nor for pregnant women.

Tetracycline may help to shorten the illness, but adequate fluids are required to save lives.

Dengue Fever Occurring in parts of southern China, this mosquito-spread disease can be fatal in children. There is no preventative drug available. A sudden onset of fever, headaches and severe joint and muscle pains are the first signs before a rash develops. Recovery may be prolonged.

Filariasis This is a mosquito-transmitted parasitic infection found in many parts of Africa, Asia, Central and South America and the Pacific. Possible symptoms include fever, pain and swelling of the lymph glands; inflammation of lymph drainage areas; swelling of a limb or the scrotum; skin rashes and blindness.

Treatment is available to eliminate the parasites from the body, but some of the damage already caused by the infection may not be reversible. Medical advice should be obtained promptly if filariasis is suspected.

Japanese B Encephalitis This viral infection of the brain is transmitted by mosquitoes. Most cases occur in rural areas as the virus exists in pigs and wading birds.

Symptoms include fever, headache and alteration in consciousness. Hospitalisation is needed for correct diagnosis and treatment. There is a high mortality rate among those who have symptoms; of those that survive many are intellectually disabled.

Leishmaniasis A group of parasitic diseases transmitted by sandfly bites, found in China, as well as many parts of the Middle East, Africa, India, Central and South America and the Mediterranean.

Cutaneous leishmaniasis affects the skin tissue causing ulceration and disfigurement and visceral leishmaniasis affects the internal organs. Seek medical advice as laboratory testing is required for diagnosis and correct treatment.

Avoiding sandfly bites is the best precaution. Bites are usually painless, itchy and are yet another reason to cover up and apply repellent.

Rabies Rabies is a fatal viral infection found in many countries and is caused by a bite or scratch by an infected animal, such as a dog, cat or monkey. Any bite, scratch or even lick from a warm-blooded, furry animal should be cleaned immediately and thoroughly. Scrub with soap and running water, and then clean with an alcohol or iodine solution.

If there is any possibility that the animal is infected medical help should be sought immediately to prevent the onset of symptoms and death. In a person who has not been immunised against rabies this involves having six injections over 28 days starting as soon as possible after the exposure.

Tetanus Tetanus occurs when a wound becomes infected by a germ which lives in soil and in the faeces of horses and other animals.

It enters the body via breaks in the skin. All wounds should be cleaned promptly and adequately and an antiseptic cream or solution applied. Use antibiotics if the wound becomes hot, throbs or pus is seen.

The first symptom may be discomfort in swallowing, or stiffening of the jaw and neck; this is followed by painful convulsions of the jaw and whole body. The disease can be fatal.

Typhus Typhus is spread by ticks, mites or lice. It begins with fever, chills, headache and muscle pains followed a few days later by a body rash. There is often a large painful sore at the site of the bite and nearby lymph nodes are swollen and painful.

Typhus can be treated under medical supervision. Seek local advice on areas where ticks pose a danger and always check your skin (including hair) carefully for ticks after walking in a danger area such as a tropical forest.

A strong insect repellent can help, and serious walkers in tick areas should consider having their boots and trousers impregnated with benzyl benzoate and dibutylphthalate.

Women's Health

Gynaecological Problems Sexually transmitted diseases are a major cause of vaginal problems. Symptoms include a smelly discharge, painful intercourse and sometimes a burning sensation when urinating. Male sexual partners must also be treated.

Medical attention should be sought and remember in addition to these diseases HIV or hepatitis B may also be acquired during exposure. Besides abstinence, the best thing is to practise safe sex using condoms.

Antibiotic use, synthetic underwear, sweating and contraceptive pills can lead to fungal vaginal infections when travelling in hot climates. Maintaining good personal hygiene, and wearing loose-fitting clothes and cotton underwear will help prevent these infections.

Fungal infections, characterised by a rash, itch and discharge, can be treated with a vinegar or lemon-juice douche, or with yoghurt. Nystatin, miconazole or clotrimazole pessaries or vaginal cream are the usual prescribed treatment.

Pregnancy It is not advisable to travel to some places while pregnant as some vaccinations normally used to prevent serious diseases are not advisable in pregnancy eg yellow fever. In addition, some diseases are much more serious for the mother (and may increase the risk of a stillborn child) in pregnancy, eg malaria.

Most miscarriages occur during the first three months of pregnancy. Miscarriage is not uncommon, and can occasionally lead to severe bleeding. The last three months should also be spent within reasonable distance of good medical care. A baby born as early as 24 weeks stands a chance of survival, but only in a good modern hospital.

Pregnant women should avoid all unnecessary medication, though vaccinations and malarial prophylactics should still be taken where needed. Additional care should be taken to prevent illness and particular attention should be paid to diet and nutrition. Alcohol and nicotine, for example, should be avoided.

TOILETS

Some travellers have given up eating (for a while at least) just to avoid having to use Chinese toilets. Unfortunately, unless your stay in China is extremely brief, you'll have to learn to cope.

Public toilets in China are hardly the healthiest-looking places – basically they're holes in the ground or ditches over which you squat, and some look like they haven't been cleaned since the Han Dynasty. Many cannot be flushed at all while others are flushed with a conveniently placed bucket of water. Public toilets can often be found in railway stations and the side streets of the cities and towns – many now charge a fee of one or two jiao. Some have very low partitions (without doors) between the individual holes and some have none. Toilet paper is never provided – always keep a stash with you. Dormitory-style hotel rooms are also not equipped with toilet paper.

While it takes some practice to get proficient at balancing yourself over a squat toilet, at least you don't need to worry about whether the toilet seat is clean. Furthermore, experts who study such things claim that the squatting position is better for your digestive system. Tourist hotels have western-style 'sit-down' toilets, a luxury you will come to appreciate. The issue of what to do with used toilet paper has caused some concern. One traveller writes:

We are still not sure about the toilet paper ... in two hotels they have been angry with us for flushing down the paper in the toilet. In other places it seems quite OK though.

In general, if you see a wastebasket next to the toilet, that is where you should throw the toilet paper. The problem is that in many hotels, the sewage system cannot handle toilet paper. This is especially true in old hotels where the antiquated plumbing system was designed in the pre-toilet paper era. Also, in rural areas there is no sewage treatment plant – the waste empties into an septic tank and toilet paper will really create a mess in there. For the sake of international relations, be considerate and throw the paper in the wastebasket.

Remember:

women: 女

men: 男

WOMEN TRAVELLERS

In general, foreign women are unlikely to suffer serious sexual harassment in China, but there have been reports of problems in Xinjiang (a Muslim area). Wherever you are, it's worth noticing what local women are wearing and how they are behaving and making a bit of an effort to fit in, as you would in any other foreign country.

We've heard of foreign women being harassed by Chinese men in Beijing's parks or while cycling alone at night, but rape (of foreign women) is not common. This doesn't mean it cannot happen, but most Chinese rapists appear to prefer Chinese victims.

The police tend to investigate crimes against foreigners much more closely and more severe penalties (like execution) are imposed if the perpetrator is caught – this provides foreign women with a small but important aura of protection.

Wearing see-through blouses, skimpy shorts or bikinis, and going topless at the beach is asking for trouble. While city people in China are hip to the latest fashions (including miniskirts), the countryside is much more conservative. If you want to play safe, wear trousers or a below-the-knee skirt, with a shirt that covers your shoulders.

GAY & LESBIAN TRAVELLERS

The official attitude to gays and lesbians in China is ambiguous, with responses ranging from draconian penalties to tacit acceptance.

Certainly there is greater tolerance in the big cities than in the more conservative countryside. However, even the big cities are not good places for gays and lesbians to flaunt their sexual preferences in public, as police or local officials might respond to this 'provocation' with a crackdown on local meeting places.

In 1996 British organisation War on Want reported that China was jailing gays for up to five years for 'disturbance[s] against the social order' (a violation of Penal Code section 158). Other gays are reportedly treated with electric shocks to 'cure' their homosexuality.

Similarly, Chinese writers and film producers who try to deal with the topic of homosexuality routinely see their works banned.

Gender Games

As with many places in the world, a woman travelling alone in China is often an object of surprise, followed closely by pity. 'You need a companion', is one of the most frequent observations made by people sharing your train compartment or bus seat.

The intense feelings of alienation that can afflict foreigners who clearly don't look Chinese in appearance can affect all lone travellers in China – regardless of whether they are male or female. For women it can be a double whammy as the inevitable questions, 'Husband? Children?' begin to grate on one's nerves, especially if they are not applicable to your life. Of course, the other side is that you get the opportunity to invent scenarios for yourself.

In fact, travelling in China can be the wellspring of countless imaginary lives you will never live. It's also a way to exert revenge after countless questions from people who see little point in minding their own business.

It's been said before that China is one of the safest places in Asia – if not the world – for foreign women to travel by themselves. This may not be quite as true as it was a decade ago, particularly in places like Beijing (beware of lecherous taxi drivers), but the changes are not dramatic. The stares, shrieks, whistles and excruciating 'hellos' that burst forth at the spectacle of a foreigner may have the occasional lascivious slant (note it's a melodious whistle as opposed to the standard American wolf call), but this is generally more annoying than actually threatening. Indeed, you are in greater danger of being robbed in China than being sexually assaulted.

In many instances, the Chinese people – both women and men – will look out for your safety; there is also the fact that it's rare to find yourself in a situation where there are no other people around. In any situation, however, it is clearly better to give your intuition the benefit of the doubt if things don't feel right.

It's worth remembering that many people in China, particularly men, have the impression that westerners treat sex as casually as shaking hands. Remember too that the Chinese press never tires of pointing out western sexual decadence. On the other hand, don't be fooled into thinking that the condescending deference often given to foreigners is gender-blind. Despite the rhetoric of the revolution, Chinese women do not share the same equality as men. And as a female foreigner, neither do you.

Marie Cambon

On the other hand, there are many recognised gay discos, bars and pubs in the big cities which appear to function without official harassment, although they tend to keep a fairly low profile (see individual city entries for listings of these venues).

Despite this apparent liberalisation, China is a long way from tolerating gays and lesbians 'coming out' to family or employers, as there is still too great a risk of being rejected or fired.

As far as most Chinese people are concerned, homosexuality is a 'foreign problem' – for them, it just doesn't exist in China.

Check out the very good Website at www.utopia-asia.com/tipschin.htm for tips on travelling in China.

DISABLED TRAVELLERS

China has few facilities geared for the disabled. But that doesn't necessarily make it out of bounds for those who do have a physical disability (and a sense of adventure). On the plus side, most hotels have lifts, so booking ground-floor hotel rooms is not essential. In bigger cities, some hotels at the four and five star level have specially designed rooms for people with physical disabilities.

On the other hand, just getting up the

steps to enter the hotel lobby could present a challenge. People whose sight, hearing or walking ability is impaired must be extremely cautious of China's crazy drivers who almost never yield to pedestrians. The buses and trains are such a horror that they pose a danger to everyone. Travelling by car or taxi is probably the safest transport option.

Not surprisingly, Hong Kong is more user-friendly to the disabled than the rest of China. However, Hong Kong presents some substantial obstacles of its own such as the stairs at the subway stations, narrow crowded footpaths and steep hills.

Get in touch with your national support organisation (preferably the 'travel officer' if there is one) before leaving home. They often have travel literature to help with holiday planning and can put you in touch with travel agents who specialise in tours for the disabled.

In the UK the Royal Association for Disability & Rehabilitation (☎ 0171-250 3222; fax 250 0212), at 12 City Forum, 250 City Rd, London EC1V 8AF, produces three holiday fact packs for disabled travellers. They cost UK£2 each and cover planning, insurance and useful organisations; transport and equipment; and specialised accommodation.

In the USA, contact Society for the Advancement of Travel for the Handicapped (SATH) (☎ (212) 447-7284) at 347 Fifth Ave No 610, New York, NY 10016; or Access – The Foundation for Accessibility by the Disabled (☎ (516) 887-5798), at PO Box 356, Malverne, NY 11565.

Australians can contact NICAN (☎ (02) 6285-3713; fax 6285-3714) at PO Box 407, Curtin, ACT 2605.

In France try the CNFLRH (☎ 1 53 80 66 66) at 236 bis rue de Tolbiac, Paris.

SENIOR TRAVELLERS

The main threat to senior travellers is the dreaded 'China Syndrome', or 'chronic bronchitis' as it's commonly known in the west. See the previous Health section in this chapter for more details.

TRAVEL WITH CHILDREN

Bringing the kids to China is a mixed bag. First off, there's the dreaded 'China Syndrome' as mentioned above – nothing is worse than having sick children to take care of while travelling.

Health problems aside, there's the fact that travel in China tends to be uncomfortable – long distances by train, often in hard seat carriages where everyone smokes and spits. China's crowds can be overpowering, and blond-haired, blue-eyed or black children will often receive far more attention than they want.

Dry museums and temples are hardly likely to attract most kids. Using the TV as a babysitter doesn't work too well – programs tend to all be in Chinese. Then there's those fun squat toilets – adults even have trouble dealing with this, but children are liable to raise hell.

On the plus side, Chinese cities tend to have zoos, spacious parks with rowing boats and amusement parks with lots of cotton candy, ferris wheels, merry-go-rounds and other nauseating rides. For older children, travellers' centres like Yangshuo – with everything from watching video movies in the cafes to floating down the river in truck inner tubes – will probably be the highlight of a China visit.

Chinese food seems to go down all right with most foreign children, provided you can teach the toddlers how to use chopsticks.

For many visitors to China the national policy of extracting every possible jiao from visitors can quickly become annoying and, unfortunately, children simply offer another excuse to charge foreigners inflated prices. Children's prices are rarely available for foreign children, who simply get lumped in with foreign adults and charged at the same inflated level. Even student prices are not available for children unless they have a student card! So, ridiculous though it may seem, it's worth getting your child, even at kindergarten age, an ISIC card to wave at temple, garden and museum entrance counters.

'foreigners' who were born in Hong Kong and hold Hong Kong passports, and in fact have never lived anywhere else. Some are one-half Chinese or one-quarter Chinese, but Beijing flatly refused to grant citizenship to anyone who was not of 'pure Chinese descent'. In other words, racial purity was the deciding factor, not place of birth. This rendered all these people stateless in July 1997. Like others born in Hong Kong, they hold 'British National Overseas' (BNO) passports, which allows them to travel, but gives them no right of abode in Britain. Since a BNO passport does not confer nationality, the non-Chinese Hong Kongers are now stateless. The 30,000 Hong Kong-born Indians are the largest affected group, but there are many others born in Hong Kong who have 'mixed blood' and are thus racially unqualified to become Chinese citizens.

Gripes aside, foreigners in China are generally treated well. It is very unusual to encounter direct racism in the form of insults (although it does happen) or be refused service in China (except to be excluded from 'Chinese-only hotels'). It does help, however, if you are from a predominantly white and prosperous nation. Other Asians and blacks often encounter discrimination in China. The most famous outright racist incident occurred in 1988 when Chinese students in Nanjing took to the streets to protest black overseas students dating local Chinese women.

When a Chinese tells you that racism is a 'foreign problem', bear in mind that homosexuality too is a 'foreign problem' – in fact almost everything the Chinese government considers 'unhealthy' is a foreign problem. And if that sounds a little racist, it isn't, because there's no racism in China.

Queues

Forget queues. In China a large number of people with a common goal (a bus seat, a train ticket etc) generally form a surging mass. It is one of the more exhausting parts of China travel, and sometimes it is worth paying extra in order to be able to avoid

railway and bus stations. Otherwise, take a deep breath and leap in with everyone else. This is China – you have to accept the fact that there's nothing you can do about a billion people!

Beggars

Yes, beggars do exist in China. Some squat on the pavement beside large posters which detail their sad story. Professional beggars are common – sometimes women clutching babies who regurgitate stories about having lost their train tickets and all their money.

The adults tend not to pounce on foreigners, but it's a different situation with the children, who practically have to be removed with a crowbar once they've seized your trouser leg. Child beggars are usually an organised operation, working under the instructions from nearby older women who supervise them and collect most of the cash. There have even been stories of children being kidnapped, taken hundreds of kilometres from their homes and forced into these begging gangs.

LEGAL MATTERS
Judicial System

Only the most serious cases are tried in front of a judge (never a jury). Most lesser crimes are handled administratively by the PSB. The PSB acts as police, judge and executioner – they will decide what constitutes a crime regardless of what the law says, and they decide what the penalty will be.

If you do have a run-in with the PSB, you may have to write a confession of your guilt and pay a fine. In more serious cases, you can be expelled from China (at your own expense). In general, if you haven't done anything particularly nasty, like smuggling suitcases of dope through Customs, the PSB will probably not throw you in prison.

In China, prisons generally operate at a profit, either by using prison slave labour to manufacture goods or by forcing the prisoners' families to cough up some cash. If you do get tossed into prison, don't be surprised if the terms of your release require you to pay the cost of your imprisonment – if you don't pay, you don't get released.

Drugs

China takes a particularly dim view of opium and all of its derivatives. The Chinese suffered severely from an opium epidemic which was started by British traders in 1773 and lasted until the Communists came to power – they haven't forgotten! Indeed, China is always fond of bringing up the issue of opium every time the British criticise China's frequent human rights violations. Not much is said about the fact that China's current booming heroin trade is run exclusively by Chinese gangs, often with help from corrupt local police.

Marijuana is often seen growing by the roadside in south-western China – it's very poor quality. Hashish is smoked by some of China's minority groups, especially the Uighurs in Xinjiang Province. It's difficult to say what attitude the Chinese police will take towards foreigners caught using marijuana – they often don't care what foreigners do if Chinese aren't involved. Then again, you have to remember the old story about 'kill the rooster to frighten the monkey'. If you plan to use drugs and don't want to become the rooster, discretion is strongly advised!

BUSINESS HOURS

China officially converted to a five day work week in 1995, although some businesses still force their workers to put in six days. Banks, offices and government departments are normally open Monday to Friday. As a rough guide only, they open around 8.30 am, close for one to two hours in the middle of the day, then reopen until 5 or 6 pm. Saturday and Sunday are both public holidays, but most museums stay open on weekends and make up for this by closing for one or two days mid-week.

Travel agencies, Friendship Stores, the foreign-exchange counters in the tourist hotels and some of the local branches of the Bank of China have similar opening hours, but are generally open on Saturday and Sunday as well, at least in the morning.

Many parks, zoos and monuments have similar opening hours and are also open on weekends and often at night. Shows at cinemas and theatres end around 9.30 to 10 pm.

Restaurants keep long hours and it is always possible to find something to eat at any hour of the day, especially around railway and bus stations.

Long-distance bus stations and railway stations open their ticket offices around 5 or 5.30 am, before the first trains and buses pull out. Apart from a one or two hour break in the middle of the day, they often stay open until midnight.

PUBLIC HOLIDAYS & SPECIAL EVENTS

Both Hong Kong and Macau have separate holidays to the mainland. The rest of the PRC has nine national holidays, as follows:

New Year's Day
   1 January
Spring Festival
   Usually in February – this is otherwise known as Chinese New Year and starts on the first day of the first month in the lunar calendar. Although officially lasting only three days, many people take a week off work. Be warned: this is China's biggest holiday and all transport and hotels are booked solid. Although the demand for accommodation skyrockets, many hotels close down at this time and prices rise steeply. If you can't avoid being in China at this time, then book your room in advance and sit tight until the chaos is over! The Chinese New Year will fall on the following dates: 16 February 1999, 5 February 2000, 24 January 2001 and 12 February 2002.
International Women's Day
   8 March
International Labour Day
   1 May – a worldwide Communist holiday.
Youth Day
   4 May – commemorates the student demonstrations in Beijing on 4 May 1919, when the Versailles Conference decided to give Germany's 'rights' in the city of Tianjin to Japan
International Children's Day
   1 June

Birthday of the Chinese Communist Party (CCP)
1 July
Anniversary of the founding of the PLA
1 August
National Day
1 October – celebrates the founding of the PRC on 1 October 1949

Much of Chinese culture took a beating during the Cultural Revolution and still has not fully revived. Nevertheless, hanging around the appropriate temples at certain times will reward you with special ceremonies and colourful events.

Special prayers are held at Buddhist and Taoist temples on days when the moon is either full or just the thinnest sliver. According to the Chinese lunar calendar, these days fall on the 15th and 16th days of the lunar month and on the last (30th) day of the month just ending and the 1st day of the new month.

Other notable times when temples are liveliest include:

Lantern Festival (yuánxiāo jié)
It's not a public holiday, but it is very colourful. People take the time to make (or buy) paper lanterns and walk around the streets in the evening holding them. It falls on the 15th day of the 1st moon, and will be celebrated on the following dates: 2 March 1999, 19 February 2000, 7 February 2001 and 26 February 2002.

Guanyin's Birthday (guānshìyīn shēngrì)
The birthday of Guanyin, the goddess of mercy, is a good time to visit Taoist temples. Guanyin's birthday is the 19th day of the 2nd moon and will fall on the following dates: 5 April 1999, 24 March 2000, 13 March 2001 and 1 April 2002.

Mazu's Birthday (māzǔ shēngrì)
Mazu, goddess of the sea, is the friend of all fishing crews. She's called Mazu in Fujian Province and Taiwan. The name gets changed to Tianhou in Guangdong Province, and in Hong Kong the spelling is 'Tin Hau'. Her birthday is widely celebrated at Taoist temples in coastal regions as far south as Vietnam. Mazu's birthday is on the 23rd day of the 3rd moon, and will fall on the following dates: 8 May 1999; 27 April 2000, 16 April 2001 and 5 May 2002.

Tomb Sweep Day (qīng míng jié)
A day for worshipping ancestors; people visit the graves of their departed relatives and clean the site. They often place flowers on the tomb and burn ghost money for the departed. It falls on 5 April in the Gregorian calendar in most years, or 4 April in leap years.

Water-Splashing Festival (pō shuǐ jié)
Held in the Xishuangbanna Autonomous Prefecture in Yunnan Province, this event falls around mid-April (usually 13-15 April). The purpose is to wash away the dirt, sorrow and demons of the old year and bring in the happiness of the new. The event gets staged more often now for tourists.

Dragon Boat Festival (duānwǔ jié)
This is the time to see dragon boat races. It's a fun holiday despite the fact that it commemorates the sad tale of Chu Yuan, a 3rd century BC poet-statesman who hurled himself into the Mi Lo river in Hunan province to protest against the corrupt government. This holiday falls on the 5th day of the 5th lunar month, which corresponds to the following dates: 18 June 1999, 6 June 2000, 25 June 2001 and 15 June 2002.

Ghost Month (guǐ yuè)
The devout believe that during this time the ghosts from hell walk the earth and it is a dangerous time to travel, go swimming, get married or move to a new house. If someone dies during this month, the body will be preserved and the funeral and burial will be performed the following month. The Chinese government officially denounces Ghost Month as a lot of superstitious nonsense. The Ghost Month is the 7th lunar month, or really just the first 15 days. The first day of the Ghost Month will fall on the following dates: 22 August 1998, 11 August 1999, 31 July 2000, 19 August 2001 and 9 August 2002.

Mid-Autumn Festival (zhōngqiū jié)
This is also known as the Moon Festival, and is the time to eat tasty moon cakes. Gazing at the moon and lighting fireworks are popular activities, and it's also a traditional holiday for lovers. The festival takes place on the 15th day of the 8th moon, and will be celebrated on the following dates: 5 October 1998, 24 September 1999, 12 September 2000, 1 October 2001 and 21 September 2002.

Birthday of Confucius (kǒngzi shēngrì)
The birthday of the great sage occurs on 28 September of the Gregorian calendar. This is an interesting time to visit Qufu in Shandong Province, the birthplace of Confucius. On the other hand, all hotels in town are likely to be booked out at this time. A ceremony is held at the Confucius Temple starting around 4 am.

ACTIVITIES

Adventure Sports

Western China in particular offers the type of topography to entice mountaineers, whitewater rafters, hang gliding enthusiasts and others who want to pursue their adventurous hobbies in some of the world's highest mountains.

The problem, as always, is the faceless, sombre figures known collectively as 'the authorities'. High-ranking cadres, the PSB, the military, CITS and others in China with the power to extort money know a good business opportunity when they see it. Foreigners have been asked for as much as US$1 million for mountaineering and rafting permits. The amount demanded varies considerably depending on who you're dealing with, and the price is always negotiable.

In many cases, it's doubtful that the law really requires a permit. A Chinese person may climb the same mountain as you without having any authorisation at all and it may be perfectly legal. But many local governments simply make up the law as they go along.

In general, when foreigners do something which is deemed unusual – and hang gliding, bungy jumping, kayaking and the like are unusual in China – a permit will be required and a fee will be charged. The more unusual the activity, the higher the fee demanded.

Hiking

As opposed to mountaineering (which requires equipment such as ropes and ice axes), normal hiking activities can usually be pursued without permits. The Chinese idea of hiking is often different from the western concept – most of the peaks climbed are hardly wilderness areas. You can expect an admission gate (charging a fee), handrails, concrete steps, Chinese characters painted on the rocks, temples, pavilions, trailside souvenir vendors, loudspeakers spewing forth advertisements, camel rides, photo props, restaurants and perhaps a hotel or two.

Hiking areas of this sort include some of China's famous mountains like Taishan and Emeishan. Still, it can be good fun and exercise, and it's part of the 'China experience'.

Camel & Horse Riding

The venues are not numerous, but China does offer some opportunities of this sort. Camel rides for tourists have become popular pastimes in places like Inner Mongolia or the deserts around Dunhuang (Gansu Province).

More common are the photo-prop camels and horses (you dress up like Genghis Khan, mount your steed and have your photo taken). There are chances for beautiful trips by horses in the mountains of Xinjiang, or for that matter in the hills west of Beijing. Costs are negotiable, but in general, the further away from a big city you are, the cheaper it gets.

Exercise & Gymnastics

Swimming pools, gymnasiums and weightlifting rooms are popular ways to keep fit and enjoy yourself. While swimming pools and gymnasiums exist for the Chinese public, they are generally overcrowded and in poor condition. You'll find better facilities at the tourist hotels, but of course it won't be free (unless you're a guest at the hotel).

For a fee, most hotels in big cities like Beijing permit non-guests to join their 'health club' which entitles you to use the workout rooms, pools, saunas or tennis courts. This is not a bad idea if you're staying for a month or more – monthly membership fees typically start at around Y500 and there are discounts for married couples and families. There are even bigger discounts if you sign up long-term (up to one-year memberships are available).

Many public swimming pools in China require foreigners to have a recent certificate proving they are AIDS-free before they are allowed to swim.

Massage

Legitimate massage (as opposed to prostitution) has traditionally been performed by

Therapeutic Massage

Massage *(ànmó)* has a long history in China. It's an effective technique for treating a variety of painful ailments, such as chronic back pain and sore muscles. To be most effective, a massage should be administered by someone who has studied the techniques. An acupuncturist who also practises massage would be ideal.

Traditional Chinese massage is somewhat different from the increasingly popular do-it-yourself techniques practised by people in the west. One traditional Chinese technique employs suction cups made of bamboo placed on the patient's skin. A burning piece of alcohol-soaked cotton is briefly put inside the cup to drive out the air before it is applied. As the cup cools, a partial vacuum is produced, leaving a nasty-looking but harmless red circular mark on the skin. The mark goes away in a few days. Other methods include blood-letting and scraping the skin with coins or porcelain soup spoons.

A related technique is called moxibustion. Various types of herbs, rolled into what looks like a ball of fluffy cotton, are held close to the skin and ignited. A slight variation of this method is to place the herbs on a slice of ginger and then ignite them. The idea is to apply the maximum amount of heat possible without burning the patient. This heat treatment is supposed to be good for such diseases as arthritis.

There is no real need to subject yourself to such extensive treatment if you would just like a straight massage to relieve normal aches and pains. Many big tourist hotels in China offer massage facilities, but the rates charged are excessive – around Y180 per hour and up. You can do much better than that by inquiring locally. Alternatively, look out for the blind masseuses that work on the streets in many Chinese cities. ■

blind people in China. The Chinese can take credit for developing many of the best massage techniques which are still employed today.

Most five star hotels have massage services at five star prices (typically Y300 per hour). You can get it for around Y50 per hour at small specialist massage clinics, but you'll need a Chinese person to direct you to one.

Winter Sports

Beijing's lakes freeze over for a couple of months during winter and ice skating becomes feasible. Further north in Harbin, January temperatures dip to -40°C (-40°F) and ice-boat racing is a favourite pastime for those who can afford it. North-east China is also the venue for skiing, both the downhill and cross-country varieties.

Skiing and ice skating demand specialised shoes, and westerners with big feet often have difficulty finding the right size.

If you want to pursue winter sports, you may need to bring your own equipment, although some local stuff is available.

Golf

Golf courses have invaded the suburbs of Beijing, Shanghai and Guangzhou. As elsewhere, it's a sport of the well-to-do, but that seems to be even more true in China. While green fees are similar to what you'd pay in the west, the cost is astronomical compared with the typical Chinese salary.

COURSES

As China continues to experiment with capitalism, universities have found it increasingly necessary to raise their own funds and not depend so much on state largesse. For this reason, most universities welcome fee-paying foreign students.

Most of the courses offered are Chinese language study, but other options include

Chinese medicine, acupuncture, music and brush painting. If you've got the cash, almost anything is possible.

A bottom-end quote for four hours of instruction per day, five days a week, is US$500 per month. Some schools charge by the semester, with rates typically US$2500 to US$3500 per semester, and perhaps half that for the summer session. Dormitory housing starts at around US$15 a day for a private room, or half that amount to share. There have been complaints from students that universities try to hit foreigners with all sorts of hidden surcharges – 'study licences', health certificates and so on. Other schools try to coerce you into teaching English for little or nothing.

If possible, don't pay anything in advance – show up at the school to assess the situation yourself and talk to other foreign students to see if they're satisfied. Once you've handed over the cash, don't expect a refund.

WORK

There are opportunities to teach English and other foreign languages, or even other technical skills if you're qualified. Teaching in China is not a way to get rich – the pay is roughly Y1200 to Y2500 a month. While this is several times what the average urban Chinese worker earns, it won't get you far after you've left China. There are usually some fringe benefits like free or low-cost housing and special ID cards that get you discounts at some hotels.

In order to qualify for the high end of the salary range, you need to be declared a 'foreign expert'. It's not totally clear what makes you an expert, but points in your favour could include holding a graduate degree, a Teacher of English as a Second Language (TESL) certificate, other credentials and/or experience. The final decision is made by the State Bureau for Foreign Experts.

As a worker in China, you will be assigned to a 'work unit', but unlike the locals you'll be excused from political meetings and the God-like control over your life that the typical Chinese has to endure.

It's become fairly typical for universities to pressure foreigners into working excessive hours. A maximum teaching load should be 20 hours per week, and even this is a lot – you can insist on no more than 15 and some teachers get away with 10. Chinese professors teach far fewer hours than this – some hardly show up for class at all since they often have outside business interests.

The main reason to work in China is to experience the country at a level not ordinarily available to travellers. Unfortunately, just how close you will be able to get to the Chinese people depends on what the local PSB allows. In some towns where the local PSB is almost hysterical about evil foreign 'spiritual pollution', your students may be prohibited from having any contact with you beyond the classroom, although you may secretly meet them far away from the campus.

Foreign teachers are typically forced to live in separate apartments or dormitories – Chinese students wishing to visit you at your room may be turned away at the reception desk, or they may be required to register their name, ID number and purpose of their visit. Since many people are reluctant to draw attention to themselves like this, they may be unwilling to visit you at all.

In other words, teaching in China can be a lonely experience unless you spend all your free time in the company of other expats, but this deprives you of the 'foreign experience' you may be seeking. A lot depends on where you'll be teaching – things are fairly open in Shanghai, but it's a different story in the hinterlands of Gansu Province.

Two topics which cannot be discussed in the classroom are politics and religion. Foreigners teaching in China have reported spies being placed in their classrooms. Other teachers have found microphones hidden in their dormitory rooms (one fellow we know took revenge by attaching his

Walkman to the microphone wires and blasting the snoops with punk music!).

Rules change – China is opening up slowly, and some provinces are liberalising faster than others. In the city where you live, you may find that conditions are better than those that are described here.

If you are interested in working in China, contact a Chinese embassy or one of the universities directly.

Doing Business

In bureaucratic China, even simple things can be made difficult – renting property, getting licences, hiring employees, paying taxes etc can generate mind-boggling quantities of red tape. Many foreign business people who have worked in China say that success is usually the result of dogged persistence and finding cooperative officials.

Even when you think you've got everything all agreed to on paper, don't be surprised if things go awry when you put your agreements into practice. It's not uncommon for your Chinese joint-venture partner to change the terms of the agreement once business has commenced. Your copyrights, patents and trademarks may be pirated. Your rent and property taxes may suddenly be raised, and your Chinese employees (who know your company's secrets) may simultaneously walk out and start working for a new state-run company just across the street producing exactly same goods as you do. While the business climate has improved in recent years, there are still 1001 things that can go wrong.

If you have any intention of doing business in China, be it buying, selling or investing, it's worth knowing that most towns and – in large cities – many neighbourhoods have a Commerce Office (shāngyè jú). If you approach one of these offices for assistance, the reaction you get can vary from enthusiastic welcome to bureaucratic inertia. In case of a dispute (the goods you ordered are not what was delivered etc), the Commerce Office could assist you, provided that it is willing.

Anyone thinking of doing serious business in China and setting up a company is advised to do some serious research before going ahead. In particular, talk to other foreigners who are already doing business in China.

ACCOMMODATION

One of the main reasons the Chinese threw the door open to tourism in the 1980s is that they badly needed the foreign exchange. Despite all the government's rhetoric about 'Friendship Hotels' and 'Friendship Stores', the purpose of opening up to tourism has always been to rake in money.

In the more developed parts of China, hotel prices have risen so high that it's no cheaper than travelling in Europe or the USA. Out in the backwaters of Inner Mongolia or Qinghai it's still pretty cheap, but the trend is clear – prices are rising everywhere.

On the other hand, quality has improved – rooms are more luxurious, service has improved and hotel staff are friendlier and more used to dealing with foreigners than a few years ago. In the past, it was common for the staff to simply deny that rooms were available even when the hotel was empty.

When you check into a hotel, there is usually a question on the registration form asking what type of visa you have. Most travellers aren't sure how to answer. For most, the type of visa is 'L', from the Chinese word for travel (lǚxíng). For a full list of visa categories, see the Visas & Documents section earlier in this chapter.

Reservations

It's possible to book rooms in advance at upmarket hotels through overseas branches of CITS, CTS and some other travel agencies. Often you actually get a discount by booking through an agency – the walk-in rate is higher.

Camping

You have to get a long way from civilisation before camping becomes feasible in China. Camping within sight of a town or village in most parts of China would probably result in a swift visit by the PSB. Wilderness camping is more appealing, but most such areas in China require special permits and are difficult to reach. Many travellers have camped successfully in Tibet and remote north-western Sichuan.

The trick is to select a couple of likely places about half an hour before sunset, but keep moving (by bicycle, foot or whatever) and then backtrack so you can get away from the road at the chosen spot just after darkness falls. Be sure to get up around sunrise and leave before sightseeing locals take an interest.

Rental Accommodation

If you're going to be working for the Chinese government as a teacher or other type of foreign expert, then you'll almost certainly be provided with low-cost housing. Conditions probably won't be luxurious, but it will be cheap or even free.

Foreign students also are usually offered decent accommodation by their schools, although the price can vary from very reasonable to totally ridiculous.

If you're visiting Chinese friends for any length of time, their work unit may be able to provide you with temporary accommodation at low cost. Alternatively, you could live with your Chinese friends – in the recent past this was prohibited, but now it seems to be OK almost everywhere in China.

The news is not good for those coming to China to do business or work for a foreign company. The cheap subsidised apartments available to the Chinese are not open to foreigners, which leaves you with two choices – living in a hotel or renting a luxury flat in a compound specifically designated for foreigners.

If you live in a hotel, you might be able to negotiate a discount for a long-term stay, but that's not guaranteed. As for luxury flats and villas, monthly rents start at around US$2000 and reach US$5000 or more.

Considering the sky-high rents, buying a flat or villa might seem like a good idea for

companies with the cash. It is actually possible, but the rules vary from city to city. In Xiamen, for example, only Overseas Chinese are permitted to buy luxury villas – real estate speculators from Taiwan do a roaring trade. Shenzhen has long been in the business of selling flats to Hong Kongers, who in turn rent them out to others. Foreigners can buy flats in Beijing (at astronomical prices), and doing this can actually gain you a residence permit.

As for simply moving in with a Chinese family and paying them rent, this is possible in some cities, but don't count on it. In most of China (including supposedly 'modern' Beijing) the PSB will swoop down on you (and the hapless Chinese family) like sharks at a feeding frenzy. However, the local PSB has the final word in such matters and in some more liberal parts of China the 'impossible' becomes possible. In any case, you will need to first register with the PSB if you want to live with a Chinese family. Of course, none of the above applies in Hong Kong and Macau where you are mostly free to live where you like.

University Accommodation

In theory, university dormitories are for students, teachers and their guests, or others with business at the university. In practice, universities are trying to make money, and they are simply entering into the hotel business just like many other state-run organisations.

While staying at a university sounds like a great idea, in practice it isn't always so easy. First of all, many university dorms appear to be perpetually full, often with Chinese customers who want a cheap place to stay. Secondly, it's not necessarily going to be cheap – many universities have upgraded their facilities and charge foreigners prices similar to a three star hotel. The tendency is to give the cheaper rooms to locals and the pricier rooms to foreigners. A final problem is that many university dormitories have restrictions – lights out by 10 pm and doors locked, no visitors in your room, etc.

In short, you should probably only consider staying at a university if you have some interest in the campus itself – maybe to hang out with the students or foreign teachers, or participate in some on-campus activities.

Hostels

If you've enjoyed hostelling in Europe, Australia, Japan or wherever, you're going to find China a profound disappointment. The 'hostel experience' in China is not a good one. A handful of travellers stay at the *Mt Davis Hostel* in Hong Kong, and even fewer stay at the *Vila Dom Bosco Hostel* in Macau. The International Youth Hostel Federation (IYHF) has managed to set up one hostel in Beijing, but scarcely anyone stays there.

There are, in fact, hostels (*zhāodàisuǒ*) throughout China. The problem is that the vast majority are off limits to foreigners.

In the early days of China travel, many of the government-run hotels had dormitories (*duō rén fáng*). Such hotels still exist, but are very thin on the ground nowadays. Most budget hotels for foreigners have been renovated to luxury standards, and the dormitories have been closed.

Where dormitories do exist, the staff at the reception desk are often reluctant to tell you. Try a little friendly forcefulness. If this doesn't work, you have no choice but to look elsewhere – there are many cities in China where dormitory accommodation is just not available to foreigners.

Guesthouses

In China guesthouses (*bīnguǎn*) are usually enormous government-run hotels, often with many wings in spacious grounds. Most of them were set up in the 1950s for travelling government officials and overseas dignitaries. Most of these have been renovated over the past decade or so and are being rented out as mid-range accommodation – you no longer have to be a government official or dignitary.

Chinese guesthouses are most definitely not the kind of inexpensive, family-run guesthouses you find all over Thailand, Indonesia and other parts of Asia.

Hotels

There is no shortage of hotels in China. The problem comes if you are on a budget. In many parts of China, finding a room for less than US$35 a night can be an ordeal. Often inexpensive accommodation is in fact available – if you are Chinese. For foreigners, there are generally rules (enforced by the PSB) concerning which hotels you may or may not stay in, and of course the only ones open to foreigners are the expensive ones.

On the other hand, for travellers on midrange budgets, China's hotels have improved immensely. Service standards are better, the toilets may actually flush and sometimes there are even minibars and 24 hour hot water. Unless you are in a four or five star joint venture, however, it is wise not to expect too much, no matter how much you are spending. Many of the finer details of the hotel business still elude Chinese management and staff.

If you're studying in the PRC, you can sometimes get a discount on room prices. Students usually have to show their government-issued 'green card', which should entitle them to pay the same price as local Chinese. However, these days many hotels charge the same price to foreigners and locals, in which case the green card is of no help at all.

If you are really stuck for a place to stay, it may help to phone or visit the local PSB and explain your problem. Just as the PSB makes the rules, the PSB can break them – a hotel not approved for foreigners can be granted a temporary reprieve by the PSB and all it takes is a phone call from the right official. Unfortunately, getting such an exemption is not the usual practice.

Some definitions of hotel terminology are in order. The vast majority of rooms in China are 'twins' which means two single beds placed in one room. A 'single room' (one bed per room) is a rarity, although you may occasionally stumble across one. The

Hotel Hassles

After you've handed over your foreigner's mark-up rate, filled in the registration form in trip-licate and idly noticed that the clocks in the hotel foyer for New York, London, Paris and Beijing all display the same time, it's time to find the *xiǎojiě* (female attendant) to open the door to your room. As you search for your room down spittoon-lined corridors, you will notice that all the doors along the corridor are flung open as the occupants channel hop with the TV on full volume. Welcome to a typical Chinese budget hotel.

As you inspect the bathroom, you notice that the lavatory is draped with a ribbon that says 'sterilised'. This actually means nothing of the sort, so don't pay much attention to it. Occasionally you will find that, with space saving ingenuity, the extractor fan from your bathroom runs directly into the bathroom of the adjacent room and vice-versa. The scorch marks of ground out cigarettes on the carpet of the main room makes the room smell and look like the headquarters of the local Triad; you will find little solace in the overhead smoke alarm that probably houses a rusty battery and a cockroach nest.

As you dive into bed, the door crashes open and *xiǎojiě* marches in with a thermos flask and a technician to mend the TV. As she crashes out again, the telephone rings and a sultry voice asks if Mr Wang is still there; you say you hope not, and put the phone down. Finding a sock a moment later in your bed, you are not so sure.

They tell you that hot water is from 6 to 8 pm. When you turn on the tap at 7 pm, nothing emerges except the hiss of escaping air, or a trickle of water the colour of coffee. You hunt for *xiǎojiě*, who assures you that hot water is imminent; hot water alternates with cold till 7.30 pm, when it stops altogether.

After chasing an engorged mosquito around your room with a flip-flop (thong) in one hand, you turn off the TV at 11 pm and get ready to hit the sack. This is the signal they've been waiting for directly below in the karaoke lounge; someone snaps their fingers with a '... and a one, two, three ...', the amplifier goes on with a 'whummpf' and there's a collective clearing of throats.

Half an hour later, you run out of your room with a pillow pressed to each ear, looking for *xiǎojiě*, but she is no where to be found – she's singing downstairs.

Damian Harper

western concept of a 'double room' (a room with one large double bed shared by two people) is also extremely rare in China. In most cases, your choice will be between a twin room (*shuāng rén fáng*) or a suite (*tàofáng*), the latter obviously being more expensive. However, in most cases two people are allowed to occupy a twin room for the same price as one person, so sharing is one good way to cut expenses.

Most hotels have an attendant on every floor. The attendant keeps an eye on the hotel guests. This is partly to prevent theft and partly to stop you from bringing locals back for the night (this is not a joke).

To conserve energy, in many cheaper hotels hot water for bathing is available only in the evening – sometimes only for a few hours – or once every three days. It's worth asking when or if the hot water will be turned on.

The policy at every hotel in China is to require that you check out by noon to avoid being charged extra. If you check out between noon and 6 pm there is a charge of 50% of the room price – after 6 pm you have to pay for another full night.

Almost every hotel has a left-luggage room (*jìcún chù* or *xínglǐ bǎoguān*), and in many hotels there is such a room on every floor. If you are a guest in the hotel, use of the left-luggage room might be free (but not always).

Something to be prepared for is lack of

privacy – what happens is that you're sitting starkers in your hotel room, the key suddenly turns in the door and the room attendant casually wanders in. Don't expect anyone to knock before entering. Some of the better hotels have a bolt that will lock the door from the inside, but most budget hotels are not so well equipped. Your best protection against becoming an unwilling star in a live nude show is to prop a chair against the door.

In a big city like Beijing or Shanghai, it's wise to call ahead first to see if there are any vacant rooms. Of course, at budget hotels there's only a 50% chance that the person answering the phone will speak anything other than Chinese. When the hotel operator answers, ask to speak to the service desk (*zǒng fúwù tái*) and then ask 'Do you have a vacancy' (*yǒu méiyǒu kōng fángjiān*), to which they'll either reply *yǒu* (have) or *méiyǒu* (don't have).

The Chinese method of designating floors is the same as that used in the USA, but different from, say, Australia's. What would be the 'ground floor' in Australia is the '1st floor' in China, the 1st is the 2nd, and so on.

FOOD
See the previous Language chapter for a list of the names of regional Chinese dishes in English, pinyin and Chinese characters.

Chinese cooking is justifiably famous, a fine art perfected through the centuries. Quality, availability of ingredients and cooking styles vary by region, but you'll almost always find something to suit your tastes.

You can also put your mind at ease about food shortages – despite China's long history of famines, the country is not short of food. Famines have resulted from natural disasters (droughts, floods, typhoons) and human disasters (wars, the Cultural Revolution), but in China today the transport system is able to quickly move food to those areas that need it. Your biggest problems with food are likely to be figuring out the menus and being overcharged.

While the Chinese make outstanding lunches, dinners and snacks, many foreigners are disappointed with breakfast. The Chinese do not seem to understand the western notion of eating lightly in the morning – a typical breakfast could include fried peanuts, pickled vegetables, pork with hot sauce, fried breadsticks (*yóutiáo*), and rice porridge, all washed down with a glass of beer. Just what you had in mind at 7 am.

Outside of hotel restaurants, prices are generally low. Beware, however, of overcharging – many places think nothing of charging foreigners double or more.

The other catch is that when Chinese dine out they spend big, and foreigners are

Chopsticks
If you haven't mastered using chopsticks before going to China, you probably will by the time you leave. In upmarket restaurants, sometimes the staff will bring out the cutlery for foreign guests, but generally you will have to click your chopsticks along with the locals.

Chopsticks are relatively easy to use and are employed for picking items from communal dishes and for shovelling rice (with the bowl held to the lips) in rapid flicking motions into the mouth – that's a tricky one to master.

In rural China, table manners leave a lot to be desired, but this does not mean you can bring back to the big cities the bad habits you have acquired in the backwoods. Spitting bones on the floor and shouting through mouthfuls of food may be OK in the street stalls of Gansu or Inner Mongolia, but is frowned upon in an upmarket Shanghai restaurant.

Chinese toothpick etiquette is similar to other nearby Asian countries. One hand wields the toothpick and does the picking, the other hand shields the mouth from prying eyes. ■

Banquet Etiquette

The banquet is the apex of the Chinese dining experience. Virtually all significant business deals in China are clinched at the banquet table.

Dishes are served in sequence, beginning with cold appetisers and continuing through 10 or more courses. Soup is usually served after the main course, usually a thin broth to aid digestion.

The idea is to serve or order far more than everyone can eat. Empty bowls imply a stingy host. Rice is considered a cheap filler and rarely appears at a banquet – don't ask for it, as this would imply that the snacks and main courses are insufficient, causing embarrassment to the host.

Never drink alone. Imbibing is conducted via toasts, which will usually commence with general table toasts and then settle down to frequent toasts to individuals. A toast is conducted by raising your glass in both hands in the direction of the toastee and crying out *ganbei*, literally 'dry glass'. Chinese do not clink glasses. Drain your glass in one hit. It is not unusual for everyone to end up very drunk, though at very formal banquets this is frowned upon.

Don't be late for a formal banquet; it's considered extremely rude. The banquet ends when the food and toasts end – the Chinese don't linger after the meal. You may find yourself being applauded when you enter a large banquet. It is polite to applaud back.

There is no such thing as everyone chipping-in to pay the bill – one person (the host) settles the account with the restaurant. Even in the very rare case where the cost is going to be split, this is never done in front of the restaurant staff – to pass money to your host in front of others would cause a massive loss of face. ■

expected to do likewise. Travellers in small groups or on their own will often find themselves being pressured to order far more than they can eat. They may also find very expensive dishes landing on their tables. Even the grottiest of Chinese restaurants will often have exotic delicacies costing as much as US$100 per serving on their menus. Be sure you know the cost of what you are ordering.

The language barrier can be formidable since English menus are a rarity. A phrasebook is a big help, but the alternative is to point at something one of the other diners is eating – be sure to determine the price before you order.

In rural China many restaurants have pick-and-choose kitchens where you wander out back, select your vegetables and meat and have the chef fry it all up. Chinese are often very surprised by the ingredients foreigners choose to throw together, but they will usually oblige all the same. Unless you're vegetarian, you may get a chance to meet your dinner – choose your chicken, duck or fish and it will be slaughtered on the spot.

See the following section on Chinese Cuisine in this chapter for a discussion of regional specialities.

Main Dishes

For a discussion of regional specialities, see the special section on Chinese cuisine at the end of this chapter.

Snacks

Western-style cakes and sweetbreads are on sale everywhere – they rarely taste very good. The Chinese are considerably better at making their traditional breads – steamed buns (*mántóu*), clay-oven bread (*shāobǐng*) and fried bread rolls (*yínsī juǎn*) are notable examples. In general, the Cantonese appear to be better at baking than other Chinese. Cantonese specialities such as coconut cakes and custard tarts are excellent.

Desserts

The Chinese do not generally eat dessert, but fruit is considered an appropriate end to a good meal. Western influence has added ice cream to the menu in some upmarket establishments, but in general sweet stuff is consumed as snacks and is seldom available in restaurants.

Fruit

Canned and bottled fruit is readily available everywhere, in department and food shops as well as in railway stations. Good quality fruit – including oranges, mandarins and bananas – is commonly sold in the street markets, although you'll find that the supply and quality drop off in winter. In the deserts of the north-west, melons are abundant, while pineapples and lychees are common along the south-east coast during summer.

Sugarcane is the traditional poor person's candy in China. It is sold at railway and bus stations and is a common on-the-road snack. The idea is not to eat the purple skin (this is usually shaved off anyway) and not to swallow the pulp – chew on it until it tastes like string, then spit it out.

Western

Big Macs and pizzas have arrived in the PRC, and have gained an enthusiastic following. The Chinese attach no stigma to eating fast food, and in fact it actually has some snob appeal. Hanging out with an Egg McMuffin is considered chic.

Aside from fast food, upmarket dishes of the steak and lobster variety can be had at the more opulent hotels. Prices are at least as high as in the west, so don't expect to find Swiss cheese and caviar at street stall prices.

Opportunities to indulge in a western meal are decidedly limited in backwaters like Tibet and Qinghai, but if you've got the cash you'll have no trouble satisfying all but the strangest cravings in Shanghai or Beijing.

DRINKS

See the previous Language chapter for a list of common Chinese beverage names in English, pinyin and Chinese characters.

Nonalcoholic Drinks

Tea is the most commonly served brew in the PRC; it didn't originate in China but in South-East Asia. Indian and Sri Lankan black tea is available only in international supermarkets. Familiar brands of western instant coffee (Maxwell House, Nescafé) are for sale everywhere, but fresh-brewed coffee is virtually unknown.

Coca-Cola, first introduced into China by American soldiers in 1927, is now produced in China. Chinese attempts at making similar brews include TianFu Cola, which has a recipe based on the root of herbaceous peony. Fanta and Sprite are widely available – both genuine and copycat versions. Sugary Chinese soft drinks are cheap and sold everywhere – some are so sweet they'll turn your teeth inside out. Jianlibao is a Chinese soft drink made with honey rather than sugar – one of the better brands. Lychee-flavoured carbonated drinks are unique to China and get rave reviews from foreigners. Fresh milk is rare, but you can buy imported UHT milk at high prices from western-style supermarkets in big cities.

A surprising treat is fresh sweet yoghurt, available in many parts of China. It's typically sold in what looks like small milk bottles and is consumed by drinking with a straw rather than eating with a spoon. This excellent stuff would make a great breakfast if you can find some decent bread to go with it.

Alcoholic Drinks

If tea is the most popular drink in the PRC, then beer must be number two. By any standards the top brands are great stuff. The best known is Tsingtao (Qingdao), made with a mineral water which gives it its sparkling quality. It's really a German beer since the town of Qingdao (formerly spelled 'Tsingtao'), where it's made, was once a German concession and the Chinese inherited the brewery. Experts in these matters claim that draft Tsingtao tastes much better than the bottled stuff. Local brews are found in all the major cities of China – notable ones include Zhujiang in Guangzhou and Yanjing in Beijing. San Miguel has a brewery in Guangzhou, so you can enjoy this 'imported' beer at Chinese prices. Real western imports are sold in Friendship Stores and five star hotels at five star prices.

China has probably cultivated vines and produced wine for more than 4000 years. Chinese wine-producing techniques differ from those of the west. Quality-conscious wine producers in western countries work on the idea that the lower the yield the higher the quality of the wine produced. But Chinese workers cultivate every possible square centimetre of earth; they encourage their vines to yield heavily and also plant peanuts between the rows of vines as a cover crop for half the year. The peanuts sap much of the nutrient from the soil, and in cooler years the large grape crop fails to ripen sufficiently to produce a wine comparable to western ones.

Western producers try to prevent oxidation in the wines, but oxidation produces a flavour which the Chinese find desirable and go to great ends to achieve. The Chinese are also keen on wines with different herbs and other materials soaked in them, which they drink for their health and for restorative or aphrodisiac qualities.

The word 'wine' gets rather loosely translated – many Chinese 'wines' are in fact spirits. Rice wine – a favourite with Chinese alcoholics due to its low price – is intended mainly for cooking rather than drinking.

Hejie Jiu (lizard wine) is produced in the southern province of Guangxi; each bottle contains one dead lizard suspended perpendicularly in the clear liquid.

Wine with dead bees or pickled snakes is also desirable for its alleged tonic properties – in general, the more poisonous the creature, the more potent the tonic effects.

Tibetans have an interesting brew called *chang*, a beer or spirit made from barley. Mongolians serve sour-tasting *koumiss*, made of fermented mare's milk with lots of salt added – most westerners gag on the stuff. *Maotai*, a favourite of the Chinese, is a spirit made from sorghum (a type of millet) and it is used for toasts at banquets – it tastes rather like rubbing alcohol and makes a good substitute for petrol or paint thinner.

Outside the more sophisticated major cities, Chinese women don't drink (except beer) in public. Women who hit the booze are generally regarded as prostitutes. However, western women can easily violate this social taboo without unpleasant consequences – the Chinese expect weirdness from westerners anyway.

As a rule Chinese men are not big drinkers, but toasts are obligatory at banquets – if you really can't drink, fill your wine glass with tea and say you have a bad stomach. In spite of all the toasting and beer drinking, public drunkenness is strongly frowned upon.

Imported booze – like XO, Johnny Walker, Kahlua and Napoleon Augier Cognac – is highly prized by the Chinese for its prestige value rather than exquisite taste. The snob appeal plus steep import taxes translates into absurdly high prices; don't walk into a hotel bar and order this stuff unless you've brought a wheelbarrow full of cash. If you can't live without western spirits, be sure to take advantage of your 2L duty-free allowance on entry to China.

ENTERTAINMENT

As on all other fronts, China's entertainment options are improving rapidly. On the nightlife front, bars, discos and karaoke parlours are springing up in all the major cities. More cultural entertainment is being performed too.

Cinemas

Upmarket hotels have in-house English-language movies, but elsewhere the situation is fairly dire. Foreign movies are dubbed into Chinese, and Chinese movies – well, they're in Chinese. Hong Kong movies at least usually have inventive English subtitles – 'she my sister you call watermelon fool!' – and can be entertaining when you are in the mood for historical kungfu epics and fast-paced police dramas.

Discos

Despite being somewhat unfashionable in the west, discos are very much alive in well in China and should not be confused with nightclubs. Discos *(dísíkē)* are places for dancing, while nightclubs *(jùlèbù)* are places for drinking, usually with a floor show thrown in (and in Hong Kong often with topless waitresses).

Discos have taken China by storm. In rural China, not many Chinese are really sure of the appropriate moves to make to a pounding bass, and it's not unusual to see huge crowds dancing in formation, everyone looking over their shoulders to see what everyone else is doing. But in cities like Guangzhou, Shanghai and Beijing, there are disco complexes (look out for the JJ chain) where the music and the dancers are surprisingly hip to the latest western trends. See the entertainment entries for Guangzhou, Shanghai and Beijing for some suggestions.

Karaoke

If you don't know what karaoke *(kǎlā OK)* is by now, China will be a rude awakening. This is *the* entertainment option for moneyed Chinese. Even the plebs are leaping in, yodelling in search of a melody at roadside karaoke stalls.

The CCP propaganda department has weighed in with suitably proletarian sing-along hits, Chinese business people from Hainan to Heilongjiang slug back the XO and caterwaul with hostesses on their knees, and no doubt Party leaders get together for wine and songs after a hard day at the office sentencing dissidents and keeping the economic miracle on track. 'Let's get together and sing some songs' is

what Chinese say to each other when it's time to unwind.

Much maligned by westerners, karaoke can be fun with enough drinks under your belt and with the right people. It's not unusual for inebriated westerners who claim to hate karaoke to have to be pried loose from the microphone once they get going.

Warning One thing to watch out for in karaoke parlours is rip-offs. In some heavily touristed areas, young women work as touts. You may not even realise that they are touts – they will 'invite' any likely looking male to join them at a nearby karaoke bar, but no sooner than the bottle of XO is ordered then the woman 'disappears' and the hapless male is presented with a bill for US$200.

It is not sensible to accept invitations to clubs from young women on the streets. In clubs themselves, if you invite a hostess to sit with you, it is going to cost you money – the same rules apply in China as anywhere else in the world of paid entertainment and sex.

Crosstalk

Back in the days before karaoke and MTV, the Chinese had to entertain themselves with pun-laden stand-up comedy acts and story-telling. This is known as *xiàngshēng* (crosstalk). Unfortunately, you'd have to be extremely fluent at Mandarin to make any sense out of this – it's extremely difficult to translate because it relies to a great extent on Chinese sound-alike words. Much of the unintelligible noise emanating from the loudspeaker on the trains and buses is just this sort of crosstalk.

SPECTATOR SPORTS

If there is any spectator sport the Chinese have a true passion for, it's soccer. Games are devoutly covered in the mass media and it's possible to see live matches when the team comes to Beijing. China has dreams of taking the World Cup eventually, and the government has been throwing money into the project by importing players and coaches. The season runs approximately from April to November.

Although it hasn't quite fired the Chinese imagination the way soccer has, basketball does provide the masses with entertainment during the long winter when playing outdoors means risking terminal frostbite. There are now two professional leagues, and players have been recruited from the USA.

Perhaps of more interest to foreigners are international sporting events. Beijing hosted the Asian Games in 1990 and the China has thrown in bids (so far unsuccessfully) for upcoming Olympic Games.

THINGS TO BUY

The Chinese do produce some interesting items for export – tea, clothing, Silkworm missiles (the latter not generally for sale to the public).

Gone are the days of ration cards and empty department stores – China is in the grip of a consumer revolution. The new China looks more and more like the old Hong Kong by the day. However, it's still sensible to save your shopping for imported electronic consumer items for Hong Kong and Macau – import duties are still too high in the rest of China. For most visitors, shopping in China is restricted to souvenirs.

The so-called 'Friendship Stores' (not notable for friendly staff) were set up to cater to foreign needs back in the days when ordinary Chinese basically had no access to imported luxury items. It is a measure of just how far China has come when you think how, just 10 years ago, many Chinese dreamed of simply getting through the doors of a Friendship Store.

Nowadays, Friendship Stores are an anachronism and have become one of the many chains of department stores stacked to the rafters with consumer goodies. However, the Friendship Stores are still useful in that they carry foreign reading matter not easily obtainable elsewhere in China, and there are usually some staff

who can speak English. Some Friendship Stores are good venues for finding souvenirs, and can even arrange shipping back to your home country.

The regular Chinese department stores all stock a broad range of cheap, everyday consumer items. They are definitely worth checking out.

Hotel gift shops are still useful to pick up western and Japanese slide film and imported magazines, among other things. On the whole, they tend to be expensive places for shopping, but can be a lifesaver when you're desperate for something to read.

Blankets spread on the pavement and pushcarts in the alleys – this is where you find the lowest prices. In street markets, all sales are final; forget about warranties and, no, they don't accept American Express. Nevertheless, the markets are interesting, but be prepared to bargain hard.

Service standards have been steadily improving in China over the past few years. In the recent past it was usual to be ignored by shop assistants as they read comics and chatted over jam jars of tea. Now with some real competition, shops are pushing their staff to be polite and attend to customers. The authorities have gotten in on the act, with public campaigns urging workers in service industries not to spit and to try smiling at customers. Even railway staff now manage the occasional tight-lipped smile as they toss passengers a rice-box lunch for the afternoon meal. Still, it will be a while before visitors to China come away praising the fine service they received.

Antiques

Many of the Friendship Stores have antique sections and some cities have antique shops, but in the case of genuine antiques you can forget about bargains. Chinese are very savvy when it comes to their own cultural heritage. Only antiques which have been cleared for sale to foreigners may be taken out of the country.

When you buy an item over 100 years old it will come with an official red wax

More Than Meets the Eye ...

Once upon a time in China you got what you paid for. If the sales clerk said it was top-quality jade then it was top-quality jade. Times have changed – now there are all sorts of cheap forgeries and imitations about, from Tibetan jewellery to Qing coins, phoney Marlboro cigarettes, fake Sony Walkmans (complete with fake Maxell cassette tapes), imitation Rolex watches, even fake Garden biscuits (Garden Bakeries is Hong Kong's biggest seller of bread, cakes and biscuits).

China has implemented a major crackdown on counterfeiting, although efforts have been directed mainly towards items that flout international intellectual copyright laws: CDs, pirated software and the like. It's a big country, however, and there are still a lot of illegal consumer goods out there.

At the same time, the government has to contend with more localised problems: the manufacture of fake railway tickets, fake lottery tickets and fake Y100 RMB notes. Cadres frequently pad their expense accounts with fake receipts – one of the many reasons why state-run companies are losing money.

Take care buying anything in China, particularly if you are forking out a large sum for it. Watch out for counterfeit Y100 notes. And if you are after genuine antiques, try to get an official certificate of verification – just make sure the ink is dry. ■

seal attached. This seal does *not* necessarily indicate that the item is an antique though. A Canadian who bought 'real' jade for Y1500 at a Friendship Store in Guilin later discovered in Hong Kong that it was a plastic fake. After six months of copious correspondence and investigation, the Guilin Tourism Bureau refunded the money and closed down the offending shop. You'll also get a receipt of sale, which you must show to Customs when you leave the country; otherwise the antique will be confiscated. Imitation antiques are sold everywhere. Some museum shops sell replicas, usually at extravagant prices.

Stamps & Coins

China issues quite an array of beautiful stamps which are generally sold at post offices in the hotels. Outside many of the post offices you'll find amateur philatelists with books full of stamps for sale; it can be extraordinarily hard bargaining with these guys! Stamps issued during the Cultural Revolution make interesting souvenirs, but these rare items are no longer cheap. Old coins are often sold at major tourist sites, but many are forgeries.

Paintings & Scrolls

Watercolours, oils, woodblock prints, calligraphy – there is a lot of art for sale in China. Tourist centres like Guilin, Suzhou, Beijing and Shanghai are good places to look out for paintings.

Prices are usually very reasonable – even some of the high quality work available in galleries. In the eyes of connoisseurs, the scrolls selling for Y200 are usually rubbish, but remain popular purchases all the same.

Oddities

If plaster statues are to your liking, the opportunities to stock up in China are abundant. Fat buddhas appear everywhere, and 60cm-high Venus de Milos and multi-armed gods with flashing lights are not uncommon.

Lots of shops sell medicinal herbs and spices. Export tea is sold in extravagantly decorated tins – you can often get a better deal buying the same thing at railway stations.

Chinese Cuisine

China harbours a diverse range of culinary styles, and between them all somehow almost everything ends up in the pot. As the Cantonese proudly declaim: 'If it's got four legs and it's not a table, we'll eat it'. For the most part, however, the pangolins, raw monkey brains and bear paws of legend rarely find their way on to the tables of Chinese restaurants (very few people can afford such delicacies), and the Chinese trick is doing ingenious things with a limited number of basic ingredients.

Chinese cuisine can broadly be divided into four major regional categories which follow a north, south, east, west orientation: Beijing and Shandong (sometimes called Mandarin), Cantonese and Chaozhou, Eastern (Shanghainese and Jiangzhenese) and Sichuan.

Beijing & Shandong

Beijing and Shandong cuisine comes from one of the coldest parts of China. Since this is China's wheat belt, steamed bread and noodles are the staples rather than rice. Basically, northern cuisine combines very simple cooking techniques (stir-frying and steaming) with the sophistication of imperial dishes.

China's most famous northern speciality is Beijing duck, served with pancakes and plum sauce. Another specialty is beggar's chicken, supposedly created by a beggar who stole a chicken earmarked for the emperor and secretly cooked it buried underground (the chicken that is, not the beggar) – the dish is wrapped in lotus leaves and baked all day in hot ashes.

Cantonese & Chaozhou

This is southern Chinese cooking – lots of steaming, boiling and stir-frying. It's the best of the bunch if you're worried about cholesterol, as it uses the least amount of oil. It's lightly cooked and not as highly spiced as the other three, with lots of seafood, vegetables, roast pork, chicken, steamed fish and fried rice.

Dim sum is a snack-like variation, served for breakfast and lunch (but never dinner) and consisting of all sorts of little delicacies served from pushcarts wheeled around the restaurant floor. It's justifiably famous and something you should experience at least once, but like many visitors you'll probably get addicted.

The Cantonese are famous for making just about anything palatable: specialities are abalone, dried squid, 1000 year eggs (traditionally made by soaking eggs in horse's urine), shark's fin soup, snake soup and dog stew.

Other culinary exotica include anteaters, pangolins, cats, rats, owls, monkeys, turtles and frogs.

JULIET COOMBE/LA BELLE AURORE

GLENN BEANLAND

Top: Eggs for sale at a street stall in Suzhou (Jiangsu Province).

Bottom: Wuxi spare ribs, a speciality of Jiangsu Province, are cooked in a stock of soy sauce and rice wine.

CHINESE CUISINE

JULIET COOMBE/LA BELLE AURORE

Top: Fish cakes, noodles, chillies and vegetables stir-fried on the street in Shanghai.

Bottom: Shark fin soup, a popular Cantonese speciality.

GLENN BEANLAND

JULIET COOMBE/LA BELLE AURORE

GLENN BEANLAND

Top: Buns steaming in bamboo trays in Ji'nan (Shandong Province).

Bottom: Northern China's most famous dish, Beijing Duck, served with pancakes and plum sauce.

CHINESE CUISINE

JULIET COOMBE/LA BELLE AURORE

MARIE CAMBON

GLENN BEANLAND

Top: Chillies are a familiar offering at street markets.

Middle: Noodles handmade on the street in a Kaifeng (Henan Province) night market.

Bottom: Chicken with peanuts and chilli (gōngbǎo jīdīng) is one of Sichuan's best known and most popular dishes.

Eastern

The cuisine of eastern China is probably the least understood of China's regional cuisines – by foreigners at least. It encompasses Shanghai, Zhejiang, Fujian and the so-called lower-Yangzi region of Jiangsu. It is undoubtedly the most diverse of China's regional cuisines and has produced many famous dishes. Wuxi spare ribs is one to look out for; it features the common eastern technique of 'red cooking' in a stock of soy sauce and rice wine to produce a tasty stew. Soups are a celebrated aspect of eastern cuisine, and there are hundreds of varieties. In the coastal regions, seafood is an important ingredient and is generally cooked simply to enhance the natural taste.

It is true that stir-fried dishes in this part of China (famously Shanghai) tend to overdo the oil or lard, but in many restaurants nowadays this is becoming less the case. Cooking standards in major eastern cities have improved immensely over the last 10 years or so, and anyone with some money to throw around can enjoy some of the best cooking in China.

Sichuan

Sichuan cuisine is world-famous and in a class of its own. The Chinese claim that it comprises more than 4000 dishes, of which over 300 are said to be famous. It's easily China's hottest and spiciest cuisine, often using *huājiāo*, literally 'flower pepper', a crunchy little item that leaves a numbing and strangely unfamiliar aftertaste – some compare it to spicy detergent.

Sichuan chefs have a catch-cry that draws attention to the diversity of Sichuanese cooking styles: '*bǎicài, bǎiwèi*', literally 'a hundred dishes, a hundred flavours'. Whether 'a hundred flavours' is a characteristic Chinese exaggeration or not is difficult to say. There is, nevertheless, a bewildering cornucopia of Sichuanese sauces and culinary-preparation techniques.

Some of the more famous varieties are *yúxiāng wèi*, a really tasty fish-flavoured sauce that draws heavily on vinegar, soy sauce and mashed garlic and ginger; *málà wèi*, a numbingly spicy sauce that is often prepared with bean curd; *yānxūn wèi*, a 'smoked flavour' sauce, of which the most justifiably famous is that used with smoked duck; and, perhaps most famous of all, the hot and sour sauce *(suānlà wèi)*. The hot and sour soup, *suānlà tāng*, is eaten throughout China and is great on a cold day.

A famous dish is spicy chicken fried with peanuts *(gōngbào jīdīng)*. Equally well known is *mápō dòufu*, which is bean curd, pork and chopped spring onions in a chilli sauce. A favourite with travellers and worth trying simply for the novelty value is *guōbā ròupiàn*. Guoba refers to the crispy bits of rice, uncannily similar to Rice Krispies, that stick to the bottom of the rice pot – they are put on a plate, and pork and gravy added in front of the diner.

CHINESE CUISINE

Getting There & Away

AIR

Airports & Airlines

China has 115 ports of entry and exit, offering you a wide choice of travel options. However, the majority of travellers still make their approach and getaway via Hong Kong.

The attitude of the Chinese government has always been to keep lucrative business for itself. Foreigners are just thrown a few scraps, and even this is done grudgingly. This attitude certainly applies to the airline business – very few foreign carriers are permitted to fly into China, and even this was only reluctantly conceded so that China's own airlines could gain access to foreign markets. The lion's share of the market has been given to China's state-owned airlines, and one result is that prices are high and discounts hard to come by.

The grand exception of course is Hong Kong, where there is considerable free market competition and therefore lower prices. Now that Hong Kong has been re-unified with China, there is speculation that airfares will rise to Chinese levels, but that has not (as yet) happened. Macau is another option for cheapish fares, although the actual number of flights to Macau is very small.

The Civil Aviation Administration of China (*zhōngguó mínháng*), also known as CAAC, is the official flag carrier of the PRC. On most international routes, CAAC is known as Air China. In the very recent past, Air China's standard of service and safety record was abysmal, but the past few years have seen significant improvements.

Cathay Pacific (*guótài hángkōng*) is a Hong Kong-based company partly owned by British Airways and (recently) CAAC. Except for Hong Kong, Cathay doesn't fly into China under its own name, but runs a joint venture with CAAC to operate Hong Kong's other airline, Dragonair.

Dragonair (*gǎnglóng hángkōng*) started operations in 1985 with a single aircraft. Owned 100% by the PRC, there was much speculation that it would go bankrupt, and it probably would have if Cathay Pacific hadn't bought into it in 1990. Cathay apparently did this to please the Chinese government and to gain air routes to China. Cathay's influence is certainly visible – these days Dragonair's service is top-notch.

As Dragonair is closely integrated with

Warning

The information in this chapter is particularly vulnerable to change: China's continued economic growth has been accompanied by steadily advancing inflation, prices for international travel are volatile, routes are introduced and cancelled, schedules change, special deals come and go, and rules and visa requirements are amended.

Airlines and governments seem to take a perverse pleasure in making price structures and regulations as complicated as possible. You should check directly with the airline or a travel agent to make sure you understand how a fare (and the ticket you may buy) works. In addition, the travel industry is highly competitive and there are many lurks and perks.

The upshot of this is that you should get opinions, quotes and advice from as many airlines and travel agents as possible before you part with your hard-earned cash. The details given in this chapter should be regarded as pointers and are not a substitute for your own careful, up-to-date research. ■

Cathay Pacific, you can book Dragonair flights from Cathay Pacific offices around the world. Also, you can book combined tickets – a seat from Beijing to Vancouver, for example, flying Dragonair from Beijing to Hong Kong and then switching to a Cathay Pacific flight to Canada. Both flights can be included on a single ticket and luggage checked all the way through. If you're a member of Cathay's frequent-flier programme (known as the 'Marco Polo Club'), flights on Dragonair can be credited to your mileage total.

Buying Tickets

The air ticket alone can gouge a great slice out of anyone's budget, but you can reduce the cost by finding discounted fares. These days, stiff competition has resulted in widespread discounting – good news for travellers! The only people likely to be paying full fare are travellers flying in first or business class. Passengers flying in economy can usually weasel some sort of discount.

But not in China! Tickets purchased within China are invariably more expensive (usually much more) than those purchased elsewhere. A London-Beijing return-trip ticket may cost twice as much if bought in Beijing than if bought in London. Again, Hong Kong and Macau are exceptions – air fares from those two cities are as cheap as anything you can find in western countries.

Even when you buy the ticket outside of China, it's still going to cost more than it should. Tickets to Hong Kong and Macau are significantly cheaper than tickets to other parts of China, but flying to Hong Kong won't be much of a bargain if you have to purchase an additional air ticket to get to Beijing.

There are plenty of discount tickets which are valid for 12 months, allowing multiple stopovers with open dates. These tickets allow maximum flexibility. Few such tickets are available in China, but look out for these bargains in Hong Kong and Macau. All sorts of special packages are available that allow you a prolonged stopover in Hong Kong on the way to somewhere else. The Hong Kong stopover may cost nothing, or perhaps US$50 extra. Return-trip tickets are usually significantly cheaper than one way.

When you're looking for bargain air fares, you have to go to a travel agent rather than directly to the airline, which can only sell fares at the full list price. But watch out – many discount tickets have restrictions (the journey must be completed in 60 days, no flights during holidays, and so on). It's important to ask the agent if restrictions apply to your ticket.

The danger with ticket discounters is that some of them are unsound. Sometimes backstairs, over-the-shop travel agents fold up and disappear after you've handed over the money and before you've got the tickets. When purchasing a ticket from a small-time operator, it's wise to take a few precautions. You're safer if you pay with a credit card – if they don't accept credit cards, that's a danger sign, although it's not absolute proof of dishonesty. Agents who only accept cash should hand over the tickets straight away, and not tell you to 'come back tomorrow'. After you've made a booking or picked up the tickets, call the airline and confirm that the booking was made. All this might sound like excessive paranoia – and perhaps it is – but remember that it's your money on the line.

If you purchase a ticket and later want to make changes to your route or get a refund, you need to see the original travel agent. Airlines only issue refunds to the purchaser of a ticket – if you bought from a travel agent, then that agent is the purchaser, not you. Many travellers do in fact change their route halfway through their trip, so think carefully about buying a ticket which is not easily refunded.

Group Tickets The so-called 'group tickets' are well worth considering. You usually do *not* need to travel with a group. However, once the departure date is booked it may be impossible to change – you can only depart when the 'group' departs, even if you never meet or see another group member.

Air Travel Glossary

Apex Apex (Advance Purchase EXcursion) is a discounted ticket which must be paid for in advance. There are penalties if you wish to change it.

Baggage Allowance This will be written on your ticket and usually includes one 20kg item to go in the hold, plus one item of hand luggage.

Bucket Shop This is an unbonded travel agency specialising in discounted airline tickets.

Budget Fare These can be booked at least three weeks in advance, but the travel date is not confirmed until seven days prior to travel.

Bumped Just because you have a confirmed seat doesn't mean you're going to get on the plane (see Overbooking).

Cancellation Penalties If you have to cancel or change an Apex ticket there are often heavy penalties involved; insurance can sometimes be taken out against these penalties. Some airlines impose penalties on regular tickets as well, particularly against 'no-show' passengers (see No-Shows).

Check In Airlines ask you to check in a certain time ahead of the flight departure (usually one to two hours on international flights). If you fail to check in on time and the flight is overbooked, the airline can cancel your booking and give your seat to somebody else.

Confirmation Having a ticket written out with the flight and date you want doesn't mean you have a seat until the agent has checked with the airline that your status is 'OK' or confirmed. Meanwhile you could just be 'on request' (see On Request).

Courier Fares Businesses often need to send urgent documents or freight securely and quickly. Courier companies hire people to accompany the package through Customs and, in return, offer a discount ticket which is sometimes a phenomenal bargain. In effect, what the companies do is ship their freight as your luggage on the regular commercial flights. This is a legitimate operation, but there are two shortcomings – the short turnaround time of the ticket (usually not longer than a month) and the limitation on your luggage allowance. You may have to surrender all your allowance and take only carry-on luggage.

Discounted Tickets There are two types of discounted fares – officially discounted (see Promotional Fares) and unofficially discounted. The lowest prices often impose drawbacks like flying with unpopular airlines, inconvenient schedules or unpleasant routes and connections. Discounted tickets only exist where there is fierce competition.

Economy Class Tickets Economy-class tickets are usually not the cheapest way to go, although they do give you maximum flexibility and they are valid for 12 months. If you don't use them, most are fully refundable, as are unused sectors of a multiple ticket.

Full Fares Airlines traditionally offer 1st class (coded F), business class (coded J) and economy class (coded Y) tickets. These days there are so many promotional and discounted fares available from the regular economy class that few passengers pay full economy fare.

ITX An 'independent inclusive tour excursion' is often available on tickets to popular holiday destinations. Officially it's a package deal combined with hotel accommodation, but many agents will sell you one of these for the flight only and give you phoney hotel vouchers in the unlikely event that you're challenged at the airport.

Lost Tickets If you lose your airline ticket an airline will usually treat it like a travellers cheque and, after inquiries, issue you with another one. Legally, however, an airline is entitled to treat it like cash and if you lose it then it's gone forever. Take good care of your tickets.

MCO A 'miscellaneous charge order' is a voucher that looks like an airline ticket, but carries no destination or date. It can be exchanged through any International Association of Travel Agents (IATA) airline for a ticket on a specific flight. It's a useful alternative to an onward ticket in those countries that demand one, and is more flexible than an ordinary ticket if you're unsure of your route.

No-Shows No-shows are passengers who fail to show up for their flight. Full-fare passengers who fail to turn up are sometimes entitled to travel on a later flight. The rest of us are penalised (see Cancellation Penalties).

On Request This is an unconfirmed booking for a flight (see Confirmation).

Open Jaws This is a return ticket where you fly out to one place, but return from another. If available, this can save you backtracking to your arrival point.

Overbooking Airlines hate to fly with empty seats and since every flight has some passengers who fail to show up (see No-Shows), airlines often book more passengers than they have seats. Usually excess passengers make up for the no-shows, but occasionally somebody gets bumped. Guess who it is most likely to be? The passengers who check in late.

Point-to-Point This is a discount ticket that can be bought on some routes in return for passengers waiving their rights to stopover.

Promotional Fares These are officially discounted fares like Apex fares, available from travel agents or directly from the airline.

Reconfirmation At least 72 hours prior to departure time of an onward or return flight, you must contact the airline and 'reconfirm' that you intend to be on the flight. If you don't do this the airline can delete your name from the passenger list and you could lose your seat.

Restrictions Discounted tickets often have various restrictions on them – advance purchase is the most usual one (see Apex). Others are restrictions on the minimum and maximum period you must be away, such as a minimum of 14 days or a maximum of one year (see Cancellation Penalties).

Round-the-World An RTW ticket is just that. You have a limited period in which to circumnavigate the globe and you can go anywhere the carrying airlines go, as long as you don't backtrack. These tickets are usually valid for one year, the number of stopovers or total number of separate flights is worked out before you set off and they often don't cost much more than a basic return flight.

Stand-By This is a discounted ticket where you only fly if there is a seat free at the last moment. Stand-by fares are usually only available on domestic routes.

Tickets Out An entry requirement for many countries is that you have a ticket out of the country. If you're unsure of your next move, the easiest solution is to buy the cheapest onward ticket to a neighbouring country or a ticket from a reliable airline which can later be refunded if you do not use it. (See also MCO.)

Transferred Tickets Airline tickets cannot be transferred from one person to another. Travellers sometimes try to sell the return half of their ticket, but officials can ask you to prove that you are the person named on the ticket. This is unlikely to happen on domestic flights in most countries (except China, where passports *are* checked on domestic flights), but on an international flight tickets are usually compared with passports.

Travel Agencies Travel agencies vary widely and you should choose one that suits your needs. Some simply handle tours, while full-service agencies handle everything from tours and tickets to car rental and hotel bookings. If all you want is a ticket at the lowest possible price, then go to an agency specialising in discounted tickets.

Travel Periods Some officially discounted fares, Apex fares in particular, vary with the time of year. There is often a low (off-peak) season and a high (peak) season. Sometimes there's an intermediate or shoulder season as well. Usually the fare depends on your outward flight – if you depart in the high season and return in the low season, you pay the high-season fare. ■

The good news is that the return date can usually be left open, but there could be other restrictions – you might have to complete the trip in 60 days, or perhaps can only fly off season or during weekdays. As always, it's important to ask the travel agent what conditions and restrictions apply to any tickets you intend to buy.

Student, Teacher & Youth Fares Some airlines offer discounts of up to 25% holders for holders of student cards, youth cards and teacher cards. In addition to the card, some airlines may even ask for a letter from your school. These discounts are generally only available on ordinary economy-class fares. You wouldn't get one, for instance, on an APEX or a RTW ticket since these are already discounted.

For information about fares for children see Travellers with Special Needs further on in this chapter.

Frequent Flier Most airlines offer frequent flier deals that can earn you a free air ticket or other goodies. To qualify, you have to accumulate sufficient mileage with the same airline.

First, you must apply to the airline for a frequent-flier account number (some airlines will issue these on the spot or by telephone if you call their head office). Every time you buy an air ticket and/or check in for your flight, you must inform the clerk of your frequent-flier account number, or else you won't get credit. Save your tickets and boarding passes, since it's not uncommon for the airlines to fail to give proper credit.

You should receive monthly statements by post informing you how much mileage you've accumulated. Once you've accumulated sufficient mileage to qualify for freebies, you are supposed to receive vouchers by mail.

Many airlines have 'blackout periods', or times when you cannot fly for free (Christmas and Chinese New Year are good examples). The worst thing about frequent flier programs is that these tend to

lock you into one airline, and that airline may not always have the cheapest fares or most convenient flight schedule.

Courier Flights Courier flights are a great bargain if you're lucky enough to find one. The way it works is that an air freight company takes over your entire checked baggage allowance. You are permitted to bring along a carry-on bag, but that's all. In return, you get a steeply discounted ticket.

There are other restrictions – courier tickets are sold for a fixed date and schedule changes can be difficult or impossible to make. If you buy a return trip ticket, your schedule will be even more rigid. You need to get it all clear beforehand just what restrictions apply to your ticket, and don't expect a refund once you've paid.

Booking a courier ticket takes some effort. They are limited in availability, and arrangements have to be made a month or more in advance. You won't find courier flights on all routes either – major routes like London–Hong Kong or New York–Shanghai offer the best possibilities.

Courier flights are occasionally advertised in the newspapers, or you could contact air freight companies listed in the phone book. You may even have to go to the air freight company to get an answer – they aren't always keen to give out information over the phone. Another possibility (at least for US residents) is to join the International Association of Air Travel Couriers (IAATC). The membership fee of $45 gets members a bimonthly update of air courier offerings, access to a fax-on-demand service with daily updates of last minute specials and the bimonthly newsletter, *The Shoestring Traveler*.

For more information contact IAATC (☎ (407) 582-8320), 8 South J Street, PO Box 1349, Lake Worth, FL 33460, USA. However, be aware that joining this organisation does not guarantee that you'll successfully get a courier flight.

Buying Tickets Online The big Internet boom has created a new market for air tickets which can be purchased online. However, our experience with online ticket sales has been less than impressive. You can spend an awful amount of time tracking down the ticket you want, only to find you could have gotten something cheaper by visiting your nearest travel agent.

Nevertheless, a few hours Web surfing can help you find out approximately what you can expect in the way of budget fares. At least it's a good start for when you're ready to start negotiating with your favourite travel agency.

The airlines also have their own Web sites. This is no place to look for discounts, but airline Web sites can be interesting nonetheless. A few to try include British Airways (www.british-airways.com/), Canadian Airlines (www.cdnair.ca), Air France (www.airfrance.fr), Air New Zealand (www.airnz.com) and Singapore Airlines (www.newasia-singapore.com).

To find some useful travel Web sites, see the listings for individual countries in this chapter.

Back-to-Front Tickets These should be avoided. Back-to-front tickets are best explained by example. If you are living as an expat in Beijing (where tickets are very expensive) and you want to fly to London for a holiday (where tickets are much cheaper), you can (theoretically) pay by cheque or credit card and have a friend or travel agent in London mail the ticket to you.

The problem is that the airlines have computers and will know that the ticket was issued in London rather than Beijing and they will refuse to honour it. Consumer groups have filed lawsuits over this practice with mixed results, but in most countries the law protects the airlines, not consumers. In short, the ticket is only valid starting from the country where it was issued. The only exception is if you pay the full fare, thus forgoing any possible discounts that London travel agents can offer.

Be careful that you don't fall foul of these back-to-front rules when purchasing air tickets by post or through the Internet.

Second-Hand Tickets You'll occasionally see advertisements on various youth hostel bulletin boards and sometimes in newspapers for 'second-hand tickets'. That is, somebody purchased a return ticket or one with multiple stop-offs, and now wants to sell the unused portion of the ticket.

The prices offered look very attractive indeed. Unfortunately, these tickets are usually worthless. The name on the ticket must match the name on the passport of the person checking in. Some people reason that the seller of the ticket can check you in with his or her passport, and then give you the boarding pass – wrong again! Usually the immigration people want to see your boarding pass, and if it doesn't match the name in your passport then you won't be able to board your flight.

This begs the question – what happens if you purchase a ticket and then change your name? It can indeed happen – some people change their name when they get married (or divorced) and some people change their name because they feel like it. If the name on the ticket doesn't match the name in your passport, you could have problems. In this case, be sure you at least have documentary proof (your old passport, perhaps) to prove that the old you and the new you are the same person.

Travellers with Special Needs
Most international airlines can cater to special needs – travellers with disabilities, people with young children and even children travelling alone.

Special dietary preferences (vegetarian, kosher etc) can also be catered for with advance notice. However, the 'special meals' usually aren't very special – basically you get a salad and fruit plate.

Airlines usually carry babies up to two years of age at 10% of the relevant adult fare, although a few may carry them free of charge. Reputable international airlines usually provide nappies (diapers), tissues, talcum and all the other paraphernalia needed to keep babies clean, dry and half-happy. For children between the ages of two and 12 the fare on international flights is usually 50% of the regular fare or 67% of a discounted fare.

USA

There are some very good open tickets which remain valid for six months or one year (opt for the latter unless you're sure), but don't lock you into any fixed dates of departure. For example, there are cheap tickets between the US west coast and Hong Kong, with stopovers in Japan, Korea or Taiwan, and for very little extra money the departure dates can be changed and you have one year to complete the journey.

However, be careful during the high season (summer and Chinese New Year) because seats will be hard to come by unless reserved months in advance.

Discounters in the USA are known as 'consolidators' (although you won't see a sign on the door saying 'Consolidator'). Usually, and not surprisingly, the cheapest fares to China are offered by consolidators owned by the ethnic Chinese. San Francisco is the ticket consolidator capital of America, although some good deals can be found in Los Angeles, New York and other big cities. Bucket shops can be found through the Yellow Pages or the major daily newspapers. Those with listings in both Roman and Chinese scripts are usually discounters.

A more direct way is to wander around San Francisco's Chinatown, where most of the shops are located, especially in the Clay St and Waverly Place area. Many of these are staffed by recent arrivals from Hong Kong and Taiwan who may speak little English. Inquiries are best made in person, and be sure to compare prices, as cheating is not unknown.

It's not advisable to send money (even cheques) through the post unless the agent is very well established – some travellers have reported being ripped off by fly-by-night mail-order ticket agents.

Council Travel (☎ (800) 226-8624; www.ciee.org) is America's largest student travel organisation, but you don't have to be a student to use it. Council Travel has an extensive network in all major US cities – look in the phone book or check out their Web site.

One of the cheapest and most reliable travel agents on the US west coast is Overseas Tours (☎ (415) 692-4892; www.overseastours.com) in Millbrae, California. Another good agent is Gateway Travel (☎ (214) 960-2000, (800) 441-1183). It's headquartered in Dallas, Texas, but has branches in many major US cities.

From the US west coast, budget one way fares to Hong Kong start at around US$385 and return tickets begin at US$660 – these fares increase dramatically during the summer and Chinese New Year. To Beijing, return fares from San Francisco begin at US$858. From New York to Hong Kong, fares start at US$408 one way and US$770 return. New York-Beijing fares start at US$1100 return.

Canada

As in the USA, Canadian discount air ticket sellers are known as 'consolidators'. Airfares from Canada tend to be about 10% higher than from the USA.

Travel Cuts is Canada's national student travel agency and has offices in all major cities. You don't have to be a student to use their services. You can find them in the phone directory, ring the Toronto office (☎ (416) 977-5228), or visit their Web site (www.travelcuts.com).

Other agencies that have gotten good reviews are Avia (☎ (514) 284-5040) in Montreal, and Mar Tours (☎ (416) 536-5458) in Toronto.

Canadian Airlines is worth trying for cheap deals to Hong Kong, although Korean Air may still be able to undercut it. Canadian Airlines has long had the cheapest flights from Vancouver to Beijing.

Besides numerous flights to Hong Kong, CAAC has two flights a week which originate in Toronto, then fly onward to Vancouver, Shanghai and Beijing (in that order).

Australia

Australia is not a particularly cheap place to fly out of, but from time to time there are some good deals going. Shop around, as ticket prices vary.

The high season for most flights from Australia to Asia is from 22 November to 31 January; if you fly out during this period expect to pay more for your ticket.

Generally speaking, buying a round-trip air ticket works out cheaper than paying for separate one way tickets for each stage of your journey, although return tickets are more expensive the longer their validity. Most return tickets to Asia have 28 day, 90 day or 12 month validity.

Cheap flights from Australia to China generally go via one of the South-East Asian capitals, such as Kuala Lumpur, Bangkok or Manila. If a long stopover between connections is necessary, transit accommodation is sometimes included in the price of the ticket, but if it's at your own expense, it may work out cheaper buying a slightly dearer ticket.

Quite a few travel offices specialise in discount air tickets. Some travel agents, smaller ones particularly, advertise cheap air fares in the travel sections of weekend newspapers, such as *The Age* and the *Sydney Morning Herald*.

Two well known discounters are STA Travel and the Flight Centre. STA Travel (www.sta-travel-group.com) is one of the more reliable travel agents and has offices in all major cities and on many university campuses, but you don't have to be a student to use its services. The Sydney branch (☎ (02) 9212 1255) is at 855 George St, Ultimo, NSW 2007, and the Melbourne branch (☎ (03) 9349 2411) is at 222 Faraday St, Carlton, VIC 3053. Flight Centre (☎131 600; www.flightcentre.com. au) has dozens of offices throughout Australia and New Zealand. Both companies regularly publish brochures with their latest deals.

The minimum low-season air fare from Australia to Hong Kong is about A$840 one way, or A$1100 return. Air China flies direct from Melbourne and Sydney to Beijing (via Guangzhou) for $A1100/1320 return low/high season.

New Zealand

The Flight Centre has a large central office (☎ 309-6171) at 3A National Bank Tower, 205-25 Queen St, Auckland.

Currently, low-season one way/return fares to Hong Kong were NZ$989/1345. Garuda Airlines has lately been offering the cheapest fare to Beijing – NZ$1360 round-trip during low season.

UK

Air-ticket discounters are affectionately known as 'bucket shops' in the UK. Despite the somewhat disreputable name, there is nothing under-the-counter about this business. There are a number of magazines in the UK which have good information about flights and agents. These include: *Trailfinder*, free from the Trailfinders Travel Centre in Earl's Court; and *Time Out*, a London weekly entertainment guide widely available in the UK. The best deals are available in London.

When purchasing a ticket from a bucket shop that looks a little unsound, make sure they are bonded and belong to the Association of British Travel Agents, as well as the Air Travel Organiser's Licensing (ATOL) government agency.

Some recommended London bucket shops include: Trailfinders Travel Centre (☎ (0171) 938-3939) in Kensington High St; Council Travel (☎ (0171) 437-7767); Platinum Travel (☎ (0171) 937-5122); and STA Travel (☎ (0171) 938-4711). Campus Travel (☎ (0171) 730-7285; www.campus travel.co.uk) has 44 offices in the UK and 150 worldwide. Flight Bookers (☎ (0171) 757-2444; www.flightbookers.co.uk) is another biggie.

Internet Travel Services (www.its.net/ta/ home.htm) has a very good Web site with many travel agencies listed. The list includes courier companies in the UK.

A one way, direct London-Hong Kong ticket will cost around £330 and a return ticket around £550 in the low season. Indirect flights are less expensive. The competitive nature of this route ensures that carriers bring out regular specials, with prices from as low as £420 return.

Air China has fares from London to Beijing for around £275 one way and £450 return. It's also possible to fly to Melbourne or Sydney via Hong Kong for as low as £385 one way or £690 return.

Continental Europe

Western Europe Fares similar to those from London are available from other Western European cities.

Austrian Airlines offers an open-jaw ticket from Vienna that allows you to fly to Ürümqi (in China's Xinjiang Province), travel overland and fly back from Beijing.

The Netherlands, Belgium and Switzerland are good places for buying discount air tickets. In Antwerp, WATS has been recommended. In Zurich, try SSR (☎ (01) 297-1111). In Geneva, there's Stohl Travel. In the Netherlands, NBBS (☎ (071) 253333) is a reputable agency.

In France, OTU is a student organisation with 42 offices around the country. You can contact its Paris office (☎ 1 43 36 80 47). Another recommended agent in Paris is Council Travel (☎ 1 42 66 20 87).

CAAC has flights between Beijing and Berlin, Frankfurt, London, Milan, Moscow, Paris, Rome, Stockholm and Zurich. Other international airlines operate flights out of Beijing, but there are very few, if any, cut-rate fares from the Chinese end.

Eastern Europe Eastern European countries with functioning airlines that fly to China include Poland (LOT Polish Airlines) and Serbia (JAT Yugoslav Airlines). Both are reputed to be cheap, but travellers have reported problems with lost luggage.

Russia Any air ticket you buy in Russia is likely to be expensive. You're not paying for fine service, you're paying for the lack of competition. The situation is much like in China. British Airways flies London-

Moscow, but the ticket costs twice as much if you buy it in Moscow as it costs in London. The Russian airline, Aeroflot, flies the same route – again, the purchase price in Moscow is just ridiculous.

No matter what you pay for the ticket, be forewarned that the Russian airline, Aeroflot, has a reputation for frequent cancellations, poor safety and lost luggage.

Foreigners are required to pay in dollars even for domestic flights within Russia – forget any rumours you've heard about cheap rouble-denominated tickets.

CAAC and Aeroflot have flights connecting Irkutsk (Siberia) with Shenyang (in China's Liaoning Province). Both airlines offer flights between Khabarovsk (Siberia) and Harbin (Heilongjiang Province). Both CAAC and Aeroflot offer weekly flights between Moscow and Ürümqi (via Novosibirsk) for US$260 – much cheaper than flying Moscow-Beijing!

Asia

Indonesia CAAC has flights originating in Jakarta which continue onwards to Surabaya and then to Guangzhou, Xiamen or Beijing. In Jakarta, Jalan Jaksa is the place to look for travel agencies specialising in discount tickets.

Japan CAAC has frequent flights from Beijing to Tokyo, Osaka, Fukuoka and Sendai. Some of these flights are direct and others are via Shanghai. Japan Airlines flies from Beijing and Shanghai to Tokyo, Osaka and Nagasaki. There are flights between Dalian and Fukuoka/Tokyo on All Nippon Airways. In Tokyo, you can try Council Travel (☎ (03) 3581-5517).

Kazakhstan CAAC has two flights a week between Ürümqi in Xinjiang Province and Almaty in Kazakhstan.

Malaysia CAAC has direct flights from Kuala Lumpur to Beijing, Guangzhou, Shanghai and Xiamen. There are also flights connecting Penang to Guangzhou and Xiamen.

Mongolia MIAT (Mongolia's airline) and CAAC run flights between Beijing and Ulaan Baatar for US$200/380 one way/return. The flight schedule is considerably reduced during the winter months.

Myanmar (Burma) There is a weekly flight from Beijing to Rangoon (Yangon) with a stopover in Kunming. You can pick up the flight in Kunming too, but you must have a visa for Myanmar – available in Beijing, not Kunming.

Nepal There are direct flights between Lhasa and Kathmandu three times a week costing US$200 one way.

Pakistan CAAC has direct flights from Beijing to Karachi once weekly. There are also CAAC flights twice a week between Ürümqi in Xinjiang Province and Islamabad.

Philippines CAAC has a twice weekly flight from Beijing to Manila and a weekly flight from Guangzhou to Manila. The cheapest option is the direct flight from Xiamen to Manila three times a week.

Singapore CAAC has flights from Singapore to Beijing, Chengdu, Guangzhou, Kunming, Shanghai and Xiamen.

South Korea Asiana Airlines, Korean Air and Air China operate routes from Seoul to Beijing, Dalian, Qingdao, Shanghai and Shenyang.

Some recommended discount travel

Paging Passenger Li

Of all the various problems that afflict China, one of the oddest is the fact that the country is running out of names.

Unlike the west, where name-giving got a new lease of life in the 1960s (think of rock star Prince, who changed his name to an ideogram which has no pronunciation), China has got stuck in a bit of a rut on the moniker front. Chinese academics point out that parents have to be more inventive with their kids' names if China is not to slip into a social quagmire of widespread mistaken identities.

Some Chinese people have four character names (two characters for the surname and two for the given name). Unfortunately, such people are the rare exception. The majority has just a one character surname and either one or two characters for the given name. On paper, China today has around 3100 surnames. Unfortunately, a quarter of the population of China share just five surnames: Li, Wang, Zhang, Liu and Chen. In Beijing alone, it's estimated that there are over 5000 individuals named Zhang Li and Liu Hui. With 1.25 billion people nationwide, it's not hard to see why so many people wind up with exactly the same name.

The problem is particularly acute in big cities, where thousands of people may share the same surname and given name, written in exactly the same characters. Chinese newspaper reports frequently bemoan wrongful arrests, bank account errors and unwanted surgery performed – all due to instances of mistaken identity.

The Chinese authorities constantly wring their hands in desperation at finding a solution. Academics have been consulted, and have proposed various ideas such as requiring children to adopt the surnames of both parents. Another proposal is to resurrect some of the 8000 surnames that were once in use in China, but have now become extinct – perhaps the authorities will assign them just like ID card numbers. Yet the easiest and undoubtedly most popular solution does not seem to have occurred to the authorities – how about just allowing individuals to change their name to whatever suits their fancy? ■

agencies in Seoul include: Joy Travel Service (☎ 776-9871; fax 756-5342), 10th floor, 24-2 Mukyo-dong, Chung-gu, Seoul (directly behind City Hall); and discounters on the 5th floor of the YMCA building on Chongno 2-ga (next to Chonggak subway station), including the Korean International Student Exchange Society (KISES; ☎ 733-9494) in room 505, and Top Travel (☎ 739-5231) in room 506. In It'aewon, you can try O&J Travel (☎ 792-2303; fax 796-2403), on the 2nd floor just above the Honey Bee Club.

Thailand CAAC offers flights between Bangkok and Beijing, Chengdu, Guangzhou, Kunming, Shanghai and Shantou.

Khao San Rd in Bangkok is budget travellers' headquarters and the place to look for bargain ticket deals.

Vietnam China Southern Airlines and Vietnam Airlines fly the China-Vietnam route. The only direct flight between Ho Chi Minh City and China is to Guangzhou. All other flights are via Hanoi. The Guangzhou-Hanoi flight (US$150 one way) takes 1½ hours; Guangzhou-Ho Chi Minh City (US$250 one way) takes 2½ hours. Return airfares cost exactly double.

The Beijing-Hanoi flight on China Southern Airlines stops at Nanning (capital of China's Guangxi Province) en route – you can board or exit the plane there.

Vietnam, like China, is not a good country for buying air tickets.

LAND
If you're starting from Europe or Asia, it's entirely possible to travel all the way to China and back without ever having to fasten your seatbelt and put out your cigarette. There are numerous interesting routes, including the Vietnam-China border crossing, the Trans-Siberian Railway from Europe, or the exotic Tibet to Nepal, Xinjiang to Pakistan and Xinjiang to Kazakhstan routes.

It is not yet possible to travel overland from Myanmar (Burma) to China. In the past you could enter Myanmar at the Ruili-

Muse checkpoint for a day trip, but the Myanmar authorities were refusing *everybody* entry when this book was being researched. See the Ruili section in the Yunnan chapter for details.

Trade between China and India occurs at the Indian bordertown of Garbyang, Uttar Pradesh, just north of the Nepalese border; unfortunately, military instability in the Kashmir region has nullified this option for travellers.

The borders with Afghanistan and Bhutan are out of bounds.

The possibility of bringing your own vehicle is a big muddle. Foreigners are not usually allowed to drive cars or motorbikes around China and are therefore not usually allowed to take them in. Bicycles are allowed on some routes, but not others – the regulations governing the use of bicycles is in a constant state of confusion. See the following Getting Around chapter for more information on cycling through China.

Hong Kong
Hong Kong is now part of China, but there is nevertheless a real border crossing at Lo Wu with Customs, immigration and the whole routine. This has long been the most popular entrance point to the PRC. For more detailed information, see the Hong Kong chapter.

Macau
On the other side of the border from Macau is the Special Economic Zone (SEZ) of Zhuhai. The Macau-Zhuhai border is open from 7 am to 9 pm, and cyclists can ride across. Most people just take a bus to the border and walk across.

For more details, see the Zhuhai section in the Guangdong chapter.

Pakistan
The Karakoram Highway stretches from Kashgar (in China's Xinjiang Province) to Islamabad. Pakistani visas are compulsory for visitors from most western countries. Visas are *not* given at the border. If going

from China to Pakistan, the closest place to get a Pakistani visa is in Hong Kong or Beijing. Chinese visas can be obtained in your own country, in Hong Kong or in Islamabad.

The following chart provides a rough guide to distances and average journey times:

Route	Distance	Duration
Kashgar-Tashkurgan	280km	6 hours
Tashkurgan-Pirali	84km	1½ hours
Pirali-Khunjerab (Sino-Pakistan border)	35km	1 hour
Khunjerab-Sust	86km	2¼ hours
Sust-Passu	35km	45 minutes
Passu-Gulmit	14km	20 minutes
Gulmit-Karimabad	37km	1 hour
Karimabad-Gilgit	98km	2 hours
Gilgit-Rawalpindi	631km	18 hours

China to Pakistan From 15 April to late October buses ply this high-altitude route. Landslides are common, and bus passengers have occasionally been killed by falling rocks. It's hard to imagine how you can protect yourself against this though – try either prayer beads or a hard hat. Also bring some warm clothes – it can be chilly at over 4000m.

Buses direct from Kashgar to the Pakistani border post at Sust (in Pakistan) leave from the Chini Bagh Hotel at about 11.30 am all through summer. From June to September buses are laid on, but earlier or later in the season there may not be buses on some days. There's an overnight stop in Tashkurgan (on the Chinese side). The same bus goes on to Sust the next day. There is an economy and high-class bus. There aren't many food stops, so bring a day's water and snacks.

Everything that goes on top of the bus is inspected by Customs at Chini Bagh and stays locked up for the entire journey. So carry on you whatever you want for the overnight stop, plus whatever you declared to Customs on entering China.

The bus stays overnight at Tashkurgan, where the Chinese Customs is located.

From Tashkurgan the road climbs higher

for the two hour stretch to Pirali (elevation 4200m), which isn't worth a stop. If you're on a Pakistani bus, you'll have no need to change buses; if you've taken the local bus from Kashgar, you'll need to change to a Pakistani bus from Pirali onwards.

Pakistan to China From Rawalpindi to Gilgit (a 15 hour trip) there are six buses daily. If you can't stand the pace of the bus ride, the flight between Rawalpindi and Gilgit runs at least once daily, weather permitting.

From Gilgit to Sust, there's a Northern Areas Transport Company (NATCO) bus; buy your ticket early on the morning of departure as the bus leaves at 8 am. In Sust, the best place to stay is the Mountain View Hotel, which has both dorms and more cushy private rooms.

From Sust to Pirali, there's a NATCO bus. Get your ticket from the NATCO office first thing in the morning – you'll need to show it to Customs.

At Pirali everyone changes to a Chinese bus to Kashgar. This bus stops overnight at Tashkurgan. Trucks offer lifts (negotiate the price); ditto for jeeps.

Some cyclists have succeeded in riding across the Pakistani border, some have had to put their bikes on a bus, and some have been refused permission altogether.

For further details, see Lonely Planet's *Karakoram Highway* guide.

Kazakhstan
Almaty to Ürümqi There is a direct daily bus service between Ürümqi (Xinjiang) and Almaty, and this is the cheapest way to travel between China and Kazakhstan.

On Monday and Saturday there is an international train from Ürümqi to Almaty, which returns the following day. Sleepers cost approximately US$75. In Ürümqi sleepers can be booked through travel agencies.

Almaty to Yining It's possible to travel overland by bus from Yining (in China's Xinjiang Province) to Panfilov in Kazakhstan, and then on to Almaty. The charge at the time of writing was US$35 by bus to Panfilov and then another US$35 on to Almaty – a ridiculous state of affairs when you consider that buses do the trip from Ürümqi for US$50. All things considered, it's probably better to organise things in Ürümqi, where you're less likely to get ripped off.

Local Kazakhs, Uighurs, Kyrgyz and others who have relatives on the other side of the border make this trip regularly and inexpensively. If you don't have a relative in Almaty, you'll find accommodation is very expensive.

Buses between Yining and Panfilov run daily from 1 May to 1 October via the border town of Korgas (hùochéng, or Khorgos in Russian). This road is actually open all year because of its low elevation, but winter storms could close it for a few days at a time. It's necessary to change buses in Panfilov to reach Almaty.

It may or may not be possible to spend the night in Panfilov, but the chances are that you will be forced to travel between Korgas and Almaty in one day. This is problematic because the border post is only open from 8.30 am to 4 pm. Crossing the other way into China should be no problem provided you have organised a Chinese visa beforehand, but at present this whole region is an unknown, with very few travellers making the trip.

Kyrgyzstan

Inquire about the possibility of a crossing between Bishkek (the capital of Kyrgyzstan) and Kashgar, via Turugart Pass (tǔ'ěrgǎtè shānkǒu). Government travel agencies have been quoting prohibitively high rates for doing the journey by car, but private entrepreneurs might be able to offer you a better deal.

Laos

From the Mengla district in China's southern Yunnan Province it is legal to enter Laos via Boten in Luang Nam Tha province if you possess a valid Lao visa. From Boten there are morning and afternoon buses onward to the provincial capitals of Luang Nam Tha and Udomxai, three and four hours away respectively.

The Lao consulate in Kunming, Yunnan, issues both seven day transit and 15 day tourist visas for Laos. These cost US$28 and US$50 respectively and take three to five days to process. You must bring four photos and already have a visa from a third country (such as Thailand) stamped in your passport. The majority of travellers from Kunming go via Jinghong to Mengla and thence to the border at Mohan. As the bus journey from Jinghong will take the better part of the day, you will probably have to overnight at Mengla. You may need a Lao visa even to enter Mengla county!

Myanmar (Burma)

The border between China and Myanmar at the Ruili-Muse checkpoint was definitely closed at the time of writing and there was no sign anything would change soon.

Nepal

The good news is that the road from Lhasa to Kathmandu reopened in 1993 after being closed to foreigners for over three years. The bad news is that there are still a few bureaucratic hurdles to clear – you will have to pay for an unwanted tour in Lhasa and there is a shortage of public transport on the Chinese side. Travel agents in Kathmandu can make all the arrangements.

The first problem is visas. Yes, you can get Chinese visas in Nepal, but you officially have to be booked on to an organised tour and you will definitely not be given more than one month. If possible, get your visa somewhere else (Hong Kong etc) and ask for a two month visa if you plan to do extensive travelling in China.

The next thing is the mandatory Lhasa tour. All foreigners wanting to visit Tibet must book a three day tour around Lhasa – whether they want it or not – for a cost of roughly US$100. This sounds cheap until you realise that the tour lasts about two hours a day for three days. The tour operator is usually unwilling to go anywhere until there are ten people in the group – if you travel solo, you may have to wait until enough other people arrive to make a quorum.

Transport is the next hurdle. Public buses operate on the Nepalese side right up to the border, but there's not much activity on the Tibetan side. People going from Lhasa to Nepal normally get to the border by rented jeep, and since the jeeps return home empty, the drivers are more than happy to find travellers waiting at the border looking for rides to Lhasa. Prices average out at Y700 to Y1000 per person to Lhasa, but there is a fair amount of latitude for bargaining. The problem is you might have to wait a while for an available jeep. There are regular bus services to Shigatse, from where there are daily buses to Lhasa, but buses between Lhasa and the border only run three or four times a month.

Walking from the border to Lhasa is not recommended, but going by bicycle might be feasible. The trouble is the Chinese authorities. Some travellers are allowed to go by bike and some aren't. The Chinese themselves do not seem to know the rules, and finding out what will be permitted next week or next month requires a knowledge of astrology, crystal ball reading or tarot cards.

For further details about transport on the Chinese side of the border, see the Tibet chapter of this book.

North Korea

You might want to see North Korea before it disappears – the country was in the grip of famine and near collapse at the time of writing. Visas are difficult to arrange, and at the time of writing it was totally impossible for US citizens.

The North Korean consulate in Beijing is worth a try, but if that doesn't work your best bet is probably Koryo Tours (☎ (10) 6595-8357; email: jgreen@iuol.cn.net), Kindly Commercial Center, 9 Jianguomenwai Dajie, Beijing 100020.

There are twice weekly trains between Beijing and Pyongyang, and at least two flights weekly on either Koryo Air or CAAC. Should you succeed in getting a North Korean visa, your time in that country will be both tightly controlled and expensive. For full details, see Lonely Planet's *Korea* guide.

Vietnam

In the finest bureaucratic tradition, travellers require a special visa for entering Vietnam overland from China. These visas cost double and take twice as long to issue as the normal tourist visas needed for entering Vietnam by air. Travellers who have tried to use a standard visa to enter Vietnam overland from China have fared poorly, and it no longer seems possible to bribe your way in.

Exiting from Vietnam to China is much simpler. The Chinese don't require anything more than a standard tourist visa, and Chinese visas do not indicate entry or exit points. However, your Vietnamese visa must have the correct exit point marked on it, a change which can easily be made in Hanoi. Ironically, it seems to be possible to bribe your way out.

The Vietnam-China border crossing is open from 7 am to 4 pm (Vietnam time) or 8 am to 5 pm China time. Set your watch when you cross the border – the time in China is one hour later than in Vietnam. Neither country observes daylight savings time. There are currently three border checkpoints, detailed below, where foreigners are permitted to cross between Vietnam and China. There is a possibility that more will open in the future.

Friendship Pass The busiest border crossing is at the Vietnamese town of Dong Dang, 164km from Hanoi. The closest Chinese town to the border is Pinxiang, but it's about 10km north of the actual border gate. The crossing point (Friendship Pass) is known as Huu Nghi Quan in Vietnamese or Youyi Guan in Chinese.

Dong Dang is an obscure town. The nearest city is Lang Son, 18km to the south. Buses and minibuses on the Hanoi-Lang

Son route are frequent. The cheapest way to cover the 18km between Dong Dang and Lang Son is to hire a motorbike for US$1.50. There are also minibuses cruising the streets looking for passengers. Just make sure they take you to Huu Nghi Quan and not to the other nearby checkpoint – this is the only one where foreigners can cross.

There is a Customs checkpoint between Lang Son and Dong Dang. Sometimes there are long delays here while officials gleefully rip apart the luggage of Vietnamese and Chinese travellers. For this reason, a motorbike might prove faster than a van since you won't have to wait for your fellow passengers to be searched. Note that this is only a problem when you're heading south towards Lang Son, not the other way.

On the Chinese side, it's a 20 minute drive from the border to Pinxiang by bus or share taxi – the cost for the latter is US$3. Pinxiang is connected by train to Nanning, capital of China's Guangxi Province. Trains to Nanning depart Pinxiang at 8 am and 1.30 pm. More frequent are the buses (once every 30 minutes) which take four hours to make the journey and cost US$4.

There is a walk of 600m between the Vietnamese and Chinese border posts.

A word of caution – because train tickets to China are expensive in Hanoi, travellers have bought a ticket to Dong Dang, walked across the border and then bought a Chinese train ticket on the Chinese side. This isn't the best way because it's several kilometres from Dong Dang to Friendship Pass, and you'll have to hire someone to take you by motorbike. If you're going by train, it's better to buy a ticket from Hanoi to Pinxiang, and then in Pinxiang get the ticket to Nanning or beyond.

Trains on the Hanoi-Dong Dang route run according to the following schedule:

No	Dep Dong Dang	Arr Hanoi
HD4	11.40 am	8 pm
HD2	5.40 pm	1.50 am

No	Dep Hanoi	Arr Dong Dang
HD3	5 am	1.30 pm
HD1	10 pm	5.10 am

There is also a twice weekly international train running between Beijing and Hanoi, which stops at Friendship Pass. You can board or exit the train at numerous stations in China. The entire Beijing-Hanoi run is 2951km and takes approximately 55 hours, including a three hour delay (if you're lucky) at the border checkpoint. Schedules are subject to change, but at present train No 5 departs Beijing at 11.20 pm on Monday and Friday, arriving in Hanoi at 6.30 am on Thursday and Monday, respectively. Going the other way, train No 6 departs Hanoi at 11 pm on Tuesday and Friday, arriving in Beijing at 9.21 am on Friday and Monday, respectively. The complete schedule follows:

Station	To Hanoi Train No 5	To Beijing Train No 6
Beijing	11.20 pm	9.21 am
Shijiazhuang	2.54 am	5.58 am
Zhengzhou	7.53 am	12.53 am
Xinyang	11.50 am	8.53 pm
Hankou (Wuhan)	2.59 pm	5.35 pm
Wuchang (Wuhan)	3.34 pm	4.56 pm
Yueyang	6.47 pm	1.46 pm
Changsha	8.56 pm	11.42 am
Hengyang	11.49 pm	8.46 am
Lengshuitan	2.07 am	6.26 am
Guilin North	5.38 am	2.31 am
Guilin	5.59 am	2.12 am
Liuzhou	8.45 am	11.07 pm
Nanning	3.10 pm	6.49 pm
Pinxiang	10.04 pm	noon
Friendship Pass	10 pm*	8 am*
Dong Dang	1 am*	5 am*
Hanoi	6.30 am*	11 pm*

* Vietnamese Time

Lao Cai-Hekou A 762km metre-gauge railway, inaugurated in 1910, links Hanoi with Kunming in China's Yunnan Province. The bordertown on the Vietnamese side is Lao Cai, 294km from Hanoi. On the Chinese side, the bordertown is called Hekou, 468km from Kunming.

At the time of writing, the Vietnamese and Chinese authorities were planning on starting a direct international train service between Hanoi and Kunming. However, at the time of writing the schedule was still not determined. If you want to take this train, make inquires in either Kunming or Hanoi. Most likely, this train will not run daily, but probably two or three times a week.

Of course, you needn't bother with the international trains. Domestic trains run daily on both sides of the border. On the Chinese side, Kunming-Hekou takes about 16 hours. Trains depart and arrive at Kunming's north railway station according to the following schedule:

No	Dep Kunming	Arr Hekou
313	9.30 pm	1.55 pm

No	Dep Hekou	Arr Kunming
314	2.45 pm	7.50 am

On the Vietnamese side, trains run according to the following schedule:

No	Dep Lao Cai	Arr Hanoi
LC4	9.40 am	8.20 pm
LC2	6 pm	4.25 am

No	Dep Hanoi	Arr Lao Cai
LC3	5.10 am	3.35 pm
LC1	9 pm	7.10 am

Mong Cai-Dongxing Vietnam's third, but little known, border crossing is at Mong Cai in the north-east corner of the country, just opposite the Chinese city of Dongxing. The two opposing bordertowns are not particularly attractive and westerners are a rare sight indeed. But if you're looking to escape the throngs of backpackers, this is one place to do it. There are no railway connections here, but buses on both sides of the border are functional.

On the Vietnamese side there are frequent minibuses between Mong Cai and Hon Gai (Halong Bay). On the Chinese side there are buses from Dongxing to Qinzhou, Nanning (via Qinzhou) or Beihai.

Trans-Siberian Railway
The Trans-Siberian Railway connects Europe to Asia. Its popularity has declined in recent years due to the general state of

chaos in Russia, plus rising prices. Nevertheless, it's an intriguing option and worth considering.

There is some confusion of terms here as there are, in fact, three railways. The 'true' Trans-Siberian line runs from Moscow to the eastern Siberian port of Nakhodka, from where one can catch a boat to Japan. This route does not go through either China or Mongolia. There is also the Trans-Manchurian line which crosses the Russia-China border at Zabaikalsk-Manzhouli, also completely bypassing Mongolia. The Trans-Mongolian line connects Beijing to Moscow, passing through the Mongolian capital city of Ulaan Baatar.

Most readers of this book will not be interested in the first option since it excludes China – your decision is basically between the Trans-Manchurian or the Trans-Mongolian; however, it makes little difference. The Trans-Mongolian (Moscow-Beijing, 7865km) is marginally faster, but requires you to purchase an additional visa and endure another border crossing, although you do at least get to see the Mongolian countryside roll past your window. The Trans-Manchurian is longer (Moscow-Beijing, 9001km).

Another option is the so-called 'Silk Route'. This involves taking a train from Moscow to Almaty in Kazakhstan, and then from Almaty to Ürümqi. This is an interesting trip, but is fraught with difficulties. For information about the Almaty-Ürümqi run, see the Kazakhstan section earlier in this chapter.

There are different classes, but all are acceptably comfortable. In deluxe class there are two beds per cabin while economy class has four beds.

Which direction you go makes a difference in cost and travelling time. The trains from Beijing take 1½ days to reach Ulaan Baatar. The journey from Moscow to Ulaan Baatar is four days.

There are delays (three to six hours) at both the China-Mongolia and the Russia-Mongolia borders. During this time, you can get off the train and wander around the station, which is just as well since the toilets on the train are locked during the whole inspection procedure. You will not have your passport at this time as the authorities take it away for stamping. When it is returned, inspect it closely – sometimes they make errors (like cancelling your return visa for China).

On the Chinese side of the Russian or Mongolian border, about two hours are spent changing the bogies (undercarriage wheels). This is necessary because Russia, Mongolia and all former Eastern Bloc countries use a wider rail gauge than China and the rest of the world. The reason has to do with security – it seems the Russians feared an invasion by train.

Tickets from Europe The best deals seem to be available in the UK from The Russia Experience (☎ (0181) 566-8846; www.travel. world.co.uk/), also known as T-rex. The people working here have all been on the Trans-Siberian and can tell you all about it.

The other main sources for budget tickets are STA Travel (www.sta-travel-group.com) and Campus Travel (www. campustravel.co.uk). Both have branches throughout Europe and can do tickets, although it's hardly likely you'll encounter any staff who have personal knowledge of the Trans-Siberian railway.

Tickets from China In theory, at least, the cheapest place to buy a ticket is at the office of China International Travel Service (CITS) in the Beijing Tourist Building (☎ 6515-8570; fax 6515-8603), at 28 Jianguomenwai Dajie, hidden behind the New Otani Hotel. Unfortunately, there are some tactical hurdles to buying a ticket from CITS. CITS offers no advance bookings – you must go to Beijing and make all your arrangements there. If you're lucky, you might get on a train a few days later. If unlucky, you will have to hang around a few weeks waiting for a vacant berth, although that is only likely to happen during the summer crunch period.

All tickets bought from CITS are straight through to Moscow (or Ulaan Baatar in Mongolia) – no stopovers are permitted. And contrary to what CITS brochures say, train tickets bought from CITS are non-refundable. If you can work within these limitations, CITS prices are as follows:

Beijing-Moscow, Chinese train (Trans-Mongolian), hard berth US$160, soft berth US$230

Beijing-Moscow, Russian train (Trans-Manchurian), hard berth US$158, luxury berth US$248

Beijing-Ulaan Baatar, hard berth US$68, soft berth US$79

These prices are deceptively cheap. You also need to arrange transport between Moscow and some point in Western Europe, and this is quite expensive for the short distance travelled. If you're coming from the direction of Beijing, you'll have three days in Moscow on a transit visa, and this is often *not* enough time to get your ticket out. You really need to book the ticket out of Moscow before you actually arrive in Moscow, otherwise you'll overstay your visa with draconian consequences. If you are forced to extend your visa in Moscow, it's going to be an expensive and bureaucratic experience. And you will pay through the nose for any tickets you purchase in Moscow, especially air tickets.

Your other alternative is to buy from a private travel agent. This will always be more expensive than CITS, but you gain a few important advantages. To begin with, you can purchase the ticket in advance without having to first go to Beijing and taking potluck. The better agencies can also arrange visas, stopover tours in Russia and Mongolia (complete with guides), local transport, food and accommodation. And they can book the Moscow-Western Europe leg of your journey too.

The best organised of the Trans-Siberian tour agents is Monkey Business, officially known as Moonsky Star (☎ 2723-1376; fax 2723-6653; www.monkeyshrine.com), 4th floor, Block E, Flat 6, Chungking Mansions, 30 Nathan Rd, Tsimshatsui, Kowloon. Monkey Business also has an information office in Beijing at Beijing Commercial Business Complex (☎ 6329-2244, ext 4406), Room 406, No 1 Building, Yulinli. However, it's best to book through its Hong Kong office as far in advance as possible. A booking can be done by telephone or fax and a deposit can be wired to them. One advantage of booking through them is that they keep all their passengers in a group (for mutual protection against theft). Furthermore, they can arrange visas and stopover tours to Mongolia and Irkutsk (Siberia). For more information, take a look at their Web site (www.monkey shrine.com).

Another Hong Kong agent selling Trans-Siberian tickets is Time Travel (☎ 2366-6222; fax 2739-5413), 16th floor, Block A, Chungking Mansions, 30 Nathan Rd, Tsimshatsui, Kowloon. Unfortunately, they offer nothing but bare-bones tickets – no visa service, no group tickets (so you might have Russian cabin-mates) and they don't offer stopover tours or onward tickets from Moscow.

You can organise tickets and visas through Wallem Travel (☎ 2528-6514), 46th floor, Hopewell Centre, 183 Queen's Rd East, Wanchai, Hong Kong. This place does organised tours, but is expensive.

Black-Market Tickets Once upon a time, black-market tickets were so common that it seemed like everyone on the train had one. Indeed, you were almost a fool not to buy one. The way it worked was that people with connections would go to Budapest and buy Beijing-Moscow tickets in bulk for around US$50 apiece, then take the tickets to Beijing and sell them for about US$150. It was a nice little business, while it lasted.

The good old days are gone. If you are approached in either Moscow or Beijing by people plugging black-market tickets on the Trans-Siberian, chances are 90% certain that you will be ripped off. Most likely, you will be sold a ticket denominated in roubles, which only Russian nationals can use.

Books A popular book about this journey is the *Trans-Siberian Handbook* by Bryn Thomas, published by Trailblazer Publications and distributed through Roger Lascelles in the UK. Another excellent book is Athol Yates' *Russia by Rail* (Bradt Publications, UK; The Globe Pequot Press, USA). Be sure to visit the Russia-Rail Web site (www.russia-rail.com).

Needs, Problems & Precautions Bring plenty of cash US dollars in small denominations for the journey – only in China can you readily use the local currency. In China, food is plentiful and readily available from both the train's dining car and vendors in railway stations. In both Russia and Mongolia, food quality is poorer, but meals are available on the train.

Once you get off the train it's a different story – food can be difficult to buy in Russia and Mongolia, especially once you get away from the capital cities. If you don't want to starve, bring along plenty of munchies like biscuits, instant noodles, chocolate and fruit. No alcohol is sold on the Russian and Mongolian trains, but a very limited selection of booze can be bought in the Chinese dining car.

Showers are only available in the deluxe carriages. In economy class, there is a washroom. You can manage a bath with a sponge, but it's best to bring a large metal cup (available in most Chinese railway stations) and use it as a scoop to pour water over yourself from the washbasin. The metal cup is also ideal for making coffee, tea and instant soup. Hot water is available on the trains.

There is much theft on the train, so never leave your luggage unattended, even if the compartment is locked. Make sure at least one person stays in the compartment while the others go to the dining car. A lot of theft is committed by Russian gangs who have master keys to the compartments, so don't assume that a 'western face' is a badge of honesty.

The luggage limit is 35kg per passenger and there is now some attempt being made to enforce this. Previously, the Trans-Siberian was little more than a freight train because traders were earning a living moving goods back and forth between Beijing and Moscow in the passenger compartments. Of course, the traders haven't given up entirely, and some will try to move their tonnes of 'luggage' into your compartment – don't allow it.

It's important to realise that food in the dining car is priced in local currency. This is true even in Mongolia or Russia. Many foreigners have the mistaken impression that they must pay in US dollars. The railway staff will gladly accept your dollars instead of local currency at some ridiculous exchange rate, which means you'll be paying many times the real price. There are black-market moneychangers at border railway stations, but all the usual dangers of black-market exchanges apply.

Visas can take several days each to issue, even longer if you can't show up at the embassy in person and want to apply through the post. If you just show up in Beijing the day before departure and think you can hop on a train without a visa, you're mistaken.

Russian Visas The burning question that many travellers ask is 'Can I stop off along the way?'. The answer is essentially 'No'. You can get a few days in Moscow on a transit visa, but stopping off elsewhere requires a tourist visa. The same problem applies to Mongolia.

Transit visas are valid for a maximum of 10 days, of which about seven days are used in the Beijing-Moscow run, leaving you only three days for the Moscow-Western Europe trip. Extending a visa in Russia is difficult and expensive – try to avoid it! To get an extension, you'll normally go through the hotel 'service bureau' (which in turn goes through Intourist) – the hotel will not help you unless you book your room for several days.

With a tourist visa, you can stay in Russia much longer, but you will pay heavily for the privilege. All hotels must be booked through Intourist in advance of arrival. Intourist insists that you stay at good hotels (read 'expensive'). The whole bureaucratic booking procedure takes about three weeks. On a transit visa, you can sleep in the railway station or in one of the rapidly proliferating cheap private hostels.

Before you can get a transit visa, you must have a ticket in hand or a ticket voucher. A transit visa can be issued in three working days for US$50; in two working days for US$80; or the same day for US$100.

Then there is also the bizarre 'consular fee' for certain nationalities. There is no logic here – Belgians pay a consular fee of US$12 for transit visas and US$33 for tourist visas, but Singaporeans pay US$9 for both kinds of visas. The Swiss pay US$18 for a transit visa, but get the tourist visa free. Israelis pay nothing for the transit visa, but must pay US$88 for a tourist visa. These fees go up and down like a toilet seat – we can't make any predictions how much you'll actually have to pay.

Someone can apply for the visa on your behalf and use a photocopy of your passport (all relevant pages must be included). If you want to change an already-issued transit visa, this will cost you US$30 (in five days) or US$50 (express service). Reasons for changing could be if you want go on a different date or change the final destination (Budapest instead of Berlin, for example).

Russian embassies are closed during all Russian public holidays: New Year's Day (1 January), Women's Day (8 March), Labour Day (1 and 2 May), Victory Day (9 May), Constitution Day (7 October) and October Revolution (7 and 8 November).

In Beijing, the Russian embassy (☎ 6532-2051, 6532-1267) is at Beizhongjie 4, just off Dongzhimen and west of the Sanlitun Embassy Compound. Opening hours are Monday to Friday from 9 am to noon. You can avoid the long queues at the Beijing embassy if you apply at the Russian consulate (☎ 6324-2682) in Shanghai, at 20

Huangpu Lu, opposite the Pujiang Hotel. However, its opening hours are brief: Tuesday and Thursday from 10 am until 12.30 pm.

The Russian consulate in Budapest is at Nepkoztarsasag utca 104, and is open Monday, Wednesday and Friday from 10 am to 1 pm. Three photos are required.

Mongolian Visas The Mongolian embassy in Beijing is open all day, but the visa section keeps short hours on Monday, Tuesday, Thursday and Friday, from 8.30 to 11.30 am. They close for all Mongolian holidays, and they shut down completely for the entire week of National Day (Naadam), which officially falls on 11-13 July. Sometimes they're closed during the visa officer's birthday, or if his wife needs to go to the dentist.

In the UK, the Mongolian embassy (☎ (0171) 937-0150, 937-5235) is at 7 Kensington Court, London W85 DL.

Transit visas cost US$15 if picked up in three days, or US$30 for express service. Tourist visas cost US$25 for three day service, or US$50 for express service. Indian and Bulgarian nationals get them free and Singaporeans can stay two weeks without a visa (figure that one out). One photo is required.

Other Visas Most travellers between Western Europe and Moscow go via Belarus and Poland, although there are alternative routes via Finland or Hungary. Depending on your situation, visas might be required for the following countries:

Belarus
On a straight-through international Russia-Poland train, no visa is required. However, a tourist visa is required (US$30 to US$50) if you stop off in Belarus, even just to change trains in Brest.
Czech Republic
A visa is not required for Europeans (except Albanians), but is needed if you're from Australia, Canada, Japan, Israel, New Zealand or South Africa. Visas cost US$22 if issued in two days, or US$33 for same-day service.

Hungary
Americans, Canadians and most Western Europeans (including UK citizens) don't need a visa for Hungary. Australians, New Zealanders, Greeks and Portuguese do (US$32); two photos are required. Get a tourist rather than a transit visa since Hungary is worth visiting.
Poland
A Polish visa is not needed by most western nationalities except Canadians and Greeks. Transit visas cost US$25 and tourist visas US$36. In China, there is a Polish embassy in Beijing and a Polish consulate in Guangzhou. Two photos are needed and your passport must be valid for at least another full year (!).
Slovakia
Western Europeans do not need a visa, but it's required if you're from Australia, Canada, New Zealand, Israel, Japan, South Africa or the USA. Visas cost US$23 and two photos are needed.

SEA
Hong Kong
There are numerous ships plying the waters between Hong Kong and the mainland, the most useful being the boats to Guangzhou and Shanghai. See the Getting There & Away section of the Hong Kong and Shanghai chapters for details.

Japan
Osaka/Yokohama to Shanghai There is a luxurious boat service between Shanghai and Osaka/Yokohama. The good ship *Suzhou Hao* departs once weekly (heading for Osaka one week and to Yokohama the next week) and takes two days. Off season it's kind of empty, but can be crowded during summer. Fares depend on class – from a low of US$140 all the way up to a staggering US$1600 for a luxury suite (but no surcharge for luggage). Departures from Shanghai are every Tuesday, while departures from Japan are every Friday. For information ring the shipping company's office in Tokyo (☎ (03) 5202-5781; fax 5202-5792), Osaka (☎ (06) 232-0131; fax 232-0211) or Shanghai (☎ (021) 6535-1713). The address of the shipping office in Shanghai is 1 Jinling Donglu.

Kobe to Tianjin Another ship runs from Kobe to Tanggu (near Tianjin). Departures

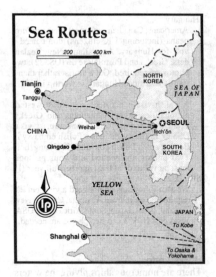

Sea Routes

from Kobe are every Thursday at noon, arriving in Tanggu the next day. Economy/1st class tickets cost US$250/350, or pay US$1400 for your very own stateroom. The food on this boat gets poor reviews so bring a few emergency munchies.

Tickets can be bought in Tianjin from the shipping office (☎ 2331-2283) at 89 Munan Dao, Hepingqu, or at the port in Tanggu (☎ 2938-3961). In Kobe, the office is at the port (☎ (078) 321-5791; fax 321-5793).

Korea

International ferries connect the South Korean port of Inch'ŏn with three cities in China: Weihai, Qingdao and Tianjin. Weihai and Qingdao are in China's Shandong Province (the closest province to South Korea) and boats are operated by the Weidong Ferry Company. Tianjin is close to Beijing and boats are run by the Jinchon Ferry Company. The boats have (horrors) a karaoke lounge.

The phone numbers for Weidong Ferry Company are: Seoul (☎ 711-9111); Inch'ŏn (☎ 886-6171); Weihai (☎ (0896) 522-6173); and Qingdao (☎ (0532) 280-3574).

Phone numbers for Jinchon Ferry Company are: Seoul (☎ 517-8671); Inch'ŏn (☎ 887-3963); and Tianjin (☎ (022) 2331-6049). In Seoul, tickets for any boats to China can be bought from Universal Travel Service, otherwise known as UTS (☎ 319-5511; fax 737-2764), room B-702, Dongyang Building.

For the Tianjin ferry only, you can also get tickets in Seoul from Taeya Travel (☎ 514-6226, 3442-4200), in Kangnam-gu by the Shinsa subway station. In China, tickets can be bought cheaply at the pier, or from CITS (for a very *steep* premium).

To reach the International Ferry Terminal from Seoul, take the Seoul-Inch'ŏn commuter train (subway line 1 from downtown) and get off at the Tonginch'ŏn station. The train ride takes 50 minutes. From Tonginch'ŏn station it's either a 45 minute walk or five minute taxi ride to the ferry terminal.

Inch'ŏn to Weihai The trip takes approximately 17 hours. Departures from Weihai are Wednesdays, Fridays and Sundays at 5 pm. Departures from Inch'ŏn are on Tuesdays, Thursdays and Saturdays at 5 pm. The fares are 2nd class US$100; 1st class US$140; royal class US$180; and royal suite class US$300. There is a 5% discount on a round-trip ticket.

Weihai is no place to hang around, so if you arrive there it's best to hop on the first bus to Qingdao. If that's not available, take a bus to Yantai and then to Qingdao.

Inch'ŏn to Qingdao Boats for Inch'ŏn leave on Mondays and Thursdays at 4 pm, take 20 hours and tickets cost Y1100. Boats leave Inch'ŏn twice a week. For details check with the Weidong Ferry Company in Seoul (☎ 711-9111), Inch'ŏn (☎ 886-6171) or Qingdao (☎ 280-3574).

Inch'ŏn to Tianjin The schedule for this ferry is a little irregular. It departs once every four or five days, usually on a Monday, Wednesday or Friday. The journey takes a minimum of 28 hours. Departures from Tianjin are at 10 am. The boat departs Inch'ŏn at 1 pm. The fares are 3B class US$120, 3A class US$140, 2B class US$150, 2A class US$160, 1st class US$180 and VIP class US$230.

The boat doesn't dock at Tianjin proper, but rather at the nearby port of Tanggu. Accommodation in Tianjin is outrageously expensive, but Tanggu has at least one economical accommodation option, the Seamen's Hotel. Tanggu has trains and minibuses directly to Beijing.

Third class on the boat is a huge vault with around 80 beds and horrid toilets.

Vietnam

A twice weekly boat service is expected to begin soon. If it goes as planned, it will connect the three Vietnamese ports of Haiphong, Halong and Mong Cai with the Chinese city of Beihai. No details were available at the time of writing, but a few enquiries from Vietnamese or Chinese travel agencies should bring you up-to-date on the status of this boat.

DEPARTURE TAX

If leaving China by air, the departure tax is Y90. This has to be paid in local currency, so be sure you have enough yuan to avoid a last-minute scramble at the airport moneychanging booth.

ORGANISED TOURS

Tour groups are still considered the darlings of the Chinese who have to deal with foreigners. It is much easier for the Chinese if you arrive in a tour group, if all your accommodation is pre-booked, and if everyone sits down at the same time to eat. If there's a government interpreter on hand, someone doesn't have to struggle with a phrasebook or broken English. Most importantly, tour groups spend more money.

Are tours worth it? Unless you simply cannot make your own way around, then probably not. Apart from the expense, they tend to screen you even more from some of the basic realities of China travel. Most people who come back with glowing

reports of the PRC have never had to travel proletariat class on the trains or battle their way on board a local bus in the whole five days of their stay. On the other hand, if your time is limited and you just want to see the Forbidden City and the hills of Guilin, then the brief tours from Hong Kong, although expensive, might be worth considering.

There are two basic kinds of tours – those for foreigners and those for Overseas Chinese. Officially, the reason for separating foreigners from Overseas Chinese is because the two groups supposedly speak different languages (often not true) and have different interests (sometimes true). Unofficially, the real reason has to do with racism. The Overseas Chinese groups usually receive about a 15% discount, so belonging to the correct gene pool can save you money.

Tours aimed at foreigners are usually organised by CITS, China Travel Service (CTS) or China Youth Travel Service (CYTS), although a few private operators are also getting in on the act. An English-speaking guide (or French, German, whatever) is supplied. Tours can be organised for very small groups, but costs are high.

Tours for Overseas Chinese are geared towards large groups and there's a heavy emphasis on shopping, feasting and posing for photos. There's also a tendency towards regimentation – the tour leader (usually female) waves a flag and uses a megaphone to keep the tourist troops in line. The tourists wear some sort of ID badge and a yellow hat.

Just what language your tour guide will speak is pot luck – some of these groups come from Australia, Canada or the USA and the guides will speak English about half the time. Groups from Hong Kong and Macau are likely to have a Cantonese-speaking guide. Groups from Taiwan might feature a guide who speaks a mixture of Fujianese (similar to Taiwanese) and Mandarin.

The prices that the Overseas Chinese pay for these tours are reasonably high, but you'll eat well and the circus atmosphere is free.

You can start the tour from your home country, or you can first fly to Hong Kong and book something from there. If you want to find out what's available, visit the Hong Kong travel agents, especially CTS. Essentially the same tours can be booked in Macau.

We could go on endlessly regurgitating all the tours to China. Here are some offered by CTS from its overseas offices:

Yangtze River Cruise Tours
13 days, including Shanghai and Beijing, from US$1,995; 15 days, including Shanghai, Xi'an and Beijing, from US$2,280; 19 days, including Shanghai, Beijing, Xi'an, Guilin and Hong Kong, from US$3,250

Silk Road Tour
18 days, from US$3,495

Other Overland Tours
14 days, including Beijing, Xi'an, Guilin and Hong Kong, from US$2,690; 20 days, including Beijing, Xi'an, Nanjing, Wuxi, Suzhou, Hangzou, Shanghai, Guilin and Hong Kong, from US$3,095

Not everyone is happy with these tours, and we've had various complaints from dissatisfied customers. Some people have booked a tour only to find that they were the sole person on the tour. Other travellers report additional charges being tacked on which were not mentioned in the original agreement. No refunds are given if you cancel – you forfeit the full amount.

Adventure Tours

Mountaineering, trekking, camping, white-water rafting, kayaking and cross-country skiing tours to China are organised by various agents in the west, but the prices are too high for low-budget travellers.

Trekking is administered and arranged by the Chinese Mountaineering Association (CMA) under the same rules that apply to mountaineering in China. The CMA makes all arrangements for a trek with the assistance of provincial mountaineering associations and local authorities. The all-important point is that CMA can get you

permits for peaks that are theoretically off limits to foreigners.

Various travel agents will book you through to these operators. Scan their literature carefully as sometimes the tours can be done just as easily on your own. What you want are places that individuals have trouble getting into.

If you can afford it, a few mountaineering, horse riding, trekking, cycling, sailing and rafting tour operators are:

Australia
Russian Passport/Red Bear Tours (☎ (03) 9867-3888; fax 9867-1055; email passport@ werple.net.au; www.travelcentre.com.au), Suite 11A, 401 St Kilda Rd, Melbourne, Vic 3004. Good for Trans-Siberian and other exotic journeys.
Tail Winds Bicycle Touring (☎ (02) 6249-6122), 1st floor, Garema Centre, Bunda St, Canberra, ACT 2601.
Taking Off Tours (☎ (03) 9521-1475), Suite 3, 618 St Kilda Rd, Melbourne, Vic 3000. Good for discount tours and Trans-Siberian Railway tickets from Beijing to Europe.
World Expeditions (☎ (02) 9264-3366), 3rd floor, 441 Kent St, Sydney, NSW 2000.

Canada
China Hiking Adventures (☎ (800) 363-0745, (416) 605-7479; fax 605-7479), PO Box 5967, Toronto, Ontario M5W 1P4.

UK
Voyages Jules Verne (☎ (0171) 723-4084; www.vjv.co.uk), 21 Dorset Square, London NW1 6QG. Good for more-upmarket tours.

USA
Access China Head Office (☎ (303) 692-8785; fax 575-0205), Suite 200, 4650 East Bails Place, Denver, CO 80222; Los Angeles Office (☎ (310) 531-9925; fax 404-7509), Suite 405-C, 14111 Freeway Drive, Santa Fe Springs, CA 90670. This place does upmarket tours with stays at four star (and upwards) hotels.
Backroads (☎ (800) 462-2848, (510) 527-1555; www.backroads.com), 801 Cedar St, Berkeley, CA 94710-1800. Offers cycling tours.
Boojum Expeditions (☎ (800) 287-0125, (406) 587-0125; fax 585-3474; email boojum @mcn.net), 14543 Kelly Canyon Rd, Bozeman, MT 59715. Mainly Horseback trips.
Earth River Expeditions (☎ (800) 643-2784; fax (914) 626-4423), 180 Towpath Rd, Accord, NY 12404. Offers rafting and trekking.

Earth Science Expeditions (☎ (970) 242-7108; email pswinn@aol.com), 202 North Ave, Grand Junction, CO 81501. Mainly rafting.

Earthwatch (☎ (617) 926-8200; fax 926-8532), 680 Mt Auburn St, PO Box 9104, Watertown, MA 02272. Provides environmental research expeditions.

Himalayan High Treks (☎ (800) 455-8735, (415) 861-2391; fax 861-2391), 241 Dolores St, San Francisco, CA 94103. Mostly Nepal, but Tibet is possible.

Ocean Voyages (☎ (800) 299-4444, (415) 332-4681; fax 332-7460; email voyages@ix.netcom.com), 1709 Bridgeway, Sausalito, CA 94965. Specialises in sailing trips.

Sierra Club (☎ (415) 977-5500; fax 977-5799; email information@sierraclub.org; www.sierra club.org/), 2nd floor, 85 2nd St, San Francisco, CA 94105-3441.

MOVING TO CHINA

If you're going to be moving something heavy like furniture or all your household goods, you will need the services of an international mover or freight forwarder. In Beijing you can try Sino Santa Fe (☎ 6467-7777) or YK Shipping International (☎ 6467-8822, ext 1726).

In Hong Kong there's Asian Express (☎ 2893-1000) and Jardine International (☎ 2563-6653).

In Shanghai you can try calling Allied Pickfords (☎ 6486-0833) or Crown Worldwide (☎ 6472-0254; email crownsha@public.sta.net.cn). Most of these companies have branch offices serving other major cities in China.

Getting Around

AIR

The Civil Aviation Administration of China (CAAC), for many years China's only domestic and international carrier, has officially been broken up and private carriers have been allowed to set up operations in China. This doesn't mean that CAAC is out of business – it now assumes the role of 'umbrella organisation' (whatever that is) for its numerous subsidiaries. Under the CAAC umbrella, you can find numerous airlines, including Air China, China Eastern, China Southern, China Northern, China Southwest, China Northwest, Great Wall, Shanghai, Shenzhen, Sichuan, Xiamen, Xinjiang, Yunnan airlines and several others.

CAAC still publishes a combined international and domestic timetable in both English and Chinese in April and November each year. These can be bought at some CAAC offices in China for Y10, but are free in Hong Kong at the CAAC office and airport service counter.

As well as the overall CAAC timetable, former CAAC units and private airlines also publish their own timetables. You can buy these in ticket offices around China.

More and more booking offices have been computerised over recent years. These offices allow you to purchase a ticket to or from any other destination on the computer reservation system. If the city you want to fly from is not on the system, however, you'll have to wait until you get there to buy your ticket from the local booking office.

You need to show your passport when reserving or purchasing a ticket, and you definitely need it to board the aircraft. Some airports will even check your Chinese visa, and if it's expired you will be prohibited from boarding.

Foreigners pay 50% more than the Chinese price. There is no way around this CAAC regulation, unless you are a foreign resident with all the excruciating paperwork. If you do somehow happen to get the Chinese price and it's discovered, your ticket will be confiscated and no refund given. Children over 12 are charged adult fare. Business class tickets cost 25% more than economy class, and 1st class tickets cost an extra 60%. At most CAAC offices it is still impossible to use credit cards to finance your transportation costs; all flights have to be paid for in cash.

There is no such thing as discounting no matter where you buy your tickets. Travel agents charge you full fare, plus extra commission for their services. The service desks in better hotels (three star and up) can reserve and even purchase air tickets for you with a little advance notice, but they will probably also tack on an additional fee.

There is an airport tax of approximately Y50 on domestic flights.

Cancellation fees depend on how long before departure you cancel. On domestic flights, if you cancel 24 to 48 hours before departure you lose 10% of the fare; if you cancel between two and 24 hours before the flight you lose 20%; and if you cancel less than two hours before the flight you lose 30%. If you don't show up for a domestic flight, you are entitled to a refund of 50%.

When purchasing a ticket, you may be asked to buy luggage insurance. It's certainly not compulsory though some staff give the impression it is – the amount you can actually claim if your bags are lost is pathetically low.

On domestic and international flights the free baggage allowance for an adult passenger is 20kg in economy class and 30kg in 1st class. You are also allowed 5kg of hand luggage, though this is rarely weighed. The charge for excess baggage is 1% of the full fare for each kilogram.

On domestic flights, you might get a real meal if you're flying on an Airbus or Boeing, but if the plane is Soviet built there will be no facilities for hot food. In that case, you'll probably be given a little bag or

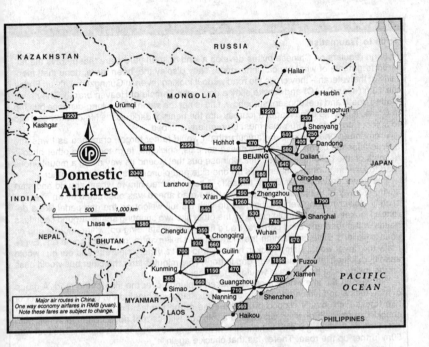

Domestic Airfares

0   500   1,000 km

Major air routes in China.
One way economy airfares in RMB (yuan).
Note these fares are subject to change.

two of sweets and a key ring as a souvenir – it almost justifies the 50% tourist surcharge!

Exiting from a Chinese aircraft is true Third World entertainment – everyone grabs their oversized hand luggage and storms for the door before the aircraft even rolls to a stop. It's best to just sit back and let them fight it out. Window seats are better because your fellow passengers won't be climbing over you in the scramble for the door.

BUS

Long-distance buses are one of the best means of getting around the country. Services are extensive and main roads are usually bumpy, but passable. Also, since the buses stop every so often in small towns and villages, you get to see parts of the countryside you wouldn't see if you travelled by train.

Of course, the buses provide stops in places you had never counted on visiting: breakdowns are frequent and can occur anywhere. This is a special treat for the locals, who are temporarily entertained by the rare spectacle of a small herd of big noses while the bus is being repaired (or stripped and sold for scrap metal). It also creates some economic opportunities – enterprising locals are quick to produce baskets of fruit, biscuits and soft drinks to sell to the waiting passengers.

Safety is another consideration. Accidents are frequent, especially on winding mountain roads. Foreigners have been injured and killed in bus crashes, and there is very little you can do to protect yourself. The government-run buses seem to be somewhat safer than the private ones – government drivers can be imprisoned for causing a bus accident.

The shock-absorbers on Chinese buses

Trips to Traumatise

Foreign regulars on Chinese buses develop a kind of 1000 yard stare that betrays the tattered fragments of what we call innocence. They display the 'been there, done that' mentality of the veteran – they cross the road without looking (even in Guangzhou), fly on Friday the 13th (even CAAC) and smoke sixty a day (even Temple of Heaven brand). They have eluded death and feel chosen, somehow. Life is not the same after a long-distance bus trip in China; it is a rite of passage, a journey into the heart of darkness, a life on the edge and to some, I am sure, a drug that must be regularly imbibed.

I remember one bus ride in particular that I would rather forget, crammed as I was into a Bruegelesque carnival of sweaty peasants, pigs, chickens, farm tools and other bucolic delights on the hulking leviathan of a Chinese bus that wound its way along a mountainous road to Dali, in Yunnan, sheer walls on one side and plunging ravines on the other.

The driver drove like Mr Death himself – I half expected him to wheel around and start scything away at the nearest passenger. If the road ahead was obstructed by an ever-so-slightly-slower moving vehicle, he'd be up with his full weight on the gas pedal like a deranged jockey. Our bus would creep by the other like two sprinting snails, around countless bends in the road and blind corners. You'd find yourself standing up, white-knuckle grip on your traveller's Bible, screaming the increasingly shrill mantra 'come on, come on'. Eventually the driver would slump back in his seat and light a victory cigarette and our bus would ease by, slotting into the hard won gap in front. Five minutes later the other bus would pass on the inside, and the process would repeat itself.

We passed the site where a car had taken a plunge over the side of the road. A group of motorists stood looking down into the ravine, hands on hips, at the point where a set of tyre tracks were neatly clipped off at the edge of the tarmac. I'm sure I heard the driver chuckle up front. Further on we passed a minibus with its roof ripped off, and an old man sat in the back singing a ditty to himself and counting his oranges in a basket. The roof was 50m further up the road. There was that chuckle again.

I remember getting to Lijiang and leafing through the travellers' book in Pete's Café (during its heyday), and coming across an entry from one poor bloke who had been in a minibus accident in the locality. The distillation of his experience yielded the tragic advice to 'sit at the back of the bus, so that when there is a collision you will have time to slow down before you hit the windscreen'.

Damian Harper

are poor (or nonexistent), and for this reason try to avoid sitting at the rear of the bus if possible. If you do sit in the back and the road is rough, expect to become airborne every time the bus hits a bump. The Chinese all know this, and there is much competition for seats at the front of the bus.

Many long-distance buses are equipped with cassette tape players and stereo speakers that allow the drivers to blast out your eardrums with screeching karaoke 'music' – select a seat as far away from these sinister speakers as possible and bring ear-plugs. Alternatively, try buying some classical music or Chinese rock tapes that you like and giving them to the driver in the hope that he'll play them.

Chinese law requires drivers to announce their presence to cyclists, and for this they use a tweeter for preliminaries, a bugle or bullhorn if they get annoyed and an ear-wrenching air horn when they're really stirred up.

While the roads and condition of the buses have improved in recent years, traffic is getting worse, making bus travel a rather slow means of transport. It's safe to reckon times for bus journeys by calculating the distance against a speed of 25km/h. Things are slowed down further by Chinese driving techniques – drivers are loath to change gears and appear to prefer coming to an almost absolute standstill on a slope rather than changing from third into second. Petrol-saving ploys include getting up to the highest speed possible and then coasting to a near standstill, before starting the process again. Engines are switched off for stops of any kind, even if it's only a matter of seconds.

Classes

In recent years night buses have become increasingly frequent. These services get mixed reviews – they are more dangerous and few but the Chinese can sleep on a crowded jolting bus. On most popular routes, sleeper buses (wòpù qìchē) have been introduced – they are usually around double the price of a normal bus service, but many travellers swear by them. Some have comfortable reclining seats, while others even have two tier bunks.

On runs of over 12 hours where sleeper buses have not been introduced there should be an overnight stop, but this is not always the case. Increasingly, buses are using two drivers and doing torturous two day excursions in a single stint – the 35 hour run between Golmud and Lhasa is a notorious example.

Privately owned minibuses are increasingly competing with public buses on medium-length routes. Although they're often a bit cramped, you always get a seat (or at least a knee to sit on), though you often have to bargain to get the Chinese price. Drivers will sometimes try to make you pay extra for bulky luggage.

Astronaut-type backpacks are a nightmare to stow on buses as there's little space under the seats, the overhead racks are hardly big enough to accommodate a loaf of bread, and there is sparse space in the aisles. If you intend doing a lot of bus travel, then travel light! In China, unlike other Asian countries, people do not ride on the roof, although luggage is sometimes stowed there.

Reservations

It's a good idea to book a seat in advance. All seats are numbered. You don't actually have a reservation until you've got a fully paid ticket in hand. While some hotels and travel agents book bus tickets, it's

---

Stunt Driving

Aside from breakdown, there are sometimes other difficulties which could delay your journey. One German traveller taking a bus from Wuzhou to Yangshuo was surprised when his bus started competing with the bus ahead for roadside passengers. After getting up perilously close to its rear bumper and blasting furiously on an armoury of horns, his driver managed, in a hair-raising exhibition of reckless abandon and dare-devilry, to sweep around the opposition on a blind bend and be first to get to a group of prospective passengers just around the corner. The other driver, determined not to let his fellow get away with such deviously unsporting behaviour, pulled up and started thumping him through the window.

A decisive knock-out proving elusive in such cramped quarters, the two soon leapt out of their buses to continue the punch-up on the roadside. Things were beginning to look grim for the German's driver, when a wailing siren announced the arrival of the boys in green. Without even a glance at the passengers of the two buses, they handcuffed the two drivers, threw them unceremoniously into the back of their van and drove off. It was five hours before new drivers were dispatched to the scene of the crime. ■

often easier and less error-prone to head for the bus station and do it yourself.

Bus stations are often large affairs with numerous ticket windows and waiting halls. There is a special symbol for a bus station which appears on local maps and is meant to resemble the steering wheel of the bus. The symbol is:

Costs

Bus travel generally works out to be comparable to hard-seat train travel in terms of expense. Gansu Province requires foreigners to purchase 'insurance' which has become a lucrative business.

In terms of how much you'll pay for meals, it's a very mixed bag out there. In about 50% of the cases, drivers take you to the filthiest and most expensive little hovels they can find with the worst food imaginable. It seems that these places are owned by their friends or relatives and the drivers get a commission. It's depressing because buses usually drive right past many perfectly acceptable restaurants, but the drivers refuse to stop. Your best defence is to stock up on sufficient munchies before you board the bus.

TRAIN

China's trains are small towns in themselves, with populations typically well over 1000. Although crowded, trains are the best way to get around in reasonable speed and comfort. The network covers every province except Tibet, and that's not for want of trying (experts have advised the Chinese that it is impossible to build a line up to Lhasa – it would involve drilling tunnels through ice). There is an estimated 52,000km of railway lines in China, most of which was built after 1949 when the system was non-existent or had been blown to bits.

The safety record of the railway system is good. Other than getting your luggage pinched or dying from shock when you see the toilets, there isn't much danger on trains. However, the Chinese have a habit of throwing rubbish out the windows even as the train moves through a station. Avoid standing too close to a passing train, lest you get hit by flying beer bottles or chicken bones.

Classes

In socialist China there are no classes; instead you have hard seat, hard sleeper, soft seat and soft sleeper.

Hard Seat Except on the trains which serve some of the branch or more obscure lines, hard seat is not in fact hard, but padded. However, it is hard on your sanity and you'll get little sleep on the upright seats. Since hard seat is the only thing the locals can afford, it's packed to the gills, the lights stay on all night, passengers spit on the floor and the carriage speakers endlessly drone news, weather, good tidings and music.

Hard seat is OK for a day trip, but some foreigners can't take more than five hours of it, although others have a threshold of 12 hours or even longer. A few brave, penniless souls have even been known to travel *long-distance* this way – some roll out a mat on the floor under the seats and go to sleep on top of the gob and cigarette butts.

As bad as it is, you should try to experience hard seat at least once, and the more crowded the better. This is China as it exists for the masses, a very different world from the glittering tourist hotels.

Hard Sleeper These are comfortable and only a fixed number of people are allowed in the sleeper carriage. The carriage is made up of doorless compartments with half a dozen bunks in three tiers. Sheets, pillows and blankets are provided and it does very nicely as a budget hotel. The best bunk to get is a middle one since the lower one is invaded by all and sundry who use it as a seat during the day, while the top one has little headroom. The top bunks are also where the cigarette smoke floats about and it's close to the endless drone from the infernal loudspeakers.

Lights and speakers in hard sleeper go out at around 9.30 to 10 pm. Competition for hard sleepers has become keen in recent years, and you'll be lucky to get one on short notice.

Soft Seat On shorter journeys (such as Shenzhen to Guangzhou) some trains have soft-seat carriages. The seats are comfortable and overcrowding is not permitted. Smoking is prohibited, a significant advantage unless you enjoy asphyxiation. If you want to smoke in the soft-seat section, you can do so only by going out into the corridor between cars. Soft seat costs about the same as hard sleeper and is well worth it. Unfortunately, soft-seat cars are a rarity.

Soft Sleeper Luxury. Softies get the works, with four comfortable bunks in a closed compartment – complete with straps to keep the top-bunk fatso from falling off in the middle of the night, wood panelling, potted plants, lace curtains, teacup set, clean washrooms, carpets (so no spitting) and often air-con. As for those speakers, not only do you have a volume control, you can turn the bloody things off!

Soft sleeper costs twice as much as hard sleeper, and almost the same price as flying (on some routes even *more* than flying!). It's comparatively easy to get soft sleeper because few ordinary Chinese can afford it. However, a growing class of *nouveaux riches* plus high-ranking party cadres (who charge it to their state expense accounts) has upped the demand for soft sleepers, so you might wind up in hard seat no matter how much cash you have.

Travelling in soft sleeper should be experienced once – it gives you a good chance to meet the ruling class.

Train Types
Train composition varies from line to line and also from day to night, and largely depends on the demand for sleepers on that

line. A typical high-frequency railway line has about 13 carriages: six hard seat, perhaps one soft seat, three hard sleeper, one soft sleeper, one dining car and one guard/baggage van.

Half or even a whole carriage may be devoted to crew quarters on the longer trips. If the journey time is more than 12 hours then the train qualifies for a dining car. The dining car often separates the hard-seat from the hard-sleeper and soft-sleeper carriages.

The conductor is in a little booth in a hard-seat carriage in the middle of the train – usually carriage No 7, 8 or 9 (all carriages are numbered on the outside). Coal-fired samovars are found in the ends of the hard-class sections, and from these you can draw a supply of hot water. On long trips, however, the water often runs out. The disc-jockey has a little booth at the end of one of the cars with a door marked 'Boyinshi', which apart from the reel-to-reel tape, radio and record player also contains the attendant's bed.

On some of the small branch lines there are various kinds of passenger carriages – some have long bench seats along the walls, others are just cattle cars without seats or windows.

Different types of trains are usually recognisable by the train number:

Nos 1-299 The 'special express' (*tèkuài*) are usually diesel-hauled. They have all classes and there is a surcharge for speed and superior facilities. With a few exceptions, the international trains are included in this group.

Nos Y1-Y299 The 'travel' (*yóu*) class trains are the same as the foregoing, though with lots of soft seat cars.

Nos K1-K299 The 'fast speed' (*kuàisù*) trains are another variation on the above theme.

Nos Z1-Z100 The 'standard high speed' (*zhǔn gāo sù*) are especially fast trains only operated on the Guangzhou-Kowloon line.

Nos 300-599 The 'direct express' (*zhíkuài*) make more stops than the special expresses. They have soft and hard sleepers, but fewer of them. The speed surcharge is half that of the special expresses, but the difference in overall price is minimal.

Nos 600-699 The 'fast passenger' (*kuàikè*) trains take short suburban routes like Shanghai-Suzhou. You won't find sleepers on these.

Nos 700-799 The 'direct passenger' (*zhíkè*) trains are slow, and stop at everything they can find. They may have hard wooden seats and no sleepers. The trains have antique fittings, lamps and wood panelling, and are usually steam-pulled. There is no speed surcharge as there is no speed.

Nos 800-801 The 'passenger' (*kè*) trains are also slowpokes, but at least have hard sleepers.

Apart from the speed breakdown, the numbers don't really tell you much else about the train. As a general rule, the outbound and inbound trains have matching numbers; thus train Nos 79/80 divide into No 79 leaving Shanghai and going to Kunming, and No 80 leaving Kunming and going to Shanghai.

Reservations & Tickets

Buying hard-seat tickets at short notice is usually no hassle, although you will not always be successful in getting a reserved seat. Buying a ticket for a sleeper can be problematic – indeed, it can be damn near impossible if you try to do it yourself.

If you try to buy a sleeper ticket at the railway station and the clerk just says *méi yǒu* ('not have'), you'll have to seek the assistance of a travel agent. This can mean CITS, CTS, CYTS or the travel booking desk in your hotel. However, many CITS and CTS offices no longer do rail bookings. If you run into this problem, the best thing is to ask at the reception desk of your hotel (unless you're staying in a grotty dump). Most hotels have an in-house travel agent who can obtain train tickets. You'll pay a service charge of perhaps Y40 or so, but it's probably worth it to avoid 30 hours in hard-seat hell.

Tickets for sleepers can easily be obtained in major cities, but not in quiet backwaters. There is a six day, advance-purchase limit, presumably to prevent tickets being hoarded by scalpers.

You can buy tickets the night before departure or on the day of departure from the railway station. This often involves formidably long queues. Some stations are surprisingly well-run, but others are bedlam. The best stations now have computers that spit out tickets quickly and efficiently, resulting in queues that move fast. Hard-seat tickets bought on the same day will usually be unreserved – you get on board and try and find a seat. If there are no seats, you'll either have to stand or find a place for your bum among the peanut shells, cigarette butts and spittle.

If you have a sleeper ticket the carriage attendant will take it from you and give you a metal or plastic chit – when your destination is close he or she will swap it back for the original ticket. Keep your ticket until you get through the barriers at the other end, as you'll need to show it there.

Platform Tickets An alternative to all the above is not to bother with a ticket at all and simply walk on to the train. To do this, you need to buy a platform ticket (*zhàntái piào*). These are available from the station's information booth for a few jiao. You then buy your ticket on the train.

This method is usually more hassle than it's worth, but may be necessary if you arrive at the station without enough time to get your ticket.

Black-Market Tickets Black-market train tickets have become something of a cottage industry in China. You simply order a ticket and pay a commission to one of the touts standing around the railway station or operating through a cafe or hotel. However, you could be buying a worthless piece of cardboard – ticket counterfeiting has also become a new growth industry in China.

The advent of computerised tickets is gradually putting a stop to the black-market ticket business.

Getting Aboard As soon as the train pulls into the station, all hell breaks loose. In the hope of getting a seat, hard-seat passengers charge at the train, often pushing exiting passengers back inside. Some would-be travellers climb through the windows.

Railway attendants attempt to keep order – sometimes using night sticks or bamboo poles.

If you have a reserved seat or sleeper, you can let the crowd fight it out for a while, then peacefully find your carriage and claim your rightful place. If you don't have a reserved seat, you're going to have to join the fray. The sensible option is to head for either the very front or the very rear of the train. Most passengers attack the middle of the train – the part closest to the platform entrance gate.

Upgrading If you get on the train with an unreserved seating ticket, you can seek out the conductor and upgrade (*bǔpiào*) yourself to a hard sleeper, soft seat or soft sleeper if there are any available. You will usually be charged foreigners' prices for this service, and there are risks involved (no sleepers left), but it is sometimes the only way to get a sleeper or even a seat. On some trains it's easy to do, but others are notoriously crowded. A lot of intermediary stations along the railway lines can't issue sleepers, making upgrading the only alternative to hard seat.

If the sleeper carriages are full then you may have to wait until someone gets off. That sleeper may only be available to you until the next major station which is allowed to issue sleepers, but you may be able to get several hours of sleep. The sleeper price will be calculated for the distance that you used it for.

Ticket Validity Tickets are valid for one to seven days, depending on the distance travelled. On a cardboard ticket the number of days is printed at the bottom left-hand corner. If you go 250km it's valid for two days; 500km, three days; 1000km, four days; 2000km, six days; and 2500km, seven days.

Thus if you're travelling along a major line you could (theoretically) buy one ticket and break the journey where you feel like it. This will only work for unreserved hard seats. The advantage of this method is

that you can keep away from railway ticket windows for a while; you can get off, find a refreshing hotel and get back on board the next day on the same ticket.

So much for theory – nothing is consistent in China. In some stations, the railway workers won't let you board unless you hold a ticket for the exact date and time of departure. If you buy a ticket for a morning train (unreserved hard seat) and try to take a later train the same day, they may refuse to let you board even though the ticket is still valid!

Given the fact that the rules are subject to the unpredictable whims of various railway workers, you'll probably wind up just buying tickets for the exact time and date you intend to depart.

Timetables
There are paperback train timetables in Chinese, but nothing in English. No matter how fluent your Chinese, the timetables are so excruciatingly detailed that it's a drag working your way through them. Even the Chinese complain about this. Thinner versions listing the major trains can sometimes be bought at major railway stations. Hotel reception desks and CITS offices have copies of the timetable for trains out of their city or town.

Most railway stations require that luggage be x-rayed before entering the waiting area. The reason has less to do with terrorism than with the fact that China has to deal with people transporting huge quantities of explosive chemicals – there have been several disastrous explosions. Occasionally, gory photographs of the results are tacked up in stations.

If the horde of starers in the waiting room is getting on your nerves, you can head to the soft-class waiting rooms if you've got a soft-seat or soft-sleeper ticket. Some soft-class waiting rooms require a Y2 ticket which includes all the tea you can drink.

Just about all railway stations have left-luggage rooms (*jìcún chù*) where you can safely dump your bags for about Y5 to Y10.

Costs

Calculation of train prices is a complex affair based on the length of the journey, speed of the train and possibly the relative position of the sun and moon. There are a few variables, such as air-con charges or whether a child occupies a berth or not, but nothing worth worrying about. The express surcharge is the same regardless of what class you use on the train. Soft-sleeper on international trains (including the *Hong Kong-Beijing express*) can clean your wallet out quickly.

Food is available on the trains and at stations. It's not gourmet style, but the prices are certainly reasonable. Aside from the dining cars, railway staff regularly walk through the trains with pushcarts offering instant noodles (*miàn*), bread (*miànbāo*), boxed rice lunches (*héfàn*), bologna (*huǒtuǐ*), beer (*píjiǔ*), mineral water (*kuàng quán shuǐ*) and soft drinks (*qìshuǐ*). After about 8 pm when meals are over you can probably wander back into the dining car. The staff may want to get rid of you, but if you just sit down and have a beer it may be OK.

As far as foreigners are concerned, many railway staff in China are exceedingly polite and can be very helpful (how they treat their fellow Chinese is another matter). The staff may bend over backwards to assist you, particularly if you smile, behave friendly and look lost. Sometimes they'll invite you to sit with them or even give you their own train seats.

Even when all the sleepers are supposedly full, they sometimes manage to find one for foreigners, so it pays to be nice. One traveller writes:

We were allowed to spend one night from Zhanjiang to Guilin in the dining car when it wasn't occupied by people eating there. We ended up there after a futile attempt to upgrade to hard sleeper. Eventually we had to pay Y15 each for the sake of staying there, but it was still less horrible than hard seat.

Unfortunately, many foreigners take out their frustrations on the railway staff – this just makes it tough for all who follow.

CAR & MOTORCYCLE

For those who would like to tour China by car or motorbike, the news is bleak – basically it's impossible unless you go with a large group (accompanied by PSB the whole way), apply for permits months in advance and pay through the nose for the privilege. It's not like India, where you can simply buy a motorbike and head off on your own.

Foreign residents may drive in China after obtaining a Chinese driver's licence. However, there are often restrictions on how far you can drive from your place of residence – the local PSB can inform you of the latest half-baked regulations.

On the other hand, it's easy enough to book a car with a driver. Basically, this is just a standard long-distance taxi. Travel agencies like CITS or even hotel booking desks can make the arrangements. They generally ask excessive fees – the name of the game is to negotiate. If you can communicate in Chinese or find someone to translate, it's not particularly difficult to find a private taxi driver to take you wherever you like for less than half of CITS rates.

Road Rules

You're more likely to get fined for illegal parking than speeding. Indeed, with China's gridlock traffic, opportunities for speeding are swiftly vanishing.

If you travel much around China, you'll periodically encounter road blocks where the police stop every vehicle and impose arbitrary fines for driving with sunglasses, driving without sunglasses, scratching your nose while driving etc. The fine must be paid on the spot or the vehicle will be impounded. Basically, these are fundraising events.

Rental

Tourists are not yet permitted to rent either cars or motorbikes in China. Rental companies do exist, but they are only for the domestic market or for foreigners armed with a Chinese driver's licence.

Purchase

Only legal residents of China can purchase a motor vehicle. The whole procedure is plagued by bureaucracy, with lots of little fees to be paid along the way.

The licence plates issued to foreigners are different from those issued to Chinese, and this is a bigger hassle than you might first imagine. Since the licence plates go with the car, this essentially means that a foreigner wanting to buy a used car must buy it from another foreigner.

BICYCLE

Probably the first time the Chinese saw a pneumatic-tyred bicycle was when a pair of globe-trotting Americans called Allen and Sachtleben bumbled into Beijing around 1891 after a three year journey from Istanbul. They wrote a book about it called *Across Asia on a Bicycle*. The novelty was well received by the Qing court, and the boy-emperor Puyi was given to tearing around the Forbidden City on a cycle.

Today there are over 300 million bikes in China, more than can be found in any other country. Some are made for export, but most are for domestic use. It's easy to see why many Chinese would be willing to spend their last yuan for a bike – anything is preferable to being at the mercy of the bus system.

The traditional Chinese bicycle and tricycle are workhorses, used to carry anything up to a 100kg slaughtered pig or a whole couch. Until very recently, Chinese bikes all looked the same – heavy gearless monsters made out of waterpipe and always painted black.

Although the black beasts are still the most popular design (because they last a long time and are relatively cheap), sleek new multi-geared models in a variety of colours are available. The Chinese are even having success in exporting these.

In western countries, travel agencies organising bicycle trips advertise in cycling magazines. Bicycle clubs can contact CITS (or its competitors) for information about organising a trip.

Rental

There are now established bicycle hire shops that cater to foreigners in most traveller centres. In touristy places like Yangshuo it's even possible to rent sharp-looking mountain bikes, but elsewhere it's the old black clunkers. The majority operate out of hotels popular with foreigners, but there are also many independent hire shops. Even in towns that don't see much tourist traffic there are often hire shops catering to Chinese who are passing through (however, they are rapidly disappearing as the increasingly affluent Chinese switch to 'modern' transport like taxis). Surprisingly, medium-size cities quite often have better bicycle-rental facilities than large metropolises.

Day hire, 24 hour hire or hire by the hour are the norm. It's possible to hire for a stretch of several days, so touring is possible if the bike is in good condition. Rates for westerners are typically Y2 per hour or Y10 to Y20 per day – the price depends more on competition than anything else. Some big hotels charge ridiculous rates, although this may get you a sharp-looking mountain bike.

If you hire over a long period you should be able to reduce the rate. Most hire places will ask you to leave some sort of ID. Sometimes they ask for your passport, which is asking a lot. Give them some other ID instead, like a student card or a driver's licence. Expired passports will do very nicely for this purpose. Some hire shops may require a deposit, but that should certainly not be more than the actual value of the bike.

If you're planning on staying in one place for more than about five weeks, it's probably cheaper to buy your own bike and either sell it or give it to a friend when you leave.

Before taking a bike, check the brakes (are there any?), get the tyres pumped up hard and make sure that none of the moving parts are about to fall off. Get the saddle raised to maximum leg power. It's also worth tying something on the bike – a handkerchief, for example – to identify your bicycle amid the zillions at the bicycle parks.

A bike licence is obligatory for Chinese, but is not necessary for a foreigner. Some cities have bicycle licence plates, and in Beijing bikes owned by foreigners have special licence plates so they can't be sold to a Chinese. Bike-repair shops are everywhere and repairs are cheap (say Y10 a shot), but overcharging of foreigners is common – ask first.

Purchase

Until very recently, there were only four basic types of bike available in China: small wheel, light roadster (14kg), black hulk (22kg) and farmers' models (25kg to 30kg).

Some travellers have saved themselves the bother of bringing bikes across the border by buying mountain bikes or racers in China. Some brands are acceptable quality and are even exported.

In Hong Kong, Flying Ball Bicycle Shop (☎ 2381-5919) at 201 Tung Choi St (near Prince Edward MTR station) in Mongkok is the place to go for both hardware and information about cycling in China.

Touring

The legalities of cycling from town to town are open to conjecture. There is absolutely no national law in China which prohibits foreigners from riding bicycles. Basically, the problem is that of 'open' and 'closed' areas. It's illegal for foreigners to visit closed areas without a permit. Fair enough, but foreigners can transit a closed area – that is, you can travel by train or bus through a closed area as long as you don't exit the vehicle in this 'forbidden zone'. The question is: Should riding a bicycle through a closed area be classified as 'transiting' or 'visiting' it?

Chinese law is as clear as mud on this issue. Most of the time, the police won't bother you, but some officials just can't stand seeing foreigners bicycling through China – they expect you to be travelling by

taxi and tour bus. After all, foreigners are universally regarded as rich and bicycles are meant for poor peasants. No respectable cadre would be caught dead riding a bicycle – they prefer limousines. Most Chinese can't figure out why foreigners would even want to cycle around China.

If you get caught in a closed area, it is unlikely to be while you are on the road. The long arm of the law keeps firm tabs on transients via hotels. If you're staying overnight in an open place, but you are suspected of having passed through a closed area, the police may pull a raid on your hotel. You can be hauled down to the police station, where you have to submit to a lengthy interrogation, sign a confession and pay a fine. Fines vary from Y50 to whatever they think you can afford. There is some latitude for bargaining in these situations, and you should request a receipt (*shōujù*). And don't expect the police to give you any tips on which areas are closed and which are open, because in fact they seldom know themselves.

It was 10 pm, it was raining, I was in the outskirts and nobody was noticing me, so I quickly hopped into a hotel. I wasn't sleeping yet and they came and took me and my stuff and my bike to the city centre, to a big hotel, of course more expensive, kept my passport and told me to come to the police station next morning.

I told them about false information and all the mismanagement. I passed through so many road blocks and nobody had stopped me, and if I asked a policeman on the street whether the place was open or not, he wouldn't know, so how should I, a tourist who can't speak Chinese, know that this is a closed city?

'No, this is an open city.' Ah? ... so what am I doing in the police station? 'You were probably in a closed area.'

I couldn't even lie, I didn't know what was open and what was not.

Ze Do Rock

Camping is possible if you can find a spare blade of grass. The trick is to select a couple of likely places about half an hour before sunset, keep pedalling and then backtrack so you can pull off the road at the chosen spot just after darkness falls.

One problem with western bikes is that they attract a lot of attention. Another problem is the unavailability of spare parts. One westerner brought a fold-up bicycle with him, but in most places it attracted so much attention that he had to give it to the locals to play with until the novelty wore off. And fold-up bikes just aren't practical for long-distance riding.

It's essential to have a kick-stand for parking. A bell, headlight and reflector are good ideas. Make sure everything is bolted down, otherwise you'll invite theft. A cage-less water bottle, even on a Chinese bike, attracts too much attention. Adhesive reflector strips get ripped off.

Hazards

It's difficult to miss the ubiquitous picture displays around Chinese cities exhibiting the gory remains of cyclists who didn't look where they were going and wound up looking like Y10 worth of fried dumplings. These displays also give tips on how to avoid accidents and show 're-education classes' for offenders who have had several accidents. Take care when you're riding and don't give the authorities the opportunity to feature a foreigner in their next display.

Night riding is particularly hazardous. Many drivers in China only use their headlights to flash them on and off as a warning for cyclists up ahead to get out of the way. On country roads, look out for those UFO-style walking tractors, which often have no headlights at all.

Your fellow cyclists are another factor in the hazard equation. Chinese bicycles are rarely equipped with lights and most Chinese cyclists have little more than an abstract grasp of basic road courtesy and traffic rules. Be prepared for cyclists to suddenly swerve in front of you, to come hurtling out of a side road or even to head straight towards you against the flow of the traffic. This is not to mention situations where you yourself are the traffic hazard:

beware of the cyclist who spots you, glides by staring gape-mouthed, crashes into something in front and causes the traffic following to topple like tenpins.

Dogs, the enemy of cyclists the world over, are less of a problem in China than elsewhere. This is because Fido is just as likely to wind up stir-fried than menacing cyclists on street corners. One exception to this rule is Tibet and parts of Qinghai. Be particularly careful if cycling around Lhasa.

In most larger towns and cities bicycles should be parked at designated places on the sidewalk. This will generally be a roped off enclosure, and bicycle-park attendants will give you a token when you park there; the charge is usually Y1. If you don't use this service, you may return to find that your bike has been 'towed' away. Confiscated illegally parked bicycles make their way to the police station. There will be a fine in retrieving it, although it shouldn't bankrupt you.

Bicycle theft does indeed exist. The bicycle parks with their attendants help prevent this, but keep your bike off the streets at night, or at least within the hotel gates. If the hotel has no grounds then take the bike up to your room. Most hired bicycles have a lock around the rear wheel which can be pried open with a screwdriver in seconds. You can increase security by buying and using a cable lock, widely available from shops in China.

Off the Road

Most travellers who bring bikes take at least a couple of breaks from the rigours of the road, during which they use some other means of transport. The best option is bus. It is generally no problem stowing bikes on the roofs of buses and there is seldom a charge involved. Air and train transport are more problematic.

Bikes are not cheap to transport on trains; they can cost as much as a hard-seat fare. It's cheaper on boats, if you can find one. Trains have quotas for the number of bikes they may transport. As a foreigner you will get preferential treatment in the luggage compartment and the bike will go on the first available train. But your bike won't arrive at the same time as you unless you send it on a couple of days in advance. At the other end it is held in storage for three days free, and then incurs a small charge.

The procedure for putting a bike on a train and getting it at the other end is as follows:

- Railway personnel would like to see a train ticket for yourself (not entirely essential).
- Go to the baggage transport section of the station. Get a white slip and fill it out to get the two or three tags for registration. Then fill out a form (it's only in Chinese, so just fill it out in English) which reads: 'Number/to station x/send goods person/receive goods person/total number of goods/from station y'.
- Take the white slip to another counter, where you pay and are given a blue slip.
- At the other end (after delays of up to three days for transporting a bike) you present the blue slip, and get a white slip in return. This means your bike has arrived. The procedure could take from 20 minutes to an hour depending on who's around. If you lose that blue slip you'll have real trouble reclaiming your bike.

Chinese cyclists spend ages at the stations mummifying their bicycles in cloth for transport. For the one scratch the bike will get, it's hardly worth going through this elaborate procedure.

The best bet for getting your bike on a bus is to get to the station early and put it on the roof. Strictly speaking, there should not be a charge for this, but in practice the driver will generally try to extort a few yuan out of you. Bypass this sort of thing by putting it on the roof and unloading it yourself. The driver probably won't like it, but you'll normally be allowed to proceed all the same.

Transporting your bike by plane can be expensive, but it's often less complicated than by train. Some cyclists have not been charged by CAAC; others have had to pay 1% of their fare per kilogram of excess weight.

HITCHING

Hitching is never entirely safe in any country in the world, and we don't recommend it. Travellers who decide to hitch should understand that they are taking a small but potentially serious risk. People who do choose to hitch will be safer if they travel in pairs and let someone know where they are planning to go.

Many people have hitchhiked in China, and some have been amazingly successful. It's not officially sanctioned and the same dangers that apply elsewhere in the world also apply in China. Exercise caution, and if you're in any doubt as to the intentions of your prospective driver, say no. A woman travelling alone would be wise to hitch with a male companion.

Hitching in China is rarely free, and passengers are expected to offer at least a tip. Some drivers might even ask for an unreasonable amount of money, so try to establish a figure early on in the ride to avoid problems later. Even when a price is agreed upon, don't be surprised if the driver raises it when you arrive at your destination and creates a big scene (with a big crowd) if you don't cough up the extra cash. Indeed, he may even pull this scam half-way through the trip, and if you don't pay up then you get kicked out in the middle of nowhere.

In other words, don't think of hitching as a means to save money – rarely will it be any cheaper than the bus. The main reason to do it is to get to isolated outposts where public transport is poor. There is, of course, some joy in meeting the locals this way, but communicating is certain to be a problem if you don't speak Chinese.

The best way to get a lift is, like anywhere else, to head out to main roads on the outskirts of town. There are usually lots of trucks on the roads, and even army convoys are worth trying. There is no Chinese signal for hitching, so just try waving down the trucks.

Unless you speak the local language, you'll need to have where you want to go written down in Chinese characters.

BOAT

For better or worse, China's boats are fast disappearing. Many services have been cancelled – victims of improved bus and air transport. In coastal areas, you're most likely to use a boat to reach offshore islands like Putuoshan (near Shanghai) or Hainan in the south.

The Yantai-Dalian ferry will likely survive because it saves hundreds of kilometres of overland travel. For the same reason, the Shanghai-Ningbo service will probably continue to operate, but elsewhere the outlook for coastal passenger ships is not too good.

There are also several inland shipping routes worth considering, but these are also vanishing. For details of each trip see the appropriate sections in this book.

The best known river trip is the three day boat ride along the Yangzi River from Chongqing to Wuhan. The Guangzhou to Wuzhou route along the West (Xi) River is popular with low-budget travellers as it is the cheapest way to get from Guangzhou to Guilin and Yangshuo, disembarking at Wuzhou and then continuing on by bus to Guilin or Yangshuo. The Li River boat trip from Guilin to Yangshuo is a popular tourist ride which takes six hours.

You can also travel the Grand Canal from Hangzhou to Suzhou on a tourist boat – the old ferry services have gone the way of the buggy whip. There are no longer passenger boats on the Yellow River.

There are still a number of popular boats between Hong Kong and the rest of China. See the Getting There & Away section of the Hong Kong chapter for details.

LOCAL TRANSPORT

Long-distance transport in China is not really a problem – the dilemma occurs when you finally make it to your destination. As in US and Australian cities where the car is the key to movement, the bicycle is the key in China and if you don't have one, life is more difficult. Walking is not usually recommended, since Chinese cities tend to be very spread out.

Bus

Apart from bikes, buses are the most common means of getting around in the cities. Services are fairly extensive and the buses go to most places you want to go. The problem is that they are almost always packed. If an empty bus pulls in at a stop then the battle for seats ensues, and a passive crowd of Chinese suddenly turns into a stampeding herd. Even more aggravating is the slow traffic. You just have to be patient, never expect anything to move rapidly, and allow lots of time to get to the railway station to catch your train. One consolation is that buses are cheap – rarely more than two jiao.

Good maps of Chinese cities and bus routes are readily available and are often sold by hawkers outside the railway stations. When you get on a bus, point to where you want to go on the map, and the conductor (who is seated near the door) will sell you the right ticket. They usually tell you where to get off, provided they remember.

You may be offered a seat in a crowded bus, although this is now a rarity. If that peculiarly Chinese politeness does manifest itself, and if you're offered a seat, it's best to accept as a refusal may offend. Whatever you do, smile and be appreciative.

Taxi

Taxis cruise the streets in most large cities, but elsewhere they may simply congregate at likely spots (such as bus stations) and hassle every foreigner who walks past. Rather than speak to you in Chinese, the drivers typically grab foreigners by the arm, get all agitated and start grunting 'Laowai, hey, ooh, aaahh, arrrghh' and so on. This seems to be a special dialect peculiar to taxi drivers.

You can always summon a taxi from the tourist hotels, which sometimes have separate booking desks. You can hire them for a single trip or on a daily basis – the latter is worth considering if there's a group of people who can split the cost. Some of the tourist hotels also have minibuses on hand.

Navigating Cities on Foot

At first glance, Chinese street names can be a little bewildering, with name changes common every few hundred metres. The good news is that there is some logic to it, and a little basic Chinese will help to make navigating much easier.

Many road names are compound words made up of a series of directions that place the road in context with all others in the city. Compass directions are particularly common in road names. The directions are: *bei* (north), *nan* (south), *dong* (east) and *xi* (west). So Dong Lu literally means East Road.

Other words which regularly crop up are *zhong* (central) and *huan* (ring, as in ring road). If you bring them together with some basic numerals, you could have Dongsanhuan Nanlu, which literally means 'east third ring south road' or the south-eastern part of the third ring road. ■

While most taxis have meters, they are a pure formality (except in large cities) and usually only get switched on by accident. Sometimes you're better off without the meter – as elsewhere in the world, Chinese taxi drivers don't mind taking you for a 20km ride to a place just across the street. Taxi prices should be negotiated before you get into the taxi, and bargaining is usual (but keep it friendly as nastiness on your part will result in a higher price!). Don't be surprised if the driver attempts to change the price when you arrive, claiming that you 'misunderstood' what he said. If you want to get nasty, *this* is the time to do it. If your spoken Chinese is less than perfect, write the price down clearly and make sure the driver agrees at the start, to avoid 'misunderstandings' later.

It's important to realise that most Chinese cities impose limitations on the number of passengers that a taxi can carry. The limit is usually four, though minibuses can take more, and drivers are usually unwilling to break the rules and risk trouble with the police.

We witnessed a vicious argument in Beijing between eight foreigners and a taxi driver – the driver refused to take all eight people in one trip, saying it was illegal and he could get into trouble. He was willing to make two trips, but the foreigners figured that was just his way of trying to charge

double and therefore rip them off. The driver was, in fact, telling the truth.

Motorcycle Taxi

The deal is that you get a ride on the back of someone's motorcycle for about half the price of what a regular four wheeled taxi would charge. If you turn a blind eye to the hazards, this is a quick and cheap way of getting around. It's required that you wear a helmet – the driver will provide one. Obviously, there is no meter, so fares must be agreed to in advance.

Motor-Tricycle
(*sānlún mótuōchē*)

The motor-tricycle – for want of a better name – is an enclosed three wheeled vehicle with a driver at the front, a small motorbike engine below and seats for two passengers behind. They tend to congregate outside the railway and bus stations in larger towns and cities. Some of these vehicles have trays at the rear with bench seats along the sides so that four or more people (plus a few chickens) can be accommodated.

Pedicab
(*sānlúnchē*)

A pedicab is a pedal-powered tricycle with a seat to carry passengers. Chinese pedicabs have the driver in front and passenger seats in the back, the opposite of some countries (Vietnam, for example).

Pedicabs are gradually disappearing in China, victims of the infernal combustion engine. However, pedicabs congregate outside railway and bus stations or hotels in many parts of China. In a few places, pedicabs cruise the streets in large numbers (Lhasa, for example).

Unfortunately, most of the drivers are so aggressive that you have to pry them off you with a crow bar. Almost without exception a reasonable fare will be quoted, but when you arrive at your destination it'll be multiplied by 10. So if you're quoted a fare of Y5 it becomes Y50, and if you're quoted Y50 it becomes Y500. Another tactic is to quote you a price like Y10 and then demand US$10 – the driver claims that you 'misunderstood'.

The best bet is to write it down (be sure to specify Renminbi, not US$), get the driver to agree three or four times and sign it, and then when he tries to multiply by 10, hand over the exact change and walk away. At this point the smiling friendly driver will suddenly be transformed into an exceedingly menacing beast – you just have to stand your ground. It's worse if there are two of them, so *never* get into a pedicab if the driver wants his 'brother' to come along for the ride (a common strategy). The 'brother' is there to threaten and bully you into paying up when you inevitably baulk at being ripped off.

The situation is less likely to turn ugly when the driver is female, but women pedicab drivers are very rare indeed. And if she happens to have a 'brother' who wants to come along for the ride, find another driver. In many cases, a taxi works out to be cheaper than a pedicab because the chances of being ripped off are much lower.

ORGANISED TOURS

Some of the one day tours are reasonably priced and might be worth the cost as they can save you a lot of trouble. Some remote spots are difficult to reach and a tour might well be your only option.

Some tours are very informal and even popular with budget travellers. For example, at Turpan in Xinjiang Province, many travellers do a one day tour by minibus of the surrounding countryside. The minibus drivers hang around the hotels and solicit business, so there is no need to get involved with CITS or other agencies.

Another low-cost option is to go on a tour with a local Chinese group. A number of travellers use this option in Beijing, for example, to reach the Great Wall. The tour bus could be an old rattletrap and you'll get to visit a few souvenir shops (which invariably pay under-the-table commissions to the bus drivers), but these tours can be interesting if you keep a sense of humour about it. Don't expect the guides to speak anything but Chinese – possibly just the local dialect.

Sometimes the buses will whiz through what westerners would consider interesting spots and make long stops at dull places for

Pedicabs Versus Rickshaws

A rickshaw is a two wheeled passenger cart pulled by a man on foot. It was invented in Japan, where the word *jin-rikusha* means 'human-powered vehicle'. It was introduced into China in the late 19th century, where it was called *yángchē* (foreign vehicle).

The rickshaw eventually became a symbol of human exploitation – one person pulling another in a cart – and disappeared from China in the 1950s. Its replacement, the pedicab – sometimes mistakenly called a rickshaw – is a tricycle with a seat for one or two passengers. ■

the requisite photo sessions. You might have difficulty getting a ticket if your Chinese isn't good and they think you're too much trouble. The Chinese tours are often booked through hotel service desks or from private travel agencies. In some cases, there is an established tour bus meeting spot – you just roll up in the morning and hop on board.

Of course, you can always let CITS, CTS, CYTS, etc do the organising. In most cases this will get you an English-speaking guide, although even that's not absolutely guaranteed. The standard of service offered by supposedly 'professional' CITS agents can vary tremendously around the country. In some cases you may be paying a lot of money for a lot of nothing.

Beijing 北京

'The mountains are high and the emperor is far away' says an ancient Chinese proverb, meaning that the further one strays from Beijing's grasp, the better. Beijing, capital of the People's Republic of China, is where they move the cogs and wheels of the Chinese universe, or try to slow them down if they're moving in the wrong direction.

As far away as Ürümqi they run on Beijing's clock; around the country they chortle in *putonghua*, the Beijing dialect; in remote Tibet they struggle to interpret the latest half-baked directives from the capital. The Chinese government has announced that if the Dalai Lama were to return he'd be posted to a desk job in (where else?) Beijing.

Those who have slugged it out in hard-seat trains and ramshackle buses through the poverty-stricken interior of China appreciate the creature comforts of Beijing. The city boasts some of China's best restaurants, recreation facilities and palatial hotels fit for an emperor. Other foreigners, having passed their time only in Beijing without seeing the rest of China, come away with the impression that everything is hunky-dory in the PRC and that the Chinese are living high. The Chinese they encounter may, in truth, be doing so.

Whatever impression you come away with, Beijing is not a realistic window on China. It's too much of a cosmetic showcase to qualify. It is, however, a large, relatively clean city, and with a bit of effort you can get out of the make-up department. In between the wide boulevards, high-rises and militaristic structures are some historical and cultural treasures.

History

Although the area south-west of the city was inhabited by cave dwellers some 500,000 years ago, the earliest records of settlements in Beijing date from around 1000 BC. It developed as a frontier trading

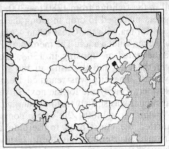

Beijing Facts & Highlights

Area: 16,800 sq km

Population: 12.6 million

Highlights

- The Forbidden City, the centre of power in the Middle Kingdom for more than 500 years.
- Tiantan, a perfect example of Ming architecture and the symbol of Beijing.
- The Summer Palace, the lovely gardens of China's imperial rulers in a stunning setting beside Kunming Lake.
- The Great Wall, ancient China's greatest public works project and now the nation's leading tourist attraction.

town for the Mongols, Koreans and tribes from Shandong and central China. By the Warring States Period it had grown to be the capital of the Yan Kingdom. The town underwent a number of changes as it acquired new warlords – the Khitan Mongols and the Manchurian Jurchen tribes among them. During the Liao Dynasty Beijing was referred to as Yanjing (capital of Yan), and this is still the name used for Beijing's most popular beer.

Beijing's history really gets under way in 1215 AD, the year that Genghis Khan set fire to Yanjing and slaughtered everything in sight. From the ashes emerged Dadu (Great Capital), alias Khanbaliq, the Khan's town. By 1279 Genghis Khan's grandson Kublai had made himself ruler of most of Asia, and Khanbaliq was his capital. With a lull in the fighting from 1280 to 1300, foreigners managed to drop in along the Silk Road for tea with the Great Khan – Marco Polo even landed a job. The mercenary Zhu Yanhang led an uprising in 1368, taking over the city and ushering in the Ming Dynasty. The city was renamed Beiping (Northern Peace) and for the next 35 years the capital was shifted south to Nanjing.

In the early 1400s Zhu's son Yong Le shuffled the court back to Beiping and renamed it Beijing (Northern Capital). Many of the structures like the Forbidden City and Tiantan were built in Yong Le's reign.

The first change of government came with the Manchus, who invaded China and established the Qing Dynasty. Under them, and particularly during the reigns of the emperors Kangxi and Qianlong, Beijing was expanded and renovated, and summer palaces, pagodas and temples were built.

In the last 120 years of the Manchu Dynasty, Beijing and subsequently China were subjected to power struggles, invaders and the chaos created by those who held or sought power: the Anglo-French troops who in 1860 marched in and burnt the Old Summer Palace to the ground; the corrupt regime under Empress Dowager Cixi; the Boxers; General Yuan Shikai; the warlords; the Japanese who occupied the city in 1937; and the Kuomintang after the Japanese defeat. Beijing changed hands again in January 1949 when People's Liberation Army (PLA) troops entered the city. On 1 October of that year Mao proclaimed a 'People's Republic' to an audience of some 500,000 citizens in Tiananmen Square.

Like the emperors before them, the Communists have significantly altered the face of Beijing to suit their own image. Down came the commemorative arches, while blocks of buildings were reduced to rubble to widen major boulevards. From 1950 to 1952 the outer walls were levelled in the interests of traffic circulation. Soviet experts and technicians poured in, which may explain the Stalinesque features on the public structures that went up. The capitalist-style reforms of the 1980s and 1990s have brought foreign money, new highrises, freeways and shopping malls. At this rate, Beijing will wind up looking similar to Los Angeles.

Orientation

With a total area of 16,800 sq km, Beijing Municipality is roughly the size of Belgium.

Though it may not appear so to the visitor in the shambles of arrival, Beijing is a city of very orderly design. Think of the city as one giant grid, with the Forbidden City at its centre. As for the street names: Chongwenmenwai Dajie means 'the avenue (dajie) outside (wai) Chongwen Gate (Chongwenmen)', whereas Chongwenmennei Dajie means 'the avenue inside Chongwen Gate' (that is, inside the old wall). It's an academic exercise since the gate and the wall in question no longer exist.

A major boulevard can change names six or eight times along its length. Streets and avenues can also be split along compass points: Dong Dajie (East Avenue), Xi Dajie (West Avenue), Bei Dajie (North Avenue) and Nan Dajie (South Avenue). All these streets head off from an intersection, usually where a gate once stood.

Officially, there are four 'ring roads' around Beijing, circumnavigating the city centre in four concentric rings. A fifth ring road exists on paper, but construction has yet to begin.

Maps English-language maps of Beijing are generally handed out free at the big hotels. They're often part of an advertising supplement for various companies whose locations are, of course, also shown on the map. It's better to fork out a few yuan for a bilingual map which shows bus routes. These are available from the Friendship Store and hotel gift shops.

If you can deal with Chinese character

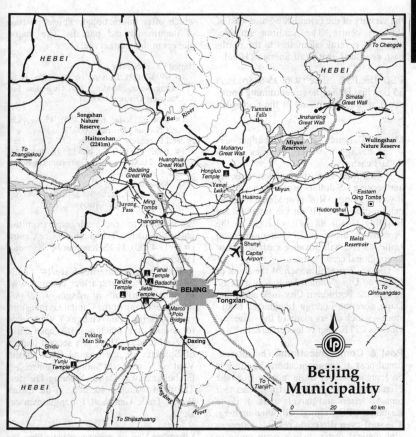

Beijing
Municipality

0   20   40 km

maps, you'll find a wide variety from which
to choose.

Information
Unless otherwise indicated, all of the places
mentioned below appear on the Central
Beijing map.

Tourist Offices The main branch of CITS
is at the Beijing Tourist Building (☎ 6515-
8562; fax 6515-8603) at 28 Jianguomenwai
Dajie, next to the Gloria Plaza Hotel and
near Scitech Plaza.

There is an English-speaking 24 hour
Beijing Tourism Hotline (☎ 6513-0828).
This service can answer questions and listen
to complaints.

Embassies Beijing is not a bad place to
stock up on visas. There are two major
embassy neighbourhoods: Jianguomenwai
and Sanlitun. For a complete list of embassies in Beijing with addresses and phone
numbers, see the Facts for the Visitor
chapter earlier in this book.

The Jianguomenwai embassy area is in

the vicinity of the Friendship Store, east of the city centre. The Sanlitun embassy cluster is several kilometres to the north-east, near the Great Wall Sheraton Hotel.

PSB The PSB office (☎ 6525-5486) is at 85 Beichizi Dajie, the street running north-south at the eastern side of the Forbidden City.

Money All hotels – even most budget ones – can change travellers cheques or US dollars cash.

If you want to cash travellers cheques and receive US dollars in return (necessary if you're going to Russia or Mongolia), this can be done at CITIC at the International Building (*guójì dàshà*), adjacent to the Friendship Store at 19 Jianguomenwai Dajie. CITIC will advance cash on major international credit cards.

There is a useful branch of the Bank of China on Dong'anmen Dajie – just to the east of the Forbidden City in Wangfujing Dajie near the Foreign Languages Bookstore – which offers many of the same services as CITIC, but is less efficient.

Post & Communications The international post & communications building is on Jianguomenwei Dajie, not far from the Friendship Store. It's open from 8 am to 7 pm. All letters and parcels marked 'Poste Restante, GPO Beijing' will wind up here. The staff even file poste restante letters in alphabetical order, a rare occurrence in China, but you pay for all this efficiency – there is a Y1.50 fee charged for each letter received.

Overseas parcels must be posted from here; a counter sells wrapping paper, string, tape and glue. There's also an international telegraph and telephone service.

There is also a small but convenient post office in the CITIC building at Jianguomenwei Dajie. Another useful post office is in the basement of the China World Trade Centre, further east on the same road.

There are a number of private couriers which offer international express posting of documents and parcels. The major players in this market are:

United Parcel Service
(☎ 6593-2932), Unit A, 1st floor, Tower B, Beijing Kelun Building, 12A Guanghua Lu, Chaoyang District, 100020
DHL
(☎ 6466-2211; fax 6467-7826), 45 Xinyuan Jie, Chaoyang District, 100027
Federal Express
(☎ 6462-3253; fax 6462-3259), 401 EAS Tower, 21 Xiaoyun Lu, Dongsanhuan Beilu, Chaoyang District, 100027
TNT Skypak
(☎ 6465-2227; fax 6462-4018), 8A Xiangheyuan Zhongli, Chaoyang, 100028

It's possible to send a telegraph from the phone company's Telegraph Service Centre (☎ 6603-4900), 11 Xichang'an Jie, Xicheng District.

The Sparkice Internet Cafe (☎ 6833-5335; email cafe@sparkice.co.cn; www.sparkice.co.cn) (*shíhuá wǎngluò kāfēi shì*) in the west wing of the Capital Gymnasium (west of Beijing Zoo) charges Y30 per hour for use of their machines. It's open daily except Monday. There is a second branch of Sparkice on the ground floor of the Vantone New World Shopping Centre, 2-8 Fuchengmenwai Dajie, Xicheng District. The third branch is located in the China World Trade Centre at 1 Jianguomenwai Dajie.

Libraries Various embassies have libraries in English and other languages. Although the selection of books is limited, it's certainly better than what you can hope to find at the Chinese libraries. Some of the more useful embassy libraries include:

American Center for Educational Exchange
(☎ 6532-2331), Room 2801, Jingguang New World Hotel, Hujialou, Chaoyang District
Australian Embassy
(☎ 6532-2331), 21 Dongzhimenwai Dajie, Chaoyang District
Canadian Embassy
(☎ 6532-3536), 19 Dongzhimenwai Dajie, Chaoyang District

Cultural & Educational Section
  (☎ 6501-1903), 4th floor, British Embassy Annex, Landmark Tower, 8 Dongsanhuan Beilu, Chaoyang District

Medical Services Asia Emergency Assistance (☎ 6462-9100; fax 6462-9111) has the biggest market share with the foreign community. The staff is mostly expats, and emergency service is available 24 hours. AEA is at 2-1-1 Tayuan Diplomatic Building, 14 Liangmahe Nanlu, in the Sanlitun embassy area. AEA offers emergency evacuation from China for the critically ill. The International Medical Centre (☎ 6465- 1561; fax 6465-1984) is in the Lufthansa Centre at 50 Liangmaqiao Lu. Emergency service is available 24 hours, but it's a good idea to call first for an appointment.

National Buildings & Monuments
For information on the Forbidden City and the New Summer Palace, see the special colour section at page 240.

Tiananmen Square (*tiān'ānmén guǎngchǎng*) This is the heart of Beijing, a vast desert of pavement and photo-booths. The square is Mao's creation, as is Chang'an

---

Accidental Terrorists

It was the evening of 3 June 1993, the night was hot, and we had escaped the clogging confinement of our shared student rooms and sauntered up to the roof of the foreign student building of Beijing Normal University. The roof was no more than a concrete expanse of broken tiling and only offered a view of smokestacks and miserable rooftops, but after a year in China's capital, it was what we were used to. Anyway, it was a place where you could sit, sink a few cheap beers, smoke a few local cigarettes and strum a few songs, if anyone had brought a guitar along.

None of us had any inkling that we would soon be terrorists. There was no heinous motive, and nothing more sinister than playfulness guided our actions that evening, but we would go down in history, anyway. The fact of the matter was that we had already downed quite a few 'five star' beers and, as we were approaching the end of our year-long stay in China, we were in a celebratory mood – a mood with a measure of rowdiness thrown in. I guess that our year-long sojourn in Beijing had made us restless, and we were all suffering from deprivations that made us dream of home.

I can't remember who threw the first bottle, but I remember it sailing through the night sky and landing with a well aimed splash in the courtyard pool below. This was the signal for everyone to join in, and altogether about eight bottles made the journey to the pond, until a window slammed open and a Chinese voice bellowed out at us. We legged it inside smartish, got our breath back and sought sanctuary in one of the student dormitories.

We duly forgot about the incident, unspectacular as it was, and busily returned to daily chore of learning the Chinese language and preparing for the examinations that awaited us on our return home. In fact the whole event would naturally have suffered the erosion of time had not we heard, through a friend, that a fellow China-watcher had read 'due to a heightened security presence, all was quiet on the eve of the anniversary of the Tiananmen massacre in China, apart from an outbreak of protest at the foreign students building in Beijing Normal University'.

How could we have overlooked the two simple facts that it was a sensitive anniversary the next day and that the throwing of beer bottles was a popular symbol of protest during the time of Deng Xiaoping? (The word 'xiaoping' is homophonous with the word 'small bottle' in Mandarin.)

Damian Harper

Jie leading up to it. During the Cultural Revolution, the chairman, wearing a Red Guard armband, reviewed parades of up to a million people here. In 1976 another million people jammed the square to pay their last respects to him. In 1989, army tanks and soldiers cut down pro-democracy demonstrators.

Today (if the weather is conducive) the square is a place for people to lounge around in the evening and to fly decorated kites and balloons for the kiddies. Surrounding or studding the square is a strange mishmash of monuments past and present: Tiananmen (Heavenly Peace Gate), the Chinese Revolution History Museum, the Great Hall of the People, Qianmen (Front Gate), the Mao Mausoleum and the Monument to the People's Heroes.

If you get up early you can watch the flag-raising ceremony at sunrise, performed by a troop of PLA soldiers drilled to march at precisely 108 paces per minute, 75cm per pace. The same ceremony in reverse gets performed at sunset, but you can hardly see the soldiers for the throngs gathered to watch. A digital sign on the square announces the times for the sunrise ceremony for the next two days.

Bicycles cannot be ridden across Tiananmen Square (apparently tanks are OK), but you can walk the bike. Traffic is one way for north-south avenues on either side of the square.

Tiananmen Gate (tiān'ānmén) Tiananmen, or Heavenly Peace Gate, is a national symbol. The gate was built in the 15th century and restored in the 17th. From imperial days it functioned as a rostrum for proclaiming to the assembled masses. There are five doors to the gate, and in front of it are seven bridges spanning a stream. Each of these bridges was restricted in its use and only the emperor could use the central door and bridge.

It was from the gate that Mao proclaimed the People's Republic on 1 October 1949. The dominating feature is the gigantic portrait of Mao – the required backdrop for any photo the Chinese take of themselves at the gate. To the left of the portrait is a slogan 'Long Live the People's Republic of China' and to the right 'Long Live the Unity of the Peoples of the World'.

You pass through Tiananmen Gate on your way into the Forbidden City (assuming you enter from the southern side). There is no fee for walking through the gate, but to go upstairs and look down on the square costs a whopping Y30 for foreigners, or Y10 for Chinese. It's hardly worth it – you can get a similar view of the square from inside Qianmen for a quarter of the price.

Qianmen (qiánmén) Silent sentinel to the changing times, Qianmen (Front Gate) sits on the southern side of Tiananmen Square. Qianmen guarded the wall division between the ancient Inner City and the outer suburban zone and dates back to the reign of Emperor Yong Le in the 15th century. With the disappearance of the city walls, the gate sits out of context, but it's still impressive.

Qianmen actually consists of two gates. The southern one is called Arrow Tower (jiàn lóu) and the rear one is Zhongyang Gate (zhōngyángmén, also called chéng lóu). You can go upstairs into Zhongyang Gate.

Great Hall of the People (rénmín dàhuì táng) This is the venue of the rubber-stamp legislature, the National People's Congress. It's open to the public when the Congress is not sitting – to earn some hard currency it's even rented out occasionally to foreigners for conventions! These are the halls of power, many of them named after provinces and regions of China and decorated appropriately. You can see the 5000 seat banquet room where US President Richard Nixon dined in 1972, and the 10,000 seat auditorium with the familiar red star embedded in a galaxy of lights in the ceiling. There's a sort of museum-like atmosphere in the Great Hall, with objets d'art donated by the provinces, plus a snack bar and restaurant.

The hall is found on the western side of Tiananmen Square and admission costs a mind-boggling Y35.

Monument to the People's Heroes (*rén-mín yīngxióng jìniàn bēi*) On the southern side of Tiananmen Square, this monument was completed in 1958 and stands on the site of the old Outer Palace Gate.

The 36m obelisk, made of Qingdao granite, bears bas-relief carvings of key revolutionary events (one relief shows the Chinese destroying opium in the 19th century), as well as appropriate calligraphy from Mao Zedong and Zhou Enlai.

Mao Zedong Mausoleum (*máo zhǔxí jìniàn táng*) Chairman Mao died in September 1976 and his mausoleum was constructed shortly thereafter.

Commonly known to Beijing expats as the 'Maosoleum', this enormous building

Mao Mania

Although he's been dead for 20 years, the legacy of Mao Zedong continues to play a major role in the contemporary political life of China and, indeed, for many mainland Chinese Mao has made the leap from emperor to god-like status.

What is more intriguing, perhaps, is how Mao has captivated the imagination beyond China's borders in a guise that is far less politically defined: 'Like, wouldn't it be cool to have matching Mao earrings?'. Maybe it all began with Andy Warhol's 1972 silkscreen portrait after Nixon's visit to China that put the chairman up alongside pop icons like Marilyn Monroe and made him fashionable, for it can't be denied that the Mao image today, along with other artefacts associated with the Cultural Revolution, has a certain trendy cachet in Hong Kong, Japan and the west. Of course, China experienced its own resurgence of Maoist kitsch in the early 90s, yet this was seen as a nostalgic and even spiritual response to disillusionment with the current leadership and uncertainty about changes brought by the economic reforms.

The fascination with Mao outside of the local context is a little more baffling, especially when seen in the light of historical realities. Compared with Mao, it's hard to think of other dictators in world history that have made such a splash in the souvenir market – Mao badges, Mao's little red books, miniature Mao statues, Mao lighters and Mao T-shirts have all done a brisk trade since China's opening in the early 80s.

It does beg the question: how can anybody with more than a passing understanding of Mao's role in Chinese history really feel comfortable walking around wearing a Mao T-shirt? It's difficult to see a similar currency among tourists for souvenirs featuring Hitler or Stalin. Perhaps the difference is that the international community, and most certainly the mainland Chinese government, have not repudiated Mao's value as the leader of China after 1949, but this does not make his crimes against humanity any less abhorrent.

Not many foreign tourists seemed interested in buying a Deng Xiaoping T-shirt after the crackdown on demonstrators in the 1989 Tiananmen Massacre. Yet that single incident pales almost into insignificance when one considers many of the events which occurred under Mao's leadership – the mass slaughter of Chinese soldiers during the Korean War, the anti-rightist purge during the One Hundred Flowers campaign, the famine following the Great Leap Forward where as many as 30 million people (if not more) died of starvation, and finally the brutality and devastation of the Cultural Revolution, from which China has yet to recover.

The complete demystification of Mao may never take place in China and no doubt he will occupy a sacred place for many years to come. Outside of China, however, Mao's image might have less appeal as an item of popular recognition if there was a greater awareness about his role in Chinese history. No matter how compelling he may appear in the official portrait hanging above the entrance to the Forbidden City, there's nothing like a good dose of Mao stories to turn you off the chairman forever. ∎

is located just behind the Monument to the People's Heroes in Tiananmen Square.

However history judges Mao, his impact on its course was enormous. Easy as it now is to vilify his deeds and excesses, many Chinese show deep respect when confronted with the physical presence of the man. CITS guides freely quote the old 7:3 ratio on Mao that first surfaced in 1976 – Mao was 70% right and 30% wrong (what, one wonders, are the figures for CITS itself?) and this is now the official Party line.

The mausoleum is open daily from 8.30 to 11.30 am and from 1 to 3.30 pm. Entry is free, though you have to pay Y10 to check your bags and camera. Join the enormous queue of Chinese sightseers, but don't expect more than a quick glimpse of the body as you file past the sarcophagus. At certain times of year the body requires maintenance and is not on view.

Whatever Mao might have done to the Chinese economy while he was alive, sales of Mao memorabilia are certainly giving the free market a boost these days. At the souvenir stalls near the mausoleum you can pick up Chairman Mao key rings, thermometers, face towels, handkerchiefs, sun visors, address books and cartons of cigarettes (a comment on his chain-smoking?).

Zhongnanhai (*zhōngnánhǎi*) Just west of the Forbidden City is China's new forbidden city, Zhongnanhai. The interior is off limits to tourists, but you can gawk at the entrance. The compound was first built between the 10th and 13th centuries as a sort of playground for the emperors and their retinues. It was expanded during Ming times, but most of the present buildings only date from the Qing Dynasty.

Empress Dowager Cixi once lived here; after the failure of the 1898 reform movement she imprisoned Emperor Guangxu in the Impregnating Vitality Hall where, ironically, he later died. After the overthrow of the imperial government and the establishment of the republic, it served as the site of the presidential palace.

Since the founding of the People's Republic in 1949, Zhongnanhai has been the site of the residence and offices of the highest-ranking members of the Communist Party.

Old Summer Palace (*yuánmíngyuán*) Located north-west of the city centre (see the Beijing map), the original Summer Palace was laid out in the 12th century. By the reign of Emperor Qianlong it had developed into a set of interlocking gardens.

The Power of Eunuchs

An interesting feature of the Ming Dynasty, and one that was principal in its eventual decline, was the ever-increasing power and number of eunuchs in the imperial court. Eunuchs, generally castrated at a young age by their families in the hope that they would attain the imperial court, had been employed by Chinese emperors as early as the Han Dynasty. Traditionally, their role was to serve the needs of the emperor and his harem in parts of the imperial palace that were off limits to all adult males barring the emperor himself.

By the early Ming, the number of eunuchs in the service of the emperor was already 10,000 and, despite imperial edicts forbidding their access to political power, they continued to grow in influence and numbers throughout the Ming.

Certain eunuchs (perhaps the most infamous of whom is Wei Zhongxian, who practically ruled all of China in the 1620s) assumed dictatorial power and siphoned off massive fortunes while their emperors frolicked with their consorts.

In the late years of Ming rule, eunuchs probably numbered somewhere between 70,000 and 100,000 and exercised enormous control over the nation. ■

Qianlong set the Jesuits to work as architects for European-style palaces for the gardens – elaborate fountains and baroque statuary.

During the second Opium War (1860), British and French troops destroyed the palace and sent the booty abroad. Since the Chinese pavilions and temples were made of wood they did not survive fires, but a marble facade, some broken columns and traces of the fountains remain.

The ruins have long been a favourite picnic spot for foreigners living in the capital and for Chinese twosomes seeking a bit of privacy. More recently, the government has decided to slowly restore the gardens, moats and buildings. It's uncertain yet just how far the restoration will go – will it be allowed to remain as ruins or will it become another tourist circus like the Ming Tombs? At present, it's a very worthwhile place to visit.

The site covers a huge area – some 2.5km from east to west – so be prepared to do some walking. There are three entrance gates to the compound, all on the southern side. The western section is the main area, Perfection and Brightness Garden (*yuánmíngyuán*). The southern compound is the 10,000 Spring Garden (*wànchūnyuán*). The eastern section is the Eternal Spring Garden (*chángchūnyuán*) – it's here that you'll find the European Garden with its Great Fountain Ruins, considered the best preserved relic in the palace and featured prominently on picture postcards.

Minibuses connect the new Summer Palace with the old one, or a taxi will take you for Y10.

Parks & Gardens
Jade Spring Mountain (*yùquán shān*)
About 2.5km west of the Summer Palace is Jade Spring Mountain (see the Beijing map), an area only recently developed as a park. The spring's name is derived from the simple observation that the water has a clear, jade-like crystalline appearance. During the Ming and Qing dynasties,

mineral water from the spring was sent daily to the Forbidden City to quench the emperor's thirst – it was believed the water had a tonic effect, an essential consideration with so many concubines to satisfy.

Jade Spring Mountain is dressed-up with the usual temples, pagodas and pavilions. At the base of the mountain is the Garden of Light & Tranquillity.

Fragrant Hills Park (*xiāngshān gōngyuán*)
Easily within striking distance of the Summer Palace are the Western Hills (*xī shān*), another former villa-resort of the emperors. The part of the Western Hills closest to Beijing is known as the Fragrant Hills (*xiāngshān*). This is the last stop for the city buses – if you want to get further into the mountains, you'll have to walk, cycle or take a taxi.

You can scramble up the slopes to the top of **Incense-Burner Peak**, or take the crowded chairlift. From the peak you get an all-embracing view of the countryside. The chairlift is a good way to get up the mountain, and from the summit you can hike further into the Western Hills and leave the crowds behind.

Within walking distance of the North Gate of Fragrant Hills Park is the **Azure Clouds Temple** (*bìyún sì*), whose landmark is the Diamond Throne Pagoda. Of Indian design, it consists of a raised platform with a central pagoda and stupas around it. The temple was built in 1366, and was expanded in the 18th century with the addition of the Hall of Arhats, containing 500 statues representing disciples of Buddha. Dr Sun Yatsen's coffin was placed in the temple in 1925 before being moved to Nanjing. In 1954 the government renovated Sun's memorial hall, which has a picture display of his revolutionary activities.

There are a couple of ways of getting to the Fragrant Hills by public transport: bus No 333 from the Summer Palace, bus No 360 from the zoo or bus No 318 from Pingguoyuan (the last stop in the west on the subway).

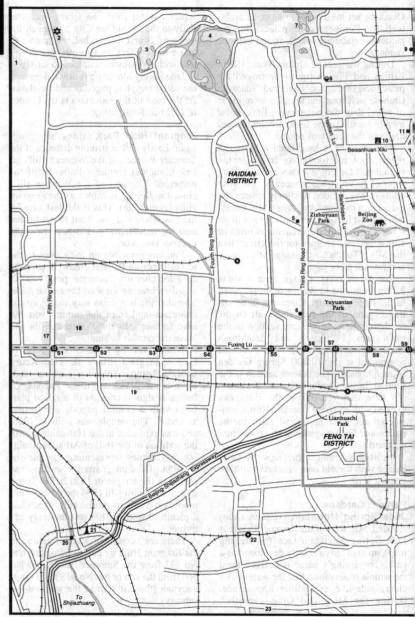

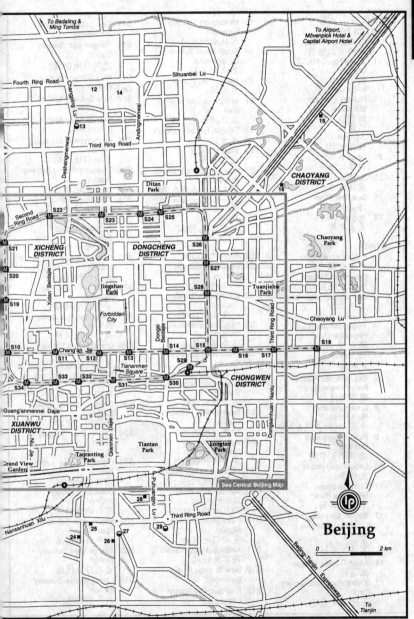

To Badaling &
Ming Tombs

To Airport,
Mövenpick Hotel &
Capital Airport Hotel

Fourth Ring Road

Sihuanbei Lu

12   14

13   Third Ring Road

Ditan
Park

CHAOYANG
DISTRICT

16

15

Chaoyang
Park

Second
Ring Road   S22   S23   S24   S25

S21

XICHENG
DISTRICT   DONGCHENG
DISTRICT   S26

S20   S27

S19   Jingshan
Park   S28

Tuanjiehu
Park

Forbidden
City   Chaoyang Lu

S10   Chang'an Jie   S14   S15   S18

S11   S12   S13   S16   S17

S33   S32   S29   CHONGWEN
DISTRICT

S34   S31   S30

Guang'anmennei Dajie

XUANWU
DISTRICT

Tiantan
Park   Longtan
Park

Taoranting
Park

Grand View
Garden

See Central Beijing Map

28

Beijing

0   1   2 km

Nansanhuan Xilu   24   25   27   29

26   Third Ring Road

To
Tianjin

BEIJING 北京
PLACES TO STAY
5 Shangri-La Hotel
香格里拉饭店

11 Jimen Hotel; NASA
Disco
蓟门饭店、
NASA迪斯可

15 Holiday Inn Lido;
Watson's
丽都假日饭店、
屈臣氏

16 Jiali Hotel
佳丽饭店

24 Lihua Hotel
丽华饭店

25 Jinghua Hotel
京华饭店

26 Sea Star Hotel
海兴大酒店

28 Jingtai Hotel
景泰宾馆

OTHER
1 Fragrant Hills Park
香山公园

2 Botanical Gardens
北京植物园

3 Jade Spring Mountain
玉泉山

4 Summer Palace;
Tingliguan Imperial
Restaurant
颐和园

6 TV Tower
电视塔

7 Old Summer Palace;
Fuhai Restaurant
圆明园遗址

8 Zhongguancun
(Bus Stop)
中关村(公共汽车站)

9 Beijing Language
Institute
北京语言学院

10 Great Bell Temple
大钟寺

12 Chinese Ethnic
Minorities Park
中华民族园

13 Beijiao (Deshengmen)
Long-Distance Bus
Station
北京(德胜门)
长途汽车站

14 Asian Games Village
亚运村

17 Shijingshan Amusement
Park
石景山游乐场

18 Motorcycle Training
Ground
摩托车训练场

19 South-West Suburban
Greenhouse
西南郊苗圃

20 Marco Polo Bridge
卢沟桥

21 Anti-Japanese War
Memorial
抗日战争纪念馆

22 Fengtai Railway Station
丰台站

23 World Park
世界公园

27 Haihutun Long-Distance
Bus Station
海户屯公共汽车站

29 Zhaogongkou Bus
Station (Buses to
Tianjin)
赵公口汽车站
(至天津)

SUBWAY STATIONS
S1 Bajiaocun Subway
Station
八角村地铁站

S2 Babaoshan Subway
Station
八宝山地铁站

S3 Yuquanlu Subway
Station
玉泉路地铁站

S4 Wukesong Subway
Station
五棵松地铁站

S5 Wanshoulu Subway
Station
万寿路地铁站

S6 Gongzhufen Subway
Station
公主坟地铁站

S7 Junshibowuguan
Subway Station
军事博物馆地铁站

S8 Muxidi Subway Station
木樨地地铁站

S9 Nanlishilu Subway
Station
南礼士路地铁站

S10 Fuxingmen Subway
Station
复兴门地铁站

S11 Xidan Subway Station
西单地铁站

S12 New Subway Station
(unnamed)

S13 New Subway Station
(unnamed)

S14 New Subway Station
(unnamed)

S15 Jianguomen Subway
Station
建国门地铁站

S16 New Subway Station
(unnamed)

S17 New Subway Station
(unnamed)

S18 New Subway Station
(unnamed)

S19 Fuchengmen Subway
Station
阜城门地铁站

S20 Chegongzhuang Subway
Station
车公庄地铁站

S21 Xizhimen Subway
Station
西直门地铁站

S22 Jishuitan Subway
Station
积水潭地铁站

S23 Gulou Subway
Station
鼓楼地铁站

S24 Andingmen Subway
Station
安定门地铁站

S25 Yonghegong Subway
Station
雍和宫地铁站

S26 Dongzhimen Subway
Station
东直门地铁站

S27 Dongsishitiao Subway
Station
东四十条地铁站

S28 Chaoyangmen Subway
Station
朝阳门地铁站

S29 Beijing Zhan Subway
Station
北京站

S30 Chongwenmen Subway
Station
崇文门地铁站

S31 Qianmen Subway
Station
前门地铁站

S32 Hepingmen Subway
Station
和平门地铁站

S33 Xuanwumen Subway
Station
宣武门地铁站

S34 Changchunjie Subway
Station
长春街地铁站

Botanical Gardens (*xiāngshān zhíwù yuán*) About 2km east of Fragrant Hills Park are the Botanical Gardens. While not spectacular, the gardens are a botanist's delight and a pleasant place for a stroll. At the northern end of the gardens is the Sleeping Buddha Temple (*wòfó sì*).

Jingshan Park (*jǐngshān gōngyuán*) Just to the north of the Forbidden City is Jingshan (Prospect Hill) Park, which contains an artificial mound made of earth excavated to create the palace moat. If you clamber to the top pavilions of this regal pleasure garden, you get a magnificent panorama of the capital and a great overview of the russet roofing of the Forbidden City.

On the eastern side of the park a locust tree stands in the place where the last of the Mings, Emperor Chongzhen, hanged himself after slaying his family, rather than see the palace razed by the Manchus. The hill supposedly protects the palace from the evil spirits – or dust storms – from the north, but it didn't quite work for Chongzhen.

Entrance to Jingshan Park is a modest Y0.30, or you can pay more than 30 times as much for a souvenir 'tourist passport ticket' – fortunately, this is optional.

Beihai Park (*běihǎi gōngyuán*) Approached by four gates, and just north-west of the Forbidden City, Beihai Park is the former playground of the emperors. The park covers an area of 68 hectares, more than half of which is a lake. The island in the lower middle is composed of the heaped earth dug to create the lake – some attribute this to the handiwork of Kublai Khan.

The site is associated with the Great Khan's palace, the belly-button of Beijing before the creation of the Forbidden City. All that remains of the Khan's court is a large jar made of green jade, in the Round City near the southern entrance.

From the 12th century onwards, Beihai Park was landscaped with artificial hills, pavilions, halls, temples and covered walkways. Dominating Jade Islet on the lake,

the White Dagoba is a 36m-high pop-art 'bottle' originally dating from 1651. It was put up for a visit by the Dalai Lama and was rebuilt in 1741.

On the north-eastern shore of the islet is the handsome and double-tiered Painted Gallery – with unusual architecture for a walkway. Near the boat dock is the Fangshan Restaurant, dishing up imperial recipes favoured by Empress Cixi. She liked 120 course dinners with about 30 kinds of desserts. The restaurant is expensive and high class, and reservations are necessary (but check out the decor!).

The main attraction on the northern side is the Nine Dragon Screen, 5m high and 27m long, made of coloured glazed tiles. The screen was built to scare off evil spirits; it stands at the entrance to a temple which has disappeared. To the south-west of the boat dock on this side is the Five Dragon Pavilion dating from 1651, where the emperors liked to fish, camp and sing songs around the campfire (an ancient form of karaoke).

Beihai Park is a relaxing place to stroll around, grab a snack, sip a beer, rent a rowing boat or, as the Chinese do, cuddle on a bench in the evening. It's crowded at weekends. Some people dive into the lake when no-one's around, but swimming is not permitted. In winter there's ice skating.

Tiantan Park (*tiāntán gōngyuán*) The most perfect example of Ming architecture, Tiantan (the Temple of Heaven) has come to symbolise Beijing. Its lines appear on countless pieces of tourist literature and as a brand name for a wide range of products from Tiger Balm to plumbing fixtures. It is set in a 267 hectare park, with four gates at the compass points, and is bounded by walls to the north and east. It originally functioned as a vast stage for solemn rites performed by the Son of Heaven, who came here to pray for good harvests, seek divine clearance and atone for the sins of the people.

The temples, seen in aerial perspective, are round and the bases are square, deriving from the ancient Chinese belief that heaven is round, and the earth is square. Thus the northern end of the park is semi-circular and the southern end is square.

Tiantan was considered highly sacred ground and it was here that the emperor performed the major ceremonial rites of the year. The least hitch in any part of the proceedings was regarded as an ill omen, and it was thought that the nation's future was thus decided.

The 5m-high **Round Altar** was constructed in 1530 and rebuilt in 1740. It is composed of white marble arrayed in three tiers, and its geometry revolves around the imperial number nine. Odd numbers were considered heavenly, and nine is the largest single-digit odd number. The top tier, thought to symbolise heaven, has nine rings of stones, with each ring composed of multiples of nine stones, so that the ninth ring has 81 stones. The number of stairs and balustrades are also multiples of nine. If you stand in the centre of the upper terrace and say something, the sound waves are bounced off the marble balustrades, amplifying your voice (nine times?).

Just north of the altar, surrounding the entrance to the Imperial Vault of Heaven, is the **Echo Wall**, 65m in diameter. This enables a whisper to travel clearly from one end to your friend's ear at the other – that is, if there's not a tour group in the middle.

The octagonal **Imperial Vault of Heaven** was built at the same time as the Round Altar, and is structured along the lines of the older Hall of Prayer for Good Harvests. It used to contain tablets of the emperor's ancestors, which were used in the winter solstice ceremony. Proceeding up from the Imperial Vault is a walkway: to the left is a molehill composed of excess dirt dumped from digging air-raid shelters, and to the right is a rash of souvenir shops.

The dominant feature of the whole complex is the **Hall of Prayer for Good Harvests**, a magnificent piece mounted on a three-tiered marble terrace. Amazingly, the wooden pillars ingeniously support the ceiling without nails or cement – for a building 38m high and 30m in diameter, that's an accomplishment unmatched until Lego was invented. Built in 1420, the Hall was burnt to cinders in 1889 and heads rolled in apportioning blame. A faithful reproduction based on Ming architectural methods was erected the following year.

Grand View Garden (*dàguān yuán*) At the south-western corner of town is Grand View Garden, also known as Daguanyuan Park. Unlike most of Beijing's parks, which date back to imperial days, this one is new – construction started in 1984 and was completed four years later.

The park was built as a replica of the family gardens described in the Chinese novel *The Dream of the Red Chamber* (see also Prince Gong's Residence further on). The book is a Chinese classic written in the late 18th century. While the park is not steeped in history, it could be of interest if you've read the novel. Otherwise, just kick back and enjoy the birds and the trees.

Museums & Galleries
Chinese Revolution History Museum (*zhōngguó gémìng lìshǐ bówùguǎn*) If you don't count the Forbidden City and other palaces, this is Beijing's largest museum. It is housed in a sombre building on the eastern side of Tiananmen Square, and access was long thwarted by special permission requirements. From 1966 to 1978 the museum was closed so that history could be revised in the light of recent events. There are actually two museums here combined into one – the Museum of History and the Museum of the Revolution. Explanations throughout most of the museums are, unfortunately, entirely in Chinese, so you won't get much out of this labyrinth unless you're particularly fluent or pick up an English-speaking student. An English text relating to the museum is available inside.

The Museum of History contains artefacts and cultural relics (many of them copies) from year zero to 1919, subdivided into primitive communal groups, slavery, feudalism, and capitalism and imperialism, laced with Marxist commentary. Without a guide you can discern ancient weapons, inventions and musical instruments.

The Chinese Revolution History Museum is split into five sections: the founding of the CCP (1919-21), the first civil war (1924-7), the second civil war (1927-37), resistance against Japan (1937-45) and the third civil war (1945-49). It's open from 8.30 am to 4 pm daily and admission costs Y2.

Military Museum (*jūnshì bówùguǎn*) Perhaps more to the point than the Chinese Revolution History Museum, this traces the genesis of the PLA from 1927 to the present and has some interesting exhibits: pictures of Mao in the early days, Socialist realist sculptures, and captured US tanks from the Korean War, warplanes, missiles and other tools of destruction. Explanations are in Chinese only.

The museum is open from 8.30 am to 5 pm daily and admission is Y5. It is on Fuxing Lu on the western side of the city; to get there take the subway to Junshibowuguan.

Natural History Museum (*zìrán bówùguǎn*) This is the largest such museum in China and gets good reviews from travellers. The four main exhibition halls are devoted to flora, fauna, ancient fauna and human evolution. Some of the more memorable exhibits include a human cadaver cut in half to show the insides and a complete dinosaur skeleton. There is also plenty of pickled wildlife, although nothing worse than what you see for sale in some of the street markets.

Some of the exhibits were donated by the British Museum, the American Museum of Natural History and other foreign sources.

The Natural History Museum is in the Tianqiao area, just north of Tiantan Park's west gate. Admission is Y15. The museum is open daily, except Monday, from 8.30 am until 4 pm.

China Art Gallery (*zhōngguó měishù guǎn*) Back in the post-Liberation days, one of the safest hobbies for an artist was to retouch classical-type landscapes with red flags, belching factory chimneys or bright red tractors. You can get some idea of the state of the arts in China at this gallery. At times, very good exhibitions of current work (including photo displays) are held in an adjacent gallery. Check the *China Daily* for listings. The arts and crafts shop inside has an excellent range of woodblock prints and papercuts.

The gallery is just north-east of the Forbidden City on Chaoyangmennei Dajie. It's open Tuesday to Sunday from 9 am to 4 pm. Admission is Y4.

Song Qingling Museum (*sòng qìnglíng gùjū*) Madam Song was the second wife of Dr Sun Yatsen (he divorced the first), who went on to become the first president of the Republic of China. After 1981, Madam Song's large residence was transformed into a museum dedicated to her memory and to that of Dr Sun. The original layout of the residence is unchanged and on display are personal items and pictures of historical interest.

The museum is on the northern side of Shisha Houhai lake. It is open daily from 9 am to 4.30 pm. Admission is Y10.

Wax Museum (*làxiàng guǎn*) This is Beijing's answer to Madame Tussaud's in London. In order to be immortalised in wax here, you have to be dead. There is a wax Mao, and rumour has it that Deng Xiaoping will soon join the exhibit.

The Wax Museum is north of the city centre in Ditan Park in the Dongcheng District, within walking distance of the Lama Temple. It's open from 9 am to 4 pm, but closed on Thursday and Friday. Admission is Y5.

Temples & Mosques
Lama Temple (*yōnghégōng*) This is by far the most colourful temple in Beijing – beautiful gardens, stunning frescoes and

tapestries, and incredible carpentry. Get to this one before you're 'templed out' – it won't chew up your day.

The Lama Temple is the most renowned Tibetan Buddhist temple in China, outside Tibet itself (a carefully worded statement!). North-west of the city centre toward Andingmen Dongdajie, it became the official residence of Count Yin Zhen after extensive renovation. There was nothing unusual in that – but in 1723 he was promoted to emperor and moved to the Forbidden City. His name was changed to Yong Zheng, and his former residence became Yonghe Palace. In 1744 it was converted into a lamasery and became a residence for large numbers of monks from Mongolia and Tibet.

In 1949 the Lama Temple was declared protected as a major historical relic. Miraculously it survived the Cultural Revolution without scars. In 1979 a large amount of money was spent on repairs and it was restocked with several dozen novices from Inner Mongolia – a token move on the part of the government to back up its claim that the Lama Temple is a 'symbol of religious freedom, national unity and stability in China'. The novices study Tibetan language and the secret practices of the Yellow Sect.

No photography is permitted inside the temple buildings (tempting as it is). The monks, and the postcard industry, are sensitive to the reproduction of Buddha images. The temple is open daily, except Monday, from 9 am to 4 pm. You can get there by subway to the Yonghegong station.

Confucius Temple & Imperial College
(kǒng miào, guózǐjiān) Just down the hutong (alley) opposite the gates of the Lama Temple is the former Confucius Temple and Imperial College.

The Confucius Temple is the second largest in the land, after the one at Qufu. The temple was reopened in 1981 after some mysterious use as a high-official residence and is now used as a museum. The forest of steles in the temple courtyard look forlorn. The steles record the names of those successful in the civil service examinations (possibly the world's first) of the imperial court.

The Imperial College was the place where the emperor expounded the Confucian classics to an audience of thousands of kneeling students, professors and court officials – an annual rite. Built by the grandson of Kublai Khan in 1306, the former college was the only institution of its kind in China; it's now the Capital Library.

Great Bell Temple
(dàzhōng sì) This, the biggest bell in China, weighs a hefty 46.5 tonnes and is 6.75m tall. The bell is inscribed with Buddhist sutras, a total of over 227,000 Chinese characters.

The bell was cast during the reign of Ming Emperor Yong Le in 1406 and the tower was built in 1733. Getting the bell from the foundry to the temple proved problematic – back in those days it wasn't possible to contract the job out to a Hong Kong company. A shallow canal had to be built which froze over in winter – the bell was moved across the ice by sled.

Within the grounds of the monastery are several other buildings (besides the Bell Tower itself). This includes the Guanyin Hall, Sutra-keeping Tower, Main Buddha Hall and Four Devas Hall. This monastery is one of the most popular in Beijing and was reopened in 1980.

The Great Bell Temple is along the north-western part of the third ring road (Beisanhuan Xilu; see the Beijing map).

White Dagoba Temple
(báitǎ sì) The dagoba can be spotted from the top of Jingshan and is similar (and close) to the one in Beihai Park. It was used as a factory during the Cultural Revolution, but reopened after restoration in 1980. The dagoba dates back to Kublai Khan's days and is now basically just a historical monument. It lies off Fuchengmennei Dajie.

Guangji Temple
(guǎngjì sì) The Guangji (Universal Rescue) Temple is on the north-western side of the Xisi Dajie intersection,

to the east of the White Dagoba Temple. It's in good shape and is the headquarters of the Chinese Buddhist Association. It is claimed to contain some of the finest Buddhist statues in China.

Dongsi Mosque (*dōngsì qīngzhēn sì*) This is one of two functioning mosques in Beijing, the other being Niujie Mosque. It's to the east of Jingshan Park at 13 Dongsi Nandajie, just south of the intersection with Chaoyangmennei Dajie.

Niujie Mosque (*niújiē lǐbài sì*) In the south-western sector of Beijing (Xuanwu District), south of Guang'anmennei Dajie, is a Muslim residential area with a handsome mosque facing Mecca. Niujie (Ox St) has a feel all its own and is worth checking out.

Fayuan Temple (*fǎyuán sì*) In a lane just east of Niujie Mosque is the Fayuan (Source of Law) Temple. The temple was originally constructed in the 7th century and is still going strong. It's now the China Buddhism College and is open to visitors.

White Cloud Temple (*báiyúnguàn*) This temple is south-west of town. It was once the Taoist centre of northern China and is now the most active Taoist temple in Beijing. Check a map for directions. Walk south on Baiyun Lu and cross the moat. Continue south along Baiyun Lu and turn into a curving street on the left; follow it for 250m to the temple entrance. Inside are several courtyards, including a pool, a bridge, several halls of worship and Taoist motifs.

Prince Gong's Residence
(*gōngwángfǔ*)
To find this, you have to get off the main roads into the small alleys running around the Shisha Hai Lakes. Prince Gong's Residence is more or less at the centre of the arc created by the lakes running from north to south. It's reputed to be the model for the mansion in Cao Xueqin's 18th century

classic, *A Dream of Red Mansions*. It's one of the largest private residential compounds in Beijing, with a nine courtyard layout, high walls and elaborate gardens. Prince Gong was the son of a Qing emperor.

Drum Tower & Bell Tower
(*gǔlóu/zhōnglóu*)
The Drum Tower was built in 1420 and has several drums which were beaten to mark the hours of the day – in effect the Big Ben of Beijing. Time was kept with a water clock. The tower is located on Gulou Dong Dajie, 1km due north of Jingshan Park.

Behind the Drum Tower, down an alley further north, is the Bell Tower which was built at the same time as the Drum Tower, but burnt down. The present structure dates from the 18th century.

Ancient Observatory
(*gǔ guānxiàngtái*)
One interesting oddity in Beijing is the observatory mounted on the battlements of a watchtower which forlornly overlooks the traffic-clogged second ring road near Jianguomennei Dajie.

The observatory dates back to Kublai Khan's days, when it was north of the present site. The Great Khan, as well as later Ming and Qing emperors, relied heavily on astrologers before making any move – as far as anyone knows, Mao and Deng Xiaoping didn't bother.

The present Beijing Observatory was built from 1437 to 1446, not only to facilitate astrological predictions, but also to aid seafaring navigators. Downstairs are displays of navigational equipment used by Chinese shipping. On the roof is a variety of astronomical instruments designed by the Jesuits.

The observatory is open Wednesday to Sunday from 9 to 11 am and from 1 to 4 pm.

Marco Polo Bridge
(*lúgōuqiáo*)
Publicised by the great traveller himself, the 260m-long Reed Moat Bridge is made of grey marble and has more than 250

BEIJING

To Summer Palace
& Beijing University

Second Ring Road

Zizhuyuan
Park

Beijing
Zoo   4

● 1

Deshengmen Xidajie

Shisha
Houhai
Lake

5

Xizhimennei Dajie

Xizhimenwai Dajie

3

13

Baishiqiao Lu

Sanlihe Lu

Zhanlan Lu

Xinjiekou Beidajie

Chegongzhuang Dajie

11

12

▼ 2

Third Ring Road

7

Fuchengmenwai Dajie

Fuchengmennei Dajie

8   9

6

Xisi Dajie

Wenjin Jie

Yuyuantan
Park

Yuetan Park

Xidan Beidajie

93

99   M   Fuxing Lu   M   Fuxingmenwai Dajie   M   M   Fuxingmennei Dajie   M

97

95 94   92   91

96

90

98

Baiyun Lu

Lianhuachi
Park   100

101   Guang'anmennei Dajie

102   103   107

Nanheng Jie

Central Beijing

0   1   2 km

See the Beijing map for subway station names

Niu Jie

Grand
View
Garden

Taoranting
Park

104   105 106

Heijing Fu Hotel
No 7. Zhang 2i Zhong Rd.
Dongcheng. (86-10 6401 7744 - 6001/6118

Hoiday Inn Hotel
10# Zhang Zi Zhong Rd
Dongcheng (86-10143174 - 64 0140

CENTRAL BEIJING
北京市中心

PLACES TO STAY
- 7 Holiday Inn Downtown
  金都假日饭店
- 12 Beihai Hotel
  北海宾馆
- 15 Bamboo Garden Hotel
  竹园宾馆
- 18 Lüsongyuan Hotel
  侣松园宾馆
- 27 Kunlun Hotel
  昆仑饭店
- 30 Hilton Hotel
  希尔顿大酒店
- 33 Great Wall Sheraton Hotel
  长城饭店
- 34 Landmark Hotel; Hard Rock Cafe
  亮马河大厦、硬石酒吧
- 38 Beijing Asia Hotel
  北京亚洲大酒店
- 39 Chains City Hotel; Owl Cafe
  城市宾馆 敦煌西餐厅
- 45 Jingguang New World Hotel
  京广新世界饭店
- 46 China World Hotel; World Trade Centre; Brauhaus
  国际贸易中心
- 47 Jinglun Hotel
  京伦饭店
- 48 Jianguo Hotel
  建国饭店
- 52 Scitech Hotel; Scitech Plaza
  赛特饭店 赛特购物中心
- 61 Ritan Hotel
  日坛宾馆
- 64 International Hotel
  国际饭店
- 68 Chongwenmen Hotel
  崇文门饭店
- 69 Xinqiao Hotel
  新桥饭店
- 70 Palace Hotel
  王府饭店
- 71 Peace Hotel
  和平宾馆
- 75 Fangyuan Hotel
  芳园宾馆
- 80 Grand Hotel Beijing
  贵宾楼饭店
- 95 Minzu Hotel
  民族饭店
- 104 Beijing Commercial Business Complex (Hotel)
  北京商务会馆
- 105 Qiaoyuan Hotel
  侨园饭店
- 107 Qianmen Hotel
  前门饭店
- 108 Far East Hotel
  远东饭店
- 109 Fengzeyuan Hotel
  丰泽园饭店
- 110 Dongfang Hotel
  东方饭店
- 111 Beiwei & Rainbow Hotels
  天桥宾馆、北纬饭店
- 115 Haoyuan Hotel
  昊园宾馆
- 116 Traffic Hotel
  交通饭店
- 117 Tiantan Sports Hotel
  天坛体育宾馆
- 118 Tiantan Hotel
  天坛饭店
- 119 Longtan Hotel
  龙潭饭店
- 121 Leyou Hotel
  乐游饭店

PLACES TO EAT
- 2 Muslim Restaurants
  百万庄西路
  (回民餐馆)
- 10 Fangshan Restaurant
  芳山饭店
- 24 Pizza Hut
  必胜客
- 29 Hong Kong Food City
  香港美食城
- 31 Subway Sandwiches; Schiller's Bar
  三明治餐厅、西乐酒吧
- 53 McDonald's; Uncle Sam's Fastfood
  麦当劳 山姆叔叔快餐店
- 67 Bianyifang Duck Restaurant
  便宜坊烤鸭店
- 74 Banpo Primitive Hotpot Beer Hut
  半坡啤酒屋
- 86 KFC; Delifrance Bakery
  肯德鸡、大磨坊面包
- 88 Qianmen Quanjude Duck Restaurant
  前门全聚德烤鸭店
- 113 Gongdelin Vegetarian Restaurant
  功德林素菜馆

OTHER
- 1 Sparkice Internet Cafe; Capital Gymnasium
  实华网络咖啡室、首都体育馆
- 3 Zhanlanguan Lu Tour Bus Station
  展览馆路旅游车售票处
- 4 Beijing Exhibition Centre
  北京展览馆
- 5 Beijing North (Xizhimen) Railway Station
  北京北火车站
- 6 Vantone New World Shopping Centre
  万通新世界商场
- 8 White Dagoba Temple
  白塔寺
- 9 Guangji Temple
  广济寺
- 11 JJ's Disco
  JJ迪斯可
- 13 Prince Gong's Residence
  恭王府
- 14 Song Qingling Museum
  宋庆龄故居
- 16 Bell Tower
  钟楼
- 17 Drum Tower
  鼓楼
- 19 Wax Museum
  蜡像馆
- 20 Confucius Temple
  孔庙
- 21 Lama Temple
  雍和宫
- 22 Russian Embassy
  苏联大使馆
- 23 Dongzhimen Long-Distance Bus Station
  东直门长途汽车站
- 25 Australian & Canadian Embassies
  澳大利亚大使馆、加拿大大使馆
- 26 Tayuan Diplomatic Building
  塔园外交办公楼
- 28 Maggie's Bar
  麦姬酒吧

32	Paulaner Brauhaus; Lufthansa Centre; Kempinski Hotel 凯宾斯基饭店、 燕莎商城	
35	Agricultural Exhibition Centre 农业展览馆	
36	Jazz Ya; Dai Sy's Pub 李波餐厅、戴昔小屋	
37	La Terasse 拉德莱斯	
40	Minder Cafe; Nashville; Hidden Tree 明大西餐馆、乡谣 俱乐部、隐蔽的树	
41	Downtown Cafe; Frank's Place; Berena's Bistro 城市咖啡、万龙 酒吧、柏瑞娜酒家	
42	TGI Friday's 星期五餐厅	
43	Poacher's Inn 团结湖公园西	
44	Chaoyang Theatre 朝阳剧场	
49	Mexican Wave 墨西哥波涛	
50	Xiushui Silk Market 秀水东街	
51	Friendship Store; CITIC 友谊商店、国际大厦	
54	CITS; Gloria Plaza Hotel 凯莱大酒店、 旅游大厦	
55	International Club 国际俱乐部	
56	International Post & Communications 国际邮电局	
57	John Bull Pub 地道的英式酒吧	
58	Sunflower Jazz Club; Sun Garden Bar 向日葵爵士俱乐部、 日园酒吧	
59	Goose & Duck Pub	

60	Elephant Bar 大象酒吧
62	Yabao Lu Clothing Market 雅宝路
63	Ancient Observatory 古观象台
65	Chang'an Grand Theatre 长安大剧场
66	Beijing Railway Station 北京火车站
72	Dongsi Mosque 东四清真寺
73	China Art Gallery 中国美术馆
76	PSB 公安局外事科
77	Bank of China; Donganmen Night Market 东安门夜市、 中国银行
78	Foreign Languages Bookstore 外文书店
79	Beijing Department Store 北京百货大楼
81	Chinese Revolution History Museum 中国革命历史博物馆
82	Tiananmen Gate 天安门
83	Great Hall of the People 人民大会堂
84	Mao Zedong Mausoleum; Monument to the People's Heroes 毛主席纪念堂、 人民英雄纪念碑
85	Qianmen Tour Bus Station 前门、旅游车发车站
87	Qianmen (Front Gate) 前门
89	Dazhalan 大栅栏街

90	Liulichang 琉璃厂
91	Telegraph Service Centre 电报局
92	Aviation Building (CAAC & Airport Bus) 民航营业大厦
93	Xidan Shopping Centre 西单购物中心
94	Nationalities Cultural Palace 民族文化宫
96	Sanwei Bookstore (Teahouse) 三味书屋
97	Parkson Department Store 百盛购物中心
98	White Cloud Temple; Taoist Family Restaurant 白云观、 道家养生餐厅
99	Military Museum 军事博物馆
100	Beijing West Railway Station 北京西火车站
101	Lianhuachi Bus Station 莲花池长途汽车站
102	Niujie Mosque 牛街礼拜寺
103	Fayuan Temple 法源寺
106	Beijing South (Yongdingmen) Railway Station 北京南站 (永定门火车站)
112	Tianqiao Bus Terminal 天桥汽车站
114	Natural History Museum 自然博物馆
120	Majuan Long-Distance Bus Station 马圈长途汽车站

marble balustrades supporting 485 carved stone lions. First built in 1192, the original arches were washed away in the 17th century. The bridge is a composite of different eras (it was widened in 1969) and spans the Yongding River near the little town of Wanping.

Long before CITS, Emperor Qianlong did his bit to promote the bridge. In 1751 he put his calligraphy to use and wrote 'Morning Moon Over Lugou Bridge', now engraved into stone tablets on the site. On the opposite bank is a monument to Qianlong's inspection of the Yongding River.

Despite the publicity campaign by Polo and Qianlong, the bridge wouldn't have rated more than a footnote in Chinese history were it not for the famed Marco Polo Bridge Incident, which ignited a full-scale war with Japan. On 7 July 1937, Japanese troops illegally occupied a railway junction outside Wanping. Japanese and Chinese soldiers started shooting, and that gave Japan enough of an excuse to attack and occupy Beijing. The Marco Polo Bridge Incident is considered by many as the date of China's entry into WWII.

A relatively recent addition to this ancient site is the Memorial Hall of the War of Resistance Against Japan, built in 1987. Also on the site is the Wanping Castle, the Daiwang Temple and a tourist hotel.

The bridge is 16km from the city centre and getting there is a nuisance. You can get to the bridge by taking bus No 339 from Lianhuachi bus station south-west of the city centre. Another option is bus No 917 which can be picked up at Tianqiao bus station (west of Tiantan Park) and goes straight to the bridge.

Places to Stay – Budget

Except for a couple of derelict hotels found mostly in the southern part of town, the grim reality is that few hotels in Beijing offer dormitories. In the winter off season you'll have no trouble getting into a dorm, but during the summer crunch you'll have plenty of competition for the limited space available.

For the sake of definition, any hotel charging under Y500 in the high season would have to be considered 'budget' in Beijing. Normally you can get a twin room for Y300, though in summer these rooms go fast. Bargaining for a room is possible in some cases – politely ask for a 'discount'. Many travellers negotiate discounts of 30% or more, at least during the winter slack season.

Beijing Area The following places to stay all appear on the Beijing map.

At present, the *Jinghua Hotel* (☎ 6722-2211) (*jīnghuá fàndiàn*) is in vogue with backpackers. It's the best place to get travel information, rent bicycles and book trips to the Great Wall. Dorm beds cost Y35 in a four-bed room, or Y26 in a 30-bed room. Twins are Y180. Bus Nos 2 and 17 from Qianmen drop you off nearby. The official address is Nansanhuan Zhonglu, Yong-dingmenwai, Fengtai District, 100077 (southern part of the third ring road).

Just around the corner from the Jinghua is the *Sea Star Hotel* (☎ 6721-8855; fax 6722-7915) (*hǎixīng dà jiǔdiàn*), 166 Haihutun, Yongwai (Muxu Yuan), Fengtai District. Dorm beds are Y35 and twins cost Y180. The rooms here are even nicer than at the Jinghua, but they tend to fill up faster.

Also close by, the *Lihua Hotel* (☎ 6721-1144) (*lìhuá fàndiàn*) is at 71 Yangqiao, Yongdingmenwai. It's another well-established backpackers' haven. Dorms cost Y35 and twins are Y182. Bus No 14, from Xidan and Hepingmen subway stations, is the easiest way to get there.

A little further north, the *Jingtai Hotel* (☎ 6722-4675) (*jǐngtài bīnguǎn*) is at 65 Yongwai Jingtaixi (a small alley running off Anlelin Lu). Though it lacks dormitories, twins are reasonable at Y180. Travellers give this place good reviews, in part because of the pleasant street market on Anlelin Lu. Bus No 39 from Beijing station will get you to the eastern end of Anlelin Lu (the bus stop name is Puhuangyu) from where it's a 10 minute walk west.

A few other budget places in the Beijing area include:

Capital Airport Hotel (☎ 6459-4466; fax 6456-4563) (*shǒudū jīchǎng bīnguǎn*), 1km from the airport terminal. Standard twins are Y312.
Jiali Hotel (☎ 6436-3399; fax 6436-3366) (*jiālì fàndiàn*), 21B Jiuxianqiao Lu, Chaoyang District, 100016. Standard twins cost Y388.
Jimen Hotel (☎ 6201-2211; fax 6201-5355) (*jìmén fàndiàn*), Huangtingzi, Xueyuan Lu, Haidian District, 100088. Twins begin at Y232.

Central Beijing The following places to stay (on page 241) all appear on the Central Beijing map.

Forbidden City

The Forbidden City, *(zǐjìn chéng)* so called because it was off limits to commoners for 500 years, is the largest and best-preserved cluster of ancient buildings in China. It was home to two dynasties of emperors – the Ming and the Qing – who didn't stray from this pleasure dome unless they absolutely had to.

The Beijing authorities insist on calling this place the Palace Museum *(gùgōng)*. Whatever its official name, it's open daily from 8.30 am to 5 pm (the last admission tickets are sold at 3.30 pm). Two hundred years ago the admission price would have been instant death, but this has dropped considerably to Y85, which allows admission to all the special exhibition halls. Your Y85 includes rental of a cassette tape for a self-guided tour, although you can enter for Y60 without the tape. For the tape to make sense, you must enter the Forbidden City from the southern gate and exit from the northern gate. The tape is available in several languages.

The basic layout of the Forbidden City was built between 1406 and 1420 by Emperor Yong Le, who commanded up to a million labourers. From this palace the emperors governed China – often rather erratically as they tended to become lost in this self-contained little world and allocated real power to the court eunuchs. One emperor devoted his entire career to carpentry – when an earthquake struck (an ominous sign for an emperor) he was delighted, since it gave him a chance to renovate.

GLENN BEANLAND

FORBIDDEN CITY

Box: Detail from the handles of gilded bronze vats found in the grounds of the Forbidden City.

Above: The distinctive red pillars of the Baohedian (Hall of Preserving Harmony), once the banquet hall for emperors, and later the site of imperial examinations.

Left: This Thomas Allom engraving from 1843 depicts Qing Dynasty Emperor Daoguang reviewing his guards at the Forbidden City.

GLENN BEANLAND

The buildings now seen are mostly post-18th century, as are a lot of restored or rebuilt structures around Beijing. The palace was constantly going up in flames – a lantern festival combined with a sudden gust of Gobi wind would easily do the trick, as would a fireworks display. The moat around the palace, now used for boating, came in handy since the local fire brigade was considered too lowly to quench the royal flames.

In 1664, the Manchus stormed in and burned the palace to the ground. It was not just the buildings that went up in smoke, but rare books, paintings and scrolls. In this century there have been two major lootings of the palace: by the Japanese forces and the Kuomintang. The latter, on the eve of the Communist takeover in 1949, removed thousands of crates of relics to Taiwan where they are now on display in Taipei's National Palace Museum. The gaps have been filled by bringing treasures (old, newly discovered and fake) from other parts of China.

Above: Detail from a doorway of the Baohedian (Hall of Preserving Harmony).

Right: Marble bridges spanning the Golden River between the Wu Men and Tai He Men gates.

DAMIEN SIMONIS

Summer Palace

One of the finest sights in Beijing, the Summer Palace *(yíhéyuán)* includes an immense park that tends to pack out during the summer months. The site had long been a royal garden and was considerably enlarged and embellished by Emperor Qianlong in the 18th century. It was later abandoned. Empress Dowager Cixi began rebuilding in 1888 using money that was supposedly reserved for the construction of a modern navy, although she did restore a marble boat that sits immobile at the edge of the lake. In 1900 foreign troops, annoyed by the Boxer Rebellion, had a go at torching the Summer Palace. Restorations took place a few years later and a major renovation occurred after 1949, by which time the palace had once more fallen into disrepair.

The original palace was used as a summer residence. It was divided into four sections: court reception, residences, temples and strolling or sightseeing areas. Three-quarters of the park is occupied by Kunming Lake, and most items of structural interest are towards the east or north gates.

The main building is the Benevolence & Longevity Hall, just off the lake towards the east gate. It houses a hardwood throne and has a courtyard with bronze animals. Along the northern shore of the lake is the Long Corridor, over 700m long, which is decorated with mythical scenes. If the paint looks new, it's because a lot of pictures were whitewashed during the Cultural Revolution.

Box: Detail from the Long Corridor.

Above: The ill-fated Audience Hall of the Summer Palace, destroyed by French and British troops in 1860. This etching is taken from Thomas Allom's 1843 book China, its Scenery, Architecture & Social Habits.

Left: The 17-arch bridge links the mainland with South Lake Island in the grounds of the Summer Palace.

GLENN BEANLAND

SUMMER PALACE

On Longevity Hill are a number of temples. The Precious Clouds Pavilion on the western slopes is one of the few structures to escape destruction by the Anglo-French forces. It contains some elaborate bronzes. At the top of the hill sits the Buddhist Sea of Wisdom Temple, made of glazed tiles; good views of the lake can be had from this spot.

GLENN BEANLAND

Other sights are largely associated with Empress Cixi, like the place where she kept Emperor Guangxu under house arrest, the place where she celebrated her birthdays and held exhibitions of her furniture and memorabilia.

Another noteworthy feature of the Summer Palace is the 17-arch bridge spanning 150m to South Lake Island; on the mainland side is a beautiful bronze ox. Also note the Jade Belt Bridge on the mid-west side of the lake and the Harmonious Interest Garden at the north-east end, which is a copy of a Wuxi garden.

The park is about 12km north-west of the centre of Beijing (see the Beijing map). The easiest way to get there on public transport is to take the subway to Xizhimen (close to the zoo), then a minibus. Bus No 332 from the zoo is slower, but will get you there eventually. Lots of minibuses return to the city centre from the Summer Palace, but get the price and destination settled before departure. You can also get there by bicycle – it takes about 1½ to two hours from the centre of town.

Admission for foreigners is a steep Y45, plus there are some additional fees for various sights inside the walls.

Above: Looking across Kunming Lake to the Buddhist Virtue Temple.

Right: Running parallel to the northern bank of Kunming Lake, the Long Corridor is 728m long and features about 8000 paintings.

GLENN BEANLAND

SUMMER PALACE

The *Far East Hotel* (☎ 6301-8811; fax 6301-8233) (*yuǎndōng fàndiàn*), 90 Tieshuxie Jie, Qianmenwai, Xuanwu District, 100050, has a fine location. Tieshuxie Jie is in fact the western end of Dazhalan (southwest of Qianmen). Twins cost Y310 to Y410.

The *Fangyuan Hotel* (☎ 6525-6331; fax 6513-8549) (*fāngyuán bīnguǎn*), 36 Dengshikou Xijie, Dongcheng District, 100006, deserves a plug even though it's relatively undiscovered by westerners. Its very central location off Wangfujing Jie is a big plus. The staff are pretty friendly and the hotel is well run. Twins cost Y158 and Y198.

The *Longtan Hotel* (☎ 6771-2244; fax 6771-4028) (*lóngtán fàndiàn*), at 15 Panjiayuan Nanli, Chaoyang District, 100021, unwisely dumped its dormitories a few years ago. Other than that, it's a good place to say, and its location on the second ring road, south-east of the city centre, makes it easy to get to the centre. Twins are Y298, Y366, Y508 and Y760.

The *Lüsongyuan Hotel* (☎ 6401-1116, 6403-0416) (*lǚsōngyuán bīnguǎn*), at 22 Banchang Hutong, north of the Forbidden City, is superb but gets relatively few foreign visitors because it's hard to find. When you approach the hutong from either end, it doesn't seem that there could be a building of such high standard halfway down. The hutong is one way and many taxi drivers are reluctant to drive down it in the wrong direction. The hotel is directly north of the China Art Gallery, second hutong north of Di'anmen and then turn left. Bus No 104 from Beijing railway station comes close. Twins cost Y298 to Y358 and dorm beds are Y60. The dormitory here is currently the only one in China officially recognised by the International Youth Hostel Federation.

On the other side of town, the *Tiantan Sports Hotel* (☎ 6701-3388; fax 6701-5388) (*tiāntán tǐyù bīnguǎn*), at 10 Tiyuguan Lu, Chongwen District, 100061, is in rather bad need of renovation. However, the location near Tiantan Park makes it almost worth it. Standard twins cost Y272.

If the Tiantan is full, try the nearby *Traffic Hotel* (☎ 6711-2288) (*jiāotōng fàndiàn*) at 35 Dongsi Kuaiyu Nanjie. The 82 comfortable rooms are priced from Y238 to Y268. The hotel is in a narrow alley running south from Tiyuguan Lu – signs in English point the way. Bus No 41 runs on Tiyuguan Lu and drops you off at the alley's entrance.

A few other budget alternatives which are worth knowing about include:

Beihai Hotel (☎ 6616-2229; fax 6616-0905) (*běihǎi bīnguǎn*), 141 Di'anmen Xidajie, Xicheng District, 100009. Standard twins are priced at Y230.

Beijing Commercial Business Complex (☎ 6329-2244) (*běijīng shāngwù huìguǎn*), Building No 1, Yulin Li, Youanmenwai, 100054. The official rate for twins is Y520 which stretches the definition of 'budget', but it seems to be fairly easy to negotiate it down to Y450 or lower.

Beiwei Hotel (☎ 6301-2266; fax 6301-1366) (*běiwěi fàndiàn*), 13 Xijing Lu, Xuanwu District (western side of Tiantan Park). Standard twins are Y460, superior Y680 and suites Y800. Two stars.

Haoyuan Hotel (☎ 6701-4499) (*hàoyuán bīnguǎn*), A9 Tiantan Donglu, Chongwen District (eastern side of Tiantan Park). Twins cost Y349. Two stars.

Leyou Hotel (☎ 6771-2266; fax 6771-1636) (*lèyóu fàndiàn*), 13 Dongsanhuan Nanlu, 100021, is east of Longtan Park (south-east Beijing). Twins go for Y288. Take bus No 28 or 52 to the terminus.

Qiaoyuan Hotel (☎ 6303-8861, 6301-2244) (*qiáoyuán fàndiàn*), Dongbinhe Lu, Youanmenwai (on the second ring road). Twins in the old grotty wing cost Y280, but it's Y420 in the new wing.

Places to Stay – middle

The following hotels cost between Y500 and Y1000, which by Beijing's pricey standards is considered to be 'mid-range'. Each of them appears on the Central Beijing map.

Bamboo Garden Hotel (☎ 6403-2229; fax 6401-2633) (*zhúyuán bīnguǎn*), 24 Xiaoshiqiao Hutong, Jiugulou Dajie, 100009. Twins cost Y520 to Y730.

Chongwenmen Hotel (☎ 6512-2211; fax 6512-2122) *(chóngwénmén fàndiàn)*, 2 Chongwenmen Xidajie, 100062. Standard twins are Y480 and suites Y600.

Dongfang Hotel (☎ 6301-4466; fax 6304-4801) *(dōngfāng fàndiàn)*, 11 Wanming Lu, 100050 (south of Qianmen). Standard twins are Y500 and superior rooms cost Y700. Three stars.

Fengzeyuan Hotel (☎ 6318-6688) *(fēngzéyuán fàndiàn)*, 83 Zhushikou Xilu, Xuanwu District (1km south of Qianmen). Twins cost Y513 – very good value for a three star hotel.

Holiday Inn Downtown (☎ 6833-8822; fax 6834-0696) *(jīndū jiàrì fàndiàn)*, 98 Beilishi Lu, Xicheng District, 100037. Standard twins cost Y750. Three stars.

International Hotel (☎ 6512-6688; fax 6512-9972) *(guójì fàndiàn)*, 9 Jianguomennei Dajie, 100005. Singles/twins start at Y830/Y1200 and suites cost Y2155 to Y9948. Four stars.

Landmark Hotel (☎ 6501-6688; fax 6501-3513) *(liàngmǎhé dàshà)*, 8 Dongsanhuan Beilu, 100004. Twins are Y750 to Y1300. Four stars.

Minzu Hotel (☎ 6601-4466; fax 6601-4849) *(mínzú fàndiàn)*, 51 Fuxingmennei Dajie, 100031 (west of CAAC and Fuxingmen subway). Twins cost Y704 to Y862 and suites are Y1194 to Y1782. Three stars.

Peace Hotel (☎ 6512-8833; fax 6512-6863) *(hépíng bīnguǎn)*, 3 Jinyu Hutong, Wangfujing Dajie. Twins are Y911 to Y1326 and suites are Y1243 to Y12,435. Four stars.

Qianmen Hotel (☎ 6301-6688; fax 6301-3883) *(qiánmén fàndiàn)*, 175 Yong'an Lu, Xuanwu District, 100050 (south-west of Qianmen). Standard twins cost Y504. Three stars.

Rainbow Hotel (☎ 6301-2266; fax 6301-1366) *(tiānqiáo bīnguǎn)*, 11 Xijing Lu, Xuanwu District, 100050 (south-west of Qianmen near the Beiwei Hotel). Twin rooms are priced from Y630 to Y766. Three stars.

Ritan Hotel (☎ 6512-5588; fax 6512-8671) *(rìtán bīnguǎn)*, 1 Ritan Lu, Jianguomenwai, 100020 (near Ritan Park). Standard twins cost Y660.

Tiantan Hotel (☎ 6711-2277; fax 6711-6833) *(tiāntán fàndiàn)*, 1 Tiyuguan Lu, Chongwen District (east of Tiantan Park). Twins cost Y832. Three stars.

Places to Stay – top end

Keeping up with the top end hotels in Beijing is like skiing uphill. No sooner does one extravaganza open its doors than the ground-breaking ceremony is held for an even more luxurious pleasure palace.

For definition purposes, anything costing over Y1000 for a standard twin room is called 'top end'.

See Lonely Planet's *Beijing* guide for a more complete list, but the following will get you started. All hotels appear on the Central Beijing map, unless otherwise indicated.

Beijing Asia Hotel (☎ 6500-7788; fax 6500-7291) *(běijīng yàzhōu dà jiǔdiàn)*, 8 Xinzhong Xijie, Gongren Tiyuchang Beilu, 100027. Standard twins cost Y1030. Three stars.

Chains City Hotel (☎ 6500-7799; fax 6500-7668) *(chéngshì bīnguǎn)*, 4 Gongren Tiyuchang Donglu, Chaoyang District, 100027. Twins are Y900 to Y1020, suites Y1280 to Y3600. Three stars.

China World Hotel (☎ 6505-2266; fax 6505-0828) *(zhōngguó dà fàndiàn)*, 1 Jianguomenwai Dajie, 100020 (inside China World Trade Centre). Twins cost Y2070 to Y3600. Five stars.

Gloria Plaza Hotel (☎ 6515-8855; fax 6515-8533) *(kǎilái dà jiǔdiàn)*, 2 Jianguomen Nandajie, 100022. It's listed on the map with the CITS entry. Twins cost Y1148 to Y1405 and suites are Y1532 to Y2171. Four stars.

Grand Hotel Beijing (☎ 6513-7788; fax 6513-0038) *(guìbīnlóu fàndiàn)*, 35 Dong Chang'an Jie, 100006. Standard twins cost Y2280. Five stars.

Great Wall Sheraton (☎ 6500-5566; fax 6500-2580) *(chángchéng fàndiàn)*, 10 Dongsanhuan Beilu, Chaoyang District, 100026. Standard twins cost Y2320. Five stars.

Hilton Hotel (☎ 6466-2288; fax 6465-3052) *(xīěrdùn fàndiàn)*, 1 Dongfang Lu, Dongsanhuan Beilu, 100027. Twins are Y2072 to Y2986. Five stars.

Holiday Inn Lido (☎ 6437-6688; fax 6437-6237) *(lìdū jiàrì fàndiàn)*, Jichang Lu, Jiangtai Lu, 100037 (on road to the airport; see the Beijing map). Standard twins cost Y1450 to Y1632, superior rooms are Y1824 and suites are up to Y7864. Officially four stars, but we give it five.

Jianguo Hotel (☎ 6500-2233; fax 6500-2871) *(jiànguó fàndiàn)*, 5 Jianguomenwai Dajie, 100020. Twins cost Y1600 to Y1760 and suites are Y1970 to Y2860. Four stars.

Jingguang New World Hotel (☎ 6501-8888; fax 6501-3333) *(jīngguǎng xīn shìjiè fàndiàn)*, Hujialou, Chaoyang District, 100020. Twins begin at Y1660. Five stars.

Jinglun Hotel (☎ 6500-2266; fax 6500-2022) *(jīnglún fàndiàn)*, 3 Jianguomenwai Dajie, 100020, also known as the *Beijing-Toronto Hotel*. Twins are Y1530 to Y1870 and suites are Y2210 to Y4080. Four stars.

Kempinski Hotel (☎ 6465-3388; fax 6465-3366) (*kǎibīnsījī fàndiàn*), Lufthansa Centre, 50 Liangmaqiao Lu, 100016. Standard twins begin at Y1370. Five stars.

Kunlun Hotel (☎ 6500-3388; fax 6506-8424) (*kūnlún fàndiàn*), 2 Xinyuan Nanlu, Chaoyang District, 100004. Standard twins cost Y2155. Five stars.

Mövenpick Hotel (☎ 6456-5588; fax 6456-5678) (*guódū dà fàndiàn*) at Capital Airport. Twins start at Y1144. Four stars.

Palace Hotel (☎ 6512-8899; fax 6512-9050) (*wángfǔ fàndiàn*), 8 Jinyu Hutong, Wangfujing Dajie, 100006. Doubles cost Y2321 to Y2652 and suites Y3316 to Y6632. Five stars.

Scitech Hotel (☎ 6512-3388; fax 6512-3542) (*sàitè fàndiàn*), 22 Jianguomenwai Dajie , 341 rooms. Twins are Y1120.

Shangri-La Hotel (☎ 6841-2211; fax 6841-8006) (*xiānggé lǐlā fàndiàn*), 29 Zhizhuyuan Lu, Haidian District, 100081 (see the Beijing map). Rates are Y1980 to Y3600. Five stars.

Places to Eat

There are so many eateries around the capital that it's hard to imagine China ever experienced a famine. On the other hand, eating on a budget is becoming more difficult. While there are still plenty of back-alley cafes and pushcarts where you can grab a cheap meal, the days are gone when any backpacker could afford to visit an upmarket restaurant and rub elbows with Beijing's bloated cadres.

If you do have a meal in one of the upmarket restaurants, be aware that rice is generally considered to be a fairly plebeian dish – a final 'fill-you-up' to be ignored until the 'real food' is finished. So, unless you act like a barbarian and demand some rice at the beginning of the meal, it will probably only appear towards the end of the meal. All of the following places to eat can be found on the Central Beijing map, unless otherwise indicated.

Chinese Food Northern cuisine specialities include Beijing duck, Mongolian hotpot, Muslim barbecue and imperial dishes.

Cheap Eats The hutongs are so packed with small eateries and foodstalls that it would take a book larger than this one to list them all. A special mention should go to the Donganmen Night Market, which gets going from around 6 to 9 pm daily. All sorts of exotic eats from pushcarts are available, including tiny four legged beasties roasted on a skewer. The night market is at the northern end of Wangfujing near the Bank of China.

Beijing Duck Beijing duck, the capital's most famous invention, is now a production line of sorts. Your meal starts at one of the farms around Beijing where the duck is pumped full of grain and soybean paste to fatten it up. The ripe duck is lacquered with molasses, pumped with air, filled with boiling water, dried, and then roasted over a fruitwood fire. The result, force-fed or not, is delicious. The duck is served in stages. First comes boneless meat and crispy skin with a side dish of shallots, plum sauce and crepes, then duck soup made of bones and all the other parts except the quack.

Otherwise known as the 'Old Duck', the *Qianmen Quanjude Roast Duck Restaurant* (☎ 6511-2418) (*qiánmén quànjùdé kǎoyādiàn*) is at 32 Qianmen Dajie, on the eastern side, near the Qianmen subway station. As the nickname implies, this is one of the oldest restaurants in the capital, dating back to 1864, although there's now around a dozen branches across the city. Price depends on which section of the restaurant you sit in. The meal begins at Y188 for one person or Y188 for two.

The *Bianyifang Duck Restaurant* (☎ 6702-0505) (*biànyífǎng kǎoyādiàn*) is another famous house at 2 Chongwenmenwai Dajie (Chongwenmen subway station). Language is not really a problem; you only have to negotiate half or whole ducks. In the cheap section the locals will show you the correct etiquette, like when to spit on the floor.

You can, in fact, order Beijing duck from almost any major hotel restaurant that does Chinese cuisine, so there is no particular need to search out a restaurant specialising in it.

Cantonese No self-respecting tourist hotel in Beijing is without a Cantonese restaurant dishing up dim sum to their Hong Kong clientele. Remember that dim sum is for breakfast and lunch only – at night it's mostly seafood.

Hong Kong Food City (☎ 6466-8886) (*xiānggǎng měishí chéng*) has several branches. The most accessible one to foreigners is just to the west of the Lufthansa Shopping Centre. It has long opening hours – 11.30 am to 2 pm and 5.30 pm to 3.30 am.

Imperial (*gōngtíng cài* or *mǎnhàn dàcān*) This is food fit for an emperor and will clean your wallet out very quickly. In 1982 a group of Beijing chefs set about reviving the imperial pastry recipes, and even went so far as to dig up the last emperor's brother to try their products out on.

Imperial cuisine is served up in the *Fangshan Restaurant* (☎ 6401-1879) in Beihai Park – the official address is 1 Wenjin Jie. The Summer Palace is home to the *Tingliguan Imperial Restaurant* (☎ 6258-1955; see the Beijing map). There is also an imperial restaurant at Fragrant Hills Park.

Mongolian Mongolian hotpot is a winter dish – a brass pot with charcoal inside it is placed at the centre of the table and you cook thick strips of mutton and vegetables, fondue fashion, spicing as you like. Look for the symbol shaped like the hotpot on little foodstalls and restaurants in the hutongs.

For something different, take a look at the *Banpo Primitive Hotpot Beer Hut* (☎ 6525-5583) at 26 Wangfujing Dajie. It's built in an artificial cave, and the menu includes some tasty side orders like ants and scorpions. It's open from 10 am to midnight.

Sichuan A place with a charming setting is the *Fuhai Restaurant* (☎ 6256-8867) within the grounds of the Old Summer Palace (see the Beijing map), but it has short hours – 10 am to 3 pm.

Muslim Muslim barbecue is dirt cheap if you know the right place to look for it. The right place is the western end of Baiwanzhuangxi Lu, a street in a neighbourhood

known as Ganjiakou (not far south of the zoo). This is where Beijing's Uighur minority congregates. Restaurants here are very specialised – the way to eat is to collect some Uighur flatbread (*náng*) from the stalls, then sit down in a tea shop or restaurant and order sweet Uighur tea (*sānpào tái* or *bābǎo chá*), some vegetable dishes, noodles (*miàn*) and kebabs (*ròuchuàn*).

You'll probably have to collect your meal from several proprietors – one restaurant won't have the full range of goodies. It's often best to eat with a small group (two to four persons) so you can get several dishes and sample everything. Alternatively, you can just drift from stall to stall sampling as you go.

Vegetarian The Yangzhou-style *Gongdelin Vegetarian Restaurant* (☎ 6511-2542) (*gōngdélín sùcàiguǎn*), at 158 Qianmen Nandajie, is probably the best in the city. It serves up wonderful vegie food with names to match. How about the 'peacock in pride' or 'the fire is singeing the snow-capped mountains'? It's open 10.30 am to 8.30 pm.

Buried behind the White Cloud Temple in the Xicheng District is the *Taoist Family Restaurant* (☎ 6346-3531, ext 28) (*dàojiā yǎngshēng cāntīng*). Open 11 am to 2 pm, and 4.30 pm to 9 pm.

Western Food All of the large tourist hotels serve western food of varying quality and price. Beijing's coffee and pastries are up there with China's best.

Fast Food From the day of its grand opening in 1992, *McDonald's* (*màidāngláo*) has been all the rage with Beijingers. Though prices are low, this is one of Beijing's most prestigious restaurants, the venue for cadre birthday parties and a popular hang-out for the upper crust. It seems like a new branch opens up every month and it's hard to keep up with them (there's now more than 40 branches across the city).

For backpackers camped out at the Jinghua Hotel in south Beijing (see the Beijing map), Ronald McDonald can be visited just half a block to the west from the hotel's front entrance. A more upmarket branch (same menu though) exists next to the Hotel New Otani (south-west of the Friendship Store) on Jianguomenwai Dajie. Most branches open from 7 am until 11 pm.

By comparison, *KFC* (*kěndéjī jiāxiāng jī*) enjoys a much longer history in Beijing, having spread its wings in 1987. At the time of its opening, it was the largest Kentucky Fried Chicken in the world. The colonel's smiling face is just across the street from Mao's mausoleum in Tiananmen Square – if this doesn't make the late Chairman turn over in his grave, nothing will. A smaller *KFC* has hatched one block east of Wangfujing Dajie on the southwestern corner of Dongsi Xi Dajie and Dongsi Nan Dajie.

Pizza Hut (*bìshèngkè*) has grabbed a large slice of the Beijing fast food market. The most conspicuous branch is just in front of the Friendship Store on Jianguomenwai. Another is on Dongzhimenwai Dajie in the Sanlitun area (next to the Australian embassy).

Uncle Sam's Fastfood (*shānmǔ shūshū kuàicān*) is on the southern side of Jianguomenwai Dajie, almost adjacent to McDonald's. Don't mistake it for the US Embassy, which is on the other side of the street.

Subway sandwiches has a branch in the north-eastern part of town on Liangmaqiao Lu (by the Lufthansa Centre).

Bakeries Chinese bread is about as tasty as a dried-out sponge, but a few entrepreneurs in Beijing have started to introduce edible baked goods to the masses. One fine effort in this direction is *Delifrance* (*dà mòfáng miànbāo diàn*), which boasts genuine croissants and prices a fraction of what you'd pay in Paris. This bakery currently has several branches – easiest to find is the one next to the Friendship Store. There is another at the Qianmen Zhengyang Market, just south-west of Chairman Mao's mausoleum and adjacent to the enormous KFC.

Within the confines of the Friendship Store, there is a *bakery* off to the right as you enter the store. Prices here are also very low, but the selection is limited.

Another place to look is in some of the big hotels – a few have sent the staff off to Europe for a wintertime crash course in making German black bread and Danish pastries. Unfortunately, hotel prices tend to be high. The deli in the *Holiday Inn Lido* (see the Beijing map) stocks delectable chocolate cake, sourdough bread and other requisite baked goods, but it's certainly not cheap.

Supermarkets One of the best stocked supermarkets is in the basement of *Scitech Plaza*, a department store on the southern side of Jianguomenwai Dajie.

On the eastern fringe of Jianguomenwai is the China World Trade Centre – go down into the basement to find a fully fledged *Wellcome* supermarket imported lock, stock and shopping cart from Hong Kong. The Wellcome slogan 'low everyday prices' doesn't quite describe the situation in Beijing, but you'll find all the familiar goodies right down to the 'No Frills Dried Lemon Peel'.

Just next to the CITIC building is the *Friendship Store* – when you enter the building turn sharply right to find the food section. The supermarket is decidedly mediocre, but you can find all the basic necessities.

Just north of the Great Wall Sheraton Hotel is the enormous *Lufthansa Centre* – yes, it is a ticket office for a German airline, but also a multi-storey shopping mall. There is a fine supermarket in the basement chock-a-block with imported goods.

Pub Grub If the truth be told, the majority of westerners in Beijing rarely indulge in dim sum, Beijing duck or Mongolian hotpot. The fact is that, outside of breakfast, most foreigners are drawn towards a collection of pubs in the Sanlitun and Jianguomenwai areas. Since these are great socialising spots often with outdoor tables, live music and closing times hovering around 2 am, we've listed these places in the following 'Entertainment' section.

Entertainment

The *China Daily* carries a listing of cultural evenings recommended for foreigners. Also worth checking are the free tourist newspapers distributed around hotels. Unless otherwise indicated, all venues appear on the Central Beijing map.

Acrobatics (*tèjì biǎoyǎn*) Two thousand years old, and one of the few art forms condoned by Mao, acrobatics is the best deal in town.

The best place to catch an acrobatics show is the *Chaoyang Theatre* (*cháoyáng jùchǎng*) at 36 Dongsanhuan Beilu (at Chaoyang Beilu) in the north-eastern part of Beijing. Shows run from 7.15 to 8.40 pm and cost Y60.

Beijing Opera Special performances of Beijing opera are put on for foreigners

nightly at 7.30 pm in the *Liyuan Theatre* (*líyuán jùchǎng*), which is part of the Qianmen Hotel. Ticket prices are Y80 to Y180 depending on seat location. A mid-priced ticket buys you a seat at a table where you can enjoy snacks and tea while watching the show. The top end tickets get you get better snacks and a table with a better location. Performances last 1½ hours with sporadic translations flashed on an electronic signboard. You can get dressed up in an opera costume (with full facial makeup) for a photo-taking session.

Another place offering Beijing opera for foreigners is the *Chang'an Grand Theatre* (☎ 6510-1308) (*cháng'ān dà jùchǎng*) at 7 Jianguomennei Dajie (just west of the International Hotel). There is speculation that the Liyuan Theatre will eventually be closed and foreigners will move to this

---

Mr Wang

His only observable credentials were that he could kick his own forehead with his foot, but even his oblique disclosure that he had studied Xingyi Quan, one of the more elusive internal forms of Chinese boxing, was enough for me. Having hunted high and low in Beijing for a teacher who would reveal to me the mysteries of this art, I was ready to throttle any opportunity. The arrangement was English lessons in exchange for education in the elements of 'body-mind boxing'. Money for old rope, I thought.

Mr Wang was a very shifty fellow given to speaking in barely audible whispers, but I suspect it was all in order to conjure up an atmosphere of mystery around the proceedings. The hour and location of the lessons added to the secrecy – we would meet at midnight in a small, forested park near Xinjiekou in Beijing. He would arrive soon after the witching hour, pushing his bike, with a bundle of swords under his arm that glinted in the moonlight. He was certainly made of rubber. Once I thought he was imitating a pretzel, only to discover that this was a strategy for escaping an arm lock.

Despite knowing that teachers of Xingyi Quan typically taught slowly and in very small increments, I was a bit miffed to find myself standing for half an hour in the basic posture while Mr Wang wandered around having a cigarette. I could see the ember floating around in the dark like a firefly, and hear the odd snatch of his whistling. When a hacking cough announced his return, that was the end of the lesson. The next lesson was a repeat of the first. The fifth lesson had the added novelty of holding the same posture – while standing on an oil drum.

It carried on like this for a while, and I realised that I would have to quit. I was returning to the UK in two months time, and I knew that I would learn nothing in that period; if I wanted to really open the door to the art, I would have to spend about ten years in Beijing. Still, that pretzel move was pretty nifty.

Damian Harper

Beijing Opera

It used to be the Marx Brothers, the Gang of Four and the Red Ballet – but it's back to the classics again these days. Beijing opera *(píngjù)* is one of the many forms of the art and the most famous, but it only has a short history. The year 1790 is the key date given; in that year a provincial troupe performed before Emperor Qianlong on his 80th birthday. The form was popularised in the west by the actor Mei Lanfang (1894-1961) who is said to have influenced Charlie Chaplin.

Beijing opera bears little resemblance to its European counterpart. The mixture of singing, dancing, speaking, mime, acrobatics and dancing can go on for five or six hours, but two hours is more usual.

There are four types of actors' roles: the *sheng, dan, jing* and *chou*. The sheng are the leading male actors and they play scholars, officials, warriors and the like. The dan are the female roles, but are usually played by men (Mei Lanfang always played a dan role). The jing are the painted-face roles, and they represent warriors, heroes, statesmen, adventurers and demons. The chou is basically the clown.

Language is often archaic Chinese and the screeching music is searing to western ears, but the costumes and make-up are magnificent. The action that really catches the western eye is a swift battle sequence – the female warriors involved are trained acrobats who leap, twirl, twist and somersault into attack. It's not unlike boarding a Beijing bus during rush hour.

Catching at least one Beijing opera is almost mandatory for visitors to the capital, and that includes the Chinese. When you get bored after the first hour or so, and are sick of the high-pitched whining, the local audience is with you all the way – spitting, eating apples, breast-feeding an infant in the balcony, or plugging into a transistor radio (important sports match?). It's a lively prole audience viewing entertainment fit for an emperor. ∎

newer theatre. Prices and show times here are identical to those at the Liyuan.

Discos The *Poacher's Inn* (☎ 6595-8357, 6500-8391) deserves top billing. Currently it's only open on Friday and Saturday nights from 9 pm to 4 am. There is live music on Saturday night starting from 9.30 pm. Poacher's is on an island in Tuanjiehu Park, which is on the third ring road in north-eastern Beijing (enter from the park's west gate). Admission costs Y50.

NASA Disco (☎ 6201-6622) advertises 'advanced designed style appealing to radicals'. It can accommodate 1500 dancers and is open from 8 pm until 2 am. It's at the corner of Xueyuan Lu and Xitucheng Lu, just north of the third ring road (see the Beijing map). It's opposite the Jimen Hotel (nearest subway station: Xizhimen).

JJ's Disco (☎ 6607-9691) is an enormous Chinese dance venue at 74 Xinjiek-ou Beidajie (Jishuitan subway station). The disco operates from around 8 pm until 2 am. The cover charge is Y50, but rises to Y80 on Friday and Saturday night.

Pubs Beijingers refer to Sanlitun Lu as the 'Golden Street', which may have as much to do with the price of real estate as the fact that business is booming here. Sanlitun Lu must account for about 75% of the expat bar-cafes in town.

Jazz Ya (☎ 6415-1227) is an enormous place and one of the busiest expat night spots in Beijing. The official address is 18 Sanlitun Beilu, although it's actually hidden in a small alley jst to the east of the main road. It's open 10.30 am to 2 am (but only gets busy after 8 pm).

Nearby, *Dai Sy's Pub* (☎ 6416-4043) at 48 Sanlitun Lu is a very popular spot and has outdoor tables. It opens early and is a good spot for lunch and dinner.

La Terrasse (☎ 6415-5578) is on the western side of Sanlitun Lu. The food is French and the ambience is Paris roadside cafe. On weekends, reservations are usually necessary. Open 11 am to 11 pm.

One block west of Sanlitun Lu is the Chain's City Hotel where there is a cluster of expat cafe/bars. On the northern side of the hotel is the *Owl Cafe* (☎ 6509-3833). On the southern side is the *Downtown Cafe* (☎ 6507-3407), *Frank's Place* (☎ 6507-2617) and *Berena's Bistro* (☎ 6592-2628).

Dongdaqiao Xiejie is a narrow lane to the east of Chain's City Hotel, but west of Sanlitun Lu (and runs parallel to it). A lot of pubs have set up shop here in the past few years and it's an extremely popular spot with expats. Some of the biggies here include *Minder Cafe* (☎ 6500-6066), *Nashville* (☎ 6502-4201) and the *Hidden Tree* (☎ 6509-3642).

The east-north-east section of the third ring road is called Dongsanhuan Beilu. Here you will find the *Hard Rock Cafe* (☎ 6501-6688, ext 2571) in the west wing of the Landmark Towers at 8 Dongsanhuan Beilu. *TGI Friday's* (☎ 6595-1380) at 19 Dongsanhuan Beilu is an excellent upmarket western restaurant with awesome food.

On the 1st floor of the cavernous Lufthansa Centre is *Paulaner Brauhaus* (☎ 6465-3388, ext 5732), which is an excellent German pub-cum-restaurant. *Schiller's Bar & Restaurant* (☎ 6461-9276) is across from the Lufthansa Centre.

Maggie's Bar (☎ 6463-1166, ext 2109), on Xinyuan Lu (opposite the Kunlun Hotel) is *the* place to go if you want to stay out all night – operating hours are typically from 6 pm to 5 am.

The Jianguomenwai Embassyland is on the northern side of Jianguomenwai Dajie.

The Karaoke Phenomenon

Nowadays karaoke requires little in the way of introduction, even in the west. The word 'karaoke' is a combination of the Japanese words *kara*, meaning 'empty', and *oke*, a Japanese contraction of the English word 'orchestra'. The idea is simple enough: the voice track is removed from a particular song, providing the audience with a do-it-yourself pop hit. The results will probably leave you with the impression that 99% of Chinese are completely tone deaf.

From small-time beginnings in Japan, karaoke first took Taiwan and Hong Kong by storm, and then inevitably slipped into China. Today it has become one of the main recreational activities for the Chinese. It's easy to recognise a karaoke parlour: they are usually lit up in neon and have a Chinese sign with the characters for *kālā* (a phonetic rendering of the Japanese) followed by the English letters 'OK'. Sometimes clubs can be identified by the acronym KTV – 'karaoke television'. The latter normally have private booths.

It's actually worth checking out a karaoke parlour or two while you are in Beijing, though they are generally not cheap. There are two menus: one for the drinks and one for the songs. Don't expect much in the way of English songs. It usually costs around Y10 to get up on stage and sing a song, and the Chinese clamour for the opportunity. It doesn't matter how badly you sing. You'll get a polite round of applause from the audience when you finish, probably a rapturous round of applause if you are a foreigner.

A recent development is the poor-person's karaoke bar, a TV (a video with a bouncing ball following the lyrics) set up by the roadside, where you pay a few jiao to sing into a small PA system. The Chinese government, with characteristic market savvy, has responded to the karaoke boom by setting up a department to produce karaoke numbers that give the public an opportunity to musically express their burning ardour for the Party. Perversely, everyone seems to prefer singing Rod Stewart numbers and the latest Taiwanese and Hong Kong pop hits. ∎

In this maze on Dongdaqiao Lu is *Mexican Wave* (☎ 6506-3961) which does all sorts of western grub and ale and stays open until 2 am.

The *Goose & Duck Pub* (☎ 6509-3777), on Ritan Donglu, is just a few blocks to the north of Jianguomenwai Dajie. The southern side of Ritan Park is the venue for several outstanding bars including the *John Bull Pub*, *Sunflower Jazz Club* (☎ 6594-0515) and *Sun Garden Bar* (☎ 6501-8942).

On the north side of the park at 17 Ritan Beilu is the *Elephant Bar* (☎ 6502-4013) which features Russian food. The *Brauhaus* (☎ 6505-2266, ext 6565) in the China World Hotel is an excellent place to get Bavarian beer.

A good gay venue is *Half and Half* (☎ 6416-6919) on Sanlitun Lu, not far from the Chains City Hotel. Other places include *JJ's* and *Nightman Disco*.

Teahouses *Sanwei Bookstore* (☎ 6601-3204), at 60 Fuxingmennei Dajie (opposite the Minzu Hotel), has a trendy bookshop on the ground floor, but hidden on the 2nd floor is a charming Chinese teahouse. Jazz bands play here on Friday evening and classical music is provided on Saturday night. Business hours are from 9.30 am until 10.30 pm, but the live music begins at around 8 pm. The cover charge is Y30.

Theme Parks China's largest theme park is **World Park** (*shìjiè gōngyuán*). Chinese who can't afford an overseas holiday come here to visit the Eiffel Tower, the pyramids of Egypt and America's Statue of Liberty. Of course, these reproductions are somewhat smaller than the originals. The park is south-west of the centre, about 3km due south of Fengtai railway station (see the Beijing map). If you don't plan to travel by taxi, you'll have to take a bus to Fengtai railway station and a minibus from there to the park. Bus Nos 309 (from the Beijing West railway station) and 406 (from the Asian Games Village) can also get you there.

If World Park is where you go to see reproductions of famous buildings, then the **China Ethnic Minorities Park** (*zhōnghuá mínzú yuán*) is where you go to see reproductions of China's 56 ethnic minorities. Han Chinese dress up in minority costumes and pretend to be Tibetans or Mongolians. Tourists can do the same (for a fee) to capture that memorable photo to show the loved ones back home. The landscape is also dressed up with small-scale imitations of famous Chinese scenic spots such as a fake Jiuzhaigou Dragon Waterfall. The park is in the north of Beijing (see the Beijing map), and double decker bus No 2 goes there. The facilities are open daily from 8 am to 10 pm and admission costs Y60.

The water slides at **Shijingshan Amusement Park** (*shíjǐngshān yóulè yuán*) are the steepest (and thus most exciting) in Beijing. There are also ferris wheels, roller coasters and other vomit-inducing contraptions. The park is in the far west of Beijing on Shijingshan Lu (see the Beijing map). Take the east-west subway line to Bajiaocun station.

Yuyuantan Park (*yùyuántán gōngyuán*) is Beijing's largest water theme park, though in truth the waterslides at Shijingshan Amusement Park are more exciting. Most of the water entertainment is on the western side of Yuyuantan (Jade Hole Pool) Park. Just to the southern side of the park is the immense TV tower, one of Beijing's most prominent landmarks. The park is just north of the Military Museum.

If you'd like to go to the beach in Beijing, don't let the lack of an ocean stop you. **Tuanjiehu Park** (*tuánjiēhú gōngyuán*) boasts a 'wave pool'. Sand and hot dog vendors have been imported to create a real beach scene. There are also a few kiddie rides here. The park is in the east of Beijing on the third ring road, very close to the Jingguang New World Hotel.

Zoo The Beijing Zoo (*běijīng dòngwùyuán*) is mostly a downer – no attempt has been made to re-create natural environments for the animals, and they live in tiny cages with little shade or water. The much-ballyhooed Panda House is even more depressing and costs extra to visit. Getting to the zoo is easy enough – take the subway to the Xizhimen station. From there, it's a 15 minute walk to the west or a short ride on any of the trolley-buses.

Things to Buy

The following is a description of some shopping districts and bargains to be had.

Wangfujing This prestigious shopping street is just east of the Forbidden City – it's a solid block of stores and a favourite haunt of locals and tourists seeking bargains.

Wangfujing's biggest emporium is the Beijing Department Store (*běijīng bǎihuò dàlóu*). Of prime interest to foreign travellers is the Foreign Languages Bookstore (No 235). This is *the* place in China to buy English-language books, but don't forget to check out the music tape section upstairs.

Dazhalan Dazhalan is a hutong running west from the top end of Qianmen, near Tiananmen Square. It's a heady jumble of silk shops, department stores, theatres, herbal medicine, food and clothing specialists and some unusual architecture.

Dazhalan has a remnant medieval flavour to it; a hangover from the days when hutongs sold specialised products – one would sell lace, another lanterns, another jade. This one used to be called Silk Street. The name Dazhalan refers to a wicket-gate that was closed at night to keep prowlers out.

Liulichang Not far to the west of Dazhalan is Liulichang, Beijing's antique street. In imperial Beijing, shops and theatres were not permitted near the city centre, but Liulichang was outside the gates. Many of the city's oldest shops can be found along or near this crowded hutong.

Although it's been a shopping area for quite some time, only recently has it been dressed up for foreign tourists. The stores here are all designed to look like an ancient Chinese village. The vast majority of the shops at Liulichang are run by the government, but that doesn't mean they are honest. Prices are mostly outrageous, but Liulichang is worth a look – some of the art books and drawings are a good deal and not easily found elsewhere.

Jianguomenwai The Friendship Store (☎ 6500-3311) (*yǒuyì shāngdiàn*) at 17 Jianguomenwai Dajie is the largest in the land – this place stocks both touristy souvenirs and everyday useful items. It's been superseded by newer shopping malls, but the book and magazine section is a gold mine for travellers starved of anything to read.

Scitech Plaza is a huge department store with an enormous selection – the best deal is the supermarket in the basement. There are, of course, lots of pricey luxuries on offer: the latest fashion, makeup and perfumes. Kitchenwares are in basement No 2. Scitech Plaza is on the southern side of Jianguomenwai, opposite the CITIC building.

The Xiushui Silk Market (*xiùshuǐ dōngjiē*) is on the northern side of Jianguomenwai between the Friendship Store and the Jianguo Hotel. Because of the prestigious location amid the luxury hotels, this place is elbow to elbow with foreign tourists at times – go early to avoid crowds and forget it on Sundays. Bargaining is imperative here, although it's often a struggle because of all the foreign tourists willing to throw money around like water.

Ritan Park is north of the Friendship Store – on the western side of the park and intersecting with it at a 90-degree angle is Yabao Lu Clothing Market. This place is enormous – no Beijing department store could hope to match the variety and low prices on offer here. Bargaining is required.

Sanlitun The Sanlitun embassy district is in north-eastern Beijing, close to the Great Wall Sheraton Hotel. Like Jianguomenwai, the stores here are decidedly upmarket.

Lufthansa Centre falls into a category by itself – it was Beijing's first flashy multistorey shopping mall. The Lufthansa Centre (*yānshā shāngchéng*) is also known as the Kempinski Hotel (*kǎibīnsījī fàndiàn*). You can buy everything here from computer floppy disks to bikinis (but who in China wears the latter?). A superb (but pricey) supermarket in the basement stocks all manner of imported goods.

Xicheng District The Vantone New World Shopping Centre *(wàntōng xīn shìjiè shāngchǎng)* at 2-8 Fuchengmenwai Dajie breaks new ground – it's an American-managed shopping mall with over 200 shops. In between the boutiques and sporting goods shops, you can sustain yourself on everything from Big Macs to Häagen-Dazs. Take the circular line subway to the Fuchengmen station.

For the locals, Xidan Bei Dajie (locals just call it Xidan) is one of Beijing's hot shopping spots. Foreigners are somewhat less impressed. The centre of activity is the high-rise Xidan Shopping Centre *(xīdān gòuwù zhōngxīn)*. Take the east-west subway line to the Xidan station.

About 1km to the west of Xidan by the Fuxingmen subway station is the plush Parkson Department Store *(bǎishèng gòuwù zhōngxīn)*.

Miscellaneous If there's anything you think is impossible to buy in Beijing, check out Watson's *(qūchénshì)* in the Holiday Inn Lido on the road heading out towards the airport. This place sells every vitamin known to humanity, sunscreen (UV) lotion, beauty creams, tampons and the widest selection of condoms in Beijing.

Getting There & Away
Air Beijing has direct air connections to most major cities in the world. Many travellers make use of the direct Beijing-Hong Kong flights on CAAC or Dragonair. Economy class one way/return tickets cost Y2450/4660. Flights tend to be heavily booked, especially on Dragonair. It's cheaper to fly from Guangzhou (one way Y1790) and Shenzhen (one way Y1890), which are both near Hong Kong and have daily direct flights to Beijing.

For more information about international flights to Beijing, see the Getting There & Away chapter earlier in this book.

The CAAC aerial web spreads out in every conceivable direction, with daily flights to most destinations. For the most current information, get a CAAC timetable. Domestic flights connect Beijing to the following cities:

Anqing, Baotou, Beihai, Changchun, Changsha, Changzhi, Changzhou, Chaoyang, Chengdu, Chifeng, Chongqing, Dalian, Dandong, Datong, Dunhuang, Fuzhou, Guangzhou, Guilin, Guiyang, Haikou, Hailar, Hangzhou, Harbin, Hefei, Hohhot, Hong Kong, Huangshan, Huangyan, Jilin, Ji'nan, Jinjiang, Jinzhou, Kunming, Lianyungang, Liuzhou, Luoyang, Mudanjiang, Nanchang, Nanjing, Nanning, Nantong, Ningbo, Qingdao, Qiqihar, Quzhou, Sanya, Shanghai, Shantou, Shenyang, Shenzhen, Taiyuan, Tongliao, Ürümqi, Weifang, Weihai, Wenzhou, Wuhan, Wulanhaote, Wuyishan, Xiamen, Xiangfan, Xilinhot, Xining, Yan'an, Yanji, Yantai, Yibin, Yichang, Yinchuan, Yiwu, Zhangjiajie, Zhanjiang, Zhengzhou and Zhuhai

CAAC goes by a variety of aliases (Air China, China Eastern Airlines etc), but you can buy tickets for all of them at the Aviation Building (domestic ☎ 6601-3336; international ☎ 6601-6667) *(mínháng dàshà)* at 15 Xichang'an Jie, Xicheng District. You can purchase the same tickets at the CAAC office in the China World Trade Centre.

The individual offices of other international airlines are:

Aeroflot
    (☎ 6500-2412), Jinglun Hotel, 3 Jianguomenwai Dajie
Air France
    (☎ 6505-1818), Room 2716, China World Trade Centre, 1 Jianguomenwai
Air Macau
    (☎ 6515-8988), Room 807, Scitech Tower, 22 Jainguomenwai
Alitalia
    (☎ 6591-8468), Room 143, Jianguo Hotel, 5 Jianguomenwai
All Nippon Airways
    (☎ 6505-3311), Room 1510, China World Trade Centre, 1 Jianguomenwai
American Airlines
    (☎ 6500-4837), c/o Beijing Tradewinds, 114 International Club, 11 Ritan Lu

Asiana Airlines
(☎ 6506-1118), Room 134, Jianguo Hotel, 5 Jianguomenwai
Austrian Airlines
(☎ 6591-7861), Great Wall Sheraton Hotel, 10 Dongsanhuan Beilu
British Airways
(☎ 6512-4070), Room 210, 2nd floor, Scitech Tower, 22 Jianguomenwai
Canadian Airlines International
(☎ 6463-7901), Unit C201, Lufthansa Centre, 50 Liangmaqiao Lu
Dragonair
(☎ 6505-4343), 1st floor, L107, China World Trade Centre, 1 Jianguomenwai
El Al Israel Airlines
(☎ 6501-4512), Room 2906, Jingguang New World Hotel
Ethiopian Airlines
(☎ 6505-0134), Room 0506, China World Trade Centre, 1 Jianguomenwai
Finnair
(☎ 6512-7180), Room 204, Scitech Tower, 22 Jianguomenwai
Garuda Indonesia
(☎ 6505-2901), Unit L116A, West Wing, China World Trade Centre, 1 Jianguomenwai
Japan Airlines
(☎ 6513-0888), ground floor, Changfugong Office Building, Hotel New Otani, 26A Jianguomenwai
KLM – Royal Dutch Airlines
(☎ 6505-3505), Suite 2432, China World Trade Centre, 1 Jianguomenwai
Korean Air
(☎ 6505-0088), Room 401, West Wing, China World Trade Centre, 1 Jianguomenwai
LOT Polish Airlines
(☎ 6500-7215), Room 2002, Chains City Hotel, 4 Gongren Tiyuchang Donglu
Lufthansa Airlines
(☎ 6465-4488), S101, Lufthansa Centre, 50 Liangmaqiao Lu
Malaysia Airlines
(☎ 6505-2681), W115A/B Level One, West Wing Office Block, China World Trade Centre, 1 Jianguomenwai
MIAT Mongolian Airlines
(☎ 6507-9297), China Golden Bridge Building, East Gate, A1 Jianguomenwai
Northwest Airlines
(☎ 6505-3505), Room 104, China World Trade Centre, 1 Jianguomenwai
Pakistan International Airlines
(☎ 6505-1681), Room 106A, China World Trade Centre, 1 Jianguomenwai

Qantas Airways
(☎ 6467-4794), Suite S120B, ground floor, East Wing Office Building, Kempinski Hotel, Lufthansa Centre, 50 Liangmaqiao Lu
Scandinavian Airlines
(☎ 6512-0575), 18th floor, Scitech Tower, 22 Jianguomenwai
Singapore Airlines
(☎ 6505-2233), Room 109, China World Trade Centre, 1 Jianguomenwai
Swissair
(☎ 6512-3555), Room 201, Scitech Tower, 22 Jianguomenwai
Tarom
(☎ 6500-2233, ext 111), Jianguo Hotel, 5 Jianguomenwai
Thai Airways International
(☎ 6460-8899), S102B Lufthansa Centre, 50 Liangmaqiao Lu
United Airlines
(☎ 6463-1111), Lufthansa Centre, 50 Liangmaqiao Lu
Yugoslav Airlines
(☎ 6500-3388, ext 414), Room 414, Kunlun Hotel, 2 Xinyuan Nanlu

Bus Many foreigners don't think so, but you can indeed arrive in or depart from Beijing by bus. The advantage over the train (besides cost) is that it's easier to get a seat on a bus. Sleeper buses are widely available and certainly recommended for those long overnight journeys. In general, arriving by bus is easier than departing, mainly because when leaving it's confusing to try and figure out which bus station has the bus you need.

The basic rule is that long-distance bus stations are on the perimeter of the city in the direction you want to go. The four major ones are at Dongzhimen (north-east), Haihutun (south; see the Beijing map), Beijiao (north – also called Deshengmen; see the Beijing map) and Majuan (east). Near the entrance to the Beijing-Tianjin Expressway is the Zhaogongkou bus station (see the Beijing map) where you get buses to (surprise) Tianjin. The Tianqiao bus station (western side of Tiantan Park) and Lianhuachi bus station (south-west of the city) are two places where you can get buses to sites south-west of Beijing.

In addition, there are a few small bus stations where tour buses and minibuses gather (usually just in the morning) looking for passengers heading to the Great Wall and other sites in the outlying areas. The most important of these is the Qianmen bus station (which has two parts) just to the south-west of Tiananmen Square. Also useful is the Zhanlanguan Lu Tour bus station which is just to the south of the Beijing Zoo. A few tour buses also depart from the car park at the Workers' Stadium and the Beijing railway station.

Train Foreigners arriving or departing by train do so at Beijing's main railway station (*běijīng huǒchē zhàn*) south-east of the Forbidden City, or the newly opened Beijing west railway station (*běijīng xī zhàn*), near Lianhuachi Park. It's the largest in China.

There are also two other stations of significance in the city, Beijing South (Yongdingmen) railway station (see the Beijing map) and Beijing North (Xizhimen) railway station, on the second ring road.

There are special ticketing windows for foreigners at Beijing railway station and Beijing West railway station – look for the small sign in English saying 'International Passenger Booking Office'. The ticketing office is open daily from 5.30 to 7.30 am and 8 am to 5.30 pm, and from 7 pm to 12.30 am. Those are the official times, but foreigners have often found the staff to arrive late and leave early. Whether or not you get a ticket here is pot luck – sometimes the staff are friendly and helpful, at other times belligerent. Tickets can be booked five or six days in advance. Your chances of getting a sleeper (hard or soft) are good if you book ahead.

See the following table for approximate travel times and train fares out of Beijing for hard seat, hard sleeper and soft sleeper. Variations may arise because of different routings of different trains. For example, the journey to Shanghai can take between 17 and 25 hours depending on the train.

Getting Around
To/From the Airport The airport is 27km from the Forbidden City, but add another 10km if you're going to the southern end of town where most of the budget hotels are.

At the airport, you'll be presented with a somewhat bewildering choice of buses all congregating by the main exit. In fact, almost any bus that gets you to a subway station will do. Inside the airport terminal is the service desk that sells tickets. All buses into town cost Y16, so just plop down the money and tell them where you want to go – somebody outside can direct you towards the right bus.

One company called 'Airbus' currently operates two routes. Route A goes to Beijing railway station (*běijīng zhàn*) and this is probably the most popular bus with travellers. Route B goes to the Xinxing Hotel on the western side of town near Yuyuantan Park. Both of these buses can drop you at a subway station.

The Anle Bus Company offers three routes. The most popular route is to Xidan, which is close to the CAAC office west of the Forbidden City. Another route is to Zhongguancun in north-west Beijing. The third route is to the China Art Gallery (*zhōng-guó měishù guǎn*) north of Wangfujing (central area).

The official schedule for all of the above buses is once every 30 minutes between 5.30 am and 7 pm, but during peak demand times they put on additional buses.

A taxi (using its meter) should cost only about Y85 from the airport to the centre. Be aware of rip-off taxi drivers who approach you inside the terminal and ask something like Y250 for the trip – don't even talk to them, just go outside and find a taxi yourself. Going the other way, drivers may ask for Y20 extra because they are not assured of getting a return passenger. They will also expect you to pay the Y10 toll if you take the airport expressway.

Bus There are a mind-boggling number of buses plying Beijing's traffic-choked boulevards. Destinations are written in Chinese only and figuring out the system will take patience – it's considerably easier if you score a bus map. The buses are packed at the best of times, and during the rush hour it's armpits and elbows all round.

Travel Times & Train Fares from Beijing

Destination	Soft Sleeper (Y)	Hard Sleeper (Y)	Hard Seat (Y)	Soft Seat (Y)	Approx Travel Time (hours)
Baotou	316	208	112	–	15
Beidaihe	–	–	62	97	6
Changchun	379	248	136	–	17
Changsha	529	344	190	–	23
Chengde	–	–	28	51	5
Chengdu	642	417	230	–	34
Chongqing	658	430	237	–	40
Dalian	369	236	121	–	19
Dandong	400	262	142	–	19
Datong	162	108	54	–	7
Fuzhou	705	457	252	–	43
Guangzhou	705	457	252	–	35
Guilin	658	429	237	–	31
Hangzhou	529	345	190	–	24
Harbin	442	289	157	–	20
Hohhot	254	169	91	–	12
Hong Kong	1027	776	–	–	29
Ji'nan	205	136	72	–	9
Kunming	890	577	319	–	59
Lanzhou	600	389	214	–	35
Liuyuan	892	511	309	–	59
Luoyang	298	196	105	–	14
Nanjing	417	273	149	–	20
Nanning	748	472	289	–	39
Qingdao	326	214	115	–	17
Qinglongqiao	–	–	14	21	2
Qiqihar	353	225	113	–	22
Shanghai	520	347	199	–	17
Shenyang	298	202	115	–	11
Shenzhen	720	466	256	–	33
Shijiazhuang	139	95	41	–	4
Suzhou	452	288	149	–	25
Tai'an	241	149	92	–	10
Taiyuan	345	183	110	–	11
Tangshan	–	–	40	61	3
Tianjin	–	–	22	34	1
Turpan	985	639	354	–	72
Ürümqi	1005	650	361	–	75
Xi'an	417	273	149	–	22
Xining	658	430	237	–	44
Yinchuan	452	270	176	–	25
Zhengzhou	264	174	93	–	12

Buses run from around 5 am to 11 pm. Bus stops are few and far between. It's important to work out how many stops you need to go before boarding.

Buses are routed through landmarks and key intersections, and if you can pick out the head and tail of the route, you can get a good idea of where the monster will travel. Major terminals are situated near long-distance junctions: the main Beijing railway station, Dongzhimen, Haihutun, Yongdingmen and Qianmen. The zoo (Dongwuyan) has the biggest pile-up, with about 15 bus lines, since it's where inner and outer Beijing get together.

One or two-digit bus numbers are city core, 100 series buses are trolleys and 300 series are suburban lines. If you work out how to combine bus and subway connections, the subway will speed up part of the trip.

Double Decker Bus The double deckers are special two tiered buses for tourists and upper-crust locals. They run in a circle around the city centre. These cost Y2 but you are spared the traumas of normal public buses – passengers are guaranteed a seat! There are four routes on offer, as follows:

1 Beijing West railway station, heading east on Fuxingmen Dajie, Xichang'an Jie, Dongchang'an Jie, Jianguomenei Dajie, Jianguomenwai Dajie, Jianguo Lu and terminating at a major bus stop called Bawangfen (intersection of Jianguo Lu and Xidawang Lu).
2 Qianmen, north on Dongdan Beidajie, Dongsi Nandajie, Dongsi Beidajie, Lama Temple, the China Ethnic Minorities Park, Asian Games Village.
3 Jijia Temple (the south-west extremity of the third ring road), Grand View Garden, Leyou Hotel, Jingguang New World Hotel, Tuanjiehu Park, Agricultural Exhibition Centre, Lufthansa Centre.
4 Beijing Zoo, Exhibition Centre, second ring road, Holiday Inn Downtown, Yuetan Park, Fuxingmen Dajie flyover, Qianmen Xidajie, Qianmen.

Subway The subway (dì xià tiě) is definitely the best way of travelling around. The Underground Dragon can move at up to 70km per hour – a jaguar compared with the lumbering buses. The subway system made its debut in 1969 for Chinese only (foreigners gained admission in 1980). After nearly three decades, the trains are showing their age – it's a pale shadow to Shanghai's spiffy new subway system.

To recognise a subway station, look for the subway symbol which is an English capital 'D' with a circle around it. Another way of recognising a substation station is to look for an enormous cluster of bicycles.

Trains run at a frequency of one every few minutes during peak times. It can get very crowded, but it sure beats the buses! The carriages have seats for 60 and standing room for 200. Platform signs are in Chinese and pinyin. The fare is a flat Y2 regardless of distance. The subway is open from 5 am to 10.30 pm. There are two lines:

Circle Line This 16km line presently has 18 stations: Beijing Zhan (railway station), Jianguomen, Chaoyangmen, Dongsishitiao, Dongzhimen, Yonghegong, Andingmen, Gulou Dajie, Jishuitan, Xizhimen (the north railway station and zoo), Chegongzhuang, Fuchengmen, Fuxingmen, Changchun Jie, Xuanwumen, Heping Lu, Qianmen and Chongwenmen.

East-West Line This line has 12 stops and runs from Xidan to Pingguoyuan, which is – no, not the capital of North Korea – a western suburb of Beijing whose name translates as Apple Orchard

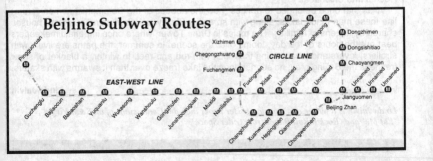

On Your Bike

It's Beijing's broad avenues, tree-lined side streets and narrow hutongs (atmospheric, winding alleyways, some of which date back 500 years) that lend the city its unique character. A taxi goes either too quickly for you to catch the details, or too slowly to sustain interest. Chronic traffic jams can make bicycle travel not just more adventurous, but more efficient as well.

Beijing city is a sprawling metropolis with six million inhabitants, but it is flat and ideal for cycling. Much of Beijing life is lived on the street, too. For an evening's entertainment, people fly kites or throw frisbees in Tiananmen Square. Elsewhere, under the Imperial Palace walls, young people dance to rock, and older ones gather for ballroom dancing. Clusters of neighbours squat under streetlights to gossip and play cards. Street stalls offer kitchenware, silk, vegetables, noodles and even banquets. Repairmen, upholsterers and house painters jostle on footpaths with their tool boxes.

You may cycle past dentists extracting teeth, barbers doing short-back-and-sides, teenage boys shooting pool, old men taking constitutionals, caged birds in hand. Magicians, 'miracle medicine' salesmen and all sorts of other street performers compete for attention. Tables spill out of restaurants onto the pavement, and brawlers tumble out of bars and karaoke clubs.

Cars, trucks, motorcycles and buses caught in the hideous traffic jams of the inner city rev their motors impatiently. Tempers flare and great bouts of cursing and counter-cursing add to the commotion.

The bustle can seem daunting. But you quickly work out how to weave around the horse-drawn carts and negotiate the buses and trams that seem to dip into the bike lanes from nowhere. You learn that crossing large intersections is best done in clusters; opportunistic alliances that are tight as the traffic policemen's white gloves. You find that, unless it's very late, there's almost nowhere you can break down, or get a flat, that's too far from the road-side stand of an itinerant bicycle repairman. With luck, you won't discover that the easiest way to get into a fight in Beijing is to run into another bicycle.

There are places in Beijing that really only ought to be seen by bicycle; places of such magic that only the breeze on your face convinces you they're for real. One is the moat around the Forbidden City, traversable around the eastern side of the palace. On one side of the path the clay-red wall of the Imperial Palace, with its crenellated battlements, rears up. Ornamental guard towers with flying eaves and roofs of gold jag into view at each corner. On the other, through weeping willows, you see lotuses and fishermen lounging as pleasure boats stir up ripples on the still water of the moat. Fabulous by day, the moat is enchanting by night. If you start at the front of the palace, by Tiananmen Square, when you come out the back you're just a short ride to the even more spectacular 'back lakes' – Houhai and Shishahai.

Villas that once belonged to princes (now the abodes of the Communist nomenklatura) line these man-made lakes, along with sprawling *dazayuar*, labyrinthine courtyard houses shared by dozens of families. The majestic Drum Tower, where once imperial timekeepers beat out the hours of the day, looms over the scene. In summer, the paths are lively with strollers, lovers and locals trying their luck with rod and reel. In winter, a blanket of snow freshens the Beijing grey; no sooner does the lake freeze over than it swarms with skaters.

Linda Jaivin

Linda Jaivin is a writer and translator. Her books include 'Confessions of an S&M Virgin', 'Eat Me' and 'Rock n Roll Babes from Outer Space'.

(unfortunately, the apple trees have long since vanished). It takes 40 minutes to traverse the length of the line. The stops are Xidan, Fuxingmen, Nanlishilu, Muxudi, Junshibowuguan (Military Museum), Gongzhufen, Wanshoulu, Wukesong, Yuquanlu, Babaoshan, Bajiaocun, Guchenglu and Pingguoyuan. Fuxingmen is where the Circle Line meets the East-West Line and there is no additional fare to make the transfer.

At the time of writing, the East-West Line was being expanded further east and will probably be open by the time you read this. However, the names of the new stations were not yet determined as we went to press.

Taxi With the number of taxis in the city reaching close to 100,000, finding one is only a problem during rush hours and rain storms.

Taxis come in different classes, and the bottom of the pecking order belongs to the yellow microbuses known as 'bread taxis' (*miàndī*) because they're shaped like a loaf of bread. Although they lack status, they're cheap at Y10 for 10km. The authorities plan to phase them out and are now replacing them with 'bullet taxis' (so-called because of their sleek shape). The bullets cost Y7 at flagfall which gets you 4km, after which you pay Y1.20 for each additional kilometre.

Next up in status and price are the *xiali* taxis, small economy cars that cost Y1.40 to Y1.80 per kilometre. Top of the line are the petrol-guzzling limousine taxis which cost Y12 for the first 4km and Y2 for each kilometre thereafter. Between 11 pm and 6 am there is a 20% surcharge added to the flagfall metered fare.

Bicycle Budget hotels are the place to rent bicycles, which cost around Y5 to Y10 per day. The cheap bikes are the black workhorse variety – a sleek mountain bike can go for Y100 per day if you rent it from an upmarket hotel!

Several shopping areas are closed to cyclists from 6 am to 6 pm; Wangfujing is one. Parking is provided everywhere for peanuts – compulsory peanuts since your

velo can otherwise be towed away. Beijing's ever-increasing traffic has made riding nerve-racking and dangerous.

Around Beijing

MING TOMBS
(*shísān líng*)
These look much like a bomb shelter, but to the Chinese the Ming Tombs are a big deal. Foreigners may be less impressed, but the scenery along the way is charming. The 7km 'spirit way' starts with a triumphal arch, then goes through the Great Palace Gate, where officials had to dismount, and passes a giant tortoise (made in 1425) bearing the largest stele in China. This is followed by a guard of 12 sets of stone animals.

Dingling was the first of the tombs to be excavated and opened to the public. In total, 13 of the 16 Ming emperors are buried in this 40 sq km area, which is why another name for this site is the Thirteen Tombs. Besides Dingling, two other tombs, Changling and Zhaoling, are open to the public.

Aware of the fact that many visitors have found the tombs disappointing, the Beijing municipal government is busy dressing up the area. New facilities include a golf course, the Dingling Museum (with a wax Genghis Khan), the Nine Dragons Amusement Park, the Aerospace Museum, an archery and rifle range, shops, cafes, a 350 room hotel, a swimming pool, an aquarium, a camping ground, a picnic area, a fountain (with 200m waterjet), a fishing pier (on the Ming Tombs Reservoir) and a velodrome.

There are also helicopter rides over the tombs and the nearby Great Wall. Admission to the Ming Tombs is Y30 (foreigners' price).

Getting There & Away
The tombs lie 50km north-west of Beijing and a few kilometres from the small town of Changping. Tour buses usually combine

them with a visit to the Great Wall. You can also get there on the local buses. Take bus No 5 or 44 to Deshengmen terminal. West of the flyover is the terminal of bus No 345, which you take to Changping, a one-hour ride (it drops you off near the Aerospace Museum). Then take bus No 314 to the tombs (or get a taxi for the last stretch).

EASTERN QING TOMBS
(qīng dōng líng)
The area of the Eastern Qing Tombs could be Death Valley, housing as it does five emperors, 14 empresses and 136 imperial consorts. In the mountains ringing the valley are buried princes, dukes, imperial nurses, and so on.

Emperor Qianlong (1711-99) started preparations when he was 30, and by the time he was 88 the old boy had used up 90 tonnes of his silver. His resting place covers half a square kilometre. Some of the beamless stone chambers are decorated with Tibetan and Sanskrit sutras; the doors bear bas-relief bodhisattvas.

Empress Dowager Cixi also got a head start. Her tomb, Dingdong, was completed some three decades before her death. The phoenix (symbol of the empress) appears above that of the dragon (the emperor's symbol) in the artwork at the front of the tomb – not side by side as on other tombs. Both tombs were plundered in the 1920s.

In Zunhua County, 125km east of Beijing, the Eastern Qing Tombs have a lot more to see in them than the Ming Tombs, although you may be a little jaded after the Forbidden City.

Getting There & Away
It's a long haul by public bus. Tour buses are considerably more comfortable than the local rattletraps and take three or four hours to get there; you have about three hours on site. Some people prefer to go from Tianjin.

BADACHU
(bādàchù)
Directly south of the Fragrant Hills is Badachu, the Eight Great Sites, also known

as Eight Great Temples (bādà sì). It has eight monasteries or temples scattered in wooded valleys. The Second Site has the Buddha's Tooth Relic Pagoda, built to house the sacred fang and accidentally discovered when the Allied army demolished the place in 1900.

Since 1994, the ancient culture has been dressed up with a new amusement park ride, a roller-toboggan course. A chairlift carries you up the hill to the top of the toboggan course. The rollerway has a length of 1700m and speeds up to 80km per hour can be achieved.

Admission to Badachu costs Y5.

Getting There & Away
The easiest way to reach the area is to take the east-west subway line to the last stop at Pingguoyuan and catch a taxi (Y10) from there. Alternatively, take bus No 347, which runs there from the zoo (it crosses the No 318 route).

TANZHE TEMPLE
(tánzhè sì)
About 45km directly west of Beijing is Tanzhe Temple, the largest of all the Beijing temples, occupying an area 260m by 160m. The Buddhist complex has a long history dating back to the 3rd century (Jin Dynasty); structural modifications date from the Liao, Tang, Ming and Qing dynasties. It therefore has a number of features – dragon decorations, mythical animal sculptures and grimacing gods – no longer found in temples in the capital.

Translated literally, Tanzhe means Pool Cudrania – the temple takes its name from its proximity to the Dragon Pool (lóng tán) and some rare Cudrania (zhè) trees. Locals come to the Dragon Pool to pray for rain during droughts. The Cudrania trees nourish silkworms and provide a yellow dye. The bark of the tree is believed to cure women of sterility, which may explain why there are so few of these trees left at the temple entrance.

The temple complex is open to the public daily from 8.30 am until 6 pm.

Getting There & Away

One option is to take bus No 336 from Zhanlanguan Lu, which runs off Fuchengmenwai Dajie (north-west of Yuetan Park), to the terminal at Mentougou and then hitch or take a taxi. A direct route is bus No 307 from Qianmen to the Hetan terminal and then a numberless bus to the temple. Alternatively, take the subway to Pingguoyuan, bus No 336 to Hetan and the numberless bus to the temple.

JIETAI TEMPLE
(*jiètái sì*)

About 10km south-east of the Tanzhe Temple is a similar but smaller compound, Jietai Temple. The name roughly translates as Temple of Ordination Terrace. The temple was built during the Tang Dynasty, around 622 AD, with major improvements made by later tenants during the Ming Dynasty. The main complex is dotted with ancient pines, all of which have quaint names – Nine Dragon Pine is claimed to be over 1300 years old.

Getting There & Away

It's roughly 35km from Jietai Temple to Beijing, and a journey out here is usually combined with a visit to nearby Tanzhe Temple.

PEKING MAN SITE
(*zhōukǒudiàn*)

The site of the primaeval Chinese, Zhoukoudian is 48km south-west of Beijing. There's an 'Apeman Cave' on a hill above the village, several lesser caves and some dig sites. There is also a fossil exhibition hall – you'd have to be a fossil yourself to stay here for more than 15 minutes. There are three sections to the exhibition hall – pre-human history, the life and times of Peking Man and a section dealing with recent anthropological research. There are ceramic models, stone tools and the skeletons of prehistoric creatures.

The exhibition hall is open daily from 9 am to 4 pm, but check before you go. Admission is Y21.

Getting There & Away

You could get a suburban train from Beijing South railway station and get off at Zhoukoudian. Bus 917 from Tianqiao bus station (western side of Tiantan Park) goes to Fangshan from where you can take a bus or taxi to the site. Another possibility is bus No 309 from Changchun Jie (the south-western corner of the second ring road); or bus No 339 from Lianhuachi bus station. If combined with a trip to Tanzhe Temple and Marco Polo Bridge, approaching the site by taxi is not unreasonable.

SHIDU
(*shídù*)

About 110km south-west of Beijing city, Shidu is Beijing's answer to Guilin. Its pinnacle-shaped rock formations, small rivers and general beauty make Shidu a favourite spot with expats. Shidu means 'ten ferries' or 'ten crossings'; before the new road and bridges were built, travellers had to cross the Juma River 10 times while going along the gorge from Zhangfang and Shidu village.

Places to Stay

The *Longshan Hotel* (*lóngshān fàndiàn*) is opposite the railway station and is the most likely place to stay. Down near Jiudu (the 'ninth ferry') there is a camping ground, conveniently located on a flood-plain.

Getting There & Away

Getting to Shidu is fastest by train, but there are only two departures daily. Departures are from the Beijing South (Yongdingmen) railway station (probably the only chance you'll have to use this station). If you take the morning train, the trip can be done in one day. The schedule is as follows:

No	From	To	Depart	Arrive
795	Yong-dingmen	Shidu	6.38 am	9.03 am
897	Yong-dingmen	Shidu	5.40 pm	8.10 pm
796	Shidu	Yong-dingmen	7.42 pm	10.02 pm
898	Shidu	Yong-dingmen	9.07 am	11.28 am

The Great Wall

Also known to the Chinese as the '10,000 Li Wall', the Great Wall stretches from Shanhaiguan Pass on the east coast to Jiayuguan Pass in the Gobi Desert. Standard histories emphasise the unity of the wall. The 'original' wall was begun 2000 years ago during the Qin Dynasty (221-207 BC), when China was unified under Emperor Qin Shihuang. Separate walls, constructed by independent kingdoms to keep out marauding nomads, were linked up. The effort required hundreds of thousands of workers, many of them political prisoners, and 10 years of hard labour under General Meng Tian. An estimated 180 million cubic metres of rammed earth was used to form the core of the original wall, and legend has it that one of the building materials used was the bodies of deceased workers.

The wall never really did perform its function as a defence line to keep invaders out. As Genghis Khan supposedly said, 'The strength of a wall depends on the courage of those who defend it'.

Legends of the Wall

The Great Wall is surely China's most famous feature, the 'symbol of the Chinese nation' to many Chinese and foreigners alike – but is it actually what it seems?

A visit to one of the world's great sights is well worth the effort; but far from providing evidence of a single people whose conception of the world is expressed through their most monumental achievement, the reality of the Great Wall appears inseparable from the claims (and myths) about it.

Reputable guidebooks, newspapers and history books confidently quote the wall's length (anywhere from 2500 to 6000km). But since China's walls and earthen ramparts have never been adequately surveyed (satellite surveying spotted a few forgotten walls in late 1997), these numbers are fanciful, even assuming the existence of a single 'wall'. The same sources often note that 'the wall is the only man-made structure visible from space'. Ironically, this claim originated in the west early this century (ie long before *Sputnik*); it gained currency in a marvellous Ripley's *Believe It Or Not* column in 1932.

Factoids aside, are we looking at one wall built for a single purpose? Visitors might imagine that the familiar crenellated Ming wall near Beijing flows on over the rest of China's old northern frontier. In fact it doesn't – the wall is no more continuous in space than it is over time. Frontier walls were built long before the Qin Dynasty, but more interesting than who built walls is who did not (eg the Tang and the Sung). In contrast to the idea of a continuous 'Chinese' approach to borders, wall

Sentries could be bribed. However, it did work very well as a kind of elevated highway, transporting men and equipment across mountainous terrain. Its beacon tower system, using smoke signals generated by burning wolves' dung, transmitted news of enemy movements quickly back to the capital. To the west was Jiayuguan Pass, an important link on the Silk Road, where there was a Customs post of sorts and where unwanted Chinese were ejected through the gates to face the terrifying wild west.

During the Ming Dynasty a determined effort was made to rehash the project, this time facing the wall with bricks and stone slabs – some 60 million cubic metres of them. This Ming project took more than 100 years, and the costs in human effort and resources were phenomenal.

The wall was largely forgotten after that. Lengthy sections of it have returned to dust. The wall might have disappeared entirely had it not been rescued by the tourist industry. Several important sections have recently been rebuilt, dressed up with souvenir shops, restaurants and amusement park rides. Oddly, the depiction of the wall as an object of great beauty is a bizarre one. It's often been a symbol of tyranny, as the Berlin Wall once was.

building was only one of several security options available to succeeding dynasties (such as trade and diplomacy).

The discontinuous array of (ineffective) fortifications occasionally and controversially deployed as a political option has only recently become 'Great'. Eighteenth century European enthusiasm for China's 'great work', which dwarfed the Egyptian pyramids in 'utility and immensity' (Voltaire), was not matched in China until the modernising Republicanism of Sun Yatsen. Until then, when conceived at all, the wall was a handy backdrop for recycled tales (eg the legend of the virtuous widow whose tears originally toppled a city wall, not a 'Great' one), or served as a metaphor for tyranny and despotism.

Allusions to Qin Shihuang and his 'despotic' wall were available to cautious critics of Mao's Cultural Revolution (which explains Qin's rehabilitation in the 1970s, especially after his terracotta army was unearthed near X'ian). Meanwhile, peasants carted off chunks of the real thing to build houses. In recent years some sections of the wall have been restored for tourism while others have been dynamited to make room for cement factories, roads and rail lines.

As the major symbol of China, 'the Great Wall' is probably better known to foreigners than it is to the people it is supposed to symbolise. Patriotic campaigners for wall renovation projects have been chagrined to learn that many people in remote regions know the wall only as 'old frontier', using the word *(bian)* employed by the Ming. As some critical historians suggest, these 'ignorant' peasants may be the only ones who've got the story right.

Russ Kerr

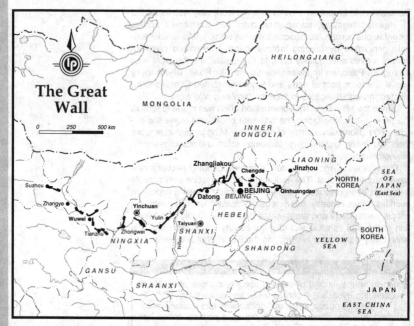

Badaling Great Wall

(bādálǐng chángchéng)

The majority of visitors see the Great Wall at Badaling, 70km north-west of Beijing at an elevation of 1000m. This section of the wall was restored in 1957, with the addition of guard rails. Since the 1980s, Badaling has become exceedingly crowded with visitors so a cable car was added to enhance the flow of tourist traffic.

The Great Wall Circle Vision Theatre was opened in 1990 – a 360° amphitheatre showing 15 minute films about the Great Wall. The latest innovation at Badaling is the millennium clock in the KFC fast-food restaurant.

There is an admission fee of Y25, which also gets you into the China Great Wall museum. You can spend plenty more for a tacky 'I Climbed the Great Wall' T-shirt, a talking panda doll, a cuckoo clock that plays 'The East Is Red' or a plastic reclining buddha statue with a lightbulb in its mouth. For an additional fee you can get your snapshot taken aboard a camel and pretend to be Marco Polo.

THE GREAT WALL

Getting There & Away

CITS, CTS, big hotels and everyone else in the tourist business does a tour to Badaling. Prices border on the ridiculous, with some hotels asking over Y300 per person.

There are cheapie Chinese tours (around Y25) departing from a number of venues. Some depart from the Qianmen tour bus station (south-west end of Tiananmen Square). The other main departure point is Zhanlanguan Lu tour bus station (just south of the Beijing Zoo). Departures are in the morning only, around 7.30 to 8 am. But first ask about the itinerary – some tour operators don't just go straight to Badaling, but instead stop at some tacky sights such as a wax museum and Chinese fun fair, with arrival at the Great Wall at nearly 5 pm (just enough time to get a photo before heading back to Beijing).

Municipal buses also ply the route to the wall. Just below Qianmen (the Arrow Tower) is a second Qianmen tour bus station where you can catch a city bus for Badaling – there is a sign in English referring to it as the 'No 1 Tourist Bus'. It costs Y11, takes 1½ hours each way. Departures are from 6.30 to 10 am, returning between 1.30 and 6 pm.

You can reach the wall by express train from Beijing railway station, getting off at Qinglongqiao. There are actually three stations within 1km of the wall – Qinglongqiao, New Qinglongqiao and Badaling, but the first is by far the closest to your destination. No trains stop at all three stations and many stop only at Qinglongqiao. You can continue from Qinglongqiao on to Datong, Hohhot and beyond. Coming from the other direction, you can get off the train at Qinglongqiao, look around, and reboard the train to Beijing on the same ticket. You can safely dump your bags in the left-luggage room at Qinglongqiao railway station while you look around.

A microbus taxi to the wall and back will cost at least Y300 for an eight-hour hire with a maximum of five passengers – you are expected to buy lunch for the driver.

Mutianyu Great Wall

(mùtiányù chángchéng)

To take some of the pressure off crowded Badaling, a second site for Great Wall viewing was opened at Mutianyu, 90km north-east of Beijing. However, it didn't take long before armadas of Japanese tour buses began to congregate, and today this part of the wall is almost as much of a carnival as Badaling.

Getting There & Away

A few Chinese tour buses go to Mutianyu – look for them near Qianmen, Zhanlanguan Lu tour bus station (by the zoo) or the Workers' Stadium. Entrance to the wall at Mutianyu costs Y30. The cable car costs Y65 one way, or Y80 for the round-trip.

Every day there is a direct bus to Mutianyu from Dongzhimen bus station at 7.30 am. Coming back, there are two buses, one at 1 pm and the other at 4 pm. You must change buses at Huairou on the return route. The total cost of the trip is Y20 and it takes about two hours to make the one way journey.

Simatai Great Wall

(sīmǎtái chángchéng)

If you prefer your wall in a relatively natural state, Simatai is the place to go. The 19km section of wall at Simatai is the most beautiful and until very recently was totally unspoiled. The first danger sign was the T-shirt vendors, who set up shop around 1994. Then a loudspeaker was added, and it now bellows music and 'nature sounds' to increase your enjoyment of the wall.

In 1996 a cable car (Y40) was installed, and it's not hard to imagine that a McDonald's or KFC will set up shop some day. But at least for the moment, Simatai is still an enjoyable outing, and if you want to do the wall in Beijing, then this is the best spot.

The Simatai section of the wall dates from the Ming Dynasty and has some unusual features like 'obstacle-walls', which are walls-within-walls used for defending against enemies who'd already scaled the Great Wall. There are 135 watchtowers at Simatai, the highest being Wangjinglou. Small cannon have been discovered in this area, as well as evidence of rocket-type weapons such as flying knives and flying swords.

Simatai is not for the faint-hearted – this section of the wall is very steep. A few slopes have a 70° incline and you need both hands free, so bring a day pack to hold your camera and other essentials. One narrow section of footpath has a 500m drop – it's no place for acrophobics. However, the steepness and sheer dropoffs help keep out the riffraff.

In the early 1970s a nearby PLA unit destroyed about 3km of the wall to build barracks, setting an example for the locals who used stones from the wall to build houses. In 1979 the same unit was ordered to rebuild the section they tore down.

The wall at Simatai is being renovated, but most of it still remains in its pristine crumbling condition. Seeing the wall au naturel is a sharp contrast to Badaling and Mutianyu, which are so well restored that you may get the impression the wall was built just yesterday to serve CITS tour groups. Perhaps it was.

Admission to the site at Simatai costs Y15.

Getting There & Away

Simatai is 110km north-east of Beijing, and due to the distance and lack of tourist facilities there is little public transport. Buses to Simatai cost Y22 for the round-trip and depart just once daily from the Dongzhimen bus station at 6.10 am. The journey takes two to three hours, and the bus departs Simatai at 3 pm (but ask to be sure).

For budget travellers, the best deal around is offered through the Jinghua Hotel – Y80 for the return journey by minibus. Ring its booking office (☎ 6761-2582 after 4 pm) for more details.

If you don't do a tour through the Jinghua Hotel, you can hire a microbus taxi for the day for about Y400. Tour operators also gather at Qianmen and charge foreigners ridiculous prices.

Jinshanling Great Wall

(jīnshānlǐng cháng chéng)

Though not as steep (and therefore not as impressive) as Simatai, the Great Wall at Jinshanling is considerably less developed than any of the previously mentioned wall sites. This section of the wall has been renovated and souvenir vendors have moved in, but so far there is no cable car and visitors are relatively few. Many of the tourists stopping here are on an excursion between Beijing and Chengde in Hebei Province, with Jinshanling thrown in as a brief stop.

Perhaps the most interesting thing about Jinshanling is that it's the starting point for a hike to Simatai. You can of course do the walk in the opposite direction, though getting a ride back to Beijing from Simatai is easier than from Jinshanling. Getting a ride should be no problem if you've made arrangements with your driver to pick you up (and didn't pay him in advance). The distance between Jinshanling and Simatai is only about 10km, but it takes nearly four hours because the trail is steep and stony.

Admission to the Great Wall at Jinshanling is Y40.

Getting There & Away

There is no public transport so access is only by chartered car, taxi or tour bus.

Walking The Wild Wall

Away from the heavily touristed areas, long sections of the Great Wall stride across the region's lofty mountain ranges. This 'Wild Wall' is remote, lonely, unspoilt, overgrown and crumbling. There are no tickets, no signposts, no hassles from trinket-sellers, no coach parks or garbage to spoil the view. Travellers can trek up narrow footpaths winding uphill from tiny villages in Beijing's backwoods and discover what for many may turn out to be the ultimate China experience.

For a genuine Wild Wall hike that is both easy to access and close to Beijing, the Huanghua (huánghuā cháng chéng, or 'Yellow Flower Fortress') section is ideal. The Great Wall at Huanghua clings to a high hillside adjacent to a reservoir. Around 60km north of Beijing, Huanghua is a classic and well preserved example of

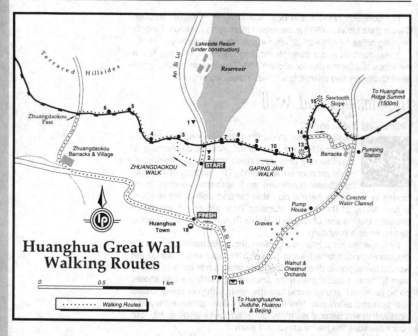

Huanghua Great Wall Walking Routes

HUANGHUA GREAT WALL WALKING ROUTES

1 Restaurant
2 Shuang Long Zhu Jin Jia Restaurant
3 Second Watchtower
4 Derelict Tower
5 Stone Ceiling Tower
6 Three Eyed Tower
7 First Tower
8 Second Tower
9 Third Tower
10 Perfectly Preserved Tower
11 Battle Platform
12 Panorama Point
13 Ming-Renovated Tower
14 Tablet Tower
15 Panorama Point
16 Post Office
17 61km Milestone
18 Buses to Huairou

Ming defence with high and wide ramparts, intact parapets and sturdy beacon towers.

It is said that one Lord Cai was responsible for building this section, and he was meticulous about its quality. Each *cun* or inch of the wall represented a whole day's work of one labourer. When the Ministry of War heard that his lordship's efforts had been so extravagant, he was beheaded and his family lost their privileges and fell into disgrace. Years later, a general judged Lord Cai's wall to be one of the best and he had the official posthumously rehabilitated.

West to Zhuangdaokou (4km; 3 hours return)

The obvious place to start this walk is at the point where the wall meets the road, however, the wall is in quite a poor state there, and it's easier to walk about 100m to the south. After passing a small, deep quarry and old toilet, you'll see a well trodden path leaving the roadside and heading up a creek. The path keeps to the left-hand side of the creek and is clear and easy to follow. After about 300m it starts to veer towards the wall, and fades among the terraces, but your first target is in sight.

Second Watch Tower

To get to this tower (the first, lower tower is derelict) make your way to an arched entranceway just past the tower itself. As you pass through the archway, straight ahead is an engraved tablet embedded in the wall. It details construction of a 150 *zhang* length of wall in the 7th year of the Wanli period (1579) by a group of commanders and their workforce. You can see the name of the stonemason who carved this tablet, Wu Zongye, in the bottom left-hand corner.

The tower itself has three windows along both its northern and southern faces. Locals describe towers by referring to the number of openings along one face, referring to them as holes *(keng)* or eyes *(yan)*. So this tower is a three hole or three eyed tower, *san keng lou* or *san yan lou*. It once had a wooden roof which supported a second story structure, but now its central area is open to the sky. You can see holes in the course of brick (half a metre above archway apexes) where roof-to-floor supporting beams were positioned.

Leaving the tower, make your way west along the ramparts towards a derelict tower. From this high point you get panoramic views of the area.

Derelict Tower

Looking east, the Huanghua reservoir is in full view. Beyond the reservoir, four towers dot the wall on its lower slopes, while a roofless battle platform can be seen near the summit. The wall then turns north and plunges out of sight. It reappears with a side view of the inverted, U-shaped stretch of wall known as the Gaping Jaw. Further on, the wall can be seen snaking up the Huanghua Ridge.

Looking north, a few seemingly solitary watchtowers can be seen in the vicinity of Fenghuangtuo Mountain (1530m). They are connected by walls, but they are small in scale and the workmanship is of inferior quality. Looking south, you can see Huanghua town and the wide river valley leading towards Huanghuazhen. The view starkly illustrates the strategic nature of the pass between the mountains here.

THE GREAT WALL

From the corner tower the wall swings north, running level through conifer woods before turning west again and dropping to a three eyed tower, notable for its stone ceiling.

Stone Ceiling Tower

Large slabs of igneous rock have been incorporated into the ceiling of this tower. Normally, rock was used only in foundations, with bricks employed throughout the upper levels. Given that the slabs are almost 1m long and about 40cm wide, it's difficult to explain their use; the effort required to hoist such heavy slabs into position would have been considerable.

Leave the tower through the western door and follow the wall as it drops through a thick conifer plantation. The parapets around here are in poor condition and the wall's pavement is overgrown and, in some places, totally derelict. After 200m and another **three eyed tower,** the ramparts cross a small valley where a pass, or gate, in the wall once existed. Almost in compensation for the condition of the ramparts here, the gate is in excellent condition.

The Zhuangdaokou pass was one of three passes built north of Beijing in the 15th century to hamper the invasion of Mongols on horseback.

Zhuangdaokou

This pass, a passageway through the wall, is about 2.5m wide in the form of a brick archway founded on large igneous blocks. It is most striking for its engraved tablets which are different on either side of the archway. On a tablet on the southern side there are the three large characters 'zhuang dao kou' from right to left. There's also a number of smaller characters recording the name of the official who put the tablet in place, Liu Xun, and the date, in the fifth year of the Wanli reign (1577). Farmers continue to use this gate to reach terraced hillsides beyond the wall to tend their fruit trees or coppice conifers for firewood.

The tablet on the northern face, also dated 1577, bears three large characters which read from right to left 'Zhen lu guan', or 'Suppress Captives Pass'.

Zhuangdaokou was originally fortified in 1404 during the early years of the Ming Dynasty. It was one of three passes (along with Juyongguan at Badaling and Gubeikou in the north-east) deemed to be critical in blocking large Mongol armies on horseback, and preventing them from reaching the capital easily. Between these passes, where sturdy walls and towers were built, there were only lines of watchtowers and beacon towers. It was left to later dynasties to connect them with walls.

Zhuangdaokou Pass to Zhuangdaokou Village

From the archway turn south and follow the path downhill. It is about 500m to the village of Zhuangdaokou, a marvellous little settlement half nestled within the walls of an ancient barracks. The path is as old as the pass itself, linking the barracks with the wall.

As you enter the village, the barracks is the large walled structure on the left; it's possible to climb its wall at the near corner. It averages seven courses of stone blocks in height, and the blocks are of the same provenance and shape as those used as foundations for the wall. About half the foundation of the structure remains; it now encloses some farmhouses.

From the top of its walls you can see carved granite water spouts protruding from inside. All other structures, and half the walls, have been removed – probably during the Cultural Revolution.

Village to Bus Stop or Restaurant

Follow your nose down through the narrow alleyways (note the Cultural Revolution slogans in yellow and faded images of Mao's head on crumbling plaster walls) to the southern edge of the village, then turn left at the bank of the stream and follow the main road for 1km to a T-junction. Buses for Huairou and Changping leave from here.

Turn left here if you want to return to the starting point, or refuel at the Shuang Long Zhu Jiu Jia restaurant (literally 'Pair of Dragons Playing with a Pearl Alcohol House').

East to Gaping Jaw (4km; 4 hours return)

From the restaurant walk north for 50m and cross the top of the dam holding back Huanghua Reservoir. The dam occupies the site of the main Huanghua Gate – only the foundations of this once-glorious structure remain.

From the far end of the dam, climb up the footpath on the northern side and enter the **First Tower** through one of its north-facing windows.

It is a short, steep climb to the **Second Tower**. Parapets have fallen down, locals have removed the bricks, and they have also taken away bricks which topped the stone block foundations of the rampart. The wall drops in height before climbing to the **Third Tower**. This is a conventional shape – more of a quadrangle than an oblong – and is offset well to the north.

Perfectly Preserved Tower

A gradual 200m climb takes you to the fourth tower. It is quite standard in shape, and is in exceptionally good condition. The ramparts before and beyond the tower are also in excellent condition (with parapets still standing and brick-work intact) as are its upper story battlements and loopholes.

The tower is a three eyed structure with its central area open to the sky. On the floor of the tower is an engraving dating from the Longqing period (1567-1572). At the time of writing, a wooden ladder in the tower gave access to the tower's top storey. Just outside the eastern door of the tower there is a flight of steps cut down into the ramparts and leading to a perfectly preserved granite archway. On the wall facing the archway is a gap which once housed a tablet.

Battle Platform

Exiting the tower, the ramparts climb to a short steep section featuring small observation platforms in front of a large battle platform. This is like a roofless watchtower, asymmetrically offset to the north for observation and enfilading (flanking) fire. Within its parapets are two rows of loopholes, each topped with bricks of different designs. The platform, close to the summit, commands a strategic position for cannon fire to the valley below. From the battle platform, the wall reaches the summit and then turns north to a tower which provides a fine place for views of the area.

Panorama Point

Looking north, you can see the distinctive shape of the section of the wall called Gaping Jaw. Looking east, the wall streaks up the Huanghua ridge towards the summit (from the south, the ridge profile looks like a camel's back and is called 'the camel's back which breaks the wind'). Heading north, the ramparts lead to a well preserved, four eyed tower.

A well preserved structure, the Tablet tower contains a 16th-century engraved tablet.

Ming-Renovated Tower

In good light, the colour of the top half-dozen courses of bricks, especially on the southern face of the tower, appears to differ from the rest. Inside, some parts of the brickwork seem to have been repaired with mortar of a different colour, suggesting that the top of the tower was rebuilt and other parts inside were repaired. The reason why these efforts were made is open to debate. It is unlikely that the tower, in such a dominant high position, was attacked and damaged. It is more likely that the tower dates from the early Ming and was repaired in the later Ming.

Tablet Tower

About 100m downhill is another fine four eyed tower. Just before the tower there are steps down from the wall leading through an archway off the wall and down the gully. The second chamber on the right (south) houses an engraved tablet from the third year of the Longqing period (1570). It is etched with 206 characters and edged with a simple vine design.

You now have two options. The shorter route is to leave by the southern door, exit the wall via the steps and archway, and head down the gully path to the valley floor. This is route is easy and reaches the valley by a small water pumping station.

If you feel like a longer walk, leave the tower by the north door and walk around the Gaping Jaw and its steep eastern limb – Sawtooth Slope. This option will appeal to those who enjoy a scramble as the Sawtooth Slope (named for its zigzag profile) is an extremely steep and slippery descent. It is possible to continue east along Huanghua Ridge, but it's a steep, tough hike.

Barracks

Both routes end up at the pumping station. From there you can walk about 50m south-west to a barracks. Its south-facing wall has an intact archway, and all its perimeter walls are standing. The barracks once housed up to 200 men stationed to guard this part of the wall, taking advantage of a sheltered position and a water source.

To the Main Road

To return to the main road, walk south on the stony track which swings gradually to the west, crossing a concrete-channelled waterway after about 600m. There is a small pump house nearby on the right, and a fork off and up a bank further to the right (west). Avoid this and keep on the main track, passing conical grave mounds on either side of the track and walking through walnut and chestnut orchards.

The track swings right all the time and eventually hits the road by a post office and beside the 61km milestone on An Si Lu. Head north to the bridge for transport to Huairou and Changping.

Places to Stay & Eat

A *resort* by the dam was under construction at the time of writing, but building had been underway for more than a year without any indication it was nearing completion. Check it out when you reach there. If you were wanting to spend a night on the wall, it's possible to sleep in the watchtowers. It's unlikely that the PSB would bother you, but we can't predict their reaction if they did find you there. As the *zhaodaisuo* (guesthouse) in Huanghuazhen doesn't accept foreigners, the nearest accommodation is in Changping or Huairou, but you'll struggle to find anything under Y100 and it's a long way away (see the following Getting There & Away section).

The *Shuang Long Zhu Jiu Jia* restaurant, just to the south of the wall, is run by a local family and serves a wide variety of cheap dishes. There's another restaurant north of the wall on the left hand side of the road. It serves similar fare. Otherwise, there is a string of restaurants on An Si Lu in Huanghuazhen.

Getting There & Away

Bus & Minibus

There is no direct bus to Huanghua, but there are two indirect routes. The first option is to take a public bus or minibus to Huairou from

Dongzhimen long-distance bus station in Beijing (near the subway station of the same name). Bus No 916 leaves every 15 minutes from 5.30 am to 6.30 pm (Y4) and takes just over an hour to get to Huairou. Minibuses *(xiao gong gong qi che)* adopt the same number (916) and run the same route for Y5, although they are a little quicker. Alight in Huairou and change to a minibus for Sihai, which passes through Huanghua. The trip takes about 75 minutes and costs Y6. The second option takes you via Changping. Hop on to minibus No 345 at Deshengmen intersection, just east of Jishuitan subway station. The ride to Changping will cost you Y8 and take up to an hour.

In Changping, change buses for Huanghua on the same street at which you pull up. (Don't take the No 345 scheduled large bus service, which is non-express with more than 20 stops.)

The route from Changping to Huanghua passes through the valley of the Ming tombs. It takes more than one hour and costs Y7.

Cycling

It is feasible and straightforward to cycle to Huanghua. Bicycles can be hired from many of Beijing's hotels or from opposite the Friendship Store. Only ride if you are in reasonable shape for the 62km distance, which includes a mountain pass.

Cycling time is four to seven hours depending on your fitness, the weather, frequency of stops and bike problems. The roads are excellent, and there are many places where punctures, rattles and squeaks can be repaired.

William Lindesay

William Lindesay has walked the length of the wall, from Jiayuguan to Shanhaiguan. This piece is based on his second book on the wall, 'Hiking on History – Exploring Beijing's Great Wall on Foot'. The illustrations in this section are based on sketches by John Macdonald.

This etching of the Great Wall outside Beijing is one of a series created by Briton Thomas Allom during his travels through China in the early 19th century.

THE GREAT WALL

Tianjin 天津

Tianjin Facts & Highlights

Area: 11,300 sq km

Population: 9.5 million

Highlights

- The Antique Market, one of China's most outstanding markets, particularly on a Sunday.
- Tianjin's 19th-century European buildings, poignant reminders of a not-too-distant past.
- Strolling, shopping and eating.

Like Beijing and Shanghai, Tianjin (*tiānjīn*) belongs to no province – it's a special municipality, which gives it a degree of autonomy, but it's also closely administered by the central government. The city is nicknamed 'Shanghai of the North', a reference to its history as a foreign concession, its heavy industrial output, its large port and its Europeanised architecture. Foreigners who live there now often call it 'TJ' – an abbreviation which mystifies the Chinese.

One of the specialities of the place is the two day kite-flying festival held in early April or late September. For business people, the big event of the year is the Tianjin Export Commodities Fair held every March. It's for invited guests only – to get an invitation, contact CITS or CTS well in advance.

The hotels are as expensive as Beijing's (but lack dormitories), so budget travellers tend to give the place a miss. However, you can travel down to Tianjin from Beijing in just 2½ hours, and one full day in this city is really quite enough.

History

The city's fortunes are, and always have been, linked to those of Beijing. When the Mongols established Beijing as the capital in the 13th century, Tianjin first rose to prominence as a grain-storage point. Pending remodelling of the Grand Canal by Kublai Khan, the tax grain was shipped along the Yangzi River, out into the open sea, up to Tianjin, and then through to Beijing. With the Grand Canal fully functional as far as Beijing, Tianjin was at the intersection of both inland and port navigation routes. By the 15th century, the town was a walled garrison.

For the sea-dog western nations, Tianjin was a trading bottleneck too good to be passed up. In 1856 Chinese soldiers boarded the *Arrow*, a boat flying the British flag, ostensibly in search of pirates. This was as much of an excuse as the British and the French needed. Their gunboats attacked the forts outside Tianjin, forcing the Chinese to sign the Treaty of Tianjin (1858), which opened the port up to foreign trade and also legalised the sale of opium.

Chinese reluctance to honour a treaty that had been foisted upon them led the British and French to start a new campaign to open the port to western trade. In 1860 British troops bombarded Tianjin in an attempt to coerce the Chinese into signing another treaty.

The English and French settled in. Between 1895 and 1900 they were joined by the Japanese, Germans, Austro-Hungarians, Italians and Belgians. Each of these concessions was a self-contained world with its own prison, school, barracks and hospital.

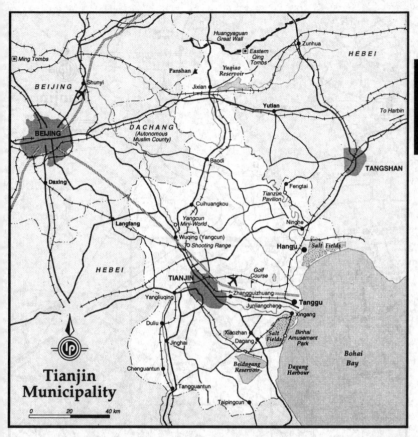

Tianjin Municipality

0   20   40 km

This palatial life was disrupted only in 1870 when the locals attacked the French-run orphanage and killed, among others, 10 of the nuns – apparently the Chinese thought the children were being kidnapped. Thirty years later, during the Boxer Rebellion, the foreign powers levelled the walls of the old Chinese city.

Meanwhile, the European presence stimulated trade and industry, including salt, textiles and glass manufacture. Heavy silting of the Hai River led to the construction of a new harbour at Tanggu, 50km downstream, and Tianjin lost its character as a bustling port.

Since 1949 Tianjin has been a focus for major industrialisation and it produces a wide range of consumer goods. Brand names from Tianjin are favoured within China for their quality – from Flying Pigeon bicycles to Seagull watches.

Orientation
Like Beijing, Tianjin is a large, sprawling municipality of which most is rural. The population of Tianjin's city and suburbs is

TIANJIN

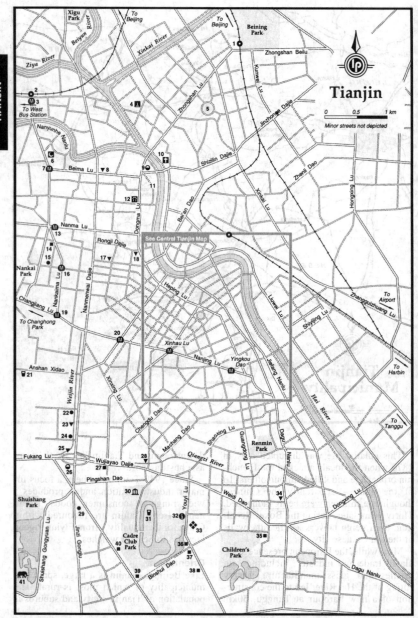

TIANJIN 天津

PLACES TO STAY
14 Cairnhill Hotel
金禧大酒店
27 Caesar's Palace Hotel
凯撒皇宫大酒店
35 Park Hotel
乐园饭店
36 Tianjin Grand Hotel
天津宾馆
37 Crystal Palace Hotel
水晶宫饭店
38 Geneva Hotel
津利华大酒店
39 Dickson Hotel
带蔷频
40 Sheraton Hotel
喜来登大酒店

PLACES TO EAT
8 Eardrum Fried
Spongecake Shop
耳朵眼炸糕店
17 Food Street
食品街
18 Quanjude Restaurant
全聚德烤鸭店
23 Alibaba Restaurant;
Internet Cafe
阿里巴巴酒家、
书香园
25 Korean Hotpot
Restaurants
韩国火锅餐厅

28 McDonald's; Bank of
China
麦当劳、中国银行
34 18th Street Dough-Twists
Shop
桂发祥麻花店

OTHER
1 North Railway Station
北火车站
2 West Railway Station
西站地铁站
3 Xi Subway Station
西地铁站
4 Dabeiyuan Monastery
大悲院
5 Zhongshan Park
中山公园
6 Great Mosque
清真寺
7 Xibeijiao Subway
Station
西北角地铁站
9 North-East Bus Station
东北角发车站
10 Wanghailou Cathedral
望海楼教堂
11 Ancient Culture Street
古文化街
12 Confucius Temple
文庙
13 Xinanjiao Subway
Station
西南角地铁站

15 Zhou Enlai
Memorial Hall
周恩来纪念馆
16 Erwei Lu Subway
Station
二纬路地铁站
19 Hai Guang Si Subway
Station
海光寺地铁站
20 Anshan Do Subway
Station
鞍山道地铁站
21 My Disco
我的迪厅
22 Tianjin University
天津大学
24 Nankai University
南开大学
26 South Bus Station
八里台发车站
29 TV Tower
电视塔
30 Natural History
Museum
自然博物馆
31 DD Disco Square
ＤＤ迪斯科广场
32 CITS
中国国际旅行社
33 Friendship Store
友谊商店
41 Zoo
动物园

some five million, although the municipality itself takes in a total of more than 10 million.

Information

Tourist Offices The Tianjin Tourism Bureau (☎ 2835-4860; fax 2835-2324) is at 18 Youyi Lu (almost opposite the Friendship Store). Just next door at 22 Youyi Lu is CITS (☎ 2835-8499; fax 2835-2619).

PSB The PSB is at 30 Tangshan Dao, and the Bank of China (☎ 2331-1559) is at 80 Jiefang Beilu.

Post & Communications You'll find the international post office, known as the Dongzhan Post Office, next to the main railway station; overseas parcels can be mailed and long-distance phone calls can be made here. For letters, there is another post office on Jiefang Beilu, a short walk north of the New World Astor Hotel.

A private courier, DHL (☎ 2328-0191; fax 2328-0376), is at 195 Machang Dao, Hexi District. TNT Skypak (☎ 2311-2365; fax 2311-2367) is at 2 Zhejiang Lu, Heping District.

Antique Market
(gǔwán shìchǎng)
Depending on your tastes, the antique market is the best sight in Tianjin even if you're not into collecting second-hand memorabilia. Just the sheer size and variety of this market makes it fascinating to stroll

TIANJIN

around. Among the many items on sale are stamps, silver coins, silverware, porcelain, clocks, photos of Mao, Cultural Revolution memorabilia (no guns though) and old books.

In China, the one thing you can be certain of is that you can't be certain of anything – especially history, since it is subject to frequent revision according to the politics of the time. Nevertheless, if true, the history behind this market is fascinating. According to the locals, much of what is on display at the antique market was seized during the Cultural Revolution and warehoused – the government is now slowly selling the stuff off to vendors who, in turn, resell it in Tianjin. These goods supposedly come from all over China. Many of the items carry stickers on the back indicating when, where and from whom the goods were seized.

Just why everything wasn't all immediately destroyed is subject to speculation – possibly it was to be used as evidence at political trials, or maybe some official was a closet antique buff. Or just maybe the Red Guards were aware of the potential resale value. Of course, not all that you see is real – there are fake antiques, fake stickers and so on.

The market is active seven days a week. On weekdays it occupies only a section of central Shenyang Dao, but on weekends it expands enormously, spilling out into side streets in every direction. It's open from 7.30 am to around 3 pm – get there at 8 am for the widest selection. Sunday morning is the best and foreigners residing in Beijing come down here for the day just to shop.

Ancient Culture Street
(gǔ wénhuà jiē)
The Ancient Culture Street is an attempt to recreate the appearance of an ancient Chinese city. Besides the traditional buildings, the street is lined with vendors plugging every imaginable type of cultural goody from Chinese scrolls, paintings and chops (name seals), to the latest heavy-metal sounds on CD. On certain public holidays, street operas are staged here.

Within the confines of the street is the small Tianhou Temple (tiānhòu gōng). Tianhou (Heaven Queen) is the goddess of the sea, and is known by various names in different parts of China (Matsu in Taiwan and Tin Hau in Hong Kong). It is claimed that Tianjin's Tianhou Temple was built in 1326, but it has seen a bit of renovation since then.

The Ancient Culture Street is a major drawcard for tourists, both foreign and local. The street is in the north-western part of town.

Confucius Temple
(wén miào)
On the northern side of Dongmennei Dajie, one block west of the Ancient Culture Street, is Tianjin's Confucius Temple. It was built in 1463 during the Ming Dynasty. The temple, and Confucianists in general, took a beating during the Cultural Revolution. In 1993 the buildings were restored and opened to the public.

Great Mosque
(qīngzhēn sì)
Although it has a distinctly Chinese look, this large mosque is an active place of worship for Tianjin's Muslim community. The mosque is on Dafeng Lu, not far south of the west railway station.

Dabeiyuan Monastery
(dàbēiyuàn)
One of the city's largest and best preserved temples, Dabeiyuan was built between 1611 and 1644, expanded in 1940, battered during the Cultural Revolution and finally restored in 1980.

The temple is on Tianwei Lu in the northern part of the city.

Catholic Church
(xīkāi jiàotáng)
This is one of the most bizarre-looking churches you're likely to see. Situated on the southern end of Binjiang Dao, the twin onion domes form a dramatic backdrop to the 'Coca-Cola Bridge' (a pedestrian

overpass crossing Nanjing Lu). It's definitely worth a look. Church services are now permitted again on Sundays, which is about the only time you'll have a chance to look inside.

Earthquake Memorial
(*kàngzhèn jìniàn bēi*)
Opposite the Friendship Hotel on Nanjing Lu is a curious, pyramid-shaped memorial. Although there's not much to see here, the memorial is a pointed reminder of the horrific events of 28 July 1976, when an earthquake registering eight on the Richter scale struck north-eastern China.

Tianjin was severely affected and the city was closed to tourists for two years. The epicentre was at Tangshan – that city basically disappeared in a few minutes.

Hai River Park
(*hǎihé gōngyuán*)
Stroll along the banks of the Hai River (a popular pastime with the locals) and see photo booths, fishing, early-morning *taijiquan*, opera-singing practice and old men toting birdcages. The Hai River esplanades have a peculiarly Parisian feel, in part due to the fact that some of the railing and bridge work is French.

Tianjin's sewage has to go somewhere and the river water isn't so pure that you'd want to drink it, but an attempt has been made to clean it up, and trees have been planted along the embankments. Tianjin's industrial pollution horrors are further downstream and are not included in the tour, but some Chinese tourists make their contribution by throwing drink tins and plastic bags into the river.

It's not Venice, but there are tourist boat cruises on the Hai River which leave from a dock not far from the New World Astor Hotel. The boats cater to Chinese tourists more than to foreigners and therefore tend to run mainly during summer weekends and other holiday periods.

At the northern end of town are half a dozen smaller rivers and canals that branch off the Hai River. One vantage point is Xigu Park. Take bus No 5, which runs from near the main railway station and passes by the west railway station.

TV Tower
(*diànshì tǎ*)
The pride and joy of Tianjin residents, the TV Tower dominates the horizon on the southern side of town. Besides its functional purpose of transmitting TV and radio broadcasts to the masses, tourists can go upstairs for a whopping Y100 fee. While the tower looks impressive from the ground, views from the top aren't spectacular in the daytime – after all, Tianjin's flat landscape of old buildings isn't exactly the eighth wonder of the world. However, the view is better at night if the sky is clear.

The TV Tower is also topped by a revolving restaurant, but you're liable to get indigestion when you see the bill.

Shuishang Park
(*shuǐshàng gōngyuán*)
This large park is in the south-western corner of town, not far from the TV Tower. The name in Chinese means water park – more than half the surface area is a lake. The major activity here is renting rowboats and pedal boats.

It's one of the more relaxed places in busy Tianjin, although not on weekends when the locals descend on the place like cadres at a banquet. The park features a Japanese-style floating garden and a decent zoo.

Getting to the park from the main railway station requires two buses. Bus No 8 to the last stop gets you close. From there, catch bus No 54, also to the last stop, just outside the park entrance.

Museums
There are five or so museums in Tianjin and none are really worth the trouble unless you're an enthusiast. The **Natural History Museum** (*zìrán bówùguǎn*) is down the fossil-end of town at 206 Machang Dao.

The **History Museum** (*lìshǐ bówùguǎn*), on the south-eastern side of the Hai River, at the edge of a triangular park called the

TIANJIN

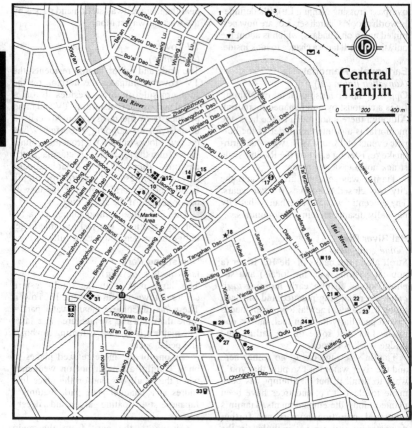

No 2 Workers' Cultural Palace (*dì èr gōngrén wénhuà gōng*), contains 'historical and revolutionary relics of the Tianjin area'.

Guangdong Guild Hall (*guǎngdōng huì guǎn*), also known as the Museum of Opera, is considered of historical relevance because Dr Sun Yatsen gave an important speech there in 1922.

Zhou Enlai Memorial Hall
(*zhōu ēnlái jìniàn guǎn*)
Zhou Enlai grew up in Shaoxing in Zhejiang Province, but he attended school in Tianjin, so his classroom is enshrined and there are photos and other memorabilia from his youth (1913-17). The memorial is on the western side of the city in the Nankai District, in the eastern building of Nankai School.

Streetscapes
Far more engrossing than any of the preceding is the fact that Tianjin itself is a museum of European architecture from the turn of the century. One minute you're in little Vienna, turn a corner and you could

CENTRAL TIANJIN
天津市中心

PLACES TO STAY
12 Huazhong Lu Hotel
   惠中饭店
13 Guomin Hotel
   国民大酒店
14 Bohai Hotel
   渤海饭店
19 Imperial Palace Hotel
   天津皇宫饭店
20 New World Astor Hotel
   利顺德大饭店
21 Tianjin First Hotel
   天津第一店
22 Hyatt Hotel
   凯悦饭店
24 Qishilin Hotel; Kiessling's
   Bakery
   天津起士林酒店
29 Friendship Hotel
   友谊宾馆

PLACES TO EAT
2 McDonald's; Wing On
   Department Store
   麦当劳、永安百货

7 Chuansu Restaurant
   川苏菜馆
8 Goubuli Restaurant
   狗不理总店
23 Cosy Cafe & Bar
   客思特西餐酒巴

OTHER
1 Buses to Beijing
   往北京汽车站
3 Main Railway Station
   天津火车站
4 Dongzhan Post Office
   东站邮局
5 Tianjin Department
   Store
   百货大楼
6 Antique Market
   古玩市场
9 Binjiang Shangsha
   Department Store
   滨江商厦
10 Shopping Area
   购物区
11 Quanyechang Department
   Store
   劝业场

15 Bus Station No 1
   (To Tanggu)
   一路汽车站（往塘沽）
16 Zhongxin Park
   中心公园
17 Bank of China
   中国银行
18 PSB
   公安局外事科
25 International Building
   国际大厦
26 Xinhua Lu Subway
   Station
   新华路地铁站
27 Isetan Department Store
   伊势丹百货
28 Earthquake Memorial
   抗震纪念碑
30 Yingkou Dao Subway
   Station
   营口道地铁站
31 International Market
   国际商场
32 Catholic Church
   西开教堂
33 Sunrise Club
   朝日俱乐部

TIANJIN

be in a London street, hop off a bus and you're looking at some vintage French wrought-iron gates or a neo-Gothic cathedral. Unfortunately, recent post-modern architectural horrors are starting to impact on Tianjin's skyline. Poking out of the post-earthquake shanty rubble is an ever-increasing number of high-rise castles made of glass and steel.

Nevertheless, if you're a connoisseur of architecture, go no further – Tianjin is a textbook of just about every style imaginable. Of course, things have been renamed, and anyone with a sense of humour will be amused by some of the uses to which the bastions of the European well-to-do have been put.

Chinatown
Sorry, but we couldn't resist this misnomer. The old Chinese sector can easily be identified on the bus map as a rectangle with buses running around the perimeter.

Roughly, the boundary roads are: Beima (North Horse), Nanma (South Horse), Xima (West Horse) and Dongma (East Horse). Originally there was one main north-south street, crossing an east-west one within that walled rectangle.

In this area you can spend time fruitfully exploring the lanes and side streets where traditional architecture remains, and perhaps even find a dilapidated temple or two. Basically, though, this is a people-watching place, where you can get glimpses of daily life through doorways. All along the way are opportunities to shop, window shop and eat to your heart's content.

Places to Stay – budget
First, the good news – Tianjin has many fine hotels of good standard at reasonable prices. The bad news is that the PSB has placed almost all cheap accommodation off limits to foreigners. Examples of the

TIANJIN

forbidden fruit include the *Changcheng Binguan*, *Tianjin Dajiudian*, *Dongfang Fandian* and the *Baihui Fandian*. However, these places *do* accept Overseas Chinese. The big noses are herded into the pricey tourist hotels.

The cheapest place that accepts foreigners is the *Guomin Hotel* (☎ 2711-3353) (*guómín fàndiàn*) on the corner of Heping Lu and Chifeng Dao. This grand old building was erected in 1923 and looks the worse for wear. Budget doubles with broken plumbing are Y164 and Y172, but more cushy rooms are Y348 to Y480.

Second-cheapest is the nearby *Bohai Hotel* (☎ 2712-3391) (*bóhǎi fàndiàn*) at 277 Heping Lu. Singles are Y258, twins cost Y240 to Y328 and suites are Y408 to Y508.

The *Huazhong Lu Hotel* (☎ 2711-0086) (*huazhōng fàndiàn*) is at 2 Huazhong Lu. Except for the central location, it hardly seems worth the Y403 tariff.

Qishilin Hotel (☎ 2331-3854) (*qǐshílín jiǔdiàn*), 33 Zhejiang Lu, is at the old Kiessling's Bakery (built in 1911). It was undergoing renovation at the time of writing so no prices were available, but it may move up into the mid-range category.

Places to Stay – middle
To all of the following mid-range and top-end places, you must add a 15% service charge.

The *Cairnhill Hotel* (☎ 2735-3143; fax 2735-4784) (*jīnxī dà jiǔdiàn*), at 2 San Malu, is a new luxury-looking high-rise where twins are Y746.

Caesar's Palace Hotel (☎ 2231-1717; fax 2337-4922), at 4 Qixiangtai Nanlu, Hexi District, is no relation to the same-named Las Vegas pleasure palace. Standard twins cost Y720.

Another new place is the *Dickson Hotel* (☎ 2836-4888; fax 2836-5018) (*dàichéng jiǔdiàn*) at 18 Binshui Dao, Hexi District. Standard twins are Y700.

The *Tianjin Grand Hotel* (☎ 2835-9000; fax 2835-9822) (*tiānjīn bīnguǎn*) is on Youyi Lu, Hexi District. And grand it is:

1000 beds in two high-rise blocks. It's benefited from considerable renovation since it was first built in 1960, and prices have been ramped up to Y640 for twins.

The *Tianjin First Hotel* (☎ 2330-9988; fax 2312-3000) (*tiānjīn dìyī fàndiàn*) is at 158 Jiefang Beilu opposite the Hyatt. The place boasts a bit of old world charm, which perhaps will make you feel better about having to fork out Y664 for a standard room. Suites cost Y747 to Y1245.

The *Imperial Palace Hotel* (☎ 2230-0888; fax 2230-0222) (*tiānjīn huánggōng fàndiàn*), at 177 Jiefang Beilu, is an old building that's been beautifully renovated. This Singapore joint venture has standard twins for Y523, plus cushier rooms from Y647 to Y1000.

The *Park Hotel* (☎ 2830-9815; fax 2830-2042) (*lèyuán fàndiàn*) at 1 Leyuan Lu is (surprise) next to a park. Standard twins cost Y620.

The *Friendship Hotel* (☎ 2331-0372) (*yǒuyì bīnguǎn*) charges rather unfriendly prices – doubles are Y700. The hotel is at 94 Nanjing Lu. The *Geneva Hotel* (☎ 2835-2222; fax 2835-9855) (*jīnlìhuá dàjiǔdiàn*), 32 Youyi Lu, is hidden behind the World Economy & Trade Exhibition Centre (one of the most perverse architectural nightmares in China). However, the hotel is fine, and twins cost Y760 to Y1514.

Places to Stay – top end
You can bask in luxury at the *Hyatt Hotel* (☎ 2331-8888; fax 2331-1234; www.hyatt.com; 542 rooms) (*kǎiyuè fàndiàn*) at 219 Jiefang Beilu. Economy rooms are a mere Y1450 while others are Y1823 to Y9948.

The *New World Astor Hotel* (☎ 2331-1112; fax 2331-6282) (*lìshùndé fàndiàn*) at 33 Tai'erzhuang Lu dates from early this century, but has been completely refurbished. Twins cost from Y1077 to Y1243, and suites are Y1823 to Y7295.

One of the most glamorous places in town is the 346 room *Crystal Palace Hotel* (☎ 2835-6888; fax 2835-8886) (*shuǐjīnggōng fàndiàn*) at 28 Youyi Lu. Facilities include a swimming pool, tennis court, health club and French restaurant. A standard room is Y1062 and suites are Y1892 to Y5544.

The *Sheraton Hotel* (☎ 2334-3388; fax 2335-8740) (*xǐláidēng dàjiǔdiàn*) is on Zijinshan Lu in the south of Tianjin. The hotel dishes up 281 rooms priced between Y1500 and Y1750, plus 49 suites ranging from Y3125 to Y6250. To that, add another 15% surcharge, but if it helps the buffet breakfast is thrown in free. Guests also qualify for a free copy of the *China Daily*.

Places to Eat

Chinese *Food Street* (*shípǐn jiē*) is a covered alley with two levels of restaurants. Old places close and new ones open all the time here, but there are approximately 40 to 50 restaurants on each level. You need to check prices – some of the food stalls are dirt cheap, but a few upmarket restaurants are almost absurdly expensive. You can find some real exotica here, like snake (expensive), dog meat (cheap) and eels (mid-range). Mexican food fans take note: there are bags of nacho chips for sale! Food Street is a couple of blocks south of Nanma Lu, about a kilometre west of the centre.

Rongji Dajie is an alley just one block north of Food Street and also boasts a fair share of restaurants. The *Quanjude* (☎ 2735-0046) is at 53 Rongji Dajie. Upstairs are banquet rooms with moderate to expensive prices. Seafood is expensive (like sea cucumber, a delicacy that chefs love to foist on foreigners). Beijing duck and Shandong food are also served.

The *Chuansu Restaurant* (☎ 2730-5142) is at 153 Changchun Dao, between Xinhua Lu and Liaoning Lu, very close to the Tianjin Roast Duck. Spicy hot Sichuan food is the speciality here, but other styles are also on the menu.

King of the dumpling shops is *Goubuli* (☎ 2730-0810) (*gǒubùlǐ*) at 77 Shandong Lu, between Changchun Dao and Binjiang Dao. The shop has a century-old history. The house speciality is a dough bun (*bāozi*), filled with high-grade pork, spices and gravy. Watch for the baozi with the red dot

since this indicates a special filling like chicken or shrimp. Frozen versions of this product can be bought from grocery stores all over Tianjin, although backpackers not carrying a microwave oven are unlikely to be customers. Goubuli has the alarming translation 'dogs won't touch them' or 'dog doesn't care'. The most satisfying explanation of this seems to be that Goubuli was the nickname of the shop's founder, a man with an extraordinarily ugly face – so ugly that even dogs were turned off by him.

A permanent cake box clipped to a bicycle rack is one of the eccentricities of Tianjin residents and a prerequisite for a visit to friends. Yangcun rice-flour cake is a pastry produced in Wuqing County suburbs since the Ming Dynasty, so they say. It's made from rice and white sugar.

The *Eardrum Fried Spongecake Shop* (*ěrduǒyǎn zhágāo diàn*) takes its name from its proximity to Eardrum Lane. This shop specialises in cakes made from rice powder, sugar and bean paste, all fried in sesame oil. These special cakes have been named (you guessed it) 'eardrum fried spongecake'.

Another Tianjin speciality that takes its name from a shop's location is the 18th Street Dough-Twists (*máhuā*). The street seems to have been renamed 'Love Your Country Street' (*àiguó dào*), and the famous shop is also referred to as *guìfā xiáng máhuā diàn*. However, the dough-twists made from sugar, sesame, nuts and vanilla can be bought all over town – try the shops at the railway station.

Kiessling's Bakery (*qǐshìlín cāntīng*), built by the Austrians back in foreign concession days (1911), is a Tianjin institution. It's at 33 Zhejiang Lu, in the same building as the Qishilin Hotel. However, you needn't go there, as the cakes are distributed all around the city at various shops and restaurants.

Foreign residents of Tianjin with a bit of cash like to pig out every Sunday at the *Sheraton Hotel*, which does a mean buffet from 11 am until 2 pm. It costs Y150 (no student cards are accepted), so don't eat breakfast if you want to get the maximum benefit. On other days there are also lunch and dinner buffets with prices which hover around Y100 – sometimes pizza is served.

The *Hyatt Hotel* also does a memorable breakfast buffet. This one costs Y70 and can fill you up for the rest of the day.

Should you wish to fortify a main meal, an ice cream or a coffee, Tianjin produces a variety of liquid substances. There's Kafeijiu, which approximates to Kahlua, and Sekijiu, which is halfway between vodka and rocket fuel.

Korean Korean hotpot (*huǒguō*) seems to be a very big hit with Tianjin's expats. There is a whole string of cheap but good Korean restaurants underneath the flyover on Fukang Lu near Nankai University in the south-western part of town.

Western Within the campus of Nankai University is *Alibaba Restaurant* (*ālǐbābā jiǔjiā*). There is Chinese food here too, but the cooks do a better job with the spaghetti, pizza and sandwiches. The restaurant doubles as an unofficial pub for foreigners studying in Tianjin, and stays open very late.

The *Cosy Cafe & Bar* (☎ 2312-7870) (*kèsītè xīcān jiǔbā*) is one of those somewhat upmarket expat havens that will make you forget you're in China. The atmosphere is very western, the menu is in English, there is MTV and popcorn is served at the beginning of every meal. The cafe has an unusual location hidden underneath the Daguangming Bridge by the Hyatt Hotel.

The *Sheraton Hotel* has a small grocery shop which sells such rare items as cheese, cereal and Diet Coke. It's not in the main building, so go into the lobby and ask.

Entertainment

Computer nerds can try the *Internet Cafe* (*shūxiāng yuán*) inside the student activity centre (*xuéshēng huódòng zhōngxīn*) on the campus of Nankai University.

DD Disco Square (☎ 2335-5800) (*DD dísīkē guǎngchǎng*) has floor shows, Chinese

dancers and Beavis & Butthead videos. It's a very large place with a Y30 cover charge. It quietens down quickly after midnight (when the raffle is finished). DD's is at 335 Machang Dao in the Industrial Exposition Centre (*gōngyè zhǎnlǎn guǎn*) which is in the park near the Cadre Club and Sheraton Hotel.

My Disco (☎ 2741-0880) (*wǒde dítīng*) is a very nice though somewhat empty dance hall. Hopefully it will slowly gain a loyal following because it's really worth an evening of your time. You'll find it in the Nankai District at 168 Anshan Dao at the intersection with Baiti Lu (inside the Lida Commercial Centre or *lìdá guǎngchǎng*).

Sunrise Club (☎ 2332-2767) (*zhāorì jùlèbù*) has live music in the evenings. There is no cover charge, but beer costs Y18 and up, plus a 6% service charge. Check out the decor – wooden floors, stained-glass windows, marble tables and very comfortable chairs. You'll find it at 64 Chongqing Dao in the Heping District. If you have the time and inclination, the Tianjin International Golf Club (*tiānjīn guójì gāo'ěrfū qiúchǎng*) is halfway between Tianjin and Tanggu.

Things to Buy

A shopping trip to Tianjin will dispel any doubts about China's commitment to the textile trade. Only Hong Kong can match Tianjin for the amount of clothing on sale, and much of Hong Kong's supply originates in Tianjin.

Adjacent to the main railway station is the Wing On department store (*yǒng'ān bǎihuò*), a branch of the Hong Kong company by the same name. It's knee-deep in everything from silk stockings to woollen overcoats.

A massive shopping drag extends from the west railway station south via Beima Lu, where it meets another shopping drag called Dongma Lu coming from the north railway station. The sprawl of shops snakes down the length of Heping Lu as far as Zhongxin Park.

The shopping street to stroll along is

Binjiang Dao, with alleyways and other commercial streets gathered around it there's something like eight whole blocks of concentrated shopping. You can find just about anything in the many boutiques, curio stores and emporiums. The area is particularly lively between 5 and 8 pm, when the streets are thronged with shoppers and theatre-goers.

On Binjiang Dao itself there are more than 100 street stalls selling mostly clothing, plus many more permanent-looking stores. The chief department store on this street is the Binjiang Shangsha.

The International Building (*guójì dàshà*) at 75 Nanjing Lu features a very good supermarket on the 2nd floor – a clone of Hong Kong's finest.

At the southern end of Binjiang Dao is the four storey International Market (*guójì shāngchǎng*). It's one of Tianjin's best department stores and features a good bakery on the ground floor. Do not confuse the

International Market with the aforementioned International Building. Almost next door is Isetan, a Japanese department store.

Also worth looking into is the Friendship Store (*yǒuyì shāngdiàn*) on Youyi Lu at the southern end of town. The ground floor has a notable supermarket – rare items on sale here include imported peanut butter and Diet Coke.

Locals look for everyday Chinese consumer products in the Tianjin department store (*bǎihuò dàlóu*) at 172 Heping Lu.

The Quanyechang (Encouraging Industrial Development Emporium) is an old but large department store on the corner of Heping Lu and Binjiang Dao. Besides selling a large variety of consumer goods, the emporium has two theatres and some electronic amusement facilities.

Specialities Tianjin is considered famous for its carpets. If you're serious about carpets (and that's serious money!) the best

Capitalist Road

Advertising for the foreign market is one area the Chinese are still stumbling around in. A Chinese-produced TV advertisement in Paris for Chinese furs treated viewers to the bloody business of skinning and to refrigerated cadavers before the usual parade of fur-clad models down the catwalk.

It would be fun to handle the advertising campaigns for China's more charming brand names. There's Pansy underwear (for men), or you can pamper your stud with Horse Head facial tissues. Wake up in the morning with a Golden Cock alarm clock (since renamed Golden Rooster). You can start your breakfast with a glass of Billion Strong Pulpy C Orange Drink, or finish your meal with a cup of Imperial Concubine Tea. For your trusty portable radio it may be best to stay away from White Elephant batteries, but you might try the space-age Moon Rabbit variety. Long March car tyres should prove durable, but what about the ginseng product with the fatal name of Gensenocide?

Out of the psychedelic 60s comes White Rabbit candy. Flying Baby toilet paper seems to have been discontinued, but you might still be able to find a pack of Puke cigarettes. The characters for Coca-Cola translate as 'tastes good, tastes happy', but the Chinese must have thought they were really on to something good when the 'Coke Adds Life' slogan got mistranslated and claimed that it could raise the dead. And as a sign of the times, one enterprising food vendor has started a chain store named 'Capitalist Road'.

Condoms provide fertile ground for creative name-branding. Asia Good Oil is an inventive local product name, while Huan Bao Multifunction Condoms gets you thinking – just how many functions *are* there for a condom? ∎

bet is to get to a factory outlet. There are eight carpet factories in the Tianjin Municipality. Making the carpets by hand is a long and tedious process – some of the larger ones can take a proficient weaver over a year to complete. Patterns range from traditional to modern. Tianjin Carpets Import-Export Corporation (☎ 2331-3708) is at 45 Baoding Dao in the Heping District. The Tianjin Carpet Corporation (☎ 2830-0894) is at 5 Xinweidi Dao in the Hexi District.

Clay figurines are another local speciality. The terracotta figures originated in the 19th century with the work of Zhang Mingshan; his fifth-generation descendants train new craftspeople. The small figures take themes from human or deity sources and the emphasis is on realistic emotional expressions. Master Zhang was reputedly so skilful that he carried clay up his sleeves on visits to the theatre and came away with clay opera stars in his pockets. In 1900, during the Boxer Rebellion, western troops came across satirical versions of themselves correct down to the last detail in uniforms. These voodoo dolls were ordered to be removed from the marketplace immediately! The workshop is at 270 Machang Dao, Hexi District (southern end of Tianjin). The Art Gallery on Jiefang Lu has a collection of earlier Zhang family figurines.

Tianjin is also known for its New Year posters. Such posters first appeared in the 17th century in the town of Yangliuqing, 15km west of Tianjin proper. Woodblock prints are hand-coloured, and are considered to bring good luck and happiness when posted on the front door during the Lunar New Year, which is OK if you like Day-Glo pictures of fat babies. Rarer are the varieties that have historical, deity or folk-tale representations.

Getting There & Away

Air CAAC (☎ 2490-2950) is at 242 Heping Lu. Dragonair (☎ 2330-1234) has a booking office in the Hyatt Hotel. Korean Air (☎ 2319-0088, ext 2800) has a booking office in room 2415 of the International Building (guójì dàshà) at 75 Nanjing Lu. CITS can book tickets on most airlines.

Korean Air flies the Tianjin-Seoul route. Dragonair and CAAC both offer daily direct flights between Hong Kong and Tianjin. Tianjin has flights to the following destinations (the number in parentheses is the frequency of flights per week):

Changchun (one), Changsha (one), Chengdu (three), Chongqing (two), Dalian (five), Fuzhou (three), Guangzhou (10), Guilin (two), Haikou (one), Harbin (two), Huangshan (one), Kunming (three), Mudanjiang (two), Nanjing (four), Ningbo (two), Qingdao (seven), Shanghai (14), Shantou (two), Shenyang (two), Shenzhen (10), Simao (one), Taiyuan (one), Ürümqi (two), Wenzhou (five), Wuhan (two), Xi'an (three), Xiamen (four), Xishuangbanna (two) and Zhengzhou (one)

Bus The opening of the Beijing-Tianjin Expressway has greatly reduced travel time between the two cities – the journey takes about 2½ hours. Buses to Beijing depart from in front of Tianjin's main railway station (Y30). In Beijing, catch the bus to Tianjin from the Zhaogongkou bus station on the southern side of town, but be careful you get a bus to Tianjin railway station (tiānjīn huǒchē zhàn) and not to the outlying districts of Kaifa or Tanggu (unless you want to go to Tanggu). Buses run roughly every 15 minutes throughout the day.

There is a direct bus linking Beijing's Capital airport with Tianjin. The cost is Y70.

There are four long-distance bus stations, with buses running to places that the average foreign traveller may have little interest in. Bus station No 1 (yīlù qìchē zhàn) is opposite the Bohai Hotel and is the place to get buses to Tanggu.

Other bus stations are usually located at intervals along the direction of travel. The south bus station (bǎlǐtái fāchē zhàn) is on the north-eastern edge of Shuishang Park, which is south-west of the city centre – this is where you get buses to points south. The west bus station (xīzhàn fāchē zhàn) is at 2 Xiqing Dao near Tianjin's west railway station.

Of possible interest to travellers is the north-east bus station (*dōngběijiǎo fǎchē zhàn*), which has the most destinations and the largest ticket office. It's very close to the Ancient Culture Street, just west of the Hai River in the north of Tianjin. Bus No 24 from the city centre will land you in the general vicinity. From the north-east bus station you can get buses to Jixian, Fengtai (Tianzun Pavilion) and Zunhua (to name just a few places). If you're the sort of person who likes to see everything along the way, a road route worth considering is from Tianjin to Beijing via Jixian.

Train Tianjin is a major north-south train junction with frequent trains to Beijing, extensive links with the north-eastern provinces, and lines southwards to Ji'nan, Nanjing, Shanghai, Fuzhou, Hefei, Yantai, Qingdao and Shijiazhuang.

There are three railway stations in Tianjin: main, north and west. Ascertain the correct station. For most trains you'll want the main railway station. Some trains stop at both the main and west stations, and some only go through the west railway station (particularly those originating in Beijing and heading south). Trains heading for north-eastern China often stop at the north railway station.

If you have to alight at the west railway station, bus No 24 connects the west railway station with the main railway station, passing through the central shopping district.

The main railway station has a 'soft-seat booking office' which foreigners can use even for hard-seat tickets. To find it, go into the main station entrance (by the x-ray machines) and up the escalator to the 2nd floor – it's off to the right. There are usually no queues here.

Express trains take just under two hours for the trip between Tianjin and Beijing. Local trains take about 2½ hours.

Car Expats with their own cars are permitted to drive almost anywhere within a day trip of Tianjin.

Boat Tianjin's harbour is Tanggu, 50km (30 minutes by train) from Tianjin proper. This is one of China's major ports, offering a number of possibilities for arriving and departing by boat. See the Tanggu section later in this chapter for details.

Getting Around

To/From the Airport From the city centre, it's about 15km to Tianjin's Zhangguizhuang airport. Taxis ask for Y50 or more for the trip, and there is a bus from the CAAC ticket office.

There are plans afoot to open the newly built Binhai international airport which is further out from town (by the sea). There's no word yet on when this momentous event will happen.

Bus A pox on local transport in this city! Tianjin is one of the most confusing places you can take on in China, and things are compounded by the fact that your visit there may turn, by economic necessity, into a very short one.

Key local transport junctions are the areas around the three railway stations. The main railway station has the biggest collection: bus Nos 24, 27 and 13, and further out toward the river are Nos 2, 5, 25, 28 and 96. At the west railway station are bus Nos 24, 10 and 31 (Nos 11 and 37 run past the west railway station); at the north railway station are bus Nos 1, 7 and 12.

Another major bus terminal point is around Zhongxin Park, at the edge of the central shopping district. From here you'll get bus Nos 11 and 94, and nearby are bus Nos 9, 20 and 37. To the north of Zhongxin Park are bus Nos 1, 91, 92 and 93.

A useful bus to know is the No 24, which runs between the main and west stations 24 hours a day. Also noteworthy is No 8 – it starts at the main railway station then zigzags across town before finally terminating at Nankai University in the southern part of town.

With the exception of bus No 24, buses run from 5 am to 11 pm.

TIANJIN

Train The subway (*dìxià tiělù*) can be useful – it runs all the way from Nanjing Lu to the west railway station and costs Y1 per ride. Tianjin's subway opened in 1982 and has seen no improvement since then; the cars shuttle back and forth on a single track.

There's nothing to see down in the depths except the subterranean bathroom tiling, but it saves some trauma with the buses.

Taxi Taxis can be found most readily near the railway station and around tourist hotels. Most drivers prefer not to use the meters, but the fare is generally Y10 to anywhere within the city centre.

Tianjin has many motor-tricycles – these cost about Y10 for anywhere in the city. They are particularly useful for manoeuvring through the narrow, traffic-clogged streets in the city centre.

Around Tianjin

Tianjin could make a staging point for trips directly north to Jixian and the Great Wall at Huangyaguan, as well as Zunhua, Tangshan and Beidaihe in Hebei. It's also a launching pad for roaring into the north-east (Manchuria). About the only place within the Tianjin Municipality that sees any foreign tourists is Tanggu.

TANGGU
(*tánggū*)
There are three harbours on the Tianjin Municipality stretch of coastline: Hangu (north), Tanggu-Xingang (centre) and Dagang (south). Tanggu is about 50km from Tianjin proper. The Japanese began the construction of an artificial harbour during their occupation (1937-45) and it

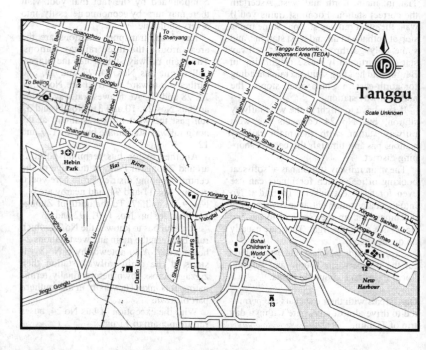

TIANJIN

was completed by the Communists in 1952, with further expansions in 1976 for container cargo. The Tanggu-Xingang port now handles one of the largest volumes of goods of any port in China.

This is one of China's major international seaports, kept open by ice-breakers in winter. The harbour is where 'friends from all over the world' come to drop anchor and get ripped off by overpriced hotels and mercenary taxi drivers.

As for sightseeing, the best advice we can give is to go no further than the ferry pier – the further you go, the worse it gets. Tanggu is a forest of cranes, containers and smokestacks – it's no place to linger.

Nevertheless, you will find foreigners lingering here – not travellers, but business people. Tanggu is booming and many export-oriented industries have set up shop here. The chief focus of all this activity is the **Tianjin Economic & Development Area** (*jīngjì jìshù kāifā qū*), or TEDA.

TANGGU 塘沽

1 Tanggu Main Railway Station
   塘沽火车站
2 Victory Hotel
   胜利宾馆
3 Tanggu Hospital
   塘沽医院
4 Haijing Amusement Centre
   海晶游乐场
5 Golden Sail Hotel
   金帆大厦
6 Hot Springs Hotel
   温泉大酒店
7 Chaoyin Temple
   潮音寺
8 Tianjin View Hotel
   北方宾馆
9 Harbour Hotel
   港口宾馆
10 International Seamen's Club
    国际海员俱乐部
11 Friendship Store
    友谊商店
12 Passenger Ferry Terminal
    天津港客运站
13 Dagu Fort
    大沽炮台

Should you decide to wander around this area in the northern part of Tanggu, you'll see plenty of factories, but also expensive residences and shops catering for the predominantly foreign and Overseas Chinese investors and technical experts.

If you insist on seeking out some touristy sights, the city is most proud of its **Bohai Children's World** (*bóhǎi értóng shìjiè*). It's actually a little better than it sounds – almost attractive buildings in a park setting on an island in the middle of the harbour. Unfortunately, the harbour itself is pretty grotty.

The other famous 'scenic spot' in town is **Dagu Fort** (*dàgū pàotái*), on the southern bank of the Hai River. The fort was built during the Ming Dynasty, some time between 1522 and 1567. The purpose was to protect Tianjin from foreign invasions. It may have worked for a while, but considering how easily the Europeans overran the place during the 19th century, it was not exactly a smashing success.

If you need to fritter away some time while waiting for a boat, you could check out the goods on sale at the Friendship Store, or sample the drinks at the International Seamen's Club just next to the harbour.

For reasons not fully understood (by us), Tanggu has a very heavy public security presence. Many of the cops are in plain clothes, but if you're astute you'll notice the PSB vehicles – they have long, white licence plates with black lettering, except for the first two letters which are red. For what it's worth, there is a local rumour that Tanggu is the PSB headquarters.

Places to Stay

As in Tianjin, you can forget about dormitories and cheap hotels. If arriving in Tanggu by ship, it's best to hop on the first train to Beijing or Beidaihe.

Most travellers stay at the *International Seamen's Club* (☎ 2589-3897) (*guójì hǎiyuán jùlèbù*). The simple reason for this is because it's within walking distance of the ferry pier. Unfortunately, for this same reason it is often full just when you are most likely to need a room here.

About 2km away from the pier is the *Harbour Hotel* (*gǎngkǒu bīnguǎn*) which was under renovation at the time of writing.

The *Hot Springs Hotel* (☎ 2588-6611) (*wēnquán dà jiǔdiàn*) is at 82 Xingang Lu. This is a Hong Kong joint-venture hotel with 156 rooms. There is an in-house travel agency that can book ferry, plane and railway tickets. Rooms cost Y350 for standard, Y600 for deluxe.

The *Golden Sail Hotel* (☎ 2532-6666) (*jīnfān dàshà*) on Huanghai Lu has rooms for Y520.

The closest hotel to the main railway station which accepts foreigners is the *Victory Hotel* (☎ 2589-5833; fax 2589-4470) (*shènglì bīnguǎn*) at 11 Jintang Lu. With 300 rooms, it happens to be the largest hotel in town. Standard twins cost Y450. Facilities include an indoor swimming pool and bowling alley.

The *Tianjin View Hotel* (☎ 2531-1301; fax 2531-1322) (*běifāng bīnguǎn*) is a Japanese joint venture at 1 Dongguzha Beilu in an especially ugly part of town far removed from anything. By way of compensation, the facilities are fine. Standard/deluxe rooms are Y480/620.

Getting There & Away

There are minibuses to Tanggu from Tianjin's south bus station and these cost Y15. In Tanggu, departures are from the main railway station. Buses leave when full – about once every 30 minutes throughout the day.

The main railway line to north-eastern China runs from Beijing to Harbin via Tianjin and Tanggu. In other words, it's a heavily travelled route with frequent services. Trains cover the 50km from Tianjin to Tanggu in just 30 minutes. The route passes by saltworks which furnish roughly a quarter of the nation's salt.

Tanggu's harbour has been renamed New Harbour (*xīngǎng*) – you catch ferries at the New Harbour passenger ferry terminal (*xīngǎng kèyùn zhàn*).

For travellers, probably the most interesting ships are the international passenger ferries. There is one plying the route between Inch'ŏn (South Korea) and Tianjin, while another goes to Kobe, Japan. See the Getting There & Away chapter for more details about prices and times.

Boats to Dalian depart once every four days and the journey takes 16 hours. Boats to Yantai depart about four times a month. The trip takes about 30 hours. Because of the large number of passengers on the boats, it's recommended that you stick to 4th class or higher. The liners are comfortable, can take up to 1000 passengers, and are equipped with a bar, restaurant and movies.

Tickets can be purchased at Tanggu port opposite the Tanggu Theatre, but if you're in Tianjin it's safer to buy in advance. In Tianjin, tickets can be bought at 5 Pukou Jie. Difficult to find, Pukou Jie runs west off Tai'erzhuang Lu and is roughly on the same latitude as the enormous smokestack which stands on the opposite side of the river.

JIXIAN
(*jìxiàn*)

Rated as one of the 'northern suburbs' of Tianjin, although it's actually 120km from Tianjin city, the Jixian area is about 90km due east of Beijing.

Near the city's west gate is the **Temple of Solitary Joy** (*dúlè sì*). At 1000 years' vintage, the main multi-storey wooden structure, the Avalokitesvara Pavilion, qualifies as the oldest such structure in China. It houses a 16m-high statue of a bodhisattva with 10 heads which rates as one of China's largest terracotta statues. The buddha dates back to the Liao Dynasty and the murals inside are from the Ming Dynasty. The complex has been restored in the interests of mass tourism.

Just east of Jixian is **Yuqiao Reservoir** (*yúqiáo shuǐkù*), easily the most attractive body of water (not counting the sea) in Tianjin Municipality.

Getting There & Away

One way of getting to Jixian is to join a tour

from Beijing to the Eastern Qing Tombs and Zunhua (see the Around Beijing section in the Beijing chapter for details). However, this will normally only give you a brief lunch stop in Jixian before pushing on to the tombs. There are also regular long-distance buses from Beijing.

Buses from Tianjin's north-east bus station go to Jixian. There is also a direct Tianjin-Jixian train link.

PANSHAN
(*pánshān*)
To the north-west of Jixian is Panshan, a collection of hills ranked among the 15 famous mountains of China. Emperor Qianlong was claimed to have been so taken with the place that he swore he never would have gone south of the Yangzi River had he known Panshan was so beautiful.

The emperor aside, don't expect the Himalayas. Nevertheless, it's still a lovely area, dotted with trees, springs, streams, temples, pavilions and various other ornaments. On the summit of the peak is the Dingguang Stupa. There are 72 temples here.

Getting There & Away
The hills are 12km north-west of Jixian, 150km north of Tianjin and 40km west of the Eastern Qing Tombs in Hebei Province. A suburban-type train runs to Jixian from Tianjin; you can also get there by bus from Tianjin's north-east bus station.

GREAT WALL AT HUANGYAGUAN
(*huángyáguān chángchéng*)
At the very northern tip of Tianjin Municipality (bordering Hebei Province) is Huangyaguan (Yellow Cliff Pass). This is where Tianjin residents head to view the Great Wall. This section of the wall is 41km long before it crumbles away on each end – the part open to tourists was restored in 1984.

Some new features have been added to the original structures, including the Eight Diagrams Labyrinth (*bāguà chéng*), Great Wall Museum (*chángchéng bówùguǎn*), the Forest of Steles (*shíkèbēi lín*) and Water Pass (*shuǐ guān*).

Getting There & Away
Huangyaguan is 140km north of Tianjin city. Buses go to the wall mostly on weekends, with early-morning departures from Tianjin's north-east bus station or sometimes from the main railway station.

TIANZUN PAVILION
(*tiānzūn gé*)
You'd have to be a real temple and pavilion enthusiast to come way out here to see this place. Nevertheless, it's rated as one of Tianjin's big sights.

The Tianzun (Heaven Respect) Pavilion is three storeys tall – locals are proud to tell you that the pavilion remained standing when everything else nearby was reduced to rubble by the 1976 Tangshan earthquake.

Getting There & Away
The pavilion is near Fengtai in Ninghe County, on the eastern border of Tianjin Municipality and Hebei Province. Buses to Fengtai depart from Tianjin's north-east bus station.

WUQING
(*wǔqīng*)
The country seat of Wuqing County, the town of Wuqing (also called Yangcun) is nothing to get excited about. However it is home to the **Yangcun Mini-World** (*yángcūn xiǎo shìjiè*). This latest addition to Tianjin's tourist potpourri was formerly known as the Yongyang Ancient Gardens (a recreated Han Dynasty village). That didn't go over too well, so it's been transformed into a model of 170 famous landscapes around the globe each reduced to miniature size. Some of the models are 1/15 life size, while others had to be shrunk to 1/30 of the original.

Shrinking people and buildings is becoming very fashionable in the Middle Kingdom – you'll find more and more mini-worlds popping up all over China these days.

Perhaps of greater interest to frustrated travellers is the **International Shooting**

TIANJIN

The PLA, Incorporated

In China's new socialist market economy, everything is pay as you go. Even the armed forces have to pay their own way. Not that they're complaining. The People's Liberation Army is doing very well out of China's economic reforms, thank you.

The PLA first raked in foreign exchange by exporting arms, and later by operating shooting galleries for the enjoyment of tourists. Since then, the number of PLA-run businesses has mushroomed. Even the military itself claims to have no idea how vast its business empire has grown. Conservative estimates put the figure at about 20,000 separate enterprises. How much money these businesses are raking in is either unknown or is a state secret. But for an idea of the scale of things, the Poly Group – the most successful of China's PLA businesses – built the Poly Plaza, a business and hotel complex in Beijing, for US$70 million.

The PLA has dabbled in all sorts of money-making schemes not related to its original mission of defending China. Cigarette machines, pharmaceuticals, spacecraft launchers, TV sets, wallpaper, mountain bikes, hotels, tourist shops, luxury buses and ovens all roll off PLA production lines, and much is exported. In Guangzhou, the military has even been known to conduct war games on TV that allow viewers to bet on the results.

The good news is that the PLA is successfully paying its own way. The problem now is that the government has lost control of this creature which it has spawned. No Chinese civilian leader could last long in office without appeasing the military. And these days, appeasing the military means letting the generals run their own financial empires, with virtually no legal controls.

Human rights groups in the west have warned that much of the clothing and cute toys for children labelled 'Made in China' may in fact be made by Chinese inmates in PLA-run prison camps. The theory was basically confirmed by Harry Wu (Wu Hongda), a former Chinese prisoner who emigrated to the USA and documented the use of forced prison labour in China. His riveting book, *Bitter Winds: A Memoir of My Years in China's Gulag*, eloquently exposed the whole scandalous business.

No government could sensibly be amenable to the idea of vast money-making corporations backed by their own armies, but this is what the PLA has in effect become. China's trading partners have noted, with alarm, that PLA-controlled businesses churn out pirated CDs and fake Rolex watches. Even more alarming is evidence that Hong Kong's triads (mafia) have high-level links with some PLA units in Guangdong Province. The mob is known to run dope, prostitution rings, gambling dens, plus loan sharking and cash counterfeiting operations. But who is going to stop them when they have generals as business partners? A mafia with access to tanks, troops and even nuclear weapons is almost too frightening to think about.

The Hainan fiasco of 1993, when Japanese cars worth US$500 million were imported duty free and resold on the mainland at enormous profits, was done so in collusion with the PLA. The Hong Kong police have shown video tapes indicating that PLA marine units are providing armed cover for smuggling outfits. As PLA businesses extend their interests into Hong Kong, many Hong Kong public figures have expressed concern that the former colony will inherit the problem of armed money-making machines that ride roughshod over all legal processes.

To be fair, not all PLA units are involved in illegal activities. Furthermore, the average PLA soldier has no idea of the enormous profits that the army is raking in. Unfortunately, a few corrupt generals are doing very well indeed, and who would dare oppose them? Even China's civilian leaders don't know what to do about the situation. China has had a long and bitter history with warlords, and it would appear that history is once again repeating itself. ■

Range (☎ 2934-5757) (*guójì shèjì cháng*). It's operated by Norinco, China's weapons manufacturer which is in fact run by the PLA.

A more benign activity practised here is table tennis (don't shoot at the balls). The 43rd World Table Tennis Championships were played here.

Getting There & Away

Wuqing is about 30km north of central Tianjin and just off the Beijing-Tianjin expressway. Catch a bus at Tianjin's north-east bus station.

BINHAI AMUSEMENT PARK
(*bīnhǎi yúlè chéng*)

If you're getting bored, you can join the Chinese tourists here and enjoy cotton candy, vomit-inducing rides and water slides. Perhaps the most interesting feature is the large open-air hot spring baths (there are also indoor facilities). Sand has been trucked in to build an artificial beach here.

Getting There & Away

The amusement park is by the seashore, about 45km from central Tianjin. Take a bus from the north-east bus station in Tianjin.

Hebei 河北

Hebei Facts & Highlights

Area: 190,000 sq km

Population: 64.9 million

Capital: Shijiazhuang

Highlights

- Chengde, a small town full of history, including one of the most startling collections of buildings in China.
- The beachside resort of Beidaihe for trendy holiday-makers from Beijing.
- Shanhaiguan, where the Great Wall meets the sea.

Wrapping itself around the centrally administered municipalities of Beijing and Tianjin is the province of Hebei (*hébĕi*). It is often viewed either as an extension of Beijing, the red-tape maker, or of Tianjin, the industrial powerhouse. This is not far off the mark since, geographically speaking, Beijing and Tianjin take up a fair piece of the pie. In fact, Tianjin used to be Hebei's capital, but when it came under central government administration, it was replaced by the next largest city, Shijiazhuang.

Topographically, Hebei falls into two distinct parts: the mountain tableland to the north, where the Great Wall runs, and the monotonous southern plain. Agriculture (mainly wheat and cotton) is hampered by

dust storms, droughts (five years in a row from 1972 to 1977) and flooding. These natural disasters will give you an idea of the weather. It's scorching and humid in summer, and freezing in winter, with dust fallout in spring and heavy rains in July and August.

Coal is Hebei's main resource and most of it is shipped through Qinhuangdao, an ugly port town with iron, steel and machine industries.

As far as tourist sights go, there's the beach resort of Beidaihe, and Chengde with its palaces and temples. Shijiazhuang, the capital city, is a waste of time.

Apart from all these, the best thing to see is the Great Wall, which spans the province before meeting the sea at Shanhaiguan.

SHIJIAZHUANG
(*shíjiāzhuāng*)

Shijiazhuang is a railway junction town about 250km south-west of Beijing and, in spite of being the capital of the province, it's a cultural desert. Its population is around one million, but at the turn of the century it was just a small village with 500 inhabitants and a handful of buildings. Railways constructed in this century brought the town relative prosperity and a consequent population explosion.

Shijiazhuang has the biggest PLA officer training school in China; it's about 2km west of the city. After the Beijing protests and subsequent killings in 1989, all the new students from Beijing University were taken to this re-education camp for a one year indoctrination.

Shijiazhuang is an industrial city known chiefly for its smokestacks. For some travellers it might be a useful transit point, but it's no place to linger.

Information

Both CITS (☎ 601-4766) and CTS (☎ 601-4570) are in the Hebei Grand Hotel at 23 Yucai Jie.

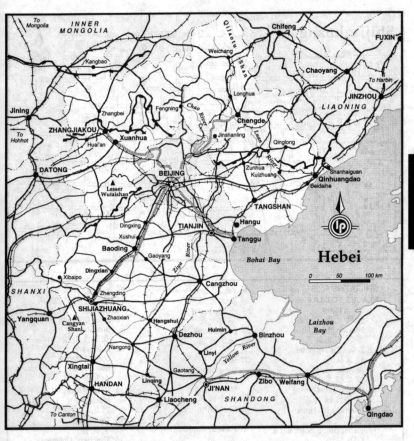

HEBEI

The post office is on Zhongshan Lu, near the railway station.

Revolutionary Martyrs' Mausoleum
(*lièshì língyuán*)
The Martyrs' Mausoleum (☎ 702-3028) is on Zhongshan Lu, west of the railway station. The guerrilla doctor Norman Bethune (1890-1939) is interred here; there is also a photo and drawing display depicting his life and works, and a white memorial.

Following the Communists' victory in 1949, Bethune (*bái qiú'ēn*) became the most famous foreigner in China since Marco Polo. Even today, most Chinese don't know who Marco Polo is, but they all know Bethune. He goes down in modern Chinese history as the man who served as a surgeon with the Eighth Route Army in the war against Japan, having previously served with the Spanish Communist forces against Franco and his Nazi allies.

Bethune is even eulogised in the reading of Mao Zedong Thought – 'We must all learn the spirit of absolute selflessness from Dr Norman Bethune'.

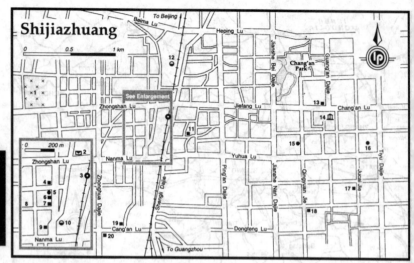

Shijiazhuang

0   0.5   1 km

To Beijing
Beima Lu
Heping Lu

12

Zhongshan Lu
See Enlargement

11
Nanma Lu

Jiefang Lu

13
Chang'an Lu

14

15
16

Chang'an
Park

0   200 m

Zhongshan Lu
2

4
3
6 5
7
8
9   10

19
Cang'an Lu
20

Yuhua Lu

17

18

Dongfeng Lu

To Guangzhou

SHIJIAZHUANG 石家庄	18 Yatai Grand Hotel	8 Yong'an Market
PLACES TO STAY	亚太大酒店	永安步行商业街
4 Bailin Hotel	19 Huadu Hotel	10 Central
柏林大厦	华都大厦	Long-Distance
6 Hualian Hebei Hotel	20 Luyou Hotel	Bus Station
华联河北饭店	旅游宾馆	长途汽车站
7 Silver Spring Hotel		12 Xiangyang
银泉饭店	**OTHER**	Long-Distance
9 Jinghua Hotel	1 Revolutionary	Bus Station
京华饭店	Martyrs'	向阳长途汽车站
11 Wujing Hotel	Mausoleum	14 Hebei Provincial
武警宾馆	烈士陵园	Museum
13 International Hotel	2 Post Office	河北省博物馆
国际大厦	邮局	15 TV Tower
17 Hebei Grand Hotel; CITS;	3 Railway Station	电视台
CTS	火车站	16 Teachers' University
河北宾馆、中国国际	5 Airport Centre (CAAC)	师范大学
旅行社、中国旅行社	河北华联旅行社	

In China, 'Bethune' is also synonymous with 'Canada' – it's about all the Chinese tend to know about the country, and bringing up the name makes for instant friendship if you're Canadian.

Buried in the cemetery are more than 700 army cadres and heroes who died during the Resistance against Japan, the War of Liberation and the Korean War.

The area is a large park, and in the central alley is a pair of bronze Jin Dynasty lions dating from 1185. There is also a statue of Dr Norman Bethune in the courtyard of the Bethune International Peace Hospital, a little way to the west of the cemetery.

Hebei Provincial Museum

This large museum (☎ 604-5642) (*hébĕi shĕng bówùguăn*) is opposite the International Hotel. All explanations are in Chinese.

Places to Stay

Shijiazhuang's hotel prices are strange indeed – many dumps charge more than the upmarket hotels. Always take a look at the room first before putting down the cash or you may be disappointed.

Wujing Hotel (☎ 603-2713) (*wǔjǐng bīnguǎn*) is the cheapest place that accepts foreigners – the reason why it can take foreigners probably has something to do with the fact that the building is owned by the military. Beds cost Y35 and up; the one inconvenience being that toilets are on the 2nd floor only. The place was recently renovated and is quite clean. The building is on Guangming Lu just behind the railway station – you can walk there in 10 minutes. When you exit the station, turn left and walk to Yuhua Lu – use the underpass to get past the railway tracks then up the steps (to your left) to reach Guangming Lu. As yet, the hotel has no English sign.

The best deal in the railway station area is the *Bailin Hotel* (☎ 702-1398) (*bǎilín dàshà*), at 24 Chezhan Jie. Rooms are very clean and the staff have impeccable manners. Triples with shared bath cost Y120. A double with private bath is Y200 to Y250, or you can get a suite for Y300 to Y350.

The *Silver Spring Hotel* (☎ 702-6981; fax 702-6360) (*yínquán fàndiàn*) is also near the railway station. Although the lobby looks fancy, the rooms are a disappointment and not worth the Y270 price tag for a double.

Just next door is the *Hualian Hebei Hotel* (☎ 702-5991) (*huálián héběi fàndiàn*). This place is horribly overpriced – Y280 for a filthy double with broken plumbing. On the positive side, at least the rooms are fairly spacious – consider this a last resort.

The *Jinghua Hotel* (*jīnghuá fàndiàn*), further down the same street, is also grotty. In fact, it wasn't accepting foreigners at the time of writing. However, a renovation is planned which could catapult this into a cushy mid-range place to stay.

The *Lüyou Hotel* (☎ 383-4559) (*lǚyóu bīnguǎn*) is a fair way from the railway station and a bit tattered, but reasonably priced at Y170 for a twin. There is no English sign identifying the hotel, but there are plenty of bright lights illuminating the building at night. The hotel is on the south-eastern corner of Zhonghua Dajie and Cang'an Lu. Bus No 3 from the railway station stops nearby.

Huadu Hotel (☎ 383-1040) (*huádū dàshà*) is the tallest building in town and the pride and joy of Shijiazhuang. Room prices are very cheap for the plush facilities – twins are Y250 to Y300, and suites are Y480 to Y600. You'll need a taxi to get here as it's a long walk from the railway station.

The *Hebei Grand Hotel* (☎ 601-5961; fax 601-4092) (*héběi bīnguǎn*) is surprisingly good value. The fully renovated guesthouse is the darling of tour groups and home to CITS and CTS. Doubles in the old block are Y300 – in the new block rates are Y350 to Y600. The hotel is at 23 Yucai Jie near the No 6 bus stop.

The *International Hotel* (☎ 604-7888; fax 603-4787) (*guójì dàshà*), at 23 Chang'an Xilu, has long been a haven for geriatric tour groups. Doubles cost from Y310 to Y740. The *Yatai Grand Hotel* (☎ 601-2901; fax 601-1071) (*yàtài dà jiǔdiàn*), at 48 Qing-yuan Lu, is the new place in town. It's a three star hotel with twins priced from Y340.

Places to Eat

Close to the Silver Spring Hotel is a long commercial street called the Yong'an Market. Here you'll find lots of good eats at rock-bottom prices from both *street stalls* and *indoor restaurants*. There is another line-up of street stalls just in front of the railway station, but these seem to operate only in the evening.

Upstairs in the railway station itself is a large karaoke and *restaurant* which supplies much of Shijiazhuang's nightlife.

Getting There & Away

CAAC connects Shijiazhuang to: Changsha (one flight weekly), Chengdu (five), Chongqing (two), Dalian (four), Fuzhou (one),

Guangzhou (10), Haikou (one), Harbin (three), Hohhot (three), Hong Kong (one), Kunming (two), Nanjing (two), Qingdao (two), Qinhuangdao (five), Shanghai (six), Shenyang (four), Shenzhen (two), Wenzhou (three), Wuhan (one), Xiamen (two), Xi'an (two) and Zhengzhou (one).

Shijiazhuang is a major rail hub with comprehensive connections: there are lines to Beijing (about four hours), Taiyuan (five hours), Dezhou (five hours) and Guangzhou (30-plus hours).

The Xiangyang long-distance bus station is north-east of the railway station and within walking distance. From there you can get buses to sights outside Shijiazhuang.

Getting Around
To/From the Airport Shijiazhuang's airport is 40km from town. The CAAC bus costs Y35 and departs from the Airport Centre (booking office) opposite the railway station. The bus is supposed to depart 2½ hours prior to flight time, although from experience we've found it departs 10 minutes earlier than that! A taxi to the airport will cost about Y120 and the ride takes about an hour.

Bus Within the city there are 10 bus lines, but buses tend to be horribly overcrowded.

AROUND SHIJIAZHUANG
There's nothing spectacular in this part of Hebei, but there are a few places that you can visit.

Zhengding
(*zhèngdìng*)
This town, 10km north of Shijiazhuang, has several magnificent temples and monasteries. The largest and oldest is the **Longxing Monastery** (*lóngxīng sì*), noted for its huge, 20m-high bronze buddha dating from the Song Dynasty almost 1000 years ago. The multi-armed statue is housed in the Temple of Great Mercy, an impressive structure with red and yellow galleries.

Minibuses to Zhengding cost Y4 and are

marked 'Great Buddha Temple' (*dà fó sì*) in Chinese. In Shijiazhuang they congregate in front of the Bailin Hotel opposite the railway station. Bus No 201 from Shijiazhuang also goes to the temples. The ride takes a full hour.

Zhaozhou Bridge
(*zhàozhōu qiáo*)
The bridge is in Zhaoxian County, about 40km south-east of Shijiazhuang and 2km south of Zhaoxian town. It has spanned the Jiao River for 1300 years and is possibly the oldest stone-arch bridge in China (another, possibly older bridge, has been unveiled in Linying County, Henan Province).

Putting the record books aside, Zhaozhou Bridge is remarkable in that it still stands. It is 50m long and 9.6m wide, with a span of 37m; the balustrades are carved with dragons and mythical creatures. Credit for this daring piece of engineering goes to a disputed source, but according to legend the master mason Lu Ban constructed it overnight. Astounded immortals, refusing to believe that this was possible, arrived to test the bridge. One immortal had a wagon, another had a donkey, and they asked Lu Ban if it was possible for them both to cross at the same time. He nodded. Halfway across, the bridge started to shake and Lu Ban rushed into the water to stabilise it. This resulted in donkey-prints, wheel-prints and hand-prints being left on the bridge.

Several more old stone bridges are to be found in Zhaoxian County.

Cangyanshan
(*cāngyánshān*)
About 78km south-west of Shijiazhuang is a scenic area of woods, valleys and steep cliffs dotted with pagodas and temples. The novelty here is a bizarre, double-roofed hall sitting on a stone-arch bridge spanning a precipitous gorge. It is known as the **Hanging Palace**, and is reached by a 300 step stairway. The palace dates from the Sui Dynasty. On the surrounding slopes are other ancient halls.

Xibaipo
(*xībǎipō*)

In Pingshan County, 80km north-west of Shijiazhuang, was the base from which Mao Zedong, Zhou Enlai and Zhu De directed the northern campaign against the Kuomintang from 1947 to 1948. The original site of Xibaipo village was submerged by the Gangnan Reservoir and the present village has been rebuilt close by. In 1977 a **Revolutionary Memorial Museum** was erected. Xibaipo has become a tourist trap, but it's still fun to visit.

CHENGDE
(*chéngdé*)

Chengde is an 18th century imperial resort area 255km from Beijing. It was once known as Jehol. It's billed as somewhere to escape from the heat (and now the traffic) of summers in the capital, and boasts the remnants of the largest regal gardens in China.

Chengde remained an obscure town until 1703 when Emperor Kangxi began building a summer palace here, with a throne room and the full range of court trappings. More than a home away from home, Chengde became a sort of government seat, since where the emperor went his seat went too. Kangxi called his summer creation Bishu Shanzhuang (Fleeing-the-Heat Mountain Villa).

By 1790, during the reign of his grandson Qianlong, it had grown to the size of Beijing's Summer Palace and the Forbidden City combined. Qianlong extended an idea started by Kangxi, to build replicas of minority architecture in order to make envoys feel comfortable. In particular he was keen on promoting Tibetan and Mongolian Lamaism, which had proved to be a useful way of debilitating the meddlesome Mongols. The Mongolian branch of Lamaism required one male in every family to become a monk – a convenient method of channelling manpower and ruining the Mongol economy.

This helps explain the Tibetan and Mongolian features of the monasteries north of the summer palace, one of them a replica of the Potala Palace in Lhasa.

So much for business – the rest was the emperor's pleasure, which included the usual bouts of hunting, feasting and orgies. Occasionally the outer world would make a rude intrusion into this dream life. In 1793 British emissary Lord Macartney arrived and sought to open trade with China. Qianlong dismissed him with the statement that China possessed all things and had no need of trade.

Chengde has very much slipped back into being the provincial town it once was, its grandeur long decayed, and its monks and emperors long gone. The population of 700,000 is engaged in mining, light industry and tourism.

Thanks to the Cultural Revolution, the priceless remnants of Qing Dynasty culture were allowed to go to seed – palaces and monasteries became tattered, Buddhist statues were disfigured, windows were bricked up, columns reduced to stumps and so on.

All this is being restored, in some cases from the base up, in the interests of promoting mass tourism. Chengde is poor, and tourism is its only real hope of obtaining a quick transfusion of cash.

The dusty, small-town ambience of Chengde is nice enough and there's some quiet hiking in the rolling countryside. Chinese speakers are apparently delighted with the clarity of the local dialect (maybe because they can actually hear it in the absence of traffic).

Information
The PSB (☎ 223091) is on Wulie Lu. The Bank of China is on the northern side of Zhonghua Lu, near the intersection with Nanyingzi Lu, and the post office is further south on Nanyingzi Lu.

Imperial Summer Villa
(*bìshǔ shānzhuāng*)

This park covers 590 hectares and is bounded by a 10km wall. Emperor Kangxi decreed that there would be 36 'beauty

HEBEI

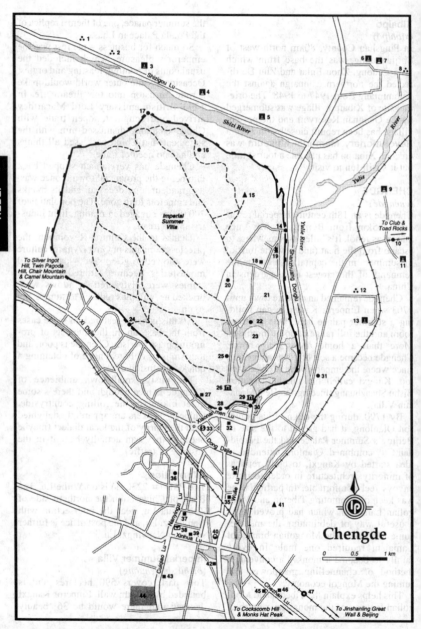

Chengde

0   0.5   1 km

CHENGDE 承德

PLACES TO STAY
18 Mongolian Yurt Hotel
蒙古包渡假村
27 Qiwanglou Hotel
绮望楼
32 Mountain Villa Hotel
山庄宾馆
34 Yindu Hotel
银都宾馆
35 Guesthouse for Diplomatic
Missions
外交人员宾馆
37 Chengde Guesthouse
承德宾馆
39 Xinhua Hotel
新华饭店
42 Yunshan Hotel
云山饭店
43 Lulu Hotel
露露宾馆
45 Chengde Hotel
承德大厦
46 Huilong Hotel
会龙大厦

OTHER
1 Arhat Hall (ruins)
罗汉堂
2 Guang'an Temple (ruins)
广安寺
3 Shuxiang Temple
殊像寺

4 Putuozongsheng Temple
普陀宗之庙
5 Xumifushou Temple
须弥福寿之庙
6 Puning Temple
普宁寺
7 Puyou Temple
普佑寺
8 Guangyuan Temple (ruins)
广缘寺
9 Anyuan Temple
安远寺
10 Chairlift
棒槌峰索道
11 Pule Temple
普乐寺
12 Pushan Temple (ruins)
溥善寺
13 Puren Temple
溥仁寺
14 Huidiji Gate
惠迪吉门
15 Beizhen Twin Peaks
北枕双峰
16 Ancient Pavilion
古俱亭
17 North-West Gate
西北门
19 Yongyou Pagoda
永佑寺塔
20 Wenjin Chamber
文津阁
21 Forest Grove
万树园

22 Misty Rain Tower
逃冔
23 Ideal Island
如意洲
24 Bifeng Gate
碧峰门
25 Fragrant Garden House
芳园居
26 Front Palace
正宫
28 Lizhengmen (Main Gate)
丽正门
29 East Palace
东宫
30 Dehui Gate
德汇门
31 Jinhe Amusement Centre
金禾游乐中心
33 Bank of China
中国银行
36 Xinhua Bookstore
新华书店
38 Post Office
邮局
40 Long-Distance Bus Station
长途汽车站
41 Arhat Hill
罗汉山
44 Revolutionary Martyrs'
Shrine
革命烈士纪念馆
47 Railway Station
火车站

spots' in Jehol; Qianlong delineated 36 more. That makes a total of 72, but where are they? At the northern end of the gardens the pavilions were destroyed by warlords and Japanese invaders, and even the forests have suffered cutbacks. The park is on the dull side, and hasn't been very well maintained.

With a good deal of imagination you can perhaps detect traces of the original scheme of things, with landscaping borrowed from the southern gardens of Suzhou, Hangzhou and Jiaxing, and from the Mongolian grasslands. There is even a feature for resurrecting the moon, should it not be around – a pool shows a crescent moon created by the reflection of a hole in surrounding rocks.

Passing through Lizhengmen, the main

gate, you arrive at the **Front Palace**, a modest version of Beijing's palace. It contains the main throne hall, the Hall of Simplicity & Sincerity, built of an aromatic hardwood called *nanmu* and now a museum displaying royal memorabilia, arms, clothing and other accoutrements. The emperor's bedrooms are fully furnished. Around to the side is a door without an exterior handle (to ensure privacy and security for the emperor), through which the lucky bed partner for the night was ushered before being stripped and searched by eunuchs.

The double storey **Misty Rain Tower**, on the north-western side of the main lake, was an imperial study. Further north is the **Wenjin Chamber**, built in 1773 to house a copy of the *Sikuquanshu*, a major anthology of classics, history, philosophy and literature commissioned by Qianlong. The anthology took 10 years to put together. Four copies were made, but three have disappeared; the fourth is in Beijing.

About 90% of the compound is taken up by lakes, hills, mini-forests and plains, with the odd vantage-point pavilion. At the northern part of the park the emperors reviewed displays of archery, equestrian skills and fireworks. Horses were also chosen and tested here before hunting sorties. Yurts were set up on the mock-Mongolian prairies (a throne, of course, installed in the emperor's yurt) and picnics were held for minority princes. So, it's a good idea to pack a lunch, take your tent and head off for the day ... the yurts have returned for the benefit of weary tourists.

Eight Outer Temples
(*wàibā miào*)
Outside the walls of the imperial garden, to the north and north-east, are several former temples and monasteries. So how many are there? The count started off at 11 many years ago, then plummeted to five (Japanese bombers, Cultural Revolution), and now the number varies between five and nine. The outer temples are from 3km to 5km from the garden's front gate; a bus No 6 taken to the north-eastern corner will drop you in the vicinity.

The surviving temples were all built between 1750 and 1780. The Chinese-style **Puren Temple** and the vaguely Shanxi-style **Shuxiang Temple** have been totally rebuilt. Get there in the early morning when the air is crisp and cool and the sun is shining on the front of the temples – it's the best time to take photos. Some of the temples are listed here in clockwise order.

Putuozongsheng Temple (*pǔtuózōng shèng zhī miào*)
Putuozongsheng (Potaraka Doctrine), the largest of the Chengde temples, is a mini-facsimile of Lhasa's Potala. It was built for the chieftains from Xinjiang, Qinghai, Mongolia and Tibet to celebrate Qianlong's 60th birthday and was also a site for religious assemblies. It's a solid-looking fortress, but unfortunately it is in bad shape – parts are inaccessible or boarded up and gutted by fire. Notice the stone column in the courtyard inscribed in Chinese, Tibetan, Mongolian and Manchurian scripts.

Xumifushou Temple (*xūmǐfúshòu zhī miào*)
Xumifushou (the Temple of Sumeru, Happiness and Longevity) was built in honour of the sixth Panchen Lama, who stayed here 1781. It incorporates elements of Tibetan and Han architecture and is an imitation of a temple in Shigatse, Tibet. At the highest point is a hall with eight gilded copper dragons commanding the roof ridges, and behind that sits a glazed-tile pagoda.

Puning Temple (*pǔníng sì*)
Puning (the Temple of Universal Tranquillity) is also modelled on a Tibetan temple. It was built to commemorate Qianlong's victory over Mongol tribes when the subjugated leaders were invited to Chengde. A stele relating the victory is inscribed in Tibetan, Mongol, Chinese and Manchu. The main feature is an Avalokitesvara towering 22m; this wooden buddha has 42 arms with an eye on each palm. The temple appears to be used as an active place of worship.

Anyuan Temple (*ānyuǎn miào*)
Only the main hall remains of Anyuan (Far Spreading Peace), a copy of a Xinjiang temple. It contains Buddhist frescoes in a very sad state.

Pule Temple (*pǔlè sì*)
Pule (the Temple of Universal Happiness) is definitely the most interesting. You can scramble along the banks of the nearby rivulet to a road that leads off near a pagoda at the garden wall.

The temple was built in 1776 for visits of minority envoys (Kazaks among them). It's in much better shape than the other temples and has been retiled and repainted. At the rear of the temple is the unusual Round

Pavilion, reminiscent of Beijing's Temple of Heaven.

You can hike to **Club Rock** (*bàngchuí fēng*) from Pule – the rock is said to resemble a club used for beating laundry dry. Nearby is **Toad Rock** (*hámá shí*). There are commanding views of the area from here. The hiking is pleasant and the scenery is good. You can save yourself a steep climb to the base of Club and Toad rocks by taking the chairlift, but it's more fun to walk if you're reasonably fit.

Other Hills
Other hills which are regarded as famous beauty spots (and possibly climbable) include: **Arhat Hill** (*luóhàn shān*), almost in the centre of town; **Monk's Hat Peak** (*sēngguān fēng*), 4km south of town; **Silver Ingot Hill** (*yuánbǎo shān*), 10km southwest of town; **Twin Pagoda Hill** (*shuāng tǎ shān*), 15km to the south-west; **Chair Mountain** (*yǐzi shān*), 14km to the south-west; **Camel Mountain** (*luòtuó shān*), 20km south-west; and **Cockscomb Hill** (*jīguān shān*), 15km south-east.

Jinshanling Great Wall
It's a good 113km drive from downtown Chengde to the Great Wall at Jinshanling, but some tourists like to do it. It's back in the direction of Beijing, and if you're travelling by car or tour bus then you could stop off here on a Beijing-Chengde excursion. Admission costs Y40.

It is possible to hike (about four hours) along the wall between Jinshanling and Simatai. For information about the Great Wall at Simatai, see the special section in the Beijing chapter.

Organised Tours
The only practical way to see all the tourist sights in one day is to take a tour by minibus. Most of these tours start out at 8 am, but a few begin in the afternoon just after lunch, around 1.30 pm. The cheapest sightseeing bus tours cost around Y30, but are Chinese-speaking only. Foreigners are usually welcome to tag along, but the tour leaders would be much happier if you could speak Chinese.

All hotels can make arrangements, but you'll almost certainly get offers as soon as you arrive at the railway station. You may even get offers on the train itself – some tour touts have arrangements with railway staff to solicit business. Every tout will insist that he or she has the best deal, and you'll never get it so cheap if you don't grab their special offer right now.

Pricey tours are available from CITS in Beijing. A complete tour to Chengde costs around Y3000 (two days) for one person, but it gets cheaper as the size of the group increases.

Places to Stay
The *Xinhua Hotel* (☎ 206-5880) (*xīnhuá fàndiàn*), at 4 Xinhua Lu, is a reliable cheapie with rooms for Y200. The Xinhua Travel Service is also reasonable for budget tours of Chengde.

The *Chengde Guesthouse* (☎ 202-2551) (*chéngdé bīnguǎn*) on Nanyingzi Dajie has comfortable doubles for Y300, Y500 and Y600. Bus No 7 from the railway station drops you right outside the hotel.

The *Chengde Hotel* (☎ 208-8808) (*chéngdé dàshà*) is a newish place at 5 Chezhan Lu near the railway station. Twins cost Y220 to Y280.

The *Yunshan Hotel* (☎ 215-6171; fax 215-3256) (*yúnshān fàndiàn*) at 6 Nanyuan Donglu is one of the better hotels in town and a favourite with tour groups. The brochure says 'Let warm and pleasure accompany you everywhere hope excellent service in Yunshan give you happy memory'. You'd probably have happier memory if prices were lower; standard rooms are Y420 in the off season and Y520 during the summer crunch.

The *Huilong Hotel* (☎ 208-5369) (*huìlóng dàshà*) on Chezhan Lu was under renovation at the time of writing. Room rates are expected to be Y300 and up after it reopens.

The *Yindu Hotel* (☎ 202-9597) (*yíndū bīnguǎn*) on Wulie Lu is nothing special,

HEBEI

but charges Y400 to Y800 for twins. The *Lulu Hotel* (*lùlù bīnguǎn*) on Cuiqiao Lu has twins for Y240.

The *Guesthouse for Diplomatic Missions* (☎ 202-1976) (*wàijiāo rényuán bīnguǎn*), on Wulie Lu, is in the upmarket league. Standard twins are Y480 and suites are Y790.

The *Mountain Villa Hotel* (☎ 202-3501; fax 202-2457) (*shānzhuāng bīnguǎn*) is at 127 Xiaonanmen Lu. The Stalinist architecture evokes mixed reactions, but this place certainly has character and gets good reviews from travellers. Standard twins cost Y280. The more expensive rooms are large enough to hold a party in – perhaps that's why they come equipped with mahjong tables. Take bus No 7 from the railway station and from there it's a short walk.

There are two hotels just within the walls of the Imperial Summer Villa. On the western side is the *Qiwanglou Hotel* (☎ 202-2196) (*qǐwànglóu bīnguǎn*) built in Qing Dynasty style with palatial gardens. Twins cost Y500.

Further north and on the eastern side is the *Mongolian Yurt Hotel* (☎ 202-2710) (*ménggǔbāo dùjiàcūn*), where doubles cost between Y300 and Y500. It's designed in yurt style with air-con, carpet, telephone and TV – not even Genghis Khan had it this good.

Getting There & Away
Bus Although there are long-distance buses between Chengde and Beijing, this is generally not the way to do it – most travellers go by train.

Train There are trains connecting Chengde to Beijing, and also to Shenyang in Liaoning Province. Most comfortable is the *Beijing-Chengde express* (train Nos 225 and 226) which have a plush soft-seat section – it's no-smoking and tea is served to passengers for a small fee. The one way trip takes less than five hours. There are slower trains which take over seven hours. The schedule is as follows:

Beijing to Chengde

Train No	Depart	Arrive
225	7.29 am	12.10 pm
591	1.28 pm	6.32 pm
613	11.08 pm	4.21 am
853	4.27 pm	11.25 pm

Chengde to Beijing

Train No	Depart	Arrive
226	2.29 pm	7.23 pm
592	6.16 am	11.24 am
614	10.48 pm	4.48 am
854	6.32 am	1.50 pm

Shenyang to Chengde

Train No	Depart	Arrive
520/521	7.50 am	9.44 pm
592	4.04 pm	6.01 am

Chengde to Shenyang

Train No	Depart	Arrive
519/522	7.01 am	8.38 pm
591	6.47 pm	8.43 am

Getting Around
Taxis and motor-tricycles are widely available – bargaining is necessary, especially with the tricycles. There are half a dozen minibus lines, but the only ones you'll probably need to use are the No 7 from the station to the Chengde Guesthouse, and the No 6 to the outer temples grouped at the north-eastern end of town. The service is infrequent – you might have to wait 30 minutes or more.

Another good way to get around town and to the outer temples is on a bicycle – ask at your hotel.

TANGSHAN
(*tángshān*)
Just on the eastern side of the Tianjin Municipality (but in Hebei proper) is Tangshan, a city of about 1.5 million. In July, 1976, Tangshan was devastated by an earthquake registering 8.0 on the Richter Scale. More than 240,000 people (almost a fifth of Tangshan's population at that time) were killed in the quake and over 160,000 seriously injured; with casualties from Beijing and Tianjin added, the total figures are considerably higher.

It was the greatest natural disaster of the

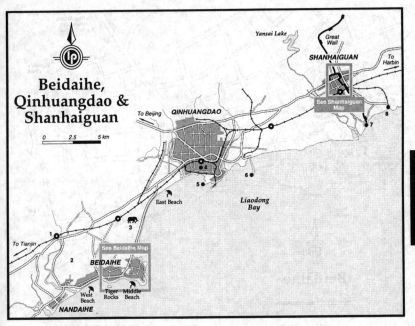

Beidaihe, Qinhuangdao & Shanhaiguan

0   2.5   5 km

To Beijing   QINHUANGDAO
Yansai Lake
Great Wall
SHANHAIGUAN
To Harbin
See Shanhaiguan Map
8
7
East Beach
Liaodong Bay
To Tianjin
1
3
2
See Beidaihe Map
BEIDAIHE
West Beach   Tiger Rocks   Middle Beach
NANDAIHE
5
4
6

HEBEI

decade, but a new Tangshan has risen from the rubble. As early as 1978 it was claimed that industrial output (steel, cement and engineering) was back to 1976 levels. There is not much to see now, but you could stop off in Tangshan for a few hours en route by train from Tianjin to Beidaihe.

BEIDAIHE, QINHUANGDAO & SHANHAIGUAN

A 35km stretch of coastline on China's east coast, this region borders the Bohai Sea. Getting There & Away and Getting Around information on the region appears at the end of the section.

Beidaihe

(běidàihé)

This seaside resort was built by westerners, but is now popular with the Chinese. The simple fishing village was transformed when English railway engineers stumbled

HEBEI

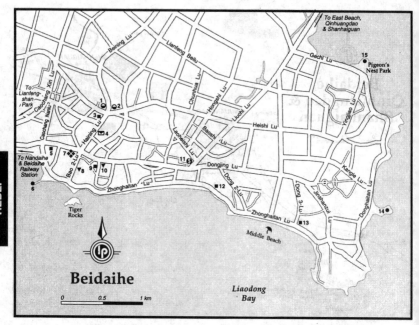

Beidaihe

across it in the 1890s. Diplomats, missionaries and business people from the Tianjin concessions and the Beijing legations hastily built villas and cottages in order to indulge in the new bathing fad.

The original golf courses, bars and cabarets have disappeared, although there are signs that these will be revived in the interests of the nouvelle bourgeoisie. Then, as now, Beidaihe is an escape from the hassles of Beijing or Tianjin. Kiessling's, the formerly Austrian restaurant, still sells its time-honoured pastries and seafood. The cream of China's leaders congregate at the summer villas, also continuing a tradition – Jiang Qing and Lin Biao had villas here and Li Peng and Jiang Zemin are said to have heavily guarded residences.

Just to make sure nothing nasty comes by in the water, there are shark nets. It's debatable whether sharks live at this latitude – maybe they're submarine nets. Army

members and working heroes are rewarded with two week vacations at Beidaihe. There are many sanatoriums where patients can get away from the noise of the city.

That's probably all you need to know about Beidaihe. The Chinese have worked the place over trying to categorise the rocks and deciding whether they're shaped like camels or tigers or steamed bread, or immortalising the rocks where Mao sat and wrote lines about fishing boats disappearing.

Information The village comes to life only in the summer (from June to September), when it's warm and fanned by sea breezes and the beaches are jammed.

The average June temperature is 21°C (70°F). In January, by contrast, temperatures rest at -5°C (23°F).

Things to See There are various hikes to vantage points with expansive views of

BEIDAIHE 北戴河

1 Minibus Stop
   中巴站
2 Bus Station
   海滨汽车站
3 Qibei Hotel
   齐北宾馆
4 Hebei Post Office
   河北邮电
5 Central Beach Hotel
   中海滩宾馆
6 Haibin Pier
   海滨码头
7 Friendship Store
   友谊商店
8 Seafood Restaurants
   海鲜餐厅
9 Guesthouse for
   Diplomatic Missions
   外交人员宾馆
10 Kiesslings Restaurant
   起士林餐厅
11 Bank of China
   中国银行
12 Dongwan Hotel
   东湾宾馆
13 Jinshan Guesthouse
   金山宾馆
14 Emerald Shell Tower
   碧螺塔
15 Eagle Pavilion
   望海亭

villas or the coast. The Sea-Viewing Pavilion (wànghǎi tíng) is at **Lianfengshan
Park** (liánfēngshān gōngyuán), about 1.5km
north of Middle Beach (halfway between
Beidaihe and Nandaihe). Right on the shoreline is the **Eagle Pavilion** at Pigeon's Nest
Park (gēziwō gōngyuán). People like to
watch the sunrise over **Tiger Rocks** (lǎohǔ
shí). At the eastern end of Beidaihe is the
Emerald Shell Tower (bìluó tǎ).

The tide at the **East Beach** recedes dramatically and tribes of kelp collectors and
shell-pickers descend upon the sands. In
the high season you can even be photographed in cardboard-cutout racing
boats, with the sea as a backdrop.

To the south-west of Beidaihe is
Nandaihe (nándàihé), an up-and-coming
resort that is already starting to look tacky.

It's less popular than its older cousin, but
you may want to come here to see the
difference. It's also another option for accommodation.

Places to Stay Many places are open for
business only during the brief summer
season, and many cheaper hotels do not
accept foreigners.

The Qibei Hotel (☎ 404-1497) (qíběi
bīnguǎn) is a reliable budget place to stay.
Room rates are Y120, Y180 and Y240.

Perhaps the cheapest beach-side hotel is
the new Central Beach Hotel (☎ 404-1445,
404-1934) (zhōnghǎitān bīnguǎn). The
large, spacious grounds (complete with a
wall around it) makes you feel slightly like
the ruling elite who stay in their guarded
compounds. Twins are Y280 and Y380.

The Guesthouse for Diplomatic Missions (☎ 404-1287) (wàijiāo rényuán
bīnguǎn) is the splashy place in town. It
seems to get renovated every two years and
prices predictably raised. At the moment it
costs Y400 in winter and Y700 in summer.

Also big with moneyed tourists is the
Jinshan Guesthouse (☎ 404-1338, 404-
1678) (jīnshān bīnguǎn) on the shore front
on Zhonghaitan Lu. Twins cost Y450.

Another beach-front possibility is the
Dongwan Hotel (dōngwān bīnguǎn) with
twins for Y300.

Rather few foreigners stay in Nandaihe,
but there are several places there which
cost around Y300 for a twin room. The
possibilities include:

Nandaihe Friendship Hotel (☎ 405-0122)
   (nándàihé yǒuyì bīnguǎn), 12 Youyi Lu
Nandaihe Guesthouse (☎ 405-0370) (nándàihé
   bīnguǎn), 11 Guangming Lu
Nandaihe Orient Holiday Hotel (☎ 405-1394)
   (nándàihé dōngfāng jiàrì jiǔdiàn), 11 Linhai
   Dao

Places to Eat There's a whole string of
seafood restaurants along Bao 2-Lu near
the beach. You won't have to look for
them, as the persistent restaurant owners
will be looking for you.

Near the Guesthouse for Diplomatic

HEBEI

Missions is *Kiessling's Restaurant* (*qǐshìlín cāntīng*), a relative of the Tianjin branch, which only operates from June to August – the bakery is outstanding.

Things to Buy The markets near the beaches have the most amusing kitsch collection of sculpted and glued shellwork this side of Dalian. Handicrafts such as raffia and basketware are on sale in the stores.

Qinghuangdao
(*qínhuángdǎo*)
Qinhuangdao is an ugly port city that you'd have to squeeze pretty hard to find tourist attractions in. It has an ice-free harbour, and petroleum is piped in from the Daqing oilfield to the wharves.

Water pollution makes the beach a non-starter – this is *not* the place to get your feet wet. The locals will be the first to suggest that you move along to Beidaihe or Shanhaiguan.

Shanhaiguan
(*shānhǎiguān*)
Shanhaiguan is where the Great Wall meets the sea. In the 1980s this part of the wall had nearly returned to dust, but it has been rebuilt and is now a first-rate tourist drawcard.

Just 10 years ago, Shanhaiguan was a city of considerable charm. Now it has been slowly absorbed into the Qinhuangdao megalopolis, with lots of traffic and new ugly buildings. Making it worse are persistent taxi drivers, souvenir vendors and touts using loudspeakers to plug their wares. On summer weekends, throngs of camera-clicking Beijingers overrun the place, but things are much mellower during the winter months. The scenic hills to the north offer a possible refuge from the chaos.

Shanhaiguan was a garrison town with a square fortress, four gates at the compass points and two major avenues running between the gates. The present village is within the substantial remains of the old walled enclosure. Shanhaiguan has a long

and chequered history – nobody is quite sure how long or what kind of chequers, but plenty of pitched battles and blood it seems.

First Pass Under Heaven (*tiānxià dìyī guān*) Also known as the East Gate (*dōngmén*), this magnificent structure is topped with a two storey, double-roofed tower (Ming Dynasty, rebuilt in 1639).

The calligraphy at the top (attributed to the scholar Xiao Xian) reads 'First Pass Under Heaven'. The words reflect the Chinese custom of dividing the world into civilised China and the 'barbarians'. The barbarians got the better of civilised China when they stormed this gate in 1644.

A Y10 ticket buys you admission to the top of the wall, and from this vantage point you can see decayed sections trailing off into the mountains. At the watchtower are souvenir shops selling First Pass Under Heaven handkerchiefs, and a parked camel waiting for photos. How about a pair of 'First Pass Under Heaven Wooden Chopsticks' or some 'Brave Lucky Jewellery'?

Nearby, the **Great Wall Museum** (*chángchéng bówùguǎn*) displays armour, dress, weaponry and pictures.

Old Dragon Head (*lǎo lóng tóu*) This is where the Great Wall meets the sea (see the Beidaihe, Qinghuangdao & Shanhaiguan map). What you see now has been reconstructed – the original wall has long since crumbled away. The name is derived from the legendary carved dragon head that once faced the ocean.

It's a 4km hike or taxi ride from the centre of Shanhaiguan. A more viable route is to follow (by road) the wall to the first beacon tower.

Yansai Lake (*yànsāi hú*) The lake is also known as Stone River Reservoir (*shíhé shuǐkù*). It's just 6km to the north-west of Shanhaiguan. The reservoir is 4km to 5km long and tourists can go boating there. Give them a few years and it could be another Guilin.

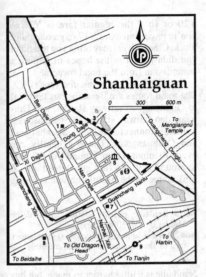

Shanhaiguan

SHANHAIGUAN 山海关

1   North Street Hotel
    北街招待所
2   Jingshan Hotel
    京山宾馆
3   First Pass Under Heaven
    天下第一关
4   Street Market
    南大商业街
5   Great Wall Museum
    长城博物馆
6   Bank of China
    中国银行
7   Shangye Hotel
    商业宾馆
8   Dongfang Hotel
    东方宾馆
9   Railway Station
    火车站

HEBEI

Mengjiangnü Temple (*mèngjiāngnǚ miào*)
Six kilometres east of Shanhaiguan (with a regular bus service from the South Gate) is the Mengjiangnü Temple, a Song-Ming reconstruction. It has coloured sculptures of Lady Meng and her maids, and calligraphy on Looking for Husband Rock.

Meng's husband, Wan, was press-ganged into wall building because his views conflicted with those of Emperor Qin Shihuang. When winter came the beautiful Meng Jiang set off to take her husband warm clothing, only to discover that he had died from the backbreaking labour. Meng tearfully wandered the Great Wall, thinking only of finding Wan's bones to give him a decent burial. The wall, a sensitive soul, was so upset that it collapsed, revealing the skeleton entombed within. Overcome with grief, Meng hurled herself into the sea from a conveniently placed boulder.

Places to Stay Most popular with foreigners is the *Jingshan Hotel* (☎ 551130) (*jīngshān bīnguǎn*) on Dong Dajie. This beautiful place has twin rooms for Y140 to Y300. Among the papers you get when you check in is a voucher for a free breakfast at the hotel's restaurant.

The nearby *North Street Hotel* (*běijiē zhāodàisuǒ*) is slightly cheaper, although somewhat less aesthetic. Twins cost Y100, but if you ask for a dormitory they'll put you in with another traveller at Y50 per bed.

The *Shangye Hotel* (☎ 505-1681) (*shāngyè bīnguǎn*) at 139 Guancheng Nanlu is definitely not worth the 100% surcharge for foreigners. Doubles for the big noses cost Y240.

The *Dongfang Hotel* (*dōngfāng bīnguǎn*) on Guancheng Nanlu was under renovation at the time of writing, but looks like a reasonable possibility if the other places are full.

Getting There & Away
Air Qinhuangdao's little airport offers flights to:

Dalian (11 per week), Guangzhou (two), Harbin (two), Hohhot (two), Kunming (two), Qingdao (three), Shanghai (three), Shenyang (two), Shijiazhuang (six), Xi'an (two) and Yantai (three)

Train The three stations of Beidaihe, Qinhuangdao and Shanhaiguan are accessible by train from Beijing, Tianjin or Shenyang (Liaoning Province). The trains are frequent, but don't always stop at all three stations or always arrive at convenient hours. The usual stop is Shanhaiguan; several trains skip Beidaihe.

One factor to consider is that the hotels at Shanhaiguan are within walking distance of the railway station, whereas at Beidaihe the nearest hotel is at least 10km from the station. This is no problem if you arrive during daylight or early evening – there are plenty of minibuses meeting incoming trains at Beidaihe railway station. However, you can't count on this at night and a taxi could be quite expensive. If you're going to arrive in the dead of night, it's better to do so at Shanhaiguan.

The fastest trains take five hours to Beidaihe from Beijing, and an extra 1½ hours to Shanhaiguan. From Shenyang to Shanhaiguan is a five hour trip. Tianjin is three to four hours away.

Alternatively, you could get a train that stops at Qinhuangdao and then take a minibus from there to Beidaihe.

Getting Around
Bus Minibuses are fast and cheap, and can be flagged down easily. At the Beidaihe railway station you'll be greeted by numerous screaming minibus drivers. Look for one that screams '*haibin*' (the beach). To be more specific, tell him you want to get off at the Beidaihe bus terminal (*hǎibīn qìchē zhàn*). The fare varies, but should be around Y3. Watch out for the minibus drivers who like to drop foreigners off at the front door of their hotel for an extra

Y20 or so – the regular fare is Y3, so you're paying an extra Y17 to go one more block. Other drivers may bring you to a hotel you didn't want in the hopes of getting a commission from the hotel owners.

On all other minibuses, the fare is Y2. The main routes are Beidaihe bus terminal to Qinhuangdao railway station, and Qinhuangdao railway station to Shanhaiguan.

Buses connect Beidaihe, Shanhaiguan and Qinhuangdao. These generally run every 30 minutes from around 6 or 6.30 am to around 6.30 pm (not guaranteed after 6 pm). Some of the useful public bus routes are:

No 5 Beidaihe railway station to Beidaihe Middle Beach (30 minutes)

Nos 3 & 4 Beidaihe to Qinhuangdao (45 minutes), then to Shanhaiguan (another 15 minutes)

Nandaihe is a little harder to reach, but bus No 22 goes there from the Beidaihe bus terminal. Otherwise, you'll have to shell out Y10 for a taxi.

Motor-Tricycles These are popular in Shanhaiguan. It's Y5 to anywhere within town. As a general formula, the real price is usually half the asking price.

Bicycle There are a couple of bicycle rental places in Beidaihe and Shanhaiguan – look for rows of bikes. The hotels are a possible source – in Shanhaiguan the Shangye Hotel is good for bike rentals (and nothing else).

Shandong 山东

Across the Yellow Sea from Korea, Shandong *(shāndōng)* has a history that can be traced back to the origins of the Chinese state; Confucius, China's great social philosopher, was born here and lived out his days in Lu, one of the small states in the south of today's province (the Chinese character for 'Lu' is still associated with Shandong). His ideas were further championed by the great Confucian philosopher, Mencius, who hailed from the same region.

Great persons aside, the Yellow River finishes its long journey from tributaries in Qinghai here, emptying into the Bohai Sea, and Taishan (Mount Tai), the most revered of China's sacred mountains, drags huge numbers of devotees from all over China up to its summit.

From the earliest record of civilisation in the province (furnished by the black pottery remains of the Neolithic Longshan culture), Shandong has had a tumultuous history. It was victim to the capricious temperament of the oft-flooding Yellow River, with consequent mass death, starvation and ruinous effect on the provincial economy, and in more recent years, it suffered the humiliation of foreign encroachment upon its territory.

In 1899, the Yellow River (also aptly named 'China's Sorrow') flooded the entire Shandong Plain; a sad irony in view of the two scorching droughts which had swept the area that same year and the year before. The flood followed a long period of economic depression, a sudden influx of demobilised troops in 1895 after China's humiliating defeat in her conflict with Japan, and droves of refugees from the south moving north to escape famines, floods and drought.

To top it all off, the Europeans arrived with their peculiar ways (Qingdao was snatched by the Germans and the British obtained a lease for Weihai), including the building of railroads and some feverish missionary work which angered the gods

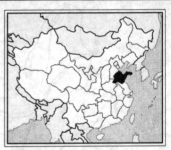

Shandong Facts & Highlights

Area: 153,000 sq km

Population: 87.3 million

Capital: Ji'nan

Highlights

- Taishan, one of China's sacred Taoist peaks.
- Qufu, the birthplace of Confucius.
- The remnant colonial architecture of Qingdao, home of China's most famous brew.

and spirits and meddled with the sacred laws of fengshui.

All this created a perfect breeding ground for rebellion, and in the closing years of the 19th century the Boxers arose out of Shandong, armed with magical spells, headbands and broadswords, only to run into a hail of bullets that was the west's inevitable response.

The port of Qingdao fell into the clutches of the Germans in 1898, who marched the place into the 20th century, adding an industrial infrastructure, cobbled streets and Bavarian architecture. This kick in the pants that shoved Qingdao into the modern age still gives it a momentum that drags the rest of the province behind it. Jinan, the provincial capital in the interior, plays second

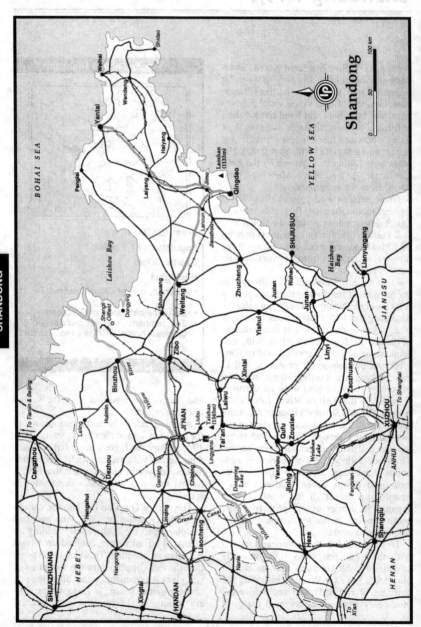

The Fists of Righteousness & Harmony

The popular movement known as the Boxers, or the Boxer Rebellion, erupted in China in the last few years of the 19th century. The Boxers, or Yihetuan (Group of Righteousness and Harmony), was a loose confederation of anti-foreign elements who took their beliefs and practices from secret societies.

Many reasons fused together to spur the Boxers on to the massacres they were to perform, and top of the list was resentment of foreigners due to the recent humiliating defeats for the Qing court at the hands of the powers, the scramble for land in China by the 'barbarians', and the general dislike of Christian missionaries and their practices.

There was a widespread feeling that China was about to be sliced up among the powers, and Chinese culture trampled underfoot.

Emerging initially in Shandong (where it found support from those suffering in great poverty and still reeling from the recent flooding of the Yellow River in 1898), the Boxers protected themselves with charms, superstitions and martial arts techniques, gradually becoming more daring in their attacks upon missionaries and their families, and eventually espousing a creed dedicated to wiping out all foreigners, or 'hairy men' (and women).

The policy of the Qing court (as represented by Cixi, the empress dowager) toward the Boxers vacillated. At first the court considered them to be no different from the usual peasant uprisings, but later viewed them as an ally in their agenda to fight back against the foreign powers and restore the integrity of the Manchu administration. The aspirations of the Qing court gradually paralleled those of the rebels when the Boxers started to attack and massacre foreigners at random in the capital and the famous 50 day siege of the foreign legations in Beijing began. The empress dowager then effectively declared war on the foreign powers on 21 June 1900.

The folly of this alliance was recognised by most provincial authorities, who refused to rally behind the court, knowing the weakness of a China pitted against the powers and doubting the Boxers claims to be impervious to the bullets of the westerners. Thus the movement was limited in scale, allowing the westerners the chance to focus attacks on the capital, Beijing, and the heart of the Boxers' cause. An international relief force of 8000 Japanese, 4800 Russians, 3000 British, 2100 Americans, 800 French, 58 Austrians and 53 Italians descended on Beijing, lifting the siege of the legations, while Cixi and the court fled to Xian.

The Boxers were destroyed and China found itself the recipient of a huge indemnity known as the Boxer Protocol. Among the 12 conditions included in the protocol was a bill of 450 million taels of gold (to be paid off yearly with interest), which would effectively cripple China's economy for many years. This endemnity contributed to the eventual collapse of the Manchu court and the Qing Dynasty. ∎

fiddle to Qindao's tune, while other economic foci like Shengli Oilfield, which is China's second-largest producer of oil, further take up the rear. By 1994, Shandong was ranked among the top four provincial economies in China (alongside Guangdong, Jiangsu and Sichuan).

The sights of Qufu and Taishan are worth a look, although they have far more significance for Chinese and Japanese tourists. If you want to sink a decent beer, scoff excellent seafood, breathe the sea air and wander the streets of a fascinating museum of colonial relics, then make a refreshing bee-line to Qingdao on the coast.

JI'NAN
(jǐ'nán)
Ji'nan (population approximately two million), the capital of Shandong Province,

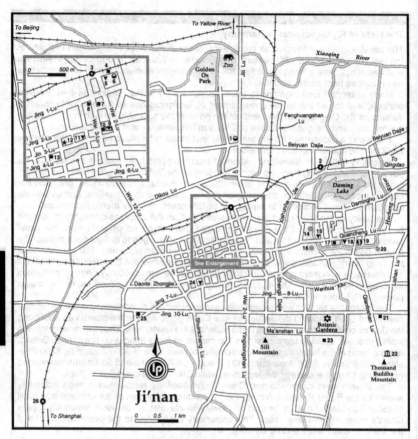

is for most travellers a transit point on the road to other destinations around Shandong. The city is not unattractive, and wandering the streets at night offers a pleasant selection of night markets, lights, hole-in-the-wall restaurants and atmosphere, but if you miss out on the official sights it won't be the end of the world.

The area has been inhabited for at least 4000 years, and some of the earliest reminders of this are the eggshell-thin pieces of black pottery unearthed in the town of Longshan, 30km east of Ji'nan. These

provide the first link in a long unbroken chain of tradition and artistic endeavour that culminates in the beautiful ceramics of later dynasties.

Modern development in Ji'nan stems from 1899, when construction of the Ji'nan to Qingdao railway line began. The line gave the city a major communications role when completed in 1904. The Germans had a concession near the railway station after Ji'nan was opened up to foreign trade in 1906. The huge German building on Jing 1-Lu opposite the Shandong Hotel now

JI'NAN 济南	PLACES TO EAT	9 Main Post Office 邮局
PLACES TO STAY	5 Tianlong Fastfood 天龙快餐	12 PSB 公安局外事科
4 Ji'nan Railway Hotel 济南铁路大厦酒店	11 Jufengde Restaurant 聚丰德饭店	14 Five Dragon Pool Spring 五龙潭公园
7 Guidu Hotel 贵都大酒店	15 Huiquan Restaurant 汇泉饭店	16 Gushing-from-the-Ground Spring; CAAC 趵突泉、中国民航
8 Shandong Hotel 山东宾馆	18 KFC 肯德鸡	19 Bank of China 中国银行
10 Xixi Hotel 习习居接待处	24 Yuedu Restaurant 粤都酒楼	20 Black Tiger Spring 黑虎泉
13 Ji'nan Hotel 济南饭店	**OTHER**	22 Shandong Provincial Museum 山东省博物馆
17 Quancheng Hotel 泉城饭店	1 Long-Distance Bus Station 长途汽车站	25 China Eastern Airlines 东方航空公司
21 Qilu Hotel; CITS 齐鲁宾馆 中国国际旅行社	2 East Railway Station 火车东站	26 South Railway Station 济南南站
23 Nanjiao Guesthouse 南郊宾馆	3 Ji'nan Railway Station 济南火车站	
	6 Tianqiao Bus Station 天桥汽车站	

SHANDONG

houses a railway sub-office; it is made of the same stone, and in the same style, as so much of Qindgdao's architecture. Foreign missions also were set up here and industrialisation took place under the Germans, the English and the Japanese.

Information
Tourist Office There is a branch of CITS (☎ 296-5858) at 88 Jing 10-Lu, near the Qilu Hotel.

PSB The PSB is a block east of the Jufengde Restaurant on Jing 3-Lu.

Money The Bank of China is in Building 10, Shangye Jie, in the eastern part of town. There are exchange services available at the centrally located Pearl and Guidu hotels.

Post & Communications The post office can be found on the corner of Jing 2-Lu and Wei 2-Lu.

Thousand Buddha Mountain
(qiānfóshān)
The statues here were disfigured or just dis-

appeared during the Cultural Revolution, but new ones are gradually being added; there's also a grotto with copies of the four famous Buddhist caves of China (unfortunately, the buddha is big business and they will sting you for Y15 to get in).

A cable car can take you to the top of the mountain for a further horrendous fee (Y18 return). Thousand Buddha Mountain is on the south side of town; entry is Y6. Bus Nos 2 and 31 go there – get off at Qianfoshan Lu.

Shandong Provincial Museum
(shāndōng bówùguǎn)
The museum is adjacent to the Thousand Buddha Mountain. It is divided into history and nature sections, including tools, objets d'art, pottery and various musical instruments.

Daming Lake
(dàmíng hú)
This lake is decorated with small temples, teahouses and, for military aircraft enthusiasts, the preserved shell of a MiG fighter. Otherwise the lake is populated by tour groups sidling about.

Mystery of the Springs

Ji'nan's 100-plus springs are often quoted as the main attraction, and most maps of Ji'nan feature gushing, idealist photos of the springs, so before you jump in a cab, let's set the record straight on this one.

The four main parks-cum-springs are Black Tiger Spring *(hēihǔquán)*, Pearl Spring *(zhūquán)*, Five Dragon Pool *(wǔlóngtán)* and Gushing-from-the-Ground Spring *(bàotūquán)*, which sound wonderful; however, the only time they display any vestige of activity is during the heavy rain season in August.

The reasons for their drying up vary – drought, pollution, increased water usage and even the building of air-raid shelters within the city. These shelters can be seen on Jing 4-Lu, near the intersection of Wei 2-Lu; they were built three decades ago at the height of Sino-Soviet tension and remain, choked with rubbish, testament to the fragility of international socialist friendship. ∎

Places to Stay

Just a stone's throw from the railway station is the *Shandong Hotel* (☎ 691-0797; fax 691-0797) *(shāndōng bīnguǎn)*, a cheap and civilised place with small doubles starting at Y150 and larger ones for Y160.

Just to the south of the Shandong Hotel is the *Xixi Hotel* (☎ 605-7886) *(xíxíjū jiēdàichù)* which is a very Chinese affair with doubles starting at Y160.

Looking just like a Victorian asylum is the *Ji'nan Hotel* (☎ 793-8981) *(jǐ'nán fàndiàn)* at 240 Jing 3-Lu. They keep you on your toes at the Ji'nan Hotel – what looks like the reception is not in fact, and you have to follow a labyrinthine route to find it. Doubles cost Y200.

Next to the railway station is the *Jinan Railway Hotel* (☎ 601-2118; fax 601-2188) *(jǐ'nán tiědào dàshà jiǔdiàn)*, a conveniently located three star option that has recently opened. Doubles start at Y280 and go up to Y680.

Also close to the railway station is the *Guidu Hotel* (☎ 690-0888; fax 690-0999) *(guìdū dàjiǔdiàn)* at 1 Shengping Lu. The cheapest rooms are in the auxiliary building next door to the hotel, and these come in at Y298 for a standard double. The main building has prices ranging from Y428.

The *Nanjiao Guesthouse* (☎ 295-3931; fax 295-3957) *(nánjiāo bīnguǎn)* at 2

Ma'anshan Lu, to the south of the Botanic Gardens, has doubles from Y310 to Y380 and suites from Y480 to Y580. Getting to the hotel by public transport is an effort – take bus No 34 from the centre and then hike up a hill. The hotel was, so the story goes, flung up for an impending visit by Mao, who then decided to skip Ji'nan.

Surrounded on all sides by the parched springs of Ji'nan is the *Quancheng Hotel* (☎ 692-1911; fax 692-3187) *(quánchéng dàjiǔdiàn)* at 2 Nanmen Dajie – a three star hotel with standard facilities. Doubles start at Y380, and deluxe suites cost Y650.

The *Qilu Hotel* (☎ 296-6888; fax 296-7676) *(qílǔ bīnguǎn)* is the prime tourist hotel in town. Doubles start at Y880. It's at 8 Qianfoshan Lu, right next to Thousand Buddha Mountain park.

Places to Eat

The area around the station is the best place to seek out cheap eats – it's dotted with bargain restaurants selling Shandong and Sichuan food. Fast food Chinese can be found directly opposite the railway station at the *Tianlong Fastfood (tiānlóng kuàicān)*; a meal for two can cost as little as Y12. Try the fried dumplings *(guōtiē)*.

One of the better known eating establishments in town is the *Huiquan Restaurant (huìquán fàndiàn)* at 22 Baotuquan

Beilu. Be aware that it features sweet and sour carp from the Yellow River which is served while still breathing. While it may be fresh, you could find this more offensive than appetising.

Good Beijing Duck can be had at *Jufengde Restaurant (jùfēngdé fàndiàn)* at the intersection of Wei 4-Lu and Jing 3-Lu. There is another branch (☎ 692-4106) at the intersection of Jing 5-Lu and Wei 2-Lu which sells a good range of Shandong food.

Decent Cantonese cuisine is served at the *Yuedu Restaurant (yuèdū jiǔlóu)* at the south-eastern intersection of Jing 7-Lu and Wei 8-Lu. You can make your choice from shrink-wrapped plates, pre-prepared but uncooked, which are arranged on chilled shelves. You know what you are getting and the food is good.

If you are in need of tacky cover-band music, *KFC* is at Quancheng Lu (beer is served as well, if it all gets too much). Some taxi drivers swear there's a *McDonald's* in Ji'nan, but they can't put their finger on where it is, or they end up driving you to KFC. Maybe things will be less equivocal by the time you read this.

Getting There & Away
Air There are four flights a week (Monday, Tuesday, Friday and Sunday) between Hong Kong and Ji'nan (Y2550). Domestic flights are available between Ji'nan and all major Chinese cities. Destinations include Beijing (Y500, daily), Shanghai (Y610, Wednesday and Thursday) and Guangzhou (Y1270, daily).

The CAAC ticket office (☎ 601-8145) is opposite the southern entrance to Gushing-from-the-Ground Spring. China Eastern Airlines (☎ 796-4445, 796-6824) is at 408 Jing 10-Lu. Both offices can sell the same tickets. Larger hotels can also supply airline tickets.

Bus Ji'nan has at least three bus stations. The main long-distance bus station *(chángtú qìchē zhàn)* in the north of town has buses to Beijing and Qingdao. The Tianqiao bus station *(tiānqiáo qìchē zhàn)* is

next door to the main railway station and has minibuses to Tai'an. Minibuses to Tai'an also depart from the huge parking lot in front of the railway station. There is another minibus station in front of the east railway station *(huǒchē dōngzhàn)*, where you catch minibuses to Qufu and rural areas near Ji'nan.

Train Be aware that there are two railway stations in Ji'nan: most trains use the main railway station *(jǐ'nán huǒchēzhàn)*, but a handful arrive and depart from the east railway station *(huǒchē dōngzhàn)*. No trains leave from the south railway station.

Ji'nan is a major link in the east China rail system. From Ji'nan there are direct trains to Beijing (Y120), which take about nine hours, and Shanghai (Y225). Trains pass through nearby Tai'an. Direct trains go to Changchun (Y298) in Jilin Province and to Qingdao (Y46) and Yantai; tickets to Tianjin cost Y90. Other destinations include Hangzhou (Y270) and Harbin (Y340). There are also direct Qingdao-Ji'nan-Xi'an-Xining trains.

Getting Around
To/From the Airport Flights depart from the Xijiao airport, 40km east of the city – a new freeway makes it possible to cover the distance in just 40 minutes. You can catch an airport bus from the CAAC ticket office – try not to miss it because a taxi will cost around Y130.

Bus & Motor-Tricycle The buses are the usual nightmare, but there are plenty of motor-tricycles and taxis. Taxis are only Y5 for the first 2.5km.

AROUND JI'NAN
Four Gate Pagoda
(sìméntǎ)
Near the village of Liubu, 33km south-east of Ji'nan, are some of the oldest Buddhist structures in Shandong. Shentong Monastery holds the Four Gate Pagoda, possibly the oldest stone pagoda in China which dates from the 6th century.

The Pagoda of the Dragon & the Tiger (*lónghǔtǎ*) was built during the Tang Dynasty. It stands close to the Shentong Monastery and is surrounded by stupas. Higher up is the Thousand Buddha Cliff (*qiānfóyá*), which displays carved grottoes containing buddhas.

Bus No 22 from the city centre heads due south on Yingxiongshan Lu to Four Gate Pagoda. Tourist buses also ply this route, departing from Ji'nan at 8 am and returning at 3 pm.

TAI'AN
(tài'ān)

Tai'an is the gateway town to the sacred Taishan, a place where most Chinese come at least once in their lifetime. You'll probably need the better part of a day to take in the mountain, so be prepared to spend the night. Nearby Qufu, Confucius' birthplace, can be taken in by minibus in much less time.

On an incidental note, Tai'an is the home town of Jiang Qing, Mao's fourth wife, ex-film actress and notorious spearhead of the Gang of Four, on whom all of China's ills are sometimes blamed. She was later airbrushed out of Chinese history and committed suicide in May 1991.

Information

The CITS office (☎ 822-3259) is in a compound just down the road from the Taishan Guesthouse, at 22 Hongmen Lu.

The PSB (☎ 822-4004) is just up the road from the main post office on Qingnian Lu. Across the road is the main post office.

Dai Temple
(dài miào)

This huge temple complex is south of the Taishan Guesthouse, at the foot of Mount Tai. Traditionally a pilgrimage stop on the road to Taishan (and a resting spot for hiking emperors), the temple was also the site of huge sacrifices to the god of Taishan. The temple covers an area of 96,000 square metres, and is enclosed by high walls. The main hall is the Temple of

---

TAI'AN 泰安

PLACES TO STAY
2 Taishan Guesthouse
  泰山宾馆
5 Taishan Grand Hotel
  泰山大酒店
10 Longtan Hotel
  龙潭宾馆
11 Liangmao Dasha (Hotel)
  粮贸大厦
15 Overseas Chinese Hotel
  华侨大厦

PLACES TO EAT
6 California Beef Noodles King
  USA
  美国加州牛肉面
17 Duck Restaurant
  惠宾餐厅

OTHER
1 Martyrs' Tomb
  烈士陵园
3 Daizong Archway
  岱宗坊
4 CITS
  中国国际旅行社
7 Museum
  博物馆
8 Dai Temple
  岱庙
9 PSB
  公安局外事科
12 Minibuses to Ji'nan; Bus No 3
  (to Taishan)
  往济南汽车、
  三路汽车
13 Railway Station
  火车站
14 Bank of China
  中国银行
16 Post Office
  邮局
18 Long-Distance Bus
  Station
  长途汽车站

Heavenly Blessing (*tiankuang*) dating back to 1009 AD. It is some 22m high and is constructed of wood with double-eaved yellow tiling.

The Tiankuang was the first built of the 'big three' halls (the others being Hall of Supreme Harmony at the Forbidden City

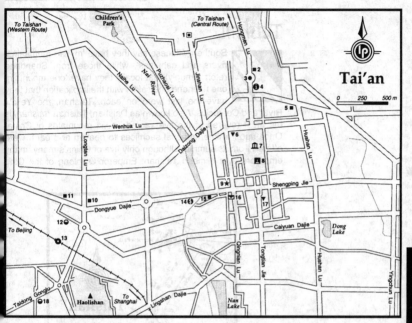

and Dacheng Hall at Qufu). Inside the poorly lit interior is a 62m-long fresco running west to east depicting the god of Taishan on his outward and return journeys. In this case the god is Emperor Zhen Zong, who had the temple built. Zhen Zong raised the god of Taishan to the rank of emperor and there is a 7m-high stele to celebrate this in the western courtyard.

The fresco has been painstakingly retouched by artisans of succeeding dynasties and, although recently restored, is in poor shape – but a majestic concept nonetheless. You may also be rewarded with the spectacle of music, dance and theatre in front of the hall.

The temple complex has been repeatedly restored, however in the late 1920s it was stripped of its statues and transmogrified into offices and shops. Later it suffered damage under the Kuomintang. It

now functions not as a temple, but as an open-air museum with a forest of 200-odd steles. One inscribed stone, originally at the summit of Taishan, is believed to be over 2000 years old (Qin Dynasty). It can be seen at the Eastern Imperial Hall, along with a small collection of imperial sacrificial vessels.

Around the courtyards are ancient, twisted cypresses, gingkos and acacias. Some of the cypresses appear partially ossified. By the cypress in front of Tiankuang Hall, visitors can indulge in a game of luck. A person is blindfolded next to a rock, has to go around the rock three times anticlockwise, then three times clockwise, and try and grope towards the cypress, 20 steps away. They miss every time.

Entry to the temple costs Y10.

Tai'an section continued on page 326 ...

Taishan

Southern Chinese say they have 'myriad mountains, rivers and geniuses', while those from Shandong retort (smugly) that locally they have 'one mountain, one river and one saint', with the implication that they have the last word on each: Taishan, the Yellow River and Confucius. Also known as Daishan, Taishan *(tàishān)* is the most revered of the five sacred Taoist mountains of China. Once upon a time, imperial sacrifices to heaven and earth were offered from its summit, although only five of China's many, many emperors ever climbed Taishan. Emperor Qianlong of the Qing

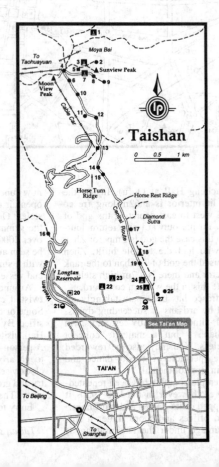

Dynasty, on the other hand, scaled it 11 times. From its heights Confucius uttered the dictum, 'The world is small'; Mao lumbered up and commented on the sunrise, 'The East is Red'. You too can climb up and say, 'I'm knackered'.

Today the mountain is a victim of its popularity, with pilgrims running the usual gauntlet of hoarse T-shirt and trinket sellers who claw at anything that moves. Sections of the mountain even echo to the strains of karaoke, the final indignity. Furthermore, devotees fling empty water bottles and film wrappers into the gullies and rivers, festooning the sacred mount with trash.

Taishan is a uniquely Chinese experience – its supernatural allure (legend, religion and history rolled into one) drags them over in droves. The Princess of the Azure Clouds (Bixia), a Taoist deity whose presence permeates the temples dotted along the route, is a powerful cult figure for the peasant women of Shandong and beyond.

Tribes of wiry grandmothers trot up the steps with frightening ease, their target the cluster of temples at the summit, where you

---

TAISHAN 泰山

1 Rear Temple
后石坞
2 Gongbei Rock
拱北石
3 Jade Emperor Temple
玉皇顶
4 Nantianmen
南天门
5 Shenqi Guesthouse
神憩宾馆
6 Archway to Immortality
开仙坊
7 Azure Clouds Temple
碧霞祠
8 Bridge of the Gods
仙人桥
9 Zhanlu Terrace
占鲁台
10 Pine Facing Pavilion
对松亭
11 Five Pine Pavilion
五松亭
12 Cloud Bridge
云步桥
13 Zhongtianmen Guesthouse; Cable Car
中天门宾馆、空中索道
14 Skywalk Bridge
步天桥
15 Hutian Pavilion
壶天阁

16 Longevity Bridge
长寿桥
17 Doumu Hall
斗母宫
18 Monument to Revolutionary Heroes
革命烈士纪念碑
19 10,000 Immortals Pavilion
万仙楼
20 Tomb of Feng Yuxiang; Everyman's Bridge
大众桥、冯玉祥墓
21 Trailhead for Western Route (No 3 Bus West Terminal or No 2 Bus)
三路汽车西终站
22 Puzhao Monastery
普照寺
23 Memorial Temple
纪念寺
24 Red Gate Palace
红门
25 Guandi Temple
关帝庙
26 Tiger Mountain Reservoir
虎山水库
27 Cloud Empress Pool
云母池
28 Trailhead for Central Route (No 3 Bus East Terminal)
三路汽车东终站

can see them burning money and incense, praying for their progeny (and their blisters). It's said that if you climb Taishan you'll live to be 100, and some of the grandmothers look pretty close to that already. Sun-worshippers – foreign and Chinese – muster wide-eyed on the peak, straining for the first flickers of dawn. In ancient Chinese tradition, it was believed that the sun began its westward journey from Taishan.

Taishan is not a major climb, but with 6660 steps to the summit,

it can be gruelling. All the while, look around you: one egged cripples claw their way up, goaded on by mysterious forces and the pull of the summit, and porters with calloused shoulders and misshapen backs plod ever upwards with crates of drinks, bedding and the occasional Chinese tourist. One wonders how many backs were broken in the building of the temples and stone stairs on Taishan over the centuries – a massive undertaking accomplished without any mechanical aids.

Climate

The tourist season peaks from May to October. But remember that conditions on the mountain vary considerably compared with Tai'an. Clouds and mist frequently envelop the mountain, particularly in summer. The best times to visit are in spring and autumn when the humidity is low, although old-timers say that the clearest weather is from early October onwards. In winter the weather is often fine, but very cold.

On average, there are 16 fine days in spring, eight in summer, 28 in autumn and 35 in winter. But take care – due to weather changes, you're best advised to carry warm clothing in a small day pack with you, no matter what the season. The summit can be very cold, windy and wet; army overcoats are available there for rental. If you don't have a waterproof, you can buy one (a converted dustbin liner) from one of the ubiquitous vendors (Y2).

Climbing Taishan

The town of Tai'an lies at the foot of Taishan and is the gateway to the mountain (see the Tai'an section earlier in this chapter). The entry fee is Y30, which includes Y1 insurance.

On Foot

Upon arrival you have several options, depending on your timing. There are three rest stops to bear in mind: Taishan Guesthouse at the base of the trail (in Tai'an); Zhongtianmen Guesthouse halfway up; and the Shenqi Guesthouse on top of Taishan.

Allow at least two hours for climbing between each of these points – a total of eight hours up and down, at the minimum. Allowing several more hours would make the climb less strenuous and give you more time to look around on top. If you want to see the sunrise, then dump your gear at the railway station or the Taishan Guesthouse in Tai'an and time your ascent so that you'll reach the summit before sundown. Stay overnight at one of the summit guesthouses and get up early next morning for the famed sunrise, which could well be a damp squib. It is possible to scale the mount at night, and some Chinese do this, timing it so that they arrive before sunrise. The way is lit by lamps, but it is advisable to take a torch, as well as warm clothes, food and water.

There are two main paths up the mountain: the central and the western, converging midway at Zhongtianmen. Most people slog up the central path (which used to be the imperial route and is littered with cultural relics) and down by the western path. Other trails run through orchards and woods. Taishan is 1545m above sea level, with a climbing distance of 7.5km from base to summit on the central route. The elevation change from Zhongtianmen to the summit is approximately 600m. The route is populated by stalls and individuals selling fruit, buns, water and so forth.

By Minibus & Cable Car

Minibuses run from the Tai'an railway station to Zhongtianmen, halfway up Taishan, several times each morning. Occasional group tour minibuses run from the Taishan Guesthouse. Buses come down the mountain hourly between 1 and 5 pm (Y10), but don't count on the schedule or the seats.

It's about a five minute walk from Zhongtianmen to the cable car (kōng zhōng suǒ dào), which holds 30 passengers and takes eight minutes to travel from Zhongtianmen to Yueguanfeng (Moon View Peak), near Nantianmen. The fare is Y40 up, and Y30 down. Be warned, if you climb Taishan in the peak season or at weekends, the queues here may force you to wait for up to two hours for a cable car. Check the length of the queue first before you buy a ticket, as getting a refund is tricky.

The same applies when you want to descend from the summit; fortunately, there is another, far more efficient cable car which only carries six passengers (Y30) and is regular as clockwork. It takes you from north of Nantianmen down to Taohuayuan, a scenic area behind Taishan that is also well worth exploring. From here you can take a minibus to Taishan, which takes about forty minutes (Y15). You can reverse this process by first taking a minibus from Tai'an railway station to Taohuayuan and then ascending by cable car.

Central Route

On this route you'll see a bewildering catalogue of bridges, trees, rivers, gullies, towers, inscriptions, caves, pavilions and temples. Taishan, in fact, functions as an outdoor museum of calligraphic art, with the prize items being the Diamond Sutra (or Stone Valley Sutra) along the first section of the walk and the Moya Bei at the summit, which commemorates an imperial sacrifice. Lost on most foreigners are the literary allusions, word games and analogies spelt out by the characters decorating the journey.

The climb proper begins at **No 1 Archway Under Heaven** at the mountain base. Behind that is a stone archway overgrown with wisteria and inscribed 'the place where Confucius began to climb'. **Red Gate Palace**, standing out with its wine-coloured walls, is the first of a series of temples dedicated to the Princess of the Azure Clouds, daughter of the god of Taishan.

Doumu Hall was first constructed in 1542 and has the more magical name of Dragon Spring Nunnery; there's a teahouse next door.

Continuing through the tunnel of cypresses known as Cypress Cave is **Horse Turn Ridge**, where Emperor Zhen Zong had to dismount and continue by sedan chair because his horse refused to go further. Another emperor rode a white mule up and down the mountain and the beast died soon after the descent; it was posthumously given the title of general and its tomb is on the mountain.

Zhongtianmen (Midway Gate to Heaven) is the second celestial gate. From here you can look north to the distant stream of the faithful on the final stretch to the summit. A little way on is **Five Pine Pavilion** where, one day back in 219 BC, Emperor Qin Shihuang was overtaken by a violent storm and was sheltered by the kind pines. He promoted them to the 5th rank of minister.

On the slopes higher up is the **Welcoming Pine**, with a branch extended as if to shake hands. Beyond that is the **Archway to Immortality**. It was believed that those passing through it would become celestial beings. From here to the summit, emperors were carried in sedan chairs – eat your hearts out!

The final leg-wobbling stretch, **The Path of Eighteen Bends**, takes you to **Nantianmen** (South Gate to Heaven), the third celestial gate. Together they are symbolic of Taishan and of Shandong itself; the picture pops up on covers of books and on maps.

On arrival at Taishan Summit *(dàidǐng)* you will see the **Wavelength Pavilion** (a radio and weather station) and the **Journey to the Stars Gondola** (the cable car). If you continue along Paradise Rd, you'll come to **Sunset Statue** where a frozen photographer sits slumped over a table with the view beyond dutifully recorded in sunrises and clipped in front of him.

The grandmothers' long march ends at the **Azure Clouds Temple** *(bìxiácí)*, where small offerings of one sort or another are made to a bronze statue, once richly decorated. The iron tiling on the buildings is intended to prevent damage by strong wind currents, and on the bronze eaves are *chiwen*, ornaments meant to protect against fire. The temple is absolutely splendid, with its location in the clouds, but its guardians are a trifle touchy about you wandering around, and parts of it are inaccessible. The bronze statuette of the Princess of the Azure Clouds is in the main hall.

Perched on the highest point (1545m) of the Taishan Plateau is **Jade Emperor Temple**, with a bronze statue of a Taoist deity. In the courtyard is a rock inscribed with the elevation of the mountain. In front of the temple is the one piece of calligraphy that you can really appreciate – the **Wordless Monument**. This one will leave you speechless. One story goes that it was set up by Emperor Wu 2100 years ago – he wasn't satisfied with what his scribes came up with, so he left it to the viewer's imagination.

The main sunrise vantage point is a springboard-shaped thing called **Gongbei Rock**; if you're lucky, visibility could extend to over 200km, as far as the coast. The sunset slides over the Yellow River side. At the rear of the mountain is **Rear Rocky Recess**, one of the better-known spots for viewing pine trees; there are some ruins tangled in the foliage. It's a good place to ramble and lose the crowds for a while.

Western Route

On this route there's nothing of note in the way of structures, but there's considerable variation in scenery, with orchards, pools and flowering plants. The major scenic attraction is **Black Dragon Pool**, which is just below **Longevity Bridge** (between the bridge and West Brook Pavilion) and is fed by a small waterfall. Swimming in the waters are some rare, red-scaled carp which are occasionally cooked for the rich.

Mythical tales revolve around this pool, which is said to be the site of underground carp palaces and of magic herbs that turn people into beasts. Worth looking into is the **Puzhao Monastery**, founded 1500 years ago along the base of the mountain.

Places to Stay & Eat

The *Zhongtianmen Guesthouse* (☎ 822-6740) *(zhōngtiānmén bīnguǎn)* is a halfway house at Zhongtianmen. Rooms are comfortable, but expensive at Y280 for a double. When we were last there we saw overwhelming evidence of a karaoke lounge which will put paid to any tranquil communion with nature you were expecting.

The *Shenqi Guesthouse* (☎ 822-3866) *(shénqí bīnguǎn)* is a three star hotel on the summit costing Y400 for doubles and Y500 for triples – expensive, but you're paying for the view. There are also quads with beds for Y60/80, but these are often full. The hotel provides extra blankets and rents out PLA-style overcoats. There's even an alarm bell which tells you when to get up for sunrise. (If you wonder where all those amazing old women go, it seems that there are lodgings – possibly former monasteries – tucked down side trails. They are off limits to foreigners.)

Tai'an section continued from page 319

Places to Stay

Budget travellers should head for the three star *Taishan Guesthouse* (☎ 822-4678; fax 822-1432) *(tàishān bīnguǎn)*, superbly located at 26 Hongmen Lu at the foot of Taishan. The three-bed dorms, which cost Y50 per person, make it a good place to round up a small group for an assault on the mountain. But if the cheap rooms are full, you'll have to fork out Y300 for a double. Dump your bags in the hotel's luggage room while you climb the mountain.

To get to the hotel, take bus No 3 or the No 3 minibus from the railway station to the second-last stop. A taxi is Y10, or grab one of the ubiquitous yellow minivans, called 'Yellow Insects' *(huángchóng)*, for the same price. Hotel touts at the railway station may drag you off to view cheap local dives – always look at the room first as they are often scuzzy.

The *Liangmao Dasha* (☎ 822-8212) *(liángmào dàshà)* is one block from the railway station. It's an OK place with a be-wildering choice of rooms, from triples at Y35 per bed to singles/doubles with bath for Y60/140. The *Longtan Hotel* (☎ 822-6511) *(lóngtán bīnguǎn)* is an average hotel in an average location; doubles are Y60 and Y80 per person.

The *Taishan Grand Hotel* (☎ 822-7211) *(tàishān dàjiǔdiàn)*, at 210 Daizhong Dajie, has doubles for Y180, Y240 and Y400. The best hotel in town is the *Overseas Chinese Hotel* (☎ 822-8112; fax 822-8171) *(huáqiáo dàshà)* on Dongyue Dajie. Equipped with four-star facilities, standard doubles cost Y788 and suites Y988.

Places to Eat

Tai'an doesn't have a great selection of places to eat, but there's some good food around all the same. Hongmen Lu, particularly the section of it between the Dai Temple and the Taishan Guesthouse, is a good area to seek out restaurants. None of them has an English menu, but you can always peek at what other diners are eating.

One of the best treats in town is the *Duck Restaurant (huìbīn cāntīng)*, south of the Dai Temple. There's no English sign, but just look out for the big restaurant with a cartoon duck on the window. You can get a whole Beijing duck for Y50, expertly carved in front of you by the chef – a bargain. The restaurant also does other dishes.

Other restaurants to look out for around town include a *California Beef Noodles King USA (měiguó jiāzhōu niúròumiàn)*, where a bowl of beef noodles *(jiāzhōu niúròumiàn)* will cost just Y6.

For more expensive cuisine, the *Overseas Chinese Hotel* caters for the international palate, with a selection of western and Chinese dishes in its many restaurants.

Getting There & Away

Bus Tai'an can be approached by road from either Ji'nan or Qufu and is worth combining with a trip to the latter.

The Tai'an-Qufu buses depart from the long-distance bus stations in both cities (two hours, roughly every hour). Only the large public buses work this route. The highway is in good condition.

Although there are a few large public buses connecting Tai'an to Ji'nan, these are overcrowded horrors and you're better off travelling by minibus (Y10, 1½ hours). In Ji'nan, departures are from the Tianqiao bus station. In Tai'an, minibuses to Ji'nan depart from in front of the railway station.

Train There are more than 20 express trains running daily through Tai'an, with links to Beijing, Harbin, Ji'nan, Nanjing, Qingdao, Shanghai, Shenyang, Xi'an and Zhengzhou.

Tai'an railway station is about 1¼ hours down the line from Ji'nan, but some special express trains don't stop at Tai'an. The town is a nine hour ride from Beijing, 11 hours from Zhengzhou and nine from Nanjing. Check the schedule to avoid arriving at some unpleasant hour like 3 am.

Tai'an and Taishan make good stopovers on the way south from Qingdao to Qufu and Shanghai. The trip takes about 9½ hours.

Getting Around
Getting around is easy. The long-distance bus station is just south of the railway station, so all local transport is directed towards these two terminals.

There are three main bus routes. Bus No 3 runs from the Taishan central route trailhead to the western route trailhead via the railway station, so that just about covers everything. Bus Nos 1 and 2 also end up near the railway station. Minibuses run on the same routes and are more comfortable, but they will leave the station only when full. You can commandeer a minibus and use it as a taxi.

Taxis and pedicabs can be found outside the railway station – the drivers practically kidnap any foreigner they see. Expect the usual problems of overcharging – most destinations around town cost Y10 to Y12.

AROUND TAI'AN
Divine Rock Temple
(língyánsì)
This temple is set in mountainous terrain in Changqing County, 20km from Tai'an. It used to be a large monastery that served many dynasties (the Tang, Song and Yuan, among others) and had 500 monks in its heyday. On view is a forest of 200 stupas and a nine storey octagonal pagoda, as well as the Thousand Buddha Temple (qiān-fódiàn), which contains 40 fine, highly individualised clay arhats – the best Buddhist statues in Shandong.

Buses to Divine Rock Temple depart from in front of the railway station in Tai'an.

QUFU
(qūfù)
Of monumental significance to the Chinese is Qufu, birthplace of Confucius, with its harmonies of carved stone, timber and fine imperial architecture. Unfortunately, Qufu has suffered a blight of tourism that would have the Great Sage pulling out the remains of his beard; prepare to wander the streets of Qufu frog-marched by map-sellers and trinket-vendors.

Following a 2000-year-old tradition, there are two fairs a year in Qufu – in spring and autumn – when the place comes alive with craftspeople, healers, acrobats, pedlars and poor peasants. Twenty-eight September is Confucius' birthday and, as you can imagine, it's a huge party. Vast phalanxes of tourists wheel around town, pursued by the local tourist industry.

The direct descendants of Confucius, the Kong family, resided in Qufu until 1948.

Information
CITS (☎ 441-2491; fax 441-2492), formerly located out of town, is back under new management, right in front of the Confucius Temple.

Confucius Temple
(kǒng miào)
The temple started out as a simple memorial hall and mushroomed into a complex one-fifth the size of Qufu. Huge extensions in the Ming and Qing dynasties are mainly responsible for its present scale. It is laid on a north-south axis, and is over 1km long. The main entrance is **Star Gate** (língxīngmén) at the south, which leads through a series of portals emblazoned with calligraphy. The third entrance gateway, with four bluish characters, refers to the doctrines of Confucius as heavenly bodies which move in circles without end; it is known as the Arch of the Spirit of the Universe.

Magnificent gnarled, twisting pines occupy the spaces between the buildings and rows of steles in the courtyards to the Confucius Temple. There are more than 1000 steles in the temple grounds, with inscriptions from Han to Qing times – the largest such collection in China. The creatures bearing the tablets of praise are actually not tortoises but bixi, dragon offspring legendary for their strength. The tablets at Qufu are noted for their fine calligraphy; a rubbing once formed part of the dowry for a Kong lady. In earlier dynasties, women were not allowed to set foot in the temple grounds; one tablet records the visit of

Confucianism

Qufu is the birth and death place of the sage Confucius (551-479 BC) whose impact was not felt in his own lifetime. He lived in abject poverty and hardly put pen to paper, but his teachings were recorded by dedicated followers (in the *Analects*). His descendants, the Kong family, fared considerably better.

Confucian ethics were adopted by subsequent rulers to keep the populace in line, and Confucian temples were set up in numerous towns run by officials. Qufu acquired the status of a holy place, with the direct descendants of Confucius as its guardian angels.

The original Confucian Temple at Qufu (dating from 478 BC) was enlarged, remodelled, added to, taken away from and rebuilt. The present buildings are from the Ming Dynasty. In 1513, armed bands sacked the temple and the Kong residence, and walls were built around the town between 1522 and 1567 to fortify it. These walls were recently removed, but vestiges of Ming town planning, like the Drum and Bell towers, remain.

More a code that defined hierarchical relationships than a religion, Confucianism has had a great impact on Chinese culture. It teaches that son must respect father, wife must respect husband, commoner must respect official, official must respect ruler, and vice versa. The essence of its teachings are obedience, respect, selflessness and working for the common good.

One would think that this code would have fitted nicely into the new order of Communism; however, it was swept aside because of its connections with the past. Confucius was seen as a kind of misguided feudal educator, and clan ties and ancestor-worship were viewed as a threat. In 1948 Confucius' direct heir, the first-born son of the 77th generation of the Kong family, fled to Taiwan, breaking a 2500-year tradition of Kong residence in Qufu.

During the Cultural Revolution the emphasis shifted to the youth of China (even if they were led by an old man). A popular anti-Confucian campaign was instigated and Confucius lost face. Many of the statues at Qufu also lost face (literally) amid cries of 'Down with Confucius, down with his wife!'. In the late 1960s a contingent of Red Guards descended on

Emperor Wuzong of the Yuan Dynasty, who brought his sister along – the first women ever to enter the Confucius Temple.

Roughly halfway along the north-south axis is the **Great Pavilion of the Constellation of Scholars**, a triple-roofed, Jin Dynasty wooden structure of ceremonial importance dating from 1190. Further north through Dacheng Gate and to the right is a juniper planted by Confucius – or so the tablet in front of it claims. The small Xingtan Pavilion up from that commemorates the spot where Confucius is said to have taught under the shade of an apricot tree.

The core of the Confucian complex is **Dacheng Hall** which, in its present form, dates from 1724; it towers 31m on a white marble terrace. The reigning sovereign permitted the importation of glazed yellow tiling for the halls in the Confucius Temple, and special stones were brought in from Xishan. The craftspeople carved the dragon-coiled columns so expertly that they had to be covered with red silk when Emperor Qianlong came to Qufu lest he felt that the Forbidden City's Taihe Hall paled in comparison. The superb stone they are carved from is called 'Fish roe stone'.

The hall was used for unusual rites in honour of Confucius. At the beginning of the seasons and on the great sage's birthday, booming drums, bronze bells and musical stones sounded from the hall as dozens of officials in silk robes engaged in 'dignified dancing' and chanting by torchlight. The rare collection of musical instruments is displayed, but the massive stone the sleepy town of Qufu, burning, defacing and destroying. Other Confucian edifices around the country were also attacked. The leader of the Guards who ransacked Qufu was Tan Houlan. She was jailed for that in 1978 and was not tried until 1982. The Confucius family archives appear to have survived the assaults intact.

Confucian ethics have made something of a comeback, presumably to instil some civic-mindedness where the Party had failed. Confucianism is finding its way back into the Shandong school system, though not by that name. Students are encouraged once again to respect their teachers, elders, neighbours and family. If there's one thing you discover quickly travelling in China, it's that respect among the Chinese has fallen to pieces. With corruption at the top of the system, the cynical young find it difficult to reciprocate respect; the elderly remain suspicious of what has passed and afraid of the street fights and arguments.

In 1979 the Qufu temples were reopened and millions of yuan were allocated for renovations and repairs. Tourism is now the name of the game; if a temple hasn't got a fresh coat of paint, new support pillars, replaced tiling or stonework, a souvenir shop or photo merchant with a Great Sage cardboard cutout, they'll get around to it soon. Some of the buildings even have electricity, with speakers hooked up to the eaves playing soothing flute music. (Emanating from the eaves is some real music – you have to stop and listen twice to make sure – yes, real birds up there!) Fully a fifth of Qufu's 50,000 residents are again claiming to be descendants of the Great Sage, though incense-burning, mound-burial and ancestor-worship are not consistent with the Party line.

Whether Confucianism can take fresh root in China is a matter for conjecture, but something is needed to fill the idealist void. A few years ago a symposium held in Qufu by Chinese scholars resulted in careful statements reaffirming the significance of Confucius' historical role, and suggesting that the 'progressive' aspects of his work were a valuable legacy which had also been cited in the writings of Mao Zedong. Confucius too, it seems, can be rehabilitated. ■

SHANDONG

statue of the bearded philosopher has disappeared – presumably a casualty of the Red Guards.

At the extreme northern end of the Confucius Temple is **Shengjidian**, a memorial hall containing a series of stones engraved with scenes from the life of Confucius and tales about him. They are copies of an older set which date back to 1592.

In the eastern compound of the Confucius Temple, behind the Hall of Poetry & Rites, is **Confucius' Well** (a Song-Ming reconstruction) and the **Lu Wall**, where the ninth descendant of Confucius hid the sacred texts during the anti-Confucian persecutions of Emperor Qin Shihuang. The books were discovered again during the Han Dynasty (206 BC-220 AD) and led to a lengthy scholastic dispute between those

who followed a reconstructive version of the last books, and those who supported the teachings in the rediscovered ones.

Entry to the Confucius Temple is Y20.

Confucius Mansions
(*kǒng fǔ*)

Situated to the east of the Confucius Temple, the Mansions date from the 16th century Ming Dynasty, with recent patchwork. The place is a maze of 450 halls, rooms and buildings, and getting around it requires a compass – there are all kinds of side passages to which servants were once restricted.

The Mansions are the most sumptuous aristocratic lodgings in China, whch is indicative of the Kong family's former great power. From the Han to the Qing dynasties,

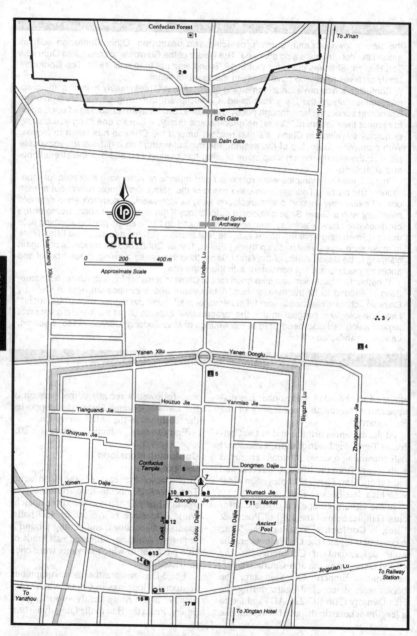

Confucian Forest

□ 1

● 2

To Ji'nan

Erlin Gate

Dalin Gate

Highway 104

Eternal Spring
Archway

Qufu

0   200   400 m
Approximate Scale

Huancheng Xilu

Lindao Lu

∴ 3

■ 4

Yanen Xilu   Yanen Donglu

🛈 5

Houzuo Jie   Yanmiao Jie

Tianguandi Jie

Shuyuan Jie

Ximen – Dajie

Zhouigongmiao Lu

Bingzha Lu

Confucius
Temple

■ 6

🛆 7

10 ■ 9
▲ 12
Zhonglou Jie

Ouqli Jie

■ 8

Wumaci Jie

Dongmen Dajie

▼ 11 Market

Gulou Dajie

Narmen Dajie

Ancient
Pool

14 ■
■ 13

Jingxuan Lu

To Railway
Station

To
Yanzhou

🛈 15

16 ■   17 ■

To Xingtan Hotel

QUFU 曲阜

1 Tomb of Confucius
  孔子墓
2 Hall for Memorial
  Ceremony
  祭奠堂
3 Ruins of the Ancient Lu
  State
  鲁国址
4 Zhougong Temple
  周公庙
5 Yanhui Temple
  颜庙
6 Confucius Mansions
  孔府
7 Drum Tower
  鼓楼
8 Xinhua Bookstore
  新华书店
9 Queli Hotel
  阙里宾舍
10 Bell Tower
   钟楼
11 Restaurants; Street Market
   餐厅、商业街
12 Tourist Souvenir Market
   旅游事业市场
13 Star Gate
   棂星门
14 CITS
   中国国际旅行社
15 Bus Station
   汽车站
16 Lüyou Hotel
   旅游宾馆
17 Confucius Mansions Hotel
   孔府饭店

the descendants of Confucius were enno-bled and granted privileges by the emper-ors. They lived like kings themselves, with 180 course meals, servants and consorts. Confucius even picked up some posthu-mous honours.

The town of Qufu, which grew around the Mansions, was an autonomous estate administered by the Kongs, who had powers of taxation and execution. Emperors could drop in to visit – the Ceremonial Gate near the south entrance was opened only for this event. Because of this royal protection, copious quantities of furniture, ceramics, artefacts, costumery and personal effects

survived and some may be viewed. The Kong family archives, a rich legacy, also seem to have survived, and extensive reno-vations of the complex have been made.

The Mansions are built on an 'interrupt-ed' north-south axis. Grouped by the south gate are the former administrative offices (taxes, edicts, rites, registration and exam-ination halls). To the north on the axis is a special gate – Neizhaimen – that seals off the residential quarters (used for weddings, banquets and private functions). East of Neizhaimen is the Tower of Refuge where the Kong clan could gather if the peasants turned nasty. It has an iron-lined ceiling on the ground floor, and a removable staircase to the 1st floor. Grouped to the west of the main axis are former recreational facilities (studies, guest rooms, libraries and small temples). To the east is the odd kitchen, an-cestral temple and the family branch apart-ments. Far to the north is a spacious garden with rockeries, ponds and bamboo groves. Kong Decheng, the last of the line, lived in the Mansions until the 1940s, when he hightailed it to Taiwan.

Entry to the Confucius Mansions is Y30.

Confucian Forest
(kǒng lín)
North of the Confucius Mansions, about 2km up Lindao Lu, is the Confucian Forest, the largest artificial park and best preserved cemetery in China. This timeworn route has a kind of 'spirit-way' lined with ancient cypresses.

It takes about 40 minutes to walk or 15 minutes to go by pedicab, or you can take bus No 1 (infrequent!). On the way, look into the Yanhui Temple *(yán miào)* which is off to the right and has a spectacular dragon head embedded in the ceiling of the main hall, plus a pottery collection. The route to the forest passes through the Eternal Spring Archway, its stone lintels decorated with coiled dragons, flying phoenixes and galloping horses dating from 1594 (Ming Dynasty). Visitors, who needed permission to enter, had to dis-mount at the Forest Gates.

SHANDONG

The pine and cypress forest of over 20,000 trees (it is said that each of Confucius' students planted a tree from his birthplace, resulting in a wide diversity) covers 200 hectares and is bounded by a wall 10km long. Buried here is the Great Sage himself and all his descendants. Flanking the approach to Confucius' Tomb are a pair of stone panthers, griffins and larger-than-life guardians. The Confucian tumulus is a simple grass mound enclosed by a low wall, and faced with a Ming Dynasty stele. Nearby are buried his immediate sons. Scattered through the forest are dozens of temples and pavilions, and hundreds of sculptures, tablets and tombstones. Even today, descendants of Confucius can still be buried in the Confucian Forest (shekels up front).

Mausoleum of Shao Hao
(shǎo hào líng)
Shao Hao was one of the five legendary emperors supposed to have ruled China 4000 years ago. His pyramidal tomb, 4km north-east of Qufu, dates from the Song Dynasty. It is made of large blocks of stone, 25m wide at the base and 6m high, and has a small temple on top. Some Chinese historians believe that Qufu was built on the ruins of Shao Hao's ancient capital, but evidence to support this is weak.

Places to Stay
There are cheap guesthouses in Qufu that *may* take you, but they are fickle. What's more, they are often difficult to find, as they display only Chinese signs – try one of the hotel touts that linger around the bus station area.

The budget option that admits foreigners, the *Confucius Mansions Hotel* (☎ 441-2686; fax 441-3786) (kǒngfǔ fàndiàn), is not far from the bus station, at 9 Datong Lu. Dorm beds are Y60 and doubles start at Y140. The words over the entrance, 'Is it not a joy to have friends come from afar?' are the opening lines of the *Analects*, a compilation of Confucius' musings by his

students. Point at it if the staff are unhelpful or insist the dorm is full.

The traditional Chinese architecture of the *Queli Hotel* (☎ 441-1956; fax 441-2022) (quèlǐ bīnshè) at 1 Queli Jie, blends in with the adjacent Confucius Temple. The hotel has comprehensive facilities with Y298 singles and Y398 doubles.

The *Xingtan Hotel* (☎ 441-2688) (xìngtán bīnguǎn) at 1 Xuequan Lu was built with tour groups in mind, and as such is badly located (far in the south of town) for individual travellers.

The *Luyou Hotel* (☎ 441-1625; fax 441-6207) (lǚyóu bīnguǎn) is a decent hotel opposite the bus station, with doubles at Y234 and suites for Y800.

Places to Eat
There is a dearth of good food in Qufu. Stalls and cheap restaurants can be found along Zhonglou Jie, and its extension, Wumaci Jie, leading off from the east of the Confucius Temple.

The *Confucius Restaurant* in the Confucius Mansions Hotel serves reasonable food. You can get coffee (Y2) and snacks at the Xinhua Bookstore, just to the south of the Drum Tower.

The name of the Great Sage is invoked in unexpected ways – Sankong (Three Confucius) beer is the local brew. Can Confucius Fried Chicken be very far behind?

Getting There & Away
Bus Buses and minibuses regularly shuttle between the railway station and the bus station in Qufu. The large buses only cost Y2, but are usually jam-packed – the minibus alternative is more comfortable for Y7. The minibuses run later, sometimes as late as 11 pm if there are passengers. Minibuses will also serve as taxis if you pay them enough.

Only the large buses go from Qufu to Tai'an (Y15, two hours, eight departures daily) and there are buses to Ji'nan every half an hour (three different types of bus at three different prices, Y14, Y17 and Y20).

Train The situation is a little confused – there's no railway station in Qufu itself. When a railway project for Qufu was first brought up, the Kong family petitioned for a change of routes, claiming that the trains would disturb the Great Sage's tomb. They won – the clan still had clout in those days – and the nearest tracks were routed to Yanzhou, 13km to the west of Qufu. But the railway builders didn't give up, and finally constructed another station about 6km east of Qufu, although still nothing in Qufu itself. Only slow trains stop here, so it is more convenient to go to Yanzhou.

When you want to buy a train ticket to Qufu, just say 'Qufu' and if the ticket clerk says '*méi yǒu*' ('don't have'), try saying 'Yanzhou'. Qufu (Yanzhou) is on the line from Beijing to Shanghai. There's a fair selection of trains, but some special express trains don't stop here; others arrive at inconvenient times like midnight. Qufu is somewhat less than two hours by train from Tai'an, three from Ji'nan, about seven from Nanjing, and about nine hours from Kaifeng.

Getting Around
There are only two bus lines and service is not frequent. Probably most useful for travellers is bus No 1 which travels along Gulou Dajie and Lindao Lu in a north-south direction, connecting the bus station area with the Confucian Forest. Bus No 2 travels east-west along Jingxuan Lu.

Pedicabs, bizarre motor-tricycles and decorated tourist horse-carts (Y15 to the Confucian Forest for the latter) swarm around, but expect to haggle.

The Luyou Hotel has bike rental: Y3 for four hours, or Y6 for eight hours.

ZOUXIAN
(zōuxiàn)
This is the home town of Mengzi (formerly spelled Mencius; 372-289 BC) who is regarded as the first great Confucian philosopher. He developed many of the ideas of Confucianism as they were later understood. Zouxian is an excellent place to visit

– far more relaxed than Qufu. Zouxian is just to the south of Qufu, a short hop on the train from Yanzhou or by bus from Qufu. A visit can easily be done as a day trip.

ZIBO
(zībó)
Zibo is a major coal-mining centre on the railway line east of Ji'nan. Over two million people live in this city, which is noted for its glassworks and porcelain. Not far from Zibo, at Linzi, a pit of horses dating back some 2500 years was excavated. They are older than the horses at Xi'an and with one big difference – they are the remains of actual animals. So far, 600 horse skeletons, probably dating from Qi times (479-502 AD), have been discovered. Horses and chariots indicated the strength of the state, so it's not surprising that they were buried (their throats slashed first) in the course of their master's funeral. About 90 horse skeletons are on display in the pit.

QINGDAO
(qīngdǎo)
Perched on the southern seaboard of the Shandong Peninsula, the picturesque town of Qingdao (Green Island) is a welcome breather from the clogging conformity of socialist town planning. Its German legacy more or less intact, Qingdao takes pride in its Bavarian appearance – the Chinese call the town 'China's Switzerland'. With its cool sea breezes, clear air, balmy evenings (in summer) and excellent seafood, this is where party cadres come to build sand castles, lick ice cream and dream of retirement. Why not do the same – foreigners who live in Qingdao unanimously love the place.

History
Qingdao was a simple fishing village until the Kaiser decided that it was high time to add to his fledgling empire in China (the killing of two German missionaries having given him sufficient pretext). In 1898, China ceded the town to Germany for 99 years and German trappings arrived

SHANDONG

Wives for Sale

As China continues to shed the austerities of the hardline Communist years, many of the old ways are returning. The Chinese are going back to their temples, burning paper money for their ancestors, playing mahjong and, in time-honoured tradition, the sale of wives in rural China is once again coming back into fashion.

Actual figures are difficult to obtain, but China's Xinhua News Agency admitted that in 1990, courts prosecuted 10,475 cases of women abducted for sale into the rural marriage market. Chinese sources admit that this number probably represents only a small percentage of actual cases.

The central problem seems to be the gangs of Chinese men who abduct young women and take them thousands of kilometres from their home towns and then sell them to rural families as brides. The going price: US$450 to US$550. The women are often drugged and raped by the gangs. It is suspected that the shame prevents many of the women from reporting what has happened to them.

Strong efforts are presently being made in China to stamp out the practice. Men who buy brides are liable to prison sentences of five to 10 years, while the traffickers face a life sentence or execution. Gang members have been publicly shot in Shandong Province for abducting women. ∎

wholesale: the famous brewery opened in 1903, electric lighting was installed, a garrison of 2000 men was stationed, missions and a university established and the railway to Ji'nan was laid.

For a city with such a short history, Qingdao has seen a lot of ping pong. In 1914, the Japanese moved into town after a successful joint Anglo-Japanese naval bombardment of the port, only to be sent packing by the Chinese in 1922. They were back in 1938, after the start of the Sino-Japanese war, but got their final marching orders in 1945; Qingdao has been Chinese ever since.

Qingdao is now China's fourth largest port and the second largest town in Shandong. Sporting both heavy and light industry, there is an entrepreneurial spirit fostered by the relative political liberalism in town. It has a population of 1.5 million, although its jurisdiction spreads over 5900 sq km and another 3.5 million people.

Orientation

Qingdao is situated on a peninsula with small bays and beaches constituting its southern coastline. The northern and eastern districts are the industrial zones, while the central district, and the area around the beaches in the south have great charm.

Information

Tourist Office The CITS office (☎ 287-9215) is in the Huiquan Dynasty Hotel at 9 Nanhai Lu, but the staff are not particularly helpful to individual travellers. Try them for tours of the brewery, shell-carving factory and locomotive factory.

For a colourful and exhaustive treatment of Qingdao's historic architecture, turn to *Far from Home: Western Architecture in China's Northern Treaty Ports* by Tess Johnston & Deke Erh (Old China Press, Hong Kong).

PSB The PSB office (☎ 286-2787) is at 29 Hubei Lu, very close to the Overseas Chinese Hotel.

The entrance to the compound is a beautiful old German building with a clock tower, but the ugly office block behind it is where the PSB does its business.

Money You can change money in any of the large hotels. The Bank of China is at 62 Zhongshan Lu.

Post & Communications The main post office is just south of the Bank of China on Zhongshan Lu.

Things to See
The wonderful castle-like villa at the eastern end of the No 2 Beach is **Huashilou** (huāshílóu), the former German governor's residence, a replica of a German palace. Built in 1903, it is said to have cost 2,450,000 taels of silver. When Kaiser Wilhelm II got the bill, he immediately recalled the extravagant governor and sacked him. The Chinese call it the 'Chiang Kaishek Building', as the generalissimo secretly stayed here in 1947. Around the back is a terrace where the German governor used to play tennis with his lackeys, and the garage where they used to park the Mercedes. It's well worth the Y5 entry fee to patrol the gardens, the reception rooms and climb to the roof for an excellent view of the sea (to really get in the mood, smuggle in a miniature of schnapps to have on the balcony).

To the right of Xinhaoshan Park remains one of Qingdao's most astounding pieces of German architecture, the **Xinhao Hill Hotel** (xìnhàoshān yíng bīnguǎn), overdone in the chunky Bavarian style. Not only did the German governor hang out here, but Chairman Mao did as well, although not simultaneously. Take a peek at the interior which has a gorgeous wooden staircase and balcony – the German grand piano was made in 1876 (the factory that made it was blitzed in WWII).

The twin-spired **Catholic Church** (tiānzhǔ jiàotáng), up a steep hill off Zhongshan Lu, is an imposing edifice with a light bulb-encrusted cross on the roof. The crosses were torn off the steeples during the Cultural Revolution, but God-fearing locals snaffled them and buried them in the hills. The church still has regular Sunday services. The area around the church is rich in architectural textures and is worth exploring. A daily fish market, featuring colourful exotica from the depths, sets up on the cobbled street of Feicheng Lu that leads up to the church.

The other main church is the **Protestant Church** (jīdū jiàotáng), opposite the southwestern entrance to Xinhaoshan Park. This German structure is simple yet attractive; the white clock face on the green tower is still inscribed with the manufacturer's name, 'J.F.Weule, Bockenem am Harz'. If you knock on the door, the Chinese priest will probably show you round and inform you that he has a congregation of 1000 people every Sunday. The interior is typically spartan, but worth a look.

Beaches
(hǎishuǐ yùchǎng)
Qingdao is famous for its beaches, numbering six in all, which are extremely popular with the Chinese. The beaches are not bad, and can make for a pleasant stroll, but don't go expecting a surfer's paradise. June to September is the main swimming season, when 60,000 to 70,000 sunseekers gather on the sand. The beaches are sheltered and are equipped with changing sheds. Shark nets, lifeguards, lifeboat patrols and medical stations conspire to make you feel safe.

Just around the corner from the railway station is the **No 6 Bathing Beach**. A lively area in the morning, jostling with Taiji exponents, frisbee-throwers and joggers, it neighbours **Zhanqiao**, a pier reaching out into the bay and overlooking the lighthouse on **Little Green Island** which lends its name to Qingdao (the pier is a famous landmark that crops up on the label of Tsingtao beer). Next to the jetty sit sunburned boat ticket vendors for tours around the bay and beyond (Y10).

Continuing east, around the headland and the lighthouse is Lu Xun Park (lǔ xùn gōngyuán), where hard-sell types will try to force you on to dangerous-looking speedboats for greased lightning tours of the beaches (Y60). This area is also chock-a-block with lifeless museums such as the

SHANDONG

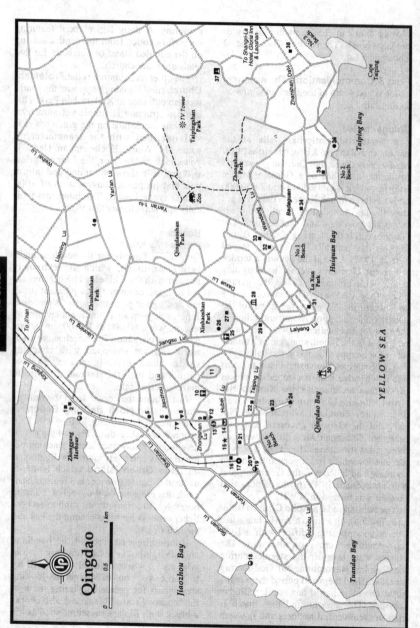

QINGDAO 青岛

PLACES TO STAY
1 Friendship Hotel;
   Store
   友谊宾馆、商店
2 Peace Hotel
   和平宾馆
9 Qingdao Hotel
   青岛饭店
16 Jinhai Hotel
   金海大酒店
21 Overseas Chinese Hotel
   华侨饭店
22 Zhanqiao Guesthouse
   栈桥宾馆
27 Xinhao Hill Hotel
   信号山迎宾馆
29 Dongfang Hotel
   东方饭店
31 Rongshao Hotel
   荣韶宾馆
32 Huiyuan Hotel
   汇原饭店
33 Huanghai Hotel;
   China Eastern Airlines
   黄海饭店、东方航空
34 Huiquan Dynasty Hotel;
   CITS
   汇泉王朝大酒店、
   中国国际旅行社

35 Badaguan Hotel
   八大关宾馆
38 Haitian Hotel
   海天大酒店

PLACES TO EAT
7 Chunhelou Restaurant
   春和楼饭店
8 Qinghai Muslim
   Restaurant
   青海穆斯林饭庄
12 KFC
   肯德鸡
20 KFC
   肯德鸡

OTHER
3 Passenger Ferry
   Terminal
   青岛港客运站
4 Brewery
   青岛啤酒厂
5 Foreign Language
   Bookstore
   外文书店
6 Xinhua Bookstore
   新华书店
10 Catholic Church
   天主教堂
11 Guanhaishan Park
   观海山公园

13 Bank of China
   中国银行
14 Main Post Office
   邮电局
15 PSB
   公安局外事科
17 Railway Station;
   Railway Hotel
   铁道大厦、火车站
18 Local Ferry
   青岛轮渡站
19 Long-Distance Buses
   长途汽车站
23 Zhanqiao
   栈桥
24 Huilan Pavilion
   回澜阁
25 Protestant Church
   基督教堂
26 Longshan Underground
   Market
   龙山地下商场
28 Qingdao Museum
   青岛博物馆
30 Little Green Island
   小青岛
36 Huashilou
   花石楼
37 Zhanshan Temple
   湛山寺

SHANDONG

Marine Museum & Aquarium and the Naval Museum.

The sand of **No 1 Bathing Beach** is coarse-grained, engulfed in seaweed and bordered by concrete beach huts and bizarre statues of dolphins. Past the Huiquan Dynasty Hotel and the Ocean Research Institute is the **Badaguan** (*bādà-guān*) area, well known for its sanatoriums and exclusive guesthouses. The spas are scattered in lush wooded zones off the coast, and the streets, named after passes (Badaguan literally means Eight Passes Area), are each lined with a different tree or flower. On Jiayuguan Lu it's maple and on Zhengyangguan it's myrtle. The locals simply call them Peach St, Snowpine St or Crab Apple St. This is a lovely area in which to stroll.

As you head out of the Eight Passes

Area, Nos 2 and 3 bathing beaches are just east, and the villas lining the headlands are exquisite. **No 2 Bathing Beach** is cleaner, quieter and more sheltered than No 1 Beach.

Parks

Qingdao has a splendid collection of parks that are worth exploring. Wandering from park to park is an excellent way of escaping the bustle and offers a diversion down Qingdao's lovely streets. The charm of **Guanhaishan Park** (*guānhǎishān gōngyuán*) lies in finding it – the way winds up a small hill through restful lanes; just keep going up as the park sits at the top. The park used to be a golf course for the Germans, although the park is minute. The white trigrams marked out on the paving

stones at the top are for the practise of a secretive internal martial art called Bagua
zhang (Eight trigram palm).

Down the hill and to the east is Xinhaoshan Park *(xìnhàoshān gōngyuán)*, whose
summit is graced with the carbuncular golf-
ball-shaped towers known as the mushroom buildings *(mógu lóu)*. Beneath the
park is the Longshan Underground Market
(lóngshān dìxià shāngyè jiē), a tunnel complex given over to selling tacky clothes.
Minibus No 26 can take you to Xinhaoshan
Park.

North of the Huiquan Dynasty Hotel is
Zhongshan Park *(zhōngshān gōngyuán)*,
which covers 80 hectares, has a teahouse
and temple and in springtime is a heavily
wooded profusion of flowering shrubs and
plants.

The mountainous area north-east of
Zhongshan Park is called **Taipingshan
Park** *(tàipíngshān gōngyuán)*, an area of
walking paths, pavilions and Qingdao's
largest temple, Zhanshan Temple *(zhànshān
sì)*. The park also houses the TV Tower
(diànshìtǎ), which has an express lift up to
fabulous views of the city (Y40). You can
reach the tower via cable car. This is the
best area in town for hiking.

Just west of Taipingshan Park is **Qing-
daoshan Park** *(qīngdǎoshān gōngyuán)*.
A notable feature of this hilly park is Jingshan Fort *(jǐngshān pàotái)*.

Brewery
(qīngdǎo píjiǔchǎng)
No guide to Qingdao would be complete
without a mention of the brewery, tucked
into the industrial part of town, inland and
east of the main harbour. Tsingtao beer
(Tsingtao is the old spelling for Qingdao)
has gained a worldwide following.

The brewery was established early this
century by the Germans who still supply
the parts for 'modernisation' of the system.
The flavour of the finest brew in Asia
comes from the mineral waters of nearby
Laoshan. Unfortunately, unless you are on
a tour, it's almost impossible to get into the
brewery for a look.

Special Events
The summer months see Qingdao overrun
with tourists, particularly in the second and
third weeks of July, when the annual trade
fair is held. Other festivals to look out for
are the Beer Festival in August. Gardeners
may be interested to note that Qingdao's
Radish Festival is in January, the Cherry
Festival is in May, while grapes get their
say in September (Qingdao is a major producer of wine).

Places to Stay – budget
If you arrive during the trade fair, be prepared to be forced into accommodation
more expensive than you bargained for.

The *Railway Hotel* (☎ 286-9963) *(tiědào
dàshà)*, 2 Tai'an Lu, is the ugly duckling
that adjoins the railway station. Dorm beds
cost from Y40. If these are fully booked,
you may be forced into standard doubles
which costs Y200 to Y280.

The hulking building further up on the
left at 2 Tai'an Lu is the *Jinhai Hotel*
(☎ 288-7788) *(jīnhǎi dàjiǔdiàn)*. They
decided, after much tutting and frowning,
that they take foreigners, so it might be
worth a look. Dorm beds start at Y35 and
doubles come in at Y200.

The *Friendship Hotel* (☎ 282-8165)
(yǒuyì bīnguǎn) is next door to the passenger ferry terminal on Xinjiang Lu. Dorm
beds are Y40. It has doubles at Y80 (no
bathroom), doubles with shower for Y120
and doubles with air-con and bathroom for
Y160. To get there from the railway
station, take bus No 8, which passes the
hotel. Alternatively, a taxi costs Y7.

The *Peace Hotel* (☎ 283-0154) *(hépíng
bīnguǎn)* is down an alley to the left of the
passenger ferry terminal – almost behind
the Friendship Hotel. Doubles with no
bathroom cost Y110, and with bathroom
Y270 to Y300. It's a reasonably popular
place and has a restaurant.

Finally, not far from No 1 Beach, the
Huiyuan Hotel (☎ 288-4233) *(huìyuán
dàjiǔdiàn)*, at 1 Qixia Lu, has a limited
number of budget rooms in an annex next
to a kindergarten. It's a quiet pension-like

place and showers are available in the Huiyuan Hotel at 7 pm. A bed in a simple double costs Y40. Ask for the *hòupèilóu* at the front desk of the Huiyuan. From the station, take a No 6 bus to the *xiǎoyúshān gōngyuán* stop. A taxi costs Y7.

Places to Stay – middle

Most of the accommodation that should be mid-range is dangerously upmarket in price, especially during peak season, and the range of hotels leaves a lot to be desired. Other mid-range hotels have priced themselves into the top-end bracket, where they don't belong.

Just across the road from Lu Xun Park is a glorified cottage called the *Rongshao Hotel* (☎ 287-0710) (*róngshào bīnguǎn*). You will probably need a torch for the incredibly murky reception area – shine it at the tariff board to reveal doubles from Y300. Not revealed is the 50% surcharge for foreigners.

The *Qingdao Hotel* (☎ 289-1888) (*qīngdǎo fàndiàn*) is at 53 Zhongshan Lu, but the entrance is around the corner on Qufu Lu. Very much for the Chinese, it has recently been refurbished, but the gloss is skin-deep and the tack shows through. Doubles come in at Y380. The cheaper and more down-at-heel hotel of the same name is next door.

Places to Stay – top end

Qingdao is swarming with top-end accommodation, most of it overpriced and aimed at Chinese on expense accounts and Chinese tourists who think having a holiday involves blowing your life savings on a hotel room. Furthermore, some hotels are set up overnight by inexperienced entrepreneurs eager to make a fast buck, and the resulting top-end look is veneer at best.

Just about to open when we were in Qingdao was the *Shangri-La Hotel* (☎ 388-3838; fax 388-6868) (*xiānggélǐlā jiǔdiàn*) which can be found at 9 Zhanliugan Lu. The hotel will almost certainly offer the best services and facilities in town.

Probably the hotel with the most charac-

ter and history is the *Xinhao Hill Hotel* (☎ 286-6209; fax 286-1985) (*xìnhàoshān yíng bīnguǎn*) at 26 Longshan Lu, next to Xinhaoshan Park. A converted former German mansion, it is splendid inside and out. Doubles start at Y600 (see the earlier Things to See section).

Other top-end options include:

Badaguan Hotel (☎ 387-2168; fax 387-1383) (*bādàguān bīnguǎn*), 19 Shanhaiguan Lu; rooms from US$80, villas also available
Dongfang Hotel (☎ 286-5888; fax 286-2741) (*dōngfāng fàndiàn*), 4 Daxue Lu; doubles from Y800
Gloria Inn (☎ 387-8855; fax 386-4640) (*kǎilái guójì jiǔdiàn*), 21 Donghai Lu
Haitian Hotel (☎ 387-1888; fax 387-1777) (*hǎitiān dàjiǔdiàn*), 39 Xianggang Xilu; doubles from US$110
Huanghai Hotel (☎ 287-0215; fax 287-9795) (*huánghǎi fàndiàn*), 75 Yan'an 1-Lu; doubles from Y550
Huiquan Dynasty Hotel (☎ 287-3366; fax 287-1122) (*huìquán wángcháo dàjiǔdiàn*), 9 Nanhai Lu; singles Y670, doubles from Y840
Overseas Chinese Hotel (☎ 287-9738; fax 287-0739) (*huáqiáo fàndiàn*), 72 Hunan Lu; good location, doubles from Y374
Zhanqiao Guesthouse (☎ 287-0936) (*zhànqiáo bīnguǎn*), 31 Taiping Lu; doubles from US$60

Places to Eat

Qingdao is overrun with good food. The locals are crazy about kebabs, which is understandable as they are delicious! You can buy them (Y1.5 each) from the ubiquitous street stalls – they are usually made from pork (*zhūròuchuàn*), or sometimes lamb (*yángròuchuàn*), and you get about five crisp chunks per skewer, all done to a nice crisp. You can get them spicy (*là*) or not (*bùlà*). These places usually sell beer and soft drinks as well, as well as giving you a stool to perch on while you feast. Go for the popular ones where the crowds gather (especially on Zhongshan Lu). Another favourite is squid on a stick (*diànkǎo yóuyú*).

The waterfront area is brimming with restaurants, from No 6 Beach almost all the way to No 1 Beach. The area around No 1 Beach is the best place to come up with

SHANDONG

cheap eats, however. Any of the seaside restaurants serve up fresh seafood; the mussels *(gǎ la)* are excellent, and a plate of these will cost you about Y12. Sea snails *(hǎiluó)* are also popular (Y20 per plate).

Zhongshan Lu is also a good area for restaurants. Just up the road from the very prominent *KFC* (there's another branch opposite the railway station) is a Muslim restaurant, the *Qinghai Muslim Restaurant (qīnghǎi mùsīlín fànzhuāng)*. It's at 31 Dexuan Lu.

There's no English sign, but you can't miss the Islamic script. Again, there's no English menu, but try the *yángròu pàomó*, a dish that involves breaking chapatti-like bread into a bowl and then adding a mutton broth – delicious and cheap.

More expensive options include the *Chunhelou* (☎ 282-7371) *(chūnhélóu)*, at 146 Zhongshan Lu, which is one of Qingdao's most famous eateries. The revolving restaurant in the *TV Tower (diànshìtǎ)* in Taipingshan Park offers reasonable food and great views of Qingdao, although the lift to the restaurant costs Y40 (the food has a preset charge of Y60 per person).

The *Shangri-La Hotel* (☎ 388-3838) will no doubt offer a wide range of Chinese and international cuisine, all done to a high standard.

Getting There & Away

Air The CAAC office (☎ 287-0057) is at 29 Zhongshan Lu. The booking office of China Eastern Airlines (☎ 287-0215) is adjacent to the Yellow Sea Hotel at 75 Yan'an 1-Lu. Larger hotels like the Huiquan Dynasty Hotel have airline ticket offices. Another useful phone number is airport enquiries (☎ 484-3331, 484- 2139).

There are five flights a week between Qingdao and Hong Kong (Y2560), and there are also direct flights to Seoul (Y1950). Air Macau flies three times a week to Macau (Y2120).

Destinations in China include Shanghai (Y680), Beijing (Y640), Shenzhen (Y2140), Zhuhai (Y1990) and Haikou (Y2200).

Bus Buses and minibuses depart from the area next to the massive Hualian Building just across from the railway station. Minibuses to Yantai (Y28) leave every 30 minutes and take 3½ hours for the journey. There are also departures every 30 minutes to Ji'nan (Y50) which take 4½ hours (which is cheaper and faster than by train). Daily sleeper buses leave at midday to Shanghai (Y150); sleepers to Beijing are also available.

Train All trains from Qingdao go through the provincial capital of Ji'nan, except for the direct Qingdao-Yantai trains. Tickets to Ji'nan cost Y27. There are two direct trains daily to Beijing (Y101). Sleepers can be bought with some persistence at the railway station – at least Qingdao has a wonderful old German ticket office! Bear in mind, if you are travelling to Yantai or Ji'nan it is quicker and cheaper to take a bus.

Direct trains to Shenyang (about 26 hours) pass through Ji'nan and Tianjin, sidestepping Beijing. There are direct trains to Xi'an (about 31 hours) which continue to Lanzhou and Xining. Trains to Guangzhou take 39 hours and cost Y152.

There is one daily train to Shanghai (Y149) which takes 24 hours; it goes via Nanjing and takes almost the same time as the boat. There is one train daily to Shanghai. It's worth bearing in mind that the train is more expensive than the boat.

One train daily goes to Yantai (Y21) which take four hours. There are more regular departures by bus so it makes more sense to do it that way.

Boat There are regular boats from Qingdao to Shanghai and Inch'ŏn in South Korea. Boats for Inch'ŏn leave on Monday and Thursday at 4 pm, take 20 hours and tickets cost Y1100. The boat to Shanghai leaves on even days of the month at noon and tickets range from Y60 to Y300; the trip takes 26 hours and you can upgrade once on the boat. Bookings for all of these can be made at the passenger ferry terminal in the north of town. Inch'ŏn ferries can also be booked at the Huiquan Dynasty Hotel.

The boat service to Dalian has been suspended, so the best way to get there is to take the train or bus to Yantai and then continue by boat – see the Yantai section later in this chapter for details.

Getting Around

To/From the Airport Qingdao's antiquated airport is 30km from the city. Taxi drivers ask Y100 (or whatever they think you might possibly pay) for the journey. Buses leave from the China Eastern Airlines ticket office, but ask first about the schedule – it's not frequent.

Bus Most transport needs can be catered for by the bus No 6 route, which starts at the northern end of Zhongshan Lu, runs along it to within a few blocks of the main railway station and then east to the area above No 3 Beach. Bus No 26 from the railway station runs along the coast, past Zhongshan Park before heading north at the end of No 3 beach. Minibuses also follow these routes (Y2).

Taxi Qingdao taxis are among the cheapest in China; Y7 will get you almost anywhere around town.

AROUND QINGDAO

Forty kilometres east of Qingdao is **Laoshan** (láoshān), a famous Taoist retreat equipped with cable-car facilities, temples and plunging waterfalls. Covering some 400 sq km, this is where Laoshan mineral water starts its life and it's an excellent place to go hiking or climbing. The mountain is associated with Taoist legend and myth, with the central attraction being the Song Dynasty Taiqing Palace (a Taoist monastery); there are paths leading to the summit of Laoshan from there. With such a large area there's plenty to explore.

Due north of the Taiqing Palace is Jiushui, noted for its numerous streams and waterfalls. An early-morning bus runs from Qingdao railway station to the Taiqing Palace. Bus No 304 also goes to Laoshan from Taiping Lu.

About 20 minutes away by boat from Qingdao and a further 20 minutes by minibus is the lovely beach of **Huangdao** (huángdǎo or Yellow Island), which is very popular with locals, but not well known to outsiders. Much cleaner and of higher quality than the rest of Qingdao's beaches, Huangdao is the place to go if you want to escape the crowds. The ferry (Y5) leaves from the local ferry terminal (qīngdǎo lúndùzhàn) to the west of the railway station.

YANTAI
(yāntái)
Yantai, alias Zhifu (at one time spelled Chefoo), is a busy ice-free port on the northern coast of the Shandong Peninsula. It's a very dull town, and the only real reason to come here would be to take a boat to Pusan in South Korea.

History
Like Qingdao, Yantai started life as a defence outpost and fishing village. It opened for foreign trade in 1862, but had no foreign concessions. Several nations, Japan and the USA among them, had trading establishments here and Yantai was something of a resort area at one time. Since 1949 the port and naval base at Yantai have been expanded and, apart from fishing and trading, the town is a major producer of wines, spirits and fruits. Yantai means Smoke Terrace: wolf-dung fires were lit on the headland to warn fishing fleets of approaching pirates.

Information
There is a CTS office (☎ 624-5625) in the crumbling edifice next to the Overseas Chinese Guesthouse, but it's unlikely the staff will be able help you.

There is a branch of the Bank of China just south of Yantaishan Park near No 1 Beach. The main post office is on the roundabout at the junction of Nan Dajie and Dahaiyang Lu.

SHANDONG

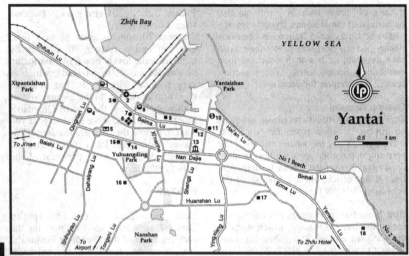

Things to See

Yantai has a few nondescript beaches that can fill an afternoon if you are stranded here. However, the beaches aren't as good as Qingdao's – they're unsheltered and prone to heavy wind-lashing. No 1 Beach has dirty water, gritty sand, ghastly modern statues and speedboats for hire (Y10). No 2 Beach, out by the Zhifu Hotel, is smaller and more pleasant, but difficult to get to.

Elsewhere, the odd colonial remnant pitches a last struggle against an encroaching mass of workers' flats.

Places to Stay

The *Tiedao Hotel* (☎ 625-6588) *(tiědào dàshà)*, is on your right as you exit the railway station. There's no English sign, but you can't miss it – it's the vast shape on the right with the clock tower. It has good facilities and service. A bed in a basic dorm goes for Y30 to Y40, although you will probably have to be in a group for these. Basic doubles are Y120 (without bathroom), and standard doubles (bathroom, air-con etc) come in at Y220. The nearby International Seaman's Club is the focus of

interest for Yantai's prostitutes, who lounge around painting their nails and adjusting their outrageous wigs in the vicinity of the Tiedao Hotel.

The *Golden Shell Hotel* (☎ 621-6495) *(jīnxiáng dàjiŭdiàn)* at 172 Beima Lu is a 10 minute walk from the railway station. There are two buildings – the first you come to has cheap doubles from Y148 and triples for Y228, while the one next door is more plush and has luxury rooms starting at Y198.

· The best hotel in Yantai is the *Shandong Pacific Hotel* (☎ 620-6888; fax 621-5204) *(tàipíngyáng dàjiŭdiàn)*, which features a bowling alley, billiards room and other four star facilities and has doubles from Y660.

Other possibilities include:

Asia Hotel (☎ 624-7888; fax 624-2625) *(yàxìyà dàjiŭdiàn)*; doubles from Y488
Overseas Chinese Guesthouse (☎ 622-4431; fax 621-6124) *(huáqiáo bīnguǎn)*, 30 Huanshan Lu; doubles from Y280
Yantai Hotel (☎ 688-8468; fax 688-8169) *(yāntái dàjiŭdiàn)*, 1 Huanshan Lu; doubles from Y388

YANTAI 烟台

PLACES TO STAY
9 Golden Shell Hotel
金翔大酒店
12 Shandong Pacific Hotel
太平洋大酒店
15 Asia Hotel
亚细亚大酒店
16 Yuhuangding Hotel
毓璜顶宾馆
17 Overseas Chinese
Guesthouse; CTS
华侨宾馆、中国旅行社
18 Yantai Hotel
烟台大酒店

PLACES TO EAT
14 Not KFC
烟台之肯德鸡

OTHER
1 Buses to Penglai
去蓬称娴
2 Railway Station;
Tiedao Hotel
火车站、铁道大厦
3 CAAC
中国民航
4 Long-Distance Bus Station
长途汽车站
5 Main Post Office
电信大楼
6 Friendship Store
友谊商店
7 International Seamen's
Club
国际海员俱乐部
8 Boat Ticket Office;
Departures
烟台港客运站
10 Bank of China
中国银行
11 Foreign Languages
Bookstore
外文书店
13 Museum
博物馆

Yuhuangding Hotel (☎ 624-4401; fax 624-2788) *(yùhuángdǐng bīnguǎn)*, 17 Yuhuangding Xilu; doubles from Y298

Zhifu Hotel (☎ 688-8288; fax 688-8289) *(zhīfú bīnguǎn)*, 1 Yingbin Lu; doubles from Y320

Places to Eat
The railway station area has a reasonable selection of restaurants. The *'fast-food' restaurant* next to the Asia Hotel serves up decent Chinese food.

Locals insist there's a KFC in town – when you take a taxi there you find it's a greasy stall with spitting rotisseries laden with whole chickens. We have called the place *Not KFC*. Don't be put off, the *kebab outlet* next door is finger-lickin' good, especially if you've picked up the habit from Qingdao. The crowds here can be unbelievable – the finished kebab skewers are poked into a bucket on the pavement, which looks like a huge porcupine. You can find it on the corner of Sida Jie and Nanda Jie, opposite a department store.

Getting There & Away
Air One flight a week goes to Seoul (Y1990) and two flights a week go to Hong Kong. A large number of domestic destinations includes two flights daily to both Beijing and Shanghai, three flights a week to Guangzhou, and regular flights to Shenzhen. Flight bookings can be made next door to the Tiedao Hotel or at the CAAC office (☎ 622-5908) on the corner of Dahaiyang Lu and Beima Lu.

Bus There are frequent minibuses between Yantai and Qingdao (Y28). In both Qingdao and Yantai, buses congregate in front of the railway stations and depart when full. The journey takes 3½ hours on an excellent highway (the roads in Shandong are the best in China).

Train The Yantai-Qingdao (Y21) train takes four hours and there is only one service daily. The train terminates in Qingdao – it does not carry on to Ji'nan. Two trains daily terminate in Ji'nan, while the trains to Beijing (once daily) and Shanghai (once daily) pass through.

Boat At the ferry office next to the railway station it is possible to book tickets for express boats to Dalian (Y149) which have

SHANDONG

Yantai KFC

Was there a KFC in Yantai? Pumping her arms like a chicken and even going so far as to stand on one foot, the aged map-seller outside the railway station assured us there was. Unfortunately, she couldn't put her finger on where it was.

You mean the greasy chicken place? The taxi driver knew exactly where it was and said he would get us there in five minutes. The streets of Yantai streamed by and we found ourselves dumped in the centre of town, standing in a cloud of dust as the taxi pounced on another fare. The familiar red and white logo of KFC and the colonel's reassuring smile were nowhere to be seen; even the tacky strains of an instrumental cover of 'I Just Called to Say I Love You' were curiously absent.

Asking at the nearest shop, we were directed up the road and further along we were directed back again. The table tennis continued for a while until a wave of disappointment deposited us on the pavement outside a hole-in-the-wall parlour, where a chef stood, cross-armed, overseeing rows of copper-skinned oily roast chickens sizzling on sheets of aluminium foil. He had obviously been watching us with mounting anticipation.

Despite knowing how the conversation would inevitably fall into place, I wearily asked if this was KFC. It certainly was, came the confident reply. Parrying his self-assured words and demonstrating that his greasy shack wasn't quite on a par with the fast-food emporium found in Beijing, he came back with the indisputable words, 'Well, it's KFC to us'. ■

---

five departures daily; the trip takes 3½ hours. There are also three slow boats a day to Dalian (Y108 to Y162). Boats for Tianjin leave at 4 pm, on even days of the month. Boats to Pusan in South Korea (US$120 to US$200) leave every Thursday at 11 am. Another destination in Korea is Qunshan; boats leave every Monday (US$120 to US$200).

Getting Around

Yantai's airport is 15km south of the city. A taxi should cost about Y70 from the railway station area. Airport buses cost Y10.

The city bus system is for the most part frustrating; the basic fare for a taxi is Y6.

PENGLAI

(pénglái)

About 65km north-west of Yantai by road is the coastal castle of Penglai, a place of the gods often referred to in Chinese mythology. China's ancient legend of the Eight Immortals Crossing The Sea originated here. The castle *(pénglái gé)* is perched on a clifftop overlooking the sea and is about a thousand years old. Here you can discover a fascinating array of small castles and temples and wonderful views of flotillas of fishing boats bouncing out to sea. Many of the temples, adjoining walls and pavilions are delightfully overgrown with ivy and creepers. The natural harmonies of the place are unfortunately jarred by foraging tour groups.

Besides the castle, Penglai is famous for an optical illusion which the locals claim appears every few decades. The last full mirage seen from the castle was in July 1981 when two islands appeared, with roads, trees, buildings, people and vehicles. This phenomenon lasted about 40 minutes.

There are some pebbly beaches in the area, but Penglai isn't considered ideal for bathing. A cable car crosses from the castle to the cliffs opposite.

There are a few hotels for those who can't handle the return trip to Yantai. The *Penglai Hotel* (☎ 564-2411) *(pénglái bīnguǎn)* has doubles from Y180. The *Pengxiang Hotel* (☎ 565-6788) *(péngxiáng dàshà)* has doubles from Y220.

It's a bit of a haul getting to Penglai – it's a two hour bus ride from Yantai. Minibuses to Penglai (Y8) depart from a bus station on the corner of Bei Malu and Qingnian Lu, about a five minute walk to the right from the railway station. Entry to the castle and its environs is Y40.

WEIHAI
(wēihǎi)
About 60km east of Yantai by road is the obscure port city of Weihai. The British had a concession here, although little remains today to remind you of its colonial heritage.

If you arrive in Weihai, you will probably want to exit swiftly – there is nothing to see. The only reason to come here is to avail yourself of its passenger ferry service to Inch'ŏn in South Korea, but you can do this in Qingdao. The boat leaves at 5 pm on Wednesday, Friday and Sunday, arriving in Inch'ŏn at 8.30 am the next day. There are a variety of ticket prices (2nd class costs Y930; the suite costs Y3360). In the other direction, the boat leaves Inch'ŏn for Weihai at the same time on Tuesday, Thursday and Saturday, arriving in Weihai at 8 am (then you can jump on a bus and vamoose).

If you arrive in Weihai without having purchased a ferry ticket in advance, the place to go is CITS (☎ 522-6210), at 44 Dongcheng Lu. Minibuses run from the long-distance bus station in Weihai directly to Yantai (Y12), Qingdao (Y40) and Ji'nan (Y62). Sleeper coaches also run to Shanghai (Y198) and Beijing (Y140).

SHANDONG

Jiangsu 江苏

Jiangsu Facts & Highlights

Area: 102,600 sq km

Population: 71.1 million

Capital: Nanjing

Highlights

- Nanjing's Zijinshan, with its wealth of historical sights.
- Suzhou, a city of canals and beautiful traditional gardens, despite the ravages of redevelopment.
- Lake Tauhu, a large shallow lake with some 90 islands.

With China's most productive land, Jiangsu *(jiāngsū)* is symbolic of agricultural abundance and has long been known as 'the land of fish and rice' – these two pictographs are even contained in the original Chinese character for the province. The southern part of Jiangsu lies within the Yangzi Basin, a tapestry landscape of greens, yellows and blues contrasting with whitewashed farmhouses. Woven into this countryside is a concentration of towns and cities with one of the highest levels of industrial output in China.

As far back as the 16th century, the towns on the Grand Canal set up industrial bases for silk production and grain storage, and are still ahead of the rest of the nation. While heavy industry is based in Nanjing and Wuxi, the other towns concentrate more on light industry, machinery and textiles. They're major producers of electronics and computer components, and haven't been blotted out by the scourges of coal mining or steelworks.

Today, southern Jiangsu is increasingly being drawn into the rapidly expanding economy of nearby Shanghai, aided in part by the completion of a new expressway between Nanjing and Shanghai. It's one of the most rapidly developing provinces in China, evident in the fast rate of construction in the major cities.

The stretch from Nanjing down to Hangzhou in Zhejiang Province is heavily touristed, but north of the Yangzi there's not really much to talk about; it's a complete contrast – decayed, backward and lagging behind the rest of the province. In the north the major port is situated at Lianyungang and there's a big coal works in Xuzhou.

Jiangsu is hot and humid in summer, yet has overcoat temperatures in winter (when visibility can drop to zero). Rain or drizzle can be prevalent in winter, but it's gentle rain, adding a misty, soft touch to the land. The natural colourings can be spectacular in spring. Heavy rains fall in spring and summer, but autumn is fairly dry.

NANJING
(nánjīng)

Nanjing (population approximately 4.5 million) is one of China's more attractive major cities. It sports a long historical heritage and has twice served briefly as the nation's capital, firstly in the early years of the Ming Dynasty (1368-1644) and secondly as the capital of the PRC in the early years of the 20th century. Most of Nanjing's major attractions are reminders of the city's former glory under the Ming.

Like many other major Chinese cities, Nanjing is rapidly developing; cranes dom-

inate the skyline as skyscrapers are constructed at a swift pace. Nanjing is home to several colleges and universities, and a large foreign student population. There is an abundance of western-style restaurants, a lively nightlife and access to just about any amenity from around the world.

Just east of the city is Zijinshan (Purple Mountain), where it's possible to spend a pleasant day hiking and swimming.

History
The Nanjing area has been inhabited for about 5000 years, and a number of prehistoric sites have been discovered in or around the city. Recorded history, however, begins in the Warring States Period (453-221 BC), when Nanjing emerged as a strategic object of conflict. The arrival of a victorious Qin Dynasty (221-207 BC) put an end to this, allowing Nanjing to prosper as a major administrative centre.

The city's fortunes took a turn for the worse in the 6th century, however, when it was successively rocked by floods, fires, peasant rebellions and military conquest.

Where are You From?

As an Asian American with ethnic roots in China's Jiangsu Province, the prospect of travelling to the land of my ancestors to research this book brought up a lot of cultural identity issues for me. Previous experiences travelling in China and living in Hong Kong led me to anticipate being unfairly judged by those with a narrow definition of what it means to be Chinese. In my case, being of Chinese descent but having grown up in the west and not able to speak Chinese, I've been described as a 'banana', a derogatory term meaning 'white' on the inside and 'yellow' on the outside. I expected feelings of guilt and inadequacy to rise to the surface; however, I was pleasantly surprised by my experiences on this trip.

Travellers are often asked where they are from, and China is no exception. Instead of answering, I would ask people to guess. Their answer was usually Korean or Japanese, sometimes Chinese. When I would tell them that I'm American, the response was always, 'No, you don't look American'. I'd explain that my father was originally from China, and that I was born in the USA. 'Oh', people would say, 'you're Chinese'. I learned there was a much shorter way of conveying all this information – *meiji huayi*, meaning someone of Chinese descent who was born and raised outside China. The term for Chinese like my father is *huachao*, or *meiji huachao*, meaning born in China, but now living abroad in the USA. *Hua ren* refers to all people of Chinese ancestry, no matter where they were born, grew up or live.

While in China I met a lot of huayi with different backgrounds. It reminded me that more and more Chinese are living further away from China, and that it's becoming more common to meet people with complex ethnic and racial backgrounds. On my short trip I met someone who was born in Vietnam, raised in Belgium and whose parents were originally from China. I also met someone who grew up in Denmark, whose father is Chinese, and mother is of Russian and Italian descent. In my case, my father is originally from China, my mother is from the Philippines, and I grew up in the Netherlands and the USA.

Chinese in China are also being increasingly exposed to images from around the world. I was heartened to see Star TV broadcasting Channel V (a sort of Chinese MTV). Their most popular host, David Woo, a meiji huachao I am told, nightly teaches American slang.

Culture isn't static, but the radical rate of change in China is starting to compel people to examine oversimplified classifications of culture, race and ethnic identity. When people used to ask me where I was from, I'd sometimes answer Hawaii, the Philippines, or some other area that would simplify my explanation. Now I'd be more open, and have higher expectations that others would also be more open, to a discussion of 'where I'm from'.

Caroline Liou

With the advent of the Sui Dynasty (589-618) and the establishment of Xi'an as imperial capital, Nanjing was razed and its historical heritage reduced to ruins. Although it enjoyed a period of prosperity under the long-lived Tang Dynasty, it gradually slipped into obscurity.

Then in 1356, a peasant rebellion led by Zhu Yuanzhang against the Mongol Yuan Dynasty (1271-1368) was successful. The peasants captured Nanjing, and 12 years later claimed the Yuan capital, Beijing. Zhu Yuanzhang took the name of Hong Wu and set himself up as the first emperor of the Ming Dynasty, with Nanjing as its capital. A massive palace was built and huge walls were erected around the city.

However, Nanjing's glory as imperial capital was short-lived. In 1420, the third Ming emperor, Yong Le, moved the capital back to Beijing. From this time, Nanjing's fortunes variously rose and declined as a regional centre, but it was not until the 19th and 20th centuries that the city again entered the centre stage of Chinese history.

In the 19th century, the Opium Wars brought the British to Nanjing, and it was here that the first of the 'unequal treaties' were signed, opening several Chinese ports to foreign trade, forcing China to pay a huge war indemnity, and officially ceding the island of Hong Kong to Britain. Just a few years later, Nanjing became the Taiping capital during the Taiping Rebellion (1851-64), which succeeded in taking over most of southern China. In 1864, the combined forces of the Qing army, British army and various European and US mercenaries surrounded the city. They laid siege for seven months, before finally capturing it and slaughtering the Taiping defenders.

In the 20th century, Nanjing has variously been the capital of the PRC; the site of the worst war atrocity in Japan's assault on China (the 1937 'Rape of Nanjing' in which as many as 300,000 people may have died); and the Kuomintang capital from 1928 to 1937 and 1945 to 1949, before the Communists 'liberated' the city and made China their own.

Orientation

Nanjing lies entirely on the southern bank of the Yangzi River, bounded in the east by Zijinshan. The centre of town is a traffic circle called Xinjiekou, where some of the hotels, including the Jinling Hotel, and most tourist facilities are located. Nanjing railway station and the main long-distance bus station are in the far north of the city.

The historical sights, including the Sun Yatsen Mausoleum, Linggu Temple and the tomb of the first Ming Emperor Hong Wu, are on Zijinshan on Nanjing's eastern fringe.

The city has experienced long periods of prosperity, evident in the numerous buildings which successive rulers built – their tombs, steles, pagodas, temples and niches lay scattered throughout the city. If you can get hold of a copy, *In Search of Old Nanking* by Barry Till & Paula Swart (Joint Publishing Company, Hong Kong, 1982) will give you a thorough rundown. Unfortunately, much has been destroyed or allowed to crumble into ruins.

Maps Several different versions of local maps are available from the Foreign Languages Bookstore, as well as newspaper kiosks and street hawkers around Nanjing. The Jinling Hotel has free English-language maps of the city.

Information

Tourist Offices CITS (☎ 342-8999; fax 342-8954; otcits@nj.col.co.cn) is at 202/1 Zhongshan Beilu. You can buy air, train and boat tickets here, although there's a service charge for each ticket. CTS (☎ 342-0920) at 313 Zhongshan Beilu offers similar services.

Money The Bank of China is at 3 Zhongshan Donglu, just east of Xinjiekou traffic circle. You can also change money at the Jinling and other top-end hotels.

Post & Communications The main post office is at 19 Zhongshan Lu, just north of Xinjiekou. The more upmarket tourist hotels also offer postal services. There is a large telephone and telegram office just north of the Drum Tower traffic circle. The Net Bar (☎ 359-3567; netbar@public-1ptt.js.cn), in the same building as the Nanjing University Foreign Students Dormitory, offers Internet access for about Y20 per hour (Y50 deposit).

Historical Sights

Ming City Wall Nanjing enjoyed its golden years under the Ming, and there are numerous reminders of the period. One of the most impressive is the Ming city wall measuring over 33km – the longest city wall ever built in the world. About two-thirds of it still stands. It was built between 1366 and 1386, by more than 200,000 labourers.

The layout is irregular, an exception to the usual square walls of these times, as much of it is built on the foundations of

JIANGSU

earlier walls which took advantage of strategic hills. Averaging 12m high and 7m wide at the top, the wall was built of bricks supplied from five Chinese provinces. Each brick had stamped on it the place it came from, the overseer's name and rank, the brick-maker's name and sometimes the date. This was to ensure that the bricks were well made; if they broke they had to be replaced.

Ming City Gates Some of the original 13 Ming city gates remain, including Heping Gate *(hépíng mén)* in the north and Zhonghua Gate *(zhōnghuá mén)* in the south. The city gates were heavily fortified and, rather than being the usual weak points of the defences, they were defensive strongholds. The Zhonghua Gate has four rows of gates, making it almost impregnable; it could house a garrison of 3000 soldiers in vaults in the front gate building. Today some of these vaults are used as souvenir shops. Zhonghua Gate can be visited, but Heping Gate is now used as a barracks.

Ming Palace Ruins Built by Hong Wu, the Ming Palace *(mínggùgōng)* is said to have been a magnificent structure after which the Imperial Palace in Beijing was modelled. Basically all that remains of it is five marble bridges lying side by side and known as the Five Dragon Bridges, the old ruined gate called Wu Men and the enormous column bases of the palace buildings.

The palace suffered two major fires in its first century and was allowed to fall into ruins after the Ming court moved to Beijing. Later the Manchus looted it. During the Taiping Rebellion, bombardments by Qing and western troops finished it off.

Early Remains Nanjing has been inhabited since prehistoric times. Remains of a prehistoric culture have been found at the site of today's Drum Tower in the centre of the city and in surrounding areas. About 200 sites of small clan communities, mainly represented by pottery and bronze

artefacts dating back to the late Shang and Zhou dynasties, have been found on both sides of the Yangzi.

In 212 AD, towards the end of the Eastern Han period, the military commander in charge of the Nanjing region built a citadel on Qinglingshan in the west of Nanjing. At that time the mountain was referred to as Shitoushan (Stone Head Mountain) and so the citadel became known as the Stone City. The wall measured over 10km in circumference. Today, some of the red sandstone foundations can still be seen.

Drum Tower Built in 1382, the Drum Tower *(gǔlóu)* lies roughly in the centre of Nanjing, on a traffic circle on Beijing Xilu. Drums were usually beaten to give directions for the change of the night watches and, in rare instances, to warn the populace of impending danger. Only one large drum remains today.

Bell Tower North-east of the Drum Tower, the Bell Tower *(zhōnglóu)* houses an enormous bell, cast in 1388 and originally situated in a pavilion on the western side of the Drum Tower. The present tower dates from 1889 and is a small two storey pavilion with a pointed roof and upturned eaves.

Chaotian Palace Chaotian Palace *(cháotiān gōng)* was originally established in the Ming Dynasty as a school for educating noble children in court etiquette. Most of today's buildings, including the centrepiece of the palace, a Confucius temple, date from 1866 when the whole complex was rebuilt. Today the buildings are being used for a range of endeavours, including a qigong institute and a pottery centre.

Off a tiny alley on the eastern side of the palace and marked by two red flags is the Jiangsu Province Kunju Theatre *(jiāngsū shěng kūnjùyuàn)*, where excellent – if rather infrequent – performances are held. *(Kunju* is a regional form of classical Chinese opera which developed in the Suzhou-Hangzhou-Nanjing triangle. It is similar to, but slower than, Peking opera and is performed with colourful and elaborate costumes.)

The palace entrance gate is on Mochou Lu on bus route No 4, two stops west of Xinjiekou.

Museums & Memorials

Taiping Museum (*tàipíng tiānguó lìshǐ bówùguǎn*) Hong Xiuquan, the leader of the Taipings, had a palace built in Nanjing, but the building was completely destroyed when Nanjing was taken in 1864. All that remains is a stone boat in an ornamental lake in the Western Garden, inside the old Kuomintang government buildings on Changjiang Lu.

There are maps showing the northward progress of the Taiping army from Guangdong, Hong Xiuquan's seals, Taiping coins, weapons, and texts which describe the Taiping laws on agrarian reform, social law and cultural policy. Other texts describe divisions in the Taiping leadership, the attacks by the Manchus and foreigners, and the fall of Nanjing in 1864. Most of the literature is copied, the originals being kept in Beijing. For background information on the Taipings see the history section (Decline of the Qing) in the Facts about the Country chapter.

The museum is open daily from 8.30 am to 5.30 pm.

Nanjing Museum Just inside the eastern city walls on Zhongshan Donglu, the Nanjing Museum (*nánjīng bówùguǎn*) houses an array of artefacts from Neolithic times right through to the Communist period. The main building was constructed in 1933 in the style of an ancient temple with yellow-glazed tiles, red-lacquered gates and columns.

An interesting exhibit is the burial suit made of small rectangles of jade sewn together with silver thread, dating from the Eastern Han Dynasty (25-220 AD) and excavated from a tomb discovered in the city of Xuzhou in northern Jiangsu. Other exhibits include bricks with the inscriptions of their makers and overseers from

the Ming city wall, drawings of old Nanjing, an early Qing mural of old Suzhou and relics from the Taiping Rebellion. The museum is open from 9 am to 5 pm.

Just east of the museum is a section of the Ming city wall with steps leading up to it from the road. You can walk along the top only as far as Qianhu Lake, where a section of wall has collapsed into the water. However, one reader reported that while at this section of the wall he was detained by police and his film confiscated supposedly because of the sensitive nature of a nearby military base.

Nanjing Treaty History Museum The Nanjing Treaty History Museum (*nánjīng tiáoyuē shǐliào chénliè guǎn*) houses a small collection of photographs, maps and newspaper clippings (no English captions) related to the Nanjing Treaties, but the real reason to come here is the building itself, which is where the first of the 'unequal treaties' was signed.

It's in the Jing Hai Temple, near the west railway station, on Chao Yue Lou off Re Hou Lu. The museum is open daily from 8.30 am to 5 pm.

Memorial of the Nanjing Massacre The exhibits at the memorial hall (*dàtúshā jìniànguǎn*) document the atrocities committed by Japanese soldiers against the civilian population during the occupation of Nanjing in 1937. They include pictures of actual executions, many taken by Japanese army photographers, and a gruesome viewing hall built over a mass grave of massacre victims. Also on display is furniture used at the signing of Japan's surrender to China – the disproportionately smaller and lower table and chairs given to the Japanese officers carried an unmistakable message.

The exhibits conclude on a more optimistic note, with a final room dedicated to the post-1945 Sino-Japanese reconciliation. The memorial hall is open daily from 8.30 am to 5 pm. It's in the city's southwestern suburbs on bus route No 7.

JIANGSU

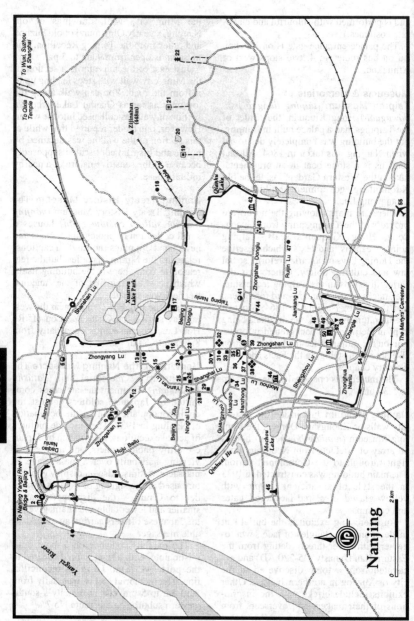

JIANGSU

Nanjing

0 1 2 km

To Wuxi, Suzhou
& Shanghai

To Qixia
Temple

▲ Zijinshan (448m)

Cable Car

Qianhu
Lake

✈ 55

Rujin Lu 47

The Martyrs' Cemetery

×

Zhongshan Donglu

Jiankang Lu

Changle Lu

Shengzhou Lu

Zhongshan Lu

Zhongshan Nanlu

Zhongyang Lu

Beijing Donglu

Xuanwu
Lake Park

Shanshan Lu

Taiping Nanlu

Mochou
Lu

Hanzhong Lu

Shanghai Lu

Yanan Lu

Guangzhou Lu

Ninghai Lu

Beijing Xilu

Huaqiao
Lu

Mochou
Lake

Qinhuai He

Hujiu Beilu

Zhongshan Lu

Jianning Lu

Daqiao Nanlu

To Nanjing Yangzi River
Bridge & Beijing

Yangzi River

JIANGSU

Monument to the Crossing of the Yangzi River Standing in the north-west of the city on Zhongshan Beilu, this monument *(dùjiāng jìniàn bēi)* erected in April 1979 commemorates the crossing of the river on 23 April 1949 and the capture of Nanjing from the Kuomintang by the Communist army. The characters on the monument are in the calligraphy of Deng Xiaoping.

Xuanwu Lake Park
(xuánwǔ gōngyuán)
This park is almost entirely covered by the waters of a large urban lake, but you can walk along causeways or take a boat out to its central forested islands.

A long path goes around the shores of Xuanwu Lake, beside the old city walls for much of its length. However, the park has an urban feel to it; if you're looking to get away from it all this is not the place to do it. You can enter Xuanwu Lake Park from the main gate off Zhongyang Lu.

Nanjing Yangzi River Bridge
(nánjīng chángjiāng dàqiáo)

One of the great achievements of the Communists, and one of which they are justifiably proud, is the Yangzi River Bridge at Nanjing. Opened on 23 December 1968, it's one of the longest bridges in China – a double-decker with a 4500m-long road on top and a railway line below.

The story goes that the bridge was designed and built entirely by the Chinese after the Russians marched out and took the designs with them in 1960. Given the immensity of the construction it really is an impressive engineering feat, before which there was no direct rail link between Beijing and Shanghai.

Fuzimiao
(fūzǐ miào)

Fuzimiao is in the south of the city, centred on the site of an ancient Confucius temple that was a centre of Confucian study for more than 1500 years. Fuzimiao has been damaged and rebuilt repeatedly, and what you see here today are newly restored late Qing Dynasty structures or wholly new buildings reconstructed in traditional style. The main Temple of Confucius is behind them on the small square in front of the canal. A five minute walk north-west from here are the Imperial Examination Halls, where scholars spent months – or years – in tiny cells studying Confucian classics in preparation for civil service examinations.

Today, Fuzimiao has become Nanjing's main amusement quarter and is a particularly lively and crowded place on weekends and public holidays. There are restaurants, souvenir shops, tacky side-shows in old halls and a bookseller stocking ancient Chinese manuscripts. Buildings surrounding the canal on the small square are lit up at night, adding to the area's kitsch ambience. This atmosphere extends into the Confucius temple itself, which now houses a tacky display of dressed-up mannequins.

You can get to the Fuzimiao area from the docks by trolley-bus No 31 and from Xinjiekou by bus No 1.

Zijinshan
(zǐjīnshān)

Most of Nanjing's historical sights are scattered over the southern slopes of this high forested hill at the city's eastern fringe.

Sun Yatsen Mausoleum For many Chinese, a visit to Sun Yatsen's Tomb *(zhōngshān líng)* is something of a pilgrimage. Sun is recognised by the Communists and the Kuomintang alike as the father of modern China. He died in Beijing in 1925, leaving behind an unstable Chinese republic. He had wished to be buried in Nanjing, no doubt with greater simplicity than the Ming-style tomb which his successors built for him. But less than a year after his death, construction of this immense mausoleum began.

The tomb itself lies at the top of an enormous stone stairway, 323m long and 70m wide. At the start of the path stands a stone gateway built of Fujian marble, with a roof of blue-glazed tiles. The blue and white of the mausoleum were meant to symbolise the white sun on the blue background of the Kuomintang flag.

The crypt is at the top of the steps at the rear of the memorial chamber. A tablet hanging across the threshold is inscribed with the 'Three Principles of the People', as formulated by Dr Sun: nationalism, democracy and people's livelihood. Inside is a seated statue of Dr Sun. The walls are carved with the complete text of the *Outline of Principles for the Establishment of the Nation* put forward by the Nationalist government. A prostrate marble statue of Sun seals his coffin.

Tomb of Hong Wu This tomb *(míng xiàolíng)* also lies on the southern slope of Zijinshan. Construction began in 1381 and was finished in 1383; the emperor died at the age of 71 in 1398. The first section of the avenue leading up to the mausoleum is lined with stone statues of lions, camels, elephants and horses. There's also a mythical animal called a *xiezhi* which has a mane and a single horn on its head; and a *qilin* which has a scaly body, a cow's tail, deer's hooves and one horn.

As you enter the first courtyard, a paved pathway leads to a pavilion housing several steles. The next gate leads to a large courtyard where you'll find the 'Altar Tower' or 'Soul Tower' – a mammoth rectangular stone structure. To get to the top of the tower, go to the stairway in the middle of the structure. Behind the tower is a wall, 350m in diameter, which surrounds a huge earth mound. Beneath this mound is the tomb vault of Hong Wu, which has not been excavated.

Linggu Temple One of the most interesting buildings in Nanjing is the **Beamless Hall**. In 1381, when Hong Wu was building his tomb, he had a temple on the site torn down and rebuilt a few kilometres to the east. Of this temple only the Beamless Hall (so called because it is built entirely of bricks) remains. The structure has an interesting vaulted ceiling and a large stone platform where Buddhist statues used to be seated. In the 1930s the hall was turned into a memorial to those who died in the 1926-28 revolution. One of the inscriptions on the inside wall is the old Kuomintang national anthem.

A road leads either side of the Beamless Hall and up two flights of steps to the **Pine Wind Pavilion**, originally dedicated to the goddess of mercy as part of the Linggu Temple. Today it houses a small shop and teahouse.

The Linggu Temple *(línggǔ sì)* itself and its memorial hall to Xuan Zang is close by; after you pass through the Beamless Hall, turn right and follow the pathway. Xuan Zang was the Buddhist monk who travelled to India and brought back the Buddhist scriptures. Inside the memorial hall is a 13 storey wooden pagoda model which contains part of his skull, a sacrificial table and a portrait of the monk.

Close by is the **Linggu Pagoda** *(línggǔ tǎ)*, which was built in the 1930s under the direction of a US architect as a memorial to Kuomintang members who died in the 1926-28 revolution. It's a nine storey octagonal building 60m high.

Scenic Spot of Ming Xiaoling *(míng xiàolíng fēng jǐng qū)* Just west of the Sun Yatsen Mausoleum, this quiet area has a tree-lined, stone pathway that winds around pavilions and picnic grounds and ends at **Zi Xia Lake** *(zǐ xiá hú)*, a small lake that you can swim in – a very relaxing way to spend a hot afternoon.

Day Tour It's possible to see Zijinshan's three main sights (Tomb of Hong Wu, the Sun Yatsen Mausoleum and Linggu Pagoda) in a single day.

Take bus No 9 from west of Xinjiekou (opposite the Jinling Hotel) to its terminus in front of the Sun Yatsen Mausoleum. From there you can walk or take a minibus or taxi to Linggu Pagoda. You can then head back west to the mausoleum and tomb. You can also take a half-hour cablecar ride to the top of Zijinshan, but other than looking at a hazy view of Nanjing, there's not much to do. The most convenient way to see several of the sights in one day is to rent a bike in town and cycle from sight to sight.

Places to Stay – budget
The cheapest beds are at the *Nanjing University Foreign Students Dormitory (nánjīng dàxué/wàiguó liúxuéshēng sùshè)*, a large white-tiled building on Shanghai Lu, just south of Beijing Xilu. Doubles with communal facilities, including kitchen, cost Y65 per person. Beds in a double with attached bathroom cost Y200 (for one or two people). The best way to get there is to take the No 13 bus from the railway station or the long-distance bus station (get off at Beijing Xilu at Shanghai Lu, near Jack's Place).

JIANGSU

A 10 minute walk from the Nanjing University dormitory is the *Nanjing Normal University Nanshan Hotel* (fax 373-8174) *(nánjīng shīfàn dàxué nánshān bīnguǎn)*. It's slightly more expensive, but its location in the middle of campus is quiet and relaxing. Just outside the main gates of the university are several inexpensive street food vendors. Doubles with shower cost from Y120.

To get there from the Nanjing University dorm, walk south along Shanghai Lu. Turn right into the second or third alleyway, then take the first road left to the main gate of Nanjing Normal University (next to a McDonald's). The dormitory is inside the campus compound, up to the left from the large grassy quadrangle.

Places to Stay – middle

Most Nanjing accommodation is middle to top end in price; in fact, it's fairly difficult to find a decent room for under Y350.

On a pretty, tree-lined street close to Nanjing University is the *Jingli Hotel* (☎ 331-0818) *(jīnglì jiǔdiàn)* at 7 Beijing Xilu. Singles/doubles start at Y380/575. Like the Jiangsu Hotel, it's a new hotel and offers the amenities of a luxury hotel.

Just north of the Drum Tower is the new *Jiangsu Hotel* (☎ 332-9888; fax 330-3308) *(jiāngsū dàjiǔdiàn)* at 28 Zhongshan Beilu. This 34 storey high-rise has the amenities of an upmarket hotel, and is good value with standard rooms starting at Y420.

The *Yue Hua Hotel* (☎ 221-3888; fax 221-3995) *(yuèhuá dàjiǔdiàn)*, across from the Mandarin Garden Hotel on Jiankang Lu in Fuzimiao, has standard rooms from Y360. Rooms are clean, but slightly run-down.

The *Hongqiao Hotel* (☎ 340-0888; fax 663-5756) *(hóngqiáo fàndiàn)*, at 202 Zhongshan Beilu, caters largely to tour groups and only just creeps into the middle category. Doubles cost from Y480.

Places to Stay – top end

The 36 storey *Jinling Hotel* (☎ 445-5888; fax 470-3396) *(jīnlíng fàndiàn)*, at Xin-

jiekou, is the best and most well known of Nanjing's top-end hotels. Standard doubles cost Y1245 and executive rooms cost Y2155. The hotel's numerous amenities include a sauna, fitness centre and swimming pool, and at street level there's a shopping arcade stocking just about any consumer item you're likely to want to buy.

Popular with foreign tour groups is the *Dingshan Garden Hotel* (☎ 880-2888; fax 882-1729) *(dīngshān huāyuán jiǔdiàn)* at 90 Chahaer Lu. Standard doubles cost Y815. Although there's a free shuttle-bus service, its location at the top of a hill makes it inconvenient to get to and from the city. On the plus side, there's a great view of the city and Xuanwu Lake from here.

Two standard luxury hotels are the *Grand Hotel* (☎ 331-1999; fax 331-9498) *(gǔnándū fàndiàn)*, at 208 Guangzhou Lu (near Nanjing Normal University), and the *Central Hotel* (☎ 440-0888; fax 441-4194) *(zhōngxīn dàjiǔdiàn)* at 75 Zhongshan Lu, near the corner of Huaqiao Lu. Both have doubles from US$100.

Behind a restaurant and across the road from the Hongqiao Hotel is the city's oldest tourist establishment, *Nanjing Hotel* (☎ 341-1888; fax 342-2261) *(nánjīng fàndiàn)* at 259 Zhongshan Beilu. Its newly renovated rooms start at US$78, although there are some older rooms available for US$40.

The *Xuanwu Hotel* (☎ 330-3888; fax 663-9624) *(xuánwǔ fàndiàn)*, a tower block at 193 Zhongyang Lu opposite the Jiangsu Exhibition Hall, is one of the cheaper top-end options. It may not quite hit the spot as a luxury hotel, but the smaller corner rooms are good value at US$64. Standard doubles start at US$80. There's also a rotating restaurant atop the hotel.

The *Mandarin Garden Hotel* (☎ 220-2555; fax 220-1876) *(zhuàng yuán lóu jiǔdiàn)*, at 9 Zhuang Yuan Lu, has single rooms from Y730 and doubles from Y996. The most useful thing about this new luxury hotel is its location in the northern part of Fuzimiao.

Places to Eat

Some of Nanjing's livelier eating houses are in the Fuzimiao quarter. The *Lao Zhengxing Restaurant (lǎo zhèngxīng càiguǎn)*, at 119 Gongyuan Jie, just east of the main square by the river, serves typical lower Yangzi cuisine and was a favourite of Kuomintang officers before the war.

On the opposite side of the Qinhuai River from the main square is *Wan Qing Lou* (☎ 224-9877) *(wǎnqínglóu)*. Here you can try delicious Nanjing dim sum; a preset, 20 dish dim sum feast costs Y60 and is definitely good value.

Anyone who has arrived in Nanjing from the backwoods of China and wants to forget all about local delicacies can head over to one of the cluster of restaurants that have sprung up around Nanjing University which cater to adventurous locals and foreign students. Down the alley near the Nanjing University Foreign Students Dormitory, east of Shanghai Lu, are several cheap places to eat including *Gold & Silver, Jack's Place* and *Blue Rain.*

Also close to Nanjing University is *Swede & Kraut* (☎ 663-8020) *(lǎowàilè)*, 137 Ninghai Lu (2nd storey). It serves great vegetarian lasagne and pizza, as well as chicken and steak dishes, and the bread and pasta are homemade. A 20% discount is given to students.

The place to go for cheap street food is just outside the main gate of Nanjing Normal University on Ninghai Lu. *Street stalls* and *restaurants* serve dumplings and steamed buns or you can get a tasty bowl of noodles for Y6 at the *Muslim noodle restaurant* (across the street from McDonald's). In a small alleyway off Ninghai Lu you can get Chinese pastries, still warm from the oven, for 50 fen each. Also on Ninghai Lu is *Red Door,* which has an English menu and serves affordable stir fries.

Henry's Home Cafe (☎ 470-1292) *(hēnglì zhī jiā)*, at 33 Huaqiao Lu, has friendly service and occasionally shows movies. It serves pasta, pizza and steak dishes.

The *Black Cat Cafe (hēimāo cānguǎn)*, at 1 Ci Bei She down an alley off Han Zhong Lu (a couple of blocks west of Xinjiekou), is popular with foreign students and locals. Pasta, pizza and meat dishes are served here as well. There's also a basic salad bar and good chocolate cake.

On the 6th floor of the *GE Shopping Centre* on Hangzhou Lu, one block west of Xinjiekou, a food court sells western fast food.

The *Sprite Outlet (wǔzhōu jiǔjiā)* (foreign students also call it the Treehouse) on Guangzhou Lu, 20m west of the intersection with Zhongshan Lu, is also popular with foreigners and locals. The food is cheap and there's an English menu. Don't be deceived by the small street-front dining area – there is more seating out the back and in some small rooms.

Worth visiting more for the view than for its food is the *vegetarian restaurant* at Jiming Temple, high on a hill overlooking Xuanwu Lake Park. It's very cheap and is open daily from 8 am to 5.30 pm.

A good place to sample local specialities is the *Jiangsu Restaurant* (☎ 662-3698) *(jiāngsū jiǔjiā)* at 26 Jiankang Lu near the Taiping Museum. Nanjing pressed, salted duck is slathered with roasted salt, steeped in clear brine, baked dry and then kept under cover for some time; the finished product should have a creamy-coloured skin and red, tender flesh. The *Sichuan Restaurant* (☎ 664-3651) *(sìchuān fàndiàn)*, at 171 Taiping Lu, is not bad either.

Finally, *KFC* and *McDonald's* have invaded Nanjing in a big way; you'll see outlets all over town.

Entertainment

Nanjing has an active nightlife, with a range of bars, pubs and discos to choose from. The best place to ask about entertainment is the foreign student dormitories. At the time of writing, the disco in the *Zhongshan Hotel* was the place to be on Friday nights.

Getting There & Away

Air Nanjing has regular air connections to all major Chinese cities. There are also daily flights to/from Hong Kong.

JIANGSU

The main CAAC office (☎ 664-9275) is at 52 Ruijin Lu (near the terminal of bus route No 4), but you can also buy tickets at the CITS and CTS offices or at most of the top-end hotels. China Eastern Airlines has daily flights to Hong Kong; its office is just north of Xinjiekou. Dragonair (☎ 332-8000) also has daily flights to Hong Kong; there's an agent in the CITS office.

Bus The long-distance bus station is west of the main railway station, south-east of the wide-bridged intersection with Zhong-yang Lu. It's a big chaotic place and even if you can read the posted information (in Chinese) it is all wildly inaccurate. There are direct buses to destinations all over Jiangsu and to major destinations around China. Have the name of the place you want to go written in Chinese to be sure. You can also buy bus tickets at a bus ticket office (☎ 334-3966) at 204 Zhongshan Beilu, near CITS. The new expressway between Nanjing and Shanghai and Nan-jing and Lianyungang has made transport by bus much quicker than before.

Train Nanjing is a major stop on the Beijing-Shanghai railway line, and the station is a disaster area; there are several trains a day in both directions. Heading eastwards from Nanjing, the line to Shang-hai connects with Zhenjiang, Changzhou, Wuxi and Suzhou.

An efficient daily express service runs between Nanjing and Shanghai, using two modern double-decker trains:

Train No.	From	To	Departs	Arrives
T1	Nanjing	Shanghai	8.54 am	12.20 pm
Y215	Nanjing	Shanghai	10 am	2.41 pm
T2	Shanghai	Nanjing	9 am	11.50 am
Y216	Shanghai	Nanjing	3.48 pm	6.38 pm

Train T1 runs directly to Shanghai, while T2 stops at Wuxi. The Y215 and Y216 also stop at Suzhou. Train numbers starting with T are the most luxurious and Y is con-sidered second best (regular trains have numbers only). All cars are air-conditioned and a no-smoking rule is vigorously en-forced.

There is no direct rail link to Hangzhou; you have to go to Shanghai first and then catch a train or bus. Alternatively, there is a direct bus from Nanjing to Hangzhou. Likewise, to get to Guangzhou by rail you must change trains at Shanghai.

Heading west, there is a direct rail link to the port of Wuhu on the Yangzi River. If you want to go further west along the river, then the most sensible thing to do is take the ferry.

You can buy train tickets at CITS, CTS or the train ticket office on Zhongshan Lu, just south of the China Eastern Airlines booking office.

Boat There are several departures daily from Nanjing's Yangzi River port down-river (eastward) to Shanghai and upriver (westward) to Wuhan (two days), including a few boats to Chongqing (five days). Most ferries leave from No 4 dock *(sìhào mǎtóu)*, 1km north of Zhongshan dock, which is at the western end of Zhongshan Beilu. For full details on Yangzi River cruises, see the Chongqing section in the Sichuan chapter.

Getting Around
To/From the Airport Nanjing airport is not far from the centre of town, in the south-east of the city. There is a CAAC bus service, and many of the hotels also have minibuses that run to and from the airport. Taxis charge around Y30 to Xinjiekou, al-though as a foreigner you may be hard-pressed to get a ride at this price.

Other Transport Taxis cruise the streets of Nanjing and are very cheap – most des-tinations in the city are Y7, but make sure that the meter is switched on. You can get around in motor-tricycles as well; be sure to agree on a price beforehand. Private minibuses ply the main thoroughfares; wave one down and ride for Y1.

You can get to Xinjiekou, in the heart of town, by jumping on a No 1 bus or a No 33

The Grand Canal

With other, faster, modes of transport now available, tourists are about the only thing being shipped on the Grand Canal (*dàyùnhé*).

The old Beijing-Hangzhou Canal meandered almost 1800km. Today perhaps half of it remains seasonally navigable. The Party claims that, since liberation, large-scale dredging has made the navigable length 1100km. This is an exaggeration. Canal depths are up to 3m and canal widths can narrow to less than 9m. Put these facts together, think about some of the old stone bridges spanning the route, and you come to the conclusion that it is restricted to fairly small, flat-bottomed vessels.

The section of the canal from Beijing to Tianjin has been silted up for centuries. A similar fate has befallen most sections from the Yellow River to Tianjin. The stretch from the Yellow River to Peixian (in northern Jiangsu Province) is also probably silted up.

As a tourist concern, the Grand Canal comes into its own south of the Yangzi, where there is year-round navigation. The Jiangnan section of the canal (Hangzhou, Suzhou, Wuxi, Changzhou, Danyang, Zhenjiang) is a skein of canals, rivers and branching lakes.

Passenger services on the canal have dwindled to a trickle; they are unpopular with locals now that there are faster ways to get around. If you want a canal journey, the only option (apart from chartering your own boat) is the overnight service that travels between Hangzhou and Suzhou. By all accounts it's a very pleasant trip, and improvements have been made on the much-maligned sanitation front. (See the Suzhou Getting There & Away section later in this chapter for more details.) ■

---

trolley-bus from the railway station, or a No 10 or No 34 trolley-bus from the Yangzi docks.

It's possible to rent a bike from a small stall on Zhongshan Lu, between Huaqiao Lu and Guangzhou Lu (look for the 'hire bicycle' sign). The cost is Y15 per day or Y1 per hour; a Y200 deposit is required.

AROUND NANJING
Qixia Temple
(*qíxiá sì*)

Qixia Temple lies 22km north-east of Nanjing. It was founded by the Buddhist monk Shao Shezhai, during the Southern Qi Dynasty, and is still an active place of worship. Qixia has long been one of China's most important monasteries, and even today is one of the largest Buddhist seminaries in the country. There are two main temple halls: the Maitreya Hall, with a statue of the Maitreya Buddha sitting cross-legged at the entrance, and behind this the Vairocana Hall, housing a 5m-tall statue of Vairocana.

Behind the temple is the Thousand Buddha Cliff. Several small caves housing stone statues are carved into the hillside, the earliest of which dates from the Qi Dynasty (479-502 AD), although there are others from succeeding dynasties through to the Ming. There is also a small stone pagoda built in 601 AD, and rebuilt during the late Tang period. The upper part has engraved sutras and carvings of the Buddha; around the base, each of the pagoda's eight sides depicts Sakyamuni.

You can reach Qixia from Nanjing by public bus from the Drum Tower bus station or by private minibus from in front of the Nanjing railway station. It's about a one hour ride.

Yangshan Quarry
(*yángshān bēicái*)

The quarry at Yangshan, 25km east of Nanjing, was the source of most of the stone blocks cut for the Ming palace and statues of the Ming tombs. The attraction here is a massive tablet partially hewn from

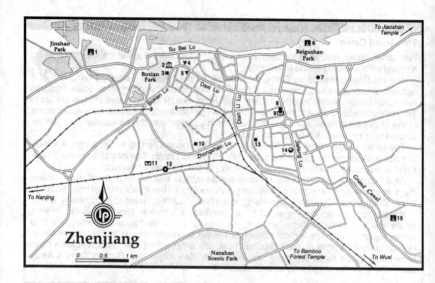

Zhenjiang

the rock. Had the tablet been finished it would have been almost 15m wide, 4m thick and 45m high! The base stone was to be 6.5m high and 13m long.

One story goes that Ming Dynasty Emperor Hong Wu wished to place the enormous tablet on the top of Zijinshan. The gods had promised their assistance to move it, but when they saw the size of the tablet, even they gave up and Hong Wu had to abandon the project. It seems, however, that Yong Le, the son of Hong Wu, ordered the tablet to be carved; he planned to erect it at his father's tomb. When the tablet was almost finished he realised there was no way it could be moved.

You can get to Yangshan from the bus station on Hanfu Jie (east of Xinjiekou) on bus Nos 9 and 20. Buses to the thermal-springs resort at Tangshanzhen pass Yangshan on the way.

ZHENJIANG
(zhènjiāng)

Just an hour from Nanjing, Zhenjiang is a town of over 300,000 people. The main attraction is Jinshan Park, where an active

Buddhist temple attracts large crowds of worshippers.

The Daxi Lu area – the oldest part of the city – is an interesting area to wander around.

Information

Zhenjiang has two post offices: one close to the railway station and the other on Jiefang Lu, on the beach side of the main roundabout.

Jinshan Park
(jīnshān gōngyuán)

Jinshan Park packs in the crowds, who congest the flights of stairs that lead up through a Buddhist temple to the seven storey octagonal Cishou Pagoda. Many monks at this temple are young, and it's interesting to see Buddhism 'come back' in the area.

There are four caves at the mount; of these Buddhist Sea *(fáhǎi)* and White Dragon *(báilóng)* feature in the Chinese fairy tale *The Story of the White Snake.* Take bus No 2 to Jinshan (this is the last stop).

ZHENJIANG 镇江

1 Jinshan Temple
金山寺
2 Museum
博物馆
3 Royal Hotel
大皇家酒店
4 Yan Chun
宴春酒楼
5 KFC
肯德鸡
6 Ganlu Temple
甘露寺
7 Martyrs' Shrine
烈士墓
8 Arts & Crafts Store
工艺品大楼
9 Post Office
邮电局
10 Zhenjiang Hotel
镇江宾馆
11 Post Office
邮局
12 Railway Station
火车站
13 Jingkou Hotel
京口饭店
14 Long-Distance Bus Station
汽车站
15 Douyao Temple
都天庙

Jiaoshan

(jiāoshān)

Also known as Jade Hill because of its dark green foliage, Jiaoshan is to the east of Zhenjiang on a small island. There's good hiking here with a number of pavilions along the way to the top of the 150m-high mount, from where Xijiang Tower gives a view of activity on the Yangzi. At the base of Jiaoshan is an active monastery.

Take bus No 4 to the terminal, then a short walk and a boat ride, or you can take a cable car to the top of the hill, walk down and take the boat back.

Beigushan Park

(běigùshān gōngyuán)

Also on the No 4 bus route, Beigushan Park is home to Ganlu Temple (gānlù sì), which features a Song Dynasty pagoda.

The pagoda was once six storeys high, but was reduced to four by overzealous Red Guards.

Museum

(bówùguǎn)

Between Jinshan Park and the centre of town is the old British consulate, which is now a museum. It houses pottery, bronzes, gold, silver, Tang Dynasty paintings, and photographs and memorabilia of the Sino-Japanese war. The ornate, red and black-brick building, situated atop a small hill, is a fascinating sight in contrast to the surrounding area.

Bus No 2 lets you off close to the museum. The museum is closed Wednesday and Thursday.

Daxi Lu & Song Jie Area

(dàxī lù, sòng jiē)

Well worth investigating on foot is the area surrounding the museum, the oldest section of Zhenjiang. Winding, cobblestone-laid alleys give views over a maze of tiled rooftops and go down to boat docks on the Yangzi.

The staircase to the east of the museum leads to Song Lu, where a small stone pagoda above an archway is said to date from the Yuan Dynasty.

Bamboo Forest Temple

(zhúlín sì)

At the southern end of town in an area known as Nanshan Scenic Park (nánshān fēngjǐng qū) is the Bamboo Forest Temple. As temples go, it won't qualify as the biggest or best in China, but its setting among the trees and hills makes it a relaxing spot.

Unfortunately buses don't go there; bus Nos 6 and 21 come close, but you'll also have to walk a couple of kilometres, hitch, or get a taxi or minibus.

Places to Stay

The *Jingkou Hotel* (☎ 522-4866; fax 523-0056) (*jīngkǒu fàndiàn*), at 407 Zhongshan Donglu, is one of the cheapest options around; it has doubles for Y120 in the old wing, although you may need to exert some pressure to get one of these. Standard renovated doubles start at Y480. The hotel can be a little tricky to find – entry is via a gate on Binhe Lu, which borders a small river. From the bridge over the river look south and you'll see a big 'J' on top of the hotel.

Not far from the station is the *Zhenjiang Hotel* (☎ 523-3888; fax 523-1055) *(zhènjiāng bīnguǎn)*, at 92 Zhongshan Xilu, which has standard doubles from US$30 in an older building, or US$60 in the new building at the front.

The *Royal Hotel* (☎ 527-1438) *(dàhuángjiā jiǔdiàn)*, at 35 Boxian Lu, is in a great location in the old section of town. White columns, gold statues and wrought iron decorate the front, making it a bizarre sight. Doubles start at Y260. The hotel is being renovated, but could be open by the time you read this. From the railway station it's a 15 minute ride on bus No 2.

Places to Eat

The most famous restaurant in town is *Yan Chun* (☎ 527-1615) *(yànchūn jiǔlóu)*, at 17 Renmin Lane (an alley north of Daxi Lu). The 1st floor serves wonton soup and other dim sum. The 2nd floor serves cold dim sum and other local specialities, along with eight treasure tea.

Hot water for the tea is poured at your table by an attendant standing several feet away using a kettle with a very long spout. The 1st floor is open from 3 to 6.30 pm. The 2nd floor is open from 11 am to 1.30 pm and 5 to 8.30 pm.

Things to Buy

There's a very fine Arts & Crafts Shop (☎ 522-2332) *(gōngyìpǐn dàlóu)* at 191 Jiefang Beilu which stocks embroidery, porcelain, jade and other artefacts. It may have some antiques.

Getting There & Away

Bus The long-distance bus station is in the south-eastern corner of the city centre.

There are hourly buses from Zhenjiang to Nanjing and Wuxi (two hours) and a bus-ferry combination to Yangzhou (1½ hours). You can get more frequent buses to Yangzhou from the eastern side of the main railway station.

Train Zhenjiang is on the main Nanjing-Shanghai line. It's 3½ hours by fast train to Shanghai and an hour to Nanjing. Some of the special express trains don't stop at Zhenjiang. Otherwise, there is a grand choice of schedules, so check the timetable at the station. Most hotels offer a train booking service and can book sleepers.

Getting Around

Almost all the transport (including local buses, buses to Yangzhou, taxis, pedicabs and motor-tricycles) is close to the railway station.

Bus No 2 is a convenient tour bus. It goes east from the station along Zhongshan Lu to the city centre where the department stores and post office are. It then swings west past the former British consulate and continues on to Jinshan, the terminal.

Bus No 4, which crosses the No 2 route in the city centre on Jiefang Lu, runs to Ganlu Temple and Jiaoshan in the east.

YANGZHOU
(yángzhōu)

Yangzhou, near the junction of the Grand Canal and the Yangzi River, was once an economic and cultural centre of southern China. It was home to scholars, painters, storytellers, poets and merchants in the Sui and Tang dynasties.

Today it is a fairly pleasant city with broad, tree-lined boulevards, canals, bridges and gardens dotting the city. It has enough sights to keep the traveller busy for a couple days, but it's not the major attraction that local tourist literature would have you believe. The main attraction, Shouxi Lake Park, tends to get swamped with tour groups. Yangzhou can be visited as a day trip from Nanjing; on a good run it only takes around 1½ hours.

Information

CTS (☎ 734-5777), on Wenhe Lu, sells rail and air tickets.

The Bank of China has two branches in Yangzhou – one on Shita Lu, not far from CTS, and the other on Yanfu Lu, across the canal from the History Museum.

Canals

Yangzhou once had 24 stone bridges spanning its network of canals. Although the modern bridges are concrete, they are still sometimes good vantage points from which to view canal life.

You might like to investigate the environs a short way out of town. The Grand Canal actually passes a little to the east of Yangzhou. The bus No 2 terminal in the north-east is a boat dock. Bus Nos 4 and 9 run over a bridge on the canal. There are two ship locks to the south of Yangzhou.

Ge Garden
(gèyuán)

On Dongguan Lu, this garden was landscaped by the painter Shi Tao for an officer of the Qing court. Shi Tao was an expert at making artificial rocks; the composition here suggests the four seasons. The entrance is on Yanfu Donglu.

He Garden
(héyuán)

Alias Jixiao Mountain Villa, the He Garden was built in the 19th century. It contains rockeries, ponds, pavilions and walls inscribed with classical poetry.

Wenfeng Pagoda
(wénfēng tǎ)

This graffiti-ridden pagoda is in an eerie state of disrepair. It offers a bird's-eye view of the flotsam, jetsam and sampans along a canal. Made of brick and wood, it's been rebuilt several times.

Shouxi Lake Park
(shòu xīhú)

This, the top scenic spot in Yangzhou, is in the western suburbs on the bus No 5 route.

Shouxi (Slender West) is a slim version of West Lake in Hangzhou. Mass local tourism has done much to restore this garden and, if you are lucky enough to visit it on a quiet day (sub-zero temperatures and lashing hail might guarantee this), it's a worthwhile excursion.

It offers an imperial dragon-boat ferry, a restaurant and a white dagoba (dome-shaped shrine) modelled after the one in Beihai Park in Beijing. The highlight is the triple-arched, five pavilion Wutang Qiao bridge, which was built in 1757.

Emperor Qianlong's fishing platform is also in the park. It is said that the local divers used to put fish on the poor emperor's hook so he'd think it was good luck and provide some more funding for the town.

Admission is Y18. There are two entrances; the southern entrance is close to the Hongqiao Hotel and the northern entrance is close to Daming Monastery.

Daming Monastery
(dàmíng sì)

The name means 'Great Brightness Temple', although Emperor Qianlong renamed it Fajing Temple in 1765 when he dropped in for a visit. The monastery was founded more than 1000 years ago and was subsequently destroyed and rebuilt. Then it was destroyed right down to its foundations during the Taiping Rebellion; what you see today is a 1934 reconstruction.

The original temple is credited to the Tang Dynasty monk Jianzhen, who studied sculpture, architecture, fine arts and medicine, as well as Buddhism. In 742 AD two Japanese monks invited him to Japan for missionary work. It turned out to be mission impossible. Jianzhen made five attempts to get there, failing due to storms. On the fifth attempt he ended up in Hainan. On the sixth trip, aged 66, he finally arrived. He stayed in Japan for 10 years and died there in 763. Later, the Japanese made a lacquer statue of Jianzhen, which in 1980 was sent to Yangzhou.

The Chinese have a wooden copy of this

statue on display at the Jianzhen Memorial Hall. Modelled after the chief hall of the Toshodai Temple in Nara (Japan), the Jianzhen Memorial Hall was built in 1974 at Daming Monastery and was financed by Japanese contributions. Special exchanges are made between Nara and Yangzhou; even Deng Xiaoping, returning from a trip to Japan, came to the Yangzhou Monastery to strengthen renewed links between the two countries.

Near the monastery is **Pingshan Hall** (*píngshān táng*), the former residence of the Song Dynasty writer Ouyang Xiu, who served in Yangzhou.

Tomb of Puhaddin
(*pǔhādīng mùyuán*)

This tomb contains documents regarding China's contacts with the Muslims. It's on the eastern bank of a canal on the bus No 2 route. Puhaddin came to China during the Yuan Dynasty (1271-1368) to spread the Muslim faith. There is an active mosque in Yangzhou, but it's currently closed for renovations.

YANGZHOU 杨州

PLACES TO STAY
7 Hongqiao Hotel
   虹桥宾馆
8 Xiyuan Hotel
   西园饭店
10 Yangzhou Hotel
   杨州宾馆
14 Lantian Hotel
   蓝天大厦

PLACES TO EAT
13 KFC
   肯德鸡
17 Caigenxiang Restaurant
   菜根香饭店
19 Fuchun Teahouse
   富春茶社

21 Gonghechun Dumpling &
   Noodle Restaurant
   共和春饺面店

OTHER
1 Tang Dynasty Ruins
   唐城遗址
2 Han Dynasty Tomb
   Museum
   汉墓博物馆
3 Martyrs' Shrine
   烈士墓
4 Daming Monastery
   大明寺
5 Pingshan Hall
   平山堂
6 Shouxi Lake Park
   Entrance
   瘦西湖

9 History Museum
   杨州市博物馆
11 Ge Garden
   个园
12 Bank of China
   中国银行
15 CTS
   中国旅行社
16 Bank of China (Main
   Branch)
   中国银行（大同支行）
18 Xinhua Bookstore
   新华书店
20 Tomb of Puhaddin
   普哈丁墓园
22 He Garden
   何园
23 Long-Distance Bus Station
   杨州汽车站

History Museum

(yángzhōu shì bówùguǎn)

The museum lies to the west of Guoqing Lu, near the Xiyuan Hotel. It's in a temple originally dedicated to Shi Kefa, a Ming Dynasty official who refused to succumb to his new Qing masters and was executed.

On display are large wooden coffins dating to the Han and Northern Song dynasties, a 1000-year-old wooden boat and a Han Dynasty jade funeral suit. A small collection of calligraphy and paintings of the 'Eight Eccentrics' is displayed in another small museum just off Yanfu Lu.

Places to Stay

On the Yangzhou Teacher's College campus, across from the southern entrance to Shouxi Lake Park, is the *Hongqiao Hotel* (*hóngqiáo bīnguǎn*) (☎ 736-5275). Clean, standard doubles are good value at Y120. From the bus station take bus No 3 to the corner of Huaihai Lu and Yanfu Lu. From there it's about a 10 minute walk. Walk west, then turn north (the first right). Cross over the stone bridge, then take the first left on to Da Hongqiao Lu. After crossing over a stone bridge take the first left. Enter

through the gate in the white wall running along the small street.

The town's two main hotels are next door to each other behind the museum. The garden-style *Xiyuan Hotel* (☎ 734-4888; fax 723-3870) *(xīyuán fàndiàn)* at 1 Fengle Shanglu is said to have been constructed on the site of Qianlong's imperial villa. Doubles are from Y280 in the older building and Y680 in the new main building.

The *Yangzhou Hotel* (☎ 734-2611; fax 734-3599) *(yángzhōu bīnguǎn)* at 5 Fengle Shanglu has standard doubles from Y448.

The new *Lantian Hotel* (☎ 736-0000; fax 731-4101) *(lántiān dàshà)* on Wenhe Lu has singles/doubles starting at Y200/240.

Places to Eat

The most famous culinary export of Yangzhou is Yangzhou fried rice and, as most travellers who have tried it will aver, it tastes just like fried rice – don't expect too much.

The *Fuchun Teahouse* *(fùchūn cháshè)*, on a lane just off Guoqing Lu, is the place to go to sip tea and eat local snacks. Order *sǔn ròu zhēng jiǎo* for a delicious sampling of dumplings *(jiǎozi)* and steamed buns *(bāozi)*. There's a new branch of the Fuchun Teahouse next to Ge Garden.

The *Caigenxiang Restaurant (càigēn-xiāng fàndiàn)* is one of Yangzhou's more famous establishments, but it's not the place to be if you have no-one to help share the costs. It's currently closed for renovations, but should be open by the time you read this.

The *Gonghechun Dumpling & Noodle Restaurant (gònghéchūn jiǎomiàndàn)*, in the south of town on Ganquan Lu, is a better option for inexpensive dining.

Getting There & Away
The nearest airport is in Nanjing. The railway line also gives Yangzhou a miss, which perhaps explains why the city is missing out on China's current tourist and industrial tidal wave. The railway station nearest Yangzhou is in Zhenjiang.

From Yangzhou there are buses to Nanjing (two hours), Wuxi, Suzhou and Shanghai, all via Zhenjiang. Minibuses from Zhenjiang (1½ hours) run every 15 minutes and depart from the eastern side of Zhenjiang railway station. Buses from Zhenjiang and Nanjing first stop at the Yangzhou west bus station. Stay on the bus and get off at the east bus station, which is closer to the centre of town. Buses cross over the Yangzi on a ferry.

Getting Around
The sights are at the edge of town. If you're in a hurry, you might consider commandeering a taxi. The central area can easily be covered on foot. Bus Nos 1, 2, 3, 5, 6 and 7 terminate near the long-distance bus station.

Bus No 1 runs from the bus station up Guoqing Lu and then loops around the perimeter of the inside canal, returning just north of the bus station. Bus No 4 is an east-west bus and goes along Ganquan Lu.

YIXING COUNTY
(yíxīng xiàn)
Yixing County is famed for its tea utensils, in particular its pots. Delicious tea can be made in an aged Yixing teapot simply by adding hot water, or so it is claimed. The potteries of Yixing, especially in Dingshan, are a popular excursion for Chinese tourists, but see very few foreign visitors.

The town of Yixing is *not* an attraction, although most visitors end up passing through the place en route to the nearby karst caves or to Dingshan.

Karst Caves
(shíhuī yándòng)
There are karst caves to the south-west of Yixing township, and if you are in the area, it is worth visiting one of them. The drab interiors are lit by the standard selection of coloured neon, but you may wish to supplement this with a torch for navigation. The caves are wet and cold, so take a jacket.

Shanjuan Cave *(shànjuǎn dòng)* This cave is embedded in Snail Shell Hill (Luoyanshan), 27km south-west of Yixing. It covers an area of roughly 5000 square metres. Entry is via the middle cave, a stone hall with a 1000m floor space. From here you can mount a staircase to the snail's shell, the upper cave, or wander down to the lower caves and the water cave. In the water cave, you can jump in a rowing boat for a 120m ride to the exit called 'Suddenly See the Light'.

From Yixing take a bus heading to Dingshan and get off about midway between the two (about a 15 minute ride). Ask the driver to let you know when to get off. From there take another minibus heading west; it's about a 20 minute ride. Admission is Y19.

Zhanggong Cave *(zhānggōng dòng)* Nineteen kilometres south of Yixing town, Zhanggong Cave is the most impressive of the three caves. It's similar in scale to Shanjuan Cave, but there are more possibilities to explore smaller caves.

From inside you scale a small hill called Yufengshan; you emerge at the top amidst a temple from which there is a splendid view of the surrounding countryside with hamlets stretching as far as Lake Taihu.

From Yixing take a bus heading toward Dingshan. Ask the driver to let you know when to get off (it's about a 20 minute ride from Yixing). From there you must take a motorcycle taxi or motor-tricycle. Admission is Y23.

Linggu Cave *(línggǔ dòng)* Three kilometres down the road from Zhanggong Cave, Linggu is the largest and least explored of the three caves. The cave has six large halls arrayed roughly in a semicircle.

Near the Linggu Cave is the Yanxian Tea Plantation *(yánxiàn cháchǎng)*, with bushel-lots laid out like fat caterpillars stretching into the horizon, and the odd tea villa in the background. The trip is worth it for the tea fields alone.

To get to Linggu follow the same directions as Zhanggong. Linggu is about five minutes down the road from Zhanggong. Admission is Y16.

Places to Stay

The *Yixing Hotel* (☎ 2179-2811) *(yíxīng fàndiàn)* is at the end of Renmin Lu on the southern edge of Yixing town. It's a large building, with gardens and some luxury living. The guesthouse is a half-hour walk from Yixing bus station; turn right from the station, follow the main road south along the lakeside and cross three bridges. The hotel entrance is marked by a large archway.

The long stretch across the bridges is the same road that runs to Dingshan, so if your bus goes to Dingshan ask the driver to let you off in front of the hotel. If you don't mind the stroll, and want to see the main drag of Yixing town, another way of getting to the guesthouse is to walk three blocks straight ahead from the bus station, turn right onto Renmin Lu and keep walking until you come to the guesthouse.

The most upmarket hotel in town is the 24 storey *International Hotel Yixing* (☎ 791-6888; fax 790-0767) *(yíxīng guójì fàndiàn)* at 52 Tongzhenguan Lu. It has singles/doubles for US$25/40.

Also in the city centre is the smaller *Taodu Grand Hotel* (☎ 790-9348; fax 790-9149) *(táodū dàfàndiàn)*, at 134 Renmin Nanlu, where doubles are Y200.

Getting There & Away

There are buses from Yixing to Wuxi (1½ hours), Shanghai, Nanjing, Suzhou and Hangzhou.

Getting Around

Private minibuses ply the streets of Yixing and all of them end up in the bus stations of either Yixing town or Dingshan. There are frequent connections between the two stations.

DINGSHAN
(dīngshān)

Dingshan is the pottery centre of Yixing County, and has enjoyed that reputation since the Qin and Han dynasties; some of the scenes you can witness here, especially at the loading dock that leads into Lake Taihu, are timeless.

Almost every local family is engaged in the manufacture of ceramics, and behind the main part of town half the houses are made of the stuff. The area is extremely dusty, and everywhere you look there are vehicles hauling rocks from the mountains outside of town.

Dingshan is about 15km south of Yixing town and has two dozen ceramics factories producing more than 2000 varieties of pottery – quite an output for a population of 100,000. Among the array of products are the ceramic tables and garbage bins that you find around China, huge jars used to store oil and grain, the famed Yixing teapots, and the glazed tiling and ceramic frescoes that are desperately needed as spare parts for tourist attractions – the Forbidden City in Beijing is one of the customers. The ornamental rocks that you see in Chinese gardens are also made here.

Dingshan's pottery factories and occasional exhibition spaces are scattered around town: you will have to do a lot of walking if you want to see everything.

JIANGSU

Judging an Yixing Teapot

Buying a teapot in Dingshan or the surrounding area can be a memorable experience. To help convince you of the high quality of their teapots, shopkeepers can be extremely animated. You'll encounter shopkeepers standing on the pot, blowing through its spout, striking a match on it, showing you that the inside is the same colour as the outside or rubbing their hand against the side and showing you their palm. Unfortunately, none of these antics give you much of an indication of whether a pot is good quality.

So what should you look for? First, make sure the teapot is stable – the body, spout, handle, lid and knob should all be balanced. Also, the lid should be deep-seated and firm (it shouldn't rattle or jam). The clay should be naturally shiny and slightly rough rather than glazed smooth. Finally, ask if you can put water in the pot; the water should shoot out straight from the spout instead of dribbling.

Prices can range wildly, from just a few dollars to US$20,000 for a pot made by a renowned artist. Some say that unless you are buying a teapot made by a well known artist, don't pay more than Y30. You may want to visit the Ceramics Research Institute (on the grounds of the Pottery Exhibition Hall) to view high-quality teapots before venturing to the market across the street where a dizzying variety of generally low-quality teapots are for sale. ■

Also, many factories require prior arrangements for a visit. Main attractions include the **Pottery Exhibition Hall** (*táocí zhǎnlǎnguǎn*) and a host of factories in the east of town next to Lake Taihu.

Getting There & Away

There are direct buses from Dingshan to Yixing (minibus No 6 departs every 20 minutes for the 20 minute journey), Wuxi (1½ hours), Zhenjiang and Nanjing.

WUXI & LAKE TAIHU
(*wúxī, tàihú*)

Wuxi and nearby Lake Taihu are possible stopovers between Suzhou and Nanjing. Wuxi itself has little to recommend it (it's a typical sprawling Chinese urban development with some dirty industry thrown in for good measure), but Lake Taihu is a popular tourist destination, although more for Chinese tourists than western ones.

Lake Taihu is a freshwater lake with a total area of 2200 sq km and an average depth of 2m. There are some 90 islands, large and small, within it. The fishing industry is very active, netting more than 30 varieties of fish.

Orientation

The city centre proper is ringed by Jiefang Lu. The railway station and main bus station are about a 10 minute walk north of Jiefang Beilu. A network of canals cuts through the city, including the Grand Canal itself.

Information

The CTS office is in a building facing the square in front of the main railway station. It sells train and plane tickets.

The Bank of China is just off Renmin Zhonglu, near the Ba Bei Ban department store. The post office is on the corner of Remin Zhinglu and Jiefang Xilu.

Xihui Park
(*xīhuì gōngyuán*)

The vast Xihui Park is west of the city. The highest point in the park, Huishan Hill, is 75m above sea level, and if you climb the Dragon Light Pagoda (*lóngguāng tǎ*), the seven storey octagonal structure at the top, you'll be able to take in a panorama of Wuxi and Taihu. The brick and wood pagoda was built during the Ming Dynasty, burned down during the Qing Dynasty and rebuilt many years later. For sunrises, try

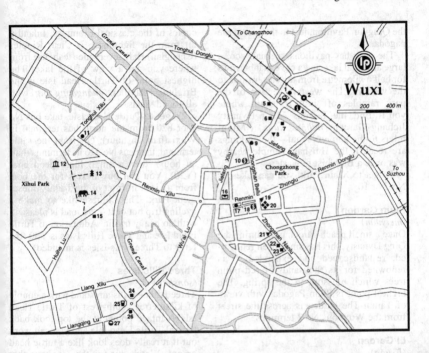

WUXI 无锡

PLACES TO STAY

5 Taishan Hotel
泰山饭店
6 Tianma Hotel
天马大酒店
7 Jinhua Hotel
锦华大饭店
15 Qinggongye University;
Foreign Experts Hotel
轻工业大学专家楼
22 New Liangxi
Grand Hotel
新梁溪大酒店
23 Liangxi Hotel
梁溪饭店
24 Holiday Inn Milido Hotel
美丽都假日酒店
26 Wuxi Grand Hotel
无锡饭店

PLACES TO EAT

8 Zhongguo Restaurant
中国饭店
19 Wuxi Roast Duck
无锡烤鸭馆
21 Wangxingji
王兴记

OTHER

1 Bicycle Rental
租自行车店
2 Railway Station
火车站
3 North Bus Station
无锡汽车客运中心站
4 CTS
中国旅行社
9 Wuxi Antiques Store
文物商店
10 Bank of China
中国银行

11 Huishan Clay Figurine
Factory
惠山泥人厂
12 Museum
博物馆
13 Dragon Light Pagoda
龙光塔
14 Zoo
动物园
16 Main Post & Telephone
Office
市邮电局
17 Wuxi International Book
Centre
无锡国际书店
18 Bank of China
中国银行
20 Ba Bai Ban Department
Store
八佰伴商场
25 Barberry's Pub Cafe
27 South Bus Station
无锡汽车站

JIANGSU

the Qingyun Pavilion, just to the east of the pagoda.

The park has pavilions, a small zoo, a large artificial lake and a cave that burrows for half a kilometre from the eastern side to the western. The western section of the park rambles off into Huishan, where you'll find the famous Ming Dynasty Jichang Garden *(jìchàng yuán)* ('Ming' refers to the garden layout – the buildings are recent); the Huishan Temple nearby was once a Buddhist monastery.

To get to Xihui Park, you can take bus No 2 or 10.

Plum Garden
(méiyuán)
Once a small peach garden built during the Qing Dynasty, this has since been renovated, re-landscaped and expanded. It is renowned for its thousands of red plum trees which blossom in the spring. The highest point is Plum Pagoda, with views of Taihu. The garden is across the street from the Wuxi bus No 2 terminus.

Li Garden
(lǐyuán)
Often crowded, this garden goes beyond bad taste – a concrete labyrinth of fish ponds, walkways, mini-bridges, a mini-pagoda, and souvenir vendors hawking garish plaster and gilded figurines. Inside the garden, on the shore of Taihu, is a tour-boat dock for cruises to other points.

Turtle Head Isle
(yuán tóuzhǔ)
So named because it appears to be shaped like the head of a turtle, Turtle Head Isle is not actually an island, but a peninsular. This is the scenic strolling area where you can watch the junks on Lake Taihu.

You can walk a circuit of the area. If you continue along the shore, you come to the ferry dock for the Three Hills Isles, passing Taihujiajue Archway and Perpetual Spring Bridge *(chángchūn qiáo)*. A walkway leads to a small lighthouse. The architecture here, like that in the Li Garden, is mostly

copies of the classical examples. Inland a bit from the lighthouse is Clear Ripples (Chenglan) Hall, a very nice teahouse from where you get a view of the lake. The highest point of Turtle Head Isle is the Brightness Pavilion *(guāngmíng tíng)* with all-round vistas.

To get to Turtle Head Isle, take bus No 1 or 820 from the north bus terminal in Wuxi (half an hour). Or, from the same terminal, take bus No 2 to its terminus (half an hour), then a small high-speed boat (Y20). You can buy tickets for the boat from a kiosk in front of the Taihu Amusement Park. The Chinese like to make a cycling trip out of it – the road is pleasant, with no heavy traffic. Admission to Turtle Head Isle and Three Hills Isles is Y30 (the ferry to Three Hills Isles is included).

Three Hills Isles
(sānshān)
Three Hills Isles is an island park a couple of kilometres south-west of Turtle Head Isle. Vantage points at the top look back toward Turtle Head Isle and you can work out if it really does look like a turtle head or not. Watch out for the monkeys that inhabit the isles.

Places to Stay – budget
Qinggongye University Foreign Experts Hotel (☎ 586-1034) *(qīnggōngyè dàxué zhuānjiālóu)* on Huihe Lu has doubles with private bath in the foreign students' dormitory for Y100. From the railway station take bus No 2. After crossing the Grand Canal get off at the second stop. The university is a few metres down the road on the other side of the street.

Places to Stay – middle
Touts around the railway station will take travellers to the *Jinhua Hotel* (☎ 272-0612; fax 271-1092) *(jìnhuá dàfàndiàn)*, where the cheapest doubles cost Y280. Rooms are slightly run-down, but clean. To get here, cross the bridge across the street from the railway station then take the first small street on your left.

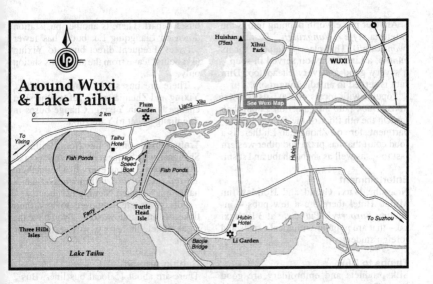

Around Wuxi & Lake Taihu

0   1   2 km

Huishan (75m)

Xihui Park

WUXI

See Wuxi Map

Plum Garden

Liang Xilu

Hubin Lu

To Yixing

Taihu Hotel

Fish Ponds

High-Speed Boat

Fish Ponds

Turtle Head Isle

Ferry

Three Hills Isles

Hubin Hotel

To Suzhou

Baojie Bridge

Li Garden

Lake Taihu

Even closer to the railway station is the *Taishan Hotel* (☎ 230-3888; fax 230-1069) *(tàishān fàndiàn)*, at 15 Tonghui Donglu, with doubles from Y248.

The new *Tianma Hotel* (☎ 272-7668; fax 272-7878) *(tiānmǎ dàjiǔdiàn)*, at 18 Liangxi Xilu, has doubles for Y350. To get here follow the same directions to the Jinhua Hotel, except go right after the bridge.

Closer to the city centre is the *Liangxi Hotel* (☎ 272-6812; fax 271-9174) *(liángxī fàndiàn)* at 63 Zhongshan Nanlu. Doubles cost from Y270. Take bus No 12 from the railway station. Next door is the more upmarket *New Liangxi Grand Hotel* (☎ 272-6878; fax 270-1207) *(xīn liángxī dàjiǔdiàn)* where the cheapest doubles are Y372.

Places to Stay – top end

In Wuxi itself is the *Holiday Inn Milido* (☎ 676-5665; fax 670-1668) *(měilìdū jiàrì jiǔdiàn)*, on the traffic circle where Liang Xilu and Liangqing Lu intersect. Rooms start at Y882. On the opposite side of the circle is the four star *Wuxi Grand* (☎ 670-6789; fax 270-0991) *(wúxī dàfàndiàn)*, with rates from Y955. Neither of these

places is worth the exorbitant rates charged. A new Sheraton was under construction at the time of writing.

All the other tourist hotels are around the lakeside, about 12km from the railway station in Wuxi (half an hour). The best hotel is the *Hubin Hotel* (☎ 510-1888; fax 510-2637) *(húbīn fàndiàn)*. Standard rooms in the main building are Y580 to Y996. Rooms in an older building at the back start at Y200. From the main bus terminal in Wuxi take bus No 1 or 820.

. The remotely located *Taihu Hotel* (☎ 551-7888; fax 551-2771) *(tàihú fàndiàn)* has standard doubles from Y298 to Y660. From Wuxi take bus No 2 to its terminus, then it's a half-hour walk or short taxi ride.

Places to Eat

Wuxi has no shortage of restaurants. For an excellent and economical lunch try the *Zhongguo Restaurant (zhōngguó fàndiàn)*, just south of the railway station. One entrance leads into an à la carte dining area, but look for the rough and ready section where dumplings are served – ask for *xiǎolóngbāo*.

Another place worth popping into is the cafeteria-style *Wangxingji Restaurant* (*wángxìngjì*). This place is famous for its *húntun*, a kind of ravioli served in soup – it's very good and very cheap too. Dim sum is served in an adjoining room.

Popular with locals and expats is *Wuxi Roast Duck* (*kǎo yā guǎn*) on Zhongshan Lu. On the 6th floor of the *Ba Bai Ban* department store on Zhongshan Lu there is a food court that has pizza and other western fast food, as well as shabu shabu and sushi.

Entertainment

Near the Wuxi Grand and Holiday Inn Milido Hotel there are a few pubs – including *Barberry's Pub Cafe* at 3 Liangxi Lu – that are popular with local expats and foreign students.

Things to Buy

Silk products and embroidery are good buys. There are also some remarkably ugly clay figurines for sale around the place. A peasant folk art, they were usually models of opera stars. Look out for models of obese infants – symbols of fortune and happiness and just the thing to fill up your mantelpiece.

The Wuxi Antiques Store (*wúxī wénwù shāngdiàn*) is a good place to stock up on souvenirs. The Huishan Clay Figurine Factory (*huìshān níǒu gōngchǎng*) is near Xihui Park; here you can buy clay figurines and overpriced Yixing teapots. If you walk outside the gates of the factory there's a street stall that sells clay figurines at better prices.

Every Sunday there is a jade market (*yù shìchǎng*) near the Jinhua Hotel and railway station that sells jade and local handicrafts, including Yixing teapots.

Getting There & Away

Air Wuxi has no airport, but you can book flights out of Shanghai from the CTS branch adjacent to the railway station or any major hotel.

Bus The north bus station, next to the railway station, is where most long distance buses depart. There is another bus station down on Liangqing Lu, but it has fewer services. Frequent direct buses to Yixing (1½ hours) leave from the south bus station only.

There are buses to Shanghai, Suzhou, Yixing and Zhenjiang. To get to Dingshan change buses in Yixing. Change buses in Zhenjiang to get to Yangzhou.

Train Wuxi is on the line from Beijing to Shanghai, with frequent express and special-express trains. About every two hours there are trains to Suzhou (40 minutes), Shanghai (1¾ hours) and Nanjing (2¾ hours).

Foreigners are supposed to buy their tickets from Window No 2. If you have the right ticket, there is a soft-seat waiting room.

Getting Around

There are about 15 local bus lines. Bus 2 runs from the railway station, along Jiefang Lu, across two bridges to Xihui Park, then way out to Plum Garden, stopping short of the Taihu Hotel. Bus No 2 almost crosses the bus No 1 route at Gongnongbing Square.

Bus No 1 starts on Gongnongbing Lu and runs to Li Garden and the Hubin and Shuixiu hotels. The actual terminal of bus No 1 is further on across a bridge to the scenery on Turtle Head Island.

A good tour bus is No 10, which does a long loop around the northern part of the city area, taking in four bridges, Xihui Park and the shopping strip of Renmin Lu.

You can rent a bike from behind the bus station (west of the railway station). Look for a public telephone sign, which is on the same building. The cost is Y7 per day or Y1 per hour; a deposit is required.

SUZHOU
(*sūzhōu*)
Jiangsu's most famous attraction, Suzhou (population about 600,000) is a famed silk production centre and a celebrated retreat brimming with gardens and canals. However, this hasn't done anything to hold back

the gathering tide of urban renewal. Unfortunately, much of the city's charm is being swept away by new road, housing and hotel developments. Nevertheless, Suzhou's charming gardens and other historical attractions are worth a visit.

History

Dating back some 2500 years, Suzhou is one of the oldest towns in the Yangzi Basin. With the completion of the Grand Canal in the Sui Dynasty, Suzhou found itself strategically located on a major trading route, and the city's fortunes and size grew rapidly.

Suzhou flourished as a centre of shipping and grain storage, bustling with merchants and artisans. By the 12th century the town had attained its present dimensions, and if you consult the map, you'll see the layout of the old town.

The city walls, a rectangle enclosed by moats, were pierced by six gates (north, south, two in the east and two in the west). Crisscrossing the city were six north-south canals and 14 east-west canals. Although the walls have largely disappeared and a fair proportion of the canals have been plugged, central Suzhou retains its 'Renaissance' character.

A legend was spun about Suzhou through tales of beautiful women with mellifluous voices, and through the famous proverb 'In heaven there is paradise, on earth Suzhou and Hangzhou'. The story picks up when Marco Polo arrived in 1276. He added the adjectives 'great' and 'noble', although he reserved his finer epithets for Hangzhou.

By the 14th century Suzhou had established itself as China's leading silk producer. Aristocrats, pleasure-seekers, famous scholars, actors and painters were attracted to the city, constructing villas and garden retreats for themselves.

At the height of Suzhou's development in the 16th century, the gardens, large and small, numbered over 100. If we mark time here, we arrive at the town's tourist formula today – 'Garden City, Venice of the East', a medieval mix of woodblock guilds and embroidery societies, whitewashed housing, cobbled streets, tree-lined avenues and canals.

The wretched workers of the silk sweatshops, protesting against paltry wages and the injustices of the contract hire system, were staging violent strikes even in the 15th century, and the landlords shifted. In 1860 Taiping troops took the town without a blow. In 1896 Suzhou was opened to foreign trade, with Japanese and international concessions. During WWII, it was occupied by the Japanese and then by the Kuomintang. Somehow Suzhou slipped through the worst ravages of the Cultural Revolution relatively unscathed.

Information

Tourist Offices Both CITS (☎ 522-2681) and CTS (☎ 522-5583) are in a separate building in the Suzhou Hotel compound. There is also a CITS at the railway station.

PSB The PSB office is at 7 Dashitou Xiang, on the corner of Renmin Lu. Enter through a red door on Renmin Lu.

Money The Bank of China is at 490 Renmin Lu, but all of the major tourist hotels have foreign-exchange counters as well.

Post & Communications The post office is on the corner of Renmin Lu and Jingde Lu. The Internet Bar (☎ 529-6278), also on Renmin Lu, offers Internet access through Netscape. Call ahead to make sure its connection is up and running. It's open from 7 pm to 2 am.

North Temple
(běi sìtǎ)

The North Temple has the tallest pagoda south of the Yangzi – at nine storeys it dominates the northern end of Renmin Lu. You can climb it for a fine aerial view of the town and the farmland beyond, where tea, rice and wheat are grown. The factory chimneys, the new pagodas of Suzhou,

JIANGSU

loom on the outskirts, and so does the haze and smoke they create.

The temple complex goes back 1700 years and was originally a residence. The pagoda has been burnt, built and rebuilt. Made of wood, it dates from the 17th century. Off to the side is Nanmu Hall, which was rebuilt in the Ming Dynasty with some of its features imported from elsewhere. There is a teahouse with a small garden out the back.

Suzhou Museum
(sūzhōu bówùguǎn)
Found near the Humble Administrator's Garden, the museum was once the residence of a Taiping leader, Li Xiucheng.

The museum offers some interesting old maps (Grand Canal, Suzhou, heaven and earth), Qing Dynasty steles forbidding workers' strikes, and relics unearthed or rescued from various sites around the Suzhou District (funerary objects, porcelain bowls and bronze swords). There are no English captions.

Suzhou Silk Museum
(sūzhōu sīchóu bówùguǎn)
Also close to the pagoda, the silk museum is worth a visit. It has some fascinating exhibitions, including a section on old looms and weaving techniques and a room with live silk worms in various stages of life. A second building displays clothing made of silk from the early 1900s.

Temple of Mystery
(xuánmiàoguàn)
The heart of what was once Suzhou Bazaar – an area that is being rapidly developed – is the Taoist Temple of Mystery. It was founded in the 3rd century (during the Jin Dynasty and laid out between 275 and 279 AD) with additions during Song times.

From the Qing Dynasty onwards, the bazaar fanned out from the temple with tradespeople and travelling performers using the grounds. The enormous Sanqing Hall, supported by 60 pillars and capped by a double roof with upturned eaves, dates

from 1181. It was burnt and seriously damaged in the 19th century. During the Cultural Revolution, the Red Guards squatted here, and it was later transformed into a library. Today the temple is surrounded by Suzhou's main shopping area, Guanqian Jie.

Museum of Opera & Theatre
(xìqǔ bówùguǎn)
In the old city of Suzhou, this small museum is worth going to for the surrounding area of small cobblestone lanes lined with stalls selling vegetables and inexpensive snacks. The museum houses a moveable stage, old musical instruments, costumes and photos of famous performers. From Linden Lu go east on Daru Hang. At the end of the road go right, then take the first left.

Gardens
(huāyuán)
Suzhou's gardens are looked upon as works of art – a fusion of nature, architecture, poetry and painting designed to ease, move or assist the mind.

Unlike the massive imperial gardens, the classical landscaping of Suzhou reflects the personal taste of officials and scholars south of the Yangzi. Rich officials, once their worldly duties were performed, would find solace here in kingdoms of ponds and rockeries. The gardens were meant to be enjoyed either in solitary contemplation or in the company of a close circle of friends with a glass of wine, a concert, poetry recital or a literary discussion.

Each garden is meant to be savoured at a snail's pace, but it's difficult to wax contemplative when there are thousands of other visitors taking photos of each other or sketching the foliage. Old-timers come here to relax.

The size of the crowds depends on the weather, the day of the week and the garden. The gardens are usually open from early morning to dusk (from 7.30 am to 5 pm) and, unless otherwise noted, admission is under Y10.

Suzhou's Gardens

The key elements of the gardens are rocks and water. There are surprisingly few flowers and no fountains – just like the Zen gardens of Japan, they give one an illusion of a natural scene with only moss, sand and rock. These microcosms were laid out by master crafts-people and changed hands many times over the centuries.

The gardens suffered a setback during the Taiping Rebellion in the 1860s, and under subsequent foreign domination of Suzhou. Efforts were made to restore them in the 1950s, but during the so-called Horticultural Revolution gardeners downed tools, as flowers were frowned upon.

In 1979 the Suzhou Garden Society was formed, and an export company was set up to promote Suzhou-designed gardens. A few of the gardens have been renovated and opened to the public. ∎

Humble Administrator's Garden *(zhuó-zhèng yuán)* Many consider this Suzhou's second-best garden (after the Garden of the Master of the Nets).

The five hectare garden features streams, ponds, bridges and islands of bamboo; it dates from the early 1500s. There's also a teahouse and a small museum that explains Chinese landscape gardening concepts. In the same area are the Suzhou Museum and several silk mills. Entry costs Y20.

Lion Grove *(shīzilín)* Just up the street from the Humble Administrator's Garden, this one hectare grove was constructed in 1350 by the monk Tian Ru and other disciples, as a memorial to their master, Zhi Zheng. The garden has rockeries that evoke leonine forms. The walls of the labyrinth of tunnels bear calligraphy from famous chisels.

Garden of Harmony *(yíyuán)* A small Qing Dynasty garden owned by an official called Gu Wenbin, this one is quite young for a Suzhou garden. It has assimilated many of the features of other gardens and blended them into a style of its own. In the east are buildings and courtyards. The western section has pools with coloured pebbles, rockeries, hillocks and pavilions.

Blue Wave Pavilion *(cānglàngtíng)* A bit on the wild side with winding creeks and luxuriant trees, this is one of the oldest gardens in Suzhou. The buildings date from the 11th century, although they have been rebuilt on numerous occasions since.

Originally the home of a prince, the property passed into the hands of the scholar Su Zimei, who gave it its name. The one hectare garden attempts to create optical illusions with the scenery both outside and inside – you look from the pool immediately outside to the distant hills.

Enlightened Way Hall *(míngdào táng)*, the largest building, is said to have been a site for delivery of lectures during the Ming Dynasty. On the other side of Renmin Lu, close by, is the former Confucius Temple.

Garden of the Master of the Nets *(wǎngshī yuán)* This is the smallest garden in Suzhou – half the size of the Blue Wave Pavilion and one-tenth the size of the Humble Administrator's Garden. It's small and hard to find, but well worth the trouble as it's better than all the others combined.

This garden was laid out in the 12th century, abandoned, then restored in the 18th century as part of the residence of a retired official. According to one story, he announced that he'd had enough of bureaucracy and would rather be a fisherman. Another explanation of the name is that it was simply near Wangshi Lu. The eastern part of the garden is the residential area –

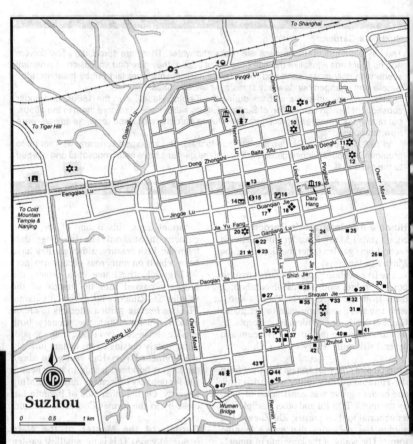

Suzhou

0   0.5   1 km

originally with side rooms for sedan-chair lackeys, guest reception and living quarters. The central part is the main garden. The western part is an inner garden where a courtyard contains the Spring-Rear Cottage *(diànchūn yí)*, the master's study. This section and the study, with its Ming-style furniture and palace lanterns, was duplicated and unveiled at the Metropolitan Museum of Art in New York in 1981.

A miniature model of the whole garden, using Qingtian jade, Yingde rocks, Anhui paper, Suzhou silk and incorporating the halls, kiosks, ponds, blossoms and rare plants of the original design, was produced especially for a display at the Pompidou Centre in Paris in 1982.

The most striking feature of this garden is its use of space. Despite its size, the scale of the buildings is large, but nothing appears cramped. A section of the buildings is used by a cooperative of woodblock artists who find the peaceful atmosphere congenial to work.

The entrance is via a narrow alley just west of the Suzhou Hotel. Going east on

SUZHOU 苏州

PLACES TO STAY
13 Overseas Chinese Hotel
华侨大酒店
25 Gloria Plaza Hotel
凯莱大酒店
26 Suzhou University Foreign
Students Dormitory
苏州大学
外国留学生宿舍
28 Nanlin Hotel
南林饭店
30 Dongwu Guesthouse
东吴饭店
31 Gusu Hotel
姑苏饭店
32 Suzhou Hotel; CITS; CTS
苏州饭店，中国国际
旅行社，中国旅行社
35 Nanyuan Guesthouse
南园宾馆
37 Suzhou Medical School
Guesthouse
苏州医学院招待所
38 Canglang Hotel
沧浪宾馆
40 Bamboo Grove Hotel
竹辉宾馆
41 Xiangwang Hotel
相王宾馆
42 Friendship Hotel
友谊宾馆

PLACES TO EAT
17 Songhelou Restaurant
松鹤楼

33 Yong He Soya-Bean Milk
Shop
永和豆浆
39 Bamboo Grove Snack Bar
竹园餐厅
43 Taipei Refreshments
Centre
锁阆菜

OTHER
1 West Garden Temple
西园
2 Garden for Lingering In
留园
3 Railway Station
火车站
4 Long-Distance Bus Station
南门汽车站
5 Suzhou Silk Museum
丝绸博物馆
6 Bicycle Rental
租自行店
7 North Temple Pagoda
北寺塔
8 Suzhou Museum
苏州博物馆
9 Humble Administrator's
Garden
拙政园
10 Lion Grove
狮子林
11 East Garden
东园
12 Coupling Garden
耦园
14 Post Office
邮局
15 Bank of China
中国银行

16 Temple of Mystery
玄妙观
18 Suzhou Shang Sha
苏州商厦
19 Museum of Opera &
Theatre
戏曲博物馆
20 Garden of Harmony
怡园
21 PSB
公安局外事科
22 Suzhou Antiques Store
文物店
23 China Eastern Airlines
Booking Office
东方航空售票处
24 Twin Pagoda Park
双塔院
27 Internet Bar
网络吧
29 Bicycle Rental
租自行车店
34 Garden of the Master
of the Nets
网师园
36 Blue Wave Pavilion
沧浪亭
44 Long-Distance
Bus Station
南门汽车站
45 Grand Canal Boats
Ticket Office
轮船站
46 Ruiguang Pagoda
瑞光塔
47 Pan Gate
盘门三景

JIANGSU

Shiquan Lu, take a right onto Daichengqiao Lu, then left onto the first alley.

Garden for Lingering In (liúyuán) Extending over an area of three hectares, the Garden for Lingering In is one of the largest Suzhou gardens, noted for its adroit partitioning with building complexes.

It dates from the Ming Dynasty and managed to escape destruction during the Taiping Rebellion. A 700m covered walkway connects the major scenic spots, and the windows have carefully selected per-

spectives. The walkway is inlaid with calligraphy from celebrated masters. The garden has a wealth of potted plants.

Outside Mandarin Duck (Yuanyang) Hall is a 6.5m-high Lake Tai piece – it's the final word on rockeries. The garden is about 3km west of the old city walls. The bus there will take you over bridges that look down on the busy water traffic.

West Garden Temple
(xīyuán sì)
Approximately 500m west of the Garden

for Lingering In, this temple was built on
the site of a garden laid out at the same
time as the Garden for Lingering In and
then donated to the Buddhist community.
The temple was destroyed in the 19th
century and entirely rebuilt; it contains
some expressive Buddhist statues.

Cold Mountain Temple
(hánshān sì)
One kilometre west of the Garden for Lingering In, this temple was named after the
poet-monk Hanshan, who lived in the 7th
century. It was repeatedly burnt down and
rebuilt, and holds little of interest except
for a stele by poet Zhang Ji immortalising
nearby Maple Bridge and the temple bell
(since removed to Japan). However, the
fine walls and the humpback bridge are
worth seeing.

The temple was once the site of lively
local trading in silk, wood and grain. Not
far from its saffron walls lies the Grand
Canal. To get to the temple take bus No 4
to the terminal, cross the bridge and walk
to the No 6 bus route; or take bus No 5 and
then connect with No 6.

Tiger Hill
(hǔqiūshān)
In the far north-west of town, Tiger Hill is
extremely popular with Chinese tourists,
but less so with those from overseas. The
hill itself is artificial, and is the final resting
place of He Lu, founding father of Suzhou.
He Lu died in the 6th century BC, and
myths have coalesced around him – he is
said to have been buried with a collection
of 3000 swords and to be guarded by a
white tiger.

Built in the 10th century, the leaning
Yunyan Pagoda stands atop Tiger Hill. The
octagonal seven storey pagoda is built entirely of brick, an innovation in Chinese
architecture at the time. The pagoda began
tilting over 400 years ago, and today the
highest point is displaced over 2m from its
original position.

To get to Tiger Hill, take bus No 5 to its
terminus. Admission is Y25.

Pan Gate
(pánmén)
At the south-western corner of the city,
straddling the outer moat, this stretch of
the city wall contains Suzhou's only remaining original city gate. From the top of
the gate there are good views of the moat,
surrounding houses and **Ruiguang Ta**, a
crumbling pagoda that dates from the third
century and is reputedly the oldest pagoda
in Jiangsu Province.

Near the southern end of Renmin Lu
cross over the humpbacked Wumen Qiao
Bridge and take the first right.

Boat Tours
By the canal, south of the railway station
(opposite the soft-seat waiting room), you
can hire a boat that will take you along the
canal either south to Pan Gate or north to
Tiger Hill. If you are with a group the cost
is Y30, or if you hire a boat alone it's
Y150. The trip takes about an hour. Boats
depart from the Foreign Travellers Transportation Company Pier (☎ 752-6931)
(wàishì lǚyou chē chuán gōngsī mǎtóu).

Places to Stay
Hotel touts outside the railway station can
be especially aggressive here. Some travellers reported going with touts, only to be
brought to hotels that don't accept foreigners. A couple of hours later they hadn't
found a place to stay and were stuck with a
large taxi bill.

Places to Stay – budget
On Suzhou University campus, the *Dongwu
Guesthouse (dōngwú fàndiàn)* has new,
clean, air-conditioned doubles for Y180.
From Renmin Lu Head east on Shiquan
Jie; the guesthouse is on the left bordering
the outer moat (prior to crossing over the
bridge). Also on campus, the *Suzhou University Foreign Students Dormitory (sūzhōu
dàxué wàiguó liúxuéshēng sùshè)* has
doubles available for Y60 to Y200. It's
next to the Institute of East West Cul-
tures/Foreign Affairs building.

The *Nanlin Hotel* (see Places to Stay –

top end) has doubles with shared bath in an older building (Building F) for Y140.

The *Suzhou Medical School Guesthouse* *(sūzhōu yīxuéyuàn)* has grotty doubles with no bath for Y80. It's in an alley off Wuqueqiao, just north of the Canglang Hotel.

Places to Stay – middle

The south-eastern corner of town is a gold mine of mid-range accommodation. The new *Canglang Hotel* (☎ 520-1557; fax 510-3285) *(cānglàng bīnguǎn)*, at 53 Wuqueqiao, has clean doubles for Y250. The *Friendship Hotel* (☎ 529-1601; fax 520-6221) *(yǒuyì bīnguǎn)* on Zhuhui Lu has standard doubles from Y240.

Just down the street, the *Xiangwang Hotel* (☎ 529-1162; fax 529-1182) *(xiāngwáng bīnguǎn)* offers a similar deal. Standard doubles are Y220 or Y280. The hotel is on the north-western corner of Xiangwang Lu and Zhuhui Lu.

Walk around the corner and you'll reach the entrance of the *Gusu Hotel* (☎ 519-5127; fax 519-9727) *(gūsū fàndiàn)*, at 5 Xiangwang Lu off Shiquan Jie, a sprawling place with standard doubles from Y260 to Y360. It was closed for renovations at the time of writing, but should be open by the time you have this book.

A final possibility is the *Overseas Chinese Hotel* (☎ 720-2883) *(huáqiáo dàjiǔdiàn)* at 518 Renmin Lu, just north of Guanqian Jie. It has standard doubles at Y300.

Places to Stay – top end

The *Bamboo Grove Hotel* (☎ 520-5601; fax 520-8778) *(zhúhuī fàndiàn)*, on Zhuhui Lu, is the pick of Suzhou's top-end accommodation with all the facilities you would expect of a five star hotel. Room rates start at US$120.

The *Suzhou Hotel* (☎ 520-4646; fax 520-5191) *(sūzhōu fàndiàn)*, at 115 Shiquan Jie, does a brisk trade in tour groups, and is a fairly dull place. Rooms start at US$70.

The *Nanlin Hotel* (☎ 522-4641) *(nánlín fàndiàn)* is at 22 Gunxiufang, off Shiquan Jie. Its very pleasant gardens include a small section with outdoor ceramic tables and chairs. Doubles cost from US$80.

The *Nanyuan Guesthouse* (☎ 519-7661; fax 519-8806) *(nányuán bīnguǎn)*, at 249 Shiquan Jie, is inside a walled garden compound. Room prices range from US$50 for a standard twin room to US$200 for a deluxe suite.

Close to the old city of Suzhou, the up-market *Gloria Plaza Hotel* (☎ 521-8508; fax 521-8533) *(kǎilái dàjiǔdiàn)*, at 535 Ganjiang East Road, offers Internet connections, email and voicemail. Rooms start at Y765.

Places to Eat

Suzhou is a tourist town, and consequently there is no shortage of expensive places serving up tourist cuisine. There are several restaurants geared toward tourists on Shiquan Jie. Open 24 hours is *Yong He Soya-Bean Milk Shop (yǒnghé dòujiāng)* at 167 Shiquan Jie (opposite the back gate of the Garden of the Master of the Nets). It serves tasty rice, noodle and soup dishes; for breakfast there is sweet soya bean milk *(yóutiáo)* and fried bread sticks *(dòujiāng)*.

The *Taipei Refreshments Centre (táiběi diǎnxīn chéng)* at 29½ Renmin Lu has an English menu and is worth popping into for a quick and inexpensive bowl of noodles or a rice dish. There's also shaved ice and green or red bean deserts.

You can fill up for Y5 in the food court on the 3rd floor of the *Suzhou Shang Sha (sūzhōu shāngshà)* department store at 57-69 Guanqian Jie. Buy food tickets at the entrance, then redeem them by choosing from the wide array of Chinese dishes and deserts, including dumplings, steamed buns, snails and 100-year-old eggs. It's hard to miss this large store, with its ornate tiled roof.

Opposite the Friendship Hotel look out for the *Bamboo Grove Snack Bar (zhúyuán cāntīng)*, which has affordable stir fries.

A half block north of the Garden of Harmony is Jia Yu Fang, a street lined with several fairly upmarket *Chinese restaurants*.

JIANGSU

If money is no object, you might try the *Songhelou Restaurant (sōnghè lóu)*, at 141 Guanqian Jie, rated as the most famous restaurant in Suzhou: Emperor Qianlong is said to have eaten there. The large variety of dishes includes squirrel fish, plain steamed prawns, braised eel, pork with pine nuts, butterfly-shaped sea cucumber, watermelon chicken and spicy duck.

The waiter may insist that you be parcelled off to the special 'tour bus' cubicle at the back where an English menu awaits. The Songhelou runs from Guanqian Jie to an alley behind, where tour minibuses pull up. Travellers give it mixed reviews.

Entertainment

Very popular is the nightly performance of dance and song at the Garden of the Master of the Nets. The audience moves from pavilion to pavilion to watch a variety of traditional Chinese performing arts. The show lasts from 7.30 to 10.30 pm and tickets can be bought from CITS for Y60. Alternatively, turn up shortly before the performance and buy your ticket on the spot.

Things to Buy

Suzhou-style embroidery, calligraphy, paintings, sandalwood fans, writing brushes and silk underclothes are for sale nearly everywhere. For souvenir items, you may want to try the Suzhou Antiques Store on Renmin Lu. Check prices against those in the small souvenir shops on Shiquan Jie before making any purchases, however.

For silk try the cloth shops on Guanqian Jie; most cloth shops have tailors on hand who can make simple clothing in about three days. Next to the Temple of Mystery there's a night market that sells very reasonably priced silk.

The newsagent in the Bamboo Grove Hotel has a good selection of foreign books.

Getting There & Away

Air Suzhou does not have an airport, but China Eastern Airlines (☎ 522-2788)

(dōngfāng hángkōng gōngsī) has a ticket office at 192 Renmin Lu for booking flights out of Shanghai.

Bus There are two long-distance bus stations. The main one is at the northern end of Renmin Lu, next to the railway station, and the other one is at the southern end of Renmin Lu. There are connections between Suzhou and just about every major place in the region, including Shanghai, Hangzhou, Wuxi, Yangzhou and Yixing.

Travelling by bus on the new Nanjing-Suzhou highway takes about the same amount of time as the train, but tickets are generally slightly more expensive.

Train Suzhou is on the railway line from Nanjing to Shanghai. To Shanghai takes about 1¼ hours, to Wuxi 40 minutes and to Nanjing 3¼ hours. For long-distance sleepers, ask your hotel or try CITS.

Boat There are boats along the Grand Canal to Hangzhou. It's basically only foreigners and Overseas Chinese who use them these days – locals prefer to travel by bus or train.

Boats from Suzhou to Hangzhou depart daily at 5 pm and arrive the next morning at 7.30 am. The fare is Y80 for a sleeper in a four berth room or Y150 in a double. Tickets can be bought through CITS or at the 'civilisation unit' window at the boat booking office. CITS adds a Y20 service charge.

Getting Around

Bus The main thoroughfare is Renmin Lu with the railway and main bus stations just off the northern end, and a large boat dock and another long-distance bus station at the southern end.

Bus No 1 runs the length of Renmin Lu and bus No 2 is a kind of around-the-city bus. Bus No 5 is a good east-west bus and can be picked up in either direction on Renmin Lu near the Bank of China or Overseas Chinese Hotel. Bus No 4 runs from Changmen directly east along Baita

Lu, turns south and runs past the eastern end of Guanqian Jie and then on to the Suzhou Hotel.

Taxi Taxis and pedicabs congregate outside the main railway station, down by the boat dock at the southern end of Renmin Lu, and at Jingmen (Nanxin Bridge) at the western end of Jingde Lu. They also tend to hover around tourist hotels. Drivers generally use their meters. Like elsewhere in China, the pedicab drivers are almost more trouble than they are worth.

Bicycle There are several bicycle rental shops scattered around the city, including one opposite the Silk Museum, one across from the Suzhou Hotel, one next door to the Suzhou Hotel and another next to the railway station. Hire costs are about Y10 to Y20 per day, plus deposit.

AROUND SUZHOU
Some of the local buses go for a considerable distance, such as bus No 11. You could hop on one for a ride to the terminal to see the enchanting countryside.

Grand Canal
(dà yùnhé)
The canal proper cuts to the west and south of Suzhou, within a 10km range of the town. Suburban bus Nos 13, 14, 15 and 16 will get you there. In the north-west, bus No 11 follows the canal for a fair distance.

Once you arrive, it's simply a matter of finding yourself a nice bridge, getting out your deck chair and watching the world go by. Unfortunately, parking yourself for too long could make you the main tourist attraction.

Precious Belt Bridge
(bǎodài qiáo)
This is one of China's best, with 53 arches, the three central humpbacks being larger to allow boats through. It straddles the Grand Canal, and is a popular spot with fisherfolk.

The bridge is not used for traffic – a modern one has been built alongside – and

is thought to be a Tang Dynasty construction named after Wang Zhongshu, a local prefect who sold his precious belt to pay for the bridge's construction for the benefit of his people. Precious Belt Bridge is south-east of Suzhou.

You can get there by taxi or a 40 minute bike ride. Head south on Renmin Lu, past the south moat, then left at the TV towers.

Lake Taihu Area
The following places can all be reached by long-distance buses from the station at the southern end of Renmin Lu (north of the bridge) or the minibus station south of the bridge over the south moat on Renmin Lu.

Lingyanshan *(língyán shān)* This is 15km south-west of Suzhou. There are weirdly shaped rocks, a temple and pagoda (molested by Red Guards), and panoramas of mulberry trees, fertile fields and Lake Taihu in the distance.

The now active Buddhist monastery has a Tibetan feel. It's set atop a large hill, although in these parts 'large' is relative to totally flat. The monastery dates back to the Ming Dynasty. It was shut down during the Cultural Revolution, but was permitted to reopen in 1980.

Lingyanshan is a lovely place to cycle to, although along the way you pass some nightmarish scenes of industrial pollution (these can be intriguing in their own bizarre way). From the railway station take bus No 16 to its terminus.

Tianpingshan *(tiānpíng shān)* This is 18km south-west of Suzhou and has more of the same – plus some medicinal spring waters.

Guangfu *(guāngfú)* About 25km to the south-west, bordering the lake, Guangfu has an ancient seven storey pagoda and is dotted with plum trees.

Dongshan *(dōngshān)* Forty kilometres to the south-west of Suzhou, this place is

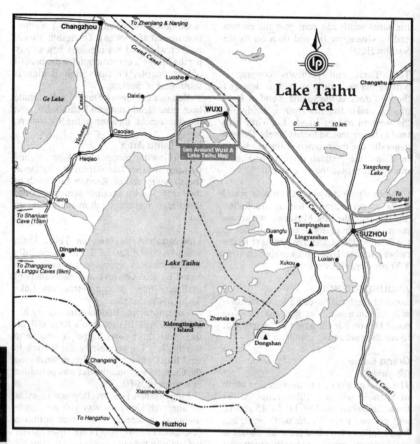

noted for its gardens and the Purple Gold (Zijin) Nunnery, which contains 16 coloured clay arhats and is surrounded by Lake Taihu on three sides.

Xidongtingshan Island *(xīdòngtíng shān)* This town, also called Xishan, is a large island 60km south-west of Suzhou. Getting there involves a 10km ferry ride. Eroded Taihu rocks are 'harvested' here for landscaping. Take a bus from opposite Suzhou railway station to Luxian, then catch a ferry across to Zhenxia.

Changshu *(chángshú)* Fifty kilometres north-east of Suzhou, this town is noted for its lace making. To the north-west of the town is Yushan, with historical and scenic spots, including a nine storey Song pagoda.

Luzhi *(lùzhí)* In this town on the water, 25km east of Suzhou, the canals provide the main means of commuting – in concrete flat-bottomed boats. The old Baosheng Temple has arhats. To get here take a bus from the station at the eastern end of Shiquan Lu (before you cross the moat).

XUZHOU
(xúzhōu)

At the junction of four provinces (Henan, Anhui, Shandong and Jiangsu), Xuzhou has a recorded history of more than 2000 years. Liu Bang, the first emperor of the Han Dynasty, was from here. More than 200 wars have been fought in the area, the most recent being one of the three major battles between the Kuomintang and the Communists (the former lost). Today Xuzhou is a fairly ordinary industrial city and a major railway junction.

Things to See

The **Xuzhou Terracotta Army Museum** *(xúzhōu bīngmǎyǒng bówùguǎn)* contains a miniature army of terracotta soldiers and horses (each under 40cm) that are more than 2000 years old.

Discovered in 1984, four pits display 3000 well preserved clay horses, foot soldiers, chariot soldiers, archers and servants all headed by a commander, and all with varying facial expressions.

The army dates from the Han Dynasty and is believed to have been built to guard the tomb of a general or warrior prince. It's in the south-eastern part of the city; bus No 5 will get you there.

In the northern part of the city is the **Han Dynasty Tomb** *(gūishānhànmù)*, the tomb of the third Chu duke, Liu Wu. There are several underground rooms, including a stable, kitchen, armoury, bathroom, coffin room and antechambers for the prince and princess. This is where the jade burial suit, on display in the Nanjing Museum, was discovered. Take bus No 37.

Half the scenery of Xuzhou is found on **Dragon in the Clouds Hill** *(yúnlóng shān)*: the Xinghua Temple, several pavilions and a stone carving from the Northern Wei Dynasty. Set in a grotto off the mountainside is a giant gilded buddha head, the statue of the Sakyamuni Buddha. The hill is a 10 minute walk west of the Nanjiao Hotel, or take bus No 2 or 11.

In a 100 acre park filled with pine and cypress trees at the southern edge of town is the **Monument to Huaihai Campaign Martyrs** *(huáihǎi zhànyì lièshì jìniàntǎ)*, a revolutionary war memorial and obelisk. The Huaihai battle was a decisive one fought by the People's Liberation Army from November 1948 to January 1949. The nearby Memorial Hall contains an extensive collection of weaponry. The park is on the bus No 11 route.

Places to Stay

The upmarket *Nanjiao Hotel* (☎ 384-7000; fax 384-4995) *(nánjiāo bīnguǎn)* has doubles starting at Y280. It's in the south-eastern part of town, within walking distance of a couple parks. Nearby there's a small night market where you can get a cheap bowl of noodles and a beer to wash it down.

Getting There & Away

Xuzhou is at the junction of two major train lines. There are frequent trains to Beijing, Nanjing and Lianyungang. The railway station is located in the north-eastern corner of the city.

LIANYUNGANG
(liányúngǎng)

The town is divided into port and city sections. Yuntai Hill is the 'scenic spot' overlooking the ocean, and there are some salt mines along the shores, as well as a Taoist monastery. A couple of hours from the city there are beaches for swimming.

Things to See

Few travellers find themselves passing through this out-of-the-way city, but if you should find yourself here there are a couple of interesting sights to pass the time. Fifteen kilometres south of the city is **Flowers and Fruit Mountain** *(huāguǒshān)*, a 625m-high mountain reputed to be the inspiration for the mountain of the same name in the Ming Dynasty classic *Journey to the West* (although three other places make the same claim).

About a third of the way up the mountain there's a 1300-year-old Taoist monastery,

JIANGSU

Sanyuan Gong, where there are two impressive 1000-year-old gingko trees.

A short walk up a footpath from the monastery is **Water Curtain Cave** *(shuǐlián dòng)*, the fictional home of Sun Wukong, the King of the Monkeys. A number of footpaths wind around this picturesque mountain, making it a pleasant place for hiking.

You can take a minibus here from 103 Tongguan Lu (a five minute walk from the Kangping Hotel); the ride takes about half an hour.

The other major sight here is **Kong-wangshan** *(kǒngwàngshān)*, where there are 110 2000-year-old (Eastern Han) stone carvings. Take the path to the left (west) of the temple; continue to take the path down to the cliff-side engravings.

Look for sculptures of a toad in a nearby field and an elephant, which also date from the Eastern Han Dynasty. Kongwangshan is located about 2km south of the city.

Places to Stay

Near the Xinpu railway station is the *Kangping Hotel* (☎ 551-1888; fax 550-0888) *(kāngpíng jiǔdiàn)* at 220 Tongguan Lu. Singles/doubles are Y168/298, with breakfast included.

Getting There & Away

CAAC and other domestic airlines fly between Lianyungang and Beijing, Guangzhou and Shanghai. Buses along the eastern coast connect Lianyungang with Shanghai. There's a new highway that connects Lianyungang and Nanjing.

From Xuzhou, a branch line runs east to Lianyungang (a three hour ride). Get off the train at Xinpu, the station closest to the city centre.

Anhui 安徽

The provincial borders of Anhui (ānhuī) were defined by the Qing government and, except for a few changes to the boundary with Jiangsu, have since remained unchanged. Northern Anhui forms part of the North China Plain, settled by the Han Chinese in large numbers during the Han Dynasty. The Yangzi River cuts through the southern quarter of Anhui and the area south of the river was not settled until the 7th and 8th centuries.

Anhui's historical and tourist sights are mainly in the south, and hence more accessible from Hangzhou or Shanghai than from the provincial capital, Hefei. Most famous are the spectacular Huangshan (Yellow Mountains), in the far south of the province, and nearby Jiuhuashan. The Yangzi River ports of Guichi and Wuhu are convenient jumping-off points for the Jiuhuashan and Huangshan mountains.

HEFEI
(héféi)

Although the capital of Anhui Province, Hefei is well off the beaten track. The city was a quiet market town before 1949 and has since expanded to become an industrial centre, with a population of over 500,000. It is a pleasant city and the people are friendly. There's not a lot to see, but the system of parks and lakes surrounding the city centre is a particularly nice touch.

Orientation

Hefei has a new railway station that opened on 1 May 1997; it's about 4km from the city centre in the north-east. The long-distance bus station is on the eastern side of town on Mingguang Lu. Shengli Lu leads down to the Nanfei River (which, along with a series of ponds to the south, forms a circle around the city centre), then meets up with Shouchun Lu to cross the river.

Changjiang Lu, a thoroughfare which cuts east-west through the city, is the main

Anhui Facts & Highlights

Area: 139,000 sq km
Population: 60.1 million
Capital: Hefei
Highlights
- Huangshan Mountains, definitive natural beauty for most Chinese.
- Jiuhuashan mountain, a Buddhist sacred mountain and a good antidote to the crowds at Huangshan.

commercial district. Most accommodation for foreigners is concentrated in the city centre and on Meishan Lu in the south-west of town overlooking Yuhua Pond.

Hefei is also home to the University of Science and Technology, where one of China's more famous dissidents, Fang Lizhi, was vice president until he sought asylum in the west after the 1989 Tiananmen Massacre.

Information

CITS (☎ 282-1418) is beside the Anhui Hotel at 8 Meishan Lu on the 5th floor. There's a big sign out the front in English that says China Anhui Overseas Tourist Corporation.

The PSB is on the northern side of

Anhui

Shouchun Lu just west of the intersection with Fuyang Lu.

The Bank of China is at 155 Changjiang Lu, although money can also be changed at the Anhui Hotel. The post office can be found on Huaihe Lu.

Things to See & Do

If you have some time to kill in Hefei, there are some pleasant parks around town. **Xiaoyaojin Park** (xiāoyáojīn gōngyuán), in the north-eastern corner of town, is the most expansive and has a small, rather depressing zoo. The living conditions for the African lions and the bears from northern China are particularly disturbing.

Baohebin Park (bāohé gōngyuǎn), to the south, is much nicer and has a series of small tombs and a temple. Finally, if you're really stuck, there's the **Provincial Museum** (shěng bówùguàn), the good old stand-by of every Chinese provincial capital. Entry for foreigners is Y10; Chinese Y2.

Places to Stay

Hefei gets very few foreign visitors (other than expenses-paid businesspeople) and consequently doesn't make much of an effort to cater to them. There are, however, two inexpensive hotels that accept foreigners near the long-distance bus station.

The *Yinlu Hotel* (☎ 262-8303; fax 261-5506) (yínlù dàjiǔdiàn) is on the southern side of the triangle where Huaihe Lu crosses the river to run into Ma'anshan Lu (it's around 10 minutes walk from the long-distance bus station). Clean air-con twins cost Y188.

The *Aoxing Hotel* (☎ 265-7661) (aòxīng bīngǔan) is on Mongguang Lu about 200m north-west from the intersection with Shengli Lu. Singles and twins without bath are Y80/50 and triples are Y54, but these rooms are hard to get. Twins with attached bath are Y140 and Y160.

In the south of town, the *University of Science and Technology* (zhōngguó kēxué jìshù dàxué) has accommodation for foreigners in the *Foreign Experts' Building* (☎ 360-2585) (zhuānjiā lóu). Beds are Y50 with shared bathrooms and twins with at-

tached bath are Y120/140. It is located in the eastern section of the university. To get there, take bus No 1 from the railway station to the university bus stop. The university entrance is on the other side of the street; go through the entrance and down the main street, turn left at the first road then left again. The guesthouse is a five storey grey building.

The *Meishan Hotel* (☎ 281-3555) (méishān fàndiàn) is set on beautiful grounds off Meishan Lu and it's possible to get twins and triples with attached bath and air-con for Y120/150. It's a sprawling place that also has expensive villas. To find the cheap rooms, head in through the gate and bear left, looking out for the reception area in a building on your right. The No 10 bus runs from the railway station and stops outside the hotel; alternatively, a taxi costs Y8 to Y10 from the city centre.

Most other accommodation has mid-range prices. The *Overseas Chinese Hotel* (☎ 265-2221; fax 264-2861) (huáqiáo fàndiàn) is central at 68 Changjiang Lu and has a bewildering host of rooms in three separate buildings. Foreigners are only allowed to stay in B block, located at the back. Standard twins are Y420. The *Fuhao Hotel* (fùháo dàjiǔdiàn) is in the same compound as the Anhui Hotel, just down the road from the Meishan Hotel, and has doubles at Y268 and Y308, plus 10% service charge. The telephone and fax number are the same as for the Anhui Hotel.

The *Anhui Hotel* (☎ 281-1818; fax 281-7583) (ānhuī fàndiàn) is a joint-venture grab at three star elegance, with the full complement of services, including English-speaking staff, health centre and coffee shop. Rooms range from Y660 to Y930 and beyond for suites and the like. Its position as the best hotel in Hefei may soon be usurped when the new Holiday Inn opens at the intersection of Shengli Lu and Shouchun Lu.

Places to Eat

Hefei is not exactly the culinary capital of China, but there are a number of reasonable sit-down restaurants in the streets and alleys

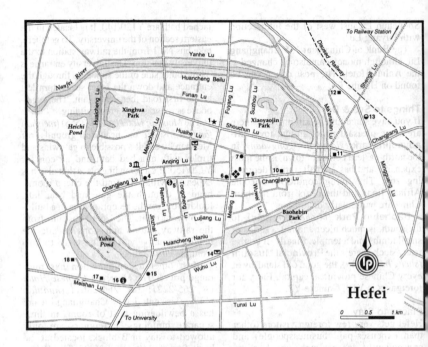

behind the Bank of China on Changjiang
Lu. The *KFC* on Changjiang Lu near the
intersection with Suzhou Lu does a roaring
trade as Hefei's premier fast-food outlet.

There's a good restaurant in the *Aoxing
Hotel*, with cheap meals, but no English

menu. Fried rice and egg is Y6 and a
pitcher of draught beer is Y20.

Getting There & Away
Air Hefei has daily flights to Beijing,
Guangzhou, Huangshan and Shanghai,

plus less regular flights to Changchun, Chengdu, Fuzhou, Haikou, Hangzhou, Shenzhen, Shenyang, Wenzhou, Wuhan, Xiamen, Xi'an and Hong Kong.

Bookings can be made at the China Eastern Airlines booking office (☎ 282-2357) at 246 Jinzhai Lu. The airport bus leaves from this office and the tickets are Y5. There are also ticket offices scattered throughout town. There's one beside the advance train ticket booking office on the northern side of Changjiang Lu at the intersection with Jinzhai Lu.

Bus The long-distance bus station is situated just down the road from the intersection of Shengli Lu and Mingguang Lu. There are daily departures to nearby destinations such as Hangzhou (nine hours), Jiujiang (eight hours), Wuhan (12 hours), Bozhou (seven hours) and Huangshan (12 hours).

The new freeway to Nanjing has shortened travel times considerably; air-con buses take 2½ hours to Nanjing (Y55) and six hours to Shanghai (Y145). Similarly, the new freeway connection south to Jiujiang (Y70) in Jiangxi province allows that journey to be done in about eight hours.

There are also frequent air-con Iveco minibuses departing for Wuhu (Y25); the trip takes 2½ hours.

Train Hefei is connected by direct train to Shanghai (8½ hours), Beijing (18 hours), Zhengzhou (10½ hours, via Kaifeng), Xiamen (38 hours) and Jiujiang (six hours).

Hard-seat tickets can be purchased at the railway station ticket office and you can try your luck with hard-sleeper tickets at windows No 14 and 15, or soft-sleeper at window No 13. You're better off going to the advance ticket booking office where you can book sleepers three days in advance. It's on the northern side of Changjiang Lu at the intersection with Jinzhai Lu and is open daily from 7.30 am to noon and 1 to 6.30 pm.

CITS can also book sleepers, but they say they need a week's notice.

BOZHOU
(bózhōu)

Bozhou lies in Anhui's far north-west, near the border with Henan. It's not a particularly attractive place, but this small regional city has long been one of the most important trading centres for traditional medicine in central China, and attracts merchants and Chinese herbalists from a wide area.

The 5th century BC founder of Taoism, Laotzu, was supposedly born near Bozhou.

Things to See

Bozhou's main attraction is its very large **Medicinal Market** *(zhōngyào shìchǎng)*, which has some interesting merchandise. Wandering through the rows of stalls, each specialising in a particular substance, you'll see mounds of pressed herbs and flowers, roots of obscure origin, rocks and other minerals, as well as wasp nests, animal skins, tortoise shells, dried insects and snakes – it's not for the faint-hearted. The market used to be in the middle of town, but it's now housed in a large, white-tiled exhibition hall on Mulan Lu near the railway station.

The **Underground Pass** *(cáocāo yùnbīngdào)* is a 600m-long subterranean passageway that runs parallel to Renmin Zhonglu and was built by the famous Han general Cao Cao as a secret route for soldiers to surprise the enemy.

You can walk right through the damp narrow tunnel, although anyone tall or prone to claustrophobia may find the going a bit confined; entry is Y10.

The **Guandi Temple** *(huāxìlóu)* has an ornate tiled gate which was built in the Qing Dynasty, and a small museum whose collection includes a Han Dynasty burial suit unearthed in 1973 and made from pieces of jade held together with silver thread. It's in the north-east section of town, which is also the most interesting part to wander around.

Places to Stay

Most places seem willing to accept foreigners. The *Bozhou Hotel* (☎ 552-4841) *(bózhōu bīnguǎn)* on Banjie Lou off Xinhua Lu in the middle of town is Bozhou's main tourist hotel. Twins in the same wing as reception cost Y220, but you may be able to bargain them down to Y160. You also get a free Chinese buffet breakfast. The other wing has very grotty twins for Y140 and you'll be blasted by karaoke all night.

About 100m up from the Bozhou Hotel, north towards Heping Lu, the *Lido Building* (☎ 552-3008) *(lìdū dàshà)* has beds in clean doubles with attached bath and air-con for Y48, and beds in triples without bath for Y18.

The *Gujing Hotel* (☎ 552-1298; fax 552-3244) *(gǔjǐng dàjiǔdiàn)* is a white-tiled attempt at modern architecture on the main corner, 1km south of the long-distance bus station. Standard doubles range from Y168 to Y228.

Directly opposite on Qiaoling Nanlu, the *Lantian Hotel* (☎ 552-3115) has beds in clean twins and triples with attached bath and air-con for Y60/45. Beds in triples without bath are Y18.

Getting There & Away

There's not a lot going on at Bozhou's long-distance bus station. Buses go to Zhengzhou (10 hours) and Hefei (nine hours), but other than that you'll have to wait around for buses that pass through town on their way to other cities.

Bozhou is also on the Zhengzhou-Hefei railway line, but trains that stop in Bozhou do so at very inconvenient hours – either very early in the morning or around midnight.

There is a daily slow train to Hefei (8½ hours) that leaves in the morning. The railway station is about 4km south-east of the city.

HUANGSHAN
(huángshān)

Huangshan (Yellow Mountain) is the name of the 72 peak range lying in the south of Anhui Province, 280km west of the coastal city of Hangzhou. For the Chinese, Huang shan, along with Guilin, is probably the most famous landscape attraction in the country – a local tourist map declares

---

Huangshan – A Tradition of Tranquillity and Inspiration

In good weather Huangshan *(huángshān)* is truly beautiful, and the surrounding countryside, with its traditional villages and patchwork paddy fields, is among the best in China. Huangshan has a 1200-year history as a tourist attraction. The Tang Dynasty emperor Tian Biao gave it its present name in the 8th century.

Countless painters and poets have since trudged around the range seeking inspiration and bestowing the peaks with fanciful names, such as Nine Dragons, Taoist Priest, Ox Nose, Fairy Capital and Hunchback.

Nowadays, the reclusive artists seeking an inspirational retreat from the hustle and bustle of the temporal world have been replaced by crowds of tourists, who bring the hustle and bustle with them. Still, with a little effort, you might be rewarded with a small moment of tranquillity, and the views are quite breathtaking.

Some travellers have escaped the well trodden tourist trails and returned thrilled with what they discovered. It is also worth noting that, given the amount of people who pass through this area, the park management does a commendable job trying to keep the place litter-free.

The highest peak is Lotus Flower Peak *(liánhuā fēng)* at 1864m, followed by Bright Summit Peak *(guāngmíng dǐng)* and Heavenly Capital Peak *(tiāndū fēng)*. Some 30 peaks rise above 1500m. ∎

ANHUI

solemnly that it is the 'marvellousest mountain on earth'.

Orientation & Information

Public buses from Tunxi (Huangshan Shi) drop you off at the terminal near Huangshan Gate in upper Tangkou *(tāngkǒu)*, the main village at the foot of the range. Maps, raincoats (frequently a necessity), snacks and accommodation are available here.

There's more accommodation available around the hot springs 4km further up the valley, although this is a more expensive place to be based. The road ends halfway up the mountain at the Yungusi cable car station (890m above sea level), where the eastern steps begin. Other hotels are scattered on various trails around the summit area.

Another cable car goes from the Jade Screen Peak area to just above the hot springs resort. A third cable car approaches Huangshan from the north-west going to Pine Forest Peak and is accessible from the southern side of the Taiping reservoir.

Routes to the Summit

There are three basic routes to the top: the short, hard way (eastern steps); the longer, harder way (western steps); and the very short, easy way (cable car). The eastern steps lead up below the Yungusi cable car line and the western steps lead up from the parking lot near the Mercy Light Temple, about 3km above the hot springs. Another cable car also goes from here to the Jade Screen Peak area, bringing you about halfway up the mountain.

Regardless of how you get up Huangshan, you'll first have to pay the entrance fee of Y65. Pay at the start of the eastern steps near the Yungusi cable car station, or at the entrance gate in the forest where the western steps begin. Minibuses run to both places from Tangkou for Y10.

Eastern Steps The 7.5km eastern steps route can be climbed comfortably in about three hours. It can be a killer if you push yourself too hard, but it's definitely easier than going up the western steps.

Purists can extend the eastern steps climb by several hours by setting out from Huangshan Gate, where a stepped path crosses the road at several points before connecting with the main eastern steps trail at the Yungusi cable car station.

If you have the time, the recommended route is a 10 hour circuit hike taking the eastern steps to the top, then descending to the hot springs resort via the western steps, but don't underestimate the the level of hardship involved. While Huangshan's cut-stone stairways undoubtedly make climbing a little easier, the extremely steep gradients will turn even an experienced walker's legs to jelly in around six to seven hours.

Western Steps The 15km western steps route has some of Huangshan's most spectacular scenery, following a precarious route hewn out of the sheer rock cliffs. It is, however, double the length and at least twice as strenuous as the eastern steps and much easier to enjoy if you're clambering down rather than gasping your way up.

The western steps descent begins at the Flying Rock *(fēilái shí)*, a rectangular boulder perched on an outcrop half an hour from the Beihai Hotel, and goes over Bright Summit Peak *(guāngmíng dǐng)*, where there is an odd-shaped weather station and a hotel.

Not to be missed on the western steps is the exhilaratingly steep and exposed stairway to Heavenly Capital Peak *(tiāndū fēng)*, directly adjacent to the Jade Screen Tower Hotel. Young lovers bring locks engraved with their names up here and fix them to the chain railings, symbolising that they're 'locked' together. The western path continues down past the Mid-Level Temple *(bànshān sì)* and back to the hot springs resort.

Halfway between the Mid-Level Temple and the hot springs resort is a parking lot with a cluster of minibuses. For Y10, it is possible to skip the last 1½ hours of walking and get a lift down to the hot springs resort.

ANHUI

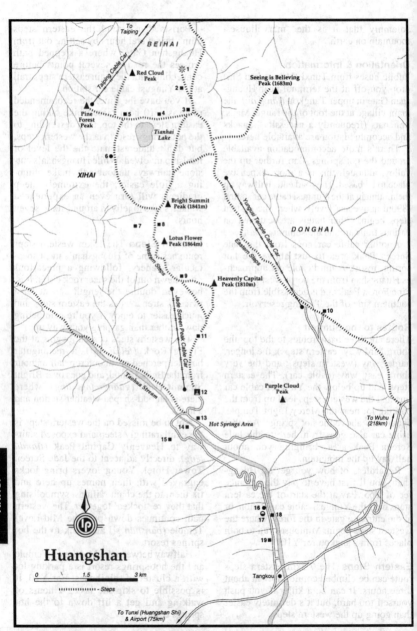

To Taiping

BEIHAI

Taiping Cable Car

Red Cloud
Peak

1

2

Seeing is Believing
Peak (1683m)

Pine
Forest Peak

5

4

3

Tianhai
Lake

6

XIHAI

Bright Summit
Peak (1841m)

Yungus Temple Cable Car

Eastern Steps

DONGHAI

7

8

Western Steps

Lotus Flower
Peak (1864m)

9

Heavenly Capital
Peak (1810m)

Jade Screen Peak Cable Car

11

Taohua Stream

Purple Cloud
Peak

12

To Wuhu
(218km)

13

14

Hot Springs Area

15

16

17

18

19

Tangkou

ANHUI

Huangshan

0   1.5   3 km

••••••••••• - Steps

To Tunxi (Huangshan Shi)
& Airport (75km)

HUANGSHAN 黄山	7 Baiyunlou Hotel 白云楼宾馆	14 Huang Mountain Wenquan Hotel 黄山温泉大酒店
1 Refreshing Terrace Lookout 清凉台	8 Tianhai Hotel 天海宾馆	15 Peach Blossom Hotel 桃源宾馆
2 Shilin Hotel 狮林饭店	9 Jade Screen Tower Hotel 玉屏宾馆	16 Huangshan Gate 黄山门
3 Beihai Hotel 北海宾馆	10 Yungu Hotel 云谷山庄	17 Long-Distance Bus Station 长途汽车站
4 Xihai Hotel 西海宾馆	11 Mid-Level Temple (Hotel) 半山寺	18 Government Hostel 镇政府招待所
5 Baiyun Hotel 白云宾馆	12 Mercy Light Temple 慈光阁	19 Tiandu Hotel 天都山庄
6 Flying Rock 飞来石	13 Huangshan Hotel 黄山宾馆	

Cable Car The eight minute cable car ride from Yungusi is the least painful way up. For Y10, minibuses take you from Huangshan Gate to the Yungusi cable car station. From here the one way cable car fare is Y40. Either get here very early in the day (the service starts at 5.30 am) or later in the day (if you're staying overnight). Queues of more than one hour are the norm, and in peak season many people wait as long as two or three hours for a ride – you may as well walk.

There's another cable car station that goes from just below the Jade Screen Tower Hotel to the parking lot above the hot springs resort. Tickets are Y35.

Guides & Porters

If you think you're having a hard time, spare a thought for the daily army of lean and agile porters lugging someone else's cargo of 50kg or more up the mountain – crates of drink bottles, baskets of food, even the odd flabby tourist.

Guides are not really necessary since the mountain paths are very easy to follow. CITS can organise an English-speaking guide for around Y400 per day. Private individuals sometimes offer their services as guides too, but virtually none speak any English besides 'hello'. The truly decadent might make their ascent in a makeshift sedan chair strung between bamboo poles and bounced (literally) along by two porters.

The price? Around Y200 to Y300 one way or Y1000 for the whole day depending on how hard you bargain.

On the Summit

Paved trails meander around the lookout points of Huangshan's summit area. Imagine a Chinese ink landscape and you will have an idea of what the Chinese tourists are referring to in their admiration – gnarled pines, craggy rocks, a rolling sea of clouds, perhaps an ant line of pinprick tourists in the distance toiling up some pointing finger of a peak.

The agreed highlight of Huangshan is the Beihai sunrise: a 'sea' of low cloud blanketing the valley to the north with 'island' peaks hazily reaching for the heavens. Fresh Breeze Terrace (five minutes from the Beihai Hotel) attracts daily sunrise crowds (hotels supply thick padded jackets for the occasion). It's communal sightseeing at its best and the noise generated by several hundred tourists is almost as incredible as the sunrise itself. Fortunately, most of them hurry back to eat breakfast shortly afterwards, leaving you to enjoy the mountains in peace.

Places to Stay & Eat

There are five locations with hotels and restaurants in the Huangshan area. Prices and availability of beds can vary a lot according to seasonal demand.

ANHUI

Tangkou *(tāngkǒu)* Tangkou is the best place to be based for an assault on Huangshan.

Accommodation up on the mountain and in the hot spring resort is expensive. There are lots of private guesthouses, but unless you look Chinese, the owners will get into trouble because all the foreigners are supposed to stay in designated places. The three main hotels taking foreigners are on the side road leading down to the village and there is also a government hostel up near the main gate.

The *Free and Unfettered Hotel* (☎ 556-2571; fax 556-1679) *(xiāoyáo bīnguǎn)* is probably the best deal in town. The staff are friendly, speak a little English and have beds in triples and quads with attached bath for Y60, but make sure you are adamant or they will give you a more expensive room. Standard twins with attached bath cost Y200. There is an English sign pointing down to the hotel from the main road (about five minutes walk), which reads 'Xiaoyao Hotel'.

The *Tangkou Hotel* (☎ 556-2400) *(tāngkǒu bīnguǎn)* is just up the hill from the Free and Unfettered Hotel, 200m off the main road. Beds in economy four-bed rooms are Y50, but they're not always easy to get. Standard twins cost Y180, but foreigners also have to pay a Y100 surcharge.

Further up the hill again and close to the main road is the *Huangshan Yinqiao Hotel* (☎ 556-2969). It has dorm beds for Y20, but again, they are difficult to get. They have standard twins with attached bath for Y200 and with air-con for Y260.

The *Tiandu Hotel* (☎ 556-2160) *(tiāndū shānzhuāng)*, about 700m downhill from Huangshan Gate, charges Y60 for a bed in a three-bed room, and Y240 for an air-con twin room. Closer to the bus terminal, the *Government Hostel* (☎ 556-1525) *(zhèn zhèngfǔ zhāodàisuǒ)* has dorm beds in quads and twins for Y40 without bath and Y60 with attached bath. Beds in air-con dorms are Y90 in quads, Y120 in triples and Y180 in twins.

There is no problem finding food in Tangkou (the restaurant owners will chase you down the street making vivid eating gestures). There is a small *restaurant* directly opposite the Free and Unfettered Hotel with an English menu. Watch out for overcharging in Tangkou – many places specialise in expensive local treats such as mountain frogs and preserved meats. You should be able to get simple meals for Y10 to Y15 a dish.

The *Happy Restaurant (kuàilè cāntīng)* is a good place about 150m along the road leading directly out from (not parallel to) the Free and Unfettered Hotel; it's beside the little footbridge and there's a white signboard with the menu in Chinese in red characters out front. Further down this street, under the main bridge and past the market, there's a small supermarket that sells bread and other goodies.

Hot Springs The hot spring resort, 4km further uphill, is a quiet, attractive place to stay, but accommodation tends to be a little overpriced. If you would like a good soak after coming down the mountain, hot spring baths are available next door to the Huangshan Hotel. A private bath is Y60 and a communal bath Y30. There's also a swimming pool. The Y45 ticket includes a bathing suit if you haven't brought yours. The pools and baths close at 9 pm.

The *Huangshan Hotel* (☎ 556-2357; fax 556-2121) *(huángshān bīnguǎn)* used to have cheap rooms, but they have been renovated out of the price range. The cheapest twins are Y300 with shower and air-con. Other twins are Y340 and up. Guests can also use the hot spring next door, which is run by the hotel.

Just across the bridge, the *Huang Mountain Wenquan Hotel* (☎ 556-2196; fax 556-2788) *(huángshān wénquán dàjiǔdiàn)* has also been renovated and now charges Y480 for twins, although you may be able to bargain them down. Higher up the hillside is the overpriced *Peach Blossom Hotel* (☎ 556-2666; fax 556-2888) *(táoyuán bīnguǎn)*, with twins from US$47 to US$72 and suites for US$120 and US$235.

The Huang Mountain and Peach Blossom hotels each have *restaurants*; as in Tangkou, restaurant touts prowl the streets in pursuit of hungry travellers. Again, watch out for overcharging.

Yungusi Cable Car Station There is one hotel here, the *Yungu Hotel* (☎ 556-2466; fax 556-2346) *(yúngǔ shānzhuāng)* and it's probably the best place to stay if you've got the money and are looking for a secluded, if somewhat inconvenient, setting within the pine and bamboo forest. This is where Chinese officials come to stay on visits to Huangshan. It's down the steps from the car park in front of the cable car station. Twins are Y580 and the luxury suites go for Y4200.

Summit Area Ideally, a visit to Huangshan should include a stay on the summit and there is a lot of accommodation available. The cheapest place near the top is the *Shilin Hotel* (☎ 556-2801) *(shílín fàndiàn)*, which has beds in eight-bed dorms for Y60/100 and twins with attached bath for Y720. They are putting up a new building that they were hoping would be open by this book's publication. It's a short walk down from the Beihai Hotel.

The *Beihai Hotel* (☎ 556-2552; fax 556-2708) *(běihǎi bīnguǎn)* is overpriced but comfortable and has the best location for seeing the sunrise. Twins are Y640 and Y720 and you can get beds in quads with attached bath for Y140.

The joint-venture *Xihai Hotel* (☎ 556-2712; fax 556-2988) *(xīhǎi bīnguǎn)*, further west along the trail, is a real 'mountain hotel' designed by Swedish architects. Twins start at over US$100. All rooms have heating and 24 hour hot water.

The *White Cloud Hotel* (☎ 556-1708; fax 556-1602) *(báiyún bīnguǎn)* is just up from Tianhai Lake and west of the Xihai Hotel, but it's not cheap. Twins start at Y580.

The Xihai and the Beihai both have bars and full-service restaurants serving western and Chinese food, but as they tend to cater to tour groups it is sometimes difficult to get service outside of meal times. Cheaper meals are available from stalls and simple restaurants nearby.

Western Steps Highest up is the *Tianhai Hotel* (☎ 556-2201) *(tiānhǎi bīnguǎn)*, just down from Bright Summit Peak beside the path on your left as you come down the mountain. Standard twins with attached bath are Y580, but they have beds in very basic dorms for Y60.

If you are looking for a little more luxury, take the right turn-off from the main path here (if heading down the mountain) to the *Baiyunlou Hotel* (☎ 556-1558; fax 556-2906) *(báiyúnlóu bīnguǎn)*. This hotel should not be confused with the White Cloud Hotel mentioned above (Baiyun means 'white cloud'). It's secluded and set right on the edge of the mountain. Beds in twins, triples and quads with attached bathrooms are Y340/200/120.

Further down the mountain at a spectacular 1660m-high lookout near Heavenly Capital Peak is the *Jade Screen Tower Hotel* (☎ 556-2317; fax 556-2258) *(yùpínglóu bīnguǎn)*. The rates and conditions reflect this hotel's relative inaccessibility: a simple twin is Y380, and washing arrangements are basic indeed. Be prepared for a lack of water supply. They also have beds in dorms for Y90 and Y70.

The next place you'll come to is the small *Mid-Level Temple (bànshān sì)* at 1340m. It only has bunk bed accommodation in small rooms for Y60 and is best considered as emergency accommodation.

There is only a couple of eating options on this route. Considering its location, the Jade Screen Tower Hotel has a very cheap *dining hall* beside the tiny courtyard, and a better *restaurant* upstairs. The Mid-Level Temple has a *teahouse* serving simpler meals and refreshments.

Getting There & Away
Air The airport serving Huangshan is at Tunxi (see the following Tunxi entry). There are flights to Beijing (twice weekly), Guangzhou (six a week), Hefei (daily),

ANHUI

Kunming (via Guilin; twice weekly), Wuhan (daily), Shanghai (daily) and Zhuhai (twice weekly), and less frequent flights to Fuzhou, Xiamen, Yichang and Xi'an. There's also a weekly flight to Hong Kong.

The CAAC office (☎ 953-4111) is on Huangshan Lu beside the International Hotel. The airport bus leaves from here for the 5km ride to the airport; tickets cost Y5. A taxi to the airport will cost about Y25. You can also book airline tickets at various outlets near the railway station.

Bus A new paved road means that buses from Tunxi (Huangshan Shi) now take around 1½ hours to reach Huangshan Gate. Minibuses to Tunxi leave from the bridge area in Tangkou and tickets are Y10.

In summer, other direct buses to Tangkou come from Hefei (eight hours), Shanghai (12 hours), Suzhou (11 hours) and Jingdezhen (six hours). There are also buses from Jiuhuashan (five hours) and the Yangzi River ports of Wuhu (six hours) and Guichi (six hours). The bus station in Tangkou is located just below Huangshan Gate.

Train Trains from Hefei and Nanjing via Wuhu pass through Tunxi (Huangshan Shi). For connections from southern destinations, first go to Yingtan (Jiangxi Province) and change trains there. Northern destinations are at window No 2 and southern destinations at window No 3 at the railway station. You can book sleeper tickets at the window in the far end of the courtyard which is reached through a doorway to the right as you exit the waiting room. The waiting room is beside the main ticket office.

If you're planning to leave from Tunxi after visiting the mountain, it's a good idea to book your ticket right away. CITS may have difficulty booking sleepers at short notice. The travel agency in the Senlin Hotel (see the following Tunxi section) can also book sleepers for a Y50 service charge.

Getting Around

The easiest and cheapest way to get to the various places around Huangshan is by minibus, although they usually don't budge an inch until there is a sufficient number of people to make it worthwhile for the driver. Minibuses head out to the eastern steps and western steps in the morning. You can usually find one by wandering the streets of Tangkou, but they usually congregate on the highway across the bridge. Likewise, there are minibuses waiting at the bottom of the routes up the mountain in the afternoon.

Minivan taxis and motorised trishaws also abound, but you'll have to bargain.

TUNXI (HUANGSHAN SHI)
(túnxī (huángshān shì))

The old trading town of Tunxi (Huangshan Shi) is roughly 70km south-east by road from Huangshan. As indicated by its new Chinese name (meaning Huangshan City), Tunxi is the main jumping-off point for the Huangshan area. It's a pleasant town to explore if you find yourself here for a day or two. The area where the two rivers meet is the most interesting.

Information

CITS (☎ 251-2771) is at 6 Xizhen Lu, on the 3rd floor of the building opposite the Huaxi Hotel. They can arrange English-speaking guides for tours of Huangshan and the surrounding area.

The PSB is in the eastern section of Tunxi at 108 Changgan Lu.

The Bank of China is at 9 Xinan Lu opposite the Xinhua Bookstore.

Places to Stay & Eat

Many of the hotels in Tunxi, especially the cheaper ones, don't accept foreigners.

The *Senlin Hotel* (☎ 252-0750) *(sēnlín jiǔdiàn)* is the cheapest place near the railway station that will accept foreigners. Twins and triples with attached bath are Y120/150. There is no English sign, but it's west of the roundabout in front of the railway station. Look for the building with the English sign that says 'Changying Hotel' (although they don't accept foreigners) on the corner. The Senlin Hotel is beside the Changying.

Another hotel near the railway station is the *Huangshan Jingwei Hotel* (☎ 252-5659; fax 251-7178) *(huángshān jīngwěi jiǔdiàn)*, on the south-eastern corner of the main street running past the railway station. Standard rooms are Y400.

Across from the Jingwei Hotel, on the south-western corner of the main street, the *Jiangnan Hotel* (☎ 251-1067) *(jiāngnán dàjiǔdiàn)* has singles and twins for Y130/170 and up, but foreigners have to pay a 50% surcharge.

Across the Hengjiang River, in the old part of town south-west of the railway station, the *Huaxi Hotel* (☎ 251-4312; fax 251-4990) *(huāxī fàndiàn)* is in the midst of putting on a new section, but has older twins for Y320. Its location, where the Hengjiang and Xinan rivers meet, is very pleasant.

The *Huangshan International Hotel* (☎ 252-6999; fax 251-2087) *(huángshān guójì dàjiǔdiàn)* is a joint venture and by far the best place to stay if you have the cash. Standard twins start at US$80.

There are numerous restaurants and food stalls around the railway station and the fare is not bad. The International Hotel has a western-style *restaurant*.

Things to Buy

Running a block in from the river, there is a souvenir street called Laojie. Besides the usual trinkets, it has a lot of the same sort of stuff that's sold in the Shanghai antique market, but you may be able to get better prices here, especially for the antique furniture.

Getting There & Away

The long-distance bus station in Tunxi is 400m east of the railway station. Regular buses run between Tunxi and Tangkou in the Huangshan mountains. There are also bus services to Shanghai, Hangzhou, Hefei, Nanjing and Jingdezhen, and direct trains

to Hefei, Yingtan (via Jingdezhen) and Wuhu. The local airport receives many flights from Beijing, Guangzhou and Shanghai, as well as other regional Chinese cities (see Huangshan section earlier).

See the previous Huangshan Getting There & Away section for more travel details.

AROUND TUNXI
Shexian & Yixian
(shèxiàn, yīxiàn)

The countryside around Huangshan has some of the most beautiful rural scenery in China and it also has some fine examples of residential architecture from the Ming and Qing dynasties. The towns of Shexian and Yixian, near Tunxi, have some interesting merchant houses, old narrow streets and memorial arches *(páifāng)*.

Formerly known as Huizhou, this region produced a number of wealthy merchants during the Ming and Qing dynasties who brought back the profits of their trading to build houses in their home towns. Both Shexian and Yixian can be done as day trips from Tunxi, although in order to see the sights in Yixian you will need to get a travel permit from the PSB in Tunxi, or have the permit arranged by CITS for Y50.

The **Memorial Arches of Tangyue** are 1.5km off the highway on the way to Shexian; you can get off the bus and walk or take a motor-tricycle.

In Shexian, the street area known as **Doushanjie**, in the centre of the old town, has a fine collection of old houses in narrow, stone-lined alleys. There's a Y8 guided tour that takes you inside the houses and it's well worth it.

At Yixian there are three main villages, **Xidi**, **Hongcun** and **Nanping**, all located outside the main town. The best way to get to them is to hire a minivan taxi in Yixian. Foreigners normally need a travel permit to get into the villages, but if you don't have a permit, your taxi driver might be able to help you with a little incentive.

Xidi also has a memorial arch – the only one remaining of the original nine. The rest

ANHUI

were destroyed during the Cultural Revolution and this one only survived because it was covered with Mao slogans.

Nanping was the location for Zhang Yimou's acclaimed film *Judou* and the set has been preserved along with photographs of the production. Many of the houses have exquisite wood carvings, although many of the human figures have had their heads sliced off, courtesy of the Red Guards. Entry to all the villages is about Y20 each.

Getting There & Away

Shexian is 15km north-east of Tunxi on the railway line and Yixian is 35km north-west of Tunxi.

You can catch minibuses to both towns from near the roundabout in front of Tunxi railway station, where the ticket-collectors lean out the doors of passing buses calling out the names of the towns. Tickets to Shexian are Y4 and the trip takes 30 minutes. The journey to Yixian takes one hour and tickets are Y7.

JIUHUASHAN

(*jiǔhuáshān*)

One way to avoid the carnival crowds on Huangshan is to skip it in favour of Jiuhuashan. The scenery here is less spectacular, but it is certainly quieter.

Jiuhuashan is one of China's four sacred Buddhist mountains (the others are Putuoshan in Zhejiang, Emeishan in Sichuan and Wutaishan in Shanxi). Third century Taoist monks built thatched temples at Jiuhuashan, but with the rise of Buddhism these were gradually replaced by stone monasteries.

Jiuhuashan owes its importance to a Korean Buddhist disciple, Kim Kiao Kak (*jīn qiáojué*), who arrived in 720 and founded a worshipping place for Ksitigarbha, the guardian of the earth. Annual festivities are held on the anniversary of Kim's death (the 30th day of the 7th lunar month), when pilgrims flock to Jiuhuashan.

In its heyday during the Tang Dynasty, as many as 5000 monks and nuns, living in more than 300 monasteries, worshipped at Jiuhuashan. Today only 70 temples and monasteries remain in the hills around Jiuhuashan, but there is still a palpable feeling of spirituality in this place that is often lacking at China's other 'holy' sites.

Jiuhuashan is also an important place for believers to come and bless the souls of the recently deceased to ensure them a passage to Buddhist heaven.

Orientation & Information

Jiuhua Village lies at 600m above sea level, about halfway up the mountain (or, as the locals say, at roughly navel height in a giant Buddha's potbelly). The bus stops just below the main gate where you must pay an entrance fee to Jiuhuashan (Y45 between March and November; Y35 the rest of the year).

From here, Jiuhua Jie, the narrow main street, leads up past cheap restaurants, souvenir stalls and hotels. The village square is built around a large pond along a side street off to the right.

It's worthwhile taking a hike up the ridge behind the Qiaoyuan Monastery at the bottom of Jiuhua Jie. The **Baisui Temple** is at the top and from there you can walk south along the ridge and come back down the path to the town or go east across the valley to **Tiantai Peak**. A cable car goes up to the top of the peak. Several 'pictorial' maps in Chinese showing mountain paths can be bought in the village.

Places to Stay & Eat

At the bottom of the village is the beautiful, palace-style *Qiyuan Monastery* (☎ 501-1281) (*qíyuán sì*). There is very basic dorm accommodation for Y5 a bed, but you might be wise to get the more comfortable bed for Y20. You may have difficulty getting in here if you can't explain yourself in Chinese.

The monks might send you to the hotel within the monastery, the *Buddhism Hotel* (☎ 501-1608) (*fójiào bīnguǎn*). Beds in six person rooms with shared bath cost Y60. Standard twins are Y140.

Directly across the square from the

monastery is the *Julong Hotel* (☎ 501-1368; fax 501-1022) *(jùlóng bīnguǎn)*, a standard Chinese tourist operation where damp and stuffy twins with attached bath cost Y180. There are better twins on the upper floors of the hotel complex, where the prices range from Y398 to Y598.

The *Bell Tower Hotel* (☎ 501-1251) *(jiǔhuáshān zhōnglóu fàndiàn)*, at the top of the main street, is a better option. Twins cost Y140 with attached bath and beds in triples without bath are Y20, if you get them to give one to you.

Behind the Bell Tower Hotel to the left is the family-run *Nanyuan Guesthouse* (☎ 501-1122) *(nányuàn lǚguǎn)* which has two small buildings with clean twins and basic washing facilities for Y30 per bed. It's right at the bottom of the trail leading down from the ridge.

There's a number of inexpensive restaurants clustered at the top of main street below the Bell Tower Hotel.

Getting There & Away

There are two daily buses to Jiuhuashan from Huangshan via Qingyang (Y25, six hours) that follow the new road built alongside the Taiping Reservoir. There are also buses to Shanghai (10 hours), Nanjing (six hours) Wuhu (four hours) and Guichi (1½ hours).

WUHU & GUICHI

(wúhú, guìchí)

For most travellers, these towns are treated mainly as transport hubs. Wuhu is a Yangzi River port and a useful railway junction. Railway lines branch off south to Tunxi, east to Shanghai (via Nanjing) and, from the northern bank of the river, north to Hefei. There are also buses to Huangshan

(five hours) and Jiuhuashan (five hours) from Wuhu.

To the west of Wuhu is the Yangzi port of Guichi, which also has buses to Huangshan (five hours) and Jiuhuashan (1½ hours). You can also go between the two towns by catching one of the Yangzi River ferries. The trip takes about five hours (for full details on Yangzi River cruises, see the Chongqing entry in the Sichuan chapter).

Places to Stay

Wuhu There's a fancy new hotel near the long-distance bus station, to your left as you exit the station. The *Wuhu Yingkesong Hotel* (☎ 385-7788; fax 385-1799) *(wúhú yíngkèsōng dàjiǔdiàn)* has standard twins for Y248.

Right next door to the bus station, the *Dongyuan Hotel* (☎ 382-9041) *(dōngyuàn bīnguǎn)* has twins without bath for Y60 and twins with attached bath and air-con for Y150. Down by the dock, the convenient *Ganglong Hotel* (☎ 383-1319) *(gǎnlóng bīnguǎn)* is down the street to the right as you exit the ferry terminal. Beds in twins and triples with attached bath and air-con are Y60/30. There are also beds in four-person dorms. The hotel has great views of the river. Bus No 4 from the railway and bus stations drops you off near the ferry terminal.

The area around the ferry terminal has a number of fruit stands and food stalls.

Guichi The *Jiuzi Guesthouse* (☎ 202-2648) *(jiǔzi bīnguǎn)* is to your left as you exit the bus station. Twins with attached bath range from Y70 to Y90. You could also try to talk them into giving you a bed for Y35. The bus station is a short motor-trike ride from the dock.

Shanghai 上海

Shanghai Facts & Highlights

Area: 6200 sq km

Population: 14.2 million

Highlights

- The Bund, the single most evocative symbol of the 'Paris of the East'.
- Nanjing Lu, where socialism with Chinese characteristics shakes hands with shop-till-you-drop commercialism.
- Getting lost on the backstreets of Frenchtown.
- Yuyuan Gardens, tacky but fun, with some delicious lunchtime snacks.

Whore of the east, Paris of China and Queen of the Orient; city of quick riches, ill-gotten gains and fortunes lost on the tumble of dice; the domain of adventurers, swindlers, gamblers, drug runners, idle rich, dandies, tycoons, missionaries, gangsters and backstreet pimps; the city that plots revolution and dances as the revolution shoots its way into town – Shanghai *(shànghǎi)* was a dark memory during the long years of forgetting that the Communists visited upon their new China.

Shanghai put away its dancing shoes in 1949. The masses began shuffling to a different tune – the dour strains of Marxist-Leninism and the wail of the factory siren; and all through these years of oblivion, the architects of this social experiment firmly wedged one foot against the door on Shanghai's past; until the effort started to tell.

Today Shanghai has reawakened and is busy snapping the dust off its cummerbund. The sun rises every day to a city typifying the huge disparities of modern China – monumental building projects push skywards, glinting department stores swing open their doors to the stylish elite, while child beggars, prostitutes and the impoverished congregate among the champagne corks and burst balloons of the night before. History is returning to haunt Shanghai and, at the same time, to put it squarely back on the map.

As the pulse of this metropolis quickens, its steps are firmer, and at this point we make an apology. A lot of what you read here will have changed by the time you have this book in your hands. Shanghai is evolving at a pace so unmatched by any other Chinese city that even the morning ritual of flinging open one's hotel curtains reveals new facets to the skyline and new sounds on the streets. Shanghai is racing towards the future and has little time for yesterday.

History

As anyone who wanders along the Bund or through the backstreets of Frenchtown can see, Shanghai (the name means 'by the sea') is a western invention. As the gateway to the Yangzi, it was an ideal trading port. But when the British opened their first concession in 1842 after the first Opium War it was little more than a small town supported by fishing and weaving. The British changed all that.

The French followed in 1847, an International Settlement was established in 1863 and the Japanese arrived in 1895 – the city was parcelled up into autonomous settlements, immune from Chinese law. It became

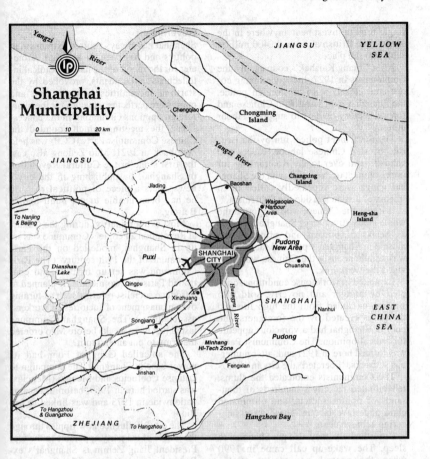

Shanghai Municipality

Yangzi River

JIANGSU

YELLOW SEA

Chengqiao

Chongming Island

0   10   20 km

JIANGSU

Yangzi River

Changxing Island

Jiading

Baoshan

Waigaoqiao Harbour Area

Heng-sha Island

To Nanjing & Beijing

Dianshan Lake

Puxi

Qingpu

SHANGHAI CITY

Pudong New Area

Chuansha

Xinzhuang

Huangpu River

SHANGHAI

Nanhui

EAST CHINA SEA

Songjiang

Pudong

Minhang Hi-Tech Zone

Jinshan

Fengxian

To Hangzhou & Guangzhou

ZHEJIANG   To Hangzhou

Hangzhou Bay

in effect China's first fully fledged Special Economic Zone.

By 1853, Shanghai had overtaken all other Chinese ports. Mid-18th century Shanghai had a population of just 50,000; by 1900 the figure had jumped to one million. By the 1930s, the city claimed some 60,000 foreign residents and was the busiest international port in Asia. Shanghai had more motor vehicles than all the rest of China put together and the largest buildings in the east.

This city that was built on the trade of opium, silk and tea, also lured the world's great houses of finance, who descended on the city to erect grand palaces of plenty. The city became a byword for exploitation and vice; its countless opium dens, gambling joints and brothels managed by the gangs at the heart of Shanghai life. And guarding it all were the American, French and Italian marines, British Tommies and Japanese bluejackets.

Foreign ships and submarines patrolled the Yangzi and Huangpu rivers and the coasts of China. They patrolled the biggest single foreign investment anywhere in the world – the British alone had £400 million sunk into the place.

After Chiang Kaishek's coup against the Communists in 1927, the Kuomintang cooperated closely with the foreign police, the Shanghai gangs and with Chinese and foreign factory owners to suppress labour unrest.

The Settlement police, run by the British, arrested Chinese labour leaders and handed them over to the Kuomintang for imprisonment or execution, and the Shanghai gangs were repeatedly called in to 'mediate' disputes inside the Settlement.

If it was the Chinese who supported the whole giddy structure of Shanghai, worked as beasts of burden and provided the muscle in Shanghai's port and factories, it was simultaneously the Chinese who provided the weak link.

Exploited in workhouse conditions, crippled by hunger and poverty, sold into slavery, excluded from the high life and the parks created by the foreigners, the poor of Shanghai had a voracious appetite for radical opinion. The Communist Party was formed here in 1921 and, after numerous setbacks, 'liberated' the city in 1949.

The Communists eradicated the slums, rehabilitated the city's hundreds of thousands of opium addicts, and eliminated child and slave labour. These were staggering achievements.

Unfortunately, they also put Shanghai to sleep. The wake-up call came in 1990 when the central government started throwing money at the municipality, and the city hasn't looked back since.

Climate

The best times to visit Shanghai are spring and autumn. In winter, temperatures can drop well below freezing, with a blanket of drizzle. Summers are hot and humid with temperatures as high as 40°C (104°F). So, in short, you'll need silk long johns and down jackets for winter, an ice block for each armpit in summer and an umbrella wouldn't go astray in either season.

Government

Shanghai has always courted extremism in politics and has been an accurate barometer for the mood of the nation. Radical intellectuals and students, provoked by the startling inequalities between rich and poor, were perfect receptacles for the many foreign opinions circulating in the concessions; the meeting which founded the Chinese Communist Party (CCP) was held here back in 1921. Mao Zedong also cast the first stone of the Cultural Revolution in Shanghai, by publishing in the city's newspapers a piece of political rhetoric he had been unable to get published in Beijing.

Most extraordinarily, during the Cultural Revolution a People's Commune was set up in Shanghai, modelled on the Paris Commune of the 19th century. (The Paris Commune was set up in 1871 and controlled Paris for two months. It planned to introduce socialist reforms such as turning over management of factories to workers' associations.) The Shanghai Commune lasted just three weeks before Mao ordered the army to put an end to it.

The so-called Gang of Four had its power base in Shanghai. The campaign to criticise Confucius and Mengzi (Mencius) was started here in 1969, before it became nationwide in 1973 and was linked to Lin Biao.

The city's influence now ripples through the whole of the party apparatus to the top: President Jiang Zemin is Shanghai's ex-Party chief and ministers Zhu Rongji and Wu Bangguo also hail from the municipality. Furthermore, Hong Kong's new chief executive, Dong Jianhua, is a Shanghai man. Ironically, Jiang Zemin has recently called for a return to Confucian values in an attempt to turn the tide on worsening social disorder and greed.

Economy

Shanghai's long malaise came to an abrupt end in 1990, with the announcement of plans to develop Pudong on the eastern side of the Huangpu River, although there have been teething problems. Foreign investors complain that costs have risen so sharply that they have been forced to shift production out of Shanghai. Nevertheless, Shanghai is a major financial centre and an emerging economic powerhouse.

By 1998 local planners reckon Pudong will have half as much office space as Singapore. Lujiazui, the area that faces off the Bund on the Pudong side of the Huangpu River, will be a modern high-rise counterpoint to the austere, old-world structures on the Bund.

Shanghai has a unique opportunity, and the savvy with which locals have grabbed it have many shaking their heads knowingly, saying that Shanghai always had the potential to be a great city. Massive freeway projects crisscross the city, the subway system is proceeding apace, and the indications are that this forward planning will circumvent the infrastructure problems that face other Asian cities such as Bangkok, Jakarta and Taipei.

As part and parcel of the great facelift that is transforming Shanghai, plans are under way to build the tallest building in the world here, the Shanghai Shimao Building.

Shanghai's burgeoning economy, its forward thinking and intrinsic self-confidence have put it miles ahead of other cities in China. Neither Beijing nor Guangzhou can match its sheer modernity: foreigners here don't feel the stresses and strains of fighting against a user-hostile service structure. The city knows that tourism makes money, so it spends a little bringing it in; this simple logic is apparently lost on the rest of the country.

An appropriate millennial feel grips Shanghai, as if a milestone is within reach. Growing self-belief and a sense of style illuminate the city, drawing investors from afar. Nothing would satisfy the central government more than for Shanghai to replace Hong Kong as China's frontier on the future, swinging the spotlight of attention from the ex-colony on to a home-grown success story.

Population

Shanghai has a population of around 13.4 million people, but that figure is deceptive since it takes into account the whole municipal area of 6100 sq km.

Nevertheless, the central core of some 220 square kilometres has more than 7.5 million people, which must rate as one of the highest population densities in China, if not the world.

Orientation

Shanghai municipality covers a substantial area, but the city proper is a more modest size. Within the municipality is the island of Chongming. It's part of the Yangzi River delta and is worth a footnote because it's the second largest island in China (or third if you recognise China's claim to Taiwan).

Broadly, central Shanghai is divided into two areas: Pudong (east of the Huangpu River) and Puxi (west of the Huangpu River). The First Ring Road does a long elliptical loop around the city centre proper, which includes all of commercial west-side Shanghai, the Lujiazui Finance and Trade Zone and the Jinqiao Export Processing Zone of Pudong.

A second (Outer) Ring Road will link Hongqiao international airport (in the west of town) with the new Gaoqiao Free Trade Zone, a port on the Yangzi River in Pudong.

For visitors, the attractions of Shanghai are in Puxi. Here you will find the Bund, the shopping streets, the foreign concessions, hotels, restaurants, sights and nightclubs. Street names are given in Pinyin, which makes navigating easy, and many of the streets are named after cities and provinces.

In the central district (around Nanjing Lu) the provincial names run north-south, and the city names run east-west. Some roads are split by compass points, such as Sichuan Nanlu (Sichuan South Rd) and Sichuan Beilu (Sichuan North Rd). Some of the monstrously long roads are split by sectors, such as Zhongshan Dong Erlu and Zhongshan Dong Yilu, which mean

SHANGHAI

Shanghai City
上海市

SHANGHAI CITY
上海市

PLACES TO STAY
5 Haijia Hotel
海佳饭店
6 Changyang Hotel
长阳饭店
13 Galaxy Hotel; Hongqiao
State Guesthouse
银河宾馆
虹桥迎宾馆
14 Yangtze New World;
Westin Taipingyang Hotels
扬子江大酒店、
太平洋大饭店
17 Cypress Hotel
龙柏饭店
22 Sheraton Huating Hotel
华亭宾馆

OTHER
1 West Railway Station
西火车站

2 Zhabei Park
闸北公园
3 Hongkou Park;
Tomb of Lu Xun
鲁迅陵、虹口公园
4 Peace Park
和平公园
7 Beixinjing Nursery Garden
北新泾苗圃
8 Changfeng Park
长风公园
9 Shanghai University
上海大学
10 Changning Railway
Station
长宁火车站
11 Zhongshan Park
中山公园
12 Tianshan Park
天山公园
15 Hongqiao Airport
虹桥机场
16 Shanghai Zoo
上海动物园

18 Wanguo Cemetery; Song
Qingling's Tomb
万国公墓；
宋庆龄陵园
19 St Ignatius Cathedral
天主教堂
20 Xujiahui Railway
Station
徐家汇火车站
21 Guangqi Park
光启公园
23 Longhua Pagoda;
Longhua Hotel
龙华塔、龙华迎宾馆
24 Martyrs' Cemetery
烈士陵园
25 Caoxi Park
漕溪公园
26 Xinlonghua Railway
Station
新龙华火车站
27 Shanghai Botanical
Gardens
植物园

Zhongshan East 2nd Rd and Zhongshan East 1st Rd.

There are four main areas of interest in the city: the Bund from Suzhou Creek to the Shanghai Harbour Passenger Terminal (Shiliupu Wharf); Nanjing Donglu (a very colourful neighbourhood); Frenchtown, which includes Huaihai Zhonglu and Ruijin Lu (an even more colourful neighbourhood); and the Jade Buddha Temple and the side trip along Suzhou Creek.

Maps English maps of Shanghai are available at the Foreign Languages Bookstore (see Bookshops later in this section), the Jinjiang Hotel bookshop and occasionally from street hawkers. Watch out for the map sellers on the Bund who squawk 'English map' (the only English they know), but when you look at them they are usually just a maze of characters. The best of the bunch is the bilingual *Shanghai Official Tourist Map*, which is produced by the Shanghai Municipal Tourism Administration – unfortunately, it's not easy to track down. Try the Tourist Information Centres listed below in the Tourist Offices section (they issue their own free map as well).

The *Shanghai Map* (Zhongguotong Publishing Co) features both English and Chinese, as does the *Geocenter Map of Shanghai* which is decent, but not very detailed. It's expensive in China so buy it abroad if you can.

An alternative bilingual map is the Hong Kong published *Map of Shanghai*, which is sometimes available in China (you can buy it in Hong Kong from most large bookshops). This map has streets and destinations in Chinese characters (traditional), as well as in English.

Information
Tourist Offices The main office of CITS (☎ 6321-7200) is on the 1st floor of the Guangming building at 2 Jinling Donglu. This is probably the most efficient of the CITS network, and they even publish their own guide to Shanghai, the *Shanghai Travel Guide*, which is free.

Train, plane and boat tickets can be booked here, but this is obviously subject to availability. CITS will often need at last three days to get tickets for destinations further than Hangzhou or Suzhou; if you're in a hurry, try your hotel, which will almost surely be able to help you.

Boat tickets are easier to book at CITS, but often a lot more expensive than doing it yourself across the road at the boat ticketing office.

Shanghai operates Tourist Information Centres in the metro station at the railway station, another at the metro station in Renmin Square (☎ 6438-1693) and a third in the arrivals hall of Hongqiao airport (☎ 6268-7788, ext 6750). Professional and polite, the staff provide free maps and free guides to Shanghai in a wide array of languages, including English, Japanese, Korean and French (although they are often sold out of the English versions). The assistants are keen to speak English and are very helpful.

The Tourist Hotline (☎ 6252-0000) has a useful English-language service.

Foreign Consulates There is a growing band of consulates in Shanghai. If you're doing the Trans-Siberian journey and have booked a definite departure date, it's much better to get your Russian visa here than face the horrible queues at the Russian embassy in Beijing.

Your own country's consulate is worth a visit – not just if you've lost your passport, but also for up-to-date newspapers from home.

Australia
  (☎ 6433-4604; fax 6437-6669) Room 401, Shanghai Centre, 1376 Nanjing Xilu
Austria
  (☎ 6279-7196; fax 6279-7198) Suite 514, Shanghai Centre, 1376 Nanjing Xilu
Canada
  (☎ 6279-8400; fax 6279-8401) Suite 604, West Tower, Shanghai Centre, 1376 Nanjing Xilu
Denmark
  (☎ 6209-0500; fax 6209-0504) Room 701, International Trade Centre, 2200 Yan'an Xilu

France
(☎ 6472-3631; fax 6472-5247) Room 2008, Ruijin Building, 205 Maoming Nanlu
Germany
(☎ 6433-6951; fax 6471-4448) 181 Yongfu Lu
Hungary
(☎ 6320-2004; fax 6320-2855) Room 1810, Union Building, 100 Yan'an Donglu
India
(☎ 6275-8885; fax 6275-8881) 2200 Yan'an Xilu
Italy
(☎ 6471-6980; fax 6471-6977) 11th floor, Qihua Tower, 1375 Huaihai Zhonglu
Japan
(☎ 6433-6639; fax 6433-1008) 1517 Huaihai Zhonglu
Netherlands
(☎ 6209-9082) 4th floor, East Tower Sun Plaza, 88 Xianxia Lu
New Zealand
(☎ 6471-1108; fax 6431-0226) 15B, Qihua Tower, 1375 Huaihai Zhonglu
Poland
(☎/fax 6433-9288) 618 Jianguo Xilu
Russia
(☎ 6324-2682; fax 6306-9982) 20 Huangpu Lu
Singapore
(☎ 6437-0776; fax 6433-4150) 400 Wulu-muqi Zhonglu
South Korea
(☎ 6219-6417; fax 6219-6918) 2200 Yan'an Xilu
Switzerland
(☎ 6248-0000) Room 1224, Hilton Hotel, 250 Huashan Lu
UK
(☎ 6279-7650; fax 6279-7651) Room 301, Shanghai Centre, 1376 Nanjing Xilu
USA
(☎ 6433-6880; fax 6433-4122) 1469 Huaihai Zhonglu

PSB The office (☎ 6321-5380) is at 210 Hankou Lu, one block north of Fuzhou Lu, near the corner of Henan Zhonglu.

Money There are money-changing counters at almost every hotel, even cheapies like the Pujiang and the Haijia. Credit cards are more readily accepted in Shanghai than in other parts of China.

Most tourist hotels will accept major credit cards such as Visa, American Express, MasterCard, Diners and JCB, as will banks and friendship stores (and related tourist outlets like the Shanghai Antique and Curio Store).

The enormous Bank of China right next to the Peace Hotel tends to get crowded, but is better organised than Chinese banks elsewhere around the country (it's worth a peek for its grand interior). There is a branch of Citibank next door on the Bund which is open 24 hours.

American Express (☎ 6279-8082) has an office at Room 206, Retail Plaza, Shanghai Centre, 1376 Nanjing Xilu.

Post & Communications The larger tourist hotels have post offices from where you can mail letters and small packages, and this is by far the most convenient option.

The express mail service and poste restante is at 276 Bei Suzhou Lu. Letters to London take just two days, or so it advertises. The international post and telecommunications office is at the corner of Sichuan Beilu and Bei Suzhou Lu. The section for international parcels is in the same building, but around the corner at 395 Tiantong Lu.

Express parcel and document service is available with several foreign carriers. Contact DHL (☎ 6536-2900), UPS (☎ 6248-6060), Federal Express (☎ 6275-0808) or TNT Skypak (☎ 6419-0000).

Long-distance phone calls can be placed from hotel rooms and do not take long to get through. Long-distance calls also can be made from the post office next to the Peace Hotel on Nanjing Donglu; international telegrams and telexes also can be sent from here. Try at the larger hotels for email facilities; an Internet cafe had just opened when we were last in town on the northern side of Jinling Lu, soon after the corner with Henan Lu as you head west. There will certainly be more in the future, so ask at your hotel for any developments.

Useful Telephone Numbers Handy numbers include the Shanghai Tourism Association (☎ 6275-5880), Tourist Hotline

(☎ 6252-0000), International Operator (☎ 103) and Hotline for Women (☎ 6404-6765). There's even an Art Hotline (☎ 6248-5823) if you suddenly *have* to buy a Kandinsky and don't know where to start.

Bookshops Shanghai is one of the better places in China to stock up on reading fodder. Coupled with the tourist hotel bookshops, Shanghai's bookstores have a reasonable, if gagged, selection.

The main Foreign Languages Bookstore is at 390 Fuzhou Lu. The 1st floor has a good but pricey range of maps and the 2nd floor has a range of western literature that breaks the usual Jane Austen mould, but still inhabits a narrow and safe horizon of science fiction, fantasy and trash fiction. Fuzhou Lu has traditionally been the bookshop street of Shanghai and is well worth a stroll.

The Shanghai Museum bookshop has an excellent range of books on Chinese art, architecture, ceramics and calligraphy and is definitely worth a visit if you are in the museum. It also has a wide selection of cards and slides.

Get a copy of Pan Ling's *In Search of Old Shanghai* for a rundown on who was who and what was what back in the bad old days.

For where they lived, consult *A Last Look: Western Architecture in Old Shanghai* by Tess Johnston & Deke Erh which offers a fascinating photographic record of buildings in the city. It's usually available at the Shanghai Museum bookshop.

If you're in need of pens or paper, a blistering range of quality stationary can be found on the ground floor of the China Science and Technology Book Company on the corner of Fuzhou Lu and Henan Lu.

Newspapers & Magazines A small range of foreign newspapers and magazines is available from the larger tourist hotels (eg Park, Jinjiang, Sheraton Huating) and some shops.

Publications include the *Wall Street Journal, International Herald Tribune,* *Asiaweek, South China Morning Post, The Economist, Time* and *Newsweek.* They are expensive, however, with *Newsweek* and *Time* usually costing about Y35.

Shanghai is trying hard when it comes to English-language papers and periodicals, and apart from the *Shanghai Star* which is a crashing bore, there are many freebie trade and tourism publications where you can check out events and places to eat, drink and dance. These include *Travel China, Culture and Recreation* and, the best of the lot, *Welcome to China – Shanghai.* They are generally available from the larger hotels.

Medical Services Shanghai is credited with the best medical facilities and most advanced medical knowledge in China. Western medicines are sold at the Shanghai No 8 Drugstore at 951 Huaihai Zhonglu.

Foreigners are referred to the Shanghai Emergency Centre (☎ 6324-4010) at 68 Haining Lu. Hospital treatment is available at the Huashan Hospital (☎ 6248-9999) at 12 Wulumuqi Zhonglu, which has a Hong Kong joint-venture section, and at the Shanghai First People's Hospital (☎ 6306-9478) at 585 Jiulong Lu in Hongqiao.

World Link (☎ 6279-7688; fax 6279-7698) offers private medical care and can be found at Suite 203 in the Shanghai Centre.

The New Pioneer Medical Centre (☎ 6469-3898; fax 6469-3897), the self-appointed 'Specialists in Expatriate Healthcare', is on the 2nd floor of the Ge Ru building at 910 Heng Shan Lu, in the Xujiahui area near St Ignatius Cathedral.

What was What
Until recently, Shanghai was a vast museum, housing an inheritance of foreign trophies. Now, with both eyes on the future, Shanghai wants a face-lift. While state-protected landmark buildings on the Bund and elsewhere are safe from the ball-and-chain, in other parts of town chunks of history are giving way to department stores and office blocks.

SHANGHAI

Language Touts

Those trying to negotiate their way down the bustling corridor of commerce known as Nanjing Donglu may be unexpectedly pounced upon by an annoying breed of limpet-like 'English Language Learners'.

What's wrong with a bit of communication with the locals, considering it's normally so difficult, you may say. That's true – it can be a blessed relief to find someone in China who is competent in the English language; however, the breed I am talking about has a hidden agenda in the form of dragging you off to expensive cafes and getting you to foot the bill. Meanwhile they get a commission from the cafe owner.

I was walking along a side street off Nanjing Donglu, when I saw a jovial American speaking animatedly to two Chinese men who were frogmarching him along the pavement. It stuck in my mind as I had rarely seen such camaraderie in China.

As I turned the corner into Nanjing Donglu, I was pounced on by a bespectacled student of the English language who said, 'You are English'. Although I realised that our conversation was never really going to progress beyond such child-like gestures, out of curiosity I followed this apprentice to a cafe where I saw the American, still with his two friends, sharing a motley assortment of expensive drinks.

As I entered the cafe, a group of exiting Chinese whispered in my ear 'watch out'. Needless to say, I gave the whole thing a miss. The next day I was in the same area, and two attractive girls tried the same trick. They were decked out in the latest Hong Kong fashions, dripping with cosmetics and fluttering their eyelashes.

Not relishing the prospect of forking out for three rounds of creme de menthe and possibly having my wallet lifted, I managed to stun them with a few words of Polish. I left them searching for the next single man to come along.

Damian Harper

Shanghai is shackled to a past it is both suspicious and proud of, so who knows what the city will look like by the next century. But as the Chinese like to say, '*Jiùde búqù, xīnde bùlái*' ('if the old doesn't go, the new won't come').

For the time being, old Shanghai can still be enjoyed. The ancient buildings have an old-world grumpiness about them, scowling at the fresh-faced upstarts surrounding them. The **Chinese city**, for example, is still a maze of narrow lanes, lined with closely packed houses and laundry hanging from windows. It lies on the south-western bank of the Huangpu, bounded to the north by Jinling Donglu and to the south by Zhonghua Lu. The **Yuyuan Gardens** are in this part of town and are well worth a visit.

The **International Settlement** (*shànghǎi zūjiè*), in its time a brave new world of co-operation between the British, Europeans and Americans (the Japanese were also included, but were considered suspect), cuts a broad swathe through the north of the city centre. It extends from the intersection of Yan'an Xilu and Nanjing Xilu north to Suzhou Creek and east to the Huangpu River. Nanjing Lu and the Bund shared pride of place in this settlement. West of Xizang Lu was the Beverly Hills of Shanghai, an elite residential district cluttered with opulent villas.

South of Yan'an Lu and squeezed north of the Chinese city was the **French concession** (*fǎguó zūjiè*). Yan'an Lu was known as Avenue Foch in the west, and Avenue Edward VII in the east; the French strip of the Bund (south of Yan'an Lu) was known as the Quai de France. Despite the names, there were never all that many French people in the concession – 90% of the residents were Chinese, and the most numerous foreigners were Russians. Nevertheless, Frenchtown remains one of the most interesting parts of Shanghai. The premier district (around the Jinjiang Hotel and on Huaihai Lu) is once again being gentrified, and department stores and boutiques are springing up everywhere. But for Frenchtown at its best, simply strike off on the side streets that head south off Yan'an Lu (see Frenchtown later in this section for more information).

Nanjing Lu & the Central District

Nanjing Donglu (Nanjing Road East), from the Peace to the Park hotels, has long been China's golden mile. Once supreme, it's looking a bit frayed and has slipped a few notches to the emerging luxury option of Huaihai Lu, but laden shoppers still traipse past its cathedrals of commerce, gawped at by gaggles of out-of-towners.

Even back in the dull Communist era (and let's face it, *that's* long gone), Nanjing Donglu had a distinctly 'shop 'til you drop' feel about it. Nowadays, Esprit, Benetton and McDonald's have shouldered Marx and Mao into the draughty halls of little-visited museums – which was where the capitalist state was meant to end up.

Nanjing Xilu takes over where Nanjing Donglu ducks beside **Renmin (People's) Park**. The park and the adjacent Renmin Square were once the site of the Shanghai Racecourse and now proudly display the Shanghai Museum. Nanjing Xilu itself was previously Bubbling Well Road. Picturesque they may be, but bubbling wells are an inconvenience on busy avenues of commerce, and this one was sealed over.

The crowds evaporate as you head west along Nanjing Xilu. At Renmin Square a clutch of fast-food outlets and faddish emporiums conspire to invade the 'Workers Cultural Palace' and other neighbouring anachronisms. Beyond the Chengdu Lu Expressway, which thunders down the centre of Shanghai, Nanjing Xilu gives way to office blocks, more shops and hotels, all of which join forces in the impressive Shanghai Centre.

The Shanghai Museum

This stunning new building was built in 1994 at a cost of 570 million yuan, and can be seen as a completely new approach to museum design in China. The Shanghai Museum (*shànghǎi bówùguǎn*) is symbolic of the many changes that are afoot in China – gone are airy corridors, dry exhibits, yawning security guards and stale air – the new Shanghai museum is as impressive outside as in.

Designed to recall the shape of an ancient Chinese *ding* vessel, as architectural statement and as home to one of the most impressive collections of art in China, the Shanghai Museum is a must-see.

Take your pick from the galleries which house some fantastic specimens – from the archaic green patina of the Ancient Chinese Bronze Gallery through the silent solemnity of the Chinese Sculpture Gallery, from the exquisite beauty of the ceramics in the Zande Lou Gallery to the measured and timeless flourishes captured in the Chinese Calligraphy Gallery. Chinese painting, seals, jade, Ming and Qing furniture, coins and ethnic art are also on offer, intelligently displayed in well-lit galleries. Furthermore, the exhibits are generously spaced out, giving you the opportunity to stroll leisurely and unhurriedly through the galleries.

While guiding you through the craft of millennia, the museum simultaneously takes you through the pages of Chinese history. Expect to spend half if not the whole day here.

Originally located on Henan Nanlu, the museum can now be found at 201 Renmin Dadao, near Renmin Square Metro station, and is open daily from 9 am to 5 pm; entrance is Y20. ∎

The Bund

The Bund (wàitān) is an Anglo-Indian term for the embankment of a muddy waterfront. The term is apt: mud bedevils the city. Between 1920 (when the problem was first noticed) and 1965, Shanghai sank several metres. Water was pumped back into the ground, but the Venetian threat remains. Concrete rafts are used as foundations for high-rises in this spongy mass.

Its muddy predicament aside, the Bund is symbolic of Shanghai. In faraway Kashgar and Lhasa, local Chinese pose for photographs in front of oil-painted Bund facades. Constant throngs of Chinese and foreign tourists pad past the porticos of the Bund's grand edifices with maps in hand. The buildings themselves loom serenely, oblivious to the march of revolutions; a vagabond assortment of neoclassical 1930s downtown New York styles, with a pompous touch of monumental antiquity thrown in for good measure.

To the Europeans, the Bund was Shanghai's Wall Street, a place of feverish trading, of fortunes made and lost. One of the most famous traders was Jardine Matheson & Company. In 1848 Jardine's purchased the first land offered for sale to foreigners in Shanghai and set up shop shortly after, dealing in opium and tea.

The Bank of China, which dwarfs its better known neighbour, the Peace Hotel, is one of the striking examples of architecture characteristic of the Bund.

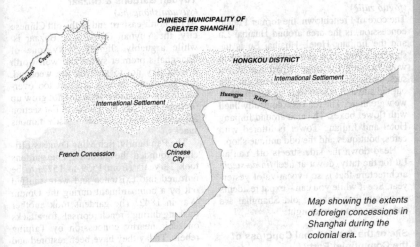

CHINESE MUNICIPALITY OF
GREATER SHANGHAI

HONGKOU DISTRICT

International Settlement

Huangpu River

International Settlement

French Concession

Old
Chinese
City

Suzhou Creek

*Map showing the extents
of foreign concessions in
Shanghai during the
colonial era.*

THE BUND

The company grew into one of the great *hongs* (a 'hong' is literally a business firm), and today it owns just about half of Hong Kong.

At the north-western end of the Bund were the British Public Gardens (now called Huangpu Park). Famously, a sign at the entrance announced 'No Dogs or Chinese Allowed'. Or at least that is how posterity remembers it; in actual fact the restrictions on Chinese and dogs were listed in separate clauses of a whole bevy of restrictions on undesirables. The slight, however, will probably never be forgotten.

The Bund today is in the process of yet another transformation. The building identified by a crowning dome is the old Hongkong & Shanghai Bank, completed in 1921 with much pomp and ceremony. The Hongkong & Shanghai Bank has long been negotiating to get it back, and probably will. For many years it has housed the Shanghai People's Municipal Government. Other Bund fixtures are being sold off, and will no doubt be dusted off and cleaned up.

The statues that once lined the Bund no longer exist; the pair of bronze lions that once stood outside the Hongkong & Shanghai Bank are now housed in the Bund History Museum.

The Tung Feng Hotel, at the bottom of the Bund near Shiliupu Wharf, only hints at its former grandeur and conveys nothing of its former exclusivity. It was once home to the Shanghai Club, the snootiest little gang this side of Trafalgar Square. Membership was confined to upper-crust male Brits. They sat around the club's 110 foot bar (the longest in the world at the time), sipping chilled champagne and comparing fortunes.

Frenchtown
(fǎguó zūjiè)

The core of Frenchtown, the former French concession, is the area around Huaihai Lu and the Jinjiang Hotel. Huaihai Lu is the shopper's Pudong, a glittering alternative to worn Nanjing Lu; huge department stores such as Isetan, Printemps and Parkson blot out the sun and others were going up when we were there. The road is colourfully lined with flower boxes. The area around Jinjiang Hotel and Jinjiang Tower is littered with cafes, boutiques and the odd antique shop.

Head down the side streets off Yan'an Lu for the tatty, down-at-heel *fin de siècle* architecture that is so evocative of yesteryear. See it while you can – expat residents complain that slabs of old Shanghai are vanishing almost overnight.

Site of the 1st National Congress of the Communist Party
(zhōnggòng yīdàhuìzhǐ)

The CCP was founded in July 1921 in a French concession building at 76 Xingye Lu. Given the significance of the occasion, the museum has a very low profile. There are some photographs and the like with English captions. Opening hours are 8.30 to 11 am and 1 to 4 pm, and it's closed Monday and Thursday mornings. Entry is Y3.

Sun Yatsen's Residence
(sūn zhōngshān gùjū)

China is simply brimming with Sun Yatsen memorabilia, and here is one of his former residences (he got around) at 7 Xianshan Lu, formerly the Rue Molière. He lived here for six years, supported by Overseas Chinese funds. After Sun's death, his wife, Song Qingling (1893-1981), continued to live here until 1937, constantly watched by Kuomintang plain-clothes police and French police. The two storey house is set back from the street and furnished as it was back in Sun's days, even though it was looted by the Japanese.

The entry price of Y7 gets you a brief tour of the house. It is open daily from 9 am to 4.30 pm.

Yuyuan Gardens & Bazaar
(yùyuán shāngshà)

At the north-eastern end of the old Chinese city, the Yuyuan Gardens & Bazaar is, while arguably slightly tacky, one of Shanghai's premier sights and well worth a visit. Try not to visit on the weekend, though, as the crowds are just too overwhelming for anyone who did not grow up in Shanghai. (See the Places to Eat section for details on the bazaar's justly famous snacks.)

The Pan family, rich Ming Dynasty officials, founded the gardens. The gardens took 18 years (from 1559 to 1577) to be nurtured into existence and were snuffed out by a bombardment during the Opium War in 1842. The gardens took another trashing during French reprisals for attacks on their nearby concession by Taiping rebels. Today they have been restored and attract hordes of Chinese tourists. Opening hours are 8.30 am to 4.30 pm daily.

The **Temple of the Town Gods** *(chénghuángmiào)* is a recently restored and overrated attraction in the bazaar area. In fact, the Yuyuan Bazaar itself, a Disneyland version of historical China, is altogether more interesting. More than 100 speciality shops and restaurants jostle shoulders over narrow laneways and small squares in a mock 'olde Cathay' setting. It's a great stop for lunch and some souvenir shopping.

Jade Buddha Temple
(yùfó sì)

The Jade Buddha Temple is one of Shanghai's few Buddhist temples. It is active and attracts large numbers of visitors – largely local and overseas Chinese tourists.

Built between 1911 and 1918, the centrepiece is a 2m-high white jade buddha around which the temple was built. The story goes that a monk from Putuoshan travelled to Myanmar (Burma) via Tibet, lugged the buddha back to its present site and then went off in search of alms to build a temple for it.

This seated buddha, encrusted with

jewels, is said to weigh 1000kg. A smaller buddha from the same shipment reclines on a mahogany couch.

No photography is permitted. The temple closes for lunch between noon and 1 pm, and is open daily except on special occasions such as the Lunar New Year in February, when some 20,000 Chinese Buddhists descend on the place.

The temple is in the north-west of town, near the intersection of Anyuan Lu and Jiangning Lu. One way to get there is to take the subway out to the Shanghai railway station and then walk (about 1km), or take a taxi or motor-tricycle.

Bus No 19 runs from around the corner of Shanghai Mansions, along Tiantong Lu and eventually on past the temple.

Pudong New Area
(pǔdōng xīnqū)

Larger than Shanghai itself, the Pudong New Area is on the eastern bank of the Huangpu River. Before 1990 – when development plans were first announced – Pudong constituted 350 sq km of boggy farmland supplying vegetables to Shanghai's markets. Now the vegies are grown elsewhere as Pudong has become a Special Economic Zone (SEZ).

It all reads like a catalogue of excess: Shanghai plans to spend US$36 billion on infrastructure projects over the next years, and much of this is related to Pudong. Two massive bridges have been constructed to connect Puxi (central Shanghai) with Pudong, as well as numerous tunnels; there are even plans for a cable car link across the Huangpu River.

Shanghai's second metro line will connect with Pudong when it opens in 1998. The Waigaoqiao harbour area is being upgraded into a major container port and work has begun on the US$2 billion Pudong airport which will supplement Hongqiao airport when it opens in 1999. At weekends, 350,000 visitors pass through the portals of Nextage, Asia's largest (and the world's second largest) department store.

The gargantuan economic strides in Pudong have created a vast city out of nothing, but culture was never an issue. Its purpose is the creation of wealth. The tourist will, for the most part, feel dwarfed and alienated by the scale of the place, and attractions are few and far between.

The **Oriental Pearl Tower** (the *Dan Dare* air traffic control tower visible from the Bund) is a uniquely uninspiring piece of architecture, although the views of Shanghai from its lookout halfway up are sensational. The drawback is that you have to queue forever to get into the high-speed elevator and the privilege costs Y50 (Y100 if you want to go to the top bauble).

Other Sights

South-west of central Shanghai, close to the Huangpu River, is the **Longhua Pagoda** (lónghuá tǎ). It is said to date from the 10th century and has recently been restored for tourism. It is a hassle to get to. The easiest way is to take the metro to the Caobao Lu metro station, then walk or take a taxi.

The Xujiahui area bordering the western end of Frenchtown once had a Jesuit settlement, with an observatory (which is still in use). **St Ignatius Cathedral**, whose spires were lopped off by Red Guards, has been restored and is open once again for Catholic services. It's at 158 Puxi Lu, in the Xujiahui district; the best way to get there is to take the underground to Xujiahui station, and then it's a short walk south to the church.

Further south-west of the Longhua Pagoda are the **Shanghai Botanical Gardens** (shànghǎi zhíwùyuán), with an exquisite collection of 9000 miniatures.

The **Shanghai Exhibition Centre** is south of the Shanghai Centre. Architectural buffs will appreciate the monumentality and unsubtle, bold Bolshevik strokes – there was a time when Pudong was set to look like this. There are irregular displays of local industrial wares and heavy machinery.

Out near the airport is **Shanghai Zoo**, which has a roller-skating rink, children's

Central Shanghai

0   250   500 m

Changshou Lu

Suzhou Creek

Hengfeng Lu

Tianmu Xilu

Tianmu Lu

Xizang Beilu

Changshu Lu Expressway

Anyuan Lu

Jiangning Lu

Changshou Lu

Kangding Lu

Xinzha Lu

Wuning Nanlu

Wanhangdu Lu

Yuyuan Lu

Beijing Xilu

Nanjing Xilu

Taixing Lu

Shimen Lu

Dalian Lu

Nanjing Lu

Jiangyin Lu

Weihai Lu

Yan'an Zhonglu

Changle Lu

Shaanxi Nanlu

Maoming Nanlu

Yan'an Xilu

Huashan Lu

Changshu Lu

Huaihai Zhonglu

Fenyang Lu

Fuxing Zhonglu

Fuxing Xilu

Yongjia Lu

Shaanxi Nanlu

Jianguo Xilu

Huaihai Zhonglu

Zhaojiabang Lu

Zhaojiabang Lu

Hengshan Lu

1
2
3
4
5
37
38
39
40
41
42
43
44
45
46
47
48
49
50
51
52
53
54
55
56
57
58
59
60
81
82
83
84
85
86
87
88
89
90
91
92
93
94
95
96
97
98
99
100

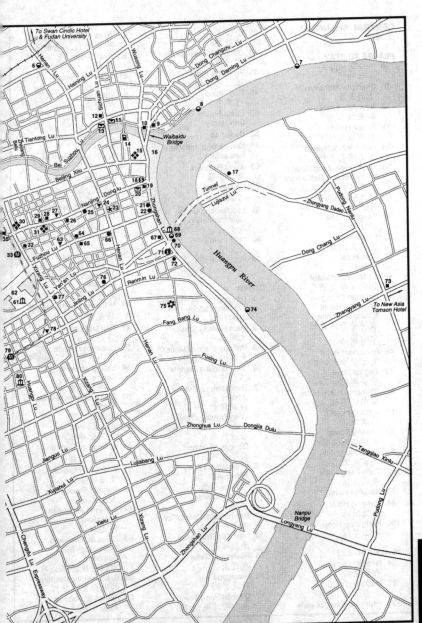

CENTRAL SHANGHAI
上海市中心

PLACES TO STAY
9 Pujiang Hotel
浦江饭店
10 Shanghai Mansions
上海大厦
12 New Asia Hotel
新亚饭店
19 Peace Hotel
和平饭店
26 Hotel Sofitel Hyland
上海海仑宾馆
28 Chun Shen Jiang Hotel;
Shendacheng Restaurant
春申江宾馆、沈大成
29 East Asia Hotel
东亚饭店
32 Yangtze Hotel
扬子饭店
35 Pacific Hotel
金门大酒店
37 Park Hotel
国际饭店
42 JC Mandarin Hotel
锦沧文华大酒店
43 Portman Shangrila
Shanghai Hotel;
Shanghai Centre
波特曼香格里拉
大酒店
上海商城
48 Equatorial Hotel
国际贵都大饭店
49 Jing'an Hotel
静安宾馆
50 Shanghai Hilton Hotel
希尔顿酒店
59 Jinjiang Hotel
锦江饭店
60 Jinjiang Tower
新锦江大酒店
65 Wu Gong Hotel
吴宫大酒店
67 Tung Feng Hotel
东风饭店
73 Nextage Hotel
98 Nanying Hotel
南鹰饭店
100 Hengshan Hotel
衡山宾馆

PLACES TO EAT
24 Häagen Dazs
哈根达斯
27 McDonald's
麦当劳
36 Espresso Express Cafe

39 KFC
肯德鸡
40 Gongdelin Restaurant
宫德林
45 Frankie's Place
法兰奇餐厅
46 Red Rhino
红犀牛餐厅
52 Pasta Fresca Da
Salvatore
53 Badlands
58 Kanetanaka Japanese
Restaurant
Xinya Restaurant
新雅饭店
63
78 LA Café
滚石一族
81 Laodachang Bakery &
Confectionery
老大昌
82 McDonald's
麦当劳
92 Pizza Hut; KFC
必胜客、肯德鸡

OTHER
1 Longmen Hotel (Railway
Ticketing Office)
龙门饭店
2 Main Railway Station
火车站
3 Railway Station (Metro)
火车站（地铁站）
4 Jade Buddha Temple
玉佛寺
5 Hangzhou Lu Station
(Metro)
杭州路站
6 Long-Distance Bus
Station
长途汽车站
7 Gongpinglu Wharf
公平路码头
8 International Ferry
Terminal
外虹桥码头
11 Poste Restante
邮局
13 International Post Office
国际邮局
14 New York New York
迪斯可
15 Friendship Store
友谊商店
16 Huangpu Park
黄浦公园
17 Oriental Pearl Tower
东方明珠电视塔

18 Bank of China; Citibank
中国银行、花旗银行
20 Post Office
邮局
21 Customs House
海关楼
22 City Hall
市政府
23 PSB
公安局
25 Xinhua Bookstore
新华书店
30 No 1 Department Store
第一百货
31 Hua Lian Department
Store
华联百货
33 Renmin Square Station
(Metro)
人民广场站
34 Renmin Park
人民公园
38 Xinzha Lu Station (Metro)
新闸路站
41 Jingdezhen Porcelain
Artware
景德镇瓷器店
44 Malone's American Cafe
马龙咖啡店
47 Jing'an Park
静安公园
51 Huashan Hospital
华山医院
54 Shanghai Exhibition
Centre
上海展览中心
55 China Eastern Airlines
(CAAC)
民航售票处
56 Jurassic Pub
恐龙世界
57 JJ Dickson Centre
锦江迪生商厦
61 Shanghai Museum
上海博物馆
62 Renmin Square
人民广场
64 Foreign Languages
Bookstore
外文书店
66 China Science and
Technology Book
Company
中国科技图书公司
68 Bund History Museum
外滩历史博物馆
69 Ferries to Pudong
码头（至浦东）

SHANGHAI

70 Huangpu Tour Boats 黄浦上游船	80 Site of 1st National Congress of CCP 一大会址	90 Cathay Theatre 国泰电影院
71 CITS (Guangming Building) 中国国际旅行社	83 Isetan 伊势丹	91 Parkson Department Store; McDonald's 百盛、麦当劳
72 Boat Ticketing Office 船售票处	84 Fuxing Park 复兴公园	93 Printemps 上海巴黎春天百货
74 Shiliupu Wharf 十六浦码头	85 Former Residence of Sun Yatsen 中山故居	94 Shaanxi Nanlu Station (Metro) 陕西南路站
75 Yuyuan Gardens; Bazaar 豫园、市场	86 Shanghai Sally's 上海沙莉	95 Conservatory of Music 音乐学院
76 Internet Cafe 网络咖啡店	87 Tequila Mama 巴哈马村庄	96 Changshu Lu Station (Metro) 常熟路站
77 Great World 大世界	88 Watson's Pharmacy 屈臣氏	97 US Consulate 美国领事馆
79 Huangpi Nanlu Station (Metro) 黄陂南路站	89 Danny's Pub 豪名酒店	99 Hengshan Lu Station (Metro) 衡山路站

playground and other recreational facilities (it's shut on Tuesdays); to get there, take the red No 831 bus from Jinling Lu off the Bund (Y4) or bus No 505 from Renmin Square. To the west of the zoo is the former **Sassoon Villas**.

On the way to the town of Jiaxing, by rail or road, is Songjiang County, 20km south-west of Shanghai. The place is older than Shanghai itself. On Tianmashan, in Songjiang County, is the **Huzhou Pagoda**, built in 1079 AD. It's the leaning tower of China, with an inclination now exceeding the tower at Pisa by 1.5°. The 19m-high tower started tilting 200 years ago. Other sights in the area include the **Fangta**, a square pagoda entirely made of wood.

Huangpu River Trip
(huángpǔ jiāng yóulǎn chuán)
The Huangpu River offers some remarkable views of the Bund and the riverfront activity. Huangpu tour boats depart from the dock on the Bund, a few blocks south of the Peace Hotel. There are several decks on the boat, but foreigners are forced upmarket into special class A or special class B. The boat takes you on a 3½ hour, 60km round trip, northwards up the Huangpu to the junction with the Yangzi River (Wusongkou) and back again along the same route.

Departure times are 9 am and 2 and 7 pm (Monday to Friday), and 11 am and 3.30 and 8 pm (Saturday and Sunday). The schedule may become erratic in winter due to bad weather. Tickets cost between Y50 and Y100. Tickets can only be purchased at the boat dock; you can try your luck phoning them (☎ 6374-4461), but we can't promise an intelligible reply.

Shanghai is one of the world's largest ports; 2000 ocean-going ships and about 15,000 river steamers load and unload here every year. The tour boat passes an enormous variety of craft – freighters, bulk carriers, roll-on roll-off ships, sculling sampans, giant praying-mantis cranes, the occasional junk and Chinese navy vessels (which aren't supposed to be photographed).

Special Events
The Shanghai Music Festival is in May and the Shanghai International Tea Culture Festival is usually at the end of April. The Shanghai Marathon Cup is in March and is one of the top sporting events in the country.

The Shanghai Beer Festival staggers into

town around the end of July, while the Shanghai Tourism Festival kicks off in late September. It is worth bearing these dates in mind as hotel accommodation can become scarce – during the Chinese New Year (usually in February) Shanghai is packed out.

Places to Stay – budget

Shanghai has the highest real estate values in China, and lower-end accommodation has felt the squeeze for a while now. There are no real cheap hotels, although there are a few that represent value for money.

Take note that budget accommodation can be swamped during the summer and on holidays, leaving you with little choice but to upgrade to pricey doubles that cost Y300 or more.

The distinguished *Pujiang Hotel* (☎ 6324-6388; fax 6324-3179) *(pǔjiāng fàndiàn)* at 15 Huangpu Lu was originally called the Astor House Hotel and was Shanghai's first hotel. This is *the* place for those counting their shekels – it's central, has loads of style and the rooms are vast. Although the galleries upstairs look like they belong in a Victorian asylum, there's a nobility about the place that makes Y55 for a dorm bed a bargain and a half. Bus No 64 leaves from in front of the main railway station to the corner of Nanjing Donglu and Jiangsu Zhonglu. Walk east along Nanjing Donglu, turn left at the Bund and walk over Suzhou Creek to the hotel.

The *Conservatory of Music* (☎ 6437-2577) *(yīnyuè xuéyuàn)*, at 20 Fenyang Lu off Huaihai Zhonglu, is an old stand-by. Unfortunately, renovations have pushed prices up to Y200 for a standard double. The conservatory only has 16 rooms and is often fully booked. Take a subway from the main railway station to Changshu Lu station. To find the rooms walk through the entrance to the conservatory and bear left.

Out of the way in the north-east is the excellent *Changyang Hotel* (☎ 6543-4890; fax 6543-0986) *(chángyáng fàndiàn)* at 1800 Changyang Lu. Doubles range from Y210 to Y290, but push for a discount as they were offering 20% off when we last asked. Bus No 22 from the Bund area runs right past the hotel.

Another option is the *Haijia Hotel* (☎ 6541-1440) *(hǎijiā fàndiàn)* at 1001 Jiangpu Lu in the north-eastern part of town. It was closed for renovations at the time of writing – give them a call and see if they're ready for business.

Places to Stay – middle

Mid-range accommodation in Shanghai will cost between Y300 and Y400 for a double.

The *East Asia Hotel* (☎ 6322-3233; fax 6322-4598) *(dōngyà fàndiàn)* at 680 Nanjing Donglu, on the corner with Zhejiang Lu, has a great location and reasonable singles for Y250 and doubles for Y352. It's hidden away above a shopping centre which you have to amble through to get to the stairs. A big white clock tower on the corner of the block gives it away.

Opposite is the *Chun Shen Jiang Hotel* (☎ 6320-5710; fax 6351-6512) *(chūnshēnjiāng bīnguǎn)*, at 626 Nanjing Donglu, which has long been known as a good midrange hotel with central Shanghai at its doorstep. Doubles start at Y330.

Quite a hike out and difficult to reach, but scenically located next to the Longhua Pagoda, is the *Longhua Hotel* (☎ 6457-0570; fax 6457-7621) *(lónghuá yíng bīnguǎn)*, which has singles at Y240 (plus 10%) and doubles from Y380. The nearest metro station is Caobao Lu station.

The *Yangtze Hotel* (☎ 6322-5115; fax 6351-6974) *(yángzǐ fàndiàn)* is at 740 Hankou Lu, facing Renmin Park. It was built back in 1934 and is an old American-style hotel in a good area. Singles go from Y360 and doubles from Y440. It is near the metro station at Renmin Square.

The *Nanying Hotel* (☎ 6437-8188; fax 6437-8593) *(nányīng fàndiàn)* at 1720 Huaihai Zhonglu is in the south-western part of the city. Very comfortable doubles cost Y388.

The *Wu Gong Hotel* (☎ 6326-0303; fax 6328-2820) *(wúgōng dàjiǔdiàn)* at 431

Fuzhou Lu is centrally located and has nice rooms, but is pricey for what you get. Singles and doubles start at Y320.

Places to Stay – top end

Shanghai is virtually built up from hotels in the top-end (over Y400) category. They generally fall into two categories: the noble and aristocratic hotels of old Shanghai and the slick new towers bursting with modern amenities.

Business travellers will probably opt for modern facilities like the Portman Shangri-la Shanghai or the Jinjiang Tower, while those with a sense of history might want to stay at one of the more urbane options, such as the Peace Hotel, where they can wrap themselves in history and fumble for the bell-pull in the middle of the night.

Interior renovations have robbed the Park, Shanghai Mansions and Jinjiang of character and history, but if there's one place left in Shanghai that will give you a sense of the past, it's the *Peace Hotel* (the old Cathay) (☎ 6321-6888; fax 6329-0300) *(hépíng fàndiàn)* at 20 Nanjing Donglu. On the ground floor of this 12 storey edifice is a sumptuous lobby, shops, bookshop, bank, video games parlour, snooker tables, cafe and barber. In a bid to grab on to the coat-tails of the future, the hotel has a touch-screen computer tourist information service in the lobby.

The cost of all this history is US$120/160 for standard singles/doubles and, if that's not enough, there are suites starting at US$250. The national deluxe suites (US$380) are laid out in 1930s Art Deco style to represent the concessions of the time – French, British, American and Japanese, not to mention Chinese.

The *Tung Feng Hotel* (☎ 6321-8060; fax 6321-0261) *(dōngfēng fàndiàn)*, 3 Zhongshan Dong 1-Lu, is a grand but lesser

---

The Cathay Hotel

The Peace Hotel is a ghostly reminder of the immense wealth of Victor Sassoon. From a Baghdad Jewish family, he made millions out of the opium trade and then ploughed it back into Shanghai real estate and horses.

Sassoon's quote of the day was 'There is only one race greater than the Jews, and that's the Derby'. His office-cum-hotel was completed in 1930 and was known as Sassoon House, incorporating the Cathay Hotel. From the top floors Victor commanded his real estate – he is estimated to have owned 1900 buildings in Shanghai.

Like the Taj in Bombay, the Stanley Raffles in Singapore and the Peninsula in Hong Kong, the Cathay was *the* place to stay in Shanghai. Sassoon himself resided in what is now the VIP section below the green pyramidal tower, complete with Tudor panelling. He also maintained a Tudor-style villa out near Hongqiao airport just west of the zoo. The likes of Noel Coward (who wrote *Private Lives* in the Cathay) wined and dined in the hotel's Tower Restaurant.

Back in 1949 the Kuomintang strayed into the place, awaiting the arrival of the Communists. A western writer of the time records an incident in which 50 Kuomintang arrived, carrying their pots and pans, vegetables and firewood, and one soldier was overheard asking where to billet the mules. After the Communists took over the city, the troops were billeted in places like the Picardie (now the Hengshan Guesthouse on the outskirts of the city), where they spent hours experimenting with the elevators, used bidets as face-showers and washed rice in the toilets – which was all very well until someone pulled the chain.

In 1953 foreigners tried to give the Cathay to the CCP in return for exit visas. The government refused at first, but finally accepted after the payment of back taxes'. ■

known establishment right on the Bund at Yan'an Donglu. The marbled interior of the lobby still hints at what was, although the KFC is a bit gauche to say the least. Doubles cost Y450 while deluxe doubles are Y800. There is also another branch (☎ 6323-5304) at Sichuan Zhonglu.

The *Park Hotel* (☎ 6327-5225; fax 6327-6958) *(guójì fàndiàn)*, at 170 Nanjing Xilu, overlooks Renmin Park. Erected in 1934, the building is one of Shanghai's best examples of Art Deco architecture from the city's cultural peak. With recent renovations, however, the interior has lost all its old-world charm. Doubles start at Y870. The rooms are quite comfortable and the service is efficient.

Shanghai Mansions (☎ 6324-6260; fax 6393-7477) *(shànghǎi dàshà)* is at 20 Suzhou Beilu, near the Pujiang Hotel on the same side of Huangpu River at the junction with Suzhou Creek. The hotel used to be called Broadway Mansions, a block of apartments used to house American officers just after WWII. Standard double rooms (no singles) start at Y550.

The *Pacific Hotel* (☎ 6327-6226; fax 6372-3634) *(jīnmén dàjiǔdiàn)*, 104 Nanjing Xilu, was previously called the Overseas Chinese Hotel *(huáqiáo fàndiàn)* and most Shanghai residents still call it that. The hotel is easily recognisable by the distinctive clock tower marked with a big red star, and by the fabulously opulent foyer. Singles start at US$55 and doubles cost US$70 to US$95. This is one of Nanjing Lu's more historic hotels.

The traditional-style *Jinjiang Hotel* (☎ 6258-2582; fax 6472-5588) *(jǐnjiāng fàndiàn)* is at 59 Maoming Nanlu. Singles here start at US$155, plus 15%. Its annexe, the adjacent and similarly named *Jinjiang Tower* (☎ 6433-4488; fax 6415-0048) *(xīn jǐnjiāng dàjiǔdiàn)*, at 161 Changle Lu, is home to a stunning interior equipped with a ballroom. Singles start at US$190, plus 15%.

The *Shanghai New Asia Tomson Hotel* (☎ 5831-8888; fax 5831-7777) *(shànghǎi-xīnyà tāngchén dàjiǔdiàn)* is a five star hotel

near Nextage in Lujiazui, the finance and trade district of Pudong. Among other top-notch facilities it has 11 bars/restaurants and two ballrooms. Singles and doubles start at US$120, plus 15%.

The best of Shanghai's modern hotels is probably the *Portman Shangrila Shanghai* (☎ 6279-8888; fax 6279-8999) *(bōtèmàn xiānggélǐlā dàjiǔdiàn)* in the massive Shanghai Centre. Singles start at US$210 and doubles at US$240, plus 15%.

The Shangrila Hotel, Pudong, is under construction and should be open by the time you read this.

The following Shanghai hotels all have modern facilities and charge from US$50 upwards:

City Hotel (☎ 6255-1133; fax 6255-0211) *(chéngshì jiǔdiàn)*, 5-7 Shanxi Nanlu
Cypress Hotel (☎ 6268-8868) *(lóngbǎi fàndiàn)*, 2419 Hongqaio Lu
Dahua Guesthouse (☎ 6251-2512; fax 6251-2702) *(dáhuá bīnguǎn)*, 914 Yan'an Xilu
Equatorial Hotel (☎ 6248-1688; fax 6248-1773) *(guójì guìdū dàfàndiàn)*, 65 Yan'an Xilu
Galaxy Hotel (☎ 6275-5888; fax 6275-0039) *(yínhé bīnguǎn)*, 888 Zhongshan Xilu
Gaoyang Hotel (☎ 6541-3920; fax 6545-8696) *(gāoyáng bīnguǎn)*, 879 Dong Daming Lu
Garden Hotel (☎ 6415-1111; fax 6415-8866) *(huāyuán fàndiàn)*, 58 Maoming Nanlu
Hengshan Hotel (☎ 6437-7050; fax 6433-5732) *(héngshān bīnguǎn)*, 534 Hengshan Lu
Hilton Hotel (☎ 6248-0000; fax 6248-3848) *(jìng'ān xī ěrdùn jiǔdiàn)*, 250 Huashan Lu
Holiday Inn Yinxing (☎ 6280-8888; fax 6280-2788) *(yínxīng jiàrì jiǔdiàn)*, 388 Panyu Lu
International Airport Hotel (☎ 6268-8866; fax 6268-8393) *(guójì jīchǎng bīnguǎn)*, 2550 Hongqiao Lu, Hongqiao airport
JC Mandarin Hotel (☎ 6279-1888; fax 6279-1822) *(jǐncāng wénhuà dàjiǔdiàn)*, 1225 Nanjing Xilu
Jianguo Hotel (☎ 6439-9299; fax 6439-9714) *(jiànguó bīnguǎn)*, 439 Caoxi Beilu
Jing'an Hotel (☎ 6248-1888; fax 6248-2657) *(jìng'ān bīnguǎn)*, 370 Huashan Lu
Jinshajiang Hotel (☎ 6257-8888; fax 6257-4149) *(jīnshājiāng dàjiǔdiàn)*, 801 Jinshajiang Lu
Novotel Shanghai Yuanlin (☎ 6470-1688; fax 6470-0008) *(nuòfùtè yuánlín bīnguǎn)*, 201 Baise Lu

Olympic Hotel (☎ 6439-1391; fax 6439-6295)
(*àolínpǐkè jùlèbù*), 1800 Zhongshan Nan 2-Lu
Rainbow Hotel (☎ 6275-3388; fax 6275-7244)
(*hóngqiáo bīnguǎn*), 2000 Yan'an Xilu
Ruijin Hotel (☎ 6433-1076; fax 6437-4861)
(*ruìjīn bīnguǎn*), 118 Ruijin 2-Lu
Shanghai Hotel (☎ 6471-2712; fax 6433-1056)
(*shànghǎi bīnguǎn*), 505 Wulumqi Beilu
Silk Road Hotel (☎ 6542-9051; fax 6542-6659)
(*sīchóuzhīlù dàjiǔdiàn*), 777 Quyang Lu
Sofitel Hyland Hotel (☎ 6320-5888; fax 6320-
4088) (*hǎilún bīnguǎn*), 505 Nanjing Donglu
Swan Cindic Hotel (☎ 6325-5255; fax 6324-
8002) (*tiān'é xìnyí bīnguǎn*), 111 Jiangwan
Lu, Hongkou
Tianma Hotel (☎ 6275-8100; fax 6275-7139)
(*tiānmǎ dàjiǔdiàn*), 471 Wuzhong Lu
West Garden Hotel (☎ 6255-7173) (*xīyuán
fàndiàn*), 2384 Hongqiao Lu, Changning District
Westin Taipingyang (☎ 6275-8888; fax 6275-
5420) (*wēisīfīng tàipíngyáng*), 5 Zunyi Nanlu
Xianxia Hotel (☎ 6259-9400; fax 6251-7492)
(*xiānxiá bīnguǎn*), 555 Shuicheng Lu
Xijiao Guesthouse (☎ 6433-6643; fax 6433-
6641) (*xījiāo bīnguǎn*), 1921 Hongqiao Lu
Xingguo Guesthouse (☎ 6437-4503; fax 6251-
2145) (*xīngguó bīnguǎn*), 72 Xingguo Lu
Yangtze New World (☎ 6275-0000; fax 6275-
0750) (*yángzǐjiāng dàjiǔdiàn*), 2099 Yan'an
Xilu
Yunfeng Guesthouse (☎ 6432-8900; fax 6432-
8954) (*yúnfēng bīnguǎn*), 1665 Hongqiao Lu

Places to Eat

Like everything else in Shanghai, the restaurant industry has witnessed an upheaval
over the last five years; sky-rocketing rents
and the wholesale arrival of international
fast food and classy cuisine have sent many
of the old favourites packing. Connoisseurs
of good food will appreciate this culinary
revolution, but your average backpacker
may grow weary of endless fast food and
snacks.

Keep your eyes open for the new restaurants that are springing up with increasing
frequency. The side streets around town all
feature small restaurants serving cheap,
local food.

Also look out for Shanghai's No 1
favourite dumpling *xiǎolóngbāo*, which is
copied everywhere else in China, but is
only true to form here. For Y5, you should

get a steamer with four of these. They are
wonderful, but there's an art to eating them
– they're full of scalding oil and the interi-
or is hotter than McDonald's apple pies. In
the Bund area, Sichuan Zhonglu is a good
place to look, as are the side streets in the
old French concession.

Fast-food outlets are everywhere in
genuine and counterfeit form. KFC has
spawned a brood of lookalikes including
Popeyes, *CFC* and *Hartz Chicken Buffet*,
while *Nancy's*, a Chinese fast-food variant,
uses a McDonald's-type logo. The raging
fast-food war creates new dimensions in
service: McDonald's offers freebie coffee
refills and free delivery of meals over Y50
to destinations within five minutes' cycle
ride of the outlet.

The Bund Area & Nanjing Lu We don't
recommend the *Petrol Restaurant* just
north of Suzhou Creek unless your doctor
says it's OK, but if you're looking for
cheap eats near the Huangpu then why not
try the *World of Snack* (*xiǎochī shìjiè*),
along and to the right on Jiujiang Lu. This
is bargainsville, with a small alley of cheap
dumpling restaurants. Ask for xiaolongbao
(see the Places to Eat introduction).

If you need to sink your teeth into fast
food, *KFC* can be found on the ground
floor of the Tung Feng Hotel.

A good street for restaurants close to the
Bund is Fuzhou Lu. Head in the direction
of Renmin Square and look out for the
prominent mosque-like structure on the
left: the *Daxiyang Moslem Restaurant*
(☎ 6322-4787) (*dàxīyáng qīngzhēn*) at 710
Fuzhou Lu. Like most big Shanghai restaurants, it has a cheaper downstairs section
and high-class dining upstairs.

For quality Cantonese, try *Xinghua Lou*
(*xìnghuā lóu*) at 343 Fuzhou Lu which
serves quality dim sum and was established
in the reign of Xianfeng. Not far from the
Foreign Languages Bookstore, also on
Fuzhou Lu, is the *Xinya Restaurant* (*xīnyǎ
fàndiàn*), which is famous for its Cantonese
dishes.

Nanjing Donglu is not what it used to be

when it comes to restaurants, and many of the old establishments have moved; *Shendacheng (shěndàchéng)* still clings to the corner of Zhejiang Zhonglu and Nanjing Donglu, opposite the East Asia Hotel; it serves up Shanghai snacks and dumplings.

Häagen Dazs has arrived for those who hanker after excellent ice cream and good coffee. It's also an escape from the sometimes unbearable bustle of Nanjing Lu. You can find it on the corner of Nanjing Donglu at the intersection with Henan Lu.

Nanjing Donglu fades into Nanjing Xilu with a further withering of decent restaurants and the triumph of fast-food outlets. Between the towering Park and Pacific hotels can be found the tiny *Espresso Express Café*; it's a friendly place steeped in the rich aroma of espresso and coffee grinds.

Yuyuan Bazaar Area If for no other reason than you are hungry, it is worth heading down to the Yuyuan Gardens & Bazaar. There are a couple of fast-food outfits here (*TCBY* and *Mos Burger*), but the real attraction is the excellent snack food. It ranks among the best in China.

These snacks are available in the big-name Yuyuan restaurants such as the *Old Shanghai Restaurant* (☎ 6328-9850) *(shànghǎi lǎo fàndiàn)* and the *Green Wave Gallery* (☎ 6373-7020) *(lǜbōlàng cāntīng)*, but these places tend to charge extortionate amounts for food that is only marginally better than the stuff served downstairs by streetside vendors. There's one advantage: they do have English menus.

Certain stalls are famed for a particular snack, and these inevitably have long queues snaking from the counters. The *Hefeng Lou (héfēng lóu)* is a canteen-style operation (no English sign outside unfortunately) with a wide range of savoury snacks on sale, including Yunnan cross-bridge noodles, wanton soup and *guōtiē* (fried dumplings). There are photo-menus and some Japanese-style plastic food displays to make ordering easier. Getting a seat can be a hassle, and watch out you

don't accidentally order smelly tofu (*chòudòu fǔ*) which is an acquired taste if ever there was one.

Old French Concession Area This area is rapidly emerging as the best part of town for places to eat. A good starting point is Changle Lu opposite the Jinjiang Tower. There is a string of cheap restaurants and pubs serving foreign food of the pizza variety and Chinese fare; they are not difficult to find as the owners all rush out to usher you around a table. The area is bursting with character, even though the food is nothing special.

Charlie, the American owner of *Badlands* (☎ 6279-4334), a popular Mexican bar-cum-restaurant, serves up good-value nachos, tacos and burritos at 939 Yan'an Zhonglu. Nearby, the *Red Rhino*, also on Yan'an Zhonglu, does an interesting mix of Chinese and French cuisine in hole-in-the-wall, ambient surroundings, although it gets mixed reviews.

Just north of Yan'an Zhonglu at 81 Tongren Lu is *Frankie's Place* (☎ 6247-0886), a Malaysian restaurant which is very popular with Malaysian residents.

Huaihai Lu once had a reputation for its confectioneries and bakeries. Many of these have disappeared, as the area steadily dresses up and is invaded by department stores and fast-food joints. The *LA Café* (☎ 6358-7097), 4th floor, 188 Huaihai Lu, is a disco by night, but by day operates as an upmarket burger joint, in the Hard Rock Cafe mould. Figure on spending around Y70 per head for your burgers.

There are branches of *McDonald's* and the Japanese chain, *Mos Burger*, close by if Y70 seems a little over the odds for a burger.

On the ground floor of the Parkson building, next to the Shaanxi Nanlu metro station, is *Gino Café* which serves up a decent, value-for-money selection of pizza and pasta. Attached is a branch of *New Zealand Natural Ice Cream*. In this area you can also find branches of *Pizza Hut*, *McDonald's* and *KFC*.

See Bars & Clubs in the following Entertainment section for details on other eateries in the area.

International & Hotel Cuisine If money is no object, international food can be enjoyed at Shanghai's larger hotels. The *Blue Heaven Revolving Restaurant* (☎ 6433-4488) in the Jinjiang Tower offers American cuisine, as does *Shanghai Jax* (☎ 6279-3888, ext 8847) in the Portman Shangrila.

The Shanghai Centre (in the same building as the Portman Shangrila) has a branch of *Tony Roma's* (☎ 6279-7129) which specialises in ribs. The *Shanghai American Club* in the Shanghai Bund International Tower is due to open by the time you read this.

French cuisine is available at a wide range of international hotels around town. Possibilities include the *Teppan Grill* (☎ 6248-0000) in the Shanghai Hilton.

Ch Euro's (☎ 6439-6010), Shanghai's first privately owned German restaurant, has opened in the Olympic Hotel at 1800 Zhongshan Nan 2-Lu.

The only place in town serving decent curries and tandoori is the *Tandoor Indian Restaurant* (☎ 6472-5494) in the New South building of the Jinjiang Hotel – both the food and decor are excellent.

For Italian food, *Pasta Fresca Da Salvatore* (☎ 6248-1705) can be found at 115 Changshu Lu, near the Equatorial Hotel. *Da Vinci's* (☎ 6248-0000) in the Shanghai Hilton also serves high-quality Italian fare. *Pizza Hut* can be found at a number of locations, including a branch near the Printemps department store on Huaihai Lu, another at 700 Xizang Lu, and a further one at 88 Nanjing Xilu, near the Pacific Hotel.

Japanese constitute by far the largest group of foreigners which comes to Shanghai (almost 50%) so it is hardly surprising that there is a host of Japanese restaurants to choose from, including *Kanetanaka* (☎ 6258-7882) at 57 Maoming Nanlu opposite the JJ Dickson Centre, which serves quality food in authentic surrounds (half-price on Sunday).

Inside the JJ Dickson Centre itself, on the 2nd floor, can be found *Itoya*. Others include the *Inagiku Restaurant* (☎ 6275-8888) at the Westin Taipingyang hotel or the *Shanghai Miyako Club* (☎ 6248-0000, ext 8580) at the Shanghai Hilton.

Traditional Korean food is served up at the *Korean Garden Restaurant* (☎ 6248-1688, ext 2333) in the Equatorial Hotel.

Many of the large hotels have restaurants specialising in cuisine from Shanghai, Guangdong, Chaozhou and Beijing.

Vegetarian Food Vegetarianism became something of a snobbish fad in Shanghai at one time; it was linked to Taoist and Buddhist groups, then to the underworld, and surfaced on the tables of restaurants as creations shaped like flowers or animals.

Khi Vehdu, who ran the Jing'an Temple in the 1930s, was one of the most celebrated exponents. The nearly 2m-tall abbot had a large following and each of his seven concubines had a house and a car. The Jing'an Temple was eventually divested of its Buddhist statues and turned into a factory.

The *Gongdelin* (☎ 6327-0218) (*gōngdélín shūshíchù*) at 445 Nanjing Xilu is probably Shanghai's most famous vegetarian restaurant. This is the original one that has also set up a branch in Beijing. All the food is designed to resemble meat, and is convincingly prepared. It is open until midnight. The food and atmosphere are well worth exploring, even if you are not a vegetarian.

The *Juelin Restaurant* (☎ 6326-0115) (*juélín shūshíchù*) at 250 Jinling Donglu is another vegetarian restaurant. It closes early at 7.30 pm. Lunch runs from 11 am to 1.30 pm.

Pub Grub See Bars & Clubs in the Entertainment section below for information on such venues as the *Hard Rock Cafe* and *Malone's American Cafe*, which cook up burgers, pizzas, steak and chips and the like. This is cooking for the seriously homesick, but bear in mind that the prices are equally serious.

SHANGHAI

Entertainment

Shanghai is emerging as the most spiritually polluted city in China. All the old evils are creeping back with a vengeance. Over the last couple of years there's been an explosion of nightlife options, with everything from sleazy karaoke parlours to comfy expat bars and discos. None of it comes cheaply, however. A night on the town in Shanghai is comparable to a night out in Hong Kong or Taipei.

Bars & Clubs The bars and clubs scene in Shanghai is proceeding apace, although many of the venues are by now old names with a tried and true formula. No doubt the increasing numbers of expats washing up on the shores of the Huangpu will encourage more variety and originality. Furthermore, be warned that a round of drinks at some of these watering holes can cost more than your hotel room and unless your backpack is full of bank notes, we recommend having a few stiff ones at the local corner stall before venturing in.

Hard Rock Cafe (☎ 6279-8133) struts into town at the Shanghai Centre offering all the usuals - buffalo wings, BBQ ribs and BLT sandwiches, all to a backdrop of live bands and music memorabilia. It's open till 3 am on Saturday and Sunday and 2 am the rest of the week. A small, neglected sign says that patrons under the age of 18 have to leave after 10.30 pm.

Certainly a good deal cheaper than the Hard Rock Cafe is *Malone's American Cafe* (☎ 6247-2400), at 257 Tongren Lu, a Canadian-run sports bar which is very popular with the expat crowd. It's a smart and preppy sort of place, with a friendly atmosphere, and chips in with live jazz on Thursdays.

In a different vein altogether is the *Jurassic Pub* (☎ 6258-3758) at 8 Maoming Nanlu. It's a dinosaur theme bar, complete with an over-arching Brontosaurus skeleton, live squawking parrots and dino-skull urinals in the gents. They've got a stage for live bands, but it's worth phoning up to see what they have in store. There's a restaurant on the 1st floor.

Shanghai Sally's (☎ 6327-1859), at 4 Xiangshan Lu, is a popular English pub opposite the former residence of Sun Yatsen. Despite having live bands five nights a week, Y45 for a small bottle of beer *during* happy hour is pushing it. Other alternatives are the *Long Bar* (☎ 6279-8268), on Level 2 of the Shanghai Centre on Nanjing Xilu, *Danny's Pub & Café* (☎ 6473-2849) at 141 Maoming Nanlu (open 24 hours!) and *Tequila Mama* (☎ 6433-5086), at 24a Ruijin Erlu, which serves up Mexican snacks and tequila slammers to a soul/reggae beat (open from 4 pm to 5 am).

Popular dance venues include *New York New York* (☎ 6321-6097), at 146 Huqiu Lu, which features a rave party every Sunday and has its ladies' night on Wednesday. Buy two shots and get one free at the shooter bar; it's open till 5 am Friday and Saturday. The dancing at *LA Café* (☎ 6358-7097), 4th floor, 188 Huaihai Lu, starts at 9.30 pm and goes on until 2.30 am; Sunday to Thursday is free for women while the rest pay Y65 (Y80 at weekends); features include the 'Disco de John Wayne' and the 'Elvis Pub'. Expect to pay about Y35 for a small bottle of beer.

No doubt there will be other clubs opening their doors to the bright young things of Shanghai, so ask at your hotel for the latest offerings and consult the trade magazine *Welcome to China – Shanghai* (see Newspapers & Magazines in the Information section earlier in this chapter).

The *Peace Hotel* bar features an ancient jazz band which has been strumming since time immemorial. There is a Y42 cover charge and activity is from 8 to 11 pm.

Drinkers on a budget should head up to the Fudan University area where there is a selection of cheap bars that serve local beer. Places like these are a good for meeting both Chinese and foreign students, but be aware that it's a long way from the centre of the city.

Gay Bars & Clubs *Eddy's Bar* (☎ 6437-8913), at 1 Yueyang Lu, is a friendly place patronised by a mix of young professionals, expats and Asians from neighbouring countries. It is open nightly, and has a pool table, karaoke and dancing.

Near the Shanghai Exhibition Centre at 90 Wei Hai Lu, is the small, friendly *Hawaii Bar* (☎ 6247-7868).

Performing Arts Along with Beijing, Shanghai is one of the great cultural centres of China. Unfortunately, Beijing and Cantonese opera and Chinese drama (which is often an extravagant display of costumes, make-up and acrobatics) are almost exclusively delivered in Chinese and therefore inaccessible to most foreigners. Getting hold of schedules for movies and musical performances is also a headache. It will probably still be some time before Shanghai emerges as an international city on this front.

One exception is the *Shanghai Centre Theatre* (☎ 6279-7132; fax 6279-8610) at the Shanghai Centre, which presents a whole gamut of cultural events from east and west. The international series includes musicians from all over the world; when we were there it featured appearances from such artists as Joni Mitchell, the Crash Test Dummies and Magic Slim.

Traditional Chinese drama and opera and interpretations of western opera, ballet and theatre are presented by such establishments as the Shanghai Opera House, the Shanghai Ballet Troupe and the Shanghai Theatre Academy. Classical music is performed by the Shanghai Symphony Orchestra and the Shanghai Philharmonic Orchestra.

Under construction at the time of writing is a huge opera house in Renmin Square, north of the Shanghai Museum. This will undoubtedly become a major venue in the city, due to its scale and its prestigious location.

Another venue for those interested in Beijing and Cantonese opera and Chinese modern drama is the *Lanxin Theatre* (☎ 6217-8530) *(lánxīn jùyuàn)*, a three storey building at 57 Maoming Nanlu.

The *Conservatory of Music* (☎ 6437-2577) *(yīnyuè xuéyuàn)*, at 20 Fenyang Lu off Huaihai Zhonglu in Frenchtown, is a treat not to be missed by classical music lovers. Performances take place on Sunday evenings at 7 pm. Tickets are usually sold out a few days beforehand so get in quick.

Cinemas In China, foreign movies are generally dubbed into Chinese and Chinese movies very rarely have English subtitles; for those who understand Chinese, or for the plain curious, there are a number of cinemas worth trying.

Check out the *Cathay Theatre (guótài diànyǐngyuàn)* at 870 Huaihai Lu for crumbling Art Deco interiors and a taste of yesteryear. It has a very gloomy cafe in the upstairs area.

The *Huangguan Yongle Cinema (huángguān yǒnglè diànyǐngyuàn)* costs hardly anything to get in (Y15), and you can stay as long as you like crashed out on the banks of leather sofas they have instead of seats. It's just like being in your own living room. You walk through the projectionist's room to get to your sofa, and before the film starts, you are exhorted not 'to smoke, spit, swear or be anti-environmentalist'. You can find it on Nanjing Donglu, next to the East Asia Hotel.

Acrobatics Chinese acrobatic troupes are among the best in the world, and Shanghai is a good place to see a performance. The *Shanghai Acrobatics Troupe (shànghǎi zájì tuán)* has performances at the Shanghai Centre (☎ 6279-8600; fax 6279-8610) every night at 7.30 pm. Tickets sell for around Y60.

Things to Buy

Shanghai offers a plethora of choice for the shopper: all Chinese products and popular souvenirs find their way here. The city is catching up with commercial centres like Hong Kong, but still has a long way to go. The shopping metropolis focuses on Nanjing Lu and Huaihai Lu, although there are signs that Pudong will also siphon off vast amounts of shoppers in the future.

SHANGHAI

The Chinese Circus

Circus acts go back 2000 years to the original Middle Kingdom. Effects are obtained using simple props such as sticks, plates, eggs and chairs. Apart from the acrobatics, there's magic, vaudeville, drama, clowning, music, conjuring, dance and mime thrown into a complete performance. Happily, it's an art which gained from the Communist takeover and did not suffer during the Cultural Revolution. Performers used to have the status of gypsies, but now it's 'people's art'.

Most of the provinces have their own performing troupes, sponsored by government agencies, industrial complexes, the army or rural administrations. About 80 troupes are active in China and they're much in demand. You'll also see more bare legs, star-spangled costumes and rouge in one acrobat show than you'll see anywhere else in China.

Acts vary from troupe to troupe. Some traditional acts haven't changed over the centuries, while others have incorporated roller skates and motorbikes. One time-proven act that's hard to follow is the 'Balancing in Pairs', with one man balanced upside down on the head of another and mimicking every movement of the partner below, mirror image, even drinking a glass of water!

Hoop jumping is another: four hoops are stacked on top of each other and the person going through the very top hoop may attempt a backflip with a simultaneous body twist.

The 'Peacock Displaying its Feathers' involves an array of people balanced on one bicycle. According to the *Guinness Book of Records*, a Shanghai troupe holds the record at 13 people, though apparently a Wuhan troupe has done 14.

The 'Pagoda of Bowls' is a balancing act where the performer, usually a woman, does everything with her torso except tie it in knots, all the while casually balancing a stack of porcelain bowls on foot, head or both – and perhaps also balancing on a partner. ■

Department Stores Shanghai has some of the best department stores in China. The latest development has been the arrival of flashy Tokyo-style operations that bring boutiques and generic brands together under one roof. Check out Isetan at 527 Huaihai Zhonglu for Japanese shopping at its best.

At the corner of Shaanxi Nanlu and Huaihai Zhonglu stands the elegant Printemps with six floors of international boutiques. Parkson has a huge department store on the opposite side of the road.

The two most popular department stores are the venerable Hua Lian Department Store (formerly No 10, and before that Wing On), at 635 Nanjing Donglu, and the No 1 Department Store, at 830 Nanjing Donglu. They are fascinating places to browse in if you can stand the crowds. Manhattan Plaza, 437 Nanjing Donglu, is a seven storey smorgasbord of joint-venture shops selling expensive imports – it's probably of more interest to Shanghai residents than to visitors.

The JJ Dickson Centre on Changle Lu is an incredibly expensive shopping centre with nothing but topnotch western names, including Gieves and Hawkes, Versace, Ralph Lauren, Escada and Guy Larouche. For more boutique shopping, Maison Mode at 1312 Huaihai Zhonglu is probably the last say. Brands featured include Yves Saint Laurent and Christian Dior.

Asia's largest department store arrives in the form of Nextage (only second in size to Macy's), on the corner of Pudong Lu and Zhangyang Lu in Pudong. There are 150 retail outlets selling from 100,000 square metres of floor space to countless customers. And by the time you read this, there will probably be a whole host of other choices available around Shanghai.

SHANGHAI

Another place is Great World, near the intersection of Xizang Lu and Yan'an Lu. Once a famous emporium, its best days are probably behind it.

The Friendship Store can be found on Beijing Xilu, near Suzhou Creek.

Supermarkets & Pharmacies If you're craving anything from home or need western pharmaceutical items, the best place to stock up is the Shanghai Centre. Wellcome is a Hong Kong supermarket chain packed with imported biscuits, chocolates, pasta, cheeses and beverages.

Also in the Shanghai Centre is a branch of Watson's, a pharmacy with cosmetics, over-the-counter medicines and health products. Watson's has another branch just down from the Cathay Theatre on Huaihai Zhonglu. Neither of these places is cheap – prices are similar to those you would pay in Hong Kong.

Photographic Supplies For photographic supplies, check the shops in the major hotels. Shanghai is one of the few places in China where slide film is readily available. Shanghai's foremost photographic supplies shop is Guan Long at 190 Nanjing Donglu.

Porcelain The best place to find decent porcelain is the Shanghai Museum. The shop there sells imitations of the pieces they display in the Zande Lou Ceramics Gallery; the imitations are fine specimens and far superior to the mediocre pieces you see in the tourist shops. Be prepared to pay a hefty whack, however.

The Yuyuan Bazaar is also a good place to rummage around in the hope you might find a gem or two; if you are hunting for rare pieces, you will not need reminding that the market is flooded with fakes.

Souvenirs On the arts and crafts, souvenirs and antiques front, one of the best places to go is the Yuyuan Bazaar. There are a number of shops here selling ceramics, 'antique' posters, pocket watches, paintings and a host of other collectibles.

Haggle hard as it's all overpriced – if you wander around you will see the same stuff at a variety of prices which means a lot of it is fake. At one shop we experimentally managed to beat the price down from Y120 to Y20.

Expensive alternatives are the designated tourist shops which are for the large part haggle-free zones. Their range is good, but again, there's a lot of rubbish so you need a shrewd eye if you don't want to pay too much over the odds. An example is the Shanghai Tourist Shopping Emporium at 239 Fuyou Lu (in the Yuyuan Bazaar area); another is the Shanghai Antique and Curio Store (☎ 6321-4697) at 218-226 Guangdong Lu.

Tea & Teapots Tea and the dainty teapots and cups used by the Chinese make excellent gifts, and Shanghai is a good place to buy them. The Yuyuan Bazaar is one of the best places in Shanghai to make purchases. Otherwise, look out for the exclusive Shanghai Huangshan Tea Co at 853 Huaihai Zhonglu. Prices can be surprisingly reasonable. Yixing ware, the most valued of all Chinese teapots, is available here.

Getting There & Away

Shanghai has rail and air connections to places all over China, ferries travelling up the Yangzi River, many boats along the coast, and buses to destinations in adjoining provinces.

Air CAAC's useful international flights include those to Bangkok, Brussels, Hong Kong, London, Los Angeles, Madrid, Munich, Nagasaki, Nagoya, New York, Osaka, Paris, San Francisco, Singapore, Sydney, Tokyo, Toronto and Vancouver. Dragonair also flies between Shanghai and Hong Kong (Y2000). Northwest and United fly to the USA, Canadian Airlines International can get you to Canada and Qantas can fly you to Australia.

Daily (usually several times daily) domestic flights connect Shanghai to every major city in China. Prices include Beijing

SHANGHAI

(Y1100), Guangzhou (Y1220) and Guilin (Y1290). Minor cities are less likely to have daily flights, but the chances are there will be at least one flight a week, probably more, to Shanghai. The domestic departure tax is Y50.

China Eastern Airlines' main office (domestic ☎ 6247-5953, international ☎ 6247-2255) is at 200 Yan'an Zhonglu, and is open 24 hours a day. There are also ticket sales counters at most of the major hotels around town and at the main CITS office in the Guangming building.

Shanghai Airlines (☎ 6255-8558) is at the airport, but travel agents peddle their tickets in the city centre. All domestic flights can also be booked at CITS. At Novel Plaza, in between the Park and Pacific hotels, you can buy tickets with Xiamen Airlines, Hainan Airlines and China Southwest Airlines (☎ 6350-8127). Several other international airlines have Shanghai offices:

Aeroflot
 (☎ 6471-1665) East Lake Hotel, Donghu Lu
Air France
 (☎ 6268-8817) Hongqiao airport
All Nippon Airways (ANA)
 (☎ 6279-7000) 2F, East Wing, Shanghai Centre, 1376 Nanjing Xilu
Canadian Airlines International
 (☎ 6415-3091) 6th floor, New Jinjiang Tower
Dragonair
 (☎ 6279-8099) Room 202, 2F, Shanghai Centre, 1376 Nanjing Xilu
Japan Airlines
 (☎ 6472-3000) 2F, Ruijin Building, 205 Maoming Lu
Korean Air
 (☎ 6248-1777) Room 104-5, Equatorial Hotel, 105 Yan'an Xilu
Lufthansa
 (☎ 6248-0000) Shanghai Hilton Hotel, 250 Huashan Lu
Malaysia Airlines
 (☎ 6279-8657) Suite 209, East Wing, Shanghai Centre, 1376 Nanjing Xilu
Northwest Airlines
 (☎ 6279-8088) Suite 207, Level 2, East Podium, Shanghai Centre, 1376 Nanjing Xilu
Qantas
 (☎ 6279-8660) Suite 203a, West Wing, Shanghai Centre, 1376 Nanjing Xilu
Singapore Airlines
 (☎ 6279-8000) Room 208, East Wing, Shanghai Centre, 1376 Nanjing Xilu
Thai Airways International
 (☎ 6279-8600) 2F, Shanghai Centre, 1376 Nanjing Xilu
United Airlines
 (☎ 6279-8009) Suite 204, West Podium, Shanghai Centre, 1376 Nanjing Xilu

Bus The long-distance bus station is on Qiujiang Lu, west of Henan Beilu. There are several buses a day to Hangzhou, Wuxi, Suzhou and Nanjing. Sleeper coaches also go to more distant destinations from the railway station.

There is another ticket office at Renmin Square, opposite the junction of Fuzhou Lu and Xizang Zhonglu, which has tickets for buses to Suzhou. The boarding points for the buses are marked on the ticket in Chinese (at the time of writing there were two boarding points for the Suzhou bus: one on Gongxing Lu near Renmin Square, and one on Huangpu Beilu Kou near the main railway station), so check where to board the bus when you buy your ticket.

Because the Shanghai-Nanjing highway corridor is so busy, rail is a better option for getting to towns along this route.

Train Shanghai is at the junction of the Beijing-Shanghai and Beijing-Hangzhou railway lines. Since these branch off in various directions, many parts of the country can be reached by direct train from Shanghai. The problem is getting hold of tickets.

In Shanghai it can be nightmare trying to get tickets yourself at the railway station, particularly for less frequent services. The best bet is to first try CITS, which can organise tickets with enough notice, but they often need three days. For destinations such as Nanjing, Suzhou and Hangzhou, CITS can generally rustle up tickets for the next day, however, for such close destinations it's often easier to go to the railway station and get a ticket yourself as there are frequent daily departures.

If you need a ticket in a hurry, the best

place is the ticketing office in the Longmen Hotel (☎ 6317-0000, ext 5315), next to the railway station, at 777 Hengfeng Lu. The office only sells soft-seat and soft-sleeper tickets. It is open from 7 am to 9 pm, with a break for tea (5 to 6.30 pm).

Compared with the railway station, it is a very civilised place to buy train tickets, and you rarely have to wait long in line. Y5 is charged for the privilege of buying your ticket here. Remember to take your passport, as they will ask to see it as the ticket office is for foreign guests only.

Advance ticket bookings can also be made at the ticket office at 230 Beijing Donglu, but it's a hassle. A final possibility for rail ticket purchases is CYTS at 2 Hengshan Lu. It is open Monday to Saturday from 9 to 11.30 am and 1 to 4 pm.

Most trains depart and arrive at the main railway station (see the Central Shanghai map), but some depart and arrive at the west station (see the Shanghai City map). Be sure to find out which one you should leave from.

Travel times from Shanghai are: Beijing 15 hours, Fuzhou 22½ hours, Guangzhou 33 hours, Guilin 29 hours, Hangzhou 2½ hours, Kunming 62 hours, Nanjing 2½ hours, Qingdao 24 hours and Xi'an 27 hours.

There are special double-decker 'tourist trains' operating between Shanghai and Hangzhou, and Shanghai and Nanjing (with stops at Wuxi, Suzhou, Changzhou and Zhenjiang). They are all comfortable soft-seat trains and smoking is forbidden; attendants bring around drinks and food and, if you're going to Hangzhou or Nanjing, it is even possible to book your hotel room aboard the train.

Boat Boats are definitely one of the best ways of leaving Shanghai and they're often also the cheapest. For destinations on the coast or inland on the Yangzi, they may even sometimes be faster than trains, which have to take rather circuitous routes. Smaller, grottier boats handle numerous inland shipping routes.

Boat tickets can be bought from CITS, which charges a commission, or from the ticket office at 1 Jinling Donglu. The situation with tickets is very confusing. CITS charges foreigners a large percentage over the local price, so it's a much better idea to buy your ticket at the boat ticket office, or at least compare prices before you fork out. Boat tickets can also be bought on the 2nd floor of the Dongfang Hotel at 12 Zhongshan Dong 2-Lu by the Bund.

The Shanghai-Hong Kong route was re-opened in 1980 after a gap of 28 years. The passenger ferry, the *Haihua*, takes 68 hours to reach Hong Kong and leaves on the 10th, 20th and 30th of each month. Ticket prices start from Y1020 and climb to Y2190; it's worth paying more for the privilege of not having to share with hordes of snoring companions in cramped conditions. A lot of travellers leave China this way and the 2½ day trip gets rave reviews. Ferries also leave twice a month for Osaka (Y1150 to Y1900) and Yokohama (Y1150 to Y1900).

Ships depart from the international passenger terminal to the east of Shanghai Mansions. The address is Wai Hong Qiao Harbour at 1 Taiping Lu. Passengers are requested to be at the harbour three hours before departure. Tickets can be bought from CITS or from the 2nd floor ticket office at 1 Jinling Donglu.

Boats to Putuoshan run every day departing at 5 pm and taking 12 hours. Tickets cost Y80 to Y500 depending on class. A seven hour rapid ferry service also departs daily at 8 am and costs Y210 or Y300 deluxe. If you take the latter service, you must first take a 7 am bus from inside the Shiliupu Wharf, which is at 111 Zhongshan Dong 2-Lu, on the Bund.

The main destinations of ferries up the Yangzi River from Shanghai are Nantong, Nanjing, Wuhu, Guichi, Jiujiang and Wuhan. From Wuhan you can change to another ferry which will take you to Chongqing. If you're only going as far west as Nanjing, take the train, which is much faster than the boat. Daily departures are from Shiliupu Wharf (for full details on Yangzi River cruises, see the Chongqing section in the Sichuan chapter).

If money is more important than time, the most sensible way to head west from Shanghai is along the river. Wuhan, for example, is over 1500km by rail from Shanghai. For about half the hard-sleeper train fare you can get a berth in 4th class on the boat. For a bit more than a hard-sleeper ticket on a train you'd probably be able to get a bed in a two person cabin on the boat.

There are also frequent boats to Xiamen (Y220 to Y250), Wenzhou (Y204 to Y265) and Qingdao (Y191 to Y345). Regular boats to Guangzhou (Y310 to Y360) had been temporarily suspended when we last asked, but may be back in action.

The frequency of coastal shipping varies according to destination. Ticket classes are split into 1st class with no further subdivisions, while 2nd class (four people together) and 3rd class (eight people together) are divided into A and B, with A being marginally better than B. Boats leave from Shiliupu Wharf.

Unfortunately, many of the coastal shipping services are being superseded by planes, trains and automobiles – many routes have been shut down completely.

Getting Around

Shanghai is not a walker's dream. There are some fascinating areas to stroll around, but new road developments, building sites and shocking traffic conditions conspire to make walking an exhausting and often stressful experience.

The buses, too, are hard work; they're not easy to figure out, and difficult to squeeze into and out of. The subway system, on the other hand, is a dream. Unfortunately, so far it only does a north-south sprint through central Shanghai. Travellers with money to spare can at least hop into a taxi.

To/From the Airport

Hongqiao airport is 18km from the Bund and getting there takes about 30 minutes if you're lucky, or

over an hour if you're not. You can get bus No 505 from Renmin Square all the way to the airport, or No 911 (double-decker) from Huaihai Zhonglu.

The small red bus No 831 also speeds to the airport from Jinling Lu, just off the Bund. There is a bus from the CAAC office on Yan'an Lu to the airport. Major hotels like the Jinjiang have an airport shuttle. Taxis from the centre of town cost approximately Y50, depending on the kind of taxi, the route taken and the traffic conditions.

Tour Bus If you want to see Shanghai in a hurry, or you want to go to Pudong, then the best way is to jump aboard one of the red Jinjiang Shanghai Tour buses that leave every half an hour from the Jinjiang Hotel on Maoming Nanlu. They are comfortable, speedy and cheap, with a one day ticket costing Y18. They stop at a number of tourist destinations, including Renmin Square, the Oriental Pearl Tower in Pudong and Nanpu bridge and then return to the Jinjiang Hotel. You can get off, go and see the sight and wait for the next bus to come along and pick you up, using the same ticket.

For those wanting to go to Pudong, this is probably the best way, as few buses head there and taxis are expensive.

Bus Buses are often packed to the hilt and, at times, impossible to board. The closest thing to revolutionary fervour in Shanghai today is the rush-hour bus ambushes. Once on board, keep your valuables tucked away since pickpocketing is easy under such conditions, and foreigners make juicy targets.

Contrary to popular belief, buses are not colour coded – the bus map is. Routes 1 to 30 are for trolley-buses (now supplemented by regular buses). Buses 1 to 199 operate from 5 am to 11 pm. Buses in the 200 and 400 series are peak-hour buses, and 300 series buses provide all-night service. Suburban and long-distance buses don't carry numbers – the destination is in characters. Some useful buse routes are listed opposite:

No 18 This bus runs from the front of the main railway station (it originates further north-east at Hongkou or Lu Xun Park) and proceeds south down Xizang Lu, and then south to the banks of the Huangpu.

No 20 This bus takes you to Renmin Square from the Bund.

No 64 This bus gets you to the railway station from the Pujiang Hotel. Catch it near the Pujiang on Beijing Donglu close to the intersection with Sichuan Zhonglu. The ride takes 20 to 30 minutes.

No 65 The No 65 runs from behind the main railway station, passes Shanghai Mansions, crosses Waibaidu bridge, and then heads directly south along the Bund (Zhongshan Lu) as far as the Bund can go.

No 49 From the PSB terminal, this bus heads west along Yan'an Lu. Nos 48 and 42 follow similar routes from Huangpu Park, travel south along the Bund, west around the Dongfeng Hotel, then link westbound along Yan'an Lu. No 26 starts in the city centre a few streets west of the Bund, drops to the Yuyuan Bazaar, and then goes west along Huaihai Lu.

No 16 This is a good linking bus for all those awkward destinations. It runs from the Jade Buddha Temple to Yuyuan Bazaar, and then on to a ferry hop over the Huangpu River.

No 11 This bus travels the ring road around the old Chinese city.

No 71 This bus can get you to the CAAC office, from which you can catch the airport bus. Catch No 71 from Yan'an Donglu close to the Bund.

No 831 This bus goes all the way from Jinling Lu, around the corner from the Bund, to the airport via Huanghai Zhonglu.

No 904 This bus goes from the railway station past the Shanghai Mansions, down to the Bund to the Shiliupu Wharf and ends up at Nanpu bridge.

No 903 This bus goes from the railway station past the Portman Shangrila, the Equatorial Hotel, the Hilton Hotel and the Jianguo Hotel.

Train The Shanghai Metro is being constructed at a feverish pace. The first section runs from the railway station in the north through Renmin Square and down to the Xinzhuang metro station in the southern part of town.

A second line connecting Hongqiao and Pudong airports (running east-west through the centre of town) is expected to open at the end of 1999.

Trains run from 5 am to 10 pm – once every nine minutes at rush hours and every 12 minutes during off-peak hours. Tickets cost Y1 to Y2.

Taxi Shanghai taxis are reasonably cheap and easy to flag down, but try to avoid the peak hours of 7 to 9 am and 5 to 7 pm. Fares vary slightly depending on the taxi – flag fall is Y10.80 or Y14.40 depending on the size of the vehicle.

It is possible to travel to most destinations within central Shanghai for around Y20 to Y25. In a bid to ease traffic congestion, during peak hours taxis with odd last registration numbers are not allowed on to certain roads in central Shanghai on Tuesdays, Thursdays and Saturdays, and the same applies to taxis with even numbers on Mondays, Wednesdays and Fridays. Bear this in mind when hailing a cab.

Car Although it is possible to hire a car in Shanghai, it's really not worth the hassle unless you are familiar with the nightmare of Shanghai's one way system and the appalling conditions on the roads.

Your chances of having an accident, being fined or arrested are astronomical unless you have experience of driving in China.

Hotel Transport Most large, opulent hotels like the Sheraton Huating have a free shuttle bus to the Bund and the airport for their guests.

Zhejiang 浙江

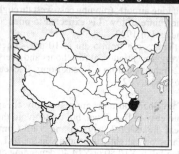
Zhejiang is one of the smallest provinces in China. Traditionally one of the most prosperous, Zhejiang *(zhèjiāng)* has always been more important than its size might indicate.

The region is mainly divided between the area north of Hangzhou, which is part of the lush Yangzi River delta cut with rivers and canals, and the mountainous area to the south, which continues the rugged terrain of Fujian Province. The jagged coastline of Zhejiang has 18,000 islands – more than any other province.

Intensely cultivated for a thousand years, northern Zhejiang has lost most of its natural vegetation and is a flat, featureless plain with a dense network of waterways, canals and irrigation channels. The Grand Canal also ends here – Zhejiang was part of the great southern granary from which food was shipped to the depleted areas of the north.

The growth of Zhejiang's towns was based on their proximity to the sea and to some of China's most productive farmland. Hangzhou, Ningbo and Shaoxing have all been important trading centres and ports since the 7th and 8th centuries. Their growth was accelerated when, in the 12th century, the Song Dynasty moved court to Hangzhou in the wake of an invasion from the north.

Ningbo was opened up as a treaty port in the 1840s, only to fall under the shadow of its great northern competitor, Shanghai. Chiang Kaishek was born near Ningbo, and in the 1920s Zhejiang became a centre of power for the Kuomintang.

Silk was one of the popular exports and today Zhejiang is known as the 'land of silk', producing a third of China's raw silk, brocade and satin. The province is also famous for its tea production.

A major import today is Christianity, which is apparently thriving off associations made between Protestantism and capitalism. This is in response to the huge economic strides the province has made in recent years – in Wenzhou alone, more than 1000 churches were built in the 1980s!

Hangzhou is the provincial capital. To the south-east of the city are several places you can visit without backtracking. The major destination for travellers, however, is the island of Putuoshan, with its monasteries, nunneries, crags, beaches, myths and legends.

In many ways the stuff of dreams, the island is easily reached from the port of Ningbo, or from Shanghai. An excellent boat trip awaits those who take the overnight ferry to Shanghai from Putuoshan; it chugs into Shanghai down the Huangpu River to the Bund at 5 am, as the huge city stirs beneath the first flickers of the morning sun.

HANGZHOU

(hángzhōu)

For the Chinese, Hangzhou (along with Guilin) is the country's most famous tourist attraction. Indeed, you can book your hotel room from on board the train as you ease into Hangzhou railway station, while announcements on the platform welcome you to the 'tourist capital of China'. This is a warning. Droves of tour groups descend on the city during all seasons, peaking on holidays and weekends and resulting in a blight of tacky tourist amenities and costly hotels.

West Lake is a large freshwater lake, bordered on three sides by hills. Its banks and islands are blanketed with small gardens and temples.

The lake gives rise to what must be one of China's oldest tourist blurbs: 'In heaven there is paradise, on earth Suzhou and Hangzhou'. Be this as it may, the earthly paradise of Hangzhou is marshalled by tour group leaders waving flags and loud-hailers, and the 50% foreigner surcharge slapped onto some hotel bills may dilute your bliss.

History

History notes Hangzhou as existing from the start of the Qin Dynasty (221 BC). By the time Marco Polo passed through Hangzhou in the 13th century he described it as one of the finest and most splendid cities in the world.

Other travellers such as Odoric of Pordenone also visited the city (he referred to it as Camsay), returning with tales of the majesty of the place. Although Hangzhou prospered greatly after it was linked with the Grand Canal in 610, it really came into its own after the Song Dynasty was overthrown by the invading Jurchen.

The Jurchen were ancestors of the Manchus, who conquered China five centuries later. The Song capital of Kaifeng, along with the emperor and the leaders of the imperial court, was captured by the Jurchen in 1126. The rest of the Song court fled south, finally settling in Hangzhou and establishing it as the capital of the Southern Song Dynasty.

China had gone through an economic revolution in the preceding years, producing huge and prosperous cities, an advanced economy and a flourishing inter-regional trade. With the Jurchen invasion, the centre of this revolution was pushed south from the Yellow River Valley to the lower Yangzi Valley and to the coast between the Yangzi River and Guangzhou.

While the north remained in the hands of the invaders (who rapidly became Sinicised), in the south Hangzhou became the hub of the Chinese state. The court, the military, the civil officials and merchants all congregated in Hangzhou, whose population rose from half a million to 1¾ million by 1275. The city's large population and its proximity to the ocean promoted the growth of river and sea trade, and of ship building and other naval industries.

When the Mongols swept into China they established their court at Beijing. Hangzhou, however, retained its status as a prosperous commercial city. It did take a beating in the Taiping Rebellion: in 1861 the Taipings laid siege to the city and captured it, but two years later the imperial armies took it back. These campaigns reduced almost the entire city to ashes, led to the deaths of over half a million of its residents through disease, starvation and warfare, and finally ended Hangzhou's significance as a commercial and trading centre.

Few monuments survived the devastation, and most of those that did became victims of the Red Guards a 100 years later during the Cultural Revolution. Much of what may be seen in Hangzhou today is of fairly recent construction.

Orientation

Hangzhou is bounded to the south by the Qiantang River and to the west by hills. Between the hills and the urban area is the large West Lake, the region's premier scenic attraction. The eastern shore of the lake is the developed touristy district; the western shore is quieter.

Information

Tourist Office The CITS office (☎ 515-2888; fax 515-6667) is at 1 Shihan Lu in a charming old building (wànghú lóu) near the Wanghu Hotel. They deal mainly with tour groups and are not very useful for the individual traveller.

PSB The PSB office is at 35 Ding'an Lu.

Money There are moneychanging counters at most tourist hotels. The main Bank of China branch is at 140 Yan'an Lu, near Qingchun Lu.

Post & Communications The post office and telephone office are opposite each other on Yan'an Lu.

Temple of Inspired Seclusion
(língyǐn sì)

Lingyin Si, roughly translated as either Temple of Inspired Seclusion or Temple of the Soul's Retreat, is really Hangzhou's main attraction.

It was built in 326 AD and, due to war

A Close Shave

During the Cultural Revolution, Lingyin Si might have been razed for good, but for the intervention of Zhou Enlai. Accounts vary as to what exactly happened, but it seems there was a confrontation between those who wanted to save the temple and those who wanted to destroy it.

The matter eventually went all the way up to Zhou, who gave the order to save both the temple and the sculptures on the rock face opposite. This is hardly surprising considering that Zhou gave the final nod of approval way back in 1953 for the carving of the huge Buddha inside the temple, and twice allocated funds for the statue's completion. The monks, however, were sent to work in the fields.

In the early 1970s a few of the elderly and invalid monks were allowed to come back and live out their last few years in a small outbuilding on the hillside behind the temple. ∎

and calamity, has been destroyed and restored no fewer than 16 times.

The present buildings are restorations of Qing Dynasty structures. The Hall of the Four Heavenly Guardians at the front of the temple is inscribed with the couplet, 'cloud forest buddhist temple', penned by the Qing emperor Kangxi, who was a frequent visitor to Hangzhou and was inspired on one occasion by the sight of the temple in the mist and trees.

Inside the hall is a statue of the laughing buddha who can 'endure everything unendurable in the world and laugh at every laughable person in the world'.

Behind this hall is the Great Hall, where you'll find the magnificent 20m-high statue of Siddhartha Gautama. This was sculpted from 24 blocks of camphor wood in 1956 and was based on a Tang Dynasty original.

Behind the giant statue is a startling montage of 150 small figures which charts the journey of 53 children on the road to buddhahood; also represented are Ji Gong, a famous monk who secretly ate meat, and a character known as the 'mad monk'. During the time of the Five Dynasties about 3000 monks lived here.

Facing the temple is Feilai Feng (*fēilái fēng*), the 'Peak that Flew from Afar'. The name, so the story goes, comes from an Indian monk named Huili who visited

Hangzhou in the 4th century and, upon seeing the mound, exclaimed that it looked exactly like one he knew in India.

Believing the place to be abounding with spirits, the locals put up the temple opposite. The rocky surface of the hill is chiselled with 330 sculptures and graffiti from the 10th to the 14th centuries.

The place is normally crawling with tourists who scramble here and there; the 'sky crack' cave is often packed out with people straining to see a sliver of sunlight penetrating the roof; you can only see it from one angle. If you go through the caves to the back you will discover some vast, recently carved Buddhist statues. A vegetarian restaurant is situated beside the temple.

To get to the temple take bus No 7, 507 (both from the railway station) or 505 (from the zoo) to the terminal at the foot of the hills west of Hangzhou. Behind the Lingyin Temple is Northern Peak, which can be scaled via cable car. From the summit there are sweeping views across the lake and city.

Zhejiang Provincial Museum
(*zhèjiāng bówùguǎn*)
This interesting museum is on Solitary Hill Island (*gǔshān*), a short walk from the Hangzhou Shangri-La Hotel. Its buildings were part of the holiday palace of Emperor Qianlong in the 18th century.

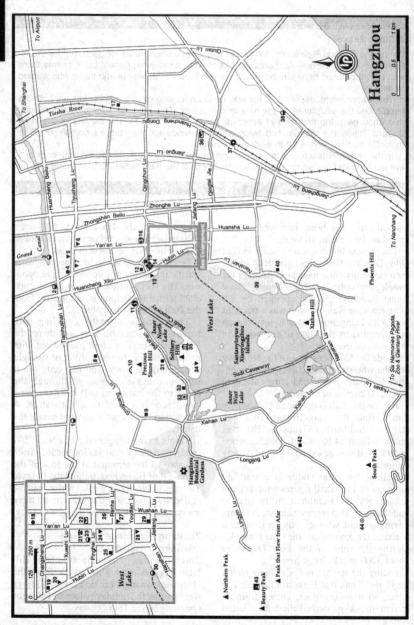

Hangzhou

HANGZHOU 杭州

PLACES TO STAY
8 Yellow Dragon Hotel
黄龙饭店
9 Foreign Student Dormitory
外国留学生楼
12 Wanghu Hotel
望湖宾馆
15 Hangzhou Haihua Novotel
Hotel
海华大酒店
17 Huajia Hotel
华家饭店
19 Hangzhou Overseas
Chinese Hotel
华侨饭
25 Xihu Hotel
西湖饭店
29 Xinqiao Hotel
新桥饭店
31 Xinxin Hotel
新新饭店
32 Hangzhou Shangri-La
Hotel
杭州香格里拉饭店
40 Qingbo Hotel
清波饭店
42 Zhejiang Hotel
浙江宾馆

PLACES TO EAT
5 KFC
肯德鸡
6 KFC
肯德鸡

7 Boston Fish & Fries
波士顿快餐
13 Casablanca Country Pub
卡萨布兰卡乡村俱乐
20 Paradise Rock
天上人间
24 Xi'an Dumpling Restaurant
西安饺子馆
27 KFC
肯德鸡
28 Roast Duck Restaurant
便宜坊烤鸭店
34 Louwailou Restaurant
楼外楼菜馆

OTHER
1 West Bus Station
长途汽车西站
2 Wulinmen Long-Distance
Bus Station
长途汽车站
3 Hangzhou Passenger
Wharf
客运码头
4 CAAC
民航售票处
10 Yellow Dragon Cave
黄龙洞
11 CITS
中国国际旅行社
14 Friendship Store;
Croissants de France
友谊商店、可颂坊
16 Bank of China
中国银行

18 Overseas Chinese Store
华侨商店
21 International Telephone
Office
国际长途电话
22 Post Office
邮局
23 Bus No 308 to Six
Harmonies Pagoda
308路车至六和塔
26 Market Street
市场
30 Boats to Santanyinyue
至三潭印月
33 Yue Fei Mausoleum
岳飞墓
35 Zhejiang Provincial
Museum
浙江省博物馆
36 Main Post Office
邮电局
37 Railway Station
火车站
38 South Bus Station
长途汽车南站
39 Liulangwenying Park
柳浪问莺公园
41 Red Carp Pond
花港观鱼
43 Temple of Inspired
Seclusion
灵隐寺
44 Dragon Well
龙井

Most of the museum is concerned with natural history; there's a large whale skeleton (a female *Rhachianectos glaucus cope)* and a dinosaur skeleton.

Mausoleum of General Yue Fei
(yuè fēi mù)
During the 12th century, when China was attacked by Jurchen invaders from the north, General Yue Fei (1103-41) was commander of the Song armies.

Despite his successes against the invaders, he was recalled to the Song court where he was executed after being deceived by Qin Hui, a treacherous court official. More than 20 years later, in 1163,

Song emperor Gao Zong exonerated Yue Fei and had his corpse reburied at the present site.

Iron statues of Qin Hui and his wife, Wang Shi, are cursed at and spat upon by Chinese tourists, leaving the pair festooned with gob. Not passing on a good opportunity, some visitors really hawk it up, so bring an umbrella.

The mausoleum of this soldier-patriot is in a compound bounded by a red-brick wall a few minutes' walk west of the Hangzhou Shangri-La Hotel. It was ransacked during the Cultural Revolution, but has since been restored. Inside is a large statue of the general and the words, 'return the mountains and rivers to us', a reference to his patriotism and resistance to the Jurchen.

Chinese martial arts connoisseurs will be interested to note that Yue Fei is the supposed founder of the internal art Xingyi quan (body-mind fist), which is the sister art of Taiji quan (supreme ultimate fist) and Bagua zhang (eight-trigram palm).

Six Harmonies Pagoda
(liùhé tǎ)

To the south-west of the city stands an enormous rail-and-road bridge which spans the Qiantang River. Close by is the 60m-high octagonal Six Harmonies Pagoda named after the six codes of Buddhism. The pagoda also served as a lighthouse, and was supposed to have magical power to halt the tidal bore which thundered up the Qiantang River in mid-September every year.

Behind the pagoda is a charming walk through terraces dotted with sculptures, bells, shrines and inscriptions. The pagoda can be reached by taking bus No 308 from Yan'an Lu.

West Lake
(xī hú)

There are 36 lakes in China called Xi Hu, but this one is by far the most famous. Indeed it is the West Lake on which all other west lakes are modelled.

West Lake is the symbol of Hangzhou, and can make for a pleasant outing, but unfortunately a lot of its charm has fallen victim to the plundering of tour groups and tacky facilities. Twilight and evening can be a better time to view the lake, especially when it is layered with mist.

West Lake was originally a lagoon adjoining the Qiantang River. In the 8th century the governor of Hangzhou had it dredged; later a dike was built which cut it off from the river completely. The resulting lake is about 3km long and a bit under 3km wide. Two causeways, the Baidi and the Sudi, split the lake into sections.

The causeways each have a number of arched bridges, large enough for small boats and ferries to pass under. The sights are scattered around the lake; a motley collection of gardens, bridges and pavilions. Many have literary associations which are unfortunately lost on most foreigners.

The largest island in the lake is **Solitary Hill** *(gūshān)* – the location of the Provincial Museum, the Louwailou Restaurant and Zhongshan Park *(zhōngshān gōngyuán)*. The Baidi causeway links the island to the mainland.

Most of the other sights are connected with famous people who once lived there – poets, emperors who visited (Hangzhou was very popular with the ruling elite) or Chinese patriots. **Red Carp Pond** *(huāgǎng guānyú)* is a chief attraction, home to a few thousand red carp and studded with earthen islets. According to the blurb, 'one can onjoy (sic) a poctic (sic) sight of red carp clothed with petals sucking petals'. I didn't, but you might be lucky.

Hangzhou's **botanical gardens** even have a sequoia pine presented by Richard Nixon on his 1972 visit.

From Xiaoyingzhou Island on the lake you can look over at **Santanyinyue** *(sāntán yìnyuè)*, a string of three small towers in the water, each of which has five holes that release shafts of candlelight on the night of the moon cake festival in mid-autumn, when the moon is full. The moon is an important part of Chinese culture and is often represented by poets and in legends.

If you want to contemplate the moon in the privacy of your own boat there are a couple of places around the lake where you can hire paddle boats and go for a slow spin. Boats can also be chartered for a lake cruise from the small docks along the eastern side of the lake.

Other Sights

The **Hangzhou Zoo** has Manchurian tigers, which are larger than their southern counterparts and are a protected species.

About 60km north of Hangzhou is **Moganshan**. Pleasantly cool at the height of summer, Moganshan was developed as a resort for Europeans living in Shanghai and Hangzhou during the colonial era.

To reach Moganshan, take a minibus from the west bus station (Y40 return); there is a selection of hotels there, with doubles starting at Y250.

Places to Stay – budget

Hangzhou's status as a mecca for tourists has pushed accommodation prices up near the stratosphere. If you are bargain hunting, the best advice is to avoid the peak season, weekends and holidays. Furthermore, the cheaper rooms are often booked out, so getting there early in the day helps.

The only real budget place is the *Foreign Student Dormitory* (☎ 795-1207) *(liúxuéshēng lóu)*, behind the Lingfeng Hotel, at Zhejiang University which has single rooms for Y60 (with bathroom) and doubles for Y120. Take bus No 16 from Hubin Lu, Huangcheng Xilu or Shuguang Lu all the way to the last stop, and look for the Lingfeng Hotel around the corner. To find the student accommodation, walk through the foyer of the Lingfeng Hotel into the courtyard area and go straight ahead.

On the eastern shores of the lake, on Hubin Lu, is the *Xihu Hotel* (☎ 706-6933) *(xīhú fàndiàn)* which has cheapish singles (without bathroom) for Y90 and similar doubles for Y145 (these prices include a foreigner's 50% surcharge).

Places to Stay – middle

Hangzhou accommodation is pretty much middle to top end. The rooms are overpriced, but there's no real alternative as the hotels have collectively agreed a price and you have to pay.

Cheapish mid-range accommodation is generally the province of grotty outfits.

One good possibility is the *Huajia Hotel* (☎ 604-1511; fax 603-3709) *(huájiā fàndiàn)*, which has decent singles for Y165 and doubles for Y200. It's a bit of a hike, but they rent bikes for an hourly rate of Y1.5 and it's in a street packed with cheap restaurants.

South of Hubin Lu, the *Qingbo Hotel* (☎ 707-9988; fax 707-3984) *(qīngbō fàndiàn)*, at 109 Qingbo Jie, is one of the few places in town that comes close to representing value for money, although at Y320 to Y360 for standard doubles it is still over the odds. It's easy to miss this place as it is on a turn-off and has no English sign – look for the ground floor ochre finish.

The *Xinxin Hotel* (☎ 798-7101; fax 705-3263) *(xīnxīn fàndiàn)*, at 58 Beishan Lu, has doubles from Y180 to Y380 and is pleasantly located on the northern shore of the lake, but it is often fully booked.

Places to Stay – top end

There is no shortage of top end accommodation in Hangzhou, most of it situated around West Lake. The northern and western edges of the lake have the best places to stay. Taxis from the railway station to any of these hotels should cost between Y20 and Y25.

The best of the lakeside hotels is the *Hangzhou Shangri-La Hotel* (☎ 707-7951; fax 707-3545) *(hángzhōu xiānggé lǐlā fàndiàn)*, also called the *Hangzhou Hotel (hángzhōu fàndiàn)*. It's on the northern side of the lake, next to the Mausoleum of General Yue Fei and surrounded by spacious forested grounds. Doubles here start at Y1360 (plus a 15% service charge).

The spick-and-span and impressive *Hangzhou Hai Hua Novotel Hotel* (☎ 721-5888; fax 721-5108) *(hǎihuá dàjiǔdiàn)* at 298 Qingchun Lu is a treat, with doubles from US$140. The restaurants are excellent and the facilities superb.

On the western side of the lake is the *Zhejiang Hotel* (☎ 797-7988; fax 797-1904) *(zhèjiāng bīnguǎn)*, a sprawling, mildly disorganised place in a quiet woodland setting. Standard doubles range from Y580 to Y790 and there are singles available from Y360 (breakfast included).

On the eastern side of the lake is the *Hangzhou Overseas Chinese Hotel* (☎ 707-4401; fax 707-4978) *(huáqiáo fàndiàn)* at 15 Hubin Lu – a vast, unappealing place with singles and doubles from Y498. In a similar vein and to the north on Wangcheng Xilu is the *Wanghu Hotel* (☎ 707-1024; fax 707-1350) *(wànghú bīnguǎn)*, where doubles start at Y650. Bike rental is available at Y5 per hour.

Other options include the *Yellow Dragon Hotel* (☎ 799-8833; fax 799-8090) *(huánglóng fàndiàn)*, where standard doubles are Y1300 (with the possibility of a 30% discount) and the *Xinqiao Hotel* (☎ 707-6688) *(xīnqiáo fàndiàn)*, where standard doubles cost US$60 to US$80.

Places to Eat

There are lakeside restaurants north of Hubin Lu and Beishan Lu, but bear in mind that these tend to be expensive.

Hangzhou's most famous restaurant is the *Louwailou Restaurant (lóuwàilóu càiguǎn)* on Solitary Hill, right on West Lake. Apart from excellent views of the lake, it has many local dishes including *xīhú cùyú* (West Lake vinegar fish) which is mainly noted for the fact that it turns up on the table still gasping for breath, mouthing at you and twitching.

Other dishes to look out for are *dōngpō ròu*, pork slices flavoured with Shaoxing wine and named after the Song Dynasty poet, Sudong Po, and another local delicacy that apparently was a firm favourite with the Qianlong emperor, *shāguō yútóu dòufu* (earthenware pot fish head tofu).

For Chinese cheap eats, check out Yan'an Lu, a street to the east of Hubin Lu. Parallel to Yun'an Lu further east, Wushan Lu is a haven for bargain restaurants with snappy service; there are a few popular dumpling restaurants here.

You can also order à la carte cheaply at the *Roast Duck Restaurant (kǎoyā diàn)* if you can read the menu. Otherwise ask for the Beijing duck *(kǎoyā)*, which costs Y36 per serving (enough for two). Downstairs is the cheaper, more down-at-heel option while upstairs is pricier.

Top end hotels dish out a wide range of superior cuisine. The Hangzhou Hai Hua Novotel Hotel features a fine western restaurant in the form of *Le Paris*. The Shangri-La Hotel chips in with a classy *Cantonese restaurant* and *coffee bar*.

KFC rears its head at various locations

(there's a branch next to the Mausoleum of General Yue Fei), and *CFC*, a mutant offspring chain, is at numerous locations around town. *Boston Fish & Fries* turns out average fast food fare opposite CAAC. The *Casablanca Country Pub* on the northeastern shores of West Lake goes for the all-wood rustic effect and offers good views over the water.

A *vegetarian restaurant* can be found next to the Temple of Inspired Seclusion. Another one to try is the *Paradise Rock Restaurant* on Hubin Lu, overlooking the eastern shore of the lake.

Things to Buy

Hangzhou is well known for its tea, in particular Longjing green tea (grown in the Longjing District, west of West Lake), silk, fans and, of all things, scissors.

Shops around the lake sell all of these, but at high, touristy prices. One of the best places to look, however, is the market street on Wushan Lu in the evenings. The stalls go up in the early evening and are piled high with a fascinating confusion of collectables. Fake ceramics jostle with Chairman Mao memorabilia, ancient pewter tobacco pipes, silk shirts and pirated CDs. Get the gloves off and bargain hard if anything catches your eye.

Getting There & Away

Air The CAAC office (☎ 515-4259) is at 390 Tiyuchang Lu, opposite the China National Rice Research Institute. Dragonair (☎ 799-8833, ext 6061) has a representative in the Yellow Dragon Hotel on Shuguang Lu, as does Silk Air.

Both CAAC and Dragonair offer daily flights to/from Hong Kong for Y1580 (discounted rate). CAAC and Silk Air (☎ 799-8833, ext 6072) offer direct connections with Singapore for Y3200.

Hangzhou has regular domestic connections with all major Chinese cities, including Beijing (Y1120), Guangzhou (Y1040), Shanghai (Y250) and Qingdao (Y770).

Bus If anything is designed to drive you up

the wall, it's the bus station situation in Hangzhou. The Wulinmen *(wŭlínmén)* long distance bus station in the north deals with destinations such as Nanjing (Y98), Qingdao (Y192), Suzhou, Wuxi and Heping (plus others), while the West bus station has vehicles to Shanghai, Shaoxing and Ningbo. The South bus station, which is less convenient to reach (although bus Nos 39 and 501 go there) has buses to Ningbo, Shaoxing and Wenzhou.

Train There are direct trains from Hangzhou to Fuzhou, Nanchang, Shanghai and Guangzhou, and east to the towns of Shaoxing and Ningbo. For most trains to the north, you must first go to Shanghai, but there is a direct train to Beijing which takes 24 hours.

Hangzhou railway station has a separate ticket booking office for foreigners. It's not that easy to find – stand around looking perplexed until someone either offers to sell you a ticket to your destination or takes you to the foreigners' ticket window *(wàibīn shòupiàochù)*. CITS will not book rail tickets, but most hotels will and this is probably the quickest option.

From Hangzhou to Shanghai takes about three hours, and there are numerous trains each day. Some trains continue through to Suzhou. Trains from Hangzhou to Guangzhou take around 28 hours (depending on the service) and go via Nanchang, the capital of Jiangxi Province, or via the railway junction of Yingtan.

From Yingtan a branch line extends to Fuzhou and Xiamen (both in Fujian Province on the south-east coast). There are direct trains from Hangzhou to Fuzhou. There is no direct train from Hangzhou to Xiamen; you must first go to Shanghai. However, you can catch a train to Fuzhou and then catch a bus to Xiamen.

Boat You can get to both Wuxi and Suzhou by boat up the Grand Canal from Hangzhou. There is one boat a day for Suzhou, departing at 5.30 pm, which takes 13 hours. Tickets range from Y40 to Y130.

The boat to Wuxi leaves at 6 pm, also takes 13 hours and tickets range from Y48 to Y114. Tickets can be bought at the wharf itself which is not far from the Wulinmen bus station in the north of the city.

Getting Around

To/From the Airport Hangzhou's airport is 15km from the city centre; taxi drivers ask around Y50 for the trip. There are shuttle buses to the airport from the CAAC office; they also leave from the larger hotels, such as the Hangzhou Hai Hua Novotel Hotel, although these are for guests only.

Bus Bus No 7 is very useful as it connects the railway station to the major hotel area on the eastern side of the lake. Bus No 1 connects the long-distance bus station to the eastern shore and bus No 28 connects it to the lake's western side. Bus No 27 is useful for getting between the eastern and western sides of the lake.

To get from the railway station to Yan'an Lu, take bus No 151. Bus No 153 takes you from the railway station to the Huajia Hotel area, as does bus No 11.

Taxi Metered taxis are ubiquitous, but often not that easy to flag down. Keep a map handy and watch out for lengthy detours. Prices for taxis depend on the size of the vehicle. Rates are cheap; figure on around Y10 to Y12 from the railway station to Hubin Lu.

Bicycle Bicycle rental is available from the Huajia Hotel for Y1.5 per hour plus a Y200 deposit; the Wanghu Hotel also rents bikes for Y5 per hour plus a similar deposit.

The bikes are the usual hulking 'flying pigeon' variety, made of cast iron with dodgy brakes, so take it easy on the bends and watch out for the fleets of tour buses that flout traffic laws, Doppler shifting from one scenic spot to another.

Boat The boating industry on West Lake is the usual throng of boat operators jostling

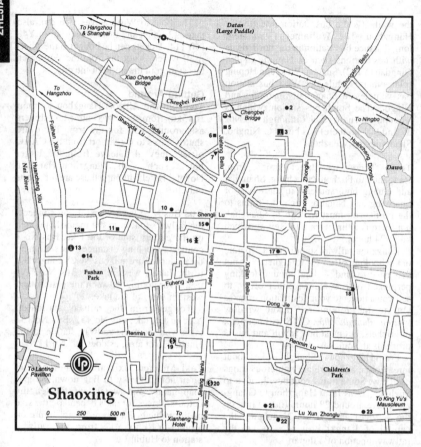

Shaoxing

To Hangzhou
& Shanghai

Datan
(Large Puddle)

Xiao Chengbei
Bridge

Chengbei River

Chengbei
Bridge

To Ningbo

Dawo

Fushan Park

Children's
Park

To King Yu's
Mausoleum

To Lanting
Pavillon

To Xianheng
Hotel

0   250   500 m

with each other to get you on board; just stand on the eastern shore and they will home in on you.

SHAOXING
(shàoxīng)

Just 67km south-east of Hangzhou, Shaoxing is the centre of the waterway system on the northern Zhejiang plain. The waterways are part of the city's charm – and although we wouldn't go as far as the tourist brochures, which sing the praises of 'China's Venice', Shaoxing is an atmos-

pheric place, notable for its rivers (subject to flooding), canals, boats and arched bridges.

For the Chinese, Shaoxing is important as a city of 500 bridges (another exaggeration), as well as the birthplace of China's first great modern novelist, Lu Xun, and Shaoxing wine, a ferocious spirit that doubles as nail-polish remover.

Since early times, Shaoxing has been an administrative centre and an important agricultural market town. From 770 to 211 BC, Shaoxing was capital of the Yue Kingdom.

SHAOXING 绍兴

1 Railway Station
火车站
2 Television Tower
电视塔
3 Jiezhu Temple
戒珠寺
4 Long-Distance Bus Station
长途汽车站
5 Goldfish Hotel
金鱼宾馆
6 Shaoxing Hostel
绍兴旅馆
7 KFC
肯德鸡
8 Overseas Chinese Hotel
华侨饭店

9 Dazhong Hostel
大众旅馆
10 City Hall
市政府
11 Shaoxing Hotel
绍兴饭店
12 Longshan Hotel
龙山宾馆
13 CITS
中国国际旅行社
14 Wanghai Pavilion
望海亭
15 Xinhua Bookstore
新华书店
16 Dashanta Pagoda
大善塔

17 Zhou Enlai's Ancestral
Home
周恩来祖居
18 Eight-Character Bridge
八字桥
19 Bank of China
大众旅馆
20 Bank of China
中国银行
21 Lu Xun's Former Home;
Memorial Hall
鲁迅故居
22 Sanwei Ancient Library
三味书屋
23 Taiping Murals
太平天国壁

Orientation

Encircled by large bodies of water and rivers, and crossed by canals, Shaoxing concentrates most of its hotels conveniently near the railway station and long-distance bus station in the north of the city. The sights are quite widely spaced, making travel between them difficult.

Information

There is a CITS office (☎ 515-3454; fax 516-5766) at 360 Fushan Xilu.

Tourist hotels should be able to change money – if not, the Bank of China has a branch at 225 Renmin Lu, and another on Jiefang Nanlu.

Lu Xun's Former Home

(lǔ xùn gùjū)
Lu Xun (1881-1936), one of China's best known modern writers and influential author of such stories as *Diary of a Madman* and *Medicine* was born in Shaoxing and lived here until he went abroad to study. He later returned to China, teaching at Guangzhou's Zhongshan University in 1927 and having to hide out in Shanghai's French Concession when the Kuomintang decided his books were too dangerous. His tomb is in Shanghai.

You can visit Lu Xun's former residence

at 208 Lu Xun Zhonglu, where his living quarters are faithfully preserved. Nearby, and also on Lu Xun Zhinglu, is the Lu Xun Memorial Hall *(lǔ xùn jìniàn guǎn)* and opposite is the school where the novelist and essayist was a pupil (his desk is still there). Opening hours 8 am to 5 pm daily.

This area is a treat, not just for the buildings associated with Lu Xun, but also for its scenic charm; wander around here and follow the river south along Fuhe Jie (which runs parallel with Jiefang Nanlu towards Xianheng Hotel) for delightful views of Shaoxing.

Fuhe Jie is home to **Guwan Market**, which consists of rows of antique stalls and shops which sell ceramics and calligraphy. It makes for a lovely walk beside dry stone walls and arched bridges.

To get to Lu Xun's former home, take bus No 2 or minibus No 7 from Jiefang Beilu.

King Yu's Mausoleum

(yǔ líng)
According to legend, the first Chinese dynasty held power from the 21st to the 16th century BC, and its founder was King Yu, who is credited with having engineered massive flood-control projects.

A temple and mausoleum complex to

honour the great-grandfather of China was first constructed in the 6th century, but has been added to over the centuries. It is composed of several parts: the huge 24m-tall Main Hall, the Memorial Hall, the Meridian Gate *(wǔmén)* and Goulou Pavilion. A statue of Yu graces the Main Hall.

A No 2 bus will get you to King Yu's Mausoleum from the railway station area (get off at the last stop). See the following East Lake entry for boat transport from King Yu's Mausoleum to the lake.

Zhou Enlai's Ancestral Home
(zhōu ēnlái zǔjū)
Zhou Enlai was born in the small town of Huai An in Jiangsu Province, but his ancestral home (a matter of great consequence in the Chinese scheme of things) was here in Shaoxing.

East Lake
(dōng hú)
East Lake is around 6km east of the city centre, and is an attractive place of sculpted rock formations. There is a temple *(dōng hú sì)* by the lake. The lake can be reached by a No 1 bus (it's the last stop). It is possible to travel by 'pedal boat', a local form of transport, from East Lake to King Yu's Mausoleum. The trip takes around one hour.

Places to Stay
Intrepid exploration work unearthed the *Dazhong Hostel (dàzhòng lǚguǎn)* at 45 Xiaoshan Jie off Jiefang Beilu, which looks like it shouldn't take foreigners, but does. Very grotty, and *very* Chinese, its saving grace is that it has dorm beds for Y14 and is thus perfect for students out of pocket.

The *Shaoxing Hostel* (☎ 513-2814) *(shàoxīng lǚguǎn)* is another budget option with singles from Y28 and doubles from Y80 (with bathroom).

The *Shaoxing Hotel* (☎ 515-5888; fax 515-5565) *(shàoxīng fàndiàn)* at 9 Huanshan Lu has doubles from Y180, as well as more expensive suites. It's a rambling place in traditional style, approached by a

small arched bridge. The *Goldfish Hotel* (☎ 512-6688; fax 513-6033) *(jīnyú bīnguǎn)* is conveniently located near the bus station and has singles at Y120 and doubles at Y210.

The *Overseas Chinese Hotel* (☎ 513-2323) *(huáqiáo fàndiàn)* at 91-5 Shangda Lu is the main tourist place, with rooms starting at Y240. The *Longshan Hotel (lóngshān fàndiàn)*, close to Fushan Park, also takes foreigners and has rates from Y170.

The best hotel in Shaoxing is the four star *Xianheng Hotel* (☎ 806-8688; fax 805-1028) *(xiánhēng dàjiǔdiàn)* at 680 Jiefang Nanjie, down in the south of town. The hotel has a tennis court, swimming pool, billiards room and has doubles from Y280.

Places to Eat
Adventurous types can try the *food stalls* that go up at night on the intersection between Dong Jie and Jiefang Lu; it's a case of pointing at what others are eating and ordering, and it's dirt cheap. Other stalls of the stir-fry variety go up at night along Xiada Lu.

If you wonder what the smell of old, unwashed socks is, it's smelly tofu *(chòudòufu)*, which is all the rage in Shaoxing. You can always beat a retreat to *KFC,* on Jiefang Beilu.

Decent Sichuan, Shaoxing and Cantonese cuisine can be found at the Xianheng Hotel; they also dish up western food at their *Tulip Western Restaurant.*

Getting There & Away
Hangzhou-Ningbo trains and buses all stop in Shaoxing. Luxury buses speed to Ningbo (Y35) in 1½ hours from the long-distance bus station's luxury waiting room – a further thrust to the stake in the heart of socialism and egalitarian standards.

AROUND SHAOXING
Considered one of Shaoxing's 'must see' spots, the **Lanting Pavilion** *(lántíng)* doesn't get many foreign visitors. There are actually several pavilions here, set in pleasant gardens which are worth visiting if you

don't mind the trek out there. The gardens were built in 1548.

Lanting Pavilion is around 10km southwest of the city and is reached by a No 3 bus.

NINGBO
(níngbō)

Like Shaoxing, Ningbo rose to prominence in the 7th and 8th centuries as a trading port. Ships carrying Zhejiang's exports sailed from here to Japan, the Ryukyu islands and along the Chinese coast.

By the 16th century, the Portuguese had established themselves as entrepreneurs in the trade between Japan and China, since the Chinese were forbidden to deal directly with the Japanese.

Although Ningbo was officially opened to western traders after the first Opium War, its once-flourishing trade gradually declined as Shanghai boomed. By that time the Ningbo traders had taken their money to Shanghai and formed the basis of its wealthy Chinese business community.

Ningbo today is a bustling city of more than 250,000 people, with fishing, textiles and food processing as its primary industries. Travellers come here mainly in transit on the way to nearby Putuoshan, one of Zhejiang's premier tourist attractions.

Information
There's a CTS office (☎ 732-4145) at 70 Mayuan Lu, adjacent to the Friendship Store, the Asia Gardens and Ningbo Hotel.

The PSB office is near the intersection of Jiefang Lu and Zhongshan Lu, and the Bank of China has a branch on the western side of Moon Lake.

The post office is just south of the Xinjiang Bridge, where the Fenghua River forks into the Yu Yao and Yong rivers.

Things to See
Ningbo is hardly studded with places of interest, yet it is not an unpleasant city. **Moon Lake** makes for a pleasant walk in the right weather. It features one of Ningbo's many temples that have become convenience stores; the roof decorations still

intact. Another collection of these temples exists behind the old bell tower near KFC on Zhongshan Lu.

If you are in the passenger ferry terminal part of town, the old Portuguese **Catholic Church** *(tiānzhǔ jiàotáng)* is well worth a visit. It was built in 1628, destroyed and rebuilt in the 19th century. It is an active church, with a Mediterranean-style whitewashed interior displaying prints of the Twelve Stations of the Cross, colourful icons and a vaulted ceiling. The whole impression is a meticulous preservation of European Catholicism. The church is at 40 Zhongma Lu, just a few minutes' walk down from the ferry terminal.

Places to Stay
The best budget place accepting foreigners is the *Yuehu Hotel* (☎ 736-3370) *(yuèhú fàndiàn)* at 59 Yanhu Jie. The hotel is in an interesting neighbourhood along the shores of Moon Lake. Doubles cost Y110.

The *Ningbo Erqing Building* (☎ 730-2288; fax 730-8794) *(níngbō èrqīng dàshà)*, at 2 Changchun Lu, is a good two star hotel with doubles from Y250. Mini-buses to the passenger ferry terminal go right by the hotel, and it's within walking distance of the railway station.

The hulking *Ningbo Hotel* (☎ 712-1688) *(níngbō fàndiàn)*, at 65 Mayuan Lu, is two blocks north of the railway station and has singles from Y270 and doubles from Y360.

The *Ningbo Huaqiao Hotel* (☎ 736-3175) *(níngbō huáqiáo fàndiàn)*, at 130 Liuting Jie, is within walking distance of the railway station and is easily recognised by the huge pine trees growing outside. Overpriced singles and doubles start at Y500.

Places to Eat
Despite its size, Ningbo really suffers from having nowhere decent to eat. This is not a great problem, as few foreigners pass through, but we had a few dreadful meals which put us off. One such meal was in a hotel's 'western' restaurant; the cream of mushroom soup was sliced mushrooms in water with powdered milk and the steak

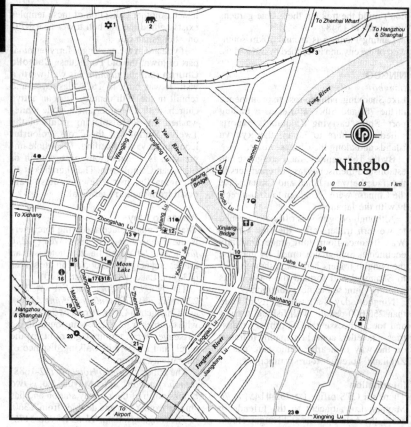

Ningbo

was cold and had some human hair attached – not pleasant at all.

Getting There & Away

Air The CAAC ticket office (☎ 783-4202) is at 91 Xingning Lu. There are international flights to Hong Kong four times weekly. Most major Chinese cities have air connections with Ningbo.

Bus There are two bus stations in town. Most long-distance buses depart from the South bus station (qìchē nánzhàn), just one block from the railway station. From here you can get buses to Wenzhou (nine hours), Hangzhou (three hours) and Shanghai. Tickets are fairly easy to obtain, although the buses are often crowded.

Train Train services between Shanghai and Ningbo are very frequent, but the Ningbo railway station ticket office is a nightmare. Ask the staff at your hotel if they can buy the ticket for you – most will do so with at least one day's notice. It's well worth the small service charge. Alternatively, try CTS.

NINGBO 宁波

PLACES TO STAY
14 Yuehu Hotel
  月湖饭店
15 Ningbo Hotel
  宁波饭店
17 Ningbo Huaqiao Hotel
  宁波华侨饭店
21 Ningbo Erqing Building
  宁波二轻大厦
22 Yonggang Hotel
  甬港饭店

PLACES TO EAT
13 KFC
  肯德鸡

OTHER
1 Baiguo Garden
  白果园
2 Zoo
  动物园
3 North Railway Station
  火车北站
4 Radio & TV Tower
  电台发射塔
5 Zhongshan Park
  中山公园
6 North Bus Station
  汽车北站
7 Passenger Ferry Terminal
  轮船码头
8 Catholic Church
  天主教堂

9 East Bus Station
  汽车东站
10 Main Post Office
  邮电局
11 City Hall
  市政府
12 PSB
  公安局外事科
16 CTS
  中国旅行社
18 Bank of China
  中国银行
19 South Bus Station
  汽车南站
20 Railway Station
  火车南站
23 CAAC
  中国民航

Boat Most useful departures are from the passenger ferry terminal (*lúnchuán mǎtóu*) near the North bus station. A few boats depart from Zhenhai Wharf (*zhènhǎi mǎtóu*), which is 20km (40 to 50 minutes by bus) north-east of Ningbo.

Boats to Putuoshan depart from the passenger ferry terminal. See the following Putuoshan section for details. There's also a twice monthly boat to Hong Kong (50 hours).

Getting Around
To/From the Airport Ningbo's Lishe airport is a 20 minute ride from town. A taxi should cost around Y40.

Other Transport The bus network is extensive, and good bus maps are for sale at the railway station. Frequent minibuses (Y1) connect the railway station with the passenger ferry terminal and the North bus station. A taxi across town costs about Y12. Pedicabs swarm the streets, but be wary of over-charging.

PUTUOSHAN
(*pǔtuóshān*)
Putuoshan is the China we all dream about – temples, pagodas, arched bridges, narrow alleys, fishing boats, artisans and monks –

the China we see on postcards and in coffee-table books. Here you feel miles away from the noise, pollution, concrete-block housing developments, billboards, political slogans and bustle that characterise modern Chinese cities.

The best way to see the island is to amble about from temple to crag and from beach to monastery, rather than rush about in imitation of Chinese tour groups. The serenity of the island lies in its unhurriedness, and that is an essential element if you want to enjoy the place to its utmost.

While there is no need to see everything, you can jump aboard one of the numerous minibuses that charge to and fro across the island, stopping at the sights.

The two large beaches, **One hundred step beach** (*bǎibùshā*) and **One thousand step beach** (*qiānbùshā*) on the east of the island, are attractive and largely unspoilt, although you have to pay to get in (Y2 and Y4 respectively). Go at twilight when the ticket office is empty and it's more atmospheric. **Sanskrit Tidings Cave** (*fányīn dòng*), on the far eastern tip of the island, has a temple dedicated to Guanyin perched between two cliffs with a seagull's view of craggy rocks and crashing waves.

The area around the **Puji Temple** (*pǔjì sì*) is a treat, and from here it is easy to plan

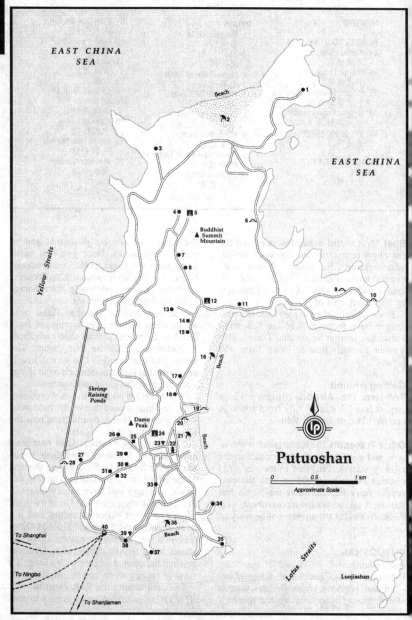

EAST CHINA SEA

Beach

EAST CHINA SEA

Yellow Straits

Buddhist Summit Mountain

Shrimp Raising Ponds

Beach

Damo Peak

Putuoshan

0   0.5   1 km

Approximate Scale

Beach

To Shanghai

To Ningbo

To Shenjiamen

Beach

Lotus Straits

Luojiashan

PUTUOSHAN 普陀山

PLACES TO STAY
14 Jinping Villa
锦屏山庄
15 Shuangquan Hotel
双泉饭店
25 Xilai Hotel
西来小庄
30 Sanshengtang Hotel
三圣堂饭店
31 Putuo Hotel
普陀山庄
32 Ruyi Hotel
如意山庄

PLACES TO EAT
23 Restaurants; Market
餐厅，市场
39 Shuixin Restaurant
水鑫菜馆

OTHER
1 Dragon Head
龙头
2 Houao Beach
后岙沙
3 Ridge Mound
岗墩
4 Putuo Goose's Ear
普陀鹅耳枥

5 Wisdom Benefit Meditation
Temple
慧济禅寺
6 Ancient Buddhist Cave
古佛洞
7 Sea Sky Buddhist Nation
海天佛国
8 Fragrant Cloud Pavilion
香云亭
9 Wisdom & Wealth Cave
善财洞
10 Sanskrit Tidings Cave
梵音洞
11 Viewing Sea Pavilion
望海亭
12 Way Rain Meditation
Temple
法雨禅寺
13 Poplar Branch Convent
杨枝庵
16 One Thousand Step
Beach
千步沙
17 Great Multiply Convent
大乘庵
18 Literary Material Hall
文物馆
19 Chaoyang Cave
朝阳洞
20 Fairy's Cave
仙人洞

21 One Hundred Step Beach
百步沙
22 Many Treasures Pagoda
多宝塔
24 Puji Temple
普济禅寺
26 Round Open Convent
圆通庵
27 Two Turtles Listen to the
Law Stone
二龟听法石
28 Western Sky Cave
西天洞
29 Administrative Office
管理局
33 Main Interest Pavilion
正趣亭
34 Cannot Agree to Leave
Guanyin Hall
不肯去观音院
35 Guanyin Leap
观音跳
36 Golden Beach
金沙
37 South Sky Gate
南天门
38 Seashore Gate
海岸牌坊
40 Passenger Ferry Terminal
轮船码头

an attack on the rest of the island. Most of the minibuses go via here.

Annoyingly, there is a Y20 entrance fee to the island itself upon arrival and on top of that you have to pay for all the other sights as well. Deng Xiaoping's maxim, 'To get rich is glorious', must have been aimed specifically at Putuoshan's ticket collectors.

Places to Stay
It is difficult to provide reliable information on Putuoshan's accommodation as prices vary seasonally and according to demand. There's nothing in the way of budget accommodation, and many hotels do not take foreigners, preferring instead to live off the packs of Chinese tourists who make pilgrimage to the island.

The *Sanshengtang Hotel (sānshèng táng*

fàndiàn) is *the* place to stay. A converted nunnery (probably haunted) it has retained all of its character, it's well in keeping with the spirit of the island and is not too far from the ferry to boot. Singles start at Y150 and doubles at Y198. To get to the hotel from the ferry terminal, first take a minibus to Puji Temple and then ask one of the hotel touts who will be swarming around you. Alternatively, if you want to walk (about 10 minutes), take the road leading up on the left after the shops and restaurants to the right of the ferry terminal. The road winds its way up a hill to the hotel.

The nearby *Putuo Hotel* (☎ 609-1666; fax 609-1667) *(pǔtuó shānzhuāng)* has doubles for Y505, while its annex opposite, the *Ruyi Hotel* (☎ 609-6166) *(rúyì shānzhuāng)*, has doubles for Y253 and triples for Y303.

Places to Eat

The hotel food is both expensive and appalling in Putuoshan, so avoid it and head for the *seafood restaurants* down near the ferry terminal. They line the left-hand side of the road to the right of the pier and offer an extensive selection of creatures (some hauled from great depths, judging from their flattened and ghoulish appearance).

Try the *Shuixin Restaurant (shǔixīn caìguǎn)* which serves excellent mussels and clams, and also offers the usual chicken, pork and aubergine dishes.

Getting There & Away

As Putuoshan is a small island with no airport, boats are the only option, short of swimming. You can approach from either Ningbo or Shanghai, but Ningbo is closer and offers more frequent services.

Many travellers prefer to enter the island from Ningbo and exit to Shanghai, or vice versa. Whichever ship you take, there is a Y20 entry fee to Putuoshan, payable on arrival at the pier.

To/From Shanghai There are two daily slow boats from Putuoshan to Shanghai; they leave at 4 and 5 pm for the 12 hour voyage to Shanghai. This is an excellent way to enter Shanghai, as the boat chugs its way into the great metropolis along the Huangpu River in the early hours of the morning. You will be woken by the booming of ships' horns – go out on deck and watch the Bund slowly sail into view.

Tickets range from Y80 to around Y500; it's easy to upgrade once you are on board. The most expensive ticket basically gets you a hotel room on the boat, with your own TV and bathroom.

A rapid ferry leaves Putuoshan at 10 am and takes seven hours to reach Shanghai. Tickets cost Y210 or Y300 deluxe.

See the Getting There & Away section of the Shanghai chapter for information on how to reach Putuoshan from Shanghai.

To/From Ningbo The simplest is the fast ferry, departing from Ningbo's passenger ferry terminal *(lúnchuán mǎtóu)* at 8.30 am and 1.20 pm. In the other direction, departures from Putuoshan are at 8 am and 2 pm.

The journey takes three hours and tickets cost Y58 – there are slower boats available, but it's a grind.

You can also get a boat from the port of Shenjiamen *(shěnjiāmén)* on the island of Zhoushan, which is separated from Putuoshan by a narrow strait. The bus from Ningbo gets to Zhoushan by vehicular ferry. This route is much more of a hassle than the fast ferry route from Ningbo and the only advantage of it is that there are several departures throughout the day.

Buses to Shenjiamen depart from Ningbo's North bus station and take four hours *(qìchē běizhàn)*. Ferries depart hourly from Shenjiamen and Putuoshan. Be careful at Shenjiamen – there are several ferries going to other neighbouring islands, so make sure you get on the one that's going to Putuoshan.

Getting Around

Walking is the most relaxing option if you have time, but if not, minibuses zip from the ferry terminal to the Puji Temple (Y5), Sanskrit Tidings Cave (Y6) and Buddhist Summit Mountain (Y5).

ZHUJIAJIAN

(zhūjiājiān)

Just south of Putuoshan is a larger island called Zhujiajian. It has a collection of small temples and fine rural scenery, but it's certainly not the magical sort of place that Putuoshan is.

Nevertheless, it might be worth a visit, particularly if you are travelling during the peak summer season when Putuoshan is packed out. Foreigners of any kind are a rarity in Zhujiajian – expect to be a tourist attraction for the locals.

To reach Zhujiajian, take a bus from Ningbo's North bus station to Shenjiamen (four hours, Y12), then a short ferry ride; if you are on Putuoshan already, you have to take a ferry to Shenjiamen first, and then a boat to Zhujiajian.

EAST CHINA SEA

Column Hill

Standing Goat Hill

To Shenjiamen

Fairy Peak

Zhujiajian

Camphor Isle Bay

Big Hill

Old Hill

Four Column Hill

Back Gate Hill

Big Green Hill

West Peak Island

EAST CHINA SEA

ZHUJIAJIAN 朱家尖

1 Sisu
   泗苏
2 Ferry Terminal
   轮船码头
3 Cool Hat Pond
   凉帽潭
4 Catch Fish Reef
   钓鱼礁
5 White Cloud Strange Stone
   白云奇石
6 Moon Valley
   月岙
7 Bird Turtle Cave
   乌龟洞
8 Camphor Tree Isle
   外樟州
9 Full Pond Bird Rock
   满塘鸟石
10 Big Cave Valley
   大洞岙
11 Outer Pond
   外塘
12 Bird Stone Pond
   小鸟石塘
13 Temple Foundation
   寺基
14 Big Isle
   大岙
15 Fishing Lake to Reflect the Moon
   渔湖映月
16 Ten-Mile Golden Sand
   十里金沙
17 King's Crag
   大王岩
18 Little Splash
   小澎安

XIKOU
(xīkǒu)

About 60km south of Ningbo is the small town of Xikou, the home of Chiang Kai-shek. It has, surprisingly, become a Chinese tourist destination. Not so surprisingly, many visitors from Taiwan also come here.

Despite local rumours that Chiang's body was secretly returned to China for burial at Xikou, his remains in fact reside in Taiwan at Cihu, south of Taipei. Chiang's relatives have persistently maintained that when the Kuomintang 'retakes the mainland', the body will be returned to its proper resting place at Xikou.

TIANTAISHAN
(tiāntái shān)

Tiantaishan is noted for its many Buddhist monasteries, which date back to the 6th century. While the mountain itself may not be considered sacred, it is very important

as the home of the Tiantai Buddhist sect, which is heavily influenced by Taoism.

From Tiantai it's a 3.5km hike to the **Gouqingsi Monastery** at the foot of the mountain (you can stay overnight here). From the monastery a road leads 25km to **Huadingfeng** (over 1100m high), where a small village has been built. On alternate days public buses run up to Huadingfeng. From here you can continue by foot for 1 or 2km to the **Baijingtai Temple** on the summit of the mountain.

On the other days the bus goes to different parts of the mountain, passing **Shiliang**

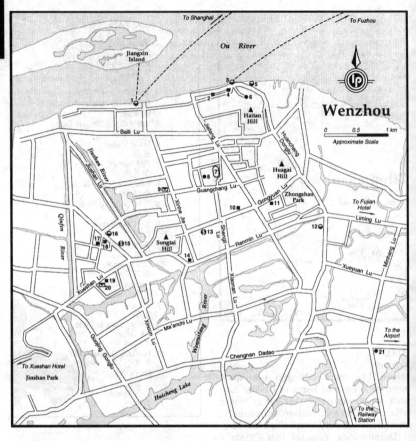

Waterfall. From the waterfall it's a good 5 to 6km walk along a series of small paths to Huadingeng.

Tiantaishan is in the east of Zhejiang. Buses link it with Hangzhou, Shaoxing, Ningbo and Wenzhou.

WENZHOU
(wēnzhōu)
Wenzhou is basically a grim stop-over on the eastern coast and offers the curious traveller little more than crushed expectations. The city is very much for those in transit.

Things to See
The only scenic site is **Jiangxin Island** *(jiāngxīn dǎo* or *jiāngxīn gūyǔ)* in the middle of the Ou River. The island is a park dotted with pagodas, a lake and footbridges. You can easily reach Jiangxin Island by ferry from the pier *(máháng mǎtóu)* just west of the passenger ferry terminal.

Gang fighting between mobs of urban-angst driven youths seems to be the rage in Wenzhou. Fighting on Renmin Lu took place when we were there. Weapons included staves and beer bottles, and everyone

WENZHOU 温州

PLACES TO STAY
2 Wangjiang Hotel
   望江旅馆
4 Dongou Hotel
   东瓯大厦
10 Xin'ou Hotel
   新瓯饭店
11 Wenzhou Grand Hotel
   温州大酒店
14 Wenzhou Huaqiao Hotel
   华侨饭店
17 Jiushan Hotel
   九山饭店

18 Yinghua Hotel
   樱花饭店
19 Ouchang Hotel
   瓯昌饭店

OTHER
1 Mahang Pier
   麻行码头
3 Passenger Ferry Terminal
   温州港客运站
5 East Bus Station
   汽车东站
6 Seamen's Club
   国际海员俱乐部
7 Renmin Stadium
   人民广场

8 City Hall
   市政府
9 Post & Telephone Office
   邮电局
12 South Bus Station
   汽车南站
13 Bank of China
   中国银行
15 Bank of China
   中国银行
16 West Bus Station
   汽车西站
20 Post Office
   邮局
21 CAAC
   民航售票处

looked on as if this was quite normal. Apparently it is a regular fixture.

Places to Stay

There are few cheap places open to *lǎowài* (foreigners) in Wenzhou, but those on a budget can find solace in the *Wangjiang Hotel* (☎ 822-2806) *(wàngjiāng fàndiàn)* opposite the passenger ferry terminal, which has dorm beds for Y17, singles from Y40 and doubles from Y50. The rather grotty *Yinghua Hotel* (☎ 852-8588) *(yínghuā fàndiàn)* has dorm beds for Y33 and doubles from Y78.

The best mid-range hotel in terms of value and location is the *Wenzhou Huaqiao Hotel* (☎ 822-3911; fax 822-9656) *(wēnzhōu huáqiáo fàndiàn)* at 77 Xinhe Jie. Singles/doubles start at Y220, breakfast is included and the swimming pool is free.

The *Dongou Hotel* (☎ 822-7901) *(dōng'ōu dàshà)* is well located on the Ou River and has singles from Y176 and doubles from Y220.

Other possibilities, all with rates of Y320 and upwards, include:

Ouchang Hotel (☎ 852-8888; fax 852-8777) *(oūchāng fàndiàn)*, 71 Xueshan Lu
Wenzhou Grand Hotel (☎ 823-5991) *(wēnzhōu dàjiǔdiàn)*, 61 Gongyuan Lu
Xueshan Hotel (☎ 822-3981) *(xuěshān fàndiàn)*, very inconveniently located in Jinshan Park and can be reached only by taxi

Getting There & Away

Air Wenzhou has reasonably good connections with other Chinese cities, but the airport is notoriously bad for heavy fog – pilots often end up flying at ridiculously low altitudes trying to find the runway. Air tickets can be bought at the Ouchang Hotel and at other large hotels.

Bus There are three bus stations in Wenzhou, and even locals are sometimes not sure which station is appropriate for a particular destination.

As a general rule, southbound buses arrive at and depart from the South bus station, northbound buses at the West bus station and some (no certainty which) use the East bus station.

Train There are trains to Hangzhou via Jinhua on the Guangzhou-Shanghai line to the north-west of Wenzhou.

Wenzhou's recently completed railway station is to the south of the city, but at the time of writing there were no buses that connected with it. A taxi to the station will cost around Y15.

Boat There are passenger ferries to Fuzhou and Shanghai. Boats to Shanghai go from the Mahang Pier *(máháng mǎtóu)* twice daily and prices range from 5th class (Y81) to 1st class (Y369); bear in mind that 2nd class means four people together and 4th class means 16 together. You can always upgrade once you're on the boat.

Boats to Fuzhou leave from the passenger ferry terminal.

Getting Around

To/From the Airport Wenzhou airport is 27km south-west of town and taxis charge between Y80 and Y100 for the trip. Bus No 301 can take you there from Renmin Lu.

Taxi & Pedicab Taxis are cheap (Y10 to most destinations) and easy to flag down. Pedicabs, on the other hand, are usually more trouble than they are worth and are not much cheaper.

CHUN'AN COUNTY
(chún'ān xiàn)

Chun'an County, in western Zhejiang, is known for its Lake of a Thousand Islands.

One route worth investigating would be a trip starting from Hangzhou. You could arrange to cross the lake by boat and then perhaps take a bus to Huangshan in Anhui Province.

Fujian 福建

The coastal region of Fujian (*fújiàn*), also known in English as Fukien or Hokkien, has been part of the Chinese empire since the Qin Dynasty (221-207 BC), when it was known as Min.

Sea trade transformed the region from a frontier into one of the centres of the Chinese world. During the Song and Yuan dynasties, the coastal city of Quanzhou was one of the main ports of call on the maritime silk route, along which travelled not only silk, but textiles, precious stones, porcelain and a host of other valuables. The city was home to more than 100,000 Arab merchants, missionaries and travellers. Even today, some residents display features of Middle Eastern origin.

Despite a decline in the province's fortunes after the Ming Dynasty restricted maritime commerce in the 15th century, the resourcefulness of the Fujianese people proved itself in the huge numbers that emigrated to South-East Asia. Ports like Xiamen were stepping stones for droves of Chinese heading for Taiwan, Singapore, the Philippines, Malaysia and Indonesia. This diaspora forged overseas links that have continued from the 16th century to today, contributing much to the modern character of the province.

In 1718 the Manchus attempted to halt Chinese emigration with an imperial edict recalling all subjects who were in foreign lands. Finding this ineffectual, in 1728 the court issued another proclamation declaring that anyone who did not return to China would be banished and those captured would be executed. Chinese emigration was only made legal by the Convention of Peking, which ended the fourth Opium War in 1860.

Nowadays, many descendants of the original emigrants send money to Fujian, and the Chinese government is trying to build up a sense of patriotism in the Overseas Chinese to get them to invest more money in their 'homeland'.

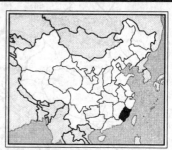

Fujian Facts & Highlights

Area: 120,000 sq km

Population: 32.6 million

Capital: Fuzhou

Highlights

- Xiamen's Gulangyu Island, with one of China's most charming pockets of colonial architecture.
- Nanputuo Temple, just outside Xiamen
- The earth buildings of the Hakka people in remote south-western Fujian.
- The walled town of Chongwu, not far from Quanzhou.

Just as most Hong Kongers trace their cultural roots to Guangdong Province, most Taiwanese consider Fujian to be their ancestral home. Fujian's local dialect, *minnanhua* (south-of-the-Min-River-language), is essentially the same as Taiwanese, although both places officially speak Mandarin Chinese. Not surprisingly, the Taiwanese are the biggest investors in Fujian and the most frequent visitors.

FUZHOU
(fúzhōu)

Capital of Fujian province, Fuzhou is an industrial hinterland, choked with concrete dust and shorn of interest. It can serve as an

overnight pit-stop for travellers en route to Xiamen or Quanzhou, but offers few diversions.

History

Fuzhou dates back to the 3rd century AD, when it was known as Yecheng ('smelting city'). Later it emerged as a major commercial port specialising in the export of tea.

Marco Polo, who passed through Fuzhou towards the end of the 13th century, described Fuzhou as being so 'well provided with every amenity' as to be a 'veritable marvel'. One can only assume that he was referring to the McDonald's on Wusi Lu and the KFC near the Yushan Hotel.

Today, Fuzhou is second only to Xiamen as a centre of Taiwanese investment. The money that the town has attracted is reflected in a lot of pricey new hotels and restaurants.

Orientation

Fuzhou city centre sprawls northward from the Min River. Walking from one end of town to the other will take you more than an hour.

The railway station is situated in the north-east of town, while most of the accommodation is on Wuyi and Wusi Lu, sandwiched between Hualin Lu and Gutian Lu.

Information
Tourist Office CITS (☎ 337-0073) can be found on the 7th floor of the Tianma building (*tiānmǎ dàshà*) on the corner of Wuyi Lu and Dongda Lu. CITS can book air, bus and train tickets.

PSB This office (☎ 755-7705) is on Xianta Lu, which runs south off Dongda Lu.

Money The most central branch of the Bank of China is near the KFC on Gutian Lu. Top-end hotels, such as the Hot Spring Hotel, have moneychanging facilities.

Post & Communications The post and telecommunications building is on the corner of Dongda Jie and Bayiqi Lu. DHL (☎ 781-1111) operates just up from the Taiwan Hotel on Hualin Lu.

Things to See
Fuzhou's sights are minor attractions and the city boasts few places of historical interest. Areas worth seeing are, for the most part, scattered about which makes travel between them difficult.

In the centre of town a vast **Mao Zedong statue** presides over a sea of cyclists. The statue was erected to commemorate the 9th National Congress of the Communist Party where Maoism was enshrined as the new state religion and Lin Biao was officially declared Mao's successor. A huge Coca-Cola advert frames the white statue in red.

Right behind Mao is the **Yushan scenic area** (*yúshān fēngjǐngqū*) which boasts the ruins of the old city walls and makes for pleasant enough walks when the sun has got his hat on.

In the north-west of Fuzhou is **West Lake Park** (*xīhú gōngyuǎn*) on Hubin Lu, where you'll find the **Fujian Provincial Museum** (*fújiànshěng bówùguǎn*). Next to the lake is the zoo, home to an unremarkable collection of our furry friends, and **Panda World** (*xióngmāo shìjiè*) where you can watch this protected species riding bicycles and 'eating western food'.

Immediately east of the town, on **Drum Hill** (*gǔ shān*), is **Yongquan Monastery** (*yǒngquán sì*). The hill takes its name from a large, drum-shaped rock at the summit which apparently makes a racket when it's rainy and windy. The monastery dates back 1000 years and is said to house a collection of 20,000 Buddhist scriptures of which almost 700 are written in blood. Bus No 39 can take you there from Wuyi Zhonglu or from Gutian Lu.

Places to Stay – budget
Budget travellers are better off not staying in Fuzhou. If you want to stay in the railway station area, it's worth trying one of the small hotels nearby, as many seem unable to decide whether they take foreigners or not. Flashing some money tends to get the ball rolling.

Just up from the north long-distance bus station is the *Jinshan Hotel* (☎ 759-4008) (*jīnshān fàndiàn*) where dorm beds are Y45, singles are Y78 and doubles Y158. It's quite seedy, but convenient for buses and trains.

A little bit further down and opposite the bus station is the *Fuzhou Guesthouse* (☎ 759-0584) (*fúzhōu fēnjú zhāodàisuǒ*) which has dorm beds for Y65; it's cheapish but scuzzy.

There are singles/doubles for Y90/120 at the *Yushan Hotel* (☎ 335-1668) (*yúshān bīnguǎn*), a pleasantly located Bauhaus building south of Yushan, but these prices are subject to a 30% foreigners' surcharge. It's nice on the outside, but it's a tip inside – you can imagine a sign on the outside saying 'Barton Fink stayed here'.

Places to Stay – middle
On the south-eastern corner of Hualin Lu and Wusi Lu is the cavernous *Material Hotel* (☎ 784-3168; fax 784-3662) (*wùzhì dàshà*). It was having a facelift when we

FUJIAN

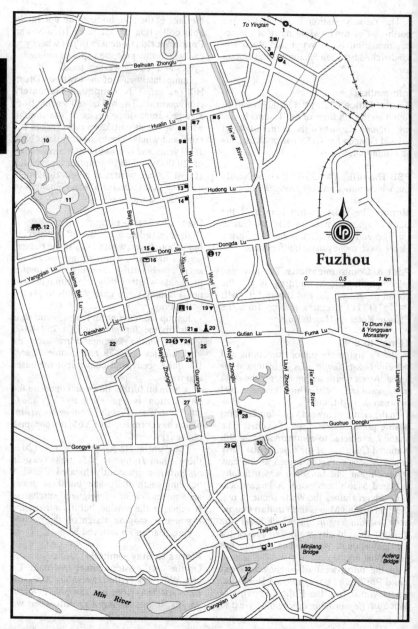

To Yingtan
1
2
3
4
Beihuan Zhonglu

Fuhe Lu

Hualin Lu
6
7
5
8
9
10

11

12
Bayiqi Lu

Wusi Lu

13
14
Hudong Lu

Jin'an River

15 Dong Jie
16
Xianta Lu
17 Dongda Lu

Fuzhou

0   0.5   1 km

Yangqiao Lu

Baima Bei Lu

18 19
Daoshan Lu
21 20
22
Gutian Lu   Fuma Lu
23 24
25
26
Bayiqi Zhonglu

Guangda Lu

Wuyi Lu

To Drum Hill
& Yongquan
Monastery

Liuyi Zhonglu

Jin'an River

Lianjiang Lu

27
28
Guohuo Donglu

Gongye Lu
29 30

Taijiang Lu

Minjiang
Bridge

Aofeng
Bridge

31
32

Min River

Cangqian Lu

FUZHOU 福州

PLACES TO STAY
2 Jinshan Hotel
金山饭店
3 Fuzhou Guesthouse
福州分局招待所
5 Taiwan Hotel
台湾饭店
7 Material Hotel
物质大厦
8 Success Link International
Hotel
成龙国际大酒店
9 Hot Spring Hotel
温泉大饭店
13 Tianfu Hotel
天福大酒店
14 Minjiang Hotel
闽江饭店
21 Yushan Hotel
于山宾馆

PLACES TO EAT
6 McDonald's
麦当劳

19 McDonald's; Friendship
Store
麦当劳、友谊商店
24 KFC
肯德鸡
26 Shanghai Restaurant
上海西餐厅

OTHER
1 Fuzhou Railway Station
火车站
4 North Long-Distance Bus
Station
长途汽车北站
10 Zuohai Park
左海公园
11 West Lake Park
西湖公园
12 Zoo
动物园
15 City Library
省图书馆
16 Post &
Telecommunications
Building
邮电大楼

17 CITS
中国国际旅行社
18 Fahai Temple
法海寺
20 Mao Statue
毛主席像
22 Wushan Scenic Area
乌山风景区
23 Bank of China
中国银行
25 Wuyi Square
五一广场
27 Tea Pavilion Park
茶亭公园
28 CAAC
民航售票处
29 South Long-Distance Bus
Station
福州汽车(南)站
30 South Park
南公园
31 Jiangbin Park (Ferry for
River Tours)
江滨公园
(上游客运码头)
32 Jiefang Bridge
解放桥

last visited; singles and doubles start at
Y160.

The *Taiwan Hotel* (☎ 757-0570) *(táiwān
fàndiàn)* calls itself the 'Home of Taiwan
Compatriots', but all are welcome. Doubles
range from Y295 to Y338 and are good
value. Facilities include a sauna, bar and
disco.

Just south of the intersection between
Hudong Lu and Wusi Lu is the three star
Minjiang Hotel (☎ 755-7895) *(mǐnjiāng
fàndiàn)*, where singles cost Y460 and
doubles are Y480. Nearby, the *Tianfu Hotel*
(tiānfú dàjiǔdiàn) has very good standard
doubles from US$42 to US$50 and suites
from US$80.

Places to Stay – top end
Hot Spring Hotel (☎ 785-1818) *(wēnquán
dàfàndiàn)*, on Wusi Lu, is one of the best
in town. Standard doubles start at US$110,
and executive suites at US$145.

The new and very impressive *Success*

Link International Hotel (☎ 782-2888; fax
782-1888) *(chénglóng guójì dàjiǔdiàn)* has
standard doubles starting at US$68 and
suites starting at US$128. The hotel fea-
tures a billiards room, sauna and weights
room.

Places to Eat
Digging up cheap eats is no problem in
Fuzhou. The railway station area is
teeming with restaurants serving steamed
dumplings or pick-and-choose stir-fries.

The *Shanghai Restaurant* *(shànghǎi
xīcāntīng)* opposite Wuyi square on
Guangda Lu, is part of a chain and serves
excellent dim sum and Shanghai dumplings *(xiǎolóng bāo)*; just point at the plates
and steamers as they come round on trolleys. Pass on the pig's trotters if you like,
but the boiled clams are great, as is the
service.

KFC has come to roost opposite the
Yushan Hotel and there's a *McDonald's* on

Wuyi Lu, next to the Friendship Store; another is on the intersection of Hualin Lu and Wusi Lu.

Getting There & Away
Air The CAAC office (☎ 334-5988) is on Wuyi Lu, and tickets can be bought here or at a few other locations around town. Flights are available to major destinations such as Beijing, Guangzhou, Hangzhou, Shanghai, Tianjin and Hong Kong.

Bus There are two long-distance bus stations in town: a north long-distance bus station near the railway station, and one at the southern end, down from the CAAC office.

There are buses north and south to all important destinations in Fujian and Zhejiang and the bus stations have services to the same destinations.

Economy ticket prices include Beijing (Y251), Guangzhou (Y91), Shanghai (Y148), Hangzhou (Y123) and Xiamen (Y39). There are buses to Wuyishan every night at 6 pm. Keep your eyes open for the ever-increasing band of very clean luxury sleepers that are cropping up; at the time of writing destinations included Wenzhou (Y155) and Hangzhou (Y195).

Train The railway line from Fuzhou heads north-west and connects the city with the main Shanghai-Guangzhou line at the Yingtan junction. A branch line splits from the Fuzhou-Yingtan line and goes to Xiamen.

There are direct trains from Fuzhou to Beijing, Shanghai, Nanchang and Xiamen. The rail route to Xiamen is circuitous, so you'd be better off taking the bus.

Getting Around
Fuzhou is a sprawling city, which makes it difficult to get around by foot. Pedicabs will go anywhere in the central part of the city for Y5 to Y7, while taxis cover similar distances for Y8.

The bus network is good and bus maps are available at the railway station or hotels. Bus No 51 travels from the railway station down Wuyi Lu; bus No 8 reaches the West Lake from Gutian Lu.

XIAMEN
(xiàmén)
Xiamen (population 1 million), or at least the part that huddles the harbour, has a relaxing charm.

The neighbouring island of Gulangyu is an enchanting retreat of meandering lanes and shaded backstreets, set in an architectural twilight of colonial villas and crumbling remains. It is well worth spending a day or so exploring the place.

History
Xiamen, also known as Amoy, was founded around the mid-14th century, in the early years of the Ming Dynasty. There had been a town here since Song times, but the Ming built the city walls and established Xiamen as a major seaport and commercial centre.

In the 17th century it became a place of refuge for the Ming rulers fleeing the Manchu invaders. Xiamen and nearby Jinmen were bases for the Ming armies who, under the command of the pirate-general Koxinga, had as their battle-cry, 'resist the Qing and restore the Ming'.

The Portuguese arrived in the 16th century, followed by the British in the 17th century and later by the French and the Dutch, all of whom were bent on establishing Xiamen as a trade port. They all met with very limited success.

The port was closed to foreigners in the 1750s and it was not until the Opium War that the tide turned. In August 1841 a British naval force of 38 ships carrying artillery and soldiers sailed into Xiamen harbour, forcing the port to open. Xiamen then became one of the first treaty ports.

Japanese and western powers followed soon after, establishing consulates and making the island of Gulangyu a foreign enclave. Xiamen turned Japanese in 1938 and remained that way until 1945.

Just offshore from Xiamen, the islands of Jinmen and Xiao Jinmen have been occupied by Taiwan Nationalist troops since the Communist takeover in 1949. When the People's Liberation Army (PLA) began bombing them in 1958, the USA's Mutual Security Pact with Taiwan very nearly led to war between China and the USA. Tensions remain high. When China conducted missile tests off Taiwan's shores in early 1996, the USA reacted by sending ships to the area, and Taiwanese forces dug in further. Taiwan spends huge amounts on defence in a bid to tip the balance.

Not that you will sense any of this in Xiamen itself. It's a vibrant place, with shops packed with all kinds of consumer goodies. The city has significantly benefited from Taiwanese, overseas Chinese and foreign investment and its designation as a Special Economic Zone in 1980.

Orientation

The town of Xiamen is on the island of the same name. It's connected to the mainland by a long causeway bearing a railway line, road and footpath.

The interesting part of Xiamen is the western (waterfront) district directly opposite the small island of Gulangyu. This is the old area of town, known for its quaint architecture, parks and winding streets.

The central district includes the railway station. Everything about 1km east of the railway station is regarded as the eastern district. Both the central and eastern districts are soulless places, a jumble of high-rises and featureless, numbing architecture.

Information

Tourist Offices There are several CITS offices around town. Probably the most convenient is the one next door to the Bank of China on Zhongshan Lu next to the harbour. They are only really good for booking air tickets, which you can do at countless other places around town.

PSB Opposite the Xinqiao Hotel is a large, red-brick building; the wide footpath on the right-hand side (as you face it) leads to the PSB (☎ 202-5502).

Money The Bank of China is at 10 Zhongshan Lu, near the Lujiang Hotel. Be wary of the ubiquitous black-market money-changers. There's an American Express office (☎ 212-0268) in Room 212 on the 2nd floor of the Holiday Inn.

Gulangyu Island
(gŭlàngyŭ)

A five minute boat trip takes you to this sleepy island of winding paths, creeper-laden trees, Christian cemeteries and almost Mediterranean flavours. By 1860, the foreign powers had well-established residencies on Gulangyu and, as the years rolled by, churches, hospitals, post and telegraph offices, libraries, hotels and consulates were built.

In 1903 the island was officially designated an International Foreign Settlement, and a municipal council with a police force of Sikhs was established to govern it. Today, memories of the settlement linger in the charming colonial buildings which blanket the island and the sound of classical piano wafting from shuttered windows. Many of China's most celebrated musicians have come from Gulangyu.

The best way to enjoy Gulangyu is to wander among the numerous streets, absorbing the charm and character of the place. Exploration is easy, and even the walk up to **Sunlight Rock** *(rìguāng yán)* – the highest point on Gulangyu (93m) – is a leisurely climb. On a clear day you can see the island of Jinmen.

Carrying on around the rock and following the paths to Jishan Lu (Chicken Mountain Road) and then on down Quanzhou Lu is atmospheric and soothing; the area fascinates with its medley of building styles.

The large colonial building at the foot of Sunlight Rock is the **Koxinga Memorial Hall** *(zhèngchénggōng jìniànguǎn)*. Inside is an exhibition which is partly dedicated to the Dutch in Taiwan, and partly to Koxinga's throwing them out. The hall is open daily from around 8 to 11 am and 2 to 5 pm.

FUJIAN

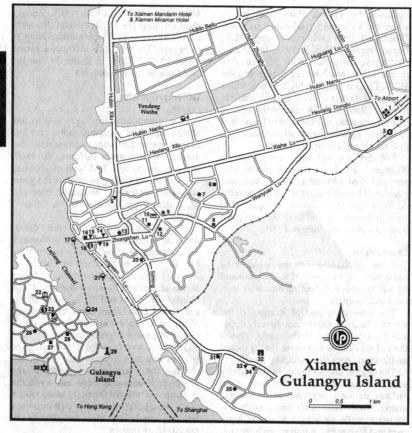

Xiamen & Gulangyu Island

0   0.5   1 km

When we were last on the island, construction work was being done on **Xiamen Seaworld** *(xiàmén hǎidǐ shìjiè)*, which will no doubt feature dolphin acts and other marine distractions. It can be found near the ferry terminal.

The ferry to Gulangyu leaves from the pier just west of Xiamen's Lujiang Hotel. The ferry is Y0.5 on the lower deck, and Y1.5 upstairs. A separate boat charges Y8 (return), including admission to many places on the island.

Once on the island, all transport is by

foot; there are no buses, cars or pedicabs, but electric buggies buzz across the island for about Y30.

Nanputuo Temple
(nánpǔtuó sì)

On the southern outskirts of Xiamen town, this Buddhist temple was built during the Tang Dynasty more than 1000 years ago. It was ruined in a battle during the Ming Dynasty, but rebuilt during Qing times.

You enter the temple through Tian Wang (Heavenly King) Hall, to be met by the

XIAMEN & GULANGYU
厦门、鼓浪屿

PLACES TO STAY
2 Xiamen Plaza Hotel
东南亚大酒店
6 Singapore Hotel
新加坡酒店
8 Xiamen Hotel
厦门宾馆
11 Xiaxi Hotel
夏溪旅社
12 Xinqiao Hotel
新侨酒店
16 Lujiang & East Ocean Hotels
鹭江大厦、东海大厦酒店
20 Holiday Inn
假日皇冠海景大酒店
25 Beautiful Island Hotel of Gulangyu
丽之岛酒店
27 Gulangyu Guesthouse
鼓浪屿宾馆
31 Dujia Hotel
渡假宾馆

PLACES TO EAT
5 Chicken Treat Restaurant
奇肯帝

14 Chicken Treat Restaurant
奇肯帝
15 KFC
肯德鸡
19 McDonald's
麦当劳
33 Dafang Vegetarian Restaurant
大方素菜馆
34 McDonald's
麦当劳

OTHER
1 Friendship Store
友谊商场
3 Railway Station
厦门火车站
4 Long-Distance Bus Station
长途汽车站
7 Zhongshan Park
中山公园
9 PSB
公安局外事科
10 Main Post & Telephone Office
邮电局
13 Xinhua Bookstore
新华书店

17 Ferry Terminal (to Gulangyu)
轮渡码头（往鼓浪屿）
18 Bank of China; CITS
中国银行 中国国际旅行社
21 Heping Pier (to Hong Kong)
和平码头（往香港）
22 Museum
博物馆
23 Bank of China
中国银行
24 Ferry Terminal (to Xiamen)
轮渡码头（往厦门）
26 Sunlight Rock
日光岩
28 Musical Hall
音乐厅
29 Statue of Koxinga
郑成功塑像
30 Shuzhuang Garden
菽庄花园
32 Nanputuo Temple
南普陀寺
35 Xiamen University
厦门大学

laughing buddha (*mílèfó*), with the four heavenly kings on either side. The classical Chinese inscription on the pillars reads: 'When entering, regard the buddha and afterwards pay your respects to the four kings of heaven'.

Standing behind the laughing buddha is Wei Tuo, another Buddhist deity who safeguards the doctrine. He holds a stick which points to the ground – this traditionally indicates that the temple is rich and can provide visiting monks with board and lodging (if the stick is held horizontally it means the temple is poor and is a polite way of saying find somewhere else to stay).

Behind this is a courtyard and on either side are the drum and bell towers. In front of the courtyard is Daxiongbao (Great Heroic Treasure) Hall, a two storey building containing three buddhas which represent Buddha in his past, present and future lives.

The biography of Buddha and the story of Xuan Zang, the monk who made the pilgrimage to India to bring back the Buddhist scriptures, are carved on the lotus-flower base of the buddha figure. In the corridors flanking the temple are the 18 arhats (monks who reach nirvana) in their customary positions.

The Dabei (Great Compassion) Hall contains four statues of Guanyin (the goddess of compassion). The original hall was made of wood, but was destroyed by fire in 1928. Worshippers cast divining sticks at the feet of the statues to seek heavenly guidance. Behind the temple complex is a pavilion built in 1936 which stores Buddhist scriptures (some written in blood),

FUJIAN

calligraphy, jade buddhas from Burma, ivory sculptures and other works of art; unfortunately it's closed to visitors.

Behind the temple is a rocky outcrop gouged with poetic graffiti – the large red character carved on one of the boulders simply means 'Buddha'.

The temple has a vegie restaurant where you can dine in the company of resident monks. To reach the temple, take either bus No 21 from the intersection of Zhongshan Lu and Siming Lu, or bus No 2 from the ferry terminal.

Xiamen University
(xiàmén dàxué)
The university is next to the Nanputuo Temple, and was established with Overseas Chinese funds. It features an attractive lake and makes for a pleasant stroll. The campus entrance is next to the terminal for bus Nos 1 and 21.

Places to Stay
The western district around the harbour has the best sights, food and atmosphere. Anything further east is inconvenient and a dead loss.

It's definitely worth considering staying on Gulangyu Island. There aren't any real budget places to stay on the island, but it will make your stay in Xiamen both memorable and relaxing.

Places to Stay – budget The *Xiaxi Hotel* (☎ 202-4575) *(xiàxī lǚshè)*, inside Xiaxi Market off Zhong-shan Lu, combines economy with an excellent location. It has a wide range of rooms, starting with singles at Y32. Cheap doubles sans bathroom are available for Y74; swisher doubles are Y120. To get there from the railway station take a minibus (Y1). From the bus station you can walk (about 20 minutes). Taxis from either the railway station or bus station cost Y9 to Y10.

Across from the Nanputuo Temple, the *Dujia Hotel (dùjià bīnguǎn)* has grotty doubles from Y120, but it does bring you within range of McDonald's.

Staying on Gulangyu island is a great idea as the scenery is splendid, the air clean and it is very quiet. The *Gulangyu Guesthouse (gǔlàngyǔ bīnguǎn)* is a converted colonial building on a hilltop, and has singles from Y75, doubles from Y150 and triples from Y200.

The quaintly named *Beautiful Island Hotel of Gulangyu* (☎ 206-3409) *(lìzhīdǎo jiǔdiàn)* is airy, bright and clean and has cosy rooms from Y100 (without window) to Y160 (with).

Places to Stay – middle Most accommodation in Xiamen is mid-range, shading into top end. It's really only worth considering the hotels near the harbour. The *Xiamen Hotel* (☎ 202-2265; fax 202-1765) *(xiàmén bīnguǎn)* is a stately place with a certain colonial elegance. Doubles start at Y640.

The *Lujiang Hotel* (☎ 202-2922; fax 202-4644) *(lùjiāng dàshà)* is opposite the Gulangyu ferry terminal. It is a 1940s Chinese-style building that caters predominantly to Taiwanese businessmen. Doubles start at US$40 (add a 10% service charge).

The *Xinqiao Hotel* (☎ 203-8883) *(xīnqiáo jiǔdiàn)* is a classy old place at 444 Zhongshan Lu. Rooms are US$28 for singles and US$48 for doubles.

The *Singapore Hotel* (☎ 202-6668; fax 202-5950) *(xīnjiāpō jiǔdiàn)* is conveniently located next to Zhongshan Park. Prices start at Y370.

Places to Stay – top end There is a wide range of top-end accommodation in Xiamen, but much of it is badly located in the eastern part of town.

The best place to stay is the *Holiday Inn* (☎ 202-3333; fax 203-6666) *(jiàrì huángguān hǎijǐng dàjiǔdiàn)*. It's straightforward to reserve a room from overseas, the hotel boasts some of the best restaurants in town, and staff can arrange for keen golfers to get into the swing of things at the Orient Golf Country Club. Standard doubles start from US$160.

Some other top-end hotels with rates of US$80 and upwards include:

GLENN BEANLAND

DALLAS STRIBLEY

GLENN BEANLAND

The East
Top: Circular entrance to the Yuyuan Gardens in Shanghai.
Bottom Left: Ornate embellishment on a Shanghai building wall.
Bottom Right: View from a guard tower at the Mutianyu Great Wall, north of Beijing.

DIANA MAYFIELD

GLENN BEANLAND

GLENN BEANLAND

The East
Top: A floral extravaganza at Tiger Hill in Suzhou (Jiangsu Province) which commemorates the town's founder, He Lu.
Bottom Left: An intense game of checkers at Tiantan Park in Beijing.
Bottom Right: A common sight in China's cities ... a bicycle parking lot, this one from Beijing.

Xiamen Mandarin Hotel (☎ 602-3333; fax 602-1431) *(xiàmén yuèhuá jiǔdiàn)*, Foreigners' Residential District, Huli

Xiamen Miramar Hotel (☎ 603-1666; fax 602-1814) *(xiàmén měilìhuá dàjiǔdiàn)*, Xinglong Lu, Huli

Xiamen Plaza (☎ 505-8888; fax 505-8899) *(xiàmén dōngnányà dàjiǔdiàn)*, 908 Xiahe Lu

Places to Eat

Xiamen is brimming with places to eat. Zhongshan Lu is peppered with small Muslim restaurants. Just opposite KFC, at 26 Zhongshan Lu, is the *Xibei Lamianguan (xīběi lāmiànguǎn)* where you can get lamb and Xinjiang bread for next to nothing.

All the alleys off Zhongshan Lu harbour cheap eats. Look out for Jukou Jie, near the intersection with Siming Lu, which harbours a plethora of seafood restaurants.

If you haven't had your Sichuan baptism of fire yet, then the *Shuweiyuan Chuanguan Restaurant (shǔwèiyuán chuānguǎn)* further down Jukou Jie will do the trick. The positively volcanic dish of pork slices and chilli *(shuǐzhǔ ròupiàn)* is excellent; order flagons of beer. There are a few other cheap Sichuan eateries nearby.

Chicken Treat, a Western Australian fast-food chain, has set up shop on Siming Lu. They also have a branch just across the road from *McDonald's* on Zhongshan Lu. *Pizza Hut* is hidden away in the park next door to the Gulangyu ferry terminal.

Vegetarians can find sanctuary in the string of restaurants facing the Nanputou Temple. Try the *Dafang Vegetarian Restaurant (dàfāng sùcàiguǎn)* which serves monk's vegetables *(luóhàn zhāifàn)* for Y5. There are also a few Taiwanese restaurants further down.

You'll find pricey, good food at the *Holiday Inn*, which has Malaysian, Japanese and Cantonese cuisine, plus poolside barbeques. The 24 hour *coffee shop* has lunch/dinner buffets, and the *Lao Sichuan* has dim sum breakfasts (about Y40 to Y50 per head).

Try the absolutely charming tea shop simply called *Yuan (yuán)*, down a small alley on the first turning to the right after the intersection between Zhongshan Lu and Siming Lu (heading west). Here you can sit in small cubicles, drink from a wide range of teas and listen to relaxing Chinese instrumental music.

Gulangyu Island is the place to go for seafood. Fresh is best and the meals swim around in buckets and trays outside the restaurants, but they're not cheap. For budget eats, wander up the hill a little from the Gulangyu Guesthouse, to the square formed by an intersection of roads. A few places here sell beef noodle dishes for Y3 to Y8.

Getting There & Away

Air CAAC calls itself Xiamen Airlines in this part of China. There are innumerable ticket offices around town, many of which are in the larger hotels like the Holiday Inn. Ask at your hotel.

CAAC offers flights to Hong Kong, Jakarta, Kuala Lumpur, Manila, Penang and Singapore. You can also fly between Xiamen and Manila with Philippine Airlines (☎ 202-3333, ext 6742), on the 2nd floor of the Holiday Inn. Silk Air (for flights to Singapore) has an office next door to Philippine Airlines. Dragonair (☎ 202-5433) is in the Seaside Building on the waterfront, near the Bank of China. Flights between Taiwan and Xiamen are still on the drawing board, but ask CAAC about recent developments.

Xiamen airport has flights to all major domestic destinations around China.

Bus Buses leave from the long-distance bus station and the ferry terminal. Destinations include Fuzhou (Y50), Quanzhou (Y25) and Shantou. Departures are frequent and there are express buses to Guangzhou (Y140) and Shenzhen (Y120). Luxury air-con buses also leave from the larger hotels.

Train Fujian has a meagre rail system. There's a line from Guangzhou to Shantou (close to the Fujian border), but still no link-up with any cities in Fujian. The line from Xiamen heads north and connects with the main Shanghai-to-Guangzhou line at the Yingtan junction. Another line runs from Yingtan to Fuzhou.

From Xiamen there are direct trains to destinations including Hangzhou (Y71), Shanghai (Y168) and Fuzhou (Y39). The train to Fuzhou takes a circuitous route – the bus is cheaper and quicker.

Boat Ships to Hong Kong leave from the Amoy Port Administration passenger station at Heping Pier on Tongwen Lu, about 10 minutes' walk from the Lujiang Hotel. There is a ticket office at the passenger station.

There are regular services to Hong Kong at 3 pm on Monday, Wednesday, Thursday and Saturday. There are also nine ships per month to Shanghai (Y220 to Y250) and three per month to Guangzhou.

Getting Around
To/From the Airport The airport is 15km east of the waterfront district, or about 8km from the eastern district. Taxis cost around Y50. Bus No 27 goes from the airport to the ferry terminal via the railway station.

Other Transport Frequent minibuses run between the railway station and ferry terminal for Y1. Bus Nos 6, 54 and 21 go to the railway station; the buses are the usual scrum. Taxi fares for most places in town cost around Y12.

The interesting western district can be seen on foot. On Gulangyu Island it's easy to navigate by foot, although electric buggies cater to those with bunions and the very slothful.

AROUND XIAMEN
The **Jimei School Village** (*jíměi xuéxiào cūn*) is a much-touted tourist attraction on the mainland north of Xiamen Island. The school was set up in 1913 by Tan Kahkee, a native of the area who migrated to Singapore and became a rich industrialist. He returned some of that wealth to the mother

country, and the school now has around 20,000 students.

The Chinese architecture has a certain appeal and the waters in front of the school are the site of a dragon-boat race at the feast of Quyuan (usually mid-June). Minibuses go to Jimei from the long-distance bus station, and pedicabs go from there to the school. Some slow trains stop at Jimei railway station.

YONGDING
(*yǒngdìng*)
Yongding is an out-of-the-way place in south-west Fujian. Set in a rural area dominated by small mountains and farmland, it wouldn't be worth a footnote, but for its unusual architecture. Known as 'earth buildings' (*tǔ lóu*), these large, circular edifices resemble fortresses and were probably designed for defence. They were built by the Hakka, one of China's ethnic minorities.

Coming from Henan Province in northern China, the Hakka people first moved to the Guangdong and Fujian provinces in the south to escape severe persecution in their homelands. The name Hakka means 'guests'; today Hakka communities are scattered all over South-East Asia.

For some reason, Japanese tourists are drawn like magnets to view the earth buildings – perhaps they know something we don't. New hotels are being built in Yongding for the Japanese tour groups, but prices might be on the high side.

To reach the earth buildings, first take a train or bus to Longyan or Kanshi, and from there a bus to Yongding.

QUANZHOU
(*quánzhōu*)
Quanzhou was once a great port city and an instrumental stop on the maritime silk route. Marco Polo, back in the 13th century, called it Zaiton and informed his readers that '... it is one of the two ports in the world with the biggest flow of merchandise'. It's slipped a few pegs since then, but Quanzhou still has a few products

of note, including the creamy-white *dehua* (or 'blanc-de-Chine' as it is known in the west) porcelain figures, and locally crafted puppets.

Prettier and cleaner than Fuzhou, Quanzhou's prime attraction is Kaiyuan Temple, which offers a relaxing retreat.

Orientation

The long-distance bus station is in the southern cozrner of the city on the intersection of Wenling Lu and Quanxiu Jie. Wenling Lu has a rash of hotels.

The Kaiyuan Temple is in the north-west of town on the corner of Xinhua Lu and Xi Jie, 2km from the bus station.

Information

The PSB office and post office are on Dong Jie. There's a Bank of China branch on Jiuyi Jie.

Things to see

The **Kaiyuan Temple** (*kāiyuán sì*) is distinguished by its pair of tall **pagodas** and the huge grounds in which it is set.

It was founded in the 7th century during the Tang Dynasty, but reached its peak during Song times when 1000 monks lived here. The present buildings, including the pagodas and the main hall, are more recent. The main courtyard is the refuge of some huge, ancient trees, one of which has a drooping branch supported by a carved pillar.

The main hall contains five large, gilded buddhas and on the ceiling above are peculiar winged apsaras – celestial beings similar to angels. Behind the main hall stands the **Guanyin Temple** with its saffron-robed goddess of compassion; the 18 arhats sit in two rows on either side.

Within the grounds of the Kaiyuan Temple behind the eastern pagoda is a **museum** containing the enormous hull of a Song Dynasty seagoing junk which was excavated near Quanzhou. The temple is on Xi Jie, in the north-western part of town. A ride on a motorbike from the bus station will cost Y5 or less.

There are charming side streets off Xi Jie; if you're in a hotel in the south of Quanzhou then get a pedicab to the Kaiyuan Temple and the driver will probably take you down the maze of winding streets that lead there.

Quanzhou is studded with small temples and can make for an interesting ramble. The **Qingjing Mosque** (*qīngjìng sì*) is evidence of the once large Muslim community; it's on Tumen Jie, but only accessible to Muslims.

Places to Stay

There is nothing particularly cheap in Quanzhou, but those watching their money are better off staying in the area around the long-distance bus station.

The *Golden Asia Hotel* (☎ 258-6788) (*jīnzhōu dàjiǔdiàn*) on Quanxiu Jie, is just around the corner from the bus station and was offering 30% discounts when we were in town; dorm beds are Y45, while pricier doubles come in at Y180. The *Jianfu Hotel* (☎ 228-3511) (*jiànfú dàshà*) on Wenling Lu is reasonably priced at Y170 for singles and Y260 for doubles.

Just down from there is the *Quanzhou Overseas Chinese Home* (☎ 228-3559) (*quánzhōu huáqiáo zhījiā*) which has singles for Y188 and doubles for Y195 (with a possible 20% discount).

There are more expensive options with rates of Y300 and upwards in town. The *Overseas Chinese Hotel Quanzhou* (☎ 228-2192; fax 228-4612) (*quánzhōu huáqiáo dàshà*) is one of these.

Places to Eat

The are loads of small restaurants and bakeries in the Kaiyuan Temple area. If spicy food is what you hanker for, there's a terrific *Sichuan restaurant* in the Quanzhou Overseas Chinese Home.

Getting There & Away

The long-distance bus station has buses to destinations as far away as Shanghai and Guangzhou. To Xiamen (three hours) it's Y13, and to Fuzhou it's Y15.

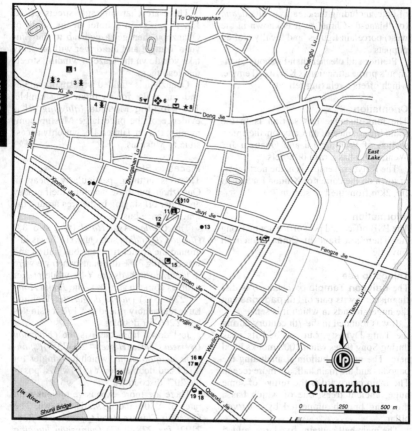

To Qingyuanshan

East Lake

Jin River

Shunji Bridge

Quanzhou

0   250   500 m

Getting Around

There are city buses, but on a short stopover it's far better to travel by motorbike or pedicab. You'll have no trouble finding them – just step out of the bus station.

AROUND QUANZHOU
Qingyuanshan
(qīngyuánshān)

Qingyuanshan translates as the 'pure water-source mountains'. Regardless of water quality, it's a reasonably scenic

mountain area dotted with a few caves, tombs and statues.

The **Buddhist caves** *(qīngyuán dòng)* in the mountain were destroyed during the Cultural Revolution, although some people still pray in front of the spaces where the statues used to be. According to an old woman who lives on the mountain, two Red Guard factions fought each other here during the Cultural Revolution, using mortars.

Also found on the mountain is the 'rock that moves' (there's a large painting of it

QUANZHOU 泉州	OTHER	9 City Hall
	1 Kaiyuan Temple	市政府
PLACES TO STAY	开元寺	10 Bank of China
12 Overseas Chinese Hotel	2 Renshou Pagoda	中国银行
Quanzhou	仁寿塔	11 Tongfo Temple
华侨大厦	3 Zhenguo Pagoda	铜佛寺
16 Jianfu Hotel	镇国塔	13 Workers' Cultural Palace
建福大厦	4 Chengxin Pagoda	工人文化宫
17 Quanzhou Overseas	诚心塔	14 Post &
Chinese Home	6 Zhonglou Department	Telecommunications
华侨之家	Store	Building
18 Golden Asia Hotel	钟楼百货	邮电大楼
金州大酒店	7 Post &	15 Qingjing Mosque
	Telecommunications	清净寺
PLACES TO EAT	Building	19 Long-Distance Bus Station
5 Pizza Hut	实缔	泉州汽车站
必胜客	8 PSB	20 Tianhou Temple
	公安局	天后宫

hanging in the dining room of the Overseas Chinese Hotel Quanzhou). It's one of these nicely shaped and balanced rocks which wobbles when you give it a nudge; we're told that to see it move you have to place a stick or a piece of straw lengthways between the rock and the ground and watch it bend as someone pushes on the rock.

The **Muslim tomb** (*língshān shèngmù*) is thought to be the resting place of two Muslim missionaries who came to China during the Tang Dynasty. There are a number of Muslim burial sites on the north-eastern and south-eastern outskirts of Quanzhou for the thousands of Muslims who once lived in Quanzhou. The earliest tombstone dates back to 1171. Many tombstone inscriptions are written in Chinese, Arabic and Persian, giving names, dates of birth and quotations from the Koran.

The largest statue on the mountain is a stubby Song Dynasty effigy of Laotzu (*lǎojūn yán*), legendary founder of Taoism. Locals say Kuomintang troops used the statue for target practice, but there's no sign of bullet holes; maybe they were bad shots.

Getting There & Away From Quanzhou, you can jump on bus No 3 by the clock tower at the intersection between Xi Jie and Zhongshan Lu. This bus will take you all the way to Qingyuanshan.

Chongwu
(*chóngwǔ*)
One of China's best preserved walled cities, Chongwu is a little-visited marvel, to the east of Quanzhou on the coast. The granite city walls are around 2.5km long and average 7m in height. Scattered around the walls are 1304 battlements; there are four gates into the city.

The town wall was built in 1387 by the Ming government as a front line defence against marauding Japanese pirates, and it has survived the last 600 years remarkably well. Koxinga also took refuge here in his battle against Qing forces.

There are daily bus services from Quanzhou to nearby Hui'an from the long-distance bus station. From Hui'an there are infrequent services to Chongwu.

MEIZHOU
(*méizhōu*)
About halfway between Quanzhou and Fuzhou is Putian County. Just offshore is the island of Meizhou, known for its scenic beauty and dotted with temples.

Taoists credit Meizhou as being the birthplace of Mazu, goddess of the sea. Mazu is known by a number of names: Tin Hau in Hong Kong, Thien Hau in Vietnam, and so on. As protector of sailors and fishing folk, she enjoys VIP status in coastal provinces like Fujian.

Mazu's birthday is celebrated according to the lunar calendar, on the 23rd day of the third moon, and at this time the island comes alive with worshippers. In summer, it's also a popular spot for Taiwanese tourists.

You reach Meizhou by taking a bus to Putian city, then a minibus to Wenjia on the Zhongwen peninsular and a ferry to the island. The temple is simply called the Mazu Temple (*māzŭ miào*).

WUYISHAN
(wŭyíshān)

Far in the north-west corner of Fujian is Wuyishan, an attractive region of rivers, crags and forests. While not really spectacular, it's pretty and has become the prime scenic spot for Taiwanese tour groups, who descend on the place by the busload. This means there are now high-standard (but expensive) hotels in the area. It can get crowded during holiday times; the off season (when it's cold) can be a good time to visit.

From Fuzhou, you can reach Wuyishan by taking a train to Nanping. From Nanping to Wuyishan takes three hours by bus. Wuyishan is now also connected to a number of cities by air.

Liaoning 辽宁

The southernmost province of the historic land of Manchuria, Liaoning (liáoníng) leaves its north-eastern neighbours behind, largely through the dynamism of the city of Dalian on the tip of the Liaodong peninsula. This city alone makes a trip to Liaoning worthwhile, even if it's the only part of the north-east you visit.

Borderland fanatics and Korea watchers will enjoy the pilgrimage to Dandong, on the Yalu River, adjacent to North Korea, while in industrial Shenyang, the provincial capital, some nuggets of Manchu history still gleam. But for most travellers, Dalian is the most tempting refuge. The 'Hong Kong of the North', as it's called, is an innovative and fast-developing city complemented by grand, historic architecture.

SHENYANG
(shěnyáng)

Shenyang was a Mongol trading centre from as far back as the 11th century, becoming the capital of the Manchu empire in the 17th century. With the Manchu conquest of Beijing in 1644, Shenyang became a secondary capital under the Manchu name of Mukden, and a centre of the ginseng trade.

Industrialisation was begun by the Russians, who occupied the city at the turn of the century, and continued by the Japanese, the victors of the Russo-Japanese War (1904-05); Shenyang was the site of the last major land battle of the war. Shenyang rapidly changed hands, in turn dominated by warlords, the Japanese (1931), the Russians (1945), the Kuomintang (1946) and the Chinese Communist Party (1948). The city was looted of its industrial hardware at the end of WWII.

Today's Shenyang is, for the most part, a grim mess of socialist town planning, solidified by ice in winter and roasting in summer. History buffs will find solace in some well-preserved relics of the Manchu

Liaoning Facts & Highlights

Area: 145,700 sq km
Population: 41 million
Capital: Shenyang
Highlights
- The North Tomb in Shenyang, the burial place of the founder of the Qing Dynasty, dating back to the start of the Manchu era.
- The dynamic port city of Dalian, which promises to become the Hong Kong of the north.
- Dandong, the gateway to North Korea.

era, but sensible travellers leap-frog Shenyang for other destinations.

Orientation
Shenyang is bordered to the south by the Hun River; most convenient accommodation is clustered around the railway stations, whilst for the most part the sights are scattered around town.

Information
Tourist Office You'll find CITS (☎ 680-5858; fax 680-8772) in a building about 100m north of the Phoenix Hotel; its official address is 113 Huanghe Nan Dajie.

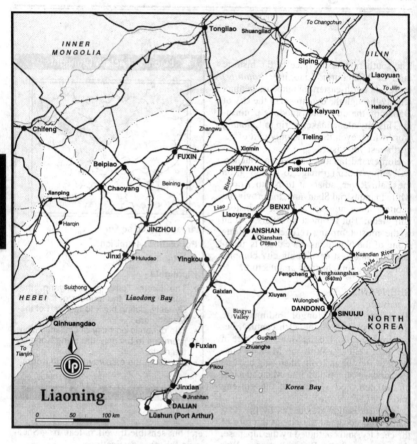

Liaoning

0   50   100 km

Consulates Consulates in Shenyang include the US consulate (☎ 282-0057; fax 282-0074) at 52 Shisi Wei Lu, Heping District, the Japanese consulate (☎ 322-7647) and the North Korean consulate (☎ 685-2742).

PSB The PSB is just off the traffic circle on Zhongshan Lu near the Mao statue.

Money There is a Bank of China conveniently located in Room 301 of the Traders Shopping Centre, next to the Traders Hotel.

Post & Communications The main post office is in the Youzheng Dasha Hotel; most large hotels have postal facilities.

Mao Statue (Zhongshan Square)
(zhōngshān guǎngchǎng)
This statue will bring a lump to the throats of art historians, socialist iconographers and students of bad taste. North-east China is littered with Mao paraphernalia, but this puts them all in the shade. Mao stands cheerily aloft, flanked by ecstatic intellectuals, vociferous peasants, miners and soldiers.

Details to look out for: the figure at the very front is thrusting up a copy of Mao's selected quotations while the peasant at the rear stomps on a traditional Chinese lion. In true tragicomic style, the merry band appear to be reaching for a bottle of Coke on an advertisement opposite.

The phenomenon is in Zhongshan Square at the intersection of Zhongshan Lu and Nanjing Jie.

North Tomb
(běilíng)
The finest sight in Shenyang, the North Tomb is the burial place of Huang Taiji (1592-1643), the founder of the Qing Dynasty (although he did not live to see the conquest of China).

Set in the huge Beiling park, the tomb took eight years to build, and the impressive animal statues on the approach to it are reminiscent of the Ming tombs. The central grassy mound area is known as Zhaoling.

To get to the North Tomb take bus No 220 from the railway station, bus No 213 from the Imperial Palace or bus No 6.

East Tomb
(dōnglíng)
Also known as Fuling, this tomb is set in a forested area 8km from Shenyang. Entombed here is Nurhachi, grandfather of Emperor Shunzhi who launched the Manchu invasion of China in 1644. Nurhachi is entombed with his mistress.

Started in 1626, construction took several years to complete, with subsequent additions and renovations. It's similar in layout to the North Tomb, but is smaller and perched on a wooded hilltop overlooking a river.

To get to the East Tomb take bus No 218 from the Imperial Palace.

Imperial Palace
(gùgōng)
This is a mini-Forbidden City in layout, although it's far smaller and the features are Manchu. The main structures were started by Nurhachi and completed in 1636 by his son, Huang Taiji. It is currently in the throes of restoration.

Straight through the main gate at the far end of the courtyard is the main structure, the octagonal Dazheng Hall with its coffered ceiling and elaborate throne. It was here that Emperor Shunzhi was crowned before setting off to cross the Great Wall in 1644.

In the courtyard in front of the hall are the Banner Pavilions, formerly administrative offices used by tribal chieftains. They now house displays of 17th and 18th century military equipment such as armour, swords and bows.

The central courtyard west of Dazheng Hall contains a conference hall, living quarters and some shamanist structures (one Manchu custom was to pour boiling wine into the ear of a sacrificial pig, so that its cries would attract the devotees' ancestors).

The courtyard to the western fringe is a residential area added on by Emperor Qianlong in the 18th century, and the Wensu Pavilion to the rear housed a copy of the Qianlong anthology.

The palace functions as a museum, with exhibitions of ivory and jade artefacts, furniture, and Ming and Qing paintings. There is also a decent display of enamels and ceramics and an excellent collection of musical instruments. Unfortunately, exhibit captions are in Chinese.

It's in the oldest section of the city; take bus No 7 from Shenyang's South railway station.

Places to Stay
If you arrive at Shenyang's North railway station, the cheapest and most convenient place to stay is the *Railway Hotel* (☎ 252-2888) (*shěntiě dàshà*). Dorm beds range from Y20 to Y50, and doubles from Y120 to Y170. The *Youzheng Dasha Hotel* (☎ 252-8717) (*yóuzhèng dàshà bīnguǎn*), next door to the Railway Hotel, has doubles for Y205.

To the east of the North railway station is the *Dongfang Hotel* (☎ 252-7388; fax 252-4520) (*dōngfāng dàshà*) at 112 Beizhan Lu; it looks like it should be expensive, but

LIAONING

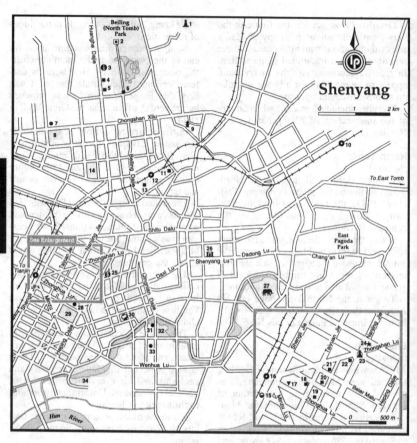

Shenyang

Beiling
(North Tomb)
Park

Huanghe Dajie

Chongshan Xilu

Beiling Dajie

To East Tomb

Shifu Dalu

East
Pagoda
Park

Shenyang Lu   Dadong Lu   Chang'an Lu

Zhongshan Lu

Daxi Lu

Qingnian Dajie

See Enlargement

Nanjing Jie

Taiyan Jie

Zhonghua Lu

To
Tianjin

Zhonghua Jie

Minzu

Heping Dajie

Shengli Jie

Wenhua Lu

Hun River

Shengli Jie   Taiyuan Jie   Nanjing Jie   Zhongshan Jie

Zhongshan Lu

Beier Malu

Heping Dajie

Minzu

Zhonghua Lu

0   500 m

---

singles come in at Y130 and doubles at
Y160.

The *Dongbei Hotel* (☎ 386-8120; fax
340-4972) *(dōngběi fàndiàn)* at 100 Tianjin
Beijie is a huge old hotel not far from the
South railway station and in the main shopping zone. It used to be called the Dongning Hotel. Singles/doubles are good value
at Y150/Y180.

The *Zhongxing Hotel* (☎ 383-8188; fax
383-1972) *(zhōngxīng bīnguǎn)* is at 86
Taiyuan Jie, right in the main market area
a couple of blocks east of the railway

station. You can't miss the hotel – it's a
brick-red pyramid-shaped skyscraper towering over the market. Vast suite-sized
doubles come in at Y298 (check them out!).
Breakfast is included.

The giant statue of Mao in Zhongshan
Square faces the castle-like *Liaoning Hotel*
(☎ 383-9166; fax 383-9103) *(liáoníng bīnguǎn)*. Full of character, this hotel was
built in 1927 by the Japanese and boasts 77
suites, a billiard room with slate tables,
and art nouveau windows – in short, old but
elegant. Singles/doubles are Y300/Y450.

SHENYANG 沈阳

PLACES TO STAY
4 Phoenix Hotel
凤凰饭店
5 Liaoning Mansions
辽宁大厦
11 Dongfang Hotel
东方大厦
13 Youzheng Dasha Hotel;
Main Post Office
邮政大厦宾馆、
邮电局
18 Zhongxing Hotel
中兴宾馆
19 Traders Hotel; Traders
Shopping Centre
商贸饭店、商贸中心
20 Dongbei Hotel
东北饭店
21 Zhongshan Hotel
中山大酒店
22 Liaoning Hotel
辽宁宾馆

PLACES TO EAT
17 KFC
肯德鸡

OTHER
1 Hang Dynasty Memorial
烈士陵园
2 Zhaoling (North Tomb)
昭陵
3 CITS
中国国际旅行社
6 Park Entrance
公园门口
7 Liaoning University
辽宁大学
8 Bainiao Park
百鸟公园
9 North Pagoda
北塔
10 East Railway Station
东站
12 North Railway Station;
Railway Hotel
北火车站、
沈铁大厦宾馆
14 Bitang Park
碧塘公园
15 South Long-Distance
Bus Station
长途汽车南站
16 South Railway Station
火车南站

23 Mao Statue
毛主席像
24 PSB
公安局外事科
25 Bank of China
中国银行
26 Imperial Palace
故宫
27 Zoo
动物园
28 CAAC
中国民航
29 Zhongshan Park
中山公园
30 US Consulate
美国领事馆
31 TV Tower; Foreign
Languages Bookstore
电视塔、外文书店
32 Qingnian (Youth)
Park
青年公园
33 Liaoning Stadium
辽宁体育馆
34 Nanhu (South Lake)
Park
南湖公园

The *Liaoning Mansions* (☎ 680-9502) *(liáoníng dàshà)* is at 105 Huanghe Dajie, near the North Tomb. This enormous Soviet-style place has echo-chamber acoustics and looks like Communist Party headquarters (maybe it is). Rooms are Y510, although low season discounts of 30% are available with a little bargaining.

The *Phoenix Hotel* (☎ 680-5858; fax 680-7207) *(fènghuáng fàndiàn)*, at 109 Huanghe Dajie, is just north of the Liaoning Mansions. This is a major staging area for tour groups, with all the modern amenities and prices to go with it. Doubles are Y458.

The *Zhongshan Hotel* (☎ 383-3888; fax 383-9189) *(zhōngshān dàjiǔdiàn)* at 65 Zhongshan Lu is one of the smartest hotels in town with an international range of facilities. Doubles start at Y580.

The best place in town is the *Traders Hotel* (☎ 341-2288; fax 341-3838) *(shāng-mào fàndiàn)*, at 68 Zhonghua Lu. This place is owned by, and indistinguishable from, the Shangri-La Hotel chain. Top-notch standards in all aspects of hotel management can be expected and the facilities are excellent. Superior doubles will cost US$165 and the 'Presidential Suite' is US$1200.

Places to Eat
Both the North and South railway stations are cheap restaurant zones; *KFC* is on Zhonghua Lu, just near the South railway station.

There is a great *bakery* and *cafe* on the second floor of the Traders Shopping Centre on Zhonghua Lu. Excellent coffee, croissants *(niújiǎo)* and fresh bread are served here.

The *Traders Hotel* next door offers a wide variety of international cuisine, including Korean and western food.

LIAONING

Things to Buy
Next to, and part of, the Traders Hotel is the Traders Shopping Centre which is a three storey emporium of international names like Dunhill, Esprit and Sisley. In the same area is Taiyuan Jie, the major shopping street of Shenyang, where you can stock up on the latest clothing at Giordano and Bossini.

Getting There & Away
Air The CAAC office (☎ 386-4605) is at 117 Zhonghua Lu, Heping District. CAAC runs four flights a week between Shenyang and Hong Kong (Y3230). There are also a number of flights to Seoul (Y2160) and Irkutsk (Y2230).

Aeroflot has a ticket office in the Phoenix Hotel and also offers flights to Irkutsk. Compared with a direct Moscow-Beijing flight, a combined Moscow-Irkutsk-Shenyang-Beijing air ticket offers considerable savings.

There are a huge number of domestic destinations, including Beijing (Y560), Shanghai (Y1040), Harbin (Y410) and Shenzhen (Y1820).

Bus If you come out of the South railway station (a Byzantine structure with a miniature tank on a pillar in front of it), turn right and walk about 200m along Shengli Jie, you will come across a line of buses. This is the South long-distance bus station; services include two buses a day to Tianjin (Y60 seat, Y100 sleeper), three a day to Dalian (Y50) and two departures a day to Beijing (sleepers; Y90). There are also regular departures to Anshan (Y12).

There are also departures from in front of the South railway station, which include Beijing (Y130 sleeper, Y75 seat) and Changchun (Y50 sleeper, Y35 seat). Similar destinations are also serviced by buses from the North railway station.

Minibuses shuttle between the South and North railway stations.

Train The situation with railway stations is tricky – there is a North station (*běi zhàn*) and a South station (*nán zhàn*). (The East railway station is a local station, used mainly for freight.)

If you buy your ticket through a hotel or travel agency, check which station you need to go to.

Buying sleepers anywhere in the northeast is a headache, and Shenyang is no exception; it is advisable to purchase your ticket out of Shenyang as soon as you arrive.

Generally, the South railway station includes trains to Harbin (Y32), Changchun (Y19), Anshan (Y5.50), Dandong (Y17), Tonghua (Y21), Beijing (Y47) and Tianjin (Y40), while express trains go from the North railway station to places including Guangzhou (Y130) and Shanghai (Y96).

Regular minibuses ply the route from the South to the North railway station and back again.

Getting Around
Buses in Shenyang are the usual unpleasantness, but taxis start at Y7. (Try to avoid turning up in the depths of winter. In 1996 there was waist-deep snow and consequently taxi drivers were charging Y200 for a trip around the block.)

AROUND SHENYANG
Qianshan
(qiānshān)
These hills are about 80km south of Shenyang. The name is an abbreviation for Qianlianshan (Thousand Lotuses Mountain).

You can hike around the hills, which have a scattering of Tang, Ming and Qing temples. The mountain, which gets very crowded on Sundays and public holidays, is steep in parts; it takes about three hours to reach the summit.

At the southern foot of the mountain (approached along a different bus route) are the **Tanggangzi Hot Springs**. The last Qing emperor, Puyi, used to bathe here with his empresses.

Tanggangzi's hot springs are piped into ordinary baths, and there's a sanatorium for those with chronic diseases. There is some hotel accommodation here.

Thousand Lotuses Mountain

According to legend, there was once a fairy who wanted to bring spring to the world by embroidering pretty clouds on lotuses. Just as she was making the 999th lotus, the gods found it, accused her of stealing the clouds and had her arrested.

The fairy put up a fight and during the struggle all the lotuses dropped to earth, where they immediately turned into green hills. In memory of the fairy, people began to call the mountain 'Thousand Lotuses Mountain', or just Qianshan.

Later, a monk arrived and actually counted the peaks and discovered there were only 999, so he built an artificial one to make a round number. ∎

Getting There & Away Regular buses from the Shenyang South long distance bus station leave for Anshan (Y12), 60km away, where you change buses to Qianshan. The whole journey takes two hours. The bus drops you off at the entrance to the Qianshan park.

Food, drink, Qianshan T-shirts, locally made clickers and knobbly walking sticks are available from hawkers. Maps can be bought from hawkers near the gate or from the ticket office.

DALIAN
(dàlián)

Dalian has been known by several names – Dalny, Dairen, Lüshun and Luda. Today, Lüshun (formerly Port Arthur) is the part further south and Lüshun and Dalian comprise Lüda.

In the late 19th century the western powers were busy carving up pieces of China for themselves. To the outrage of Tsar Nicholas II, Japan gained the Liaodong Peninsula under an 1895 treaty (after creaming Chinese battleships off Port Arthur in 1894). Nicholas II gained the support of the French and Germans and managed to get the Japanese to withdraw from Dalian; the Russians got the place as a concession in 1898, and set about constructing the port of their dreams and an alternative to the only partially ice-free port of Vladivostok.

Itching for a war with Japan (to whip up nationalist feelings at home and distract from internal difficulties), but underestimating Japanese strength, the Tsar pushed the two countries to the brink of war in 1904.

The Japanese navy pre-emptively attacked Port Arthur in February 1904, crippling and blockading the Russian fleet. The Russians lurched from one blunder to another, culminating in the serious defeat of the Russian Baltic Fleet off Korea in May 1905. The same year, Dalian passed back into Japanese hands, and the Japanese completed the port facilities in 1930.

In 1945, the Soviet Union reoccupied Dalian and did not withdraw definitively until 10 years later.

Today, Dalian has the largest harbour in the north-east, and is also one of the most prosperous cities in China. Criss-crossed by old, colourful trams, the city exhibits some wonderful architecture and has refreshing acres of grass and lawns.

The city also harbours 256,700 intellectuals (according to a recent survey), so pack your pipe and beret and sit frowning in one of Dalian's numerous bars or cafes if you want serious conversation. Dalian is also home to China's most successful football team, unbeaten (at the last count) in 39 matches. As the city is by the sea, the weather in Dalian is much more clement than in Shenyang.

Orientation
Dalian is perched on the Liaodong Peninsula and borders the Yellow Sea to the north; many of the sights can be found in

Northern Warlords

Once known as Manchuria, north-eastern China has historically been the birthplace of conquerors. Perhaps it was the harsh climate that caused the Mongols and Manchus to turn their eyes southwards.

At the turn of this century Manchuria was a sparsely populated region, but it had rich, largely untapped resources. Both the Russians and the Japanese eyed it enviously. After the Chinese were defeated by the Japanese in the Sino-Japanese War of 1894-5, the Liaoning Peninsula was ceded to Japan. Japan's strength alarmed the other foreign powers, Russia among them, and Japan was forced to hand the peninsula back to China. As a reward for this intervention, the Russians were allowed to build a railway across Manchuria to their treaty port of Port Arthur (Lüshun), near present-day Dalian. The Russians moved troops in with the railway, and for the next 10 years effectively controlled north-east China.

The Russo-Japanese War of 1904-05 put an end to Russia's domination of Manchuria. Overall control of Manchuria moved into the hands of Zhang Zuolin, a bandit-leader in control of a large and well-organised private army. By the time the Qing Dynasty fell he had the power of life and death in southern Manchuria, and between 1926 and 1928 ran a regional government recognised by foreign powers.

Zhang's policy had been to limit Japan's economic and political expansion, and eventually to break Japan's influence entirely. But by the 1920s the militarist Japanese government was ready to take a hard line on China.

Zhang Zuolin was killed by the Japanese in a bomb attack, and control of Manchuria passed to his son, Zhang Xueliang, with the blessing of the Kuomintang.

The Japanese invasion of Manchuria began in September 1931, and the weak Kuomintang government in Nanjing couldn't do anything about it. Chiang Kaishek was too obsessed with his annihilation campaigns against the Communists to challenge the Japanese militarily. Manchuria fell to the Japanese, who renamed it the independent state of Manchukuo – a Japanese puppet state. The exploitation of the region began in earnest: heavy industry was established and extensive railway lines were laid.

The Japanese occupation of Manchuria was a fateful move for the Chinese Communist forces locked up in Shaanxi. The invasion forced Zhang Xueliang and his 'Dongbei' (North-Eastern) army out of Manchuria – these troops were eventually moved into central China to fight the Communists. Up until the mid-1930s Zhang's loyalty to Chiang Kaishek never wavered, but he gradually became convinced that Chiang's promises to cede no more territory to Japan and to recover the Manchurian homeland were empty ones. Zhang made a secret truce with the Communists, and when Chiang Kaishek flew to Xi'an in December 1936 to organise yet another extermination campaign against the Communists, Zhang had Chiang arrested. Chiang was released only after agreeing to call off the extermination campaign and to form an alliance with the Communists to resist the Japanese. Chiang never forgave Zhang and later had him arrested and taken to Taiwan as a prisoner – he wasn't permitted to leave Taiwan until 1992.

the eastern part of town, around Zhongshan Square. The ferry terminal is in the east of the city and the Dalian railway station is centrally located.

The main shopping zones and sights are not far from each other and the scale of Dalian is such that walking about is reasonably easy.

Information

Tourist Offices CITS (☎ 368-7956) is on the 4th floor, 1 Changtong Jie, on the

When WWII ended, the north-east suddenly became the focus of a renewed confrontation between the Communist and Kuomintang troops. At the Potsdam Conference of July 1945 it was decided that all Japanese forces in Manchuria and North Korea would surrender to the Soviet army; those stationed elsewhere would surrender to the Kuomintang.

After the A-bombs obliterated Hiroshima and Nagasaki in August 1945 and forced the Japanese government to surrender, the Soviet armies moved into Manchuria, engaging the Japanese armies in a brief but bloody conflict. The Americans started transporting Kuomintang troops by air and sea to the north, where they could oversee the surrender of Japanese forces and regain control of north and central China. The US navy moved in to Qingdao and landed 53,000 marines to protect the railways leading to Beijing and Tianjin and the coal mines which supplied those railways.

The Communists, still in a shaky truce with the Kuomintang, also joined the rush for position. Although Chiang Kaishek told them to remain where they were, the Communist troops marched to Manchuria on foot, picking up arms from abandoned Japanese depots as they went. Other Communist forces went north by sea from Shandong. In November 1945 the Kuomintang attacked the Communists even while US-organised peace negotiations were taking place between the two. That attack put an end to the talks.

The Communists occupied the countryside, setting in motion their land-reform policies, which quickly built up support among the peasants. There was a tremendous growth of mass support for the Communists, and the force of 100,000 regulars who had marched into Manchuria rapidly grew to 300,000, as soldiers of the old Manchurian armies that had been forcibly incorporated into the Japanese armies flocked to join them. Within two years the Red Army had grown to 1½ million combat troops and four million support personnel.

On the other side, although the Kuomintang troops numbered three million and had Soviet and US arms and support, its soldiers had nothing to fight for and either deserted or went over to the Communists, who took them in by the thousands. The Kuomintang armies were led by generals Chiang had chosen for their personal loyalty to him rather than for their military competence; Chiang ignored the suggestions of the US military advisers who he himself had asked for.

In 1948 the Communists took the initiative in Manchuria. Strengthened by the recruitment of Kuomintang soldiers and the capture of US equipment, the Communists became both the numerical and material equal of the Kuomintang. Three great battles led by Lin Biao in Manchuria decided the outcome. In the first battle, in August 1948, the Kuomintang lost 500,000 people. In the second battle (from November 1948 to January 1949) whole Kuomintang divisions went over to the Communists, who took 327,000 prisoners.

The Kuomintang lost seven generals through fighting, capture or desertion, and seven divisional commanders crossed sides. The third decisive battle was fought in the area around Beijing and Tianjin; Tianjin fell on 23 January and another 500,000 troops came across to the Communist camp. It was these victories which sealed the fate of the Kuomintang and allowed the Communists to drive southwards. ∎

western side of Laodong Park not far from the Civil Aviation Hotel and CAAC. On the 5th floor of the same building is the Dalian Overseas Tourism Corporation (☎ 368-0857; fax 368-7831), which may be more useful than CITS.

Visit Dalian – a free monthly English magazine – lists a range of things to see and places to go.

It is a useful guide for those new to the city and is available on request from most large hotels.

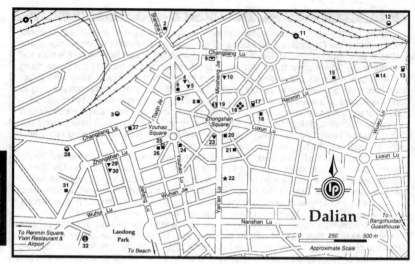

PSB The PSB is on Yan'an Lu, south of Zhongshan Square.

Money The Bank of China is the stately green-roofed building at 9 Zhongshan Square.

Post & Communications The main post and telephone office is on Changjiang Lu, however, most of the large hotels provide a postal service.

TNT Skypak (☎ 280-0524; fax 280-0520) is a private courier service with an office at 35 Changjiang Lu, Zhongshan District. DHL (☎ 272-5882) is at 10 Mingong Lu.

Ask at your hotel for information about sending or receiving email (the larger ones are far more likely to be able to help) or try the Charles Translation Company (☎ 462-1884), who advertise that they can help. There were no Internet cafes open when we were last in Dalian, but ask at your hotel for any developments.

Zhongshan Square
(zhōngshān guǎngchǎng)
This is the hub of Dalian – a panorama of grand buildings encircling a roundabout. The square (in fact a circle) in the middle comes alive at night with ambient music and lights – half of the city turns up to dance and play badminton.

The classical edifice opposite the excellent Dalian Hotel is the People's Cultural Hall. The Bank of China is next door in the triple green-domed building – pop inside and take a peek at its interior. Other historic buildings around the square have been converted to kindergartens, hotels and government offices.

Recently built structures in the area have been designed to harmonise with Zhongshan Square, testimony to the adulation it receives from locals and architects.

Renmin Square
(rénmín guǎngchǎng)
Formerly known as Stalin Square, this huge square displays a huge effigy of a Russian soldier, usually crowned with pigeons.

Behind the statue is a new residential development designed convincingly in the Russo-European style that can be seen all

DALIAN 大连

PLACES TO STAY

2 Dalian Victory Hotel
  大连胜利大酒店
8 Dalian Hotel (Fandian)
  大连饭店
14 Friendship Hotel; Store
  友谊宾馆，友谊商店
15 Furama Hotel
  富丽华大酒店
16 International Hotel
  国际大酒店
20 Dalian Hotel
  (Binguan)
  大连宾馆
21 Grand Hotel
  大连博览大酒店
24 Gloria Plaza Hotel
  凯莱大酒店
26 Eastern Hotel
  东方饭店
27 Holiday Inn
  九洲饭店
31 Civil Aviation Hotel; CAAC
  民航大厦，民航宾馆

PLACES TO EAT

4 KFC
  肯德鸡
5 McDonald's
  麦当劳
10 Dachongqing Restaurant
  大重庆酒楼
23 Barila Pizza Hall
  百和雅
29 KFC
  肯德鸡
30 McDonald's
  麦当劳

OTHER

1 North Railway Station
  大连北站
3 Dalian Railway Station;
  Long-Distance
  Bus Station
  大连火车站，
  长途汽车站
6 Xinhua Bookstore
  新华书店

7 Foreign Languages
  Bookstore; Golden Voice
  外文书店
  金嗓子唱片店
9 Post Office
  邮局
11 East Railway Station
  大连东站
12 Ferry Passenger Terminal
  大连港客运站
13 JJ's Nightclub
  JJ's俱乐部
17 Greenery Beerhouse
  君悦来啤酒屋
18 Friendship Shopping
  Centre
  友谊商城
19 Bank of China
  中国银行
22 PSB
  公安局外事科
25 Polo Bar
  波罗酒吧
28 Long-Distance Bus Station
  长途客运站
32 CITS
  中国国际旅行社

LIAONING

over Dalian. Some truly horrendous crimes against good taste conspire on either flank in the form of government buildings. It would be most excellent if you could crash out on the lawns, which are well watered and lush, but signs say you can't.

Bus No 15 can take you to Renmin Square from Zhongshan Square (Y0.5). On the way, you will pass Youhao Square (*yŏuhăo guăngchăng*) with its vast illuminated (at night) spheroid.

Places to Stay – budget

As anyone can see, Dalian has Shanghai as its model and that includes the exorbitant hotel prices. Cheapies are generally off limits to those of a foreign disposition, but Dalian is opening up rapidly and by the time you read this even the grotty Chinese guesthouses may be shovelling foreigners in.

One delightful relic of the Russian era exists just over the railway bridge in the form of the *Dalian Victory Hotel* (☎ 281-8032) (*dàlián shènglì dàjiŭdiàn*) at 61

Shanghai Lu. The jovial manager insisted they took foreigners, and dorm beds in a double room were going for Y40. If you head up Shanghai Lu from Zhongshan Square, it's the quaint old building on your right after crossing the railway bridge.

Places to Stay – middle

The *Friendship Hotel* (☎ 263-4121) (*yŏuyì bīnguăn*) is on the 3rd floor, above the Friendship Shopping Centre at 91 Renmin Lu. In Dalian, this is considered cheap, but the doubles are not worth it at Y210.

The *Eastern Hotel* (☎ 263-4161; fax 263-6859) (*dōngfāng fàndiàn*) is at 28 Zhongshan Lu, centrally located and not far from the railway station. The hotel has a relaxed atmosphere and a colourful ceramic cat on the reception desk (probably worth a bit). The cat is a good luck charm designed to rake in lolly; it succeeds when it comes to the foreigners' 20% mark up. Doubles come in at Y292. The hotel is popular and often full.

Looking like an old 1930s warehouse,

the *Dalian Hotel (Fandian)* (☎ 263-3171; fax 280-4197) *(dàlián fàndiàn)* is at 6 Shanghai Lu. Doubles go for Y468. This is not the same hotel as the more illustrious example of the same name on Zhongshan Square.

Places to Stay – top end

The *Dalian Hotel (Binguan)* (☎ 263-3111) *(dàlián bīnguǎn)* is at 7 Zhongshan Square. The wrought iron entrance leads to a fabulous marbled interior, done to a high shine. This hotel was used in a scene in the movie *The Last Emperor*. Treat yourself to an emperor's double (Y818).

Just behind the Dalian Hotel is the *Grand Hotel* (☎ 280-6161; fax 280-6980) *(bólán dàjiǔdiàn)* at 1 Jiefang Jie. It isn't very grand inside, although the prices certainly are – singles/doubles are US$78/US$88.

Nearby is the luxurious *Gloria Plaza Hotel* (☎ 280-8855; fax 280-8533) *(kǎilái dàjiǔdiàn)* at 5 Yide Jie. Standard doubles are Y595, and suites come in at Y800 (plus 15% service).

The *International Hotel* (☎ 263-8238; fax 263-0008) *(guójì dàjiǔdiàn)*, at 9 Renmin Lu, has doubles for Y1127 and suites for Y1343 (plus 15% service).

The five star *Furama Hotel* (☎ 263-0888; fax 280-4455; email: framahtl@pub. dl.inpta.net.cn) *(fùlìhuá dàjiǔdiàn)* at 60 Renmin Lu is an excellent hotel. Featuring an Executive Floor, the hotel has standard doubles for Y1549; the presidential suite is a mere Y21,750. The hotel comes complete with its own Cartier and Dunhill outlets.

The *Dalian Shangri-La Hotel* was being constructed next to the Furama at the time of writing, and another huge hotel was going up opposite.

The *Civil Aviation Hotel* (☎ 363-3111) *(mínháng dàshà)*, at 143 Zhongshan Lu, is run by CAAC and is next to its ticket office. Singles/doubles cost a whopping Y1062/1147 plus 15% surcharge.

The *Holiday Inn* (☎ 280-8888; fax 280-9704) *(jiǔzhōu fàndiàn)* at 18 Shengli Square (just off Tianjin Jie) has 'budget' singles for Y1120. It's unique among Dalian's luxury hotels in that it is conveniently placed right next to the railway station.

Out of town to is the *Bangchuidao Guesthouse* (☎ 263-5131) *(bàngchuídǎo bīnguǎn)*, set in a beautiful area by the coast. It's next to a beach and there is no way to reach it except by taxi. Many top ranking party members and cadres stay here.

Places to Eat

Tianjin Jie is a great area for small, cheap restaurants that specialise in fried dumplings and pancakes. If you walk east along to the end of Tianjin Jie, (to where it intersects with Minsheng Jie) diagonally opposite you will see *Da Chongqing (dàchóngqìng)* a Sichuan hotpot restaurant that is very popular in winter. You can divide the hot pot into spicy and bland and proceed to dip shreds of lamb *(yángròu)*, pork *(zhūròu)*, mushrooms *(mógu)*, tofu, crab and whatever else into the scalding broth. The crabs usually turn up on the table alive so give them a miss if you want. The food is not cheap (Y120 for two), but it's excellent if you're a group.

Excellent kebab-style grills can be had at the *Yixin restaurant* (☎ 362-9230) *(yīxīn kǎoròudiàn)* on Tangshan Jie, in between Laodong Park and Renmin Square. You can order plates of meat and vegetables and throw them onto a grill over a fire. Order flagons of beer and sweat it out. You may have to queue to get in as this is a popular place; next door is a copycat restaurant that siphons off waiting customers. Beer brewed in Dalian is very good indeed; try Keller, which has a crisp taste that's a cut above the rest.

Pizza can be found just south of Zhongshan Square at the *Barila Pizza Hall* *(bǎihéyǎ)*. The food isn't bad and they also do apple pie. *KFC* and *McDonald's* crop up together on Shanghai Lu and also up from the Eastern Hotel off Zhongshan Lu. Look out also for *Peter Burger*, *Williams Burger* and *MicLionel & King* which all do good fast food. *DQ* do decent hot dogs and ice cream. *Orient Express* is the local Chinese fast food variant.

Western breakfast can be had for a price at the *Captain Nemo* restaurant on the ground floor of the Grand Hotel. Excellent international and Chinese cuisine can be found in one of the many restaurants at the *Holiday Inn* and *Furama Hotel*.

Entertainment
Dalian has enjoyed an upsurge in bars, pubs and clubs in recent years. A lot of these are targeted at the Japanese business divisions with loose ties that sweep through the city, but others aim more at younger folk.

The area around Youhao Square is worth exploring. The *Polo Bar* (☎ 264-4023) is on the corner of Zhongshan Lu and Youhao Square. Very much the prop-up-the-bar-and-swig-it-from-the-bottle bar, it is cheap, the staff speak English and they try hard. Definitely for students.

More expensive is the *Casablanca Café and Bar* (☎ 264-6598) at 35 Renmin Lu, a popular hangout for the expat set. Also on Renmin Lu, on the left as you come down from Zhongshan Square, is the *Greenery Beerhouse* (☎ 263-7285); they serve western snacks as well as beer. Budweiser and Tennents come in at Y20 a bottle.

JJ's, the nightclub chain, has a setup in the Shenjiang entertainment centre (*shēnjiāng yúlèzhōngxīn*) at the northern end of Wuwu Lu.

Things to Buy
Tianjin Jie is the main shopping thoroughfare in Dalian, a huge jumble of shops and stalls. Here you can find the Dalian Foreign Languages Bookstore and next door (downstairs) is possibly the best-stocked music shop in China, Golden Voice (*jīnsǎngzi*), where you can discover a treasure trove of music beyond Richard Clayderman.

Just on the left down Renmin Lu, coming out of Zhongshan Square, is the Friendship Shopping Centre with big-name shopping and a great shop for stocking up on imported spirits. The Furama Hotel has its own shopping mall featuring such names as Gieves & Hawkes and Aquascu-

tum. *Time* and *Newsweek* can be found in the business centre of the same hotel.

The Holiday Inn has a decent supermarket that stocks items such as Cadbury's chocolate, Pampers disposable nappies, milk and other essentials.

Getting There & Away
Air Dalian has domestic and international air connections. CAAC and Dragonair fly to/from Hong Kong for Y2870. CAAC and All Nippon Airways fly to Osaka (Y3780), Fukuoka, Sendai and Tokyo (Y4490). CAAC also flies to Seoul (Y1890). Dragonair (☎ 263-8238, ext 601) has an office on the 6th floor of the International Hotel, 9 Renmin Lu.

All Nippon Airways (☎ 263-9744) also has its office in the International Hotel, but you can book through CITS. CAAC is at 143 Zhongshan Lu next to the Civil Aviation Hotel. The huge range of flights to domestic destinations include Beijing (Y620), Shanghai (Y990) and Guangzhou (Y2070).

Bus Buses leave from the square in front of the Dalian railway station. There are buses to Shenyang (Y45), Dandong (Y60), Lüshun (Y10) and the odd overnight coach to Beijing (Y130). Buses to Dandong take nine hours and leave every fifteen minutes between 4.50 am and 9.30 am. Other destinations include Tianjin and Harbin.

There is also a private bus station just next to CITS. Book your ticket peacefully the day before or arrive at the last minute and fight for it.

Train Most departures are from Dalian railway station (*dàlián huǒchēzhàn*) rather than from the East railway station (*dàlián dōng zhàn*). Ten trains leave daily for Shenyang (Y80, sleeper). The trip takes six hours, although two of these departures are express trains which take four hours.

Overnight sleepers are also available on the Dandong run (Y98). They leave at 7.30 pm and arrive at 5.30 am. Other destinations include Beijing, Harbin, Changchun, Jilin and Lüshun.

Boat Tickets can be bought at the ferry terminal in the east of Dalian, not far from the Friendship Hotel. Tickets are also sold at a booth in front of the railway station. Boats are a sensible way to leave Dalian as the trains and buses are a long haul.

There is an international service to Inch'ŏn in South Korea which leaves on Tuesdays and Fridays at noon. Ticket prices range from US$120 to US$230.

Boats to Shanghai leave on even days of the month, at 2 pm; tickets range from Y230 to Y488. There are four express departures to Yantai (Y149) daily which take 3½ hours. Slower boats also cover the route. There are two daily boats to Weihai (Y128), leaving at 7 and 9 pm. Boats to Tanggu (the port of Tianjin) depart on even days of the month at 6 pm. Boats to Qingdao depart once every four days at 7 pm and take 22 hours.

Bus No 13 goes from the railway station to the passenger ferry terminal.

Getting Around

The central district of Dalian is not large and can mostly be covered on foot, although you may have to resort to using the bus, depending on where you are staying.

To/From the Airport The airport is 12km from the city centre and can be reached on bus No 701 from Zhongshan Square.

Bus The city of Dalian has splashed out big money upgrading its fleet of buses and they are now among the best in China. Bus No 13 runs from the railway station to the passenger ferry terminal. Colourful trams also glide around the city, and run until 11 pm. Minibuses follow the same routes and charge Y2.

Taxi Taxis in Dalian will cost about Y15 for most places in the city.

AROUND DALIAN
Parks & Beaches

Dalian has a reputation for its health resorts, and beaches with their attached parks are the main attraction. Five kilo-

metres to the south-east is the **Bangchuidao Scenic Area** (*bàngchuídǎo jǐngqū*) which has an attractive pebbly beach – you can only get there by taxi and it's mainly for those staying at the Bangchuidao Guesthouse.

A good idea, if the weather's fine, is to head out there, by cab, and then follow the road along the coast on foot to **Laohutan Park** (*lǎohǔtān gōngyuán*). This stretch of coastline provides some excellent views of the ragged cliffs and crashing waves. From Laohutan Park you can return on Bus No 4 or No 12 which takes you back to Dalian.

Small **Fujiazhuang Beach** (*fùjiāzhuāng hǎishuǐ yùchǎng*) is the best – it has fine sand and rock outcrops in the deep bay, and is excellent for swimming, but has few facilities. The beach is a fair way out of town – take bus No 102 and then change to bus No 5.

Five kilometres to the south-west of the city is **Xinghai Park** (*xīnghǎi gōngyuán*), which also has a popular beach. Inside the park is Dalian's Ocean World which is an exorbitant Y110 to get in. Bus No 22 from the city centre can get you there, as can tram No 202.

Jinshitan (Golden Stone Beach), 60km north of Dalian, has a number of natural scenic wonders and is an attractive beach area with splendid coves and rock formations. There is also a golf course, cross-country motorcycling, an amusement park and hunting grounds within a forest. The area is called 'Little Guilin' locally, but that's pushing it. Buses to Jinshitan leave from the square in front of the Dalian railway station.

The town of Lüshun (Port Arthur) is probably of more interest to scholars of the Russo-Japanese war, however, the preserved remains of the former Japanese prison (*rì'éjiānyù*) make for an interesting trip. You can inspect the cells (and the ones designed for solitary confinement), the workshops and the execution chambers. Also displayed are the remains of large numbers of Chinese killed by their captors.

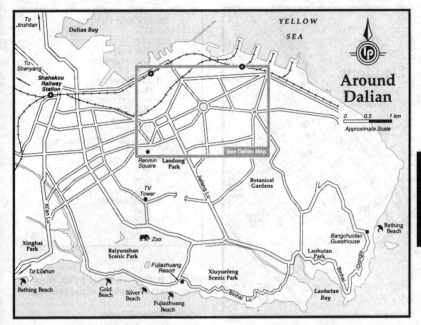

LIAONING

and buried in wooden buckets. It makes for grim viewing.

Areas of Lüshun are off limits to foreigners as they are part of a naval base. You can reach Lüshun from Dalian either by train or by bus (Y10) from in front of the railway station. One day tours also leave from the same area, although the guides speak only in Chinese.

BINGYU VALLEY
(bīngyù gōu)

According to CITS, this is Liaoning's answer to Guilin and Yangshuo. The valley has a number of towering, vertical rock formations with a river meandering between them. It's pretty, but it's not likely to replace Guilin on the travellers' circuit. Still, you might want to have a look.

The valley is 250km north-east of Dalian. Take a bus from the square in front of the Dalian railway station to Zhuanghe

(zhuānghé), a town about halfway between Dalian and Dandong. Then take another bus to Bingyu Scenic Area *(bīngyù fēngjǐn qū)*. Alternatively, you can take a train from Dalian to Zhuanghe (Y20) and then take a bus.

DANDONG
(dāndōng)

Dandong lies at the border of Liaoning Province and North Korea. Dandong's tourist industry thrives on its one asset, the views of North Korea across the Yalu River. Some travellers come here to continue onwards to Tonghua and the Changbaishan Nature Reserve in Jilin Province.

Budget travellers be warned that there is nowhere cheap to stay in Dandong, so it's wise to move on after you've seen the sights.

If you are planning to go to Sinuiju on the other side of the Yalu River, forget it.

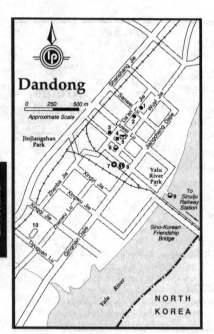

Dandong

0   250   500 m
Approximate Scale

Jinjiangshan Park

Yalu River Park

To Sinuiju Railway Station

Sino-Korean Friendship Bridge

Yalu River

NORTH KOREA

DANDONG 丹东

1 CAAC
中国民航
2 Xinhua Bookstore
新华书店
3 Yalu River Hotel
鸭绿江大厦
4 Oriental Cherry Hotel
樱花宾馆
5 Post Office
邮局
6 Long-Distance Bus Station
长途汽车站
7 Railway Station
丹东火车站
8 CITS
中国国际旅行社
9 Tour Boat Pier
旅游码头
10 Stadium
体育场

Foreigners (at the time of writing American, Israeli and South Korean nationals need not apply) can join tour groups to Pyongyang, but are not allowed into Sinuiju.

Even going to Pyongyang from Dandong via CITS means a wait of 25 days (two weeks at least) for the paperwork to grind its way through the vast cogs of the North Korean bureaucracy. You could try applying for a visa in the North Korean embassy in Shenyang or Beijing, which will be quicker.

If you have exhausted Dandong's sights, entertainment can be had by going to CITS and inquiring about visas to North Korea. Watch them foam at the mouth as they list regulations and prise your passport from your hands.

Information
The CITS office (☎ 212-7721) is the big building on your right as you exit the railway station. The post office is on the intersection of Liuwei Lu and Wuyi Lu.

North Korean Border
(*běi cháoxiǎn biānjiè*)
The **Yalu River Park** (*yālù jiāng gōngyuán*) is a favourite picnic site, full of photographers trying to squeeze mum, dad, kids, grandma and grandpa into the standard 'I visited the Sino-Korean border' shot which has to include the bridge as a backdrop. You can even get your portrait taken in the cockpit of a Chinese MiG fighter.

Yalu River Boat Cruise
(*yālù jiāng guānguāng chuán*)
Those without a North Korean visa can get pretty close by trotting down to the Yalu River Park and jumping onto one of the boats that cruise the border. The large boats (Y5) are a waste of time – you have to wait for them to fill up with passengers (which takes for ever) and the trip is laborious.

Board one of the speed boats (Y13) and zip along the river right up flush with the North Korean side. You are not supposed to take photos, but everyone does. On the Korean side are motionless fun fairs, soldiers rolling cigarettes, decrepit boats and vintage trucks; it all looks like China did about 30 years ago. If you keep paying the pilot, he will take you as far as you want, but once you are beyond the outskirts of Sinuiju, there's not much to see.

The original steel-span bridge was 'accidentally' strafed in 1950 by the Americans, who also accidentally bombed the airstrip at Dandong. The Koreans have dismantled this bridge as far as the mid-river boundary line. All that's left is a row of support columns on the Korean side and half a bridge (still showing shrapnel pockmarks) on the Chinese side. The Sino-Korean Friendship Bridge runs parallel to the remains of the old one.

Other Sights

The huge **Mao Statue** (*maózhǔxí xiàng*) that greets you as you exit the railway station is no doubt designed to fool visiting North Koreans that China is still guided by Marxist dogma and shouldering the onerous burden of a personality cult.

The **Jinjiangshan Park** (*jǐnjiāng shān gōngyuán*), in the north-west of Dandong, offers a panoramic view of the city and North Korea across the river.

Places to Stay

The *Oriental Cherry Hotel* (☎ 213-6541; fax 213-4141) (*yīnghuā bīnguǎn*) at 8 Qijing Jie, not far from the railway station, is a hotel that mainly caters for the holidaying Chinese; doubles start at Y168.

The *Yalu River Hotel* (☎ 212-5901; fax 212-6180) (*yālùjiāng dàshà*), at 87 Jiuwei Lu, is a standard two star establishment that strives to look a cut above the rest, but doesn't make it. Prices are steep, with doubles starting at Y480.

Getting There & Away

Air There are three flights each week to Beijing (Y820), plus two flights each week to Shanghai (Y820) which continue on to Shenzhen (Y2340). There are also twice weekly flights to Guangzhou (Y2530).

Other destinations include Ji'nan, Dalian,

Yantai and Qingdao. The CAAC office can be found on Da'an Jie, not far from the Yalu River Hotel.

Bus The bus station is not far from the railway station. A bus leaves daily for Tonghua at 6.30 am and takes 10 hours. As there is only one bus per day, it is often full, so book your ticket as soon as you arrive in Dandong. Buses also leave from outside the railway station for Shenyang (Y40) and Changchun (Y100). Sleeper buses to Harbin (Y150) also leave from here every other day at noon. Several buses leave daily between 6 and 8.30 am for the nine-hour trip to Dalian.

Train There are direct trains to Dandong from Shenyang and Changchun. The combination train from Moscow to Pyongyang and Beijing to Pyongyang passes through Dandong; if you have the requisite visa, you can jump on the train and head for Pyongyang for US$19.

AROUND DANDONG
Fenghuangshan

About 52km north-west of Dandong is the town of Fengcheng. The nearby mountain, Fenghuangshan, is 840m high and dotted with temples, monasteries and pagodas from the Tang, Ming and Qing dynasties.

The Fenghuang Mountain Temple Fair takes place in April and attracts thousands of people. Fenghuangshan is one hour from Dandong by either train or bus. The express train does not stop here, but you do get a view of the mountain.

Wulongbei Hot Springs
(*wǔlóngbèi wēnquán*)

The springs are about 20km north of Dandong. There's a guesthouse here and you could try the springs.

Dagushan

Dagushan, where there are several groups of Taoist temples dating from the Tang Dynasty, lies close to the town of Gushan about 90km south-west of Dandong.

Jilin 吉林

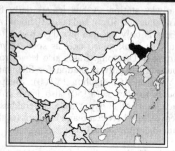

Jilin Facts & Highlights

Area: 187,000 sq km
Population: 26.1 million
Capital: Changchun
Highlights

- Tianchi, a crater lake in the stunning Ever-White Mountains – China's largest nature reserve.
- Songhuahu Qingshan and Beidahu, two of China's leading skiing venues.
- Jilin, a city to visit in the cold of winter when the ice-rimmed trees transform an industrial landscape into a snap-frozen wonderland.

Bordering Russia, North Korea and Inner Mongolia, Jilin is part of the historic territory of the Manchus, founders of the Qing Dynasty (1644-1911). Industrialised under the Japanese, who seized Manchuria and shaped it into the puppet state of Manchukuo (1931-45), Jilin's main attraction for tourists is Tianchi. This volcanic lake is only accessible for a few months of the year, when its sublime landscape is revealed by the receding snow and ice.

CHANGCHUN
(chángchūn)
Changchun was developed by the Japanese as the capital of Manchukuo between 1933 and 1945. In 1945 the Russians arrived in Changchun on a looting spree; when they departed in 1946 the Kuomintang moved in to occupy the cities of the north-east, only to find themselves surrounded by the Communists in the countryside.

The Communists had assembled a formidable array of scrounged and captured weaponry – even former Japanese tanks and US jeeps. The Communists took over the city in 1948.

China's first car-manufacturing plant was set up here in the 1950s with Soviet assistance, starting with 95-horsepower Jiefang (Liberation) trucks, and moving on to make bigger and better things like the now-defunct Red Flag limousines. If you have ever wondered why every other car on the streets of China's cities is a Volkswagen, the answer is that the company has a factory in Changchun (as well as one in Shanghai).

Travellers will see no reason to linger in Changchun. The sights are uninspiring and cheap hotels are off-limits to foreigners; it mainly functions as a transit point.

Orientation
Roughly bisected from north to south by the Yitong River, most of the facilities and sights can be found on the western side of the river. The long-distance bus station and railway station are situated in the north of the city. The city sprawls from north to south which makes communication between points arduous.

Information
Tourist Offices CTS (☎ 297-1040) has an office inside the Chunyi Guesthouse at 2 Renmin Dajie, one block from the railway station.

CITS (☎ 564-7052; fax 564-5069) is on the 7th floor of the Yinmao Building, 14 Xinmin Dajie, which is adjacent to the Changbaishan Hotel.

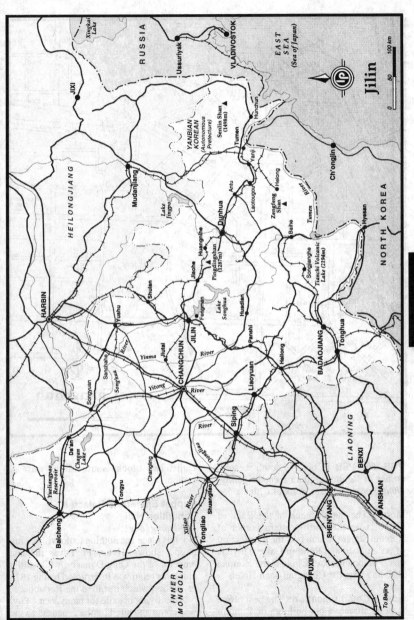

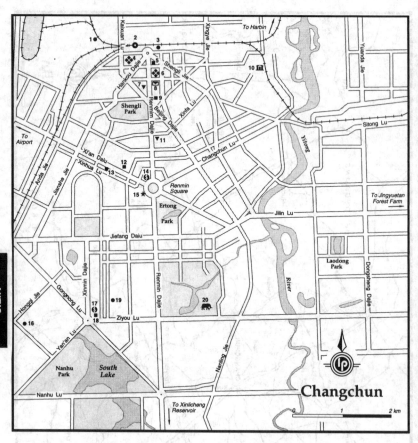

PSB The PSB is on the south-western corner of Renmin Square (rénmín guǎng-chǎng) near the main Bank of China.

Money The main branch of the Bank of China is on the north-western corner of Renmin Square, which is at the intersection of Xi'an Dalu and Renmin Dajie. There is also a branch Bank of China in the Yinmao Building near the Changbai-shan Hotel.

Post & Communications The post office is in an attractive old building on Renmin Dajie, two blocks south of the railway station.

Puppet Emperor's Palace & Exhibition Hall
(wěihuánggōng)

No, this place has nothing to do with seeing puppet shows. Henry Puyi was the last emperor of the Qing Dynasty; while still a child, his reign was interrupted by the 1911 revolution which installed the Republic.

After living in exile for many years, Puyi was commandeered by the Japanese as the

CHANGCHUN 长春

PLACES TO STAY
5 Chunyi Guesthouse;
   Long-Distance Bus
   Station; CTS
   春谊宾馆、
   客运中心、中国旅行
9 Paradise Hotel
   乐府大酒店
12 Shangri-La Hotel
   香格里拉大酒店
13 Changchun Hotel
   长春宾馆
18 Changbaishan Hotel
   长白山宾

PLACES TO EAT
7 Beijing Kaoya Restaurant
   北京烤鸭店

11 Hanguoguan Restaurant
   韩国馆

OTHER
1 Railway Carriage Factory
   客车工厂
2 Railway Station;
   Railway Hotel
   火车站、铁联大厦
3 CAAC
   中国民航
4 Underground Shopping
   Mall
   春华商城
6 Changchun Shopping
   Centre
   长春商业城
8 Post Office
   邮电局

10 Puppet Emperor's
   Palace; Exhibition
   Hall
   伪皇宫、展览馆
14 Bank of China
   中国银行
15 PSB
   公安局外事科
16 Film Studio
   长春电影制片厂
17 Bank of China;
   CITS
   中国银行
   中国国际旅行社
19 Foreign Language
   Bookstore
   外文书店
20 Zoo
   动物园

'puppet emperor' of Manchukuo in 1934. Captured by the Russians at the end of WWII, Puyi returned to China in 1959 and died in 1967, thus ending a life which had largely been governed by others. His story was the basis for the award-winning film *The Last Emperor*.

The palace is a place of threadbare carpets and sad memories. The puppet's study, bedroom, temple, his wife's quarters and his lover's quarters are all on view, eliciting sighs and tuts from visiting Chinese.

Extracts from his diary are stapled to the walls (chronicling his unhappiness in love and life) alongside period photos of the luckless Puyi and his entourage. Puyi buffs will love the sense of history, but all the captions are in Chinese. At the back of the palace is a grisly exhibition of Japanese atrocities in Manchuria.

The palace is open from 9 am to 3.50 pm; entry for foreigners is Y20. Shower caps are issued to be worn on visitor's feet to protect the carpets. Bus No 10 goes to the palace from the railway station.

Nanhu Park
(*nánhú gōngyuán*)
The largest park in the city is Nanhu Park. It has the usual ponds, pavilions and

wooden bridges and is near the Changbaishan Hotel. From the railway station, take trolley-bus No 62 or Bus No 25 or 6.

Changchun Film Studio
(*chángchūn diànyǐng zhìpiànchǎng*)
Those expecting Hollywood, or even Bollywood, will vent a few yawns sauntering around the sprawling estate of this film studio. They make documentaries and low-budget flicks here, but most of what's on show is tacky and vapid. It's only for the extremely bored.

It's Y5 to get in through the door, and from then on each spectacle has its own entry fee, or you can buy an all-inclusive ticket for Y75. Bus No 13 goes to the studio from Renmin Square.

Places to Stay
The *Railway Hotel* (☎ 298-1318) (*tiělián dàshà*) is inside the railway station itself. You can get triples for Y120, or mammoth doubles – the size of a small flat – for Y160. There are two wings to the building with two separate service desks – if one is 'all full' then try the other. Breakfast is included.

Also conveniently located is the *Chunyi Guesthouse* (☎ 297-9966; fax 896-0171) *(chūnyí bīnguǎn)* at 2 Renmin Dajie. It's one block south of the railway station and doubles come in at Y280.

The *Changchun Hotel* (☎ 892-9920; fax 892-2661) *(chángchūn bīnguǎn)* at 18 Xinhua Lu has reasonably priced doubles starting at Y210.

Near Nanhu Park is the *Changbaishan Hotel* (☎ 566-9911; fax 564-3194) *(chángbáishān bīnguǎn)* at 16 Xinmin Jie. Doubles are Y200 and Y300.

The *Paradise Hotel* (☎ 891-7071; fax 891-5709) *(yuèfǔ dà jiǔdiàn)*, at 46 Renmin Dajie, is a smart hotel opposite Shengli Park. Doubles start at US$50 with suites available from US$220. The more expensive rooms are sometimes available at half-price.

The best hotel in Changchun is the *Shangri-La Hotel* (☎ 898-1818; fax 898-1919) *(xiānggélǐlā jiǔdiàn)* at 9 Xi'an Lu, which offers sterling service and accommodation. Doubles start at US$160; the presidential suite is available at US$1200.

Places to Eat

On the north of the Renmin Dajie entrance to Shengli Park is a wonderful restaurant. The *Beijing Kaoya* (☎ 279-7093) *(běijīng kǎoyā)* serves excellent Beijing Duck among other dishes. It's not that cheap, with half a duck coming in at about Y40, but the food and the service is great. The chef nonchalantly slices the duck up in front of you with a few expert flicks of the wrist.

Decent Korean food can be had at the *Hanguoguan (hánguóguǎn)* on the corner of Xinfa Lu and Renmin Dajie. Excellent Chinese and international cuisine can be found at the *Shangri-La Hotel*, at a price. The shopping arcade in this hotel is splendid; it features an excellent delicatessen where you can stock up on the likes of Lea & Perrins, HP Sauce, Vegemite, Corona Beer and a plethora of cheeses. They also have a great bakery that sells, among other things, croissants and banana bread. Heaven.

Getting There & Away

Air The new-look CAAC office (☎ 297-7777; fax 295-2333) can be found on the eastern side of the railway station. This modern and efficient office can deliver tickets to your hotel room and even has a bar.

There is one flight a week to Hong Kong (Y2860), two a week to Seoul (Y2160) and one a week to Vladivostok (Y1330).

Domestic destinations include Beijing (Y770), Shanghai (Y1280), Shenzhen (Y1990) and Guangzhou (Y1950).

Bus The long-distance bus station *(kèyùn zhōngxīn)* is south of the railway station and adjacent to the Chunyi Guesthouse. You can catch buses from here to Jilin (Y20) – these depart about once every 20 minutes throughout the day.

Train There are frequent trains to Harbin (Y23) and Jilin (Y13). Other destinations include Beijing (Y81), Tianjin (Y81), Dalian (Y59), Shanghai (Y156), Ji'nan (Y102) and Nanjing (Y140).

An overnight train travels to Tumen – this is the train you want for Changbaishan and Tianchi (get off the train at Dunhua station).

Getting Around

To/From the Airport Changchun airport is only a few kilometres to the east of the city centre; CAAC provides a shuttle bus that goes to the airport from their ticket office (Y5).

JILIN
(jílín)

The city of Jilin, originally established as a fortress in 1673, was severely damaged during WWII and suffered the usual wholesale looting by Russian soldiers.

Despite the industrial grip on the city today, a few sights remain to challenge the backdrop of workers' flats and factories, but for the most part the city is noted for its winter scenery.

Information

The CITS office (☎ 245-7721) is in the Jiangcheng Hotel at 4 Jiangwan Lu. CTS

(☎ 245-9204) can be found in the Dong-guan Hotel at 2 Jiangwan Lu.

The Bank of China is next to the Milky Way Hotel on Somngjiang Lu.

The PSB in Jilin can be found at 10 Beijing Lu.

Ice-Rimmed Trees
(shù guà) (wù sōng)
Three large chemical plants are fuelled by the Fengman Hydroelectric Station. Built by the Japanese, disassembled by the Russians and put back together by the Chinese, the station provides Jilin with an unusual tourist attraction. Water passing from the artificial Songhua Lake through the power plant becomes a warm, steamy current that merges with the Songhua River and prevents it from freezing.

Overnight, vapour rising from the river meets the -20°C (-4°F) weather, causing condensation on the branches of pines and willows on a 20km stretch of the bank. During the Lunar New Year (late January to mid-February), hordes of Japanese and Overseas Chinese come for the resulting icicle show.

The best time to see the ice effects is in the morning; the stretch of the river in front of the Dongguan Hotel is a good place to start.

Wen Temple
(wén miào)
Just east of the Jiangcheng Hotel is the impressive Wen Temple. It's also known as the Confucius Temple *(kǒng miào)*. Temples dedicated to Confucius were built so that the Great Sage would bestow good luck on local hopefuls taking the notoriously difficult imperial examinations *(huìkǎo)*.

An exhibition details this examination, describing how examinees were confined to solitary cells during examinations. Examples of ingenious cheating devices are on show, including undershirts covered in minuscule characters (despite the fact that the ultimate penalty for cheating was death).

The temple to Confucius features a statue of the sage, his favourite students and a statue of Mencius (the Confucian philosopher). Also arrayed are a host of sacrificial animal figures. Entry to the temple is Y10. From the main railway station take bus No 13.

Beishan Park
(běishān gōngyuán)
If you need a little exercise, go to Beishan Park, a hilly area on the western side of town with temples, pavilions, forests and footpaths. The scenery is mellow enough and is certainly preferable to Jilin's industrial smokestacks. On the western side of the park is **Taoyuan Mountain**, which is worth a short hike.

Bus No 7 from the railway station terminates right in front of the park entrance. If you're on a local train, the Beishan Railway Station is near the park.

Catholic Church
(tiānzhǔ jiàotáng)
This Catholic church, which has become a symbol for Jilin City, was built in 1917. Ransacked of all its icons and finery during the Cultural Revolution, its small library of religious works was also torched. The church was reopened in 1980 and has regular services.

It is not far from the Dongguan Hotel, on the northern bank of the Songhua River.

Meteorite Shower Museum
(yǔnshí yǔ bówùguǎn)
In March 1976, the Jilin area received a heavy meteorite shower, and the largest bit, weighing 1770kg, is on view in the museum (it is apparently the largest chunk anywhere in the world). The museum is open from 9 am to 4.30 pm and admission is Y20. Take trolley-bus No 3 from outside the Dongguan Hotel.

Ice Lantern Festival
(bīngdēng jié)
Jilin, like Harbin, has an Ice Lantern Festival, held at Jiangnan Park on the southern side of the Songhua River. Locals claim

JILIN

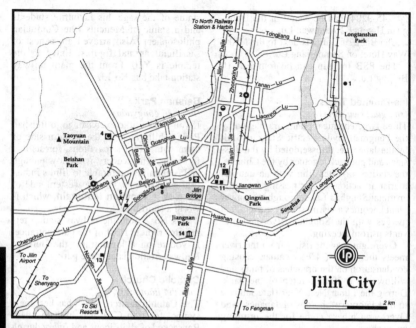

Jilin City

that Jilin invented the Ice Lantern Festival and Harbin copied it (Harbin's festival is much more famous though, so it's probably sour grapes). Other attractions in the park at winter time include an ice-skating rink.

Places to Stay

There are no cheap hotels open to foreigners in Jilin, and the lowest prices are midrange. Getting hold of a cheap room during January and February is tricky, as the city is bristling with icicle watchers. The rates quoted are off season – expect large increases when snow starts to fall.

The *Dongguan Hotel* (☎ 245-4272; fax 244-5208) *(dōngguān bīnguǎn)*, at 2 Jiangwan Lu, is the cheapest, with threadbare rooms at Y280. The restaurant on the 2nd floor serves reasonable food. CTS can be found here. Take trolley-bus No 3 from the railway station (about 3km).

Adjacent to the Dongguan Hotel is the upmarket *Jiangcheng Hotel* (☎ 245-7721; fax 245-8973) *(jiāngchéng bīnguǎn)* at 4 Jiangwan Lu. CITS makes this its HQ. This hotel mainly takes tour groups – the cheapest doubles are Y320.

The *Milky Way Hotel* (☎ 484-1780; fax 484-1621) *(yínhé dàshà)* at 79 Songjiang Lu is a reasonable option, although quite a hike from the main railway station. At least it's a good deal if you get one of the standard rooms for Y340. Suites cost Y460. Take bus No 1 and ask to be told by the driver when the bus has reached the Linjiangmen stop *(línjiāngmén)* by the bridge over the river, which is very close to the hotel.

The *Xiguan Hotel* (☎ 484-3141) *(xīguān bīnguǎn)*, at 155 Songjiang Lu, is even further away, but you can get there on bus No 1 from the station which stops outside the hotel. Doubles start at Y360.

JILIN CITY 吉林

1 Longtanshan Deer Farm
龙潭山鹿场
2 Main Railway Station
吉林火车站
3 Long-Distance Bus Station
岔路乡汽车站
4 Mosque
清真寺
5 Beishan Railway Station
北山火车站
6 PSB
公安局外事科
7 Milky Way Hotel;
Bank of China
银河大厦、中国银行
8 City Hall
市政府
9 Catholic Church
天主教堂
10 Dongguan Hotel;
CTS; CAAC
东关宾馆、中国旅行社、
中国民航
11 Jiangcheng Hotel; CITS
江城宾馆、中国国际旅行社
12 Confucius Temple
文庙
13 Xiguan Hotel
西关宾馆
14 Meteorite Shower Museum
陨石雨博物馆

Getting There & Away

Air CAAC (☎ 245-4260) can be found at 1
Chongqing Jie, next door to the Dongguan
Hotel. There are flights between Jilin and
Beijing (Y760), Shanghai (Y1170), Chang-
chun, Dalian, Guangzhou, and Shenyang.

Bus The long-distance bus station (*chà lù
xiāng*) is one long block west of the railway
station. There are buses between Jilin and
Changchun approximately once every 20
minutes throughout the day. The trip takes
2½ hours. There are also services to Shenyang and Harbin. One bus a day leaves for
Dunhua at 9 am; change at Dunhua to reach
Baihe and Tianchi.

Train The main railway station is to the
north of the city. There is a regular direct

train service between Jilin and Changchun.
There are also direct trains to Harbin (four
hours), Tumen (via Dunhua), Shenyang
and Dalian. There are also direct trains to
Beijing and Tianjin, but you have to buy
these well in advance if you want any hope
of getting a sleeper. It's easier to go to
Changchun and do it from there.

Getting Around

There's usually a virtual taxi festival happening around the railway station. Cab fares
are a flat Y20 anywhere within the city.

To/From the Airport Jilin airport is about
10km west of the city. A taxi will cost you
about Y50. Private minibuses leave the
airport after planes arrive, but don't operate
the other way. Shuttle buses run from
CAAC to the airport, once a day.

AROUND JILIN
Songhuahu Qingshan Ski Resort
(*sōnghuā hú qīngshān huáxuě chǎng*)
This resort is at 934m elevation, 25km
south-east of Jilin and just east of Fengman.
Opened in 1982, the resort features a 270m
main piste and a 1800m cableway. Also on
hand is a 5km section devoted to cross-
country skiing, and a 50m-high ski jump.
Beginners and intermediate skiers can pick
up a few skills on the 2km practice piste.

The emphasis is on beginners, and the
season is from December to February. Entry
is Y50, equipment can be hired at the resort,
and there is also a cafe, a restaurant and
shopping arcade.

Ask at any hotel in Jilin for information
concerning snow conditions, accommodation
and so on.

Bus No 9 goes to the ski resort from the
main railway station. In the south of the
province at **Tonghua**, there is a ski field
where championships have been held.

Beidahu Ski Resort
(*běidàhú huáxuě chǎng*)
This ski area 20 km from Jilin is perhaps
the best place in China to practice the art of
sliding downhill.

JILIN

TIANCHI

(tiānchí)

Tianchi (Lake of Heaven) is a volcanic lake in the Changbaishan (Ever-White Mountains) Nature Reserve. The reserve is China's largest, covering 210,000 hectares of dense virgin forest.

Because of elevation changes, there is wide variation in animal and plant life. From 700 to 1000m above sea level there are mixed coniferous and broad-leaf trees (including white birch and Korean pines); from 1000 to 1800m, there are cold-resistant coniferous trees such as dragon spruce and fir; from 1800 to 2000m is another forest belt; above 2000m it's alpine tundra – treeless and windy.

For the budding natural scientist there's plenty to investigate. Some 300 medicinal plants grow within the reserve (including winter daphne, Asia bell and wild ginseng) and entomologists will have a field day by the shores of Tianchi at the end of June when the snow finally melts and an explosion of insect life results. Some very shy animal species also make their home in the

mountain range (the rarer ones being the protected cranes, deer and Manchurian tiger).

Tianchi itself, at an elevation of 2194m, is the prime scenic spot. It's a volcanic crater lake, 5km from north to south, 3.5km from east to west, and 13km in circumference. It's surrounded by jagged rock outcrops and 16 mountainous peaks, the highest of which soars to 2691m. Three rivers run off the lake, with a rumbling 68m waterfall the source of the Songhua and Tumen rivers. The lake is also said to be home to a monster that has yet to be photographed.

Between 11 am and noon the tour buses roll up to disgorge day-trippers who pose heroically for photos in front of the waterfall, stampede up the mountain, take a lakeside breather and then rush down again between 1 and 2 pm. The beauty of the place is badly marred by picnic detritus, smashed glass and discarded film wrappers. Even so, there are opportunities to leave the crowds behind and this is a peaceful and sublime place to stay for a couple

Tianchi Legends

Enchanting scenery like that of Tianchi would not be complete in the Chinese world without a legend or mystery of some sort. Of the many myths, the most intriguing is the origin of the Manchu race, in which three heavenly nymphs descended to the lake in search of earthly pleasure. They stripped off for a dip in the lake; along came a magic magpie which deposited a red berry on the dress of one of the maidens. When she picked it up to smell it, the berry flew through her lips into her stomach. The nymph became pregnant and gave birth to a handsome boy with an instant gift of the gab. He went on to foster the Manchus and their dynasty.

Dragons, and other things that go bump in the night, were believed to have sprung from the lake. In fact, they're still believed to do so. There have been intermittent sightings of unidentified swimming objects – China's own Loch Ness beasties or aquatic yetis or what have you. Tianchi is the deepest alpine lake in China at a depth estimated at between 200 and 350m. Since it is frozen over in winter and temperatures are well below zero, it would take a pretty hardy monster to make this place home (even plankton can't). Sightings from the Chinese and North Korean sides point to a black bear, fond of swimming and oblivious to the paperwork necessary for crossing these tight borders. On a more profound note, Chinese couples throw coins into the lake, pledging that their love will remain as deep as Tianchi and as long-lived. ■

GLENN BEANLAND

JULIET COOMBE/LA BELLE AURORE

The East
Top: Greeting the dawn ... dancers on the Bund in Shanghai.
Bottom: Sunset scene on Hangzhou's West Lake (Zhejiang Province).

MARIE CAMBON

MARIE CAMBON

CLEM LINDENMAYER

Central China
Top: Chinese tourists at a Taoist temple at Wudangshan (Hubei Province).
Bottom Left: Detail of a Buddha statue in the Gongyi Caves (Henan Province).
Bottom Right: Fire buckets at the Great Mosque in Xi'an (Shaanxi Province).

of days and hike around. However, hiking at the lake itself is limited by the sharp peaks and their rock-strewn debris, and by the fact that the lake overlaps the Chinese-North Korean border – though the border isn't signposted, it isn't wise to walk any further east of the weather station below the summit of Changbaishan or you may be arrested. Cloud cover starts at 1000m and can be prevalent.

It's advisable to bring dried food, sunscreen lotion and other medical supplies, good hiking gear and go as a group. High altitude weather is very fickle no matter how warm and sunny it is in the morning – sudden high winds, rain, hail and dramatic drops in temperature are entirely possible by afternoon. In other words, hope for the best, but prepare for the worst. For those just keen to see the lake, you can rent overcoats and waterproofs from the scrum of women encircling you as you get off the bus at Tianchi. Construction helmets are issued to protect tourists from falling rocks.

Take note: foreigners are charged a massive Y120 at the main gate, plus a further Y40 to get up to the lake, totalling an extortionate Y160, while the Chinese pay only Y35. You should be aware of this as you may already have forked out a hefty sum for transport from Baihe (if you hire a driver); knowledge of the pricing system may make you think twice about going. Those who can speak reasonable Chinese and have dark hair can insist they are from Xinjiang province and get a Chinese price ticket. The word on the streets is that this two tier pricing system is going to be scrapped, but only time will tell.

Places to Stay

Budget travellers are best off staying in Baihe, and travelling to Tianchi by bus. There is no PSB is Baihe, so you can stay wherever you want. Numerous households have flung open their doors to travellers who can stay on rickety beds for Y10.

You'll probably be pounced on at the railway station by 'hoteliers'; but feel free to make your own choice from one of the many local, cheap guesthouses.

The *Tielu Zhaodaisuo (tiělù zhāodàisuǒ)* has simple doubles for Y15 per bed. It's to the right as you come out of the railway station. On the left of the railway station as you exit is the official hotel of Baihe, the *Baiyun Binguan (báiyún bīnguǎn)* where you can find doubles for Y180.

Alternatively, you can stay in the Changbaishan region and fork out big time in tacky, Chinese tour group hotels. One example is the *Changbaishan Tianchi Binguan* (☎ 574-2069) *(chángbáishān tiānchí bīnguǎn)*, by the main Tianchi gate, a tasteless villa-style hotel for visiting South Koreans. Doubles start at Y500.

Another one is the *Mount Changbai Cuckoo Villa* (☎ 571-2574; fax 571-2376) *(chángbáishān dùjuān shānzhuāng)*, a Swiss-style, all-wood affair near Lesser Tianchi Lake, complete with hot spring baths, cheesy night club and ski hire. Doubles are Y445.

Much of the same can be found at the *Changbai Athletes Village* (☎ 571-2574; fax 571-2376) *(chángbáishān yùndòngyuán cūn)*, which has doubles for Y485.

If you have a sleeping bag, camping is certainly a possibility, although it's technically against the rules. Be prepared for thunderstorms and try to find a place far away from curious spectators and those stern-faced figures collectively known as 'the authorities'.

Although Baihe is just a step up from a village and the facilities are primitive, the place is famous for being the only part of China where you can find a beautiful type of pine tree called a *Meiren Song*. They are extremely tall, elegant and photogenic, with only the tops of the trees reserved for their graceful branches.

Getting There & Away

The *only* season when there's public transport access (when the road from Baihe to Changbaishan isn't iced over) is from late June to September. Phone up one of the hotels in the area to get a weather check and status report before trekking out to be met by a white out.

JILIN

There are two main directions from which you can tackle Changbaishan; one is from Shenyang to Baihe, via Tonghua, and the other is from Dunhua to Baihe (it is also possible to fly to Yanji, then backtrack to Antu and get a bus to Baihe, but this is very expensive).

Via Tonghua This is the preferable route as you can, if you want, arrive early in the day in Baihe and tackle the mountain on the same day. There are two trains per day from Tonghua to Baihe – one leaves at 8.45 am and arrives in Baihe at 5.15 pm, and the other leaves at 9.05 pm and arrives in Baihe at 4.36 am. Sleepers are available at Y59 and seats are Y25.

The train takes about eight hours to cover the 277km between Tonghua and Baihe, so it's worth getting a sleeper. If you have to spend the night in Tonghua, dorm beds are available for Y16 in the *Guomao Hotel (guómào dàjiǔdiàn)* opposite the railway station; doubles are Y52.

If you arrive at Baihe in the evening, you will have missed all possible transport and will have to stay the night there (see the previous Places to Stay section). If you arrive in the morning, you can jump on to one of the minibuses that race up to the mountain (the service stops at noon).

From Dandong, there are buses to Tonghua departing at 6.30 am and regular buses to Tonghua from Shenyang.

Via Dunhua There are six buses a day from Dunhua to Baihe (Y14), with the earliest bus leaving at 7.45 am; the journey takes four hours. Dunhua has many places where you can stay for the night, including the *Zhonghua Yichun Hotel (zhōnghuá yìchūn bīnguǎn),* to the west of the long-distance bus station, which has doubles for Y180.

By the time you arrive in Baihe, you will probably have missed all transport to Changbaishan 40km away, and will have to wait until the next day. To catch a bus from Baihe to Dunhua, walk up the road facing the railway station, past all the restaurants

and pine trees, to the end, and buy tickets in the shop directly facing you. Buses to Dunhua stop here.

There are direct trains to Dunhua from both Changchun and Jilin. Alternatively, you can take the train to Tumen and get off at Dunhua.

Getting Around
Buses leave for Changbaishan from the square in front of the railway station at Baihe from about 6 am to noon. They cost Y40 which includes the return trip, allowing you a few hours to scramble up to the lake and back again.

If you want more time to hike around and you're in a group, it's worth considering hiring a car with a driver for the trip (just pop into one of the restaurants and ask, as some of the restaurant owners provide transport). The driver will wait for you to return from the lake and will also offer to drive you to the highest peak (by road) for an additional fee. It is worth doing this if the weather is fine – the view is spectacular.

The trip to Tianchi for a group should cost about Y300, although they will automatically ask foreigners for Y500. Get the bargaining gloves on, look them in the eye, and say 'Y300' *(sānbǎi kuài).* Be aware that both the buses and the hired cars will drop you off at a point where it is still another hour's hike to the lake.

No buses cover the route from Baihe when there's snow and ice, but you may find a local driver who can navigate the icy roads with tyre chains. This will probably set you back a small fortune and maybe the odd broken rib, followed by the possibility of frostbite, so weigh it up carefully.

An alternative route for getting from the hotels to Tianchi is to backtrack north for about 1km to the crossroads and take the road right (east). It winds on higher and higher, finally turning south, bringing you up onto the ridge of the east side of the valley.

The road ends by the meteorological station where you have a splendid view of the lake. From here you head west towards a triangular peak – beyond that small peak it's possible to scramble down to the lake and ford the stream above the waterfall, but take care! Now you are at the end of the main track and can join the crowd back to the hot springs at the start of the climb. This walk can be easily completed in one day, but it's always best to get an early start.

AROUND TIANCHI

The Changbaishan region presents you with some possibilities for shaking off the cities and traipsing through the wilderness, and gives you some good reasons for doing so: virgin forest and babbling brooks – and some rough travel and rough trails, as well as rough toilets if you can find one.

The whole zone is the Yanbian (Chaoxian) Korean Autonomous Prefecture. The local people of Korean descent are often indistinguishable in dress from their Chinese counterparts. If you visit this area around mid-August, you can join in the 'Old People Festival'. The Koreans are a fairly lively lot, who enjoy eating spiced cold noodles and dog meat, singing and dancing and offering hospitality. They can also drink you under the table.

Yanbian has the greatest concentration of Korean and Korean-Han groups in China, mostly inhabiting the border areas north and north-east of Baihe, extending up to Yanji.

Getting around by rail is safer compared with the winding roads. Apart from public buses, the only other means of transport is by jeep or logging truck.

Off the main track, the trains are puffing black dragons, possibly of Japanese vintage. The fittings are old and the trains have no sleepers.

Food has improved in recent years, and in Korean areas you can sample delicious cold noodles topped with a pile of searing hot spices.

Heilongjiang 黑龙江

Heilongjiang Facts & Highlights

Area: 469,000 sq km

Population: 37.3 million

Capital: Harbin

Highlights

- If you can survive temperatures of -40°C (-40°F), come in January to witness the amazing Ice Lantern Festival in Harbin.
- Yabuli, site of the 1996 Asian Winter Games, looks set to become China's leading ski resort.
- Jingbo Lake, an alpine lake that shines like a mirror, from which it takes its name.

Heilongjiang (Black Dragon River) is China's northernmost province and is known for its subarctic climate. Come January, with its -30°C (-22°F) weather and howling Siberian gales, the locals sensibly huddle round their stoves, swathed in blankets, quaffing the local firewater. When the strong stuff runs out, it takes a numbing waddle in thickly padded clothes to the corner shop. Activity slows to a crunch in this snowflake-spitting weather, while the animals bypass the season completely by hibernating.

Welcome, believe it or not, to the tourist season. Inquisitive Hong Kongers and Taiwanese fly up to fulfil their childhood ambition of seeing snow, and are reportedly so blown away by the cold that they never set foot north of the Tropic of Cancer again. Don't be put off, because if you come prepared for weather conditions like winter on Pluto, the city of Harbin offers a sparkling spectacle of ice-encrusted Russian buildings, winter sports and its famous Ice Lantern Festival. May to September opens up the rest of the province to exploration.

Mohe, in northern Heilongjiang, holds the record for China's lowest plunge of the thermometer, a mere -52.3°C (-61.1°F). Be there! As a result of living in these conditions, the people of Heilongjiang are hewn from rough material and have a reputation for being hardy and bellicose. It's worth noting that the hard stuff available on shelves all over Harbin is called 'hand grenade', which comes in an appropriately shaped bottle. It may not be for connoisseurs of wines and spirits, but is possibly a collector's item none the less.

HARBIN
(hāěrbīn)

Originally a quiet village on the Songhua River, Harbin derives its name from 'Alejin', the Manchu word for 'honour' or 'fame'.

In 1896, the Russians negotiated a contract to build a railway line through Harbin to Vladivostok (and Dalian). The Russian imprint on the town remained in one way or another until the end of WWII. By 1904 the 'rail concession' was in place, and with it came other Russian demands on Manchuria. These were stalled by the Russo-Japanese War (1904-05), and with the Russian defeat the Japanese gained control of the railway.

In 1917 large numbers of Russian refugees flocked to Harbin, fleeing the Bolsheviks; in 1932 the Japanese occupied the city; and in 1945 the Soviet army wrested it

Heilongjiang

RUSSIA

Mohe
Gulian
Heilong River
Bishui
Huma
Belogorsk
Jagdaqi
Heihe
Blagoveshcensk

INNER MONGOLIA
Nenjiang
Sunwu
Heilong
Wudalianchi Nature Reserve
Longzhen
Wuyiling
KHABAROVSK
Fuyuan
Dedu
Keshan
Bei'an
Tongbei
YICHUN
Songhua River
Tongjiang
QIQIHAR
Zhalong Nature Reserve
Mingshui
HEGANG
Jiamusi
Fujin
DAQING
Anda
Suihua
Shuang-yashan
Zhaodong
HARBIN
Qitaihe
Baicheng
Shuangcheng
Acheng
Fangzheng
Yanshou
JIXI
Mishan
Qian
Yuquan
Shangzhi
Xingkai Lake
Yabuli
Mudanjiang
Suifenhe
RUSSIA
Dongjing
Dongning
Ussurlysk
CHANGCHUN
JILIN
JILIN
Jingbo Lake
VLADIVOSTOK

0   75   150 km

back for a year and held it until 1946, when the Kuomintang troops were finally installed, as agreed by Chiang Kaishek and Stalin.

Harbin today is largely an industrial city, but improving relations with Russia has resulted in flourishing trade and a mini-boom in cross-border tourism. The vast majority of foreign faces on the streets of Harbin today are Russian; the Chinese call them 'lao maozi' *(lǎo máozi)* or 'hairy ones'. They will no doubt call you this as well, or speak to you in Russian, rather than

Chinese or English. The Russians generally come over to holiday and to buy all manner of consumer goods: clothing, coffee, cosmetics and other items which Russia no longer seems capable of producing. They bring with them all manner of items that will fetch a price in China, including Russian army surplus (for 'surplus' read 'anything that sells') like night-vision goggles and possibly the odd warhead.

Harbin is a graceful Chinese city possessing a number of architectural gems handed down from the Russian era, which hopefully will survive the mass construction/demolition mentality in vogue. Some of the old areas of Russian origin are coming down – having long fallen into neglect – while other sections are being restored.

Orientation

The main railway station is in the centre of town, surrounded by a cluster of hotels; the Songhua River is in the north, separating the city from Sun Island.

The Daoli District, in the section towards the banks of the Songhua River, houses the main shopping zone of Harbin and displays most of the historical buildings that give the city its character.

Information

Tourist Offices CITS (☎ 233-4925) is in a separate building in the grounds of the Swan Hotel, at 73 Zhongshan Lu on the No 3 bus route.

Far more useful and also conveniently located is the China Harbin Overseas Tourist Corporation (☎ 468-7875; fax 461-4259) on the 2nd floor of the charming Modern Hotel at 89 Zhongyang Dajie. It can arrange all sorts of tours and activities including hunting, skiing, 'cold water' fishing (on the vast Xingkai Lake in the east of the province) and tours to the Heilong River area. See the Heilong River Borderlands section later in this chapter for details.

Money The Bank of China is at 19 Hongjun Jie near the International Hotel. Any of the large hotels, including the nearby International Hotel, will change money for you.

Post & Communications There is a post office on the corner of Fendou Lu and Dongda Zhijie.

Daoliqu
(dàolǐqū)

Put wandering around the market areas and the streets high on your list. There's a very different kind of architectural presence in Harbin – Russian spires, cupolas, scalloped turrets and cobblestone streets. Walking along Zhongyang Dajie, and the side streets that run off it in the heart of the area known as Daoliqu, provides you with a museum of showcase buildings.

Harbin has many Orthodox churches *(dōngzhèng jiàotáng)*, but most were ransacked during the Cultural Revolution and have fallen into disrepair.

The **Church of St Sofia** is certainly worth a visit. When we were last in town, the buildings surrounding it were being pulled down to expose the church in all its glory. The brick church itself was boarded up, saplings were growing from the roof and there was no way to enter the structure, but it should be more accessible in the future. You can find the church on Toulong Jie, in between Zhaolin Jie and Diduan Jie.

Children's Railway
(értóng gōngyuán)

This railway in the Children's Park was built in 1956. It has 2km of track plied by a miniature diesel pulling seven cars with seating for 200; the round trip ('Beijing' to 'Harbin') takes 20 minutes. The train driver, ticket collectors, rail guards and support personnel are all kids under the age of 13.

You can take your kids there on bus No 8 from the southern end of Zhongyang Dajie.

Stalin Park
(sīdàlín gōngyuán)

Down by the river, this is a tacky strip stacked with statues; it's the main perambulating zone, with recreation clubs for the locals. A 42km embankment was constructed along the edge to curb the unruly Songhua River, hence the bizarre Flood Control Monument *(fánghóng shènglì jìniàn tǎ)*, which was built in 1958.

A resort feel holds sway in summer, with ice-cream stands, photo booths and boating trips along the river. Vendors sell cooked river snails, crickets in cages and boat tickets across to Sun Island and along the

Species Under Threat

China has four subspecies of tiger: the Bengal tiger *(Panthera tigris tigris)*, the South China tiger *(Panthera tigris amoyensis)*, the Indo-China tiger *(Panthera tigris corbetti)* and the North-Eastern, or Manchurian, tiger *(Panthera tigris altaica)*. All told there are probably no more than 100 left in the wilds of China.

The South China subspecies is among the most endangered and numbers only a few dozen in the wild and about 30 in zoos in both China and abroad. (Even when India launched its Project Tiger in 1973, there were 1800 tigers left in the territory – a number that was considered perilously low.) Unlike the Bengal and Manchurian tigers, which are found in several countries, the South China tiger is peculiar to China. Its plight began in the 1950s, with indiscriminate hunting and deforestation. At that time tigers were still fairly numerous in many southern provinces, especially in Hunan, Fujian, Guizhou and Jiangxi. Throughout the 50s and early 60s there were 'anti-pest' campaigns and many areas had their entire tiger populations wiped out. Today the subspecies exists only in the mountainous regions of south-west and south-east Hunan, and in northern Guangdong.

The Indo-China tiger has met a similar fate, and now numbers no more than 10, all of which are currently protected in Yunnan Province's Xishuangbanna Reserve.

The Manchurian tiger is also under serious threat, numbering no more than 50 in the wilds of north-eastern China, although there are larger numbers in Russia and North Korea. The Chinese government has set up a captive breeding programme which aims at raising Manchurian tigers in captivity, with the possibility of releasing them into the wilds at a later date. Currently, the programme has about 70 tigers in captivity; Siberia Tiger Park in Harbin, the capital of Heilongjiang Province, is part of this programme.

There's probably fewer than 10 Bengal tigers in China, but the figure is difficult to calculate as they often lope over borders. They live in the Xishuangbanna Autonomous Region and southern Yunnan near Myanmar (Burma) and Laos, in a few countries in western Yunnan bordering Myanmar, and in the subtropical mountainous region of south-eastern Tibet and neighbouring Assam. ■

Songhua River; all sorts of weird vessels claim to be able to ferry you here and there – even fibreglass monstrosities resembling chickens and sharks.

The river itself comes alive in winter, with ice-skating, ice-hockey, tobogganing and even ice sailing – vessels that sail on the ice surface, assisted by wind power and reaching speeds of 30 km/h. Equipment for each of these sports can be hired. Slightly madder folk astound visitors by swimming in gaps in the ice.

Sun Island
(tàiyángdǎo gōngyuán)
Facing Stalin Park and a ferry hop away is Sun Island, a sanatorium/recreational zone

covering 3800 hectares. Parks, gardens, forested areas and a 'water world' serve to siphon off tourists from the other side of the river. Helicopters can be hired here for short flights over Harbin (Y150).

Siberia Tiger Park can also be found in the north of the island. In summer there's swimming, picnics and camping; in winter it's skating and other sports. There are a number of restaurants and other facilities on Sun Island (see the boxed story on the following page). Boat tickets are available from sellers in Stalin Park. Buy a ticket from one of the government-run boat ticket vendors *(guóyíng chuánpiào)* as these only cost Y2 return. The private operators will fleece you.

Siberia Tiger Park

My first inkling that this was no boring day trip to the zoo came as I saw the cow being trussed up on the back of a pick-up when buying tickets. We all boarded a small minibus that was wrapped with wire caging, which slowly trundled through the tall portals of Siberia Tiger Park. I didn't notice that the pick-up had slipped in behind, sandwiched between us and another vehicle. The tigers were ahead of us now on a patch of grass, about six of them, huge and menacing and carefully examining the parade of vehicles in front; the cow was freed and it stumbled away, eyes bulging, as two tigers flashed towards it. It made a terrible noise as it was torn apart.

You could well get more than you bargained for at Siberia Tiger Park, a reserve dedicated to the breeding and conservation of the huge Manchurian tiger. There are currently about 30 at the park, and the ultimate aim is to release them into the wild so that they can fend for themselves and multiply. (Let's just hope that the 'wild' doesn't turn out to be Harbin's main street!)

The park, an offshoot of a Siberian tiger-breeding project, invites worrying comparisons with Jurassic Park – ashen-faced spectators locked in flimsy minivans, eyes darting for an escape route in case one of the burly beasts turns nasty.

The laughing drivers, displaying an edgy bravado, sit in front of a windscreen that is unprotected; so is the rear window. Worst of all, the side door, that even the weight of a stumbling drunk could fling open, is devoid of caging. (The minivans are the same as the ones that ply routes from city to town all over China, simply wrapped in a bit of chicken wire.) You can't help thinking that the tigers, who periodically give the vehicles a long, studied look, seem to know that the side door (which regularly opens on other vehicles so that the driver can throw out chicken appetisers) is the way out, and consequently, the way in.

You are reassured by the drivers that the tigers are bred in captivity and are harmless, that they are regularly fed and that they are not aggressive (unless you are a cow). But what if one of the tigers has a bad toothache, or a thorn it its paw, or is just plain psychotic? The whole enterprise needs careful regulation and security, but this is unlikely in a country that is increasingly a bandwagon of 'openess' and experiment.

Siberia Tiger Park can be reached by taking a boat to Sun Island, and then by either bus (Y40) or minibus/taxi (Y40) from beside the pier, which is a 20 minute drive from the enclosure. Entry is Y30. Don't take the kiddies along, unless you want them to experience nature's savagery, up close and personal.

Damian Harper

Japanese Germ Warfare Experimental Base – 731 Division

(rìběn xìjūn shíyàn jīdì – 731 bùduì)

If you haven't visited concentration camps such as Belsen or Auschwitz, a similar lesson in the horrors of extermination can be learnt at this base.

In 1939, the Japanese army set up a top-secret, germ-warfare research centre here. Japanese medical experts experimented on Chinese, Soviet, Korean, British and other prisoners. Over 4000 were exterminated in bestial fashion: some were frozen or infected with bubonic plague, others were injected with syphilis and many were roasted alive in furnaces.

When the Soviets took back Harbin in 1945, the Japanese blew up the base. The secret could have remained buried forever, but a tenacious Japanese journalist dragged out the truth in the 1980s.

Japan's medical profession was rocked by the news that some of its leading members had a criminal past which had hitherto escaped detection. Another disturbing angle to the story was the claim that the Americans had granted freedom to the perpetrators of these crimes in return for their research data.

As you walk in, you are met by a sign in Chinese which naturally says 'The friendship between the Japanese and Chinese people is everlasting'. Right. Despite the importance of such monuments, the exhibition consists only of two rooms with captions in Chinese, plus a nearby vestige of the original base.

Opening times are 8.30 to 11.30 am and 1 to 4 pm. The ticket price for foreigners is Y10. To get to the base, take bus No 338 from the main railway station to the terminal, which is close to Pingfang District (about 10km).

Ice Lantern Festival
(bīngdēng jié)
If you don't mind the cold, then you shouldn't miss Harbin's main drawcard, the Ice Lantern Festival in Zhaolin Park. Officially, it's held from 5 January to 15 February, although in reality it may start a week earlier and glisten into March.

Fanciful sculptures are produced in the shapes of animals, plants, buildings or motifs taken from legends. Some of the larger sculptures have included a miniature Great Wall of China and a scaled-down Forbidden City. At night the sculptures are illuminated from the inside with coloured lights, turning the place into a temporary fantasy land. Ticket prices vary from year to year, but are costly.

Music Festival
(yīnyuèhuì)
In warmer times, there's the Harbin Music Festival, a 12 day event that takes place in July (it was suspended during the Cultural Revolution).

Places to Stay
During Harbin's Ice Lantern Festival (January and February) hotel prices are at least 20% higher than those listed here and rooms of any sort can be difficult to find. As you exit the railway station, you will be pounced upon by hotel touts who will drag you off to some cheap dive in the locality. If what you want is budget accommodation, then tag along, but scope the room first.

For those of you who want to camp (yěyíng), there are cheap tents flung up on the southern shores of Sun Island which cost Y25 a night. Conditions are primitive and it's a bit nippy in winter.

It seems that the PSB cares less and less in Harbin as to who stays where. They even have their own hostel which is a first. Imaginatively named *The Hostel of the PSB* (☎ 360-6055) (gōng'ānchù zhāodàisuǒ) it's near the railway station and has dorm beds from Y25 to Y80. It's seedy and makeshift and trains go by every five minutes, but you get what you pay for. As you come out of the railway station turn right and it's on a small turning to the right off Tielu Jie.

As you exit the main railway station, just off to your right is the 19 storey *Tianzhu Hotel* (☎ 363-4266; fax 364-3720) (tiānzhú bīnguǎn) at 6 Songhuajiang Jie. This is an excellent place to stay, well located and with cheap rooms; it's normally bursting with Russians. Doubles start at Y150 and breakfast is included, although you may need to remind them of this.

Similarly besieged by Russian contingents is the *Beiyuan Hotel* (☎ 364-2529; fax 362-931) (běiyuàn fàndiàn) which directly faces the railway station. Cheap doubles are Y150 and Y180.

The *Overseas Chinese Hotel* (☎ 364-1341; fax 362-3429) (huáqiáo fàndiàn) is at 52 Hongjun Jie, within walking distance of the main railway station. A refuge of Hong Kongers and southerners coming to build snowmen in Harbin, it's often full. Doubles start at Y200.

The *International Hotel* (☎ 364-1441; fax 362-5651) (guójì fàndiàn), at 124 Xidazhi Jie, is just off Hongjun Jie and less than 1km from the railway station. Overpriced doubles are Y468, but breakfast is thrown in free as a consolation.

HEILONGJIANG

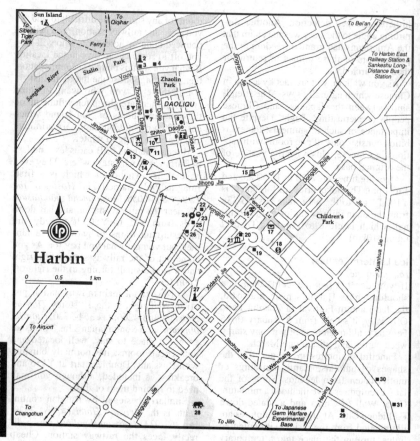

The *Modern Hotel* (☎ 4615-846; fax 4614-997) *(mǎdiēěr bīnguǎn)* at 89 Zhongyang Dajie was, in fact, built in 1906. This is a wonderful hotel, full of character and style and the staff are polite and friendly. It's also in a stunning location, in Daoliqu. The rooms are gorgeous, with the cheapest double costing Y480.

Not far away and towards the Songhua River is the *Songhuajiang Gloria Inn* (☎ 463-8855; fax 463-8533) *(sōnghuājiāng kǎilái shāngwùjiǔdiàn)* at 257 Zhongyang Dajie. It offers decent rooms and service in a

prime location, with prices to match. Rooms start at Y588. Next door is the *Nationality Hotel* (☎ 467-4668; fax 467-4058) *(mínzú bīnguǎn)*, at 111 Youyi Lu, which has doubles from Y364 (plus 10% service).

The *Swan Hotel* (☎ 230-0201; fax 230-4895) *(tiān'é fàndiàn)* is in a far-flung part of town at 73 Zhongshan Lu. Doubles start from Y450. Minibus No 103, which runs down Zhongshan Lu, can take you to the hotel for Y2.

Also far-flung is the *CAAC Hotel of Heilongjiang* (☎ 230-6188; fax 230-3458)

HARBIN 哈尔滨

PLACES TO STAY
1 Camping Zone
 野营区
3 Songhuajiang Gloria Inn
 松花江凯莱商务酒店
4 Nationality Hotel
 民族宾馆
6 Modern Hotel
 马迭尔宾馆
14 Holiday Inn
 万达假日酒店
19 International Hotel;
 Beifang Hotel
 国际饭店、北方大厦
20 Overseas Chinese Hotel
 华侨饭店
22 Beiyuan Hotel
 北苑饭店
25 Tianzhu Hotel
 天竹宾馆
26 The Hostel of the PSB
 公安处招待所

29 Flamingo Hotel
 双鹤宾馆
30 CAAC Hotel; CAAC
 民航大厦、中国民航
31 Swan Hotel; CITS
 天鹅饭店
 中国国际旅行社

PLACES TO EAT
5 Huamei Western
 Restaurant
 华梅西餐厅
7 KFC
 肯德鸡
10 Futailou Restaurant
 福泰楼饭店
11 Laodu Yichu Restaurant
 老都一处

OTHER
2 Flood Control Monument
 防洪胜利纪念塔
8 Foreign Languages
 Bookstore
 外文书店

9 Church of St Sophia
 圣索菲亚教堂
12 PSB
 公安局外事科
13 Oriental City
 东方娱乐城
15 Martyrs' Museum
 东北烈士馆
16 Telephone Office
 电信局
17 Post Office
 邮局
18 Bank of China
 中国银行
21 Provincial Museum
 省博物馆
23 Long-Distance Bus Station
 公路客运站
24 Main Railway Station
 哈尔滨火车站
27 Mao Statue
 毛主席像
28 Harbin Zoo
 哈尔滨动物园

(hēilóngjiāngshěng mínhángdàshà), at 101 Zhongshan Lu, where doubles cost from Y460 and you can also book air tickets.

The *Flamingo Hotel* (☎ 263-6698; fax 265-7028) (shuānghè bīnguǎn) is also a long way from the action at 118 Minsheng Lu. It's a lot of effort to pay Y510 for a double with a 15% service charge.

Just on the cusp of Harbin's attractive Daoliqu district is *Holiday Inn* (☎ 422-6666; fax 422-1661) (wàndá jiàrì jiǔdiàn) at 90 Jingwei Jie. The hotel is at hand for those in need of four star service and expert hotel management, plus a decent range of restaurants. Rooms start at Y814.

Places to Eat
A practice almost exclusive to Harbin is that red lanterns hang above the door outside every restaurant. It's a rating system – the more lanterns, the higher the standard and price. Red lanterns mean Chinese food, and blue denotes pork-free cuisine from the Muslim Hui minority (mainly lamb dishes).

Harbin has also long been famous for expensive culinary exotica, such as grilled bear paws, deer nostrils and Siberian tiger testicles. Fortunately, Beijing now takes a dim view of serving up endangered species and substitutes have taken their place.

If you want crispy Beijing duck washed down with scrumptious beer, the *Futailou Restaurant* (☎ 461-4721) (fútàilóu fàndiàn) at 25 Xi Shisandao Jie comes prepared with its own brew (German formula). The fruity beer alone is a welcome release from the standard Chinese stuff, although it's not cheap at Y26 for a medium-sized flagon.

Opposite the Futailou is the *Laodu Yichu* (lǎodū yīchù), a well known dumpling (jiǎozi) restaurant. A large plateful of these will cost you Y24.

Next to the Modern Hotel in Xiba Daojie is *Bomba Hamburger* which serves up western food such as burgers, fries, fried chicken and banana splits. *KFC* can be found nearby. Also in the vicinity, on Zhongyang Dajie, are a few *bakeries* that serve excellent bread and croissants.

HEILONGJIANG

Despite the name, the *Huamei Western Restaurant* (☎ 461-7368) *(huáméi xī cān-tīng)*, just opposite the Modern Hotel on Zhongyang Dajie, is the place to go for Russian food.

Getting There & Away

Air CAAC (☎ 262-7070) can be found in the hotel of the same name at 101 Zhong-shan Lu. It also has a ticketing office next to the International Hotel on Hongjun Jie. Twice weekly flights go to Hong Kong (Y290). CAAC and Aeroflot (☎ 364-1441) both offer international flights to Kha-barovsk in Siberia and twice-weekly flights to Vladivostok (Y1330).

A huge number of domestic destinations can be reached from Harbin including Beijing (Y770), Shanghai (Y1410), Guang-zhou (Y2030), Shenzhen (Y2760), Heihe (Y390) and Shenyang (Y380).

Bus The main long-distance bus station is located directly opposite the railway station.

Destinations include Tianjin (Y180), Jilin (Y28), Jiamusi (Y63, sleeper), Shenyang (Y84, sleeper), (Y188, sleeper), Qiqihar (Y47) and Dalian (Y147, sleeper).

Train There are departures to Jiamusi (Y40), Qiqihar (Y32), Mudanjiang (Y39), Suifenhe (Y59), Changchun (Y19, four hours), Dalian (Y123), Beijing (Y98, 18 hours) and Ji'nan (Y93), among others. Rail connections to Qiqihar, Mudanjiang and Jiamusi are regular, but slow.

For travellers on the Trans-Siberian Railway, Harbin is a possible starting or finishing point, but it is very tricky getting hold of tickets. For more information try CITS (☎ 233-4925), the China Harbin Overseas Tourist Corporation (☎ 468-7875) or ask directly at the railway station. You could also try the Tianzhu Hotel or the Beiyuan Hotel near the railway station – because so many Russians stay at these hotels, they should be able to either help you procure a ticket or provide you with information.

Getting Around

To/From the Airport Harbin's airport is 46km from town and the journey takes at least one hour, half of which is spent in the traffic-clogged streets near the city centre.

Shuttle buses depart for the airport from the CAAC office and cost Y10; buy tickets on the bus, not inside the office. Buses depart about 2½ hours before scheduled flight departure times. The CAAC shuttle bus is far preferable to taxis, which charge around Y150 to reach the airport.

Bus Harbin's many buses start running at 5 am and finish at 10 pm (9.30 pm in winter). Trolley-bus Nos 103 and 101 can take you from Stalin Park to the railway station. Minibuses also follow this route and cost Y2.

Boat From May to September it is possible to travel by boat to Jiamusi and Tongjiang and points in between on the Songhua River. Jet-cats take five hours for the journey to Jiamusi, while large, slow boats take 16 to 20 hours. Ask at the China Harbin Overseas Tourist Corporation in the Modern Hotel or CITS for tickets and details.

Tickets are also available in Stalin Park for boat cruises up and down the Songhua River (Y30).

AROUND HARBIN
Ski Resorts
(huáxuě chǎng)

The **Yuquan** hunting grounds, 65km from Harbin, have skiing facilities, but the em-phasis is mainly on beginners. If you want to go hunting instead, you pay for the animals you've slaughtered, rather than an entrance fee. Make inquiries at the China Harbin Overseas Tourist Corporation in the Modern Hotel or ask at CITS.

Yabuli is about 200km (four hours by train) east of Harbin and was the site of the 1996 Asian Winter Games. Dagoukui Mountain, the actual ski area, is a 25km ride by jeep from the main town of Yabuli.

The main hotel is the *Windmill Hotel*

(☎ 339-0088) (*fēngchē shān-zhuāng*), in the town itself, which has doubles from Y420 (expect a price increase during peak season). Information and room bookings can also be acquired in Harbin (☎ 367-8616). Accommodation, meals and ski rental are available at a lodge near the ski area. A package including meals, lodging, ski rental and lift passes costs Y250 to Y400 per day. Facilities also exist for cross-country skiing.

MUDANJIANG
(*mŭdānjiāng*)

A nondescript city of more than one million people, Mudanjiang's only interest to travellers is its function as a staging post for visits to nearby Jingbo Lake (see next section).

Places to Stay

The *Beishan Hotel* (☎ 652-5788) (*bĕishān bīnguăn*) is on Xinhua Lu (opposite the park) about 1km north of the railway station. Dorm beds are Y80, although foreigners can expect a 100% surcharge. CITS is installed here.

The other place accepting foreigners is the *Mudanjiang Hotel* (☎ 622-5633; fax 622-7947) (*mŭdānjiāng bīnguăn*) at 85 Guanghua Jie, 1km east of the railway station. Doubles are Y265.

Getting There & Away

There are flights from Mudanjiang to Beijing, Dalian, Guangzhou, Shanghai, Shenyang and Yantai. The usual approach by rail to Mudanjiang is from Harbin.

JINGBO LAKE
(*jìngpò hú*)

The name means mirror lake, and covers an area of 90 sq km; it's 45km long from north to south, with a minimum width of 600m and a maximum of 6km. Studded with small islands, the lake is extremely popular with visiting Russians, and the place has been developed as a resort, with hotels, recreation centres and even a post office.

Unfortunately, the natural charm of the

area has been destroyed by the discarded rubbish left behind by foraging tribes of tourists. The place has little majesty left and the surrounding greenery is pockmarked with red-roofed resort-style hotels and villas.

Apart from speeding about from island to islet by boat, or turning off the beaten path and escaping into the woods that ring the lake, the main pastime is fishing. The season is from June to August, and tackle and boats can be hired (prices negotiable). Different varieties of carp (silver, black, red-tailed, crucian) are the trophies. Autumn is an attractive season to visit the lake, when the leaves change colour.

Diaoshuilou Waterfall (20m high, 40m wide) is an attractive spectacle that swells in size during the rainy season (late summer). Some foreigners like to come here and amaze the Chinese by diving into the pools.

The buses from Dongjing and Mudanjiang will drop you off at a point occupied by hotels and ticket vendors who will try and strong-arm you on to one of the speedboats as you get off the bus. Summer constitutes a battle against vendors of every conceivable shape and size who prey off the visiting hordes – try and avoid it.

Places to Stay

A myriad of hotels encircles the lake, though many of them are out of bounds to foreigners. Cheap rooms are available at the *Shanzhuang Binguan* (☎ 627-0012) (*shānzhuāng bīnguăn*) which has beds for Y80. Buses from Dongjing will drop you off near the hotel.

The *Jingbo Lake Hotel* (☎ 627-0091) (*jìngbóhú bīnguăn*) is the more upmarket option with doubles from Y450.

Getting There & Away

The best approach is by rail from Harbin. First take a train to Mudanjiang (Y42) and then change trains to Dongjing (Y4). From there, it's one hour by minibus (Y6) to the lake.

If you get off at Mudanjiang, it's three hours by bus to Jingbo Lake. Buses depart between 6 and 7 am from the square in front of Mudanjiang railway station, in summer only (from June to September). There are three connections a day between Mudanjiang and Dongjing.

There are also slower connections by rail from Tumen (one train daily, about six hours), Suifenhe (one train daily, five hours from Mudanjiang) and Jiamusi (two trains a day, about 10 hours).

If you are on a tour of the lakes of the north-east, it is possible to take the bus from Baihe, near Tianchi in Jilin Province, to Dunhua and from there take the bus to Dongjing. The bus from Dunhua will pass Jingbo Lake, but it is better to carry on to Dongjing and backtrack as you will be dropped off miles from any transport at the edge of the lake.

SUIFENHE
(suífēnhé)

This town achieved commercial importance in 1903 with the opening of the South Manchurian Railway, which was a vital link in the original Trans-Siberian route running from Vladivostok to Moscow via Manchuria.

The railway was later re-routed via Khabarovsk to Vladivostok and Nakhodka. After the demise of the USSR in 1991, Suifenhe has, like other borderland outposts, enjoyed a spasmodic growth in cross-border trade and tourism. The self-flattering nickname of 'Little Moscow of the East' harbours an element of truth as most of the buildings are Russian leftovers in the elegant, turn-of-the-century ginger-bread style – reminders of pre-revolutionary times. Apart from that, however, there is not much left in the way of sights.

The prize for many is Vladivostok on the other side of the border and, with the right paperwork, it is attainable. However, you will need to have sorted out a Russian visa in Beijing and, if you plan to re-enter China, a re-entry visa as well.

Getting There & Away
The Harbin to Suifenhe train leaves Harbin at 8.45 pm and passes through Mudanjiang at 3.30 am, arriving in Suifenhe at 7.34 am. Unless you are a night owl, it is eminently sensible to depart from Harbin.

An international passenger train departs for Vladivostok twice a week (Friday and Monday), leaving at 9.30 am and passing through Pogranichny (Grodekovo). Pogranichny is a small town which borders China near Suifenhe, 210km from Vladivostok. Pogranichny is also connected by bus and taxi with Ussuriysk and Vladivostok.

WUDALIANCHI
(wǔdàliánchí)

Wudalianchi (Five Large Connected Lakes) is a nature reserve and health spot which has also been turned into a 'volcano museum'. Despite being voted one of the top 40 sights in China in 1992, Wudalianchi is still primarily the province of geologists, vulcanologists and the infirm.

This area, in the north of the province, has a long history of volcanic activity. The most recent eruptions were during 1719 and 1720, when lava from craters blocked the nearby Bei River and formed this series of five barrier lakes. The malodorous mineral springs are the source of legendary cures and thus the main attraction for hordes of chronically ill, who slurp the waters or slap mud onto themselves. To increase blood pressure, immerse your feet in a basin of the water; to decrease blood pressure, immerse your head. Baldness, cerebral haemorrhages, skin diseases and gastric ulcers are a few of the ailments miraculously cured by drinking the water or applying mudpacks, although some of the cures are only temporary.

As for the volcanoes themselves, don't come expecting Mt Fuji or Krakatoa. Basically, the volcano museum has steam fumaroles, hot springs and a little geothermal activity here and there, but not much else.

To liven up the scenery, there is a sort of Ice Lantern Festival like the one in Harbin, only this one is year-round. The ice sculptures are inside caves which have a steady temperature of -10°C (14°F), even during

The Oroqen

Traditionally, the Oroqen minority live the nomadic life of forest hunters. Recent estimates put their numbers at about 4000, scattered over a vast area of north-western Heilongjiang and Inner Mongolia.

Their traditional tent, called a *xianrenzhu*, is covered with birch bark in the summer and deerskin in the winter. Hunting as well raising reindeer are still their main activities. A major source of income is deer hunting since the deer's embryo, antlers, penis and tail are highly prized in Chinese medicine.

The Oroqen lifestyle is changing rapidly, although they retain their self-sufficiency. Boots, clothes and sleeping bags are made from deerskins; baskets, eating utensils and canoes are made from birch bark; and horses or reindeer provide transport. Their food consists mostly of meat, fish and wild plants. Oroqens are particularly fond of raw deer liver washed down with fermented mare's milk. Meat is often preserved by drying and smoking.

Interesting facets of their religion included (and probably still do to some degree) a belief in spirits and in consulting shamans. It was once taboo to kill bears. If this happened, perhaps in self-defence, a complicated rite was performed to ask the bear's 'forgiveness' and its bones were spread in the open on a tall frame of willow branches. This 'wind burial' was also the standard funeral for a human. Our word shaman means an 'agitated or frenzied person' in the Manchu-Tungus language. Such persons could enter a trance, become 'possessed' by a spirit and then officiate at religious ceremonies.

It's hard to determine how much of Oroqen culture has remained intact. Official publications trumpet stories of a wondrous change from primitive nomadism to settled consumerism complete with satellite TV. Meng Pinggu, a probably fictional Oroqen, was quoted in the *China Daily* as saying, 'Now we Oroqens can see movies at home'.

The Oroqens – China's Nomadic Hunters by Qiu Pu is a very informative publication, provided you skip the political salad dressing. ∎

summer. Coloured lights inside the sculptures create a psychedelic effect.

A month long festival, the 'water drinking festival', is held at the start of May every year by the local Daur minority. Activities include music, dance and unbridled drinking of the local waters.

Hotels such as the *Dragon Spring Hotel* (*lóngquán bīnguǎn*) are becoming more and more expensive, but there is a choice of 38 sanatoriums where you can stay.

To reach Wudalianchi, take a six hour train ride northwards from Harbin to Bei'an, where there are regular minibuses covering the 60km to the lakes (Y12); large buses also cover the route for Y8. Alternatively, if you are coming from the north, there are buses every morning from Heihe to the lakes. Entry to the lakes is Y23.

HEILONG RIVER BORDERLANDS
(*hēilóngjiāng biānjìng*)

Much of the north-eastern border between China and Siberia follows the course of the Heilong River (Black Dragon River), also known to the Russians as the Amur River. Most places along this river are open to foreigners, but ask the PSB anyway just to be sure – international borders and ethnic minority areas are sensitive places. It should be possible to see some Siberian forest and the dwindling settlements of northern tribes, such as the Oroqen, Daur, Ewenki and Hezhen.

Ask in Harbin at either CITS or the China Harbin Overseas Tourist Corporation in the Modern Hotel for details about boat tours along the Songhua River to Tongjiang and then on to Heihe, Huma and beyond on the Heilong River. Opportunities exist for looking at Russian settlements, especially Blagoveshchensk, a large Russian port opposite Heihe.

Assuming you have at least two weeks to spare and are flexible about transport, an independent trip should also be viable during the summer – take a small medical kit and insect repellent. Apart from the boat, other connections with the borderlands include flights to Heihe from Harbin and daily trains and buses.

Mohe
(mòhé)
Natural wonders are the attraction at Mohe, China's northernmost town, sometimes known as the Arctic of China. In mid-June, the sun is visible in the sky for as long as 22 hours. The northern lights (aurora borealis) are another colourful phenomenon seen in the sky at Mohe. China's lowest absolute temperature of -52.3°C (-62°F) was recorded here in 1965; on normal winter days temperatures of -40°C (-40°F) are common.

During May 1987 this area was devastated by China's worst forest fire in living memory. The towns of Mohe and Xilinji were completely gutted, more than 200 people died and over one million hectares of forest were destroyed.

Try for a permit at the PSB in Jagdaqi *(jiāgédáqí)* in Inner Mongolia. Getting to Mohe requires a train trip north from Jagdaqi to Gulian, followed by a 34km bus ride.

Heihe
(hēihé)
Heihe's claim to fame is that it borders Russia. Due to the recent thawing in relations between the two countries, there is a steadily increasing amount of cross-border trade and even a fledgling tourist industry. Chinese tour groups are now able to cross the border to Blagoveshchensk.

Street stalls in Heihe sell Russian army greatcoats, boots, helmets, binoculars and other Cold War surplus. Chinese tourists don't find much to buy in Russia, but are impressed to see a city where nobody spits and people actually stand in line.

There are problems for foreigners wishing to visit Blagoveshchensk. A Russian tourist visa is needed, and a re-entry visa for China would also be necessary. All this must be arranged in Beijing, not in Heihe. In theory, one could cross the border at Blagoveshchensk and take a train to link up with the Trans-Siberian Railway at Belogorsk, 109km away, continue to Moscow and then on to Europe. This would require a tourist visa.

Those without a Russian visa can console themselves with hour-long cruises of the Heilong River from Heihe (Y10); binoculars can be rented on board with which you can survey the far side.

The main hotel in Heihe accepting foreigners is the *Heihe International Hotel* (☎ 227-013) *(heīhé guójì fàndiàn)* at 48 Wangsu Jie; doubles are Y230.

Flights between Harbin and Heihe run four times weekly. Boats also connect Heihe with Mohe and Tongjian. Daily trains run to and from Harbin, but be aware that the railway station is 5km from Heihe and tickets for Harbin must be bought in the city centre from the ticket office at the junction between Xinghua Jie and Guandu Lu. Buses also run to and from Heihe from Harbin (Y62), Beian (Y30), Wudalianchi (Y36) and Qiqihar (Y50).

Tongjiang
(tóngjiāng)
Tongjiang lies at the junction of the Songhua and Heilong rivers. They swell to a combined width of 10km, but their respective colours, black for the Heilong and yellow for the Songhua, don't mix until later.

The Hezhen minority, a mere 1300 people, lives almost entirely from fishing in this region. A local delicacy is sliced, raw fish with a spicy vinegar sauce. Apart from carp and salmon, the real whopper here is the huso sturgeon *(huáng yú)*, which can grow as long as 3m and weigh up to 500kg!

Tongjiang has boat and bus connections with Jiamusi; boats also connect with Heihe and Harbin. Trains reach nearby Fujin, from where buses connect with Tongjiang.

QIQIHAR
(qíqíhā'ěr)
Qiqihar (the name is taken from the Daur word for 'borderland') is the gateway to the Zhalong Nature Reserve, a bird-watching area 35km to the south-east. It's also one of the oldest settlements in the north-east and was established in 1684. Highest and lowest temperatures over the year achieve a nice symmetry with 39°C (102.2F) in July and -39°C (-38.2°F) in January. The town itself is industrialised, with a population of more than one million, and produces locomotives, mining equipment, steel, machine tools and motor vehicles. There's not much to see here – a zoo, the riverside and the ice-carving festival from January to March.

Information
The CITS office (☎ 271-5836) is in the Hubin Hotel and the staff are very friendly. They can give you a lot of advice about the best places for watching birds.

Places to Stay
The *Hubin Hotel* (☎ 271-3121) *(húbīn fàndiàn)* at 4 Wenhua Dajie is one of the cheapest places that accepts foreigners; doubles are Y304. An alternative is the

---

Rare Cranes Find Sanctuary

The Zhalong Nature Reserve, one of China's first, was set up in 1979. In 1981 the Chinese Ministry of Forestry invited Dr George Archibald (director of the International Crane Foundation – ICF) and Wolf Brehm (director of Vogelpark Walsrode, Germany) to help set up a crane centre at Zhalong.

Of the 15 species of cranes in the world, eight are found in China and six are found at Zhalong. Four of the species that migrate here are on the endangered list: the red-crowned crane, the white-naped crane, the Siberian crane and the hooded crane. Both the red-crowned and white-naped cranes breed at Zhalong (as do the common and demoiselle cranes), while hooded and Siberian cranes use Zhalong as a stopover.

The centre of attention is the red-crowned crane, a fragile creature whose numbers at Zhalong (estimated to be only 100 in 1979) were threatened by drainage of the wetlands for farming. The near-extinct bird is, ironically, the ancient symbol of immortality and has long been a symbol of longevity and good luck in the Chinese, Korean and Japanese cultures. With some help from overseas experts, the ecosystem at Zhalong has been studied and improved, and the number of these rare birds has risen.

Several hand-reared (domesticated) red-crowned and white-naped cranes are kept in a pen at the sanctuary for viewing and study.

On the eve of their 'long march' southwards in October, large numbers of cranes can be seen wheeling around, as if in farewell. The birds have been banded to unlock the mystery of their winter migration grounds (in either Korea or southern China).

Since the establishment of the ICF, George Archibald and Ron Sauey have managed to create a 'crane bank' in Wisconsin, USA, stocking 14 of the 15 known species. They've even convinced the North Koreans to set up bird reserves in the mine-studded demilitarised zone between North and South Korea, and the travel baggage of these two countries includes suitcases full of Siberian crane-eggs picked up in Moscow (on one trip a chick hatched en route was nicknamed 'Aeroflot'). Last on the egg list for the ICF is the black-necked crane, whose home is in remote Tibet and for whom captive breeding may be the final hope. ■

Crane City Hotel (☎ 272-2541; fax 271-3367) *(hèchéng bīnguǎn)*, behind the Hubin, which has doubles at Y330. You can reach the Hubin Hotel on trolley-bus No 15 – it's seven stops from the railway station.

Getting There & Away

There are flights between Qiqihar and Beijing, Dalian, Guangzhou, Shanghai and Shenyang. Qiqihar is linked directly by rail to Beijing (about 22 hours) via Harbin (about four hours); Qiqihar is also connected by rail to the northern towns of Bei'an and Heihe. Look after your valuables when travelling this route, as it's a notorious route for theft. There are also buses to Harbin, but it's easier to purchase train tickets.

ZHALONG NATURE RESERVE

(zhālóng zìrán bǎohùqū)

The Zhalong Nature Reserve is at the north-west tip of a giant marsh, and is made up of about 210,000 hectares of reeds, moss and ponds. It lies strategically on a bird-migration path which extends from the Russian Arctic, around the Gobi Desert and down into South-East Asia, and some 236 different species of bird are found there, including storks, swans, geese,

ducks, herons, harriers, grebes and egrets. The tens of thousands of winged migrants arrive from April to May, rear their young from June to August, and depart from September to October.

Birds will be birds – they value their privacy. While some of the red-crowned cranes are more than 1.5m tall, the reed cover is taller. The best time to visit is in spring before the reeds have a chance to grow.

Places to Stay

The modest *Zhalong Hotel* is relatively cheap and offers tours through the freshwater marshes of the reserve in flat-bottom boats. The area is mainly of interest to the patient binoculared and rubber-booted ornithologist.

Getting There & Away

Zhalong is linked to Qiqihar by a good road, but there's not much traffic along it. Buses leave for Zhalong (Y5) from the bus station at the western end of Longhua Lu in Qiqihar. Departures are at 6 am, 12.20 and 3.30 pm and the journey takes one hour. Try and avoid the 3.30 pm bus as it returns soon after from Zhalong and is the last bus returning to Qiqihar.

Shanxi 山西

Shanxi (*shānxī*) was one of the earliest centres of Chinese civilisation and formed the state of Qin. After Qin Shihuang unified the Chinese states, the northern part of Shanxi became the key defensive bulwark between the Chinese and the nomadic tribes to the north.

Despite the Great Wall, the nomadic tribes still managed to break through and used Shanxi as a base for their conquest of the Middle Kingdom.

When the Tang Dynasty fell, the political centre of China moved away from the north-west. Shanxi went into a rapid economic decline, although its importance in the northern defence network remained paramount.

It was not until the intrusion of the foreign powers into China that any industrialisation got under way. When the Japanese invaded China in the 1930s they carried out development of industry and coal mining around the capital of Taiyuan. True to form, Shanxi was a bastion of resistance to this invasion from the north, this time through the Communist guerrillas who operated in the mountainous regions.

After 1949, the Communist government began to exploit Shanxi's mineral and ore deposits, and developed Datong and Taiyuan as major industrial centres. China's biggest coal mines can be found near these cities, and the province accounts for a third of China's known iron and coal deposits.

Shanxi means West of the Mountains, the mountains being the Taihang Range, which forms the province's eastern border. To the west it is bordered by the Yellow River. The province's population of about 31 million people is surprisingly small by Chinese standards, unless you consider the fact that almost 70% of the province is mountainous.

Along with its mineral deposits, Shanxi is rich in history. This is especially true of the northern half, which is a virtual gold

Shanxi Facts & Highlights

Area: 156,000 sq km

Population: 31.1 million

Capital: Taiyuan

Highlights

- Yungang Buddhist Caves, crowded with figures and frescoes.
- The 1400-year-old Hanging Monastery, 75 km south-east of Datong.
- Taihuai, a peaceful monastic village in the picturesque Wutaishan mountain range.

mine of temples, monasteries and cave-temples – a reminder that this was once the political and cultural centre of China. Among these, the main attraction for travellers is the Yungang Buddhist Caves at Datong.

TAIYUAN
(tàiyuán)

Taiyuan, provincial capital and industrial sprawl often shrouded in fog, no doubt thick with all kinds of nasty particulate matter, has a few attractions, but little to make it worth a special trip. It is, however, more cosmopolitan than its northern neighbour, Datong.

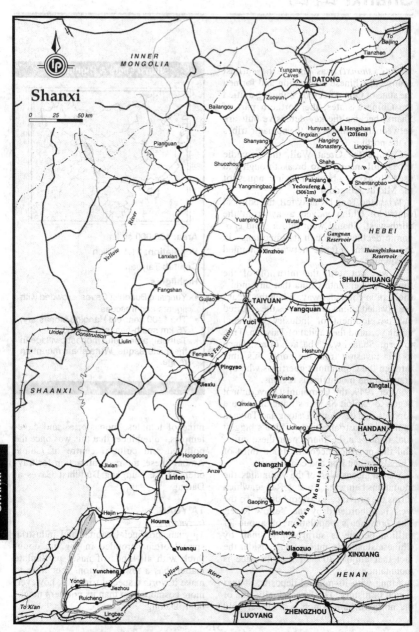

Shanxi

0   25   50 km

History

The first settlements on the site of modern-day Taiyuan date back 2500 years. By the 13th century it had developed into what Marco Polo referred to as 'a prosperous city, a great centre of trade and industry'. But it was also the site of constant armed conflict, sitting squarely on the path by which successive northern invaders entered China. There were once 27 temples here dedicated to the god of war.

In the latter part of the 19th century, Taiyuan moved rapidly towards industrialisation. Between 1889 and 1910 Taiyuan gained a train link to Hebei, electricity and a telephone system, not to mention a university and military academy. Development was pushed along by the warlord Yan Xishan, who ruled Shanxi virtually as his own private empire after the fall of the Manchu Dynasty.

Today, the city looks much like its modern counterparts Zhengzhou and Luoyang, with wide, tree-lined avenues and large residential blocks. Industry is concentrated north of the city.

Information

Tourist Office CITS (☎ 704-2125) is in the south of town on Pinging Lu in the Guolü building *(guólǚdàshà)*.

PSB The PSB foreign affairs office is at No 9 Houjia Lane, near May 1st Square, and is open Monday to Friday from 8 am to noon and 2.30 to 5.30 pm.

Money The Bank of China has its main branch on Yingze Dajie, east of Xinjian Lu, and can change money, including travellers cheques, daily from 8.30 am to noon and 2.30 to 5.30 pm. The tourist hotels also change money.

Post & Communications The main post and telephone office is in a white multi-storey building diagonally opposite the railway station. There is also a modern telecommunications centre on the corner of Yingze Dajie and Jiefang Lu.

Chongshan Monastery

(chóngshàn sì)

This Buddhist monastery was built towards the end of the 14th century on the site of a monastery, said to date back to the 6th or 7th century. The main hall contains three impressive statues; the central figure is Guanyin, the goddess of mercy with 1000 hands and eyes.

Beautifully illustrated book covers show scenes from the life of Buddha. Also on display are some Buddhist scriptures of the Song, Yuan, Ming and Qing dynasties. The monastery is on a side street running east off Wuyi Lu. Hours are 8 am to 5 pm daily (admission Y6).

Twin Pagoda Temple

(shuāngtǎ sì)

This temple has two Ming Dynasty pagodas, each a 13 storey octagonal structure almost 55m high. The pagodas are built entirely of bricks carved with brackets and cornices to imitate ancient Chinese wooden pagodas.

You can get halfway there by taking the No 19 bus from in front of the railway station and getting off one stop after the railway bridge. From there walk the few steps back to Shuangta Beilu, turn left (south) and follow this road for 20 minutes to the temple. It's open daily from 8 am to 5 pm (admission Y6).

Provincial Museum

(shānxī shěng bówùguǎn)

This is on Qifeng Jie, north-west of May 1st Square. The museum is in the Chunyang Palace *(chúnyáng gōng)*, which used to be a temple for offering sacrifices to the Taoist priest Lu Dongbin, who lived during the Tang Dynasty. The temple was built during the Ming and Qing dynasties. Hours are 9 am to 6 pm daily and entry is Y3.

Places to Stay & Eat

For budget travellers, Taiyuan is bad news. It's almost as if the PSB hunted down all the cheap hotels that took foreigners and threatened them with dire consequences if they did so again.

SHANXI

You might try the *Tianhe Hotel* (☎ 407-5054) *(tiánhé dàshà)*, at No 11 Gongyu Lane, a small street leading south from the railway station. Officially, it can't accept foreigners, but seems willing to take the occasional backpacker. There are dorm beds in quads/triples for Y15/32 and doubles with attached bath for Y120. There's a few similar places around the railway station where you may be able to talk your way into a cheap dorm bed.

Failing that, the next cheapest option is the *Shanxi Electric Power Hotel* (☎ 404-

1784) *(shānxī diànlì dàshà)*, about 300m west of the railway station on Yingze Dajie. Doubles/triples with shared bath are Y80/120, but you have to take the whole room: you can't just rent a bed. Doubles with attached bath are Y160 and Y200, which unfortunately is a pretty good price for Taiyuan. At least the hotel is fairly new and clean.

A bit further west on the same road, the *Yunshan Hotel* (☎ 404-1351) *(yúnshān bīnguǎn)* has doubles with private bath for Y132, the lowest official foreigner price in

TAIYUAN 太原	7 Railway Booking Office 火车轮联航售票处	14 Shanxi Electric Power Hotel
1 Shanxi Grand Hotel 山西大酒店	8 Bingzhou Hotel 并州饭店	山西电力大厦
2 Dumpling World Restaurant 饺子大世界	9 Provincial Musuem 山西省博物馆	15 Post & Telephone Office 邮电大楼
3 Bank of China 中国银行	10 May 1st Square 五一广场	16 Long-Distance Bus Station 长途汽车站
4 Telecommunications Centre 市邮电局	11 PSB 公安局	17 Railway Station 火车站
5 Yingze Hotel 迎泽宾馆	12 Chongshan Monastery 崇善寺	18 Tianhe Hotel 天和大厦
6 Airline Booking Office 通航售票处	13 Yunshan Hotel 云山饭店	19 Twin Pagoda Temple 双塔寺
		20 CITS 中国国际旅行社

town. There are more upmarket rooms for Y186.

After that it's strictly middle to top end. The three star *Bingzhou Hotel* (☎ 404-2111) *(bìngzhōu fàndiàn)*, opposite May 1st square, has well-kept singles/doubles for Y268/368. Service seems friendly and efficient, and all rooms have air-con and satellite TV.

The *Yingze Hotel* (☎ 404-3211) *(yíngzé bīnguǎn)* incorporates two massive buildings. The east block has doubles for Y210, but only for Chinese guests. The west block has recently been turned into a glittering four star hotel, complete with sauna, gym, medical clinic and swimming pool (a rarity in this part of China). Doubles cost Y530, plus 15% service charge, and come equipped with English-language satellite TV and refrigerators.

The joint venture *Shanxi Grand Hotel* (☎ 404-3901) *(shānxī dàjiǔdiàn)* is a well run, four star outfit with facilities similar to the Yingze Hotel (minus the pool). Singles/doubles cost Y600/680.

On the Taiyuan street-food menu are local favourites like pigs' trotters *(zhūjiǎo)* stewed in cauldrons, and a savoury pancake called *làobǐng*. The local variant of Chinese noodles, called *liángpí*, is often served in steaming bowls of spiced soup.

Those craving western food should head over to the Shanxi Grand Hotel. The ground-floor coffee shop does good hamburgers, salads and almost certainly the best cup of coffee in Shanxi, although it's a bit steep at Y20 per cup. The restaurant in the Tianhe Hotel is good and cheap: if you can't get a room, console yourself with a nice meal.

Getting There & Away

Air The airline booking office (☎ 404-2903) is at 158 Yingze Dongdajie and is open daily from 8 am to 8 pm. Useful direct flights include Beijing (daily, Y530), Chengdu (thrice weekly, Y1100), Guangzhou (daily, Y1580), Shanghai (daily, Y1160) and Xi'an (four times weekly, Y550). There are also flights to most other major domestic destinations.

Bus Buses to Datong (Y31, eight hours) leave at 8 am from the long-distance bus station. Minibuses to Datong leave when full from outside the southern end of the railway station; regular minibuses cost Y30 and take seven hours, while imported Iveco buses make the trip in five hours for Y50.

There are six buses to Wutaishan (Y17, seven hours) from the bus station between 6.20 and 10 am, and private buses and minibuses run from the northern end of the railway station between 6.30 am and 1 pm.

From in front of the west side of the long-distance bus station there are express buses to Beijing every 30 minutes from

SHANXI

6.30 am to 11 pm. Some departures feature Mercedes-Benz and Volvo buses, which make the trip in six hours. Tickets cost Y120 regardless of the type of bus, so you may want to hold out for a good one.

There is one daily sleeper bus to Xi'an (Y81, 16 hours) from the bus station at 4 pm, and sleepers to Zhengzhou (Y68, 10 hours) twice each afternoon. There are also one or two afternoon sleeper buses to Luoyang (Y83, 13 hours).

Train It's fairly easy getting sleeper tickets for trains originating from Taiyuan, but difficult for those that don't. There is a special foreigner's ticket window (No 14) at the railway station where you can buy same-day tickets; it's open from 8.30 am to noon and 2.30 to 6.30 pm.

For advance purchases go to the advance railway booking office (☎ 412-6657) at 138 Yingze Dajie, which is open daily from 8.30 am to 8 pm.

You may be able to get sleeper tickets for *some* trains originating outside Taiyuan, but not others, notably trains bound for Xi'an. Services starting off from Taiyuan include express trains to Beijing, Baoji, Chengdu, Luoyang, Qingdao, Shanghai and Tianjin.

If you're headed to Xi'an, your best bets are train No 535 (leaving at 4.40 pm) or 485 (departing at 1.30 pm): both trains start from Taiyuan. Train No 475 (Baotou-Xi'an), which leaves Taiyuan at 12.15 am and arrives in Xi'an at 11 am, is the most convenient in terms of timing, but you'll have to try your luck with upgrading once you get on board. The ride to Xi'an takes 12 hours.

Other travel times include Beijing (nine hours), Chengdu (31 hours), Datong (eight hours), and Zhengzhou (10 hours).

AROUND TAIYUAN
Jinci Temple
(jìncí sì)
This ancient Buddhist temple is at the source of the Jin River by Xuanwang Hill, 25km south-west of Taiyuan. It's thought

that the original buildings were constructed between 1023 and 1032 AD, but there have been numerous additions and restorations over the centuries, right up to Qing Dynasty times.

As you enter the temple compound the first major structure is the Mirror Terrace, a Ming building used as an open-air theatre. The name is used in the figurative sense to denote the reflection of life in drama.

Zhibo's Canal cuts through the temple complex and lies west of the Mirror Terrace. Spanning this canal is the Huixian (Meet the Immortals) Bridge, which provides access to the Terrace for Iron Statues, which displays figures cast in 1097 AD.

Further back is the Goddess Mother Hall, the oldest wooden building in the city and one of the most interesting in the temple complex. Inside are 42 Song Dynasty clay figures of maidservants standing around a large seated statue of the sacred lady, said to be the mother of Prince Shuyu of the ancient Zhou Dynasty.

Next to the Goddess Mother Hall is the Zhou Cypress, an unusual tree which has supposedly been growing at an angle of about 30° for the last 900 years.

In the north of the temple grounds is the Zhenguan Baohan Pavilion, which houses four stone steles inscribed with the handwriting of the Tang Emperor Tai Zong. In the south of the temple grounds is the Sacred Relics Pagoda, a seven storey octagonal building constructed at the end of the 7th century.

The temple is open daily from 8 am to 6 pm and admission is Y15 (Y18 if you want a map of the complex).

To get to Jinci Temple you can take a No 8 bus from in front of the Taiyuan railway station. The ride takes one hour and costs Y1.

Shuanglin Monastery
(shuānglín sì)
Shuanglin Monastery, 110km south-west of Taiyuan, is worth the effort of getting to. It contains exquisite painted clay figurines and statues dating from the Song, Yuan,

Ming and Qing dynasties. Most of the present buildings date from the Ming and Qing dynasties, while the majority of the sculptures are from the Song and Yuan dynasties. There are something like 2000 figurines in total.

A visit to Shuanglin can be done as a day trip from Taiyuan by train. Take a train to Pingyao, then a motor-tricycle out to the temple. Two good train connections are the No 675, departing from Taiyuan at 11.26 am and arriving in Pingyao at 1.06 pm, and the No 676, which heads back from Pingyao at 6.15 pm.

WUTAISHAN & TAIHUAI
(wǔtáishān)

Wutaishan, centred on the beautiful monastic village of Taihuai *(táihuái)*, is one of China's sacred Buddhist mountain areas. Taihuai lies deep in an alpine valley enclosed by the five peaks of Wutaishan, the highest of which is the 3061m northern peak, Yedoufeng, known as the roof of northern China. Taihuai itself has 15 or so old temples and monasteries, and some 20 others dot the surrounding mountainsides.

The relative inaccessibility of Wutaishan spared it the worst of the Cultural Revolution. Improved roads have now made it possible to reach Taihuai in seven hours from either Datong or Taiyuan, and the area sees a steady flow of Chinese tourists, which rises to a flood in July and August. But at other times of the year it's a charming, relaxing spot.

In addition to the temples, the surrounding scenery is great, and there are quite a few mountain trails leading out from near Taihuai.

Information
Tourist Office CITS (☎ 654-2142) has an office at No 18 Mingqing Jie, a small road on the eastern side of the Qingshui River, south of Taihuai village. It can arrange

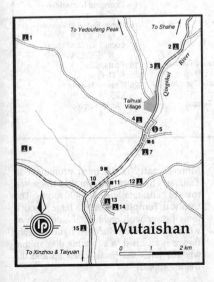

WUTAISHAN 五台山

1 Fenglin Temple
  风林寺
2 Bishan Temple
  碧山寺
3 Qifo Temple
  七佛寺
4 Shuxiang Temple
  殊像寺
5 CITS
  中国国际旅行社
6 Liangcheng Hotel
  凉城山庄
7 Puhua Temple
  普化寺
8 Longquan Temple
  龙泉寺
9 Friendship Hotel
  友谊宾馆
10 Yunfeng Hotel
   云峰宾馆
11 Qixiange Hotel
   栖贤阁宾馆
12 Guanyin Cave Temple
   观音洞
13 Nanshan Monastery
   南山寺
14 Youguo Temple
   佑国寺
15 Zhenhai Temple
   镇海寺

tours of the outlying temples, but unless you want an English-speaking guide, you can take one of the Chinese tours from Taihuai for far less money (see Organised Tours later in this section).

PSB If you need to reach the PSB for any reason, talk to the owner of the hotel you're staying at. The official who deals with foreigners seems to move around quite a bit, so it's best to get a local to help track him down.

Money There is no Bank of China in Taihuai, so it would be best to change money before coming here. Some of the expensive tourist hotels south of town have money-changing facilities, but you may have to be a guest to use them, especially if you are wanting to change travellers cheques.

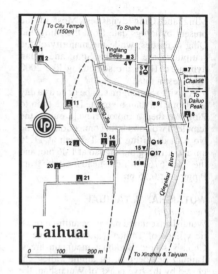

Taihuai

TAIHUAI 台怀

PLACES TO STAY
3 Yuejin Hotel
  汽运公司跃进招待所
7 Jinjie Hotel
  金界宾馆
9 Honglou Hotel
  红楼宾馆
10 Gongyi Meishu Hotel
  工艺美术招待所
18 Wutaishan No 5 Hotel
  五台山第五招待所

PLACES TO EAT
4 Ruyi Restaurant
  如意饭店

5 Liji Restaurant
  里吉酒家
15 Noodle Stands
  路边面摊

OTHER
1 Pusa Peak
  菩萨顶
2 Guangzong Temple
  广宗寺
6 Public Buses to Datong
  大同国营汽车站
8 Shancai Cave Temple
  善财洞
11 Yuanzhao Temple
  园照寺

12 Xiantong Temple
  显通寺
13 Luohou Temple
  罗侯寺
14 Guangren Monastery
  广仁寺
16 Public Buses to Taiyuan
  太原国营汽车站
17 Local Tour Minibuses
  一日游中巴站
19 Post Office
  邮政局
20 Tayuan Temple
  塔院寺
21 Wanfo Temple
  万佛寺

Temples

You'd have to either be a sincerely devout Buddhist or utterly temple-crazed to take in every temple and monastery in the Wutaishan area. Most people will probably just stroll around Taihuai, although there are some outside town that are worth visiting.

The **Tayuan Temple** with its large, white, bottle-shaped pagoda built during the

Ming Dynasty is the most prominent in Taihuai. The **Xiantong Temple** has seven rows of halls, totalling over 400 rooms. The **Luohou Temple** contains a large wooden lotus flower with eight petals, on each of which sits a carved Buddhist figure; the big flower is attached to a rotating disk so that when it turns the petals open up and the figures appear.

SHANXI

Just next door, the small **Guangren Monastery**, run by Tibetan and Mongolian monks, contains some fine examples of early Qing woodcarvings.

For a more secluded, spiritual visit, try the **Cifu Temple**, several hundred metres beyond the Pusa Peak Temple on the ridge overlooking the town. Here there are no hawkers, just a few pleasant monks, one or two of whom speak English. If you're polite, they may let you up to the 2nd floor of the main temple (normally closed to the public) which houses several Tibetan Buddhist figures.

To get a bird's-eye view of Taihuai, you can make the somewhat strenuous trek up to **Dailuo Peak**, on the eastern side of the Qingshui River. If you want to spare your legs, and lighten your wallet, there's a chairlift (Y16 one way).

About 2.5km south of Taihuai is the sprawling **Nanshan Monastery**, which offers nice views of the Wutaishan valley. Just above it, the **Youguo Temple** contains frescoes of the fable *Journey to the West*.

Other sights include the marble archway of the **Longquan Temple** and the 26m-high buddha and carvings of 500 arhats in the **Shuxiang Temple**.

Organised Tours

Privately operated minibuses make half-day and full-day tours of the outlying temples. A sample route might include the Qifo, Guanyin Cave, Shuxiang, Longquan and Youguo temples and the Nanshan Monastery, among others. For a group of four to six people, this kind of tour costs Y45 per person, but if there is a larger number of tourists taking the same bus you may only have to pay Y38.

Buy your ticket at the small blue booth near the minibus stand. Show up between 7 and 7.30 am: after that most of the Chinese tourists will be gone, making it hard to join a tour.

You can also hire a minibus for Y200 for a private half-day tour, or a jeep for around Y150.

Places to Stay

Taihuai is teeming with small hotels that cater mainly to Chinese tourists, although many seem willing to take the occasional foreigner. In any case, there are a few that are actually allowed to have foreign guests, which at least means you don't have to worry about being kicked out in the middle of the night by the PSB. Rates for all hotels generally go up around 30% during the peak season (July to August).

One of the best bets is the *Gongyi Meishu Hotel* (☎ 654-2531) (*gōngyì měishù zhāodàisuǒ*), which has dorm beds in quads and triples with shared bath for Y20, and beds in doubles with private bath for Y50. The latter includes all the little amenities like towels, soap, toilet paper etc. It's at 25 Taiping Jie. As with all the small places in Taihuai, there's no English sign.

The tiny *Yuejin Hotel* (☎ 654-2586) (*qìyùngōngsī yùejìn zhāodàisuǒ*), at 32 Yingfang Beijie, is a friendly spot with clean rooms and a nice courtyard. The asking price of Y50 for a bed in a double with sink and bath (but no toilet) is a bit steep, but you should be able to talk the price down. The hotel is tucked away down the small lane heading west off the main road, opposite the bridge to the Jinjie Hotel (which doesn't take foreigners, by the way).

On the main road near the Qingshui River is the *Honglou Hotel* (☎ 654-2520) (*hónglóu bīnguǎn*), which has dorm beds from Y10 and doubles/triples with private bath for Y100/150. The rooms aren't bad, although the hotel lacks the charm of the smaller places.

Further south along the main road is the *Wutaishan No 5 Hotel* (☎ 654-2373), which should be accepting foreigners by the time this book is in print. Beds in relatively clean triples with shared bath are Y30, while doubles with private bath go for Y80 and Y100.

Wutaishan's luxury hotels are several kilometres south of the village. When we last visited, there were 10 large tourist hotels, with more under construction – another

SHANXI

typical case of excess top-end supply at a Chinese resort.

Of these, the best choice is probably the *Qixiange Hotel* (☎ 654-2400) *(qīxiángé bīnguǎn)*, which enjoys a peaceful setting at the foot of the mountains, and is a short walk from Nanshan Monastery. Nicely furnished doubles/triples cost Y380/428, and there are also dorm beds in triples with shared bath for Y80.

Also pleasant is the *Liangcheng Hotel* (☎ 654-2418) *(liángchéng bīnguǎn)*, 1km south of Taihuai village. It's close to the mountains, and has basic doubles for Y198 and fancier ones for Y360. Dorm beds in triples with private bath are available for Y64: not a bad deal.

Two kilometres south of Taihuai, the *Friendship Hotel* (☎ 654-2678) *(yǒuyì bīnguǎn)*, one of the official tourist spots, charges a ridiculous Y486 for doubles – definitely not worth it. A bit further south, the *Yunfeng Hotel* (☎ 654-2566) *(yúnfēng bīn-guǎn)* is a fairly soulless place, but has more reasonable rates, with doubles/triples from Y256/330.

Places to Eat

Taihuai has almost as many small restaurants as it does hotels, and again they are largely similar. Prices tend to be higher here, as nearly all food has to be trucked in from the plains. Expect vegie and tofu dishes to be around Y10, and meat dishes to be around Y20. Except for the pricey tourist hotels, there's not an English menu to be found in the area.

The *Ruyi Restaurant (rúyì fàndiàn)*, opposite the Yuejin Hotel, has great food and the prices are slightly cheaper than most places. On the main road, next to the Datong public bus stop, the *Liji Restaurant (lǐjí jiǔjiā)* is quite good, although dishes are a bit more expensive.

There are some noodle stands along the main road near the southern end of the village serving tasty cold noodles *(liáng pí)*, fried noodles, dumplings etc. Beware of overcharging: a bowl of cold noodles shouldn't be more than Y3.

Getting There & Away

From Taiyuan's long-distance bus station there are six departures to Wutaishan (Y17, eight hours) between 6.20 and 10 am. Private minibuses also leave from in front of the railway station (northern end) when full – the last bus is around 1 pm. They claim to do the trip in seven hours, but often take as long as the public buses. The fare is Y20.

From Datong, there's one bus to Wutaishan departing the new bus station at 7.20 am, although it's best to get there at 7 am in case it leaves early. The trip, via Hunyuan, Shahe and over the scenic pass near Yedoufeng, takes seven hours (Y30). There's also a bus from Datong's old bus station at 7.30 am.

From Taihuai, buses to Datong (Y30) leave from the northern part of the village. There is one departure daily, at 6.30 am. Public buses to Taiyuan (Y20) leave at 6 and 7 am from a small stop near the middle of the village. Sometimes there's also a 2 pm departure.

Private buses and minibuses also make the run to Taiyuan. Most leave in the morning, although sometimes there are afternoon departures. Private buses generally loiter between the two public bus stops. These services are condemned by locals as unreliable and slow, so you may want to opt for the public bus.

Getting Around

Taihuai town can be covered on foot, and you can make day hikes out to some of the temples in the surrounding area.

Unfortunately, at the time of writing there was no place to rent bicycles, although maybe some entrepreneur will catch on in the next few years.

DATONG

(dàtóng)

Datong's chief attraction is the nearby Yungang Buddhist Caves. The city itself is not very attractive, although it has a few interesting historical sights. An ancient imperial capital, modern Datong has little to show for its former greatness – it's basically yet another crowded, polluted Chinese industrial city.

Local authorities have at least been trying to spruce up the city centre. It's be-come a pretty lively place, with rows of upmarket shops and restaurants, but you still probably won't want to stay any longer in Datong than you need to.

History

In the 5th century AD, the Toba, a Turkic-speaking people, succeeded in unifying all of northern China and forming the Northern Wei Dynasty. Adopting Chinese ways, they saw trade, agriculture and Buddhism flourish. Their capital was Datong. It remained as such until 494 AD, when the court moved to Luoyang.

Outside the modern-day city is the greatest icon of the period, the impressive Yungang Buddhist Caves.

Orientation

The pivotal point of Datong is the intersection just north of the Drum Tower in the large old city. Apart from the Yungang Caves, the historic sights such as Huayan Monastery and the Nine Dragon Screen are inside the crumbling old city walls. This is where you'll also find most of the shops and nightlife.

At Datong's northern end is the railway station, and several of the few hotels open to foreigners. There are also two tourist hotels at the southern end of town.

Maps Maps of Datong with some English on them are available at the Xinhua Bookstore, diagonally opposite the main post office. You can also pick up maps from hawkers around the railway station.

Information

Tourist Offices Datong has two CITS offices: a branch at the railway station and another at the Yungang Hotel (☎ 502-4176). They broker accommodation, can purchase train tickets and run regular tours of the city and Yungang Caves.

PSB The PSB office is on Xinjian Beilu, north of the large department store.

Money The Bank of China's main branch on Yingbin Xilu is the only place to change travellers cheques, unless you're staying at the Yungang or Datong hotels. Money-changing hours are 8 am to noon and 2.30 to 6 pm from Monday to Friday.

Post & Communications The main post and telephone office is the large central building with the clock tower at the intersection of Da Xijie and Xinjian Nanlu.

Nine Dragon Screen
(jiǔlóng bì)
This is one of Datong's several 'dragon screens' – tiled walls depicting fire-breathing dragons. The Nine Dragon Screen was originally part of the gate of the palace of Ming Dynasty Emperor Hong Wu's 13th son, and is 8m high, over 45m long and 2m thick.

The Nine Dragon Screen is a short way east of the intersection of Da Dongjie and Da Beijie; you can get there on bus No 4 from the railway station. Admission is Y6 and it's open daily from 8 am to 6.30 pm.

Huayan Monastery
(huáyán sì)
The Huayan Monastery is on the western side of the old city. The original monastery dates back to 1140 AD and the reign of Emperor Tian Ju'an of the Jin Dynasty.

Mahavira Hall is one of the largest Buddhist halls still standing in China. In the centre of the hall are five gilded Ming Dynasty buddhas seated on lotus thrones. Around them stand Bodhisattvas, soldiers and mandarins. The ceiling is decorated with colourful paintings originally dating from the Ming and Qing dynasties, but recently restored and supported by massive wooden beams.

Bojiajiaocang Hall (Hall for the Conservation of Buddhist Scriptures of the Bojia Order) is smaller but more interesting than the main hall. It contains 29 coloured clay

SHANXI

figures made during the Liao Dynasty (916-1125 AD), representing the Buddha and Bodhisattvas. The figures give the monastery a touch of magic lacking in other restored temples.

Huayan Monastery is about 500m east of the post office at the end of Xiasipo Lane, which runs south off Da Xijie. Bus No 4 passes here. Entry costs Y18 and hours are 8 am to 5.30 pm.

Shanhua Temple
(shànhuà sì)
The Shanhua Temple is in the south of Datong just within the old city walls. Built during the Tang Dynasty, it was destroyed by fire during a war at the end of the Liao Dynasty.

In 1128 AD more than 80 halls and pavilions were rebuilt, and further restoration was done during the Ming Dynasty. The main hall contains statues of 24 divine generals. There is a small dragon screen within the monastery grounds. Admission is Y12. The temple is open daily from 8.30 am to 5 pm.

Datong Locomotive Factory
(dàtóng jīchē chǎng)
This factory was the last in China to make steam engines for the main railway lines. In 1989 it finally switched to diesel and electric engines. However, the factory maintains a museum housing several steam locomotives. After wandering through the factory you enjoy the ultimate train-buff dream – a ride in the cabin of one of the locomotives.

The factory is on the city's south-western outskirts. You can only see it as part of a CITS tour. It's rare that large groups wish to go, but CITS will arrange small group tours – these should cost around Y150 per person if there are only two of you.

Places to Stay
Datong offers little for the budget traveller. The cheapest deal you can get is a dorm bed for Y40, and you may need to book through CITS at the railway station to get this price.

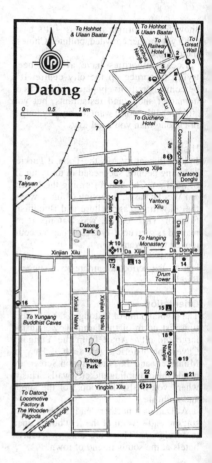

Outside of the CITS net, the only semi-budget option is the *Gucheng Hotel* (☎ 602-3585) *(gǔchéng bīnguǎn)*, which has doubles with private bath for Y104. The bathrooms are a bit grimy, and the location is not that convenient, but it's still not a bad deal. It's at 14 Huanghua Jie, 1.5km from the railway station. There's no public bus, but a taxi there costs only Y5.

A good mid-range choice is the *Hongqi Hotel* (☎ 206-8405) *(hóngqí bīnguǎn)* just across from the northern end of the railway station. Fairly new, clean doubles go for

DATONG 大同

1 Hongqi Hotel
  红旗大饭店
2 Chezhan Restaurant
  车站快餐
3 Railway Station; CITS
  火车站
  中国国际旅行社
4 Feitian Hotel
  飞天宾馆
5 Post & Telephone Office
  邮电局
6 Old (North) Bus Station
  汽车北站(旧站)
7 New Children's Park
  新儿童乐园
8 Bank of China
  中国银行

9 New Bus Station
  新汽车站
10 PSB
  公安局
11 Department Store
  百货大楼
12 Post & Telephone Office
  邮电大楼
13 Huayan Monastery
  华严寺
14 Nine Dragon Screen
  九龙壁
15 Shanhua Temple
  善化寺
16 Xinkaili Bus Station (for Yungang Caves)
  新开里汽车站
17 Datong Stadium
  大同体育场

18 Datong Air Service Company
  大同航空服务公司
19 Foreign Languages Bookstore
  外文书店
20 Yonghe Restaurant
  永和大酒店
21 Yungang Hotel; CITS
  云冈宾馆
  中国国际旅行社
22 Datong Hotel
  大同宾馆
23 Bank of China (Main Branch)
  中国银行
  (大同支行)

Y160, and the price includes three meals a day, a rather rare perk. Triples with shared bath are Y162, but you need to take the entire room: no dorm beds.

Opposite the Hongqi lies the *Feitian Hotel*, which asks a ridiculous Y240 for very average doubles with attached bath. If you book through CITS you get the same room for Y160. The same deal goes for the *Railway Hotel*, which is about 750m north of the railway station, and also has some of the Y40 dorm beds. You'll have to go through CITS to get a room here.

At the southern end of town are Datong's two traditional tourist hotels. The *Yungang Hotel* (☎ 502-1601) (*yúngāng bīnguǎn*) is a three star operation with well appointed doubles from Y405, although CITS may be able to get you a better rate. The hotel's east wing also has beds in triples with shared bath for Y40: the reception is to the right as you enter the main gate. You can, but don't have to, book through CITS to get these dorm beds.

The *Datong Hotel* (☎ 203-2476) (*dàtóng bīnguǎn*) is also three star, although it doesn't feel as upmarket as the Yungang. Doubles start from Y308 and there are dorm beds in triples with private bath for Y80. To reach the Datong and Yungang hotels take

bus No 15 from the railway station. For the Datong Hotel get off at the 12th stop (just after the bus turns sharply left). For the Yungang Hotel, get off at the stop after that. Taxis cost Y15 to either hotel.

Places to Eat
The best place to go restaurant hunting is around Da Nanjie and Nanguan Nanjie. Cheap hole-in-the-wall places vie with fancy banquet halls for business. At the time of writing *the* place to go was the *Yonghe Restaurant* (*yǒnghé dàjiǔjiā*) which serves great food to Datong's upper crust. It's a fun spot if you get there between 6 and 8 pm. Dinner for four with beer costs about Y20 to Y40, depending on how many meat dishes you order.

At the opposite end of the spectrum, next to the railway station, is *Chezhan Restaurant* (*chēzhàn kuàicān*). It's a tiny, five table affair serving tasty and cheap noodles and dumplings.

The restaurants at the *Hongqi* and *Gucheng* hotels are both pretty good, and the latter is quite reasonably priced.

Getting There & Away
Air Datong has an airport south of the city, but when we last visited flights had stopped

SHANXI

due to insufficient demand. If they start up again they will probably go to Beijing and Guangzhou. The Datong Air Service Company (☎ 204-4039) is at 1 Nanguan Nanjie, and can also book flights for air routes other than to/from Datong. It's open daily from 8.30 am to 6.30 pm.

Bus Datong has two bus stations: the old, or north station, near the railway station, and the new station on Yantong Xilu. Departures mostly start from the new station and pass by the old one before heading out, although some routes have separate departures from each station.

Officially, foreigners are forbidden to travel by bus from Datong, but in practice there seems to be no trouble buying tickets.

Buses to Taiyuan leave the new station at 7.30 am (8.20 am from the old station), cost Y31 and take eight hours. Privately run buses to Taiyuan also leave frequently throughout the day from in front of the railway station. Ordinary buses cost Y30, while Iveco minibuses, which make the trip in around five hours, cost Y50.

There is one daily bus to Wutaishan from the new station at 7.20 am, although it's best to get there at 7 am, as it sometimes leaves early. The ride takes around seven hours and costs Y30. There is also a separate bus from the old station departing at 7.30 am.

Train A railway line north-east to Beijing and a northern line to Inner and Outer Mongolia meet in a Y-junction at Datong. (Trans-Siberian trains via Ulaan Baatar come through here.)

There are daily express trains to Beijing (seven hours), Lanzhou (23 hours), Taiyuan (seven hours) and Xi'an (17 hours). Tickets to Xi'an can be hard to get, mainly because there's only one direct train, No 475. It starts in Baotou and leaves from Datong at 5.04 pm.

If you have no luck at the ticket windows, try the group tour window on the 2nd floor of the main waiting hall. Failing that, the staff at the CITS office at the railway station might be able to get you a

ticket: they charge a Y40 commission per hard-sleeper berth.

AROUND DATONG
Yungang Buddhist Caves
(yúngāng shíkū)
These are the main reason most people make it to Datong. The caves are cut into the southern cliffs of Wuzhoushan, 16km west of Datong, next to the pass leading to Inner Mongolia. The caves contain over 50,000 statues and stretch for about a kilometre east to west.

On top of the mountain ridge are the remains of a huge, mud-brick, 17th century Qing Dynasty fortress. As you approach the caves you'll see the truncated pyramids which were once the watchtowers.

Admission to the caves is Y25, and they are open from 8.30 am to 5.30 pm. There are no guides at the caves, but there are good English descriptions and explanations throughout.

For details, see the special section starting on page 530.

Getting There & Away Bus Nos 3 and 10 from the terminal at Xinkaili, on the western edge of Datong, go past Yungang Caves. You can get to Xinkaili on bus No 2 from the railway station or bus No 17 from outside the Datong Hotel. From Xinkaili it's about one hour's ride to the caves.

Many travellers take a CITS tour out to the caves, which costs Y100 per person (minimum of five people) or Y195 with lunch and entrance fees included. The tour also includes the Hanging Monastery.

Hanging Monastery
(xuánkōng sì)
The Hanging Monastery is just outside the town of Hunyuan, 75km south-east of Datong. Built precariously on sheer cliffs above Jinlong Canyon, the monastery dates back more than 1400 years. Its halls and pavilions were built along the contours of the cliff face using the natural hollows and outcrops. The buildings are connected by corridors, bridges and boardwalks and

contain bronze, iron, and stone statues of gods and buddhas.

Notable is the Three Religions Hall where Buddha, Laotzu and Confucius sit side by side. Some long-overdue repairs have been made to the monastery in recent years and some sections have been closed off. Admission costs Y20.

The CITS tour to the Yungang Caves (see that entry on the previous page) will include the Hanging Monastery. Chinese tours costing Y30 and taking four to five hours leave from both the old and new bus stations from 7.30 to 8.30 am.

You can also take a public or private bus from Datong to Hunyuan, just 5km from the Hanging Monastery. Public buses to Hunyuan leave from the old bus station at 7.30 am, take two hours and cost Y5. Private minibuses leave from near the bus station and cost Y8. The last bus back from Hunyuan leaves at around 4 pm. Another option is the bus to Wutaishan, which goes directly past the monastery. A taxi from Hunyuan to the monastery costs Y30 return.

You can stay overnight in Hunyuan, and either return to Datong the next day, or continue on to Wutaishan. (The bus to Wutaishan usually rolls into Hunyuan around 9 to 9.30 am.) The *Hengshan Guesthouse* (☎ 832-2045) *(héngshān bīnguǎn)* is 150m to the right (as you come out of the bus station), and has mouldy doubles for Y160.

A cheaper option is the *Hunyuan Jiguan No 1 Hotel* (☎ 832-3778) *(húnyuán jīguān dìyī zhāodàisuǒ)*, where dorm beds start from Y15 and doubles are Y80. From the bus station, turn left and walk about 500m to the intersection and then turn right. The hotel is about 400m along the road on the left-hand side: the entrance gate is just past a four storey white building.

Wooden Pagoda
(mùtǎ)
This 11th century pagoda at Yingxian *(yìngxiàn)*, 70km south of Datong, is one of the oldest wooden buildings in the world. It's said that not a single nail was used in the construction of the nine storey, 97m structure.

Tours of the Hanging Monastery sometimes include the Wooden Pagoda. You can also get there by taking a minibus from near the old bus station in Datong (Y10, two hours).

YUNCHENG
(yùnchéng)
Yuncheng is in the south-western corner of Shanxi Province, near where the Yellow River completes its great sweep through far northern China and begins to flow eastwards. The small city is famed for the gutsy little orange tractors that are assembled here and often seen chugging along country roads.

At Jiezhou *(jièzhōu)*, 13km south of Yuncheng, is the large **Guandi Temple**, originally constructed during the Sui Dynasty, but destroyed by fire in 1702 AD and subsequently rebuilt. Bus No 11 from Yuncheng railway station drops you right at Guandi Temple in Jiezhou.

Places to Stay
The *Huanghe Hotel* (☎ 202-3135) *(huánghé dàshà)*, near the first street corner on the left as you leave the railway station, has good doubles for Y124 and dorm beds from Y25.

The *Yuncheng Hotel* (☎ 202-4481) *(yùnchéng bīnguǎn)*, on Hongqi Lu, has twins/triples with an attached bath for Y64/96. There's fancier twins from Y162 to Y222.

Getting There & Away
Yuncheng is on the Taiyuan-Xi'an railway line; all trains, including daily express trains, stop here. You probably won't be able to get sleeper tickets in Yuncheng, so if you want one you'll need to buy a hard-seat ticket and upgrade once on board.

There are direct bus connections from Yuncheng to Luoyang (Y22, six hours), leaving every 30 minutes between 6.30 am and 3 pm from the long-distance bus station. There's also one sleeper bus to Xi'an leaving at 10 pm, but the train is a far more comfortable way to go.

Yungang Buddhist Caves

Most of the caves were carved during the Northern Wei Dynasty between 460 and 494 AD. Yungang (Cloud Ridge) is the highest part of Wuzhoushan's sandstone range and is on the north bank of the river of the same name. The Wei rulers once came here to pray to the gods for rain.

The Yungang Caves appear to have been modelled on the Dunhuang Caves of Gansu Province, which were dug in the 4th century AD and are some of the oldest in China. At the Dunhuang Caves the statues are terracotta since the rock was too soft to be carved, but here at Datong are some of the oldest examples of stone sculpture to be seen in China. Various foreign influences can be seen in the Yungang Caves: there are Persian and Byzantine weapons, Greek tridents, and images of the Indian Hindu gods Vishnu and Shiva. The Chinese style is reflected in the robust Bodhisattvas, dragons and flying *apsaras* (celestial beings rather like angels).

Work on the Yungang Caves fizzled out when the Northern Wei moved their capital to Luoyang in 494 AD. In the 11th and 12th centuries the Liao Dynasty, founded by northern invaders, saw to some repairs and restoration. More repairs to the caves were carried out during the Qing Dynasty. From east to west the caves fall into three major groups, although their numbering has little to do with the order in which they were constructed.

Caves 1-4

These early caves, with their characteristic square floor plan, are at the far eastern end, and are separated from the others. Caves 1 and 2 contain carved pagodas. Cave 3 is the largest in this group, although it contains only a seated buddha flanked by two Bodhisattvas.

Caves 5-13

Yungang art is at its best in this group, especially caves 5 and 6, which boast walls of wonderfully carved Buddhist tales and processions. Cave 5 also contains a colossal seated buddha almost 17m high. Cave 6 contains a richly carved pagoda, and an entrance flanked by fierce guardians. In the centre of the rear chamber stands a two storey pagoda-pillar about 15m high. On the lower part of the pagoda are four niches with carved images, including one of the Maitreya Buddha (the future Buddha). Gautama Buddha's life story from birth to his attainment of nirvana is carved in the east, south and west walls of the cave and on two sides of the pagoda.

Caves 7 and 8 are linked and contain carvings with Hindu influences. Shiva, with eight arms and four heads and seated on a bull, is on one side of the entrance to Cave 8. On the other side is the multi-faced Indra, perched on an eagle. Caves 9 and 10 are notable for their front pillars and figures bearing musical instruments. These instruments appear again in Cave 12, while Cave 13 has a 15m-high buddha statue, its right hand propped up by a figurine.

Caves 16-20

These caves were carved in 460 AD and the buddha in each one represents an emperor from the Northern Wei Dynasty. The buddha in Cave 18 represents Emperor Taiwu, who was once a great patron of Buddhism, but later (through the influence of a minister) came to favour Taoism.

After a revolt which he blamed on the Buddhists, Taiwu ordered the destruction of Buddhist statues, monasteries and temples, and the persecution of Buddhists. This lasted from 446 to 452 AD, when Taiwu was murdered. His son is said to have died of a broken heart, having been unable to prevent his father's atrocities, and was posthumously awarded the title of emperor.

Taiwu's grandson (and successor) Emperor Wencheng, who restored Buddhism to the dynasty, is represented by the 14m-high seated buddha of Cave 20.

The caves from No 21 onwards are small, in poor condition and can't compare to their better preserved counterparts.

While not as spectacular as the Magao Caves in Gansu, the statuary at Yungang is of the same period and the caves are far easier to reach.

YUNGANG BUDDHIST CAVES

RUICHENG
(ruìchéng)
At Ruicheng, 93km south of Yuncheng, is
Yongle Taoist Temple, which has valuable frescoes dating from the Tang and
Song dynasties. In the 1960s the temple
was moved to Ruicheng from its original
site beside the Yellow River, when the
Sanmenxia Dam was built.

Places to Stay
The *Yongle Hotel* (☎ 302-2171) *(yónglè
fàndiàn)*, at the town's main intersection,
has clean basic doubles with shared bath

for Y30 and Y40, and dorm beds for Y20.
(Yongle Temple is 3km directly south
along this road.)

Getting There & Away
From Yuncheng's long-distance bus station
there are half-hourly departures to Ruicheng (Y8, 2½ hours). On the way, the bus
passes Jiezhou before climbing the cool
subalpine slopes of Zhongtiaoshan; it's a
nice trip.

From Ruicheng you can get an early-
morning bus to Xi'an: the first (and sometimes only) departure is at 5.30 am!

Shaanxi 陝西

The northern part of Shaanxi *(shǎnxī)* is one of the oldest settled regions of China, with remains of human habitation dating back to prehistoric times. This was the homeland of the Zhou people, who eventually conquered the Shang and established their rule over much of northern China. It was also the homeland of the Qin, who ruled from their capital of Xianyang near modern-day Xi'an and formed the first dynasty to rule over all of eastern China.

Shaanxi remained the political heart of China until the 9th century. The great Sui and Tang capital of Chang'an (Xi'an) was built there and the province was a crossroads on the trading routes from eastern China to central Asia.

With the migration of the imperial court to pastures further east, Shaanxi's fortunes declined. Rebellions afflicted the territory from 1340 to 1368, again from 1620 to 1644, and finally in the mid-19th century, when the great Muslim rebellion left tens of thousands of the province's Muslims dead. Five million people died in the famine from 1876 to 1878, and another three million in the famines of 1915, 1921 and 1928.

It was probably the dismal condition of the Shaanxi peasants that provided the Communists such willing support in the province in the late 1920s and during the subsequent civil war. From their base at Yan'an the Communist leaders directed the war against the Kuomintang and later against the Japanese, before being forced to evacuate in the wake of a Kuomintang attack in 1947.

Some 35 million people live in Shaanxi, mostly in the central and southern regions. The northern area of the province is a plateau covered with a thick layer of windblown loess soil which masks the original landforms. Deeply eroded, the landscape has deep ravines and almost vertical cliff faces.

The Great Wall in the far north of the

Shaanxi Facts & Highlights

Area: 205,000 sq km

Population: 35.4 million

Capital: Xi'an

Highlights

- The Army of Terracotta Warriors, one of China's premier attractions.
- Huashan, one of the less-touristed sacred mountains.
- Xi'an, with its cultural sites, great food and interesting mix of Chinese and Islamic culture.

province is something of a cultural barrier, beyond which agriculture and human existence were always precarious ventures.

Like so much of China, this region is rich in natural resources, particularly coal and oil. The Wei River, a branch of the Yellow River, cuts across the middle of the province. This fertile belt became a centre of Chinese civilisation.

The south of the province is quite different from the north; it's a comparatively lush, mountainous area with a mild climate.

XI'AN
(xī'ān)
Xi'an (population six million) once vied with Rome and later Constantinople for the

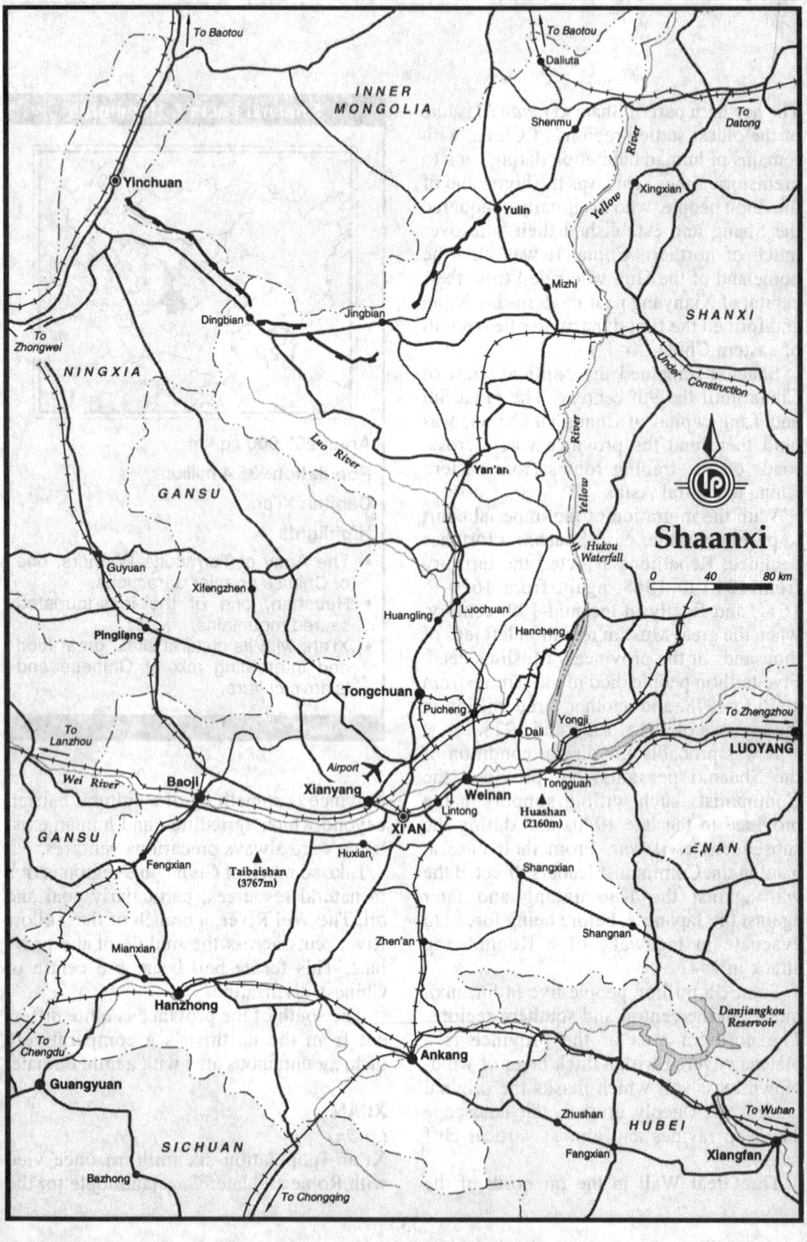

Shaanxi
0
40
80 km
To Baotou
To Baotou
Daliuta
INNER MONGOLIA
Shenmu
To Datong
Yellow River
Xingxian
Yinchuan
Yulin
Mizhi
SHANXI
Dingbian
Jingbian
To Zhongwei
Under Construction
NINGXIA
Luo River
Yan'an
Yellow River
GANSU
Hukou Waterfall
Guyuan
Xifengzhen
Huangling
Luochuan
Hancheng
Pingliang
Tongchuan
Pucheng
To Zhengzhou
Yongji
Dali
To Lanzhou
LUOYANG
Airport
Wei River
Baoji
Xianyang
Weinan
Tongguan
Huashan (2160m)
Lintong
XI'AN
GANSU
Huxian
Fengxian
Taibaishan (3767m)
Shangxian
Zhen'an
Shangnan
Mianxian
Hanzhong
Danjiangkou Reservoir
To Chengdu
Ankang
Guangyuan
To Wuhan
Zhushan
HUBEI
SICHUAN
Fangxian
Xiangfan
Bazhong
To Chongqing

Xi'an

title of greatest city in the world. Over a period of 2000 years Xi'an has seen the rise and fall of numerous Chinese dynasties, and the monuments and archaeological sites in the city and the surrounding plain are a reminder that once upon a time Xi'an stood at the very centre of the Chinese world.

Today Xi'an is one of China's major attractions. The big drawcard is the Army of Terracotta Warriors, but there are countless other sights scattered in and around the city. There is also an Islamic element to Xi'an, found in tucked-away mosques and busy marketplaces, that lends the city a touch of the exotic rarely found in Chinese cities further east.

History

The earliest evidence of human habitation in the Xi'an area dates back 6000 years to Neolithic times, when the then lush plains proved a perfect area for primitive Chinese tribes to establish villages. In time, the legendary Zhou established a capital on the banks of the Fen River near present-day Xi'an.

Xianyang Between the 5th and 3rd centuries BC, China split into five separate states locked in perpetual war, until the state of Qin conquered everyone and everything. Emperor Qin Shihuang became the first emperor of a unified China and established his capital at Xianyang, near modern-day Xi'an. His longing for immortality gave posterity a remarkable legacy – a tomb guarded by thousands of terracotta soldiers.

The Qin Dynasty crumbled shortly after the death of Qin Shihuang. In 207 BC it was overthrown by a revolt led by a commoner, Liu Pang. Pang established the Han Dynasty, which lasted a phenomenal 400 years, during which time the boundaries of the empire were extended deep into central Asia. But the dynasty was never really secure or unified. It collapsed in 220 AD, making way for more than three centuries of disunity and war.

Nevertheless, the Han empire set a precedent that lingered on in the dreams of would-be empire builders, a dream that came to fruition in the Sui and Tang dynasties, which ruled from the city of Chang'an.

Chang'an After the collapse of the Han, the north of China was ruled by foreign invaders, and the south by a series of weak and short-lived Chinese dynasties. When the Sui Dynasty united the country, it built the new capital of Chang'an in 582 AD as a deliberate reference back to the glory of the Han period, a symbol of reunification.

The Sui was short-lived and in 618 it was replaced by the Tang. Under the Tang, Chang'an became the largest city in Asia, if not the world. It attracted courtiers, merchants, foreign traders, soldiers, artists, entertainers, priests and bureaucrats, and embarked the Tang on a brilliant period of creativity.

The city's design encompassed outer walls which formed a rectangle, 10km east-west and just over 8km north-south, enclosing a neat grid system of streets and wide avenues. The walls, punctuated by 11 gates, were made of pounded earth faced with sun-dried bricks, and were probably about 5.5m high and between 5.5m and 9m thick at the base. Within these walls the imperial court and government conducted their business inside yet another walled city.

Communications between the capital and the rest of China were developed, mainly by canals which linked Chang'an to the Grand Canal and to other strategic places – another system that was also developed and improved by the Tang. Roads radiated from the capital, with inns for officials, travellers, merchants and pilgrims.

This transport infrastructure enabled Chang'an to draw in taxes and enforce its power. The city became a centre of international trade, and a large foreign community established itself. Numerous foreign religions built temples and mosques, including Muslims, the Zoroastrians of Persia, and the Nestorian Christian sect of Syria.

The growth of the government elite and the evolution of a more complex imperial court drew vast numbers of people to serve it. By the 8th century the city had a phenomenal population of two million.

Towards the end of the 8th century the Tang Dynasty and its capital began to decline. From 775 onwards the central government suffered reverses at the hands of provincial warlords and Tibetan and Turkic invaders. The setbacks exposed weaknesses in the empire, and although the Tang still maintained overall supremacy, they gradually lost control of the transport networks and the tax-collection system on which their power depended.

The dynasty fell in 907 AD and China once again broke up into a number of independent states. Chang'an was eventually relegated to the role of a regional centre.

Orientation

Xi'an retains the same rectangular shape that characterised Chang'an, with streets and avenues laid out in a neat grid pattern.

The central block of the modern city is bounded by the city walls. The centre of town is the enormous Bell Tower, and from here run Xi'an's four major streets: Bei, Nan, Dong and Xi Dajie. The railway station stands at the north-eastern edge of the central city block. Jiefang Lu runs south from the station to intersect with Dong Dajie.

Most of the tourist facilities can be found either along or in the vicinity of Jiefang Lu or Xi and Dong Dajie. However, many of the city's sights like the Shaanxi History Museum, the Big Goose and Little Goose pagodas and Banpo Neolithic Village are outside the central block.

Further afield on the plains surrounding Xi'an are sights such as the Entombed Warriors at Xianyang, Famen Temple, the Tomb of Qin Shihuang and the Army of Terracotta Warriors near Lintong.

Maps Pick up a copy of the widely available *Xi'an Tourist Map*. A bilingual production, it is exhaustive in its listings and is regularly updated – even the bus routes are correct.

Information

Tourist Offices CITS (☎ 524-1864) has its main office on Chang'an Lu, a short walk south of the Xi'an Hotel. There is a more central branch at the Bell Tower Hotel (☎ 727-9200, ext 2842). These offices mainly organise tours, although other services such as rail ticket bookings are available.

PSB The PSB (☎ 727-5934) is at 138 Xi Dajie, a 10 minute walk west of the Bell Tower. It's open Monday to Friday from 8 am to noon and 2.30 to 6 pm.

Money The main Bank of China branch is at 223 Jiefang Lu, just up from Dong Wulu. It's open from 8.30 to 11.45 am and from 2 to 5.30 pm Monday to Friday and from 9 am to 3 pm on weekends. There's also a branch on Dong Dajie where foreigners can change money.

Many of the hotels also have money-changing services, but they often refuse to serve non-guests.

Post & Communications The most convenient post and telephone offices are next to the railway station and opposite the Bell Tower on Bei Dajie. Hours are 8.30 am to 8 pm daily.

Travel Agencies One of the best choices in town is Golden Bridge Travel, on the 2nd floor of the Bell Tower Hotel (☎ 725-7975; fax 725-8863). Staff are friendly and willing to dole out information even if you don't end up using their services. Their local sightseeing tours tend to be a bit more personalised, and the agency can provide substantial discounts on mid-range and top-end hotel bookings in Xi'an: call or stop by here before checking in anywhere. Golden Bridge can also arranged discounted airline tickets, a rarity in China.

Staff at Mum's Home Cooking and Dad's Home Cooking can also provide some useful information on booking train tickets and getting to major sights in the area.

Bell Tower
(zhōnglóu)

The Bell Tower is a huge building in the centre of Xi'an that you enter through an underpass on the north side of the tower. The original tower was built in the late 14th century, but was rebuilt at the present location in 1739 during the Qing Dynasty. A large iron bell in the tower used to mark the time each day, hence the name.

Drum Tower
(gǔlóu)

The Drum Tower, a smaller building to the west of the Bell Tower, marks the Muslim quarter of Xi'an. Foreigners pay an entry price of Y15 and opening hours are 8 am to 6 pm. Beiyuanmen is an interesting restored street of traders and craftspeople running directly north from the Drum Tower.

City Walls
(chéngqiáng)

Xi'an is one of the few cities in China where old city walls are still visible. The walls were built on the foundations of the walls of the Tang Forbidden City during the reign of Hong Wu, first emperor of the Ming Dynasty.

They form a rectangle with a circumference of 14km. On each side of the wall is a gateway, and over each stand three towers. At each of the four corners is a watchtower, and the top of the wall is punctuated with defensive towers. The wall is 12m high, with a width at the top of 12m to 14m and at the base of 15m to 18m.

Air-raid shelters were hollowed out of the walls when the Japanese bombed the city, and during the Cultural Revolution caves were dug to store grain. Most sections have been restored or even rebuilt, but others have disappeared completely (although they're still shown on the maps), so unfortunately it's not possible to walk right around Xi'an along the city walls.

There are access ramps up to the wall just east of the railway station, near Heping Lu and at South Gate *(nánmén)* beside the

Provincial Museum. There are also some obscure steps at the eastern end of the south wall. Tickets generally cost around Y10.

Big Goose Pagoda
(dà yàn tǎ)

This pagoda stands in what was formerly the Temple of Great Maternal Grace in the south of Xi'an. The temple was built around 648 AD by Emperor Gao Zong (the third emperor of the Tang Dynasty) when he was still crown prince, in memory of his deceased mother. The buildings that stand today date from the Qing Dynasty and were built in a Ming style.

The original pagoda was built in 652 AD with only five storeys, but it has been renovated, restored and added to many times. It was built to house the Buddhist scriptures brought back from India by the travelling monk Xuan Zang, who then set about translating them into 1335 Chinese volumes. This impressive, fortress-like wood-and-brick building rises to 64m. You can climb to the top for a view of the countryside and the city.

The Big Goose Pagoda is at the end of Yanta Lu, at the southern edge of Xi'an. Bus No 41 from the railway station goes straight there. The entrance is on the southern side of the temple grounds. Foreigners pay Y13 at the main gate, plus Y20 to climb the pagoda (student concessions are available).

On the eastern side of the temple is the **Tang Dynasty Arts Museum** *(tángdài yìshù bówùguǎn)* with a collection specifically devoted to the Tang period in Xi'an. Entry is Y15. Both the pagoda and museum are open from 8.30 am to 5.30 pm.

Little Goose Pagoda
(xiǎo yàn tǎ)

The Little Goose Pagoda is in the grounds of the Jianfu Temple. The top of the pagoda was shaken off by an earthquake in the middle of the 16th century, but the rest of the structure, 43m high, is intact.

The Jianfu Temple was originally built in 684 AD as a site to hold prayers to bless the afterlife of the late Emperor Gao Zong. The pagoda, a rather delicate building of 15 progressively smaller tiers, was built from 707 to 709 AD and housed Buddhist scriptures brought back from India by another pilgrim.

You can get to the Little Goose Pagoda on bus No 3, which runs from the railway station through the South Gate of the old city and down Nanguan Zhengjie. The pagoda is on Youyi Xilu just west of the intersection with Nanguan Zhengjie.

Entry to the grounds is Y10 for foreigners, plus Y10 more to climb to the top of the pagoda for a panorama of Xi'an's apartment blocks and smokestacks. It's open from 8.30 am to 5 pm.

Great Mosque
(dà qīngzhēnsì)
This is among the largest mosques in China. The present buildings only date back to the middle of the 18th century, although the mosque might have been established several hundred years earlier.

It stands north-west of the Drum Tower and is built in a Chinese architectural style with most of the grounds taken up by gardens. Still an active place of worship, the mosque holds several prayer services each day.

The mosque is open from 8 am to 7 pm. The courtyard of the mosque can be visited, but only Muslims may enter the prayer hall. Entry is Y15.

The Great Mosque is a five minute walk from the Drum Tower: go under the arch, then take the second tiny lane leading left to a small side street. From here the mosque is a few steps along to the right past souvenir shops.

Shaanxi Provincial Museum
(shǎnxī shěng bówùguǎn)
Once the Temple of Confucius, the museum houses a fine collection devoted largely to the history of the Silk Road. Among the artefacts is a tiger-shaped tally from the Warring States Period, inscribed with ancient Chinese characters and probably used to convey messages or orders from one military commander to another.

One of the more extraordinary exhibits is the Forest of Steles, the heaviest collection of books in the world. The earliest of these 2300 large engraved stone tablets dates from the Han Dynasty.

Most interesting is the Popular Stele of Daiqin Nestorianism, which can be recognisable by the small cross at the top and engraved in 781 AD to mark the opening of a Nestorian church. The Nestorians were an early Christian sect who differed from orthodox Christianity in their belief that Christ's human and divine natures were quite distinct.

Other tablets include the Ming De Shou Ji Stele, which records the peasant uprising led by Li Zhicheng against the Ming, and the 114 Stone Classics of Kaichen from the Tang Dynasty inscribed with 13 ancient classics and historical records. Because of this collection, the museum is sometimes referred to as the Forest of Steles Museum.

All of the important exhibits have labels in English. The museum entrance is on a side street which runs west off Baishulin Lu, close to the South Gate of the old city wall. It's open from 8.30 am to 5.30 pm. Admission for foreigners is Y30.

Shaanxi History Museum
(shǎnxī lìshǐ bówùguǎn)
Built in huge, classical Chinese style, the museum was opened in 1992 and is rated by some as the best museum in China. The collection is chronologically arranged and includes material previously housed in the Provincial Museum, although many objects have never been on permanent display before.

The section on the ground floor deals with Chinese prehistory and the early dynastic period, starting with Palaeolithic Langtian Man and the more recent New Stone Age settlements at Lintong and Banpo between 7000 and 5000 years ago. Particularly impressive are several enormous Shang and Western Zhou Dynasty bronze cooking tripods, Qin burial objects, bronze arrows and crossbows, and four original terracotta warrior statues taken from near the Tomb of Qin Shihuang.

Upstairs, the second section is devoted to Han, Western Wei and Northern Zhou Dynasty relics. There are some interesting goose-shaped bronze lamps and a set of forged-iron transmission gears, which are surprisingly advanced for their time.

The final, third section has mainly artefacts from the Sui, Tang, Ming and Qing dynasties. The major advances in ceramic-making techniques during this period are most evident, with intricately crafted terracotta horses and camels, fine pale-green glazed *misi* pottery and Buddhist-inspired Tang Dynasty statues.

To get there from the railway station, take bus No 5 or 14. Photography is strictly prohibited and you must deposit (free of charge) any hand luggage in the lockers provided. Admission is Y38, but holders of a valid student card pay only Y10. All exhibits include labels and explanations in English. The museum is open every day from 8.30 am to 5.30 pm.

Muslim Quarter
This area near the Great Mosque has retained much of its original character. The backstreets to the north and west of the mosque have been home to the city's Hui community for centuries.

Walking through the narrow laneways lined with old mud-brick houses, you pass butcher shops, sesame oil factories, smaller mosques hidden behind enormous wooden doors and proud, stringy-bearded men wearing white skullcaps. Good streets to explore are Nanyuan Men, Huajue Xiang and Damaishi Jie, which runs north off Xi Dajie through an interesting Islamic food market.

The Temple of the Eight Immortals
(bā xiān ān)
This is Xi'an's largest Taoist establishment and an active place of worship. Scenes from Taoist mythology are painted around the temple courtyard.

To get there take a No 10 bus east along Changle Lu and stops past the city walls, then 100m on foot and turn right (south a green-painted iron gateway into a m lane. Follow this, turning briefly right th left again into another small street leading past the temple. The entrance is on the southern side of the temple grounds. You can also reach the temple by following the street running directly east from Zhong-shan Gate.

Places to Stay – budget
For such a major travel destination, Xi'an has a depressingly limited selection of true budget spots. In recent years the main backpacker crash pad has been *Flats of Renmin Hotel* (☎ 622-7644) *(rénmín dàshà gōngyù)* at No 9 Fenghe Lu, about 4km north-west of the city centre. It's not a convenient location, and the hotel's popularity stems solely from its *relatively* cheap dorm beds and the presence of two traveller cafes across the street, where you can meet other travellers and fill up on banana pancakes.

Beds in mini-dorm quads (with free breakfast) go for Y40, while shabby aircon doubles with bathroom cost Y110. There's 24 hour hot water for showering, bicycle rental and a relatively cheap laundry service. Rooms aren't particularly clean, and service can be curt, although the latter may be partly because some staff are shy about using their limited English. If no-one from one of the restaurants meets you at the station, take bus No 9 and get off after six stops. A taxi from the station should cost between Y10 and Y12.

Another old stand-by is the *Victory Hotel* (☎ 789-3040) *(shènglì fàndiàn)*, just south of Heping Gate, but unfortunately all the dorm beds have been ripped out. Aircon doubles with bathroom cost Y140; more expensive than the Flats, but also cleaner. Bus Nos 5 and 41 (among others) go past the hotel from the railway station.

An alternative worth considering is the *Petroleum Hotel* (☎ 823-7381, ext 3300) *(shíyóu bīnguǎn)*, which is run by the Xi'an

0, 11, 28 or 42
get off two
continue
under
ket
en

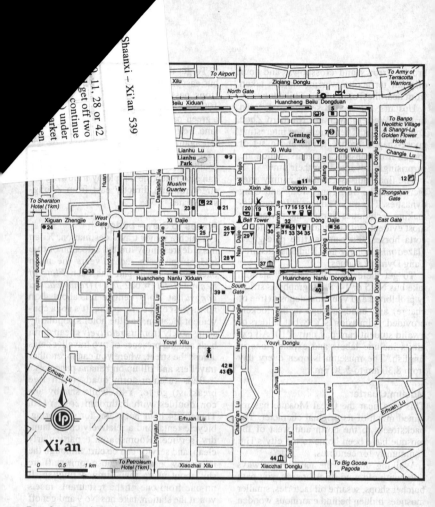

Xi'an

0   0.5   1 km

To Petroleum
Hotel (1km)

To Airport
Xilu   Ziqiang Donglu
North Gate   To Army of
Terracotta
Warriors
Beilu Xiduan   Huancheng Beilu Dongduan
Geming
Park   To Banpo
Neolithic Village
& Shangri-La
Golden Flower
Hotel
Lianhu Lu   Xi Wulu   Dong Wulu
Lianhu
Park   Changle Lu
Muslim
Quarter   Bei Dajie   Jiefang   Renmin Lu
Damaishi Jie   Xixin Jie   Dongxin Jie
Zhongshan
Gate
To Sheraton
Hotel (1km)   Duanlumen Nanxin Jie
Xiguan Zhengjie   West
Gate   Xi Dajie   Bell Tower   Dong Dajie   East Gate
Laodong Nanlu   Huancheng Xilu Nanduan   Nan Dajie   Heping Lu   Huancheng Donglu Nanduan
Hongguang Jie
Huancheng Nanlu Xiduan   South
Gate   Huancheng Nanlu Dongduan
Lingyuan Lu   Nanguan Zhengjie   Wenyi Lu   Yanta Lu
Youyi Xilu   Youyi Donglu
Erhuan Lu   Changan Lu   Cuihua Lu   Yanta Lu   Erhuan Lu
Lingyuan Lu
Erhuan Lu   Xiaozhai Xilu   Xiaozhai Donglu   Cuihua Lu   To Big Goose
Pagoda

SHAANXI

Petroleum Institute. It's about 4km south of
the South Gate, but is cleaner and cheaper
than either of the above two places, and
staff seem quite friendly. Beds in doubles/
triples with attached bath cost Y36, and
fairly plush air-con doubles/triples cost
Y120/150. There is a cheap restaurant
nearby, and bicycles can be rented from
near the north gate of the Petroleum Institute: staff will show you how to get there.

The best way to reach the hotel by public
transport is to take bus No 3 from the
railway station to the South Gate, and then
change there to bus No 204, which departs
from the street just north of the ANA
Grand Castle Hotel. From here it's about
eight stops – tell the driver you want to
get off at the *shíyóu xuéyuàn* or *shíyóu
bīnguǎn*. From the bus stop walk south and
turn right: the hotel is located on the north-
western corner of Linyuan Lu and Dianzi
Erlu.

Places to Stay – middle
Before checking into a mid-range or top-
end place, it's worth calling Golden Bridge

[Handwritten note at top of page: "Silk Road Hotel. Behind Sheraton (in same compound) 300Y per night for double with bath"]

XI'AN 西安

PLACES TO STAY
1 Flats of Renmin Hotel
   人民大厦公寓
5 Jiefang Hotel
   解放饭店
10 Grand New World Hotel
   古都新世界大酒店
11 People's (Renmin) Hotel
   人民大厦
19 May First Hotel
   五一饭店
26 Bell Tower Hotel; Golden
   Bridge Travel
   钟楼饭店
32 Hotel Royal Xi'an
   西安皇城宾馆
36 Hyatt Regency Xi'an
   西安凯悦饭店
39 ANA Grand Castle Hotel
   Xi'an
   长安城堡大酒店
40 Victory Hotel
   胜利饭店
42 Xi'an Hotel
   西安宾馆

PLACES TO EAT
2 Mum's Home Cooking;
   Dad's Home Cooking
8 Singapore Fast Food
   新加坡快餐
13 KFC
   肯德鸡

16 Baiyunzhang Dumpling
   Shop
   白云章饺子馆
17 Bob & Betty's (Fast Food)
   堡之碧
27 Indian Restaurant
   印度餐厅
28 Minsheng Grand Hotel
   Food Village
   民生大酒店
29 East Asia Restaurant
   东亚饭店
30 Singapore Fast Food
   新加坡快餐
31 Laosunjia Restaurant
   老孙家饭庄
34 Xi'an Restaurant
   西安饭庄

OTHER
3 Railway Station
   火车站
4 Post Office
   邮电局
6 Long-Distance Bus Station
   长途汽车站
7 Bank of China (Main
   Branch)
   中国银行
9 Advance Rail Booking
   Office
   铁路售票处
12 Temple of the Eight
   Immortals
   八仙安
14 Old Gun Club
   老枪酒吧

15 Fashion Bar
   福喜会酒吧
18 Foreign Languages
   Bookstore
   外文书店
20 Post &
   Telecommunications
   Building
   邮电大楼
21 Drum Tower
   鼓楼
22 Great Mosque
   大清簃
23 City God's Temple
   城隍庙
24 China Northwest Airlines
   Xi'an Booking Centre
   中国西北航空公司
   西安售票处
25 PSB
   公安局
33 Bank of China
   中国银行
35 Ferry Man Bar
   摆渡客酒吧
37 Shaanxi Provincial
   Museum
   陕西省博物馆
38 Xi'an West Bus Station
   西安汽车西站
41 Little Goose Pagoda;
   Jianfu Temple
   小雁塔
43 CITS
   中国国际旅行社
44 Shaanxi History Museum
   陕西历史博物馆

Travel to see what kind of discounts they can arrange: you may be able to save up to 50% off the walk-in rate.

The *Jiefang Hotel* (☎ 742-8946) (*jiěfàng fàndiàn*), diagonally across the wide square to your left as you leave the railway station, has a convenient location which is the deciding factor for some travellers. Comfortable doubles cost Y240, triples Y280 and quads Y320.

A short distance from the Bell Tower, the *May First Hotel* (☎ 721-6063) (*wǔyī fàndiàn*) is at 351 Dong Dajie. A recent renovation has pushed prices up to Y300 a double, and these may rise even further

if the hotel attains the three star rating it's seeking. Whether the service can match the prices was questionable at the time of writing, but things may improve. The location is definitely a plus.

The enormous *People's (Renmin) Hotel* (☎ 721-5111) (*rénmín dàshà*) is at 319 Dongxin Jie. Designed in the classic early 1950s Stalinist architectural style (with Chinese characteristics), it's been renovated into a fairly upmarket accommodation option. The cheapest doubles (which do look quite nice) cost Y470, although if the hotel isn't full you may get the price down to Y380.

SHAANXI

Places to Stay – top end

This is the category most Xi'an hotels aim for, and there are dozens of choices. There are some that stand out from the crowd.

For location and luxury you can't beat the *Hyatt Regency Xi'an* (☎ 723-1234; fax 721-6799) *(kǎiyuè fàndiàn)*. Its service and facilities have garnered it a five star rating, and it's just a few minutes' walk to Xi'an's restaurant and nightlife scene. Standard doubles are US$130, and luxury doubles are US$150. Regency club rooms, which are better equipped for business travellers, are US$170 per night.

Also enjoying a fine location, and a bit cheaper, is the *Hotel Royal Xi'an* (☎ 723-5311; fax 723-5884) *(xī'ān huángchéng bīnguǎn)*, which is a member of Japan's Nikko Hotels group. Twin rooms start at US$90, while suites cost US$180. Service seems fairly efficient, although perhaps not always up to the standard one would normally expect from a Nikko hotel.

The prize for best position among Xi'an's hotels has to go to the *Bell Tower Hotel* (☎ 727-9200; fax 721-8767) *(zhōng-lóu fàndiàn)*. Managed by the Holiday Inn group, it's quite a pleasant place, and is among the more reasonably priced top-end choices with rates starting at Y600. The service and amenities don't match the Hyatt or other luxury hotels, but should still make for a comfortable stay.

A bit further from the city centre, *Grand New World Hotel* (☎ 721-6868; fax 721-9754) *(gǔdū xīnshìjiè dàjiǔdiàn)* is another well run international operation – standard/ superior rooms cost US$100/110.

Outside the city walls are several other options. The best of these is probably the *Shangri-La Golden Flower (xiānggélǐlā jīnhuā fàndiàn)* which, like the Hyatt, enjoys a five star rating. Facilities include an indoor heated swimming pool, health club, satellite TV and in-house movies. Rates for double rooms start at Y1020, those for suites at Y1785. The hotel is about 2.5km east of the city walls, near the intersection of Changle Xilu and Jinhua Lu.

On the opposite edge of the city is the *Sheraton Xi'an Hotel* (☎ 426-1888; fax 426-2986) *(xī'ān xīláidēng dàjiǔdiàn)*, yet another five star, although it doesn't feel quite as luxurious as the Hyatt or Shangri-La. Still, service standards and amenities are excellent, which they should be for the price: doubles start at US$110.

Just south of the South Gate is the *ANA Grand Castle Hotel Xi'an* (☎ 723-1800; fax 723-1500) *(cháng'ān chéngbǎo dàjiǔdiàn)*, which appears to cater mainly to Japanese tour groups. It has a fairly impressive lobby/atrium, and although outside the city walls the hotel is still fairly close to the city centre. Standard rooms are US$110, superior rooms US$120.

Note that all the above hotels levy a 15% service charge on room rates and all food and services.

Places to Eat

There's a lot of good street food in Xi'an. In winter the entire population seems to get by on endless bowls of noodles, but at other times of the year there are all kinds of delicious snacks to be had.

Much of the local street food is of Islamic origin, and some common dishes are: *fěnrèròu*, made by frying chopped mutton in a wok with fine-ground wheat; *héletiáo (*dark brown sorghum or buckwheat noodles); and *ròujiāmó*, fried pork or beef stuffed in pita bread, sometimes with green peppers and cumin.

Another dish worth trying is *yángròu pàomó*, a soup dish that involves breaking (or grating) a flat loaf of bread into a bowl and adding a delicious mutton stock. You will first be served a bowl and one or two pieces of flat bread: try and break the bread into tiny chunks, the better to absorb the broth.

For Muslim-Chinese 'haute cuisine' try the 3rd floor section of the *Laosunjia Restaurant (lǎosūnjia fànzhuāng)* on the corner of Duanlumen and Dong Dajie. The restaurant is opposite the Friendship Store and is readily identified by its green dome roof with an crescent moon on top. It serves a delicious local hotpot called *shuànguōzi*, made by dipping uncooked meat and vegetable slices into a boiling chafing dish. Downstairs, an extremely filling serving of yangrou paomo will cost you Y12.

The cheap downstairs restaurant in the *May First Hotel (wǔyī fàndiàn)* is good for staple northern Chinese food like pork dumplings and hearty bowls of noodles. It's popular with locals and always busy.

The *East Asia Restaurant (dōngyà fàndiàn)* was founded in 1916 in Shanghai, but moved to Xi'an in 1956. The restaurant's better sections on the 2nd and 3rd floors have long been known for having some of Xi'an's best Chinese cuisine. The East Asia is south-east of the Bell Tower at 46 Luoma Shi, a lane running off Dong Dajie.

The *Xi'an Restaurant (xī'ān fànzhuāng)* is at 298 Dong Dajie. In the cheap section downstairs, the house speciality is salty fried dumplings called *guōtiē*. There are also steamed and boiled dumplings, fried dishes and a wide assortment of cold appetisers to choose from.

An excellent spot for dumplings is the *Baiyunzhang Dumpling Restaurant (báiyúnzhāng jiǎozǐguǎn)*, diagonally opposite the Hotel Royal Xi'an. Mutton or beef dumplings are made fresh, which sometimes means a bit of a wait: it's worth it.

For a little bit of everything, you can head down Nan Dajie to the *Minsheng Grand Hotel Food Village (mínshēng dàjiǔdiàn shícūn)*, on the 4th floor of the Minsheng Grand Hotel. Sort of a mini food court, you can buy Y20 worth of coupons and take your pick of local and regional specialities. There are no English signs, but everything is plainly on display, making ordering fairly easy. The food is reasonably priced and quite tasty. It's open from 11 am to 2 pm and from 5.30 to 9.30 pm. Access is via the north stairwell of the hotel, one floor above the 'deluxe' restaurant/nightclub.

Around the Flats of Renmin Hotel, the travellers' restaurant scene centres on two restaurants: *Dad's Home Cooking* and *Mum's Home Cooking*. These are separate establishments and competition between them is fierce. Service and food are almost exactly the same, so spread your business around if possible. Both are pleasant places to meet up with other backpackers, trade travellers' tales and knock back more beer than is good for you.

Xi'an also has a few fast-food options. There are branches of *KFC* all over town. Another, more palatable, option is *Singapore Fast Food*, a hawker-style variation on the fast-food theme – air-con and laminex – but the food isn't bad. Also worth checking out is *Bob & Betty's* at 285 Dong Dajie. It has good burgers, pizzas and coffee at affordable prices.

Entertainment
Although not on a par with Beijing or Shanghai, Xi'an does have an increasingly lively nightlife scene. In addition to the usual karaoke and hostess clubs, a number of small bars featuring live music have sprung up, and are worth popping into.

The *Old Gun Club (lǎoqiāng jiǔbā)* on Dong Dajie, is one of the friendliest and relaxing spots, and has live folk/rock music (Chinese and western) nightly. Across the street, the *Ferry Man Bar (bǎidùkè jiǔbā)* has a similar rustic feel to it. There's also live music nightly here and it's popular with the local expat community.

A bit further west along Dong Dajie is the *Fashion Bar (fúxǐhuì jiǔbā)*. The entrance doesn't look like much, but once you reach the top of the stairs you may feel you've stepped into Hong Kong or even New York. A circular burnished pine bar, Art Deco design, a high-quality sound system and catwalk balconies make this one of the flashiest bars you're likely to find in town. At the time of writing it had just opened, and there were plans to have Chinese rock bands play fairly regularly. Drop by to see what's developed.

Things to Buy
Huajue Xiang *(huàjuè xiàng)* is a narrow alley running beside the Great Mosque with many small souvenir and 'antique' shops – they're great for browsing. This is one of the best places in China to pick up

souvenirs like name chops or a pair of chiming steel balls. Bargaining is the order of the day.

An interesting place to visit is the City God's Temple *(chéng huáng miào)*, an old-style wooden structure that possibly dates from the early Qing period. It's actually no longer a temple, but now houses a small wares market that looks like the China of the early 1980s: lots of older consumer goods, some interesting porcelain ware, Chinese musical instruments and calligraphy implements.

The temple is a 10 minute walk west of the Drum Tower at the end of a long covered market running north off Xi Dajie. There's no English sign, so look for the large red Chinese characters above the entrance immediately east of the Xijing Hotel.

Around town you'll also find worthy conversation pieces like carved-stone ink trays used in Chinese calligraphy and a wide range of jade products from earrings to cigarette holders. There are plenty of silks too, but you're probably better off buying these closer to their source (Suzhou, Shanghai etc). Street hawkers sell delicate miniature wire furniture and ingenious little folded bamboo-leaf insects such as crickets and cicadas, which make cheap and attractive souvenirs.

If you're interested in Chinese and Buddhist classical music, there's an interesting selection at the Little Goose Pagoda.

Getting There & Away

Air Xi'an is one of the best-connected cities in China – it's possible to fly to almost any major Chinese destination, as well as several international ones.

The China Northwest Airlines Xi'an Booking Centre (☎ 870-2299) is a modern, efficient operation, although somewhat inconveniently located on the south-eastern corner of Xiguan Zhengjie and Laodong Lu, 1.5km from West Gate. It may be worth the time to get here though: you can get discounts on most domestic flights if you purchase directly from this office, but not if you go through CITS or any of the

booking offices in the major hotels around town. Office hours are 8 am to 9 pm daily.

Daily flights include Beijing (Y980), Chengdu (Y640), Guangzhou (Y1400), Guilin (Y1040), Shanghai (Y1260) and Qingdao (Y2090). There are two flights a week to Lhasa (Y2340), although this service seems to come and go.

On the international front, there are flights to Hong Kong for Y2300 with both Dragonair and China Northwest, although at the time of writing the latter was offering the flight for Y1860 through direct purchase from their booking centre. Dragonair (☎ 426-9288) has an office in the lobby of the Sheraton Hotel.

China Northwest also has flights to Macau, and to Nagoya and Hiroshima in Japan.

Bus The most central long-distance bus station is opposite Xi'an railway station. From here you can get buses to Huashan (Y12, 3½ hours) and Yan'an (Y32, 10 hours), as well as sleeper buses to more distant destinations such as Zhengzhou (Y96, 12 hours), Luoyang (Y60, 10 hours) and Yinchuan (Y113, 15 hours).

Buses to Zhengzhou leave around noon, those to Luoyang at 6 pm, while sleepers to Yinchuan leave hourly from noon to 6.30 pm. There's also a large bus station on Huancheng Nanlu, west of the South Gate.

If you're headed to Huashan, private minibuses leave when full from the east parking lot in front of the railway station from 7 am to 6 pm. If they go via the highway the ride takes 2½ hours and costs Y20.

Train There are direct trains from Xi'an to Beijing, Chengdu, Guangzhou, Hefei, Qingdao, Shanghai, Taiyuan, Ürümqi and Wuhan. For Chongqing and Kunming change at Chengdu.

While you can sometimes get same-day tickets in the main ticket hall, most counters will probably refer you to the foreigners' ticket window on the 2nd level: look for the staircase near the English sign directing foreigners and Overseas Chinese to the '1st floor'. You'll need to bring your passport in order to register at the small window at the western end of the 2nd level. The ticket clerk will then give you a registration slip which you take to window No 2, at the eastern end of the floor: this is where you actually buy the ticket. The foreigner's window is open from 8.30 to 11.30 am and from 2.30 to 5.30 pm.

There's an Advance Rail Booking Office on Lianhu Lu, but it only sells hardseat tickets. Hours are 8 am to 11.30 pm and 1 to 5.30 pm. CITS can organise tickets with a minimum of fuss, providing you give two or three days' notice.

Direct trains to Beijing take around 16 hours, to Guangzhou around 27 hours and to Chengdu around 17 hours. For travellers to Luoyang and Zhengzhou, there is an aircon tourist train (No Y201) that leaves at 11.54 am and arrives in Zhengzhou at 9.09 pm the same day.

Getting Around

To/From the Airport Xi'an's Xiguan airport is around 40km north-west of Xi'an. China Northwest Airlines runs shuttle buses hourly from 5 am to 6 pm between the airport and its Xi'an booking centre (Y15, 50 minutes), from where you can pick up a taxi or local bus to your hotel.

Small Daihatsu taxis charge at least Y120 in either direction, while larger Santannas cost around Y160.

Bus Xi'an's packed public buses are a pickpocket's paradise, so watch your wallet when you ride them. More comfortable minibuses run on the same routes and charge around Y2 for most central destinations.

Local buses go to all the major sights in and around the city, such as Banpo Neolithic Village and the Army of Terracotta Warriors.

Taxi Taxis are abundant and reasonably cheap: flag fall is around Y6. Although most drivers use the meter in town, for more distant destinations, such as the airport, you'll have to negotiate a price.

Bicycle Bicycle hire is available at the Flats of Renmin, Victory and Bell Tower hotels for around Y1 to Y2 per hour.

AROUND XI'AN

Most of the really interesting sights are outside the city. The two biggest drawcards are the Army of Terracotta Warriors near the Tomb of Qin Shihuang, and the Banpo Neolithic Village.

Tomb of Qin Shihuang
(qín shǐhuáng líng)

It may not amount to much as a tourist attraction, but in its time the Tomb of Qin Shihuang must have been one of the grandest mausoleums the world had ever seen.

In the year 246 BC, at the age of 13, Ying Zheng ascended the throne of the state of Qin and assumed the title 'Shi Huang', or First Emperor. One by one he defeated his enemies, until in 221 BC the last of them fell. Qin Shihuang united the country, and standardised the currency and written script.

On the downside, he acquired a reputation for purges, mass book-burning parties, enforced labour in massive construction projects, and other tyrannical behaviour. His rule lasted until his death in 210 BC. His son only held out for four years, before being overthrown by the revolt which established the Han Dynasty.

Historical accounts describe Qin's tomb as containing palaces filled with precious stones and ingenious defences against intruders. It housed ceilings vaulted with pearls, statues of gold and silver, and rivers of mercury. It is said that the artisans who brought it all into being were buried alive within, taking its secrets with them.

Despite the legends and the impressive statistics, basically all there is to see nowadays is a mound. Unless you have a good sense for Chinese history this place probably won't do much for you. However, if you're still interested, the tomb is about 1.5km east of the Army of Terracotta Warriors, and can be reached by the No 306 bus. Entry costs Y12.

SHAANXI

ARMY OF TERRACOTTA WARRIORS

Army of Terracotta Warriors

Ranking up there with the Great Wall and the Forbidden City as one of China's top historical sights, the 2000-year-old Army of Terracotta Warriors (bīngmǎyǒng) remains stunningly well preserved: a perpetually vigilant force standing guard over an ancient imperial necropolis. In 1974 peasants digging a well uncovered what turned out to be perhaps the major archaeological discovery of the 20th century: an underground vault of earth and timber that eventually yielded thousands of life-size terracotta soldiers and their horses in battle formation. In 1976, two other, smaller vaults were discovered close to the first one.

The first underground vault measures about 210m east to west and 60m from north to south. The pit varies in depth from 5m to 7m. Walls were built running east to west at intervals of 3m, forming corridors. In these corridors, on floors laid with grey brick, are arranged the terracotta figures. Pillars and beams once supported a roof.

The 6000 terracotta figures of warriors and horses face east in a rectangular battle array. The vanguard appears to be three rows of 210 crossbow and longbow bearers who stand at the easternmost end of the army. Close behind is the main force of armoured soldiers holding spears, dagger-axes and other long-shaft weapons, accompanied by 35 horse-drawn chariots (the latter, made of wood, have long-since disintegrated). Every figure differs in facial features and expressions.

The horsemen are shown wearing tight-sleeved outer robes, short coats of chain mail and wind-proof caps. The archers have bodies and limbs positioned in strict accordance with an ancient book on the art of war. There is speculation that the sculptors used fellow workers, or even themselves, as models for the warriors' faces.

Many of the figures originally held real weapons of the day, and over 10,000 pieces have been sorted to date. Bronze swords were worn by the figures representing the generals and other senior officers. Surface treatment made the swords resistant to rust and corrosion so that after being buried for more than 2000 years they were still sharp. The weapons are now kept in storage, out of public view.

The second vault, excavated in 1976, contained about 1000 figures. The third vault contained only 68 warriors and one war chariot, and appeared to be the command post for the soldiers in the other vaults. Archaeologists believe the warriors discovered so far may be part of an even larger terracotta army still buried around Qin Shihuang's Tomb. Excavation of the entire complex and the tomb itself could take decades.

Almost as impressive is a pair of bronze chariots and horses unearthed in 1980 just 20m west of the Tomb of Qin Shihuang and now housed in a small museum *(qín yǒng bówùguǎn)* within the enclosure of the warriors site.

Visitors are not permitted to take photos at the site and people who break this rule can expect to have their film confiscated. If you decide to take a few sly shots and get caught, try to remember that the attendants are just doing their job.

Ticket prices have risen steadily in recent years. It costs Y80 to see the vaults, Y15 for the museum, and Y40 for a 'Circle Vision' documentary on the warriors and their excavation. Student discounts are available. Hours for all the exhibits are from 8.30 am to 5.30 pm daily.

Getting There & Away

You can see the site as part of a tour from Xi'an (see Organised Tours in the earlier Xi'an entry). Alternatively, it is possible to do it yourself by public bus. From the parking lot just east of the railway station take a No 306 bus, which travels via Huaqing Pool, for Y5. Some buses don't go all the way: ask for *bīngmǎyǒng* to make sure. The No 307 bus does the return journey to Xi'an via Banpo Neolithic Village.

One of the timeless attractions in China, the 2000-year-old Army of Terracotta Warriors is astonishingly well preserved.

Around Xi'an

Huaqing Pool

(huáqīng chí)

The Huaqing Pool is 30km east of Xi'an below Lishan. Water from hot springs is funnelled into public bathhouses that have 60 pools accommodating 400 people.

During the Tang Dynasty these natural hot baths were a favoured retreat of emperors and their concubines. The Huaqing Pool leaves most visitors cold. If you don't fancy strolling around the gardens with swarms of excited Chinese tourists, try the museum up the road or take a walk on one of the paths leading up through the forest behind the complex.

There is a Taoist temple on Lishan dedicated to the 'Old Mother' Nu Wa, who created the human race and patched up cracks in the sky after a catastrophe. On the mountain's summit are beacon towers built for defence during the Han Dynasty. A cable car will whiz you up there for Y25,

and Y20 to come down. Admission to Huaqing Pool is Y30 for foreigners.

The No 306 bus, which runs from the Xi'an railway station to the Army of Terracotta Warriors, stops at Huaqing Pool. The Eastern Tour, organised from Xi'an, visits the Huaqing Pool (see Organised Tours later in this section), but some tours stop for an excessively long two hours.

Banpo Neolithic Village

(bànpō bówùguǎn)

Officially rated as Xi'an's No 2 attraction, surpassed only by the Army of Terracotta Warriors, the Banpo Neolithic Village gets mixed reports from travellers. The general consensus is that it's tacky and boring, but the occasional traveller comes away singing its praises.

The best advice is to limit your visit to the Neolithic village itself (also referred to as the Banpo Museum) and avoid the adjacent

Matriarchal Clan Village, where matriarchs in Neolithic garb, high heels and reinforced stockings merely reinforce the feeling that you're in modern, not ancient, China.

Banpo is the earliest example of 'Yang-shao culture', named after the village where the first of these was discovered. It appears to have been occupied from 4500 BC until around 3750 BC. The village was discovered in 1953 and is on the eastern bank of the Chan River in a suburb of Xi'an.

A large hall has been built over what was part of the residential area of the village, and there are adjacent buildings housing pottery and other artefacts. Pottery found south of the Qinlingshan mountains has suggested that even earlier agricultural villages may have existed here.

The Banpo ruins are divided into three parts: a pottery-manufacturing area, a residential area and a cemetery. These include the remains of 45 houses or other buildings, over 200 storage cellars, six pottery kilns and 250 graves.

The residential part of the village was surrounded by an artificial moat, 300m long, about 2m deep and 2m wide. It protected the village from attacks by wild animals and from the effects of heavy rainfall in what was originally a hot and humid environment. To the east of the residential area is the pottery kiln centre. To the north of the village lies the cemetery, where the adult dead were buried along with funerary objects like earthen pots. The children were buried in earthen pots close to the houses.

Entry to the Neolithic village costs Y20, while the Matriarchal Clan Village is another Y40. Both are open daily from 8 am to 6.30 pm.

Getting There & Away The Eastern Tour to the Army of Terracotta Warriors usually includes Banpo Neolithic Village. 'Unorganised' travellers generally visit by way of bus No 307, which stops at Banpo on the return journey from the Terracotta Warriors to Xi'an. Electric bus No 105 will get you there directly from the railway station.

Xianyang
(xiányáng)
This little town is half an hour's bus ride from Xi'an. The chief attraction is Xianyang City Museum *(xiányáng shì bówùguǎn)*, which houses a remarkable collection of 3000 miniature terracotta soldiers and horses, discovered in 1965. Each figure is about half a metre high. They were excavated from a Han Dynasty tomb. Admission is Y12 and the museum is open from 8.30 am to 5 pm.

Getting There & Away To get to Xianyang Museum from Xi'an, take bus No 611 from the railway station to the terminal and then get bus No 59. Get off at the terminal in Xianyang. Up ahead on the left-hand side of the road you'll see a clock tower. Turn right at this intersection and then left at Xining Jie.

The museum is housed in a former Ming Dynasty Confucian temple on Zhongshan Jie, which is a continuation of Xining Jie. The entrance is flanked by two stone lions. It's about a 20 minute walk from the bus terminal.

Imperial Tombs
Apart from the tomb of Qin Shihuang, a large number of other imperial tombs dot the Guanzhong plain surrounding Xi'an. The easiest way to get there is by tour from Xi'an (see the Organised Tours section for details).

In these tombs are buried the emperors of numerous dynasties, as well as empresses, concubines, government officials and high-ranking military leaders. Construction of an emperor's tomb often began within a few years of his ascension to the throne and didn't finish until he died.

Entry fees to the tombs range from Y15 to Y20. All tombs are open from 8.30 am to 5 pm.

Zhao Tomb *(zhāo líng)* The Zhao Tomb set the custom of building imperial tombs on mountain slopes, breaking the tradition of building tombs on the plains with an artificial hill over them. This burial ground on Jiuzongshan, 70km north-west of Xi'an, belongs to the second Tang emperor, Tai Zong, who died in 649 AD.

Of the 18 imperial mausoleums on the Guanzhong plain, this is probably the most representative. With the mountain at the centre, the tomb fans out to the south-east and south-west. Within its confines are 167 lesser tombs of the emperor's relatives and high-ranking military and government officials. Burying other people in the same park as the emperor was a custom dating back to the Han Dynasty.

Buried in the sacrificial altar of the tomb were six statues known as the 'Six Steeds of Zhaoling', representing the horses which the emperor used during his wars of conquest. Some of the statues have been relocated to museums in Xi'an.

Qian Tomb (*qián líng*) This is one of the most impressive tombs, 85km north-west of Xi'an on Liangshan. This is the joint resting place of Tang Emperor Gao Zong and his wife Empress Wu Zetian.

Gao Zong ascended the throne in 650 AD after the death of his father, Emperor Tai Zong. Empress Wu, actually a concubine of Tai Zong, also caught the fancy of his son, who made her his empress. Gao died in 683 AD, and the following year Empress Wu dethroned her husband's successor, Emperor Zhong Zong. She reigned as an all-powerful monarch until her death around 705 AD.

The tomb consists of three peaks; the two on the southern side are artificial, but the higher northern peak is natural and is the main part of the tomb. Walls used to surround the tomb, but these are gone. South-west of the tomb are 17 smaller tombs of officials.

The grounds of the imperial tomb boast a number of large stone sculptures of animals and officers of the imperial guard. There are 61 (now headless) statues of the leaders of minority peoples of China and of the representatives of friendly nations who attended the emperor's funeral. The two steles on the ground each stand more than

6m high. The 'Wordless Stele' is a blank tablet; one story goes that it symbolises Empress Wu's absolute power, which she considered inexpressible in words.

Prince Zhang Huai's Tomb (*zhāng huái mù*) Zhang was the second son of Emperor Gao Zong and Empress Wu. For some reason the prince was exiled to Sichuan in 683 AD and died the following year, aged only 31.

Empress Wu posthumously rehabilitated him. His remains were brought to Xi'an after Emperor Zhong Zong regained power. Tomb paintings show horsemen playing polo, but these and other paintings are in a terrible state.

Princess Yong Tai's Tomb (*yǒng tài gōng zhǔ mù*) Near Prince Zhang Huai's Tomb is the Tomb of Princess Yong Tai, which features tomb paintings depicting palace servants. The line engravings on the stone outer coffin are extraordinarily graceful.

Yong Tai was a granddaughter of Tang Emperor Gao Zong, and the seventh daughter of Emperor Zhong Zong. She was put to death by Empress Wu in 701 AD, but was rehabilitated posthumously by Emperor Zhong Zong after he regained power.

Mao Tomb (*mào líng*) The Mao Tomb, 40km from Xi'an, is the resting place of Emperor Wu, the most powerful ruler of the Han Dynasty, who died in 87 BC. The cone-shaped mound of rammed earth is almost 47m high, and is the largest of the Han imperial tombs. A wall used to enclose the mausoleum, but now only the ruins of the gates on the eastern, western and northern sides remain.

It is recorded that the emperor was entombed with a jade cicada in his mouth and was clad in jade clothes sewn with gold thread, and that buried with him were live animals and an abundance of jewels.

Famen Temple
(*fǎmén sì*)
Famen Temple, 115km north-west of Xi'an,

was built during the Eastern Han Dynasty in about 200 AD.

In 1981, after torrential rains had weakened the temple's ancient brick structure, the entire western side of the 12 storey pagoda collapsed. The subsequent restoration work produced a sensational discovery. Below the pagoda in a sealed crypt (built during the Tang Dynasty to contain four sacred finger bones of the buddha, known as *sarira*) were over 1000 sacrificial objects and royal offerings, including stone-tablet Buddhist scriptures, gold and silver items and some 27,000 coins. These relics had been completely forgotten for over 1000 years.

A museum housing part of the collection has been built on the site. After the excavations had finished the temple was reconstructed in its original form.

The best way to visit Famen Temple is to take a Western Tour from Xi'an (see the following Organised Tours section). Some tours don't include the temple so check before you book. Foreigners' entry prices are Y25 to the temple, Y20 to the crypt and Y20 to the museum; the pagoda itself is not open to the public.

Organised Tours

One day tours allow you to see all the sights around Xi'an more quickly and conveniently than if you arranged one yourself. Itineraries differ somewhat, but there are two basic tours: a 'Western Tour' and an 'Eastern Tour'. There are also Chinese tours that leave from the square in front of the railway station.

Travel agency tours are more expensive than those run by other operators, but the railway station operators don't leave until they have enough people and tend to give you less time at each place.

Eastern Tour The Eastern Tour *(dōngxiàn yóulǎn)* is the most popular as it includes the Army of Terracotta Warriors as well as the Tomb of Qin Shihuang, Banpo Neolithic Village and Huaqing Pool.

CITS offers an Eastern Tour for Y280 including lunch and all entry tickets: it also throws in a visit to the Big Goose Pagoda. The coach leaves Xi'an around 9 am and returns by 5 pm. An English-speaking guide is provided and you usually get two hours at the warriors and Qin Shihuang's Tomb.

Golden Bridge Travel does the same tour (minus the Big Goose Pagoda). At Y340 per person it costs more, but groups are usually limited to five or six people and the bus leaves directly from the Bell Tower Hotel, rather than making rounds of the city's hotels to pick up passengers as CITS does.

Essentially the same tour can be done for far less by taking one of the Chinese minibus tours; you can buy tickets for Y44 at a kiosk in front of the railway station. Just remember that in this case, you get what you pay for.

If you don't mind waiting for public buses, you can reach the Eastern Tour sights on your own for less than Y200: see the Around Xi'an section for transport and entry ticket details.

Western Tour The longer Western Tour *(xīxiàn yóulǎn)* includes the Xianyang City Museum, some of the imperial tombs, the Qian Tomb and sometimes also Famen Temple.

It's far less popular than the Eastern Tour and consequently you will have to get a group of people to make your own tour with either Golden Bridge Travel or CITS – the cost for one person alone is around Y800, although you could just hire a vehicle without a guide for around Y500.

HUASHAN
(huáshān)

The 2200m-high granite peaks of Huashan, 120km east of Xi'an, tower above the plains to the north, forming one of China's sacred mountain areas. Although not as famous as, say, Huangshan or Emeishan, it's a beautiful area and less touristed than its better known counterparts.

A 6km path leads to the North Peak, the

first of four summit peaks. The first 4km are pretty easy going, but after that it's all steep stairs, and from the North Peak on to the other summits is also fairly strenuous. But the scenery is great; along Green Dragon Ridge, which connects the North Peak with the East, South and West peaks, the way has been cut along a narrow rock ridge with sheer cliffs on either side.

The South Peak is the highest at 2160m, but all three rear peaks afford great views when the weather cooperates.

From Huashan village at the base of the mountain it usually takes between three to five hours to reach the North Peak, and another hour or so to get to any one of the others. Several narrow and almost vertical 'bottleneck' sections are dangerous when the route is crowded, particularly under wet or icy conditions. If your legs aren't feeling up to the task, an Austrian-built cable car can get you from the eastern base of the mountain to the North Peak in just 10 minutes (Y45 one way, Y80 return).

There is accommodation on the mountain, most of it quite basic and overpriced, but it does allow you to start in the afternoon, spend the night and catch the sunrise from the East Peak. Many Chinese tourists actually make the climb at night, aided by torches (flashlights) and countless tea and refreshment stands. The idea is to start off at around 11 pm to midnight, which should get you to the East Peak at sunrise. In summer this is certainly a much cooler option, but you do miss the scenery on the way up.

The gate ticket price is Y40, plus another Y5 'registration fee'. When heading out from Huashan village, be careful not to hit the trail via the Yuquan Temple, unless you're interested in seeing it, and paying another Y10 entry fee. There's a path that skirts the temple to the left and reconnects with the main Huashan trail.

Places to Stay & Eat

There are plenty of cheap places to stay in Huashan village along the road leading up to the trailhead and Yuquan Temple. About 100m from the Yuquan Temple, on the right-hand side of the street is the *Xiyue Hotel* (☎ 436-3145) *(xīyuè fàndiàn)*, an ornate yellow and red traditional-style building. Beds in a fairly clean triple with shared bath cost Y18, while doubles with bath attached go for Y80 to Y140.

The nearby *Huashan Banking Hotel* (☎ 436-3119) *(huáshān jīnróng bīnguǎn)* is the top spot in town, and offers upmarket doubles from Y200 to Y300. It also has air-con triples/quads with shared bath for Y150/200.

Opposite the Huashan Banking Hotel is the *Kaiyue Hotel (kǎiyuè dàjiǔdiàn)*, a small family-run operation that has beds in nice triples with shared bath for Y20, and doubles with (tiny) attached bathrooms for Y120. There's no English sign.

Just over 4km up the mountain trail at Maonü Cave *(maónǚ dòng)* is a small hostel with very basic rooms, all with shared bath. Rates range from Y15 for a bed in a 10 person dorm to Y30 in a double. Although nothing special, it's better value than what you'll find at the summit.

The next place is the *Beifeng Hotel* (☎ 436-3203) *(běifēng fàndiàn)*, just below the North Peak, which has doubles/quads with private bath for Y220/240 and beds in eight-person dorms for Y45.

All the other summits have accommodation of one sort or another. The *Xifeng Hostel (xīfēng lǚshè)* sits atop the West Peak, and charges a usurious Y60 for a bed in grimy, draughty quads with shared bath. Beds in similar doubles are Y80.

A slightly better deal is the small temple/hostel on the way up to the West Peak, which has beds in cleaner rooms for Y40 to Y60. Also on the West Peak is the *Dianli Hotel* (☎ 436-2961) *(diànlì bīnguǎn)*, the mountain's high-end option, where doubles/triples with attached bath start at Y480/530. This is not an especially good deal, and unless you really crave the creature comforts, it's probably best skipped. On the South and East peaks are places similar to the Xifeng Hostel in terms of both conditions and prices (although the East Peak hostel is a bit cleaner).

Getting There & Away

The nearest railway station is at Mengyuan, on the Xi'an-Luoyang line, about 15km east of Huashan. This station is also referred to as Huashan, and is served by nearly a dozen trains daily in either direction. Minibuses run between the railway station and Huashan village, usually stopping near the Huashan Banking Hotel. The 30 minute ride costs Y3.

Occasionally there will be minibuses direct to the cable car, but usually you'll need to take a taxi (Y20), as it's about 5km south-east of Huashan village.

Minibuses to Xi'an (Y10, 2½ hours) leave when full from opposite the Huashan Banking Hotel from 7 am to around 6 pm. Coming from Xi'an, buses leave from the east parking lot in front of the railway station. Public buses (Y11) also make the run, leaving from Xi'an's long-distance bus station, but the ride takes 3½ to four hours, as these buses don't take the highway.

The Huashan bus station is a few hundred metres east of the intersection of the main road with the street leading up to Yuquan temple and the trailhead.

YAN'AN

(yán'ān)

Yan'an, 270km from Xi'an in northern Shaanxi Province, is a small city of 40,000 people, but together with Mao's birthplace at Shaoshan it has special significance as a major Communist pilgrimage spot.

Between the years 1936 and 1947 this was the headquarters of the fledgling Chinese Communist Party. The Long March from Jiangxi ended in 1936 when the Communists reached the northern Shaanxi town of Wuqi. The following year they moved their base to Yan'an.

Apart from the revolution history sites, there's not a whole lot to see in Yan'an, although just making it up to this remote section of the province is in itself pretty interesting. Despite its status as the 'birthplace' of the revolution, Yan'an has been largely neglected by the Chinese Communist government, and it remains a fairly poor, underdeveloped place.

Even Mao himself turned his back on Yan'an: after living here for nearly a decade, he left in 1947, never to revisit.

Orientation

Yan'an is spread out along a Y-shaped valley formed where the east and west branches of the Yan River meet. The town centre is clustered around this junction, while the old Communist army headquarters is at Yangjialing on the north-western outskirts of Yan'an. The railway station is at the far southern end of town, 4.5km from the centre.

Things to See

During their extended stay, the Communist leadership moved house quite a bit within Yan'an. As a result there are numerous former headquarters sites.

One of the most interesting is the **Yangjialing Revolution Headquarters Site** *(yángjiālíng gémìng jiùzhǐ)*, 3km north-west of the town centre. Here you can see the assembly hall where the first Central Committee meetings were held, lincluding the 7th national plenum, which formally confirmed Mao as the leader of the party and the revolution.

Nearby are simple dugouts built into the loess earth where Mao, Zhu De, Zhou Enlai and other senior Communist leaders lived, worked and wrote. Further uphill are caves that used to house the secretariat, propaganda and personnel offices. Admission to the site is Y10 and hours are 7.30 to 11.30 am and 2.30 to 5.30 pm.

About 1km south-east is the **Yan'an Revolution Museum** *(yán'ān gémìng jìniànguǎn)* which has an extensive collection of revolutionary paraphernalia – old uniforms, weaponry and many photographs and illustrations. There's even a stuffed horse that was allegedly ridden by Mao himself. Unfortunately, there are no English labels. The museum is open daily from 7.30 am to 6 pm and entry costs Y10.

Just a few minutes' walk south is the

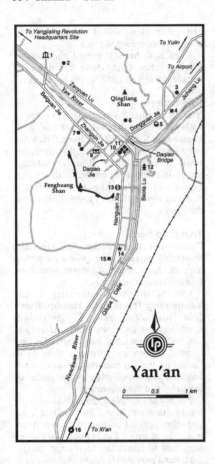

Yan'an

0   0.5   1 km

To Xi'an

PLACES TO STAY

4 Jialing Hotel
   嘉岭宾馆
7 Yan'an Hotel
   延安宾馆
15 Yan'an Jiaoji Hotel
   延安交际宾馆

OTHER

1 Yan'an Revolution Museum
   延安革命纪念馆
2 Wangjiaping Revolution
   Headquarters Site
   王家坪革命旧址
3 Airline Booking Office
   民航售票处
5 Long-Distance Bus Station
   延安汽车站
6 Qingliangshan Entry Gate
   清凉山售票口
8 Fenghuangshan Revolution
   Headquarters Site
   凤凰山革命旧址
9 Post & Telephone Office
   邮电大楼
10 Xinhua Bookstore
   新华书店
11 Yan'an Department Store
   延安百货大楼
12 Baota Pagoda
   宝塔
13 Bank of China
   中国银行
14 PSB
   公安局
16 Railway Station
   火车站

last site occupied by the Communist leadership in Yan'an, the **Wangjiaping Revolution Headquarters Site** *(wángjiāpíng
gémìng jiùzhǐ)*. There's not quite as much
to see here, although it's interesting to note
the improvement in living standards enjoyed by Mao and top-ranking comrades.
Entry costs Y5 and hours are 7.30 am to 6
pm daily.

All the above stops can be reached by
taking the No 1 bus, which runs from the
railway station along the road east of the
river and then heads up Zaoyuan Lu. From

the station it's 11 stops to Wangjiaping and
the museum, and 14 stops to Yangjialing.

More accessible from the city is the
**Fenghuangshan Revolution Headquar-
ters Site** *(fēnghuángshān gémìng jiùzhǐ)*,
about 100m south of the Yan'an Hotel.
This was the first site occupied by the
Communists after their move to Yan'an, as
reflected by the relatively primitive lodgings of the leading cadres. Entry is Y3 and
hours are 7.30 am to 6 pm.

The **Baota Pagoda** *(bǎotǎ)*, built during
the Song Dynasty, stands on a prominent

hillside south-east of the river junction. Entry costs Y10, plus an additional Y5 to climb the pagoda, which is open from 7 am to 8 pm daily.

Qingliangshan *(qīngliángshān)* is a pleasant hillside park with some nice trails and a few sights, including a **Ten Thousand Buddha Cave** *(wànfó dòng)* dug into the sandstone cliff beside the river. The cave has relatively intact Buddhist statues and wall inscriptions. The park is open daily from 7 am to 7 pm and entry is Y20.

Places to Stay & Eat
There are only two hotels officially allowed to take foreign guests. Of these the cheaper option is the *Yan'an Jiaoji Hotel* (☎ 211-3862) *(yán'ān jiāojì bīnguǎn)*, which has triples with shared bath for Y72 and doubles with private bath for Y100 and Y120. It's a pretty comfortable place, but is often full as it is the official reception hotel for visiting officials and is also popular with tour groups. To get there from the railway station take the No 3 five stops, get off and walk back 200m.

The other official choice is the *Yan'an Hotel* (☎ 211-3122) *(yán'ān bīnguǎn)*, the top spot in town. Doubles range from Y200 in the old north wing to Y280 in the new south wing. There may be a little latitude for bargaining if the tour groups aren't swarming about. From the railway station it's nine stops on the No 3 bus.

The *Jialing Hotel* (☎ 231-5470) *(jiālíng bīnguǎn)*, on the eastern side of town, is not supposed to accept foreigners, but you may be able to talk your way in. If so, you can get dorm beds for Y26 and slightly dingy but comfortable doubles with private bath for Y120.

Yan'an doesn't seem to have any really outstanding restaurants (although maybe you will stumble across one), but there are quite a few cheap, fairly good places near the long-distance bus station. There are also a few more upmarket *restaurants* near the Yan'an Hotel. *Night markets* set up on the western side of the Daqiao Bridge and near the long-distance bus station.

Getting There & Away
Air There are two weekly flights between Xi'an and Yan'an (Y350), although service is sometimes reduced or suspended depending on demand. There are also flights to Beijing (Y800).

The airline booking office (☎ 211-3854) is on Jichang Lu, diagonally opposite the Jialing Hotel, and is open daily from 8 am to noon and 2.30 to 5.30 pm. A free bus service connects the office with the airport, 7km north-east of the city.

Bus From the long-distance bus station in Xi'an, buses to Yan'an run every 30 to 60 minutes from 6 to 11.30 am. The ride takes nine hours and costs Y32 (Y50 for a sleeper). The schedule is the same in the reverse direction.

From Yan'an there are four buses in the morning to Yulin (Y31, eight hours) and one daily departure at 5.30 am to Yinchuan, in Ningxia Province (Y44, 12 hours).

Train A railway line links Yan'an with Xi'an via an interesting route along the Luo River. There are two trains daily in either direction: an overnighter which leaves Xi'an at 10.20 pm and Yan'an at 10.30 pm (eight hours), and a day train that departs either station around 8.30 am (nine hours).

Getting sleeper tickets to Xi'an is usually no problem, but getting them back can be quite difficult: either get down to the station by 7.30 am to line up, or contact CITS at the Yan'an Hotel a day or two in advance and see if they can get one for you.

YULIN
(yúlín)
Yulin lies on the fringe of Inner Mongolia's Mu Us Desert in far northern Shaanxi. During the Ming Dynasty, Yulin was a fortified garrison town and patrol post serving the Great Wall.

Yulin's remoteness and relative poverty have kept the old town somewhat insulated from the 'white-tile' trend in Chinese architecture, which is rapidly destroying what remains of the country's older buildings. Along the narrow brick lanes near the un-restored bell tower are traditional family houses with tiny courtyards hidden behind low enclosure walls and old stone gates. The city's old Ming walls are mainly still standing, although in places their original outer brick layer has been removed.

A large three tiered **fortress** and beacon tower *(zhènběitái)* lie 7.5km north of town.

Places to Stay & Eat

In Yulin, two hotels (out of a total of three) accept foreigners. The *Yulin Hotel* (☎ 328-3835) *(yúlín fàndiàn)*, 2km north of the bus station on Xinjian Lu, charges Y25 per person for beds in doubles with attached bath. Beds in triples/quads with shared bath are Y10/8.

The *Yulin Hotel* (☎ 223-974) *(yúlín bīnguǎn)*, on Xinjian Lu, just north of the city walls, is the appointed abode for the

occasional foreigner who turns up, and charges Y200 for a double. Both hotels have good, cheap dining halls.

Getting There & Away

The are several flights a week linking Yulin with Xi'an (Y500), but this service tends to come and go depending on demand, so don't count on it.

There's one direct sleeper bus daily between Xi'an and Yulin (Y87, 14 hours), but it's more convenient and less tiring to stop in Yan'an. There are also four buses each day between Yan'an and Yulin (Y31, eight hours), with departures between 6 am and noon.

There is one daily bus at 5.30 am to Yinchuan (Y46, 14 hours) following a route close to the Great Wall. There are also half-hourly buses to Daliuta, from where you can catch a train to Baotou in Inner Mongolia.

Henan 河南

Henan *(hénán)*, or at least the northern tip of it which is intersected by the Yellow River, is allegedly where it all began. The beginnings of the Chinese civilisation can be traced back here, about 3500 years ago, when primitive settlements began to coalesce into a true urban sprawl.

Today, Henan is one of China's smallest provinces, and also one of the most densely populated, with more than 80 million people jostling for living space and train tickets. Only Sichuan Province has more human mouths to feed. For the traveller, Henan's charms are limited. The province is at its best in the city of Kaifeng, a delightful old-world surprise, and at the Longmen Caves near Luoyang.

History
It was long thought that the Shang Dynasty (1700-1100 BC) was founded by tribes who migrated from western Asia. Excavations of Shang Dynasty settlements in Henan, however, have shown these towns to be built on the sites of even more ancient settlements. The Shang probably emerged from a continuous line of development that reaches back into prehistoric times.

The first Shang capital, perhaps dating back 3800 years, is believed to have been at Yanshi, west of modern-day Zhengzhou. Around the middle of the 16th century BC the capital was moved to Zhengzhou, where the walls of the ancient city are still visible. Later the capital moved to Yin, near the modern town of Anyang, in the north of Henan.

The only clues as to what Shang society was like are found in the remnants of their cities, in divining bones inscribed with a primitive form of Chinese writing, and in ancient Chinese literary texts. Apart from the walls at Zhengzhou, all that has survived of their cities are the pounded-earth foundations of the buildings, stone-lined trenches where wooden poles once support-

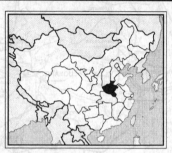

Henan Facts & Highlights

Area: 167,000 sq km

Population: 91.7 million

Capital: Zhengzhou

Highlights
- Kaifeng, a delightful blast from the past.
- Shaolin Monastery, for those with an interest in kungfu.
- Buddhist Longmen Cave complex near Luoyang.

ed thatched roofs, and pits used for storage or as underground houses.

Henan once again occupied centre stage during the Song Dynasty (960-1279 AD), but political power deserted it when the government fled south from its capital at Kaifeng in the wake of an invasion from the north in the 12th century. Nevertheless, with such a large population on the fertile (although periodically flood-ravaged) plains of the unruly Yellow River, Henan remained an important agricultural area.

Henan's urban centres dwindled in importance and population with the demise of the Song. It was not until the Communist takeover in 1949 that they once again expanded. Zhengzhou was transformed into a sizeable industrial city, as was Luoyang.

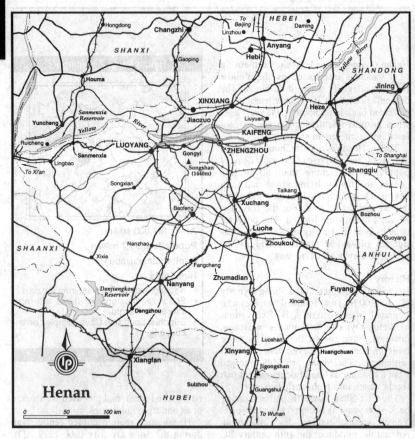

Henan

0   50   100 km

Kaifeng and Anyang have been slower to respond to the call of the hammer and anvil.

ZHENGZHOU
(zhèngzhōu)

Provincial capital of Henan since 1949, Zhengzhou is a sprawling paradigm of ill-conceived town planning. It sports broad, neatly intersecting boulevards, a people's park, a towering anachronistic Mao statue and a brand-new provincial museum to replace the old one.

While Zhengzhou lags far behind Guang-zhou, Shanghai and Beijing, it is neverthe-less valiantly holding up its end in the latest Chinese revolution: there's a high technol-ogy science park on the outskirts of town and a reasonably large number of expats are in town working on a massive World Bank-funded dam project close to Luoyang. For the traveller, however, Zhengzhou is at best an overnight stop en route to more worth-while attractions.

Orientation

All places of interest to travellers lie within

the section of the city east of the railway line.

The liveliest part of town is around the railway and long-distance bus stations, with street stalls, restaurants and markets. North-east of the railway station, five roads converge at the prominent Erqi Pagoda (or February 7th Memorial Tower) to form a vast messy traffic circle that marks the commercial centre of Zhengzhou. Erqi Lu runs north from the Erqi Pagoda to intersect with Jinshui Lu near Renmin Park; the new premises of the Provincial Museum is in the northern section of city along Nongye Lu, and the Holiday Inn is east on Jinshui Lu.

Information

Tourist Office CITS (☎ 595-2072) has an office at 15 Jinshui Lu, in the courtyard reached by a small alley leading off the street.

PSB The PSB is at 70 Erqi Lu, near the intersection with Xili Lu.

Money The Bank of China is at 16 Huayuankou Lu in the northern section of the city. There is also a branch that changes travellers cheques and cash on Jinshui Lu across the T-intersection with Chengdong Lu.

Post & Communications The main post and telecommunications centre is in the building at the far right of the square as you exit the railway station.

Shang City Ruins
(shāngdài yízhǐ)

On the eastern outskirts of Zhengzhou lie the remains of an ancient city from the Shang period. Long, high mounds of earth indicate where the city walls used to be, although they're now cut through by modern roads. This is one of the earliest relics of Chinese urban life.

The first archaeological evidence of the Shang period was discovered near the town of Anyang in northern Henan. The city at Zhengzhou is believed to have been the

second Shang capital, and many Shang settlements have been found outside the walled area.

Excavations here, and at other Shang sites, suggest that a 'typical' Shang city consisted of a central walled area containing large buildings (presumably government buildings or the residences of important people, used for ceremonial occasions) surrounded by a ring of villages. Each village specialised in such products as pottery, metalwork, wine or textiles. The village dwellings were mostly semi-underground pit houses, while the buildings in the centre were rectangular and above ground.

Excavations have also uncovered Shang tombs. These are rectangular pits with ramps or steps leading down to a burial chamber in which the coffin was placed and surrounded with funerary objects such as bronze weapons, helmets, musical instruments, inscribed oracle bones and shells, silk fabrics, and ornaments of jade, bone and ivory. Some also contained the skeletons of sacrificial animals and humans. Study of these human skeletons suggests they were of a different ethnic origin from the Shang – possibly prisoners of war. This and other evidence has suggested that Shang society was not based on the slavery of its own people. Rather, it was a dictatorship of the aristocracy with the emperor/father-figure at the apex.

There are two sites where you can see part of the ruins. The portion that still has some of the wall standing is in the south-eastern section of the city. Bus No 2 stops nearby – get off at the stop called East Gate *(dōng mén kǒu)*. Bus No 3 also runs near the old Shang City.

The other set of ruins is in Zijingshan Park *(zǐjīngshān gōngyuán)* near the Novotel Hotel.

Henan Provincial Museum
(hénán shěng bówùguǎn)

The museum, originally at the intersection of Renmin Lu and Jinshui Lu, has moved to an impressive new building in the northern section of the city on Nongye Lu across

HENAN

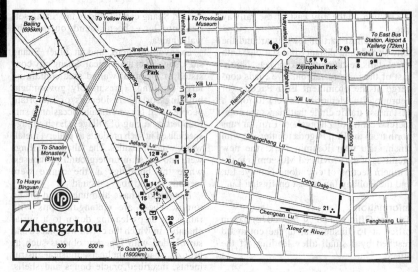

from the intersection with Jingqi Lu; it should be open by the time you read this.

The museum has an interesting collection of artefacts discovered in Henan Province, including some from the Shang period. There's also an exhibition on the February 7th revolt. The Erqi Pagoda, in the centre of Zhengzhou, commemorates the 1923 strike organised by workers build-

ing the railway from Wuhan to Beijing. The strike was bloodily suppressed.

Yellow River
(huánghé)

The Yellow River is just 24km north of Zhengzhou and the road passes near the village of Huayuankou, where in April 1938 Kuomintang general Chiang Kaishek ordered his troops to blow up the river dikes to halt the Japanese advance. This desperately ruthless tactic was successful for only a few weeks and came at the cost of drowning some one million Chinese people and making another 11 million homeless and starving.

The dike was repaired with American help in 1947 and today the point where it was breached has an irrigation sluice gate and Mao's instruction, 'Control the Yellow River', etched into the embankment. The river has always been regarded as 'China's sorrow' because of its propensity to flood. It carries masses of silt from the loess plains and deposits them on the riverbed, causing the water to overflow the banks. Consequently, the peasants along the riverbank have had to build the dikes higher and higher each century. As a result, parts of the river flow along an elevated channel which is sometimes more than 15m in height.

The river has been brought partially under control through the building of upstream dams and irrigation canals which divert the flow. The largest of these is the Longyang Dam in Qinghai Province, which is also a principal source of hydroelectric power.

You can catch bus No 16 out to the Yellow River Park from outside the Zhengzhou Hotel.

Renmin Park
(rénmín gōngyuán)
This park is interesting not for its scenic beauty, but for the entrance which looks like someone's attempt to recreate either the Lunan Stone Forest or the Tiger Balm Gardens. The park itself has little to offer, but family circuses sometimes set up here, performing such feats as wrapping their bodies in wire or lying down with a concrete block on their stomach while dad takes to it with a sledgehammer.

You can play that venerated Chinese sport of ping pong on the concrete tables in the park if you've got some bats and a ball. The entrance to the park is on Erqi Lu.

Places to Stay – budget
The cheapest place that accepts foreigners is near the southern gate of Zhengzhou University, west of the railway station and Taoyuan Lu. The *Huayu Hotel* (☎ 793-5234, ext 3182) *(huáyù bīnguǎn)* has twins with attached bath for Y90 and Y100. Beds in triples without bath are Y30. To get there take bus No 201 from the railway station and get off at the 13th stop. The hotel is about 50m east of the bus stop, just past the university's southern gate.

Closer to the railway station, the *Golden Sunshine Hotel* (☎ 696-9999; fax 871-2921) *(tàiyángguāng dàjiǔdiàn)* is a new upmarket place, but has very comfortable singles with air-con for Y60 and Y80, although the cheaper ones are in windowless rooms. Standard twins go for Y328. There are also rooms for Y298, but these are often occupied by tour groups. The hotel is immediately to your left as you exit the railway station, at 6 Erma Lu.

Directly opposite the railway station is *Zhongyuan Mansions* (☎ 696-6172) *(zhōngyuán dàshà)*, a cavernous white tower with untold numbers of rooms in two adjoining hotels. Both are more than a bit run-down, but handy if you're only passing through. There's twins/triples with shared bath for Y84/111, and singles/twins with attached bath and air-con are Y110/120.

The *Zhengzhou Hotel* (☎ 696-9941) *(zhèngzhōu fàndiàn)* is on Xinglong Jie, across the street and to the left as you leave the railway station. Basic doubles without bath are Y80, plus a 50% surcharge for foreigners, so it is best to avoid this place unless the other hotels are full. Standard twins with attached bath are Y130 and Y160.

Not far from the station near the Erqi Pagoda, the *Erqi Hotel* (☎ 696-1169) *(èrqī bīnguǎn)* has doubles for Y124 and Y140 with attached bath, but foreigners have to pay 40% extra.

Places to Stay – middle
Good mid-range accommodation is thin on the ground in Zhengzhou, but the marble-infested *Red Coral Hotel* (☎ 698-6688;

fax 699-3222) *(hóngshānhú jiǔdiàn)* on Erma Lu has singles for Y360/390 and standard twins for Y420. The hotel also offers a free Chinese-style breakfast with each room, and there is the added bonus of a swimming pool.

The *Friendship Hotel* (☎ 622-8807; fax 622-4728) *(yǒuyì fàndiàn)* has clean twins from Y280 to Y380. It also has a limited number of cheap twins without bath for Y70, or Y100 with attached bath. Bus Nos 6, 24 and 32 from the railway station all will get you there. Minivan taxis cost Y10 to Y15.

Places to Stay – top end

The *Asia Hotel* (☎ 698-8866; fax 696-9877) *(yàxìyà dàjiǔdiàn)*, a joint venture facing the Erqi Pagoda, has singles and twins for Y358/398, but foreigners pay Y100 more for their rooms. It's close to the station, but has little else to recommend it.

Over in the city's eastern suburbs, on 114 Jinshui Lu, is the *Novotel International Hotel Zhengzhou* (☎ 595-6600; fax 595-1526) *(hénán guójì fàndiàn)*. Rooms start at Y470 for a twin and Y920 for a small suite, plus a 15% service charge.

The *Holiday Inn Crowne Plaza Zhengzhou* (☎ 595-0055; fax 599-0770) *(hénán zhèngzhōu huángguān jiàrì bīnguǎn)* is next door. This place started life as the Russian Foreign Experts' Hotel back in the 50s and after three years of renovations is now being managed by the Holiday Inn group. Rates start from US$103 for singles and US$118 for twins, plus a 20% service charge.

Places to Eat

There's not a lot of good stuff to eat in Zhengzhou, unless you enjoy slurping down bowls of opaque noodles called *liáng fěn*. Popular in Henan, as in many parts of north-western China, it's fairly pedestrian fare. Try it in soup with a tossing of vinegar or hot chilli.

The station area is the best for cheap eats. Opposite the Sunshine Hotel, there's a bustling *canteen* of no discernible name

that has various noodle, dumpling and rice dishes that you can choose from behind the counter. Next door to the Erqi Hotel, look for a sign resembling a truncated version of the McDonald's golden arches that is the *Red Sorghum (hónggāoliang)* chain of fast-food joints which specialises in lamb dishes.

The classier restaurants are clustered in the fashionable end of town, on Jinshui Lu between Chengdong Lu and Huayuankou Lu. The *Flower Restaurant (huāyuán fàndiàn)* has good Cantonese dishes in the Y20 to Y60 range. There is no English sign, but look for the large glass window in front.

Nearby, the *Richmond Brewery (zhūqímén)* specialises in Canadian-style draught beer and has both western and Chinese dishes, as well as pictures to help you choose what you want to eat. Prices are in the Y20 to Y30 range, but a pint of beer is a bit steep at Y30. Look for the Canadian flag on the sign out the front.

The Holiday Inn has a *patisserie* and a western *restaurant* in the foyer serving reasonably inexpensive hamburgers, steaks and the like. The Novotel also has a *coffee shop*.

Getting There & Away

Air The CAAC office (☎ 696-4789) is at 51 Yi Malu, but there are ticket outlets scattered all over town, notably in the Holiday Inn Crowne Plaza, Novotel International Hotel, and even in the Zhongyuan Mansions.

From Zhengzhou there are scheduled flights to more than 20 Chinese cities. Daily services include Beijing, Guangzhou and Shanghai, and there's less frequent flights to Guilin, Kunming, Wuhan, Qingdao and even Ürümqi. There are also three flights a week to Hong Kong.

Bus From the Zhengzhou long-distance bus station (diagonally opposite the railway station) there are comfortable air-con Iveco minibuses to Luoyang (Y25, two hours) that leave every 20 minutes and ply the new freeway between Zhengzhou and Luoyang.

The ordinary bus (Y14, 3½ hours) takes the old road. Buses leave every half hour for the four hour trip to Anyang (Y25). Buses leaving for Kaifeng (Y8) from here don't take the freeway, so the trip takes a little over an hour. There are also overnight sleeping-berth coaches *(wòpùchē)* to Beijing, Wuhan, Xi'an and numerous other destinations, although these long hauls are better done by train if possible. Minibuses leave irregularly from the square in front of the railway station for Shaolin (Y10).

From the east bus station, Iveco minibuses do the trip to Kaifeng in 45 minutes on the freeway. Buses depart every 20 minutes and tickets are Y10. There is also a car service from here to Kaifeng in Peugeot sedans for Y15.

Train Zhengzhou is one of the most important junctions in the Chinese rail network, and numerous express and rapid trains run via the city, so you could well find yourself here 'in transit' for a few hours. The ticket office at Zhengzhou railway station is often crowded and tickets are easier to buy at the advance booking office at 134 Erqi Lu. CITS and many of the hotels also can book tickets for you.

Express trains can now do the journey to Beijing in 8½ hours and there are trains to Guangzhou (20 hours), Luoyang (two hours), Shanghai (14 hours), Wuhan (6½ hours), Xi'an (eight hours) and Taiyuan (12 hours). The Beijing-Kowloon express train also stops in Zhengzhou.

Travellers to Xi'an are best off taking the two-tiered 'tourist train' which leaves Zhengzhou daily at 11.02 am and arrives in Xi'an just before 8 pm.

Getting Around
To/From the Airport The airport is 3km from the city centre and is a short taxi ride from the city centre.

Bus & Taxi Since most of the sights and tourist facilities are well away from the city centre, you can forget walking. Unfortu-

nately, no bicycle rental is available, but the bus system is pretty straightforward.

Bus No 2 gets you from the railway station to the Novotel, while the No 3 runs near the Shang City Ruins.

Taxis (both red sedan and yellow minivan) are readily available. The red taxis have meters, but drivers rarely use them (most journeys around town should be Y10 to Y15); minivans generally cost between Y7 and Y10.

AROUND ZHENGZHOU
Shaolin Monastery
(shàolín sì)
David Carradine never trained here, but China's most famous martial arts tradition was indeed developed by Buddhist monks at the Shaolin Monastery, 80km west of Zhengzhou.

Each year, thousands of Chinese enrol at Shaolin's martial art schools. Large classes of enthusiastic young trainees, many no older than nine or 10, can often be seen in the monastery grounds ramming a javelin through their imaginary opponent's body or kicking into a sparring dummy with enough force to wind an elephant.

According to the legend, Shaolin was founded in the 5th century AD by an Indian monk, Bodhidharma, who preached Chan (Zen) Buddhism. The story goes that for relief between long periods of meditation, Bodhidharma's disciples imitated the natural motions of birds and animals, developing these exercises over the centuries into a form of unarmed combat.

The monks have supposedly intervened continually throughout China's many wars and uprisings – always on the side of righteousness, naturally – and, perhaps as a result, their monastery has suffered repeated sackings. The most recent episodes were in 1928, when a local warlord had a go, and in the early 70s, courtesy of bands of Red Guards.

In spite of the fires and vandalism, many of the monastery buildings are still standing, although most have had any original charm restored out of them. One of the

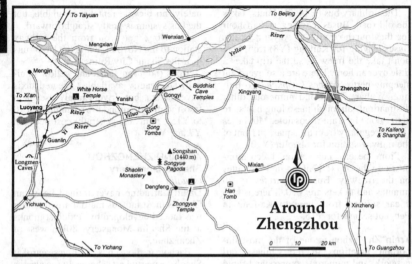

Around Zhengzhou

more interesting sights is the **Forest of Dagobas** (shàolín tǎlín) outside the walls past the temple; each dagoba was built in memory of a monk.

Nowadays Shaolin is a tourist trap catering to crowds of Chinese tourists who are bussed in every day. The way from the main bus parking area to the monastery is thick with food stalls, ice-cream sellers, street photographers and small souvenir shops selling imitation scimitars along with other junk. Try to visit on a weekday when there are less people. There's also a better chance of seeing some of the martial arts classes in action. You may bump into the occasional foreigner studying at Shaolin.

The monastery sits on Songshan, a mountain sacred to Taoists. On the same mountain is the Taoist **Zhongyue Temple**, thought to be founded during the Qin Dynasty, and the site of the oldest surviving pagoda in China.

The main gate ticket is Y55, and that covers entrance to sites around Shaolin, including a mediocre panoramic film that is screened in the round building near the entrance.

Places to Stay It's possible to spend the night at Shaolin at the *Wushu Hotel* (☎ 274-9016) (wǔshù bīnguǎn). Standard twins with attached bath and air-con are Y160 and there are more expensive rooms in building No 2. The hotel sometimes has martial arts demonstrations for Y15.

Closer to the bus parking area and beside one of the main schools, the *Songshan Hotel* (☎ 274-9050) (sōngshān bīnguǎn) has beds in clean doubles with attached bath for Y60/65, but it is often full by the afternoon.

Getting There & Away Shaolin is well off the major road between Zhengzhou and Luoyang. One way of getting there is to take one of the frequent but unscheduled private minibuses from in front of the railway station in either city. Tickets will cost you Y10 from Zhengzhou and Y8 from Luoyang.

Many of the hotels in Zhengzhou also have day tours to Shaolin that include sites along the way, but among these only the Han tombs at Dahuting are of any interest. The tour price (Y40) does not include entry

Gongyi City

Gongyi City *(gǒngyìshi)*, formerly called Gongxian County, is between Zhengzhou and Luoyang and is home to a series of Buddhist caves and tombs built by the Northern Song emperors.

Construction of the caves began in 517 AD. Additions continued through the Eastern and Western Wei, Tang and Song dynasties, and today there are 256 shrines containing more than 7700 Buddhist figures.

The Song Tombs are scattered over an area of 30 sq km, and within them repose seven of the nine Northern Song emperors (the other two were carted off by the Jin armies who overthrew the Northern Song in the 12th century). Some 800 years on, all that remain of the tombs are ruins, burial mounds and the statues which line the sacred avenues leading up to the ruins amid fields of wheat.

About 700 stone statues are still standing, and together they comprise the main attraction of the tombs. Experts see a progression of styles from the simplicity of late-Tang forms to the life-like depiction of public figures and animals. Both the tombs and the caves are worth visiting.

Buses running on the old highway (not the freeway) from Luoyang to Gongyi pass by one of the tomb sites, simply called *sòng líng* (Song tombs). You can get off the bus there and visit the tombs, or you can continue on into Gongyi and hire a taxi to go back to the tombs and then visit the Buddhist caves, which are known as *shíkūsì*. It's possible to do this in half a day; expect to pay about Y80 for the taxi. If you're coming from the direction of Zhengzhou, get off at Gongyi.

Entry to the tomb site and caves is Y5. From Gongyi there are frequent buses between Luoyang and Zhengzhou. ∎

fees for the sites or Shaolin itself. You can also buy return tickets to Shaolin (Y25) at the reception in the Zhengzhou Hotel.

LUOYANG
(luòyáng)

Founded in 1200 BC, Luoyang was the capital of 10 dynasties until the Northern Song Dynasty moved its capital to Kaifeng in the 10th century AD. In the 12th century Luoyang was stormed and sacked by Jurchen invaders from the north and never quite recovered from the disaster.

For centuries it languished with only memories of greatness. By the 1920s it had just 20,000 inhabitants. It took the Communists to bring life back to Luoyang, constructing a new industrial city that now houses more than a million people.

In other words, today it's hard to imagine that Luoyang was once the centre of the Chinese world and home to more than 1300 Buddhist temples. There are reminders of Luoyang's historical greatness scattered about town, but the main point of interest is the Longmen Caves, 16km out of town.

Orientation

Luoyang is spread across the northern bank of the Luo River. Luoyang railway station, a large new white-tiled building with a loudly chiming clock, is in the north of the city. Luoyang's chief thoroughfare is Zhongzhou Lu, which meets Jinguyuan Lu leading down from the railway station at a central T-intersection.

The old city is in the eastern part of town, beyond the old west gate at Xiguan, where sections of the original walls can still be seen. Throughout the maze of narrow streets and winding laneways stand many older houses. Using the Wenfeng Pagoda as a landmark, it is an interesting area to explore on foot.

Information

The CITS office (☎ 432-5061) is on Changjiang Lu diagonally opposite Xiyuan Park, not far from the Friendship Hotel. There is also a branch on the 2nd floor of the Peony Hotel. The PSB is on the corner of Kaixuan Lu and Tiyuchang Lu.

The Bank of China is on the corner of Yanan Lu and Zhongzhou Xilu (opposite the Friendship Store). The main post and telephone office is at the T-intersection of Zhongzhou Lu and Jinguyuan Lu.

White Horse Temple
(báimǎ sì)

Founded in the 1st century AD, the White Horse Temple was the first Buddhist temple constructed on Chinese soil. Today, Ming and Qing structures stand at the site of the original temple.

Five hundred years before the journey of Xuan Zhuang, the Tang Dynasty monk whose travels are fancifully immortalised in the classic *Journey to the West*, two envoys of the Han Dynasty court went in search of Buddhist scriptures.

In Afghanistan they met two Indian monks and together they returned to Luoyang. The story goes that they carried Buddhist scriptures and statues on the backs of two white horses. In due course the temple was founded to house the scriptures and statues, and it was named after the horses. The temple is 13km east of Luoyang. The sensible way to get there is to take a minibus from in front of the station for Y5. Alternatively, take bus No 5 or 9 to Xiguan traffic circle at the edge of the old city walls and then walk east to the stop for bus No 56, which will take you to the temple. Entry is Y6 for Chinese and Y12 for foreigners.

Wangcheng Park
(wángchéng gōngyuán)

The Jian River runs through the park. In the

north-western section, across the river, there's a tiny and depressing zoo that contains an emaciated tiger, among other animals. There's also an underground 'theme park' with moving dinosaur models and an assortment of polystyrene ghouls.

The Peony Festival, centred on Wangcheng Park, is held from 15 to 25 April when thousands of Chinese tourists descend on Luoyang to view the peony flowers. If nature fails to provide sufficiently resplendent blooms, fake peonies are attached to the bushes.

Luoyang Museum
(luòyáng bówùguǎn)

The museum is next to Wangcheng Park and houses a collection of early bronzes, Tang figurines and implements from the Stone Age. There are some eye-catching pieces, especially in jade, and there are brief English captions in some of the exhibits.

Bus No 2 from the railway station area goes to the museum. Entry is Y6 for Chinese and Y12 for foreigners.

Luoyang Museum of Ancient Tombs
(luòyáng gǔmù bówùguǎn)

This is a new museum that has a number of restored tombs ranging from the Han to the Song dynasties and includes the Han tombs formerly located in Wangcheng Park. The museum is underground and basically consists of brick-lined vaults with painted murals, carvings and burial items that were discovered when the tombs were excavated. While there is some English explanation, there are no detailed English captions for each exhibit. Entry is Y12.

The museum is on the road to the airport, north of the city. Take bus No 83 from the stop opposite the long-distance bus station and ask the driver to let you off at the turnoff to the museum. A minivan taxi will take you there for Y10.

Longmen Caves
(lóngmén shíkū)

In 494 AD the Northern Wei Dynasty moved its capital from Datong to Luoyang.

At Datong the dynasty had built the impressive Yungang Caves. Now in Luoyang, the dynasty commenced work on the Longmen Caves. Over the next 200 years, more than 100,000 images and statues of Buddha and his disciples were carved into the cliff walls on the banks of the Yi River, 16km south of the city. It was an ideal site. The hard texture of the rock, like that at Datong, made it eminently suitable for carving. The caves of Luoyang, Dunhuang and Datong represent the peak of Buddhist cave art.

Apart from natural erosion, at Luoyang there has been much damage done to the sculptures during the 19th and 20th centuries by western souvenir hunters who beheaded just about every figure they could lay their saws on. These heads now grace the museums and private paperweight collections of Europe and North America. Among these were two murals which were entirely removed and can now be seen at the Metropolitan Museum of Art in New York and the Atkinson Museum in Kansas City. The Cultural Revolution also took its toll when the Red Guards arrived with hammers. The Ten Thousand Buddha Cave was particularly damaged during this period.

The art of Buddhist cave sculpture largely came to an end around the middle of the 9th century as the Tang Dynasty declined. Persecution of foreign religions in China began, with Buddhism as the prime target. Although Buddhist art and sculpture continued in China, it never reached the heights it had enjoyed previously.

Binyang Caves *(bīnyáng dòng)* The main caves of the Longmen group are on the western bank of the Yi River. They stretch out along the cliff face on a north-south axis. The three Binyang Caves are at the northern end, closest to the entrance. All were begun under the Northern Wei and, although two were finished during the Sui and Tang dynasties, the statues all display the benevolent expressions which characterised the Northern Wei style.

Ten Thousand Buddha Cave *(wànfó dòng)* Just south of the Binyang Caves is the Tang Dynasty Ten Thousand Buddha Cave, built in 680. In addition to the legions

Cave Dwellings

The road between Zhengzhou and Luoyang provides a unique opportunity to see some of China's cave dwellings. Over 100 million Chinese people live in cave houses cut into dry embankments, or in houses where the hillside makes up one or more walls. These are not peculiar to Henan Province: a third of these dwellings are found in the dry loess plain. Some communities use both caves and houses; the former are warmer in winter and cooler in summer, but also tend to be darker and less ventilated than ordinary houses.

Sometimes a large square pit is dug first and then caves are hollowed into the four sides of the pit. A well is sunk in the middle of the yard to prevent flooding during heavy rains. Other caves, such as those at Yan'an, are dug into the side of a cliff face.

The floors, walls and ceilings of these cave dwellings are made of loess, a fine yellowish-brown soil which is soft and thick and makes good building material. The front wall may be made of loess, mud-brick, concrete, bricks or wood, depending on the availability of materials.

Ceilings are shaped according to the quality of the loess. If it is hard then the ceiling may be arched; if not, the ceiling may rise to a point. Besides the doors and windows in the front wall, additional vents may let in light and air. ∎

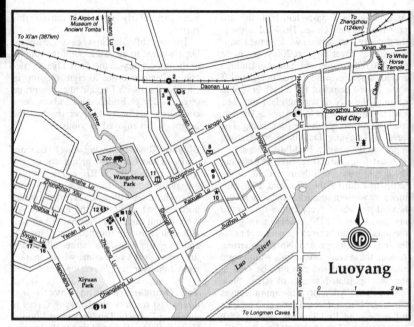

Luoyang

To Airport &
Museum of
Ancient Tombs
To Xi'an (387km)
To Zhengzhou (124km)
To White Horse Temple
Xinan Jie
Daonan Lu
Old City
Zhongzhou Donglu
Zoo
Wangcheng Park
Jianshe Lu
Zhongzhou Xilu
Jinghua Lu
Yanan Lu
Xiyuan Lu
Xiyuan Park
Changjiang Lu
Luo River
Longmen Lu
To Longmen Caves
0   1   2 km

of tiny bas-relief buddhas which give the cave its name, there is a fine big buddha and images of celestial dancers.

Other images include musicians playing the flute, the *pípá* (a plucked stringed instrument), the cymbals and the *zheng* (a 13 to 14 stringed harp).

Lotus Flower Cave (*liánhuā dòng*) This cave was carved in 527 AD during the Northern Wei Dynasty and has a large standing buddha, now faceless. On the ceiling are wispy apsaras drifting around a central lotus flower. A common symbol in Buddhist art, the lotus flower represents purity and serenity.

Ancestor Worshipping Temple (*fèng-xiān sì*) This is the largest structure at Longmen and contains the best works of art. It was built between 672 and 675 AD, during the Tang Dynasty. The roof is gone

and the figures lie exposed to the elements. The Tang figures tend to be more three-dimensional than the Northern Wei figures, standing out in high relief and rather freer from their stone backdrop.

Their expressions and poses also appear to be more natural, but unlike the other-worldly figures of the Northern Wei, the Tang figures are meant to be awesome.

The seated central buddha is 17m high and is thought to be Vairocana, the supreme, omnipresent divinity. The face is thought to be modelled on that of the all-powerful Empress Wu Zetian of the Tang Dynasty.

As you face the buddha, to the left are statues of the disciple Ananda and a bodhisattva wearing a crown, a tassel and a string of pearls.

To the right are statues (or remains) of another disciple, a bodhisattva, a heavenly guardian trampling on a spirit and a guardian of the buddha.

the first cave of the Longmen group to be built.

Shiku Cave This cave is a Northern Wei construction. It is the last major cave in the Longmen complex and features carvings depicting religious processions.

Getting There & Away The caves are 13km south of town and can be reached from the Luoyang railway station area by bus No 81 or from the Friendship Hotel by bus No 60, which leaves from the stop opposite the hotel across the boulevard. Bus No 53 from the Xiguan traffic circle also goes past the caves. Minibuses go to the caves from the railway and bus station area for Y2. Get off before the bus crosses the bridge and walk down the steps to the entrance. Entry is Y16 for Chinese and Y25 for foreigners. The caves are open daily from 6 am to 8 pm. It's a good idea to go in the early morning both to avoid the crowds and to enjoy the best light as the morning sun hits the cliff side. To get a comprehensive view, cross the river and view the caves from the other side.

Places to Stay

Directly opposite the railway station is the *Luoyang Hotel* (☎ 393-5181) *(luòyáng lüshè)*, where twins and triples without bath cost Y50/60 and singles cost Y40. It's a depressing, noisy place. The friendly *Huacheng Hotel* (☎ 491-3400) *(huāchéng fàndiàn)* at 49 Zhongzhou Xilu, has twins without bath for Y50 and twins/triples with attached bath for Y90/105. Bus Nos 2, 4 and 11 run past it – get off at the stop after the Peony Hotel.

The *Tianxiang Hotel* (☎ 394-0600) *(tiānxiāng lüshè)* is around the corner from the Luoyang Hotel and has singles/twins without bath for Y45/44, and air-con twins with attached bath for Y180. The rooms are comfortable, but foreigners have to pay a 100% surcharge.

Over in the west of town, on Xiyuan Lu, are two Friendship Hotels. Catering largely to tour groups, both have standard twins

Medical Prescription Cave South of the Ancestor Worshipping Temple is the tiny Medical Prescription Cave. The entrance to this cave is filled with 6th century stone steles inscribed with remedies for common ailments.

Guyang Cave Adjacent to the Medical Prescription Cave is the much larger Guyang Cave, cut between 495 and 575 AD. It's a narrow, high-roofed cave featuring a buddha statue and a profusion of sculpture, particularly of flying apsaras. This was probably that start at Y480 (foreigners' price). The older of the two, the *Friendship Hotel* (☎ 491-2780; fax 491-3808) *(yǒuyì bīnguǎn)* is a better deal and also has a swimming pool. The *New Friendship Hotel* (☎ 493-1445; fax 491-2328) *(xīn yǒuyì bīnguǎn)* is just down the road. Bus No 9 from the main railway station terminates close to the hotels (get off at the seventh stop). For a taxi, expect to pay around Y40 from Luoyang airport or Y15 to Y20 from the main railway station.

The *Peony Hotel* (☎ 485-6699; fax 485-6999) *(mǔdān dàjiǔdiàn)* is a high-rise joint venture at 15 Zhongzhou Xilu. It's popular with foreign tour groups and expats, although it falls short of delivering international standards. Room rates start at Y550, plus 5% tax.

Places to Eat

Luoyang is situated far enough west to give the local street food a slight Islamic touch. Cheap common snacks include *jiǎnpào*, small fried pastries filled with chopped herbs and Chinese garlic, and *dòushāgāo*, a sweet 'cake' made from ground yellow peas and jujubes (Chinese dates), sold by street vendors for about Y0.50 a slice. At night the *street stalls* around the railway station sell cheap and very good *shāguō*, a kind of meat and vegetable casserole cooked with bean noodles in a small earthenware pot. In the summer *outdoor restaurants* (and outdoor karaoke) set up along northern sections of Jiefang Lu and Jinguyuan Lu and serve cheap draught beer for Y5. A couple of these restaurants beside the Tianxiang Hotel have English menus.

You'll find better 'sit-down' *restaurants* along Zhongzhou Lu. The Peony Hotel has a good *coffee shop* (Y10 for a bottomless cup) with passable western-style meals.

Getting There & Away

Air The CAAC office is on Daobei Lu north of the railway line, but it's not really necessary to go there because it's possible to book air tickets at various places around town. Luoyang is not so well connected by air with the rest of China (consider flying to or from Zhengzhou). The Peony Hotel has a small ground-floor office, as does the Tianxiang Hotel and the Friendship hotels.

There are flights to Beijing, Guangzhou, Shenzhen, Shenyang, Dalian and Chengdu. There are also charter flights to Hong Kong.

Bus The long-distance bus station is diagonally opposite the main railway station. Aircon Iveco buses do the trip to Zheng-zhou on the freeway in about two hours for Y25, departing every 20 minutes. There are also ordinary buses to Zhengzhou (Y17, 2½ hours). Buses to Shaolin depart every half hour (Y8, one hour). You can also get direct buses to Anyang (eight hours) and Ruicheng in south-western Shanxi Province (eight hours) from here.

Coach buses fitted with sleeping berths leave in the evening from outside the railway station for Xi'an (10 hours), Taiyuan (11 hours), Wuhan (15 hours) and Yantai in Shandong Province (23 hours). There are also frequent minibuses to Gongyi City from here (one hour).

Train From Luoyang there are direct trains to Beijing (13 hours), Shanghai (18 hours) and Xi'an (eight hours). Note that there is also a two tiered tourist train running between Zhengzhou and Xi'an daily – it stops in Luoyang en route to Xi'an at 12.25 pm and arrives in Xi'an around 7 pm the same day.

There are some direct trains north to Taiyuan (14 hours) and south to Xiangfan (7½ hours) and Yichang (13 hours). Yichang is a port on the Yangzi River, where you can pick up the Chongqing to Wuhan ferry.

Getting Around

To/From the Airport The airport is 12km north of city. Bus No 83 leaves from the stop opposite the long-distance bus station to the airport. A taxi ride will cost about Y15 to Y20 from the railway station.

Other Transport You can rent bicycles from in front of the Luoyang Hotel for Y5 a day. Red-cab and yellow-minivan taxis are abundant and rarely cost more than Y10. The bus system is also less crowded than in many Chinese cities.

ANYANG

(ānyáng)

Anyang, north of the Yellow River near the Henan-Hebei border, is now believed to be the site of Yin, the last capital of the ancient Shang Dynasty and one of the first centres of an urban-based Chinese civilisation.

Peasants working near Anyang in the late 19th century unearthed pieces of polished bone inscribed with an ancient form of Chinese writing, which turned out to be divining bones with questions addressed to the spirits and ancestors. Other inscriptions were found on the plastrons of tortoises, as well as on bronze objects, suggesting that the late Shang capital once stood here in the 14th century BC.

The discoveries attracted the attention of both Chinese and western archaeologists, although it was not until the late 1920s that work began on excavating the site. These excavations uncovered ancient tombs, the ruins of a royal palace, and workshops and houses – proof that the legendary Shang Dynasty had indeed existed.

Museum of the Yin Ruins

(yīnxū bówùyuàn)

There is a museum at the Yin site, but its collection is disappointingly limited. It includes reassembled pottery and oracle bone fragments, as well as jade and bronze artefacts, but there are no English captions and it's all a bit mystifying unless you're really into this stuff. There are some pits in the back, but some might find the best part of this museum to be the beautiful rose garden.

Bus No 1 from near the corner of Jiefang Lu and Zhangde Lu goes past the museum turn-off, then you have to walk across the railway tracks and head along the river until you come to the museum. Admission is Y5.

Tomb of Yuan Shikai

(yuán shìkǎi mù)

A more recent remnant of Chinese history is the Tomb of Yuan Shikai. He had it built in the style of the tomb of the American Civil War general and president, Ulysses S Grant, adding some Chinese touches as well. It reflects, more than anything else perhaps, the Napoleonic aspirations of this man who started out as a Qing military official and then went on to support Sun Yatsen, only to wrest the presidency from him and attempt a restoration of the imperial system, crowning himself emperor in 1916! His coup was short-lived, however, and he was buried shortly afterwards in this tomb of his own design. It's about 3km east of the Yin museum, or you can take bus No 2 from the railway station. Get off at the bridge and walk north to the site. Entry is Y3 for Chinese; foreigners are supposed to pay more, but you can argue for clemency.

Other Sights

It's well worth walking around the old part of town which is a few blocks east of the railway station and south of Jiefang Lu. Look for the **Wenfeng Pagoda**, a hexagonal Buddhist tower topped by a stupa. You can climb up the pagoda for a good view of the city.

Places to Stay & Eat

The *Fenghuang Hotel* (☎ 593-7207) *(fēnghuáng bīnguǎn)*, on Jiefang Lu near its intersection with Xihuancheng Lu, charges Y70 for rather grotty twins without bath and Y96 for twins with attached bath and air-con. There is a good restaurant on the ground floor, but beware of rats paying you a surprise visit in your room during the night.

The *Anyang Guesthouse* (☎ 592-2219; fax 592-2244) *(ānyáng bīnguǎn)*, up the road and across the street at 1 Youyi Lu, is a much nicer place to stay. Twins with attached bath cost Y128 and up.

There are a number of *restaurants* in the old town, particularly on Hongqi Lu south of Jiefang Lu near the restored gate tower. The food isn't great in Anyang, but you can't beat the price of draught beer for Y2 a pint.

Getting There & Away

From Anyang long-distance bus station there are connections to Zhengzhou (4½ hours), Linzhou City (leaving every 10 minutes), Taiyuan (a rough 10 hour ride across the Taihangshan) and Luoyang (eight hours). The long-distance bus station is a large orange-tiled building close to the railway station. Turn right down the street after exiting the station. Anyang is on the main Beijing-Zhengzhou railway line and most express trains make a stop here.

AROUND ANYANG

About 50km west of Anyang, in the foothills of the Taihangshan close to Henan's border with Shanxi Province, lies **Linxian County** (*línxiàn*), although the name of the main town has been changed to Linzhou City (*lìnzhōushí*).

Linxian is a rural area which rates with Dazhai and Shaoshan as one of the 'holy' places of Maoism, since this is the location of the famous Red Flag Canal. To irrigate the district, a river was re-routed through a tunnel beneath a mountain and then along a new bed built on the side of steep cliffs. The Communists insist that this colossal job, carried out during the Cultural Revolution, was done entirely by the toiling masses without the help of engineers and machines.

The statistics are impressive: 1500km of canal were dug, hills were levelled, 134 tunnels were pierced, 150 aqueducts were constructed and enough earth was displaced to build a road 1m high, 6m wide and 4000km long. All this was supposedly done by hand in keeping with Mao's vision of a self-reliant China.

You can take the daily bus from Anyang that goes to Changzhi in Shanxi Province and get off when it goes past the canal site. Otherwise take a bus to Linzhoushi and change for buses to the canal.

JIGONGSHAN
(*jīgōngshān*)

Jigongshan, on the Henan-Hubei border, was developed as a hill station resort by American missionaries in the early 20th century. It soon became popular with westerners living in Hankou as a relief from the hot summers. Like Lushan in Jiangxi Province, it's full of old European-style stone houses and has a refreshing setting, but is smaller and less inundated with tourists.

Jigongshan is dominated by **Dawn Heralding Peak** (*bàoxiǎo fēng*), a large stone outcrop resembling a crowing rooster, which is how Jigongshan (Rooster Mountain) got its name. It's an easy climb to the top and gives a nice view of the surrounding area. Across the valley to the east, the former **American School** (*měiguóshì dàlóu*) is well preserved and worth a look. To the south, **Chiang Kaishek's Air Raid Shelter** (*jiǎng jièshí fángkōng dòng*) is part of his former residence and is open to visitors. The main village in Jigongshan, known as **Nanjie**, is on the western flank of the mountain overlooking the Beijing-Zhengzhou railway below.

The entry fee to Jigongshan is Y12.

Places to Stay & Eat

Although less crowded than Lushan, Jigongshan is a popular weekend getaway for local tourists from Wuhan and Zhengzhou, but there's plenty of accommodation choices.

On the road to the main peak, the *Yunzhong Park Guesthouse* (☎ 621-2030) (*yúnzhōng gōngyuán zhāo-dàisuǒ*) is an old stone villa that has grotty triples for Y20 per bed and basic washing facilities.

Further up the hill, a hotel with a similar name, the *Yunzhong Hotel* (☎ 621-2004) (*yúnzhōng bīnguǎn*) has beds in clean twins and triples with attached bath for Y90 and Y60. The suites are Y360 and have a terrific view.

The *Friendship Hotel* (☎ 621-2067) (*yǒuyì bīnguǎn*) is near Chiang Kaishek's former house and has twins with attached bath for Y180 and dorm beds for Y30.

All these hotels also have *restaurants*. Nanjie village also has a number of private *restaurants* with beds upstairs for Y20.

Getting There & Away
The station for Jigongshan (with the same name) is on the Beijing-Zhengzhou railway line. Normally you can take a train from Wuhan (four hours), but services have been temporarily suspended, although they may have resumed by the time you read this. Buses from Wuhan leave from the Hankou long-distance bus station and take about four hours. There are frequent minibuses to Xinyang (45 minutes) where it's easy to catch trains to Wuhan or Zhengzhou..

It's 11km from the railway station to Jigongshan and minibuses make the trip for Y5. It's also possible to approach Jigongshan from the south-east where a cable car takes people up for Y24.

KAIFENG
(kāifēng)
Once the prosperous imperial capital of China during the Northern Song Dynasty (960-1126 AD), Kaifeng is a charming city with a population of around 600,000. It doesn't see a great deal of tourist traffic and it deserves more than it gets. Kaifeng has been somewhat left behind in China's modernisation drive. While the locals tut with embarrassment about the lack of fast-food outfits and five star hotels, for the foreign visitor there is much in Kaifeng that has disappeared from other parts of China.

It would be a good idea to get there soon, however. Even Kaifeng is slowly being nudged into the modern world, and whole blocks are being demolished to make way for the dreams of China's civic planners. The old city walls surround Kaifeng on all sides, but these are frequently interrupted by roads or new buildings.

A small Christian community also lives in Kaifeng alongside a much larger local Muslim minority; you may come across their churches and mosques in Kaifeng's backstreets.

Orientation
The long-distance bus station and the railway station are both outside (about 1km south) of the old city walls; the rest of Kaifeng is mostly within the walled area. The city's pivotal point is the intersection of Sihou Jie and Madao Jie; the street market here is particularly lively at night. The surrounding restaurants, shops and houses are of mainly traditional Chinese wooden architecture. Nearby is the Kaifeng Guesthouse and the Xiangguo Temple.

Information
CITS (☎ 595-5130) has an office at 14 Yingbin Lu, next to the Dongjing Hotel. There is also a CITS counter in the Dongjing Hotel. The PSB is at 14 Shengfu Jie on the southern side of the street at the Zhongshan Lu corner.

The Bank of China is on Gulou Jie diagonally opposite the Daijintai Hotel. There are post and telephone offices near the corner of Zhongshan Lu and Ziyou Lu, and on the corner of Mujiaqiao Jie and Wusheng Jiao Jie.

Xiangguo Temple
(xiàngguó sì)
This temple is next door to a large Chinese-style market. Founded in 555 AD, but frequently rebuilt over the following 1000 years, Xiangguo Temple was completely destroyed in 1644 when the Yellow River floodgates were opened in a disastrous attempt to halt a Manchu invasion. The current buildings date from 1766 and have had a thorough going-over since then. There's an enormous old cast-iron bell on the right as you go in; entry costs Y15.

Iron Pagoda
(tiě tǎ)
Built in the 11th century, the Iron Pagoda is actually made of normal bricks, but covered in specially coloured tiles that look like iron. You can climb to the top of this impressive structure. The tiles on the lower levels have damaged buddha images, possibly thanks to Red Guard sledgehammers.

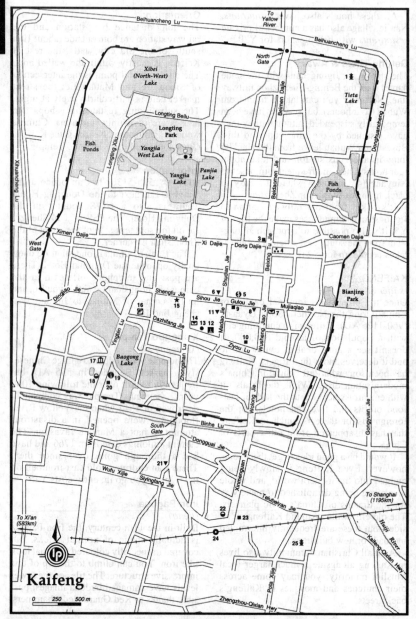

Kaifeng

0   250   500 m

To Xi'an
(583km)

To Shanghai
(1195km)

KAIFENG 开封

PLACES TO STAY
3 Bianjing Hotel
汴京饭店
9 Dajintai Hotel
大金台旅馆
10 Kaifeng Guesthouse
开封宾馆
20 Dongjing Hotel
东京大饭店
23 Bian Hotel
汴大旅社

PLACES TO EAT
6 Jiaozi Guan
Restaurant
饺子馆
8 California Beef
Noodles
加州牛肉面

11 Li's California Beef
Noodle King
李先生加州
牛肉面大王
21 Di Yi Lou Dumpling
Restaurant
第一楼饺子馆

OTHER
1 Iron Pagoda
铁塔
2 Longting (Dragon Pavilion)
龙亭
4 Ruins of Kaifeng
Synagogue
开封犹太教堂遗址
5 Bank of China
中国银行
7 Post Office
邮电局
12 Xiangguo Temple
相国寺

13 Xiangguosi Market
相国寺市场
14 Post Office
邮电局
15 PSB
公安局
16 Yanqing Taoist Temple
延庆观
17 Museum
博物馆
18 West Bus Station
汽车西站
19 CITS
中国国际旅行社
22 Long-Distance
Bus Station
长途汽车站
24 Railway Station
火车站
25 Fan Pagoda
繁塔

Take bus No 3 from near the long-distance bus station to the route terminus; it's a short walk to the park's entrance from there. Entry to the park is Y15 and it's an additional Y3 to climb the tower.

Other Sights

The large local **museum** (*kāifēng bówùguǎn*) on Yingbin Lu, just south of Baogong Lake, might once have been worth a look, but it is now virtually empty (apart from a workmanlike display on Kaifeng's revolutionary history) – 'no money', the staff complain.

Longting Park (*lóngtíng gōngyuán*) is covered mostly by lakes; on its drier northern rim near the **Longting** (Dragon Pavilion) there is a small children's fun park with sideshows and bumper-car rides; old men often sit here playing Chinese chess in the shade.

The very small **Yanqing Taoist Temple** (*yánqìng guàn*) has interesting architecture and a strange, 13m-high pagoda. The oldest existing building in Kaifeng is **Fan Pagoda** (*fán tǎ*), south-east of the railway station.

Unfortunately, there is almost nothing left of the **Kaifeng Synagogue** (see the boxed story on the following page) now the boiler room of the No 4 People's Hospital. You can see the remains of an iron cover over an old well, which still has water. The staff at the hospital have seen so many visitors coming through, they'll know what you're looking for. The hospital is diagonally opposite the Bianjing Hotel on Beixing Tu Jie, on the route for bus No 3.

You can visit the **Yellow River**, which is about 10km north of the city, although there isn't much to see because the water volume has shrunk considerably in recent years. About 1km east of where the bus terminates, there's a statue called the **Iron Rhinoceros** (*tiěniú*) which dates from the Ming Dynasty and was meant to guard against floods. To get to the Yellow River, take bus No 6 from the bus terminal near the Iron Pagoda to Liuyankou. It only does the trip twice a day, however, so a taxi might be more practical (about Y50, including the return trip).

Places to Stay

Kaifeng is one of those rare things in modern China – a place where budget travellers get a wider range of accommodation

Kaifeng's Israelites

Father Nicola Trigault translated and published the diaries of the Jesuit priest Matteo Ricci in 1615, and based on these diaries he gives an account of a meeting between Ricci and a Jew from Kaifeng. The Jew was on his way to Beijing to take part in the imperial examinations, and Trigault writes:

When he (Ricci) brought the visitor back to the house and began to question him as to his identity, it gradually dawned upon him that he was talking with a believer in the ancient Jewish law. The man admitted that he was an Israelite, but he knew no such word as 'Jew'.

Ricci found out from the visitor that there were 10 or 12 families of Israelites in Kaifeng. A 'magnificent' synagogue had been built there and the five books of Moses had been preserved in the synagogue in scroll form for more than 500 years.

The visitor was familiar with the stories of the Old Testament, and some of the followers, he said, were expert in the Hebrew language. He also told Ricci that in a province which Trigault refers to as 'Cequian' at the capital of 'Hamcheu' there was a far greater number of Israelite families than at Kaifeng, and that there were others scattered about. Ricci sent one of his Chinese converts to Kaifeng, where he confirmed the visitor's story.

Today several hundred descendants of the original Jews live in Kaifeng and though they still consider themselves Jewish, the religious beliefs and customs associated with Judaism have almost completely died out. The original synagogue was destroyed in a Yellow River flood in 1642. It was rebuilt but destroyed by floods again in the 1850s. This time there was no money to rebuild it. Christian missionaries 'rescued' the temple's scrolls and prayer books in the late 19th century, and these are now in libraries in Israel, Canada and the USA. ■

than those with lots of money to throw around. There seem to be absolutely no constraints on where foreigners can choose to stay.

The *Bian Hotel* (☎ 595-1893) *(biàn dàlüshè)* is the white, four storey building you see to the left as you leave the bus station. It's very basic inside (none of the rooms comes with private bathroom), but has singles from Y20 and twins from Y36, so one can hardly complain.

Another good value place is the *Dajintai Hotel* (☎ 595-6677) *(dàjīntái lüguǎn)* on Gulou Jie, nearly opposite the Bank of China. It has a central yet quiet location in a small courtyard just behind the street front, and offers twin rooms with attached bath (including 24 hour hot water) for Y100. Basic no-frills twins are available for Y30 and Y44 per room.

In the mid-price range is the *Bianjing Hotel* (☎ 595-2012; fax 596-2449) *(biànjīng fàndiàn)* on the corner of Dong Dajie and Beixing Tu Jie, at the north-eastern edge of town in the Muslim quarter. It's an older prefab concrete building with little character of its own, but the rooms are clean and there's plenty of activity on the surrounding streets. There's also a popular restaurant in the back of the hotel compound. Singles with attached bathroom and air-con are Y160 and beds in similar twins and triples are Y60. There are also dorm beds for Y20. To get there take bus No 3 from the long-distance bus station and get off at the sixth stop.

The *Kaifeng Guesthouse* (☎ 595-5589; fax 595-3086) *(kāifēng bīnguǎn)* on Ziyou Lu, right in the centre of town, is a Russian-built structure, but done in a rather ornate style of traditional Chinese architecture. It has an unusual amount of charm, and there is a bewildering array of rooms in the various buildings around a central square. Standard twins range from Y110 to Y168 in the pleb wings. There are more up-market rooms in Building 2 where twins start at 220. There's also a range of suites starting at Y294.

South of Baogong Park on Yingbin Lu is the *Dongjing Hotel* (☎ 398-9388; fax 595-6661) *(dōngjīng dàfàndiàn)*. It's one of those Chinese attempts to bring international comforts to the weary traveller and to throw in some local colour at the same time. The result is akin to a caring prison complex with souvenir shops. The staff speak some English and do their best. Twins in the newer rooms are Y288 and Y298. There are also twins for Y98 in the older rooms, but you can do better elsewhere. Bus No 9 from the railway station goes past here. The hotel is opposite the west long-distance bus station.

Places to Eat
Despite its small size, Kaifeng offers a fair variety of street food, which is particularly good at the *night market* near the corner of Sihou Jie and Madao Jie. Worth sampling there is *ròuhé*, a local snack of fried vegetables and pork (or mutton in its Islamic version) stuffed into a 'pocket' of flat bread.

The eating places around the railway station offer the same generic slop that railway stations all over China serve up. The simple *Di Yi Lou Dumpling Restaurant (dìyīlóu bāoziguǎn)* is a 10 minute walk up Zhongshan Lu from the station and specialises in dumplings. Try the *xiǎolóng bāo*, small dumplings filled with pork, for Y6.

As its name suggests, the government-run *Jiaozi Guan Restaurant (jiǎozi guǎn)* specialises in jiaozi, Chinese dumplings with a meat or vegetable filling. The dumplings here are tasty and very cheap. Upstairs there's a much wider selection of dishes. It's on the corner of Shudian Lu and Sihou Jie in a three storey traditional Chinese building with a quaint old wooden balcony where you can get good views of the bustling night market.

For fast food with a Chinese touch, try *California Beef Noodles (jiāzhōu niúròumiàn)* on Gulou Jie up from the Dajintai Hotel. In the opposite direction, on Madao Jie just off Gulou Jie, *Li's California Beef Noodle King (lǐ xijiāzhōu niúròu dàwáng)* has similar fare, as well as curry and rice dishes.

Getting There & Away
Bus Private minibuses to Zhengzhou collect passengers from in front of the railway station. The best option, however, is to head over to the west bus station, opposite the Dongjing Hotel and take one of the air-con Iveco minibuses (Y15, 45 minutes). Peugeot sedans also leave from here for Y15. There are also frequent Iveco minibuses to Luoyang that do the trip on the freeway in 2½ hours for Y30.

From the bus station in front of the railway station, there are three regular daily buses to Anyang (five hours) via Zhengzhou hours and a somewhat irregular bus service to Bozhou (10 hours) in Anhui Province. You can also get to Bozhou by taking the Kaifeng-Wenzhou bus (it passes through Bozhou).

Train Kaifeng lies on the railway line between Xi'an and Shanghai and trains are frequent. Expresses to Zhengzhou take about 1½ hours, to Shanghai 13 hours and to Xi'an nine hours. You can also get trains south to Bozhou and Hefei in Anhui Province from here, but the departure times are not very convenient.

Getting Around
Buses are less crowded than in many other parts of China and cover all sights of likely interest to tourists. Pedicabs and minivans are also widely available and fairly cheap.

Hubei 湖北

Hubei Facts & Highlights

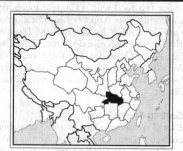

Area: 187,400 sq km
Population: 58.3 million
Capital: Wuhan
Highlights

- Wuhan, a major port on the Yangzi and probably the most cosmopolitan and lively of China's interior cities.
- Yichang, access point for the massive Three Gorges Dam project and cruises upriver to Chongqing via the soon to be submerged Three Gorges.
- Shennongjia district, a relatively untravelled mountainous region boasting some of Hubei's wildest scenery.

Site of the great industrial city and river port of Wuhan, slashed through by the Yangzi River and its many tributaries, and supporting a population of almost 50 million, Hubei (*húběi*) is one of China's most important provinces. For most travellers, however, it's mainly a transit point, or the end point of the Yangzi cruise down from Chongqing (see Yangzi River section in the Sichuan chapter for full details on that journey).

The province actually comprises two quite different areas. The eastern two-thirds

is a low-lying plain drained by the Yangzi and its main northern tributary, the Han River, while the western third is an area of rugged highlands with small cultivated valleys and basins dividing Hubei from Sichuan.

The plain was settled by the Han Chinese in 1000 BC. Around the 7th century AD it was intensively settled and by the 11th it was producing a rice surplus. In the late 19th century it was the first area in the Chinese interior to undergo considerable industrialisation.

WUHAN
(wǔhàn)

Not many people go out of their way to get to Wuhan, but a lot of people pass through the place since it's the terminus of the Yangzi ferries from Chongqing. Livelier, less grimy and more modern than Chongqing, Wuhan is now enjoying a boom in foreign and local investment that may help it catch up to the comparatively sparkling cosmopolitan citadels of Nanjing and Shanghai.

With a population of nearly four million, Wuhan is one of China's largest cities. It's actually a conglomeration of what were once three independent cities: Wuchang, Hankou and Hanyang.

Wuchang was established during the Han Dynasty, became a regional capital under the Yuan and is now the seat of the provincial government. It used to be a walled city, but the walls have long since gone. Hankou, on the other hand, was barely more than a village until the Treaty of Nanjing opened it to foreign trade. There were five foreign concession areas in Hankou, all grouped around present-day Zhongshan Dadao.

Arriving in 1861, the British were the first on the scene, followed by the Germans in 1895, the Russians and the French in 1896 and the Japanese in 1898. With the building of the Beijing-Wuhan railway in

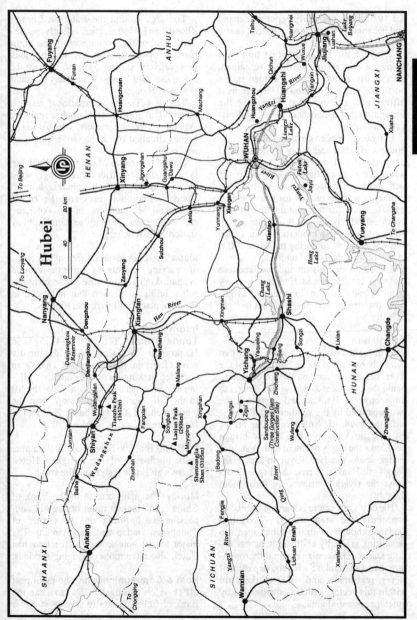

the 1920s, Hankou really began to expand and became the first major industrial centre in the interior of China.

Many of the European-style buildings from the concession era have remained, particularly along Yanjiang Dadao in the north-eastern part of town. Government offices now occupy what were once the foreign banks, department stores and private residences.

Hanyang has been outstripped by neighbouring Hankou and today is the smallest municipality. It dates back to 600 AD, when a was town first developed on the site. During the second half of the 19th century it was developed for heavy industry. The plant for the manufacture of iron and steel which was built at Hanyang in 1891 was the first modern one in China and it was followed during the early 1900s by a string of riverside factories.

The 1930s depression and the Japanese invasion totally ruined Hanyang's heavy industry and since the Communist Revolution the main activity has been light industry.

Orientation

Wuhan is the only city on the Yangzi that can truly be said to lie on both sides of the river. From Wuchang on the south-eastern bank, the city spreads across the Yangzi to the sectors of Hankou and Hanyang, the two separated by the smaller Han River.

In the south of Wuhan an older bridge crosses the Yangzi, while a new bridge now links the city's northern end. A shorter bridge spans the Han River to link Hanyang with Hankou. Ferries and speedboats cross the rivers continuously throughout the day.

The city's real centre is Hankou (hànkǒu), especially the area around Zhongshan Dadao, although 'central' Wuhan seems to be shifting gradually northwards, across Jiefang Dadao, Hankou's principal thoroughfare. Most of Hankou's hotels, department stores, restaurants and street markets are within this sector, which is surrounded by quieter residential areas.

The area around the Jianghan Lu and Zhongshan Lu intersection is lively, particularly during the evening when the night markets open. Hankou has an enormous new railway station 5km north-west of town; the main Yangzi River ferry terminal is also in Hankou.

The new Tianhe international airport, about 30km north of Hankou, has replaced Wuchang's Nanhu airport, which is now being parcelled off as lucrative blocks of real estate.

On the other side of the river, Wuchang is a modern district with long, wide avenues lined by drab concrete blocks. Many recreational areas and the Hubei Provincial Museum are on the Wuchang side of the river. The city's second railway station is in Wuchang.

Maps There are several different city maps of varying usefulness on sale around Wuhan. Xinhua Bookstore and some hotels sell a bilingual version that indicates, in English, places of interest to tourists.

Information

Tourist Office CITS (☎ 578-4125) is in Hankou at 26 Taibei Yilu, diagonally across from the Ramada Hotel. There's an enclosed parking lot outside and the building entrance has a CITS sign. Take the lift to the 7th floor. Bus No 9 stops near the western end of Taibei Yilu on Xinhua Lu: from there it's a five minute walk.

PSB This is at 206 Shengli Jie, a 10 minute walk north-east of the Jianghan Hotel. There's an English sign out the front.

Money The main branch of the Bank of China is in Hankou in an ornate old concession-era building on the corner of Zhongshan Dadao and Jianghan Lu. The major tourist hotels, such as the Jianghan Hotel, also have moneychanging services.

Post & Communications The main post office is on Zhongshan Dadao near the Bank of China. If you're staying at either the Yangtze Hotel or the Hankou Hotel there is a more convenient post office on the corner of Qingnian Lu and Hangkong Lu.

Guiyuan Temple
(guīyuán sì)
Doubling as a curiosity shop and active place of worship, this Buddhist temple has buildings dating from the late Ming and early Qing dynasties.

The main attractions are the statues of Buddha's disciples in an array of comical poses. A few years ago the statues were out in the open, and the incense smoke and sunshine filtering through the sky-lights gave the temple a rare magic. Alas, no longer. The incense is considered a fire hazard, so now visitors have to make do with unlit offerings; entry is Y3.

To get there, take bus No 45 down Zhongshan Dadao and over the Han River bridge; there's a stop near the McDonald's within walking distance of the temple. The temple is on Cuiweiheng Lu at the junction with Cuiwei Lu. A trinket market sets up along Cuiwei Lu.

Yangzi River Bridge
(wǔhàn chángjiāng dàqiáo)
Wuchang and Hanyang are linked by this great bridge – it's more than 1100m long and 80m high. The completion of the bridge in 1957 marked one of Communist China's first great engineering achievements, because until then all road and rail traffic had to be laboriously ferried across the river. A second trans-Yangzi bridge in northern Wuhan was completed in mid-1995.

Hubei Provincial Museum
(húběishěng bówùguǎn)
The museum is a must if you're interested in archaeology. Its large collection of arte-facts came from the Zenghouyi Tomb, which was unearthed in 1978 on the out-skirts of Suizhou City, about halfway along the railway line between the cities of Wuhan and Xiangfan.

The tomb dates from around 433 BC, in the Warring States Period. The male in-ternee was buried with about 7000 of his favourite artefacts, including bronze ritual vessels, weapons, horse and chariot equip-ment, bamboo instruments and utensils, and gold and jade objects.

There is also an interesting exhibit of lacquerware and musical instruments, in-cluding a display of bronze bells. Various examples of musical recordings are for sale at one of the counters. Another room has displays on the ambitious project to cata-logue and preserve cultural relics that will be lost after the Three Gorges Dam is com-pleted. Unfortunately there are no English captions. Entry to the museum is Y10. It is open daily from 8.30 am to noon and 2 to 4 pm.

The museum is beside Donghu (East Lake) in Wuchang, one of the most pleasant areas in Wuhan. Take bus No 14 from the Zhonghua Lu ferry pier (the dock closest to the old bridge) to the last stop, then walk back along the road about 10 minutes, where there's a sign for Mao Zedong's villa. The museum is down that road.

Day Trip In summer you can do a scenic day trip that includes the museum, taking a ferry over from Hankou to the Zhonghua Lu pier in Wuchang, then boarding bus No 36 to Moshan Hill. Take another ferry across the lake to East Lake Park, walk to the museum, then get bus No 14 to Yellow Crane Tower, and finally get a ferry back to Hankou.

Mao Zedong's Villa
(máozédōng biéshù)
If you've just come up from Hunan, you may have had your fill of Mao by now. But if not, you may find a stroll through this bucolic hideaway of the Chairman worth your time and the Y20 entrance fee. Chinese pay Y10.

The tour takes in his living quarters, offices, private swimming pool and a meeting room where key decisions were made during the Cultural Revolution. Mao

HUBEI

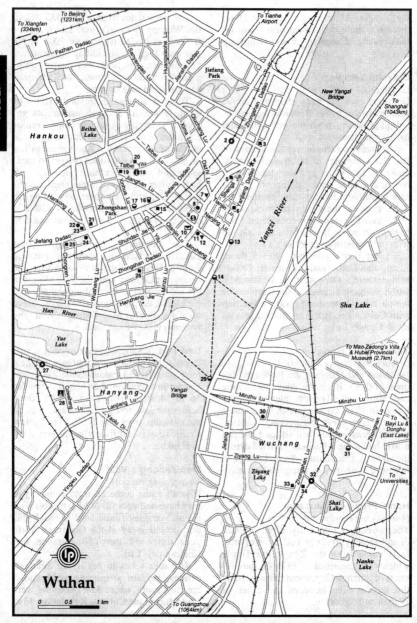

To Xiangfan
(334km)

To Beijing
(1231km)

To Tianhe
Airport

Fazhan Dadao

Samtandao Lu

Qingdao Lu

Huangpu Dadao

Jiefang
Park

Jiang
lie Dadao

Jiefang Dadao

Beihu
Lake

Hankou

Qingdao Lu

Xima Lu

Zhongshan Dadao

New Yangzi
Bridge

To
Shanghai
(1043km)

Talbei Lu

Talbei Yilu

Dazhi Lu

20

19 **18**

Jianghan Lu

Xinhua Lu

Jiefang Dadao

Hankong Lu

Zhongshan
Park

17 **16**

15

Qianjin Yilu

Shengli Jie

5

7

8

Hanjin Lu

Nanjing Lu

Tanjiang Dadao

2

3

4

6

Yangzi River

22
23

21

Qianjin Lu

10

9

11 **12**

13

Jiefang Dadao

25 **24**

Shundao Jie

Zhongshan Dadao

Minsheng Lu

Wusheng Lu

Chongren Lu

26

Zhongshan Dadao

Linan Lu

Hanzheng Jie

14

Sha Lake

Han River

*Yue
Lake*

Yangzi
Bridge

To Mao Zedong's Villa
& Hubei Provincial
Museum (2.7km)

29

27

Qintai
Lu

Hanyang

Lanjiang Lu

Yaolu Di

28

Minzhu Lu

Minzhu Lu

Wuluo Lu

Zhongnan Lu

To
Bayi Lu &
Donghu
(East Lake)

Jiefang Lu

30

Wuchang

Ziyang Lu

31

To
Universities

Yingwu Dadao

*Ziyang
Lake*

Zhongshan Lu

33

32

34

*Shai
Lake*

*Nanhu
Lake*

Wuhan

0   0.5   1 km

To Guangzhou
(1064km)

WUHAN 武汉	PLACES TO EAT	14 Hankou-Wuchang Ferries 汉口武昌渡船
PLACES TO STAY	7 Laotongcheng Restaurant 老通城酒楼	16 JJ's Disco JJ的士高广场
3 Victory Hotel 胜利饭店	12 McDonald's 麦当劳	17 Long-Distance Bus Station 长途汽车站
5 Jianghan Hotel 江汉饭店	**OTHER**	18 CITS 中国国际旅行社
6 Xieli Hotel 协力宾馆	1 New Hankou Railway Station 汉口新火车站	22 China Southern Airlines Office 中国南方航空公司
15 Holiday Inn 武汉天安假日酒店	2 Old Hankou Railway Station 汉口旧火车站	24 CAAC Office 中国民航售票处
19 Xinhua Hotel 新华酒店	4 PSB 公安局外事科	27 Hanyang Railway Station 汉阳火车站
20 Ramada Hotel Wuhan 华美达酒店	8 Advance Booking Office (Train Tickets) 火车预售票处	28 Guiyuan Temple 归园寺
21 Hankou Hotel 汉口饭店	9 Bank of China 中国银行	29 Zhonghua Lu Pier 中华路码头
23 Yangtze Hotel 长江大酒店	10 Main Post Office 邮局	30 Former Headquarters of the 1911 Revolution 武昌起义纪念馆
25 Wuhan Asia Hotel 武汉亚州大酒店	11 Xinhua Bookstore 新华书店	31 Wuchang Long-Distance Bus Station 武昌长途汽车站
26 Yin Feng Hotel 银丰宾馆	13 Yangzi Ferry Terminal 武汉港客运站	32 Wuchang Railway Station 武昌火车站
33 Marine Hotel 航海宾馆		
34 Jiuzhou Hotel 九洲饭店		

stayed here more than 20 times between 1960 and 1974, including nearly 18 months between 1966 and 1969. Jiang Qing joined him, but only three times: apparently she didn't like the place. If you're lucky, you may get a guided tour from one of the frosty, politically correct female guides.

The buildings are in pretty poor shape and have obviously been neglected for decades. But the tree-filled grounds and the gardens are quite nice and have become a haven for a variety of birds. To get there, keep going past the provincial museum for about 10 minutes: there are plenty of signs to show you the way.

Wuhan University
(wǔhàn dàxué)
Wuhan University is beside Luojia Hill in Wuchang. It was founded in 1913, and many of the charming campus buildings originate from that period.

The university was the site of the 1967

'Wuhan Incident' – a protracted battle during the Cultural Revolution with machine gun nests on top of the library and supply tunnels dug through the hill. For a bit of Cultural Revolution nostalgia take bus No 12 to the terminal.

Former Headquarters of the 1911 Revolution
(xīnhàigémìng wǔchāng qǐyì jìniànguǎn)
At the beginning of Wuluo Lu below the Yellow Crane Tower, there is a small square with a statue of Sun Yatsen. Behind the statue there is a colonial-style red brick building which was the headquarters for the Wuchang uprising of 10 October 1911 which toppled the Qing Dynasty. Sun Yatsen wasn't even in China at that time, but he returned as president of the new republic. Like the revolution itself, the exhibit is rather pathetic, but the building is interesting. Entry is Y10 for foreigners, but it is possible to argue for the Chinese price of Y5.

HUBEI

Places to Stay – budget

Nearly all the really bottom-end places in Wuhan have slammed their doors to foreigners, leaving few options. While a bit difficult to get to, accommodation at the universities is the cheapest. The *Foreign Student Dormitory* (☎ 788-2712, ext 2813) *(liúxuéshēnglóu)* at Wuhan University has spartan rooms for Y30 per bed.

Up the road from there, the *Foreign Experts Guesthouse* (☎ 788-2712, ext 2930) *(wàiguó zhuānjiā zhāodàisuǒ)* has large twin rooms with attached bath and air-con for Y180. Both these places will accept travellers, but it's best to phone first. They are located in the eastern part of the campus and it's a long 20 minute slog up the hill. You might be better off hiring a motorcycle with side-car at the entrance that will take you up for Y4.

The *Foreign Guesthouse* (☎ 787-8444, ext 3183) *(wàibīnlóu)* at Wuhan Normal University *(wǔhàn shīfàn dàxué)* has beds in twins for Y60 with shared bathrooms. There is not a lot of space available, so it's better to phone first (if you're lucky enough to get someone to answer the phone). The easiest way to get there is to take bus No 601 to the eastern gate of the university on Zhuodaoquan Lu. No 601 runs from the bottom of Jianghan Lu near the Hankou-Wuchang ferry terminal. From the eastern gate it's a short walk to a white sign with red characters. Turn right and head up the hill for about 50m, then take the left fork. The guesthouse is the first building you come to. The No 66 bus runs from the Wuchang railway station to the university's main gate, but it's a long walk to the dormitory. Either walk up Wuluo Lu and turn right at Zhuodaoquan Lu and proceed to the eastern gate, or take a taxi from the main gate to the eastern gate.

The next cheapest, and a far more convenient choice in Wuchang, is the *Marine Hotel* (☎ 804-3395; fax 807-8717) *(hánghǎi bīnguǎn)*, diagonally across from the railway station and underneath the overpass on Zhongshan Lu. Singles/doubles are Y110/130.

In Hankou, the *Victory Hotel* (☎ 270-7241; fax 270-7604) *(shènglì fàndiàn)*, an old British-built guesthouse on the corner of Shengli Jie and Siwei Lu, has standard twins for US$48, but at the back they have a few cheap rooms around a leafy courtyard for Y100 if you ask for them. The place is a bit out of the way, but there are plenty of buses along Shengli Jie.

Places to Stay – middle

Pretty much in central Hankou, the *Xinhua Hotel* (☎ 579-0333) *(xīnhuá jiǔdiàn)* is on a side street off Jianghan Beilu just around the corner from Xinhua Lu. It looks uninspiring from the outside, but the rooms are OK. The hotel has air-con singles/triples without bath for Y88/150 and singles/twins with attached bath for Y128/168.

Just north of and across from the massive Yangzi ferry terminal at 2 Tianjin Lu, the *Xieli Hotel* (☎ 280-3903) *(xiélì bīnguǎn)* has decent twins for Y204. It's good to keep in mind for those late-night Yangzi River cruise arrivals.

Costing a bit more, but definitely worth it, is the *Yin Feng Hotel* (☎ 589-2711; fax 589-3011) *(yínfēng bīnguǎn)*, which is centrally located at 400 Zhongshan Dadao. Twins are Y268/328 and feature clean wooden floors, sparkling bathrooms and great water pressure for excellent showers.

Over in Wuchang and very convenient to the railway station, the *Jiuzhou Hotel* (☎ 804-2120; fax 804-2784) *(jiǔzhōu fàndiàn)* has twins for Y168. The hotel is at the far left of the square as you exit the station.

Places to Stay – top end

The *Jianghan Hotel* (☎ 281-1600; fax 281-4342) *(jiānghàn fàndiàn)* at 245 Shengli Jie, near the old (now disused) Hankou railway station, is the place to stay if you can afford it. Built by the French in 1914 as the Demin Hotel, it's one of the best examples of colonial architecture in this part of China. It looks a bit run-down from the outside, but the interior is impressive. Room rates range from US$90 for a twin to

US$280 for a suite, plus a 15% surcharge. The hotel has its own post office, shops and an excellent restaurant.

The *Yangtze Hotel* (☎ 363-2828; 364-4110) *(chángjiāng dàjiǔdiàn)*, on the corner of Jiefang Dadao and Qingnian Lu, has singles and doubles for US$70/88 and up (plus 15%). Immediately opposite is the *Hankou Hotel* (☎ 579-7846; fax 579-5565) *(hànkǒu fàndiàn)* which is similar, but somewhat cheaper, with standard twins for Y388 and a 10% service charge. Both are quite good hotels, but this intersection now resembles a freeway junction due to an adjacent noisy traffic overpass.

Although its location is a bit inconvenient, the US-style *Ramada Hotel Wuhan* (☎ 578-7968; fax 578-9171) *(huáměidá jiǔdiàn)* at 9 Taibei Yilu offers four star service for around US$79 for a twin (plus 15%), although prices seem negotiable. It's also a good spot for western food (see the Places to Eat section below).

The *Wuhan Asia Hotel* (☎ 380-0777; fax 380-8080) *(wǔhànyàzhōu dàjiǔdiàn)* at 616 Jiefang Dadao is another four star hotel where a twin room will set you back Y893 (plus 15%).

The newly opened *Wuhan Tianan Holiday Inn* (☎ 586-7888 fax; 584-5353) *(wǔhàn tiān'ān jiàrì jiǔdiàn)* is the best hotel in town; standard singles/twins are US$110/120. It's located at 868 Jiefang Dadao, about 100m south-west of the intersection with Jianghan Lu.

Holiday Inn will also manage the revamped *Qingchuan Hotel (qíngchuān jiàrì fàndiàn)*, due to open in the spring of 1998 on a prime location on the edge of the river north of the old Yangzi River bridge in Hanyang.

Places to Eat
Wuhan has some pretty good eating houses in all price ranges. Popular local snacks include fresh catfish from the nearby Donghu (East Lake) and charcoal-grilled whole pigeons served with a sprinkling of chilli. You can try some of these dishes on the *floating restaurants* at the end of Bayi Lu on the shore of Donghu, where you can pick your catfish before they cook it.

Good streets for night food are Minsheng Lu and Jianghan Lu, both running off Zhongshan Dadao. If you have a craving for western food, there's no better spot than the Ramada Hotel's *coffee shop* and the *Holiday Inn*, where prices are still fairly reasonable.

If you're really desperate for a hamburger that is considerably cheaper, there's a *McDonald's* on Jianghan Lu south-east of the intersection with Zhongshan Dadao, as well as one up on Zhongshan Dadao near the intersection with Minzu Lu. Altogether, there are about five McDonald's and a number of *KFC* outlets scattered around Wuhan.

Bakeries with western-style bread are also fairly common. There's a good one beside the Holiday Inn.

The *Laotongcheng Restaurant (lǎotōngchéng jiǔlóu)* at 1 Dazhi Lu on the corner with Zhongshan Dadao serves a tasty snack called *dòupí*. While it may look like a stuffed omelette, it's actually made with a bean curd base – its name translates as 'bean skin' – and is served rolled around a filling of rice and diced meat. The Laotongcheng was apparently a favourite of Mao's, although presumably he didn't have to push and shove with the proletariat to get his doupi. Doupi is no great delicacy, but at Y4 a serving you can't go wrong. There are a number of different fillings, including egg and rice *(dànguāng dòupí)* or vegetable *(shuāngdōng dòupí)*.

Entertainment
Wuhan nightlife is beginning to take off, with discos and nightclubs opening all over Hankou. The proverbial JJ's is popular with locals. In fact, the manager, Mr Zhang, says his JJ's is one of the originals, along with the one in Guangzhou, and all the others in China are copies. He brings in bands and DJs from the Philippines. Entrance is Y50, which includes one nonalcoholic drink. The disco is right across from the Holiday Inn.

Getting There & Away

The best way of getting to eastern destinations such as Nanjing and Shanghai is by air or river ferry, rather than the circuitous rail route.

Air CAAC has its main ticket office in Hankou at 151 Liji Beilu, but it is better to go to the China Southern Airlines (☎ 362-4600) ticket outlet at 3 Hangkong Lu right near the Yangtze Hotel. It offers air connections to virtually all major cities in China, including daily flights to Beijing, Guangzhou, Kunming, Shanghai and Shenzhen, and several each week to Nanjing, Fuzhou, Xi'an, Chengdu and Hong Kong.

You can also find a number of air ticket outlets in the area around the Wuchang railway station.

Bus The main long-distance bus station is in Hankou on Jiefang Dadao, between Xinhua Lu and Jianghan Lu. There are daily departures to Nanchang (seven hours), Changsha (five hours), Zhengzhou (12 hours), as well as other major cities.

They also have buses to Jigongshan (southern Henan) and Bozhou (northern Anhui). The best way to get to Yichang is on one of the comfortable air-con buses run by the Jianlong bus company leaving every hour throughout the day (Y81). The journey takes four hours on the new freeway.

You can also get buses to Yichang and other destinations from the bus station in Wuchang which is south-east of Zhongshan Lu on Wuluo Lu, and marked by a pedestrian bridge crossing. A Korean joint-venture bus company, Hanguang, does the four hour trip to Yichang for Y80, leaving every hour.

Train Wuhan is on the main Beijing-Guangzhou line; express trains to Kunming, Xi'an and Lanzhou run via the city. All trains that go through Wuhan to other destinations usually stop at both Hankou and Wuchang railway stations.

At Hankou station, hard and soft sleepers must be booked in the small ticket office between the waiting hall and the main ticket office.

There is also a railway ticket office in central Hankou where Zhongshan Dadao briefly divides into Baohua Jie at the intersection with Nanjing Lu. You can book sleepers three days in advance.

Note that many southbound trains originating at Wuhan actually depart from Wuchang station rather than Hankou. Tickets for these must be bought at Wuchang. Window 14 is for foreigners, but you can go to any of the other windows as well. CITS can also book sleepers for a Y50 service charge.

The Beijing-Kowloon express train also goes through Wuchang, but it does not stop in Hankou.

Some sample hard-sleeper tickets are Beijing (Y325), Guangzhou (Y290) and Kunming (Y285).

Boat You can catch ferries from Wuhan along the Yangzi River either east to Shanghai or west to Chongqing (see the Yangzi River section in the Sichuan chapter for full details).

Getting Around

To/From the Airport Buses to Tianhe international airport leave four to five times throughout the day from the China Southern Airlines office on Hangkong Lu. The fare is Y10. A taxi to the airport should cost between Y100 and Y120.

Bus & Ferry Bus routes criss-cross the city, but getting where you want to go may mean changing at least once. A useful bus is the No 38, which passes the Jianghan Hotel to and from the new Hankou railway station. Bus No 9 runs from the railway station down Xinhua Lu to the Yangzi River ferry terminal.

In Wuchang, bus No 12 runs from Wuhan University to the Zhinghua Lu ferry pier, and Nos 503 and 601 go from the Hankou ferry terminal across to Wuchang. Motor-tricycles and pedicabs wait outside the two main railway stations and the Yangzi ferry terminal, as well as the smaller ferry docks.

The Hankou-Wuchang ferries are normally a more convenient, and always a much faster, way of crossing the river than taking a bus over the Yangzi bridge. The large boats take 15 to 20 minutes to make the crossing, while smaller speedboats, which carry around 15 people, do it in five minutes for Y5.

WUDANGSHAN
(wǔdāng shān)
The Wudangshan mountains stretch for 400km across north-western Hubei Province. Situated south-east of Shiyan, the highest summit is the 1612m Tianzhu Peak, whose name translates as 'Pillar Propping Up the Sky', or 'Heavenly Pillar Peak'.

The Wudangshan is a sacred range to the Taoists, and a number of Taoist temples were built here during the construction sprees of the Ming emperors Cheng Zu and Zhen Wu. Noted temples include the Golden Hall on Tianzhu Peak, which was built entirely of gilded copper in 1416; the hall contains a bronze statue of Zhen Wu, who became a Taoist deity.

The Purple Cloud Temple stands on Zhanqifeng Peak, and the Nanyan Temple perches on the South Cliff. Wudangshan is also famous for the Wudangshan style of martial arts developed here, and there are numerous schools in and around the town.

The railway station is called Wudangshan, but the town used to go by the name of Laoying. The entrance gate to the mountain is about 1km east of the town; entry costs Y21 and then it's another Y10 to view the Golden Hall when you get to the top.

It's 10km from the entrance gate to the parking lot up the mountain, then another two hours hike up to Tianzhu Peak. There are walking paths up from the entrance gate, but most people take a minivan taxi up to the parking lot for Y10. A cable car is also being constructed.

Places to Stay & Eat
On the main street directly down from the railway station, the *Xuanwu Hotel* (☎ 566-6013) *(xuánwǔ dàjiǔdiàn)* has beds in twins with attached bath for Y25 and better twins for Y80. There's no English sign, but it's right beside an ornate Chinese-style arch.

The best value in town is the *Laoying Hotel* (☎ 566-5347) *(laǒyīng fàndiàn)* with clean twins/triples for Y60/50 per bed. It's east down the main street past the intersection with Yongle Lu.

At the end of Yongle Lu, beside the martial arts school, the *Wudangshan Hotel* (☎ 556-5548; fax 556-5560) *(wǔdāngshān bīnguǎn)* is the most luxurious place in town with twins for Y200.

You can also stay on the mountain. The *Jinding Hotel (jīndǐng lǚguǎn)* below the temple on Tianzhu Peak has beds in twins and triples for Y60/40, as well as bunk beds for Y25. Bathroom and eating facilities are basic, but there are some fantastic views and you might get to know some of the Taoist priests who live up there.

Down at the parking lot, the best place to stay is the *Baihui Hotel (bǎihuì shānzhuāng)* with nice twins for Y78 and Y120. If you contact the hotel before you arrive in town they can send down a car to pick you up for Y10.

In town, there are a couple of good private restaurants on Yongle Lu near its intersection with the main road. The hotels in town and at the parking lot also have restaurants.

Getting There & Away
Wudangshan is on the railway line from Wuhan to Chongqing, but few trains make the stop and you may have to take a bus to Shiyan (one hour). There are daily trains from Wuhan and Xiangfan. There are also sleeper buses to Wuhan (12 hours) leaving from the bus station that is diagonally opposite the Xuanwu Hotel.

Minibuses to Shiyan go up and down the main street collecting passengers; tickets cost Y5.

HUBEI

SHENNONGJIA
(shénnóngjià)

The Shennongjia district in remote north-western Hubei has the wildest scenery in the province. With heavily forested mountains of fir, pine and hemlock – including something rare in China, old-growth stands – the area is known as a treasure trove of more than 1300 species of medicinal plants. Indeed, the name for the area roughly translates as 'Shennong's Ladder' to commemorate a legendary emperor, Shennong, believed to be the founder of herbal medicine and agriculture. According to the legend, he heard about some special plants growing up high on a precipice, so he cut down a great tree and used it to climb to the site and reach the plants, which he added to his medical collection.

As part of a more modern legend, Shennongjia is also famous for the sightings of wild, ape-like creatures – a Chinese equivalent of the Himalayan Yeti or the North American Bigfoot. The stories are interesting, but the creatures seem to be able to distinguish between peasants and scientists – molesting the former and evading the latter. Nevertheless, there is a small base station set up in the reserve with displays of 'evidence' of sightings. More real, but just as elusive perhaps, are species of leopard, bear, wild boar and monkey (including the endangered Golden Snub-Nosed Monkey) that reportedly inhabit the area.

Foreigners are only allowed into the area of the Shennongjia district near the town of **Muyuping**, 200km north-west of Yichang. There are two high peaks in the area, Shennongjiashan at 3105m and Laojunshan at 2936m. It's a 10 hour bus ride to Muyuping from Yichang, or you can take a boat to Xiangxi (five hours) on the Three Gorges and from there it's a 90km ride to Muyuping. From Muyuping you will have to hire a car to get into the reserve.

The CITS in Yichang arranges a three day tour that includes visits to botanical sites, rafting and Shennongjiashan, but be prepared to pay up to Y2000 per person. The tour includes accommodation, although much of the time is taken up with transportation. Other travel agencies around the railway station in Yichang also offer tours to Shennongjia, but you should specify the Muyuping area unless you want some adventures with the police.

Even though the bus station in Yichang will merrily sell you a ticket, foreign travellers who go to Songbai in the Shennongjia reserve will be sent back on the bus the next morning and can expect to be fined up to Y1000. The PSB in Yichang and Wuhan will not issue travel permits for this part of the district unless you have a special invitation.

YICHANG
(yíchāng)

Sited just below the famous Three Gorges, Yichang is the gateway to the upper Yangzi and was a walled town as long ago as the Sui Dynasty. The city was opened to foreign trade in 1877 by a treaty between Britain and China and a concession area was set up along the riverfront south-east of the old city.

Today Yichang is best known for the nearby Gezhou Dam, and the city's economy has taken off due to the massive Three Gorges hydroelectric project now being built at Sandouping, 40km upstream.

A steady flow of Yangzi River tourists passing through town is also swelling local coffers. Unless you have a special fondness for dams, there's really not much worth seeing in Yichang, but it's a useful jumping-off point for more interesting places.

CITS offers tours of the Three Gorges that include rafting trips, but you'll need four or more people to make it worthwhile in terms of price. If you want visit the Three Gorges Dam construction site, mini-buses and minivan taxis leave from the bottom of the steps leading down from the railway station. The trip takes an hour and tickets are Y10, or if you go by the new freeway being built to Chongqing, it's only half an hour. Security is very tight and the police are constantly stopping people to check their identity cards.

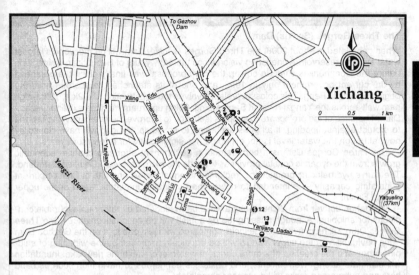

HUBEI

YICHANG 宜昌

1 Three Gorges Hotel
三峡宾馆
2 Charles' Fast Food
查理堡快餐
3 Railway Station
火车站
4 Sunshine Hotel
阳光大酒店
5 Post Office
邮局

6 Long-Distance Bus
Station
长途汽车站
7 Children's Park
儿童公园
8 CITS
中国国际旅行社
9 Taohualing Hotel
桃花岭饭店
10 PSB
公安局

11 CITS Air Ticket Centre
国际旅行社票务中心
12 Bank of China
中国银行
13 Dagong Hotel
大公饭店
14 Dagongqiao Bus/Ferry
Terminal
大公桥客运站
15 Yichang Ferry Terminal
宜昌港

The gap was closed in November 1997 and, while there may not be a lot to see at the dam site except piles of cement and dirt for the time being, a visit does bring home the absolute audacity of this project and its consequences.

Information

Tourist Offices CITS (☎ 646-5856) is at 25 Yunji Lu near the entrance to the Taohualing Hotel. There is also a branch at the bottom of the steps leading from the railway station.

Money You can change money at the Bank of China on Shengli Silu near the Dagong Hotel.

Post & Communications The main post office is at the corner of Yunji Lu and Yiling Dadao.

Places to Stay

Across from the Dagongqiao bus and ferry terminal, the *Dagong Hotel* (☎ 622-4532) *(dàgōng fàndiàn)* is the cheapest place in town that takes foreigners. Twins are Y80/90

The Three Gorges (Sanxia) Dam

When completed in about 2008, the Three Gorges *(sānxiá)* Dam will be the world's largest water storage reservoir. A cherished vision since the early years of Republican China, long before the Communists came to power, the dam proposal was finally given the go-ahead by the current government only in 1992, and one of its staunchest supporters from the beginning was Li Peng. This colossal project involves the construction of a 2km, 185m-high dam wall across the Yangzi River at Sandouping, 38km upstream from the existing Gezhou Dam. The aims of the project are to supply electricity, to improve the river's navigability and to protect against flooding. If all goes according to schedule, the gap will have closed by now, although the water level is not expected rise significantly for a few more years.

The Three Gorges Dam is a cornerstone in government efforts to channel economic growth from the dynamic coastal provinces towards the more backward Chinese hinterland. The dam's hydroelectric production – reckoned to equal almost one-fifth of China's current generating capacity – is intended to power the continuing industrialisation of the upper Yangzi Basin.

Navigation upriver from Yichang has always been hindered by rather unfavourable conditions for shipping. Although passing the dam itself will be an inconvenience – the Three Gorges Dam will have five passage locks compared with just one lock on the Gezhou Dam – the navigability of the upper Yangzi will be drastically improved by the widening of shipping lanes and the creation of a more constant water level within the new lake. Inundation will eliminate strong river currents, and obstacles dangerous to navigation such as sand bars and submerged rocks will disappear completely.

At least as important will be the dam's role in flood control. The Yangzi is prone to repeated flooding, often causing great loss of life. Several catastrophic floods have occurred this century, in 1931, 1935, 1954 and more recently in 1991, when more than 2000 people are believed to have perished.

However, the massive scale of the Three Gorges Dam project has caused disquiet among environmentalists and economists, arousing some of the most outspoken criticism

and triples Y90/105 per room with attached bath. The hotel is up a small driveway set back from Yanjiang Dadao and has no English sign, but there's a big, red-lit sign in Chinese at night that's easy to spot.

Just down the steps from the railway station and to the left, the *Sunshine Hotel* (☎ 644-6075; fax 644-6086) *(yángguāng dàjiǔdiàn)* has clean, although slightly tattered, twins for Y180 and up, but foreigners pay a 30% surcharge. There are a number of other hotels around here, but none of them seems to welcome foreign friends.

The best hotel to date is the recently renovated *Taohualing Hotel* (☎ 644-2244; fax 644-5701) *(táohuālíng bīnguǎn)* in the middle of town at 29 Yunji Lu. Nice twins

with wooden floors are Y248 and up, with an added 20% service charge for all guests. The hotel also has a bowling alley and swimming pool, and very nice grounds.

The *Three Gorges Hotel* (☎ 673-9888; fax 673-8165) *(sānxiá bīnguǎn)* is a fair way north at 38 Yanjiang Dadao and has twins for slightly higher prices, but the rooms and atmosphere are not as nice. Take bus No 11 from the station or No 2 from the dock.

Places to Eat

Yichang has a variety of restaurants around town, but try the bustling area of Yunji Lu between the intersection of Zhenzhu Lu and the river.

For fast food and passable hamburgers

of government policy in China since 1989. Protests also centre on what will be a significant loss of cultural artefacts and important sites marking various periods of China's cultural history. Despite an ambitious plan of relocation and preservation, time is running out and the technocrats in charge of the dam project have not given this issue the attention it deserves.

The social and environmental implications of the dam, which will create a vast 550km-long lake stretching deep into Sichuan Province, are profound indeed. When the backwaters build up behind the dam wall, the great inland port of Chongqing will become the world's first metropolis situated on the banks of a major artificial lake.

An estimated two million people living in the inundated areas will need to be relocated. Some destruction of the natural and scenic splendour of the Three Gorges is unavoidable, though how the dam will affect Yangzi River tourism – still in its infancy – is uncertain. Tour operators in Yichang are optimistic there will still be great demand, 'for a different type of scenic tour' they say. Nevertheless, boat trips of the Three Gorges are running overtime as local and foreign tourists rush to see one of China's most famous sights before the concrete slabs begin to spell the demise of a great river.

Construction of the dam will be enormously expensive, with a final cost probably somewhere in the vicinity of US$20 billion. Economists both in China and abroad have warned that it may be imprudent for the government to concentrate such investment into one single project.

Fears about the dam project were also heightened when information was released about two dams that collapsed in Henan Province in 1975. After 20 years as a state secret, it is now apparent that as many as 230,000 people died in the catastrophe.

Planners insist that the Three Gorges Dam will be constructed according to safety regulations that would make a similar disaster impossible – still, the collapse of the walls holding back the world's largest storage reservoir in one of the world's most densely populated pieces of real estate is a thought that must give even the most gung-ho supporters of the Three Gorges project nightmares. ∎

there are two outlets of *Charles' Fast Food* (*chálǐbǎo kuàicān*) – one at the bottom of the steps leading from the railway station and the other at the intersection of Zhenzhu Lu and Yunji Lu. There is also a lively *night market* for dining that sets up on Taozhu Lu.

Getting There & Away

Air Yichang has an airport with flights to major cities, as well as three flights a week to Zhangjiajie City (formerly Dayong) in Hunan Province. There are a number of ticket places around town; check out the area around the railway station and ferry terminals.

The CITS ticket centre that books flights (☎ 622-8915) is at 2 Erma Lu.

Bus The long-distance bus station is south of the railway station along Dongshan Dadao. There are day buses and night sleepers to Wuhan. The Hanguang air-con bus to Wuhan (four hours) leaves from here every hour. There is also a daily morning bus to Muyuping. Buses to Wuhan, including the Jinlong service, also leave from the Dagongqiao bus and ferry terminal on Yanjiang Dadao.

Train The town is linked by a 40km section of track to the rail junction at Yaqueling (*yāquèlǐng*).

There are direct trains daily between Yichang and Beijing, Zhengzhou, Xi'an, Wuhan and Huaihua. Trains to Huaihua stop en route at Zhangjiajie City. If you can't get on these, you will probably have to change trains at Yaqueling.

The long-distance bus station also has buses to Yaqueling. Make sure to somehow let the driver know you're headed to the railhead, as it is located far outside the town of Yaqueling. You'll probably then be dropped off next to the railway tracks and pointed in the direction of the station. Walk along the tracks for 10 minutes and you'll get there.

Boat All passing river ferries call in at Yichang ferry terminal. Travellers often find the two day boat trip through the Yangzi gorges between Chongqing (Sichuan Province) and Yichang quite long enough, and some disembark or board here rather than spend an extra day on the river between Yichang and Wuhan.

There is also a hydrofoil service that goes

to Wanxian in Sichuan Province at the western end of the Three Gorges; the trip takes six hours. Tickets are Y200, but foreigners have to pay a 50% surcharge. The boats don't leave from the ferry terminal, but a bus picks up passengers to the point of embarkation above the Gezhou Dam.

For full details on Yangzi River cruises, see the Yangzi River section in the Sichuan chapter.

Getting Around

To/From the Airport The airport bus leaves from the Three Gorges Hotel and tickets are Y20.

Bus & Motorcycle Bus Nos 3 and 4 run from Yunji Lu near the railway station to the ferry terminal. Motorcycles are abundant and the best way to get around, at Y5 a ride.

Jiangxi 江西

Jiangxi *(jiāngxī)* was incorporated into the Chinese Empire at an early date, but remained sparsely populated until the 8th century. Before this, the main expansion of the Han Chinese had been from the north into Hunan and then into Guangdong. When the building of the Grand Canal from the 7th century onwards opened up the south-eastern regions, Jiangxi became·an important transit point on the trade and shipment route overland from Guangdong.

Before long the human traffic was diverted into Jiangxi, and between the 8th and 13th centuries the region was rapidly settled by Chinese peasants. The development of silver mining and tea growing allowed the formation of a wealthy Jiangxi merchant class. By the 19th century, however, the province's role as a major transport route from Guangzhou was much reduced by the opening of coastal ports to foreign shipping, which forced the Chinese junk trade into a steady decline.

Jiangxi also bears the distinction of having been one of the most famous Communist guerrilla bases. It was only after several years of war that the Kuomintang were able to drive the Communists out onto their 'Long March' to Shaanxi.

NANCHANG
(nánchāng)
A fairly nondescript capital of a province that sees little in the way of foreign visitors, Nanchang has been called 'the poor person's Beijing'. There is little to see, and the city can be a very miserable place on a cold, rainy day. Still, there are far worse Chinese cities, and the side streets that run off the broad boulevards can make for interesting exploring.

History
Nanchang is largely remembered in modern Chinese history for the Communist-led uprising of 1 August 1927.

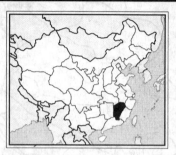

Jiangxi Facts & Highlights

Area: 166,600 sq km

Population: 41.1 million

Capital: Nanchang

Highlights

- Jingdezhen, China's most famous area for the production of porcelain and ceramics.
- Lushan, a hill resort where mountain vistas have inspired Communist leaders and artists alike.

After Chiang Kaishek staged his massacre of Communists and other opponents in March 1927, what was left of the Communist Party fled underground and a state of confusion reigned. At this time the Party was dominated by a policy of urban revolution, and the belief was that victory could only be won by organising insurrections in the cities.

Units of the Kuomintang Army led by Communist officers happened to be concentrated around Nanchang at the time, and there appeared to be an opportunity for a successful insurrection.

On 1 August (known as *bāyī* in Chinese) a combined army of 30,000 under the leadership of Zhou Enlai and Zhu De seized the

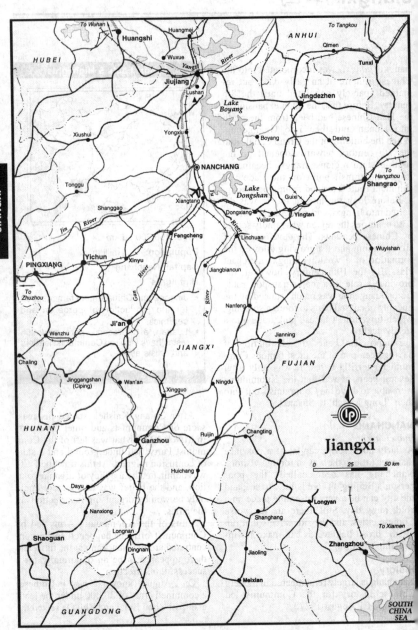

Jiangxi

city and held it for several days until they were driven out by troops loyal to the Nanjing regime.

The revolt was largely a fiasco, but it is remembered in Chinese history as the beginning of the Communist Army. The army retreated south from Nanchang to Guangdong, but part of it, led by Zhu De, circled back to Jiangxi to join forces with the ragtag army that Mao Zedong had organised in Hunan and then led into the Jinggangshan mountains.

Orientation

Nanchang is bounded in the north by the Gan River and in the west by the Fu River, which branches off the Gan. Zhanqian Lu heads leads directly west from the railway station to the Fushan traffic circle and overpass.

Bayi Dadao goes north-west from the Fushan traffic circle and is the main north-south artery through the centre of town; another main strip is Yangming Beilu, which cuts east-west to the old and new Bayi Bridges over the Gan River.

Most of the sights and tourist facilities are on or in the vicinity of Bayi Dadao. The centre of town is Renmin Square at the intersection of Bayi Dadao and Beijing Lu.

Maps City transport maps (in Chinese) are sold around the bus and railway stations. Otherwise, try the two Xinhua Bookstores on Bayi Dadao: one at Renmin Square and the other on the western side of the street between the long-distance bus station and the Fushan traffic circle.

Information

Tourist Offices The CITS office (☎ 621-7536) is in the building behind the rear car park at the Jiangxi Hotel (Binguan). They also have a counter in the lobby of the hotel near the shopping arcade.

PSB This is in the new cream-tiled highrise building on Shengli Lu, about 100m north of Minde Lu.

Money The main Bank of China is opposite the Nanchang Hotel on Zhanqian Xilu. The Jiangxi Hotel (Binguan) also has a money-changing service, but only for cash.

Post & Communications There is a post office on the ground floor of the Jiangxi Hotel (Binguan), and another on the corner of Bayi Dadao and Ruzi Lu, just south of the Exhibition Hall.

Things to See

On Bayi Dadao in the heart of Nanchang is **Renmin Square**. Here you'll find the **Monument to the Martyrs**, a sculpture of red-tiled flags and a stone column topped with a rifle and fixed bayonet. Opposite the square is the **Exhibition Hall**, an immense building adorned with a giant red star – a nostalgic tribute to Stalinist architecture now somewhat obscured by advertising billboards.

The pride of the city is the massive **Tengwang Pavilion**, erected in 1989, allegedly on the same site as 28 previous reconstructions. Originally built during the Tang period, the modern nine storey granite pavilion is situated on the banks of the Fu River and houses exhibition rooms, teahouses and the inevitable souvenir shops.

On the top floor is a traditional Chinese music and dance theatre. There are performances every hour and it's open daily from 8 am to 5.30 pm; entry is Y20 for Chinese and foreigners.

Most of the other sights are reminders of the Communist Revolution and include the **Memorial Hall to the Martyrs of the Revolution** on Bayi Dadao, north of Renmin Square; the **Residence of Zhou Enlai & Zhu De** on Minde Lu; and the **Former Headquarters of the Nanchang Uprising**, now a museum, near the corner of Shengli Lu and Zhongshan Lu.

Places to Stay

The best deal in Nanchang is the *Xiangshan Hotel* (☎ 678-1402, ext 2366) *(xiàngshān fàndiàn)*, on Xiangshan Beilu, although it is a long way from the bus and railway stations.

JIANGXI

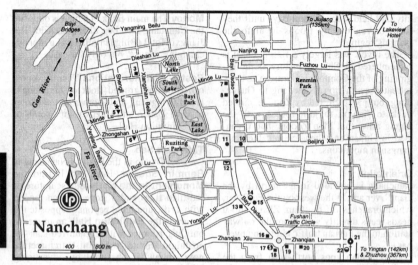

Nanchang

NANCHANG 南昌

1 Nanchang Port
南昌港客运站
2 Tengwang Pavilion
腾王阁
3 Xiangshan Hotel
象山宾馆
4 PSB
公安局外事科
5 Rosa Bakery
罗沙蛋糕
6 St Hark Country Chicken
美国胜哈客乡村炸鸡
7 Jiangxi Hotel (Binguan)
江西宾馆

8 Jiangxi Hotel (Fandian)
江西饭店
9 Memorial Hall to the
Martyrs of the Revolution
烈士纪念馆
10 Renmin Square
人民广场
11 Exhibition Hall
展览馆
12 Post Office
邮电局
13 Ganjiang Hotel
赣江宾馆
14 Long-Distance Bus Station
长途汽车站

15 CAAC Booking Office
中国民航
16 Nanchang Hotel
南昌宾馆
17 Bank of China
中国银行
18 Poyanghu Hotel
郵阳湖大酒店
19 Lucky Hotel
九洲大酒店
20 Jingjiu Hotel
京九宾馆
21 Railway Station
火车站
22 Minibuses to Jiujiang
往九江小型车

Beds in basic quads are Y27.50, and Y54.50 in triples with attached bath and air-con. They also have twins ranging from Y133 to Y225. Take bus No 5 for nine stops from the railway station; the bus stop is diagonally opposite the hotel entrance.

The *Nanchang Hotel* (☎ 621-9698) (*nánchāng bīnguǎn*) is within walking distance of the railway station. At the time of writing, the hotel was undergoing massive renovations, but beds in quads will be available for Y60 and twins from Y125 to Y290 with attached bath and air-con. Foreigners can expect to pay a 60% surcharge.

The *Poyanghu Hotel* (☎ 622-9688; fax 622-6562) (*póyánghú dàjiǔdiàn*), on the south-western side of the Fushan traffic circle, is also undergoing renovation and has twins with attached bath for Y166 and Y280, although for the cheaper doubles foreigners will pay a 50% surcharge. It's quite convenient for the bus and railway stations.

Further up Bayi Dadao, just opposite the long-distance bus station, the *Ganjiang Hotel* (☎ 622-1159; fax 626-2480) *(gànjiāng bīnguǎn)* has twins for Y100 per room, and beds in triples and quads for Y100 and Y80 per bed, but you normally have to book the whole room. Foreigners are supposed to pay a 50% surcharge for these rooms, but you may be able to talk them out of it. There are also twins with attached bath for Y280 and Y480, with no surcharge.

There are a couple of mid-range hotels just down from the railway station: the *Lucky Hotel* (☎ 622-8840; fax 621-9733) *(jiǔzhōu dàjiǔdiàn)* has standard twins with attached bath for Y238.

Further towards the railway station, the *Jingjiu Hotel (jīngjiǔ bīnguǎn)* was in the midst of renovation at the time of writing, but it can be expected to have similar prices.

Two local establishments go by the English name Jiangxi Hotel, although their names in Chinese use different words (and characters) for hotel. The *Jiangxi Hotel* (☎ 622-1131; fax 622-4388) *(jiāngxī bīnguǎn)*, at 78 Bayi Dadao, is where most foreign tourists stay. The building's exterior is still recognisable as a relic of early 1960s socialist architecture, but the interior has been recently renovated. Standard rooms start at US$80.

The other *Jiangxi Hotel* (☎ 621-2123) *(jiāngxī fàndiàn)* is a large complex around the corner and down Bayi Dadao. Triples are Y90 per room with air-con. Singles and twins with attached bath are Y180/210 and up.

A new hotel becoming popular with overseas business travellers is the Hong Kong joint-venture *Lakeview Hotel* (☎ 852-1888; fax 852-1999) *(wǔhú dàjiǔdiàn)*, located in the north-east section of the city at 33 Hongdu Lu on Qingshan Lake. Rooms start at US$85.

Places to Eat
As usual, the railway station area is a good hunting ground for cheap eats. For street snacks try *xiànbǐng* – fried pancakes stuffed with vegetables. The ones cooked in the electric fryers are less oily than the deep-fried variety.

The Hong Kong-style *Rosa Bakery* chain *(luóshā dàn'gāo)* also has shops scattered around town, with good bread and cakes. There's one beside the PSB on Shengli Lu and another on Zhongshan Lu opposite the Former Headquarters of the Nanchang Uprising.

For KFC-style fast food try the Taiwanese-run *St Hark Country Chicken* *(měiguó shènghākè xiāngcūn zhájī)* at 378 Zhongshan Lu near the intersection with Shengli Lu. The Jiangxi Hotel (Binguan) also has western-style food and English menus.

Getting There & Away
Air The airport is at Xiangtang, 28km south of the city centre, and scheduled flights go to Beijing, Guangzhou, Hong Kong, Kunming, Ningbo, Shanghai, Wenzhou, Xi'an and other destinations.

The most convenient CAAC office is on Bayi Dadao, next to the long-distance bus station, and there are various ticketing outlets on Zhanqian Lu near the railway station.

There is also a Chinese Eastern Airlines (☎ 627-0881) office at 87 Minde Lu opposite the Jiangxi Hotel (Binguan).

Bus Nanchang's long-distance bus station is on Bayi Dadao between Renmin Square and the Fushan traffic circle. From here there are air-con buses to Changsha (Y70, four daily, eight hours), Jiujiang (Y30, leaving every 40 minutes, 1½ hours) and the porcelain-producing centre of Jingdezhen (Y29, leaving every hour, 6½ hours). There are also direct buses to Jinggangshan in Jiangxi's south-western mountains (Y40, nine hours) and Lushan hill station to the north (Y27.30, leaving every two hours, 2½ hours). The bus station is open from 4 am to 10 pm.

Minibuses to Jiujiang (Y20) run throughout the day as soon as there are enough passengers to make the trip worthwhile. They depart from in front of the railway station. You can also buy tickets for sleeper buses to various destinations such as Guangzhou (18 hours) or Shenzhen (20 hours) on the right as you exit the railway station area.

Train Counter No 19 at Nanchang railway station is for foreigners. Nanchang lies just off the main Guangzhou-Shanghai railway line, but most trains make the short detour north via the city. There are also direct trains to Fuzhou once daily. Express trains run daily to the Yangzi River port of Jiujiang (2½ hours), although the new freeway between Nanchang and Jiujiang makes it quicker and cheaper to do the trip by bus.

Boat The small Nanchang ferry terminal is just south of the two Bayi Bridges. An alternative way of getting to Jingdezhen is to catch a 6.30 am boat across Lake Boyang to the town of Boyang, then a bus to Jingdezhen. Tickets are Y26 and the trip takes seven hours to Boyang, then another two hours to Jingdezhen. There are two daily fast boats that do the trip in three hours; tickets cost Y61. In summer, tourist cruise boats also leave from here.

Getting Around
To/From the Airport Buses to the airport leave from the main CAAC office (☎ 627-8246) at 37 Beijing Xilu near Renmin Square. Tickets are Y10.

Bus & Taxi From the Nanchang railway station, the most useful public transport routes are the No 2 bus, which goes up Bayi Dadao past the long-distance bus station, and the No 5 bus, which runs north along Xiangshan Beilu.

Pedicabs and motor-tricycles are common and there are plenty of meter taxis available at reasonable rates.

JINGDEZHEN
(jǐngdézhèn)
Jingdezhen is an ancient town once famous for the manufacture of much-coveted porcelain. The city has maintained its position as a major producer of Chinese ceramics, but quality seems to have been compromised by mass production.

The skyline of Jingdezhen is dominated by chimney stacks belching out coal smoke from countless firing kilns. While the centre of town is pleasant enough, the outskirts are depressing.

In the 12th century the Song Dynasty fled south in the wake of an invasion from the north. The Song court moved to Hangzhou and the imperial potters moved to Jingdezhen, near Gaolin village and the rich supply of kaolin clay. Today some 10% of Jingdezhen's 400,000 people are employed in the ceramics industry. For a rundown on the history of pottery in China, see the Arts section in the Facts About the Country chapter.

Orientation
Most of Jingdezhen lies on the eastern bank of the Chang River, and the main arteries are Zhongshan Lu and Zhushan Lu. Various restaurants and hotels can be found in the city centre.

Good bus maps are available from newspaper stands, the Xinhua Bookstore and around the railway station.

Information
The CITS office is at 8 Lianhuatang Lu to the north of the city, the post office is on Zhushan Lu and the Bank of China is on Maanshan Lu, towards the railway station.

Things to See & Do
The best parts of the town to wander around are the side streets which lead off Zhongshan Lu, particularly those in the older area between Zhongshan Lu and the river. In the tiny streets, barely 1.5m wide, washing is strung out between the old houses. The large wooden doors are removed in summer for ventilation.

To Airport (10km) & Jiujiang (151km)

To Tunxi (Huangshan Shi) (167km)

To Yingtan (159km)

JINGDEZHEN 景德镇

PLACES TO STAY

1 Jingdezhen Hotel (Binguan)
   景德镇宾馆
2 Jingdezhen Guesthouse
   景德镇宾馆（合资）
8 Jingdezhen Hotel (Fandian)
   景德镇饭店
11 Wen Yuan Grand Hotel
   文苑大饭店
13 Huaguang Hotel
   华光饭店

OTHER

3 CITS
   中国国际旅行社
4 New Century Restaurant
   新世纪餐厅
5 CAAC Ticket Office
   中国民航
6 Xinhua Bookstore
   新华书店
7 Post Office
   邮电局
9 Dermatology Hospital
   市皮肤病医院
10 Bank of China
   中国银行
12 Railway Station
   火车站
14 Museum of Ceramic History
   陶瓷历史博览区
15 Long-Distance Bus Station
   长途汽车站

The **Museum of Ceramic History** (*gǔ táocí bólǎnqū*) is on the western edge of the city. Most of the buildings are reconstructed traditional stone-and-wood structures housing a modest collection taken mainly from ancient kiln sites. A second section (right from the main gate) is set up as an open workshop demonstrating traditional Qing and Ming porcelain-making technologies.

To get there take bus No 3 past the long-distance bus station to the terminus near Cidu Dadao. Then walk under the stone gate and follow the road through forest and tea groves for about 800m to the museum entrance. Entry to the museum costs Y10 for foreigners and Y5 for Chinese. An additional Y10 for foreigners and Chinese alike is charged for entry to the workshop area.

There are **pottery factories** all over the city, many of them being run as cottage industries within enclosed courtyards. If you're interested in a tour, contact CITS (☎ 822-2905) at 8 Lianhuatang Lu, but don't expect it to be cheap, unless you are with a group of 10 or more. Tours may include the Art Porcelain Factory (*yìshù*

táochǎng), the Porcelain Sculpture Factory (*měidiāo táochǎng*) or the modern Weimin Porcelain Factory (*wèimín táochǎng*), where you can see the whole process of porcelain production.

Places to Stay

The rock-bottom cheapest deals in town are clustered in the miserable railway station area.

The inappropriately named *Wen Yuan Grand Hotel* (☎ 822-4898) (*wényuàn dàfàndiàn*) is next door to the railway station and has twins with decrepit bathrooms for Y50 per room, and beds in triples for Y40 per person. There are somewhat better twins available for Y70 and Y80 per room.

Directly opposite the railway station, the low-budget *Huaguang Hotel (huáguāng fàndiàn)* was closed for renovations at the time of writing, but was expected to open by this book's publication.

The best place in town to stay is a modern Hong Kong-China joint venture called the *Jingdezhen Guesthouse* (☎ 822-5010; fax 822-6416) *(jǐngdézhèn bīnguǎn (hézī))* on Lianhuatang Lu, a quiet lake park about 15 minutes' walk from the centre of town. Porcelain-buyers from abroad often stay here. The guesthouse charges Y480 for a standard air-con twin with TV, phone and refrigerator. It has a couple of restaurants, a bar, a cafe and a shop, as well as a post office and a money-changing counter.

Literally in the shadow of the guesthouse is the *Jingdezhen Hotel (Binguan)* (☎ 822-4927) *(jǐngdézhèn bīnguǎn)*. This is the older place right behind; standard twins range from Y150 to Y240. Compared with its neighbour of the same name, this hotel is a trifle run-down, but it's reasonable value for your money.

Another *Jingdezhen Hotel (Fandian)* (☎ 822-2301) *(jǐngdézhèn fàndiàn)* is at No 1 Zhushan Lu in central Jingdezhen. It has standard twins for Y48, Y100 and upwards to Y240. Bus No 2 goes past the hotel.

Places to Eat

There is no shortage of cheap eats in Jingdezhen, particularly the tasty thick rice noodles known locally as *liángbàn mǐfěn*.

On the restaurant front, one place that deserves a special mention is the *New Century Restaurant (xīn shìjì cāntīng)* on Lianshe Beilu, about five minutes' walk up the hill from the Jingdezhen Hotel (Fandian). The food is excellent and reasonably priced, and there is an English menu. A plate of fried rice or an egg sandwich cost about Y10 each. Mr Zheng is the owner and resident English-speaker – he is starved of opportunities to use his English.

Things to Buy

Porcelain products are sold everywhere around the city, piled up on pavements, lined up on street stalls and tucked away in antique shops, particularly those on Lianshe Beilu, up from the Jingdezhen Hotel (Fandian).

The Porcelain Friendship Store *(yǒuyì shāngdiàn)* is at 13 Zhushan Lu, but you are probably better off heading to the large market spreading down the road and side streets opposite the Jingdezhen Hotel (Fandian). Huge blue and white summer teapots sell for as low as Y15 or you can purchase a 2m-high mega-vase for Y1000 and up. Also worth checking out are the hand-painted tiles *(cíbǎn)* which come in a variety of sizes and prices. Dinner sets are also a bargain, ranging from Y60 to Y90.

Getting There & Away

Jingdezhen is a bit of a bottle-neck as far as transportation is concerned, but things have improved recently with the opening of the Luojia airport and expanded bus services.

Air Luojia airport is about 10km north-west of the city centre. There is a CAAC ticket office on Lianshe Beilu across from the Jingdezhen Hotel (Fandian) and just up from the Xinhua Bookstore. There are two flights a week to Shanghai and Guangzhou and one flight a week to Shenzhen.

Bus Minibus services for Jiujiang and Nanchang leave from the northern end of Maanshan Lu, a couple of minutes' walk from the Jingdezhen Hotel (Fandian). You can also buy tickets for an early morning minibus to Nanchang at the hotel reception.

The long-distance bus station has services to Yingtan (four hours), Jiujiang (4½ hours) and Nanchang (6½ hours), as well as to more distant destinations such as Shanghai, Hangzhou and Guangzhou. Sleeper buses to Tunxi (Huangshan) leave in the afternoon after 3 pm and cost Y48. The trip takes three hours. There is another long-distance bus station near the railway station that has similar routes.

Train Jingdezhen railway station is rather like a vast, deserted crypt, and there is little in the way of tickets available either. Everything but hard-seat tickets (no seat allocation) is reserved for those with connections with the ticket sellers.

This is one town where it is worth calling in to CITS, where you can organise hard-sleeper and soft-sleeper tickets, although you may have to book quite a few days in advance.

If you're heading north there are trains to Shanghai and Nanjing via Tunxi (Huangshan, 3½ hours) and Wuhu (seven hours).

There is one daily express train to Nanchang (5½ hours), but for better connections first go to the railway junction at Yingtan (three hours).

Getting Around

To/From the Airport A bus to the airport supposedly leaves from the entrance of the Dermatology Hospital (shì pífūbìng yīyuàn) on Zhushan Donglu, but check for departure times when you book your ticket. Tickets are Y5.

Bus Jingdezhen must hold the record for the slowest buses in China. Bus No 2 crawls at a snail's pace from the long-distance bus station, through the centre of town past the Jingdezhen Hotel (Fandian) and out to the railway station.

Taxi Taxis are reasonable, although you will have to bargain. There are also plenty of pedicabs, motor-tricycles and motorcycles for hire. The centre of town is small enough to walk around anyway.

JIUJIANG
(jiǔjiāng)

Jiujiang is a stopover on the road to Lushan; if you are travelling from Nanchang, you can safely miss the place altogether by taking a direct bus. Travellers arriving in Jiujiang by ferry from Chongqing or Shanghai may need to stay overnight, but Jiujiang is most definitely not a place to linger, although many locals labour happily under the misapprehension that the two lakes in the centre of town

make their city something of a scenic wonder.

Situated close to Lake Boyang, which drains into the Yangzi, Jiujiang has been a port since ancient times. It was once a leading market town for tea and rice in southern China. After it was opened to foreign trade in 1862, the city developed into a port serving nearby Hubei and Anhui provinces. Today, Jiujiang is a medium-sized city, second in importance to Nanchang on a provincial level.

Orientation

Jiujiang stretches out along the southern bank of the Yangzi River. Two interconnected lakes divide the older north-eastern part of the city from a newer industrial sprawl off to the south. The long-distance bus station is on the city's eastern side and the new railway station is on the southern edge of the city, while the main river port is more conveniently situated close to the heart of town.

Information

There is a CITS office (☎ 855-5702) on the 2nd floor of a building in the back courtyard of the Nanhu Guesthouse. A branch of the Bank of China is near the western shore of the Gantang Lake, and the post office is close to the intersection of Liaotong Lu and Xunyang Lu.

Things to See

The small **Nengren Temple** (néngrén sì) on Yuliang Nanlu is worth a short visit. In the temple grounds is a disused Yuan Dynasty pagoda (dàshèngtǎ) and a delightful garden. About 20 monks moved back to the temple in 1988 after it was closed down during the Cultural Revolution. On the same street, at the corner with Gantang Nanlu, is an old Catholic church that was reopened for worship in 1984.

A **museum** is housed in quaint old buildings on **Yanshuiting** (yánshuǐtíng), a tiny island in Gantang Lake. It's near the centre of town and is connected to the shore by a short bridge. The museum has

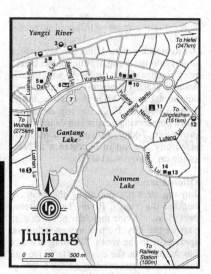

Jiujiang

small exhibits of clothing, ceramics and imperial knights' armour and weaponry, but there are no captions in English. There are also a few interesting old photographs of Jiujiang during the treaty port days; entry costs Y5.

Places to Stay
Jiujiang is a bit of a nightmare for budget travellers. Beware of the touts disguised as harmless old ladies who prowl the wharf area. They will inevitably lead you to hotels that do not take foreigners or demand high surcharges.

The cheapest hotel that accepts foreigners is the *Yangzi Jiang Hotel* (☎ 822-3985) *(yángzǐ jiāng dàfàndiàn)*, but this place is a real dump. Beds in grotty twins with attached bath and air-con are Y40 and Y60. Dorm beds in a four person room cost Y20, and Y30 in a twin. It's near the No 2 Hospital just off Dazhong Lu near the harbour.

A better deal is the *Beigang Hotel* (☎ 822-5582; fax 822-4459) *(běigǎng bīnguǎn)*, conveniently located on Binjiang Lu opposite the ferry terminal. They have twins/triples for Y186/Y280 with air-con.

There are a number of other mid-range hotels on Xunyang Lu about 10 minutes' walk from the ferry terminal. The *Wuzhou Hotel* (☎ 811-3796) *(wǔzhōu fàndiàn)* has singles for Y180 and twins for Y200 that are good value. Beside it, the *Kuanglu Hotel* (☎ 822-8893) *(kuānglú bīnguǎn)* has similar prices, with singles/twins at Y150/Y180.

Across the street, the *Bailu (White Deer) Hotel* (☎ 822-2818; fax 822-1915) *(báilù bīnguǎn)* is a Chinese version of a luxury hotel with twins from Y200 to Y280 and suites for Y480. With the more expensive room, you also get a free Chinese meal. The Bailu also has tours to Lushan – see the following Lushan section for details.

At the western end of Xunyang Lu, at 75 Lushan Lu, the *Jiulong Hotel* (☎ 823-6779; fax 822-8634) *(jiǔlóng bīnguǎn)* has twins for Y242, but try to bargain them down.

Further away from the harbour in a pleasant setting on the shores of Nanmen Lake, the *Nanhu Guesthouse* (☎ 858-5041; 858-2998) *(nánhú bīnguǎn)*, at 28 Nanhu Lu, has twins for Y180 and Y210. Foreigners are required to pay a 50% surcharge.

Next door, the *Jiujiang Hotel* (☎ 856-0018; fax 856-6677) *(jiǔjiāng bīnguǎn)* is the best hotel in Jiujiang with standard twins for Y380 and various suites ranging from Y500 to Y800. Foreigners pay a Y100 surcharge.

Getting There & Away

Air Jiujiang's new airport is 30km south of the city. The CAAC office (☎ 823-7010) is in the Jiulong Hotel and there are flights to Guangzhou three times a week and a weekly flight to Shanghai.

Bus Minibuses for Lushan leave from the car park next to the ferry terminal whenever they have enough passengers. Scheduled public buses to Lushan leave from the long-distance bus station between 7.30 am and 1.30 pm. The fare for all Lushan buses is about Y10.

Most of the hotels in town offer guided one-day tours of Lushan for Y100. You can also buy tickets for the same tour from the parking lot in front of the ferry terminal.

Minibuses depart for Jingdezhen (Y25) every half-hour from the long-distance bus station. The 4½ hour trip includes a short ferry ride across the mouth of Lake Boyang. There are frequent buses to Nanchang (1½ hours) and daily buses to Wuhan (five hours), among other places.

Minibuses to Nanchang (Y20) can also be picked up at the parking lot in front of the ferry terminal and at the railway station.

Train There are several Jiujiang-Nanchang express trains each day; the train takes 2½ hours, which is slightly slower than the minibus service. Jiujiang has a brand-new railway station in the southern section of the city.

A Jiujiang-Hefei railway link opened in 1995 and the journey takes six hours. Trains to Wuhan, however, now depart from the Lushan station (not to be confused with the hill station) on the southern outskirts of Jiujiang; it's easier to take the bus or boat. CITS can book sleepers, but with a Y50 service charge.

Boat There is a massive ferry terminal in Jiujiang, and most long-distance boats plying the Yangzi call in here. Ferry tickets upriver to Chongqing cost Y605 (2nd class), Y254 (3rd class) and Y182 (4th class); downriver fares to Shanghai are Y234 (2nd class), Y98 (3rd class) and Y71 (4th class). First class exists only on the Wuhan to Chongqing route.

CITS can book boat tickets, but it's easy enough to buy them at the dock, although foreigners are generally charged 50% more at both places.

Getting Around

To/From the Airport The airport bus leaves from the Jiulong Hotel and tickets cost Y12.

Bus & Taxi Bus No 1 and minibuses ply the route between Xunyang Lu, the long-distance bus station and the new railway station. You can get pedicabs and motortricycles from around the bus and railway stations, and the dock.

LUSHAN
(lúshān)

Lushan, or Kuling, as it was called in English, was established as a mountain resort town by European and American settlers late last century as an escape from lowland China's sweaty summers.

They left a fascinating hotchpotch of colonial buildings, from quaint stone cottages reminiscent of southern Germany to small French-style churches and more grandiose hotels built in classical Victorian style.

Despite this, Lushan is not a particularly attractive proposition as a travel destination. For much of the year it is bitterly cold and shrouded in heavy fog, and then for the summer season, which sees it at its best, it is inundated with tourists from all over the country.

For the Chinese, however, Lushan is rich with significance. Its mountain vistas have been the subject of poems and paintings, and on the historical front it has been the site of some epoch-making events.

China's post-1949 revolutionaries found Lushan's cool uplands a good place for Party conferences. It was here in 1959 that the Central Committee of the Communist Party held its fateful meeting which eventually ended in the dismissal of Peng Dehuai, sent Mao almost into a political wilderness and provided the seeds of the rise and fall of Liu Shaoqi and Deng Xiaoping.

In 1970, after Mao had regained power, another meeting was held in Lushan, this time of the Politburo. Exactly what happened is shrouded in as much mist as the mountains, but it seems that Lin Biao clashed with Mao, opposed his policies of *rapprochement* with the USA and probably proposed the continuation of the xenophobic policies of the Cultural Revolution. Whatever happened, by the following year Lin was dead.

Orientation & Information

The point of arrival in Lushan is the charming resort village of Guling *(gǔlǐng)*, perched 1167m high at the northern end of the range. Two kilometres before Guling is the entrance gate, where you must pay a fee of Y50.

Guling village is where the shops, post office, bank and the long-distance bus station are located. Nestled into the surrounding hills are scores of tourist hotels, sanatoriums and factory work-units' holiday hostels.

The CITS office (☎ 828-2497), uphill

from the Lushan Hotel, is quite well organised and helpful.

Detailed maps of Lushan showing roads and walking tracks are available from shops and hawkers in Guling.

Things to See

Lushan has enough sites of historical and scenic interest to keep you here for a couple of days. The entry fee for most of the places mentioned below is Y10, but the best way to enjoy Lushan is to avoid the tourist areas and go exploring on your own.

Built by Chiang Kaishek in the 1930s as a summer getaway, **Meilu Villa** *(měilú biéshù)* was named after the general's wife, Song Meiling. It's not a particularly grand house, but well worth a visit. Although the original gardens were probably much more spacious and better maintained than today, the villa has evidently been kept much as it was and there are some interesting items on display, like the American fridge which operated on kerosene.

The **People's Hall** *(rénmín jùyuàn)*, built in 1936 and the venue for the Communist Party's historic 1959 and 1970 get-togethers, has been turned into a museum. On display are photos of Mao, Zhou and other members of the Party elite taking it easy between meetings. The main auditorium is decked out with the predictable red flags and Mao-era decor.

At Lushan's north-western rim, the land falls away abruptly to give some spectacular views across the densely settled plains of Jiangxi. A long walking track south around these precipitous slopes passes the **Xianren Dong Cave** *(xiānrén dòng)* and continues to **Dragon Head Cliff** *(lóng-shǒuyá)*, a natural rock platform tilted above a vertical drop of hundreds of metres.

A place of interest to Chinese visitors is the **Three Ancient Trees** *(sānbǎoshù)*, not far by foot from Lulin Lake; 500 years ago Buddhist monks planted a ginkgo and two cedar trees near their temple. Tourists used to climb on to the branches to have their photos taken, but a fence now protects the trees from this indignity.

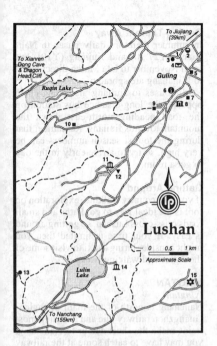

LUSHAN 庐山

PLACES TO STAY
5 Guling Hotel
牯岭饭店
7 Lushan Villa Hotel
庐山别墅村
9 Lushan Hotel
庐山宾馆
10 Yunzhong Guesthouse
云中宾馆

OTHER
1 Jiexin Park
街心公园
2 Long-Distance Bus Station
长途汽车站
3 Xinhua Bookstore
新华书店
4 Post Office; Bank
邮局、银行
6 CITS
中国国际旅行社
8 Meilu Villa
美庐别墅
11 People's Hall
人民剧院
12 Sanhe Restaurant
三合饭店
13 Three Ancient Trees
三宝树
14 Lushan Museum
博物馆
15 Botanical Garden
植物园

The **Lushan Museum** (*bówùguǎn*) beside Lulin Lake commemorates the historic 1970 meeting with a photo collection and Mao's huge bed. Scrolls and inscribed steles displaying the poetry and calligraphy of Li Bai and other Chinese poet-scholars who frequented Lushan also can be seen, as well as exhibits on local geology and natural history. Unfortunately, the explanations in English are limited.

The **Botanical Garden** (*zhíwùyuán*) is mainly devoted to sub-alpine tropical plants that thrive in the cooler highland climate. In the open gardens there are flowering rhododendrons, camellias and conifers, as well as hothouses with a cactus collection and a number of species of palm and hibiscus.

Organised Tours
From Jiujiang, return day trips cost Y100 and give you about five hours in Lushan;

one hotel in Jiujiang that has regular tours is the Bailu (White Deer) Hotel.

Tours normally include several of the pavilions, a nature hike and the museum. These tours are much more bearable if there is more than one of you.

Places to Stay
Hotel prices in Lushan vary considerably according to season. Off season (from October to May), when Lushan is usually cold, drizzly and miserable, very few people stay overnight and there are some good deals to be had. In the high season it's a different matter.

In the height of summer, budget travellers can forget about Lushan – it would probably be cheaper to stay in Jiujiang and do a day trip.

The best place to try for reasonably priced accommodation is the *Guling Hotel* (☎ 828-2200; fax 828-2209) *(gŭlĭng fàndiàn)*. It's right in Guling village around the corner from the bank, shops, restaurants and bus terminal. Twins with attached bath are Y50, but expect to pay four times this price in the summer.

Most other places open to foreigners are more upmarket, although it is worth checking around Guling village if you are looking for a bargain. You can also book villa accommodation through CITS.

There's three other places you might consider. The *Lushan Hotel* (☎ 828-2060; fax 828-2843) *(lúshān bīnguǎn)* is a large colonial-era hotel now managed as a joint venture. It has twins ranging from Y120 to Y580 in the off season.

Lushan Villa Hotel (☎ 828-2927; fax 828-2275) *(lúshān biéshù cūn)* has cottages scattered throughout a lovely old pine forest. Suites range from Y480 to Y3000, and there's usually a 20% discount in the off season.

Yunzhong Guesthouse (☎ 828-2547; fax 828-2657) *(yúnzhōng bīnguǎn)* has various villas for rent, as well as rooms in villas for Y360 and up.

Places to Eat

There are plenty of places to eat in Lushan. Remember that Lushan is a prime tourist attraction for Chinese, who like to spend big on meals; if you are on a budget, check the prices first.

Don't expect any English menus, but you will find one of sorts at the *Sanhe Restaurant (sānhé fàndiàn)*, run by Mr Liu, a transplanted Shanghaiese. It's housed in a quaint little stone building with blue windows and you can find it on the road to the People's Hall.

There is a variety of vegetarian and meat dishes available at reasonable prices, including the proverbial fried rice and fried eggs with tomatoes. Try the delicious lemon chicken for Y28.

Getting There & Away

In summer there are daily buses to Nanchang (Y27.30) and Jiujiang (Y10), but from November to late March direct buses to Nanchang are sporadic.

Minibuses to Jiujiang also congregate opposite the long-distance bus station on the road heading north-east down the mountain towards Jiujiang. Remember that during the tourist season numbers can be very high, so try to arrive early in the day to get a room.

Getting Around

If you like country walking, exploration on foot is the ideal way to go. Paths and small roads criss-cross Lushan, so getting around is easy. If your time is limited then you might consider hiring a taxi to visit some of the sights and walking back.

YINGTAN
(yīngtán)

Nanchang is north of the main Shanghai-Guangzhou railway line and although most trains make the short detour to Nanchang, you may have to catch some at the railway junction town of Yingtan.

If you do stop here and have some time to kill, walk down the main street leading from the railway station. The street ends in a T-intersection in front of a park. Turn right for the old part of town by the river. You might try getting a boat to the other side and exploring.

Places to Stay & Eat

There are two hotels near the railway station that allow foreigners. The joint-venture *Overseas Chinese Hotel* (☎ 622-1344; fax 622-1149) *(huáqiáo fàndiàn)* is the large 15 storey building on the main street down from the station. Standard twins are Y288.

If you're looking for something cheaper, try the *Dongfang Hotel* (☎ 622-1245) *(dōngfāng fàndiàn)* where dorm beds are available for Y30. It's diagonally opposite the Overseas Chinese Hotel towards the station. There are lots of *food stalls* and small *restaurants* on this same street.

Getting There & Away

The long-distance bus station is on the main street opposite the railway station. There are buses to Jingdezhen (three hours) and Nanchang (two hours), as well as other destinations like Guangzhou.

There are trains from Yingtan to Fuzhou (9½ hours), Guangzhou (16 hours), Shanghai (11½ hours) and Xiamen (15 hours). Trains to Nanchang take two hours and there is also a branch line to Jingdezhen (2½ hours) via Guixi.

JINGGANGSHAN (CIPING)

(jǐnggāngshān)

The remote Jinggangshan region, in the Luoxiao mountains along the Hunan-Jiangxi border, played a crucial role in the early Communist movement.

After suffering a string of defeats in an urban-based revolution in the cities, Mao led a core of 900 men into the refuge of these misty hills in 1927. They were soon joined by other companies of the battered Communist Army led by Zhu De, and from here began the Long March.

Orientation & Information

The main township, Ciping (also called Jinggangshan), up in the mountains at 820m, is an attractive place built around a small lake.

The local CITS (☎ 655-2504) is in the Jinggangshan Hotel (Binguan). The Xinhua Bookstore near the museum sells a Chinese tourist map of Ciping which also shows hiking trails in the hills. Local tour companies have tours to the main sights and expect them to knock on your door in the evening or early morning. The tours usually cost Y30 for the day.

Things to See

The **Jinggangshan Revolutionary Museum** *(jǐnggāngshān gémìng bówùguǎn)* is devoted to the Kuomintang and Communists' struggle for control of the Hunan-Jiangxi area in the late 1920s.

The collection includes Nationalist and Communist Army war paraphernalia and has exhibits showing military strategies and troop movements. The explanations are all in Chinese, but the collection is graphic enough for you to get the gist of things. Admission is Y4, but expect the price to increase once the renovations are completed.

The **Former Revolutionary Quarters** *(gémìng jiùzhǐ qún)* in Ciping served as the Communist centre of command between 1927 and 1928. Mao lived temporarily in one of the four crude mud-brick buildings; entry is Y2.

Jinggangshan is a major scenic area with large expanses of natural highland forest; the area boasts an interesting species of square-stemmed bamboo, (some examples of which you can find growing near the toilets in the Former Revolutionary Quarters compound) and some 26 kinds of alpine azaleas that bloom from late April.

There are some good walks into the hills around Ciping, such as to **Five Fingers Peak** *(wǔzhǐfēng)*, a mountain featured on the back of the Y100 banknote, and to the **Five Dragon Pools** *(wǔlóngtán)*.

Places to Stay & Eat

The *Jinggangshan Hotel* (☎ 655-2328) *(jǐnggāngshān fàndiàn)*, a short walk down from the bus station, provides clean, basic accommodation. Four-person dorms go for Y60, and twins with attached bath for Y165. Beds are also available in triples with attached bath for Y45 each.

The other *Jinggangshan Hotel* (☎ 655-2272; fax 655-2221) *(jǐnggāngshān bīnguǎn)* is where the Party top brass choose to stay – Mao, Lin Biao, Deng and Li Peng have all put up here. Renovations have made this hotel expensive – Y200 and up-wards for a twin – and there is a mind-boggling variety of rooms and villas from which to choose, including one called the Nuclear Power Villa *(hédiàn shānzhuāng)* (it was apparently built by the group involved in the Daya Bay project near Hong Kong). The hotel is 15 minutes' walk from the bus station; go downhill, turn right at the first road, and then right again. There's

JIANGXI

no English sign on the main entrance to the driveway.

Up the road from the Jinggangshan Hotel (Binguan) is a another monolithic enterprise, the *Jinggangshan Plaza* (☎ 655-2251; fax 655-2428) *(jǐnggāngshān dàshà)*. A sign also refers to the hotel as the Jinggangshan Grand Hotel, as if they couldn't make up their minds what to call it in English. It's very popular with roving tour groups on government-sponsored jaunts, and rooms are often unavailable. Twins are Y60/80 and triples are Y150. Beds are available for Y20 and Y25 in dorms. Prices go up by about 20% during the peak season.

There are good cheap *restaurants* on the main street down from the bus station. For something a bit more romantic, try the place on the island in the middle of the lake.

Things to Buy
Shops by the museum sell a number of different bamboo products – most of them

pretty tacky – but there are nice summer mats made of bamboo cubes and some comfortable bamboo rocking chairs.

You can find these products all over south-central China, but the chairs in particular are a good buy here, ranging from Y45 to Y70.

Getting There & Away
From Nanchang there are five direct buses to Ciping/Jinggangshan each day (nine hours). It's a pleasant ride through lush countryside with high bamboo fences, old stone bridges, lots of water buffalo, and flocks of ducks in the rice paddies.

A bus from Ganzhou to Hengyang in Hunan Province stops in Ciping and then continues to Hunan via the beautiful Huangyang Pass, but the service is sporadic. The overnight bus to Changsha (11 hours) also goes through the pass and is more reliable. The road is prone to icing over in cold weather, however.

Hunan

Most people pass through Hunan on their way to somewhere else, but the province has its attractions. The Zhangjiajie nature reserve in the western part of the province offers some of the most bizarre mountain scenery in China, rivalling the karst peaks of Guangxi. Shaoshan, birthplace of Mao Zedong, makes for an interesting visit and is a beautiful, relaxing village as well. Up north, Yueyang is a major stop for Yangzi River cruises, and the city has a unique port feel to it.

Hunan *(húnán)* lies on some of the richest land in China. Its main period of growth occurred between the 8th and the 11th centuries when the population increased five-fold, spurred on by a prosperous agricultural industry and migrations from the north. Under the Ming and Qing dynasties it was one of the empire's granaries, and vast quantities of Hunan's rice surplus were shipped to the depleted northern regions.

By the 19th century Hunan was beginning to suffer from the pressure of population. Land shortage and landlordism led to widespread unrest among the Chinese farmers and the hill-dwelling minority peoples. The increasingly desperate economic situation led to the massive Taiping Rebellion of the mid-19th century and the Communist movement of the 1920s.

The Communists found strong support among the poor peasants of Hunan, and also a refuge on the mountainous Hunan-Jiangxi border in 1927. Some of the most prominent Communist leaders were born in Hunan: Mao Zedong, Liu Shaoqi (both of whose villages can be visited), Peng Dehuai, Hu Yaobang and others. Hua Guofeng, a native of Shanxi, became an important provincial leader in Hunan.

Most of the inhabitants are Han Chinese. Hill-dwelling minorities can be found in the border regions of the province. They include the Miao, Tujia, Dong (a people related to the Thais and Lao) and Yao. In

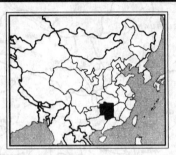

Hunan Facts & Highlights

Area: 210,000 sq km

Population: 64.3 million

Capital: Changsha

Highlights

- Shaoshan, birthplace of Mao Zedong and a fascinating look at 'Mao Mania'.
- Zhangjiajie/Wulingyuan Scenic Area, home to bizarre and beautiful rock formations.
- Yeuyang, a principal Yangzi port with interesting back alleys.
- Changsha, a chance to retrace the Chairman's footsteps and get a feel for the formative years of Chinese Communism.

the far north of the province there is, oddly enough, a pocket of Uighurs.

CHANGSHA
(chángshā)

The site of Changsha has been inhabited for 3000 years. By the Warring States Period a large town had grown up here. The town owes its prosperity to its location on the fertile Hunan plains and on the Xiang River, where it rapidly grew as a major trading centre of agricultural produce.

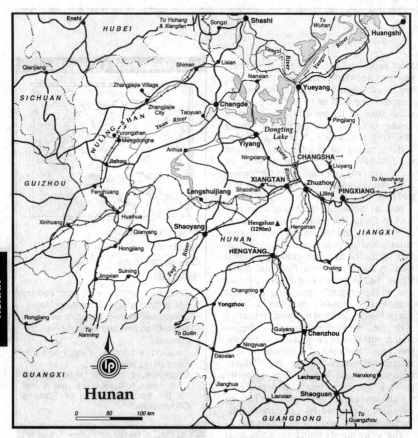

Hunan

In 1904 the city was opened to foreign trade as a result of the 1903 Treaty of Shanghai between Japan and China. The 'most-favoured nation' principle allowed foreigners to set themselves up in Changsha, and large numbers of Europeans and Americans came to build factories, churches and schools. The medical centre was originally a college established by Yale University.

Today greater Changsha has a population of 5.6 million people.

Orientation

Most of Changsha lies on the eastern bank of the Xiang River. The railway station is in the far east of the city. From the station Wuyi Lu leads to the river, neatly separating the city's northern and southern sections.

From Wuyi Lu you cross the Xiang River bridge to the western bank, passing over Long Island in the middle of the river. Most of the sights are on the eastern side of the river.

Maps Several colourful variations of the local city transport map are on sale at kiosks around the railway station and in shops at some of the hotels.

Information

Tourist Office The local CITS office (☎ 446-7356) is among the row of travel agencies in the parking lot to the left of the Lotus Hotel lobby entrance. The staff speak some English. The Xiangjiang Hotel and the Huatian Hotel can assist with transport bookings, as well.

PSB This is in a big cream-tiled building on Huangxing Lu, at the western end of town just south of Jiefang Lu.

Money The Bank of China is next to the CAAC office on Wuyi Donglu. You can also change money at the Xiangjiang Hotel and the Lotus Hotel.

Post & Communications The main post and telecommunications office is on the north-eastern corner of Wuyi Zhonglu and Cai'e Lu in the centre of town. There are other post offices at the railway station and the Xiangjiang Hotel.

Hunan Provincial Museum
(húnán bówùguǎn)

The Hunan Provincial Museum is on Dongfeng Lu within walking distance of the Xiangjiang Hotel. The exhibits are in three main buildings. The first section covers revolutionary history while the two other buildings are devoted to the 2100-year-old Western Han tombs at Mawangdui, some 5km east of the city centre, which were fully excavated by 1974.

Not to be missed are the mummified remains of a Han Dynasty woman. Her preserved body, which was found wrapped in more than 20 layers of silk and linen, is housed in the basement and is viewed from the floor above through Perspex. The organs have been removed and are laid out on display. Another building houses the enormous solid outer timber casks.

Large quantities of silk garments and fabrics were found in the tomb, as well as stockings, shoes, gloves and other pieces of clothing. One of the most interesting objects, now on display in the museum, is a painting on silk depicting the underworld, earth and heaven.

To counteract all these references to death, the museum also provides visitors with a display of various live reptiles and other auspicious symbols of long life on the 2nd floor of the smaller building outside. Entry is Y1.

The museum is open Monday to Friday from 8 am to noon, and from 2.30 to 5 pm. On weekends the hours are 8.30 am to 5 pm. Entry to all three sections is Y10 for students and Chinese and Y30 for foreigners. The No 3 bus heads north on Dongfeng Lu past the museum from the intersection of Yingbin Lu and Wuyi Zhonglu.

Maoist Pilgrimage Spots

Scattered about the city are a number of Maoist pilgrimage spots. The **Hunan No 1 Teachers' Training School** *(dìyī shīfàn xuéxiào)* is where Mao attended classes between 1913 and 1918, and where he returned as a teacher in 1920-21. The school was destroyed during the civil war, but has since been restored. Follow the arrows for a self-guided tour of Mao's dorm room, study areas, halls where he held some of his first political meetings and even an open-air bathing well where Mao was fond of taking cold baths. There's a quote from him above the well, where he said it was a good way to 'exercise fearlessness'. Given the recent revelations about Mao's sex life, no doubt he found the cold water helpful for less heroic reasons as well.

The school is still in use, so you also get a chance to see China's educational system in action. At the same time, one can't help considering the irony of the place, given how much its famous former student did to destroy China's educational system during the Cultural Revolution. To get there take the No 1 bus from outside the Xiangjiang Hotel.

HUNAN

The **Former Office of the Hunan (Xiang District) Communist Party Committee** *(zhōnggòng xiāngqū wěiyuánhuì jiùzhǐ)* is now a museum that includes Mao's living quarters and an exhibition of photos and historical items from the 1920s. Nearby is a long wall with carved large-scale versions of Mao's poems that reproduce his characteristic expansive brushstrokes. The entrance is on Bayi Lu on the No 1 bus route. In the museum grounds there is a large statue of Mao.

Other Sights

If the rabid excesses of Communist propaganda suit your sense of humour, try to fit in a visit to the **Lei Feng Memorial Museum** (☎ 810-5014) *(léifēng jìniànguǎn)*, about one hour's bus ride west of Changsha. Lei Feng was a young soldier who in 1963, one year after dying in a traffic accident at age 22, was lionised by the Communist Party as a model worker, warrior, Party member and all-round PRC citizen.

The masses were urged by top Party officials to, 'learn from Comrade Lei', whose feats included washing his fellow soldiers' laundry in his spare time, helping old ladies cross the street and making sure everyone in his home town and army platoon was up-to-date on the latest Party doctrine.

Lei was dredged up again by the Beijing leadership in 1990, in an attempt to counter the widespread disillusionment with the Party that followed the Tiananmen Square massacre. The revival is still in place, especially in Hunan where Lei's face adorns walls and can be found plastered on bus windshields.

Although the museum exhibits have no English captions, such photos as Lei gently smiling over a washtub of dirty socks or the cartoon-like renderings of him and his parents facing down evil landlords and Japanese invaders speak for themselves. In all, the museum has somehow managed to assemble five rooms of photos, diary entries and objects to catalogue Lei's life, which is quite a feat when one considers that no-one had really heard of this guy until a year

after he died. The head of the museum has admitted that some of the photos were 'later restaged', although it's not clear if this was before or after Lei's death.

To get there, take the No 12 bus from the railway station to the terminus at Rongwanzhen, where you can switch to the No 15 minibus, which makes its final stop just two minutes' walk south of the museum; entry is Y4.

Back in Changsha, Yuelu Park is a pleasant place to visit on the western bank of the Xiang River, along with the beautiful campus of **Hunan University**. The university evolved from the site of the **Yuelu Academy** which was established during the Song Dynasty for scholars to prepare for the civil examinations. In 1903, the Confucian classics were replaced by more practical subjects as the Qing government made a belated attempt at educational reform to foster modernisation. In 1926, Hunan University was established. The Yuelu Academy is on the hillside area behind the Mao statue and is well worth a visit. There's a teashop inside, as well as a good Chinese bookshop in the back.

From the university you can hike up to the **Loving Dusk Pavilion** *(àiwǎntíng)*, from where you can get a good view of the town. **Long Island** *(júzizhōu)*, or Long Sandbank, from which Changsha takes its name, lies in the middle of the Xiang River. To get to the university, take the No 206 bus from Wuyi Xilu and get off at the last stop, past the Mao statue.

The only remaining part of the old city walls is **Tianxin Pavilion** *(tiānxīngé)* south-west of Jiefang Lu. This is also one of the most interesting parts of Changsha to walk around and explore.

Places to Stay

Unhappily for backpackers, the hotels in Changsha that take foreigners are mostly upmarket places. There's plenty of good, cheap accommodation for locals, of course, but they're quite determined in excluding non-Chinese from their registers. This includes the Binhua Hotel, which used to

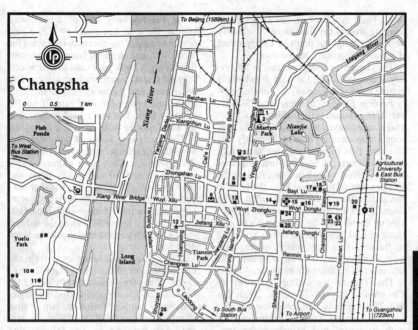

HUNAN

CHANGSHA 长沙

PLACES TO STAY

5 Xiangjiang Hotel
湘江宾馆
8 Hunan Normal
University Foreign
Experts' Building
湖南师范大学专家楼
10 Wangjiang Building
望江楼
13 Cygnet Hotel
小天鹅大酒店
16 Lotus Hotel; CITS
芙蓉宾馆
中国国际旅行社
17 Binhua Hotel
宾华宾馆
18 Nanhai Hotel
南海宾馆
20 Chezhan Hotel
车站大厦

25 Huatian Hotel
华天大酒店

PLACES TO EAT

14 George's Fast Food
乔治快餐
19 Kaiyunlou Restaurant
开云楼

OTHER

1 Hunan Provincial Museum
省博物馆
2 Monument to the Martyrs
烈士纪念碑
3 JJ's Disco
湖南太空世界
娱乐中心
4 Former Office of the
Hunan Communist Party
Committee
中共湘区委员会旧址
6 Post Office
邮局

7 Rongwanzhen Bus
Terminus
溶湾镇终站
9 Loving Dusk Pavilion
爱晚亭
11 Yuelu Academy
岳麓书院
12 PSB
公安局
15 Friendship Store
友谊商店
21 Railway Station
火车站
22 Bank of China
中国银行
23 CAAC Office
中国民航售票处
24 Xinhua Bookstore
新华书店
26 Hunan No 1 Teachers'
Training School
第一师范学校

turn a blind eye, but now has a PSB guard hanging around the front door. It still may be worth trying, but don't be disappointed if you are vigorously waved away.

The cheapest option is to stay in university accommodation; the only drawback is getting there. The *Hunan Normal University Foreign Experts' building* (☎ 888-3131, ext 2211) *(húnán shīfàn dàxué zhuānjiālóu)* accepts travellers and has beds in twin rooms with attached bath for Y75. It's best to phone first because they are often full. The university is located just north of Hunan University, below Yuelu Park on the western side of the river. Take the No 206 bus and ask the driver to let you off at *shīfèn dàxué*. From the entrance, it's about a 750m slog up the hill and the building is a bit difficult to find. Keep to the left as you head up the hill. It's a large white building with a circular driveway. You might be better off taking a taxi up from the entrance.

The *Hunan Agricultural University Guesthouse* (☎ 461-2770, ext 2060; fax 461-2870) *(húnán nóngyè dàxúe waì bīn lóu)* has beds for Y60 in nice twin rooms with balconies and private bathrooms. Again, it is better to phone to make sure they have space. The university is located in the eastern outskirts of the city past the east long-distance bus station. Take the No 10 bus or minibus from the south parking lot beside the railway station. The ride takes about 40 minutes to the last stop in front of the university entrance. From the entrance, walk straight beside the playing field, turn left at the first intersection, then right and left again at the small garden circle. Go straight for about 75m. At the bottom of a short set of stairs there is a sign for the guesthouse in English.

In the city centre, the next best deal is the *Nanhai Hotel* (☎ 229-7888; fax 229-6771) *(nánhǎi bīnguǎn)* on Bayi Lu. They have comfortable twins for Y200. The best rooms are on the 4th floor. The *Lotus Hotel* (☎ 440-1888; fax 446-5175) *(fúróng bīnguǎn)* has singles and twins for Y268/298 and standard twins for Y398 with free semi-western breakfast.

On the northern side of the railway station, the *Chezhan Hotel* (☎ 229-3366) *(chēzhàn dàshà)* has decent twins/triples for Y200/180, and an added bonus: if you stay there, they'll book your train tickets which they get direct from the railway station. The hotel even has a doorway on to the platform, just before the exit gate. If you're taking a train, this one's hard to beat, but the hotel is often full.

The *Xiangjiang Hotel* (☎ 440-6888; fax 444-8285) *(xiāngjiāng bīnguǎn)* is at 36 Zhongshan Lu. They have ordinary twins available for Y180 and newly renovated twin rooms for Y280 and up. The more expensive rooms add a 10% service charge, but include a free Chinese-style breakfast. To get there, take bus No 1 from the railway station, which has a stop just past the hotel driveway.

If you don't mind being away from the city centre, one of the nicest places to stay is the *Wangjiang Building* (☎ 882-1246; fax 882-4287) *(wàngjiāng lóu)* on the Hunan University campus. Twins and triples with attached bath are Y240/360. It's in a new red-brick building on the hillside just behind the Yuelu Academy. It's a good idea to phone and make sure there are rooms available.

The *Cygnet Hotel* (☎ 441-0400; fax 442-3698) *(xiǎotiān'é dàjiǔdiàn)* is a new three star, joint venture on the corner of Wuyi Zhonglu and the Furong Lu overpass. Standard twins are Y508 plus 14% service charge.

The best luxury deal in town is the four star *Huatian Hotel* (☎ 444-2888; fax 444-2270) *(huátiān dàjiǔdiàn)* at 380 Jiefang Donglu, just off Shaoshan Lu. Business travellers praise the Huatian for its service and clean rooms. Rates range from US$58 for a standard twin room to US$388 for a deluxe suite. All rooms come with a 15% service charge.

Places to Eat

Hunanese food, like that of neighbouring Sichuan Province, makes use of plenty of chilli and hot spices. The *Kaiyunlou*

Restaurant (kāiyúnlóu jiǔjiā) is on Wuyi Donglu near the corner of Chaoyang Lu. Although government-run, it's cheap and surprisingly good, but it doesn't have an English menu. There are also several good Hunan-style fast-food places on Chezhan Lu just south of the railway station. For fast food, *George's Fast Food (qiáozhì kuàicān)* has passable hamburgers and fried chicken. It's at the corner of Shaoshan Lu and Wuyi Zhonglu.

The bigger hotels, such as the Lotus and Xiangjiang, have good restaurants and there is a branch of the famed Beijing *Quanjude Roast Duck Restaurant (quánjùdé kǎoyādiàn)* on the 2nd floor of the roadside buildings beside the Lotus Hotel. The *coffee shop* of the Huatian has standard western fare for reasonable prices. Right next door to the hotel, the *Oasis (ōuxiāng wū)* is a Taiwan-style coffee house with good-value meals of meat, rice and vegetables for Y35, including tea or coffee.

The Cygnet Hotel has a western bar and restaurant called *John's Cafe (wànlóng xīcāntīng)* which serves draught beer and steak dishes. The adventurous might like to sample betel nut *(bīngláng)*, sold at small street stalls all around town. When chewed, the woody flesh, which has an overpowering, spicy-sweet taste, produces a mild, semi-narcotic effect. Once should be enough to satisfy your curiosity.

Entertainment

Unfortunately, Changsha's first western-style bar, the *Ocean-shore Music Bar (hǎi'ànxiàn yīnyuè jiǔláng)*, which once featured live bands playing Chinese and western rock 'n' roll, has closed down.

There are numerous Taiwan-style bars and teahouses in the vicinity of Jiefang Zhonglu and Chaoyang Lu, but if you're looking for loud music, the best disco in town is *JJ's* in the grounds of the Exhibition Hall on Zhanlanguan Lu; entry is Y40.

Getting There & Away

Air The main CAAC office (☎ 229-9821) is at 5 Wuyi Donglu, one block west of the railway station. The Lotus Hotel also has a CAAC booking office. Together, CAAC and its associated local airline, China Southern Airlines, has daily flights to Beijing, Chengdu, Guangzhou and Shanghai. Other useful flights include Kunming, Nanjing, Shenzhen and Xi'an.

There are also flights to Hong Kong on Mondays and Thursdays with Chinese Southern and Tuesdays and Fridays with Dragonair. The airport is 26km from the city centre and CAAC buses leave about two hours before scheduled flights. The fare is Y13.

Bus The are no less than three separate long-distance bus stations in Changsha and they are all inconveniently located outside the city centre. The general rule is that buses heading west depart from the west bus station, points east and north depart from the east bus station and for the south, it's (you guessed it!) the south bus station. You can reach all the bus stations from the railway station which has both public bus and minibus services.

To get to the east bus station take the No 26 bus from the railway station, for the west bus station No 212, and for the south bus station No 701. Buses for Yueyang (2½ hours), Wuhan (eight hours), Nanchang (eight hours), Fuzhou (24 hours), Nanjing (20 hours) and Jinggangshan (11 hours) leave from the east bus station. Buses for Huaihua (11 hours) and Zhangjiajie (11 hours) leave from the west bus station.

Buses for Shaoshan (2½ hours), Hengyang (five hours) and Guangzhou (24 hours) leave from the south bus station. All the stations are open from 6 am to at least 9 pm. You can also catch minibuses to Yueyang from the railway station for Y20.

Train There are two Guangzhou-Changsha-Beijing express trains daily in each direction, as well as a daily train to Shanghai. Other important routes via Changsha are Beijing-Guilin-Kunming and Guangzhou-Xi'an-Lanzhou. Not all trains to Shanghai, Kunming and Guilin stop in Changsha, so

HUNAN

it may be necessary to go to Zhuzhou first and change there.

If you're heading to Hong Kong, there's an overnight Changsha-Shenzhen air-conditioned express train that gets into Shenzhen around 9.30 am. A hard-sleeper berth costs around Y185. The Beijing-Kowloon express train also passes through Changsha. There is a daily train to Shaoshan (Y11), leaving at 7.25 am. Counter No 6 at the Changsha railway station is for foreigners, but you can also book tickets with CITS for a Y40 service charge.

SHAOSHAN
(sháoshān)

The village of Shaoshan, about 130km south-west of Changsha, has a significance to Chinese Communism which far overshadows its minute size, for this is where Mao Zedong was born. In the 1960s, during the Cultural Revolution's headier days, three million pilgrims came here each year, and a railway line and a paved road were built from Changsha to transport them.

After Mao's death, the numbers declined. But in recent years, as memories of the Cultural Revolution's excesses gradually fade, the village has seen a tourist revival. In 1993 Shaoshan held celebrations to mark the centenary of Mao's birth.

Shaoshan is hardly typical of Chinese villages, considering the number of tourists who have passed through since it was established as a national shrine. Despite the obvious impact of tourism, however, the surrounding countryside has retained its original rural charm. Traditional adobe houses dot this landscape of mountains and lush rice paddies.

Apart from its historical significance, Shaoshan is a great place to get away from those grim, grey cities, although the atmosphere is somewhat compromised by loudspeakers blaring out recordings of Mao's speeches.

Orientation

There are two parts to Shaoshan: the new town clustered around the railway and bus stations and the original Shaoshan village about 5km away.

From the railway station you can catch minibuses to the main sites. Minibuses and motor-tricycles also meet the train from Changsha. The minibus to the village should only cost Y1, but some drivers may try to charge you more. Normally, they proceed directly to the Dripping Water Cave, so make sure you indicate to the driver you want to get off at the village when you pass through. The long-distance bus station is on Yingbin Lu, just north of the railway station.

Mao's Childhood House
(máozédōng tóngzhì gùjū)

This is the first building you come to as you reach Shaoshan, and it is the village's principal shrine. It's a fairly large structure with mud walls and a thatched roof. It's no different from millions of other mud-brick dwellings in China, except for the painstaking restoration.

Exhibits include a few kitchen utensils and original furnishings and bedding, as well as photos of Mao's parents. In front of the house is a pond, and on the other side is a pavilion where Chinese tourists pose for photos with the house in the background; entry is Y3.

Museum of Comrade Mao
(máozédōng tóngzhì jìniànguǎn)

Devoted to the life of Mao, the museum opened in 1967 during the Cultural Revolution. Unfortunately there are no English captions, but the exhibits are graphic enough. There were originally two wings, exact duplicates, so that more visitors could be accommodated at the same time. Today only one set of exhibits exists. The best part of the museum is the vendors with computers who can create digital reproductions of you lighting Mao's cigarette, shaking his hand etc. Admission is Y7.

Other Sights

If you came looking for Mao souvenirs, there are **tourist markets**, both uphill

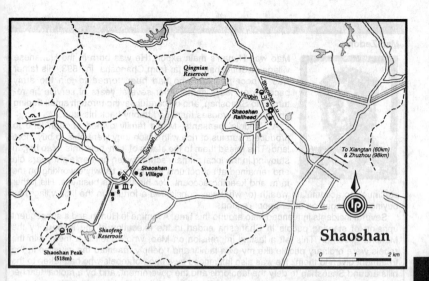

Shaoshan

SHAOSHAN 韶山

1 Dripping Water Cave
  滴水洞
2 Long-Distance Bus Station
  长途汽车站
3 Railway Station
  火车站
4 Yinfeng Hotel
  银峰宾馆
5 Mao's Childhood House
  毛泽东同志故居
6 Shaoshan Guesthouse
  韶山宾馆
7 Museum of Comrade Mao
  毛泽东同志纪念馆
8 Hongri Hotel
  红日饭店
9 Xiangyue Hotel
  湘粤酒店
10 Cable Car Station
  韶峰游览索道

from Mao's childhood house and diagonally across from the Shaoshan Guesthouse, which should satiate any craving for Maoist kitsch. Fancy a Chinese fan that

unfolds to reveal a jolly profile of the Chairman? Or how about a set of Mao chopsticks decorated with His picture?

Of course, there is also more conventional Maobilia such as Mao badges, Mao rings and Mao bracelets, as well as those Mao portrait good-luck charms that Chinese drivers attach to their windscreens and car mirrors.

Dripping Water Cave (*dīshuǐdòng*) is 3km up from Shaoshan village. Retreating to his native Shaoshan in June 1966, Mao lived in this cave for 11 days, probably thinking up new slogans for the Cultural Revolution that he had just begun. Nearby are the Mao clan's family tombs. You can get a bus up here from the parking lot opposite the Shaoshan Guesthouse.

Shaoshan Peak (*sháofēng*) is the prominent, conical-shaped mountain visible from the village. There is a lookout pavilion on the summit, and the 'forest of steles' on the lower slopes has stone tablets engraved with Mao's poems. The area is less frequented than other sites in Shaoshan and has some nice walks along quiet paths through pine forests and stands of bamboo.

Mao Zedong

Mao was Hunan's main export. He was born in the Hunanese village of Shaoshan, not far from Changsha, in 1893. His father was a poor peasant who had been forced to join the army because of heavy debts. After several years of service he returned to Shaoshan, and by careful saving through small trading and other enterprises managed to buy back his land.

As 'middle' peasants, Mao's family owned enough land to produce a surplus of rice with which they were able to buy more land. This raised them to the status of 'rich' peasants. Mao began studying in the local primary school when he was eight years old and remained at school until the age of 13, while working on the farm and keeping accounts for his father's business. His father continued to accumulate wealth (or what was considered a fortune in the little village) by buying mortgages on other people's land.

Several incidents influenced Mao around this time. A famine in Hunan and a subsequent uprising of starving people in Changsha ended in the execution of the leaders by the Manchu governor. This left a lasting impression on Mao, who '... felt that there with the rebels were ordinary people like my own family and I deeply resented the injustice in the treatment given to them'. He was also influenced by a band of rebels who had taken to the hills around Shaoshan to defy the landlords and the government, and by a radical teacher at the local primary school who opposed Buddhism and wanted people to convert their temples into schools.

At the age of 16, Mao left Shaoshan to enter middle school in Changsha, his first stop on the path to power. At this time he was not yet an anti-monarchist. He felt, however, even at an early age, that the country was in desperate need of reform. He was fascinated by stories of the ancient rulers of China, and learned something of foreign history and geography.

In Changsha, Mao was first exposed to the ideas of revolutionaries and reformers active in China, heard of Sun Yatsen's revolutionary secret society and read about the abortive Canton Uprising of 1911. Later that year an army uprising in Wuhan quickly spread and the Qing Dynasty collapsed. Yuan Shikai made his grab for power and the country appeared to be slipping into civil war. Mao joined the regular army, but resigned six months later, thinking the revolution was over when Sun handed the presidency to Yuan and the war between the north and south of China did not take place.

Mao became an avid reader of newspapers and from these was introduced to socialism. He decided to become a teacher and enrolled in the Hunan Provincial First Normal (Teachers' Training) School, where he was a student for five years. During his time at the Teachers' Training School, he inserted an advertisement in a Changsha newspaper 'inviting young men interested in patriotic work to make contact with me ...'. Among them was Liu Shaoqi, who later became president of the PRC; Xiao Chen, who became a founding member of the Communist Party; and Li Lisan.

'At this time', says Mao, 'my mind was a curious mixture of ideas of liberalism, democratic reformism and utopian socialism ... and I was definitely anti-militarist and anti-imperialist.' Mao graduated from the Teachers' Training School in 1918 and went to Beijing, where he worked as an assistant librarian at Beijing University. In Beijing he met future co-founders of the Chinese Communist Party: the student leader Zhang Guodao, Professor Chen Duxiu and university librarian Li Dazhao. Chen and Li are regarded as the founders of Chinese Communism. It was Li who gave Mao a job and first introduced him to the serious study of Marxism.

Mao found in Marxist theory a programme for reform and revolution in China. On returning to Changsha, he became increasingly active in Communist politics.

He became editor of the *Xiang River Review*, a radical Hunan students' newspaper, and also took up a post as a teacher. In 1920 he was organising workers for the first time and from that year onwards considered himself a Marxist. In 1921, Mao went to Shanghai to attend the founding meeting of the Chinese Communist Party. Later he helped organise the first provincial branch of the Party in Hunan, and by the middle of 1922 the Party had organised trade unions among the workers and students.

Orthodox Marxist philosophy saw revolution spreading from the cities as it had in the Soviet Union. The peasants, ignored through the ages by poets, scholars and political soothsayers, had likewise been ignored by the Communists; however, Mao took a different stance and saw the peasants as the lifeblood of the revolution. The Party had done very little work among them, but in 1925 Mao began to organise peasant trade unions. This aroused the wrath of the landlords and Mao had to flee to Guangzhou (Canton), where the Kuomintang and Communists held power in alliance with each other. Mao proposed a radical redistribution of the land to help the peasants, and supported (and probably initiated) the demands of the Hunan Peasants Union to confiscate large landholdings. Probably at this stage he foresaw the need to organise and arm them for a struggle against the landlords.

In April 1927, Chiang Kaishek launched his massacre of the Communists. The Party sent Mao to Changsha to organise what became known as the 'Autumn Harvest Uprising'. By 1 September, units of a peasant-worker army had been formed, with troops drawn from the peasantry, Hengyang miners and rebel Kuomintang soldiers. Mao's army moved south through Hunan and climbed up into the Jinggangshan mountains to embark on a guerrilla war against the Kuomintang. This action eventually culminated in the 1949 Communist takeover.

Mao became the new chairman of the People's Republic of China, and was to retain the title until his death in 1976. Faced with a country exhausted from civil war, yet jubilant with victory, Mao embarked on a number of radical campaigns to repair his war-ravaged country. During the formative years of the Chinese Communist state, Mao was inclined to conform to the Stalinist model of 'constructing Socialism'. In the mid-1950s, however, he and his advisers became more disillusioned with the Soviets and began to implement Mao's preferred peasant-based and de-centralised socialist development. The outcome was the ill-fated Great Leap Forward and, later, the Cultural Revolution (for details, see the History section in the Facts About the Country chapter at the beginning of this book).

The current regime in Beijing still remembers Mao as being 70% correct and 30% wrong, and for many Chinese they will never forget both sides of their Chairman. Today, Mao is a bag of contradictions. He is hated for the torturous memories and experiences that he dragged many Chinese through, but at the same time, he is revered like a god who united the Chinese people and put China on the map as a world power. For many Chinese he will always be remembered as the 'Great Leader', 'Great Teacher', 'Great Helmsman', 'Great Commander-in-chief' and 'supremely beloved Chairman Mao'.

Despite the ever-present image of Mao looking down upon Tiananmen Square, the most common position Mao holds is hanging from the rear view mirror of Beijing's taxis. As China moves away from its revolutionary past and into its current capitalist zeal, Mao has slowly been replaced by his successors – and has been transformed from the people's idol into a saint who will protect them from a crash or financial bankruptcy.

Detailed biographies of Mao Zedong include Ross Terrill's *Mao*, Jerome Ch'en's *Mao and the Chinese Revolution* and Stuart R Schram's *Mao Tse-tung*. An interesting account of Mao's earlier years is recorded in Edgar Snow's *Red Star Over China*. The five volume *Selected Works of Mao Tse-tung* provide an abundant collection of materials on Mao Zedong's thoughts. ■

HUNAN

From Shaoshan village take a minibus south to the end of the road at the cable car station, or hop on the back of a motorcycle for about Y5. The walk to the top takes about an hour, or you can take the cable car for Y20.

Places to Stay & Eat

The recently renovated *Shaoshan Guesthouse (sháoshān bīnguǎn)* (☎ 568-5127) in Shaoshan village is in a convenient location on the main street into town across from the parking lot. The guesthouse has twins/triples for Y140/150. Another extension of the hotel (☎ 568-5064) is around the corner to the right up a small hill and has very nice grounds, although the reception, with its portraits of Marx, Mao et al, is rather austere. Doubles are Y140.

Up the road from the Mao statue is the cheaper *Hongri Hotel (hóngrì fàndiàn)*, a smaller, family-run hotel. They have no-frills accommodation with very basic bathroom facilities for Y10 per bed in small dorms, and twins without bath for Y30.

Right behind the Hongri, the *Xiangyue Hotel (xiángyuè jiǔjiā)* has similar prices and rooms. Both of these places provide cheap meals. There is also a row of little *restaurants* on the road across from the parking lot and the Shaoshan Guesthouse. Meals are a bit pricey in Shaoshan, as the steady flow of tourists means food must be shipped in.

Back in the new town, just south of the railway station, the *Yinfeng Hotel* (☎ 568-1080) *(yínfēng bīnguǎn)* has beds in triples for Y50 with attached bath and air-con, and twins for Y168.

Getting There & Away

Bus Changsha has two daily buses to Shaoshan, one in the morning and one in the afternoon, leaving from the south bus station. From the Shaoshan bus station there is one morning bus and one afternoon bus back to Changsha daily. The trip costs Y11.50 and takes about three hours.

There are also frequent minibuses to Xiangtan (Y6). The trip takes about 1½

hours and from there you can catch a train or bus to Changsha or Huaihua.

Train There is one train daily from Changsha. The train leaves at 7.25 am and departs from Shaoshan station at 4.16 pm, so you can easily do Shaoshan as a day trip. The one-way fare is Y11 and the journey takes three or more hours. There are hard seats only. Coming back, the second to last car offers 'tea seating' *(cházuò)*: for only a few yuan, you get a steady supply of tea and a bit of extra elbowroom, although they may be discontinuing this service.

YUEYANG
(yuèyáng)

Yueyang is a port of call for river ferries plying the Yangzi between Chongqing and Wuhan. The Wuhan-Guangzhou railway passes through this small provincial city, so if you're heading to Guangzhou you can get off the boat here instead of going all the way to Wuhan.

Orientation & Information

Yueyang is situated just south of the Yangzi River on the north-eastern shore of Dongting Lake, where the lake flows into the river. Yueyang has two quite separate sections. Yueyang proper is really the southern part, where you'll find the railway and bus stations, as well as most of the hotels and sights. Some 17km away to the north at Chenglingji *(chénglíngjī)* is the city's main port. Most Yangzi ferries dock here, but there are also two smaller local docks in the main (southern) part of Yueyang, where long-distance ferries also call in.

The CITS office (☎ 832-0106) is on the 3rd floor of the *Yueyang Hotel* at 26 Dongting Beilu. Boat and train tickets can be booked at the ticket centre in the lobby.

Things to See

Yueyang has a 'port city' atmosphere, and its backstreets make interesting exploring. The city's chief landmark is the **Yueyang Pavilion** *(yuèyáng lóu)*, a temple complex and park originally constructed during the Tang Dynasty and subsequently rebuilt. Housed within the pavilion is a gold replica of the complex. The park is something of a mecca for Japanese tourists, apparently because of a famous poem written in its praise which Japanese kids learn at school. It is difficult to say if it is worth the Y21 entrance fee, however.

Also on the shoreline, but more to the south, the **Cishi Pagoda** *(císhì tǎ)* is a brick tower dating back to 1242. To get there, take the No 22 bus down Baling Lu to the lake, get off and walk south on Dongting Nanlu. Keep to the left-hand side of the street so the buildings don't block your line of sight and, after about 10 minutes, you'll see the pagoda which lies up a lane to the right in a residential courtyard. This the oldest part of town and is worth exploring.

Yueyang borders the enormous **Dongting Lake** *(dòngtíng hú)*. At 3900 sq km, it is the second largest body of fresh water in China. There are several islands in the lake; the most famous is **Junshan Island** *(jūn-shān dǎo)*, where the Chinese grow 'silver needle tea' *(yínzhēn chá)*. When the tea is added to hot water, it's supposed to remain on the surface, sticking up like tiny needles and emitting a fragrant odour.

You can board boats for the 45 minute ride to Junshan Island at either Nanyuepo dock *(nányuèpō mǎtou)*, centrally located at the end of Baling Lu (bus No 22 more or less gets you there), or at the Yueyang Pavilion ferry dock *(yuèyáng lóu lúnchuán kèyùnzhàn)*, just north of the pavilion on Dongting Beilu. The latter has more frequent departures.

For both docks, the earliest boats leave around 7.30 am and the last boat back from the island departs at 4.30 pm. The return fare is only Y15, and it's worth a visit not only for the tea plantations, but for the other farming activity on the island. Be prepared for a rather steep entrance fee of Y30 once you get off the boat. There are also fast boats which get there in 10 minutes for Y60 return.

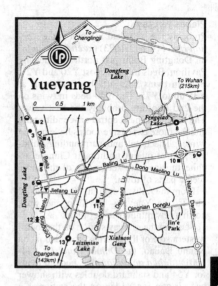

YUEYANG　岳阳

1　Yueyang Pavilion
　　Ferry Dock
　　岳阳轮船客运站
2　Xuelian Hotel
　　雪莲宾馆
3　Yueyang Pavilion
　　岳阳楼
4　Yueyang Tower Hotel
　　岳阳楼宾馆
5　Yueyang Hotel; CITS
　　岳阳宾馆
　　中国国际旅行社
6　Nanyuepo Dock
　　南岳坡码头
7　Daizu Restaurant
　　傣家村
8　New Railway Station
　　新火车站
9　Long-Distance Bus Station
　　长途汽车站
10　Dahua Hotel
　　大华大酒店
11　Yunmeng Hotel
　　云梦宾馆
12　Cishi Pagoda
　　慈氏塔
13　Old Railway Station
　　(not in use)
　　旧火车站

Places to Stay

Probably the best deal in town is the *Xuelian Hotel* (☎ 832-1633) *(xuělián bīnguǎn)* on Dongting Beilu just north of Yueyang Pavilion. Beds in quads cost Y20 and Y25. Beds in twins with attached bath start at Y35 up to Y75. The Y40 beds in twins on the 2nd floor are probably the best value. The hotel also has central air-conditioning and the more expensive rooms have heat in winter. The hotel and surrounding buildings are of quaint traditional Chinese architecture and are set in one of the more scenic parts of town.

From the railway station, take the No 22 bus to the Yueyang Pavilion and walk north a few minutes to get there.

South of the railway station on the southwestern side of the overpass roundabout on Nanhu Dadao, the *Dahua Hotel* (☎ 824-1001) *(dàhuá dàjiǔdiàn)* has beds in twins for Y54 and standard doubles with shower and air-con for Y148. As the station is a long way east of the lakeshore, this place is really only convenient if you need to catch an early train.

On a side street just off Dongting Beilu, the *Yueyang Tower Hotel* (☎ 832-2188) *(yuèyáng lóu bīnguǎn)* is a friendly place offering twins and triples with private bath for Y148/188. The No 22 bus to the Yueyang Pavilion will get you there. The *Yunmeng Hotel* (☎ 822-1115) *(yúnmèng bīnguǎn)* is east of the lakeshore and across the railway tracks at 25 Chengdong Lu. It has twins for Y220 and triples for Y180/210. There is also a CITS (☎ 823-2010) outlet at this hotel.

The classiest and probably most central place in town is the *Yueyang Hotel* (☎ 832-0011; fax 832-0235) *(yuèyáng bīnguǎn)* at 26 Dongting Beilu. Singles/twins cost Y200/248 and up. From the railway station, take bus No 22 and get off just after turning right onto Dongting Beilu.

Places to Eat

There are some good fish and seafood restaurants, particularly on Dongting Beilu, which also has a swathe of cheap spots for dumplings, noodles and breakfast. You can get refreshing drinks and ice cream as well as full meals at the *High-stepping Restaurant (bùbùgāo dàjiǔjiā)*. The name is in Chinese, but there's an English sign that says 'cold drinks'. They'll also pour you out a cup of *bābǎo chá*, 'eight-treasure' spiced and fruity tea, even if you don't ask for it, then make you pay Y4. It's across from the Yueyang Hotel.

Somewhat far from home, but tasty nevertheless, is the *Daizu Restaurant (dǎi-jiācūn)*, specialising in Dai minority food from Yunnan. Try the *bōluó fàn*, rice served up in a carved-out pineapple for Y20, or the *héyè dòufu*, tofu wrapped in lotus leaves for Y25. It's on the corner of Jiefang Lu and Nanzheng Jie, which leads into Dongting Nanlu. The entrance is done up in rustic wood with waterwheels out the front as decoration. If you're really on the cheap, there are plenty of outside *food stalls* and small *restaurants* near the Nanyuepo dock and just south of the new railway station.

Things to Buy

About the only thing of interest to buy in Yueyang is the 'silver needle tea' to amaze your friends back home. It's not cheap – the best quality goes for Y120 for 50g – but you can also buy the same amount of lesser quality for Y48. It's sold in a variety of places, but try the shop across from the Yueyang Pavilion.

Getting There & Away

Yueyang is on the main Guangzhou-Beijing railway line. There are trains to Wuhan (2½ hours), Changsha (two hours) and Guangzhou (12 hours). There are also daily buses to Changsha (2½ hours) and Wuhan (four hours) from the long-distance bus station.

Most of the large Yangzi ferries dock at Yueyang's northern port at Chenglingji. Private minibuses to Yueyang railway station regularly meet arriving boats. Bus Nos 1 and 22, which leave from an intersection about 200m inland from the ferry terminal, also take you to the trains.

There are usually four boats daily to

Chongqing from Chenglingji. Boats to Wuhan leave twice daily, in the morning. The Yueyang Pavilion ferry dock usually has one to two departures daily in either direction. Although boats are less frequent, sailing from the Pavilion ferry dock is more convenient if you're in town, not to mention aesthetically more pleasing: Chenglingji is a pit.

Upriver to Chongqing usually takes four full days. Chinese ticket prices from Yueyang are: 2nd class Y478, 3rd class Y202, and 4th class Y145. Although not available on all boats, there are also 1st class cabins for Y952. Sailing to Chongqing, you'll find prices out of Chenglingji are a bit lower.

Downriver to Wuhan normally takes just under 10 hours. Chinese ticket prices from Yueyang are: 2nd class Y100, 3rd class Y48, and 4th class Y36. You may be able to buy a Chinese-price ticket. Normally foreigners are charged 50% more, but Yueyang seems to be the exception.

You can book both train and boat tickets at the ticket counter in the lobby of the Yueyang Hotel, as well as CITS, and there doesn't seem to be any problem getting Chinese-price tickets prices for the boat. For more information on the Chongqing to Shanghai boat trip, see the Yangzi River cruises section in the Sichuan chapter.

ZHUZHOU
(zhūzhōu)

Formerly a small market town, Zhuzhou underwent rapid industrialisation following the completion of the Guangzhou-Wuhan railway line in 1937. As a major railway junction and a port city on the Xiang River, Zhuzhou has since developed into an important coal and freight reloading point, as well as a manufacturing centre for railway equipment, locomotives and rolling stock.

The only reason foreigners usually come here is to change trains. Although there's really nothing much in Zhuzhou to see, it is a pleasant enough place for a short stopover.

Places to Stay & Eat

The joint-venture *Qingyun Hotel* (☎ 822-4851; fax 822-5356) *(qìngyún dàshà)* opposite the railway station has triples for Y198 and twins for Y268 and up, which include a free breakfast.

More affordable is the *Zhuzhou Guesthouse* (☎ 821-9888; fax 821-0399) *(zhūzhōu bīnguǎn)* on Xinhua Xilu. The clean and spartan triples in the building fronting the street are very good value at Y45 per room. Twins with attached bath are Y190 in the middle building and Y258 in the new building furthest from the road. To get there from the railway station head right past the Qingyun Hotel. At the next main intersection turn left and continue past the traffic roundabout. The hotel is just before the bridge off a little side street to the right.

Across from the long-distance bus station, the shabbily upmarket *Hongdu Hotel* (☎ 822-3760) *(hóngdūgúojì dàjiǔdiàn)* has singles/twins starting at Y148/158. To get there, walk past the Qingyun Hotel to the intersection at Xinhua Xilu, turn right, cross the bridge across the railway lines and go straight for another 10 minutes. It's on the right.

The *Qingyun Hotel* has good, if somewhat pricey, dim sum on the 2nd floor, as well as a rather expensive rooftop restaurant. Just up the street from the Qingyun is the basic *Garden Restaurant (huāyuán jiǔjiā)* that has good noodles and an ebullient manager from Beijing. You can recognise the place by the man making noodles out the front.

There is also a shopping complex to the left of the Qingyun as you exit the hotel that has a *bakery* and good ice cream.

Getting There & Away

Zhuzhou is at the junction of the Beijing-Guangzhou and the Shanghai-Kunming railway lines. From Changsha it's just one hour by express train.

You can catch buses to Xiangtan (from where you can then get a bus to Shaoshan) at the long-distance bus station on Xinhua Xilu. It's a 15 minute walk to the railway

HUNAN

station: turn right and cross the railway bridge, then turn left again at the next intersection. Taxis are cheap and there are plenty of motor-tricycles and motorcycles for hire.

HENGYANG
(héngyáng)
With a population of over 800,000 Hengyang is Hunan's second largest city. It's on the railway junction where the Guilin-Changsha and Beijing-Guangzhou lines intersect, and those travelling from Guangzhou to Guilin often find themselves here briefly between train connections.

Hengyang has important lead and zinc-mining industries, but was badly damaged during WWII. Despite post-1949 reconstruction, Hengyang still lags noticeably behind its neighbour down the Xiang River, Zhuzhou.

If you find yourself here for a full day, you might want to go to Nan Yue Mountain, better known as **Hengshan**, one of China's five sacred Buddhist mountains. It's a little over an hour away by bus, which departs from the long-distance bus station every 25 minutes. Tickets are Y6.

There is a CITS (☎ 825-4160) office in Hengyang with some very obliging English-speakers. It's around the corner from the Yan Cheng Hotel at 26 Huancheng Nanlu. They can help with booking train tickets and also arrange a guide to visit Hengshan.

Places to Stay & Eat
Hengyang, like Zhuzhou, is quite strict about where foreigners can stay. Close to the railway station is the *Huiyan Hotel* (☎ 833-2331) *(huíyàn bīnguǎn)*, at 26 Guangdong Lu, which charges Y188 for a nice twin room with wooden floors. You may be able to bargain the price down. From the railway station it's a 10 minute walk straight along the main road.

Across the river, where the city centre lies, another option is the *Yan Cheng Hotel* (☎ 822-6921) *(yànchéng bīnguǎn)* at 91 Jiefang Lu, where twins start at Y160. Bus No 1 runs past the hotel, but a taxi might be best for the first time, as the main sign is only in Chinese and construction around the area makes it a bit difficult to find.

The *Suifeng Building* (☎ 823-9998; fax 823-9998) *(suīfēng dàshà)* is a new hotel with very friendly staff who speak some English. It's at 101 Jiefang Lu, near the Yan Cheng Hotel. Twins are Y188 and Y218 with a 4% service charge.

Upon emerging from the railway station, you may be besieged by touts promising to get you into cheaper local hotels. Think twice about this, as you may well end up walking with them only to get turned back when the hotel staff discover that you're not Chinese.

The *Huiyan Hotel* has a restaurant next door that serves great steamed dumplings and some other fairly cheap dishes. Check prices first, though, as they have a few seafood delights priced at Y200 and up.

On Guangdong Lu near the railway station and beside the Xinhua Bookstore, there's a nice, clean, cheap restaurant, the *Everyone Loves It Noodle House (rénrén'ài dàmìanguǎn)* that has good beef noodle soup, fried eggs, and vegetable dishes. There's no English sign, or menu, but take a look at what the other diners are eating, or head into the kitchen.

Getting There & Away
Hengyang is a major railway junction with direct trains to Wuhan, Guangzhou and Guilin, among other places. Trains to Changsha take 2½ hours and hard seats cost Y28. Buses for Changsha (three hours) leave once an hour and cost Y22.

There's also a bus that goes to Jinggangshan (10 hours) in Jiangxi Province, departing at 6.20 am. To get to the long-distance bus station, take the No 1 bus from the railway station to the last stop on Jiefang Lu.

HUAIHUA
(huáihuà)
Huaihua is a small, drab town built around a railway junction in western Hunan. It's not the sort of place you'd choose to come

SHAUN McVICAR

RICHARD I'ANSON

The South
Top: Coils of incense hanging from the ceiling of the Man Po Temple – one of Hong Kong's oldest and finest.
Bottom: The familiar sight of a Star Ferry departing Kowloon Pier for Hong Kong Island.

MARTIN MOOS

GLENN BEANLAND

GLENN BEANLAND

The South
Top: The ruins of St Paul's church, the symbol of Macau. Built in 1602, the church was destroyed during a typhoon in 1853.
Middle: Watching the world go by in a Shamian Island park in Guangzhou (Guangdong Province).
Bottom: Detail from a handpainted fan, typical of those for sale on Cat St (Hong Kong Island).

to, but if you're on the way to or from Zhangjiajie, Yaqueling or Liuzhou there are train connections from here.

The *Railway Hotel* (☎ 225-1888) *(tiědào bīnguǎn)* is the first hotel on your right as you exit the railway station and has twins/triples for Y168/Y150, but they will charge up to 70% more for foreigners. A much better deal is the *Tianfu Hotel* (☎ 225-1988) *(tiānfù fàndiàn)* which is right beside the Railway Hotel. You may have to look a little forlorn to elicit their pity and persuade them give you a room. Beds in twins are available for Y48 or Y68 per person, and in triples for Y40 or Y50, with bath and air-con.

On the left side as you exit the railway station, the *Jindu Hotel* (☎ 223-6198) *(jīndū dàjiǔdiàn)* has singles and twins for Y98/138, but they may insist on a 50% surcharge for foreigners.

You can find better value at the *Lido Hotel* (☎ 223-8888; fax 223-9988) *(lìdū bīnguǎn)* which has standard twins for Y268. Some of the staff speak English. It's at 156 Yingfeng Xilu. Turn left at the first intersection off the main street leading from the railway station and walk about 50m.

There's a good Sichuan-style restaurant along the bustling side street to your left as you exit the railway station, just down from the Jindu Hotel. The *Sichuan Restaurant (dàsìchuān cānguǎn)* has no English sign, but there is a big white sign outside with 'KTV' written on it. The women that run the place are very friendly and their meals are inexpensive and delicious.

Getting There & Away

Beijing-Kunming, Chengdu-Guangzhou and Shanghai-Chongqing express trains run via Huaihua. There are also a number of slower trains from Guiyang, Guangzhou, Zhengzhou and Liuzhou, terminating in Huaihua.

There is a daily train to Zhangjiajie (5½ hours) which leaves at 11.25 am. You can also catch a train to Sanjiang (5½ hours), in northern Guangxi Province.

WULINGYUAN SCENIC AREA/ ZHANGJIAJIE
(wǔlíngyuán fēngjǐngqū)

Parts of the Wuling mountains *(wǔlíngshān)* in north-western Hunan were set aside in 1982 as nature reserves collectively known as the Wulingyuan Scenic Area, encompassing the localities of Zhangjiajie, Tianzishan and Suoxiyu. Of these, Zhangjiajie is the best known, and many Chinese refer to this area by that name.

The first area of its kind in China, Wulingyuan is home to three of the province's minority peoples – the Tujia, Miao and Bai – many of whom continue to speak their languages and maintain their traditional cul-ture.

The mountains have gradually eroded to form a peculiarly spectacular landscape of craggy peaks and huge rock columns rising out of the luxuriant subtropical forest. There are waterfalls, limestone caves (including Asia's largest chamber), fresh clear streams, and rivers suitable for organised rafting trips. There are many possible short and extended hikes, but even if you don't intend doing any walking it's a nice place to spend some time.

Several towns serve as access points to Wulingyuan, but the most popular way in is via **Zhangjiajie City** (formerly known as Dayong) and Zhangjiajie Village. The city is near the railway line, while Zhangjiajie Village is situated nearly 600m above sea level in the Wuling foothills, surrounded by sheer cliffs and vertical rock outcrops.

A fee of Y49 (for both locals and foreigners alike) must be paid at the main entrance gate to the Zhangjiajie forest reserve just past the village. Chinese maps showing walking trails, some with key tourist sites marked in English, are on sale in both Zhangjiajie City and Village. The scenery is spectacular, but don't expect to view it alone: Wulingyuan has been targeted as a major national tourist area and is usually swarming with both Chinese and overseas tour groups.

The local government recently opened an airport to further the tourist trade, and more hotels and karaoke nightspots are being continually added to the already considerable number both inside and outside the park. You'll almost certainly be approached by locals who hire themselves out as guides, but you don't really need one. Just follow the crowds up the mountain paths.

Things to See & Do

The highest area closest to Zhangjiajie Village is **Huangshizhai** and, at 1048m, it's a strenuous hike up 3878 stone steps. Like other sights that require a certain amount of exertion in China, a cable car is being built for the less physically inclined.

In the northern section of the reserve, **Tianzishan** is another good hike. Like Huangshan and Guilin, every rock, crag and gully has been given an elaborate name and if you're with a guide your progress will be considerably slowed by them pointing out each item ad nauseam.

Outside the reserve proper, 15km west of Sangzhi, **Jiutiandong** is Asia's largest cave, covering an area of more than 20,000 sq m. It's a bit difficult to get there unless you latch on to a tour. Cave aficionados might find it interesting, but you have to join a guided tour of the cave and these can last up to three hours. Entry is Y48 and you have to pay an extra Y10 for a boat ride across a subterranean pond. If you arrive with a tour, these fees should be included in the cost.

Organised tours to the park and Jiutiandong often include a **rafting trip**, or you can join a tour and just do the rafting trip. While there are some good white-water rafting possibilities north-west of Zhangjiajie near the Hubei border, you would have to make special arrangements for the equipment and transport.

In Wulingyuan, most of the rivers the tours go on are pretty tame, so don't expect

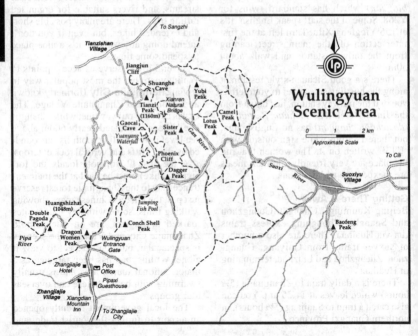

Wulingyuan Scenic Area

To Sangzhi
Tianzishan Village
Jiangjun Cliff
Shuanghe Cave
Xianren Natural Bridge
Yubi Peak
Tianzi Peak (1160m)
Gaocai Cave
Camel Peak
Lotus Peak
Sister Peak
Yuanyang Waterfall
Phoenix Cliff
Gan River
Dagger Peak
Suoxi River
Suoxi
Suoxiyu Village
To Cili
Huangshizhai (1048m)
Jumping Fish Pool
Double Pagoda Peak
Conch Shell Peak
Baofeng Peak
Pipa River
Dragon Women Peak
Wulingyuan Entrance Gate
Zhangjiajie Hotel
Post Office
Pipaxi Guesthouse
Zhangjiajie Village
Xiangdian Mountain Inn
To Zhangjiajie City
0   1   2 km
Approximate Scale

Accidents Do Happen

'Do the rafts ever capsize?' I asked the tour operator for the third time, before putting down my deposit. 'Never' he said, shaking his head. 'Believe me, all these times we've taken people on rafting trips, we've never had one capsize!' He looked vaguely like Johnny Depp and had all the persuasive conviction of a man born to sell.

By the time our incongruous group gathered on the shore to get into the rafts, tempers were already frayed. The two girls from Zhuhai had held everyone up for half an hour arguing about the ticket price for a section of the cave tour. When we arrived at the river, the placidity of the water elicited more grumbling. This river was flat. Where were the rapids?

I was separated from my group as there wasn't enough room in the raft, and was instead placed with a carousing band of Hunanese who broke into song every five minutes. There were three sets of what could hardly even be called rapids, but the scenery was nice. Our guide took his work very seriously. As the semi-turbulent water loomed he yelled out like an army sergeant 'Sit down! Sit down! Keep your camera covered! Don't lean over like that!'. Before we knew it, the trip was over: 'I thought it was supposed to be longer', someone complained.

The Hunanese scrambled up the bank and piled into their waiting bus. They drove off and I was left in the van with the grandmother who had stayed behind with the baby while the parents went off on their adventure. The baby bawled incessantly, but there was no sign of the other rafters. Grandmother was very worried. 'They're fine', I said. 'They're just around the corner.' An hour later, the sodden remains of my group clambered up the bank. On the third set of rapids, the inflatable raft had reared up and deposited its contents unceremoniously in the water. Luckily all were wearing life-jackets because none of them could swim. Everyone was talking at once, hurling acrimonious insults at the guide, whose careless steering technique had apparently caused the accident. Evidently he had been up the night before drinking and playing mahjong. Before skulking off to another vehicle, he admitted sheepishly that his concentration was off. One of the Zhuhai girls held up her injured little finger as if mortally wounded. 'Our plane tickets are all wet, where's our compensation?' she cried. 'My mobile phone is ruined', grumbled the portly man from Henan.

In the van on the way back, the girls from Zhuhai harangued the other guides who blasted out angry retorts then sulked in the front seat. 'Who will compensate us?' the girls kept demanding, 'This is outrageous!'. Finally, getting no more response from the guides, they passed around a piece of paper for us to put down our names and addresses. That way, they explained, they would have witnesses when they took the rafting company to court. You couldn't help but be impressed by the girls from Zhuhai.

The woman who was the wife of the man from Henan was sitting beside me. In her soaking clothes she leaned over and told me she was a Protestant. 'I knew I would be safe', she said a little breathlessly, the colour high in her cheeks. 'I knew God would protect me', she said. Divine intervention on a river in western Hunan ...

Marie Cambon

great thrills; but it's still a good way to get away from the crowds and the scenery is beautiful. The actual rafting usually lasts about two hours with about the same amount of time taken up in travel to the launch area.

You can join tours or arrange your own through the hotels in Zhangjiajie or better still, at one of the many travel agencies in Zhangjiajie City. The Dongsheng Travel Agency (☎ (0744) 822-8711) *(dōngshēng lǚxíngshè)* offers better rates than CITS, at

Y400 per person for an individualised tour or Y180 per person to join a group. They're at 18 Jiefang Lu near the Wuling Guesthouse.

Places to Stay

You'll probably find it more convenient and interesting to stay in Zhangjiajie Village, but in Zhangjiajie City a number of hotels also take foreigners.

Diagonally opposite the bus station is the *Dule Hotel* (☎ 822-2872) (*dùlè bīnguǎn*), where a spartan twin with shower is Y120 a night and beds in a triple are Y40 with shower and Y15 without.

The *Wuling Guesthouse* (☎ 822-2630) (*wǔlíng bīnguǎn*) on Jiefang Lu (past the Puguang Temple) charges Y240 for very nice twin rooms with bathroom, TV and lots of hot water.

At 46 Jiefang Lu, the *Dragon International Hotel* (☎ 822-6888; fax 822-2935) (*xiánglóng guójì jiǔdiàn*) is a glittering marble and chrome establishment masquerading as a four star hotel. The cheapest rooms are twins in the older wing at Y280. In the renovated building twins start at Y420, plus a 15% service charge, and go up steadily from there.

The *Taiwan Barbecue Village (bābǐ Q taíwāncūn cāntīng)* on the corner of Tianmen Lu and Jiaochang Lu has great atmosphere and good meals featuring barbecued chicken and so on. Draught beer is available in the afternoon and evening. The restaurant was started up by Mr Ding, who is of Tujia nationality, but was born in Taiwan where his father retreated with Kuomintang troops after 1949.

In Zhangjiajie Village most places seem willing to take foreigners. Just uphill from where the buses stop is the *Zhangjiajie Hotel* (☎ 571-2388) (*zhāngjiājiè bīnguǎn*), which has basic but clean twins for Y150. You may be able to bargain them down to Y120 if you're very persistent. The hotel also has a new three star addition next door which offers more upmarket air-con twins for Y300. They also have beds for Y75 in dorms, but you will have to push to get these. The hotel can also book train tickets

three days in advance for a Y30 service charge.

Better value can be found at the *Xiangdian Mountain Inn* (☎ 571-2266; fax 571-2172) (*xiāngdiàn shānzhuāng*), uphill from the bridge, 50m off the main road. This hotel has beds in clean twins and triples with attached bathrooms for Y70. There are also more luxurious twins for Y280. The hotel is nicely laid out and there are nice touches such as towels and balconies. It's also quieter than the Zhangjiajie Hotel, which sits amid several karaoke clubs.

The *Pipaxi Guesthouse* (☎ 571-8888; fax 571-2257) (*pípāxī bīnguǎn*) also offers a quiet setting and has somewhat fancy twins for Y200 and Y320 and suites for Y800. This is where a lot of the overseas tour groups come to stay. The Pipaxi is situated just outside Zhangjiajie Village, so you can save yourself a 10 minute walk back uphill by getting dropped off here.

For those hiking overnight in Wulingyuan, there are places to stay inside the park along the popular trail routes. As the park tickets are only good for one entry, local visitors often do a two to three day circuit hike, going in at Zhangjiajie Village and hiking out to villages within the park boundaries such as Tianzishan and Suoxiyu, both of which have a bewildering choice of hotels and hostels.

If you're just interested in day hiking, a stay in Zhangjiajie will do just fine. One way to skirt the crowds and the entrance fee is to walk up the road past the Xiangdian Mountain Inn and several other hotels, and follow the stream up past the reservoir into the foothills. It takes a bit of bushwhacking, but there are nice views to be had, and some peace and quiet in which to enjoy them. There are poisonous snakes in the area, so take care if you take the bushwhacking route.

Places to Eat

Like most tourist resorts in China, you'll be chased down the street by people wanting you to eat in their restaurants. There are many to choose from in the village. The places on the other side of the small stream opposite the Zhangjiajie Hotel on the road towards the park entrance have good *húndùn* dumplings. There are simple *eating houses* scattered around the village, and the better hotels also have their own *restaurants*.

Things to Buy
Besides the usual tourist trinkets, the best thing about Zhangjiajie is the tightly woven baskets with a simple black line pattern that the Tujia women carry on their backs. You can find them at markets in Zhangjiajie City and particularly in a row of shops on Huilong Lu west of Beizheng Lu. These aren't the coloured baskets sold to tourists but the real thing, and cost about Y20. There are also other items sold in these shops that cater to local families, like wooden buckets and bamboo cradles.

Getting There and Away
With the opening of the new airport in late 1994, there are now direct flights linking Zhangjiajie City with Beijing, Changsha, Chongqing, Guangzhou, Shanghai, Wuhan and Shenzhen.

There are direct trains from Zhangjiajie City to Changsha (16 hours), Zhengzhou (30 hours) and Guangzhou (24 hours). The Changsha train leaves around 6.30 pm and gets you in the next morning at 10.30 am. You can also get trains from the Yangzi port of Yichang that pass through Zhangjiajie on their way to Huaihua, including the daily train from Xiangfan in Hubei Province that passes through Sanjiang and terminates at Liuzhou in Guangxi Province. The CTS in Zhangjiajie City (☎ 822-7718) is opposite the Dragon Hotel on Jiefang Lu. They can help you book hard and soft sleepers, as well as air tickets.

Buses leave the Zhangjiajie City bus station for Changsha in the early morning. The 10 hour trip costs Y49 and Y83 for air-con buses, which are also faster by a couple of hours. Sleeper buses are also available for Y83, leaving at around 5, 6 and 7 pm and arriving in Changsha 10 hours later.

Minibuses to Zhangjiajie Village pick up incoming passengers at the parking lot in front of the railway station. The trip takes over an hour and costs Y10. The minibuses first stop at the bus station in Zhangjiajie City, which lies across the river, 14km from the railway station. They then continue on to the Zhangjiajie Village. At the Zhangjiajie City bus station, you can also get buses to Tianzishan and Suoxiyu villages.

MENGDONGHE
(měngdònghé)
An hour and a half south of Zhangjiajie by train, the small station of Mengdonghe is nestled between the hills and rivers of western Hunan.

From here you can take a 45 minute boat ride to the village of Wangcun, which is better known as **Furongzhen**, or Hibiscus Town, after it was the location for Xie Jin's 1986 film of the same name. The film, adapted from the novel by Gu Hua, portrayed how the political turbulence of the 50s and 60s unsettled the lives of ordinary villagers and is probably Xie Jin's best film. It turned the town into a tourist destination; unfortunately, as is often the case, the stone streets and wooden buildings came out much better on film than in real life.

Today, the village has little character and most of the buildings are so dilapidated that it seems the whole town could well slide into the river and only remains propped up by the tourist trade.

There's a private museum of **Tujia Culture** in an old house on the main street that's worth visiting, but one of the main reasons to go to Furongzhen is to try out the rafting. Trips here are better organised than in Zhangjiajie and you can buy tickets at the rafting ticket office at the dock. The cost is Y70 and includes transport to the launch site. Be prepared to get wet. Vendors in the village sell plastic ponchos and bags.

Places to Stay & Eat
Overlooking the river and ferry dock, the *Mengdonghe Hotel* (☎ 585-3358) *(měngdònghé bīnguǎn)* looks perfect, but it's a real dump. Inside, the twins with balconies

HUNAN

and attached bath are not worth the Y160 charged. There's more spartan accommodation in the back, with doubles and triples without bath for Y34/45.

Up the stone steps and to the left side of the main street of the village, a private establishment, with the wonderful name of *First Snail Under Heaven Restaurant* (☎ 585-3418) *(tiānxià dìyī jiǔlóu)* has small clean rooms upstairs for Y8, although washing facilities are very basic. They can also arrange the rafting trip tickets, and they throw in a free hat as well.

On the southern side of the stream that runs by the village, the *Tingtao Hotel* (☎ 585-3372) *(tīngtāo shānzhuāng)* has a nice view, even if it is dominated by the cement factory on the other side of the river. Singles and twins with attached bath are Y128/156.

It's already quite obvious where you should go if you like to eat snails. There are lots of other restaurants lining the main street as well. In the film *Hibiscus Town* the main protagonist is renowned for making *mǐdòufu*, a tasty snack that looks like cubes of tofu, but is actually milled rice flour topped with pickles and chilli sauce. The stalls down by the dock sell it for about Y2 a bowl.

Getting There & Away
Trains from Zhangjiajie, Huaihua and Liuzhou all stop in Mengdonghe. From the railway station, walk down the steps to the ferry boat dock. Tickets to Furongzhen are Y4, but beware of overcharging. Boats go back to the railway station roughly an hour before the train arrives.

Hong Kong & Macau

Hong Kong is a curious anomaly. It's an energetic paragon of the virtues of capitalism and yet is now part of what is officially the largest Communist country in the world. A British colony since the middle of the 19th century, Hong Kong was handed back to China on 1 July 1997 amid much fanfare and anticipation.

Sixty kilometres west of Hong Kong, on the other side of the Pearl River's mouth, is the oldest European settlement in the east – the tiny Portuguese territory of Macau. Its 16 sq km consists of a peninsula joined to the Chinese mainland, and the islands of Taipa and Coloane, which are joined together by a causeway and linked to central Macau by two bridges. Macau is slated to be handed back to China in 1999.

Hong Kong 香港

Despite its return to the 'motherland', Hong Kong's political and economic system is still significantly different from that of the PRC. Thus, much of what you've read elsewhere in this book (about visas, currency, accommodation, international phone calls etc) does not apply to Hong Kong.

HISTORY

Hong Kong must stand as one of the more successful results of drug dealing. The drug was opium and the runners were backed by the British government. European trade with China goes back more than 400 years. As the trade mushroomed during the 18th century and European demand for Chinese tea and silk grew, the balance of trade became more and more unfavourable to the Europeans – until they started to run opium into the country.

The Middle Kingdom grew alarmed at this turn of events and attempted to throw the foreigners out. Opium was affecting the

Hong Kong Facts & Highlights

Area: 1092 sq km
Population: 6.31 million
Highlights

- A sampan ride in Aberdeen harbour.
- Riding the Peak Tram to Victoria Peak.
- A dim sum feast in a top-notch restaurant.
- Retail therapy in the many shopping centres.

economy to an alarming degree and creating a society of addicts. The war of words ended when British gunboats were sent in. There were only two of them, but they managed to demolish a Chinese fleet of 29 ships. The ensuing first Opium War went much the same way and, at its close in 1841, the island of Hong Kong was ceded to the British.

Following the second Opium War in 1860, Britain took possession of the Kowloon Peninsula. Finally, in 1898, a 99 year lease was granted for the New Territories. What would happen after the lease ended in 1997 was the subject of considerable speculation. Although the British supposedly had possession of Hong Kong Island and the Kowloon Peninsula for all eternity, it was pretty clear that if they

Unequal Treaties

The first of the many unequal treaties foisted on the Chinese by the Europeans (and later the Japanese) was the Treaty of Nanjing. It brought the Opium wars to a close with a humiliating slap in the face for the Qing court.

According to its terms (there were 12 articles altogether) the ports of Guangzhou, Xiamen, Fuzhou, Ningbo and Shanghai were to be opened to foreign trade; British consuls were to be established in each of the open ports; an indemnity of 21 million Mexican dollars was to be paid to the British; the Cohong was to be disbanded; and, perhaps most humiliating, Hong Kong was to be ceded to the British 'in perpetuity'.

Unequal treaties followed thick and fast once a precedent had been established in Nanjing. The Treaty of Tianjin, originating in a Chinese refusal to apologise for having torn a British flag and culminating in a combined British-French occupation of Tianjin, provided a further 10 treaty ports and more indemnities.

Subsequent complications led to the burning of the Summer Palace by the British and the ceding of the Kowloon Peninsula. Further unequal treaties won the French the Chinese vassal state of Vietnam, gave the Japanese Taiwan, the Pescadores and the Liaodong Peninsula, and eventually opened 50 treaty ports from as far south as Simao in Xishuangbanna to Manzhouli on the Russian frontier.

In the space of some 50 years or so, a spate of unequal treaties effectively turned China into a colony of the imperial forces of the day. ∎

handed back the New Territories, China would want the rest as well.

In late 1984, an agreement was reached: China would take over the entire colony on 1 July 1997, but Hong Kong's unique free enterprise economy would be maintained for at least 50 years. Hong Kong would become a Special Administrative Region (SAR) of China with the official slogan, 'One country, two systems'.

China repeatedly reassured Hong Kong's population that 'nothing will change', but few believed this. Well aware of China's previous record of broken promises and harsh political repression, Hong Kongers began looking for escape routes, especially after the 1989 massacre in Tiananmen Square.

Nervousness about 1997 also caused capital to flee to safe havens overseas. A belated attempt by Britain to increase the number of democratically elected members of Hong Kong's Legislative Council (Legco) caused China to threaten to dismiss the council and appoint leaders approved by Beijing. Indeed, during the years leading up to the handover, the denunciations of Britain by the Chinese leadership bordered on the hysterical.

The last governor and instigator of the reforms, Chris Patten, was vilified as China's No 1 enemy. Despite protests up to the last minute, LEGCO was dissolved days before the handover and on 1 July, the new Provisional Legislative Council took office, composed of Hong Kong representatives appointed by Beijing. Former shipping magnate, Tung Chee-hwa, himself a refugee to Hong Kong after 1949, was given the post of Chief Executive.

In spite of the uncertainties, Hong Kong continues to prosper and confidence in its future was running high in the months after the handover. Many who emigrated in the late 80s and 90s have returned (with a foreign passport, just in case).

Trade with both the west and the rest of China is booming. Service industries such as banking, insurance, telecommunications and tourism employ almost 75% of Hong Kong

Handover or Hangover?

In the months leading to 1 July 1997, mainland China geared itself up for what must have been one of the biggest propaganda drives since the Cultural Revolution.

You couldn't turn on the TV without coming across some show celebrating the 'return to the motherland'. The evening news started out by informing viewers how many days were left before Hong Kong returned to China. Every museum had an exhibit outlining the history of Hong Kong, crowned with a large portrait of the late Deng Xiaoping.

Many, of course, were enthralled, but not everyone agreed with all the hoopla and grumbled (privately) that maybe it was a bit excessive after all.

In Hong Kong, the anticipatory build-up was a bit more imaginative and low-key, sort of like the way everyone hopes Hong Kong, vis a vis China, will be in the years to come. Nevertheless, in the week before the handover there was a sense of excitement in the air, like a storm brewing.

An inordinate number of TV crews loitered on the streets in Central looking bewildered as the business crowds swirled around them on their way to lunch. The last session of Legco, the elected legislature, was held. Remaining figureheads of the Royal emblem were erased from public buildings. Prince Charles arrived. Then, on the afternoon of 30 June, it started raining.

In the mainland, the impending handover was highlighted by the slogan 'washing away 100 hundred years of shame'. This provoked mixed feelings for many Hong Kong Chinese. As one man put it, 'I'm proud of the fact that Hong Kong will no longer be a British colony, but I have nothing to be ashamed about. This is a prosperous place'.

Countless viewers in mainland China and Hong Kong could relive the shame every night on TV in dramatic adaptations of the Opium Wars. Better yet, they could go see Xie Jin's epic, *The Opium War*, the most expensive mainland film ever made, and sneer at the foreign invaders, or sniffle at the tragic patriotism of Lin Zexu, the upright official who was dismissed by the corrupt Qing regime.

In any case, there were a few tears around, but most of them seemed to be falling from British eyes. As Chris Patten left the Governor's house for the last time, he defied that 'keep a stiff upper lip' tradition and showed his emotions openly to the people of Hong Kong, a very fitting parting gesture from a man who genuinely cared about the place.

That night the crowds fringed the harbour to watch the fireworks exploding like sodden flowers. At midnight, in a wonderful tableau of Chinese and British protocol, the solemn ritual ending 156 years of British rule took place inside the new Hong Kong Exhibition and Convention Centre.

A small group of protesters chanting 'Down with Li Peng' was drowned out by Beethoven blaring out of police speakers so the Chinese premier wouldn't lose face. After midnight, the ousted Legco democrats climbed up to the balcony of the Legco building and the crowd was addressed in a rousing speech by their leader, Martin Lee, who vowed 'we shall return!'. Small herds of expat men wandered around with cans of beer in their hands and the occasional British flag was waved.

Throughout it all the rain kept falling. Indeed, in the month following the handover, the rainfall volume broke all previous records. The first week of the new Special Administrative Region was marked by flooding and landslides. Perhaps this was part of 'washing away 100 years of shame' or was it a more ominous sign from the heavens?

Most of the journalists went home disappointed that nothing spectacular happened. There was no mass hysteria, the PLA moved into the barracks formerly occupied by the British and, after a couple of days, Hong Kong resumed its normal frenetic pace.

Marie Cambon

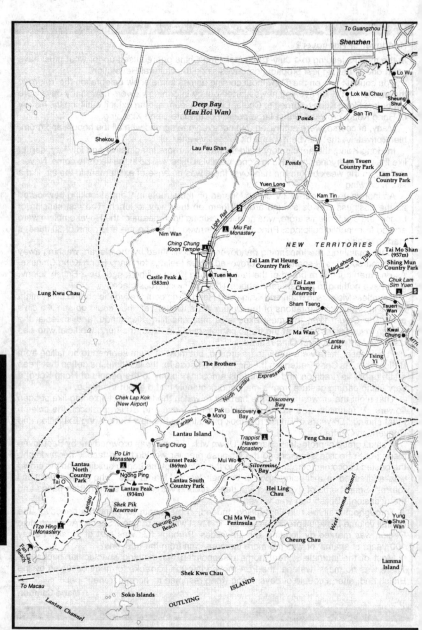

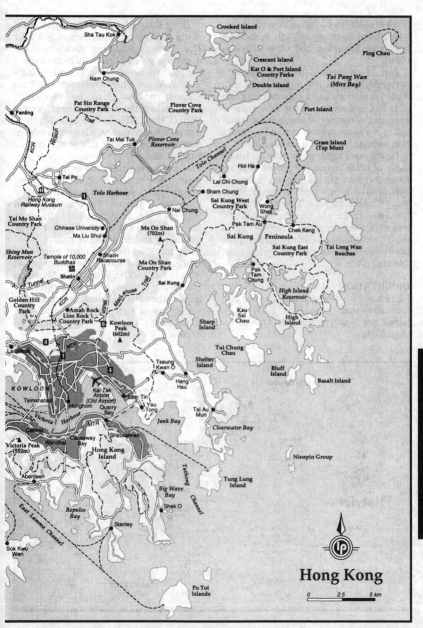

Hong Kong

0   2.5   5 km

residents. All the polluting sweatshop factories have been moved just across the border to Shenzhen and other cities in China.

Part of the reason for Hong Kong's prosperity is that it is a capitalist's dream; it has lax controls and a maximum tax rate of 15%. Combine this with its new status as a member of the largest nation in the world, and it's not surprising that many Hong Kong business people are optimistic.

On the other hand, while there's a strong sense of pride among the people of Hong Kong that they are no longer a colony of Britain, and a new consciousness about being Chinese, they don't want to lose their freedoms. In the end, despite the colossal power of their overseer, it will be up to them to determine whether Hong Kong can keep its position as one of the world's most dynamic cities.

ORIENTATION

Hong Kong's 1070 sq km are divided into four main areas – Kowloon, Hong Kong Island, the New Territories and the outlying islands.

Hong Kong Island is the economic heart of the colony, but comprises only 7% of Hong Kong's land area. Kowloon is the densely populated peninsula to the north – the southern tip of the Kowloon Peninsula is Tsimshatsui, where herds of tourists congregate. The New Territories, which officially include the outlying islands, occupy 91% of Hong Kong's land area. Much of it is rural and charming, but tourists seldom take the time to visit this scenic part of Hong Kong.

Western visitors should have few problems getting around Hong Kong – English is widely spoken and most street signs are bilingual. If you've been brushing up on your Mandarin, be aware that less than half the population can speak it – most speak Cantonese as their native tongue.

On the other hand, so many people are studying Mandarin since the handover that it's often a good bet to try it out. Mandarin is currently in vogue and it also helps break the ice when you are talking to people who are shy about their English or have been linguistically assaulted by too many rude expats.

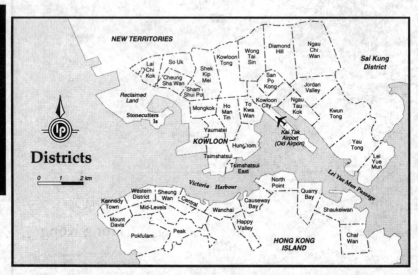

INFORMATION
Tourist Offices
The enterprising Hong Kong Tourist Association (HKTA) is definitely worth a visit. They're efficient and helpful and have reams of printed information – most of which is free. They also have general and specialised tours, as well as brochures on walks you can do on your own.

You can call the HKTA hotline (☎ 2807-6177) from 8 am to 6 pm Monday to Friday, or from 9 am to 5 pm on weekends and holidays. If you're coming in from mainland China, you'll find the helpful attitude of this organisation nothing short of miraculous. If they haven't got it covered in their brochures, they'll do their best to answer any of your questions, including shopping advice and inquiries about retailers who are HKTA members.

HKTA Offices Overseas The homepage of HKTA is www.hkta.org on the Internet. Overseas branches of the HKTA can be found in most European and Asian countries, as well as Australia, New Zealand and the USA.

The China Travel Service (CTS) has numerous outlets around Hong Kong and is also a good place to get visas and book tickets to China, although occasionally their service will make you think you're already on the mainland.

They have a hotline and email (☎ 2851-1700; email: ctsdmd@hkstar.com) and two main branches, one in Kowloon at 1st floor, Alpha House, 27-33, Nathan Rd, Tsimshatsui (enter from Peking Rd), and one in Central at 4th floor, CTS House, 78-83 Connaught Rd.

Foreign Consulates
Hong Kong is a good place to pick up a visa for elsewhere or to replace a stolen or expired passport. There is still some uncertainty surrounding the fate of the Chung Hwa Travel Service which issues visas for Taiwan, but it was still functioning at the time of writing. The following consulates could come in handy:

Australia
 (☎ 2827-8881) 23rd and 24th floor, Harbour Centre, 25 Harbour Rd, Wanchai
Canada
 (☎ 2810-4321) 11th-14th floor, Tower One, Exchange Square, 8 Connaught Place, Central
France
 (☎ 2529-4316) 26th floor, Tower Two, Admiralty Centre, 18 Harcourt Rd, Central
India
 (☎ 2527-2186) 5th floor, Tower One, Admiralty Centre, 18 Harcourt Rd, Central
Indonesia
 (☎ 2890-4421) 6-8 Keswick St and 127 Leighton Rd, Causeway Bay
Japan
 (☎ 2522-1184) Exchange Square, Central
Malaysia
 (☎ 2527-0921) 24th floor, Malaysia Building, 50 Gloucester Rd, Wanchai
Myanmar (Burma)
 (☎ 2827-7929) Room 2421-2425, Sung Hung Kai Centre, 30 Harbour Rd, Wanchai
Nepal
 (☎ 2667-7813) Room 2, 6th floor, 30-32 Cameron Rd, Cammer Commercial Building, Tsimshatsui
New Zealand
 (☎ 2525-5044) Room 3414, Jardine House, 1 Connaught Place, Central
Pakistan
 (☎ 2827-1950) Room 3806, 38th floor, China Resources Building, Harbour Drive, Wanchai
Philippines
 (☎ 2823-8500) Room 602, United Centre, 95 Queensway, Central
Portugal
 (☎ 2802-2585) Harbour Centre, 25 Harbour Rd, Wanchai
South Africa
 (☎ 2577-3279) 27th floor, Sunning Plaza, 10 Hysan Ave, Causeway Bay
South Korea
 (☎ 2529-4141) 5th floor, Far East Finance Centre, 16 Harcourt Rd, Central
Sri Lanka
 (☎ 2866-2321) 22nd floor, 43 Queen's Rd East, Wanchai
Switzerland
 (☎ 2522-7147) Room 3703, Gloucester Tower, The Landmark, 11 Pedder St, Central
Taiwan
 (☎ 2525-8315) Chung Hwa Travel Service, 4th floor, Lippo Tower, 89 Queensway, Central

Life After the Handover

What's changed for the traveller to Hong Kong, now it's reverted to Chinese control (becoming the Hong Kong Special Administrative Region)? While the situation may change in the future, the short answer is 'not much'. Some of the changes are:

Consulates The British have opened up a new consulate, while the Australian, Canadian and other Commonwealth-country commissions will become consulates.

Currency The Chinese government has promised to honour Hong Kong's capitalist system and way of life for the next 50 years; thus Hong Kong's currency does not change.

Emergencies Free emergency medical service for visitors is no longer available – everyone now pays. (The UK/Hong Kong Reciprocal Health Arrangement also ended with the handover: Brits should now have travel insurance for Hong Kong.)

Flag The new flag (a white Bauhinia flower with five red stars on a red field) replaces the Union Jack.

Holidays Queen Elizabeth's birthday no longer will be celebrated from 1998; neither will Remembrance Day. Two new holidays celebrate the handover of Hong Kong at the beginning of July and Victory over Japan Day (18 August).

Names Victoria Park will be renamed Hong Kong Central Park; most names that included the word Royal will lose that title and be known without it, eg The Royal Post Office becomes The Post Office.

Transport A new express train between Kowloon and Beijing began service in July 1997, taking about 30 hours.

Visas Some Hong Kong travel agencies, eg Phoenix Services and Shoestring Travel, will still arrange visas to mainland China. The border between Hong Kong and mainland China will remain in place. Delays at the Hong Kong-Shenzhen crossing have occurred; in 1998 authorities began looking at streamlining it. ■

Thailand
(☎ 2521-6481) 8th floor, Fairmont House, 8 Cotton Tree Drive, Central
UK
(☎ 2901-3111) 1 Supreme Court Rd, Central
USA
(☎ 2523-9011) 26 Garden Rd, Central
Vietnam
(☎ 2591-4517) Visa Office, 15th floor, Great Smart Tower, 230 Wanchai Rd, Wanchai

Visas

Even under Chinese rule, most visitors to Hong Kong still do not need a visa. But beware – these visa regulations could very well change in the next few years.

British passport holders are permitted to stay visa-free for six months, but this can be expected to change and they are no longer given the automatic right to work.

Citizens of most Western European nations can stay for three months, while citizens of the USA and most other countries get one month. Visas are still required for Eastern Europeans and citizens of Communist countries (including mainland China, where a special travel permit is still required). Visas for Hong Kong are now issued through Chinese consulates.

For tourist visa extensions, you should inquire at the Immigration Department (☎ 2824-6111), 2nd floor, Wanchai Tower Two, 7 Gloucester Rd, Wanchai. In general, they do not like to grant extensions unless there are special circumstances – cancelled flights, illness, registration in a legitimate course of study, legal employment, marriage to a local etc.

Hong Kong is still the best place to pick up a visa for China, and this will probably continue for a while. See the Facts for the

Visitor chapter at the beginning of this book.

Money

Costs Hong Kong is an expensive place and it gets more expensive every year. If you stay in dormitories, eat budget meals and resist the urge to shop, you can survive (just barely) on under HK$250 per day. However, most travellers will spend more.

In general, tipping is not expected in Hong Kong. A 10% service charge is usually added to restaurant bills in upmarket establishments, and this is a mandatory 'tip'. In taxis you should round the fare up to the nearest HK$0.50 or dollar.

If you shop for cameras, electronics and other big ticket items in the Tsimshatsui tourist zone, bargaining is essential because the shops will try to charge double. However, bargaining is *not* the norm in Hong Kong. It's only normal in places where tourists congregate.

Out in the suburban shopping malls or in the street markets of Mongkok and Shamshuipo, everything has a price tag and there is little scope for bargaining. Always try to bargain for your accommodation, however, if you're staying at a private guesthouse or smaller hotel.

Currency Exchange The unit of currency in Hong Kong is the HK dollar, which is divided into 100 cents. Bills are issued in denominations of $10, $20, $50, $100, $500 and $1000. Coins are issued in denominations of $5, $2, $1, 50 cents, 20 cents and 10 cents. Exchange rates are as follows:

Australia	A$1	=	HK$5.20
Canada	C$1	=	HK$5.46
China	Y1	=	HK$0.93
France	FF1	=	HK$1.27
Germany	DM1	=	HK$4.26
Japan	¥100	=	HK$5.98
New Zealand	NZ$1	=	HK$4.51
UK	UK£1	=	HK$12.97
USA	US$1	=	HK$7.74

Hong Kong has no exchange controls – locals and foreigners can send large quantities of money in or out as they please with no restrictions, and even play the local stock market while they're at it.

Hong Kong is, in fact, the financial centre of Asia simply because it is so unregulated. Whether or not China will interfere with this financial freedom in the coming years is the big question that keeps bankers awake at night.

Hong Kong is also a dream come true for money changing. All major and many minor foreign currencies can be exchanged. Foreigners can open bank accounts in various currencies (or in gold!), and international telegraphic transfers are fast and efficient. International credit cards are readily accepted.

Banks give the best exchange rates, but they vary from bank to bank. Excellent rates can be found at Wing Lung Bank, 4 Carnarvon Rd, Tsimshatsui, next to the New Astor Hotel. It also charges the lowest fee for the service, HK$20 per transaction. There's also an automatic exchange machine outside, although the rates won't be as good as in the bank.

Another good bank for changing money is the Hang Seng Bank, which has numerous branches all over the city (the small branches in the MTR stations do not change money). However, the Hang Seng charges HK$50 per transaction, so the rates are good only if you change more than US$200. Its parent company, the Hong Kong Bank, offers slightly lower rates.

Licensed moneychangers in the tourist districts operate 24 hours a day, but give relatively poor exchange rates, which are clearly posted. However, you can often get a better rate by bargaining (but be sure to ask politely).

The moneychangers in Chungking Mansions in Tsimshatsui are known to give the best exchange rates. Try not to change more money than necessary at the airport as the exchange rate there is poor (although there are ATMs there).

Bank hours are generally from 9 am to 4.30 pm Monday to Friday, and from 9 am to 12.30 pm on Saturday. You can also

The People's Liberation Army Liberates Hong Kong

On 1 July we got up at 5.30 am to watch the PLA roll into Hong Kong – one Canadian, two Japanese, a Brit and our friend from Hong Kong.

Each of us had some connection with this place; it was part of the history of our respective homelands. The rain was coming down hard, in sheets. We planned to stand on the pedestrian overpass overlooking the highway. It was deserted except for two policemen in black capes who emerged from nowhere to tell us we couldn't stay on the overpass. This was an historic occasion, but who wanted to argue with police in the pouring rain at six in the morning?

Then our friend arrived and said, 'That's ridiculous, of course we can watch from the overpass, let me talk to them, this is where I grew up, I live here'. Maybe the policemen saw the fervent desire to witness history in our eyes, for they relented and we watched the trucks coming in on the empty highway, the men in uniform standing ramrod straight, followed by the armoured personnel carriers, each with a man standing in the hatch, saluting. Despite the downpour, a huge silence filled the air. The last truck went past and it was over. We thanked the policemen and returned to bed, exhausted from the night before; the speeches, the pomp and circumstance, and the novelty of riding the Hong Kong subway at 3 am. Yet all it amounted to was the beginning of another new order; the next army had arrived. It was, in the end, like the letdown of a New Year's morning, where a resolution is but a broken promise and nothing ever really changes.

Marie Cambon

withdraw cash by credit card or bank card at ATMs throughout the city, as long as the machine displays your card's logo (on the back of the card), such as Global Access, Cirrus etc.

Post & Communications

Sending Mail All post offices are open Monday to Friday from 8 am to 6 pm, and 8 am to 2 pm on Saturday. They are closed on Sunday and public holidays.

The main post office is where you go to collect poste restante letters – it's in Central just to the west of the Star ferry terminal.

In Tsimshatsui, there are two convenient post offices just east of Nathan Rd: one at 10 Middle Rd and another in the basement of the Albion Plaza, 2-6 Granville Rd.

Telephone If you want to call overseas, it's cheapest to use an International Direct Dialling (IDD) telephone. You can place an IDD call from most phone boxes, but you'll need lots of coins.

A better alternative is to use phonecards, which come in denominations of HK$50, HK$100 and HK$250.

Every 7-Eleven store in Hong Kong has an IDD phone and sells the requisite phonecards. You can also find card phones at Hong Kong Telecom offices. There's a Hong Kong Telecom at 10 Middle Rd in Tsimshatsui and another in the basement of Century Place on the corner of D'Aguilar and Wellington Sts in Central (Lan Kwai Fong area).

To make an IDD call from Hong Kong, first dial ☎ 001, then the country code, area code and number. When calling Hong Kong from abroad, the country code is ☎ 852.

For calls to countries that do not have IDD service, you can call from a Hong Kong Telecom office – first pay a deposit and they will hook you up (minimum three minutes) and give you your change after the call is completed.

If you don't have the cash on hand, an easy way to make collect calls or bill to a credit card is to use a service called Home

Country Direct. This service connects you immediately to an operator in your home country, so there is no language barrier. See the Facts for the Visitor chapter at the beginning of this book for details.

Some useful phone numbers include:

Ambulance, fire, police, emergency	☎ 999
Directory assistance	☎ 1081
Operator-assisted calls	☎ 10010
International dialling assistance	☎ 10013
Credit card calls	☎ 011
Police business & taxi complaints	☎ 2527-7177
Time	☎ 18503
Weather	☎ 187-8066

Fax, Telex & Telegraph All your telecommunications needs can be taken care of at Hong Kong Telecom offices.

Many hotels and even hostels have fax machines and will allow you to both send and receive material for quite reasonable service charges.

Travel Agencies

There are lots of travel agencies, but some agencies we've personally tried and found to offer competitive prices include:

Phoenix Services (☎ 2722-7378; fax 2369-8884), Room B, 6th floor, Milton Mansion, 96 Nathan Rd, Tsimshatsui

Shoestring Travel (☎ 2723-2306; fax 2721-2085), Flat A, 4th floor, Alpha House, 27-33 Nathan Rd, Tsimshatsui

Traveller Services (☎ 2375-2222; fax 2375-2233), Room 1012, Silvercord Tower One, 30 Canton Rd, Tsimshatsui

Bookshops

Hong Kong is an excellent place to stock up on books, although English-language books are very expensive.

Books critical of China could still be found on the shelves after the handover, but it remains to be seen how much an issue censorship will become in the next few years.

At present, some of Hong Kong's notable bookshops include:

Bookazine Company (☎ 2523-1747), Basement, Jardine House, 1 Connaught Place, Central

Cosmos Books (☎ 2866-1677), 30 Johnston Rd, Wanchai

Hong Kong Book Centre (☎ 2522-7064), 25 Des Voeux Rd, On Lok Yuen Building, Central

South China Morning Post Bookshop (☎ 2522-1012), Star Ferry Terminal, Central; (☎ 2366-8001), 13 Lock Rd, Tsimshatsui

Times Books (☎ 2722-6583), Basement, Golden Crown Court, corner Carnarvon and Nathan Rds, Tsimshatsui

Cultural Centres

The HKTA can give you the latest schedule of events, or check out the upcoming events in *bc magazine* or *HK Magazine*. You can pick up copies (they're free) at the Hong Kong Book Centre in Central or Swindon Books in Tsimshatsui and in various expat gathering places around town.

You can reserve tickets by calling the URBTIX hotline (☎ 2374-9009) and pick them up from any URBTIX outlet within three days. A convenient way to book and pay for movie tickets by credit card is by phoning Cityline (☎ 2317-6666).

Films

Hong Kong produces many times more films than the rest of China put together. Censorship under the British did exist, but it was very light and Hong Kong grew up to be one of the movie capitals of Asia. Unfortunately, this freewheeling entertainment industry could suffer a major setback as a result of the handover to China.

Some well known Hong Kong directors include John Woo, Eric Tsang, Tsui Hark, Wong Jing, Wong Kar Wai and Ringo Lam. Jackie Chan has directed some of his own films.

One area where the Hong Kong film industry really does excel is in comedies. In terms of quantity, the number of comedies is not large by world standards, but some are of excellent quality. Certainly there is no other place in Asia that comes close to matching the quality of Hong Kong's humorous flicks.

Some well known examples include: *Aces Go Places 1, 2, 3, 4* and *5 (zuì jiā pāi dǎng); God of Gamblers 1, 2* and *3 (dǔ shèng); Golden Girls (shān shuǐ yǒu xiāng féng); Haunted Cop Shop 2 (měng guǐ xué táng); Love on Delivery (pò huài zhī wáng);* and *Mack the Knife (liú máng yī shēng).*

Hong Kong produces a large number of films of the human interest sort. Love stories, often ending in tragedy, are probably second only to kungfu dramas. A variation on the theme is ghost stories, although Chinese ghosts scarcely resemble their western counterparts.

Good ones to check out include: *Au Revoir Mon Amour (hé rì jūn zài lài); C'est la Vie, Mon Cherie (xīn bù liǎo qíng); Cageman (lóng mín); Green Snake (qīng shé); He's a Woman, She's a Man (jīn zhī yù yè);* and *Tom, Dick, and Hairy (fēng chén sān xià).*

Epic historical dramas are often co-productions between Hong Kong and the mainland. Ones to look for include: *A Chinese Odyssey Part One – A Pandora's Box (xīyóujì dì yìbǎilíng yī huí zhī yuè guāng bǎohé); All Men Are Brothers – Blood of the Leopard (shuǐ hǔ zhuàn zhī yīng xióng běn sè);* and *The Great Conqueror's Concubine (xī chǔ bà wáng).*

Hong Kong is best known for its action-packed kungfu films. These are usually spectacularly bloody, and definitely not for everyone. Mao Zedong was a loyal fan and set up a screen in his study for viewing Hong Kong kungfu movies, even though he prohibited the masses from watching them.

Some of the better ones feature good acting and actually have an interesting plot, but the majority are rubbish by any standard.

Actor Bruce Lee *(lǐ xiǎo lóng)* essentially started it all and his films tend to be much better than average. Jackie Chan *(chéng lóng)* is another star, notable for both serious and funny kungfu dramas. A more recent kungfu star is Jet Li *(lǐ liánjié)* who is from the mainland.

Standard kungfu plots revolve around the triads (mafia), loan sharks, casinos (with a few scenes in Macau) and personal acts of revenge. Notable characters include at least one macho walking death machine hero, a sadistic triad chieftain, an evil Japanese soldier, kungfu women and sometimes kungfu children.

Look out for: *Chinese Connection (jīng wǔ mén); Fist of Legend (jīng wǔ yīng xióng); Licence to Steal (lóng fèng zéi zhuō zéi); Police Story (jǐngchá gùshì);* and *The Twin Dragons (shuāng lóng huì).*

Media

Hong Kong has two local English-language daily newspapers, the *South China Morning Post* and the *Hong Kong Standard.* Also printed in Hong Kong are the *Asian Wall St Journal,* the *International Herald Tribune* and *USA Today International.* Imported news magazines are readily available.

There are two English-language and two Cantonese TV stations. Star TV offers satellite TV broadcasting that has some English programming. There is also a variety of English radio stations from which to choose.

Medical Services

There are some excellent private hospitals in Hong Kong, but their prices reflect the fact that they are required to operate at a profit. Some of the better private hospitals include Canossa (☎ 2522-2181), Grantham (☎ 2518-2111), Hong Kong Central (☎ 2522-3141), Matilda & War Memorial (☎ 2849-0111) and St Paul's (☎ 2890-6008).

Public hospitals are cheaper, although foreigners pay more than Hong Kong residents. Public hospitals include Queen Elizabeth Hospital (☎ 2958-8888), Princess Margaret Hospital (☎ 2990-1111), Queen Mary Hospital (☎ 2819-4111) and Prince of Wales Hospital (☎ 2632-2211).

Emergency

The general emergency phone number for ambulance, fire and police is ☎ 999. You can dial this without a coin.

KOWLOON

Kowloon, the peninsula pointing out towards Hong Kong Island, is packed with shops, hotels, bars, restaurants, nightclubs and tourists. Nathan Rd, the main drag, has plenty of all.

Start your exploration from Kowloon's southern tip, the tourist ghetto known as Tsimshatsui. Adjacent to the Star ferry terminal is the **Hong Kong Cultural Centre** with its controversial windowless facade facing one of the most spectacular views in the world. Just next door is the **Museum of Art**. Both are closed on Monday, otherwise operating hours are weekdays and Saturday from 10 am to 6 pm, and Sunday and holidays from 1 to 6 pm.

Adjacent to the Cultural Centre is the **Space Museum**, which has several exhibition halls and a Space Theatre (planetarium). Opening times for the exhibition halls are weekdays (except Monday) from 1 to 9 pm, and from 10 am to 9 pm on weekends and holidays. The Space Theatre has about seven shows each day. Check times with the museum (☎ 2734-2722).

The lower end of Nathan Rd is known as the **Golden Mile**, which refers to both the price of real estate here and also its ability to suck money out of tourist pockets. If you continue north up Nathan Rd you come into the tightly packed Chinese business districts of Yaumatei and Mongkok.

Hidden behind Yue Hwa's Park Lane Store on Nathan Rd is **Kowloon Park**, which every year seems to become less of a park and more of an amusement ground. The swimming pool is perhaps the park's finest attribute – it's even equipped with waterfalls.

The **Museum of History** is in Kowloon Park near the Haiphong Rd entrance. It covers Hong Kong's existence from prehistoric times (about 6000 years ago, give or take a few) to the present and contains a large collection of old photographs. The museum is open Tuesday to Saturday from 10 am to 6 pm, and Sunday and public holidays from 1 to 6 pm. Admission is HK$10.

The **Kowloon Mosque** stands on Nathan Rd at the corner of Kowloon Park. It was opened in 1984 on the site of an earlier mosque constructed in 1896. Unless you are Muslim, you must obtain permission to go inside. You can inquire by ringing ☎ 2724-0095.

The **Science Museum** is in Tsimshatsui East on the corner of Chatham and Granville Rds. This multi-level complex houses more than 500 exhibits. Operating hours are 1 to 9 pm Tuesday to Friday, and 10 am to 9 pm on weekends and holidays; entry is $HK25. The museum is closed on Monday.

The most exotic sight in the Mongkok district is the **Bird Market**. It's on Hong Lok St, an obscure alley on the southern side of Argyle St, two blocks west of Nathan Rd. There has been talk of moving this market for years and, by the time you read this, it should be at its new site on Yuen Po Street, between the Mongkok Stadium and KCR railway tracks off Prince Edward Rd.

The **Wong Tai Sin Temple** is a very large and active Taoist temple built in 1973. It's right near the Wong Tai Sin MTR station in North Kowloon. The temple is open daily from 7 am to 5.30 pm. Admission is free, but a donation of HK$1 (or more) is expected.

HONG KONG ISLAND

The northern and southern sides of the island have very different characters. The northern side is an urban jungle, while much of the south is still surprisingly rural (but developing fast). The central part of the island is incredibly mountainous and protected from further development by a country park.

Northern Side

Central is the bustling business centre of Hong Kong. A free shuttle bus from the Star ferry terminal brings you to the lower station of the famous Peak Tram on Garden Rd. The tram terminates at the top of **Victoria Peak** (552m), and the ride costs HK$15 one way or HK$23 return. The tram opens at 7 am and closes at midnight.

It's worth repeating the peak trip at night

HONG KONG & MACAU

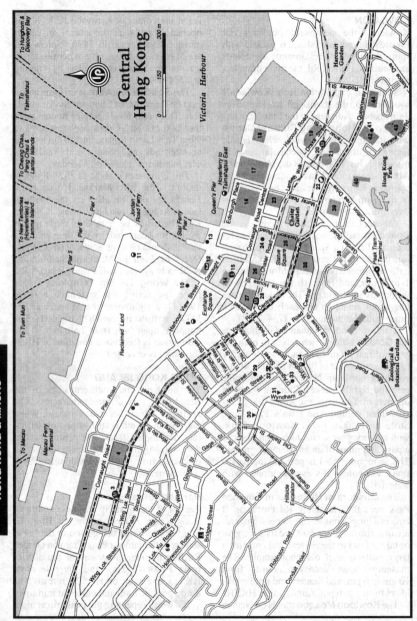

Central Hong Kong

0   150   300 m

Victoria Harbour

CENTRAL HONG KONG	5	China Travel Service	24	Cenotaph
	6	Cat Street Galleries	25	Legco Building
PLACES TO STAY	7	Man Mo Temple	27	Swire House
23 Furama Kempinski Hotel	8	Central Market	28	Central MTR Station
	9	Bus Terminal	29	Photo Scientific & Color Six
26 Mandarin Oriental Hotel	10	Site of New Railway Station to Airport	32	HK Telecom
43 Island Shangri-La Hotel	11	Bus Terminus	33	Lan Kwai Fong
	12	Post Office	34	Fringe Club
	13	South China Morning Post Bookshop	35	Hong Kong & Shanghai Bank Building
PLACES TO EAT	14	Jardine House	36	Former Government House
30 Club Sri Lanka	15	HKTA Office	
31 Ashoka Restaurant	16	City Hall	37	US Consulate
	17	HMS Tamar Naval Centre	38	St John's Cathedral
	18	Prince of Wales Building	39	Bank of China
OTHER			40	Flagstaff House Museum
1 Shun Tak Centre	19	Far East Finance Centre	41	Government Publications Centre
2 Western Market	20	Admiralty MTR Station	
3 Sheung Wan MTR Station	21	Lippo Centre	42	Queensway Government Offices
4 Wing on Department Store	22	Thai Consulate	44	Pacific Place

as the illuminated view is spectacular if the weather cooperates. Don't just admire the view from the top – wander up Mt Austin Rd to **Victoria Peak Garden** or take the more leisurely stroll around Lugard and Harlech Rds; together they make a complete circuit of the peak. You can walk right down to Aberdeen on the southern side of the island or you can try Old Peak Rd for a few kilometres (return) to Central. The more energetic may want to walk the **Hong Kong Trail**, which runs along the top of the mountainous spine of Hong Kong Island from the Peak to Big Wave Bay.

There are many pleasant walks and views in the **Zoological & Botanical Gardens** on Robinson Rd overlooking Central. Entry is free to the **Fung Ping Shan Museum** in Hong Kong University (closed Sunday) at 94 Bonham Rd.

Hong Kong Park is just behind the city's second tallest skyscraper, the Bank of China. It's an unusual park, not at all natural, but beautiful in its own weird way. Within the park is the **Flagstaff House Museum**, the oldest western-style building

still standing in Hong Kong. Inside, you'll find a Chinese teaware collection. Admission is free and the museum is closed on Mondays.

Between the skyscrapers of Central you'll find **Li Yuen St East** and **Li Yuen St West**, which run parallel to each other between Des Voeux and Queen's Rds. Both streets are narrow alleys, closed to motorised traffic and crammed with shops and stalls selling everything imaginable.

The **Hillside Escalator Link** is a mode of transport that has become a tourist attraction. The 800m moving walkway (known as a 'travelator') runs from the Vehicular Ferry Pier alongside the Central Market and up Shelley St to the Mid-Levels.

West of Central in the Sheung Wan district is appropriately named **Ladder St**, which climbs steeply. At the junction of Ladder St and Hollywood Rd is **Man Mo Temple**, the oldest temple in Hong Kong. A bit further north near the Macau ferry terminal is the indoor **Western Market**, a four storey red-brick building built in 1906 and now fully renovated.

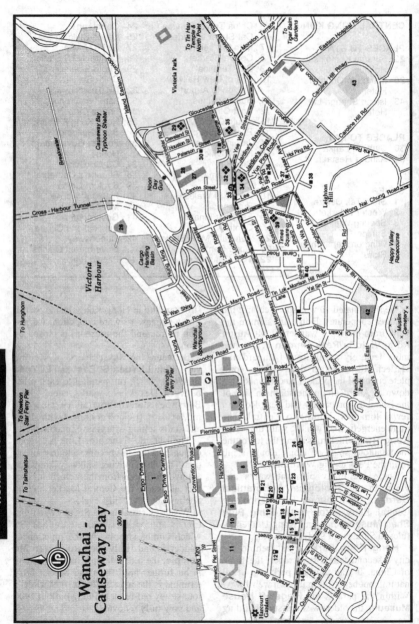

Wanchai - Causeway Bay

Victoria Harbour

To Taimshatsui
To Kowloon Star Ferry Pier
To Hunghom
To Hunghom

Cross - Harbour Tunnel

Breakwater

Causeway Bay Typhoon Shelter

Victoria Park

To Tin Hau Temple & North Point

To Tiger Balm Gardens

Island Eastern Corridor

Moreton Terrace

Tung Lo Wan Road

Eastern Hospital Rd

Cotton Park

Caroline Hill Road

Caroline Hill Rd

Link Road

Gloucester Road

Cleveland St

Houston St

Paterson St

Great George Street

Cannon Street

Lee Garden

Jardine's Bazaar

Yun Ping Road

Hoi Ping Rd.

Irving Ave

Leighton Hill

Wong Nai Chung Road

Noon Day Gun

Cargo Handling Basin

Hung Hing Road

Gloucester Road

Percival Street

Jaffe Road

Lockhart Road

Canal Road

Canal Road

Leung Tang St

Russell Street

Times Square

Sharp St

Yiu Wa St

Matheson St

Sports Rd.

Happy Valley Racecourse

Muslim Cemetery

Hung Hing Road

Wan Shing

Marsh Road

Marsh Road

Wanchai Sportsground

Tonnochy Road

Tonnochy Road

Tonnochy Road

Tin Lok Lane

Morrison Hill Road

Sharp St

Yat Sin St

Oi Kwan Road

Wanchai Park

Wanchai Ferry Pier

Stewart Road

Jaffe Road

Lockhart Road

Hennessy Road

Burrows Street

Wanchai Road

Queen's Road East

Cross Street

Harbour Drive

Fleming Road

Gloucester Road

O'Brien Road

Thomson Rd.

Johnston Road

Spring Garden Lane

Lee Tung St

Expo Drive

Expo Drive Central

Convention Road

Harbour Road

Tung King

Fenwick Pier Street

Fenwick Street

Arsenal Street

Queen's Road East

Anton St

Ship St

Thomson Road

Tai Yat St

Lun Fat St

Amoy St

Swatow St

Lee Tung St

Gresson St

Anton St

Spring Garden Lane

Wanchai Road

Kennedy Road

Queen's Road East

Star St

Harcourt Garden

WANCHAI - CAUSEWAY BAY	PLACES TO EAT	20 Big Apple Disco
	17 Saigon Beach Restaurant	22 Delaney's & Kublai's Cybercafe
PLACES TO STAY		23 Bb's
2 Grand Hyatt	**OTHER**	24 Wanchai MTR Station
3 New World Harbour View Hotel	1 Hong Kong Convention & Exhibition Centre	26 Royal HK Yacht Club
9 Harbour View International House	4 Hong Kong Convention & Exhibition Centre	27 World Trade Centre
13 Empire Hotel		29 Daimaru Household Square
14 Wesley Hotel		
15 New Harbour Hotel	5 Australian Consulate	32 Sogo Department Store
18 Wharney Hotel	6 China Resources Centre (Visas for China)	33 Causeway Bay MTR Station
21 Luk Kwok Hotel		
25 Century Hong Kong	7 Central Plaza	34 Mitsukoshi Department Store
28 Excelsior Hotel	8 Immigration Department	
30 Wang Fat Hostel		35 Matsuzakaya Department Store
31 Noble Hostel	10 Arts Centre	
36 Famous Villa	11 Academy for the Performing Arts	39 Times Square
37 Phoenix Apartments		42 Queen Elizabeth Stadium
38 Emerald House	12 The Wanch	
40 South Pacific Hotel	16 Neptune Disco	43 South China Athletic Association
41 Charterhouse Hotel	19 Joe Bananas	

At the Western Market you can hop on one of Hong Kong's delightfully ancient double-decker trams, which will take you eastwards to Wanchai, Causeway Bay and Happy Valley.

Just east of Central is **Wanchai**, known for its raucous nightlife, but relatively dull in the daytime. One thing worth seeing is the **Arts Centre** on Harbour Rd. The Pao Sui Loong Galleries are on the 4th and 5th floors of the centre and international and local exhibitions are held year-round with the emphasis on contemporary art.

Wanchai's **Police Museum**, at 27 Coombe Rd, emphasises the history of the Royal Hong Kong Police Force. Opening hours are Wednesday to Sunday from 9 am to 5 pm, and Tuesday from 2 to 5 pm. It's closed on Monday and admission is free.

The **Hong Kong Convention & Exhibition Centre** is an enormous building on the harbour and boasts the world's largest 'glass curtain' – a window seven storeys high. Just be glad you don't have to be the one to wash it. You can ride the escalator to the 7th floor for a superb harbour view. The new wing on the waterfront with its distinctive roof is where the handover to China took place at midnight on 30 June 1997.

The **Museum of Chinese Historical Relics** houses cultural treasures from China unearthed in archaeological digs. It's on the 1st floor, Causeway Centre, 28 Harbour Rd, Wanchai. Enter from the China Resources Centre. Opening hours are 10 am to 6 pm Monday to Saturday, and 1 to 6 pm on Sundays and public holidays. It's best to phone first (☎ 2827-4692) to find out about current exhibitions.

On the eastern side of Causeway Bay is **Victoria Park**, a large playing field built on reclaimed land. Early in the morning it's a good place to see the slow-motion choreography of *taijiquan* practitioners.

South-east of Causeway Bay near Happy Valley is the **Tiger Balm Gardens**, officially known as the Aw Boon Haw Gardens. The gardens are three hectares of grotesque statuary in appallingly bad taste, but are a sight to behold. Aw Boon Haw made his fortune from the Tiger Balm cure-everything medication and this was his gift to Hong Kong. He also built a similar monstrosity in Singapore. It's definitely worth visiting, at least for comic relief. Admission is free.

Southern Side

With a pocketful of change you can circumnavigate Hong Kong Island. Start in Central. You have a choice of hopping on bus No 6 at the Exchange Square bus terminal and going directly to Stanley, or taking a tram first to Shaukeiwan and changing to a bus. The bus is easier and faster, but the tram is more fun.

The tram takes you through hustling Wanchai and bustling Causeway Bay to the Sai Wan Ho ferry pier at Shaukeiwan. Look for the trams marked 'Shaukeiwan' and hop off just before the end of the line. You then take bus No 14 up and over the central hills to **Stanley**. Stanley has a decent beach, a fine market, expensive villas and a maximum-security prison.

From Stanley, bus No 73 takes you along the coast by beautiful **Repulse Bay**, which is rapidly developing into high-rises and shopping malls. The bus passes **Deep Water Bay**, which has a sandy beach, and continues to **Aberdeen**. The big attraction here is the harbour choked with boats, which are also part-time residences for Hong Kong's fishermen and their families. There will generally be several sampans ready to take you on a half-hour tour of this floating city for about HK$50 per person (it's worth seeing), or bargain a whole boat for a group (about HK$150).

Floating regally amid the confusion in Aberdeen are several palace-like restaurants, the largest being the Jumbo Floating Restaurant. The restaurant runs its own shuttle boat.

From Aberdeen, a final short ride on bus No 7 takes you back to your starting point, via the Hong Kong University.

Ocean Park, a spectacular aquarium and funfair, is also close to Aberdeen. Don't try to include it on a tour to Aberdeen – Ocean Park is worth a full day of your time.

Spread over two separate sites, and connected by a cable car, the park includes what is reputed to be the world's largest aquarium, but the emphasis is on the funfair with its roller coaster, space wheel, octopus, swinging ship and other astronaut-training machines. The **Middle Kingdom** is an ancient Chinese spin-off of Ocean Park and is included in the admission fee. The entrance fee for the whole complex is HK$140.

You can get to Ocean Park on bus No 70 from the Exchange Square bus station near the Star ferry terminal in Central – get off at the first stop after the tunnel. Alternatively, there's an air-con Ocean Park Citybus which leaves from both Exchange Square and the Admiralty MTR station (underneath Bond Centre) every half-hour from 8.45 am and costs HK$11.50 one way. You can also get a complete ticket package on the bus for HK$163 which includes entrance fee and return trip. Ocean Park is open from 10 am to 6 pm. Get there early because there is much to see.

Just next to Ocean Park is **Water World**, a collection of swimming pools, water slides and diving platforms. Water World is open from June to October. During July and August, it's open from 9 am to 9 pm. During June, September and October it opens from 10 am to 6 pm. Admission for adults/children is HK$65/33 during the day, but in the evening falls to HK$44/22. Take bus No 70 and get off at the first stop after the tunnel. If you take the Ocean Park Citybus, be sure to get off at the first stop.

Shek O, on the south-eastern coast, has one of the best beaches on Hong Kong Island. To get there, take the MTR or tram to Shaukeiwan, and from Shaukeiwan take bus No 9 to the last stop.

NEW TERRITORIES

You can explore most of the New Territories by bus and train in one very busy day, assuming that you don't take time out for hiking or swimming (both worthwhile and recommended activities).

You start out by taking the MTR to the

last stop at **Tsuen Wan**. The main attraction here is the **Yuen Yuen Institute**, a Taoist temple complex, and the adjacent Buddhist **Western Monastery** in Lo Wai village. You reach the institute by taking minibus No 81 from Shiu Wo St, which is two blocks south of the MTR station. Alternatively, take a taxi, which is not expensive.

Chuk Lam Sim Yuen is another large monastery in the hills north of Tsuen Wan. The instructions for getting there are almost the same as those for the Yuen Yuen Institute. Find Shiu Wo St and take maxicab No 85.

At Tsuen Wan you have two options. You can continue west to Tuen Mun, or north to **Tai Mo Shan** (957m), Hong Kong's highest peak. To reach Tai Mo Shan, take bus No 51 from the Tsuen Wan MTR station – the bus stop is on the overpass that goes over the roof of the station, or you can also pick it up at the Tsuen Wan ferry pier. The bus heads up Route Twisk (Twisk is derived from Tsuen Wan Into Shek Kong). Get off at the top of the pass, from where it's uphill on foot. You walk on a road, but it's unlikely you'll encounter traffic. The path is part of the **MacLehose Trail**, which is 100km long. The trail runs from Tuen Mun in the west to the Sai Kung Peninsula in the east and walking the entire length would take several days.

If you choose not to visit Tai Mo Shan, from Tsuen Wan take bus No 60M or 68M to the bustling town of **Tuen Mun**. Here you can visit Hong Kong's largest shopping mall, the Tuen Mun Town Plaza. From here, hop on the Light Rail Transit (LRT) system to reach **Ching Chung Koon**, a temple complex smack in the middle of building estates, on the northern side of Tuen Mun.

You then get back on the LRT and head to Yuen Long. From here, take bus No 54, 64K or 77K to the nearby walled villages at **Kam Tin**. These villages with their single stout entrances are said to date from the 16th century.

There are several walled villages at Kam

Tin, but most accessible is **Kat Hing Wai**. Drop about HK$5 into the donation box by the entrance and wander the narrow little lanes. The old Hakka women in traditional gear require payment before they can be photographed.

The town of Sheung Shui is about 8km north-east on bus No 77K. Here you can hop on the KCR and go one stop south to **Fanling**. The main attraction in this town is the **Fung Ying Sin Kwun Temple**, a Taoist temple for the dead, located across from the KCR station.

At Fanling, get on the Kowloon-Canton Railway (KCR) and head to the Tai Po Market station. From here, you can walk 10 to 15 minutes to the **Hong Kong Railway Museum**.

You can get back on the KCR and go south to the Chinese University, where there's the Art Gallery at the **Institute of Chinese Studies**. A shuttle bus takes passengers up the hill to the university. Admission is free.

The KCR will bring you to Shatin, a lively, bustling city where you can visit the huge **Shatin Town Centre**, one of Hong Kong's biggest shopping malls. Also, this is where you begin the climb up to the **Temple of 10,000 Buddhas** (which actually has over 12,000). The site was closed at the time of writing due to damage from landslides, so it's best to check with HKTA before you head out.

All this should fill your day, but there are other places to visit in the New Territories. The **Sai Kung Peninsula** is one of the least spoilt areas in the New Territories – it's great for hiking and you can get from village to village on boats in the Tolo Harbour.

Also, the best beaches in the New Territories are around the Sai Kung Peninsula, including **Clearwater Bay**. From the Choi Hung MTR station take bus No 91 to Clearwater Bay or No 92 to Sai Kung village.

To explore the eastern side of the peninsula, take bus No 94 from Sai Kung that ends at Wong Shek pier.

OUTLYING ISLANDS

There are 235 islands dotting the waters around Hong Kong, but only four have substantial residential communities and are thus readily accessible by ferry.

While very tranquil during the week, the islands are packed on weekends and holidays. Cars are prohibited on all of the islands except Lantau, and even there vehicle ownership is very restricted.

Cheung Chau

This dumbbell-shaped island has a large community of western residents who enjoy the slow pace of island life and relatively low rents. Were it not for the Chinese signs and people, you might think you were in some Greek island village.

The town sprawls across the narrow neck connecting the two ends of the island. The bay on the western side of the island (where the ferry lands) is an exotic collection of fishing boats much like Aberdeen on Hong Kong Island. The eastern side of the island is where you'll find Tung Wan beach, Cheung Chau's longest. There are a few tiny but remote beaches that you can reach by foot, and at the southern tip of the island is the hideaway cave of the notorious pirate, Cheung Po Tsai.

The expat nightlife spot is the Garden Cafe/Pub (☎ 2981-4610) at 84 Tung Wan Rd, in the centre of the island.

Lamma

This is the second largest of the outlying islands and the one closest to the city. Lamma has good beaches and a very relaxed pace on weekdays, but on weekends it's mobbed like anywhere else. There are two main communities here – Yung Shue Wan in the north and Sok Kwu Wan in the south. Both have ferry services to Central.

Both Yung Shue Wan and Sok Kwu Wan are lined with seafood restaurants, so you won't starve. The Waterfront Bar in Yung Shue Wan is a lively place for nightlife and good food, or you can try its quieter competition, the Island Bar, or sit outside in front of the Fountain Head (☎ 2982-2118) next to the Hong Kong Bank. The Deli Lamma (☎ 2982-1583) has a variety of healthy food dishes and Dino's (☎ 2982-6196) has hamburgers and fish and chips. Tootchka's (☎ 2982-0159) is another popular hang-out.

Lantau

This is the largest of the islands and the most sparsely populated – it's almost twice the size of Hong Kong Island, but the population is only 30,000. You could easily spend a couple of days exploring the mountainous walking trails and enjoying uncrowded beaches.

Mui Wo (Silvermine Bay) is the major arrival point for ferries. As you exit the ferry, to your right is the road leading to the beach. It passes several eateries and hotels along the way.

From Mui Wo, most visitors board bus No 2 to **Ngong Ping**, a plateau 500m above sea level in the western part of the island. It's here that you'll find the impressive **Po Lin Monastery**. It's a relatively recent construction and almost as much a tourist attraction as a religious centre. Just outside the monastery is the world's largest outdoor bronze buddha statue. It's possible to have a vegetarian lunch at the monastery dining hall and you can spend the night here. The main reason to stay overnight is to launch a sunrise expedition to climb Lantau Peak (934m). Another place to visit is Tai O, a village at the western end of the island; take bus No 1.

The 2km-long **Cheung Sha Wan** on Lantau Island is Hong Kong's longest beach. You'll have it to yourself on weekdays, but forget it on weekends.

On Lantau's northern shore is the 19th century **Tung Chung Fort**, which still has its old cannon pointing out to sea. The bad news here is that just off the coast, Hong Kong's new airport at Chek Lap Kok (due to open in July 1998) has transformed this part of the island, and turned the Tung Chung area into a new town development. It is connected to Tsuen Wan by the new

Tsing Ma road and rail bridge that opened in May 1997.

The railway, also due to open in July 1998, will shuttle airport passengers to a new station in front of the Exchange towers in Central. To get to Lantau via the bridge, take bus No E31 from the Tsuen Wan ferry pier and change at Tung Chung for buses to other destinations on Lantau.

You may also want to visit **Discovery Bay** in the north-eastern part of the island. This is a very upmarket housing development complete with high-rises, shopping mall, yacht club and golf course. Jet-powered ferries run from Discovery Bay to Central every 20 minutes, but there are no places to stay and tourism is actively discouraged. The main reason for visiting isn't to see Discovery Bay, but to walk for one hour southwards along the coastline to find the **Trappist Haven Monastery**. Walking about another 1½ hours from there over a dangerously slippery trail brings you out to Mui Wo, from where you can get ferries back to Central.

There are good places to eat and drink in Lantau. Papa Doc's Bar and Cafe (☎ 2984- 9003) at 3 Ngan Wan Rd in Mui Wo is good for western food, and there's a new bar, the China Bear (☎ 2984-7360) nearby, that has a good selection of locally brewed beer. West of Mui Wo, 5km up the road, Charlie's (☎ 2984-8329) is a popular expat place, with Chinese, Indian and western food.

Further west along the road past Cheung Sha beach at Tong Fuk, The Gallery (☎ 2980-2582) serves up a South African-style barbecue. It's open Wednesday to Friday in the evenings, and from noon onwards on weekends.

Peng Chau

This is the smallest of the outlying islands that are readily accessible. It's also the most traditionally Chinese, with narrow alleys, an outdoor meat and vegetable market and a very tiny expat community. The **Tin Hau Temple** was built in 1792. A climb to the top of **Finger Hill** (95m) will reward you with a view of the entire island and nearby Lantau.

South of the main ferry pier and right along the shoreline are the two best western restaurants and pubs – the Sea Breeze (☎ 2983-8785) and adjacent Forest Bar and Restaurant (☎ 2983-8837). There are no places to stay in Peng Chau unless you can rent a holiday flat.

ACTIVITIES

If you'd like a morning jog with spectacular views, nothing beats the path around Victoria Peak on Harlech and Lugard Rds. Part of this is a fitness trail with various exercise equipment (parallel bars and the like).

Anyone who is serious about sports should contact the South China Athletic Association (☎ 2577-6932) at 88 Caroline Hill Rd, Causeway Bay. The SCAA has numerous indoor facilities for bowling, tennis, squash, ping-pong, gymnastics, fencing, yoga, judo, karate, billiards and dancing. Outdoor activities include golf, and there is also a women's activities section. Membership is very cheap and there is a discounted short-term membership available for visitors.

Another excellent place you can contact is the Hong Kong Amateur Athletic Association (☎ 2504-8215), Room 913, Queen Elizabeth Stadium, 18 Oi Kwan Rd, Wanchai. All sorts of sports clubs have activities here or hold members' meetings.

Windsurfing has become very popular in Hong Kong, especially after local athlete, Lee Lai-San, won Hong Kong's first Olympic gold medal in Atlanta. Some popular places to windsurf are Stanley, Shek O, Cheung Chau Island and other beaches in the New Territories. At Tai Mei Tuk in the New Territories you can rent boards through the Regional Council for as low as HK$10 per hour. On Cheung Chau Island, the Windsurfing Centre (☎ 2981-8316) rents boards for HK$50 to HK$90. Phone the Hong Kong Windsurfing Association (☎ 2504-8255) for more information.

Hong Kong has a growing community of surfers, but surfing is not officially sanctioned and there were still discussions going on at the time of writing whether to ban it completely or let it continue on a beach-sharing basis with swimmers.

The main area of contention is Big Wave Bay on Hong Kong Island. Bear in mind that you could be fined, although this has not as yet been strictly enforced. Check with the Hong Kong Windsurfing Association.

Walking & Hiking Trails

There are numerous trails on Hong Kong Island, the New Territories and the outlying islands and there are some beautiful views from the peaks, although they can get crowded on weekends. The best place to get information on trails is at the Government Publications Centre, however, the HKTA sometimes has pamphlets as well if you ask for them.

The three main trails in the region are the Hong Trail (50km), which runs through the four country parks of Hong Kong Island. A good place to start is the Peak and then head west. The Wilson Trail (78km) begins above Stanley and goes across Hong Kong Island to Quarry Bay, picks up again in Lam Tin in Kowloon, and continues to Nam Chung in the New Territories.

The Friends of Country Parks publishes a good pamphlet on the route. It's an organisation run out of the office of Tam Wing Kun Holdings (☎ 2377-2068), room 4010, China Resources Centre, 26 Harbour Rd, Wanchai.

The longest trail is the MacLehose Trail (100km) that runs east-west across the New Territories. From Pak Tam, it circumnavigates the Sai Kung Peninsula and then heads west across the ridge of hills, ending up in Tuen Mun.

ORGANISED TOURS

There are dozens of these, including boat tours. All can be booked through the HKTA, travel agents, large tourist hotels or directly from the tour company.

PLACES TO STAY

For budget travellers, the situation is grim – accommodation in Hong Kong is expensive. Solo backpackers may want to seek out dormitories, some of which are very basic. There are a few YHA dormitories, which charge only HK$35 to HK$100 per bed, but all are very inconveniently located. The same is true for camping sites – they exist, but you'll spend an hour or two commuting to the city.

Guesthouses are the salvation for most budget travellers. Some guesthouses (not many) have dormitories where beds go for HK$60 to HK$80, with discounts for long-term (one week or more) rentals.

Private rooms the size of closets are available for as little as HK$160, but you can easily spend twice that. It definitely pays for two people to share a room, as this costs little or no more.

A 'mid-range' Hong Kong hotel would cost anything between HK$600 and HK$1000, but even rooms at these prices are becoming rare.

The majority of cheap accommodation is on the Kowloon side. With few exceptions, the places on Hong Kong Island are mid-range to top-end hotels. Rentals are about 20% cheaper if you pay by the week, but stay one night first to make sure that the room is acceptable – noisy neighbours and rats will not be obvious at first glance.

At mid-range and top-end hotels, you can get sizeable discounts (up to 30%) by booking through some travel agencies. One such place is Traveller Services (☎ 2375-2222), but a few other agents do it as well.

At the airport, there is a hotel reservation desk, but they deal only with the more expensive hotels. However, they always have good deals, particularly if you arrive late at night. You'll always get a better price if you book at this desk rather than straight through the hotels. Even budget travellers can use their free courtesy phone to call around and see who has vacancies.

Kowloon – Guesthouses

Chungking Mansions There is probably

no other place in the world like Chungking Mansions, the budget accommodation ghetto of Hong Kong. It's a huge high-rise dump at 30 Nathan Rd in the heart of Tsimshatsui with approximately 80 guesthouses. It's divided into five blocks labelled A to E, each with its own derelict lift.

If you stand around the lobby with your backpack, chances are that the touts from the guesthouses will find you before you find them.

With few exceptions, there is little difference in prices for private rooms, but dormitories are of course significantly cheaper. The price range for a private room is roughly HK$150 to HK$250, while dormitory beds go for about HK$60 to HK$80, although more dormitories are available in the Mirador Arcade further up Nathan Rd.

Two places that offer dormitories in Chungking Mansions are the ever-popular *Travellers' Hostel* (☎ 2368-7710), A block, 16th floor, which has beds for HK$80; and the *New World Hostel* (☎ 2723-6352), A block, 6th floor, which has beds for HK$60. The following is a sampling of cheap guesthouses.

A Block, 16th floor: *Travellers' Hostel* (☎ 2368-7710), rooms without/with attached bath for HK$160/200

A Block, 15th floor: *Park Guesthouse* (☎ 2368-1689), clean and friendly and has rooms without/with attached bath for HK$100/150

A Block, 14th floor: *Hawaii Guesthouse* (☎ 2366-6127), rooms with attached bath for HK$180

A Block, 13th floor: *Capital Guesthouse* (☎ 2366-3455), rooms with attached bath from HK$230 to HK$260

A Block, 12th floor: *Peking Guesthouse* (☎ 2723-8320), friendly management and clean rooms without bath for HK$160 and with attached bath ranging from HK$200 to HK$320

A Block, 6th floor: *London Guesthouse* (☎ 2366-5010), singles from HK$160 to HK$180

A Block, 4th and 5th floors: *Chungking House* (☎ 2366-5362; fax 2721-3570), the most up-market place in Chungking Mansions has singles/twins for HK$322/437 all with attached bath

B Block, 17th floor: *Amar Guesthouse* (☎ 2368-4869), singles/twins without bath for HK$120/130 and singles/twins with attached bath for HK$150/170

B Block, 15th floor: *Carlton Guesthouse* (☎ 2721-0720), a friendly place with singles and twins for HK$200/300 with attached bath

B Block, 12th floor: *Hong Kong Guesthouse* (☎ 2723-7842), singles for HK$170 and twins for HK$250

B Block, 10th floor: *Kowloon Guesthouse* (☎ 2369-9802), a large place with a number of room types. Singles without/with attached bath for HK$125/160 and triples for HK$350

C Block, 16th floor: *Tom's Guesthouse* (☎ 2367-9258), clean, friendly and popular, with singles/twins with attached bath for $HK250/350. They also have rooms on the 16th floor of B Block and 8th floor of A Block

C Block, 16th Floor: *Garden Guesthouse* (☎ 2368-0981), also an excellent place, with rooms with attached bath for $HK150

C Block, 13th floor: *Osaka Guesthouse* and *New Grand Guesthouse* (☎ 2311-1702), same owner, all rooms come with attached bath and range from HK$180 to HK$300

C Block, 7th floor: *Chungking Guesthouse* (☎ 2368-0981), rooms with attached bath for HK$150

C Block, 6th floor: *New Brother's Guesthouse* (☎ 2724-0135), rooms with/without attached bath for HK$180/$250

Mirador Arcade You can avoid the stigma of staying in Chungking Mansions by checking out Mirador Arcade at 58 Nathan Rd. There are numerous places here and it's a bit cleaner and less crowded.

14th floor: *Man Hing Lung* (☎ 2722-0678; fax 2311-6669), flat F2. All rooms come equipped with private bath, air-conditioning and TV, and this is our personal favourite in Mirador. Singles are HK$200 to HK$280 and twins are HK$300 to HK$360. If you arrive by yourself and want a roommate, the management can put you in with another traveller thus cutting the bill by half. The *Wide Sky Hotel* (☎ 2312-1880; fax 2317-6546), flat F3 on the same floor, has rooms from HK$300 to HK$450

13th floor: *New Garden Hotel* (☎ 2311-2523; fax 2368-5241), flat F4, has rooms without bath for HK$120 and HK$150, and with attached bath for HK$200. It's one of the largest guesthouses in the building and is quite popular

HONG KONG & MACAU

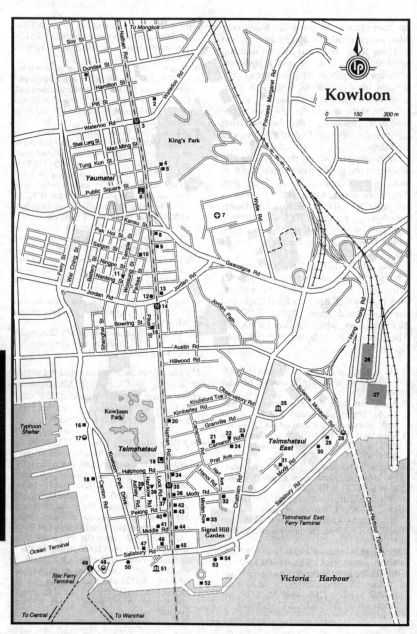

Kowloon

0   150   300 m

KOWLOON

PLACES TO STAY
1 STB Hostel
2 YMCA International House
4 Booth Lodge
5 Caritas Bianchi Lodge
8 Eaton Hotel
9 Nathan Hotel
10 Evergreen Hotel
13 New Lucky Mansions
15 Shamrock Hotel
16 Royal Pacific Hotel
18 Omni Marco Polo Hotel
20 Tourists Home
21 Star Guesthouse
22 International Hotel
23 Park Hotel
24 Lee Garden Guesthouse
29 Nikko Hotel
30 Grand Stanford Harbour View Hotel
31 Royal Garden Hotel

32 Lyton House Inn & Frank's Mody House
33 Mariners' Club
34 Golden Crown Court
36 Mirador Arcade
37 Hyatt Regency
41 Kowloon Hotel
42 Holiday Inn Golden Mile
43 Chungking Mansions
44 Imperial Hotel
45 Sheraton
46 The Peninsula
47 YMCA Salisbury
52 Regent Hotel
54 New World Hotel

PLACES TO EAT
11 Night Market
38 Java Rijsttafel
39 Orchard Court

OTHER
3 Yaumatei MTR Station
6 Tin Hau Temple

7 Queen Elizabeth Hospital
12 Yue Hwa Chinese Products
14 Jordan MTR Station
17 China Hong Kong City (Ferries to China)
19 Kowloon Mosque
25 Science Museum
26 Hunghom Railway Station
27 Coliseum
28 Cross-Harbour Bus Stop
35 Tsimshatsui MTR Station
40 China Travel Service
48 Star Ferry Bus Terminal
49 HKTA Office
50 Hong Kong Cultural Centre; Museum of Art
51 Space Museum
53 New World Centre

12th floor: *Ajit Guesthouse* (☎ 2369-1201), flat F3, is very friendly and clean, with singles without bath from HK$160 to HK$200 and twins with attached bath for HK$250

5th floor: *Loi Loi Guesthouse* (☎ 2367-2909; fax 2723-6168), flat A2, is clean and fairly new, with twins/triples with attached bath for HK$280/390

4th floor: *Star Guesthouse* (☎ 2311-9095; fax 2312-0085), flat F2B, has rooms without bath for HK$170 and HK$190, and with attached bath for HK$200

3rd floor: *Lily Garden Guesthouse* (☎ 2366-2575; fax 2312-7681), flat A9, rooms are HK$200 with shared bath and HK$250 with attached bath

Dormitories are also available in the following places:

Ajit Guesthouse (☎ 2369-1201), 12th floor, flat F3, beds for HK$50
Blue Lagoon Guesthouse (☎ 2721-0346), 3rd floor, flat F2, beds for HK$60
City Guesthouse (☎ 2724-2612), 9th floor, beds for HK$60

New Garden Hotel (☎ 2311-2523), 13th floor, flat F4, probably the best place for dormitories, beds for HK$50 and HK$60
Star Guesthouse (☎ 2311-9095), 4th floor, flat F2B, beds for HK$60

New Lucky Mansions Located at 300 Nathan Rd (entrance on Jordan Rd) in Yaumatei, this is a better neighbourhood than most of the other guesthouses, but it's also a bit more expensive.

The *Great Wall Hotel* (☎ 2388-7645; fax 2388-0084), also known as *Sky Guesthouse*, is on the 14th floor. It has singles/twins for HK$350/400.

The *Ocean Guesthouse* (☎ 2385-0125; fax 2782-6441), 11th floor, also has singles/twins for HK$350/400.

The *Hilton Inn* (☎ 2770-4880; fax 2771-1382), 3rd floor, has rooms with attached bath for HK$280.

Other Cheapies YMCA Salisbury (☎ 2369-2211; fax 2739-9315) at 41 Salisbury Rd,

Tsimshatsui, has very pricey rooms, but is attractive to travellers because of the four person dorm rooms on the 5th floor. At HK$190 per person, it's more than you'd pay for a bed on Nathan Rd, but the extra yuan is well worth it. Each room has its own bathroom and it's very clean. You can book a bed by fax or phone, but there are restrictions; guests can only stay for seven consecutive nights and they will not accept people who have already been in Hong Kong for 10 days.

On the 5th floor of Golden Crown Court, at 66-70 Nathan Rd, Tsimshatsui, the *Wah Tat Guesthouse* (☎ 2366-6121; fax 2311-7195) is spotlessly clean and highly recommended. Singles/twins cost HK$250/300 and up, but you can bargain if business is slow. It's hidden in the back part of the building.

The *STB Hostel* (☎ 2710-9199; fax 2385-0153), 2nd floor, Great Eastern Mansion, 255-261 Reclamation St, Mongkok, is run by the Student Travel Bureau. Dorm beds are HK$160, twins are HK$460 and triples are HK$540. To get there, go to Yaumatei MTR station and take the Pitt St exit.

Star Guesthouse (☎ 2723-8951; fax 2311-2275), 6th floor, 21 Cameron Rd, is immaculately clean. *Lee Garden Guesthouse* (☎ 2367-2284) is on the 8th floor, D Block, 36 Cameron Rd, close to Chatham Rd. Both guesthouses are run by the same owner, the charismatic Charlie Chan. Rooms with shared bath are HK$250 and with private bath they jump to HK$350 to HK$380.

The Lyton building, 32-40 Mody Rd, has two decent guesthouses, but neither is cheap. *Lyton House Inn* (☎ 2367-3791; 2724-2685) is on the 6th floor of Block 2 and costs HK$500 for a twin. *Frank's Mody House* (☎ 2724-4113) is on the 7th floor of Block 4 and has twins for HK$400 to HK$550.

Tourists Home (☎ 2311-2622; 2368-8580) is on the 6th floor, G Block, Champagne Court, 16 Kimberley Rd. Twins are from HK$380 to HK$430. All rooms have an attached private bath.

Kowloon – Hotels

Mid-range hotels cost generally between HK$550 and HK$1200 and include the following:

Booth Lodge (☎ 2771-9266; fax 2385-1140), 11 Wing Sing Lane, Yaumatei, 54 rooms, twins HK$644 to HK$736 – run by the Salvation Army

Caritas Bianchi Lodge (☎ 2388-1111; fax 2770-6669), 4 Cliff Rd, Yaumatei, singles HK$720, twins HK$820

Caritas Lodge (☎ 2339-3777; fax 2338-2864), 134 Boundary St, Mongkok (not far from the Prince Edward MTR station), singles/twins HK$540/620

Evergreen Hotel (☎ 2780-4222; fax 2385-8584), 42-52 Woosung St, Yaumatei, singles HK$600, twins HK$700, triples HK$820

Holy Carpenter Guesthouse (☎ 2362-0301; fax 2362-2193), 1 Dyer Ave, Hunghom, twins HK$640, triples HK$816

Imperial (☎ 2366-2201; fax 2311-2360), 30-34 Nathan Rd, Tsimshatsui, 215 rooms, twins HK$950, suites HK$1100

International (☎ 2366-3381; fax 2369-5381), 33 Cameron Rd, Tsimshatsui, 89 rooms, twins HK$782, suites HK$1012

Mariners' Club (☎ 2368-8261), 11 Middle Rd, Tsimshatsui, a hostel for sailors and members only. Singles/twins are HK$540/680

Nathan (☎ 2388-5141; fax 2770-4262), 378 Nathan Rd, Yaumatei, 186 rooms, twins HK$1250, suites HK$1500

Shamrock (☎ 2735-2271; fax 2736-7354), 223 Nathan Rd, Yaumatei, 148 rooms, singles HK$750, twins HK$850, and suites HK$1170

YMCA International House (☎ 2771-9111; fax 2771-5238), 23 Waterloo Rd, Yaumatei, 333 rooms, twins are priced at HK$958, suites HK$1430

YWCA Anne Black Guesthouse (☎ 2713-9211; fax 2761-1269), badly located near Pui Ching and Waterloo Rds in Mongkok. The official address is 5 Man Fuk Rd, up a hill behind a Caltex petrol station. There are 169 rooms for women only. Singles without bath are HK$393 and twins with attached bath are HK$595.

You can get as much as 30% off rooms in the more expensive hotels by booking through a travel agency. Some of the better known Kowloon hotels in the top-end category are:

SHAUN McVICAR

DIANA MAYFIELD

The South-West
Top: Spectacular scenery on the Li River near Guilin (Guangxi Province).
Bottom: Cabbage and rice paddies on the outskirts of Kunming (Yunnan Province).

JULIET COOMBE/LA BELLE AURORE

CHRIS TAYLOR

CHRIS TAYLOR

The South-West
Top: A scene from the Shaping Market near Dali (Yunnan Province).
Bottom Left: The rugged karst mountains of the Yangshou region (Guangxi Province).
Bottom Right: Making bamboo steamers in Ruili (Yunnan Province).

Eaton (☎ 2782-1818; fax 277-10043), 380 Nathan Rd, Yaumatei, 393 rooms, singles HK$1550, twins HK$1980, suites HK$2700

Grand Stanford Harbour View, (☎ 2721-5161; fax 2723-5121), 70 Mody Rd, Tsimshatsui East, 579 rooms, singles HK$2350 to HK$2550 (twins add HK$150), suites HK$4800 to HK$13,000

Harbour Plaza (☎ 2621-3188; fax 2621-3311), 20 Tak Fung St, Hunghom, 415 rooms, singles HK$2200 to HK$2400, twins HK$2350 to HK$2550, suites ranging from HK$4500 to HK$29,500

Holiday Inn Golden Mile (☎ 2369-3111; fax 2369-0948), 46-52 Nathan Rd, Tsimshatsui, singles are HK$2200 to HK$2450, twins are HK$2300 to HK$2550, suites are HK$5700 to HK$10,000

Hyatt Regency (☎ 2311-1234; fax 2739-8701), 67 Nathan Rd, Tsimshatsui, 723 rooms, singles and twins HK$1680 to HK$2180, suites HK$3280 to HK$7880

Kowloon (☎ 2369-8698; fax 2301-2668), 19-21 Nathan Rd, Tsimshatsui, 736 rooms, singles HK$1300 to HK$2300, twins HK$2400 to HK$2500, suites HK$3400

Kowloon Shangri-La (☎ 2721-2111; fax 2723-8686), 64 Mody Rd, Tsimshatsui East, 717 rooms, twins HK$2700 to HK$3150, suites HK$3850 to HK$17,000

New World (☎ 2369-4111; fax 2721-8594), 22 Salisbury Rd, Tsimshatsui, 543 rooms, singles HK$2200 to HK$2500, twins HK$2350 to HK$2600, suites HK$3300 to HK$5000

Nikko Hongkong (☎ 2739-1111; fax 2311-3122), 72 Mody Rd, Tsimshatsui East, 461 rooms, twins HK$2200 to HK$3100, suites HK$5000 to HK$13,500

Omni Marco Polo (☎ 2113-0888; fax 2113-0111), Harbour City, Canton Rd, Tsimshatsui, 440 rooms, singles HK$1950 to HK$2200, twins HK$2050 to HK$2300, suites HK$3450 to HK$7500

Park (☎ 2366-1371; fax 2739-7259), 61-65 Chatham Rd South, Tsimshatsui, 430 rooms, singles HK$1600 to HK$2100, twins HK$1700 to HK$2200, suites HK$2600 to HK$4800

Peninsula (☎ 2366-6251; fax 2722-4170), Salisbury Rd, Tsimshatsui, 300 rooms, twins HK$3100, suites HK$7000 to HK$38,000

Regal Airport (☎ 2718-0333; fax 2718-4111), Sa Po Rd, Kowloon (next to the old airport), 389 rooms, singles HK$1900 to HK$2100, twins HK$2050 to HK$2250, suites HK$5000 to HK$8000

Regent (☎ 2721-1211; fax 2739-4546), Salisbury Rd, Tsimshatsui, 602 rooms, twins HK$2850 to HK$3850, suites HK$4650 to HK$26,600

Royal Garden (☎ 2721-5215; fax 2369-9976), 69 Mody Rd, Tsimshatsui East, 422 rooms, singles are HK$2300 to HK$2900, twins are HK$2450 to HK$3050, suites are HK$4000 to HK$11,000

Royal Pacific (☎ 2736-1188; fax 2736-1212), China Hong Kong City, 33 Canton Rd, Tsimshatsui, 675 rooms, singles HK$1900 to HK$2300, twins HK$2100 to HK$2500, suites HK$3900 to HK$9800

Sheraton (☎ 2369-1111; fax 2368-1999), 20 Nathan Rd, Tsimshatsui, 798 rooms, singles HK$2500 to HK$3100, twins HK$2800 to HK$3400, suites HK$3900 to HK$9300

YMCA The Salisbury (☎ 2369-2211; fax 2739-9315), 41 Salisbury Rd, Tsimshatsui, singles HK$1030, twins HK$1150, suites HK$1700 to HK$2000

Hong Kong Island – Hostel

Ma Wui Hall (☎ 2817-5715), on top of Mt Davis on Hong Kong Island, offers stunning views and is the most accessible of the YHA hostels. The drawback is that it's 'centrally located' in the relative sense only. From the Star ferry pier in Central it's still a good hour's journey, but travellers say it's 'almost worth it'.

Before embarking on the trek, ring up first to be sure a bed is available. To get there, take bus Nos 5B or 47 to the 5B terminus at Felix Villas on Victoria Rd. Walk back 100m and look for the YHA sign. You've then got a 20 to 30 minute climb up the hill. Don't confuse Mt Davis Path with Mt Davis Rd! There are 112 beds here and the nightly cost is HK$65, or $95 for non-members. Family rooms are HK$260. You can buy a a YHA card at the hostel for HK$180. The hostel is open from 7 am to 11 pm.

Hong Kong Island – Guesthouses

Most of the cheaper guesthouses on Hong Kong Island are in Causeway Bay. The *Wang Fat Hostel* (☎ 2895-1015) is on the 3rd floor, flat A2, 47 Paterson St, just above the Daimaru department store. Rooms without bath are HK$280, and with attached bath HK$400. It's a friendly place and the owner speaks English.

Noble Hostel (☎ 2576-6148; 2577-0847) is surely one of the best guesthouses in Hong Kong, but it is often full. Due to popular demand, the owner has expanded to five locations. The main office is at flat A3, 17th floor, 27 Paterson St (above Daimaru). Singles/twins with shared bath are HK$260/340 and with attached bath are HK$400/450.

At the same address on Paterson St, the *Wonderful Well* (☎ 2577-1278; fax 2577-6639) is at flat A5 on the 4th floor and has twins without bath for HK$380 and with attached bath for HK$420. On the 11th floor at flat A1, the *Kai Woo Hung Wan Co* (☎ 2890-5813; fax 2890-5725) has singles/twins for HK$420/450.

Causeway Bay Guest House (☎ 2895-2013; fax 2895-2355) is at 44 A-D Leighton Rd. You can enter the building at Leighton Lane, around the corner, and the guesthouse is at flat B, 1st floor. Singles/twins/triples are HK$400/500/600 with attached bath.

The *Emerald House* (☎ 2577-2368; fax 2894-9082) is also on the 1st floor, at 44 Leighton Rd. It has clean rooms with private bath and round beds (no kidding) for HK$450. Enter the building from Leighton Lane just around the corner.

The *Phoenix Apartments*, at 70 Lee Garden Hill Rd, Causeway Bay (look for the New Phoenix shopping centre on the ground floor), has a number of elegant and reasonably priced guesthouses. The catch here is that most are short-time hotels, where rooms are rented by the hour. One hotel proudly advertises 'Avoidance of Publicity & Reasonable Rates'. Nevertheless, rooms are available for overnighters, and as long as the sheets have been changed recently it's not a bad place to stay.

One of the cheaper options is the *Wah Lai Villa Guesthouse* (☎ 2576-2768), with rooms (only one bed) for HK$500, but only HK$240 if you want it for the night after 10 pm. There are a couple of similar places on Pak Sha Rd – they're very clean, but only

really worthwhile if you arrive late in the evening.

The *Famous Villa* (☎ 2577-8118), at 18 Pak Sha Rd on the 3rd floor, will give you a room with attached bath for HK$240 from midnight to 10 am.

Hong Kong Island – Hotels

In terms of mid-range hotels, there's even less available on Hong Kong Island than in Kowloon.

Figure on HK$500 at the mini-mum and up to HK$1200. Again, check with travel agents for discounts. Some places to check out include:

Harbour View International House (☎ 2802-1111; fax 2802-9063), at 4 Harbour Rd, Wanchai, 320 rooms, twins HK$1050 to HK$1450

New Cathay Hotel (☎ 2577-8211; fax 2576-9365), 17 Tung Lo Wan Rd, Causeway Bay, 225 rooms, singles HK$700 to HK$900, twins HK$900 to HK$1130

New Harbour (☎ 2861-1166; fax 2865-6111), 41-49 Hennessy Rd, Wanchai, 173 rooms, twins HK$1080 to HK$1480, suites HK$1780

YWCA – Garden View International (☎ 2877-3737; fax 2845-6263), 1 MacDonnell Rd, Central, 130 rooms, twins HK$880 to HK$900, suites HK$1512 to HK$1815

It's a good idea go through a travel agent for top-end hotels, where it is sometimes possible to get up to 30% off. Top-end hotels on Hong Kong Island include the following:

Bishop Lei International House (☎ 2868-0828; fax 2868-1551), 4 Robinson Rd, Mid-Levels, 227 rooms, singles HK$1080, twins HK$1280, suites HK$1880 to HK$2080

Century Hong Kong (☎ 2598-8888; fax 2598-8866), 238 Jaffe Rd, Wanchai, 516 rooms, twins HK$1850 to HK$2400, suites HK$4080 to HK$8280

Charterhouse (☎ 2833-5566; fax 2833-5888), 209-219 Wanchai Rd, Wanchai, 237 rooms, twins from HK$1400 to HK$1850, suites HK$2500

City Garden (☎ 2887-2888; fax 2887-1111), 9 City Garden Rd, North Point (Fortress Hill MTR station), 615 rooms, singles HK$1500, twins HK$2300, suites HK$3550

Conrad (☎ 2521-3838; fax 2521-3888), Pacific Place, 88 Queensway, Central, 513 rooms, twins HK$3050 to HK$3350, suites HK$5200 to HK$20,000

Empire (☎ 2866-9111; fax 2861-3121), 33 Hennessy Rd, Wanchai, 341 rooms, twins HK$1700 to HK$2100, suites HK$2700 to HK$6000

Excelsior (☎ 2894-8888; fax 2895-6459), 281 Gloucester Rd, Causeway Bay, 885 rooms, twins HK$2400 to HK$3200, suites HK$4200 to HK$5000

Furama Kempinski (☎ 2525-5111; fax 2845-9339), 1 Connaught Rd, Central, 517 rooms, twins HK$2500 to HK$3500, suites HK$3700 to HK$4000

Grand Hyatt (☎ 2588-1234; fax 2802-0677), 1 Harbour Rd, Wanchai, 572 rooms, singles HK$2900 to HK$3200, twins HK$3150 to HK$3450, suites HK$5500 to HK$25,000

Grand Plaza (☎ 2886-0011; fax 2886-1738), 2 Kornhill Rd, Quarry Bay, 248 rooms, twins HK$1500 to HK$2400, suites HK$2900 to HK$4500

Island Shangri-La (☎ 2877-3838; fax 2521-8742), Pacific Place, Supreme Court Rd, Admiralty, 565 rooms, twins HK$2700 to HK$3200, suites HK$5000 to HK$25,000

JW Marriot (☎ 2810-8366; fax 2841-3027), Pacific Place, 88 Queensway, Central, 604 rooms, singles HK$3150 to HK$3400, twins HK$2650 to HK$3950, suites HK$6000 to HK$23,000

Luk Kwok (☎ 2866-2166; fax 2866-2622), 72 Gloucester Rd, Wanchai, 198 rooms, singles HK$1700 to HK$2400, twins HK$1880 to HK$2180, suites HK$4000 to HK$6000

Mandarin Oriental (☎ 2522-0111; fax 2530-0180), 5 Connaught Rd, Central, 538 rooms, singles are HK$3300 to HK$4700, twins are HK$3850 to HK$4950, suites HK$5300 to HK$22,000

New World Harbour View (☎ 2802-8888; fax 2802-8833), 1 Harbour Rd, Wanchai, 862 rooms, singles HK$2700 to HK$3100, twins HK$3000 to HK$4950, suites HK$5300 to HK$18,800

Newton (☎ 2807-2333; fax 2807-1221), 218 Electric Rd, North Point (Fortress Hill MTR station), 362 rooms, twins HK$1400 to HK$1950, suites HK$3900

Park Lane (☎ 2890-3355; fax 2576-7853), 310 Gloucester Rd, Causeway Bay, 807 rooms, singles HK$2480 to HK$2980, twins HK$2780 to HK$3280, suites HK$4880 to HK$20,880

Regal Hongkong (☎ 2890-6633; fax 2881-0777), 88 Yee Wo St, Causeway Bay, 425 rooms, doubles and twins HK$1900 to HK$2650, suites HK$3800 to HK$15,000

Ritz-Carlton (☎ 2877-6666; fax 2877-6778), 3 Connaught Rd, Central, 216 rooms, singles HK$2850 to HK$3200, twins HK$3550 to HK$3850, suites HK$4500 to HK$19,000

South Pacific (☎ 2572-3838; fax 2893-7773), 23 Morrison Hill Rd, Wanchai, 293 rooms, singles are HK$1500 to HK$1850, twins are HK$1650 to HK$2000, suites are HK$3200 to HK$5300

Wesley (☎ 2866-6688; fax 2866-6613), 22 Hennessy Rd, Wanchai, 251 rooms, twins are HK$1250 to HK$2900

Wharney (☎ 2861-1000; fax 2529-5133), 57-33 Lockhart Rd, Wanchai, 332 rooms, singles HK$1700 to HK$1850, twins HK$1800 to HK$1950, suites HK$3000 to HK$4500

New Territories

The Hong Kong Youth Hostel Association (HKYHA; ☎ 2788-1638) operates several hostels in the New Territories. All are in fairly remote locations and it isn't practical to stay in these places and commute to the city. The only reason for staying would be to enjoy the countryside and do a bit of exploring and hiking. You'll need a YHA card – these can be bought at the hostels for HK$180 (bring a photo) – otherwise you'll have to pay the non-members' price. You are strongly advised to ring first to make sure a bed is available. The following four places are all YHA-operated:

Bradbury Lodge (☎ 2662-5123), Ting Kok Rd, Tai Mei Tuk, Tai Po, is the most easily reached hostel in the New Territories. There are 80 beds costing HK$55, and HK$85 for non-members, but no camp sites. Take the KCR to Tai Po Market station, then bus No 75K to Tai Mei Tuk (last stop). Walk south (the sea will be to your right) for four minutes to reach the hostel.

Sze Lok Yuen (☎ 2488-8188) is on Tai Mo Shan Rd. There are 92 beds costing HK$35 each, HK$60 for non-members, and 200 camp sites. Take the No 51 bus (Tsuen Wan Ferry Pier-Kam Tin) at Tsuen Wan MTR station and alight at Tai Mo

Shan Rd. Follow Tai Mo Shan Rd for about 45 minutes and, after passing the car park, turn on to a small concrete path on the right-hand side, which leads directly to the hostel. This is a good place from which to climb Tai Mo Shan, Hong Kong's highest peak. Because of the high elevation, it can get amazingly cold at night, so be prepared.

Pak Sha O Hostel (☎ 2328-2327), Hoi Ha Rd, Sai Kung East Peninsula, has 112 beds priced at HK$35 and HK$55 for non-members. There are camp sites for 150 tents that are HK$16 for members and HK$25 for non-members. Take bus No 92 from the Choi Hung Estate bus terminal and get off at the Sai Kung terminal. From Sai Kung, take bus No 94 (last one is at 7 pm) towards Wong Shek Pier, but get off at Ko Tong village. From there, walk 100m along Pak Tam Rd to find Hoi Ha Rd on the left. The walk along Hoi Ha Rd to the hostel is sign-posted and takes about 40 minutes.

Also on the Sai Kung Peninsula is *Brad-bury Hall* (☎ 2328-2458) in Chek Keng. There are 100 beds costing HK$35, HK$60 for non-members, plus 100 camp sites. From Choi Hung Estate bus terminal, take bus No 92 to the Sai Kung terminal. From Sai Kung, take bus No 94 (last one is at 7 pm) to Yellow Stone Pier, but get off at Pak Tam Au. There's a footpath at the side of the road leading to Chek Keng village (a 45 minute walk). The hostel is right on the harbour just facing the Chek Keng ferry pier. An alternative route is to take the ferry from Ma Liu Shui (adjacent to the Chinese University railway station) to Chek Keng ferry pier.

Outlying Islands
Cheung Chau There is a solid line-up of booths when you come off the ferry pier that offer flats and rooms for rent, some of which can be very reasonable, but you'll have to bargain, and the price doubles on weekends and holidays.

Cheung Chau has one upmarket place to stay, the *Warwick Hotel* (☎ 2981-0081; fax 2981-9741) with 70 rooms. Doubles cost HK$1190 on weekdays and weekends.

Lamma There are several places to stay in Yung Shue Wan. Right by the Yung Shue Wan ferry pier is the *Man Lai Wah Hotel* (☎ 2982-0220) where rooms cost HK$350 on weekdays, rising to HK$650 on weekends. *Lamma Vacation House* (☎ 2982-0427) is at 29 Main St and offers coffin-sized rooms for HK$150 or with attached bath for HK$250, and sea-view rooms for HK$350 – prices double on weekends.

On nearby Hung Shing Ye beach is *Concerto Inn* (☎ 2982-1668; fax 2982-0022), an upmarket place with rooms for HK$523 to HK$716 on weekdays, and HK$748 to HK$1023 on weekends.

Lantau As you exit the ferry in Silvermine Bay, turn right and head towards the beach. Here you'll find several hotels with sea views. One of the best deals around is the *Mui Wo Inn* (☎ 2984-1916; fax 2984-1916) with twins from HK$320 to HK$480 on weekdays, and HK$650 to HK$800 on weekends.

Top of the line is the *Silvermine Beach Hotel* (☎ 2984-8295; fax 2984-1907), which has twins ranging from HK$809 to HK$901.

There are two places to stay in Ngong Ping. The *SG Davis Youth Hostel* (☎ 2985-5610; 48 beds) costs HK$45 for YHA members and HK$65 for non-members. You can buy a YHA card at the hostel for HK$180. The hostel also has a camp site for 20 tents. The *Tea Garden Hotel* (☎ 2985-5161) has grotty singles with shared bath for HK$170 and better twin rooms with attached bath for HK$250.

PLACES TO EAT
Hong Kong offers incredible variety when it comes to food. You should at least once try dim sum, a uniquely Cantonese dish served for breakfast or lunch, but never dinner. Dim sum delicacies are normally steamed in a small bamboo basket. Typically, each basket contains four identical pieces, so four people would be an ideal number for a dim sum meal. You pay by the number of baskets you order. The baskets are stacked up on pushcarts and

rolled around the dining room. You choose whatever you like from the carts, so no menu is needed.

In Cantonese restaurants, tea is often served free of charge, or at most you'll pay HK$1 for a big pot which can be refilled indefinitely. On the other hand, coffee is seldom available except in western restaurants or coffee shops and is never free.

Kowloon

There are a lot of restaurants concentrated in the tourist area of Tsimshatsui.

Breakfast If your hotel doesn't serve breakfast, you may find it difficult to eat before 9 am, when most of the restaurants open. The window of the *Wing Wah Restaurant* (☎ 2721-2947) is always filled with great-looking cakes and pastries. It's at 21A Lock Rd near Swindon Bookstore and the Hyatt Regency. Either take away or sit down with some coffee or tea. Prices are very reasonable. Inexpensive Chinese food is also served and – a rare treat for a Hong Kong budget Chinese cafe – there is an English menu.

Just down the street is *Big John* (☎ 2739-6035) at 17 Lock Rd, where you can get good breakfasts for HK$20 to HK$30.

Deep in the bowels of *every* MTR station you can find a *Maxim's Cake Shop*. The cakes and pastries look irresistible, but don't sink your teeth into the creamy delights until you're back on the street as it is prohibited to eat or drink anything in the MTR stations or on the trains – you're liable for a HK$1000 fine if you do.

If you're looking for something a little more wholesome, try *Uncle Russ* for delicious muffins and coffee, located on the northern side of Peking Rd near the intersection with Canton Rd.

The cafeteria-style *Delifrance* has numerous outlets throughout Hong Kong and serves up fresh croissants for breakfast, as well as other delicious items. In Tsimshatsui you can find one in the Hyatt Arcade at 67 Nathan Rd and another in Carnarvon Plaza at 20 Carnarvon Rd.

To really appreciate what Hong Kong has to offer in the morning, one of the best places to have breakfast is at the *Harbourside* (☎ 2313-2405) in the Regent Hotel. The view is splendid, but it's not cheap; the buffet is HK$225. The *Peninsula Hotel* (☎ 2366-6251) is another elegant place for breakfast, or, if you get up late, try the afternoon tea.

If you're up before the aforementioned places open, *7-Eleven* operates 24 hours and does coffee, packaged breads and microwave food.

American *Planet Hollywood* (☎ 2377-7888), 3 Canton Rd, claims to be 'the galaxy's ultimate dining experience'. Never mind the food – this place wins awards for its knock-out decor, but it's not a good place if you're seeking some peace and quiet. Many people buy T-shirts as souvenirs.

Dan Ryan's Chicago Grill (☎ 2735-6111), Shop 200, Ocean Terminal, Harbour City, Canton Rd, Tsimshatsui, is a trendy spot with prices to match.

Chinese – Dim Sum This is normally served from around 11 am to 3 pm, but a few places have it available for breakfast. The following places are chosen for their reasonable prices:

Canton Court (☎ 2739-3311), Guangdong Hotel, 18 Prat Ave, Tsimshatsui, dim sum served from 7 am to 3 pm

Eastern Palace (☎ 2730-6011), 3rd floor, Omni The Hongkong Hotel, Shopping Arcade, Harbour City, Canton Rd, Tsimshatsui, dim sum served from 11.30 am to 3 pm

Harbour View Seafood (☎ 2722-5888), 3rd floor, Tsimshatsui Centre, 66 Mody Rd, Tsimshatsui East, dim sum served from 11 am to 5 pm

New Home (☎ 2366-5876), 19-20 Hanoi Rd, Tsimshatsui, dim sum from noon to 3.30 pm

North China Peking Seafood (☎ 2311-6689), 2nd floor, Polly Commercial Building, 21-23 Prat Ave, Tsimshatsui, dim sum from 11 am to 3 pm

Orchard Court (☎ 2317-5111), 1st & 2nd floors, Ma's Mansion, 37 Hankow Rd, Tsimshatsui, dim sum served from 11 am to 5 pm

Tai Woo (☎ 2369-9773), 14-16 Hillwood Rd, Yaumatei, dim sum from 11 am to 3 pm

Chinese – Street Stalls The cheapest place to enjoy authentic Chinese cuisine is the *Temple St Night Market* in Yaumatei. It starts at about 8 pm and begins to fade at 11 pm. There are also plenty of mainstream indoor restaurants with variable prices.

Fast Food *Oliver's* is on the ground floor of Hong Kong Pacific Centre, 28 Hankow Rd, and in the basement at 100 Nathan Rd. It's a great place for breakfast – bacon, eggs and toast. The sandwiches are equally excellent, although it gets crowded at lunch time.

McDonald's occupies key strategic locations in Tsimshatsui. Late-night restaurants are amazingly scarce in Hong Kong, so it's useful to know that two McDonald's in Tsimshatsui operate 24 hours a day: at 21A Granville Rd, and 12 Peking Rd. There is also a McDonald's at 2 Cameron Rd, and another in Star House just opposite the Star ferry pier. McDonald's is one of the cheapest places to eat in Hong Kong.

Domino's Pizza (☎ 2765-0683), Yue Sun Mansion, Hunghom, does not have a restaurant where you can sit down to eat. Rather, pizzas are delivered to your door within 30 minutes of phoning in your order. *Pizza Hut* has three outlets in Tsimshatsui, at Shop 22, Lower Basement, Silvercord Shopping Centre, Haiphong and Canton Rds, at Carnarvon Plaza, 20-20C Carnarvon Rd, and at Shop 008, Ocean Terminal, Harbour City, Canton Rd.

Indian The greatest concentration of cheap Indian restaurants is in Chungking Mansions on Nathan Rd. Despite the grotty appearance of the entrance to the Mansions, many of the restaurants are surprisingly plush inside. A meal of curried chicken and rice, or curry with chapattis and dhal, will cost around HK$30 per person.

The mezzanine floor has a number of places from the cheaper *Nepal Fast Food* to the more upmarket *Swagat* (☎ 2722-5350), although all are good value. The *Bismillah Fast Food* and *Sher-E-Punjab* are also on this floor, and have free delivery.

Upstairs in Chungking Mansions are many other places with better food and a more pleasant atmosphere. Prices are still low, with set meals from HK$40 or so, although these are often only available at lunch. The following places are worth a try:

Delhi Club (☎ 2368-1682), 3rd floor, one of the best and it offers free delivery
Islamabad Club (☎ 2721-5362), 4th floor, C block, Indian and Pakistani halal food
Royal Club Mess (☎ 2369-7680), 5th floor, D Block, Indian and vegetarian food, with free delivery
Taj Mahal Club Mess (☎ 2722-5454), 3rd floor, B Block, excellent

Elsewhere in Tsimshatsui, the excellent *Koh-I-Noor* (☎ 2368-3065) at 3-4 Peninsula Mansion, 16C Mody Rd, has a good selection of Mughal dishes, as well as vegetarian. In East Tsimshatsui, *Woodlands* (☎ 2369-3718) Shops 5 & 6, ground floor, Mirror Tower, 61 Mody Rd, specialises in vegetarian dishes.

For tandoori, *Gaylord* (2376-1001) 1st floor, 11 Ashley Centre, 23-25 Ashley Rd, is well known in Hong Kong, but it's also a bit more expensive than the other restaurants mentioned here.

Indonesian The *Java Rijsttafel* (☎ 2367-1230), ground floor, Han Hing Mansion, 38 Hankow Rd, Tsimshatsui, is a good place to enjoy a 'rijsttafel', literally meaning a rice table, for about HK$150 per person. This place packs out with Dutch expats.

The *Indonesian Restaurant* (☎ 2367-3287) at 66 Granville Rd also has good food.

Italian A great Italian restaurant is *Valentino* (☎ 2721-6449) at 16 Hanoi Rd. *The Pizzeria* (☎ 2369-8698, ext 3322) is an Italian eatery on the 2nd floor of the Kowloon Hotel at 19-21 Nathan Rd, Tsimshatsui.

For cheaper Italian food, try *Mario* (☎ 2735-7163) at Shop 018 and 024 in

Ocean Terminal, Harbour City, Canton Rd. One of the best Italian restaurants in Hong Kong, but pricey, is the *Mistral* (☎ 2721-5161) in Tsimshatsui East, located at Basement 2, Grand Stanford Harbour View Hotel, 70 Mody Rd.

Japanese Japanese restaurants are pretty expensive in Hong Kong, but if you're looking for good fast food, try *Yoshinoya* (☎ 2721-0719) at Level B1, 5 Cameron Rd, Tern Plaza, Tsimshatsui.

Korean There are several excellent and easily accessible Korean restaurants. One that gets top marks is the *Arirang* (☎ 2956-3288) at Shop 210, 2nd floor, The Gateway, 25 Canton Rd, Tsimshatsui.

Malaysian The *Singapore Restaurant* (☎ 2376-1282), 23 Ashley Rd, Tsimshatsui, does Malaysian-style cooking. It's coffee-shop style, but forget the decor because the food is excellent and cheap (by Hong Kong standards). It's open from 11 am until midnight.

Another place for reasonably priced meals is *Banana Leaf Curry House* (☎ 2721-4821), 3rd floor, Golden Crown Court, 68 Nathan Rd, Tsimshatsui.

Thai A reasonably priced and good Thai restaurant is *Royal Pattaya* (☎ 2366-9919), 9 Minden Ave, Tsimshatsui. They also have a vegetarian menu.

Vegetarian *Bodhi* (☎ 2739-2222), ground floor, 56 Cameron Rd, Tsimshatsui, is one of Hong Kong's biggest vegetarian restaurant chains. Try the tofu dishes made to look like meat.

A popular place for locals is the *Light Vegetarian Restaurant* (☎ 2384-2833) at Shop 1, ground floor, New Lucky House, 13 Jordan Rd. They also have dim sum starting at 11 am.

Self-Catering If you're looking for the best in cheese, bread and other imported delicacies, check out the delicatessen at

Oliver's on the ground floor of Ocean Centre on Canton Rd. There's also a number of supermarkets scattered about. A few in Tsimshatsui and Yaumatei to look for include:

Park'n Shop, south-western corner of Peking Rd and Kowloon Park Drive; 2nd basement, Silvercord Shopping Centre, 30 Canton Rd

Wellcome, inside the Dairy Farm Creamery (ice-cream parlour), 74-78 Nathan Rd; north-western corner of Granville and Carnarvon Rds

Yue Hwa Chinese Products, Basement, 301 Nathan Rd, Yaumatei (north-western corner of Nathan and Jordan Rds), both western products and Chinese exotica (tea bricks and flattened chickens)

Hong Kong Central
The place to go for reasonably priced eats and late-night revelry is the neighbourhood known as Lan Kwai Fong. However, it's such a conglomeration of pubs and all-night parties that it's covered in the Entertainment section.

Breakfast To save time and money, there are food windows adjacent to the Star ferry that open shortly after 6 am. It offers standard commuter breakfasts consisting of bread, rolls and coffee with no place to sit except on the ferry itself. As you face the ferry entrance, off to the right is a *Maxim's* fast-food outlet, also with no seats.

There are three outlets of *Oliver's Super Sandwiches* in Central that open at 7.30 am, where you can get a good breakfast. The one closest to the ferry is at Shop 104, Exchange Square Two, 8 Connaught Place (see Fast Food below for other addresses). *McDonald's* is also a cheap place for breakfast in Hong Kong. You can get good coffee at various stalls in the malls and in Lan Kwai Fong.

Of course, all the big hotels serve breakfast, often a sumptuous buffet.

Chinese – Dim Sum All of the following places are in the middle to lower price range:

Luk Yu Tea House (☎ 2523-5464), 26 Stanley St, Central, dim sum served from 7 am to 4.30 pm
Tai Woo (☎ 2524-5618), 15-19 Wellington St, Central, dim sum served from 11 am to 4.30 pm
Zen Chinese Cuisine (☎ 2845-4555), Lower ground 1, The Mall, Pacific Place, Phase I, 88 Queensway, Central, dim sum served from 11.30 am to 3.30 pm

Fast Food Like Kowloon, there's an abundance of fast-food places, both Chinese and western-style. In Central, you can find *Oliver's Super Sandwiches* at Shop 201-205, 2nd floor, Prince's Building, 10 Chater Rd and Shop 102, 1st floor, Hang Seng building, 77 Des Voeux Rd, as well as one in Exchange Square (see Breakfast above).

There are *McDonald's* at 38-44 D'Aguilar St in Lan Kwai Fong, at 37 Queen's Rd and at 30-32 Connaught Rd, and a *Pizza Hut* at B37-46, B1, Edinburgh Tower, The Landmark, 11-19A Queen's Rd.

French Wine, cheese, the best French bread and bouillabaisse can be found at *Papillon* (☎ 2526-5965), 8-13 Wo On Lane. This narrow lane intersects with D'Aguilar St (around No 17) and runs parallel to Wellington St.

Indian The ever-popular *Ashoka* (☎ 2524-9623) is at 57 Wyndham St. Next door in the basement at 57 Wyndham St is the excellent *Village Indian Restaurant* (☎ 2525-4117).

Greenlands (☎ 2522-6098), 64 Wellington St, is another superb Indian restaurant offering all-you-can-eat buffets.

Club Sri Lanka (☎ 2526-6559) in the basement of 17 Hollywood Rd (almost at the Wyndham St end) has great Sri Lankan curries. Their fixed-price all-you-can-eat deal is a bargain compared with most Hong Kong eateries.

Kosher The *Shalom Grill* (☎ 2851-6300), 2nd floor, Fortune House, 61 Connaught Rd, serves up kosher and Moroccan cuisine. If you're in the mood for a Jerusalem falafel or a Casablanca couscous, this is the place.

Vietnamese The *Saigon Beach* (☎ 2529-7823) at 66 Lockhart Rd, Wanchai, is a popular establishment that serves up good food for under HK$100 per person.

Self-Catering For imported delicacies, check out *Oliver's Super Sandwiches* (see the Fast Food and Breakfast sections). The largest stock of imported foods is found at the Seibu department store, Two Pacific Place, 88 Queensway, Central (Admiralty MTR station). Besides the imported cheeses, breads and chocolates, tucked into one corner is the Pacific Wine Cellar. This is *the* place to get wine, and there are frequent sales on wine by the case. It's open from 11 am until 8 pm.

Of special interest to chocolate addicts is *See's Candies* with two stores in Central: B66 Gloucester Tower, The Landmark, 11 Pedder St; and Shop 245, Two Pacific Place, 88 Queensway, Central (Admiralty MTR station).

ENTERTAINMENT

There's as much to do in Hong Kong in the evening as during the day, but none of it comes cheap. It's impossible to list all the bars and clubs here and the following is only a selection: it's best to check out reviews and listings in *bc magazine* or *HK Magazine*.

Kowloon

Rick's Cafe (☎ 2367-2939), Basement, 4 Hart Ave, is popular with the backpacker set.

Jouster II (☎ 2723-0022), Hart Ave Court, 19-23 Hart Ave, is a fun multistorey place with wild decor. Normal hours are noon to 3 am, except on Sunday, when it's open from 6 pm to 2 am. Happy hour is any time before 9 pm.

Ned Kelly's Last Stand (☎ 2376-0562), 11A Ashley Rd, open 11 am to 2 am, became famous as a real Australian pub complete with meat pies. Now it is known mainly for its Dixieland jazz and Aussie folk bands.

Amoeba Bar (☎ 2376-0389), 22 Ashley

Rd, is a local new-wave place with live music from around 9 pm, and it doesn't close until about 6 am.

The *Kangaroo Pub* (☎ 2376-0083), 1st and 2nd floors, 35 Haiphong Rd, Tsimshatsui, is an Aussie pub in the true tradition. This place does a good Sunday brunch.

Mad Dog's Pub (☎ 2301-2222), Basement, 32 Nathan Rd, is a popular Aussie-style pub. From Monday to Thursday it's open from 7 am until 2 am, but from Friday to Sunday it's 24 hour service.

Delaney's (☎ 2301-3980), 3-7A Prat Ave, has Irish food and folk music, and great beer.

It's also worthwhile to check out the places on Knutsford Terrace, a narrow alley north of Kimberley Rd, (which is one block north of Kimberley St). The easiest way to find it is through Observatory Rd, which runs west off Chatham Rd. *Bahama Mama's* (☎ 2368-2121), the *Big Tree Pub* (☎ 2721-1686) and *Knuts Bar* (☎ 2368-8702) are located here.

Hong Kong Island
Lan Kwai Fong Running off D'Aguilar St in Central is a narrow, L-shaped alley closed to cars. This is Lan Kwai Fong, and along with neighbouring streets and alleys it is Hong Kong's No 1 eating, drinking, dancing and partying venue. Prices range from economical to outrageous.

Club 64 (☎ 2523-2801), 12-14 Wing Wah Lane, is an old favourite, although it is not as good as in the past because the authorities no longer permit customers to sit outdoors.

As you face the entrance to Club 64, off to your left are some stairs (outside the building, not inside). Follow the stairs up to a terrace to find *Le Jardin Club* (☎ 2526-2717), 10 Wing Wah Lane. This is an excellent place to drink, relax and socialise.

Facing Club 64 again, look to your right to find *Bon Appetit* (☎ 2525-3553), a Vietnamese restaurant serving up reasonably priced meals. At the other end of the price range for Vietnamese food, *Indochine 1929* (☎ 2869-7399) offers an elegant dining ex-

perience in the California Tower, 2nd floor, at 30-32 D'Aguilar St.

The *Jazz Club* (☎ 2845-8477) is next door on the 2nd floor, in the California Entertainment building, and is a good place to go after dinner. Phone first to find out what bands are playing and if there's a cover charge.

Post 97 (☎ 2810-9333), 9 Lan Kwai Fong, is a very comfortable eating and drinking spot. During the daytime it's more of a coffee shop, and you can sit for hours to take advantage of the excellent rack of western magazines and newspapers. It can pack out at night, and the lights are dimmed to discourage reading at that time.

Both vegetarian and meat dishes can be found at *Koh-I-Noor* (☎ 2877-9706), an Indian restaurant. *Il Mercato* (☎ 2868-3068) steals the show for Italian food. Both are in the California Entertainment building. Prices are mid-range.

For good Japanese food that won't completely destroy your budget, try the *Yorohachi Japanese Restaurant* (☎ 2524-1251) on the ground floor at 5-6 Lan Kwai Fong. At 50 D'Aguilar St, *Supatra's* (☎ 2522-5073) is a popular place for Thai food and there is a bar downstairs.

The *California* (☎ 2521-1345), also in the California Entertainment building, is perhaps the most expensive bar mentioned in this book. Open from noon to 1 am, it's a restaurant by day, but there's disco dancing and a cover charge Wednesday to Sunday nights from 5 pm onwards.

The American Pie (☎ 2877-9779) is *the* locale for desserts in Hong Kong – not only pies, but all sorts of killer desserts like cakes, tarts, puddings and everything else containing sinful amounts of sugar, not to mention superb coffee and tea. It's also a good place for brunch, but if you're on a diet, don't even go near the place. It's an upmarket place charging upmarket prices. You'll find it on the 4th floor of the California Entertainment building.

Al's Diner (☎ 2869-1869), at 27-37 D'Aguilar St, is a Hong Kong institution. The place looks like it was lifted lock, stock, burgers and French fries from a New York diner of the 1950s. The food is fine, but none of it comes cheaply.

Schnurrbart (☎ 2523-4700) at 29 D'Aguilar St is a Bavarian-style pub. There are a couple of other German pubs on either side.

Oscar's (☎ 2804-6561), 2 Lan Kwai Fong, is a very posh cafe and bar combination. Specialities include pizza, pasta and sandwiches on pita bread. Food is available from noon until 11 pm and the place stays open until 2 am. Bring lots of money.

Central Just outside of Lan Kwai Fong is *Fringe Club* (☎ 2521-7251), 2 Lower Albert Rd. It's an excellent pub known for cheap beer and an avant-garde atmosphere. Live music is provided nightly by various local folk and rock musicians.

The *Mad Dogs Pub* (☎ 2810-1000), 1 D'Aguilar St, Central, is just off the trendy Lan Kwai Fong. It's a big British pub that serves pub grub and drinks.

The legendary *Hard Rock Cafe* (☎ 2537-0033), 11 Chater Rd, Central, has its happy hour from 3 to 7 pm.

LA Cafe (☎ 2526-6863), ground floor, Shop 2, Lippo Centre, 89 Queensway (near the Admiralty MTR station) has a large loyal following of late-night rowdies. The mostly Mexican luncheons are not to be discounted either – great guacamole, burritos and other Tex-Mex delights, but it isn't cheap.

The *Bull & Bear* (☎ 2525-7436), ground floor, Hutchison House, 10 Harcourt Rd, Central, is a British-style pub and gets pretty lively in the evening. It is open from 8 to 10.30 am, and again from 11 am to midnight.

Wanchai Most of the action is concentrated at the intersection of Luard and Jaffe Rds. Expect to pay a cover charge of HK$100 or more at most of the places mentioned below, although it's often cheaper or free for women, and may include one drink.

Joe Bananas (☎ 2529-1811), 23 Luard Rd, has become a trendy disco nightspot

and has no admission charge, but you may have to queue to get in. Happy hour is from 11 am until 9 pm (except Sunday) and the place stays open until around 5 am.

Neptune Disco (☎ 2528-3808), Basement, 54-62 Lockhart Rd, is the place to go to dance, and to accommodate the spillover crowd, there is *Neptune Disco II* (☎ 2865-2238), 98-108 Jaffe Rd.

In a similar vein, *The Big Apple Pub & Disco* (☎ 2529-3461), 20 Luard Rd, has live music. Another popular dancing place with live music, but more expensive, is *JJ's* (☎ 2588-1234), Grand Hyatt Hotel, 1 Harbour Rd, Wanchai.

At 54 Jaffe Rd just west of Fenwick St is *The Wanch* (☎ 2861-1621). It stands in sharp contrast to the more usual Wanchai scene of hard rock and disco. This is a very pleasant little folk-music pub with beer and wine at low prices, but it can get crowded. *Delaney's* (☎ 2804-2880) at One Capital Place, 18 Luard Rd, is an Irish pub that has great atmosphere and Irish music.

For the best in Hong Kong beer, *Bb's* (☎ 2529-7702), ground floor at 114-120 Lockhart Rd, features locally brewed ales from the South China Brewing Company.

Gay Pubs & Bars *Petticoat Lane* (☎ 2973-0642), 2 Tun Wo Lane, Central, is a friendly place for the local gay and lesbian scene, although it's dropped a little in popularity. It's above Lyndhurst Terrace near the pedestrian escalator that goes up to Mid-Levels.

FLEX, at 7 Glenealy Rd, was Hong Kong's newest and trendiest gay bar at the time of writing. *Secret Party*, at 6F All-ways Centre, 468 Jaffe Rd, Causeway Bay, attracts a mostly lesbian crowd. Other options on Hong Kong Island include:

CE Top (☎ 2544-3581), 9/F 37-43 Cochrane St, Central
Club 97 (☎ 2810-9333), 9 Lan Kwai Fong, Central
Garage (☎ 2542-1488), 35 Peel St, Central
Propoganda (☎ 2868-1316), 1 Hollywood Rd, Central
Zip (☎ 2523-3595), 2 Glenealy Rd, Central (no sign)

THINGS TO BUY

It's very easy in Hong Kong to decide suddenly that you need all sorts of consumer goods you don't really need at all. Try not to let the flashy stores tempt you into an uncontrollable buying binge.

Hong Kong resembles one gigantic shopping mall, but a quick look at price tags should convince you that the city is not quite the bargain it's cracked up to be. Imported goods like Japanese-made cameras and electronic gadgets can be bought for roughly the same price in many western countries. However, what makes Hong Kong shine is the variety – if you can't find it in Hong Kong, then you don't need it.

The HKTA advises tourists to shop where they see the HKTA red logo on display. This means that the shop is an 'ordinary member' of the HKTA. From our experience, many of the 'ordinary members' charge high prices for rude service, while many non-members are quite all right. That said, the free *Official Shopping Guide,* published by the HKTA and available at their outlets, is very useful, especially if you're looking for a specific item.

The worst neighbourhood for shopping happens to be the place where most tourists shop. Tsimshatsui, the tourist ghetto of Kowloon, is the most likely place to be cheated. Notice that none of the cameras or other big ticket items have price tags. This is *not* common practice elsewhere in Hong Kong. If you go out to the Chinese neighbourhoods where the locals shop, you'll find price tags on everything.

Clothing is the best buy in Hong Kong. All the cheap stuff comes from China and most is decent quality, but check zippers and stitching carefully – there is some real junk around. You'll find the cheapest buys at the street markets at Tong Choi St in Mongkok and Apliu St in Shamshuipo.

Another good place for cut-rate clothes is the mezzanine floor of Chungking Mansions (not the ground floor). Better quality stuff is found in Tsimshatsui on the eastern end of Granville Rd. Two Chinese chain stores with Italian names, Giordano's and Bossini, offer quality clothing at reasonable prices. In Central, the two alleys known as Li Yuen St East and Li Yuen St West also have some bargains.

For these cheapo places, however, you can't try on the clothes, so bring along a tape measure. It's a bit frustrating to find a great deal on a pair of jeans only to find later you can't get them past your hips.

Yue Hwa Chinese Products at 301 Nathan Rd, Yaumatei (corner of Nathan and Jordan Rds) is a good place to pick up everyday consumer goods and one of the best places to get eyeglasses made. It's also a good place to pick up Chinese herbal medicine and other things Chinese you might have missed on the mainland.

Sometimes it's easier to find the quintessential Chinese product in Hong Kong than it is in mainland China. Try the Chinese Arts and Crafts stores that have branches in Kowloon and on Hong Kong Island. There's one at Star House (you can't miss the sign outside) at 3 Salisbury Rd in Tsimshatsui and one in Central on the ground floor, Prince's building, 3 Des Voeux Rd.

You might find cheaper mainland souvenirs at the Yue Hwa stores or CRC department stores. There's a CRC in the Chiao Shang building, 92-104, Queen's Rd, Central. For Chinese retro, both pre and post-1949, Shanghai Tang, the brainchild of maverick entrepreneur, David Tang is one of the most fashionable (and expensive) places to shop. It's worthwhile checking out just for the decor, on the ground floor, Pedder Building, 8 Theatre Lane, in Central.

If you're looking for the real thing, as in Mao badges and other cast-offs, try the street markets up near Hollywood Rd on Lascar Row, otherwise known as Cat Street. This is also the area to look for antiques.

The Golden Shopping Centre, Basement, 146-152 Fuk Wah St, Shamshuipo, has the cheapest collection of desktop computers, as does the New Capital Computer Plaza at 85-95 Un Chau St. You can find these places easily from the Shamshuipo MTR station. Another good place to explore is Mongkok Computer Centre on the corner of Nelson and Fa Yuen Sts in Mongkok.

For laptop computers, the best shopping centre in Kowloon is Star Computer City on the 2nd floor of Star House, at 3 Salisbury Rd, near the Star ferry, Tsimshatsui. Prices are generally cheaper in Kowloon, but on Hong Kong Island you can find a concentration of computer shops in Windsor House, Great George St, Causeway Bay, and at the Hong Kong Computer City at 298 Hennessy Rd, Wanchai.

If it's a camera you need, don't even waste your time on Nathan Rd in Tsimshatsui. Photo Scientific (☎ 2522-1903), 6 Stanley St, Central, is the favourite of Hong Kong's resident professional photographers. But if you're in a hurry and want to buy in Tsimshatsui, the best seem to be Kimberley Camera Company (☎ 2721-2308) and David Chan (☎ 2723-3886) located in Champagne Court, 16 Kimberley Rd. You can also find used cameras and lenses here.

Apliu St in Shamshuipo has the best collection of electronics shops selling personal stereos, CD players and the like.

HMV (☎ 2302-0122) at 12 Peking Rd in Tsimshatsui has the largest collection of CDs in Hong Kong, and prices are very reasonable. There is another branch on the 10th floor of Windsor House, Great George St, Causeway Bay, and one at Shop 107-108A, Swire House, in Central. KPS is also a good chainstore for discounted CDs and tapes with branches around the city – most convenient is the shop in the basement of the Silvercord Shopping Centre on Canton Rd, Tsimshatsui.

Tower Records (☎ 2506-0811), 7th floor, Shop 701, Times Square, Matheson St, Causeway Bay, also has a good CD collection.

Flying Ball Bicycle Shop (☎ 2381-5919), 201 Tung Choi St (near Prince Edward MTR station), Mongkok, is the best bike shop in Asia.

Hong Kong is a good place to pick up a decent backpack, sleeping bag, tent and other gear for hiking, camping and travelling. Mongkok is by far the best neighbourhood to look for this stuff, although there are a couple of odd places in nearby Yaumatei.

Finally, if you want to see a good shopping mall where the locals go, visit Cityplaza in Quarry Bay. Take the MTR to the Tai Koo station.

GETTING THERE & AWAY

Air

Hong Kong is a good place to buy discounted air tickets, but watch out – there are swindlers in the travel business. The most common trick is a request for a non-refundable deposit on an air ticket. So you pay a deposit for the booking, but when you go to pick up the tickets they say the flight is no longer available, but there is another flight at a higher price, sometimes 50% more! On the other hand, many travel agencies will simply not make a booking until you've paid a deposit. That's why it pays to go with a reputable agency.

The best way is not to pay a deposit, but rather to pay for the ticket in full and get a receipt clearly showing that there is no balance due and that the full amount is refundable if no ticket is issued.

Tickets are normally issued the next day after booking, but for the really cheapie tickets (actually group tickets) you must pick these up yourself at the airport from the 'tour leader' (whom you will never see again once you've got the ticket).

One note of caution: when you get the ticket from the tour leader, check it carefully. Occasionally there are errors, such as being issued a ticket with the return portion valid for only 60 days when you paid for a ticket valid for one year.

You can generally get a good idea of what fares are available by looking in the classified section of the *South China Morning Post* newspaper, where courier trips are also advertised. Some budget fares available in Hong Kong follow, but please note that these are discounted fares and may have various restrictions upon their use:

Destination	One Way (HK$)	Return (HK$)
Auckland	3600	5300
Bangkok	750	1500
Beijing	1500	2990
Darwin	2900	4100
Frankfurt	2650	4350
Jakarta	1500	3000
London	2600	4500
Los Angeles	2350	4650
Manila	680	1280
New York	2800	4390
Seoul	1200	1900
Singapore	1100	2200
Sydney	3500	5220
Taipei	800	1250
Tokyo	1600	3200

If you're planning to fly to a destination in China, you can also book tickets in Hong Kong leaving from Guangzhou or Shenzhen that are cheaper than flying out of Hong Kong. CAAC runs numerous direct flights between Hong Kong and every major city in China. Many of these flights are technically called 'charter flights'. It's important to know if your flight is designated a 'charter' because it means that the

tickets have fixed-date departures and are nonrefundable.

The table at the bottom of the page shows one way fares between China and Hong Kong on CAAC, and flights marked with an asterisk are 'charters'.

You can purchase a ticket from a travel agent or CAAC itself. Travel agents seldom give discounts on CAAC tickets because CAAC usually charges the agents almost full fare. This is starting to change as China's airline industry undergoes reform, especially for popular routes like Hong Kong-Shanghai and Hong Kong-Beijing so it's advisable to check in the newspaper and with travel agents. The most convenient CAAC ticketing offices in Hong Kong are in the airline list later in this section.

It is possible to buy all of your CAAC tickets from CTS in Hong Kong (both international and domestic) and even from some non-Chinese airlines that have reciprocal arrangements with CAAC. While this should work OK for international flights, this is generally *not* a good idea for Chinese domestic flights, unless you are certain your travel plans are not going to change, because it is almost impossible to get a refund on tickets issued outside of

One Way Air Fares – Hong Kong to China

Destination	Fare (HK$)	Destination	Fare (HK$)
Beihai*	1350	Luoyang*	1980
Beijing	2530	Meixian*	1150
Changchun*	2600	Nanchang*	1650
Changsha*	1480	Nanjing*	1950
Chengdu	2400	Nanning*	1400
Chongqing	2150	Ningbo	1630
Dalian	2600	Qingdao	2190
Fuzhou	1560	Shanghai	1730
Guangzhou	530	Shantou	1080
Guilin*	1340	Shenyang	2910
Guiyang*	1550	Taiyuan*	2180
Haikou*	1310	Tianjin	2450
Hangzhou	1560	Wuhan*	1650
Harbin*	2600	Xi'an	2080
Hefei*	1690	Xiamen	1270
Huangshan*	1750	Zhanjiang*	1220
Ji'nan*	2280	Zhengzhou*	2150
Kunming	1640		
Lanzhou*	1980	* charter flight	

China. Even if Hong Kong is now part of China, it's still two systems, as the government is fond of saying.

Dragonair typically charges HK$100 less than CAAC on one way tickets, and double that amount for round-trip tickets, although again it's wise to check around. Dragonair has flights from Hong Kong to 14 cities in China: Beijing, Changsha, Chengdu, Chongqing, Dalian, Guilin, Haikou, Hangzhou, Kunming, Nanjing, Ningbo, Qingdao, Shanghai, Tianjin, Xiamen and Xi'an.

In Hong Kong, any travel agent with a computer can book you onto a Dragonair flight, but you can contact the ticketing offices of Dragonair directly (see the airline list below). Within China, Dragonair tickets can be bought from CITS or a number of Dragonair representatives listed in this book.

Airport departure tax is HK$100, but you're excused from paying if you can convince them that you're under age 12. If departing by ship, departure tax is HK$26, but it's included in the purchase price of the ticket.

There are often horribly long queues at immigration, and more than a few travellers have missed their flights because of this. On departure, allow yourself an hour to clear immigration. The problem seems to be most acute during lunch hour, when there are insufficient staff to handle the stampede.

You need to reconfirm your onward or return fight if you break your trip in Hong Kong. This can be accomplished at one of the following airline offices:

Aeroflot
 (☎ 2537-2611) New Henry House, 10 Ice House St, Central
Air Canada
 (☎ 2522-1001) Room 1002, Wheelock House, 20 Pedder St, Central
Air France
 (☎ 2524-8145) Room 2104, Alexandra House, 7 Des Voeux Rd, Central
Air India
 (☎ 2522-1176) 10th floor, Gloucester Tower, 11 Pedder St, Central

Air Lanka
 (☎ 2521-0708) Room 602, Peregrine Tower, Lippo Centre, 89 Queensway, Central
Air New Zealand
 (☎ 2524-9041) Suite 902, 3 Exchange Square, 8 Connaught Place, Central
Air Niugini
 (☎ 2524-2151) Room 705, Century Square, 1-13 D'Aguilar St, Central
All Nippon Airways
 (☎ 2810-7100) Room 2512, Pacific Place, 88 Queensway, Central
Ansett Australia Airlines
 (☎ 2527-7883) Alexandra House, 7 Des Voeux Rd, Central
Asiana Airlines
 (☎ 2523-8585) Gloucester Tower, The Landmark, 11 Pedder St, Central
Biman Bangladesh
 (☎ 2721-5393) 207 Houston Centre, 63 Mody Rd, Tsimshatsui East
British Airways
 (☎ 2868-0303; information 2868-0768) 30th floor, Alexandra House, 7 Des Voeux Rd, Central; (☎ 2368-9255) Room 112, Royal Garden Hotel, 69 Mody Rd, Tsimshatsui East
CAAC
 (☎ 2973-3666) ground floor, 10 Queen's Rd, Central; (☎ 2739-0022) ground floor, 1 Mody Rd, Tsimshatsui
Canadian Airlines International
 (☎ 2868-3123) ground floor, Swire House, 9-25 Chater Rd, Central
Cathay Pacific
 (☎ 2747-1888) ground floor, Swire House, 9-25 Chater Rd, Central; Sheraton Hotel, 20 Nathan Rd, Tsimshatsui
China Airlines (Taiwan)
 ground floor, St George's Building, Ice House St and Connaught Rd, Central; (☎ 2868-2299) G5-6 Tsimshatsui Centre, Tsimshatsui East
Continental Micronesia
 (☎ 2525-7759) Room M1, New Henry House, 10 Ice House St, Central
Delta Airlines
 (☎ 2526-5875) Pacific Place, 88 Queensway, Central
Dragonair
 (☎ 2868-6777) Room 601-603, 6/Fl Wheelock House, 20 Pedder St, Central
Garuda Indonesia
 (☎ 2840-0000) 2nd floor, Sing Pao Centre, 8 Queen's Rd, Central
Japan Airlines
 (☎ 2523-0081) 20th floor, Gloucester Tower, 11 Pedder St, Central

Japan Asia
(☎ 2521-8102) 20th floor, Gloucester Tower, 11 Pedder St, Central

Korean Air
(☎ 2368-6221) 11th floor, South Seas Centre, Tower II, 75 Mody Rd, Tsimshatsui East

Malaysia Airlines
(☎ 2521-8181) 23rd floor, Central Tower, 28 Quenn's Rd, Central

Northwest Airlines
(☎ 2810-4288) 29th floor, Alexandra House, 7 Des Voeux Rd, Central

Philippine Airlines
(☎ 2369-4521) Room 6, ground floor, East Ocean Centre, 98 Granville Rd, Tsimshatsui East

Qantas
(☎ 2842-1438) Room 1422, Swire House, 9-25 Chater Rd, Central

Royal Brunei Airlines
(☎ 2869-8608) Room 1406, Central Building, 3 Pedder St, Central

Royal Nepal Airlines
(☎ 2375-9151) Room 704, Lippo Sun Plaza, 28 Canton Rd, Tsimshatsui

Singapore Airlines
(☎ 2520-2233) United Centre, 95 Queensway, Central

South African Airways
(☎ 2877-3277) 30th floor, Alexandra House, Central

Thai Airways International
(☎ 2529-5601) United Centre, Pacific Place, 88 Queensway, Central

United Airlines
(☎ 2810-4888) 29th floor, Gloucester Tower, 11 Pedder St, Central

Vietnam Airlines
(☎ 2810-6680) 10th floor, United Centre, 95 Queensway, Central

Bus

Shenzhen is the city just across the border from Hong Kong where you can get buses (and trains) to other points in Guangdong. The border checkpoint is open daily from 6 am to midnight.

A new superhighway connects Hong Kong to Guangzhou (Canton) – the bus journey takes three hours and there are a number of different bus companies making the trip.

In Kowloon, Citybus (☎ 2736-3888) has frequent departures from the bus station on the ground floor of China Hong Kong City (the same building where you get ferries to Guangzhou). Tickets are HK$180. Departures are at 7.30, 8.30, 9 and 9.30 am, and 2.30 pm. There are also departures from City One in Shatin (New Territories).

From Guangzhou, you catch these buses at the Garden Hotel, departing at 9.15 am and 2.30, 3.30, 4 and 4.30 pm. The same company also operates buses to places in Shenzhen, including Shenzhen airport, Safari Park, Windows of the World, Shenzhen Bay and Central Shenzhen.

Guangdong Tours Transportation (☎ 2576-9995) leaves from the New Cathay Hotel at 17 Tung Lo Wan Rd, Causeway Bay. Tickets are HK$150 and there are frequent departures in the morning until 10 am and in the afternoon at 2.30 and 5.15 pm. It also stops in Mongkok, at Exit A of the Prince Edward MTR station. In Guangzhou, passengers are let off at the Liuhua Hotel opposite the Guangzhou railway station.

CTS has information on other bus companies, but most of it is only available in Chinese.

Train

The KCR train takes 30 minutes to run from Hunghom station in Kowloon to the border checkpoint at Lo Wu. You walk across the border to the city of Shenzhen, and from there you can take a local train or bus to Guangzhou and beyond.

Alternatively, there are express trains straight through between Hunghom station in Kowloon and Guangzhou. Tickets start from HK$250 1st class and HK$220 2nd class. These depart four times daily in the morning starting at 8.35, 9.25 and 11.35 am ,and 12.55 pm. There is also a Kowloon-Zhaoqing train. You pass through immigration and Customs at the point of departure – therefore, you must arrive at the railway station at least 30 minutes before departure or you will not be allowed to board. The staff are very strict about enforcing this.

In May 1997, the new express route from Shanghai and Beijing to Kowloon opened and it offers one of the cheapest ways to head up north directly from Hong Kong. The trains leave alternate days to Beijing (30 hours) and Shanghai (29 hours). To Beijing, deluxe soft sleepers are HK$1191, soft sleepers HK$934 and hard sleepers HK$706. The train also stops in Changsha, Wuchang and Zhengzhou.

To Shanghai, deluxe soft sleepers are HK$1089, soft sleepers HK$825 and hard sleepers HK$627. There are no hard seats. You can book tickets through the KCR (☎ 2602-7799), CTS or other travel agencies, and you can also book return tickets.

Boat

Hong Kong has one of the most spectacular harbours in the world, so departing or arriving this way can be fun. Luxury cruise liners frequently visit Hong Kong, although this option is basically for elderly millionaires.

For those of more humble means, there are economical boats between Hong Kong and several other cities in China. There are special discounts for children on all these boats – inquire if interested. Most of the boats leave from the China ferry terminal (China Hong Kong City) in Kowloon.

Hong Kong – Guangzhou The Hong Kong-Guangzhou boat is one of the most popular ways to enter or exit China. The journey takes about nine hours, and the boats leave at 9 pm on alternate days from Kowloon, and from the Zhoutouzui Wharf in Guangzhou. There is no service on the 31st day of the month. Tickets cost HK$226 for 1st class, which is a four person cabin and HK$196 for a cabin with 10 people.

There is also a jet-powered catamaran which completes the journey in just three hours. Departures are daily at 8.15 am, and departures from Guangzhou are at 1 pm. The fare is HK$186. You can book tickets through the CTS (who add a HK$12 service charge).

Hong Kong – Shanghai This is a fine way to get to Shanghai, but the service was sus-

pended at the time of writing and there is uncertainty whether it will be resumed. Check with CTS or Phoenix Travel Agency.

You could also phone the China Merchant Shipping Company (☎ 2850-5985) which was running the service, but it may be difficult to find someone who speaks English.

Hong Kong – Shekou There are jet-powered catamarans that go to Shekou, on the eastern side of the Shenzhen Special Economic Zone. Boats depart from Kowloon at 7.50 and 10.15 am, and at 1.30 and 4 pm. Tickets are HK$110.

There are also departures from the Shun Tak Centre, but tickets are a bit more expensive at HK$120 and HK$150. The trip takes about 50 minutes.

Hong Kong – Shenzhen Airport The jet-powered catamaran departs six times daily in each direction leaving from Kowloon. The trip takes about an hour and tickets are HK$186 for economy class, HK$286 for 1st class and HK$1716 for a six seat VIP cabin. The trip from Shenzhen airport to Kowloon costs HK$5 more.

Departure times are 7.30, 9 and 10.30 am, and 12.45, 2.30 and 3.45 pm. Phone ☎ 2851-1700 for information and ☎ 2789-5421 for reservations.

Hong Kong – Taiping (Opium War Museum) The jet-powered catamaran takes at least two hours to complete the journey. Departures from Kowloon are daily at 8.35 and 8.45 am, and 2.20 and 4.15 pm. Departures from Taiping are at 9.30 am and 2.15 and 4.50 pm.

Fares from Hong Kong are HK$221 for deluxe class, HK$201 for 1st class and HK$181 for 2nd class.

Hong Kong – Wuzhou Wuzhou is the gateway to Guilin. The boat journey takes 10 hours, and departures from Hong Kong are at 8 am on even-numbered dates. Departures from Wuzhou are at 7.30 am on odd-numbered dates. The fare is HK$395.

Hong Kong – Xiamen The journey takes 22 hours. Kowloon departures are at 2 pm roughly every two days, but it's best to phone CTS to confirm times. Departures from Xiamen are at 3 pm. Tickets cost HK$550 for 1st class, HK$500 for 2nd class, HK$450 for 3rd class and HK$390 for a seat.

Hong Kong – Zhaoqing There are daily departures by jet-powered catamaran which completes the journey in four hours. Departures from Kowloon are at 8.10 am on even-numbered dates and from Zhaoqing at 2 pm. There is no service on the 31st of each month.

Fares are HK$311 for deluxe, HK$298 for 1st class and HK$281 for 2nd class.

Hong Kong – Zhuhai This is another way to get to Macau if you want to take a look at Zhuhai, or go into China from there. Jet-powered catamarans leave from both the China ferry terminal in Kowloon and the Shun Tak Centre in Central, although departures are less frequent from the latter. The trip takes about 70 minutes. Tickets are HK$183.

GETTING AROUND
To/From the Airport

One of the great things about landing in Hong Kong was the exhilarating approach from the sea or, if you were lucky, the hair-raising sweep down through the forest of Kowloon apartment buildings. Another advantage was the close proximity of Kai Tak airport to the belly of Hong Kong itself.

However, all that will have changed by now with the opening of the new airport at Chep Lap Kok in July 1998. Upon completion, the passenger terminal will be a whopping eight times larger than Kai Tak airport and, despite its location off the north side of Lantau Island, it is hoped that the rail shuttle and extensive bus services to and from the new airport will make the journey into town just as convenient as it was from Kai Tak.

The Airport Express rail line will run between Kowloon station, the new Hong Kong station in Central, Tsing Yi station and the airport. If things go according to plan, it will also be possible for passengers to check in their baggage at these stations. Trains are expected to leave every eight minutes and the service will be open from 6 am until 1 am daily. The trip will take about 25 minutes. Prices were not available at the time of writing.

There are a number of bus service options that will link up the new the airport with the rest of Hong Kong, but the most useful for travellers will probably be the Airbus routes identified by the letter A. The A21 service will go from the airport to Tsimshatsui, Jordan Rd, Yau Ma Tei, Mong Kok and the Kowloon KCR Station for HK$33. The A11 will take you to Causeway Bay, Wanchai and Central (HK$40), and the A12 will also go through these areas and east past Quarry Bay along Hong Kong island to the Sai Wan Ho ferry pier (HK$45).

Buses out to the New Territories include the A41 to Shatin (HK$20) and the A31 to Tsuen Wan (HK$17). The A22 will run from the airport to the Lam Tin MTR station near Kwun Tong. Keep in mind that none of these services had begun operating at the time of writing, so there may be changes.

Bus

Before setting out to travel anywhere by bus, ensure you have a good pocketful of small change – the exact fare normally must be deposited in a cash box and nobody has change (the new Octopus card is supposed to change all that, see below). There are plenty of buses with fares starting from HK$1.10 and going up to HK$32 for the fancy 'City Buses' which take you to the New Territories.

Most services stop around 11 pm or midnight, but the Cross-Harbour Tunnel buses Nos 121 and 122 operate from 12.45 to 5 am. Bus No 121 runs from the Macau ferry terminal on Hong Kong Island, then through the tunnel to Chatham Rd in Tsimshatsui

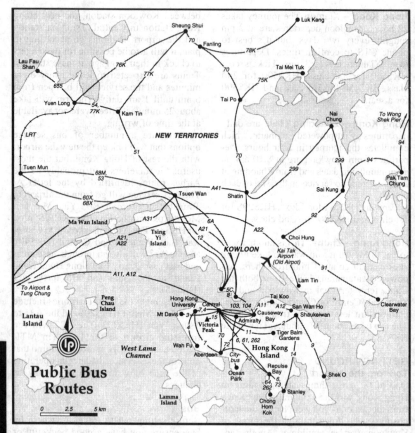

Public Bus Routes

0   2.5   5 km

East before continuing on to Choi Hung north-east of the airport.

Bus No 122 runs from North Point on Hong Kong Island, through the Cross-Harbour Tunnel, to Chatham Rd, the northern part of Nathan Rd and on to Laichikok in the north-western part of Kowloon.

There are three bus companies in Hong Kong – Citybus (☎ 2873-0818), China Motor Bus (☎ 2565-8556) and Kowloon Motor Bus (☎ 2745-4466). The HKTA offices also have leaflets on major bus routes, but you have to ask for them.

Minibus & Maxicab

Small red and yellow minibuses supplement the regular bus services. They cost HK$2 to HK$7 and you pay as you exit. They generally don't run such regular routes, but you can get on or off almost anywhere.

Maxicabs are just like minibuses except they are green and yellow and they run regular routes. Two popular ones are from the car park in front of the Star ferry in Central to Ocean Park, or from HMS Tamar (east of the Star ferry) to the Peak.

Fares are between HK$1 and HK$8 and you pay as you enter.

Train
Mass Transit Railway The MTR (☎ 2881-8888) operates from Central across the harbour and up along Kowloon Peninsula. It is very fast and convenient, but fairly pricey. The ticket machines do not give change (get it from the ticket windows or change machines) and single-journey tickets are valid only for the day they are purchased. Once you go past the turnstile, you must complete the journey within 90 minutes or the ticket becomes invalid. The MTR operates from 6 am to 1 am.

If you use the MTR frequently, it's very useful to buy a Common Stored Value Ticket for HK$70, HK$100 or HK$200. These tickets are expected to be phased out by this book's publication, when the new Octopus card is to be completely in place. Introduced in September 1997 (along with fare increases), the Octopus card can be used on MTR, KCR and Light Rail services and some buses. Eventually, passengers will be able to use the Octopus card on outlying ferries as well.

Smoking, eating and drinking are not allowed in the MTR stations or on the trains (makes you wonder about all those Maxim's Cake Shops in the stations). The fine for eating or drinking is HK$1000, while smoking will set you back HK$2000. Busking, selling and soliciting are forbidden. There are no toilets in the MTR stations.

Kowloon-Canton Railway The KCR runs from Hunghom station in Kowloon to Lo Wu, where you can walk across the border into Shenzhen. Apart from being a launch pad into China, the KCR is also an excellent alternative to buses for getting into the New Territories.

The Common Stored Value Tickets and Octopus cards which are used on the MTR are valid on the KCR too, but not for Lo Wu station, which requires a separate ticket.

Tram
There is just one major tram line, running east-west along the northern side of Hong Kong Island. As well as being ridiculously picturesque and fun to travel on, the tram is quite a bargain at HK$1.20 for any distance. You pay as you get off.

There is also a spur route off to Happy Valley. Some trams don't run the full length of the line, but basically you can just get on any tram that comes by. They pass frequently and there always seem to be half a dozen trams actually in sight.

Light Rail Transit
The LRT (☎ 2468-7788) operates only on routes in the western part of the New Territories, running between the Tuen Mun ferry pier and Yuen Long. Fares are HK$3.20 to HK$5.20.

Taxi
On Hong Kong Island and Kowloon, the flag fall is HK$14.50 for the first 2km then HK$1.30 for every 200m. In the New Territories, flag fall is HK$12.50, thereafter HK$1.20 for every 200m. There is a luggage fee of HK$5 per bag, but not all drivers insist on this.

If you go through either the Cross-Harbour Tunnel or Eastern Harbour Tunnel, you'll be charged an extra HK$20. The toll is only HK$10, but the driver is allowed to assume that he won't get a fare back so you have to pay.

Note: Taxis cannot pick up or put down passengers where there's a painted yellow line in the road.

Bicycle
Bicycling in Kowloon or Central would be suicidal, but in quiet areas of the islands or the New Territories a bike can be quite a nice way of getting around. The bike-rental places tend to run out early on weekends.

Some places where you can rent bikes and ride in safety include: Shek O on Hong Kong Island; Shatin and Tai Mei Tuk (near Tai Po) in the New Territories; Mui Wo

(Silvermine Bay) on Lantau Island; and on the island of Cheung Chau.

Boat

With such a scenic harbour, commuting by ferry is one of the great pleasures of Hong Kong. You have a wide choice of boats, although the one most familiar to tourists is the Star ferry.

Star Ferry There are three routes on the Star ferry, but by far the most popular one shuttles between Tsimshatsui and Central. The boats cost a mere HK$1.70 (lower deck) or HK$2.20 (upper deck), except for the Hunghom ferry, which is HK$2.20 and HK$2.70, respectively. The schedule for all three ferries is as follows:

Tsimshatsui – Central, every five to 10 minutes from 6.30 am until 11.30 pm
Tsimshatsui – Wanchai, every 10 to 20 minutes from 7.30 am to 11 pm
Hunghom – Central, every 12 to 20 minutes (every 20 minutes on Sunday and holidays) from 7 am to 7.20 pm

Hoverferries These are operated by the Hong Kong & Hong Kong & Yaumati Ferry Company. The schedule for hoverferries is as follows:

Tsimshatsui East – Central (Queen's Pier, beside Star ferry), every 20 minutes from 8 am to 8 pm
Tsuen Wan – Central (Outlying Ferry Pier area, Pier 6), every 20 minutes from 7 am to 6.30 pm
Tuen Mun – Central (Outlying Ferry Pier area, Pier 5) every 10 to 20 minutes from 6.45 am to 7.40 pm

There is also a ferry from Central (Outlying Ferry Pier area) to Jordan Rd, running from 6.10 am to midnight (every 15 to 20 minutes) and Wanchai to Hunghom from 7 am to 8 pm (every 15 to 20 minutes).

Kaidos A *kaido* is a small to medium-sized ferry which can make short runs on the open sea. Few kaido routes operate on regular schedules, preferring to adjust their supply

according to demand. There is sort of a schedule on popular runs like the trip between Aberdeen and Lamma Island. Kaidos run most frequently on weekends and holidays when everyone tries to get away from it all.

A *sampan* is a motorised launch which can accommodate only a few people. A sampan is too small to be considered seaworthy, but can safely zip you around typhoon shelters like Aberdeen Harbour.

Bigger than a sampan, but smaller than a kaido, is a *walla walla*. These operate as water taxis on Victoria Harbour. Most of the customers are sailors living on ships anchored in the harbour.

Outlying Island Ferries The HKTA can supply you with schedules for these ferries or phone the Hong Kong & Yaumati Ferry Company (☎ 2542-3081). Fares are higher on weekends and holidays and the boats can get crowded. From Central, most ferries go from the Outlying Islands Piers just west of the Star ferry pier on Hong Kong Island. Besides the ordinary ferries, there are also hoverferries to Lantau, Cheung Chau and Peng Chau.

Macau 澳門

The lure of Macau's casino gaming tables has been so actively promoted that its other attractions are almost forgotten, but it is a fascinating blend. Steeped in history and old-world elegance, it is prosperous and changing fast. It has a very different look and feel from Hong Kong, and is well worth the one hour boat trip to get there. Better yet, spend at least one night – this is a place to enjoy and relax.

HISTORY

Portuguese galleons visited Macau in the early 1500s, and in 1557, as a reward for clearing out a few pirates, China ceded the tiny enclave to the Portuguese. For centuries, it was the principal meeting point for

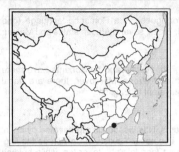

Macau Facts & Highlights

Area: 20 sq km

Population: 400,000

Highlights

- The ruins of St Paul's, the symbol of Macau.
- Monte Fort, with its great views over Macau.
- Colonial architecture.
- Gambling in one of the casinos.

trade with China. In the 19th century, European and American traders could operate in Guangzhou (just up the Pearl River) only during the trading season. They would then retreat to Macau during the off-season.

When the Opium wars erupted between the Chinese and the British, the Portuguese stood diplomatically to one side and Macau soon found itself the poor relation of the more dynamic Hong Kong.

Macau's current prosperity is given a big boost by the Chinese gambling urge; every weekend hordes of Hong Kongers shuttle off to the casinos. Although the government doesn't publicly admit it, prostitution is also a significant source of revenue. Macau suffered a blow to its tourist industry in the summer of 1997 when a number of criminal incidents related to triad gang activity kept visitors away and caused a significant drop in hotel prices.

About 95% of Macau's people are Chinese, 3% are Portuguese and 2% are foreigners employed in what is loosely called the 'entertainment industry'. Whether or not the Portuguese and foreigners will be permitted to remain after Macau is handed back to China in 1999 is a largely unanswered question.

In the meantime, Macau is pushing ahead with more reclamation projects along the waterfront, and bridge-building. There are even nascent plans to build a 38km bridge across the Pearl River Estuary to Lantau to provide a link with Hong Kong. It may be a good idea to get there before all these projects inevitably change the face of Macau.

LANGUAGE

Portuguese may be the official language, but Cantonese is the real one. Mandarin Chinese is spoken by about half the population. Bus and taxi drivers almost never speak English. On the other hand, virtually all Portuguese in Macau can speak English well.

There is no real need to learn Portuguese, but it can be helpful (and fun) to know a few words for reading maps and street signs. The following table should come in handy.

INFORMATION
Tourist Office

The Macau Government Tourist Office (MGTO; ☎ 315-566) is well organised and extremely helpful. Staff have an ample supply of printed information that provides a good background to various sights. It's well worth following some of the routes laid out in the *Walking Tours* pamphlet. The office is at Largo do Senado, Edificio Ritz No 9, near the Leal Senado building in the square in the centre of Macau. The square is immediately recognisable for the multicoloured paving bricks arranged in a wave pattern.

Tourist information on Macau can be accessed through the Internet (macau.tourism. gov.mo).

The organisation also maintains overseas tourist offices in most European and Asian countries, as well as Australia, New Zealand and the USA.

PORTUGUESE

Like French, Italian, Spanish and Romanian, Portuguese is a Romance language (one closely derived from Latin). It's spoken in Portugal, Brazil, several African states and Macau.

Pronunciation

Pronunciation of Portuguese is difficult; like English, vowels and consonants have more than one possible sound depending on position and stress. Moreover, there are nasal vowels and diphthongs in Portuguese with no equivalent in English.

Vowels

Single vowels should present relatively few problems. Nasalisation is represented by an 'n' or an 'm' after the vowel, or by a tilde (~) over it. The nasal 'i' exists in English as the 'ing' in 'sing'. For other nasal vowels, try to pronounce a long 'a', 'ah', 'e' or 'eh' while holding your nose, so that you sound as if you have a cold.

Vowel combinations (diphthongs) are relatively straightforward. For nasal diphthongs, try the same technique as for nasal vowels. To say *não*, pronounce 'now' through your nose.

Word Stress

Word stress is important in Portuguese, as it can affect the meaning of a word. Many Portuguese words have a written accent which indicates the syllable to be stressed.

Useful Phrases

Yes/No.	*Sim/Não.*
Maybe.	*Talvez.*
Please.	*Se faz favor/ por favor.*
Thank you.	*Obrigado/a.*
You're welcome.	*De nada.*
Sorry. (forgive me)	*Desculpe.*

Greetings

Hello.	*Bom dia/Olá/Chao.*
Good morning.	*Bom dia.*
Good evening.	*Boa tarde.*
Goodbye.	*Adeus/Chao.*
See you later.	*Até logo.*

Small Talk

How are you?	*Como está?*
I'm fine, thanks	*Bem, obrigado/a.*
What's your name?	*Como se chama?*
My name is …	*Chamo-me …*

Getting Around

I want to go to …	*Quero ir a …*
What time does the next … leave/arrive?	*A que horas parte/ chega o próximo …?*

boat	*barco*
bus (city)	*autocarro*
bus (intercity)	*camioneta*

Where is …?	*Onde é …?*
the bus stop	*a paragem de auto carro*
Is this the bus to ...?	*E este o autocarre para … ?*
I'd like a one way ticket.	*Queria um bilhete simples/de ida.*
I'd like a return ticket.	*Queria um bilhete de ida e volta.*
left-luggage office	*o depósito de bagagem*
platform	*cais*
timetable	*horário*
I'd like to hire …	*Queria alugar …*
a car	*um carro*
a motorcycle	*uma motocicleta*
a bicycle	*uma bicicleta*

Directions

How do I get to …?	*Como vou para …?*
What … is this?	*O que … é isto/ista?*
street/road	*rua/estrada*
town	*cidade/vila*

north/south	*norte/sul*	How much is it per	*Quanto é por noite/*
east/west	*este/oeste*	night/per person?	*por pessoa?*
		Is breakfast included?	*O pequeno almoço*

Around Town

Where is ...?	*Onde é ...?*
a bank	*um banco*
an exchange office	*um câmbio*
the city centre	*o centro da cidade/da baixa*
the hospital	*o hospital*
my hotel	*do meu hotel*
the post office	*dos correios*
the public toilet	*sanitários/casa de banho pública*
telephone centre	*da central de telefones*
the tourist office	*do turismo/posta de turismo*
What time does it ...?	*A que horas*
open	*abre*
close	*fecha*
I'd like to make a telephone call.	*Quero usar o telefone.*
I'd like to change some money/ travellers cheques	*Queria trocar dinheiro/cheques de viagem*

Accommodation

I'm looking for ...	*Procuro ...*
a youth hostel	*uma pousada de juventude/albergue de juventude*
a guesthouse	*uma pensão*
a hotel	*uma hotel*
Do you have any rooms available?	*Tem quartos livres?*
I'd like to book ...	*Quero fazer una reserva para ...*
a bed	*uma cama*
a single room	*um quarto individual*
a double room/ with twin beds	*um quarto de casal/duplo*
a dormitory bed	*cama de dormitório*
Can I see the room?	*Posso ver o quarto?*

How much is it per night/per person?	*Quanto é por noite/ por pessoa?*
Is breakfast included?	*O pequeno almoço está incluído?*
Where is the toilet?	*Onde ficam os lavabos?*

Time & Dates

What time is it?	*Que horas são?*
When?	*Quando?*
today	*hoje*
tonight	*hoje à noite*
tomorrow	*amanhã*
yesterday	*ontem*
morning	*manhã*
afternoon	*tarde*

Medical

I need a doctor.	*Preciso um médico.*
Where is a ...?	*Onde é um ...?*
hospital	*hospital*
medical clinic	*centro de saúde*
I'm pregnant.	*Estou grávida.*
I'm allergic to ...	*Sou alérgica/o a ...*
antibiotics	*antibióticos*
penicillin	*penicilina*

Numbers

1	*um/uma*
2	*dois/duas*
3	*três*
4	*quatro*
5	*cinco*
6	*seis*
7	*sete*
8	*oito*
9	*nove*
10	*dez*
100	*cem*
1000	*mil*

Emergencies

Help!	*Socorro!*
Call a doctor!	*Chame um médico!*
Call the police!	*Chame a polícia!*
Go away!	*Deixe-me em paz!*
I've been robbed.	*Fui roubado/a.*
I'm lost.	*Estou perdido/a.*

HONG KONG & MACAU

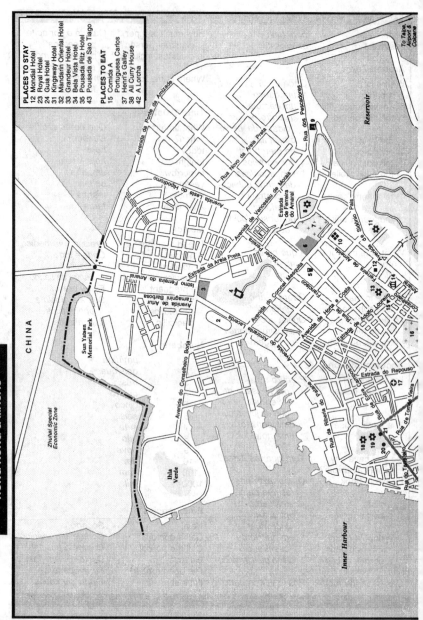

PLACES TO STAY
12 Mondial Hotel
23 Royal Hotel
24 Guia Hotel
31 Kingsway Hotel
32 Mandarin Oriental Hotel
33 Grandeur Hotel
34 Bela Vista Hotel
35 Pousada Ritz Hotel
43 Pousada de Sao Tiago

PLACES TO EAT
15 Comida A
   Portuguesa Carlos
37 Henri's Galley
38 Ali Curry House
42 A Lorcha

CHINA

Zhuhai Special
Economic Zone

Sun Yatsen
Memorial Park

Ilha
Verde

Inter Harbour

Reservoir

To Taipa,
Airport &
Coloane

HONG KONG & MACAU

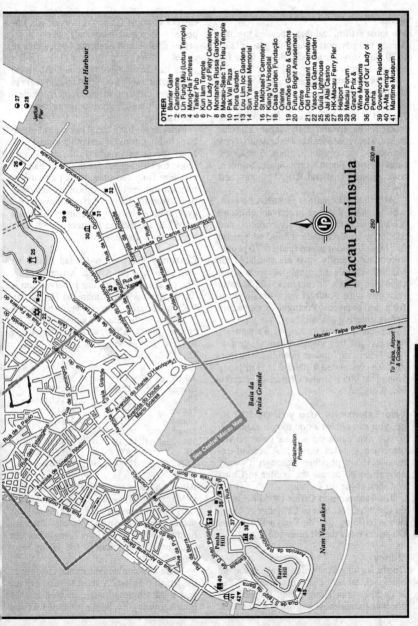

Macau Peninsula

OTHER
1 Barrier Gate
2 Canidrome
3 Lin Fung Miu (Lotus Temple)
4 Mong-Ha Fortress
5 Talker Pub
6 Kun Iam Temple
7 Our Lady of Piety Cemetery
8 Montanha Russa Gardens
9 Macau Sec Tin Hau Temple
10 Paka Vai Plaza
11 Flora Garden
13 Lou Lim Ioc Gardens
14 Sun Yatsen Memorial
   House
16 St Michael's Cemetery
17 Kiang Vu Hospital
18 Casa Garden Fundação
   Oriente
19 Camões Grotto & Gardens
20 Future Bright Amusement
   Centre
21 Old Protestant Cemetery
22 Vasco da Gama Garden
25 Guia Lighthouse
26 Jai Alai Casino
27 HK-Macau Ferry Pier
28 Heliport
29 Macau Forum
30 Grand Prix &
   Wine Museums
36 Chapel of Our Lady of
   Penha
39 Governor's Residence
40 A-Ma Temple
41 Maritime Museum

Macau - Taipa Bridge

To Taipa, Airport & Coloane

Baia da Praia Grande

Nam Van Lakes

Outer Harbour

Jetfoil Pier

Reclamation Project

See Central Macau Map

0   250   500 m

Visas

For most visitors, all that's needed to enter Macau is a passport. Everyone gets at least a 20 day stay on arrival, or 90 days for Hong Kongers.

Visas are not required for people from the following countries: Australia, Austria, Belgium, Brazil, Canada, China, Denmark, Finland, France, Germany, Greece, Hong Kong, India, Ireland, Italy, Japan, Luxembourg, Malaysia, Mexico, Netherlands, New Zealand, Norway, Philippines, Singapore, South Africa, South Korea, Spain, Sweden, Switzerland, Thailand, UK, Uruguay and USA.

All other nationalities must have a visa, which can be obtained on arrival in Macau. Visas cost M$100 for individuals and M$50 for children under 12 and per person in a bona fide tour group (usually 10 people minimum). Family visas are available for M$200. People holding passports from countries which do not have diplomatic relations with Portugal must obtain visas from an overseas Portuguese consulate before entering Macau.

An exception is made for Taiwanese, who can get free visas on arrival, despite their lack of diplomatic relations. The Portuguese consulate (☎ 2802-2585) in Hong Kong is at 905 Harbour Centre, 25 Harbour Rd, Wanchai.

Visa Extensions After your 20 days are up, you can obtain a one month extension if you can come up with a good reason (emergency poker game?). A second extension is not possible, although it's easy enough to go across the border to China and then come back again.

The Immigration Office (☎ 577-338) is on the 9th floor, Macau Chamber of Commerce building, Rua de Xangai 175, across the street from the Holiday Inn.

Money

Costs As long as you don't go crazy at the blackjack tables or slot machines, Macau is cheaper than Hong Kong. Indeed, it is cheaper than almost anywhere else on the eastern coast of China. However, it's important to avoid weekends when hotel prices double and even the ferries charge more.

As in China, tipping is not the usual custom, although hotel porters and waiters may have different ideas. Upmarket hotels hit you with a 10% service charge and a 5% 'tourism tax'.

Most stores have fixed prices, but if you buy clothing, trinkets and other tourist junk from the street markets, there is some scope for bargaining. On the other hand, if you buy from the ubiquitous pawnshops, bargain ruthlessly. Pawnbrokers are more than happy to charge whatever they can get away with – charging five times the going price for second-hand cameras and other goods is not unusual!

Currency Exchange Macau issues its own currency, the pataca, written as M$. The pataca is divided into 100 avos and is worth about 3% less than the HK dollar. HK dollars are accepted everywhere on a 1:1 basis with patacas, which means, of course, that you'll save a little by using patacas. The exchange is roughly M$8 to US$1.

Australia	A$1	=	M$5.53
Canada	C$1	=	M$5.87
China	Y1	=	M$1.01
France	FF1	=	M$1.36
Germany	DM1	=	M$4.54
Japan	¥100	=	M$6.00
New Zealand	NZ$1	=	M$4.69
UK	UK£1	=	M$13.89
USA	US$1	=	M$8.33

Although Hong Kong coins are acceptable in Macau, you'll need pataca coins to make calls at public telephones. Get rid of your patacas before departing Macau – they are hard to dispose of in Hong Kong, although you can change them at the Hang Seng Bank.

There is a convenient moneychanger at the jetfoil pier (where most tourists arrive) and at the Chinese border, as well as a 24 hour currency-exchange machine at the airport. Banks are normally open on weekdays from 9.30 am to 4.30 pm, and on Saturday from 9.30 am until noon.

If you need to change money when the banks are closed, the major casinos (especially the Lisboa) can accommodate you 24 hours a day.

There are numerous ATMs around the city where you can easily withdraw cash using Visa, MasterCard or American Express.

Post & Communications
Postal Rates Domestic letters cost M$1 for up to 20g. For international mail Macau splits the world into two zones. Zone 1 is east Asia, including Korea and Taiwan, and Zone 2 is everywhere else (although there are special rates for the rest of China and Portugal). Printed matter receives a discount of about 30% off the regular rates. Registration costs an extra M$12.

Sending Mail The main post office on Largo do Senado is open Monday to Friday from 9 am to 6 pm, and 9 am to 1 pm on Saturday. Large hotels like the Lisboa also sell stamps and postcards and can post letters for you.

Scattered around Macau are several red-coloured 'mini-post offices', which are basically machines that sell stamps. The current postal rates are posted clearly on the machines.

Telephone Companhia de Telecomunicações (CTM) runs the Macau telephone system, and for the most part the service is good. There are a lot more public pay phones around than there used to be, although they're not as common as in Hong Kong. You can find them around the Leal Senado and most large hotels have one in the lobby.

Local calls are free from a private or hotel telephone. At a public pay phone, local calls cost M$1 for five minutes. All pay phones permit IDD. The procedure for dialling Hong Kong is totally different from all other countries. You first dial ☎ 01 and then the number you want to call – you must *not* dial the country code.

The international access code for every country *except* Hong Kong is ☎ 00. To call into Macau from abroad, the country code is ☎ 853. Telephone cards from CTM are sold in denominations of M$70, M$100 and M$200. A lot of phones which accept these cards are found around Largo do Senado, the jetfoil pier and at a few large hotels.

You can also make a call from the telephone office at Largo do Senado, in the same building as the main post office, but with a separate entrance at 92 Avenida de Almeida Ribeiro. The office is open from 8 am until midnight Monday to Saturday, and from 9 am until midnight on Sunday.

Some useful phone numbers in Macau include:

Directory assistance (Macau)	☎ 181
Directory assistance (Hong Kong)	☎ 101
Time	☎ 140
Emergency	☎ 999

Fax, Telex & Telegraph Unless you're staying at a hotel that has its own fax, the easiest way to send and receive a fax is at the EMS counter at the main post office (not the telephone office) at Largo do Senado. The number for receiving a fax at this office is ☎ (853) 550-117, but check because the number can change. If you're sending a fax, you must put your name and hotel telephone number on top of the message so the postal workers can find you. The cost for receiving a fax is M$10 for one to five pages, and M$15 for six to 10 pages.

Telex messages are sent from the CTM office next to the main post office. The telephone office also handles cables (telegrams).

Travel Agencies
In all likelihood, you'll only visit a travel agent if you want to book a day tour around Macau. However, CTS and a few other agencies do visas for China in 24 hours.

There is a CTS counter at the jetfoil pier, as well as other travel agencies where you can book tours of Macau.

A day tour will cost about M$100 and is cheaper than if you book it in Hong Kong. A typical city tour (booked in Macau) of the peninsula takes three to four hours and costs about M$100 per person, often including lunch. Bus tours out to the islands cost from about M$50 per person.

You can also book a one day bus tour across the border into Zhuhai in China, which usually includes a trip to the former home of Dr Sun Yatsen in Zhongshan County. Given the dearth of interesting sights in Zhuhai, it hardly seems worth the bother.

Film & Photography

You can find most types of film, cameras and accessories in Macau, and photo processing is of a high standard. The best store in town for all photographic services, including visa photos, is Foto Princesa (☎ 555-959), at Avenida do Infante D'Henrique 55-59, one block east of Avenida da Praia Grande.

Medical Services

Medical treatment is available at the Government Hospital (☎ 514-499, 313-731), north of San Francisco Garden.

Emergency

The emergency phone number is ☎ 999, and if you want the police dial ☎ 573-333.

THINGS TO SEE

Macau has far more of historical interest than Hong Kong and, unlike the rest of China, churches are a major part of the scenery. Although Buddhism and Taoism are the dominant religions, the Portuguese influence has definitely had an impact and Catholicism is very strong in Macau.

Many Chinese have been converted and you are likely to see Chinese nuns. A good walk is the peninsula route outlined in the tourist office's Walking Tour pamphlet. Go up the hill to **St Augustine's Church** and

the **Dom Pedro V Theatre**, and then continue down to **St Lawrence's Church**.

From there, go down to Travessa do Padre Narciso, past the pink Government House, then right, along the waterfront, turning right at Calcada da Praia to head up the hill again and into the ritzy neighbourhood of the Governor's residence. From here there are signs leading to the **Chapel of Our Lady of Penha** on top of the hill overlooking Macau.

Ruins of St Paul's

This is the symbol of Macau – the facade and majestic stairway are all that remain of this old church. It was designed by an Italian Jesuit and built in 1602 by Japanese refugees who had fled anti-Christian persecution in Nagasaki.

In 1853 the church was burned down during a catastrophic typhoon. There's a small museum at the back (down the stairs) that has some interesting artefacts and paintings from the period, as well as a relic bone (the right arm) of St Francis Xavier.

Monte Fort

The fort overlooks the ruins of St Paul's and almost all of Macau from its high and central position. It was built by the Jesuits. In 1622, a cannonball fired from the fort conveniently landed in a Dutch gunpowder carrier during an attempted Dutch invasion, demolishing most of their fleet.

Kun Iam Temple

This is the city's most historic temple. The 400-year-old temple is dedicated to Kun Iam, the queen of heaven and goddess of mercy. You'll find it on Avenida do Coronel Mesquita. In the study are 18 wise men in a glass case – the one with the big nose is said to be Marco Polo.

Old Protestant Cemetery

Lord Churchill (one of Winston's ancestors) and the English artist George Chinnery are buried here, but far more interesting are the varied graves of missionaries and their families, traders and seamen with the often detailed accounts of their lives and deaths.

One US ship seems to have had half its crew 'fall from aloft' while in port. The cemetery is behind the small Protestant church, also known as the Morrison Chapel, in commemoration of Robert Morrison who translated the bible into Chinese. He is also buried here.

Camões Grotto & Gardens

This serves as a memorial to Luis de Camões, the 16th century Portuguese poet who has become something of a local hero, although his claim is not all that strong. He is said to have written his epic *Os Lusiadas* by the rocks here, but there is no firm evidence that he was ever in Macau.

A bust of Camões is in the gardens, which provide a pleasant, cool and shady place. The gardens are popular with the local Chinese and you may find old men sitting here playing chequers.

Barrier Gate

This used to be of interest because you could stand 100m from it and claim that you'd seen into China. Now you can stand on the other side and claim you've seen Macau.

Leal Senado

Known in English as the Loyal Senate, this graceful building looks out over the main town square and is the main administrative body for municipal affairs. At one time it was offered (and turned down) a total monopoly on all Chinese trade! The building also houses the National Library. It's across from the main post office.

Guía Fortress

This is the highest point on the Macau Peninsula, and is topped with a lighthouse and 17th century chapel. First lit up in 1865, the lighthouse is the oldest on the China coast.

St Dominic's Church

Arguably the most beautiful church in Macau, this 17th century building has an impressive tiered altar. There is a small museum at the back, full of church regalia, images and paintings. At the time of writing, the church was undergoing repairs so don't be surprised if you find it still swathed in tarps and scaffolding.

Lou Lim Ioc Gardens

These peaceful gardens with an ornate mansion (now the Pui Ching School) are a mixture of Chinese and European influences, with huge shady trees, lotus ponds, pavilions, bamboo groves, grottoes and odd-shaped doorways.

A-Ma Temple

Macau means the City of God and takes its name from A-Ma-Gau, the Bay of A-Ma. A-Ma Temple (Ma Kok Miu), which dates from the Ming Dynasty, stands at the base of Penha Hill near the southern end of the peninsula.

According to legend, A-Ma, goddess of seafarers, was supposed to have been a beautiful young woman whose presence on a Guangzhou-bound ship saved it from disaster. All the other ships of the fleet, whose rich owners had refused to give her passage, were destroyed in a storm. The boat people of Macau come here on a pilgrimage each year in April or May.

Macau Maritime Museum

There are a number of boats on exhibit here, including a *lorcha*, a type of sailing cargo vessel used on the Pearl River. Entry is M$8. Short cruises are offered for M$15, which includes entrance to the museum. There is also a small aquarium.

The museum is on the waterfront opposite the A-Ma Temple and is open daily except Tuesday, from 10 am to 5.30 pm.

Grand Prix Museum & Wine Museum

These two museums are located in the same premises opposite the Kingsway Hotel. The Grand Prix exhibit has various cars that have taken part in the Macau Grand Prix since it was started in 1954, as well as simulators for any armchair racing drivers.

Across the hall, the Wine Museum has displays chronicling the history of wine, but is basically a promotional exhibit for Portuguese wine. You can buy wine here and there are tasting booths as well. This strange combination celebrating both the grape and the automobile may be the only place in the world where you can safely drink and drive.

Bus No 3A or No 10 stops near the museum. The entry fee of M$20 includes both museums and they are open daily from 10 am to 6 pm.

The Islands

Directly south of the mainland peninsula are the islands of Taipa and Coloane. Two bridges connect Taipa to the mainland, and a causeway connects Taipa and Coloane. There are a number of buses that do the trip.

For Taipa take bus No 11, and for Coloane No 25. If you want to get to Coloane from Taipa you'll have to walk back to the round-about north-east of the village and get onto the highway to catch the bus to Coloane.

Taipa This island seems to have become one big construction site with the Hyatt Regency Hotel and Macau University just the first of a number of massive projects. Long blocks of apartments now sit on re-claimed land.

Taipa village, however, is pleasant and there are some fine little restaurants to sample. At the southern end of the main village street you can rent a bicycle to explore the village and further afield. There's an old church, a couple of temples and the stately Taipa House Museum east of the main village street and over the hill.

Entrance to the museum is free and it gives a good sense of how the Macanese middle-class lived at the beginning of the 20th century.

Coloane This island has a pretty village where it is possible to rent bicycles, de-pending on the mood of the man who owns

the rental place. His shop is beside the bakery by the red postal stamp vending machine.

Situated in a muddy river mouth, Macau is hardly likely to be blessed with wonderful beaches, but Coloane has a couple that are really not bad. Tiny Cheoc Van beach has white sand and Hac Sa beach has black sand. Both beaches have places that rent windsurfers, water-scooters and other sea toys. Cheoc Van beach has a yacht club and Hac Sa has a horse-riding stable. Bus No 25 terminates at Hac Sa beach, and goes past the turn off for Cheoc Van beach.

South of the causeway on Coloane, Seac Pai Van Park has a good hiking trail to the highest point in Macau, Alto de Coloane. It starts south of the park's entrance and is 8km long. There is a lot of construction going on near the entrance of the park so the place is a bit of a mess near the road. Bus No 25 goes by the park.

ACTIVITIES

Future Bright Amusement Centre (☎ 953-399) has Macau's only ice-skating rink (with skate rentals) and is also a venue for bowling. It is on Praca Luis de Camões, on the southern side of the Camões Grotto & Gardens.

Up around the Guía Lighthouse is the best track for jogging. It's also a good place to watch early-morning taiji exercises.

Bicycles are available for hire on Taipa and Coloane, but not on the Macau Peninsula. The Westin Resort on Coloane also boasts a golf course.

Hotels offering tennis facilities include the Hyatt Regency, Mandarin Oriental, New Century and Westin Resort, and there is a public tennis court at Hac Sa beach on Coloane.

Spectator sports are best seen at the Macau Forum (near the jetfoil pier) and the Taipa Stadium (next to the Jockey Club on Taipa).

SPECIAL EVENTS

Macau has its own collection of holidays, festivals and cultural events, including some imported from Portugal. It's unlikely, however, that Portuguese festivals will still be held after 1999.

An International Fireworks festival is held annually in mid-September and the International Music Festival is held during the third week of October. The Macau Marathon is held in the first or second week of December.

The biggest event of the year is without doubt the Macau Grand Prix. As in Monte Carlo, the streets of the town make up the race track. The race is a two day event held on the third weekend in November – accommodation can be scarce as a three humped camel at this time. There's myriad other Chinese, Portuguese and religious festivals and holidays. Some of the highlights are:

Chinese Lunar New Year
    As elsewhere in China, this is a three day public holiday held in late January or early February
Lantern Festival
    Not a public holiday, but a lot of fun, this festival occurs two weeks after the Chinese New Year
Dragon Boat Festival
    As in Hong Kong, this is a major public holiday held in early June
Mid-Autumn Festival
    A major public holiday in September
Cheung Yeung Festival
    A public holiday in October, also celebrated in Hong Kong
Winter Solstice
    Not a public holiday, but an interesting time to visit Macau. Many Macau Chinese consider the winter solstice more important than the Chinese New Year. There is plenty of feasting and temples are crammed with worshippers.

PLACES TO STAY

During weekends, which begin Friday night, hotel prices can double and rooms of any kind can be scarce. Some bargaining is possible during the mid-week, especially in the winter off season. All prices listed below are mid-week prices.

With the mid to upper-range places, you can get discounts of 20% or more by booking through a Hong Kong travel agent. The best places to do this are at the numerous travel agencies in the Shun Tak Centre (Macau ferry pier) at Sheung Wan, Hong Kong Island.

Places to Stay – budget

All places listed are on the following Central Macau map.

One block back from waterfront and a couple of blocks south of Avenida de Almeida Ribeiro is an alley called Rua do Bocage. At No 28 on the 3rd floor there's the *Vila Pung Loi* (☎ 574-292) that has simple rooms without bath for M$120.

A block north, at Rua da Caldeira 43, the *Hotel Tai Fat* (☎ 933-908) is a bit more expensive, but very good value with rooms for M$200. South again, near the covered market, the well managed *Pensao Kuan Heng* (☎ 573-629, 937-624) at Rua Ponte E Horta 3-4 has clean rooms with bath for M$150 and twins/triples for M$250/350.

Also down at the bottom end, the *San Va Hospedaria* (☎ 573-701) is a funky old building on the corner of Rua de Felicidade and Travessa de Felicidade, that has rooms without bath ranging from M$50 to $120, although the cheaper ones don't have any windows.

Near the corner with Travessa Auto Novo, the *Vila Universal* (☎ 573-247) has singles/twins with bath for M$190/260.

Moving to the eastern side of the peninsula, the area between the Lisboa Hotel and Avenida da Praia Grande has some budget accommodation. Intersecting with Avenida da Praia Grande is a small street called Rua Dr Pedro Jose Lobo where there's a dense cluster of guesthouses, including *Vila Meng Meng* (☎ 715-241) on the 2nd floor at No 24. If you don't mind a shared bathroom, you can get an air-con room for M$130.

Next door is the *Vila Nam Loon*, where rooms start at M$100 without a window but with air-con, and go up to twins with attached bath for $M180.

Just above Foto Princesa (a camera shop), at Avenida do Infante D'Henrique 55-59, the *Vila Kimbo* (☎ 710-010) was

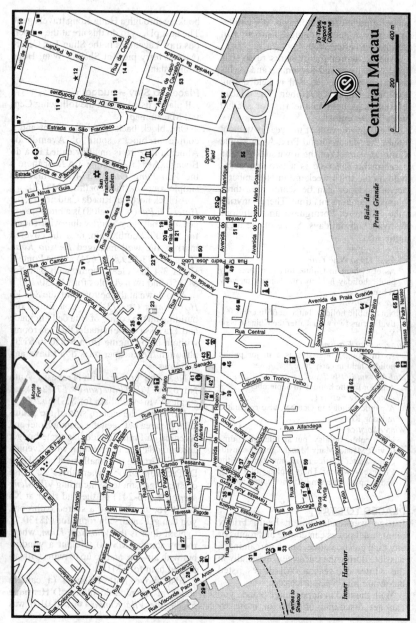

Central Macau

HONG KONG & MACAU

CENTRAL MACAU	51 Sintra Hotel	18 Chinese Library
	54 Lisboa Hotel	23 Cathedral
PLACES TO STAY	59 Pensao Kuan Heng	24 Livraria Sao Paulo
7 Vila Tak Lei	60 London Hotel	25 Livraria Portuguesa
8 Holiday Inn	61 Sun Sun Hotel	(Portuguese
9 New World Emperor		Bookshop)
Hotel	**PLACES TO EAT**	26 St Dominic's Church
13 Beverly Plaza Hotel	3 McDonald's	29 Floating Casino
14 Fortuna Hotel	22 Ze do Pipo	(Macau Palace)
15 Presidente Hotel	37 Fat Siu Lau Restaurant	32 Kee Kwan Motors
16 Vila San Vu	39 Restaurante Safari	(Buses to Guangzhou)
19 Vila Nam Pan	42 Leitaria I Son	41 Macau Government
20 Nam Tin Hotel	47 Solmar	Tourist Office
21 Pensao Nam In	53 Pizza Hut	43 GPO
27 East Asia Hotel	64 Estrela do Mar	44 CTM Telephone
28 Vila Capital		Office
30 Grand Hotel	**OTHER**	45 Leal Senado
31 Peninsula Hotel	1 St Anthony's Church	49 Foto Princesa
33 Macau Masters Hotel	2 Ruins of St Paul's	52 Bus Stop to Taipa &
34 Hou Kong Hotel	4 Watson's Drugstore	Coloane
35 Hotel Tai Fat	5 Cineteatro Macau	55 Bank of China
36 Vila Universal	6 Government Hospital	56 Jorge Alvares Statue
38 San Va Hospedaria	10 Immigration Office	57 St Augustine's
40 Central Hotel	11 Macau Exhibition	Church
46 Metropole Hotel	Centre	58 Dom Pedro V Theatre
48 Vila Kimbo	12 Main Police Station	62 St Joseph's Church
50 Vila Nam Loon;	17 Military Club &	63 St Lawrence's Church
Vila Meng Meng	Museum	65 Government House

undergoing renovation at the time writing, but will probably have rooms in the M$150 to M$200 range.

Running off Avenida D Joao IV is an alley called Travessa da Praia Grande. At No 3 you'll find *Pensao Nam In* (☎ 710-024), where singles with shared bath are M$200, and pleasant twins with private bath are M$230.

Behind the Lisboa Hotel on Avenida de Lopo Sarmento de Carvalho is a row of pawnshops and a couple of guesthouses. The *Vila San Vu* (☎ 780-779) has good rooms for M$210. There's also a sign outside in English with its translated name, the Vila Coral.

Probably one of the nicest places to stay if you can get a bed is the *Pousada de Juventude* at Cheoc Van beach on Coloane Island. It's at the top of the driveway down to the beach, but you can't just arrive and

get a bed. First you'll have to book a room at the Youth Hostel Booking Office (☎ 344-340) in Macau and pick up your voucher there. It's located near the A-Ma Temple. You'll also need to have an International Youth Hostel Federation card (see the earlier Hong Kong section for details). Mid-week prices for beds are M$40.

Places to Stay – middle
For the sake of definition, a mid-range hotel in Macau is anything priced between M$200 and M$500. Unless otherwise noted, all places are on the Central Macau map.

An excellent place to stay is the *East Asia Hotel* (☎ 922-433; fax 922-430) Rua da Madeira 1-A. This is one of the city's classic colonial buildings – the outside maintains its traditional facade, but it's been fully remodelled inside. Spotlessly clean singles/twins are M$238/268 with private bath and fierce air-conditioning. The dim sum restaurant on the 2nd floor does outstanding breakfasts.

Almost next door to the East Asia Hotel is the *Vila Capital* (☎ 920-154) at Rua Constantino Brito 3. Singles/doubles are M$200/250.

In Travessa da Praia Grande, *Nam Tin Hotel* (☎ 711-212) looks cheap, but isn't – singles are M$300 and twins M$380! *Vila Nam Pan* (☎ 572-289) on the corner has also become too pricey, with singles for M$300, but try polite bargaining.

The *Central Hotel* (☎ 373-838; fax 372-404) is, true to its name, centrally located at Avenida de Almeida Ribeiro 26-28, a short hop west of the main post office. The hotel looks better on the outside than it does on the inside – go upstairs and look at the rooms before you decide to stay. They have a mind-boggling variety of rooms starting at M$192 for singles without windows to four person rooms (with windows and attached bath) for M$328.

The *London Hotel* (☎ 937-761) is at 4 Praca Ponte e Horta, two blocks east of the waterfront, and has singles/twins for M$238/288. Rooms are comfortable and clean. Next door, the *Sun Sun Hotel* (☎ 939-393; fax 938-822; HK 2517-4273) is more upmarket, but still affordable with twins for M$360.

Closer to Avenida de Almeida Ribeiro and a block from the waterfront, is an alley called Travessa das Virtudes. On your left as you enter the alley off the waterfront is the *Hou Kong Hotel* (☎ 937-555; fax 338-884) which has singles/twins for M$220/280. Nearby, at No 146 on the northern side of Avenida de Almeida Ribeiro, the *Grand Hotel* (☎ 921-111; fax 922-397) has singles/twins for M$242/276.

A couple of blocks south of the intersection where Avenida de Almeida Ribeiro meets the waterfront at Rua das Lorchas is the multi-storey *Peninsula Hotel* (☎ 318-899; fax 344-933). Singles/twins are M$280/300. This hotel is large, clean and popular. Just down the street, the *Macau Masters Hotel* (☎ 937-572; fax 937-565; 75 rooms)

is at Rua das Lorchas 162. Twins start at M$350.

The area north of the Lisboa Hotel, on a street called Estrada de Sao Francisco, is one more place to look around You have to climb a steep hill to get up this street, but the advantage is that the hotels have a little sea breeze and it's quiet. At 2-A, the *Vila Tak Lei* (☎ 577-484) has twins for M$250.

Further up the hill, and more expensive, is the *Guia Hotel* (☎ 513-888; fax 559-822; 89 rooms) at Estrada do Eng Trigo 1-5 (see the Macau Peninsula map). Twins are priced from M$400 to M$524 and suites start at M$604.

The *Metropole Hotel* (☎ 388-166; fax 388-553; 112 rooms) has a prime location at Avenida da Praia Grande 63. Singles are M$396 and twins are M$443.

The *Mondial Hotel* (☎ 566-866; fax 514-083; 141 rooms) is on a side street called Rua de Antonio Basto, east of the Lou Lim Ioc Gardens (see the Macau Peninsula map). It's rather far from the centre. Twins are M$322. The *Sintra* (☎ 710-111; fax 510-527; HK 2546-6944), on Avenida Dom Joao IV west of the Lisboa Hotel, is borderline for mid-price, but has doubles beginning at M$488.

Similarly, the *Presidente* (☎ 553-888; fax 552-735; HK 2857-1533), on Avenida da Amizade, is among the higher-priced hotels east of the Lisboa, but has twins starting at M$495.

Places to Stay – top end

If you have the cash, then the best place to stay in Macau is the *Bela Vista* (see prices on the next page), a luxurious small hotel run by the Mandarin Oriental Hotel group. But you had better hurry, because after 1999, it will become the Portuguese consulate.

A century removed from colonial splendour, the other unique place to stay in Macau is the *Lisboa Hotel*, whose wonderfully tacky facade is one of the best examples of the American postwar aesthetic this side of Las Vegas.

Most of the hotels listed below have a telephone number in Hong Kong which you can call to make a booking. However, you can often get a better deal booking top-end places from the travel agencies inside Shun Tak Centre (the Macau ferry pier) in Hong Kong. During the summer travel season, many upmarket hotels are solidly booked, even during weekdays. Just where all these rich high-rollers come from is a mystery.

The map location for most hotels is shown as CM (Central Macau) or MP (Macau Peninsula); the others are on Taipa or Coloane Island. The list of top-end places includes:

Bela Vista (☎ 965-333; fax 965-588; HK 2881-1688), Rua Comendador Kou Ho Neng, eight rooms, twins M$2000, suites M$4850 (MP)

Beverly Plaza (☎ 782-288; fax 780-684; HK 2739-9928), Avenida do Dr Rodrigo Rodrigues, 300 rooms, twins M$820 to M$960, suites M$1800 to M$1960 (CM)

Fortuna (☎ 786-333; fax 786-363; HK 2517-3728), Rua da Cantao, 368 rooms, twins M$580 to M$749, suites M$1519 to M$1841 (CM)

Grandeur (☎ 781-233; fax 781-211; HK 2857-2846), Rua de Pequim, 350 rooms, twins M$550 to M$700, suites M$1850 to M$6050 (MP)

Holiday Inn (☎ 783-333; fax 782-321; HK 2736-6855), Rua de Pequim, 451 rooms, twins M$1380, suites M$3100 (CM) – don't confuse this place with the similarly named Holiday Hotel

Hyatt Regency (☎ 831-234; fax 830-195; HK 2559-0168), Estrada Almirante Marques Esparteiro 2, Taipa Island, 326 rooms, standard rooms M$800, suites M$3000

Kingsway (☎ 702-888; fax 702-828), Rua de Luis Gonzaga Gomes, 410 rooms, twins M$788, suites M$1271 to M$3087 (MP)

Lisboa (☎ 577-666; fax 567-193; HK 2559-1028), Avenida da Amizade, 1050 rooms, twins M$900 to M$1150, suites M$2080 to M$3100 (CM)

Mandarin Oriental (☎ 567-888; fax 594-589; HK 2881-688), Avenida da Amizade, 435 rooms, twins M$1300 to M$1900, suites M$3800 to M$20,000 (MP)

New Century (☎ 831-111; fax 832-222; HK 2581-9863), Avenida Padre Tomas Pereira 889, Taipa Island, 600 rooms, 28 apartments, twins M$688 to M$930, suites M$2200, apartments M$20,000 to M$35,000

New World Emperor (☎ 781-888; fax 752-287; HK 2724-4622), Rua de Xangai, 405 rooms, twins M$840, suites M$1160 to M$4060 (CM)

Pousada de Coloane (☎ 882-143; fax 882-251; HK 2523-5690), Cheoc Van beach, Coloane Island, 22 rooms, twins M$630 to M$690

Pousada de Sao Tiago (☎ 378-111; fax 552-170; HK 2739-1216), Avenida da República, 23 rooms, twins M$1290 to M$1620, suites M$1890 to M$3250 (MP)

Pousada Ritz (☎ 339-955; fax 317-826; HK 2739-6993), Rua da Boa Vista 2, 31 rooms, twins M$980 to M$1380, suites M$2080 to M$2280 (MP)

Royal (☎ 552-222; fax 563-008; HK 2543-6426), Estrada da Vitoria 2-4, 380 rooms, twins M$550 to M$880, suites M$1200 (MP)

Westin Resort (☎ 871-111; fax 871-122; HK 2803-2015), Estrada de Hac Sa, Coloane Island, 208 rooms, twins M$1100 to M$1950, suites M$4500 to M$16,000

PLACES TO EAT

Given its cosmopolitan past, it's not surprising that the food of Macau is an exotic mixture of Portuguese and Chinese. It also speaks of a far greater appreciation and integration of food culture on the part of the Portuguese compared with the British in Hong Kong. There is also a little influence from other European countries and Africa. The English-speaking waitresses are invariably from the Philippines.

The most famous local speciality is African chicken baked with peppers and chillies. Other specialities include *bacalhau*, which is cod, served baked, grilled, stewed or boiled. Sole, a tongue-shaped flatfish, is another Macanese delicacy. There's also ox tail and ox breast, rabbit prepared in various ways, and soups like *caldo verde* and *sopa a alentejana* made with vegetables, meat and olive oil.

The Brazilian contribution is *feijoadas*, a stew made of beans, pork, spicy sausages, potatoes and cabbage. The contribution from the former Portuguese enclave of Goa on the western coast of India is spicy prawns.

The Portuguese influence is visible in the many fine imported Portuguese red and white wines, port and brandy. Mateus Rosé is the most famous, but even cheaper are bottles of red or white wine. A long, lazy Portuguese meal with a carafe of red to wash it down is one of the most pleasant aspects of a Macau visit. The menus are often in Portuguese, so a few useful words are *cozido* (stew), *cabrito* (kid), *cordeiro* (lamb), *carreiro* (mutton), *galinha* (chicken), *caraguejos* (crabs), *carne de vaca* (beef) and *peixe* (fish).

Another Macau pleasure is to sit back in one of the many little *pastelarias* (cake shops) with a glass of *chá de limão* (lemon tea) and a plate of cakes – very genteel! These places are good for a cheap breakfast. Not surprisingly, there's good bread to be found in Macau, another legacy of its Portuguese heritage. People eat early in Macau – you can find the chairs being put away and that the chef has gone home around 9 pm.

Henri's Galley (☎ 556-251) is on the waterfront at Avenida da República 4, on the southern end of the Macau Peninsula. The adjacent *Ali Curry House* is also worth a visit.

For good, cheap Portuguese and Macanese food, the *Estrela do Mar* (☎ 322-074) at Travessa do Paiva 11, off the Avenida da Praia Grande, is the place to go, as is the *Solmar* (☎ 574-391) at Avenida da Praia Grande 512. Both places are famous for African chicken and seafood. *La Lorcha* (☎ 313-193), located down near the Maritime Museum at 289A Rua Almirante Sergio, is also highly recommended as a place to get some of the best Portuguese food in Macau at very reasonable prices.

Fat Siu Lau (☎ 573-580) serves Portuguese and Chinese food. It's at Rua de Felicidade 64, once the red-light Street of Happiness that has recently undergone a face-lift. The speciality at Fat Siu Lau is roast pigeon.

A friendly and unpretentious place is the *Comida A Portuguesa Carlos* (☎ 300-315) at Rua Bishop Medeiros 28, a block south of the Lou Lim Ioc Gardens.

Convenient, if somewhat lacking in at-mosphere, the *Restaurante Safari* (☎ 322-239) is at Patio do Cotovelo 14, a tiny square off Avenida de Almeida Ribeiro across from the Central Hotel. It has good coffee-shop dishes, as well as spicy chicken, steak and fried noodles.

Ze do Pipo (☎ 374-047), Avenida da Praia Grande 717 (near Rua do Campo), is a two storey Portuguese restaurant. It's not a bad place to eat, but check the menu prices first. For very elegant dining, the *Military Club Restaurant* (☎ 714-009) at 795 Avenida da Praia Grande has buffets for lunch and dinner.

Chinese-style yoghurt and milkshakes are dished up at *Leitaria I Son*, next to the Macau Government Tourist Office. It's a good place to go for breakfast. Also next door is a good noodle shop. Further down Avenida de Almeida Ribeiro across from the Taitung Bank, there's a Japanese fast-food place with good set meals for M$40. There's no English sign, but there's a large model of a sumo wrestler-cum-sushi chef hanging above the doorway.

Lots of people hop over to Taipa village for the excellent restaurants found there, although it's no longer cheap. One place to try is either one of *Pinocchio's* (☎ 827-128), located at both ends of Rua do Cunha. On the same street, other popular Taipa Village restaurants include the very Portuguese *Restaurante Panda* (☎ 827-338) and *Galo Restaurant* (☎ 827-318), as well as *O'Manuel* (☎ 827-571).

At Hac Sa beach on Coloane Island, the legendary *Fernando's* (☎ 882-264) deserves honourable mention for some of the best food and nightlife in Macau.

Besides these places, of course, Macau has its fair share of cheap Chinese restaurants and eight outlets of *McDonald's* if you can't go without a Big Mac.

ENTERTAINMENT
Gambling
Even if gambling holds no interest for you, it's fun to wander the casinos at night. The largest and most fun arena for losing money is the *Lisboa Hotel*. Cheating at

gambling is a serious criminal offence, so don't even think about it. The *Crazy Paris Show* at the hotel also features Las Vegas-style dancing shows every night.

There's also horse racing on Taipa Island at the *Jockey Club*. Dog races are held at the *Canidrome* (yes, they really call it that) in the north of Macau starting at 8 pm on Tuesday, Thursday, Saturday and Sunday. For the bloodthirsty, there are occasional bullfights held in Macau every 10 years or so, although they may (unfortunately) be catching on because the event has been held consecutively in the last two years and has proved popular with Hong Kongers. Check with the tourist office for information.

Pubs

A prominent part of nightlife for local and Hong Kong expats is the *Talker Pub* (☎ 550-153, 528-975) at Rua de Pedro Coutinho 104, near the Kun Iam Temple. It doesn't really get going until after 9 pm. A hot spot which is open on Friday and Saturday night only is the *Jazz Club* (☎ 596-014), Rua Alabardas 9, near St Lawrence's Church. Live music is normally performed here between 11 pm and 2 am. Go to the back of the church and turn left down Rua George Chinnery and turn right at the street at the bottom.

Other pubs include the *Billabong Bar* (☎ 355-009), run by an Aussie expat, at 2C Beco do Goncalo, off Rua Central, and *Oskar's Pub* inside the Holiday Inn.

THINGS TO BUY

Pawnshops are ubiquitous in Macau, and it is possible to get good deals on cameras, watches and jewellery, but you must be prepared to bargain without mercy. In Macau, at least, the nasty reputation of pawnbrokers is well deserved!

The MGTO has a number of good souvenir items for sale at low prices, but you'll have to ask for them because the items are all hidden away behind the counter. Some of the items to consider are Macau T-shirts, books, sets of postcards and other tourist paraphernalia.

St Dominic's Market, in the alley behind the Central Hotel, is a good place to pick up cheap clothing. If you are looking for reproductions of antique Chinese furniture, it's much cheaper to buy it in Macau than Hong Kong, and the price will include shipping to Hong Kong. The shops are concentrated in the tourist area on Rua da Palha and Rua de S Paulo near the Ruins of St Paul's.

If you've got the habit, Macau is cheap for Portuguese wine, imported cigarettes, cigars and pipe tobacco. However, Hong Kong's customs agents only allow you to bring in 1L of wine and 50 cigarettes duty free.

GETTING THERE & AWAY

Air

Macau's controversial new airport opened in December 1995. There were serious doubts that the airport would ever generate enough passengers to pay for itself, but traffic has increased in the last two years and the two million mark was reached for passenger activity in May 1997, although it doesn't seem like much when you consider that nearly 24 million air passengers go through Hong Kong each year. There are also plans to commence a jetfoil service running directly from the airport to Hong Kong.

The main airline is Air Macau, but there are also a few regional and international airlines that fly to Macau. There are flights to cities in China and Taiwan, as well as to Kuala Lumpur, Manila, Singapore, Seoul, Pyongyang and Lisbon.

For Hong Kongers in a hurry to lose their money, East Asia Airlines runs a helicopter service. Flying time from Hong Kong is 20 minutes at a cost of HK$1206 on weekdays, or HK$1310 on weekends – quite an expense just to save the extra 30 minutes required by boat. There are up to 22 flights daily.

In Hong Kong, departures are from Shun Tak Centre (☎ 2859-3359), 200 Connaught Rd, Sheung Wan; in Macau, departures are from the jetfoil pier (☎ 790-7040).

Bus

Macau is an easy gateway into China. You simply take a bus to the border and walk across. Buses No 3 and 10B run between the jetfoil pier and the Barrier Gate at the Macau-China border.

You can also catch a bus directly from Macau to Guangzhou, although this won't save any time because you've got a long stopover at the border while your fellow passengers go through the immigration queues.

Tickets for the Guangzhou bus are sold at Kee Kwan Motors (☎ 933-888) beside the Macau Masters Hotel at Rua das Lorchas 12. Buses leave from there every half-hour between 8.30 and 10.30 am, then every hour up to 6.30 pm. Tickets cost M$60 and the trip takes approximately three hours.

Boat

The vast majority of visitors to Macau make their arrival and departure by boat.

Hong Kong-Macau Macau is separated from Hong Kong by 65km of water. There are departures about once every 15 minutes during daylight hours, and every 30 minutes at night. The boats operate all night, with less frequent departures after midnight.

You have three types of boats to choose from. There are jetfoils, turbocats (jet-powered catamarans) and high-speed ferries. Jetfoils take 55 minutes. The turbocats come in two varieties: so-called jumbo-cats, which take 65 minutes, and tri-cats, which take 55 minutes.

Slowest are the high-speed ferries (95 minutes) operated by the Hong Kong & Yaumati Ferry Company, but they are also the cheapest. Smoking is prohibited on the jetfoils and turbocats.

Most of the fast boats depart from the huge Macau ferry pier next to Shun Tak Centre at 200 Connaught Rd, Sheung Wan, Hong Kong Island – this is easily reached by MTR to the Sheung Wan station. However, there are a few boats from the China Hong Kong City ferry pier in Kow-

loon and the slow boats, ie high-speed ferries, also leave from here.

Luggage space on the jetfoils is limited to what you can carry. You'll be OK just carrying a backpack or one suitcase, but oversized baggage will need to be checked in as on an aircraft.

On weekends and holidays, you'd be wise to book your return ticket in advance because the boats are sometimes full. Even Monday morning can be difficult for getting seats back to Hong Kong, but there is normally no problem on weekdays. If you can't get a seat on the jetfoil or turbo-cat, you might have a chance with the high-speed ferries, which have a lot more room.

Jetfoil tickets can be purchased up to 28 days in advance in Hong Kong at the pier and at MTR Travel Services Centres, or booked by phone (M ☎ 790-7039; HK ☎ 2859-6596) if you have a credit card. Turbocat tickets (M ☎ 790-3211; HK ☎ 2921-6688) can be purchased 28 days in advance at the pier, at China Travel Service in Hong Kong or at the Lisboa Hotel in Macau. The Jumbo-cats can also be booked by phone and credit card (M ☎ 790-3211; HK ☎ 2559-9255).

There are three different classes on the turbocats (economy, 1st and VIP). The VIP cabin seats up to six people, and the cost per ticket is the same whether one or six people occupy the cabin. The jetfoils have two classes (economy and 1st) and the Hong Kong ferries have one standard class only. All depart from the jetfoil pier in Macau.

The Hong Kong government charges HK$26 departure tax, which is included in the price of your ticket. Macau charges M$22 departure tax, also included in the ticket price. The following prices are what you pay in Hong Kong:

Vessel	Weekday (HK$)	Weekend (HK$)	Night (HK$)
Ferry	111	132	152
Jetfoil	134/148	145/158	165/179
Turbocat	129/251/ 1386	140/246/ 1476	160/259/ 1556

Shekou-Macau Ferries leave once a day from the wharf behind the Peninsula Hotel to Shekou in the Shenzhen Special Economic Zone. The boat leaves Macau at 2.30 pm and arrives in Shekou at 4 pm. Tickets are M$97.

GETTING AROUND
Macau is fairly compact and it's relatively easy to walk almost everywhere, but you'll definitely need motorised transport to visit Taipa and Coloane.

To/From the Airport
Taxis and AP1 buses take passengers to the major hotels and the jetfoil pier, and terminate at the border. The price is M$6.

Bus
There are minibuses and large buses, and both offer air-con and frequent service. They operate from 7 am until midnight. Buses on the Macau Peninsula cost M$2.30 and M$4.50 for longer rides out to the islands.

Arguably the most useful bus to travellers is the No 3, which takes in the China border crossing, the jetfoil pier and the central area near the main post office. Bus No 10 also takes you into the centre of town, and 10B goes directly from the jetfoil pier to the border. Bus No 11 goes from the square and the Lisboa Hotel to Taipa and No 25 goes to Coloane. The map handed out by the tourist office also has a list of bus routes. Unlike Hong Kong, however, minibuses take as many passengers as possible, and can be very crowded.

Car
The mere thought of renting a car for sightseeing on the Macau Peninsula is ridiculous – horrendous traffic and lack of parking space make driving more of a burden than a pleasure. However, between a group, car rental might make sense for exploring Taipa and Coloane.

As in Hong Kong, driving is on the left-hand side of the road. Another local driving rule is that motor vehicles must always stop for pedestrians at a crossing if there is no traffic light. It's illegal to beep the horn.

Happy Mokes (☎ 726-868) is in the jetfoil pier, level 1, counter 1025. They also have an office in the New Century Hotel (☎ 831-212) in Macau. Bookings can be made at its Hong Kong office (☎ 2540-8180).

Mokes or other models cost M$380 and up. You can also rent Mokes from Avis Rent A Car (☎ 336-789) at the Mandarin Oriental Hotel. It's probably not necessary on weekdays, but you can book in advance at the Avis Hong Kong office (☎ 2541-2011).

Taxi
Macau taxis all have meters, and drivers are required to use them. Flag fall is M$9 for the first 1.5km, thereafter it's M$1 every 250m. There is a M$5 surcharge to go to Taipa, and M$10 to go to Coloane, but there is no surcharge on return trips.

Taxis can be dispatched by radio through the Vang Lek Radio Taxi company if you ring up (☎ 519-519). Not many taxi drivers speak English, so it would be helpful to have a map with both Chinese and English or Portuguese. If you hire a taxi for the day or half a day, it's better to agree on a price beforehand.

Pedicab
The pedicabs are essentially for touristy sightseeing and photo opportunities. The vehicles have to be bargained for and it's hardly worth the effort – if there are two of you make sure the fare covers both. Typical fees are M$20 for a short photo opportunity, or about M$100 per hour. Don't worry about finding them; they'll find you.

Bicycle
You can hire bicycles out on the islands of Taipa and Coloane (if you're lucky). On the peninsula, there are no places to hire bikes and, anyway, it wouldn't be pleasant riding with the insane traffic.

Guangdong 广东

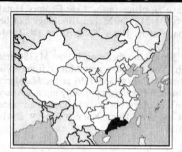

Guangdong Facts & Highlights

Area: 186,000 sq km

Population: 69.6 million

Capital: Guangzhou

Highlights

- Guangzhou's Shamian Island – sample its decaying colonial ambience.
- Fear and loathing, the bizarre and the disgusting (plus vegetables) at Qingping Market in Guangzhou.
- Zhaoqing, a poor cousin to Guilin, but with its share of sights and the nearby beauty of Dinghushan.

Guangdong's proximity to Hong Kong has made it a major gateway into China. It has also made it China's most affluent province. In 1979, Guangdong *(guǎngdōng)* was only the 10th most affluent, but the high level of economic integration between Guangdong's Pearl River Delta and Hong Kong has led to record economic growth – some economists refer to the area as Greater Hong Kong.

The Cantonese, as the people of Guangdong are called, are regarded with a mixture of envy and suspicion by many in the rest of China. Guangdong's topography, unique dialect (Cantonese) and remoteness from traditional centres of authority, coupled with long-standing contact with 'foreign barbarians', has created a strong sense of autonomy and self-sufficiency.

The Cantonese also spearheaded Chinese emigration to the USA, Canada, Australia and South Africa in the mid-19th century, spurred on by the gold rushes in those countries and by the wars and growing poverty in their own country. Bustling Chinatowns around the world are steeped in the flavours of Guangdong cuisine and ring with the sing-song sounds of the Cantonese dialect and Canto-pop melodies. Hong Kong heroes such as Bruce Lee and Jackie Chan are as famous abroad as they are at home.

The province has basked in the healthy regional economic climate encompassing Hong Kong, becoming the target for investment by overseas Chinese. Much of the manufacturing for which Hong Kong was once famous is now done in Guangdong (by 1993, more than 30,000 manufacturers from Hong Kong had set up businesses in the province) and about 15% of China's foreign trade is now conducted in Guangzhou, the province's capital.

Supping at the same table as Hong Kong has both fattened the province and cultivated a regional idiosyncrasy that finds vigorous expression in the burgeoning film and music industries. When China-watchers worry (or rub their hands in glee) about the possible decentralisation of power in China and the rise of regionalism, it is Guangdong that they look to first. After all, Guangdong was a latecomer to the Chinese Empire. While it was integrated in 214 BC (during the Qin Dynasty), it was not until the mid-12th century that large numbers of Han settlers (propelled by the Jurchen invaders) emigrated to the province from northern China.

Until then, Guangdong was considered to be a barbaric borderland fit only for exiled officials. In subsequent years, the

Guangdong
0
50
100 km
FUJIAN
JIANGXI
HUNAN
GUANGXI
GUANGDONG
SOUTH CHINA SEA
HONG KONG
KOWLOON
MACAU
Xinfengjiang Reservoir
To Hengyang
Longyan
Zhangzhou
SHANTOU
Chaozhou
Jieyang
Meixian
Fengshun
Puning
Lufeng
Haifeng
Longchuan
Heyuan
Huizhou
Huiyang
Shenzhen
Dongguan
Humen
Luofushan
Conghua
Xinfeng
Shaoguan
GUANGZHOU
Zhongshan
Zhuhai
Jiangmen
Taishan
Foshan
Sanshui
Qingyuan
Yangshan
Lianxian
Zhaoqing
Dinghu
Enping
Yangjiang
Yunfu
Luoding
Hexian
Wuzhou
Yangxi
Dianbai
Maoming
Xinyi
Gaozhou
Huazhou
Zhanjiang
Haikang
Xuwen
Yulin
Guilin
LIUZHOU
Guixian
Beihai

GUANGDONG

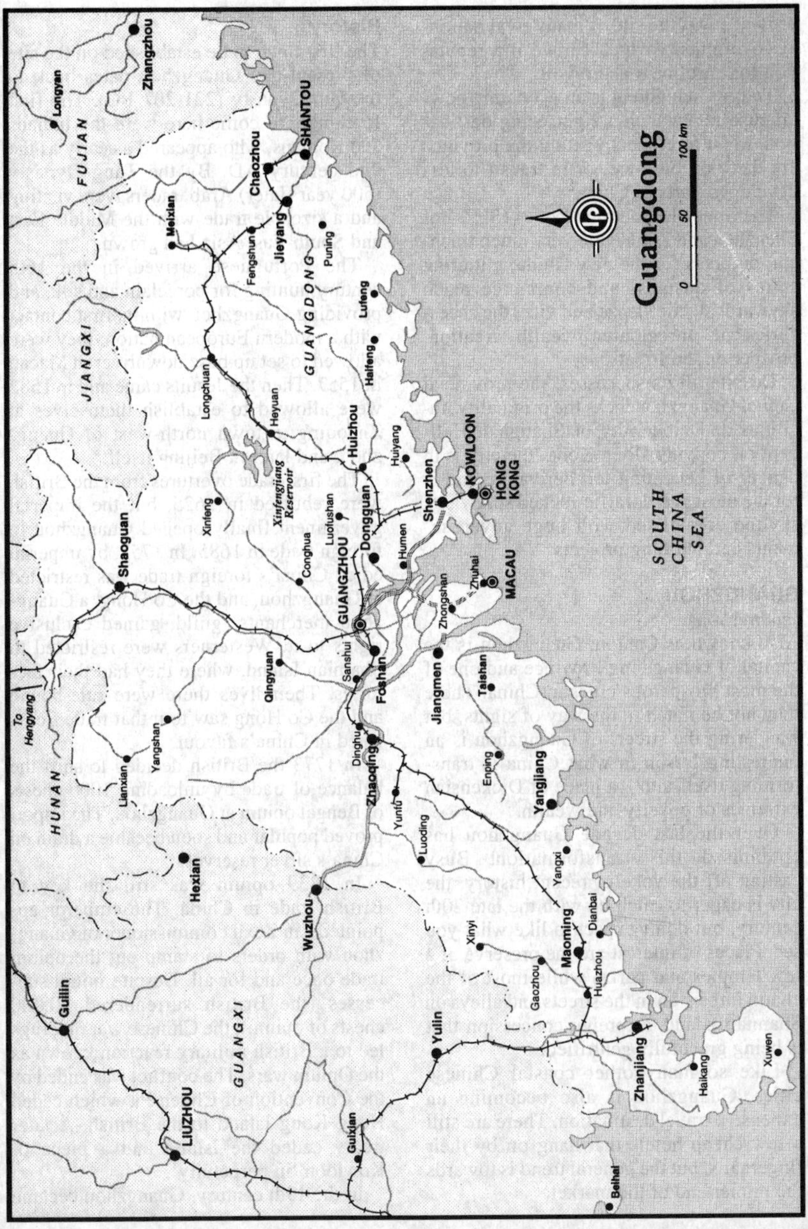

province was the site of many rival national governments which earned it a reputation for unruliness and revolt.

Today Guangdong is an economic powerhouse rather than a sightseeing destination. Most foreigners visiting the province are there on business, or in transit to less developed parts of China.

The Special Economic Zones (SEZs) of Shenzhen and Zhuhai are very much financial outposts for the new China; glittering spires of business and commerce reach skywards, while sleaze and vice, the accessories of unregulated wealth creation, prosper on the streets.

Despite all its successes, the provincial capital Guangzhou lacks the originality, facilities and modernity of Shanghai. Hellbent on copying Hong Kong, the city is in danger of becoming too derivative and is for the most part a traffic-locked sprawl, its skyline crenellated with huge advertisements and building projects.

GUANGZHOU
(guǎngzhōu)

Also known as Canton, Guangzhou is the capital of Guangdong Province and one of the most prosperous cities in China. There may not be much in the way of sights, but wandering the streets of Guangzhou is an interesting lesson in what China is transforming itself into – a place of Dickensian extremes of poverty and wealth.

Over the last decade Guangzhou has epitomised this transformation. Busy casting off the yoke of recent history, the city is eager to catch up with the late 20th century, but don't expect to like what you see. Places of interest are the preserve of a few temples and parks, while most of the charm lingers on in the streets and alleys on Shamian Island, a foreign concession that is being gracefully gentrified.

Like so many other coastal Chinese cities, Guangzhou is also becoming an expensive travel destination. There are still a few cheap hotels that hang on by their fingernails, but the general trend is towards the pricier end of the market.

History

The first town to be established on the site of present-day Guangzhou dates back to the Qin Dynasty (221-207 BC). The first foreigners to come here were the Indians and Romans, who appeared as early as the 2nd century AD. By the Tang Dynasty (500 years later) Arab traders were visiting and a sizeable trade with the Middle East and South-East Asia had grown.

The Portuguese arrived in the 16th century hunting for porcelain and silk, and providing Guangzhou with its first contact with a modern European nation; they were allowed to set up base downriver in Macau in 1557. Then the Jesuits came and in 1582 were allowed to establish themselves at Zhaoqing, a town north-west of Guangzhou, and later in Beijing itself.

The first trade overtures from the British were rebuffed in 1625, but the imperial government finally opened Guangzhou to foreign trade in 1685. In 1757, by imperial edict, China's foreign trade was restricted to Guangzhou, and the Co Hong, a Guangzhou merchants' guild, gained exclusive rights to it. Westerners were restricted to Shamian Island, where they had their factories. Their lives there were rule-bound and the Co Hong saw to it that trade flourished in China's favour.

In 1773 the British decided to shift the balance of trade by unloading 1000 chests of Bengal opium at Guangzhou. The import proved popular and soon became a drain on China's silver reserves.

In 1839 opium was still the key to British trade in China. The emperor appointed Lin Zexu commissioner of Guangzhou with orders to stamp out the opium trade once and for all. Despite initial successes (the British surrendered 20,000 chests of opium), the Chinese war on drugs led to a British military reaction known as the Opium wars. The conflict was ended by the Convention of Chuen Pi, which ceded Hong Kong Island to the British. A later treaty ceded the island and a piece of Kowloon 'in perpetuity'.

In the 19th century, Guangzhou became

The Heavenly Kingdom of the Taiping

The Taiping Rebellion in the middle of the 19th century ranks among the most frenzied and calamitous in Chinese history. What made it more remarkable was its creed: that Hong Xiuquan, the leader of the Taipings, was the brother of Jesus and the son of God. He had been sent down to exterminate 'demons' – who (coincidentally) were personified by the Qing Dynasty and its supporters.

Born into a Hakka family in eastern Guangxi and having failed the official examinations that would have taken him onto the career ladder among the Qing elite, Hong Xiuquan first came into contact with Christianity through Protestant missionaries in Canton in the mid-1830s. After failing the official examinations for the third time, Hong had a dream of a bearded man and a younger man who he later interpreted, in a flash of realisation after reading some Christian tracts, as being God the Father and Jesus, his son. He repeatedly read the character for his surname 'Hong' in the Chinese translation of the bible he possessed; the character means 'flood' and he made strong associations between the biblical flood and his mission on earth to wipe out evil.

Collecting around him a flock of believers attracted by his zeal, self-belief and drive, Hong soon had a formidable army of faithful who sought to establish the Heavenly Kingdom of Great Peace on earth, overthrowing the Qing in the process. God was the one true god and traditional Chinese beliefs (such as Confucianism) were heretical and wayward.

By 1850, Hong Xiuquan's followers numbered more than 20,000 and were a capable military force, regimented by a strict morality that forbade opium smoking, took serious measures against corruption and established separate camps to divide the sexes. A communal treasury was set up to take charge of the finances of the Taiping community and legal and agrarian reforms followed suit.

Led by capable and daring officers, the Taiping army dispatched itself on a remarkable series of conquests that took it through Hunan, Hubei and Anhui, eventually setting up the Taiping capital in Nanjing, which fell to the rebels in March 1853. The Manchu population of Nanjing was slaughtered in affirmation of Hong's plan to rid China, and the world, of demons.

For 11 years the Taiping held sway over their conquered domain, with Hong ruling over all as the Heavenly King. Hong further regimented the rules governing the Taiping faithful, creating a society ordered by spartan and inflexible decrees all intent on eliminating inequality. However, the forces that were to destroy the Heavenly Kingdom soon emerged in a power struggle among the leadership of the Taiping, which resulted in the murder of those in positions of great influence, and their supporters. Hong reasserted his authority, but in doing so eliminated his most useful advisers.

The Taiping's failure to take Peking (Beijing) and Shanghai was partly because the foreign powers (suspicious of Hong's heretical strain of Christianity) failed to respond to Hong's faith that they would not support the Qing. Their economic strategies similarly failed, and the strict codes of conduct left many bitter and complaining; Hong also failed to align himself and his cause with other contemporaneous anti-Qing rebellions. All of these factors led to an erosion of the power and influence of the Taiping.

Qing soldiers, led by Zeng Guofan, eventually retook Nanjing in 1864, soon after Hong Xiuquan's death. Zeng Guofan reported to the emperor that none of the 100,000 rebels in Nanjing surrendered, but instead took their own lives.

The fanaticism of the Taiping was incredible, and despite its strongly anti-Manchu character, the event clearly questions the theory that Christianity has no place in China. Even though Hong arrogated upon himself the heretical (to Protestants and Catholics) title of son of God, the Taiping were responsible for, among other things, a vast translation and publishing programme of Christian scriptures and writings, and it was their aim to spread these ultimately to the four corners of the earth. ■

a cradle of revolt. The leader of the anti-dynastic Taiping Rebellion, Hong Xiuquan (1814-64), was born at Huaxian, north-west of Guangzhou, and the early activities of the Taipings centred on this area.

Guangzhou was also a stronghold of the republican forces after the fall of the Qing Dynasty in 1911. Sun Yatsen, the first president of the Republic of China, was born at Cuiheng village south-west of Guangzhou. In the early 1920s, Sun headed the Kuomintang (Nationalist Party) in Guangzhou, from where the republicans mounted their campaigns against the northern warlords. Guangzhou was also a centre of activities for the fledgling Communist Party.

Contemporary Guangzhou, however, swings to the tinkle of cash registers rather than the drum roll of protest and revolt. In recent times the Cantonese have been happy to leave the turbulence of politics to their northern compatriots.

Orientation

Central Guangzhou is bounded by a circle road (Huanshi Lu – literally 'circle-city road') to the north and the Pearl River to the south. A larger ring road (the Huancheng expressway) is being constructed. This is not the full extent of the city, of course, but most hotels, commercial areas and places of interest lie within these boundaries.

Accommodation tends to be clustered around the railway station (in the north), on Huanshi Donglu (in the north-east), and in and around the old foreign concession of Shamian Island (in the south). If you don't want to leave with the impression that Guangzhou is one huge construction site, seek sanctuary on Shamian Island, which is by far the quietest and most appealing sector of the city.

According to Chinese convention, Guangzhou's major streets are usually split into numbered sectors (Zhongshan 5-Lu etc). Alternatively they are labelled by compass points: *bei* (north), *dong* (east), *nan* (south) and *xi* (west) – as in Huanshi Donglu, which will sometimes be written in English as Huanshi East Road.

Information

Travel Offices There is an enormous CITS office (☎ 8666-6271) at 179 Huanshi Lu, next to the main railway station. This office is being made increasingly redundant by all the hotel booking services and private operations in town. Its days are numbered – they even asked us for a tip before handing over information when we were last there! Occasionally it manages to find tickets lurking in the crevices of its vast bureaucracy, but don't count on it.

Most of the major hotels have ticketing agencies which can provide air, boat and train tickets with a minimum of fuss. Some of the smaller hotels are able to get hold of train and boat tickets with little hassle. Also ask at your hotel for advice on new sights and places to go.

Consulates There are several consulates which can issue visas and replace stolen passports.

Australia
  (☎ 8331-2738; fax 8331-2198) Room 1503-4, Main Building, Citic Plaza, 339 Huanshi Donglu
France
  (☎ 8667-7522; fax 8666-5390) Unit 1160, China Hotel, Liuhua Lu
Germany
  (☎ 8192-2566) 103 Shamian Beijie, Shamian Island
Japan
  (☎ 8333-8999) Garden Hotel Tower, 368 Huanshi Donglu
Poland
  (☎ 8186-1854) near the White Swan Hotel on Shamian Island
Thailand
  (☎ 8888-6968, ext 3310) Room 316, White Swan Hotel, Shamian Island
USA
  (☎ 8888-8911; fax 8886-2341) 1 Shamian Nanjie, Shamian Island
Vietnam
  (☎ 8358-1000, ext 101) 13 Taojin Beilu (behind the Guangzhou Friendship Store)

PSB The PSB (☎ 8333-1060) is at 863 Jiefang Beilu, opposite the road which leads up to the Zhenhai Tower.

Warning

While it is fairly safe to walk the streets of Guangzhou, remember that the city is inundated with poor peasants in search of riches. Some of them turn to crime. Be on the alert for pickpockets, wear a money belt if you have one, stash your passport somewhere safe and be sure you know what you are getting if buying rail tickets from touts in front of the railway station. ■

Money Every large tourist hotel cashes travellers cheques and changes Hong Kong and US dollars, and increasing numbers provide cash advances on credit cards.

If you're coming from Hong Kong then be warned that Guangzhou's residents are all too happy to receive Hong Kong dollars from you, but they will give you change in RMB; change your dollars first to RMB at the bank or at your hotel.

Guangzhou's American Express office (☎ 8331-1771; fax 8331-3535) is in the ground floor lobby of the Guangdong International Hotel.

Post & Communications All the major tourist hotels have post offices where you can send letters and packets containing printed matter. If you're posting parcels overseas, go to the post office at 43 Yanjiang Xilu, near the riverfront and Shamian Island. Get the parcel contents checked and fill out a customs form.

Adjacent to the railway station is the main post office, known locally as the Liuhua post office *(liúhuā yóu jú)*.

DHL (☎ 8664-4668) has an office in Guangzhou, as does UPS (☎ 8775-5778). Federal Express (☎ 8386-2026) can be found in the Garden Hotel, Room 1356-7, Garden Tower.

The telecommunications office is across from the railway station on the eastern side of Renmin Beilu. Most hotels have International Direct Dialling (IDD) – calls to Hong Kong are very cheap. All the main tourist hotels have 'business centres' offering domestic and international telephone, fax and telex facilities (some offer email as well).

Guangzhou's first Internet cafe had recently opened at 351 Tianhe Lu, near the Tianhe Sports Centre in the east of the city. Charges are Y8 per half-hour off peak, and Y15 during peak time. Ask at your hotel if they have an email facility or whether they know of more central Internet cafes that have opened; there will surely be more.

Bookshops The Foreign Languages Bookstore at 326 Beijing Lu has the usual drab display with nothing but highbrow fiction of the *Our Mutual Friend* and *War and Peace* mould.

For more normal reading material head off to the newsagents in the Guangdong International Hotel, the Garden Hotel or the White Swan. Some popular novels are available, as well as current issues of *Time*, *Newsweek*, *The Economist*, *Far Eastern Economic Review*, *Asiaweek* and even some French and German publications.

Medical Services The Guangzhou Red Cross Hospital has an emergency number (☎ 8444-6411) with English-speakers. For general treatment of non-emergencies, try the medical clinic for foreigners at the Guangzhou No 1 People's Hospital (☎ 8333-3090) *(dìyī rénmín yīyuàn)* at 602 Renmin Beilu.

If you're staying on Shamian Island or the riverfront, a nearby hospital is the Sun Yatsen Memorial Hospital (☎ 8188-2012) *(sūn yìxiān jìniàn yīyuàn)* at 107 Yanjiang Xilu, opposite the Aiqun Hotel. Not much English is spoken here, but the medical facilities are pretty good and the prices low.

Just next to Shamian Island and the Qingping Market is the Guangzhou Hospital of Traditional Chinese Medicine (☎ 8188-6504) *(zhōngyī yīyuàn)* at 16 Zhuji Lu. If you want to try acupuncture and herbs, this is the place to go. Many foreigners come here to study Chinese medicine rather than to be treated.

Shamian Island
(shāmiàn)

Shamian is a blessed retreat from the bustle of Guangzhou's streets. Everything is conducted in low gear – pedestrians saunter rather than walk, cars sidle rather than drive, birds sing and lazy tennis matches stretch out into the late afternoon. The island has shades of Paris' *rive gauche* in its serenity and crumbling history and is an ideal place to wander around and inhabit the past.

Shamian means 'sand surface', which is all this island was until foreign traders were permitted to set up their warehouses and factories here in the middle of the 18th century. Land reclamation has increased its

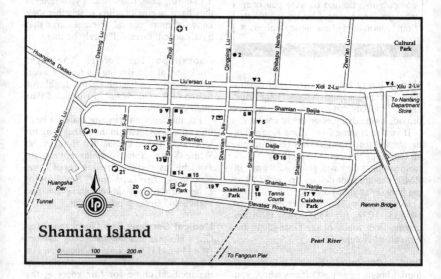

Shamian Island

0   100   200 m

To Fangcun Pier

Pearl River

SHAMIAN ISLAND 沙面	4	McDonald's; Antique Market 麦当劳、古玩市场	2	Qingping Market 清平市场

PLACES TO STAY

6 Guangdong Victory Hotel (new annexe)
   胜利宾馆（新楼）
8 Guangdong Victory Hotel
   胜利宾馆
14 Guangzhou Youth Hostel
   省外办招待所
15 Shamian Hotel
   沙面宾馆
20 White Swan Hotel
   白天鹅宾馆

PLACES TO EAT

3 Bakery
   面包店

5 New York Silver Palace Restaurant
   银宫大酒楼
9 Bakery
   面包店
11 Li Qun Restaurant
   利群饮食店
17 Chicago Coffee Shop
   芝加哥咖啡馆
19 Lucy's Bar & Restaurant
   露丝酒吧餐厅

OTHER

1 Hospital of Traditional Chinese Medicine
   中医医院

7 Post Office
   邮局
10 German Consulate
   德国领事馆
12 Polish Consulate
   波兰领事馆
13 Shamian Bar
   沙面酒吧
16 Bank of China
   中国银行
18 Lankwaifong Bar
   兰桂坊
21 US Consulate
   美国领事馆

area to its present size: 900m from east to west, and 300m from north to south. The island became a British and French concession after they defeated the Chinese in the Opium wars, and is covered with decaying colonial buildings which housed trading offices and residences.

The French Catholic church has been restored and stands on the main boulevard. The boulevard itself is a gentle stretch of gardens, trees and birdsong. Just to the west of the White Swan Hotel is the Church of Christ, which is an active church again, and is managed by the Guangdong Christian Council. Today most of the buildings are used as offices or apartment blocks – some with their front doors flung open to reveal old wooden staircases climbing into cavernous interiors. The German consulate on the far west of the island is a recent Teutonic addition to this European enclave.

Slowly but surely the island is being gentrified. Sidewalk cafes, bars and the occasional boutique have sprung up, while police patrol to keep beggars off the island.

Temple of the Six Banyan Trees
(liù róng sì huā tǎ)
The six banyan trees of the temple's name (celebrated in a poem by Su Dongpo, a renowned poet who visited the temple in 1100 AD), are no longer standing, but the temple remains a popular attraction for its octagonal Flower Pagoda.

At 55m, the pagoda is the tallest in the city – from the outside it appears to have only nine storeys, but inside it has 17. The pagoda was constructed in 1097. It's worth climbing up, although if you are tall you might end up with a collection of bruises as the doorways on the way up are very low. As you come down, go anticlockwise for the quickest descent, otherwise things can get a bit labyrinthine.

The temple, which may date as far back as 537 AD, originally was associated with Hui Neng, the sixth patriarch of the Zen Buddhist sect. Today it serves as the headquarters of the Guangzhou Buddhist Association. It is an active temple – be sensitive

about taking photographs of monks and worshippers. Inside the Guanyin Temple is a huge golden effigy of Guanyin (the goddess of compassion), to whom women burn incense and pray.

Liurong Lu, outside the temple, is a colourful array of souvenir shops selling ceramics, jade and religious ornaments and there is also a bustling fruit and meat market on Ruinan Lu, on the right just before you reach the temple itself. Entrance to the temple is Y1 and, if you want to climb the pagoda, tickets are Y5.

Bright Filial Piety Temple
(guāngxiào sì)
This temple is one of the oldest in Guangzhou. The earliest Buddhist temple on this site possibly dates to the 4th century AD and may have existed before the city was established. The place has particular significance for Buddhists because Hui Neng of the Zen Buddhist sect was a novice monk here in the 7th century.

The temple buildings are of much more recent construction, the original buildings having been destroyed by fire in the mid-17th century. The main temple is a deep and impressive construction equipped with golden figures.

Five Genies Temple
(wǔ xiān guān)
This Taoist temple is held to be the site of the appearance of the five rams and celestial beings in the myth of Guangzhou's foundation (see the section on Yuexiu Park later in this chapter for the story).

The large hollow in the rock in the temple courtyard is said to be the impression of a celestial being's foot; the Chinese refer to it by the name of Rice-Ear Rock of Unique Beauty. The great bell, which weighs five tonnes, was cast during the Ming Dynasty – it's 3m high, 2m in diameter and about 10cm thick, and is probably the largest in Guangdong Province. It's known as the 'calamity bell', since the sound of the bell, which has no clapper, is a portent of calamity for the city.

GUANGDONG

At the rear of the main tower stand life-size statues with archaic Greek smiles; these appear to represent four of the five genies. In the temple forecourt are four statues of rams, and embedded in the temple walls are inscribed steles.

The temple is just south of Huaisheng Mosque at the end of an alleyway whose entrance is on Huifu Xilu. It is open daily from 9 am to noon and from 1.30 to 5 pm; entry is Y1.

Qingping Market
(qīngpíng shìchǎng)

Qingping Market came into existence in 1979. Although such private (capitalist) markets are a feature of all Chinese cities today, it was one of Deng Xiaoping's more radical economic experiments at that time.

The market is like a take-away zoo. Near the entrance you'll find the usual selection of medicinal herbs and spices, dried starfish, snakes, lizards, deer antlers, dried scorpions, leopard and tiger skins, bear paws, semi-toxic mushrooms, tree bark and unidentifiable herbs and plants. Further up you'll find the live ones waiting to be butchered. Sad-eyed monkeys rattle at the bars of their wooden cages, tortoises crawl over each other in shallow tin trays, owls sit perched on boxes full of pigeons, and fish paddle around in tubs aerated with jets of water. There are also bundles of frogs, giant salamanders, pangolins (anteaters), dogs and raccoons, alive or contorted by recent violent death – which may just swear you off meat. This market will definitely upset the more sensitive traveller.

The market is on the north side of Liu'er-san Lu and spills out into Tiyun Lu, which cuts east-west across Qingping Lu.

Sacred Heart Church
(shí shì jiàotáng)

This impressive twin-spired church is built entirely of granite. Started in 1863 and completed in 1888 (during the reign of Guangxu), it was designed by the French architect Guillemin. The church is an imitation of a European Gothic cathedral and its spires tower to a height of 58m. Four bronze bells suspended in the building to the east of the church were cast in France; the original coloured glass was also made in France, but almost all of it is gone. It's on the northern side of Yide Xilu, west of Haizhu Circle.

The **Zion Christian Church**, at 392 Renmin Zhonglu, is another church which may be of interest. The building is a hybrid, with a traditional European Gothic outline and Chinese eaves. It's an active place of worship.

Huaisheng Mosque
(huáishèng sì guāngtǎ)

The original mosque on this site is said to have been established in 627 AD by the first Muslim missionary to China. By all accounts the original mosque was the first Islamic building in China, which illustrates the level of early communication between the two cultures.

The present buildings were built in the Qing Dynasty (1644-1911) as the original mosque was destroyed in a fire in 1343. The name of the mosque means 'Remember the Sage', in memory of the prophet. Inside the grounds of the mosque is a minaret, which because of its even appearance is known as the Guangta, or Smooth Tower. It stands on Guangta Lu, which runs eastwards off Renmin Zhonglu.

Haizhuang Park
(hǎizhuàng gōngyuán)

Haizhuang Park across the river would be a nondescript park, but for the remains of what was once Guangzhou's largest monastery, the **Ocean Banner Monastery**. It was founded by a Buddhist monk in 1662, and in its heyday the monastery grounds covered 2.5 hectares. After 1911 the monastery was used as a school and soldiers' barracks. It was opened to the public as a park in the 1930s.

Religious services stopped at the temple during the Cultural Revolution, but have resumed today. The temple is home to three huge golden buddhas and in the rear courtyard incense burning and prayers are conducted by lay visitors. An adjacent building houses thousands of miniature shrines, each with a photograph of the deceased.

The temple, the gate to the park and other fixtures are being slowly restored, and the area gradually prettified. During the day the grounds are full of old men chatting, playing cards and chequers, and airing their pet birds.

Bus Nos 10, 16 and 25 all go to the park; bus No 10 can be picked up on Liu'ersan Lu which faces Shamian Island.

Yuexiu Park
(yuèxiù gōngyuán)

This is the biggest park in Guangzhou, covering 93 hectares, and includes the Zhenhai Tower, the Sculpture of the Five Rams, a few artificial lakes and a huge swimming pool.

The **Sculpture of the Five Rams**, erected in 1959, is the symbol of Guangzhou. It is said that long ago five celestial beings wearing robes of five colours came to Guangzhou riding through the air on rams. Each carried a stem of rice, which they presented to the people as an auspicious sign from heaven that the area would be free from famine forever. Guangzhou means Broad Region, but from this myth it takes its other name, City of Rams, or just Goat City.

The **Zhenhai Tower**, also known as the Five Storey Pagoda, is the only part of the old city wall that remains. From the upper storeys it commands a view of the city to the south and the White Cloud Hills to the north. The present tower was built during the Ming Dynasty upon the highest portion of the northern city wall.

Because of its strategic location it was occupied by the British and French troops at the time of the Opium wars. The 12 cannon in front of the tower date from this time. The tower now houses the City Museum, with exhibits which describe the history of Guangzhou from Neolithic times until the early part of this century.

Bus Nos 5, 24, 29, 101 and 103 all go to the park.

Cultural Park
(wénhuà gōngyuán)

Just north-east of Shamian Island, the Cultural Park was opened in 1956. Not your average Chinese park, this one provides you with a whole medley of alternatives, including dodgem cars *(pèngpèngchē)*, a miniature funfair, a big wheel, a weights room, dolphin acts at Ocean World, a theatre and even a flight simulator which will set you back Y20 unless you're a kiddy (Y15).

Southern Yue Tomb Museum
(nán yuè wáng mù)

The Southern Yue Tomb Museum is also known as the Museum of the Western Han Dynasty of the Southern Yue King's Tomb. It stands on the site of the tomb of Emperor Wen, the second ruler of the Southern Yue Kingdom dating back to 100 BC. The Southern Yue Kingdom is what the area around Guangzhou was called during the Han Dynasty (206-220 AD).

The tomb was originally 20m under Elephant Hill and was discovered in 1983; inside were 15 funerary bodies and more than 1000 sacrificial objects made of jade. It's an excellent museum with English explanations. More than 500 rare artefacts are on display.

It can be found just to the west of Yuexiu Park and can be reached by taking bus No 5, 24, 29, 101 or 103.

Pearl River Cruises
(zhūjiāng yóulánchuán)

The northern bank of the Pearl River is one of the most interesting areas of Guangzhou – filled with people, markets and dilapidated buildings. By contrast, the southern side takes its inspiration from Victoria Harbour in Hong Kong – a growing forest of huge neon advertisements.

A tourist boat ride down the Pearl River runs daily from 3.30 to 5 pm and costs Y10. Boats leave from the pier just east of

To Beijing

Sanyuanli

TV Tower

Xicun

Orchid
Park

Yuexiu
Park

Huanshi Xilu

Zengbu River

Guangyuan Lu

Xhan Xilu

Zhanqian Lu

Renmin Beilu

Jiefang Beilu

Liuhua Lu

Liuhua
Park

Liuhua
Lake

Dongfeng Xilu

Dongfeng

Zhonglu

To
Foshan

Zhongshan 8-Lu

Zhongshan 7-Lu

Zhongshan 6-Lu

Renmin Zhonglu

Jiefang Zhonglu

People's
Park

Children's
Park

Liwan
Park

Wenchang Lu

Daihe

Xiguan

Baoyuan Lu

Changshou Lu

Duobao Lu

Dade Lu

Daxin Lu

Renmin Nanlu

Haizhu
Circle

Beijing Lu

Enning Lu

Baohua

Dishipu Lu

Xiaju Lu

Yide Xilu

Haizhu
Bridge

Tianzi
Pier

Huangsha Dadao

Datong Lu

Cultural
Park

Yanjiang Xilu

Xidi
Pier

See Shamian Island Map

Shamian
Island

Pearl River

Renmin
Bridge

Binjiang Xilu

Tongtu
Donglu

Jiangnan Dadao

Fangcun

Haizhuang
Park

Zhoutouzui
Wharf

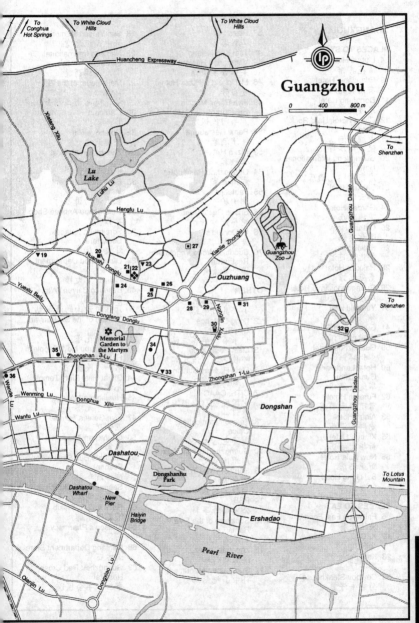

Guangzhou

0   400   800 m

To Conghua Hot Springs

To White Cloud Hills

To White Cloud Hills

Huancheng Expressway

To Shenzhen

Xiatang Xilu

Lu Lake

Lülu Lu

Hengfu Lu

Xianlie Zhonglu

Guangzhou Zoo

Guangzhou Dadao

▼19

20

Huanshi Donglu

21 22 ▼23

□ 27

Ouzhuang

Yuexiu Beilu

■ 24

25

■ 26

28

29

Nonglin

31

To Shenzhen

Dongfeng Donglu

30

Nonglin Xilu

✿ Memorial Garden to the Martyrs 3-Lu

34

32

35

Zhongshan

▼33

Zhongshan 1-Lu

Guangzhou Dadao

36

Renda Lu

Wenming Lu

Donghua Xilu

Dongshan

Wanfu Lu

Dashatou

To Lotus Mountain

Dongshanhu Park

Dashatou Wharf

New Pier

Haiyin Bridge

Ershadao

Dongbao Lu

Pearl River

Qianjin Lu

GUANGZHOU 广州

PLACES TO STAY
4 Liuhua Hotel
   流花宾馆
9 Friendship Hotel
   友谊宾馆
11 Dongfang Hotel
   东方宾馆
12 China Hotel; Hard Rock
   Cafe
   中国大酒店、
   硬石俱乐部
20 Guangdong International
   Hotel
   广东国际大酒店
21 Baiyun Hotel
   白云宾
24 Garden Hotel
   花园酒店
25 Cathay Hotel
   国泰宾馆
26 Holiday Inn
   文化假日酒店
28 Hakka's Hotel
   嘉应宾馆
29 Guangdong Jinye Hotel
   广东金叶大厦
31 Yuehai Hotel
   粤海大厦
41 Guangdong Guesthouse
   广东迎宾馆
59 Guangzhou Hotel
   广州宾馆
60 Hotel Landmark
   Guangzhou
   华厦大酒店
62 Furama Hotel
   富丽华大酒店
63 Aiqun Hotel
   爱群大酒店
65 Xinhua Hotel
   新华大酒店
66 New Asia Hotel
   新亚酒店
67 Bai Gong Hotel
   白宫酒店

PLACES TO EAT
6 Fairwood Fast Food
   快活快餐
19 KFC
   肯德鸡
23 Kathleen's
   嘉芙莲
33 Cowboy Steakhouse
   西部牛仔餐馆

37 Pizza Hut
   必胜客
45 Tsai Ken Hsiang
   Vegetarian Restaurant
   菜根香素菜馆
48 McDonald's; Pizza Hut
   麦当劳
49 Five Rams Muslim
   Restaurant
   五羊回民饭店
52 Panxi Restaurant
   泮溪酒家
53 Pizza Hut
   必胜客
54 Guangzhou Restaurant
   广州酒家
55 Taotaoju
   陶陶居
56 Snake Restaurant
   蛇餐馆
58 McDonald's
   麦当劳
70 Buddhist World Vegetarian
   Restaurant
   佛世界素食社

OTHER
1 Minibus Station
   小公共汽车站
2 Long-Distance
   Bus Station
   广东省汽车客运站
3 Main Post Office
   邮政总局（流花邮局）
5 Main Railway Station
   广州火车站
7 CITS; CAAC
   中国民航、中国国际
   旅行社
8 Telecommunications
   Office
   国际电话大楼
10 Guangzhou Gymnasium
   广州体育场
13 Southern Yue Tomb
   Museum
   南越王汉墓
14 PSB
   公安局外事科
15 Sculpture of the Five
   Rams
   五羊石像
16 Zhenhai Tower
   镇海楼
17 Sun Yatsen Monument
   孙中山纪念碑

18 Sun Yatsen Memorial Hall
   孙中山纪念堂
22 Nanfang International
   Plaza
   南方国际商厦
27 Mausoleum of the 72
   Martyrs
   黄花岗七十二烈士墓
30 L'Africain
   非洲吧
32 One Love Bar
   艳阳天酒吧
34 Zhongshan Medical
   College
   中山医科大学
35 Peasant Movement
   Institute
   农民运动讲习所
36 Guangzhou Antique Shop
   粤雅堂
38 Foreign Languages
   Bookstore
   外文书店
39 Guangzhou Department
   Store
   广州百货大楼
40 Buses to Baiyun (White
   Cloud Hills)
   开往白云山的汽车站
42 Temple of the Six Banyan
   Trees
   六榕寺花塔
43 Guangzhou No 1 People's
   Hospital
   第一人民医院
44 Bright Filial Piety Temple
   光孝寺
46 Huaisheng Mosque
   怀圣寺光塔
47 Five Genies Temple
   五仙观
50 Chen Clan Academy
   陈家祠
51 Guangfo Bus Station (for
   Foshan)
   广佛汽车站
57 Sacred Heart Church
   石室教堂
61 Rock and Roll Club
   滚石俱乐部
64 Watson's Pharmacy
   屈臣氏
68 Nanfang Department Store
   南方百货
69 Guangzhou Red Cross
   Hospital
   市红十字会医院

Renmin Bridge. They take you down the river as far as Ershadou and then turn around and head back to Renmin Bridge. From April to October there are night cruises for tourists. Departures are from Xidi Pier (☎ 8333-0397) just south of the Nanfang Department Store. These cruises are becoming increasingly colourful as more and more neon goes up on the southern shore of the Pearl River. Bookings can be made at many hotels around town, including the Shamian Hotel on Shamian Island. Tickets at the pier are Y38 and the boat runs from 7.30 to 9 pm.

The White Swan Hotel on Shamian Island also offers an evening cruise from 7.30 to 9 pm between Monday and Thursday. Tickets are Y50. At weekends dinner is included and tickets are Y250.

Other Sights

At 42 Zhongshan 4-Lu can be found the **Peasant Movement Institute** (nóngmín yùndòng jiǎngxí suǒ), a former training ground for communist aspirants to copy the good examples set by peasants; the institute is now a revolutionary museum.

Continuing up Zhongshan 3-Lu, one reaches the **Memorial Garden to the Martyrs** (lièshì língyuán) which commemorates the unsuccessful Guangzhou Communist uprising of 11 December 1927; the garden is laid out on Red Flower Hill (hónghuāgǎng) which was one of the execution grounds.

The **Chen Clan Academy** (chén shì shū yuàn; chén jiā cí) is a family shrine housed in a large compound built between 1890 and 1894. The compound encloses 19 traditional-style buildings along with numerous court-yards, stone carvings and sculptures. Bus Nos 19, 107 and 104 all pass by.

Liuhua Lake Park (liúhuāhú gōng-yuán) is an enormous park containing the largest artificial lake in Guangzhou. Or-nithologists may be interested in the bird island which is home to thousands of our feathered friends.

It was built in 1958, a product of the ill-fated Great Leap Forward. The entrance to the park is on Renmin Beilu and can be reached on bus Nos 19, 107 and 104.

Built in 1958, **Guangzhou Zoo** (guǎng-zhōu dòngwùyuán) is one of the largest and best zoos in China, although that's not saying much. It's on Xianlie Zhonglu in the north-east of the city; bus No 6 goes there.

Special Events

Guangzhou Trade Fair (zhōngguó chūkǒu shāngpǐn jiāoyì huì), otherwise known as the Chinese Export Fair, is mostly of interest to those who want to conduct trade with China. Apart from the Chinese New Year, this is the biggest event in Guangzhou. It is held twice yearly, usually in April and October, each time for 20 days. You need an invitation to attend. The Guangzhou Fair is important to travellers for one reason – accommodation becomes a real problem at that time and many hotels double room prices.

The city is unbearably crowded at the best of times, but during the Chinese New Year, usually held in February, Guangzhou is even more packed out as Chinese return to see their families.

Places to Stay – budget

This is not such a safe option, but if you're getting off the train it might be worth checking out what's on offer with the usual galaxy of touts who operate there. They will come rushing at you as you exit the station, waving photo books or simple placards advertising inexpensive rooms. Some of these places are Chinese-only, but some don't seem to care who they take.

Shamian Island, however, is a quieter and more attractive place to be; you are much more likely to meet other travellers there and the bars are better.

On Shamian Island, near the massive White Swan Hotel, is the Guangzhou Youth Hostel (☎ 8188-4298) (shěngwàibàn zhāo-dàisuǒ) at 2 Shamian 4-Jie. By default, this place wins the title of 'backpackers head-quarters' in Guangzhou since there is little else in this price range that is open to foreigners. They are not a pleasant lot at the hotel, but it's cheap (despite the foreigner's mark-up). The cheapest dorm beds are Y60 and doubles come in at Y160.

Places to Stay – middle

The vast number of Guangzhou hotels open to foreigners belong to the middle and top-end price ranges, and the trend is ever upwards.

Pearl River Area The *Shamian Hotel* (☎ 8191-2288; fax 8191-1628) *(shāmiàn bīnguǎn)*, at 50 Shamian Nanjie, is only a few steps to the east of the Guangzhou Youth Hostel on Shamian Island. Doubles with twin beds start at Y278. This is an attractive, charming and popular hotel just up from Shamian Park.

Also on Shamian Island are two branches of the *Guangdong Victory Hotel* (☎ 8186-2622; fax 8186-2413) *(shènglì bīnguǎn)*. Both are fairly upmarket, although the branch at 54 Shamian Beijie is the cheaper of the two, and has rooms from HK$250 upwards. The branch at 53 Shamian Beijie (despite the consecutive number they are on the same side of the road and around five minutes' walk from each other) has standard doubles for HK$530 and triples for HK$600.

The *Aiqun Hotel* (☎ 8186-6668; fax 8192-0119) *(àiqún dàjiǔdiàn)* is at 113 Yanjiang Xilu (on the corner of Changdi Lu). Opened in 1937, this grand old place overlooks the Pearl River. Doubles start at Y320, with the more expensive deluxe options facing the river.

The *Bai Gong Hotel* (☎ 8188-2313; fax 8188-9161) *(bái gōng jiǔdiàn)* is a pleasant and friendly place to stay, although it's in a very noisy part of town near the river at 17 Renmin Nanlu. Singles are Y198 or Y238, and doubles Y238 or Y318. From the railway station, take bus No 31 and get off at the river.

Across the street from the Bai Gong is the elegant *New Asia Hotel* (☎ 8188-4722) *(xīnyà jiǔdiàn)*, at 10 Renmin Nanlu, which has singles for Y238 and doubles for Y298. There is no English sign on the hotel, which

is an indication that most of the clientele is from Hong Kong.

Just to the south of the New Asia is the *Xinhua Hotel* (☎ 8188-2688) *(xīnhuá dàjiǔdiàn)* at 4 Renmin Nanlu. This is another large, Chinese-speaking place geared towards the Hong Kong crowd. Singles/ doubles are reasonably priced at Y198/288, and triples are Y398.

Railway Station Area Certainly one of the best deals in this neighbourhood is the *Friendship Hotel* (☎ 8667-9898; fax 8667-8653) *(yǒuyì bīnguǎn)* at 698 Renmin Beilu. On 'side B' of the hotel, doubles are Y168, while those on 'side A' cost Y300. They were also offering discounts *(zhékòu)* when we last asked, so try your luck.

The *Liuhua Hotel* (☎ 8666-8800; fax 8666-7828) *(liúhuā bīnguǎn)* is the large building directly opposite the railway station at 194 Huanshi Xilu. Like many hotels in Guangzhou, it mainly caters to Chinese. Standard doubles start at Y380.

North-Eastern Area At 422 Huanshi Donglu, *Guangdong Jinye Hotel* (☎ 8777-2888; fax 8778-7759) *(guǎngdōng jīnyè dàshà)* has standard doubles for Y238 and Y298, or Y468 for a suite. It's a nondescript kind of place with nothing in particular to recommend it.

The *Hakka's Hotel* (☎ 8777-1688; fax 8777-0788) *(jiāyìng bīnguǎn)*, at 418 Huanshi Donglu, is reasonably good value at the lower end of the business market. Singles/ doubles start at US$38/41 and range up to US$70 for a suite.

Places to Stay – top end

Pearl River Area One of the best hotels in this area is the *White Swan Hotel* (☎ 8188-6968; fax 8186-2288) *(báitiān'é bīnguǎn)*, at 1 Shamian Nanjie, which has an excellent range of facilities, including 11 restaurants and bars, Rolls-Royce rental and a complete shopping arcade. There is a range of rooms with standard/deluxe doubles at US$120/160 and executive suites at US$250 (plus a 10% service charge).

Other topnotch hotels to be found in the area are:

Furama Hotel (☎ 8186-3288; fax 8186-3388) *(fùlìhuá dàjiǔdiàn)*, 316 Changdi Lu; standard singles/doubles Y480, suites Y907

Hotel Landmark Guangzhou (☎ 8335-5988; fax 8333-6197) *(huáshà dàjiǔdiàn)*; standard singles/doubles start at Y600, suites from Y860

Railway Station Area Home to the Hard Rock Cafe is the *China Hotel* (☎ 8666-6888; fax 8667-7014) *(zhōngguó dàjiǔdiàn)*, a traditional Chinese piece of architecture built in 1948 and one of the best hotels in Guangzhou with excellent facilities. Doubles start at US$140 (plus a 10% service charge).

Other top-end hotels in the area include:

Dongfang Hotel (☎ 8666-2946; fax 8666-2775) *(dōngfāng bīnguǎn)*, 120 Liuhua Lu; singles cost Y700, doubles Y800

Guangdong Guesthouse (☎ 8333-2950; fax 8333-2911) *(guǎngdōng yíng bīnguǎn)*, 603 Jiefang Beilu; doubles Y440, suites Y539

North-Eastern Area The north-eastern part of the city has the highest concentration of top-end hotels and is probably the best area in which to base yourself. The five star *Guangdong International Hotel* (☎ 8331-1888; fax 8331-1666) *(guǎngdōng guójì dàjiǔdiàn)* is probably the pick of the pack for business travellers. It offers a full range of professional business services, coupled with luxury standards of service. Doubles are US$140 (plus 20% service).

Other excellent choices include:

Baiyun Hotel (☎ 8333-3998; fax 8333-6498) *(báiyún bīnguǎn)*, 367 Huanshi Donglu; wide range of rooms, with singles for Y398, doubles for Y548 and more

Cathay Hotel (☎ 8386-2888; fax 8384-2606) *(guótài bīnguǎn)*, 376 Huanshi Donglu; standard doubles cost Y480

Garden Hotel (☎ 8333-8989; fax 8335-0467) *(huāyuán jiǔdiàn)*, 368 Huanshi Donglu; doubles cost US$140, executive doubles US$160 (plus 20% service)

Holiday Inn (☎ 8776-6999; fax 8775-3126) *(wénhuà jiàrì jiǔdiàn)*, 28 Guangming Lu; rooms start at US$130 (plus 20% service)

Places to Eat

The Chinese have a saying that to enjoy the best in life, one has to be 'born in Suzhou, live in Hangzhou, eat in Guangzhou and die in Liuzhou'. Suzhou is renowned for beautiful women, Hangzhou for scenery and Liuzhou for its coffins. While most travellers will sensibly pass on a Liuzhou coffin, Guangzhou is certainly one of the best places in China to stuff your face.

There are restaurants scattered all over Guangzhou. The city is famous for its old, established restaurants (many of which are listed below), however, travellers on a budget will be better off tracking down the inexpensive eats that litter the streets and back alleys.

Chinese Most budget travellers still head for the old favourite, the *Li Qin Restaurant* (*lì qún yǐn shídiàn*) on Shamian Island. It's built around a tree that emerges through the roof. It's cheap and the food is excellent. Try the spicy fried dried bean curd *(làchǎo dòugān)* and the sweet and sour chicken *(tángcù jīkuài)*. For affordable dim sum on Shamian, head to the *New York Silver Palace* (*yíngōng dàjiǔlóu*).

By the river is the *Datong Restaurant* (☎ 8188-8988) *(dàtóng jiǔjiā)* at 63 Yanjiang Xilu, just around the corner from Renmin Lu. The restaurant is an eight storey building overlooking the river, and can seat 1600 customers so don't worry about space. Specialities are crisp fried chicken *(dàtóng cuìpíjī)* and roast suckling pig *(kǎo rǔzhū)*. The restaurant is very popular and it's also a great place for morning dim sum.

Probably the most famous eatery in the city, the *Guangzhou Restaurant* (☎ 8188-8388) *(guǎngzhōu jiǔjiā)*, is at 2 Wenchang Nanlu near the intersection with Dishipu Lu. Specialities include shark fin soup with shredded chicken, chopped crabmeat balls and braised dove. This is an expensive restaurant and reservations are sometimes necessary.

For excellent Muslim-Chinese cuisine, check out the *Five Rams Muslim Restaurant (wǔyáng huímín fàndiàn)*, a huge place at 325 Zhongshan Liulu right on the corner of Renmin Lu and Zhongshan Lu. Try the boiled mutton slices *(shuàn yángròu)* and the crispy goose *(cuìpí huŏé)*.

In the west of Guangzhou, the *Panxi* (☎ 8181-5718) *(pànxī jiŭjiā)*, at 151 Longjin Xilu, is one of the largest restaurants in the city. It's noted for its dumplings, stewed turtle, roast pork, chicken in tea leaves and a crabmeat-sharkfin consommé. Its famed dim sum is served from about 5 to 9.30 am, at noon and again at night.

A very popular restaurant is the *Taotaoju* (☎ 8181-5769) *(táotáojū)*, at 20 Dishipu Lu. Originally built as a private academy in the 17th century, it was turned into a restaurant in the late 19th century. Dim sum is the speciality here; you choose sweet and savoury snacks from the selection on trolleys that are wheeled around the restaurant. Other specialities include the trademark Taotao ginger and onion chicken *(táotáo jiāngcōng jī)*. Taotaoju mooncakes are very popular at the time of the Mooncake Festival in mid-autumn.

Just to the west of Renmin Lu at 43 Jianglan Lu is the *Snake Restaurant* (☎ 8188-3811) *(shé cānguǎn)*, announced by a large neon sign and the knot of snakes displayed in the window. The restaurant was originally known as the 'Snake King Moon' and has an 80 year history. If you want to sink your fangs into snake breast meat stuffed with shelled shrimp, stir-fried colourful shredded snakes, three snake thick soup or just plain, simple fried snake, this is the place for you. Wash it all down with a glass of snake's blood mixed with Chinese wine. There are English menus available.

To get to the restaurant you have to walk down Heping Lu, which runs west from Renmin Lu. After a short distance turn right into Jianglan Lu and follow it around to the restaurant on the left-hand side.

Vegetarian The *Tsai Ken Hsiang Vegetarian Restaurant* (☎ 8334-4363) *(càigēnxiāng sùshíguǎn)*, at 167 Zhongshan 6-Lu, is one of the few places in Guangzhou where you don't have to worry about accidentally ordering dog, cat or monkey brains.

Another vegetarian option south of the river is the *Buddhist World Vegetarian Restaurant (fóshìjiè sùshíshè)* on Tongfu Donglu, just up from the Guangzhou Red Cross Hospital and near Haizhuang Park.

Fast Food Guangzhou is swarming with fast-food restaurants nowadays. Finding these is no problem, as the city is slowly being paved with western names and their local derivatives. *McDonald's* had more than 20 restaurants in Guangzhou at the last count. *KFC* and *Pizza Hut* branches also can be found dotted around.

Some of the Hong Kong franchise chains, such as *Maxims Fairwood Fast Food* and *Café de Coral,* do fast food Cantonese style. They have English menus and photo-menus, and should set you back around Y25 for a meal and drink. Standard favourites are roast duck or roast pork and rice.

Pub Grub Guangzhou has a quickly shifting number of western-style bars where you can scoff pizza or burger and chips, sink a chilled imported beer and put a few yuan into the jukebox. The trouble is keeping up with them – they come and go with annoying regularity.

Shamian island has just such a population of will-o'-the-wisp bars and cafes, and you can be assured that many of those mentioned here will have either packed up and left, changed their names, gone up/downmarket or just vanished.

One deserved survivor, nestling on Shamian Park, is *Lucy's* (☎ 8187-4106), a *very* American bar that serves chunky pint glasses of almost frozen beer for Y9. The bar appears to have a 24 hour happy hour policy, which is an admirable achievement. The food is also excellent, of the grilled chicken and steak variety, and the decor (perfect for homesick Americans) is almost as retro as the price tag on the drink. If you're planning on going to Shanghai, get drunk here first as it's miles cheaper.

Other bars on Shamian Island try to hit the right note, but are for the most part tired sorts of places.

They include the *Lankwaifong Bar* (☎ 8191-9722), which tries to recreate the bustle and excitement of the Hong Kong nightspot with little success; the *Shamian*, a pricey and tacky alternative; and the *Chicago Coffee Shop*, which appears rarely to be open. Anyway, try your luck and go for a scout to see any new fixtures that have appeared.

Hard Rock Cafe (☎ 8666-6888) can be found in the basement of the China Hotel, dishing up the usual buffalo wings, steak and chips fare, albeit with hefty price tags for the experience.

Another place is *Kathleen's* (☎ 8359-8045) *(jiāfúlián)* at 60 Taojin Lu, north of Huanshi Donglu. More of the light music variety, this cafe bar serves up western food and has beer at Y40 for a small jug.

The *Cowboy Steakhouse* (☎ 8333-7634) *(xībù niúzǎi píjiǔ niúpái chéng)* is a funky place with live music (pretty awful), steaks and beer, and staff dressed in cowboy attire. It's at 90 Zhongshan 2-Lu. They have three branches altogether, and another can be found at 62 Jiefang Lu.

Hotel Cuisine Guangzhou's international hotels are among the best in China to eat elegant Chinese cuisine or to escape Chinese cuisine altogether. Naturally, which ever way you incline, you will be paying international prices for the privilege.

For Italian cuisine head over to *The Pizzeria* in the Garden Hotel. Pasta dishes are also available here and it is popular with the expat community. Barbecue with a Gallic touch can be had at *Le Grill* in the Guangdong International Hotel. *Cafe La* here has a French smorgasbord in the evenings.

For Japanese cuisine, try the *Hirata* restaurant on the 3rd floor of the White Swan Hotel. Barbecue dinners are available in the river wing of this hotel.

All the major hotels have a selection of Chinese dining options with English menus available.

Entertainment
The entertainment scene in Guangzhou is covering ground fast, however, many venues come and go almost overnight. The large hotels offer a range of late-night drinking holes and nightclubs, but it's all pretty mundane stuff. Try any of the bars listed in the Pub Grub section of Places to Eat for darts, pool, jukebox music and imported beers.

If it's dancing you want, then try the *One Love Bar* (☎ 8737-1720) *(yànyángtiān)* which has a large beer garden, dance floor and live music upstairs. Dancing starts at 10 pm and goes on until 2 am. A large beer is Y30 and it's Y10 to get in. You can find it on the north-western corner of Dongfeng Donglu and Guangzhou Dadao.

In the same area, another place to be seen in is *L'Africain* (☎ 8778-2433) *(fēizhōubā)* on the corner of Dongfeng Donglu and Nonglin Xialu. They have dancing until 2 am on weekdays and until 4 am at weekends. It's a popular gay venue.

Other gay venues include *42nd Street* at Huanshi Donglu and *Nanfang* at Renmin Zhonglu. Nanfang is back in business after being closed in March 1997 following a police raid. (Before this incident, Guangzhou's gay community had enjoyed an harassment-free police policy for a number of years – another reminder of the capricious nature of Chinese authorities.)

Hard Rock Cafe (☎ 8666-6888) in the basement of the China Hotel has a disco from 10 pm to 2 am from Sunday to Thursday and from 10.30 pm to 3 am at weekends. The cover charge is Y50, but the beer is pricey. Live music is also on the menu with New Zealand bands at the time of writing.

The *Rock and Roll Club* (☎ 8890-8088) *(gǔnshí jùlèbù)* down near the river at 101 Yanjiang Xilu was another popular dance venue at the time of writing, with live bands, floor shows, karaoke, catwalk and

GUANGDONG

disco all rolled into one. Entrance is Y60 during the week and Y80 at weekends.

Guangzhou's remaining venues are very much falling prey to the inexorable march of bad taste as exemplified by karaoke parlours. If you want to include karaoke as one of your really genuine experiences of modern China, then why not try the aptly named *Sing High Karaoke Club* at the White Swan Hotel. Knock back a few stiff ones, grab the golden microphone, swallow hard and try and remember the melody for *Desperado* as everyone cheers you on.

Things to Buy

The intersection of Beijing Lu and Zhongshan Lu was traditionally the principal shopping area in the city, but the whole of central Guangzhou is gradually being transformed into a huge shopping mall.

The section of Renmin Nanlu down by the river is crammed with fashionable boutiques, the Haizhu traffic circle has a ritzy shopping complex, and the north-eastern part of town on Huanshi Donglu, where all the best hotels are, is also emerging as a topnotch shopping district.

The large hotels often have well supplied tourist shops, but bear in mind that their prices are astronomical compared to local shops. Items on sale are often 10 times the price on the streets, so it's worth spending some time looking around.

On the left of the Cultural Park and tucked away down a small street is a fascinating antiques market full of ceramics, jade and other collectables. The owners of the stalls all trip over each other to show you the cream of their crop. Haggle hard.

On the west of Shamian Island, on Shamian Sijie, is a string of souvenir shops selling paintings, clothes and calligraphy. The road leading up to the Temple of the Six Banyan Trees is also chock-a-block with souvenir shops bursting with ceramics and jade. The Guangzhou Antique Shop at 172 Wende Beilu has a reasonable range of (not cheap) souvenir items.

Getting There & Away

Air The CAAC office is at 181 Huanshi Lu, to your left as you come out of the railway station. It has separate telephone numbers for domestic services (☎ 8666-2969), international services (☎ 8666-1803) and its counter at the airport (☎ 8666-1823). The office is open from 8 am to 8 pm daily. You can also book air tickets at various locations around town, including the White Swan Hotel and the Garden Hotel.

There are at least four daily flights (usually more) from Hong Kong (Y590) on CAAC. The flight takes 35 minutes.

There are also direct flights between Guangzhou and a number of other foreign cities, including Bangkok, Hanoi, Ho Chi Minh City, Jakarta, Kuala Lumpur, Manila, Melbourne, Penang, Singapore and Sydney.

Singapore Airlines (☎ 8335-8999) has an office on the mezzanine floor of the Garden Hotel, 368 Huanshi Donglu. Malaysia Airlines (☎ 8335-8828) is also in the Garden Hotel, Shop M04-05. Vietnam Airlines (☎ 8382-7187) also has an office in Guangzhou. International airport departure tax is Y90.

Virtually every destination in China that has an airport is connected with Guangzhou, including Beijing (Y1534) and Shanghai (Y1196). The domestic airport departure tax is Y50.

Bus Buses ply both international and domestic routes. A small sample of what's on offer includes the following:

Hong Kong The hassle-free way to get to Hong Kong is to use one of the coaches that leave the large hotels and follow the Guangzhou-Shenzhen superhighway, which can get you there in under four hours.

You could try one of the coaches that leave the Liuhua Hotel at 9.30 am and 2, 3 and 4.30 pm and pass through Kowloon Tong, Causeway Bay and go to North Point. Customs procedures are normally routine and painless. Tickets start at HK$150.

Macau The best way to get to Macau is to get a bus to Zhuhai and then walk across the border. Kee Kwan Motors, across the street from the Floating Casino in Macau, sells bus tickets direct to Guangzhou. It is necessary to change buses at the border. The trip takes about five hours in all.

It is often quicker to arrange the trip yourself: take a taxi or bus to the Macau-Zhuhai border, then change to a minibus to Guangzhou.

Shenzhen From Guangzhou to Shenzhen, you can take a luxury bus from the long-distance bus station on Huanshi Xilu near the railway station. They leave every 30 minutes from 7 am to 9 pm and cost Y55. Otherwise, buses go from in front of the Liuhua Hotel for the same amount.

Minibuses ply the route to Shenzhen from the western side of the railway station and leave when the bus is full (Y30).

The other way around, privately owned air-con minibuses line up opposite the Shenzhen railway station near the Hong Kong border. The trip takes around three hours and costs Y30.

Large luxury buses go from the Luohu bus station next to the railway station for Y55 and take two hours.

Zhuhai There are buses every half an hour from 7.30 am to 6.30 pm for Zhuhai that leave from the long-distance bus station (Y34); they take you to the Gongbei District just on the border with Macau.

Unscheduled minibuses to Zhuhai also

cruise in front of the railway station and leave when full (Y30).

Other Destinations Other buses from the long-distance bus station include the following destinations: Zhaoqing (Y17), Guilin (air-con sleeper, Y116), Fuzhou (air-con sleeper, Y198), Shantou (sleeper, Y80), Xiamen (air-con sleeper, Y167), Foshan (every 10 minutes, Y10) and Shanghai (double-decker sleepers, twice per day, Y300).

Train Both international and domestic trains service Guangzhou. Getting sleepers on the domestic routes can be difficult, but in general it is easy getting tickets at the station.

Ticket touts swarm around the station area and zero in on foreigners. Make sure you know what you are buying, and if you are not sure then give it a miss.

Beijing Trains head north from Guangzhou to Beijing, Shanghai and every province in the country except Hainan Island and Tibet. There are three departures daily to Beijing. CITS is not always able to organise advance sleeper tickets, although they are worth a try; if you have a problem at the railway station, try the travel agents in the larger hotels, although this will be more expensive.

In Hong Kong it is possible to book domestic railway tickets at CTS for more than double the price. The fastest express trains to Beijing take 33 hours (if on time), but

Guangdong-Hong Kong Train Timetable

Train No	From	To	Departs	Arrives
98	Kowloon	Guangzhou	7.50 am	10.38 am
96	Kowloon	Guangzhou	9.50 am	11.49 am
92	Kowloon	Guangzhou	12.23 pm	3.01 pm
94	Kowloon	Guangzhou	2.22 pm	5.00 pm
91	Guangzhou	Kowloon	8.15 am	10.55 am
93	Guangzhou	Kowloon	10.10 am	12.58 pm
95	Guangzhou	Kowloon	4.50 pm	6.49 pm
97	Guangzhou	Kowloon	6.15 pm	8.53 pm

GUANGDONG

most trains require 36 hours or more. The Shanghai-Kowloon route is now open and the journey takes 29 hours.

Hong Kong The express train between Hong Kong and Guangzhou is comfortable and convenient. The train covers the 182km route in 2½ hours; tickets cost HK$285 (economy) and HK$335 (1st class). It is much cheaper to take a local train to Shenzhen and then another local train to Guangzhou.

The timetable current at the time of writing appears on the previous page.

Shenzhen The local train from Shenzhen to Guangzhou is cheap and reasonably fast. Since the opening of the superhighway, tickets have become much easier to come by. The trip takes between 2½ and three hours.

If you buy a ticket in Guangzhou, check which station it leaves from. Eleven trains go from the main railway station and eight trains go from the east railway station, which is a long way from the centre of town. Express trains all leave and arrive at Guangzhou's main railway station. It is, however, simpler and cheaper to take a minibus to Shenzhen.

In Guangzhou, you can try your luck with CITS, otherwise go to the station where it is unusually easy to procure tickets.

Boat Guangzhou is the major port on China's southern coast. It offers high-speed catamaran services or slower overnight ferries to a number of destinations.

Hong Kong Two types of ship ply the route between Hong Kong and Guangzhou: jetcats (jet-powered catamaran) and slow, overnight ferries. See the Hong Kong chapter for information on departures from Hong Kong.

The jetcat takes 3½ hours to travel between Hong Kong and Guangzhou. In Guangzhou, departures are from Zhoutouzui Wharf (*zhōutóuzuǐ kèyùnzhàn*) daily at 1 pm. Tickets can be bought at the wharf and

some major hotels if you give them enough advance notice. Tickets cost HK$211.

Overnight ferries travel between Hong Kong and Guangzhou. This is an excellent way to get to Guangzhou from Hong Kong and saves you the cost of one night's accommodation. The boats alternate on the runs between Hong Kong and Guangzhou, and leave at 9 pm and arrive at 6 am from both cities.

Tickets in Guangzhou can be bought at the Zhoutouzui Wharf and they cost from HK$138 to HK$406. If you can't get a cabin or a bunk, then buy a seat ticket and go to the purser's office to upgrade (*bǔpiào*) as soon as you are on board. The purser distributes leftover bunks and cabins, but get in quickly if you want one.

Bus No 31 (not trolley-bus No 31) crosses Renmin Bridge and will drop you off near Houde Lu in Guangzhou (about half a kilometre down from the bridge), which leads to Zhoutouzui Wharf. To get from the wharf to the railway station, walk up to the main road, cross to the other side and take bus No 31 all the way to the station.

Macau At the time of writing, services to Macau had been cancelled. Ask at your hotel or at Zhoutouzui Wharf (☎ 8444-8218) for any developments.

Wuzhou/Yangshuo Ferry connections between Guangzhou and Wuzhou have improved in recent years. It is possible to buy a combined bus/boat ticket, but there are plenty of buses available in Wuzhou for Yangshuo and Guilin, and many of them are timed with the arrival of boats from Guangzhou.

The quickest way to get to Wuzhou is the rapid ferry service, which takes between 4½ and five hours. It costs Y160 and departures are at 7.30 and 9 am, and 12.30 and 2 pm. Tickets are sold at the Dashatou Wharf (☎ 8383-3691) and departures are from the Rapid Ferry Terminal, which is 100m east of Dashatou. Bus No 7 travels from the railway station to the wharf.

The old 24 hour service is still running, but most of the ferries have been upgraded, so you can do the trip in a bit more comfort than was the case in the past. Y77 will get you a two bed cabin, and Y50 a four bed cabin; penny-pinchers can sleep with the masses for Y35. Boats depart from Dashatou Wharf at 12.30, 2.30 and 9 pm.

Zhaoqing Wuzhou-bound ferries (see the previous entry) stop at Zhaoqing. The slow ferries take around 10 hours to get there, while the new rapid service takes just two hours. Tickets for the Zhaoqing rapid service cost Y80.

Other Destinations At the time of writing the service to Shanghai from Dashatou Wharf had been suspended; it might have started again by the time you read this. The same applies to the service to Dalian, Qingdao and Liuzhou. There are occasional ferries to Haikou on Hainan Island which take 25 hours.

Getting Around

Guangzhou proper extends for 60 sq km, with most of the interesting sights scattered throughout, so seeing the place on foot is impractical. None of the transport options are pleasant however, and the only alternative to riding wedged against someone's armpit on one of the public buses is to take a grid-locked taxi and watch the meter climb.

Guangzhou's traffic conditions are in a state of mob rule. Be careful when crossing the road and use 360° vision as vehicles come from all directions.

To/From the Airport Guangzhou's Baiyun airport is 12km out of town near the Baiyun Hills. There is a regular airport bus that runs from the CAAC office near the railway station to the airport (Y3).

Just outside the entrance to the airport is a taxi ramp. Taxis leaving from here are metered. Don't go with the taxi touts unless you want to be ripped off. When you get into a taxi, tell the driver *dǎ biǎo* (turn on

the meter). The cost should be between Y30 and Y40 depending on the size of the taxi and where you are headed in town.

Bus Guangzhou has an extensive network of motor and electric trolley-buses which will get you just about anywhere you want to go. Unfortunately the network hasn't figured on the sheer mass of humanity living in Guangzhou, all of whom travel by bus. As soon as a bus pulls into view, the genteel granny you were just chatting to at the bus stop is transformed into a bagswinging human tank. Bumper-to-bumper traffic also serves to slow public transport down during peak hours and can make getting around Guangzhou a frustrating experience.

It's worth getting a detailed map of the city (for the bus routes) from one of the hawkers outside the railway station or at one of the hotels. There are too many bus routes to list them all here, but a few of the important routes are:

No 31 Runs along Gongye Dadao Bei, east of Zhoutouzui Wharf, crosses Renmin Bridge and goes straight up Renmin Lu to the main railway station at the north of the city.

No 30 Runs from the main railway station eastwards along Huanshi Lu before turning down Nonglin Xialu to terminate in the far east of the city. This is a convenient bus to take if you want to go from the railway station to the Baiyun and Garden hotels.

No 5 Starting from the main railway station, this bus takes a similar route to No 31, but instead of crossing Renmin Bridge it carries on along Liu'ersan Lu, which runs by the northern side of the canal separating the city from Shamian Island. Get off here and walk across the small bridge to the island.

Minibus Minibuses seating 15 to 20 people ply the streets on set routes. If you can find out where they're going, they're a good way to avoid the crowded buses; they often slow down and shout out the destination, but it's all too often incomprehensible.

The front window usually displays a sign with the destination written in Chinese characters.

Taxi Taxis are abundant on the streets of Guangzhou, but demand is great, particularly during the peak hours: from 8 to 9 am and during lunch and dinner hours.

Taxis are equipped with meters. The per-km cost (after flag fall) is displayed on a little sticker on the right rear window. Depending on the vehicle, a trip from the railway station to Shamian Island should cost between Y15 and Y20.

Bicycle Shamian Island usually has a place where you can rent a bike. The shifting sands of the bike-rental world on Shamian move bike-rental outlets around, so ask at your hotel for details. Usually rental is Y2 per hour or Y20, plus a large deposit (Y400).

Take a look at the traffic on the streets of Guangzhou and before hiring a bike check the brakes to make sure it's not a death-trap.

AROUND GUANGZHOU
White Cloud Hills
(báiyún shān)

The White Cloud Hills, in the north-eastern suburbs of Guangzhou, are an offshoot of Dayu Ling, the chief mountain range of Guangdong Province. There are more than 30 peaks which were once dotted with temples and monasteries, although no buildings of any historical significance remain.

Famous as a resort since the Tang and Song dynasties, the area is being thematically restored to attract Hong Kong tourists and now sports water slides, a golf course, botanical gardens and a sculpture park, among other sights.

The brochure describes it as 'the first spectacular scene of Guangzhou' (the lawless traffic conditions are a close second), and it's really not bad if good weather chips in. Despite being very much for the Chinese, it can provide relaxing walks in sometimes lovely scenery.

The highest peak in the White Cloud Hills is Star Touching Hill *(mōxīng lǐng)*. On a clear day, you can see a panorama of

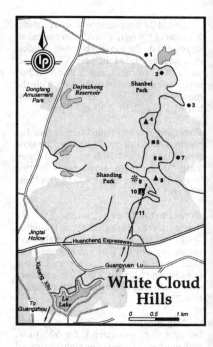

WHITE CLOUD HILLS 白云山

1 Liaoyang Clinic
  疗养院
2 Mingzhu Building
  明珠楼
3 White Cloud Billowing Pines
  白云松涛
4 Star Touching Peak
  摩星岭
5 Shanzhuang Inn
  山庄旅舍
6 Twin River Villa
  双溪别墅
7 Dripping Water Crag
  滴水岩
8 Southern Sky First Peak
  天南第一峰
9 Cheng Precipice
  白云晚望
10 Nengren Temple
  能仁寺
11 Cable Car
  白云索道

GUANGDONG

What Price Immortality?

The Cheng Precipice in the White Cloud Hills takes its name from a Qin Dynasty tale: It is said that the first Qin Emperor, Qin Shi Huang, heard of a herb which would confer immortality on whoever ate it. Cheng On Kee, a minister of the emperor, was dispatched to find it.

Five years of wandering brought Cheng to the White Cloud Hills, where the herb grew in profusion. On eating the herb, he found that the rest of it disappeared.

In dismay and fearful of returning empty-handed, Cheng threw himself off the precipice, but having been assured immortality from eating the herb, he was caught by a stork and taken to heaven. ∎

the city – the Xiqiao Hills to one side, the North River and the Fayuan Hills on the other side, and the sweep of the Pearl River. Unfortunately, clear days are becoming a rarity in Guangzhou.

The Chinese rate the evening view from Cheng Precipice as one of the eight sights of Guangzhou. The precipice was formerly the site of the oldest monastery in the area. However, these days the precipice is usually just called the White Cloud Evening View (*báiyún wǎnwàng*).

Getting There & Away The White Cloud Hills are about 15km from Guangzhou and make a good half-day excursion. Express buses leave from Guangwei Lu, a little street running off Zhongshan 5-Lu to the west of the Children's Park, about every 15 minutes. The trip takes between 30 and 60 minutes, depending on traffic.

Also, bus No 24 can take you from Dongfeng Zhonglu, just north of the People's Park, to the cable car at the bottom of the hill near Lu Lake. The cable car covers a short stretch for Y30 (return).

Lotus Mountain
(*liánhuā shān*)
Lotus Mountain is an old Ming Dynasty quarry site 46km to the south-east of Guangzhou. It is a possible day trip from Guangzhou, although it is of more interest to Guangzhou long-termers than to travellers with a busy itinerary.

The stone-cutting at Lotus Mountain

ceased several hundred years ago and the cliffs have eroded to a state where it looks almost natural. On the mountain is an assortment of temples and pagodas, including the Old Lotus Tower that was built in 1664. During the Opium wars, Lotus Mountain served as a major line of defence against the British forces.

Getting There & Away Both bus and boat connections are available, but the boat is more interesting. Boats depart from Xidi Pier (☎ 8333-0397) just south of the Nanfang Department Store on Yanjiang Xilu.

There is an individual service that leaves from Xidi Pier at 8.30 am for Y25, but probably the best option is to get the earlier luxury one day tour that leaves the same pier at 8 am and returns from Lotus Mountain at 3.15 pm. Tickets are Y38 and can be bought at Xidi Pier. The boat takes about one hour to reach Lotus Mountain.

Buses depart from the railway station area in Guangzhou. In theory the bus should be faster than the boat, but with Guangzhou's traffic jams it works out about the same.

The major hotels in Guangzhou also run tours to Lotus Mountain, as does CTS in Hong Kong. Naturally it is cheaper to do it yourself.

Conghua Hot Springs
(*cónghuà wēnquán*)
Conghua Hot Springs is unlikely to be of much interest to foreign visitors, but it has

been big business with the Chinese since the 1930s. Nowadays the hot spring water, which can reach 73°C (163.4°F), is piped into the bathrooms of fairly expensive tourist hotels, and the area has generally been developed into an ugly resort.

There is no shortage of hotels in the area, and visitors are greeted by touts representing the smaller, cheaper establishments (reckon on at least Y150 for a double). Prices of Y300 and upwards prevail at the better hotels.

Getting There & Away Buses to Conghua depart throughout the day from the long-distance bus station on Huanshi Xilu near Guangzhou railway station.

Buses are very frequent and cheap (Y10), but some buses go directly to the hot springs, while others go to the town of Conghua, from where you will have to get another bus (20 minutes) to the hot springs. Make sure you are on the right bus and ask for *wēnquán* (hot springs).

Foshan
(fóshān)

Foshan, just 28km south-west of Guangzhou, is for the most part a drab diversion that wouldn't warrant a mention were it not for its Ancestor Temple, which has emerged as a popular destination for local and Overseas Chinese tourists.

Like all tourist attractions worth their salt in China, there is a legend connected with Foshan (Buddha Hill). In this case, the story involves three buddha statues which mysteriously disappeared only to be rediscovered hundreds of years later in the Tang Dynasty (618-907 AD).

Foshan also has a reputation as a handicrafts centre.

Information CITS (☎ 335-3338; fax 335-2347) is in the Foshan Hotel at 75 Fenjiang Nanlu. CTS (☎ 222-3828) is in the Overseas Chinese Hotel at 14 Zumiao Lu.

Ancestor Temple *(zǔ miào)* Foshan's No 1 tourist attraction, the Ancestor Temple, is one of those temples that has been rebuilt

so many times that its name and function have drifted apart from each other.

The original 11th century temple may have been a place of ancestor worship, but from the mid-14th century it has enshrined a 2.5 tonne bronze statue of Beidi, the Taoist god of the water and all its denizens, especially fish, turtles and snakes. The temple itself is naturally lit.

Because southern China is prone to floods, people often tried to appease Beidi by honouring him with temples and carvings of turtles and snakes.

Outside the temple is a statue of 'the casted iron beast of flood easing' – a one horned buffalo. Statues like this were placed near the river at times of flood to hold back the waters.

Among other historical fragments are some caricatures of British imperialists on the stone plinths outside the temple and a huge ridge tile covered with a whole galaxy of ceramic figures. The temple is open daily from 8.30 am to 4.30 pm. Bus Nos 1, 9 and 11 go to the temple from the railway station.

Getting There & Away Foshan is easily visited as a day trip from Guangzhou. There are frequent minibuses from the west (Guangfo) bus station *(guǎngfó qìchē zhàn)* on Zhongshan Balu.

Alternatively, there are less frequent services from the long-distance bus terminal next to the Liuhua Hotel, near the railway station. If you are in the Shamian Island area of Guangzhou, just wait on Liu'ersan Lu and you will see minibuses heading west, many of which are going to Foshan (Y8). Put your hand out and they'll stop.

Minibuses take about an hour, but can take longer in Guangzhou's horrific traffic. Foshan is connected to a number of cities by air.

Train services between Guangzhou and Foshan are faster than the buses (30 minutes), but are only really worth it if you are living in the railway station area. If you add on the time getting to the station and queuing for a ticket, it could take a lot longer.

FOSHAN 佛山

1 Railway Station
   火车站
2 Buses to Guangzhou
   开往广州的汽车站
3 Long-Distance Bus Station
   长途汽车站
4 Renmin Athletic Field
   人民体育场
5 McDonald's
   麦当劳
6 Post Office
   邮电局
7 CTS
   中国旅行社
8 Revolving Palace Hotel
   旋宫酒店
9 Renshou Pagoda
   仁寿寺
10 Market
   莲花市场
11 Bank of China;
   New Stadium
   中国银行、新广场
12 Ancestor Temple
   祖庙
13 Rose Restaurant
   玫瑰酒家
14 McDonald's
   麦当劳
15 Foshan Hotel; CITS
   佛山宾馆
   中国国际旅行社
16 KFC
   肯德鸡

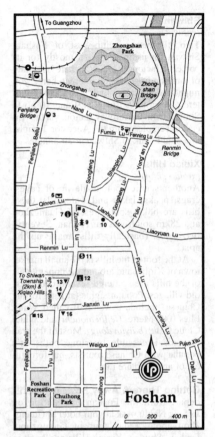

There are five buses a day from the Revolving Palace Hotel (☎ 228-5622) *(xuángōng jiǔdiàn)* at 1 Zumiao Lu in Foshan to Zhuhai (Y37), and one a day to Kowloon (HK$250).

For the busy business traveller, there are now direct express trains to/from Hong Kong. There is one service from Foshan to Kowloon which leaves at 10.39 am, and takes three hours (HK$240). Going the other way, the train departs from Kowloon at 2.45 pm.

Getting Around You won't have to look too hard for the two-wheeled taxis – they will be looking for you. Motorcycle drivers wearing red safety helmets greet minibuses arriving from Guangzhou and practically kidnap disembarking passengers. The drivers assume that every foreigner wants to head for the Ancestor Temple. If that's not where you want to go, make that clear straight away.

There aren't too many pedicabs, but you will see them about town. Foshan's pedicabs are really designed for hauling freight – there are no passenger seats, just a cargo area behind the cabin. Negotiate your fare with the driver.

Shiwan
(shíwān)

Two kilometres south-west of Foshan, Shiwan township is known mostly for its porcelain factories. Although there is nothing of outstanding scenic interest here, you might want to take a look if you have an interest in pottery. Bus Nos 9 and 10 go to Shiwan from the railway station, via the Ancestor Temple. From the Ancestor Temple, you could walk to Shiwan in 30 minutes.

Xiqiao Hills
(xīqiáo shān)

Another scenic spot, made up of caves, crags, peaks, lakes and waterfalls, these hills are 68km south-west of Guangzhou and 28km south-west of Foshan. Seventy-two peaks (basically hills) make up the area.

At the foot of the hills is the small market town of Xiqiao and around the upper levels of the hills are scattered several centuries-old villages. Popular sights (at least for the Chinese) include a waterfall called Water Flies 1000 Metres *(fēiliú qiānchǐ)* and White Cloud Cave *(báiyún dòng)*. Most of the area is made accessible by stone paths. It's popular with Chinese tourists, but foreigners of any kind are rare.

Getting There & Away Buses to the hills depart from the Foshan bus station on Jiefang Nanlu. Ask at your hotel in Guangzhou about a day tour of Guangzhou, Foshan, Shiwan, Xiqiao Hills and back to Guangzhou. These tours are usually very good value and are certainly less hassle than doing it all yourself, but the commentary will undoubtedly be delivered in Chinese.

SHENZHEN
(shēnzhèn)

'You think you're brave until you go to Manchuria, you think you're well read until you reach Beijing and you think you're rich until you set foot in Shenzhen', goes an oft-coined maxim of today's China.

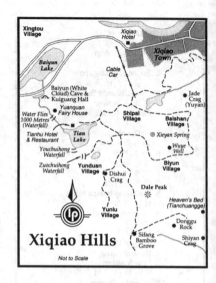

The locals of China's north-east have always been a rough-and-ready lot and Beijing's residents have a long history of learning, but you can give the knives and broken bottles a miss, forgo the books and the erudition and head straight for Shenzhen if you want to be rolling in it.

The name 'Shenzhen' refers to three places: Shenzhen City (opposite the border crossing at Lo Wu); Shenzhen Special Economic Zone (SEZ); and Shenzhen County, which extends several kilometres north of the SEZ. None of them is particularly interesting to visit, and the majority of foreigners who come here are on business. If you are coming from the north, Shenzhen City will seem like a tacky introduction to Hong Kong and if you are coming from the south, it may seem like a tacky prologue to China. Most travellers give the place a wide berth.

The northern part of the SEZ is walled off from the rest of China by an electrified fence to prevent smuggling and to keep back the hordes of people trying to emigrate illegally into Shenzhen and Hong Kong. There is a checkpoint when you leave the

SEZ. You don't need your passport to leave, but you will need it to get back in, so don't leave it in your hotel if you decide to make a day trip outside Shenzhen.

History
Shenzhen was no more than a fishing village until it won the equivalent of the National Lottery and became an SEZ in 1980. Developers added a stock market, glittering hotels, office blocks and a population of two million to the existing fish market; the only fishnets you see now are on the legs of Shenzhen's prostitutes.

Like many fortune winners, the city attracted a lot of unwanted friends (beggars throng the streets and two-thirds of its residents have no permit to live there) and its morals have gone soft, with prostitution and sleaze endemic. A surging crime rate is another of its less appealing statistics: it jumped by 66% in the mid-90s.

Shenzhen has no doubt been a fabulous commercial success, but it's a place without culture or spirit, a kit city driven on by the worst excesses of vice and avarice. In other words, if it's high-rises and the high life you want, stay in Hong Kong and if you want history, anywhere else is an improvement.

Information
Tourist Offices There are two branches of CITS. The more convenient one for arriving travellers is the office in the railway station. Otherwise there is a branch (☎ 217-6615) in the lobby of the Guangxin Hotel on Renmin Nanlu that sells train and plane tickets, while inquiries of a tourist nature are dealt with in Room 1102 (☎ 218-2660) of the same building.

CTS has a branch at the Wah Chung International Hotel (☎ 223-8060).

PSB The Foreign Affairs Branch of the PSB (☎ 557-2114) can be found at 174 Jiefang Lu.

Money Shenzhen effectively operates with a dual currency system – Chinese yuan and Hong Kong dollars. If you pay in HK dollars, you will get RMB as change and will effectively lose out on every transaction, so change some of your dollars into yuan.

Hotels change money, but this magic can also be performed at the border crossing with Hong Kong. There is a branch of the Hong Kong Shanghai Bank in the Century Plaza Hotel. The Bank of China is at 23 Jianshe Lu, outside of which assemble armies of moneychangers.

Post & Communications The main post office is at the northern end of Jianshe Lu and is often packed out. Telecommunications facilities are in a separate building on Shennan Donglu, but many hotels now offer IDD service right from your room. Rates to Hong Kong are very cheap, but not as cheap as the other way around.

For express delivery of packages, phone DHL (☎ 339-5592) for details.

Dangers & Annoyances Shenzhen acts as a mecca for beggars from all over the country. They mainly congregate on Jianshe Lu and Renmin Nanlu and tenaciously follow foreigners in search of alms. If you do give them money, this is generally the green light for the rest to pursue you. A traveller writes:

I was walking down Renmin Nanlu at night when a young girl, followed by a small posse of children, asked me if I wanted a *xiǎojiě* (young girl). Judging from her scruffy appearance, she was obviously from a village and most probably very hungry. Goodness knows what she would have charged, but you can bet it wouldn't have been much more than the price of a meal for her and the kiddies standing behind her.

Places to Stay – middle
There is no real budget accommodation in Shenzhen. Most of the cheaper hotels have rates that start at Y200 for a standard double.

You can try your luck with the hotel touts at the railway station; but they usually take you to cheap and tacky sleaze joints.

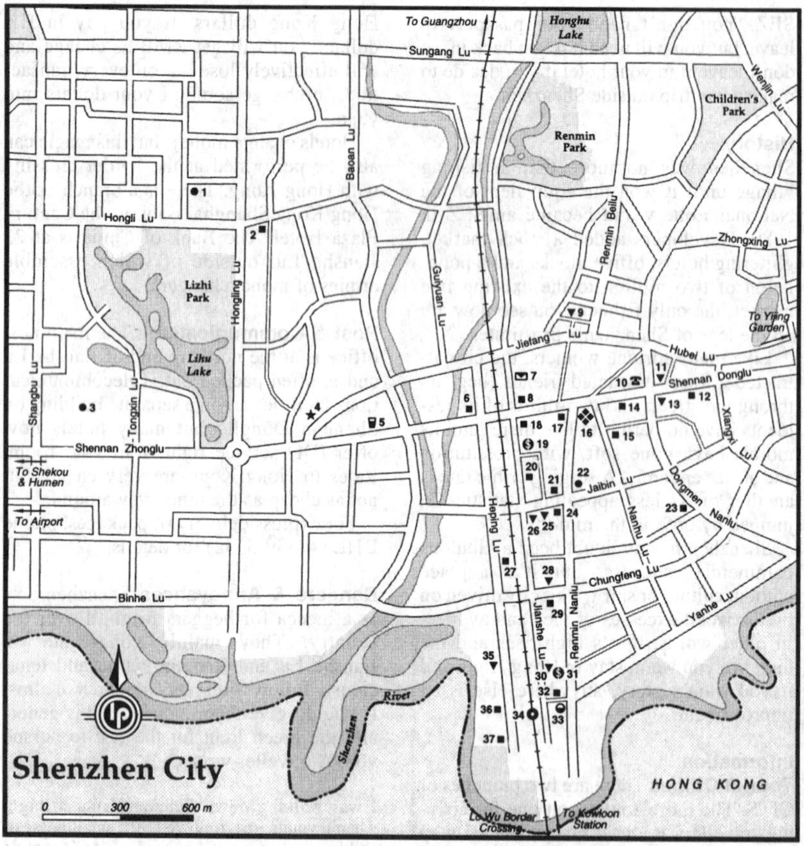

Shenzhen City

0   300   600 m

HONG KONG

There is a 10% or 15% service charge included for almost all Shenzhen hotels.

One cheapie that was grudgingly taking foreigners at the time of writing was the *Kouan Guesthouse (kǒuàn zhāodàisuǒ)*, a grotty establishment near the Bank of China on Shennan Donglu. Doubles (no toilet) go from Y110 while doubles (with toilet) start at Y160.

Nearby is the *Yat Wah Hotel* (☎ 558-8530) *(rìhuá bīnguǎn)*. You can find it next to a colourful miniature Disneyland kindergarten on the north-western corner of Shennan Lu and Heping Lu, just to the west of the railway tracks. The outside looks a bit tattered, but the rooms are large and bright. Room prices are Y168 for singles and doubles. There is a 20% discount from Monday to Friday.

The *Shen Tieh Building* (☎ 558-4248) *(shēntiě dàshà)* has more upmarket rooms, coupled with a good location and offers 20% discount on its listed price of Y268 for doubles.

Other mid-range hotels around town include:

SHENZHEN CITY 深圳市

PLACES TO STAY
2 Great Wall Hotel
  长城大酒店
6 Yat Wah Hotel
  日华宾馆
8 Kouan Guesthouse
  口岸招待所
12 Far East Grand Hotel
  远东大酒店
14 Guangdong Hotel
  粤海酒店
15 Landmark Hotel
  富苑酒店
17 Wah Chung International
  Hotel; CTS
  华中国际酒店
  中国旅行社
18 Shenzhen Hotel
  深圳酒店
20 Nanyang Hotel
  南洋酒店
21 Petrel Hotel
  海燕大酒店
23 Sunshine Hotel
  阳光酒店
24 Guangxin Hotel; CITS
  广信酒店
  中国国际旅行社
27 Shen Tieh Building
  深铁大厦

29 Century Plaza Hotel
  新都酒店
32 Shangri-La Hotel
  愀窦铟缶频
36 Forum Hotel
  富临大酒店
37 Overseas Chinese
  Hotel
  华侨大厦

PLACES TO EAT
9 McDonald's
  麦当劳
11 KFC
  肯德鸡
13 Wendy's
  云狄斯
25 Pizza Hut
  必胜客
26 Pan Hsi Restaurant
  泮溪酒家
28 Luohu Restaurant
  罗湖酒店
30 McDonald's
  麦当劳
35 Fairwood Fast Food
  大快活

OTHER
1 Xinhua Bookstore
  新华书店

3 Shenzhen City Hall
  深圳市政府
4 PSB
  公安局外事科
5 Xinxing Guangchang;
  Hard Rock Cafe
  信兴广场；
  硬石俱乐部
7 Post Office
  邮局
10 Telecommunications
  Building
  电信大楼
16 Oriental Sunshine
  Shopping Complex
  东方天虹商场
19 Bank of China
  (large)
  中国银行
22 International
  Trade Centre
  国贸大厦
31 Bank of China
  (small)
  中国银行
33 Minibuses
  小型车
34 Railway Station; Bus
  Station; Luohu
  Commercial City
  火车站、汽车站、
  罗湖商业城

Guangxin Hotel (☎ 217-6615) *(guǎngxīn jiǔdiàn);* doubles from Y250

Nanyang Hotel (☎ 222-4968; fax 223-8927) *(nányáng bīnguǎn);* doubles HK$302

Overseas Chinese Hotel (☎ 557-3811) *(huáqiáo dàshà);* doubles HK$238

Petrel Hotel (☎ 223-2828; fax 222-1398) *(hǎiyàn dàjiǔdiàn);* singles from Y288, doubles from Y391

Shenzhen Hotel (☎ 223-8000; fax 222-9422) *(shēnzhèn jiǔdiàn),* 156 Shennan Donglu; doubles from Y260

Wah Chung International Hotel (☎ 223-8060; fax 222-1349) *(huázhōng guójì jiǔdiàn),* 140 Shennan Donglu; singles/doubles from Y210 and Y308

Places to Stay – top end
Century Plaza Hotel (☎ 222-0888; fax 223-4060) *(xīndū jiǔdiàn);* standard/deluxe doubles cost HK$900/1000

Far East Grand Hotel (☎ 220-5369; fax 220-0239) *(yuǎndōng dàjiǔdiàn),* 104 Shennan Donglu; singles/doubles from Y478/498

Forum Hotel (☎ 558-6333; fax 556-1700) *(fùlín dàjiǔdiàn),* 67 Heping Lu; doubles from HK$660

Great Wall Hotel (☎ 558-3369; fax 558-0424) *(chángchéng dàjiǔdiàn),* 4 Honggui Lu; doubles from Y428

Guangdong Hotel (☎ 222-8339; fax 576-9381) *(yuèhǎi jiǔdiàn);* standard doubles start at Y660

Hotel Oriental Regent (☎ 224-7000; fax 224-7290) *(jīngdū jiǔdiàn);* singles from Y820, doubles from Y890

Landmark Hotel (☎ 217-2288; fax 229-0473) *(shēnzhèn fùyuàn jiǔdiàn);* singles/doubles from Y750

Shangri-La Hotel (☎ 223-0888; fax 223-9878) *(xiānggélǐlā dàjiǔdiàn);* doubles from Y1155

Sunshine Hotel (☎ 222-3211) *(yángguāng jiǔdiàn);* singles at HK$966

GUANGDONG

Places to Stay – resorts
These Chinese-oriented 'paradise escapes' are unlikely to be of much interest to the average foreign visitor (why not fly to Thailand or Malaysia instead?).

They offer discos, saunas, swimming pools, golf courses, horseback riding, roller coasters, supermarkets, palaces, castles, Chinese pavilions, statues and monorails. The huge dim sum restaurants become nightclubs in the evening, with Las Vegas-style floor shows.

Expect to pay upwards of Y300 for a double. Those interested might contact:

Honey Lake Resort (☎ 774-5061; fax 774-5045) *(xiāngmì hú dùjià cūn)*
Shenzhen Bay Hotel (☎ 660-0111; fax 660-0139) *(shēnzhèn wān dàjiǔdiàn)*
Shiyan Lake Hot Springs Resort (☎ 996-0143) *(shíyán hú wēnquán dùjià cūn)*
Silver Lake Resort Camp (☎ 222-2827; fax 224-2622) *(yín hú lǚyóu zhōngxīn)*
Xiaomeisha Beach Resort (☎ 555-0000) *(xiǎoméishā dàjiǔdiàn)*
Xili Lake Resort (☎ 666-0022; fax 666-0521) *(xīlì hú)*

Places to Eat
Shenzhen has a thriving upmarket dining scene, but there are also cheap eats available around town. The railway station has a number of affordable restaurants on its 3rd floor.

At the back of the railway station on Heping Lu, there are a number of cheap restaurants selling dumplings and the like. Up around the Jiefang Lu area are street vendors selling tasty chicken legs and fruit.

Those who like spicy hot food should try the *Xiangcai restaurant (xiāng càiguǎn)* on the 2nd floor of the Shen Tieh building. What's cooked up here is very cheap, extremely spicy Hunan cuisine, one of the hot regional cuisines of China (along with Sichuan and Hubei). If you haven't tasted it before, then try the hot and sour soup *(suānlà tāng)* and the spicy chicken with peanuts *(gōngbǎo jīdīng)*, which will blow you away. Order copious amounts of beer.

Dim sum breakfast is available in almost all of the hotels and can usually be found in the restaurants on the 2nd and 3rd floor. Prices are slightly lower than in Hong Kong. You'll have to pay in Hong Kong dollars in the better hotels, but you may get away with RMB elsewhere.

One of Shenzhen's best restaurants is the *Pan Hsi Restaurant* (☎ 223-8081) *(pànxī jiǔjiā)* at 33 Jianshe Lu. Opposite the Century Plaza Hotel is the *Luohu Restaurant (luóhú dàjiǔjiā)*, which is one of the most popular restaurants in the city centre. At night it's noticeable a long way off for its decorations and bright lights.

Shenzhen is fast-food city and all the usual names are represented, including *McDonald's, Wendy's, Pizza Hut* and *KFC*. Fast-food Cantonese is also available at *Fairwood Fast Food*. The McDonald's north of Jiefang Lu is absolutely enormous and almost a sight in itself considering the crowds.

Hard Rock Cafe (☎ 246-1671) is at hand for those on the run from noodles, rice and Canto-pop. You can find it in the huge Xinxing Guangchang building on Shennan Donglu.

Entertainment
Hard Rock Cafe (☎ 246-1671) flings open its doors at 11.30 am, but the dancing doesn't start until 10.30 pm. Last dancers are thrown out at 3 am. Entry is Y50 on Monday to Thursday, and Y70 on weekends. Soft drinks will set you back Y20 and beer is a cool Y40. Hard Rock can be found in the vast Xinxing Guangchang building on Shennan Donglu.

Things to Buy
On the flyovers to the east of the railway station and around the Luohu Commercial City *(luóhú shāngyè chéng)* are whole avenues of stalls selling ceramics and curios for souvenir and antique hunters. Don't expect to find trophies from the Summer Palace in Beijing here, but it's a colourful and varied selection.

There is also an assortment of art and antique shops at the western end of Chungfeng Lu, near the Century Plaza Hotel, that have a varied if pricey selection. If you see anything that sparks your interest, either haggle hard or look around for cheaper versions.

Opposite the Shen Tieh building on Heping Lu is a branch of Wellcome, the Hong Kong supermarket chain, where you can stock up on cheese, biscuits, milk and other goodies.

Getting There & Away

Air Shenzhen's Huangtian airport (Airport Hotline: ☎ 777-6789) is rapidly becoming one of China's busiest. There are flights to most major destinations around China, but it is often significantly cheaper to fly from Guangzhou.

Air tickets can be purchased from most of the larger hotels, including the Shen Tieh Building (☎ 558-4248). CITS also provides air tickets and there is a small airline ticketing office on the 2nd floor of the railway station.

Bus Services from Hong Kong to Shenzhen are run by Citybus, the Motor Transport Company of Guangdong & Hong Kong, and CTS.

For most travellers, buses are not a good option unless you are on a tour, but bear in mind that there are no single-ticket buses from Shenzhen to Hong Kong, so you have to buy a return ticket if you want to come back by bus.

Long-distance buses leave from the Luohu bus station (luóhú qìchēzhàn) next to the railway station; destinations include Shantou (Y120) and Chaozhou (Y140). There is also an air-con service to Guangzhou (Y55) which takes two hours.

There are frequent minibuses between Shenzhen and Guangzhou. In Shenzhen, departures are from just east of the railway station next to the Hong Kong border crossing. The fare is Y30 and the ride takes three hours.

Train The Kowloon-Guangzhou (Canton) Railway (KCR) offers the fastest and most convenient transport to Shenzhen from

Hong Kong. See the Hong Kong & Macau chapter for details.

There are frequent local trains between Guangzhou and Shenzhen and the journey takes around 2½ hours. Ticket prices are Y41 (hard seat) and Y65 (soft seat). There is also a fast service that takes 1½ hours and costs Y70.

The queues at the railway station can be appalling, so if you are staying overnight, see if your hotel can get you a ticket (most of them can).

Boat There are 11 jetcat departures daily between Shekou (a port on the western side of Shenzhen) and Hong Kong. Four of these go to the China Hong Kong City ferry terminal in Kowloon, while the rest go to the Macau ferry terminal on Hong Kong island. Ticket prices are HK$90 and the trip takes one hour.

There are six departures daily to the China Hong Kong City ferry terminal from the Shenzhen Fuyong ferry terminal (shēnzhèn fúyóng kèyùnzhàn) at the airport. The trip takes one hour and 10 minutes; ticket prices are Y161 (economy) and Y261 (1st class).

There is one jetcat departure daily from Shekou to Macau. It departs from Shekou at 11 am and arrives at noon. Tickets are HK$87. Ferries leave every half an hour for Zhuhai from Shekou, take one hour and cost Y65.

On even-numbered days, there's a service from Shekou to Guangzhou which leaves at 9 pm and arrives at 5 am (the boat returns from Guangzhou on odd-numbered days). There is also a daily boat to Haikou (not on Sundays) from Shekou which leaves at 3.30 pm, costs Y323 and takes 18 hours. This service was under threat at the time of writing, so check the state of play at the ferry terminal.

Getting Around

To/From the Airport Bus No 501 goes from the railway station to the airport; bus Nos 502 and 504 stop at the Guangxin Hotel en route to the airport. Minibuses and taxis are also available, but remember that in Shenzhen's traffic, getting to the airport can take a long time. Shuttle buses also leave for the airport from the Airlines Hotel at 130 Shennan Donglu.

Bus Shenzhen has some of the best public transport in China. The city bus services are dirt cheap and not nearly as crowded as elsewhere in China. The minibuses are faster. These are privately run and cheap, but if you can't read the destination in Chinese characters, you will need help.

Taxi Taxis are abundant, but not so cheap, because their drivers have been spoilt by free-spending tourists. There are meters, but drivers often demand a negotiated fee instead. Payment can be made either in RMB or Hong Kong dollars.

AROUND SHENZHEN CITY

At the western end of the SEZ, grouped together near Shenzhen Bay, are a collection of tacky attractions possibly of interest if you are stuck in Shenzhen.

Shenzhen – Splendid China (*jǐnxiù zhōnghuá*) is an assembly of China's sights in miniature; famous monuments of the world get the same treatment at **Window of the World** (*shìjiè zhī chuāng*); while the **China Folk Culture Villages** (*zhōngguó mínzú wénhuà cūn*) recreates 24 life-sized ethnic minority villages.

They are all clumped together not far from the Shekou ferry terminal and can be reached either by bus No 101 (Y4) or by minibus (both leave from the railway station). If you are entering Shenzhen by way of Shekou, then you could take a taxi.

HUMEN
(*hǔmén*)

The small city of Humen on the Pearl River is of interest only to history buffs curious about the Opium wars that led directly to Hong Kong's creation as a British colony.

At the end of the first Opium War, after the Treaty of Nanking, there was a British Supplementary Treaty of the Bogue, signed on 8 October 1843. The Bogue Forts (*shājiǎo pàotái*) at Humen is now the site of an impressive museum. There are numerous exhibits, including large artillery pieces and other relics, and the actual ponds in which Commissioner Lin Zexu had the opium destroyed.

Getting there is a hassle. No buses go directly to Humen, but buses and minibuses travelling from Shenzhen to Guangzhou go right by. You could ask to be let off at the Humen access road, and then get a taxi, hitch or walk the 5km into town.

Minibuses do however go from Guangzhou and leave from outside the Xiangjiang Hotel (to the right of the railway station as you face it). There are half-hourly departures (Y20).

ZHUHAI
(*zhūhǎi*)

Like Shenzhen to the east, Zhuhai is doing very well out of the South China Gold Coast. In true rags to riches style, Zhuhai was built from the soles up on what was farmland not long ago.

Travellers from the 1980s (even *late* 1980s) remember Zhuhai as a small agricultural town with a few rural industries and a quiet beach. Well that's all gone the way of the history books – the Zhuhai of today not only has the usual SEZ skyline of glimmering five star hotels and big-name factories, it has its own 'aerotropolis' to boot (servicing a spotless ultra-modern airport).

Zhuhai is mainly a business destination offering little in the way of interest to the independent traveller. That said, Zhuhai is a lot prettier and cleaner than Shenzhen. The city is so close to the border with Macau that a visit can be arranged as a day trip; alternatively, you can use Zhuhai as an entry or exit point for the rest of China.

Orientation

Zhuhai City is divided into three main districts. The area nearest the Macau border is called Gongbei, the main tourist zone. To the north-east is Jida, the eastern part of which has Zhuhai's harbour *(jiǔzhōu gǎng)*. A mountainous barrier separates these two sections from northern Xiangzhou – an area of worker flats and factories. The rest of Zhuhai SEZ is to the east and harbours the airport, tacky holiday resorts and infrastructure projects.

Information
There is a helpful CTS office (☎ 888-6748) next door to the Huaqiao Hotel. They are unusually keen to speak English and assist you with any inquiries. The PSB (☎ 222-2459) is in the Xiangzhou District on the south-western corner of Anping Lu and Kangning Lu, and another office exists in Gongbei on Yingbin Dadao. The most useful post office is on Qiaoguang Lu, in Gongbei. You can make IDD calls from your own room in most hotels.

Dangers & Annoyances
Zhuhai's pavements are full of gaping holes that could potentially disable you if you fell in one. Out of familiarity, the locals can steer around them at night like bats, but if you've had one tequila slammer too many, tread carefully.

Things to See
At the foot of Dashilin Mountain is a monumental symbol of where China's tourist industry is headed. The first phase of the **New Yuan Ming Palace** *(yuánmíng xīnyuán)* has been completed at a cost of Y600 million. This is a reproduction of the original imperial Yuan Ming Palace in Beijing that was torched by British and French forces during the second Opium War.

The very impressive entrance gives way to a huge adventure playground of reproduction scenic sights from around China and the world, including the Great Wall of China, Italian and German castles, halls, restaurants, temples and a huge lake.

The colossal scale of the project is reflected in the ticket price – foreigners have to pay Y140 (locals only have to cough up Y80), although children are half-price. The whole affair is clearly aimed at the Chinese market, which makes up the vast proportion of visitors. Opening hours are from 9 am to 7.30 pm. Bus No 30 can take you there from Guihua Lu.

The area around the **Jiuzhou Cheng shopping centre** *(jiǔzhōu chéng)* in Jida may be worth a trip. The shopping centre itself is a huge piece of reproduction classical Chinese architecture opposite the duty-free shopping centre.

Haibin Park, just up the road and facing the sea, makes for a pleasant walk with hills on both sides, palms, statues and a windmill. Bus No 13 takes you to Jiuzhou Cheng from Gongbei.

The bustling **markets** and side streets of the Gongbei area, close to the Macau border, offer a colourful diversion. Lianhua Lu is a lively area of hairdressers, restaurants and family-run stores.

Places to Stay – middle
As in Shenzhen, very few travellers stay in Zhuhai. Most of the accommodation is clustered close to the Macau/Zhuhai border, an area with some charm. Budget accommodation was elbowed out of Zhuhai a long time ago and prices are rocketing.

The *Zhuhai Quzhao Hotel* (☎ 888-6256) *(gǒngběi dàshà)* is the cheapest place around, with singles from Y178 and doubles from Y198.

Another hotel traditionally cheaper than the rest, the *Lianhua Hotel* (☎ 888-5673) *(liánhuā dàshà)*, at 13 Lianhua Lu, was being renovated when we were last in town. Expect to fork out at least Y200 for double rooms.

Other hotels in Gongbei in the Y200 to Y300 bracket include:

Bu Bu Gao Hotel (or *Popoko Hotel*) (☎ 888-6628) *(bùbùgāo dàjiǔdiàn)*, 2 Yuehai Donglu, doubles from Y303
Friendship Hotel (☎ 888-6683) *(yǒuyì jiǔdiàn)*, 2 Youyi Lu, doubles from Y210
Huaqiao Hotel (☎ 888-5123) *(huáqiáo bīnguǎn)*, Yingbin Dadao, doubles from Y292
Jiuzhou Hotel (☎ 888-6851; fax 888-5254) *(jiǔzhōu jiǔdiàn)*, Shuiwan Lu, singles/doubles from Y255/Y273

To Cuiheng

Yanhe Lu

Cuixiang Lu

Shahan Lu

Fengzhuang Beilu

Xingli Lu

1

Daoyang

2

3

Xiangzhou District

Fengboshan Park

4

Taoyuan Lu

Zixi Lu

Anping Lu

Kangning Lu

Dongfeng Lu

Fengzhuang Nanlu

Renmin Xilu

Ninpo Lu

Renmin Donglu

Huwan Lu

5

Mt Shijingshan ▲

Boulder Forest

Xianglu Bay

Yeli Island

Jida Reservoir

7

6

8

Haijing Beilu

Haibin Beilu

Haibin Park

9

Jida Lu

Yuanlin Lu

Jingshan Lu

Jida District

Haijing Lu

Banzhangshan Tunnel

Mt Banzhang (274m) ▲

Jiuzhou Dadao

▲ Mt Shihuashan

Haizhou Lu

10

To New Yuan Ming Palace & Airport

Shihua Xilu

Shihua Donglu

11

Yingbin Dadao

Guihua Beilu

Yuehai Xilu

Shuiwan Lu

12

Zhuhai Holiday Resort

Jiuzhou Harbour

Jiuzhou Island

14

Lian'an Lu

Lianhua Lu

13

SOUTH CHINA SEA

15

16 17

18

19

Yuehai Donglu

20

23

24

25

21

22

26

Yuehua Lu

Guihua Nanlu

Qiaoguang Lu

27

Shuiwan Lu

28

Gongbei District

32

30

29

31

Changsheng Lu

33

Zhuhai SEZ

MACAU

Zhuhai

0   400   800 m

GUANGDONG

ZHUHAI 珠海	29	Jiuzhou Hotel 九州酒店	7	Jiuzhou Cheng (Shopping Mall) 九州城

ZHUHAI 珠海

PLACES TO STAY
6 Zhuhai Hotel
珠海宾馆
13 Grand Bay View Hotel
珠海海湾大酒店
14 Huaqiao Hotel; CTS
华侨宾馆；
中国旅行社
15 Yindo Hotel
银都酒店
17 Zhuhai Quzhao Hotel
拱北大厦
18 Good World Hotel
好世界酒店
19 Guangdong Hotel
粤海酒店
23 Overseas Chinese Hotel
华侨大酒店
25 Bu Bu Gao Hotel
步步高大酒店
26 Lianhua Hotel
莲花大厦
28 Gongbei Palace Hotel
拱北宾馆

29 Jiuzhou Hotel
九州酒店
30 Traffic Hotel
交通大厦
32 Friendship Hotel
友谊酒店

PLACES TO EAT
20 McDonald's
麦当劳
24 Fairwood Fast
Food
大快活

OTHER
1 Bus Station
香州汽车站
2 Post Office
邮局
3 Xiangzhou Harbour
香州码头
4 Martyrs Museum
烈士陵园
5 PSB
公安局

7 Jiuzhou Cheng
(Shopping Mall)
九州城
8 Duty-Free Shopping
Centre
珠海免税商场
9 Zhuhai Amusement Park
珠海游乐场
10 Helicopter Pad
直升机场
11 Jiuzhou Harbour
九州港
12 Resort Reception
渡假村总服务台
16 Bank of China
中国银行
21 CAAC
中国民航
22 Gongbei Market
拱北市场
27 Post Office
邮局
31 Bus Station
长途汽车站
33 Border/Customs
海关

Overseas Chinese Hotel (☎ 888-5183) (*huáqiáo dàjiǔdiàn*), 3-5 Yuehua Lu, doubles from Y280; discounts of 30% available during weekdays

Traffic Hotel (☎ 888-4474) (*jiāotōng dàshà*), 1 Shuiwan Lu, doubles from Y255

Places to Stay – top end

Most top-end accommodation in Zhuhai includes tax of 10% to 15%, and sometimes a further tax of 10% to 15% for weekends and holidays.

The best place within striking distance of the border is the *Yindo Hotel* (☎ 888-3388; fax 888-3311) (*yíndū jiǔdiàn*) in Gongbei. Its services range from a coffee shop, bar and shopping arcade to massage centre, sauna and bowling alley. Rates start at Y690.

Other top-end hotels include:

Gongbei Palace Hotel (☎ 888-6833; fax 888-5686) (*gōngběi bīnguǎn*), standard singles/doubles Y450/Y520, 30% discount available
Good World Hotel (☎ 888-0222; fax 889-2061) (*hǎo shìjiè jiǔdiàn*), 82 Lianhua Lu, Gongbei, doubles from Y396

Grand Bay View Hotel (☎ 887-7998; fax 887-8998) (*zhūhǎi hǎiwān dàjiǔdiàn*), Shuiwan Lu, doubles from Y665
Guangdong Hotel (☎ 888-8128; fax 888-5063) (*yuèhǎi jiǔdiàn*), 30 Yuehai Donglu, Gongbei, doubles from Y690
Zhuhai Holiday Resort (☎ 333-2038; fax 333-2036) (*zhūhǎi dùjiàcūn*), Jida District, singles/twins from HK$498/538, villas from HK$498 to HK$3380

Places to Eat

Zhuhai is brimming with places to eat. The Gongbei area is the best place to seek out restaurants. Try Lianhua Lu for *bakeries* and a *Fairwood* fast-food joint. There are also a couple of restaurants serving up cheap Cantonese cuisine here. In warm weather many restaurants set up tables outside. There is a collection of these places opposite the Huaqiao Hotel up on Yingbin Dadao – most of them sell seafood. There are other similar restaurants on the side streets off Lianhua Lu.

Just to the west of the customs checkpoint is another knot of inexpensive *restaurants* with outdoor seating – single men

GUANGDONG

may be invited to have a quick dalliance with one of the waitresses (prostitution is rife in Zhuhai).

McDonald's has opened at last in Gongbei; apparently you had to queue for two hours on its opening day which kind of defeats the notion of 'fast-food'. The queues are marginally better now.

Getting There & Away

Air Zhuhai's glimmering new airport has domestic flights to most major cities in China.

Bus There are connections with Guangzhou, Foshan, Zhaoqing, Zhanjiang and Shantou. Buses leave from the main bus terminal on Youyi Lu, directly opposite the customs building (the border checkpoint). Buses from Zhuhai to Guangzhou depart regularly through the day from 6.50 am to 4 pm, and air-con services cost Y47.

Boat Jetcats between Zhuhai and Hong Kong do the trip in about 70 minutes. From the ferry terminal at China Hong Kong City on Canton Rd in Tsimshatsui, boats depart at 7.45, 9.30 and 11 am, and 2.30 and 5 pm. Boats from the Macau ferry terminal in Central depart at 8.40 am, noon and 4 pm. It is, however, only marginally slower (and less expensive) to take a ferry to Macau and then a taxi to Zhuhai.

Going the other way, departures are from Jiuzhou Harbour *(jiǔzhōu gǎng)* in Zhuhai. Boats to Tsimshatsui leave at 8 and 9.30 am, and at 1, 3 and 5 pm; to Central they leave at 10.30 am, and at 2 and 5.30 pm. The cost is Y140.

A high-speed ferry operates between the port of Shekou in Shenzhen and Jiuzhou Harbour. There are departures every 15 minutes between 7.30 am and 6 pm. The cost is Y65 and the journey takes one hour.

Zhuhai to Macau Simply walk across the border. In Macau, bus Nos 3 and 5 lead to the Barrier Gate, from where you make the crossing on foot. Taxis from the Hong Kong ferry area cost around HK$22. The Macau-Zhuhai border is open from 7.30 am to midnight.

Getting Around

To/From the Airport Zhuhai's airport is about 40km from the city centre, which makes travel to and from it a hassle. A taxi will be expensive (more than Y100), so the best option is a CAAC shuttle bus which runs reasonably frequently from the CAAC office near McDonald's (Y15). Alternatively, take bus No 201 to Sanzao *(sānzào)* from the bus station in Xiangzhou, and then change to bus No 105, which will take you directly to the airport.

Bus Zhuhai has a clean and efficient bus system. The buses are new and the routes are clearly marked on the Zhuhai city map. Minibuses ply the same routes and cost Y2 for any place in the city.

Taxi You are most likely to use taxis to shuttle between your hotel and the boats at Jiuzhou Harbour. Taxi drivers cruising the streets use their meters. From the Customs area to Jiuzhou Harbour costs around Y20.

AROUND ZHUHAI

In the village of Cuiheng *(cuìhēng cūn)*, north of the city limits of Zhuhai, is **Dr Sun Yatsen's Residence** *(sūn zhōngshān gùjū)*. Republican, enemy of the Qing Dynasty and China's most famous revolutionary, Dr Sun Yatsen was born in a house on this site on 12 November 1866. That house was torn down after a new home was built in 1892. This second house is still standing and open to the public.

There are frequent minibuses to Cuiheng departing from Gongbei near the border checkpoint.

ZHONGSHAN CITY
(zhōngshān shì)
The administrative centre of the county by the same name, Zhongshan City is also known as Shiqi. An industrial city, there is little to see or do here, although you may pass through the place if you are doing the

circuit from Cuiheng to Zhongshan Hot Springs. If you get stranded here for an hour or so, the one and only scenic spot in town is **Zhongshan Park**, which is pleasantly forested and dominated by a large hill (*yāndūn shān*) topped with a pagoda. It's visible from most parts of the city so it's easy to find.

AROUND ZHONGSHAN

The Zhongshan Hot Springs (*zhōngshān wēnquán*) resort has indoor hot springs and a golf course. If you're a real enthusiast of either activity, you might want to spend a night here. Otherwise, you'll probably just want to look around briefly and then head back to Gongbei.

Accommodation is available at the *Zhongshan Hot Springs Hotel* (☎ 668-3888; fax 668-3333) from Y300 for doubles, plus a 10% service charge. A minibus drops you by the entrance to the resort, then it's a 500m walk to the hotel. For a couple of yuan you can hire someone to carry you on the back of a bicycle. You won't have to look for them as they'll be looking for you. To get back to Gongbei, flag down any minibus you see passing the resort entrance.

ZHAOQING

(*zhàoqìng*)

Zhaoqing, home to some craggy limestone rock formations similar to those around Guilin, is rated highly among the attractions of Guangdong. Despite not having the appeal of Yangshuo, Zhaoqing is an attractive city with far more character than Guangzhou or Foshan. As the city is a major tourist destination for the Chinese (and most of them head directly for the Seven Star Crags) you could always escape to the nearby mountainous Dinghushan area, which makes for a charming walk among temples, pools, brooks and lush scenery.

Orientation

Zhaoqing, 110km west of Guangzhou on the Xi River, is bounded to the south by the river and to the north by the lakes and crags that make up Seven Star Crags Park. The main attractions can be easily seen on foot.

Information

There is a branch of CTS (☎ 227-6660) next to the Texas Cowboy Fastfood on Duanzhou Wulu. CITS (☎ 282-2091) has a branch at 46 Renmin Nanlu. There's a post office on Jianshe Lu.

Things to See

Zhaoqing's premier attraction, the **Seven Star Crags** (*qī xīng yán*), is a group of limestone towers – a peculiar geological formation abundant in the paddy fields of Guilin and Yangshuo.

The crags are home to myriad inscriptions and limestone caves that you can explore. A boat can take you from the southern tip of Zhongxin Lake (Paifang Square) and speed you across to a bridge that crosses

---

Divine Inspiration

Legend has it that the Seven Star Crags were actually seven stars that fell from the sky to form a pattern resembling the Big Dipper. Another legend dates from Ming Dynasty times:

It was said that if you stood under Stone House Crag on clear moonlit nights, you could hear the celestial strains of music played by the Jade Emperor, the supreme god of Taoism, as he gave a banquet for the rest of the gods and goddesses.

Furthermore, a tablet known as Horse Hoof Tablet, one of many inscribed tablets at the site of the crags, was dented by the hoof of an inquisitive celestial horse as he alighted on the shores of Star Lake. ∎

GUANGDONG

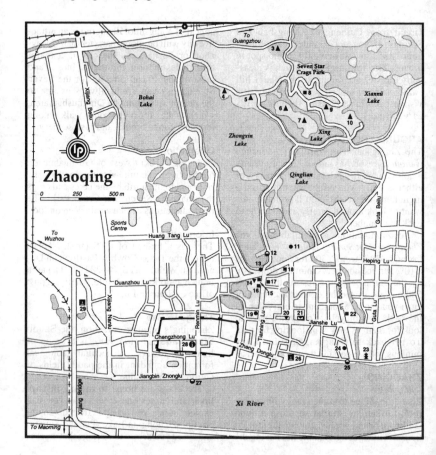

over to the crags. At this point you have to pay an entrance fee or you can just turn right and keep walking in a big circle (no charge) among the willows and kapok trees all the way around Xing Lake, looking out across at the view.

On Tajiao Lu in the south-east, the nine storey **Chongxi Pagoda** *(chóngxī tǎ)* was in a sad state after the Cultural Revolution, but was restored in the 1980s. On the opposite bank of the river are two similar pagodas.

The **Yuejiang Temple** *(yuèjiāng lóu)* is a restored temple about 30 minutes' walk

from the Chongxi Pagoda, just back from the waterfront at the eastern end of Zheng Donglu.

Places to Stay

Zhaoqing is not the place to stay for budget accommodation, but there are a few relatively cheap establishments in town.

The least expensive hotel around is the *Flower Tower Hotel* (☎ 223-2412) *(huātǎ jiǔdiàn)* at 5 Gongnong Beilu. It was renovating when were last in town – doubles start at Y120.

ZHAOQING 肇庆	**OTHER**	12 Bus Station
	1 Zhaoqing Railway Station	公共汽车站
PLACES TO STAY	肇庆火车站	13 Paifang Square
8 Star Crag Hotel	2 Seven Star Crags Railway	牌坊广场
星岩宾馆	Station	19 Xinhua Bookstore
15 Huaqiao Hotel	七星岩火车站	新华书店
华侨大厦	3 Apo Crag	21 Post Office
16 Duanzhou Hotel	阿坡岩	邮局
端州大酒店	4 Fairy-Hand Crag	23 Chongxi Pagoda
17 Jinbi Hotel	仙掌岩	崇禧塔
金碧大酒店	5 Toad Crag	24 Boat Ticketing Office
18 Star Lake Hotel	蟾蜍岩	for Hong Kong
星湖大酒店	6 Pillar of Heaven Crag	去香港船运售票处
22 Flower Tower Hotel	天柱岩	25 Zhaoqing Pier (Boats
花塔酒店	7 Stone House Crag	toHong Kong)
	石室岩	肇庆码头(去香港)
PLACES TO EAT	9 Jade Curtain Crag	26 Yuejiang Temple
14 Texas Cowboy	玉屏岩	阅江楼
Fastfood; CTS	10 Langfeng Crag	27 Passenger Ferry Terminal
德州牛仔快餐、	阆风岩	肇庆港客运站
中国旅行社	11 Star Lake Amusement	28 CITS
20 KFC	Park	中国国际旅行社
肯德鸡	星湖游乐园	29 Plum Monastery
		梅庵

In terms of sheer character and scenery, why not stay at the predictably named *Star Crag Hotel* (222-6688; fax 222-4112) *(xīngyán bīnguǎn)* slap bang in the middle of the crags. Take a boat over and walk around Xing Lake to the northern side; there you will start to see signs leading to the hotel, which is hidden behind a wall of bamboo. Go through the bamboo and you will see a crumbling flight of steps leading up to the hotel past almost vertical grass slopes. It's quite a haul with a rucksack, but it's well worth it. Doubles/triples start at Y150/Y198. You can also get there by taxi.

The *Jinbi Hotel* (☎ 222-3888; fax 222-3328) *(jīnbì dàjiǔdiàn)* is in a good location on Tianning Beilu. Singles are Y168, with deluxe doubles for Y288. A 30% discount is available.

Opposite, at 77 Tianning Beilu, is the *Duanzhou Hotel* (☎ 223-2281) *(duānzhōu dàjiǔdiàn)*, with doubles from Y180.

The *Huaqiao Hotel* (☎ 223-2952; fax 223-1197) *(huáqiáo dàshà)*, at 90 Tianning Beilu, has an excellent location and has doubles starting at Y288.

The *Star Lake Hotel* (☎ 222-1188; fax 223-6688) *(xīnghú dàjiǔdiàn)*, at 37 Duanzhou 4-Lu, is the best of Zhaoqing's hotels and has a full range of near international-class services with rooms from Y565.

Places to Eat
Just take a stroll along Duanzhou Lu for affordable eats. Look out for the restaurants selling *zòngzi* – rice, pork and other oddments steamed in a lotus leaf; these triangular snacks can be seen hanging outside the restaurants. Tianning Lu is another good area for restaurants.

Texas Cowboy Fastfood (☎ 223-29520) *(dézhōuniúzǎi kuàicān)*, next to the Huaqiao Hotel, cooks up fried chicken, pizza, hamburger, French toast and Chinese food. *KFC* has flown into town and is currently roosting on Jianshe Lu near the post office.

Things to Buy
There is a lively night market that sets up on Tianning Beilu outside the Jinbi Hotel. Stalls are flung up and on display are curios, antiques, old watches, Qing Dynasty water

pipes, woodcarvings, jade ornaments, ceramics and just about anything else you can think of.

Getting There & Away

Bus Buses to Zhaoqing leave from Guangzhou's west bus station and from the long-distance bus station near the railway station. There are five departures daily, the fare is Y17 and the trip takes about three hours. Try to avoid returning to Guangzhou on a weekend afternoon.

Privately run minibuses operate between Zhaoqing and Guangzhou. In Zhaoqing the minibus ticket office is inside the main gate of the Seven Star Crags Park; tickets are Y33 and there are 14 departures daily. The buses leave from near the local bus station to the right of Paifang Square; minibuses also leave from here for Shenzhen (Y30).

Train Be careful – there are two railway stations in Zhaoqing. All trains stop at the main railway station (*zhàoqìng huǒchē zhàn*), but only train Nos 351 and 356 stop at the Seven Star Crags railway station (*qīxīngyán huǒchē zhàn*). If you get into a taxi and say you want to go to the railway station, drivers will automatically assume you mean the main railway station.

There are four trains daily to Guangzhou (Y26). If the train is a through train, fight for your seat as your place will almost certainly be occupied by peasants from Maoming; if they refuse to budge, either call the attendant. Trains from Guangzhou take two to three hours. All trains also stop at Foshan.

Train Nos 16 and 78 connect Zhaoqing and Shenzhen – you do not need to get off at Guangzhou if you wish to go straight through. Direct trains to Kowloon cost Y319. Going eastwards, there are trains to Maoming and Zhanjiang.

Boat This is the best way to get to Zhaoqing nowadays. There are direct high-speed ferries from Guangzhou to Zhaoqing (they continue to Wuzhou) from the Dashatou ferry terminal. Ferries take two hours,

cost Y80 and there are four departures daily (the last one is at 2 pm). Slow boats from Guangzhou leave from Dashatou and take 10 hours.

Jetcats speed from Zhaoqing to Hong Kong at 2 pm, take four hours and cost Y218. Boats leave from Zhaogang pier and tickets can be bought just up the road on Gongnong Nanlu. Boats from Ducheng to Zhuhai go via Zhaoqing; you can get on board at 1.30 pm.

Getting Around

The local bus station is on Duanzhou Lu, a few minutes' walk east of the intersection with Tianning Lu and next to Paifang Square. Bus No 1 runs to the ferry dock on the Xi River.

The railway station is a long haul, but can be reached on bus No 2 which goes from the local bus station. A taxi will set you back Y12.

AROUND ZHAOQING
Dinghushan
(*dǐnghúshān*)

Twenty kilometres north-east of Zhaoqing is Dinghushan, one of the most attractive scenic spots in Guangdong. This easy-to-reach mountainous area offers myriad walks among pools, springs, ponds, temples, nunneries, and charming scenery. You can easily spend half the day here as there is a lot to cover. Qingyun Temple is the most famous temple on Dinghushan.

If you get stranded on the mountain, you can crash the night in the nearby *Qingyun Resort* (*qìngyún dùjiàcūn*). Minicab and taxi drivers await at the bus stop at Dinghushan to ferry you around. If you have time, then journey on foot and take it all in slowly, otherwise taking a minicab or hiring a taxi may be a good idea. Bus No 15 goes to Dinghushan from the bus station to the right of Paifang Square on the southern tip of Zhongxin Lake.

ZHANJIANG
(*zhànjiāng*)

Zhanjiang is a major port on the southern

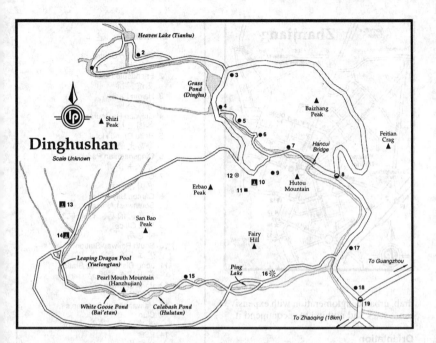

DINGHUSHAN 鼎湖山

1 Cliff-Face Plank Path
(Liantianzhandao)
连天栈道
2 No 1 Hydroelectric
Station
水电一站
3 No 2 Hydroelectric
Station
水电二站
4 Twin Rainbow Bridge
(Shuanghongfeijian)
双虹飞堑
5 Tingpu Pavilion
听瀑亭

6 Sun Yatsen Swimming
Area
孙中山游泳处
7 Half Mountain Pavilion
半山亭
8 Bus Station
鼎湖山汽车站
9 Tea Flower Pavilion
(Huachage)
花茶阁
10 Qingyun Temple
庆云寺
11 Qingyun Resort
庆云渡假村
12 Gulong Spring
古龙泉

13 White Cloud Temple
白云寺
14 Leaping Dragon Nunnery
(Yuelong'an)
跃龙庵
15 Lion's Roar Rock
(Shihoushi)
狮吼石
16 Crane Viewing Pavilion
望鹤亭
17 Archway
牌楼
18 Kengkou Store
坑口商店
19 Kengkou Bus Station
坑口汽车站

coast of China, and the largest Chinese port west of Guangzhou. It was leased to France in 1898 and remained under French control until WWII.

Today the French are back, but this time Zhanjiang is a base for their oil-exploration projects in the South China Sea. Very few foreigners come to Zhanjiang, and when they do they are usually en route to Hainan. This is eminently sensible: Zhanjiang is a

1 Shopping Centre
百货大厦
2 Friendship Hotel
友谊宾馆
3 Haibin Park
海滨公园
4 Cuiyuan Restaurant
翠园酒楼
5 Haifu Grand Hotel
海富大酒店
6 Qingshaonian Park
青少年公园
7 CTS
中国旅行社
8 Canton Bay Hotel;
Southwest Airlines
广东湾酒店、西南航空
9 Post Office
邮电局
10 South Railway Station
湛江火车站
11 Long-Distance Bus Station
霞山汽车客运站
12 Bank of China
中国银行
13 Haiwan Hotel; Seamen's
Club
海湾宾馆、海员 慑植
14 PSB
公安局
15 Zhanjiang Harbour
Passenger Terminal
湛江港客运站

drab, urban conglomeration with expensive room rates and nothing to recommend it.

Orientation

Zhanjiang is split into two districts – Chikan (chìkǎn qū) to the north and Xiashan (xiáshān qū) to the south. There is no need to bother with the northern part of town at all, as the harbour, bus station and most of the hotels are conveniently close together in the southern part of town.

Places to Stay

For budget travellers the *Friendship Hotel* (☎ 228-6622) (yǒuyì bīnguǎn) is the best option. Singles/doubles/triples are Y98/170/210. It's pretty grotty, and still had Christmas decorations up in April, but that's all in the price.

Most of the other hotels that take foreigners are mid-range in price. The *Canton Bay Hotel* (☎ 228-1966; 228-1347) (guǎngdōngwān huáqiáo bīnguǎn), at 16 Renmin Nan Dadao, is well located, and has clean air-con rooms starting from Y180 to Y240.

The *Haiwan Hotel* (☎ 222-2266) (hǎiwān bīnguǎn) on Renmin Nan Dadao is also the

location of the International Seamen's Club and boasts a karaoke bar. Singles cost Y168, while doubles range from Y198 to Y280.

The *Haifu Grand Hotel* (☎ 228-0288) (hǎifù dàjiǔdiàn) has doubles for Y290 (with city view, if you want it) or Y300 (sea view).

Getting There & Away

Air The CAAC office (☎ 222-4415) is at 23 Renmin Nan Dadao. It is also possible to make bookings from the Southwest Airline ticketing office almost next door to the Canton Bay Hotel.

There are flights out of the Zhanjiang airport to Guangzhou (Y530), Beijing (Y2180), Shanghai (Y1630), Zhuhai (Y400),

Shenzhen, Hong Kong, Kunming, Wuhan, Chengdu, Chongqing, Guiyang, Sanya and Shantou.

Bus The long-distance bus station in the south has services to Guangzhou for a range of prices (Y70, Y80 and Y90) including sleepers. Tickets for more deluxe services (reclining seats and videos) can be bought at the Haifu Grand Hotel (Y160). The trip takes 10 to 11 hours and most buses travel by night. There are also bus services to Shenzhen (Y100).

The north long-distance bus station on Shenchuan Dadaobei in the Chikan District also has services to Zhaoqing, Shantou, Zhuhai, Shenzhen, Guangzhou and combined bus-boat services to Haikou. The station is a long way from the southern part of town, but can be reached on bus No 1.

Train Trains to Guilin, Nanning, Foshan and Guangzhou leave from the south railway station. Overnight air-con fast trains connect with Guangzhou for Y250 (sleeper) and take 10 hours. From Zhanjiang to Guilin takes about 13 hours. Apart from at the railway station, if you are arriving in Zhanjiang by boat, you can purchase your ticket outside the Customs building at the ferry terminal.

Boat There are combination bus-boat tickets to Haikou on Hainan Island on sale at the bus station. However, it is more convenient – and not much more expensive – to take the express boat to Haikou (Y101) which takes three hours; tickets are on sale at the harbour. The express boats leave at 9 am and 2.30 pm.

Be aware that both these services were in doubt at the time of writing. Check out the situation at the harbour.

Getting Around
To/From the Airport Zhanjiang's airport is 5km east of the city centre. A taxi will cost Y25 to Y30.

Bus, Train & Pedicab There are two rail-way stations and two long-distance bus stations, one each in the northern and southern parts of town. The southern railway station is the main one.

Bus No 1 runs between the two districts. Taxis cost about Y10 anywhere in the Xiashan area. There are many motorcycles, some with side cars, cruising the streets; Y5 is enough for all locations within a couple of kilometres from where you embark.

Pedicabs also swarm after foreigners – Y10 will get you almost anywhere on one of these (maybe even to Guangzhou).

SHANTOU
(shàntóu)
Shantou is one of China's four original Special Economic Zones (SEZ) along with Shenzhen, Zhuhai and Xiamen. It's a little-visited port with a unique culture.

The local dialect is known as *chaoshan* in Mandarin – a combination of Chaozhou and Shantou – or *taejiu* by the people themselves and is the language of many of the Chinese who emigrated to Thailand. The language is completely different from Cantonese. These Thai-Chinese people have started to return, and it's not unusual to see Thai script in the hotels and on business signs.

Unfortunately, Shantou shows all the signs of an SEZ damp squib, with little to recommend it. History is also in serious deficit here (although there are a few pockets of interest), and the city is basically a transit point on the little-travelled haul between Guangzhou and Fujian.

History
Shantou was previously known to the outside world as Swatow. As early as the 18th century the East India Company had a station on an island outside the harbour, when the town was little more than a fishing village on a mudflat.

The port was officially opened up to foreign trade in 1860 with the Treaty of Tianjin, which ended another Opium war. The British were the first foreigners to establish themselves here, although their

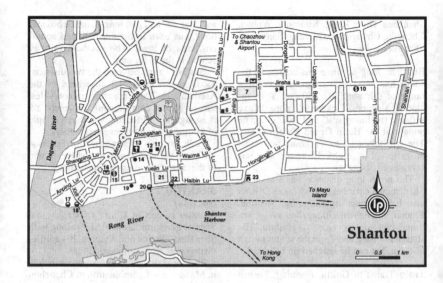

Shantou

0   0.5   1 km

SHANTOU   汕头市

PLACES TO STAY

2   Hualian Hotel
    华联酒店
4   Swatow Peninsula
    Hotel
    鮀岛宾馆
6   Huaqiao Hotel; CTS;
    Bank of China
    华侨大厦、
    中国旅行社、
    中国银行
9   International Hotel
    国际大酒店
11 Taiwan Hotel
    台湾宾馆
12 Xinhua Hotel
    新华酒店

OTHER

1   Long-Distance Bus Station
    汽车客货运站
3   Zhongshan Park
    中山公园
5   CAAC
    民航售票处
7   Jinsha Park
    金沙公园
8   Post Office
    邮电局
10 Bank of China
    (Main Branch)
    中国银行
13 Shantou Christian Church
    市西堂
14 Xinhua Bookstore
    新华书店
15 Bank of China
    中国银行

16 Post Office
    邮电局
17 Xidi Bus Station
    西堤客运站
18 Xidi Passenger Ferry
    西堤客运码头
19 International Seamen's
    Club
    国际海员俱乐部
20 Shantou Wharf
    Passenger Terminal
    汕头港客运站
21 Renmin Square
    人民广场
22 Guangchang Wharf
    Passenger Terminal
    广场码头
23 Stone Fort
    石炮台

projected settlement had to relocate to a nearby island due to local hostility.

Before 1870 foreigners were living and trading in Shantou town itself. Many of the old colonial buildings still survive, although in a state of extreme dilapidation.

Orientation

Most of Shantou lies on a peninsula, bounded in the south by the ocean and separated from the mainland in the west and the north by a river and canals. Most tourist amenities are in the western part of the peninsula.

Information

Tourist Office The CTS office (☎ 823-3966) is in the Huaqiao Hotel. It sells bus tickets to Guangzhou, Shenzhen and Xiamen, boat tickets to Hong Kong and air tickets to wherever CAAC flies.

PSB You'll find the PSB on Yuejin Lu at its eastern end, near the intersection with Nanhai Lu.

Money Right opposite the post office is a branch of the Bank of China. Another branch can be found in the Huaqiao Hotel.

Post & Communications The main post office can be found on Waima Lu, just before the turning with Yongping Lu.

Things to See

There's not much in the way of sights in Shantou, but the roundabout at the point where Shengping Lu and Anping Lu converge is interesting for its colonial remains. It's worth looking at the architecture above street level while it's still there: someone really ought to occupy the post office on the corner of Shengping Lu and Guoping Lu and turn it into a hotel; it would make such a gem.

The same goes for the Nansheng trade building. If you have time and an eye for history and buildings, then this area can come up with a few surprises.

Places to Stay

The *Swatow Peninsula Hotel* (☎ 823-1261) *(túodǎo bīnguǎn)* on Jinsha Lu is the best bargain in town. Comfortable singles with private bath are HK$78. There are also more plush doubles from HK$128 (Y141). Downstairs appears to house the trendiest disco in Shantou, or at least it looks that way from the hordes of hip teenagers lounging around in the lobby.

The *Xinhua Hotel* (☎ 827-3710) *(xīnhuá jiǔdiàn)*, at 121 Waima Lu, has basic singles (with shower) for Y170 and better rooms from Y200.

Next door, the *Taiwan Hotel* (☎ 827-6400) *(táiwān bīnguǎn)* has singles/doubles for Y208/268, and rooms 'with a view' for Y288. There is a 10% service charge.

The *Huaqiao Hotel* (☎ 831-9888) *(huáqiáo dàshà)* on Shanzhang Lu has reasonable singles for Y260 and doubles from Y298 to Y398. Opposite the long-distance bus station is the *Hualian Hotel* (☎ 822-8389) *(huálián jiǔdiàn)*, where doubles are Y258.

There are a number of top-end hotels in town. The pick of the bunch is the huge and glitzy *International Hotel* (☎ 825-1212; fax 825-2250) *(guójì dàjiǔdiàn)* on Jinsha Zhonglu. It has a scuffed and used feel, but has a great French wine shop on the 2nd floor for those who are sick of the filling-loosening super-sweet Chinese stuff. It has standard doubles from Y930, deluxe doubles from Y1200 and suites from Y2100. Discounts can go as high as 40%.

Places to Eat

Street markets set up at night and this is where you'll find the cuisine Shantou is famous for. Rice noodles (called *kwetiaw* locally) are also a speciality. All along Minzu Lu are a number of stalls specialising in delicious wonton *(húndùn)*.

If you're staying at the Swatow Peninsula Hotel, check and see if they've finished refurbishing the *Western Restaurant* in the back. It turns out good, cheap food when the decorators aren't in.

For decent cuisine, try the revolving restaurant on the 23rd floor of the *International Hotel*, which does reasonable western food at an affordable price.

Getting There & Away

Air Shantou airport, about 20km from the city centre, has international flights to Bangkok, Singapore and Hong Kong (twice daily). Domestic flights are available to Beijing, Guangzhou, Fuzhou, Guilin, Haikou, Nanjing, Shanghai and other cities.

The CAAC office (☎ 825-1915) is at 46 Shanzhang Lu, a few minutes' walk south of the intersection with Jinsha Lu. It's usually more convenient to buy from CTS next door in the Huaqiao Hotel.

Bus Buses to Guangzhou (Y40 to Y80), Xiamen (Y50 to Y90), Fuzhou (Y90 to Y120), Haikou (Y220), Zhuhai, Nanning, Quanzhou, Zhanjiang, Shenzhen and Zhaoqing leave from the Xidi bus station next to the Xidi passenger ferry terminal. There is a daily service to Kowloon that takes five hours and costs HK$260 (HK$190 for children).

Most hotels also offer bus services, including the Swatow Hotel and the Hualian Hotel. More and more private companies are operating these days and are raising the standards of service.

Train There are overnight services between Shantou and Guangzhou (Y220 hard sleeper). There are six trains a day to Chaozhou.

Boat Boats ply the route between Hong Kong and Shantou. In Hong Kong, departures are from China Hong Kong City ferry terminal in Tsimshatsui, Kowloon.

In Shantou, departures are from Shantou Wharf passenger terminal (☎ 827-1513) *(shàntóu gǎng kèyùn zhàn)*. There is a ship every two days; the price ranges from HK$260 (seat) to HK$360 (four to six people sharing a cabin) and HK$460 (one to two people in a cabin). Tickets are available at the spick-and-span ticket office at the passenger terminal.

Getting Around
To/From the Airport Buses to Shantou airport leave from the CAAC office on Shanzhang Lu. A taxi will cost Y40 to Y50.

Bus & Pedicab The local public buses are the usual horror, but there are minibuses for Y2 going anywhere in the city. Bus Nos 3 and 4 go to the Xidi passenger ferry terminal and the adjacent bus station.

Pedicabs and motor-tricycles hover outside the long-distance bus station and tourist hotels and charge about Y3 for most trips in the town centre. Generally you

won't have to bother with any of this – it doesn't take long to explore the city on foot.

AROUND SHANTOU
Not far out of the city is **Mayu Island** *(māyǔ dǎo)*, which makes a good day trip. A boat leaves from the Guangchang Wharf at 9.30 am every day and returns at 2 pm (Y20 return).

On an ordinary weekday the boat is filled with people toting bags of food and sacrificial offerings. Follow the crowd from the landing to the Temple of the Mother of the Heavenly Emperor *(tiānhòu miào)*, built in 1985 with funds supplied by Overseas Chinese.

The site has apparently always been holy to this deity, and this is where the fisherfolk burn incense before they leave in the morning. As soon as you approach Guangchang Wharf, all sorts of old witch types will surround you, trying to get you on to their boats – some of them have good deals if you are in a group.

Evidently the island has been developed to keep pace with the worshippers' enthusiasm; there are hotels and restaurants, as well as marked trails for getting around the island. A huge bridge spans the island from Shantou. There are no cars, and the beaches and views are refreshing after the large Chinese cities.

According to the villagers, the island was settled mainly during the Japanese occupation, although there were a few people living here before then.

CHAOZHOU
(cháozhōu)
Chaozhou is an ancient commercial and trading city dating back 1700 years. It is situated on the Han River and surrounded by the Golden and Calabash hills. It can be explored in a couple of hours and is best visited as a day trip from Shantou.

The chief sight is the **Kaiyuan Temple** *(kāiyuán sì)*, which was built during the Tang Dynasty to house a collection of Buddhist scriptures sent here by Emperor Qian Long. The temple was reduced almost

Chaozhou

to rubble during the Cultural Revolution, but now houses three large buddhas flanked by 18 golden arhats. The temple, noted for its colourful roof ornaments and decorations, is active and many monks are usually present at prayer.

Chaozhou's old city wall still runs along next to the Han River; preserved sections like the Guangjimen area are attractive (this is also an area full of cheap food stalls, of the pick and choose variety).

West Lake can make for pleasant strolls although it is gradually being developing into a theme park.

Hidden away among the dodgem cars and merry-go-rounds are the **Moya carvings** depicting local landscapes and the customs of the people, as well as poems and calligraphy; they date back 1000 years.

South-east of Chaozhou is the seven storey **Phoenix Pagoda** (*fènghuáng tǎ*) built in 1585.

Still further south-east of Chaozhou is the more difficult to reach **Sanyuan Pagoda** (*sānyuán tǎ*).

Getting There & Away

Minibuses run out to Chaozhou from in front of the Hualian Hotel in Shantou. The trip takes around one hour and costs Y8. There are six trains a day to Guangzhou; from the railway station in Chaozhou to the town centre is a hike and you will probably have to jump on a motor-tricycle (Y20).

Hainan Island 海南岛

Hainan Island Facts & Highlights

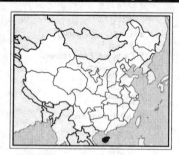

Area: 34,000 sq km

Population: 7.3 million

Capital: Haikou

Highlights

- Li and Miao minority villages around Tongzha (for the intrepid, Chinese-speaking traveller only).
- Asian Dragon Bay to the east of Sanya, a 7km stretch of beautiful sand and sun.

Hainan Island *(hǎinán dǎo)* is a large tropical island off the southern coast of China. It was administered by the government of Guangdong Province until 1988, when it became Hainan Province.

With its acres of beaches in the south, dense vegetation, balmy winds and lilting palm trees, Hainan is popular as a winter refuge; however, unless you wish to spend the Yuletide season cheek-by-jowl with the rest of China in pricey hotels, miss the rush and go between March and November when you can expect large discounts on hotel accommodation (up to 50%).

Despite mainly catering to hordes of Chinese tour groups, Hainan still manages to tempt with some of the trappings of an island paradise: golden beaches, the promise of a deep tan and (albeit muffled by posses of trinket sellers) the thud of falling coconuts.

HISTORY

Historically, Hainan has always been a backwater of the Chinese Empire, a miserable place of exile and poverty. When Li Deyu, a prime minister of the Tang Dynasty, was exiled to Hainan he dubbed it 'the gate of hell'. According to historical records, only 18 tourists came to Hainan of their own volition during the entire Song, Yuan and Ming dynasties (about 1000 years)! That's about the rate per second during winter nowadays.

Times are changing – the entire island of Hainan was established as a Special Economic Zone (SEZ) in 1988 and has emerged as an enclave of free-market bedlam operating on the periphery of the law. One of the most famous fiascos occurred when the provincial government imported 90,000 duty-free Japanese cars in 1985 and resold them on the mainland at a 150% profit. The army and navy were enlisted to transport the vehicles, which traced the chain of command to the Governor of Hainan, Lei Yu, who was subsequently relieved of his post after the official investigation. Land prices tripled in value between January and June 1992, the island opened a stock market without authorisation in the same year and recent estimates of growth for the province hover around 22%. But despite the heady economic climate, the Haikou skyline is punctuated with the shells of unfinished construction, testament to the fickleness of investors and financial overreaching.

Heavy industry is virtually absent, and some 80% of the island's economy is washed ashore by tourism.

CLIMATE

Hainan is the southernmost tip of China (Sanya, in the south, is roughly on the same latitude as the southern reaches of Hawaii),

The Spratly Spat

If it was not such a contentious piece of real estate, very few people would have heard of the Spratly Islands, and their near neighbours the Paracel Islands. To find them on a map, look for a parcel of dots in the South China Sea hemmed in by Malaysia, Brunei, the Philippines, Vietnam and China way to the north. They all claim the islands as their own.

It is tempting to ask what all the fuss is about. After all, this is a collection of 53 specks of land, many of which are reefs and shoals rather than islands. The answer is oil. Not that any oil has been discovered in the region, and some experts dispute that any will ever be found. Yet the very possibility that there *might* be oil in the Spratly Islands has set all the countries in the region at loggerheads with each other.

China, the most distant of the claimants, sees its territorial rights to the area as being validated by a historical relationship with the islands that dates back to the Han Dynasty. The ruins of Chinese temples can still be found on some of the islands. Vietnam has for long been a disputant to this claim, and in 1933 the colonial French government of Vietnam annexed the islands. They lost them to Japan in 1939. With Japan's WWII defeat, the question of the Spratly Islands was left unaddressed. It was not until a Philippine claim in 1956 that the Taiwan-based Kuomintang government reasserted the traditional Chinese claim over the island group by occupying the largest of the islands, Taiping, where they remain. Vietnam followed by hoisting a flag over the westernmost of the islands. The Chinese struck back in 1988 by sinking two Vietnamese ships and forcibly occupying the islands. In 1996, the Philippine navy destroyed a small Chinese-built radar base on Mischief Reef in the Spratlys.

With all the countries of the region embarking on programmes of updating their military capabilities, the Spratly Islands remain one of the most potentially destabilising issues in the Asian region. ∎

and can be relied on to be warm even when the rest of China is freezing.

At the height of China's frigid winter, average temperatures of 21°C (69.8°F) prevail; the yearly average is 25.4°C (77.7°F). From as early as March through to November, the weather becomes hot and humid.

Typhoons can play havoc with a tight itinerary. Usually descending on the island between May and October, there has been at least one every year for the last 50 years. They can be incredibly destructive – the September 1996 gust caused Y300 million in damage and had parts of Haikou, the island's capital, waist deep in water.

Bear in mind that typhoons can cripple all transport and communication with the mainland for several days at a time. On a good note, there is almost no heavy industry in Hainan, so the air is clean and the skies are clear.

POPULATION & PEOPLE

Thirty-nine minority groups live on Hainan Island, although only the original inhabitants of the island, the Li and Miao, are accessible, living in the dense tropical forests covering the Limulingshan mountains that stretch down the centre of the island. The Li probably settled on Hainan 3000 years ago after migrating from Fujian Province.

Although there has been a long history of rebellion by the Li against the Chinese, they aided the Communist guerrillas on the island during the war with the Japanese. Perhaps for this reason the island's centre was made an 'autonomous' region after the Communists came to power.

Until recently the Li women had a custom of tattooing their bodies at the age of 12 or 13. Today, almost all Li people except the elderly women wear standard Han dress. However, when a member of the Li dies,

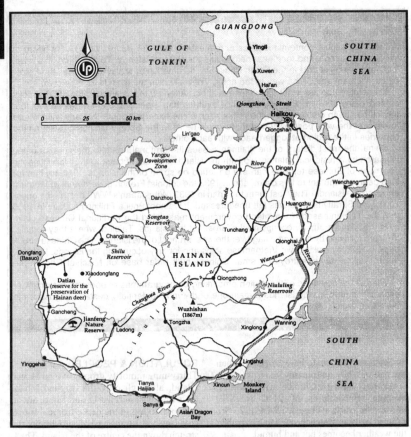

Hainan Island

GUANGDONG

GULF OF
TONKIN

SOUTH
CHINA
SEA

0   25   50 km

Yingli

Xuwen

Hai'an

Qiongzhou   **Strait**

Haikou

Qiongshan

Lin'gao

Yangpu
Development
Zone

Chengmai   *River*   Dingan

Nandu

Wenchang

Danzhou

Dinglan

Huangzhu

Songtao
Reservoir

Tunchang

Changjiang

*Shilu
Reservoir*

Qionghai

HAINAN
ISLAND

Wanquan   River

Dongfang
(Basuo)

Qiongzhong

Datian
(reserve for the
preservation of
Hainan deer)

Xiaodongfang

*Niululing
Reservoir*

Gancheng

Changhua River

Jianfeng
Nature
Reserve

Wuzhishan
(1867m)

Ledong   Tongzha

Xinglong   Wanning

SOUTH

Yinggehai

Lingshui

CHINA

Tianya
Haijiao

Xincun   **Monkey
Island**

SEA

Sanya

Asian Dragon
Bay

---

traditional Li costume is considered essential if the dead are to be accepted by ancestors in the afterworld.

The Miao (Hmong) people spread from southern China across northern Vietnam, Laos and Thailand. In China they moved south into Hainan as a result of the Chinese emigrations from the north, and now occupy some of the most rugged terrain on the island.

The coastal areas of the island are populated by Han Chinese. Since 1949, Chinese from Indonesia, Malaysia and, later, Vietnam have been settled here. All told, Hainan has a population of around 6.5 million, of which about 700,000 are Li and 40,000 are Miao.

ORIENTATION

Haikou, the capital of Hainan, and Sanya, a port with popular beaches, are the two major urban centres. They are at opposite ends of the island.

Three highways link the towns: the eastern route via Wanning (the fastest route); the central route via Tunchang and Tongzha (also known as Tongshi); and the less popular western route via Danzhou (also known as Nada), Basuo (Dongfang) and Yinggehai.

Most visitors to Hainan take the rapid eastern route from Haikou to Sanya. It's possible to stop off en route, but very few people bother, particularly now that a new motorway (currently being widened) bypasses most of the possible attractions.

A highway is also planned to replace the road that cuts across the centre of the island.

The central route takes you through the central highlands of Hainan and past the Li and Miao minority villages. Showcase villages for Chinese tour groups are not the real thing; the genuine articles lie hidden far away from convenient transport links and are, for the most part, inaccessible. Dig out a good map, a machete and mosquito repellent if you're interested.

The best mountain scenery (and it really is impressive) is between Sanya and Qiongzhong, but there's little of interest beyond that. This route tunnels through what remains of the mountainous forest regions of Hainan; the island was the scene of mass deforestation between 1950 and 1980, when up to half of the natural forest cover was felled to make way for rubber plantations.

There's little traffic on the western route

Warning

If you are planning on going to Sanya by bus, be aware that the trip back on the central route, via Tongzha, is a white-knuckle ride; the drivers drive as if fleeing an exploding volcano.

In a one hour stretch we witnessed two serious crashes and one death, all unrelated. The only alternatives are to fly back to Haikou or return by the highway in the east. A highway is planned for the central route, but it's quite a few years away from completion. ∎

and it has little in the way of amenities. Attractions include the Institute of Tropical Plants *(rèdài zhíwù yánjiūsuǒ)* near Danzhou *(dānzhōu)* and the Nature Reserve for the Protection of the Hainan Deer *(dàtián zìrán bǎohùqū)* at Datian.

To the east of Datian is the town of Xiaodongfang, the site of the Li minority's 'Loving Festival' on the third day of the third lunar month (around April).

The Jianfeng Nature Reserve *(jiānfēnglǐng zìrán bǎohùqū)* is another popular destination. A motorway is also planned to cover this route.

HAIKOU
(hǎikǒu)
Haikou, Hainan's capital, lies on the northern coastline at the mouth of the Nandu River. It's a port town and handles most of the island's commerce with the mainland.

For most travellers, Haikou is merely a transit point on the way to Sanya. The city is quite pretty, but there's little else to appeal and accommodation is pricey. Apart from a sprinkling of temples, and decaying colonial charm in the Sino-Portuguese architecture around Xinhua Nanlu, there is not much to keep you from hopping on a bus and heading for the surf and sun in the south.

Orientation
Haikou is split into three fairly separate sections. The western section is the port area. The centre of Haikou has all the tourist facilities. On the southern side of the airport is another district of little interest to travellers.

Information
Tourist Offices The main CTS office (☎ 676-6523; fax 672-2183) is in a dilapidated building hidden behind the Overseas Chinese Hotel. They mainly deal with tour groups and are not much use to individual travellers. It's worth asking about tours around the island, as these can work out much cheaper than tackling it all yourself.

The usual package is three days and four

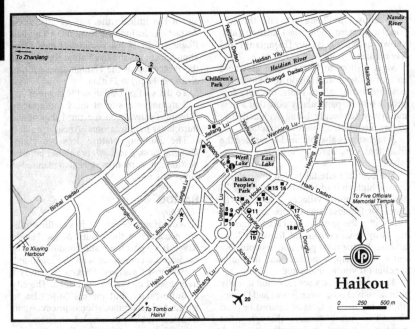

Haikou

0   250   500 m

nights, taking in Xinglong, Sanya, Tongzha and back to Haikou via the odd minority village. Prices start from Y500, and include transport, accommodation and meals (ticket prices for sights not included).

If CTS can't help, or are too expensive, ask at your hotel or at one of the numerous travel agents around town; the only problem is that you follow a strict itinerary and the tour group leader will speak Chinese, unless you are a sizeable group, in which case they will supply an interpreter. Adventurous students of Chinese will profit from the journey.

PSB The PSB (☎ 653-3166) can be found on Jinhua Lu, just after the intersection with Longhua Lu.

Money The Bank of China is in the International Financial Centre at 33 Datong Lu and there is a branch next door in the In-

ternational Commercial Centre; money-changers throng the streets outside both.

Post & Communications The post and telecommunications building is south of the long-distance bus station on Daying Lu. There is another post and telecommunications centre on Jiefang Xilu, near the Xinhua Bookstore. Most upmarket hotels also offer postal services.

Things to See
As Chinese cities go, Haikou is quite attractive, sporting palm-tree lined boulevards and a picturesque old quarter, but there is little in the way of sights.

The city's crumbling colonial remains can be covered quickly by strolling down Xinhua Lu. Take a couple of detours along the lanes that run off these streets for shades of Macau.

The **Five Officials Memorial Temple**

HAIKOU 海口

PLACES TO STAY
2 Wuhan Hotel
  武汉大厦
4 Friendship Hotel & Store
  友谊大酒店、商店
5 Overseas Chinese Hotel
  华侨大厦
8 International Financial
  Centre; Bank of China
  国际金融大厦、
  中国银行
9 CAAC Hotel; Ticket Office
  民航酒店售票处
10 International Commercial
  Centre
  海口国际商业大厦

12 Garden Hotel
  花园大酒店
13 Seaview International
  Hotel
  望海国际大酒店
14 Ocean Hotel;
  Kwaihuolin Delicious
  Food Town
  海洋宾馆、快活林
15 Haikou Hotel
  海口宾馆
16 East Lake Hotel
  东湖大酒店
17 Wuzhishan Hotel
  五指山大厦
18 Shu Hai Hotel
  蜀海酒店

OTHER
1 Haikou New
  Harbour
  海口新港
3 Xinhua Bookstore
  新华书店
6 CTS
  中国旅行社
7 PSB
  公安局
11 Long-Distance
  Bus Station
  长途汽车站
19 Post Office
  邮缇
20 Haikou Airport
  海口机场

(wǔgōngcí) is an attractive temple dedicated to five officials who were banished to Hainan in earlier times. The famous Song Dynasty poet, Su Dongpo, was also banished to Hainan and is commemorated here. The temple was first built in the Ming Dynasty, restored in the Qing Dynasty and is home to a collection of ponds, bridges and palm trees. It can be found at 169 Haifu Dao; bus Nos 13,14 and 15 all go there.

The **Tomb of Hairui** (hǎiruìmù) was mostly torn down during the Cultural Revolution, but has been put back together again. Hairui was a compassionate and popular official who lived in the 16th century; the temple is being fully restored and was being repainted in vibrant colours at the time of writing. The ceiling is particularly attractive. The tomb can be found in the west of Haikou, off Haixiu Dadao; take bus No 2.

The **Haikou People's Park** has a Y1 entry charge. The column at the centre of the park, dedicated to revolutionary martyrs, is offset by a neighbouring statue of Mickey Mouse.

Places to Stay – budget
Travellers won't find much in the way of budget accommodation in Haikou; a cheapie does exist, however, in the form of the *Wuhan Hotel* (☎ 621-1809) (wǔhàn dàshà). It's grubby, but a bargain at Y90 for doubles and Y120 for triples. It's conveniently tucked away opposite the passenger ferry terminal.

Scraping in at the bottom end, the wonderful *Garden Hotel* (huāyuán dàjiǔdiàn) at 5 Daying Houlu has singles for Y128, but pricey doubles for Y288. Ringed by classical statues, the hotel looks like a huge wedding cake left out in the rain. Behind the reception area, a spacious courtyard is home to colossal palms. It sticks out like a sore thumb on the south-western corner of Haikou Park.

Places to Stay – middle
Most of Haikou's hotels are middle to top end, but push for discounts (zhékòu) wherever you go; if you avoid the winter months, you can hammer the price down.

Cheaper hotels can be found around Jichang Donglu. The *Wuzhishan Hotel* (☎ 535-1012) (wǔzhǐshān dàshà) chips in with Y240 for serviceable singles and Y260 for doubles (there's a potential 50% discount).

Quite a bit further south on Jichang Donglu – and in an area dominated by hairdressing salons with lurid pink lighting – is the *Shu Hai Hotel* (☎ 535-1904; fax 535-2172) (shǔhǎi jiǔdiàn), where standard doubles are Y260. Big discounts are possible here.

The *Overseas Chinese Hotel* (☎ 670-8430; fax 677-2094) *(hǎinán huáqiáo dàshà)*, at 17 Datong Lu, is another possibility. All rooms come with a private bathroom, with singles from Y276, doubles from Y360, and triples from Y480. Discounts are available, but foreigners should pay in HK dollars.

The *Friendship Hotel* (☎ 622-5566; fax 622-1107) *(yǒuyì dàjiǔdiàn)*, next door to the Friendship Store at 2 Datong Lu, has higher rates, but was willing to offer a 50% discount. Posted rates were Y380 for standard doubles.

Places to Stay – top end

At the *East Lake Hotel* (☎ 535-3333; fax 535-8827) *(dōnghú dàjiǔdiàn)*, at 8 Haifu Dadao, standard doubles cost Y450.

The *Seaview International Hotel* (☎ 677-3381; fax 677-3101) *(wànghǎi guójì dàjiǔdiàn)* is a popular and impressive hotel with singles from Y385, doubles from Y498 and suites from Y994. Check for discounts.

Close by, the *Haikou Hotel* (☎ 535-0221; fax 535-0232) *(hǎikǒu bīnguǎn)* seems to be the busiest hotel in town; or at least the large and very sleazy lobby coffee shop is. Rooms range from Y588 to Y1280.

Haikou's prime location is the *Haikou International Commercial Centre* (☎ 679-6999; fax 677-4751) *(hǎikǒu guójì shāngyè dàshà)*, a modern structure that offers health club facilities, banking, shopping and restaurants. Singles start from Y528, and doubles from Y800.

The *Haikou International Financial Centre* (☎ 677-3088; fax 677-2113) *(hǎikǒu guójì jīnróng dàshà)*, at 33 Datong Lu, is a very similar setup to the Commercial Centre next door. Amenities include everything from a swimming pool to a bowling alley. Singles start at Y598 and doubles at Y668.

Places to Eat

In response to the phalanxes of tour groups that trundle through Haikou, most restaurants tend to be hot-pot affairs, although there is a clutch of cheaper restaurants on Jichang Donglu.

Hot-pot meals can be a lot of fun, but you may feel they are more suited to Mongolia than the tropics; they are not cheap either, and you can expect to pay in the region of Y60 to Y70 for two. Popular ingredients to fling into the hot-pot include crab *(pángxiè)*, mushroom *(mógu)*, cabbage *(qīngcài)*, tofu, sliced pork and lamb, and congealed duck's blood.

Traditional Hainan dishes worth looking out for include Wenchang chicken, Jiaji duck, Dongshan lamb (which has a mild flavour) and Hele crab.

If you really want to save money, there are *fruit sellers* on the street vending bananas, mangoes, sugar cane and so on. Instead of forking out for soft drinks, buy a green coconut for Y1: the vendor slices the top off with a machete, pokes in a straw and there you are.

The *Kuaihuolin Delicious Food Town* *(kuàihuólín)* is next door to the Ocean Hotel on Jichang Donglu. It serves up set meals in fast-food surroundings, with prices from around Y12. The English menu is much more limited than the Chinese menu, but still provides a couple of pages of choices.

Upmarket eats with an English menu? The Haikou International Financial Centre is your best bet. The 2nd floor *Western Restaurant (ōulù cāntīng)* serves excellent food in quiet and relaxed surroundings; the rack of lamb is particularly good, but the wine is a tad pricey. Fresh coffee can be had in the ground floor coffee shop of the Seaview International Hotel, although at Y18 per pot it is getting close to international prices.

Entertainment

Haikou has a certain reputation ... this is the balmy tropics of China and businessmen come here to do deals and loosen their ties. Hainan is a far cry from Beijing and virtually a law unto itself, but anyone who thinks they are coming to Bangkok or Manila, however, is wrong.

The entertainment scene is typically

Chinese and goes as far as karaoke parlours, which keep all and sundry awake until the early hours with grinding discords. Larger hotels have nightclubs and tacky floor shows.

Male travellers could receive regular phone calls asking if they want a sauna *(sāngnà)*; how they get the sauna up to your room, I don't know. If you don't want a sangna, unplug your phone.

Prostitution is a pervasive industry all over the island, with the coffee lounge of the Haikou Hotel being its main headquarters (apparently a tourist attraction).

Getting There & Away

Air There are daily flights between Haikou and Hong Kong (HK$1350) on CAAC and Dragonair; CAAC has flights once a week to Bangkok. Dragonair (☎ 677-3088, ext 1743) has a representative in Room 2 on the 5th floor of the International Financial Centre.

The CAAC office (☎ 677-2608), in a large building which also houses the CAAC Hotel, is on Daying Houlu. Just a few doors down is the China Southwest Airlines office. Between them they have regular flights between Haikou and many cities including Beijing, Guangzhou, Harbin, Kunming, Nanning, Shanghai and Shenzhen.

Meilan international airport is due to open at the start of 1999 with a wider range of international routes.

Bus The long-distance bus station has departures to all major destinations on the island, as well as offering combination ferry/bus journeys to many destinations on the mainland; sleeper buses to Guangzhou cost Y157, Y197 with air-con, and Y347 to Fuzhou.

Also worth looking out for are the private operators running buses to Sanya. Super-luxury buses depart from near the Ocean Hotel on Jichang Donglu, take just three hours and cost Y75. However, luxury buses from the bus station are only Y65 (ask for *háohuá*), and there are 25 departures daily; economy buses are Y42, but

are crowded and slow, taking six to seven hours.

There are 10 departures daily to Tongzha; prices are Y47 (luxury) and Y33 (economy).

Boat There are two harbours in Haikou, but most departures are from Haikou New Harbour *(hǎikǒu xīngǎng)* at the terminus of bus No 7. From the centre of town to the harbour by taxi costs around Y15.

There are 12 departures daily for the 1½ hour trip to Hai'an on the Leizhou Peninsula, where there are bus connections with Zhanjiang, but it is much simpler just to take the boat direct to Zhanjiang, unless you desperately want to go via Hai'an.

Tickets for the slow ferry to Zhanjiang (Y33) can be bought at the Haikou harbour passenger ferry ticket office opposite the East Lake Hotel. The slow ferry departs from Xiuying harbour. Alternatively, take one of the fast boat services from Haikou New Harbour, which leave at 9.30 am and 1.30 pm for Zhanjiang. Tickets cost Y100 and the journey takes 3½ hours. An overnight boat leaves daily for Beihai in Guangxi Province at 6 pm. Tickets are on sale at the harbour and cost between Y68 and Y153.

There are occasional ferries to Guangzhou from Xiuying harbour and the journey takes 25 hours. Tickets are available from the Haikou harbour passenger ferry ticket office.

Getting Around

To/From the Airport Haikou airport is 2km south of the city centre and taxi fares should be about Y20. Bus No 7 runs between the airport and Haikou New Harbour.

Bus The central area of Haikou is small and easy to walk around, but there is also a workable bus system. The fare is Y1 for any destination in the city.

Taxi Taxis are reasonably abundant in Haikou and operate on a meter system. Fares start at Y12.8 for the first 3km.

WENCHANG
(wénchāng)

The coconut plantations at Dongjiao *(dōngjiāo yēlín)* and Jianhuashan *(jiànhuáshān yēlín)* are a short ride out of town at Qinglan harbour *(qīnglán gǎng)*. The area is also well known for its seafood.

Minibuses by the riverside in Wenchang will take you to Qinglan, where you can take a ferry to the stands of coconut palms and mile after mile of beach. Another way to get to here is to take the direct bus to Dongjiao from Haikou's long-distance bus station.

Unfortunately, the beaches in this area are being developed as resorts and accommodation prices are very high.

Buses leave for Wenchang from Haikou's long-distance bus station; there are five departures daily, from 10 am to 4 pm, and tickets cost Y10. The 73km could be done as a day trip.

XINGLONG
(xīnglóng)

Since 1952, more than 20,000 Chinese-Vietnamese and Overseas Chinese refugees (mostly from Indonesia or Malaysia) have settled at the **Xinglong Overseas Chinese Farm** *(xīnglóng huáqiáo cūn)*. Tropical agriculture, rubber and coffee are important cash crops here. Xinglong coffee is famous all over China. Many of the residents speak English and may be able to organise transport to Miao villages.

It's almost worth forking out Y250 for the cheapest hotel room so that you can relax in the hot spring baths that have made Xinglong famous. The baths are typically swimming pool-sized, open-air and separated into hot and cool; you can slide from one into another endlessly and really open your pores. It's very relaxing.

Unfortunately, the hotels in Xinglong all cater to Chinese tour groups who get discounted rates; if you're not with a group then you have to pay full whack (a good reason to join a tour).

From the bus stop to the hotels costs Y2 on the back of a motorbike, or Y4 in a motorbike with sidecar.

Evidence that you are far from the conservative dictates of Beijing can be seen in the many local massage parlours glowing with garish neon, their doorways propped up by sultry women with cigarettes hanging from their lips who clearly haven't dipped into Mao's little red book for a while.

A small, functional railway in Xinglong exists for ferrying bevies of tourists around the town.

Near Xinglong is the **Indonesian Village** *(yìnnícūn)*, principally designed for tour groups and featuring Indonesian singing, dancing, snake acts and a complimentary cup of super-sweet local Xinglong coffee. It's all quite a laugh in a tacky sort of way, but transport is a problem as only tour buses head there.

XINCUN
(xīncūn)

Xincun is populated almost solely by Danjia (Tanha) minority people, who are employed in fishing and pearl cultivation (look out for large holes carved from the walls of houses in nearby Shuiling; these represent pearls and bring good luck to the owners).

In recent years, typhoons have repeatedly blown away the pearl and oyster cultivation farms. Furthermore, Xincun's main attraction, Monkey Island, is not what it used to be and can be easily skipped by those eager to reach the sands of Sanya.

Buses travelling the eastern route will drop you off at a fork in the road about 3km from Xincun. It should then be easy to get a lift on a passing minibus, or hitch or walk into Xincun. Frequent minibuses run to Xincun directly from Lingshui (15km away) and Sanya.

MONKEY ISLAND
(nánwān hóudǎo)

One thousand Guangxi monkeys *(Macaca mulatta)* live on this narrow peninsula near Xincun. The area is under state protection and a special wildlife research centre has been set up to investigate all the monkey business.

However, recent years have seen a decline in the population; many are ill, struck down with ailments people say are due to the countless scraps of dirty food thrown by tourists to the unsuspecting brood.

A shack on the beach at Xincun functions as a booking office selling return ferry tickets. The ferry putt-putts from Xincun to Monkey Island in 10 minutes. At the entrance a stall sells tickets, and peanuts for the monkeys.

Apart from feeding times at 9 am and 4 pm, it's a case of the monkeys seeing you and not vice versa. You can often hear them crashing around and chattering in the shrubs on the hillside; occasionally a wild, woolly head pops out of the top branches to see what's happening or to scream at you.

Much more active is the mating season for the local population (from February to May), however, tour groups give the place a wide berth at this time as the monkeys are, shall we say, over-hospitable and you may have to crowbar them off your leg.

SANYA
(sānyà)

Sanya is a busy port and tourist resort on the southern tip of Hainan Island. The town lies on a peninsula parallel to the coast and is connected to the mainland on one side by two bridges.

The harbour area is protected to the south-east by the hilly Luhuitou Peninsula. On the western outskirts of Sanya there's a community of around 5000 Hui, the only Muslim inhabitants of Hainan.

The Hui are traditionally considered to be shy, although your most direct contact with them, via the packs of Hui map-sellers clawing at you on the beaches, will probably put paid to that notion.

For the most part, Sanya is a bore, and there is little to stop you from grabbing a towel and jumping on to a beach-bound bus.

Things to See
The popular beaches are Asian Dragon Bay, Dadonghai, the Luhuitou Peninsula

and Tianya Haijiao. It's worth remembering that the sun is very intense at this latitude from March onwards and if you intend going to the beach, take high sun-factor lotion; sunburn is common.

The best of the lot is Asian Dragon Bay *(yàlóng wān)* to the east of Sanya, a great beach which features a 7km strip of sand (much longer than the longest beach in Hawaii). The views here are excellent and you can roam about for hours, throw your towel onto the sand and bake.

Off to the west along the beach is Dragon-Hovering Beach *(lóngxiáng wān)* which features island camping, paragliding, and motorboat and banana boat hire. There are regular minibuses from Sanya (Y5).

The crescent-shaped beach at **Dadonghai** *(dàdōnghǎi)* is much closer to Sanya, but is much smaller and consequently crowded. Entry is Y5. The best time to go is at night (no charge) – grab a beer and stroll along the sand where you can listen to the surf and watch the phosphorescent shark nets. Dadonghai is around 3km south-east of Sanya and is easily reached by bus (Y1) from Sanya bus station.

The beaches on the **Luhuitou Peninsula** *(lùhuítóu)* are poor, but they make for pleasant enough walks.

The beach at **Tianya Haijiao** *(tiānyá hǎijiǎo)* (literally 'edge of the sky, rim of the sea'), about 24km west of Sanya, is not bad, but of far more interest to Chinese tourists who crowd around the stone immortalised on the back of the Y2 note to have their photo taken. Entry to the beach is Y16. Catch any bus travelling west from Sanya bus station. The trip takes about 45 minutes. It's a bone-rattling ride.

Places to Stay
Be warned, there is hardly anywhere for travellers on a budget. Most of the hotels in and around Sanya cater mainly to package tourists, and the cheaper places don't take foreigners.

If you want to keep costs to a minimum in a good location, the best bet is the *Seaside Holiday Inn Resort* (☎ 821-3898)

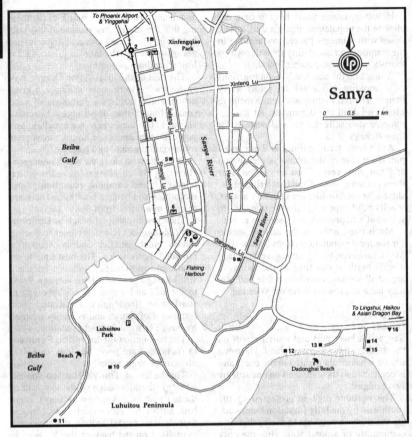

Sanya

0   0.5   1 km

To Phoenix Airport & Yinggehai

Xinfengqiao Park

Xinfeng Lu

Beibu Gulf

Sanya River

Jiefang Lu

Shengi Lu

Hedong Lu

Sanya River

Gangmen Lu

Fishing Harbour

To Lingshui, Haikou & Asian Dragon Bay

Luhuitou Park

Beibu Gulf

Beach

Dadonghai Beach

Luhuitou Peninsula

(bīnhǎi dùjiàcūn) in Dadonghai. Standard singles are Y260 and deluxe doubles are Y340. There are many other hotels in the Dadonghai area (in fact there is really nothing but hotels in Dadonghai). All sport room rates starting at Y350 for a double and there is little to distinguish one from another. The *South China Hotel* (☎ 821-3888) (*nánzhōngguó dàjiǔdiàn*) is rated as the best of the lot and has singles for Y647, and standard doubles for Y867.

Finding a hotel in Sanya itself will bring costs down slightly, but it's not a very

pleasant place to stay. The *Hongyun Hotel* (☎ 827-5036) (*hóngyùn bīnguǎn*) is quite cheap at Y70 for a single and Y90 for a twin, but it's pretty grim and is in an inconvenient location.

The *Sanya Hotel* (☎ 827-4703) (*sānyà bīnguǎn*) is in the centre of town on Jiefang Lu, and has singles from Y130, doubles from Y180 and triples for Y240. They were offering 30% discounts when we were last in town.

Sanya's luxury option is the *Sanya International Hotel* (☎ 827-3068) (*sānyà guójì*

SANYA 三亚

PLACES TO STAY
1 Hongyun Hotel
    鸿运宾馆
5 Sanya Hotel
    三亚宾馆
9 Sanya International Hotel
    三亚国际大酒店
10 Luhuitou Hotel
    鹿回头宾馆
12 Jinling Holiday Resort
    金陵渡假村
13 Seaside Holiday Inn
    Resort
    滨海渡假村
14 Dadonghai Hotel
    大东海大酒店
15 South China Hotel
    南中国大酒店

PLACES TO EAT
16 North-East Rice
    Porridge King
    东北粥王

OTHER
2 Railway Station
    火车站
3 Post Office
    邮电局
4 Sanya Bus Station
    三亚汽车站
6 Post & Telephone Office
    邮电局
7 Bank of China
    中国银行
8 Buses to Haikou
    往海口汽车站
11 Marine Research Station
    海学研究所

---

dàjiǔdiàn). It's poorly located close to town next to the Sanya River. Standard doubles start at Y520.

Places to Eat

Sanya and its environs are swarming with restaurants. Most of them are seafood restaurants like the *Jumbo Seafood Restaurant*, a huge floating affair.

Budget travellers are better off seeking out *street stalls*. Gangmen Lu has dozens of stalls that set up tables and chairs

outside, and are pleasant enough places to sit and have a meal on balmy evenings. Most are of the pick-and-choose variety, and have lots of fresh seafood.

If you buy fruit from the stalls then avoid betel nut (*bīnglàng*) unless you've developed a taste for it (it's very bitter) and want to walk around with a bright red mouth.

If you like *zhōu* (Chinese rice porridge) for breakfast, then try what's on offer at the *North-East Rice Porridge King* (*dōngběi zhōuwáng*) on Gangmen Lu. They have around 20 different types of porridge; you pay Y8 and choose as much as you want.

Things to Buy

Southern Hainan is famous for its cultured pearls, but watch out for fakes. Tourists have been known to pay 100 times the going price for authentic-looking plastic. Polished turtle shells and coral paperweights are snapped up by Chinese tourists.

Getting There & Away

Air Phoenix airport is open for domestic flights including Shenzhen (Y710), Guangzhou (Y580) and Beijing (Y1590) and international flights are also anticipated in the future.

Reception at the major hotels may be able to book plane tickets; otherwise try the Hainan airlines ticketing office (☎ 827-2946), inconveniently located in the northern reaches of Jiefang Lu.

Bus From Sanya bus station there are frequent buses and minibuses to most parts of Hainan. Deluxe buses for Haikou (Y75) also depart from the Sanya, Luhuitou and Dadonghai hotels. The express buses to Haikou take around 3½ hours to cover the 320km route.

Train The railway line is used for hauling freight and does not have a passenger service.

Boat There are currently no boat services operating from Sanya; all boat services operate from Haikou.

Getting Around

The only way to the airport is by taxi; it's a 20 minute drive from the town. Reckon on paying around Y40.

Motorbikes with sidecars cruise the streets all day. The real fare is usually half the asking price (Y5 to most places).

Given that Sanya's attractions are so widely spread out, it is worth getting together with a few people and hiring a vehicle and driver. The minibuses down by the long-distance bus station charge Y150 for a full day, six destination excursion.

TONGZHA

(tōngzhá)

Tongzha, also known as Tongshi, is also called Jade City and is the capital of the Li and Miao Autonomous Prefecture, which in itself makes it sound as if it's worth a visit. It is, however, a drab stopover on the central route between Haikou and Sanya.

Nearby villages are for tourist consumption only with Nike-wearing ethnic dancers and tidy minority children on parade. Intrepid travellers might want to try hopping on a motorbike for a small fee and seeking out the real Li and Miao villages at Maogan, Maodao or Maozhen, but it's a long haul.

Near Tongzha, at 1867m, is Wuzhistan *(wǔzhǐshān)* (Mt Five Fingers), Hainan's highest mountain. The mountain itself is off limits and can only be looked at from afar which is nothing spectacular unless you have bionic vision.

QIONGZHONG

(qióngzhōng)

The route between Tongzha and Qiongzhong passes through thick forest. Cows absent-mindedly cross the road, munching grass and staring at the traffic. Qiongzhong is a small hill town with a lively market; the nearby waterfall at Baihuashan drops more than 300m.

Guangxi 广西

Guangxi's best known attraction is Guilin – perhaps the most eulogised of all Chinese sightseeing areas. While most travellers spend some time in the nearby town of Yangshuo, few make it to other parts of Guangxi *(guǎngxī)*. For the adventurous, there are minority regions in the northern areas bordering Guizhou, as well as less touristed karst rock formations like those in Guilin on the Zuo River, not far from Nanning.

Guangxi also has a border crossing with Vietnam near the town of Pingxiang. Open to Chinese for years, this route has now been made much more accessible to western travellers.

Guangxi first came under Chinese sovereignty when a Qin Dynasty army was sent southwards in 214 BC to conquer what is now Guangdong Province and eastern Guangxi; two earlier attempts by Emperor Qin Shi Huang had wrested little effective control from the Zhuang people. Like the rest of the south-west, the region had never been firmly under Chinese control – the eastern and southern parts of Guangxi were occupied by the Chinese, while a system of indirect rule through chieftains of the aboriginal Zhuang prevailed in the west.

The situation was complicated in the northern regions by the Yao (Mien) and Miao (Hmong) tribespeople, who had been driven there from their homelands in Hunan and Jiangxi by the advance of the Han Chinese settlers. Unlike the Zhuang, who easily assimilated Chinese customs, the Yao and Miao remained in the hill regions, often cruelly oppressed by the Han. There was continuous conflict with the tribes, with uprisings in the 1830s and again during the Taiping Rebellion, which began in Guangxi.

Today the Zhuang are China's largest minority, with well over 15 million people (according to a 1990 census) concentrated in Guangxi. Although they are virtually indistinguishable from the Han Chinese (the

Guangxi Facts & Highlights

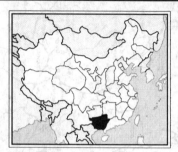

Area: 236,300 sq km
Population: 45.9 million
Capital: Nanning
Highlights

- Yangshuo, a backpacker mecca, famed for its gorgeous scenery and laid-back rural atmosphere.
- Guilin, overrated and pricey, but still one of China's more aesthetically pleasing cities.
- Longsheng/Sanjiang, mountain towns and gateways to many minority villages, spectacularly terraced fields and beautiful scenery.
- Behai, a sleepy seaside town boasting white sand beaches which attract sun-seeking Chinese tourists.

last outward vestige of their original identity being their linguistic links with the Thai people), in 1955 Guangxi Province was reconstituted as the Guangxi Zhuang Autonomous Region. Besides the Zhuang, Miao and Yao minorities, Guangxi is home to smaller numbers of Dong, Maonan, Mulao, Jing (Vietnamese Gin) and Yi peoples. Until recently, more than 75% of Guangxi's population was non-Han.

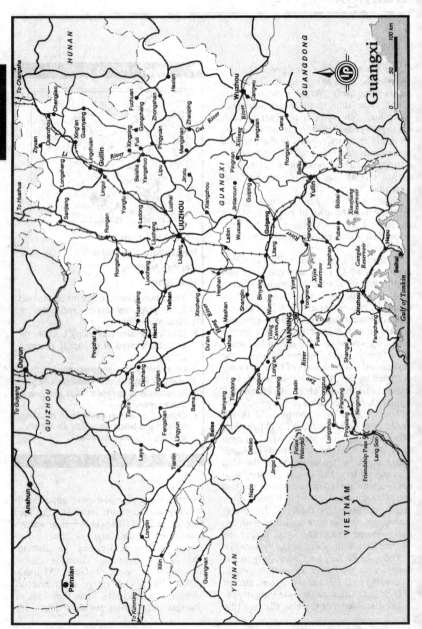

Guangxi

China's first canal was built in Guangxi after the emperor gained a foothold in the Qin Dynasty, but the scattered Han had little ability to use it to much economic advantage and the province remained comparatively poor until the present century. The first attempts at modernising Guangxi were made during 1926-27 when the 'Guangxi Clique' (the main opposition to Chiang Kaishek within the Kuomintang) controlled much of Guangdong, Hunan, Guangxi and Hubei. After the outbreak of war with Japan, the province was the scene of major battles and substantial destruction.

Guangxi remains one of China's less affluent provinces, although you might not realise this if you only visit the major centres of Nanning, Liuzhou, Wuzhou and Guilin. In these parts, industry, trade and foreign investment have brought great changes – and much neon lighting – over recent years.

NANNING
(nánníng)

Nanning (population approximately two million) is one of those provincial centres that provide an insight into just how fast China is developing. China's new affluence leaps out at the visitor at every turn. The department stores are brimming with electronic goods and fashionable clothes, and many of the old backpackers' stand-bys have transformed themselves into upmarket retreats for well heeled tour groups or Overseas Chinese investors. There's not a lot to see in Nanning, but it's an interesting place to walk around, and an important transit point for travellers moving on to Vietnam. You can even arrange a Vietnam visa here.

A mere market town at the turn of the century, Nanning has grown to become the capital of Guangxi. Apart from the urban expansion that the post-1949 railway induced in the south-west, Nanning became an important staging post for shipping arms to Vietnam in the 1960s and 1970s. It's now reprising that role, this time in the thriving border trade that has sprung from Beijing's increasingly friendly ties with Hanoi.

The railway line to the border town of Pingxiang was built in 1952, and was extended to Hanoi, giving Vietnam a lifeline to China. The link was cut in 1979 with the Chinese invasion of Vietnam. Today the line is set to open again and it's already possible, with the appropriate paperwork, to travel to Pingxiang by train, cross the Vietnam border and continue (by train or bus) to Hanoi from Lang Son just over the border.

The only colourful minorities you're likely to encounter in town are the occasional Miao and Dong people selling silver bracelets and earrings on the pedestrian overpasses near the railway station.

Information

Tourist Offices The CITS office (☎ 281-6197) is at 40 Xinmin Lu, across from the Jin Yue and Xiangyun hotels. The new Family and Individual Traveller (FIT) department here is good news for travellers. The friendly English-speaking staff can help you get the formerly elusive Vietnam visa (US$40 plus a Y50 service charge for a one month visa). It takes 10 (yes, 10!) working days.

FIT also offers five-day individual or group tours to Hanoi and Haiphong, and a nine-day tour taking in Saigon. The office is open from 8.30 to noon and from 2.30 to 5 pm, Monday to Friday.

PSB The regional Foreign Affairs office of the PSB (☎ 383-4606) is at 37 Hengyang Xilu, one large block north of the railway station along Di Donglu, then west a similar distance.

Post & Communications The post office is close to the railway station. It's open from 8.30 am to 11 pm daily.

Maps Nanning city maps are available at shops and stalls near the railway and long-distance bus stations; better ones will have a provincial map on the back.

Guangxi Provincial Museum
(guǎngxī bówùguǎn)

Down on Minzu Dadao, the museum offers

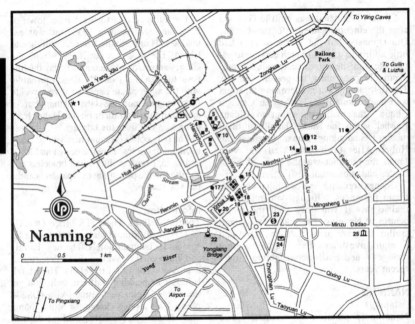

Nanning

0   0.5   1 km

a peaceful browse through 50,000 years of
Guangxi history up to the Opium wars.
There's a wealth of minority costumes and
artefacts, as well as several full-size examples of Dong and Miao architecture in the
tree-filled back yard. The museum also
makes for a quiet, relaxing break from the
hectic city streets. To get there, take a No
6 bus, which runs along Chaoyang Lu from
the railway station, into Minzu Dadao and
past the museum. Opening hours are from
8.30 to 11.30 am and 2.30 to 5.30 pm daily;
admission is Y3. You may or may not find
someone to let you in if you show up in the
off hours.

Bailong Park
(báilóng gōngyuán)
Also known as Renmin Park, this spot has
reverted to its old name, which means
White Dragon. It's pleasant enough for a
stroll and has a lake, a couple of pagodas,

a restaurant and boat hire. Close to the
main entrance is a flight of stairs leading to
a viewing platform with funny mirrors and
an old cannon. Entrance to the park is
Y0.5, and it's open until 10.30 pm daily.

Dragon-Boat Races
As in other parts of the south-west (and
Hong Kong, Macau and Guangzhou), Nanning has dragon-boat races on the fifth day
of the fifth lunar month (generally in June),
when large numbers of sightseers cheer on
the decorated rowing vessels along the
Yong River. The rowers paddle to a drum-
beat pounded out by a crewmate at one end
of the boat.

Places to Stay – budget
Nanning is getting expensive, and most
hotels are pricing themselves out of the
backpacker market, but there are still a few
cheapies around the railway station.

GUANGXI

NANNING 南宁

PLACES TO STAY

4 Yingbin Hotel
迎宾饭店
5 Milky Way Hotel;
Morning Sun Hotel
银河大厦、朝阳旅社
6 Airways Hotel;
CAAC
中国民航酒店、
中国民航
8 Tian Hu Hotel
天湖饭店
9 Phoenix Hotel
凤凰宾馆
13 Majestic Hotel
明圆饭店
14 Xiangyun Hotel
翔云大酒店

PLACES TO EAT

10 American Fried Chicken
华越美餐馆
20 Muslim Restaurant
清真饭店

OTHER

1 PSB
公安局
2 Railway Station
火车站
3 Post Office
邮局
7 Long-Distance Bus Station
南宁汽车站
11 Exhibition Hall
展览馆
12 CITS
中国国际旅行社
15 Chaoyang Square
朝阳广场

16 Electronics Store
(Friendship Store)
南宁友谊商店
17 Nightmarket Area
夜市
18 Nanning Department
Store
南宁百货大楼
19 Xinhua Bookstore
新华书店
21 Bicycle Rental
出租单车
22 Ferry Dock
南宁客运码头
23 Bank of China
中国银行
24 Main Post Office
电信大楼
25 Guangxi Provincial
Museum
广西省博物馆

Opposite the railway station is the *Yingbin Hotel (yíngbīn fàndiàn)* (☎ 282-8223), which is probably the cheapest place open to foreigners, with basic doubles starting at Y26 and dorm beds for Y10. For a splurge, the Y76 doubles are quite spacious and clean. There's no English sign for this place, but it is one of the few places where the managers exhibit good customer relations.

A little further up Chaoyang Lu, next to the CAAC booking office, is the *Airways Hotel (mínháng fàndiàn)*. It supposedly has dorm beds for Y32 and singles/doubles with attached bathrooms from Y90. However, there's the old problem of management denying the dorm's existence and pushing you towards the overpriced Y140 rooms.

If the Airways is full, try the *Phoenix Hotel (fènghuáng bīnguǎn)* (☎ 283-2400) across the road. It asks a pricey Y70 for a bed in a triple with shared bathroom; a dank double with bathroom and satellite TV starts at Y120.

Also near the Airways Hotel is the *Morning Sun Hotel (zhāoyáng lǚshè)*, with barely adequate dorm beds for Y20. It has no English sign, so find it via the mid-range Milky Way Hotel nearby.

Places to Stay – middle & top end
For Y150 and up, there are more options available. In the railway station area the *Milky Way Hotel (yínhé dàshà)* (☎ 243-8223) and the *Tian Hu Hotel (tiānhú fàndiàn)* have dingy but fairly comfy doubles with air-con, satellite TV and bathrooms for Y140 to Y150.

Less conveniently located, the three star *Xiangyun Hotel* (☎ 282-2888; fax 283-3106) *(xiángyún dàjiǔdiàn)* has triples starting at Y520, doubles starting at Y380 and singles starting at Y320. All are clean and good if you can get used to the bellboys trying to do everything for you. Next to the Xiangyun is the *Jin Yue Hotel*, similar in offerings and pricing.

Forget about the *Majestic Hotel* (☎ 283-0808) *(míngyuán xīndù fàndiàn)* across the road from the Xiangyun Hotel unless you're set to bleed cash. This recently reborn, five star monster has rooms starting at Y780 and topping out at a cool Y10,800. What they won't tell you is that there's also an older building (☎ 280-8923; fax 280-8583) which has double rooms starting at Y380 (and there's definitely *not* Y400 difference between these and the Y780 variety).

Places to Eat

If you're in the railway station area on Chaoyang Lu, you can't miss the *American Fried Chicken* restaurant. It's run by young Vietnamese-Americans of Chinese extraction, and serves up some good dishes. Their Vietnamese noodle soup is worth a try, as are the burgers. For some excellent food and cheap beer try the *Muslim Restaurant (qīngzhēn fàndiàn)*. It has a limited English menu, and the staff are friendly. To get there, walk south-west to the end of Xinhua Lu, bear left, and then take the first left again.

There's also a lively row of *restaurants* offering both northern and southern dishes on Hangzhou Lu. There's not much in the way of English menus here, but that does not stop the owners from trying to lure you off the street.

Nanning, like Guilin and Liuzhou, is famous for its dog hotpot *(gǒuròu huǒguō)*. While many travellers may turn up their noses, the canine cuisine district (just over the Chaoyang Stream, south of Chaoyang Lu) teems nightly with stalls serving dog-flavoured dishes.

Getting There & Away

Air Domestic airlines fly daily from Nanning's Wuxi airport to Guangzhou, Shanghai (Y660), Shenzhen, Kunming, and Beijing. There are also flights to Hong Kong (Y1350) on Tuesday, Friday and Sunday, and to Guilin (Y410) on Sunday and Thursday.

Other flights available include Chengdu (Y920), Shenyang, and Hanoi (Monday and Thursday, Y810). Flights to Wuzhou are constantly discussed, but were still unavailable at the time of writing.

The CAAC office (☎ 243-1459) is at 82 Chaoyang Lu and is usually efficient. You may also try the Nanning Air Service (☎ 280-2911) next to CITS at 40 Xinmin Lu. Both are open from 8.30 am to noon and from 2.30 to 5 pm.

Bus Daily sleeper buses to Wuzhou, from Nanning's long-distance bus station, cost

Y60 and take up to nine hours, with a meal stop. There are still one or two regular buses prowling the route for less, but these are few and far between. Sleepers to Guangzhou are Y105 and take 15 to 20 hours (although it's a long trip, having a place to actually lie down brightens the picture a bit, and it's the cheapest way to get to Guangzhou from Nanning).

There are also regular buses from 7 am to 4 pm to Liuzhou (Y25, five hours) and Beihai (Y23.60, five hours, although seven hours isn't uncommon). Buses to Pingxiang leave at 7.10 and 7.55 am and also take around five hours and cost Y22, while Fangcheng buses cost Y15. An interesting though rigorous option is the sleeper berth bus service to Yunnan's capital of Kunming via Guangnan. Tickets are around Y161. Regular buses to Guangnan, just over the Guangxi-Yunnan border, are Y56, but are slowly being replaced by sleepers. The roads are bad and the whole journey can take up to 36 hours, although some have made it in 28 hours.

Train Trains bound for Beijing allow for connections with Changsha, Guilin, Liuzhou, Wuhan (Hankou) and Zheng-zhou. Other major destinations with direct rail links with Nanning are Shanghai, Guangzhou and Xi'an.

There are also direct connections with Zhanjiang (eight hours) in Guangdong Province. Zhanjiang is a coastal town with ferry connections to Hainan Island. Trains to Zhanjiang leave at 8.20 and 9 am, and cost Y64.

Direct trains from Nanning to Guilin take around seven hours and cost Y64 for a hard seat. Most direct trains also pass through Liuzhou. There are trains of all sorts to Liuzhou throughout the day. Hard-seat tickets for the four hour trip cost Y40. Getting tickets doesn't seem to be too problematic; you'll be sent to Window No 5.

There's a service to Chongqing (in Sichuan) via Guiyang every other day. It's around 12 hours to Guiyang and another eight hours on to Chongqing. Hard-sleeper tickets to Guiyang are around Y200, and to

Chongqing Y345. You can also get trains to Kunming, but staff will only sell you a berth up to Guiyang. After that, it's hard seat: you have to try and upgrade to a sleeper in Guiyang. A railway line between Nanning and Kunming is nearing completion, although services are not expected to start for several years. This will not only cut travel time to Kunming, but also ease some of the pressure on the overworked Guilin-Guiyang-Kunming line.

There are two trains daily for Pingxiang. The faster one (Y30) leaves at 8.30 am and arrives at 1.30 pm. The slower train (Y20) leaves at 10.40 am and takes seven hours, so it pays to get up early.

Two trains leave daily for Beihai, at 5.40 am and 9.55 am, and both cost Y27.

Boat There used to be ferries connecting Nanning to Wuzhou as well as Guangzhou. When we last checked, the service had been suspended indefinitely due to a lack of passengers, and the ticket window had disappeared. Should service resume, the trip takes 36 hours to Wuzhou and 48 hours to Guangzhou.

Getting Around
There is an abundance of taxis and motor-cycle taxis (a ride on the back or sidecar of a motorcycle or motor-tricycle). Taxi rides usually start at Y10, the motorcycle taxis around Y5. A bicycle hire place can be found along Chaoyang Lu, north of the Yongjiang Bridge; rentals are available from 7 am to 11 pm for Y0.60 per hour.

AROUND NANNING
Yiling Caves & Wuming
(yílíng yán)
Twenty-five kilometres to the north-west of Nanning are the Yiling Caves, with their stalagmites and galactic lights. About 15 minutes is enough for the caves, but the surrounding countryside is worth exploring.

Wuming is 45km from Nanning, on the same road that leads to the Yiling Caves. A few kilometres further up is **Lingshui Springs**, which is a big swimming pool.

To get to either Wuming or the Yiling Caves, take a minibus from the square on the left-hand side of Chaoyang Lu just over the Chaoyang Stream. It's possible to do it by big public buses, but this involves disembarking at landmark buildings and such, so you'll definitely need a friend on the hotel staff to write it down in Chinese for the bus drivers.

Guiping & Jintiancun
(guìpíng/jīntiáncūn)
If you want to break up the journey between Nanning and Wuzhou, Guangxi residents recommend a stop in Guiping, said to have beautiful mountain scenery as well as places to stay overnight.

Just 25km north-west of Guiping is Jintiancun, the birthplace of Hong Xiuquan. Hong was a schoolteacher who declared himself a brother of Jesus Christ and eventually led an army of over a million followers against the Qing Dynasty in what came to be known as the Taiping Rebellion, one of the bloodiest civil wars in human history.

Minibuses run every 10 minutes from Guiping's square for the 25km, one hour trip. The round-trip fare is Y5.

Zuo River Scenic Area
(zuǒjiāng fēngjǐngqū)
The Zuo River area, around 190km south-west of Nanning, provides the opportunity to see **karst rock formations** like those in Guilin, with the added attraction that this area is home to around 80 groups of Zhuang minority **rock paintings**. The largest of these is in the area of **Huashan** (huāshān bìhuà), which has a fresco 45m high and 170m across with about 1300 figures of hunters, farmers and animals.

This area is relatively unexplored by western travellers. It may be worth considering one of the two-day tours offered by Nanning's FIT department for around Y550 per person. Alternatively, take a bus from the Nanning square on Chaoyang Lu to Ningming City Wharf (níngmíng xiànchéng mǎtóu) and from there haggle to join one of the boat tours for the one-hour ride to Huashan. These tours aren't that frequent, so you may have a bit of a wait.

The *Huashan Ethnic Culture Village* (☎ 0781 728-195) (*huāshān mínzúshānzhài dùjiàcūn*), in neighbouring Panlong, offers rooms in Dong-style wooden cabins, but at tourist prices of around Y200. You may be able to find something cheaper in the area.

Pingxiang
(píngxiáng)
Pingxiang is the staging post for onward transport to Vietnam. It's basically a border trading town, and after you've taken a wander through the bustling markets there's not a lot to see. There are places to stay, but they're no bargains. The *Xiangxiang Hotel* (*xiángxīng bīnguǎn*) on Beida Lu has doubles for Y120. Nearby on Nanda Lu, the *Nan Yuan Hotel* (*nányuán bīnguǎn*) charges foreigners Y160 for a double.

Nevertheless, there's no real need to stay in Pingxiang. An early-morning bus or train from Nanning will get you into Pingxiang around midday, and at this point you should be able to hitch a lift to the Friendship Pass (*yǒuyì guān*) on the Vietnamese border.

There are minibuses and private transport running from around the long-distance bus station – you shouldn't have to pay more than Y5 for a ride. From the Friendship Pass it's a 10 minute walk to Vietnam. Onward transport to Hanoi by train or bus is via the Vietnamese town of Lang Son. Ensure you get to the correct crossing point; some travellers have found themselves at the 'local' crossing point and have had to purchase Y2 tickets to get to the right one. You'll probably have to take a motorcycle taxi to get to the border.

Beihai
(běihǎi)
Beihai is a coastal town that sees few western travellers. This may change with the recently opened ferry service to Hainan Island and the advent of a direct rail link from Nanning. Beihai itself is worth a couple of days, providing you don't expect too much of the beaches, touted as the best in China. The town, with its shady boulevards draped with wide-branched *yùngshù*, is easy-going and people seem pretty friendly.

Silver Beach
(yíntān)
Southern Thailand it is not, but Silver Beach, which lies about 10km south-east of Beihai city, does have sparkling white sands and fairly clean water. A national tourist site, the beach and the road leading to it are also home to some of the oddest resort villas you're likely to see in China – Swiss chalets, German castles, French villas and the obligatory concrete hulk hotels all vie for space along the shoreline.

To get here from Beihai, walk west from the bus station, bear right at Jiefanglu (which branches off behind the Beihai Yingbinguan) and catch a minibus at Renmin Jǔchang. The ride takes about 20 minutes and costs Y2.

Places to Stay Beihai is up and coming enough to warrant the odd tout hanging about the bus station who will likely lead you to cruddy, but exceedingly cheap, local small hotels in the vicinity of the station. Expect to pay as little as Y40 for a double at the more fragrant options, and you can probably still bargain this down. Give cheap-looking Chinese hotels a shot, as they seem amenable to foreign friends. As you exit the bus station, there's a little guesthouse immediately to the left. It has no English sign and its staff are thoroughly confused by foreigners, but it has better doubles from Y65.

For a more upmarket stay, try the *Beihai Yingbinguan* (*běihǎi yíngbīnguǎn*) at 32 Beibuwan Zhonglu. Singles/doubles start at Y180/240, but this place is clean, quiet and well run. And well it should be: this is where the cadres stay when they come down for a dose of Beihai's sea breezes.

Places To Eat There's not much in the vicinity of the bus station, but a bit east of

Zhongshan Park there's a pleasant restaurant with some outdoor seating – the *Jinxing Restaurant (jìnxìng fàndiàn)*. There's no English menu, but there is a sweet-and-sour beancurd dish *(dānghuā rìbèn dòufǔ)* and great braised beancurd *(hóngshāo dòufǔ)*. You can sit and watch/ listen to the ballroom dance lessons by day, disco dancing by night, and even the odd beer-barrel polka in the nearby Sun Yatsen Park.

Getting There & Away Buses leave daily connecting Beihai with Nanning, Liuzhou and Guilin. To Nanning is Y29 for a regular bus on a five hour trip. A sleeper bus is Y76.80 for the 12 hour jaunt to Liuzhou (see the Getting There & Away sections on these cities for more information). There are also sleeper buses to Guangzhou for Y112.

Boats for the 11 hour journey to Haikou on Hainan Island leave daily at 6 pm from the Beihai ferry terminal *(běiháng kèyùnzhàn)*. Cabins for two are Y153 per head, while dorm-style beds are Y75. A seat will cost you Y48.

Beihai is served by flights to and from Guangzhou (daily except Friday, Y610), Shenzhen (Tuesday, Friday, Sunday, Y700), Haikou (daily), Hong Kong (Tuesday and Saturday, Y750), Beijing (Saturday, Monday, Wednesday, Thursday, Y2150), Guiyang (Tuesday and Friday, Y680), Chengdu (Monday, Thursday and Saturday, Y1140) and Guilin (Monday, Tuesday, Thursday, Friday, Y460). There are also flights to Changsha (Y990), Chongqing (Y1010), Xian (Y1480) and Shanghai (Y1530).

The railway station is also always shut up tight until just before trains leave, with throngs of people outside, so don't bother going early for tickets. One train departs at noon for Nanning, and another at 2.55 pm for Chengdu which also passes through Nanning, Liuzhou, and Chongqing. Hard seat fares are Y27 to Nanning, and Y47 to Liuzhou. Hard-sleeper fares to Liuzhou are Y110.

The best thing to do for any tickets is head a few minutes west of the bus station to the new city ticket office (☎ 202-8618) being finished at the time of writing. Its hours are scheduled to be 8 am to 4 pm and it will sell boat, bus, and plane tickets, with train tickets to be phased in eventually. Schedules are posted on the wall.

GUILIN
(guìlín)

Guilin is famous for its scenery and it has been eulogised in innumerable literary works, paintings and inscriptions since its founding as the most beautiful spot in 'the world' (ie China). Rapid economic growth and a booming tourist trade have pared some of Guilin's charm – a maddening, seemingly permanent haze hovers here as many photographers soon discover – but it's still one of China's greener, more scenic cities.

If you can handle the hectic traffic, most of Guilin's limestone karst peaks and parks are a short bicycle ride away. There's also a wealth of restaurants – particularly of the outdoor point-and-choose variety – and a few now have English menus to boot. Unfortunately, most tourist sights levy exploitative entry fees for foreigners, and many travellers tell of being grossly overcharged at restaurants throughout town. And near the train and bus stations, touts can appear at every turn. All this means you'll hear plenty of 'best of/worst of' tales about Guilin.

The city was founded during the Qin Dynasty and developed as a transport centre with the building of the Ling Canal, which linked the important Pearl and Yangzi river systems. Under the Ming it was a provincial capital, a status it retained until 1914 when Nanning became the capital.

During the 1930s, and throughout WWII, Guilin was a Communist stronghold, and its population expanded from about 100,000 to over a million as people sought refuge here. Today it's home to around 600,000 people.

If you're itching to get to the heart of karst country, you may do best to skirt the crowds, high prices and heat of the city and go straight to Yangshuo, approximately one hour south of Guilin by bus. However, for those in the mood for a bit of city life, a day or two of cycling around Guilin can be very enjoyable.

Orientation

Most of Guilin lies on the western bank of the Li River. The main artery is Zhongshan Lu, which runs roughly parallel to the river on its western side. At the southern end of this street – that is, Zhongshan Nanlu – is Guilin Railway Station, where most trains pull in. Zhongshan Lu itself is a rapidly developing stretch of tourist-class hotels, opulent department stores and expensive restaurants – a good place for a browse, but be sure to check prices before you order a bite to eat.

Closer to the centre of town is Banyan Lake, to the west of Zhongshan Lu, and Fir Lake on the eastern side. Further up around the Zhongshan Lu/Jiefang Lu intersection, you'll find the CITS office, the PSB and places to hire bicycles, as well as one of Guilin's original upmarket hotels and landmarks, the Li Jiang Hotel.

Jiefang Lu runs east over Liberation (Jiefang) Bridge to the large Seven Star Park, one of the town's chief attractions. For the best views of the surrounding karst formations you either have to climb up the hills here, or get to the top of the Li Jiang or Hong Kong hotels, which give you 360° vistas.

Information

Tourist Office The CITS office (☎ 282-2648) is north of the Li River ticket office on Binjiang Lu. The staff are friendly, reasonably helpful and are now better equipped to serve both independent travellers and tours. They'll still try to push you into the Y200 half-day city tour or the granddaddy, the Y460 Li River cruise. You can send email from this office for Y15.

PSB This office is on Sanduo Lu, a side street running west off Zhongshan Lu between Banyan Lake and Jiefang Lu.

Money The main branch of the Bank of China is on Shanhu Beilu and this is where you have to go if you want a cash advance on your credit card. For changing money and travellers cheques, you can use the branches at the corner of Shanghai Lu and Zhongshan Nanlu (next to the railway station) and at Zhongshan Lu near Yinding Lu. Tourist hotels, including the Hidden Hill, also have foreign-exchange services which you can usually use even if you're not staying at the hotel.

Post & Communications The post and telecommunications building is on Zhongshan Lu. There is a second post office on the northern corner of the large square in front of the railway station. It has a convenient International Direct Dialling (IDD) service that's considerably cheaper than dialling from the business centres of the tourist hotels. Some of the large hotels, such as the Li River Hotel, have post offices.

Dangers & Annoyances In Guilin it's always hunting season, and your wallet is the quarry. Whether it's a fourfold price hike in the cost of a meal, a wildly circuitous taxi ride or extortionate entry fees, almost every traveller can count on having to deal with overcharging. Stay alert to potential rip-offs and calmly negotiate prices first. And keep the word 'calm' in mind, no matter what, because it's easy to lose your cool and that makes things worse.

Be wary of students wanting to practice English on you. While most are sincere, some travellers have lost money to smooth-talking 'English students' selling art or offering to act as guides or arrange railway tickets. Signs of possible scam artists include a willingness to discuss ways of spending your money and a reluctance to talk near police or in hotel lobbies. Also, watch out for pickpockets, especially around the railway station. Guys, a newer hassle may be encountered in the bus/railway station area where slimy pimps offer evening escorts, something unheard of in previous years.

Solitary Beauty Peak
(dúxiù fēng)
The 152m pinnacle is at the centre of the town. The climb to the top is steep, but there are good views of the town, the Li River and surrounding hills. The nephew of a Ming emperor built a palace at the foot of the peak in the 14th century, but only the gate remains. The site of the palace is now occupied by a teachers' college. A Y4 entrance fee is charged.

Bus No 1 goes up Zhongshan Lu past the western side of the peak. Alternatively, take bus No 2, which goes past the eastern side along the river. Both buses leave from Guilin Railway Station. Bus No 18 also runs past the peak.

Wave-Subduing Hill
(fúbō shān)
Close to Solitary Beauty and standing beside the western bank of the Li River, this peak offers a fine view of the town. Its name is variously described as being derived from the fact that the peak descends into the river, blocking the waves, and from a temple that was established here for a Tang Dynasty general who was called Fubo Jiangjun, the wave-subduing general.

On the southern slope of the hill is Returned Pearl Cave *(huánzhū dòng)*. The story goes that the cave was illuminated by a single pearl and inhabited by a dragon; one day a fisherman stole the pearl, but he was overcome by shame and returned it.

Near this cave is Thousand Buddhas Cave *(qiānfó dòng)*, which has a couple of dozen statues dating from the Tang and Song dynasties. This peak costs a rather outrageous Y10, although some think it's worth it. Bus No 2 runs past the hill.

Other Hills
North of Solitary Beauty is **Folded Brocade Hill** *(diécǎi shān)*. Climb the stone pathway which takes you through the cooling relief of **Wind Cave**, with walls decked with inscriptions and Buddhist sculptures. Some of the damage to faces on the sculptures is a legacy of the Cultural Revolution. There are great views from the top of the hill, which you can skirt by taking Bus No 1.

There's a good view of **Old Man Hill** *(lǎorén shān)*, a curiously shaped hill to the north-east, from Wave-Subduing Hill. The best way to get there is by bicycle as buses don't go past it. At the southern end of town, one of Guilin's best known sights is **Elephant Trunk Hill** *(xiàngbí shān)*, which actually does resemble an elephant dipping its snout into the Li River. Another entry fee of Y10 is charged here, and the authorities have done a good job of blocking any views with fences, which means you can't see the river either.

Seven Star Park
(qīxīng gōngyuán)
One of China's nicer city parks, Seven Star Park is on the eastern side of the Li River. Cross Liberation Bridge *(jiěfàng qiáo)* and continue to the end of Jiefang Donglu to get there.

The park takes its name from its seven peaks, which are supposed to resemble the star pattern of the Ursa Major (Big Dipper or Great Bear) constellation. There are several caves in the peaks, where visitors have inscribed graffiti for centuries, including a recent one which says, 'The Chinese Communist Party is the core of the leadership of all the Chinese People'. It takes a lot of imagination to see the 'Monkey Picking Peaches' and 'Two Dragons Playing Ball' in the stalagmites and stalactites. Back outside, there are lots of trails in and around the hills, and sprawling lawns to sit or picnic on. You may want to avoid the pitiful zoo, which is enough to bring tears to any animal lover.

To get to the park take bus No 9, 10 or 11 from the railway station. From the park, bus No 13 runs back across the Li River, past Wave-Subduing Hill and down to Reed Flute Cave.

Reed Flute Cave
(lúdí yán)
Some of the most extraordinary scenery

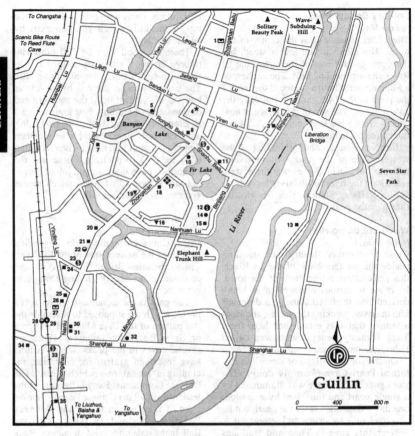

Guilin has to offer is underground at the Reed Flute Cave, where multicoloured lighting and fantastic stalactites and stalagmites resemble a set from *Journey to the Centre of the Earth*. The entrance to the cave was once distinguished by clumps of reeds used by locals to make musical instruments, hence the name.

One grotto, the Crystal Palace of the Dragon King, can comfortably hold about 1000 people, although many more crammed in here during the war when the cave was used as an air-raid shelter. The domi-nant feature of the cave is a great slab of white rock hanging from a ledge like a cataract, while opposite stands a huge sta-lactite said to resemble an old scholar. The story goes that a visiting scholar wished to write a poem worthy of the cave's beauty. After a long time he had composed only two sentences and, lamenting his inability to find the right words, turned to stone.

The other story is that the slab is the Dragon King's needle, used as a weapon by his opponent the Monkey King. The Monkey King used the needle to destroy

GUILIN 桂林

PLACES TO STAY
2 Universal Hotel
3 Sheraton Guilin Hotel
  文华大酒店
6 Ronghu Hotel
  榕湖饭店
7 Holiday Inn Guilin
  桂林宾馆
8 Hubin Hotel
  湖滨饭店
11 Li Jiang Hotel
  漓江饭店
13 Guishan Hotel
  桂山大酒店
15 Yu Gui Hotel
  玉桂饭店
18 Tailian Hotel
  台联酒店
20 Osmanthus Hotel
  丹桂大酒店
21 Taihe Hotel
  泰和饭店
24 Xingui Hotel
  新桂饭店

25 Jingui Hotel
  京桂宾馆
26 Hidden Hill Hotel
  隐山饭店
30 New City Hotel
  新城市酒店
31 South Stream Hotel
  南溪饭店
34 Hong Kong Hotel
  香江饭店
35 Overseas Chinese Hotel
  华侨大厦

PLACES TO EAT
16 Yiyuan Restaurant
  怡园饭店
19 Night-Time Food Stalls
  夜间摊子

OTHER
1 Post Office
  邮电局
4 PSB
  公安局
5 Ancient South Gate
  古南门

9 Bank of China
  中国银行
10 Xinhua Bookstore
  新华书店
12 CITS
  中国国际旅行社
14 Boat Tickets
  船售票处
17 Guilin Department Store
  桂林百货大楼
22 Long-Distance Bus
  Station
  长途汽车站
23 Bank of China
  中国银行
27 Post Office
  邮电局
28 Guilin South Bus
  Station
  城南站
29 Guilin Railway Station
  火车站
32 CAAC
  中国民航
33 Bank of China
  中国银行

the dragon's army of snails and jellyfish, leaving their petrified remains scattered around the floor of the cave.

Although the cave is worth visiting, some travellers may be put off by the laughably high entrance fee of Y44 (Y16 for locals). Also, the horde of hawkers that swarm around the exit may leave you with a deep-seated hatred of the phrase 'hello, postcard'.

The cave is on the north-western outskirts of town. Take bus No 3 from the railway station to the last stop. Bus No 13 will take you to the cave from Seven Star Park. Otherwise, it's a pleasant bike ride. Follow the route of bus No 3 along Lijun Lu, which runs into Taohua Jiang Lu. The latter parallels a small river and winds through fields and karst peaks, avoiding the traffic of Zhongshan Lu.

Other Sights

At the southern end of Guilin, **South Park** (*nán gōngyuán*) is a pretty place. You can

contemplate the mythological immortal said to have lived in one of the caves here; look for his statue.

There are two lakes near the city centre, **Banyan Lake** (*róng hú*) on the western side and **Fir Lake** (*shān hú*) on the eastern side. Banyan Lake is named after an 800-year-old banyan tree on its shore. The tree stands by the restored South City Gate (*nán mén*) originally built during the Tang Dynasty. This is one of the nicer neighbourhoods in town.

Places to Stay – budget

Guilin lacks options for those on a backpacker's budget – the lower end of the market is served primarily by Yangshuo. The old backpackers' stand-by, the *Overseas Chinese Hotel* (☎ 383-3573) (*huáqiáo dàshà*), has decided it's now a classier establishment, but it still has the cheapest beds in town. OK dorms are Y40, and usually are not full up. You may be able to wheedle an Y80 double with shared bathroom, but staff will probably push you toward the Y180 doubles.

Across from the railway station, the *South Stream Hotel (nánxī fàndiàn)* has singles for Y80, doubles for Y100 and triples for Y120. This place has cleaned up its act immensely since previous editions and gets good reports of late. Five minutes north of the railway station, on Yinding Lu, the *Xingui Hotel (xīnguì fàndiàn)* has singles/doubles starting at Y60/100. You can try and wangle a room in a reported 'secret' old wing, which has four bed rooms for Y16 each and triples for Y20 each. But don't count on it.

Nearby on Zhongshan Lu, the *Jingui Hotel (jīnguì bīnguǎn)* offers very few doubles from Y80; most have been spruced up and now cost Y160, although the management has on occasion offered (unsolicited) steep discounts. The nearby *Hidden Hill Hotel (yǐnshān fàndiàn)* isn't even worth looking at for the price.

To the north on Ronghu Lu, the *Hubin Hotel* (☎ 282-2837) *(húbīn fàndiàn)* has decidedly downmarket singles/doubles starting at Y70, but once again they'll strenuously push you toward the Y120 rooms.

There are numerous Chinese hotels north and south of the railway station on Zhongshan Lu that officially don't take foreigners, but may soon do so, or might even make an exception for you. They will probably double their price, but given the low base, it still could be worth a try.

Places to Stay – middle
Most of the low-end places mentioned above also have nicer rooms for Y100 to Y200, but there are also a couple of mid-range spots for those setting their sights a bit higher.

Quite close to the long-distance bus station is the *Taihe Hotel* (☎ 333-5504) *(tàihé fàndiàn)*. Doubles with air-con and TV cost Y120 and triples are also available from Y150. Get there quickly, as this place was planning to renovate its way to top-end status.

At the higher end of the middle range,

the *Yu Gui Hotel* (☎ 282-5499) *(yù guì bīnguǎn)* has clean singles/doubles with all the features from Y180. Some of the rooms also have nice views of the Li River and Elephant Trunk Hill.

Places to Stay – top end
There's no shortage of choice here in terms of price, but only some of the expensive spots are worth it. One new place that several readers have rated highly is the *New City Hotel* (☎ 343-2511) *(xīnchéngshì jiǔdiàn)*, which is just across from the railway station. Its immaculate singles/doubles start at US$60 and the service is reportedly great.

Just to the north of the long-distance bus station on Zhongshan Lu, the *Osmanthus Hotel* (☎ 383-4300) *(dānguì dàjiǔdiàn)* is one of the better long-standing top-end deals, with nicely furnished doubles from US$60. There are rooms for half that, but it's likely you won't get in.

The *Li Jiang Hotel* (☎ 282-2881) *(líjiāng fàndiàn)* at 1 Shanhu Beilu was once the main tourist hotel in Guilin. It's right in the middle of town and the roof provides a panoramic view of the encircling hills. Standard doubles are US$65, deluxe rooms closer to US$100; there are no singles available. It has the full works: post office, barber, bank, restaurants, tour groups and bellboys in monkey suits.

In about the same price and value range, the *Ronghu Hotel* (☎ 282-3811) *(rónghú fàndiàn)* at 17 Ronghu Lu has singles/doubles from US$68 to $180. This spot seems to be favoured by Overseas Chinese tour groups. Looking out over Banyan Lake, it's in a nice part of town, although a bit inconvenient unless you have a bicycle.

At 14 Ronghu Lu, the US four star *Holiday Inn Guilin* (☎ 282-3950) *(guìlín bīnguǎn)* has doubles posted at US$110, but when occupancy is low it offers a 20% discount, which offsets the 15% 'service charge' attached to everything. The only swimming pool in town is here as well.

The *Universal Hotel* at 1 Jiefang Lu is a fairly new luxury hotel with rooms for

US$80 to US$100, some having nice river views. You can literally still smell the paint drying here.

Although its 19th floor revolving restaurant has a great view of the city and surrounding peaks, the Hong Kong-managed *Hong Kong Hotel* (☎ 383-3889) *(xiāngjiāng fàndiàn)* is looking a bit run-down to be charging US$80 for a double. And give the western breakfast a miss – for Y65 it's a rip-off; the dim sum is much better.

Across the river, the formerly ritzy *Guishan Hotel (guìshān dàjiǔdiàn)* is showing a bit of wear and tear, but boasts a bowling alley. Doubles start at US$90, but discounts are possible if occupancy is low.

The five star *Sheraton Guilin Hotel* (☎ 282-5588; fax 282-5598) *(guìlín dàzì fàndiàn)* at 9 Binjiang Nanlu asks a minimum of US$110 for a double, although some guests have opined that a star should be pared from its ranking.

Places to Eat

Guilin is traditionally noted for its snake soup, wild cat or bamboo rat, washed down with snake-bile wine. You could be devouring some of these animals into extinction, and we don't recommend that you do. The pangolin (a sort of Chinese armadillo) is a protected species, but still crops up on restaurant menus. Other protected species include the muntjac (Asian deer), horned pheasant, mini-turtle, short-tailed monkey and gem-faced civet. Generally the most exotic stuff you should come across is eel, catfish, pigeon and dog.

For a quick bite of more down-to-earth fare, there are a couple of places between the railway station and the long-distance bus station on Zhongshan Lu with reasonable prices and English menus. Don't worry too much about finding these places; the staff will let you know where they are.

At night, on Zhongshan Lu north of Nanhuan Lu, the street comes alive with *pavement stalls* serving all sorts of wok-fried goodies. Just point at what you want, and they'll do the rest. But make sure you set prices first: too many travellers have

had a fine meal ruined by a bill for over Y100 when Y25 would do. There's also a few places that only Guilin (or Las Vegas) could support, with cowboys in full glitter, duded up Elvises, or costumed little people lounging about the outside.

Candle-lit dinners for two are rare in Guilin. Virtually every restaurant in town is *rè nào* (hot and noisy), and wide-eyed backpackers may find themselves placed at huge tables with boisterous Chinese tourists.

There's an outstanding and inexpensive Sichuan restaurant on Nanhuan Lu called the *Yiyuan Restaurant* (*yíyuán fàndiàn*). Although there is no English sign, you'll easily spot the place by its tasteful, all-wood exterior. The owner speaks excellent English and will be happy to help you choose dishes. She imports all her spices from Sichuan Province, and you can taste the difference. It serves from 11.30 am to 2.30 pm and again from 5.30 to 9.30 pm.

For an OK cup of coffee and an excellent view of Guilin, try the revolving restaurant on the 19th floor of the *Hong Kong Hotel* (but don't get the abysmal western breakfast). For pizza at Y30, try the *pizzeria* at the Universal Hotel.

For dim sum, the *Tailian Hotel* is considered by locals and Overseas Chinese as the best place in town, as long as you get there around 8 am; too much later and all the best dishes will have been snatched up.

Getting There & Away

Guilin is connected to many places by air, bus, train and boat. Give some serious thought to flying in or out of this place. Train connections are not particularly convenient.

Air CAAC has an office (☎ 384-4007) at the corner of Shanghai Lu and Minzhu Lu. Go in through the doorway on the corner and head up to the 2nd floor. Hours of operation are 7.30 am to 8.30 pm. Shanghai Airlines (☎ 282-7046) is at 93 Zhongshan Lu, and Dragonair (☎ 282-5588, ext 8895) has an office in the Sheraton Guilin Hotel.

Guilin is well connected to the rest of

China by air and destinations include: Beihai (Y460), Beijing, Changsha (Y480), Chengdu (Y930), Chongqing, Fuzhou, Haikou, Hangzhou, Hong Kong, Guangzhou (Y470), Guiyang (Y450), Kunming, Lanzhou, Qingdao, Shanghai, Shenzhen, Shenzou, Ürümqi, Xiamen, Wuhan (Y770) and Xi'an (Y1040). Whatever destination you have in mind you should purchase in advance; Guilin is one of China's most popular tourist spots and with a billion people competing for seats no amount of airlines can handle the load.

Probably the most popular travellers' option is the Guilin-Kunming flight, which can save considerable travelling time and mucking about trying to get tickets on a train that is frequently booked out; to Kunming it costs around Y850.

Bus For short local runs (ie Yangshuo, Xing'an), minibuses depart regularly from the railway station. Buses to Yangshuo should set you back Y5, no matter what anyone says, and the trip takes just over an hour. Most folks just have to exit the railway station doors before people start asking them to go to Yangshuo. In the unlikely event there are no buses, you can catch the No 21 bus down the street to the right from the railway station, which runs to the end of the line and hooks up with Yangshuo minibuses.

The long-distance bus station is north of the railway station on Zhongshan Lu. Buses to Longsheng (Y9.60) leave approximately every half-hour from 6.50 am to 5.20 pm; buses leave for Sanjiang at 7.10 and 11.30 am and 2.50 pm. There is one bus daily for Xing'an at 11.40 am.

Frequent buses leave for Liuzhou from 6.20 am until 1.40 pm, and from Liuzhou you can connect with buses to Nanning; a regular bus to Liuzhou costs Y21.90. There is also a sleeper bus to Nanning leaving daily at 6.50 am; four others depart between 5.30 and 6.50 pm. A sleeper bus to Nanning should cost around Y60.

For Wuzhou and Guangzhou, ordinary and sleeper buses are available. The sleepers may be your best bet, especially for the 16-hour marathon to Guangzhou. Sleeper buses to Guangzhou leave in the early morning and afternoon until 6.30 pm, and cost around Y98. Buses for Wuzhou leave pretty much hourly between 6.40 am and 8 pm, and cost Y56.50 for a regular bus and Y77 for a sleeper. You can also catch buses daily to Zhuhai and Shenzhen, and you should definitely get a sleeper (Y128.50) for these 20 hour marathon rides.

Behind the railway station is the Guilin South bus station. It's from here that buses and minibuses depart on a fairly regular basis for Longsheng and other relatively local destinations.

Train There are useful train connections to Guilin, but some of these (such as the Kunming-Guiyang-Guilin-Shanghai route) tend to involve long hauls on unbelievably crowded carriages.

The good news now is that you can almost always get a ticket. The bad news is that you can forget about getting a hard sleeper if booking on the day of departure. Be prepared to wait an extra day. You may be able to swing a hard-sleeper ticket from the cafes and travel outfits in Yangshuo, but this is definitely something not to count on. If you're in Yangshuo, you should consider a day trip to Guilin to book your own ticket. The Yangshuo CITS can always get you a ticket, but on the most recent trip, some travellers were paying shockingly high 'service charges' (as high as 75% above face value); still, some say it's better than knocking yourself out in Guilin getting your own.

A tip: if tickets are *méi yǒu* (literally 'don't have') request a ticket for a destination one or two stops *after* your intended stopping point. You may be surprised how often that works. If it does work, you'll have to get the ticket seller to write an explanation on the back of the ticket, or you may have trouble getting the ticket conductor on the train to return it so you can disembark.

There are two trains a day to Kunming:

one starts from Shanghai and the other from Guangzhou. In either case, the trains are generally very crowded. As mentioned, tickets are available, but these are usually for the train from Guangzhou, which stops in Guilin around 1 am. Tourist-price tickets from Guilin to Kunming are around Y265 for hard sleeper and a shocking Y540 for soft sleeper.

Other direct trains out of Guilin include those to Beijing (31 hours), Changsha (11 hours), Guangdong (13 hours), Guangzhou (15 hours), Guiyang (18 hours, Y128 for hard sleeper), Kunming (29 hours), Liuzhou (four hours), Nanning (seven hours), Shanghai (35 hours), Xi'an (36 hours, Y221 for hard sleeper), and Zhanjiang. For Chongqing, change trains at Guiyang.

Getting Around
To/From the Airport Guilin's new international airport is now open, 30km west of the city. CAAC runs buses from the Shanghai Lu office to the airport (Y20), leaving hourly or every other hour, depending on the day. A taxi will cost at least Y80.

Bus & Taxi Most of the city buses leave from the terminal at Guilin railway station and will get you to many major sights, but a bicycle is definitely better, especially in the searing summer heat.

Taxis are available from the major tourist hotels for about Y20 per trip, depending on the distance. On the street, the flagfall rate is supposed to be Y9, with an additional Y1.40 per kilometre. Pedicabs charge Y5 to Y10 per trip.

Bicycle Bicycles are the best way to get around Guilin. There are plenty of bicycle-hire shops – just look along Zhongshan Lu for the signs. There are some near the long-distance bus station and the railway station, one next to the Overseas Chinese Hotel and another on the grounds of the Li Jiang Hotel. Most charge between Y10 and Y15 per day, and require Y200 or your passport as security (try to avoid handing over your passport).

AROUND GUILIN
The **Ling Canal** *(líng qú)* is in Xing'an County, about 70km north of Guilin. It was begun in about 200 BC during the reign of the first Qin emperor, Qin Shihuang, to transport supplies to his army. The canal links the Xiang River (which flows into the Yangzi River) and the Tan River (which flows into the Pearl River), thus connecting two of China's major waterways.

You can see the Ling Canal at **Xing'an**, a market town of about 30,000 people, two hours by bus from Guilin. A daily bus departs from the long-distance bus station at 11.40 am. Minibuses to Xing'an also leave from in front of the railway station. The town is also connected to Guilin by train. Two branches of the canal flow through the town, one at the northern end and one at the southern end. The total length of the Ling Canal is 34km.

LI RIVER
(lí jiāng)
The Li River is the connecting waterway between Guilin and Yangshuo and is one of the main tourist attractions of the area.

A thousand years ago a poet wrote of the scenery around Yangshuo, 'The river forms a green gauze belt, the mountains are like blue jade hairpins'. Well, the 83km stretch between the towns is hardly that, but you do see some extraordinary peaks, sprays of bamboo lining the riverbanks, fishers in small boats and picturesque villages.

As is the Chinese habit, every feature along the route has been named. **Paint Brush Hill** juts straight up from the ground with a pointed tip like a Chinese writing brush. **Cock-Fighting Hills** stand face to face like two roosters about to engage in battle.

Mural Hill, just past the small town of Yangti, is a sheer cliff rising from the water; there are supposed to be the images of nine horses in the weathered patterns on the cliff face.

A popular tourist trip is the boat ride from Guilin down the Li River to Yangshuo, although low-budget travellers have been put off by the exorbitant ticket prices, which presently come in at Y450, including lunch and the bus trip back to Guilin from Yangshuo. This is one of Guilin's worst cases of price gouging, as the most luxurious local trip costs only Y100.

Tour boats depart from Guilin at a jetty across the road from the Yu Gui Hotel each morning at around 8 am, although when the water is low you have to take a shuttle bus to another pier downriver. For trips booked through hotels, buses usually pick you up at around 7.30 to 8 am and take you to the boat. Otherwise, the ticket office for the trip is across the road from the park entrance, on the same side of the street as the Yu Gui Hotel. The trip lasts all day, and some people find that the time drags towards the end. It's probably not worth it if you're going to be spending any length of time in Yangshuo, where you can organise local boat trips.

YANGSHUO
(*yángshuò*)

Just 1½ hours from Guilin by bus, Yangshuo has, along with Dali in Yunnan, become one of those legendary backpacker destinations that most travellers have heard about long before they even set foot in China. Set amid limestone pinnacles, it's a small town growing bigger on the back of its popularity. Although not as quaint as it once was, Yangshuo is still a great laidback base from which to explore other small villages in the nearby countryside.

With its western-style cafes, Hollywood movies, Bob Marley tunes and banana pancakes, Yangshuo may not seem like the 'real China', but who cares? It's a great spot to relax, see the scenery and grab a good cup of coffee – the perfect antidote to weeks or months on the road. Don't make this your first or second stop coming from Hong Kong. Save it for after knocking around Guangzhou or Guangxi for a spell. You'll appreciate it much more.

And either way, for sheer scenic beauty, it's hard to top a leisurely bike ride around Yangshuo and its surrounding villages. A

lot of people have even stayed overnight in the villages, and if you want to go camping in the mountains you shouldn't have any problem. It's probably not permitted to camp out, but who's going to climb a 200m peak to bring you down?

Information
Tourist Offices There's a CITS office on Xi Jie, not far from the intersection with Pantao Lu. Another office shares space with a CAAC ticket office down from the bus station along the road to the Xilang Hotel. Both are generally open from 8.30 am to noon and 2.30 to 5.30 pm.

You can get useful maps of Yangshuo and the surrounding area which show villages, paths and roads. The staff are helpful and friendly, although travellers seldom avail themselves of their services – enterprising locals working from the cafes are generally more in touch with the needs of independent travellers, and definitely levy lower service charges.

Next to Minnie Mao's, East Eagle offers an email service for Y20 a message.

Money The Bank of China on Binjiang Lu will change cash and travellers cheques, as well as receive wire transfers.

Post & Communications The post office, on the main road across from Xi Jie, has English-speaking staff and long-distance phone services that are much cheaper than those offered by the cafes and hotels. They also don't run the other way when you front up with a calling card from your home country. Its operating hours are from 8 am to 5 pm.

Things to See
The main peak in Yangshuo is **Green Lotus Peak** (*bìlián fēng*), which stands next to the Li River in the south-eastern corner of the town. It's also called Bronze Mirror Peak (*tóngjìng fēng*) because it has a flat northern face which is supposed to look like an ancient bronze mirror.

Yangshuo Park (*yángshuò gōngyuán*)

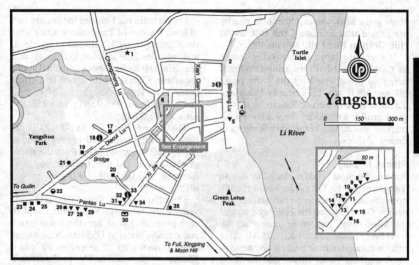

Yangshuo
Li River
Turtle Islet

To Guilin

Green Lotus Peak

To Fuli, Xingping & Moon Hill

See Enlargement

YANGSHUO 阳朔	PLACES TO EAT	OTHER
PLACES TO STAY	5 Jia Tian Xia Restaurant 甲天下餐厅	1 PSB 公安局
16 Sihai Hotel 四海饭店	7 William's Cafe	2 Market 市场
17 Xilang Hotel 西郎山饭店	8 Merry Planet Café 快乐星球	3 Bank of China 中国银行
19 Golden Dragon Hotel 金龙饭店	9 Brothers Bar & Restaurant	4 Wharf 码头
20 Yangshuo Resort Hotel 阳朔度假饭店	10 Minnie Mao's	6 Market Area 市场
23 Yangshuo Youth Hostel	12 Red Star Express 红星饭店	11 East Eagle
24 Golden Leaves Hotel 金叶饭店	13 Mei You Café 没有饭店	18 CITS 中国国际旅行社
25 Nanyang Hotel 南方大酒店	14 Susannah's	21 Bookshop 书店
26 Good Companion Holiday Inn	15 Lisa's Cafe	22 Long-Distance Bus Station 汽车总站
35 Zhuyang Hotel 珠阳饭店	27 Hard Seat Cafe	30 Post Office 邮电局
	28 Ebo's Cafe	33 CITS 中国国际旅行社
	29 Planet Yangshuo	
	31 Green Lotus Cafe	
	32 Paris Cafe	
	34 MC Blues Bar & Cafe	

---

is in the western part of the town, and here
you'll find **Man Hill** (xīláng shān), which
is meant to resemble a young man bowing
and scraping to a shy young girl represent-

ed by **Lady Hill** (xiǎogū shān). You may
just want to look from the outside – it now
costs a pretty hefty Y15 to enter the park,
although some locals may be willing to

GUANGXI

show you a back way in. Other hills nearby are named after animals: **Crab Hill**, **Swan Hill**, **Dragon Head Hill** and the like.

It's amazing how many travellers come to Yangshuo and don't see Yangshuo itself, being so preoccupied by the karst peaks (along with Pantao Lu's beer and movies). To the north and west of Pantao Lu there's great small-town trekking: back alleys, small markets, and throngs of tourists poking about tonnes of shops.

Places to Stay

Among the most popular places to stay in Yangshuo are the Yangshuo Youth Hostel, opposite the long-distance bus station, the nearby Good Companion Holiday Inn, and the Sihai Hotel, nestled in among all the travellers' hang-outs on Xi Jie. All three offer similar standards and can be noisy – the Yangshuo Youth Hostel and the Good Companion because of trucks hurtling down the main road to Guilin, and the Sihai because of late-night drinking binges by travellers in the cafes below.

The *Sihai Hotel* is popular mainly for its convenience to the cafes on Xi Jie, and, apart from the noise in the evenings and the dampness of the rooms in the winter months, it's a good spot. The Sihai has 'luxury' doubles for Y40 per person, as well as singles/doubles with shared bathroom starting at Y15/20. Not far away, popular *Lisa's* now has rooms. A bed in a triple is Y20, and in a double is Y25. Both have a shared bath. A single with private bath costs Y60.

The *Yangshuo Youth Hostel* has beds for Y15 in a five-bed dorm and for Y25 in a three-bed dorm – both with attached bath. Dorm beds in rooms without attached bath are Y10. Beds in singles and doubles range from Y30 to Y60. Despite rather recent upgrades, this place seems a tad tired, but most travellers find it to be just fine.

Just up the street, the *Good Companion Holiday Inn* still offers dorm beds for Y10 and beds in singles/doubles/triples for 80/45/25 – cheap prices, but the staff can be rather distant. Rooms in the back are quiet.

On the main road toward the eastern end of town lies one of Yangshuo's better bets: the *Zhuyang Hotel*. It's friendly, very clean, and provides little touches like towels and tea. Singles/doubles with attached bathroom are Y30/60, while a bed in a triple costs Y20. These, though, are often full, and prices from here leap up to Y150/200 for a single/double.

The *Xilang Hotel* (☎ 881-2312) is set back from the street and is very quiet at night. Unfortunately, it's also in the midst of renovation, and the cheapest rates will likely be Y50 for beds in a triple – probably not worth it.

The offspring of a Sino-Malaysian joint venture, the *Yangshuo Resort Hotel*, replete with swimming pool, bar, three-star rating and doubles starts at US$100! Nice rooms and a serious slate of amenities include a fitness centre, satellite TV, pool tables, a business centre, restaurants and lounges, and lots more. You knew it was only a matter of time ...

There are also several formerly Chinese-only hotels along the main roads which have opened up to foreign guests, including the *Golden Dragon Hotel* (☎ 882-2674) and the *Nanyang Hotel*. They're not bad, but tend to charge a bit more and offer a bit less than their more seasoned competitors. By far the best of these is the *Golden Leaves Hotel* (☎ 882-2860; fax 882-2853), at 83 Pantao Lu, which even smells antiseptically clean. Professionally run, the spotless rooms all have air-con, attached bath, and 24 hour hot water. Rates are posted as Y100/150 a single/double, but without prompting the very nice managers seemed amenable to negotiation.

Along Xi Jie, the *Buckland Hostel* is only for students and staff of the on-site language school.

Places to Eat

Xi Jie teems with cafes offering interesting Chinese/western crossovers as well as perennial travellers' favourites such as banana pancakes, muesli and pizza. For anyone who's been wandering around China for a while it's a good chance to have a break from oily stir-fried vegetables and grab a cup of coffee. Movie junkies are in heaven, since the cafes woo travellers with Hollywood flicks over dinner.

One popular cafe is *Lisa's*. Local fame has made Lisa a tad cheeky, but she and her staff are all smiles, the food is generally excellent and the place is often packed when other spots are not, although that doesn't mean the others aren't worth trying.

Across from Lisa's, the *Mei You Cafe* promises 'mei you bad service, mei you warm beer', and it delivers – the service is good and the beer is cold. Just up the street, *Minnie Mao's* has won travellers' praise for tasty dishes and some of the most attentive service in town. The paint was literally drying on the *Merry Planet Cafe* which old hands may remember as the erstwhile Sunny Side Bakery. Nearby, on a small side street, *Susannah's* also draws a steady stream of customers. Its claim to fame is that it was the first western restaurant in town and Jimmy Carter ate there in 1987! Do try the drunk duck *(zuì yā)*, a terribly appealing dish cooked in a sauce of local red wine.

Other popular places include the cluster of cafes up on the corner of Xi Jie and the main road: *Green Lotus*, *Paris Cafe* and *MC Blues Bar & Cafe*. They all have outdoor seating and are good places to sit and watch the world go by. MC Blues has the added attraction of more than 150 tapes, and the very sociable staff are usually happy to let you choose what you like.

The places on the main road are where some of Yangshuo's original cafes started. They don't enjoy the popularity of some of the places on Xi Jie, but cafes like *Ebo's*, *The Hard Seat* and *Planet Yangshuo* are all friendly spots for a meal or a cup of coffee.

There's a slew of other cafes as well, making for fierce competition – by the time you read this it's a safe bet some of names will have changed, but at least you won't be lacking for choice.

If you get tired of the 'international' spots, you'll find a number of *yóutiáo* (fried bread sticks) and noodle vendors on Xie Jie closer to the main road and around the long-distance bus station. On Binjiang Lu south of the Bank of China is the *Jia Tian Xia*, a Chinese snack joint with substantial entrees, including Taiwanese ginger chicken *(sān bēijī)*.

Things to Buy

Yangshuo is a good place to do some souvenir shopping. Good buys include silk jackets (at much cheaper prices than in Hong Kong), hand-painted T-shirts, scroll paintings and batiks (from Guizhou). Name chops cost Y10 to Y60 on average. Everything on sale should be bargained for. The paintings available in Yangshuo, for example, are generally of poor quality (even if you think they look good) and a starting price of Y150 can easily go below Y100.

If you are in the market for a chop, bear in mind that it is not the size of the stone that is important in determining a price, but the quality of the stone itself. Often the smaller pieces are more expensive than the hefty chunks of rock available.

Don't forget, too, that Yangshuo is not simply Xi Jie. Wander around the backstreets, especially north along Binjiang Lu around the Bank of China. There are tonnes of places; they're not especially better, but offer the shopper lots more comparison shopping.

Student Cards Several places around Yangshuo, most notably the Merry Planet Language Club, offer brief courses in Chinese language, t'ai chi *(taijiquan)* or medicine that will allow you to walk away with a student ID card.

Travellers who paid the Y30 fee have gleefully told of subsequently nabbing Chinese-price tickets at railway and bus stations, hotels and parks. Railway station staff in Guilin and other major cities already are wise to this scam, and it's doubtful many places accept it at all any longer. Still, it may be worth a shot, as it only needs to work a couple of times to recoup your money.

Getting There & Away

Air The closest airport is in Guilin, and the CAAC office is near the Xilang Hotel. Cafes can also drum up tickets for you. Check the Guilin Getting There & Away section earlier in this chapter for details on the flights available.

Bus There are frequent buses and minibuses running to Guilin throughout the day. The best option is the minibus service which operates from the square in front of the long-distance bus station. Buses leave as soon as they fill up, which could be anywhere from five to 15 minutes, and the trip takes a little over an hour. They charge Y5 per person, and Y1 per piece of luggage.

If you're heading to Guangzhou you can take a bus/boat combination from Yangshuo for around Y100; buses to Wuzhou leave in the morning and evening. The morning bus allows you to connect with the evening boat leaving Wuzhou; the evening bus is less convenient as it leaves you to sit out in the wee small hours of the morning waiting for the first boat of the day. From Yangshuo you can only book 3rd class tickets. If you want your own 2nd class cabin you should book in Wuzhou when you arrive – the 5 pm boat usually has beds in cabins for Y77.50. Tickets for the five hour, high-speed ferry ride to Guangzhou also must be booked in Wuzhou.

You can arrange the Wuzhou-Hong Kong high-speed ferry in Yangshuo. Combined bus/boat tickets are available from CITS and most cafes/travel outfits for around Y500. Most people catch the morning bus, a Japanese minivan at 8 am costing Y66, and stay overnight in Wuzhou, although accommodation is not included in the price of the ticket. If you opt for the overnight sleeper, the nine hour trip departs at 8 pm and costs Y78.

There are several buses a day to/from Yangshuo's long-distance bus station to Liuzhou for around Y21. Overnight sleeper buses direct to Guangzhou leave twice during the afternoon and cost around Y90 for the 15 hour ride. Although still a bumpy

ride, the sleepers have taken some of the nightmare out of this journey. Other epic journeys include a 19 hour travail to Shenzhen for Y125, and a 15 hour sleeper to Zhuhai for Y70. Less painful is the 6.10 am local bus to Nanning for around Y50.

Train The nearest railway station is in Guilin. Almost any cafe or travel outfit around Yangshuo will organise train tickets, and some offer hard sleepers for high-demand routes like Guilin to Kunming at anywhere from Y300 to Y365. When eyeing these prices, bear in mind that locals usually have to go through 'the back door' in Guilin to get the tickets. This also means that sometimes a 'guaranteed' hard-sleeper ticket can turn into a less-than-enticing hard seat, which has led some travellers to make the day-trip up to the Guilin Railway Station just to be sure.

To get any of these tickets you'll probably have to book at least two to three days in advance.

Getting Around

Yangshuo itself is small enough to walk around without burning up too many calories, but if you want to get further afield then hire a bicycle. Just look for rows of bikes and signs near the intersection of Xi Jie and the main road. The charge is about Y10 per day and a few places now don't bother securing a deposit.

AROUND YANGSHUO

The highway from Guilin turns southward at Yangshuo and after a couple of kilometres crosses the Jingbao River. South of this river and just to the west of the highway is **Moon Hill** *(yuèliang shān)*, a limestone pinnacle with a moon-shaped hole. To get to Moon Hill by bicycle, take the main road out of town towards the river and turn right on the road about 200m before the bridge. Cycle for about 50 minutes – Moon Hill is on your right and the views from the top (some 1251 steps, so reports one focused Frenchman) are incredible! You can espy Moon Hill

Village – itself worth checking out – and the ancient Big Banyan Tree (ask the hawkers to point it out).

There are weeks and weeks of possible exploration out there for travellers on bike, boat, foot, or any combination therein. Some intrepid travellers have even hefted their bikes on to a boat and ridden back from elsewhere. One sure-fire trip involves the local roads through **Baisha** town to Fuli and Dragon Bridges. Locals say the scenery along here beats the Li River. Baisha is 9km to the north of Yangshou, and probably another 4km to 5km to the bridges beyond that. All told, it'd be a whole day's trek so be sure you know where you're going first.

A series of caves have been opened up not far from Moon Hill: the **Black Buddha Caves** (hēifó dòng), **New Water Caves** (xīnshuǐ dòng) and **Dragon Cave** (jùlóng tán). If you head out to Moon Hill, you will undoubtedly be intercepted and invited to visit the caves. Tours cost around Y25 per head, although prices can drop if there are more of you. You go through the caves and then climb down a steep chimney via a rope and ladder to an underground pool fed by a river. You can walk along the river through the mountain for a few hours and come out on the other side. The Dragon Cave demands an outlandish Y46. Not cheap for a damp and muddy trek.

In Yangshou there are also several locals offering guided tours of Moon Hill, the caves and other famous spots, as well as their home villages. Some will even bring you home and cook you lunch! These mini-tours have garnered rave reviews from some travellers and may be worth a try, although you usually need to get at least three people together to make it worth your guide's while. You can get almost a whole day's tour for Y50 and you get taken on the real-deal backroads of Yangshou, through the rice paddies and everything.

River Excursions

There are many villages close to Yangshou which are worth checking out. A popular riverboat trip is to the picturesque village of **Fuli** (fùlǐ), a short distance down the Li River, where you'll see stone houses and cobbled lanes. There are a couple of boats a day to Fuli from Yangshuo for around Y40 (foreigners' price), although most people tend to cycle there – it's a pleasant ride and takes around an hour.

An alternative mode of transport to Fuli is by inner tube. Inner-tube hire is available for about Y5 per day. It takes around three or four hours to get to Fuli this way. Several places also offer rafting trips and kayak hire – both popular options in the warm summer months.

On market days in Fuli, be very careful of pickpockets; young men work in groups of three or four, brushing up against travellers in the press of the crowd and relieving their pockets of valuables.

A host of cafes and local travel agents also organise boat trips to **Yangti** (yángtí) (Y110) and **Xingping** (xīngpíng) (Y68).

About three hours upstream from Yangshuo, the mountain scenery around Xingping is breathtaking, and there are many caves. People living in some of the caves make gunpowder for a living.

Many travellers take their bicycles out to Xingping by boat and cycle back – it's a picturesque ride of about three hours, and the whole package costs Y20 to Y30 depending on how many of you there are. Any number of cafes can organise boat tickets for you.

It's possible to spend the night in Xingping. One small hotel sits on a point that juts out into the river; basic rooms are Y10 to Y20 per person. A couple of doll's house restaurants with bilingual menus keep everyone fed (take care that they don't overcharge).

If you're keen on a river trip, the best thing to do, as always, is ask around. There are literally dozens of touts and guides chatting you up on the streets of Yangshuo, so hit them up for advice on the good/bad/boring stretches of the river.

Markets

Villages in the vicinity of Yangshuo are best

visited on market days, and these operate on a three day, monthly cycle. Thus, markets take place every three days starting on the first of the month for Baisha (1, 4, 7 etc), every three days starting on the second of the month for Fuli (2, 5, 8 etc), and every three days starting on the third of the month for Yangshuo and Xingping (3, 6, 9 etc; Yangshuo is on the same cycle as Xingping). There are no markets on the 10th, 20th, 30th and 31st of the month.

LONGSHENG & SANJIANG
(lóngshèng/sānjiāng)

Around four and seven hours respectively by bus to the north-west of Guilin, Longsheng and Sanjiang are close to the border of Guizhou Province and are a good introduction to the rich minority cultures of this region. The Longsheng area is home to a colourful mixture of Dong, Zhuang, Yao and Miao minorities, while Sanjiang is mainly Dong.

Longsheng and Sanjiang are best visited with an overnight stay in each. Trying to do either as a day trip from Guilin would leave you with no time to get out of town and see the sights. Several travellers have raved about staying with locals around Longsheng's rice terraces; you can easily organise these stays in Yangshuo cafes. And if nothing else, the bus trip is engaging enough, snaking and switchbacking above a river alternately mocha and metallic green. There's plenty of landslides in these parts – get ready to dig your way through along with the rest of the passengers.

Longsheng

Longsheng's main attraction is definitely not the town – a cluster of concrete hulks that clash with the mountain backdrop. Not far out of town, however, are the Dragon's Backbone Rice Terraces *(lóngjǐ tītián)* and a nearby hot spring *(wēnquán)*. The hot spring is a tacky tourist highlight and can be safely missed, although local buses running out to the hot spring pass through rolling hills sculpted into precipitous rice terraces and studded with Yao minority vil-

lages. The area is reminiscent of Banaue in northern Luzon, Philippines. It's possible to desert the bus around 6km to 7km from the hot spring and take off into the hills for some exploring. When you return from the day's outing, Longsheng at least offers cheap accommodation and even cheaper food at its lively night market.

Things to See Although the region around Longsheng is covered with terraced rice fields, the **Dragon's Backbone Rice Terraces** sees these feats of farm engineering reach all the way up a string of 800m peaks. A half-hour climb to the top delivers an amazing vista, if the Yao women who invariably tag along to peddle their trinkets allow you to enjoy it.

Buses to the terraces leave from 7 am to 5.30 pm from opposite the Jinhui Restaurant. Although the trip is only about 20km, some of the buses stop midway at the town of Heping to try and pull in more passengers, which can make the ride last up to 1½ hours! Locals pay Y3, but you'll probably have a tough time getting your fare below Y5. Expect a Y8 per-person entry fee at the terraces.

There are some other tourist sights around Longsheng, including **forest reserves**, **Dong** and **Yao villages** and unusual **stone formations**. Staff at the Longsheng Tourist Corp, next to the Longsheng Tourist Corp Hostel, can give you a somewhat fanciful map and perhaps tell you how to get to these spots, although they'll probably want you to rent your own van, which could get pricey. And on a last visit, they were less than thrilled to do much of anything.

Places to Stay Longsheng is betting its future on tourism, and now sports a host of hotels that welcome foreign guests. Be aware that the powers that be levy some variety of 'local tax' (around Y6), so don't worry, you're not getting gouged.

Leading the low end in price is the *Longsheng Tourist Corp Hostel (lóngshèng xiàn lǚyóu zǒnggōngsī zhāodàisuǒ)*. Beds in triples start at Y10 and doubles cost Y28 to

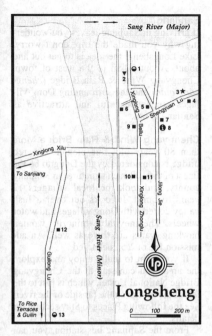

LONGSHENG 龙胜

PLACES TO STAY
4 Longsheng All-
Autonomous Government
Hotel
龙胜各族自治县政府招待所
5 Business Hotel
商业宾馆
6 Foreign Trade Hotel
外贸宾馆
7 Longsheng Tourist Corp
Hostel
龙胜县旅游公司客房部
9 Moon Hotel
月亮宾馆
10 Xiantao Hotel
仙桃大酒店
11 Hualong Hotel
华隆大酒店
12 Riverside Hotel
凯凯旅社

OTHER
1 Minibus Station
小公共汽车站
2 Jinhui Restaurant
金徽饭店
3 PSB
公安局
8 Longsheng Tourist Corp
龙胜县旅游公司
13 Bus Station
汽车站

Y48. This place isn't the Taj Mahal, but it's cheap and central.

Downhill from the bus station, just before the bridge, is the *Riverside Hotel* (*kǎikǎi lǔshè*). It's run by an English teacher who seems happy to help travellers with information on getting to the local sights. She's even made up a map of the surrounding area for her guests. Rooms are basic and cost Y10 per bed.

The best value around for mid-range lodging is definitely the *Foreign Trade Hotel* (☎ 751-2078) (*wàimào bīnguǎn*) – which you can't miss for all the signs about town. Lots of rooms are available, and a largish, clean, mid-range double costs just Y35, with good mosquito nets and ceiling fans. Dorm rooms are available from Y20. The staff seemed downright delighted to have 'foreign friends'.

The Foreign Trade's quality likely spells the end for the *Business Hotel* (*shāngyè*

bīnguǎn), just down the street from the Longsheng Tourist Corp Hostel. This place is one cockroach away from being off the list altogether. The rooms are passable (barely) and the service isn't. Singles/doubles with bathrooms are Y35/40.

The *Moon Hotel* (*yuèliàng bīnguǎn*), which is one block nearer the bridge on Xinglong Beilu, has air-con rooms, but the service is nothing to write home about.

Up the hill from the Longsheng Tourist Corp Hostel, on Shengyuan Lu, the ponderously named *Longsheng All-Autonomous Government Hotel* (☎ 751-2503) (*lóngshèng gèzú zìzhìxiàn zhèngfǔ zhāodàisuǒ*) offers a quiet refuge from the karaoke that rocks Longsheng's main streets until about midnight. This is also the place for the bathroom-conscious, as it has western-style toilets. This sanctuary costs Y120 for all rooms – singles, doubles and triples. So for three people, it's a deal; otherwise head for the Foreign Trade.

Places to Eat Longsheng is no culinary wonderland. At least within recent years plenty of restaurants have opened up. The problem is that none has any English menus or speakers.

Past the Moon Hotel, the *Jinhui Restaurant (jīnhuī fàndiàn)* doesn't look like much, but serves up some decent dishes and has an English menu, albeit one pinched from the Hong Kong Hotel in Guilin. Negotiate the prices down, and forget about ordering the sea cucumber or crab. Just past the bridge on Xinglong Xilu, street stalls appear around 8 pm, offering point-and-choose meals by lantern light. There are also some noodle shops on Xinglong Beilu.

Getting There & Away From Guilin, you can catch buses and minibuses to Longsheng from the long-distance bus station and the south bus station (behind the railway station). The long-distance bus station has buses departing approximately on the half-hour between 6.50 am and 5.20 pm. Buses from the railway station and the south bus station are less frequent, but do the trip a bit faster. Barring landslides, the trip should take around three to four hours.

From Longsheng to Guilin, buses leave the bus station every 15 to 20 minutes from 6 am to 5.40 pm. The fare is Y9.60. There is also a daily Longsheng-to-Liuzhou bus which leaves at 6.50 am and costs Y24.50.

Buses and minibuses leave from the Longsheng bus station for Sanjiang approximately every hour from 6.30 am to 5 pm. You can also catch these at the corner of Guilong Lu and Xinglong Xilu, down the road from the bus station. The fare is Y6.60 and the bumpy but scenic journey takes three hours. Oddly enough, even sleepers are making this run now, for the same price.

Sanjiang

If arriving in Sanjiang leaves you wondering why you made the trip, don't worry. Like Longsheng, the idea is to get out and about. About 20km to the west of town, Chengyang Wind & Rain Bridge *(chéngyáng qiáo)* and the surrounding Dong villages are as peaceful and attractive as Sanjiang is not.

Chengyang Wind & Rain Bridge More than 80 years old, this elegant covered bridge is considered by the Dong to be the finest of the 108 such structures in Sanjiang county, and took the local villagers 12 years to build. It looks out over a lush valley dotted with Dong villages and water wheels. The inevitable minority women hawking wares are there as well. An admission fee of Y5 is charged.

If you want to really enjoy and explore the area, you can stay at the Chengyang Bridge National Hostel, which is just to the left of the bridge on the far side of the river. See the following Places to Stay section for details.

From the Sanjiang bus station, you can catch hourly buses to Lin Xi *(lín xī)* or any bus to Gu Yi *(gǔyì)*, right past the bridge. The 45 minute ride costs Y3. If there are several of you, hire a van to take you out there for around Y60 for the round trip. You'll probably see the travel agency with an English sign opposite the bus station. Their cheapest tour is Y160, but they are nice, do speak English and you can score a map from them. Bus services stop around 5 pm, so if you need to get back to Sanjiang later than that you'll have to hitch a lift. The first bus of the day to Sanjiang passes by the bridge around 7.30 to 8 am.

Places to Stay With the advent of the Chengyang Bridge National Hostel, there's no need to stay in Sanjiang unless you're catching a very early bus out of town. If so, your quietest option is the *Guesthouse of the People's Government of the Sanjiang Dong Autonomous County (sānjiāng dòngzú zìzhìxiàn rénmín zhèngfǔ zhāodàisuǒ).*

Doubles are Y40, or Y60 with bathroom attached. To get there, follow the road that runs between the Department Store Hotel and the bus station uphill, and bear left. Walk about 10 minutes and it's on your right, across from a Dong drum tower. You'll definitely be the talk of the town along the way.

Right in town on the opposite corner of the long-distance bus station, the *Hostel of the Department Store (sānjiāng bǎihuò zhāodàisuǒ)* has cacophonous three and four-bed dorms for Y5/7, and doubles with attached bathroom for Y20. There's every chance that they'll tell you no cheap rooms are available.

Further down the street, the *Chengyang Bridge Hotel (chéngyáng qiáo bīnguǎn)* (not to be confused with the National Hostel at the bridge itself) has slightly more upmarket singles/doubles starting at about Y100.

Opened in mid-1994, the *Chengyang Bridge National Hostel* (☎ (0772) 861-2444) *(chéngyáng qiáo zhāodàisuǒ)* is an all-wood Dong-style building with beds for Y20 and nice doubles with shared bath for Y60, and friendly staff who speak some English. Even if you don't spend the night, a cup of tea or a simple meal on the hostel's riverside balcony is a great way to enjoy the scenery. The only fly in the ointment is the karaoke-crazed staff, but a few polite words may persuade them to croon softly.

Getting There & Away The Sanjiang bus station has several buses to Guilin between 7.10 am and 2.30 pm (Y15.70) and a handful of buses to Liuzhou between 6.40 am and 4 pm. Buses to Longsheng leave every 40 to 50 minutes between 6.40 am and 4 pm.

Sanjiang to Kaili If you have time on your hands, it's worth considering entering Guizhou Province through the backdoor, by local bus. From Sanjiang take the 2 pm bus to Long'e (Y9.5), which is just across the Guizhou border. Although the journey is only approximately three hours, you'll almost certainly have to stay overnight in Long'e, as the onward bus to Liping leaves at 6 am. The hotel on the square where the buses stop has beds in triples for Y5.

The four hour journey to Liping costs Y10, and passes through some beautiful mountains, as well as the town of Zhaoxing, which itself may be worth a visit. From Liping there is one bus to Kaili daily at 6 am, and sometimes buses run in the afternoon as well.

One as yet untested option might be to take a bus to Fulu, from where you can get on a boat to Congjiang. Congjiang has connections to Rongjiang and Kaili. Another possibility is to take a train to Tongdao in Hunan Province and from there travel onwards by bus to Liping (there are minibuses running to the railway station west of Sanjiang half-hourly throughout the day).

LIUZHOU
(liǔzhōu)
Liuzhou, with a population of more than 730,000, is the largest city on the Liu River and an important railway junction in southwestern China. The place dates back to the Tang Dynasty, when it was a dumping ground for disgraced court officials. The town was largely left to its mountain wilds until 1949, when it was transformed into a major industrial city. It isn't as up-and-coming as other cities in south-western China, but it thinks it is by the absurd number of banks around.

Liuzhou is Guilin's poor cousin, with similar but less impressive karst scenery on the outskirts of town. (Most mornings eagle-eyed travellers can witness t'ai chi practice sessions atop the peaks ringing the outskirts of town.) It sees few foreigners, and the locals are thus far from jaded in their dealings with travellers. Cheaper hotels that take foreign guests are also few and far between.

Information
The Bank of China is on Feie Lu. The post office, south of Liuzhou Square, is open from 8 am to 8 pm.

GUANGXI

Things to See

There are a few sights around town worth a look if you have time. Along Feie Lu near the long-distance bus station is **Yufeng Hill** *(yúfēng shān)*, or Fish Peak Mountain, in Yufeng Park. It's very small as mountains go (33m), and derives its name from the fact that it looks like a 'standing fish'. Climb to the top for a

smoggy vista of Guangxi's foremost industrial city.

Next door to Fish Peak Mountain is **Mt Ma'an** *(mǎ'ān shān)*, or Horse Saddle Mountain, which provides similar views.

Liuhou Park *(liǔhòu gōngyuán)* is a more pleasant park in the north of the city. It has a lake and a small temple erected to the memory of Liu Zongyuan (772-819), a famous scholar and poet. Bus No 2, 5 or 6 will get you to the park, or you can walk there from the long-distance bus station in around 20 minutes.

Places to Stay

Liuzhou is another Chinese city with a lack of budget lodging options. Near the main railway station down Feie Lu is the large *Nanjiang Hotel* (☎ 361-2988) *(nánjiāng fàndiàn)*, which will take foreigners. Rooms with hard beds, your own TV and mouldy bathroom start at Y30 for a bed in a triple, which they may or may not let you into and, if they do, you may have to buy the whole room. Other rooms have increased dramatically after yet another 'face lift' to the reception area. A single will set you back Y100 now, although you can probably bargain it down. The hotel purports to have 24-hour hot water ... good luck.

There is a new, lower-price (although not exactly budget) option to the east along

LIUZHOU 柳州		
PLACES TO STAY	3 Old Place Bar 老地方酒吧	13 Yufeng Park 鱼峰公园
5 Liuzhou Hotel 柳州饭店	4 CITS 中国国际旅行社	14 Foreign Language Bookstore 外文书店
11 Yu Feng Hotel 鱼蜂大厦	6 Liuhou Park 柳侯公园	15 Long-Distance Bus Station 汽车总站
19 Tiedao Hotel 铁道饭店	7 Liuzhou Square 柳州广场	16 Xinhua Bookstore 新华书店
21 Nanjiang Hotel 南疆饭店	8 Post Office 邮电局	17 CAAC 民航售票处
	9 Ferry Dock 航运码头	18 Bank of China 中国银行
OTHER	10 Riverside Park 江滨公园	20 Liuzhou Bus Station 柳州南站
1 North Railway Station 火车北站	12 Mt Ma'an 马鞍山	22 Main Railway Station 火车站
2 Xinhua Bookstore 新华书店		

Feie Lu. The *Tiedao Hotel* (☎ 361-1140) *(tiědào fàndiàn)* is across the street and east of the south bus station. It's set back a bit off the street so keep a sharp eye. The interiors sport the classic China weariness, but the rooms are kept up well. The staff was eager to have foreign guests. Triples cost Y78 for the whole room; an OK single room will set you back Y76.

Right next door to the long-distance bus station you may notice the *Transport Hotel*, but despite its English sign it does not take foreigners.

Taking a step up in price, there is a nearby middle range hotel taking foreigners. The *Yu Feng Hotel* (☎ 383-8177) *(yùfēng dàshà)* has decent, if a bit cramped, rooms starting at Y160 for a double. There is hot water 24 hours here.

The *Liuzhou Hotel (liǔzhōu fàndiàn)* rounds out the limited middle range. Its cheapest doubles start at Y100, and after that it's a quick jump up to Y460 for TV and air-con. To get there take bus No 2 to Liuhou Park, turn right into Youyi Lu and look out for the hotel on the left.

Places to Eat

Your best bet may be the lively *night market* across from the Foreign Language Bookstore. Starting around 8 pm, it has numerous stalls serving up tasty dumplings and noodles fried with your choice of fresh ingredients – just point to what you want. The railway station area also has dumpling and noodle places. The *Liuzhou Hotel* has a few restaurants, but the prices will probably put you off. A cup of coffee, albeit brewed, costs Y18.

Off Liuzhou Square towards the Liuzhou Hotel is Liuzhou's first foray into western-style bars, the *Old Place (lǎo dìfāng)* (☎ 286-9128). It serves up a few decent western dishes and has draught beer! As the few foreigners who work in Liuzhou tell it, the Old Place is becoming *the* new hang-out. The very sociable owners – a handful of eager young entrepreneurs – whip about the flyspeck-sized place.

Getting There & Away

Air The CAAC booking office (☎ 383-1604 or 382-0449) on Feie Lu was temporarily closed for remodelling at the time of writing, but should be open by press time. Flights depart four days a week to Guangzhou, and twice weekly to Beijing and Shanghai. At the time of writing, flights to Guiyang were still not beyond discussion stage, so like all other smaller cities you'll have to fly to Guilin (Y450) first and fly direct from there.

Bus The Liuzhou south bus station is actually north of the long-distance station cartographically, but let's not quibble. Along Feie Lu, it's actually much closer to budget lodgings and the railway station, so this will likely become the main one for travellers. The other station is a hefty hike from the railway station, south of Yufeng Park. The stations have different schedules entirely, so if you arrive at one station and it doesn't have a convenient departure time, check the other one. Buses for Yangshuo, likely the most popular destination, depart pretty much hourly, from 8 am to 3.30 pm, and cost Y26 for a sleeper. The trip takes five to six hours, much of it rounding eye-poppingly narrow bluffside curves, blaring the horn to warn the ubiquitous water buffalo. Frequent buses to Guilin (Y30) also pass through Yangshuo, but this may change when current construction of a direct Liuzhou-Guilin road is completed.

Other destinations include Beihai (Y36 or Y71 sleeper bus), Fangcheng (Y37.40 regular bus), Guangzhou (Y76 or Y106 sleeper bus), Guiping (Y23.40 or Y33 sleeper bus), Longsheng (Y25), Nanning (Y23), Pingxiang (Y42.70), Sanjiang (Y19 or Y22 sleeper bus), Shenzhen (Y117 or Y134 sleeper bus), Wuzhou (Y34.80 or Y64 sleeper) and Zhuhai (Y91.50 or Y136.60 sleeper bus).

Train Trains from Guilin to Kunming pass through Liuzhou. If you're coming up from Nanning you'll have to change trains in Liuzhou to get to Kunming (Y187 hard sleeper). All trains heading out of Nanning pass through Liuzhou, and you could hook up with any one of these to get to a number of major destinations. Possibilities include Beijing, Changsha, Chengdu (Y220 hard sleeper) Guangzhou (Y210 hard sleeper), Guiyang (Y91), Shanghai and Xi'an.

Besides lines passing through, trains originate in Liuzhou twice daily for Guilin (7.10 am and 5.10 pm). The hard-seat fare from Liuzhou to Guilin is around Y15, and the trip takes approximately four hours. One train departs at 7.40 am for Nanning and hard-seat tickets for the five hour trip are Y23. Express No 38 also leaves at 2.55 pm for Guangzhou.

Boat Nightly boats for Guangzhou used to leave at 5 pm, but literally on the day we stopped by, the service ran its last leg, perhaps for good, due to dwindling passenger demand. If resumed, the 12 hour journey takes you through Guiping, where you have to transfer for boats to Wuzhou and Guangzhou. To Guiping is Y40; to Guangzhou it's Y100 for a 3rd class dorm-style bed - no cabins are available. Tickets are certainly in good supply, and can be bought at the ferry dock. The dock is tough to spot – it's directly across from a bank.

Getting Around
Liuzhou is a bit large for walking around, particularly at the height of summer when the place is like a blast furnace! There is now a bike rental place almost directly across from the Nanjiang Hotel; bikes can be rented for Y0.80 per hour or Y4per day. Pedicabs, motor-tricycles, motorcycle taxis and taxis can be found at the bus station and outside the main railway station.

Bus No 2 will take you to the Liuzhou Hotel, and bus No 11 links the long-distance bus station to the main railway station. Bus maps can be bought from hawkers at both railway stations.

WUZHOU
(wúzhōu)
For most travellers, Wuzhou is a pit stop on

the road between Yangshuo and Guangzhou or Hong Kong. Although it's not one of Guangxi's major attractions, Wuzhou has some pleasant parks and interesting street life.

Not enough travellers check this place out; give it an overnight, as it's either a great first city off the boat from Hong Kong, or a calming influence after Hong Kong and Guangzhou.

In 1897 the British dived into this trading town, setting up steamer services to Guangzhou, Hong Kong and later Nanning. A British consulate was established, and the town was also used by British and US missionaries as a launching pad for the conversion of the 'heathen' Chinese.

During the period after 1949, a paper mill, food-processing factories, and machinery and plastics manufacturing were established, among other industries.

During the Cultural Revolution, parts of Guangxi appear to have become battle-grounds for Red Guard factions claiming loyalty to Mao. In something approaching a civil war, half of Wuzhou was reportedly destroyed.

Today, Wuzhou has some fine street markets (absolutely everywhere you walk, in fact), tailors, tobacco, herbs, roast duck and river life to explore. Wuzhou also has one of Guangxi's more unusual sights: the Snake Repository.

Information
CITS used to be in the Beishan Hotel, but at the time of writing it was moving to Heping Lu, which is an east-west road one giant block north of Nanhuan Lu (the main street which crosses the river at the bridge); you shouldn't have to deal with CITS at all in any event, as all onward transport is quite straightforward.

The post office is located on Nanhuan Lu, just before the bridge. Good maps of the city, with bus routes, are usually available at shops near the long-distance bus station. Failing that, try the Xinhua Bookstore on Danan Lu, up from the New World Hotel.

Snake Repository
(shécáng)

Wuzhou has what it claims is the world's largest snake repository, a major drawcard for Overseas Chinese tourists and a sight that pulls in the occasional western traveller. More than one million snakes are transported each year to Wuzhou (from places like Nanning, Liuzhou and Yulin) for export to the kitchens of Hong Kong, Macau and other snake-devouring parts of the world. To get there, walk along Shigu Lu from next to the Wuzhou Hotel; it's about 2km away. Snake and cat fights are staged for visiting groups of Overseas Chinese tourists – something you may wish to avoid. The repository is open daily from 8 am to 6 pm. Entry is Y4.

Sun Yatsen Park
(zhōngshān gōngyuán)

Just north of the river up Zhongshan Lu, which then turns into Wenhua Lu, Sun Yatsen Park is worth a look as the site of China's earliest memorial hall for the founder of the Republic of China. The hall was constructed in 1928 and commemorates an important speech given by Sun Yatsen in Wuzhou. Entry is Y1.

Western Bamboo Temple
(xīzhú yuán)

Just north of town bordering Sun Yatsen Park is the Western Bamboo Temple, where around 40 Buddhist nuns live. The vegetarian restaurant, open for breakfast and lunch, is highly rated by travellers who have taken the time to wander up here. You can walk to the temple by taking Wenhua Lu into Sun Yatsen Park. From the park gate walk for about 10 minutes until you reach an old brick building with an English sign saying 'temple' on the left-hand side. Then just follow the signs. The restaurant doesn't keep regular hours, but the earlier you get there, the better.

Places to Stay

The steady flow of Hong Kong Chinese into Wuzhou has pushed hotel prices up, and in several places room rates are quoted in HK dollars.

If you want or need to stay overnight in Wuzhou, the best budget choice is the *Yuanjiang Hotel (yuānjiāng jiǔdiàn)* on Xijiang Lu, a five minute walk down from the bus station and ferry dock area. Singles/doubles with attached bathroom range from Y60 to Y90, while singles/doubles with common washing facilities are from Y40 to Y60. Close by, the *Xinxi Hotel (xīnxī lǚdiàn)* offers similar or even slightly lower rates, you can get a triple with air-con for Y90 for example, but it's dank and gloomy.

The somewhat more upmarket *Hebin Hotel (☎ 202-2069) (hébīn fàndiàn)*, lies west across the Gui River near the bridge. Doubles cost around Y105 a night, Y135 for a triple, but it's a bit of a concrete hulk. The best reason to stay here is to catch the early morning high-speed ferry to Hong Kong (see Getting There & Away in this section).

Originally the top spot in town, the *Beishan Hotel (běishān fàndiàn)*, at 12 Beishan Lu up Dazhong Lu to the north of the city centre, is better avoided. It's overly expensive for what it offers, and is a fair trudge out of town.

Wuzhou's newest hotel, the *New World Hotel (☎ 282-8333; fax 282-4895) (xīnjiè dàjiǔdiàn)* doesn't seem worth the HK$328 (up to HK$2385!) it charges for a standard room. Across the street, the *Triumphal Arch Hotel (☎ 202-6618) (kǎixuánmén dàjiǔdiàn)* already looks as if its glory days have passed, but singles and doubles start at a more reasonable Y130/185 and the service is cheery.

The *Wuzhou Hotel (☎ 202-2193) (wúzhōu dàjiǔdiàn)* is also showing signs of wear and tear, and isn't much of a bargain either. Rooms range from Y120 to Y880, but they'll likely push you toward doubles around Y200.

Places to Eat

There's no shortage of small restaurants, especially in the vicinity of the boat docks and bus station. The illuminated mirages

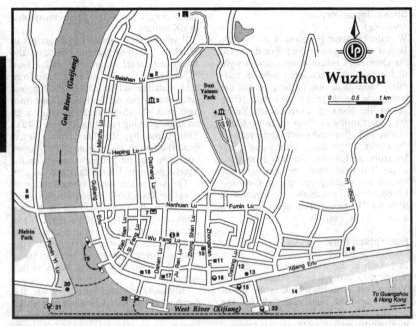

Wuzhou

by the riverbank are restaurants à la Aberdeen (Hong Kong), with extravagant names such as *Water City Paradise*. They sure ain't paradises.

There's a great underground grouping of *hotpot places* that's as *re nao* ('hot and noisy') as it gets. It's also a bit tough to find. Walk east of the ferry docks along Xijiang Erlu until you see a driveway leading down to the right into an underground market; go down, turn left and walk all the way through the market, and then bear left through the (very dark) tunnel and it'll open up into the cacophony of literally hundreds of tables. If the market has closed for the night, ask somebody for the place where they have *huǒguō*, or 'hotpot'.

If that doesn't appeal to you, there are other small restaurants along the eastern bank of the Gui River on Guijiang Erlu. For a slightly upmarket snack and a cup of coffee after a long bus or boat journey head

over to the ground-floor coffee shop at the *Wuzhou Hotel*. A good cup of coffee costs only Y6, and the food is not bad either.

Getting There & Away

Air Wuzhou has daily flights to Beijing (Y490) and Haikou (Y550). There are also flights to Shenzhen, Guangzhou, Zhuhai, Nanning and Guilin, although these may be available only on a charter basis.

Bus Buses to Yangshuo leave from the two long-distance bus stations next to the ferry dock area (on opposite sides of Xijiang Lu) and can cost as little as Y35 for a regular bus or Y53 for a sleeper. Buses leave at 7.20 and 9 am, and at 6, 7.35 and 8.30 pm, so it's possible to catch a bus after coming in on any of the boats from Guangzhou; be sure to check with ticket windows at both stations as there may be buses leaving from either side of the street. High-speed ferries

WUZHOU 梧州

PLACES TO STAY
2 Beishan Hotel
   北山饭店
6 Wuzhou Hotel
   梧州大酒店
8 Hebin Hotel
   河滨饭店
10 New World Hotel
   新世界大酒店
11 Triumphal Arch
   Hotel
   凯旋门大酒店
17 Xinxi Hotel
   新西旅店
18 Yuanjiang Hotel
   鸳江酒店

OTHER
1 Western Bamboo Temple
   西竹园
3 Museum
   博物馆
4 Sun Yatsen Memorial
   Hall
   中山纪念堂
5 Snake Repository
   蛇园
7 Post Office
   邮电局
9 Bank of China
   中国银行
12 Market
   市场
13 Ferry Tickets (for
   Guangzhou)
   梧港客运站

14 Underground Market
   地下市场
15 Long-Distance Bus Station
   客运站
16 Long-Distance Bus Station
   客运站
19 Waterside Restaurants
   河边餐厅
20 Yuanjiang Pavilion
   鸳江亭
21 Ferry Dock (for
   Hong Kong)
   往香港船
22 Ferry Dock (for
   Guangzhou)
   客运站码头
23 Ferry Dock (for
   Guangzhou)
   客轮码头

from Hong Kong connect with the evening buses. There are also bus connections to Beihai (Y69), Guangzhou (Y57), Guilin (Y68), Liuzhou (Y60), Nanning (Y65) and Shenzhen (Y84).

The bus trip from Wuzhou to Yangshuo takes a bumpy seven hours, with another two hours to Guilin. The scenically impressive Wuzhou-Nanning run takes nine hours.

To complicate things, there's a third bus station more or less across from the Yuanjiang Hotel, with departures to almost everywhere except Yangshuo.

Boat There's a high-speed ferry service between Wuzhou and Hong Kong on odd days of the month (1, 3, 5, 7 etc), leaving at 7 am and arriving in Hong Kong at around 3 pm on the same day. (From Hong Kong, boats leave at 8 am on even dates.) Tickets are around HK$450. From Yangshuo, CITS and several local hotels can arrange tickets for the trip; for more details see the Yangshuo Getting There & Away section earlier in this chapter and the Getting There & Away chapter at the start of this book.

If you do arrive via this ferry, you face either a Y20 taxi ride into the town centre, or a trudge.

Boats to Guangzhou leave at 5, 7 and 8 pm, and the cheapest tickets are for the crowded (but bearable) dorm-style accommodation atop the boat at Y44.50. Two bed and four bed cabins are Y56.50 and Y77, but are only available on one or two boats per evening. Boats leave from both the docks just past the long-distance bus stations, or from a pier diagonally across the street from the Yuanjiang Hotel. Make sure you know exactly where to go. Tickets for the high-speed boats can be bought at a ticket office east of the docks, or for all boats at the docks themselves. At the time of writing a new high-speed ferry ticket office was being opened east of the Yuanjiang Hotel on Xijiang Lu; this may signal increased service.

There are now also high-speed ferries that make the trip to Guangzhou in four to five hours. Boats leave at 7.40 am and 1.30 pm. Tickets are Y159.50. Boats no longer serve Shenzhen at all, but slow boats make the trip to Zhuhai Monday, Wednesday, and Friday for Y56.

Guizhou 贵州

Guizhou Facts & Highlights

Area: 170,000 sq km

Population: 35.6 million

Capital: Guiyang

Highlights

- Huanggoushu Falls, China's highest at 74m, scenic countryside and minority villages.
- The south-east region, home to several minority groups, offering village-hopping and festival-watching.

Pity poor Guizhou *(guìzhōu)*. A Chinese newspaper once described it as 'a place of sunless sky, endless hills, and penniless people'. The 'Southwest Coal Sea' (as it's also known) sounds more benign, but is no less ugly.

Until recent times Guizhou was both a backwater and backward. It has always been one of the most sparsely populated and poverty-stricken areas in China, and it remains among the poorest today. It is also one of the most rewarding provinces to visit. Mountains and plateaus make up some 87% of Guizhou's topography, which has an average altitude of 1000m above sea level. The star attraction close to Guiyang is the Huangguoshu Falls – China's highest.

The neighbourhood also presents many opportunities for hiking and stumbling around some of China's least-visited villages.

About 65% of Guizhou's population is Han and the rest a mixture of minorities such as Miao, Bouyei, Dong, Yi, Shui, Hui, Zhuang, Bai, Tujiao and Gelao. In all, over 80 non-Han groups populate the province. Between them these minorities celebrate nearly 1000 festivals each year, which preserve fascinating customs and elaborate skills in architecture, dress and handicrafts.

Surprisingly, for a province so rich in minority culture, Guizhou is neglected by most travellers. The very well-worn path from Guilin to Kunming bisects the province, and yet if you hop off the train in, say, Guiyang, other westerners look at you as if you're daft. According to the Guizhou Tourism Administration, the province's total number of foreign visitors to date is just over 100,000. One of the reasons is probably the difficulty of travel in the province; another is that very little English is spoken. (However, these difficulties also exist in other more popular areas – northern Sichuan for example.)

However, the south-east of Guizhou in particular deserves more attention from adventurous travellers, especially since now almost all counties and towns are open to foreigners. Around 72% of the population in this region is Miao, Dong and a mixture of other minorities. Those who strike off from Guilin to Guiyang by local buses, for example, will find themselves travelling through countless tiny villages with drum towers and wind and rain bridges. With the exception of the buses and trucks that ply the roads, life in this part of China seems to go on as it has for centuries past.

HISTORY

Although Chinese rulers established an administration in the area as early as the Han Dynasty, they merely attempted to maintain

Guizhou

some measure of control over the non-Chinese tribes who lived here and Chinese settlement was confined to the north and east of the province. The western areas were not settled until the 16th century, when the native minorities were forced out of the most fertile areas.

Another wave of Chinese immigration in the late 19th century brought many settlers in from overpopulated Hunan and Sichuan. But Guizhou remained impoverished and backward, with poor communications and transport.

When the Japanese invasion forced the Kuomintang to retreat to the south-west, the development of Guizhou began; roads to the neighbouring provinces were constructed, a rail link was built to Guangxi and some industries were set up in Guiyang and Zunyi. Most of the activity ceased with the end of WWII, and it was not until the construction of the railways in the south-west under Communist rule that some industrialisation was revived.

Chinese statistics continue to paint a grim picture of backwardness and poverty. Eight million of the province's population live below the national poverty line. Between 60% and 70% of the population is illiterate and nearly 30% of the villages are not accessible by road.

Unfairly, blame has been laid at the door of the minorities, who have been castigated by state-run media for 'poor educational quality'. More self-righteous arguments have been levelled at cave dwellers because 'the temptations of modern life have failed to lure these Miao out of their dark, unhealthy cave'. These self-sufficient minorities living without TV, radio, electricity etc are certainly poor, but they show few signs of embracing consumer life and throwing away their cultural identity as a reward for assimilation with the Han. The government, for its part, claims plans to change all this, mostly by laying down roads in every place possible, mostly to facilitate travel between Chongqing, Chengdu and Huangguoshu Falls.

The province's most famous export is Maotai liquor, named for the village of its origin in Renhuai County. This fiery white spirit is sold in distinctive white bottles with a diagonal red label. Guizhou is also, like Yunnan, a major tobacco producing area.

FESTIVALS
Festivities among the minorities in Guizhou offer plenty of scope for exploration. Festivals take place throughout the lunar calendar at specific sites and are technicolour spectaculars which can feature bullfighting, horse racing, pipe playing, comic opera, singing contests and gigantic courting parties.

There are several festivals in Guiyang during the first lunar month (usually February or March), fourth lunar month (around May) and sixth lunar month (around July). Some of these take place in Huaxi.

A good starting point for festival forays is Kaili, which is on the railway line east of Guiyang. A profusion of festivals is held in nearby minority areas such as Leishan, Xijiang, Danxi, Qingman and Panghai. The town of Zhijiang, about 50km from Kaili, is also a festival centre.

About 10km further east on the railway line is Zhenyuan, which is renowned for its festivals between April and July. This town was once an important staging point on the ancient post road from central China to South-East Asia.

GUIYANG
(guìyáng)
Guiyang, the capital of Guizhou Province, has a mild climate all year round. Its name means Precious Sun and may be a reference to the fact that the sun rarely seems to shine through the clouds and drizzle. The place remains a much underrated Chinese city.

Most travellers give the place a miss, but it's worth lingering for a day or so. There's good food available, lively market and shopping areas (more clothing boutiques than you'd ever think possible) and a few interesting sights around town.

A few old neighbourhoods and temples remain amid the mushrooming high-rise towers, and with some effort the place can be appreciated for the funky conglomeration of city and village that it is. Guiyang is also a jumping-off point for the Huangguoshu Falls (or via Kaili) to the minority areas of the south-east.

Orientation
Guiyang is a sprawling kind of place that at first glance seems to lack a centre of any kind. It doesn't take long to get on top of things, however.

Zunyi Lu heads up from the railway station and links up with Zhonghua Lu, the road that cuts through the centre of town which is home to Guiyang's main shopping area. Yan'an Lu intersects Zhonghua Lu, and it is along this road that you will find the Bank of China, CITS, the expensive Guiyang Plaza Hotel and, on the other end, the long-distance bus station. There are more hotels as you go further up Zhonghua Lu near the intersection with Beijing Lu.

Information

Tourist Offices CITS is at 20 Yan'an Zhonglu (☎ 582-5873) and is one of China's more helpful and friendly CITS branches. The staff have maps and info on minority areas. It's located on the ground floor of a crumbling white plaster and brick building.

PSB The office (☎ 682-1231) is in a white-tiled building complex on Zhongshan Xilu, quite close to the intersection with Zhonghua Lu. This is the place to report thefts or seek visa extensions. As nearly all of Guizhou is now open to foreigners, there shouldn't be any need to get permits for travel within the province.

Money The Bank of China has several branches around town that will change money: on Yan'an Donglu, near the Guiyang Plaza Hotel; across from the CAAC ticket office; and the main branch up on Ruijin Beilu. The latter can also help with credit card withdrawals and wire transfers.

The Guiyang Plaza Hotel has an efficient exchange service, although the hotel, at the end of Yan'an Donglu, is quite a trudge from the railway station.

Post & Communications The post and telecommunications building is up on the intersection of Zunyi Lu and Zhonghua Nanlu. It's posted as 24 hours, but was shut tight on at least one morning. You can make international phone calls from the international and long-distance hall, located to the left of the main doors. If the lines are really long, try the post and telecommunications office at the intersection of Zhonghua Lu and Yan'an Lu.

Bookshops There's a branch of the Foreign Languages Bookstore on Yan'an Donglu. It's not particularly well stocked, but if you're desperate for reading material there should be something worth picking up.

Several employees of the shop hold an English-speaking and lecture session there every Sunday morning and they warmly welcome foreign visitors.

Dangers & Annoyances Guiyang has a reputation among Chinese as one of China's most dangerous cities for theft. Be particularly careful at night. The railway station is a favoured haunt of pickpockets, and travellers have reported problems in the station. Take care. Most times, however, the worst you'll have to deal with is an abundance of over-ambitious motorcycle taxi drivers.

Things to See

The distinctive architectural characteristics of Guiyang's handful of Mussolini-modern buildings are the columns, like the ones at the Provincial Exhibition Hall. The main street, Zunyi Lu, leading north from the railway station, harbours one of the largest glistening white statues of Mao Zedong in China. For details on a scenic bus tour around the city, see the Getting Around section.

Qianling Park (*qiánlíng gōngyuán*) is worth a visit for its forested walks and for the late Ming Dynasty **Hongfu Monastery** (*hóngfú sì*), perched near the top of 1300m-high Qianling Mountain. The monastery has a vegetarian restaurant in the rear courtyard that's open from 11 am to around 4 pm, making the park a good place to head out to for lunch. From the Jinqiao Hotel or the railway station area take a No 2 bus. The park is open from 8 am to 10.30 pm, and admission is Y1.

Guiyang's two other park attractions, **Huaxi Park** (*huāxī gōngyuán*) and **Nanjiao Park** (*nánjiāo gōngyuán*), are nothing to get particularly excited about, and if you're short of time give them a miss. Both of them have caves and strolling areas.

Not far from the CAAC office is **Hebin Park** (*hébīn gōngyuán*), which has benches under shade trees along the river and a Ferris wheel offering good views of Guiyang for Y6.

Guiyang is a pleasant enough place to

GUIZHOU

Guiyang

stroll around (if it's not raining), and apart from the markets and shopping district there are a few pavilions and pagodas scattered around town. These include the **Wen Chang Pavilion**, **Jiaxiu Pavilion**, **Hua Jia Pavilion** and the **Qianming Temple**. Check the map for their locations. They're all within easy walking distance of the centre of town.

In the northern part of town, along Beijing Lu, there is a regional **museum**. At the time of writing it was completely gutted and closed for remodelling, how-

ever, it has since opened and attracted favourable reviews. Admission is Y5.

Places to Stay – budget
Unfortunately, budget accommodation is in short supply in Guiyang. Contrary to popular opinion the hard/soft sleeper waiting room upstairs in the railway station is not a place to crash out, and if you try it you'll be asked to leave.

Your cheapest option is a bed at the *Jinqiao Hotel* (☎ 582-9951) (*jīnqiáo fàndiàn*), somewhat inconveniently located on Ruijin

GUIYANG 贵阳

PLACES TO STAY
1 Bajiayan Hotel
  八角岩饭店
2 Guizhou Park Hotel
  贵州公园饭店
3 Yunyan Hotel
  云岩宾馆
12 Guiyang Plaza Hotel
  金筑大酒店
20 Jingdu Hotel
  京都饭店
21 Jinqiao Hotel
  金桥饭店
23 Hebin Hotel
  河滨宾馆
32 Sports Hotel
  体育宾馆

PLACES TO EAT
22 Night Market
  夜市
33 Guizhou Beijing Duck Restaurant
  贵州北京烤鸭店

OTHER
4 Museum
  博物馆
5 Bank of China
  中国银行
6 Long-Distance Bus Station
  贵阳汽车站
7 Xinhua Bookstore
  新华书店
8 CITS
  中国国际旅行社
9 Post & Telecommunications Office
  电信局
10 Foreign Languages Bookstore
  外文书店
11 Bank of China
  中国银行
13 Hua Jia Pavilion
  华家阁
14 Market
  市场
15 Wen Chang Pavilion
  文昌阁
16 Night Market
  夜市

17 PSB
  公安局
18 Advance Rail Ticket Office
  火车票预售处
19 Department Store
  百货大楼
24 Post & Telecommunications Building
  邮电大楼
25 Jiaxiu Pavilion
  甲秀楼
26 Qianming Temple
  黔明寺
27 People's Square; Mao Statue
  人民广场
28 CAAC
  中国民航
29 Guizhou Exhibition Centre
  省展览馆
30 Chaoyang Cinema
  朝阳影剧院
31 Guizhou Gymnasium
  省体育馆
34 Railway Station
  贵阳站

GUIZHOU

Zhonglu, a good 30 minute walk from the railway station. Beds in a six-person dorm room cost Y40, and although it's a long trek to the showers – you'll seriously need to get directions and perhaps leave a popcorn trail – the rooms themselves are actually pretty nice. It's a steep jump in price if you want your own bathroom, however. Doubles start at Y168 and don't seem a particularly good deal at that price. Bus Nos 1 and 2 run from the railway station past the hotel.

Not exactly low, but another lower-budget possibility, is a double for Y90 at the *Jingdu Hotel (jīngdū fàndiàn)*, located down narrow Gangzhu Gang, diagonally across from the PSB compound. The rooms come with washroom attached, so it's not a bad deal if there are two of you, although this hotel has obviously seen better days. (Ask about the Y55 rooms – they're not for foreign friends, but if you get the right person on the right day, you might even get in.)

The *Bajiaoyan Hotel* (☎ 682-2651) *(bājiǎoyán fàndiàn)* is near the corner of Zhonghua Beilu and Beijing Lu. It has clean doubles with bathroom for Y100 and Y130, and suites from Y220. Although somewhat of a concrete hulk, it's a quiet place and not a bad deal for the price.

Places to Stay – middle & top end
Most of Guiyang's accommodation is mid-range in standard, even if some of the prices quoted for rooms are definitely top end. Pick of the bunch in terms of value for money is the *Sports Hotel* (☎ 579-8777) *(tǐyù bīnguǎn)* on the grounds of the Guizhou Gymnasium. It's next door to the big restaurant on the railway station side of the complex. Enormous and very clean doubles with TV and bathroom start at Y160. If you are in need of a night of comfort, they're well worth the money. The hotel is just a short walk from the railway station.

Near the entrance to Hebin Park, the newly spruced up *Hebin Hotel* (☎ 682-2451) *(hébīn bīnguǎn)* has a few triples for Y352, and from there it's a stratospheric leap to Y220 for a single. There are some rooms in the building's glass turret, which is complete with 180° picture windows. The rooms are OK, but international direct dial phones (and not much else) don't really warrant the pricing scheme.

Up near the corner of Zhonghua Beilu and Beijing Lu are a couple hotels catering to the well heeled.

The *Yunyan Hotel* (☎ 682-3324) *(yúnyán bīnguǎn)*, a cadre-style place, has singles/doubles starting at Y176 and triples at Y240. Staying here does give you access to a swimming pool in front of the hotel, although actually swimming there will cost you extra.

The *Guizhou Park Hotel* (☎ 682-2888) *(guìzhōu fàndiàn)* is the lap of luxury, with standard doubles ranging from Y500 to Y800. Ask about the presidential suite for Y4800 – maybe they have special rates for backpackers.

Places to Eat

Guiyang, like Kunming, is a great city for snack tracking. Just follow Zunyi Lu up to Zhonghua Nanlu and peer into the side alleys for noodle, dumpling and kebab stalls. North of Zhongshan Donglu along Fushui Lu is a bustling street of outside restaurants – lots of hotpot in all its incarnations, but plenty of others as well, including grill-your-own.

There's also a decent, if small, night market on Ruijin Lu between the Jinqiao and Hebin hotels. You can select from the local varieties of *shā guō fěn*, a combination of noodles, seafood, meat and vegetables in a hotpot and fired over a flame of rocket-launch proportion. Unfortunately, nearly all the local beers in Guizhou are putrid, so be warned.

Next door to the Sports Hotel on the grounds of the Guizhou Gymnasium is a good Chinese restaurant with fairly reasonable prices. Try the chicken and peanuts

dish *(gōngbǎo jīdīng)*. There's no English menu, but give other forms of communication a try, as this place is a treat. There are literally dozens of extremely attentive staff (being trained, no doubt) and it's loads of fun trying to stop them doing things for you. You'll also get the traditional form of Eight Treasures Tea *(bābǎo chá)*, with the server swirling hot water from a long-stemmed copper kettle.

For a special night out, try the *Guizhou Beijing Duck Restaurant (guìzhōu běijīng kǎoyādiàn)*, across the road from the Sports Hotel near the railway station. The duck here is really excellent, and although you'll be looking at around Y60 for a whole duck it's money well spent.

Getting There & Away

Air The CAAC office (☎ 584-4534 to book, 581-2138 to reconfirm) is at 170 Zunyi Lu. The staff are cheerful and helpful, and a spot check found all flights with tickets available for the following morning. Flights from Guiyang include: Beijing, Changsha, Chengdu (daily, Y540), Guangzhou, Guilin (Tuesday, Friday, Sunday, Y450), Haikou, Kunming (daily, Y470), Shanghai, Shenzhen, Wuhan, Xiamen and Xi'an.

China Southwest has two flights a week to Hong Kong for HK$1450, or US$194. The office is open from 8.30 am to 9 pm. By the time you read this, Guiyang's new airport should be open, so all schedules may change.

Bus The long-distance bus station is quite a long way from the railway station, and if you want to get out of Guiyang quickly you're better off using the bus services that operate from the railway station. There are buses to Xingyi (from where there are onward buses to Kunming) between 8 am and 6 pm for Y55, although these aren't as frequent as they once were. There's also a nightly sleeper bus at 6 pm which costs around Y70, but its future is in doubt. It takes about 12 hours to get from Guiyang to Xingyi.

Buses to Anshun leave every half-hour

(or whenever they fill up) from 7 am to 6 pm, although some may leave later if demand warrants it. The journey takes two hours and costs Y8. There are some super-luxury buses now which make the run in comfort for Y10. For the five hour (if you're very lucky) trip to Kaili, there are buses approximately hourly from 6.30 am to 5.30 pm. The fare is Y25. Buses to Zunyi leave every 30 minutes from 7 am to 9 pm. The ride takes five hours and costs Y15. The travel times to both Kaili and Zunyi should improve gradually as extensive roadworks are completed. The road to Zunyi has much higher priority, as you'll discover if you try the road to Kaili.

The long-distance bus station is the closer, better option if you stay overnight in Guiyang at the Jinqiao Hotel. There are eight buses to Anshun between 7 am and 6 pm. Three sleeper buses to Xingyi leave from 6 pm and after; the fare is Y72.

To Zunyi, buses leave more or less every half hour from 6.20 am to 5 pm; the trip takes four or five hours and costs Y25. There is now one bus at 4.30 pm to Kaili, but you're better off leaving from the railway station, where there are more. The trip takes anywhere from five to 10 very painful hours on very small, bad buses and costs Y35.

It's also possible to take tour buses (don't expect much of a 'tour' though) to Huangguoshu Falls and the Longgong Caves from the railway station, the long-distance bus station and most of the hotels. They generally depart at 6 or 7 am (7 to 7.30 am in the case of the bus station) and cost Y55. If you don't want to stay overnight at the falls, this is definitely the most hassle-free way of getting out there.

Train Direct trains run to Kaili, Kunming (Yun-nan), Shanghai, Guilin (Guangxi), Liuzhou (Guangxi), Nanning (Guangxi), Zhanjiang (Guangdong) and Chongqing (Sichuan).

Some sample hard sleeper fares for for-eigners from Guiyang are: Kunming, Y150; Chengdu (Sichuan), Y170; Changsha, Y123;

and Guilin, Y112. Whatever you do, don't take the local train to Zunyi unless you have nothing special planned for the day. See the Anshun Get-ting There & Away section later in this chapter for fares and departure times to Anshun.

Foreigners are required to buy their tickets at a special booth in the soft-sleeper waiting room, located upstairs on the left hand side of the railway station. There are no crowds or lines here, making it one of the more pleasant places in China to buy a train ticket. Lines through here are popular, so this is a place where you may have to try the trick of purchasing a ticket three or four stops *after* your destination (say, Guilin) and then have the ticket seller scribble a note to the conductors, so they can return your ticket to you early.

The advance rail ticket office for locals only (if you're planning to have someone buy a ticket for you) is on the 2nd floor of a large yellow-tiled building on Gongyuan Lu.

Getting Around

If you want to do a city-loop tour, then across the square from the railway station are two round-the-city buses, Nos 1 and 2. They follow the same route, but No 2 goes clockwise while No 1 goes anticlockwise.

These buses will get you to most places; the round trip from the railway station will cost Y0.80 and takes about 45 minutes. You can get a good window seat since you get on at the terminal – the same cannot be said if you choose to alight at random for a foot-sortie.

The main shopping street is on the bus No 1 route heading north, but this area is more fun to explore on foot. Note that minibuses with route numbers on the wind-screen do not follow the same route as larger buses bearing the same numbers.

ANSHUN
(ānshùn)
Spending a day or two in Anshun isn't the worst of fates. The karst valley setting is pleasant and some of the narrow streets are

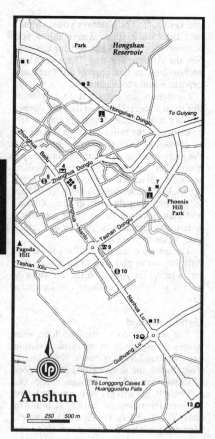

GUIZHOU

ANSHUN 安顺

1 Hongshan Hotel
   虹山宾馆
2 Dock
   码头
3 Wen Temple
   文庙
4 Post Office
   邮电局
5 Bank of China
   中国银行
6 Department Store
   百货大楼
7 Minzu Hotel; CTS
   民族饭店;
   中国旅行社
8 Donglin Temple
   东林寺
9 Telecommunications
   Building
   邮电大楼
10 Bank of China
    中国银行
11 Xixiushan Hotel
    西秀山宾馆
12 Long-Distance
    Bus Station
    长途汽车站
13 Railway Station
    火车站

lined with interesting old wooden houses.
It is also the best place from which to visit
Huangguoshu Falls and Longgong Caves.
(The only downside is a dearth of cheap
lodging.)

Once an opium-trading centre, Anshun
remains the commercial hub of western
Guizhou, but is now known for its batiks.
The town's main attraction is the **Wen
Temple** (wénmiào), north-west of the
railway station. The temple, which dates
back to the Ming Dynasty, underwent
restoration work in 1668.

Information

Tourist Offices Anshun lacks a CITS
branch, but its domestic cousin the China
Travel Service (CTS; ☎ 224-379) has an
office at the Minzu Hotel. It organises trips
to Huangguoshu and the surrounding area
and has information on minor attractions in
the region.

Post & Communications

The main post
office is at the corner of Zhonghua Nanlu
and Tashan Donglu. Another is a hike north
along Zhonghua Donglu. The former is supposed to offer 24 hour service, but it was
shut tight at 6 am on the last check.

Places to Stay & Eat

There are basically only three options for
foreigners staying in Anshun, and none is
cheap.

Near the bus station, the *Xixiushan Hotel*

(xīxiùshān bīnguǎn) has doubles with common washrooms (no showers) for Y60 and somewhat musty but OK doubles with attached bath for Y120. These prices are double what Chinese pay, but if you play tough you can usually bargain them down somewhat, usually to Y80 for a double. You'd better play hardball with them, because it's now the cheapest you'll find in town.

The *Minzu Hotel (mínzú fàndiàn)* on Tashan Donglu, on the eastern side of town near the highway to Guiyang, used to have cheap rooms, but has renovated and now has doubles costing around Y200. There are triples for around Y240 so if there's three of you it's almost worth it. There's a Muslim restaurant on the 2nd floor.

The main tourist joint, inconveniently located on the northern outskirts of Anshun, is the *Hongshan Hotel* (☎ 333-088) *(hóngshān bīnguǎn)* at 43 Hongshan Donglu. It's a bit lacking in the electricity and plumbing departments, but it's solid. The hotel gardens overlook the Hongshan Reservoir. This place has used some recent partial renovations as an excuse to hike prices for its cheapest rooms up to Y200.

Behind the bus station on Guihuang Lu, which is the highway linking Guiyang and Huangguoshu, is the *Jiaotong Hotel (jiāotōng fàndiàn)*. This place wasn't taking foreigners at the time of writing, but seems like a possible candidate, so it might not hurt to check.

For cuisine, expect nothing. Nothing other than rows of forgettable, if friendly, point-and-choose places surrounding the bus station area. But be warned – lots of doggie is served in these parts, one local sign even reading 'Lunch of Dog Counter'.

Getting There & Away

Bus The simplest option is probably the minibuses that run to Anshun from the Guiyang railway station. They leave every 30 minutes or when full, and cost Y8.

Alternatively, you can head out to the long-distance bus station, where buses run approximately every hour between 7 am and 6 pm. The trip takes about two hours along the Guihuang Expressway, Guizhou's first and only real highway, built specifically to whisk tourists up to Huangguoshu Falls. Some super-luxury liners with great comfy seats – though still precious little leg room – whip along the route from the bus and railway stations; it'll set you back all of Y10.

From Anshun, Huangguoshu Falls and Longgong Caves are 46km and 32km away, respectively. There are minibuses running from the long-distance bus station to Huangguoshu for Y8, although prices are fairly flexible and may require a little bargaining. If you arrive in the low season, be prepared for a wait and some frustrating negotiations with minibus drivers.

It is possible to take a rickety old big local bus to Huangguoshu Falls from the same place outside the bus station, but even they will try to gouge you (don't pay more than Y10).

Buses to Longgong are occasional at best, so you may have to join up with one of the local tours running from the bus station or the hotels, if you can get on.

If you don't feel like heading back to Guiyang to book a railway sleeper, you might want to consider travelling onwards from Anshun to Kunming by bus. From Anshun there is a 1 pm direct bus that arrives in Kunming around 8 am, roads permitting. There is also a regular bus during the day, but it runs intermittently if not enough passengers buy tickets; and it's a hell-ride that gets you in around midnight in any event. The day bus costs Y39, the sleeper Y80.05.

More interesting might be travelling from Anshun or Huangguoshu to Xingyi in the south-west of Guizhou. Xingyi is worth a visit in itself (see the listing at the end of this chapter), and there are direct buses from there to Kunming (12 hours). There is a daily bus from Anshun to Xingyi which leaves around 10 am. The ride takes around eight hours and costs Y21.50. There are oddly enough no sleepers yet for this route, but hopefully this will change.

GUIZHOU

Train Most of the trains running between Guiyang and Anshun currently depart from Guiyang and arrive in Anshun in the evening (usually the late evening). One exception originates in Guiyang at 7 am and stops in Anshun at around 9 am. Another leaves at 5.12 am, if you can handle it. But most people, obviously, will opt for the bus.

On the other hand, if you're going to Guiyang from Anshun, most trains leave during the day.

If you're thinking of travelling onwards from Anshun to Kunming by train, bear in mind that it's almost impossible to get hold of hard-sleeper tickets in Anshun itself. If comfort is important to you, you'll be better off heading back to Guiyang and organising your ticket there.

Getting Around
From town, the bus station and the railway station are 3km and 4km away, respectively. The No 1 minibus will take you into town for Y0.50 to Y1 depending on where you alight.

AROUND ANSHUN
Huangguoshu Falls
(huángguǒshù dàpùbù)
Located 46km south-west of Anshun, China's premier cataract reaches a width of 81m, with a drop of 74m into the Rhinoceros Pool, and is the foundation of Gui-zhou's fledgling tourist industry. If, like some travellers, you feel the falls are overrated, don't worry. Huangguoshu also provides an excellent chance to go rambling through the superb rural minority areas on foot. Although transportation is quite easy, not many travellers get here, so you'll probably be the attraction as much as anything. Yet another ridiculous entrance fee of Y30 is made more tolerable by having included in it another of those uselessly cool Chinese gold medallions.

Once you're there, you'll have no transport problems as everything you need is within walking range or, if you wish to go further, hiking range. Take a raincoat if you're off to the waterfalls and a warm jacket or sweater if you're descending into caves, which can be chilly.

The thunder of Huangguoshu Falls can be heard from some distance, and the mist from the falls carries up to Huangguoshu village during the rainy season, which lasts from May to October. The falls are at their most spectacular about four days after heavy rains. The dry season lasts from November to April, so during March and April the flow of water can become a less impressive trickle.

The main falls are the central piece of a huge waterfall, cave and karst area, covering some 450 sq km. It was explored by the Chinese only in the 1980s as a preliminary to harnessing the hydroelectric potential. They discovered about 18 falls, four subterranean rivers and 100 caves, many of which are now gradually being opened up to visitors.

At the edge of the falls is **Water Curtain Cave** *(shuǐlián dòng)*, a niche in the cliffs which is approached by a slippery (and dangerous) sortie wading across rocks in the Rhinoceros Pool – from the cave you'll get an interior view of the gushing waters through six 'windows'.

One kilometre above the main falls is **Steep Slope Falls** *(dǒupō pùbù)*, which is easy to reach. Steep Slope Falls is 105m wide and 23m high and gets its name from the crisscross patterning of sloping waters. Eight kilometres below Huangguoshu Falls are the **Star Bridge Falls** *(tiānxīng qiáo)*, known as the 'potted landscape', for which there are occasional minibuses leaving from Huangguoshu village.

Longgong Caves
About 32km from Anshun is a spectacular series of underground caverns called Longgong *(lónggōng)*, or Dragon Palace, which form a network through some 20 mountains. Charter boats tour one of the largest water-filled caves, often called the Dragon Cave. The caverns lie in Anshun County, at the Bouyei settlement of Longtan *(lóngtán zhài)* (Dragon Pool).

Other scenic caves in the vicinity include

The Bouyei People of Huangguoshu

Huangguoshu (Yellow Fruit Tree) is in the Zhenning Bouyei and Miao Autonomous County. Every 10 steps through the park, you'll have to circumnavigate camera-toting Chinese tour groups lining up shots of themselves with well dressed minority women. The Miao are not in evidence around the falls, but for the Bouyei, who favour river valleys, this is prime water country.

The Bouyei are the 'aboriginals' of Guizhou. The people are of Thai origin and related to the Zhuangs in Guangxi. They number two million, mostly spread over the south-western sector of Guizhou Province. Bouyei dress is dark and sombre, with colourful trimmings; 'best' clothes come out on festival or market days. The Bouyei marry early, usually at 16, but sometimes as young as 12. Married women are distinguished by headgear symbols.

The Bouyei are very poor, showing signs of malnutrition and wearing clothes that are grubby and tattered. The contrast with the postcard minority image of starched and ironed costumes, or the ring-of-confidence sparkling teeth, is obvious. The Bouyei tribespeople can also be shy and suspicious of foreigners.

Batik (cloth wax-dyeing) is one of the skills of the Bouyei. The masonry at Huangguoshu is also intriguing – houses are composed of stone blocks, but no plaster is used; the rooves are finished in stone slates.

There is a Bouyei festival in Huangguoshu lasting 10 days during the first lunar month (usually February or early March). The attendance is estimated at around 10,000 people. ∎

GUIZHOU

Daji Dong, Chuan Dong and Linlang Dong. Admission is Y30.

Places to Stay & Eat

At the bus park near the Huangguoshu Falls are some food stalls. Below them, down the cliff, is a teahouse and souvenir shop. The viewing area for the falls is a short downhill walk from the bus park. Further away from the bus park is *Huangguoshu Guesthouse (huángguǒshù bīnguǎn)*, which has actually become two hotels. The 'new' Huangguoshu Guesthouse is up a driveway to the right and, being the more expensive of the two, sports an English sign at the entrance to show foreigners which way to turn. Rooms here start at Y190 for a standard double. The old guesthouse, which actually doesn't look too different from the new one, has doubles for Y140, although they may try and tack on a 30% 'service charge' for foreign friends. The old guesthouse also has five to seven-bed dorms for Y86, but these are almost always booked up.

And unfortunately, that's presently your choice for lodging. The old stand-by in the village proper, the *Tianxing Hotel (tiānxīng fàndiàn)* has had a facelift and now charges well over Y100 for a room. Some travellers have managed to get beds for Y10 in the Chinese hotels, while others have been turned away. If you try, go for a hotel on the waterfall side: apparently one has a little pathway that gives you free access to the waterfall viewing area!

Along the town main road there are several restaurants that have verandas at the back where you can eat, sip a cold beer and enjoy a great view of the falls.

Getting There & Away

You can get to Huangguoshu Falls and Longgong Caves from either Guiyang or Anshun. There are a few direct buses to the falls from the Guiyang long-distance bus station and the railway station around 7 am, although these take about three to four hours to get there. Otherwise, catch a bus or a train to Anshun and hitch up with a minibus there. Minibuses and regular buses run every 30 minutes from Guiyang railway station to Anshun, a distance of 106km from Guiyang.

Alternatively, local tour buses leave from Guiyang railway station at around 7 am. They take in both the falls and Longgong Caves for Y55, depending on the type of bus. This does not include entry fees. Tours also run from nearly all the hotels listed in the Guiyang Places to Stay section. These buses will get you to Huangguoshu in around 2 to 3 hours, as opposed to the five hours required if you take public transport.

From the Anshun long-distance bus station there are one or two direct buses to Huangguoshu between 6 and 7 am. The fare is Y6 to Y8. Buses to Zhenfeng and Qinglong all pass through Huangguoshu. There are also frequent minibuses running from the bus station from 8 am to 5 pm for around Y8, although it's problematic at times for solo travellers or duos to hitch along with groups; the drivers will also try for whatever fare they can get, so be prepared. Both buses and minibuses take the local road to Huangguoshu rather than the expressway, so the 46km ride takes around 1½ hours. However, it does pass through some interesting small towns. If you do take a local bus, it may drop you along the highway instead of the bus park by the park entrance, which requires a steep, but pretty, 15 minute walk down from there.

Minibuses run from Huangguoshu to Anshun and on to Guiyang from 7 am to 7 pm. Buses leave as soon as they are full. Try to get one that takes the Guihuang Expressway rather than a local bus. These aren't that hard to find, as there are usually a fair number of visitors headed directly back to Anshun or Guiyang.

KAILI
(kǎilǐ)
Around 195km almost directly east of Guiyang, Kaili is a fairly uninspiring kind of place, but it's the gateway to the minority areas of south-eastern Guizhou. The bus

journey between here and Liping in the far south-east of Guizhou takes you through some of the most fascinating minority regions in this part of China. It should be possible to stop over in some of these towns without arousing the ire of local PSB agents as nearly all of Guizhou Province is now open to foreigners.

Particularly recommended are Leishan, Yongle and Rongjiang. Liping is a good base for exploring nearby Dong villages. Buses also run from Kaili to the Miao area of Shibing to the north, from where there are cruises on the Wuyang River, something that the local tourist authorities are promoting heavily. This whole area sees few western travellers.

Things to See
There's really not a great deal in this category. There's a pagoda in the **Dage Park** *(dàgé gōngyuán)*, which is not surprising as the park's name means Big Pagoda Park. The only other thing to check out is the drum tower down in **Jinquanhu Park** *(jīnquánhú gōngyuán)*, at the very southern end of town, where you can also find the moderately interesting **Minorities Museum** *(zhōu mínzú bówùguǎn)*.

Festivals
Kaili and the areas around it are host to a large number of minority festivals – over 130 annually, according to CITS. One of the biggest is the Lusheng Festival, held from the 11th to 18th of the first lunar month. The *lusheng* is a reed instrument used by the Miao people. Activities include playing the lusheng (of course), dancing, drumming, bull fighting and horse racing. Participants are said to number 30,000. The festival is held in Danxi.

A similar festival is held midway through the seventh lunar month in Qingman. Participants number 20,000. The Miao new year is celebrated on the first four days of the 10th lunar month in Kaili, Guading, Danxi and other Miao areas by some 50,000 people. CITS in Kaili should be able to provide you with a list of local

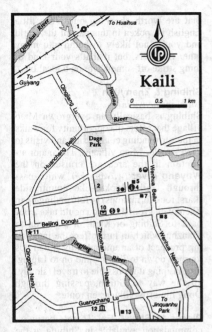

GUIZHOU

festivals and their dates. After that, you're probably better off on your own.

Places to Stay & Eat

If you're looking to save a few yuan, head for the *Zhenhua Guesthouse (zhènhuá zhāodàisuǒ)*, south of the long-distance bus station at the corner of Wenhua Nanlu and Beijing Donglu. Double/triple/quad dorm rooms cost Y14/15/16. If you want your own washroom, there are doubles available for Y30. The Zhenhua is spartan to put it nicely, and grumpy service is to be expected, but then again you can't expect too much for these prices.

Also south of the long-distance bus station is the *Shiyou Guesthouse (shíyóu bīnguǎn)* with doubles from Y40 – you'll be shown the Y68 doubles – and triples/quads for Y42/48. The triples have their own bathrooms. A few five person rooms are available. Note that this place doesn't

allow you to split up the cost; you pay for the whole room regardless.

Not far from there is the *Yingpanpo National Hotel (yìngpànpō mínzú bīnguǎn)*, which has doubles and triples for Y68, and you can't split the cost up here either. More upmarket doubles in a new wing go for Y226, although you might be able to bargain them down. To find this place, look for a big gate at the three way intersection, enter and follow the road up and to the right. CITS has an office in the hotel compound. The staff speak passable English and can fill you in on minority activities and destinations, and they have decent maps in English of the area. Be careful if they try and get you onto one of their 'minority tours' however, unless you're interested in a visit to a Dong village, complete with dance performance for a mere Y600 per head.

The only other option is the forlorn-looking *Kaili Hotel (kǎilǐ bīnguǎn)* down in the south of town, where doubles start at a 'discount price' of Y180. No bargains there.

Food options include lots of exceedingly dark restaurants. Walking west from the Shiyou Hotel and then north on Zhaoshan Nanlu there is a smallish night market where you can find any number of critters on skewer and grill. A departure from the point-and-choose tedium are the *shā guō*, convex coal-fired grills atop which you can roast your own dinner. Beancurd is available, along with lots of greens.

Getting There & Away

There are many trains departing Guiyang that pass through Kaili, including four between 8 am and noon. A hard-seat ticket is Y8 to Y12, depending on which train you take. From Kaili to Guiyang your choices are more limited: trains leave at 5.15, 5.40, 7.30 and 8.45 pm unless you want to hook up with trains around 3 or 4 am. The trip either way should take around three hours, although be warned – some take up to five hours.

Any train is preferable to the road and buses between Guiyang and Kaili. Buses to Kaili leave frequently from in front of Guiyang railway station between 6.30 am and 5.30 pm. The journey costs Y25 and takes five to seven hours – although 10 is not unheard of. If you get there in less than six hours consider yourself blessed.

The Kaili long-distance bus station has frequent buses to Guiyang between 6.30 am and 2 pm. If you are headed for Shibing and Zhenyuan, bus station staff will point you to the railway station. Liping and Congjiang are served by one to two buses daily, leaving Kaili between 6 and 7 am. There are numerous buses each morning for Leishan, up to every half hour; the trip costs Y5. Hourly buses, more or less, to Rongjiang leave between 6.30 am and 1.30 pm.

AROUND KAILI

The minority areas of south-eastern Guizhou are relatively unexplored by western travellers, and the following are some places that are worth checking out. Very little English is spoken in this part of the world and you're not likely to bump into many other travellers, but if that's your kind of thing strike off somewhere on a local bus.

Shibing & Zhenyuan

(shībīng/zhènyuán)

Shibing is basically an overgrown Miao village that offers the opportunity for walks in the surrounding countryside and visits to even smaller Miao villages. The major attraction in the area are cruises on the **Wuyang River** *(wǔyáng hé)*, which pass through Guilin look-a-like countryside (karst rock formations) before ending up in Zhenyuan. From there you could take a bus back to Shibing or Kaili, or a bus on to Tianzhu, which in turn offers the interesting prospect of an undoubtedly rough bus journey down to Jinping and on to Liping. From Liping it is possible to travel (slowly) all the way to Guilin, passing through Dong minority villages en route.

Places to Stay & Eat There's basic accommodation available in Shibing at the *Shibing Guesthouse (shībīng zhāodàisuǒ)* and in Zhenyuan at the *Zhenyuan Guesthouse (zhènyuán zhāodàisuǒ)*. Both are small towns and you'll have no problems finding the hotels.

Chong'an

(chóng'ān)

Lying about two hours north of Kaili by bus, this hamlet's claim to fame is its Friday market, and travellers who have seen it say it's one not to miss. There are also some nice walks to be had along the river and into the Miao villages nearby. There's one hotel in town taking foreigners, with dorm beds for Y5 to Y8. Buses to Shibing pass through Chong'an.

KAILI TO LIPING

Liping, in the far south-east of Guizhou, is a fairly uninteresting town, but the stretch of road between it and Kaili is crammed with sights and some beautiful countryside.

Ideally, it would be best to get off the bus and spend at least a couple of hours in some of the minority villages like **Leishan**, **Tashi**, **Chejiang**, **Rongjiang**, **Maogong** and **Gaojin**. Accommodation in these small spots is usually limited to a hotel either attached or next to the bus station. If you wander around looking lost, someone will either put you on the next bus or take you to the local hotel. Most of these towns have Dong wind and rain bridges and drum towers, many of which you'll see from the bus.

If you decide to head straight to Liping, the bus ride takes around nine hours, and costs Y20. Liping has basic accommodation in the *Liping Guesthouse (lìpíng zhāodàisuǒ)* – reckon on Y5 to Y10 for a bed. It's located at the traffic circle at the centre of town, near where the long-distance buses stop.

LIPING TO GUILIN

This is really only an option for travellers with time to kill. Buses in this part of the world are very infrequent and travel at a snail's pace over roads that only barely qualify as such. Buses run from Liping to **Diping** *(dìpíng)*, also known as Long'e *(lóng'é)*, at 7 am. To Diping, it takes around four hours, passing through the town of **Zhaoxing** *(zhàoxīng)*, an incredible Dong minority village with a total of five drum towers. There's a hotel in Zhaoxing, and a stop in the village would require you stay in it as there is only one bus a day travelling between here and Diping. Diping, another Dong village, also requires an overnight stop, as the bus on to Sanjiang in Guangxi Province doesn't leave until the next morning. The hotel at the square where the buses stop has dorm beds for Y5. From Sanjiang there are buses on to Longsheng or direct to Guilin. See the Sanjiang section of the Guangxi chapter for more information.

ZUNYI
(zūnyì)

Around 163km north of Guiyang, Zunyi is worth a mention and even possibly a visit for those who have a particular interest in Chinese Communist Party (CCP) history. For everyone else it's a fairly drab, industrialised Chinese town with few attractions.

Hemmed into the Jiangxi Soviet by Kuomintang forces, on 16 October 1934 the Communists set out on a Herculean one-year, 9600km tramp from one end of China to the other. By mid-December, having reached Guizhou, they marched on Zunyi, a prosperous mercantile town. Taking the town by surprise, the Communists were able to stock up on supplies and take a breather. On 15 to 18 January 1935, the top-level Communist leadership took stock of their situation in the now-famous Zunyi Conference. The resolutions taken largely reflected the views of Mao Zedong, who was elected a full member of the ruling Standing Committee of the Politburo and chief assistant to Zhou Enlai in military planning. It was a crucial factor in Mao's rise to power.

Things to See

The main sight is the **Zunyi Conference Site** *(zūnyì huìyì huìzhǐ)*. It's around 5km to the south-west of the railway station and is home to a collection of CCP memorabilia. The meeting rooms and living quarters are also open to the public. It is open 8.30 am to 4.30 pm daily.

Zunyi Park *(zūnyì gōngyuán)* is the park area across the road from the conference site and **Phoenix Hill Park** *(fènghuángshān gōngyuán)* is not far off. Neither is particularly exciting, but will probably make for a pleasant enough stroll if you have some time to kill.

Places to Stay & Eat

Across from the railway station is the first-rate bargain *Zuntie Hotel* (☎ 822-3266) *(zūntiě dàshà)*, a basic, friendly place with immaculate triples and quads for Y48. Doubles with attached bath start at Y35 and are definitely worth the money. Near the conference site the plush *Zunyi Guesthouse (zūnyì bīnguǎn)*, the official tourist abode, has doubles from Y120.

GUIZHOU

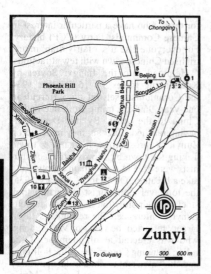

There's nothing to rave about, culinarily speaking. Beijing Lu west of the CAAC office has some groupings of alfresco hot-pot restaurants come dinnertime. South on Zhonghua Beilu there are more, along with some grill-your-own. Pickings are slim for non-meat eaters.

Getting There & Away

Zunyi is on the main northern railway line that connects Guiyang with Chongqing, Chengdu, Shanghai and basically the rest of China. It could be used as a stopover on any of these routes; a hard-seat ticket from Guiyang is Y10. Whatever you do, don't take the local 8 am No 832 train from Guiyang, unless you've got lots and lots of time to kill. The ride from Zunyi to Chongqing costs Y36.

Alternatively, buses leave Guiyang's long-distance bus station half-hourly between 6.20 am and 5 pm. You can also catch buses to Zunyi from in front of Guiyang railway station: there's one about every half-hour between 7 am and 9 pm. Zunyi's long-distance bus station is next door to the Zuntie Hotel, and there are

minibuses leaving for Guiyang throughout the day starting at 7 am, although they start to thin out around 6 pm. The ride takes five hours and costs Y25. And that's it for bus service to big places – no buses run to Chongqing or Chengdu. At least for now; the government has big plans to link Guiyang with Chengdu via Chongqing with new expressways.

XINGYI

(xīngyì)

Xingyi is mainly a stopover in the far south-west of Guizhou for those travelling between Guiyang and Kunming by bus. The main attraction in the area is the 15km-long **Maling Gorge** *(mǎlínghé xiágǔ)*, which some travellers say is more interesting than Huangguoshu Falls. There are steps and walkways cut into the gorge, which is quite precipitous in parts. It's a good idea to bring along a torch to light your way through some of the caves that the path passes through. You can hire a motorcycle to take you out to the trailhead for Y5.

Xingyi is an interesting town to wander around, and the sights include a good **minorities museum**. The *Panjiang Hotel* (*pánjiāng bīnguǎn*) is the only hotel that officially takes foreigners (don't worry, you'll get directed to it) and it costs around Y20 for a bed in a three bed dorm, or Y50 for a nice double with attached bath. Some travellers have managed to sneak a few nights in some of the Chinese-only hotels, but got hassled for it later. Keep an eye (and nose) out for the tasty warm cinnamon bread sold fresh in the mornings from street stalls and bakeries.

Getting There & Away
Buses to Xingyi leave approximately hourly

from in front of Guiyang railway station between 6 am and 6 pm. The fare is Y35. There are also three sleepers, which leave the long-distance bus station and cost Y72. The journey to Xingyi takes 12 hours.

If you're coming from Anshun, you can catch the daily bus at 10 am. The seven hour trip takes in some beautiful scenery, so it's good that it only runs in the daytime (there are no sleepers). The fare is Y21.50.

From Xingyi, buses leave the bus station at 6 am for the nine to 12 hour ride to Kunming. There is also a 6 pm bus, but it's not a sleeper, which could make for a long, dark, bumpy ride.

In addition, a number of independent bus companies around town operate services to Kunming throughout the day. Tickets range from Y25 to Y30. From Kunming's long-distance bus station there are morning buses to Xingyi.

GUIZHOU

Yunnan 云南

Yunnan Facts & Highlights

Area: 394,000 sq km
Population: 40.4 million
Capital: Kunming
Highlights

- Kunming, with its intriguing backstreets, great food and good sights (despite increasing modernisation).
- Lijiang's old town, whose narrow stone streets give a fascinating glimpse into Naxi culture and history.
- Tiger Leaping Gorge, a two to three day trek amid dramatic cliffs and waterfalls.
- Dali, one of China's best places to kick back and relax surrounded by wooden buildings and flagstone streets.
- Tengchong, a quaint town with nearby hot springs and (dormant) volcanoes.
- Ruili, a sometime wild bordertown surrounded by plenty of temples, villages and forests to explore.
- Xishuangbanna, a taste of tropical South-East Asia and home to the Dai people.

Yunnan *(yúnnán)* is without doubt one of the most alluring travel destinations in China. It's the most geographically varied of all of China's provinces, with terrain as widely divergent as tropical rainforest and icy Tibetan highlands. It is also the sixth largest province in China and home to a third of all China's ethnic minorities (nearly 50% of the province is non-Han) and half of all China's plant and animal species. If you could only go to one province, this one might well be it.

Yunnan is also well known for its mild climate year-round – its name is a reference to this reputation, meaning South of the Clouds. The provincial capital, Kunming, is similarly referred to as the 'Spring City'.

Despite the best government efforts, there are numerous pockets of the province that have successfully resisted Chinese influence and exhibit strong local identities. Even Kunming has a flavour all its own that seems more than half a world away from Beijing, although this gap is in danger of being bridged by rapid economic growth. (Yunnan's mammoth agricultural tallies account for nearly one third of the Gross National Product.)

Nicknames are affixed to everything in China, and Yunnan holds the vast majority. Since the province contains the nation's highest number of species of flora and fauna – including 2500 varieties of wild flowers and plants – it has been given monikers such as 'Kingdom of Plants (or Animals)', 'Garden of Heavenly Marvellous Flowers', and 'Hometown of Perfume'. Officials are less thrilled with the new tag: 'Treasure House of Crude Drugs'.

HISTORY

When Qin Shihuang and the Han emperors first held tentative sway over the southwest, Yunnan was occupied by a large number of non-Chinese aboriginal peoples who lacked cohesive political organisation.

By the 7th century AD, however, the Bai people had established a powerful kingdom, the Nanzhao, south of Dali. Initially allying its power with the Chinese against the Tibetans, this kingdom extended its power until, in the middle of the 8th century, it was

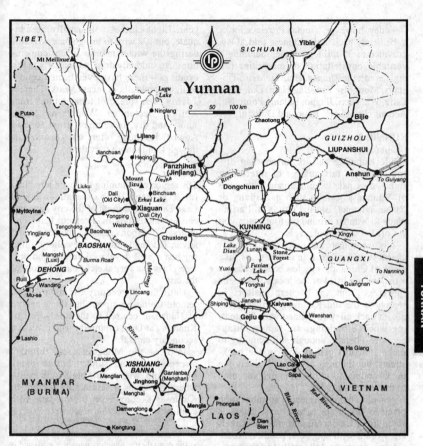

able to challenge and defeat the Tang armies. It took control of a large slice of the south-west and established itself as a fully independent entity, dominating the trade routes from China to India and Burma.

The Nanzhao kingdom fell in the 10th century and was replaced by the kingdom of Dali, an independent state which lasted until it was overrun by the Mongols in the mid-13th century. After 15 centuries of resistance to northern rule, this part of the south-west was finally integrated into the empire as the province of Yunnan.

Even so it remained an isolated frontier region, with scattered Chinese garrisons and settlements in the valleys and basins, a mixed aboriginal population occupying the highlands, and various Dai (Thai) and other minorities along the Lancang (Mekong) River.

Like the rest of the south-west, it was always one of the first regions to break with the northern government. During China's countless political purges, fallen officials often found themselves exiled here, which added to the province's rebellious character.

Today, however, Yunnan Province looks to be firmly back in the Chinese fold. It is a province of 35 million people, including a veritable constellation of minorities (25 registered): the Zhuang, Hui, Yi, Miao, Tibetans, Mongols, Yao, Bai, Hani, Dai, Lisu, Lahu, Wa, Naxi, Jingpo, Bulang, Pumi, Nu, Achang, Benglong, Jinuo and Dulong.

KUNMING
(kūnmíng)

While Kunming and its surrounding districts boast a fair number of interesting sights, they pale in comparison with some of Yunnan's jewels, such as Lijiang or Xishuangbanna. But the city is still a fine place to wander around on foot, once you get off the wide boulevards.

It is unfortunate that much of Kunming's charm is under threat: in recent years, like much of China, the city has been treated to a major face-lift. For the locals this spells 'progress', but for western visitors in search of the old Kunming it means the quaint back alleyways lined with fascinating wooden buildings are rapidly disappearing. There is enough still standing to make it worth getting lost in the backstreets, but the next decade will likely see the last remnants of old Kunming succumb to the wrecking ball.

For now the city remains an interesting place to linger for a few days. There is some great food available, and the streets are vibrant with shoppers, peddlers, roadside masseurs, karaoke stalls and the occasional street performer.

Kunming's total population is around 3.5 million, although only a million or so inhabit the urban area. At most, minorities account for 6% of Kunming's population, although the farming areas in the outlying counties are home to some Yi, Hui and Miao groups. There are also a fair number of Vietnamese refugees-turned-immigrants from the Chinese-Vietnamese wars and border clashes that started in 1977.

At an elevation of 1890m, Kunming has a milder climate than most other Chinese cities, and can be visited at any time of

year. Light clothes will usually be adequate, but it's wise to bring some woollies during the winter months when temperatures can suddenly drop, particularly in the evenings – there have even been a couple of light snowfalls in recent years. There's a fairly even spread of temperatures from April to September. Winters are short, sunny and dry. In summer (from June to August) Kunming offers cool respite, although rain is more prevalent.

History

The region of Kunming has been inhabited for 2000 years. Tomb excavations around Lake Dian to the south of the city have unearthed thousands of artefacts from that period – weapons, drums, paintings, and silver, jade and turquoise jewellery – that suggest a well-developed culture and provide clues to a very sketchy early history of the city.

Until the 8th century the town was a remote Chinese outpost, but the kingdom of Nanzhao, centred to the north-west of Kunming at Dali, captured it and made it a secondary capital.

In 1274 the Mongols came through, sweeping all and sundry before them. Marco Polo, who put his big feet in everywhere, gives us a fascinating picture of Kunming's commerce in the late 13th century:

At the end of these five day journeys you arrive at the capital city, which is named Yachi, and is very great and noble. In it are found merchants and artisans, with a mixed population, consisting of idolaters, Nestorian Christians and Saracens or Mohametans ... The land is fertile in rice and wheat ...

For money they employ the white porcelain shell, found in the sea, and which they also wear as ornaments about their necks. Eighty of the shells are equal in value to ... two Venetian groats.

In this country also there are salt springs ... the duty levied on this salt produces large revenues to the Emperor. The natives do not consider it an injury done to them when others have connection with their wives, provided the act is voluntary on the woman's part.

Here there is a lake almost a hundred miles in circuit, in which great quantities of fish are caught. The people are accustomed to eat the raw flesh of fowls, sheep, oxen and buffalo ... the poorer sorts only dip it in a sauce of garlic ... they eat it as well as we do the cooked.

In the 14th century the Ming set up shop in Yunnanfu, as Kunming was then known, building a walled town on the present site. From the 17th century onwards, the history of this city becomes rather grisly. The last Ming resistance to the invading Manchu took place in Yunnan in the 1650s and was crushed by General Wu Sangui. Wu in turn rebelled against the king and held out until his death in 1678. His successor was overthrown by the Manchu emperor Kangxi and killed himself in Kunming in 1681.

In the 19th century, the city suffered several bloodbaths, as the rebel Muslim leader Du Wenxiu, the Sultan of Dali, attacked and besieged the city several times between 1858 and 1868. A large number of buildings were destroyed and it was not until 1873 that the rebellion was finally and bloodily crushed.

The intrusion of the west into Kunming began in the middle of the 19th century when Britain took control of Burma (Myanmar), and France took control of Indochina, providing access to the city from the south. By 1900 Kunming, Hekou, Simao and Mengzi were opened to foreign trade. The French were keen on exploiting the region's copper, tin and timber resources, and in 1910 their Indochina railway, started in 1898 at Hanoi, reached the city.

Kunming's expansion began with WWII, when factories were established here and refugees fleeing the Japanese poured in from eastern China. In a bid to keep China from falling to Japan, Anglo-American forces sent supplies to Nationalist troops entrenched in Sichuan and Yunnan. Supplies came overland on a dirt road carved out of the mountains in 1937-38 by 160,000 Chinese with virtually no equipment. This was the famous Burma Road, a 1000km haul from Lashio to Kunming (today, the western extension of Kunming's Renmin Lu, leading in the direction of Heilinpu, is the tail end of the road).

In early 1942 the Japanese captured Lashio, cutting the supply line. Kunming continued to handle most of the incoming aid during 1942-45 when US planes flew the dangerous mission of crossing the 'Hump', the towering 5000m mountain ranges between India and Yunnan. A black market sprang up and a fair proportion of the medicines, canned food, petrol and other goods intended for the military and relief agencies were siphoned off into other hands.

The face of Kunming has been radically altered since then, with streets widened and office buildings and housing projects flung up. With the coming of the railways, industry has expanded rapidly, and a surprising range of goods and machinery available in China now bears the 'made in Yunnan' stamp. The city's produce includes steel, foodstuffs, trucks, machine tools, electrical equipment, textiles, chemicals, building materials and plastics.

Orientation

The jurisdiction of Kunming covers 6200 sq km, including four city districts and four rural counties (which supply the city with fruit and vegetables). The centre of the city is the traffic circle at the intersection of Zhengyi Lu and Dongfeng Lu. This is where you'll find the local trendies, cinemas, karaoke bars and department stores overflowing with the latest fashions and electronic goods. Surprisingly, it is still possible to find a few rows of old wooden houses in nearby neighbourhoods, although these are being levelled with alarming regularity. Kunming's tree-lined Jinbi Lu, the last bastion of original architecture, fell in its entirety to the wrecking ball in late 1997.

East of the intersection is Kunming's major north-south road, Beijing Lu. At the southern end is the main railway station, the long-distance bus station and the Kunhu Hotel, one of the few cheap places to stay in Kunming. At about the halfway point Beijing Lu is intersected by Dongfeng Donglu.

YUNNAN

Maps Shop around as there's a great variety; some with a smattering of English names. The *Kunming Tourist Map* has street and hotel names in English and shows bus lines, while the *Yunnan Communications and Tourist Map* has the names of nearly every town in the province written out in English.

Information

Tourist Offices CITS (☎ 314-8308) is just east of Beijing Lu in a large white-tiled building at 220 Huancheng Nanlu. Like CITS offices elsewhere in China, this one emphasises group tours and is not able to offer a lot of assistance to individual travellers. A few years back some travellers successfully made reservations by telex to Beijing for tickets on the Trans-Siberian, but CITS staff seemed shocked that such a transgression had taken place. Another office (☎ 313-3452) can be found on Dongfeng Donglu, near the Kunming Hotel.

Better for independent travellers would be CITS' new Family and Independent Traveller (FIT) office (☎ 313-8888/3104) adjoining the King World Hotel on Beijing Lu; they have another office (☎ 316-5888/6212) at the Holiday Inn.

Consulates Thailand, Laos and Myanmar (Burma) now all have visa-issuing consulates in Kunming. When we last checked, PSB officials said exit permits were not needed to go into Laos. But given the flexibility of rules in China, it would be wise to check for yourself. Visa details for each country follow.

Laos The Lao consulate (☎ 317-6623) is on the 2nd floor of Building Three at the Camellia Hotel. Unless you have a sponsor in Laos (doesn't everyone?) you'll probably only be able to get a seven day transit visa, five days if you arrive by plane. This is just enough time to cross the border at Mengla, make your way down to Vientiane and on to Thailand. The visa costs US$25 and takes four or five days to process. You must bring three photos.

In the past, you needed to already have a visa from a third country stamped in your passport, but this had been waived at the time of writing. Even though Thailand grants most nationalities a grace period of 30 days before requiring a visa, you may have to get one stamped in your passport anyway, just to satisfy the Lao officials.

Also note that these regulations have changed seemingly month to month in recent years, so by the time you read this, you may be able to show up at the border and get a 30 day visa. Or not. Office hours are Monday to Friday, 8.30 to 11.30 am and 2.30 to 4.30 pm.

Myanmar (Burma) The office (☎ 317-6609; fax 317-6309) is just above the Lao consulate, on the 3rd floor of Building Three. Myanmar seems to be really gearing up for tourists: the consulate can grant you a four week visa in 24 hours for Y85, although don't count on such speed. There are two catches: first you are required to change US$300 into Myanmar kyat at the government's scandalously low rate; and the visas are not good for land crossings: you are supposed to fly in via Yangon (Rangoon) only. The consulate is open Monday to Friday from 8.30 am to noon and 1 to 4.30 pm.

Thailand The Thai consulate (☎ 313-8888/2204; fax 313-1910) is on the 3rd floor of the building directly next to the King World Hotel and can arrange two month visas for Y110 in three working days. Travellers from most countries won't need one unless they plan to spend more than 30 days in Thailand (which actually is not all that hard to do).

PSB The Foreign Affairs Branch is a little way down an alley off 93 Beijing Lu and is open from 8 to 11.30 am and 2.30 to 5.30 pm, and until 4.30 pm on Friday. On weekends it's posted as closed, but there's usually someone about. It's a tiny office with a small plaque in English on the wall outside. The officers on duty usually speak excellent English, and are quite friendly. They also have current lists of all the open counties and cities in Yunnan (happily, the list keeps getting longer). All they can do otherwise is roll their eyes, groan, and tell you that those rumours of the road into Tibet from Yunnan opening up have been greatly exaggerated.

Money The Kunming, Green Lake, Camellia, King World, Holiday Inn and Golden Dragon hotels each have foreign-exchange counters. Changing money in the hotels is generally more convenient than trudging up to the Bank of China at 448 Renmin Donglu, although the bank recently opened a branch near the Golden Dragon Hotel on Beijing Lu. The former is open from 9 to 11.45 am and from 2.30 to 5.30 pm. Another branch on Qingnian Lu also has a foreign exchange counter.

There are still one or two hopeful money-changers in front of the Kunming Hotel, but be very careful of rip-offs, which occur frequently by sleight of hand.

Post & Communications There is an international post office on the east side of Beijing Lu. It's halfway between Tuodong Lu and Huancheng Nanlu and has a very efficient poste restante and parcel service – this is where poste restante mail ends up. Every poste restante letter or parcel that comes in is listed in a ledger that's kept on the counter. To claim a letter, you must show your passport or ID. Usually, at least one of the clerks speaks English. You can also make telephone calls here.

There is another post office to the north of this one, at the intersection of Beijing Lu with Dongfeng Donglu. The postal service hours here are from 8 am to 8 pm, and the telecommunication service operates from 8 am to 5 pm.

Medical Services The Yan'an Hospital (*yán'ān yīyuàn*) on Renmin Lu has a foreigners' clinic (☎ 317-7499, ext 311) on the 1st floor of Building 6, at the back of the compound.

Tang Dynasty Pagodas
To the south of Jinbi Lu are two Tang pagodas, of which the West Pagoda (*xīsì tǎ*) is more worth visiting. The East Pagoda (*dōngsì tǎ*) was, according to Chinese sources, destroyed by an earthquake; western sources say it was destroyed by the Muslim revolt. It was rebuilt in the 19th century, but there's little to see.

The more interesting West Pagoda is on Dongsi Jie, a bustling market street – you'll probably have to walk your bicycle through the crowds. The West Pagoda has a compound that is a popular spot for old people to get together, drink tea and play cards and mahjong. You can even get a haircut and a shave at the base of the pagoda. It's not a bad stop to catch your breath and sip a cup of tea.

It's a bit tricky to find. Look out for a red gateway hidden among the trees and karaoke signs: the pagoda is about 20m in along a narrow corridor. The temple is open from 9 am to 9 pm and admission is Y2.

Yunnan Provincial Museum
(*yúnnánshěng bówùguǎn*)
The museum, on Wuyi Lu, houses an exhibition centred on Yunnan's minorities, as well as a collection of artefacts from tomb excavations at Jinning on the southern rim of Lake Dian. All things considered, the museum is probably not worth the foreigners' entry fee of Y15.

The exhibits are for the most part fairly tacky shop mannequins dressed in minority colours, and photographs of minority festivals. However, at the time of writing there was a great exhibition on Deng Xiaoping's life. The museum is open from Tuesday to Sunday from 9 am to 5 pm.

Yuantong Temple
(*yuántōng sì*)
The Yuantong Temple, to the north-east of the Green Lake Hotel, is the largest Buddhist complex in Kunming, and is a target for pilgrims. It is over 1000 years old, and has seen many renovations. Leading up to

YUNNAN

the main hall from the entrance is an extensive display of flowers and potted landscapes. The central courtyard holds a large square pond intersected by walkways and bridges, and has an octagonal pavilion at the centre.

To the rear of the temple a new hall has been added, enshrining a statue of Sakyamuni, a gift from the king of Thailand. There's a vegetarian restaurant west of the temple entrance that serves lunch and dinner.

The temple is open from 8 am to 5 pm, although the restaurant doors don't close until 9 pm. Admission is Y5 for overseas visitors, Y1 for locals. Watch out for pickpockets outside the temple and for the elderly women inside who do their best to stop foreigners taking pictures of the Buddhist statuary.

Kunming Zoo
(dòngwùyuán)
Close to Yuantong Temple is the zoo. The grounds are pleasantly leafy and high up, and provide a bird's-eye vista of the city, but most travellers find the animals' living conditions depressing – animal lovers are better off giving the place a miss.

Cuihu Park
(cuìhú gōngyuán)
A short distance south-west of the zoo, the Cuihu Park is worth a stroll if they charge you the Chinese price of Y2; at last check they were. Sunday sees the park at its liveliest, when it is host to an English Corner and hordes of families at play. There are more of those colourful paddleboats at play too.

Mosques
(qīngzhēnsì)
Today, while Kunming's Buddhist shrines, desecrated during the Cultural Revolution, are humming with renovations for the tourist trade, the local Muslim population seems to have been left out of the action. There are a few mosques around the city centre, none of which see much activity. This has very recently begun to change. The oldest of the lot, the 400-year-old Nancheng Ancient Mosque *(nán-chéng gǔsì)* was ripped down in 1997 in order to build a larger version. The question is how much officialdom consulted the Muslim community before ramming through the project.

Completed in 1998, the mosque sits immediately north of the Kunming Department Store at 51 Zhergyi Lu. Looking vaguely

---

Kunming's Muslims

Unlike Muslims in other parts of China, who generally formed settlements at the terminus of trade routes used by Arab traders, Yunnan's sizeable Muslim population dates back to the 13th century Mongol invasion of China. Ethnically indistinguishable from the Han Chinese, the *huǒ*, as Muslims are known, have had an unfortunate history of repression and persecution, a recent low point being the years of the Cultural Revolution. The Cultural Revolution failed to spark off a revolt of any kind, though unsuccessful protests were registered in Beijing. The turbulent years of the mid-19th century, which witnessed the massive Taiping and Nian rebellions, were another matter. Heavy land taxes and disputes between Muslims and Han Chinese over local gold and silver mines triggered a Muslim uprising in 1855.

The Muslims made Dali the centre of their operations and laid siege to Kunming, overrunning the city briefly in 1863. Du Wenxiu, the Muslim leader, proclaimed his newly established kingdom Nanping Guo, or the Kingdom of the Pacified South. But the Muslim successes were short-lived. In 1873 Dali was taken by Qing forces and Du Wenxiu was captured and executed, having failed in a suicide attempt. ∎

like a Las Vegas casino, it has the appearance of a typical white-tiled office building (it does have office space) topped by bluish domes. Only in China. Not too far away is a lively strip of lots and lots of Muslim restaurants. To get there, walk north-west past the Chun Cheng Hotel and then bear left a half-block to a small alley.

There's another mosque nearby, wedged between Huguo Lu and Chongyun Jie, although it looks to be more of an historical landmark rather than a place of active worship.

Organised Tours

Several tour outfits cover the area faster than public minibuses would, but you must be prepared to pay for them. They generally feature a lot of sights that most western travellers find rather boring, like the Black Dragon Pool and various caves (a national obsession). More central sights like Yuantong Temple are just a short bicycle ride away – it hardly makes sense to join a tour to see them. Some tour operators refuse to take foreigners on their tours, claiming the language barrier causes too much trouble.

There are various tours to the Stone Forest running from in front of the railway station, and from near the Three Leaves, Golden Dragon and Kunhu Hotels on Beijing Lu – avoid them. You'll spend the whole morning rummaging around in caves where you'll be charged exorbitant foreigners' entry fees, followed by a marathon midday lunch. If you're lucky you may even get an hour or so in the Stone Forest before being whisked back to Kunming.

That said, the occasional traveller has come back satisfied with the experience – an interesting initiation into Chinese tourism rituals. The Camellia Hotel's trip gets you there the quickest and does *not* go via caves, but it too makes a couple of rather convenient 'rest stops' at jade emporiums en route.

There's also an outfit up at No 73 Renmin Xilu called Yunnan Exploration (☎ 531-2203), which can organise jeep

tours, hiking, backcountry skiing, bicycle trips and other more exotic outdoor activities, most of which take place far away from Kunming. What's on offer looks interesting, although probably beyond the budgets of many travellers.

Places to Stay – budget

Only two hotels have dormitories for Y50 or less – all other accommodation open to foreigners is mid-range, at least in terms of price.

Long frequented by budget travellers, the *Camellia Hotel* (☎ 316-3000/2198; fax 314-7033) *(cháhuā bīnguǎn)* on Dongfeng Donglu closed down its dormitory accommodation for several years. But a ceaseless barrage of backpackers apparently changed someone's mind. You can get in for Y30 per bed in a seven person room, and it can be difficult to get in sometimes. They may put you in a cramped but bright 20 person dorm in the main building, but building No 3 across the compound is quieter. Avoid No 3's 1st floor and ask for 3rd floor rooms – they're in better shape. Also in demand are the hotel's Y140 doubles, which have TV and their own bathroom. It's sad to say, but these are almost among the cheapest such rooms in Kunming. There are also standard doubles for Y220, which some travellers have resorted to in hopes they'll get a dorm bed or a Y140 double the next day.

The Camellia has bicycle hire, a foreign-exchange counter, poste restante and the cheapest laundry service you'll find. The hotel used to fill up quickly and there would be traffic jams of backpackers in peak season, but with more rooms opening up, the situation isn't quite so severe. Still, give the staff a break; they do a pretty good job with the steady stream of guests. To get there from the railway station, take a No 2 or 23 bus to Dongfeng Lu, then change to the No 5 bus heading east and get off at the second stop.

Near the railway and bus stations on Beijing Lu, the *Kunhu Hotel* (☎ 313-3737) *(kūnhú fàndiàn)* also has dorm beds in

YUNNAN

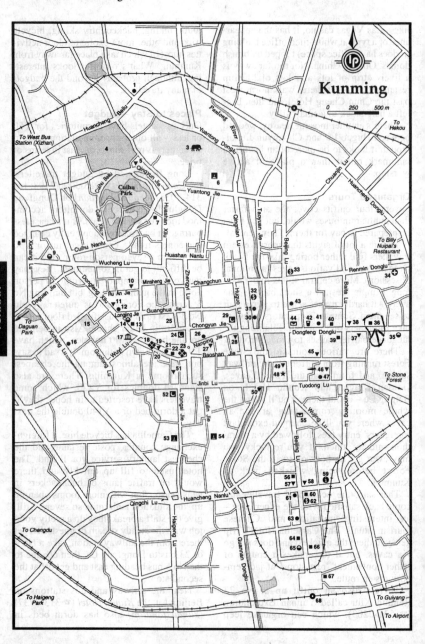

Kunming

To West Bus
Station (Xizhan)

To Hekou

To Daguan
Park

To Chengdu

To Haigeng
Park

To Billy
Nuipai's
Restaurant

To Stone
Forest

To Guiyang

To Airport

Cuihu Park

Cuihu Beilu
Cuihu Xilu

Huancheng Beilu

Yuantong Dongiu

Panlong River

Yuantong Jie

Chuanjin Lu

Huancheng Dongiu

Renmin Dongiu

Qingyun Jie
Huashan Xilu
Cuihu Nanlu
Huashan Nanlu
Wucheng Lu

Yuantong Jie

Qingnian Lu

Taoyuan Jie

Beijing Lu

Bala Lu

Dongfeng Xilu
Daguan Jie
Xichang Lu
Dongfeng Lu
Minsheng Jie
Fu An Jie
Guanghua Jie
Longjing Jie
Changchun Lu
Zhengyi Lu
Huguo Lu

Dongfeng Donglu

Wuyi Lu
Guofong Lu
Chongyun Jie
Nanping Jie
Baoshan Jie

Tuodong Lu

Jinbi Lu

Dongsi Jie
Shulin Jie

Wujing Lu

Chunchen Lu

Qingchi Lu
Huancheng Nanlu

Beijing Lu

Haigeng Lu

Guannan Donglu

KUNMING 昆明

PLACES TO STAY
7 Green Lake Hotel
翠湖宾馆
8 Golden Flower Hotel
金花宾馆
13 Yunnan Hotel
云南饭店
22 Chun Cheng Hotel
春城饭店
36 Camellia Hotel
茶花宾馆
39 Holiday Inn Kunming
樱花酒楼
40 Kunming Hotel
樱花假日酒店
56 Kunhu Hotel
昆湖饭店
60 Golden Dragon Hotel
金龙饭店
64 King World Hotel
锦华大酒店
66 Three Leaves Hotel
三叶饭店
67 Railroad Travel
Service
铁路旅行社

PLACES TO EAT
5 Tong Da Li Restaurant
通达利餐馆
10 Laozhiqing Restaurant
老知青食馆
11 Shanghai Noodle
Restaurant
上海面店
19 Qiaoxiangyuan
Restaurant
桥香园饭店
20 Muslim Restaurants
清真饭店
27 Beijing Restaurant
北京饭店
28 Minsheng Restaurant
民生饭店
37 Cooking School
学厨饭店
38 Yunnan Typical Local
Food Restaurant
根兴饭店
45 Bai Ta Dai Flavour
Restaurant
白塔傣味餐厅
46 La Piazzetta

49 Mengzi Across-the-Bridge
Noodles Restaurant
蒙自过桥米线
50 Guangshengyuan
Restaurant
冠生园饭店
51 Yunnan Across-the-Bridge
Noodles Restaurant
云南过桥米线
57 Yuelai Cafe
悦来餐厅
58 Wei's Place
哈哈餐厅

OTHER
1 Yunnan Minorities
Institute
云南民族学院
2 North Railway Station
火车北站
3 Kunming Zoo
昆明动物园
4 Yunnan University
云南大学
6 Yuantong Temple
圆通寺
9 Xiaoximen Bus Station
小西门汽车客运站
12 Arts Theatre
艺术剧院
14 Buses to Western Hills &
Bamboo Temple
往西山、筇竹寺的车
15 Guofang Sports Ground
国防体育场
16 Advance Ticket Booking
Office
火车票预售处
17 Yunnan Provincial
Museum
云南省博物馆
18 Wuhua Mansions
Department Store
五华大厦
21 Kunming United Airlines
昆明联合航空公司
23 Kunming Department
Store
昆明百货商店
24 Nancheng Mosque
南城清真古寺
25 Flower & Bird Market
花鸟市场
26 Xinhua Bookstore
新华书店

29 Mosque
清真寺
30 Yunnan Antique Store
云南 奈锷痕
31 Foreign Languages
Bookstore
外文书店
32 Bank of China
中国银行
33 Bank of China
中国银行
34 Yan'an Hospital
延安医院
35 Yunnan Tourist
Transportat Company
(Buses to Dali)
云南旅游客运中心
41 China Southern &
Shanghai Airlines
上海航空公司
42 Golden Triangle Bar
金角酒吧
43 China Southwest Airlines
西南航空公司
44 Post &
Telecommunications
Office
邮电局
47 CAAC; Yunnan Airlines
中国民航；
云南航空公司
48 PSB
公安局
52 Mosque
清真寺
53 West Pagoda
西寺塔
54 East Pagoda
东寺塔
55 International Post Office
国际邮局
59 CITS
中国国际旅行社
61 China Southwest
Airlines
西南航空公司
62 Bank of China
中国银行
63 Thai Airways
泰国航空公司
65 Long-Distance Bus
Station
长途汽车总站
68 Main Railway Station
火车站

quads for Y25. The lion's share of back-packers head here now for these reasons. Unfortunately the dorm rooms look out onto Beijing Lu, so they're quite noisy. The hotel also has singles/doubles with common bath for Y60/68. Beyond this, rooms aren't quite worth the price – dingy doubles with attached bath go for Y120. Some travellers have been more than a bit unnerved by the common washrooms *and* showers. On the plus side, the common bathrooms are fairly clean and next door to the hotel are several cafes where you can relax, sip coffee and trade tales with fellow travellers. The hotel is two stops from the railway station on bus No 2, 23 or 47.

The only other budget option is the *Golden Flower Hotel* (☎ 532-6900) *(jīnhuā bīnguǎn)* way out on Xichang Lu. A bed in a triple room is Y55, which is akin to robbery, but may have to do if you're shut out of the Camellia and Kunhu. Standard doubles are Y200. The hotel is in a courtyard set back from Xichang Lu, but there is a gateway with an English sign out front. Getting here by bus is a hassle. Take the No 3 bus to the intersection of Jinbi Lu and Xichang Lu, and change to the No 22 bus which runs up Xichang Lu and past the hotel.

Places to Stay – middle

Your best bet here is probably the *Chun Cheng Hotel* (☎ 316-3271) *(chūnchéng fàndiàn)* on Dongfeng Xilu. Also known as the Spring City Hotel, it has spacious clean doubles with attached bathroom for Y166 – pretty good value for money. There are also doubles with common washroom for Y82, which are not such a good deal. A couple of larger 'suites' for slightly higher prices are also good value. For a minor splurge, this is a good place. Friendly, attentive service is the norm here. The restaurant gets great reviews too.

Right next to the main railway station, the *Railroad Travel Service* (☎ 351-2166; fax 351-3421) *(tiělù lǚxíngshè)* has doubles with bath for Y180. There are much cheaper rooms, but they're not for you. The

hotel is fairly new, so it's not a bad place to stay as long as you don't mind wading through the railway station crowds on your way in and out of the building. The *Three Leaves Hotel* (☎ 351-2542; fax 313-8544) *(sānyè fàndiàn)* is a short walk from the railway station and directly opposite the long-distance bus station on Beijing Lu. Decent standard doubles with air-con and satellite TV are Y238.

Places to Stay – top end

Several former proletarian stand-bys have received luxury face-lifts and so, as usual, there is plenty to choose from in this category. (If Kunming's tourist authorities had their way, probably every hotel in town would be a four star or higher.)

The *Kunming Hotel* (☎ 316-2063) *(kūnmíng fàndiàn)* at 145 Dongfeng Donglu has north and south wings; both are fairly expensive, although the south wing is the cheaper of the two. Only doubles are available in the north wing, and prices start at US$118. The south wing has doubles for US$35. The hotel has some useful facilities: airline ticket bookings, poste restante, post office, photocopying, a snooker room, bike hire, several high-end restaurants, including a Chaozhou eatery, and a couple of shops. To get there from the main station, take bus No 23 to the intersection of Dongfeng Lu and Beijing Lu, and then take a bus east or walk. From the west bus station *(xīzhàn)* take bus No 5.

Diagonally opposite the Kunming Hotel is Kunming's super-luxury monster: the *Holiday Inn Kunming* (☎ 316-5888; fax 313-5199) *(yínghuā jiàrì jiǔdiàn)*. It is still the best of Kunming's hotels, sporting some excellent restaurants, a western-style pub, a super-chic disco and one of the better breakfasts in town. You can expect the usual Holiday Inn standards and room rates (US$118 to US$154 for a double, and then into the stratosphere at US$888 for a suite). Rooms come with a western buffet breakfast.

The *Green Lake Hotel* (☎ 515-8888; fax 515-3286) *(cuìhú bīnguǎn)* on 6 Cuihu

Nanlu is in an older section of Kunming. It used to be quiet and quaint, but has lost some of its character with the construction of a 20 floor, four star addition in the back. Doubles in the old building are actually pretty reasonable at Y280, especially when compared with US$100 for a room in the new section. The hotel has a bar, a coffee shop and both western and Chinese restaurants. The food in these places has a good reputation.

Down on Beijing Lu, the *Golden Dragon Hotel* (☎ 313-3015) (*jīnlóng fàn-diàn*) is a Hong Kong-China joint venture. Only doubles are on offer and these start at US$80, while suites start at US$140 and reach the giddy heights of US$600 (plus 10% service charge). A 15% discount is sometimes available on request. Dragonair has an office here and there is a business centre on the premises as well.

Down the road from the Golden Dragon is another luxury hotel: the *King World Hotel* (☎ 313-8888; fax 313-1910) (*jǐnhuá dàjiǔdiàn*). Doubles range from US$88 for a standard to US$198 for a superior suite, plus 15% service charge. The hotel features an expensive revolving restaurant (the highest above sea level in China, the hotel proudly points out) on the top floor. Rooms come with fruit baskets and a complimentary breakfast. The best rooms even have computer modules, some of the first in China. A shuttle is offered to the airport.

The *Yunnan Hotel* (☎ 361-3888) (*yúnnán fàndiàn*) on Dongfeng Xilu, near the Yunnan Provincial Museum and the Zhengyi Department Store, was Kunming's first tourist hotel. It recently made a break with its humble beginnings and now its cheapest rooms are Y288. But if you're going to spend this much, the old wings at the Cuihu or Kunming Hotel will probably give you more for your money.

Places to Eat

Local Cuisine There are several eating places near the Kunming and Camellia hotels on Dongfeng Donglu that have bilingual menus. The *Cooking School (xuéchú*

fàndiàn) specialises in local fish and vegetable dishes, but it must save its novice chefs for the foreigners: the place gets the thumbs down from most travellers who have eaten there. On the other hand, the *Yunnan Typical Local Food Restaurant (gēnxīng fàndiàn)* has a good range of dishes, including across-the-bridge noodles, and gets good reviews on its food from both locals and foreigners. Service is spotty.

Several small restaurants in the vicinity of Yunnan University's main gate are highly recommended, especially the popular *Tong Da Li Restaurant (tōngdálì cāntīng)*. Coming out of the Yunnan University gate, go left on the main road and then take the first left onto a small back street; Tong Da Li is the second restaurant on the right. There's a slew of little restaurants on this street, most of which have outdoor seating and are overflowing with happy diners. They're worth a try as well. This area is about a 15 minute walk north of the Green Lake Hotel.

Two of the better known places for steampot chicken are the *Chun Cheng Hotel* on Dongfeng Xilu and the *Dongfeng Hotel (dōngfēng fàndiàn)*, around the corner of Wuyi Lu and Wucheng Lu, in the direction of the Green Lake Hotel.

Several small, private restaurants on Beijing Lu opposite the long-distance bus station sell cheaper versions of steampot chicken. Steampot chicken is served in dark-brown Jianshui County casserole pots, and is imbued with medicinal properties depending on the spicing – caterpillar fungus *(chóngcǎo)* and pseudo-ginseng are two favourite local ingredients.

A good restaurant to try Kunming's famous noodle dish is the *Minsheng Restaurant (mínshēng fàndiàn)*. Prices are either Y5 or Y10, but you'll probably be pressured into the Y10 option – relax, it's worth it.

Close to the Yunnan Provincial Museum and set back from the main road a little is the *Qiaoxiangyuan Restaurant (qiáoxiāng yuán)*. The noodles here are also very good

Kunming Food

Kunming has some great food, especially in the snack line. Regional specialities are herb-infused chicken cooked in an earthenware steampot *(qìguōjī)*, Yunnan ham *(xuānwēi huǒtuǐ)*, across-the-bridge noodles *(guòqiáo mǐxiàn)*, goat's cheese *(rǔbǐng)*, and various Muslim beef and mutton dishes. Some travellers wax lyrical about toasted goat's cheese, another local speciality. It probably depends on how long you've been away from home – the cheese is actually quite bland and sticks to your teeth.

Gourmets with money to burn may perhaps be interested in a whole banquet based on Jizhong fungus (mushrooms) or 30 courses of cold mutton, not to mention fried grasshoppers or elephant trunk braised in soy sauce.

The chief breakfast in Kunming, as throughout most of Yunnan, is noodles (choice of rice or wheat), usually served in a meat broth with a chilli sauce.

Yunnan's best known dish is across-the-bridge noodles. You are provided with a bowl of very hot soup (stewed with chicken, duck and spare ribs) on which a thin layer of oil is floating, along with a side dish of raw pork slivers (in classier places this might be chicken or fish) and vegetables, and a bowl of rice noodles. Diners place all of the ingredients quickly into the soup bowl, where they are cooked by the steamy broth.

Across-the-bridge noodles is the stuff of which fairy tales are made, as the following story proves:

Once upon a time there was a scholar at the South Lake in Mengzi (southern Yunnan) who was attracted by the peace and quiet of an island there. He settled into a cottage on the island, in preparation for official examinations. His wife, meanwhile, had to cross a long wooden bridge over the lake to bring the bookworm his meals. The food was always cold in winter by the time she got to the study bower. Oversleeping one day, she made a curious discovery. She'd stewed a fat chicken and was puzzled to find the broth still hot, though it gave off no steam – the oil layer on the surface had preserved the temperature of the broth. Subsequent experiments showed that she could cook the rest of the ingredients for her husband's meal in the hot broth after she crossed the bridge.

It is possible to try across-the-bridge noodles in innumerable restaurants in Kunming. Prices generally vary from Y5 to Y15 depending on the side dishes provided. It's usually worth spending a bit more, because with only one or two condiments it lacks zest. ∎

and are similarly priced to those of the Minsheng Restaurant.

The *Yunnan Across-the-Bridge Noodles Restaurant (guòqiáo mǐxiàngguǎn)* on Nantong Jie serves huge bowls of food at rock-bottom prices. The decor is, shall we say, basic – the predominant noise is a chorus of hissing and slurping; tattered beggars circulate among the stainless-steel-topped tables, pursued by management. Never mind the beggars or the decor – the food is absolutely delicious!

A more recent phenomenon in Kunming is the discovery of ethnic cuisines. At present there are at least two Dai minority restaurants in Kunming. The food is spicy and uses sticky rice as its staple. Popular with overseas students studying in Kunming is the *Laozhiqing Restaurant (lǎozhīqīng shíguǎn)*, which used to be adjacent to the entrance to Cuihu Park (for old hands) but has relocated about 800m away, just off the corner of Wuyi Lu and Ru An Lu, next to the No 8 Middle School.

The *Bai Ta Dai Flavour Restaurant (báitǎdǎiwèi cāntīng)*, nestled down an alley near the Kunming Hotel, has tasty food, an English menu and cold draught beer. The prices are a bit high, but it's a good place to try Dai cuisine – an opportunity you won't get again unless you head down to Xishuangbanna.

Other Chinese Cuisine There is a string of eateries on Xiangyun Jie between Jinbi Lu and Nanping Lu. At the Nanping end at No 77 is the *Beijing Restaurant (běijīng fàndiàn)* with northern-style seafood, chicken and duck. Further down are lots of street vendors and small private restaurants.

Pick of the pleb restaurants is the *Shanghai Noodle Restaurant (shànghǎi miànguǎn)* at 73 Dongfeng Xilu, in a yellow-fronted building. To the left side you'll get cheap noodles; to the right are steampot chicken, cold cuts and dumplings.

Vegetarian Kunming's only real vegie option, the *Wucheng Vegetarian Restaurant (wǔchéng sùshí cān)*, in a small red wooden building at 162 Wucheng Lu, was bulldozed – along with the rest of the street – to facilitate road construction on Wucheng Lu. Hopefully, by time the time you read this it will be back in business in a new row of buildings. Until then, apart from the various temples in and around town, most of the restaurants near the Kunhu and Camellia Hotels which cater to westerners also have vegie selections. The *Chun Cheng Hotel* has a dim sum with good vegie items. West of the Yuantong Temple, a few doors down, is an amazing *vegetarian restaurant* which is open for lunch and dinner.

Snacks Kunming used to be a good place for bakeries, but many of these seem to be disappearing. Exploration of Kunming's backstreets might turn up a few lingerers, however.

In the vicinity of the long-distance bus station and in many of the side streets running off Beijing Lu are roadside noodle shops. Generally you get a bowl of rice noodles for around Y2 and a bewildering array of sauces with which to flavour the broth – most of them are hot and spicy.

Another place to go snack hunting is Huguo Lu, north of Nantaiqiao, for simmering noodle bars and a teahouse. The intersection of Changchun and Huguo yields lots of small eateries. Also try Shuncheng Jie, an east-west street running south of Dongfeng Xilu near the Chun Cheng Hotel. Here you'll find literally dozens of Muslim restaurants, dumpling shops and noodle stands.

Western Kunming hasn't as yet experienced the friendly invasion of KFC à la Chengdu – but there is a local approximation in front of the Kunming Department Store.

If your stomach is crying out for western food that tastes like the real thing, there is one option outside the Holiday Inn's tasty but expensive restaurants. Tucked away in the north-eastern Xinying Xiaoqu district is *Billy Niupai's* (☎ 331-1748) *(bǐlì niúpái)*, where you can get steaks, burgers, pasta and even tacos that should successfully satisfy a homesick appetite. Figure on around Y50 for a full western meal, much of it made with imported ingredients. The decor is strictly American cowboy, but pleasant for all that. It's probably best to take a taxi, if for no other reason than you'll definitely need the cab driver to help you find the place. The ride should cost around Y15 to Y20 from the Kunhu Hotel, less from the Camellia.

A few doors down from the Kunhu Hotel on Beijing Lu are several pleasant cafes catering to travellers and hip locals. Prices are very reasonable at the *Yuelai Cafe*, where the outside tables are almost always full, even though it's house policy to never hassle passing travellers by trying to drag them in off the street. Around the corner, *Wei's Place (hāhā cāntīng)* is a bit more like a hip western bar in atmosphere; it has books and lots of traveller information, as well as good food. Diners at the outdoor tables are also spared the traffic roar of Beijing Lu.

Near the Camellia Hotel are yet more places catering to foreigners. Tops is the always packed *Bluebird Cafe*, which is west of the Kunming Hotel. Between here and the Camellia are a handful of others, which are mostly indistinguishable.

The big hotels all sport coffee shops. For a no-holds-barred breakfast buffet, head down to the *Holiday Inn Kunming*, where you can eat as much as you can stuff in for Y70. If you're a caffeine addict you'll love their coffee deal – Y20 for as many refills as you can stomach, and the coffee is excellent. The ground-floor coffee shop in the *Golden Dragon Hotel* is not quite in the same league, but the coffee is good.

A giant block south of the Camellia Hotel is another brand-new cafe with outstanding food and a pleasant atmosphere of eclectic western music – *La Piazzetta*, located off Tuodong Lu in a small alley (look for arrows on the wall). In addition to the dense menu of believable Italian food, the wood-fired pizzas are unspeakably good, even with pizza popping up all over China now for travellers. You can also get Chinese dishes, such as good medicinal-herb chicken in a pot. Frosted mugs for beer top off the effect. There are plenty of magazines and newspapers to peruse as well. It's open from 8 am (theoretically) to midnight, but the breakfasts don't match the dinners in quality.

Entertainment

If you're not an ardent fan of karaoke bars, the nightlife options for Kunming are fairly dismal.

Wei's Place on Huancheng Nanlu attracts a fairly good crowd of both foreigners and locals in the evenings, and has a good western music selection. Not far from the Kunming Hotel, the *Golden Triangle Bar* sounds promising, but is an expensive place for a drink by Chinese standards. Up the street, the *Bluebird Cafe* has similar prices. Both spots fill up at night, mostly with local patrons.

Over at the Holiday Inn, *Charlie's* bar is frequented by Kunming's expat community, but prices are considerably higher – stick to beer, since a mixed drink will cost you around Y80.

You might be able to chase up minority dancing displays (more often held for the benefit of group tours), travelling troupes or Yunnan Opera. CITS sometimes has information on these events. The *Arts Theatre* on Dongfeng Xilu is a likely venue.

Things to Buy

You have to do a fair bit of digging to come up with inspiring purchases in Kunming. Yunnan specialities are jade, marble (from the Dali area), batik, minority embroidery (also musical instruments and dress accessories) and spotted brass utensils.

Other crafts to consider are some of the basic utilitarian items that are part of everyday Yunnanese life: the large bamboo waterpipes for smoking angel-haired Yunnan tobacco, local herbal medicines (Yunnan White Medicine *(yúnnán báiyào)* is a blend of over 100 herbs and is highly prized by Chinese throughout the world) and the *qìguō* or ceramic steampot.

Yunnanese tea is also an excellent buy and comes in several varieties, from bowl-shaped bricks of smoked green tea called *tuóchá*, which have been around since at least Marco Polo's time, to leafy black tea that rivals some of India's best.

One of the main shopping drags is Zhengyi Lu, which has the Zhengyi Department Store, the Overseas Chinese Department Store and the Kunming Department Store, but these mainly sell consumer goods. Other shopping areas are Jinbi Lu by the Zhengyi Lu intersection (lots of small speciality shops), and Dongfeng Donglu, between Zhengyi Lu and Huguo Lu (here renamed Nanping Jie).

The Flower and Bird Market *(huāniǎo shìchǎng)* is definitely worth a visit. It's tucked away on Tongdao Jie, one of numerous little streets and alleys lying between Zhengyi Lu and Wuyi Lu, just north of the Kunming Department Store. Pet supplies, fishing gear and flowers dominate the cramped rows of tiny stalls, but

YUNNAN

there is a bizarre assortment of other items such as old coins, wooden elephants, tacky wall murals and so-called 'antiques' on sale. Just walking around here is rewarding: if you actually find something you want to buy, consider it an added bonus. Animal lovers beware – you're apt to see lots you don't like.

The Yunnan Antique Store *(yúnnán wénwù shāngdiàn)*, on Qingnian Lu, has some pottery, porcelain and handicrafts, but it's pretty dull. Better to look among the privately run shops on Beijing Lu and Dongfeng Donglu. Outside the Kunming Hotel you will probably be ambushed by minority women flogging their handiwork – bargain if you want a sane price. Both the Green Lake and Kunming hotels sell batik which you can also find in Dali. Delve into the smaller shops around Jinbi Lu if you're into embroidery. For Yunnan herbal medicines, check the large pharmacy on Zhengyi Lu (on the east side, several blocks up from the Kunming Department Store). There is also a few herbal medicine shops at the southern end of Beijing Lu.

Kunming is a fairly good place to stock up on film, and one of the few places in Yunnan where slide film is available. Fuji and other brands are on sale.

Getting There & Away

Air CAAC (☎ 558-1466, 312-1223) also had its building bulldozed to allow another skyscraper to go up. Relocating one block south, to Tuodong Lu, it shares office space with Yunnan Airlines (☎ 316-4270, 312-1223). It's open from 8.30 am to 7.30 pm. Plans are to have another office in the Holiday Inn.

China Southern Airlines (☎ 317-4682) has its main office on the other side of the Kunming Hotel, as well as a number of branches around the city. The main branch is open from 8.30 am to 8 pm.

For internal flights, other alternatives include Shanghai Airlines (☎ 316-3687), on Dongfeng Donglu, Kunming United Airlines (☎ 316-4590) on Dongfeng Xilu, and China Southwest Airlines (☎ 317-

9696) at 36 Beijing Lu and another ticket office (☎ 317-8491) north of the Camellia Hotel at 504 Beijing Lu, both open from 8 am to 7 pm.

Kunming is well connected by air to the rest of China, and most flights (even within Yunnan) are on Boeing 737 and 757 jets. The most popular destinations include: Beijing (Y2050), Chengdu (Y700), Chongqing (Y640), Guangzhou (Y1300), Guiyang (Y470), Shantou (Y1410), Guilin (Y830), Haikou (Y990), Lanzhou (1600), Nanjing (Y1710), Nanning (Y660), Qingdao (2140), Shanghai (Y1860), Shenzhen (Y1400), Xiamen (Y1540), Xi'an (Y1150) and Wuhan (Y1270).

Within the province you can reach Baoshan (Y400), Jinghong (Y520), Lijiang (Y390), Mangshi (Dehong) (Y530), Xiaguan (Dali) (Y320) and Zhaotong (Y400).

CAAC and several foreign carriers have flights to Hong Kong (Y1710, daily), and to international destinations such as Bangkok (Y1540, daily), Yangon (Rangoon) (Y2800, weekly), Vientiane (Y1290, twice weekly), Singapore (Y2150, twice weekly), Kuala Lumpur (Y1900, twice weekly).

Bus The bus situation in Kunming can be a little confusing at first. There seem to be buses leaving from all over the place. However, the long-distance bus station on Beijing Lu is the main centre of operations, and this is the best place to organise bus tickets to almost anywhere in Yunnan or further afield. Exceptions to this are more local destinations like Lake Dian.

The most popular bus routes from Kunming are Dali, Lijiang, Jinghong (in the Xishuangbanna Prefecture in the south) and the Dehong Prefecture (in the west). The long distances involved make sleeper buses a popular option. These have double-tiered bunks. If you are looking at an overnight trip, they are definitely worth the extra cost. Very few travellers go straight from Kunming to Lijiang; it makes better sense to take a sleeper bus to Dali first and then move on to Lijiang.

Day buses from the bus station direct to

Dali leave five times between 7 and 10.20 am and cost around Y55. The trip takes around 11 hours. Most travellers opt for the sleepers, which generally leave from 6 to 8 pm and cost from Y85 to Y95. Buses leave from the station or from a number of spots on Beijing Lu. It is patently unnecessary to go to any of the ticket 'offices' near the Camellia Hotel. If your bus terminates in Xiaguan (although the signs say Dali), which isn't uncommon, it is 30 minutes by public bus from Dali. So make sure where *exactly* your bus will end up before you get on. There are numerous day buses between 7 am and 8.20 pm, costing Y41; night buses to Xiaguan leave from 7 pm, and prices are Y91 for a sleeper.

For those who absolutely cannot sleep on sleeper buses, there is a great new alternative. Just east of the Camellia Hotel on the opposite side of the road, the Yunnan Tourist Transport Company has super-luxury day buses, with reclining seats, leaving at 8 am; for Y90 you get a reliable, bump-free, eight hour ride through great scenery, a decent lunch midway, the occasional English movie, and even a bottle of mineral water and other souvenirs. This bus does not go to the old city, but lets you out at the Cangshan Hotel in Xiaguan. You need to exit the hotel's main gate, turn right and walk to the first intersection. Cross the street and wait for either the No 4 local bus (Y0.7) or a minibus (Y5).

For the 15 hour Lijiang trip, buses leave at 5.20 and 6.20 pm and cost Y101 to Y112 for the sleepers.

With road and vehicle improvements, the marathon trip to Jinghong in Xishuangbanna now takes only 18 to 22 hours, depending on the length of the numerous meal breaks and various unscheduled but inevitable stops. The trip used to include an overnight stop, but now nearly all buses drive straight through. Sleepers to Jinghong cost Y161 and leave at 2, 6 and 6.40 pm. Buses leave at 11 am and 4 pm and cost around Y150. For those on a real budget, cheaper day/night regular buses are waning and may be finished altogether by

the time you read this, but if you get one, they usually leave up until 8 am and cost around Y90 to Y100. This is for serious riders only.

Both options for getting to the Dehong region involve long hauls, so it's worth considering doing at least one leg of the trip by air (to Mangshi). Sleeper buses leave for Baoshan from the long-distance bus station four times a day between 4.30 and 6.20 pm and cost Y114. The journey takes around 15 to 18 bumpy hours. Buses – all sleepers – direct to Ruili take even longer (22 to 26 hours). They leave six times daily between 9.20 am and 7.40 pm and cost Y171. To Manshi there is a direct sleeper at 1 pm, which costs Y150. To Ninglang there is a bus at 11.40 am costing Y101.

If you're headed to Vietnam, there are night sleeper buses to the Chinese border town of Hekou, leaving at 6.40 and 8 pm. The trip takes 14 hours and costs Y86 to Y90. A rattletrap day bus leaves at 8 am and costs Y55. Travellers looking to go overland to Laos have to go to Jinghong first, from where there are buses to Mengla, near the border crossing. You'll also need a visa; see the Consulates section under Information for Kunming earlier in this chapter.

It is possible to travel by bus to several destinations in neighbouring provinces from the long-distance bus station, including Guiyang (Guizhou) and Nanning (Guangxi).

Finally, the long-distance station also has buses to the Stone Forest, with round-trip tickets costing Y37. For more information see the Stone Forest section later in this chapter.

Train Rail options out of Kunming include Beijing, Chengdu, Chongqing, Guangzhou, Shanghai and basically all points between. You can also take a train down the narrow-gauge railway to the border crossing with Vietnam at Hekou. A new rail link with Nanning has technically been completed, although direct service is not expected to start for several years yet. This should dramatically cut down travelling time between

Yunnan and the provinces of Guangxi and Guangdong. Services should be established to Xiaguan (Dali) before the turn of the millennium.

The No 12 window at the main railway station is the place to buy both sleeper and hard-seat tickets. There is a booking office at 142 Xichang Lu (open from 8 to 11.30 am and 1.30 to 5 pm), but it only sells hard-seat tickets. The main station sells both hard-sleeper and hard-seat tickets from 8.30 am, up to three days in advance. In peak season you may need to book this far ahead. The railway station ticket office is open from 6.30 am to 11.10 pm.

There are also trains to Shanghai (via Guiyang, Zhuzhou, Nanchang and Hangzhou), Beijing (via Guiyang, Changsha and Zhengzhou), Chongqing (via Guiyang), Guangzhou (via Guilin), Emei, Chengdu and Hekou.

Getting Around

Most of the major sights are within a 15km radius of Kunming. Local transport to these places is awkward, crowded and time-consuming; it tends to be an out-and-back job, with few crossovers for combined touring. If you wish to take in everything, you'd be looking at something like five return trips, which would consume three days or more.

You can simplify this by pushing Black Dragon Pool, Anning Hot Springs and the Golden Temple to the background, and concentrating on the trips of high interest – the Bamboo Temple and Western Hills, both of which have decent transport connections with special express buses in the mornings. Lake Dian presents some engrossing circular-tour possibilities on its own. Better still, buy a map, hire a good bicycle and tour the area on two wheels (although there are some steep hills lurking out there ...).

To/From the Airport A super efficient shuttle departs to and from Kunming airport and the CAAC/Yunnan Airlines office. Service is supposed to be from 6 am to 8 pm,

but these aren't to be taken too seriously. Buses run from the airport when full, and pretty much every 15 minutes to CAAC.

Alternatively, you can exit the airport, walk past the taxis, a traffic roundabout and a hotel to the main road. Bus No 52 runs along this road, terminating near the airport entrance.

Bus The best option for getting out to the Bamboo Temple and the Western Hills is to head over to the Yunnan Hotel – buses and minibuses leave from in front of the hotel in the morning. Departure times depend on how fast the bus fills up: afternoon buses can sit around for hours.

Public buses run out to most of the other major sights. Options include: No 10 to the Golden Temple and the No 9 to Black Dragon Pool, both from the North railway station; the No 44 from Kunming railway station to Haigeng Park; and the No 4 from the zoo to Daguan Park.

Bicycle Bikes are a fast way to get around town. The Camellia Hotel carries a decent selection (and requires large deposits of between Y200 and Y400!) The Kunhu also has a few bikes for rent, although they've seen better days.

AROUND KUNMING
Golden Temple
(jīndiàn)
This Taoist temple is perched amid a pine forest on Phoenix Song Mountain, 11km north-east of Kunming. The original was carted off to Dali; the present one dates from the Ming Dynasty and was enlarged by General Wu Sangui, who was dispatched by the Manchus in 1659 to quell the uprisings in the region. Wu Sangui turned against the Manchus and set himself up as a rebel warlord, with the Golden Temple as his summer residence.

The pillars, ornate door frames, walls, fittings and roof tiles of the 6m-high temple are all made of copper; the entire structure, laid on a white Dali marble foundation, is estimated to weigh more than 300 tonnes.

YUNNAN

In the courtyard are ancient camellia trees. At the back is a 14 tonne bronze bell, cast in 1423. The gardens around the temple offer secluded areas for picnicking. In the compound are teahouses and a noodle stand.

To get there, take bus No 10 from Kunming's North railway station. Many travellers ride hired bikes to the temple – it's fairly level-going all the way to the base of the hill. Once you get there, you'll have to climb an easy hill path to the temple compound. You may or may not think the Y20 entrance fee (just the beginning of these) is worth it.

Black Dragon Pool
(hēilóng tán)
Eleven kilometres north of Kunming is this uninspiring garden, with old cypresses, dull Taoist pavilions and no bubble in the springs. But the view of the surrounding mountains from the garden is inspiring. Within walking distance is the **Kunming Botanical Institute**, where the collection of flora might be of interest to specialists. Take the No 9 bus here from the North railway station.

Bamboo Temple
(qióngzhú sì)
Twelve kilometres north-west of Kunming, this temple dates back to the Tang Dynasty. Burned down and rebuilt in the 15th century, it was restored from 1883 to 1890 when the abbot employed master Sichuan sculptor Li Guangxiu and his apprentices to fashion 500 luohan (arhats or noble ones). These life-size clay figures are stunning – either very realistic or very surrealistic – a sculptural tour de force.

Down one huge wall come the incredible surfing buddhas, some 70-odd, riding the waves on a variety of mounts – blue dogs, giant crabs, shrimp, turtles, unicorns. One gentleman has metre-long eyebrows, and another has an arm that shoots clear across the hall to the ceiling.

In the main section are housed row upon row of standing figures. The statues have

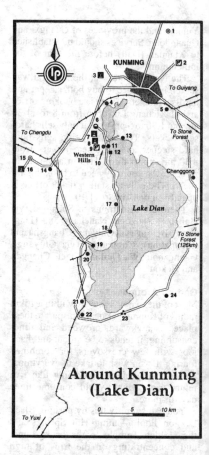

Around Kunming (Lake Dian)

been done with the precision of a split-second photograph – a monk about to chomp into a large peach (the face contorted almost into a scream), a figure caught turning around to emphasise a discussion point, another about to clap two cymbals together, yet another cursing a pet monster. The old, the sick, the emaciated – nothing is spared; the expressions of joy, anger, grief or boredom are extremely vivid.

So lifelike are the sculptures that they were considered in bad taste by Li Guangxiu's contemporaries (some of whom no

---

AROUND KUNMING (LAKE DIAN)

昆明地区（滇池）

1 Black Dragon Pool
黑龙潭
2 Golden Temple
金殿
3 Bamboo Temple
筇竹寺
4 Daguan Park
大观公园
5 Guandu
官渡区
6 Gaoyao Bus Station
高峣汽车站
7 Huating Temple
华亭寺

8 Taihua Temple
太华寺
9 Sanqing Temple
三清阁
10 Dragon Gate
龙门
11 Dragon Gate Village
(Shanyi Village)
龙门村（三邑村）
12 Xiyuan Hotel
西园宾馆
13 Haigeng Park
海埂公园
14 Anning
安宁县
15 Anning Hot Springs
安宁温泉

16 Caoxi Temple
曹溪寺
17 Guanyinshan
观音山
18 Baiyukou
白鱼口
19 Haikou
海口
20 Gucheng
古城
21 Jinning
晋宁
22 Zheng He Park
郑和公园
23 Stone Village Hill
石村
24 Jincheng
晋城镇

---

doubt appeared in caricature), and upon the project's completion he disappeared into thin air. As for the bamboo of the temple's name, there was actually none on the grounds until very recently, when bamboo was transplanted from Chengdu. The main halls were restored in 1958 and again, extensively, in 1981.

By far the easiest way to get there is to take a bus from in front of the Yunnan Hotel. Buses run from 7.30 am to around 4.30 pm (although the last often goes at around 1 pm) leaving as soon as they are full. The ride takes 30 minutes and costs around Y5. Once there, the admission is Y10 and the temple is generally considered to be worth it.

Anning Hot Springs
(ānníng wēnquán)

Most travellers sensibly give this place, 44km south-west of Kunming, a wide berth. The local tourist authorities proclaim (in their Chinese-language promotional material) the hot spring as 'No 1 under the heavens', but the hot springs and the surrounding area (which includes some Miao minority villages) sadly are not particularly interesting.

There are various hotels and guesthouses here that pipe the hot spring water into the rooms, but reports have it that couples are not accepted in some of them – this rule may have changed.

Nearby, and possibly worth a look, is the **Caoxi Monastery**. It's over the river and a couple of kilometres or so to the south in a bamboo grove on Cong Hill.

Buses to the springs run approximately hourly from the Xiaoximen bus station between 8 am and 6 pm. Returning, the last bus is at 5 pm. There is another bus station west of Xiaoximen which may also have buses. While road construction is ongoing in front of Xiaoximen bus station, large buses also sit in the Xichang Lu intersection a block west of Xiaoximen, waiting for passengers to the springs.

Lake Dian
(diān chí)

The shoreline of Lake Dian, to the south of Kunming, is dotted with settlements, farms and fishing enterprises; the western side is hilly, while the eastern side is flat country. The southern end of the lake, particularly the south-east, is industrial, but other than that there are lots of possibilities for extended touring.

The lake is an elongated one – about 150km in circumference, about 40km from north to south, and covering 300 square kilometres. Plying the waters are *fanchuan*, pirate-sized junks with bamboo-battened canvas sails. It's mainly an area for scenic touring and hiking, and there are some fabulous aerial views from the ridges up at Dragon Gate in the Western Hills.

Daguan Park
(dàguān gōngyuán)

Daguan (or Grand View) Park is at the northernmost tip of Lake Dian, 3km southwest of the city centre. It dates back to 1682, when a Buddhist temple was constructed there. Shortly after, in 1690, work began on the park and the Daguan Tower. It covers 60 hectares and includes a nursery with potted plants, children's playground, rowing boats and pavilions. The **Daguan Tower** *(dàguān lóu)* provides good views of Lake Dian. Its facades are inscribed with a 180-character poem by Qing poet Sun Ranweng rapturously extolling the beauty of the lake. Bus No 4 runs to Daguan Park from Yuantong Temple via the city centre area.

At the north-eastern end of the park is a dock where you can get boats to Dragon Gate Village and Haigeng Park. Boats leave when full and the 40 minute ride should cost Y5. From Dragon Gate Village you can hike up the trail to Dragon Gate and the Western Hills, and then catch a minibus back into town near the summit at the Tomb of Nie Er. From Haigeng, take the No 44 bus to Kunming's main railway station.

Western Hills
(xī shān)

The Western Hills spread out across a long wedge of parkland on the western side of Lake Dian; they're also known as the 'Sleeping Beauty Hills', a reference to their undulating contours, which are thought to resemble a reclining woman with tresses of hair flowing into the sea. The path up to the summit passes a series of famous temples – it's a steep approach from the north side. The hike from Gaoyao bus station at the foot of the Western Hills to Dragon Gate takes 2½ hours. If you're pushed for time, there's a connecting bus from Gaoyao to the top section, or you could take a minibus direct from in front of the Yunnan Hotel to Dragon Gate. Alternatively, it is also possible to cycle to the Western Hills in about an hour – to vary the trip, consider doing the return route across the dikes of upper Lake Dian.

At the foot of the climb, about 15km from Kunming, is **Huating Temple** *(huátíng sì)*, a country temple of the Nanzhao kingdom believed to have been constructed in the 11th century, rebuilt in the 14th century, and extended in the Ming and Qing dynasties. The temple has some fine statues and excellent gardens. There is a Y10 entry fee.

The road from the Huating Temple winds from here up to the Ming Dynasty **Taihua Temple** *(tàihuá sì)*, housing a fine collection of flowering trees in the courtyards, including magnolias and camellias. Entry here costs Y8.

Between the Taihua Temple and Sanqing Taoist Temple near the summit is the **Tomb of Nie Er** (1912-36) *(nièěr zhīmù)*, who was a talented Yunnan musician. Nie composed the national anthem of the PRC before drowning in Japan en route for further training in the Soviet Union. From here you can catch a chairlift to the top (Y20), if you want to skip the fairly steep ascent to the summit. If you decide to visit the restaurant at the top, watch that you are not overcharged.

The **Sanqing Temple** *(sānqīng gé)* near the top of the mountain was a country villa for a prince of the Yuan Dynasty, and was later turned into a temple dedicated to the three main Taoist deities.

Further up is **Dragon Gate** *(lóngmén)*, a group of grottoes, sculptures, corridors and pavilions hacked from the cliff between 1781 and 1835 by a Taoist monk and co-workers, who must have been hanging up there by their fingertips. At least that's what the locals do when they visit, seeking out the most precarious perches for views of Lake Dian. The tunnelling along the outer cliff edge is so narrow that only one or two people can squeeze by at a time, so avoid public holidays and weekends! Entry to the Dragon Gate area (which includes Sanqing Temple) costs Y20.

From Kunming to the Western Hills the most convenient mode of transport is minibus. These leave from outside the Yunnan Hotel between 7.30 am and 1 pm – although they're posted as running until 4.30 pm – leaving as they fill up. The 30 minute ride costs around Y4.

Alternatively, you can use the local bus service to get there: take bus No 5 from the Kunming Hotel to the terminus at Liang-jiahe, and then change to bus No 6, which will take you to Gaoyao bus station at the foot of the hills. Buses to the Kunming Steel Plant *(kūngāng)* also run past Gao-yao, and leave from in front of the Arts Cinema (near the Yunnan Hotel), or from Xiaoximen bus station.

From the Western Hills to Kunming you can either take the bus or scramble down from the Dragon Gate area directly to the lakeside along a zigzag dirt path and steps that lead to Dragon Gate Village, also known as Shan Yi Village *(shānyìcūn)*. When you reach the road, turn right and walk about 100m to a narrow spit of land which leads across the lake. Continuing across the land spit, you arrive at a narrow stretch of water and a small bridge. The opposite bank is one giant construction zone and will eventually be the base for a cable car being built to link Haigeng with Dragon Gate. Proceed by foot through this area along the lakeside road that runs back to Haigeng Park, where you can catch the No 44 bus to Kunming railway station.

The tour can easily be done in reverse; start with the No 44 bus to Haigeng Park, walk to Dragon Gate Village, climb straight up to Dragon Gate, then make your way down through the temples to Gaoyao bus station, where you can get bus No 6 back to Xiaoximen bus station. Alterna-tively, bus No 33 runs along the coast through Dragon Gate Village, or you can take a boat from Daguan Park.

Haigeng Park & Yunnan Nationalities Village
(hǎigěng gōngyuán/yúnnán mínzúcūn)
On the north-eastern side of the lake, the local tourist authorities have thrown to-gether a string of model minority villages with the aim of finally representing all 26 of Yunnan's minorities.

It's a rather expensive cultural experi-ence for the visitor, with a Y20 general entry fee and Y10 per village. There are also various song-and-dance performances throughout the day, some of which also cost extra. As for the villages, while they show you what the minorities' architecture and costumes look like, it's impossible to get any feel for how these people really live. Add in the hordes of gawking tourists, and the place feels a bit like a zoo. If you're at all averse to tourist-board fabrications of ethnic cultures, give the place a miss and spend an extra day in Xishuangbanna or Dehong, where you can see the real thing. However, with the advent of the Na-tionalities Village, what little remains of Haigeng Park – a narrow strip of greenery along the lakefront – has become a good place to escape the crowds and enjoy the scenery. The roller coaster is covered with weeds, and most of the lakefront restau-rants are shuttered, giving the place a ghost town feel. There are great views of the lake and the Western Hills, and plenty of spots to kick back, read a book or have a picnic. And when you're ready, you can tackle the hike up to Dragon Gate.

Bus No 44 runs to Haigeng Lu from one street north of the Kunming railway station.

Zheng He Park
(zhènghé gōngyuán)
At the south-west corner of the lake, this park commemorates the Ming Dynasty navigator Zheng He (known as Admiral Cheng Ho throughout most of the world). A mausoleum here holds tablets describing his life and works. Zheng He, a Muslim, made seven voyages to more than 30 Asian and African countries in the 15th century in command of a huge imperial fleet.

From Xiaoximen bus station take the bus to Kunyang: the park is on a hill overlooking the town. Or for a change of pace, take a train from North railway station to Haikou, and then a local bus to Kunyang. You can complete a full circuit by catching a bus on to Jincheng and Chenggong. There's also accommodation in Kunyang for around Y20 per bed if you feel like moving at a more relaxed pace.

Jinning County
(jìnníng xiàn)
This is the site of archaeological discoveries from early Kunming, and you'll find it at the southern end of the lake. Bronze vessels, a gold seal and other artefacts were unearthed at **Stone Village Hill**, and some items are displayed at the Provincial Museum in Kunming.

The bus to Kunyang runs via Jincheng to Jinning.

Chenggong County
(chénggòng xiàn)
This is an orchard region on the eastern side of the lake. Its climate has a lot to do with Kunming's reputation as the florist of China. Flowers bloom all year round, with the 'flower tide' in January, February and March. This is the best time to visit.

Camellias, azaleas, orchids and magnolias are not usually associated with China by westerners, although many western varieties derive from south-west Chinese varieties. They were introduced to the west by adventuring botanists who carted off samples in the 19th and 20th centuries. Azaleas are native to China – of the 800 varieties in the world, 650 are found in Yunnan.

During the Spring Festival (February/March) a profusion of blooming species can be found at temple sites around Kunming – notably the Taihua, Huating and Golden temples, as well as Black Dragon Pool and Yuantong Hill.

Take the No 5 bus east to the terminus at Juhuacun, and change there for the No 12 bus to Chenggong.

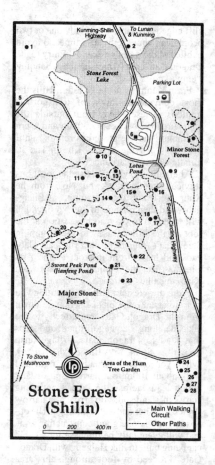

Stone Forest (Shilin)

STONE FOREST
(shílín)
The Stone Forest, around 120km south-east of Kunming, is a massive collection of grey limestone pillars, split by rain water and eroded to their present fanciful forms, the tallest standing 30m high. Marine fossils found in the area suggest that it was once under the sea. Legend has it that the immortals smashed a mountain into a labyrinth for lovers seeking some privacy – picnicking Chinese couples take heed of this myth (it can get busy in there!).

STONE FOREST (SHILIN)
石林

1 Five-Tree Village
   五木村
2 Truck Stop
   卡车
3 Bus Departures
   汽车站
4 Local Handicraft
   Stalls
   工艺摊
5 Yunlin Hotel
   云林宾馆
6 Shilin Hotel; CITS
   石林宾馆
   中国国际旅行社
7 Inscription of Mao
   Zedong's poem
   'Ode to the Plum Blossom'
   咏梅石
8 Rock Arrowhead Point
   to the Sky
   石簇擎天

9 Figure of Monk
   Tanseng
   唐僧石
10 Lion Pond
   狮子池
11 Sweet Water Well
   甜水井
12 Stone Buffalo
   小水牛
13 Stone Screen
   石屏风
14 Open Stage
   舞场
15 Resting Peak for Wild
   Geese
   落雁峰
16 Stone Prison
   石监狱
17 Phoenix Combing its
   Wings
   凤凰梳翅
18 Stone Mushroom
   灵芝石

19 Steps to the Sky
   竿天阶
20 Lotus Peak
   莲花峰
21 Two Birds Feeding Each
   Other
   双鸟渡食
22 Stone Bell
   石钟
23 Rhinoceros Looking
   at the Moon
   犀牛望月
24 Wife Waiting for Her
   Husband
   望夫石
25 Goddess of Mercy
   观音石
26 Camel Riding on an
   Elephant
   骆驼骑象
27 Swan Gazing Afar
   天鹅远嘱
28 Old Man Taking a Stroll
   漫步从容

YUNNAN

The maze of grey pinnacles and peaks, with the odd pool, is treated as an oversized rockery, with a walkway here, a pavilion there, some railings along paths and, if you look more closely, some mind-bending weeds. The larger formations have titles like Baby Elephant, Everlasting Fungus, Baby Buffalo, Moon-Gazing Rhino and Sword Pond. The maze is cooler and quieter by moonlight, and would enthral a surrealist painter.

There are actually several stone forests in the region – the section open to foreign tourists covers 80 hectares. Twelve kilometres to the north-east is a larger (300 hectare) rock series called Fungi Forest, with karst caves and a large waterfall.

The Stone Forest is basically a Chinese tourist attraction and some westerners find it grossly overrated on the scale of geographical wonders. The important thing, if you venture there, is to get away from the main tourist area – within a couple of kilometres of the centre you will find some idyllic, secluded walks.

The villages in the Lunan County vicinity are inhabited by the Sani branch of the Yi tribespeople. Considering that so many other 'ethnic' areas of Yunnan are now open, you could be disappointed if you make the trip just to see the tribespeople who live in this area. Their craftwork (embroidery, purses, footwear) is sold at stalls by the entrance to the forest, and Sani women act as tour guides for groups.

Off to the side is Five-Tree Village, which is an easy walk and has the flavour of a Mexican pueblo, but the tribespeople have been somewhat influenced by commercialism.

For those keen on genuine village and farming life, well, the Stone Forest is a big place – you can easily get lost. Just take your butterfly net and a lunch box along and keep walking – you'll get somewhere eventually.

There is a Y30 entry fee for foreigners into the main Stone Forest.

Activities
The Shilin and Yunlin hotels put on Sani song-and-dance evenings when there are

enough tourists around. Surprisingly, these events generally turn into good-natured exchanges between Homo Ektachromo and Sani Dollari, and neither seems to come off the worse for wear. The short performances display ethnic costumes and musical instruments. The hotels usually charge a fee of around Y25 for the performances, which start around 7.30 to 8 pm.

The Torch Festival (wrestling, bullfighting, singing and dancing) takes place on 24 June at a natural outdoor amphitheatre by Hidden Lake.

Places to Stay

The *Shilin Hotel* (☎ 771-1405) *(shílín bīnguǎn)*, near the main entrance to the Stone Forest, is a villa-type place with a souvenir shop and dining hall. A double room costs Y250 (Y200 in the off season, whenever that is), and triples are Y300. Before you despair, wait: there's a 'Common Room Department' *(pǔtōng kèfáng)* at the rear section of the hotel compound, with dormitory accommodation for Y30 per bed. It's on the other side of the hill, across from a restaurant and a couple of souvenir shops.

Rates are a bit cheaper at the *Yunlin Hotel (yúnlín fàndiàn)*, which is a little less than a kilometre down the road that forks to the right after you cross the bridge. In addition to Y150 doubles and Y200 triples, the Yunlin has one concrete cell with four soft beds for Y80.

Near the bus terminal are several smaller hotels with basic rooms for Y20 to Y30 per person: these have similar bathing facilities to the dorm rooms at the Shilin and Yunlin, but are not as clean. They may or may not accept foreign guests.

Places to Eat

Several restaurants next to the bus terminal specialise in duck roasted in extremely hot clay ovens with pine needles. A whole duck costs Y40 to Y50 and takes about 20 minutes to cook – have the restaurant staff put a beer in their freezer and it'll be just right when the duck comes out. Near the

main Stone Forest entrance is a cluster of food vendors that purvey a variety of pastries and noodles from dawn to dusk. The *Shilin Hotel* and *Yunlin Hotel* offer fixed-price meals that aren't bad. Western breakfasts are available at both hotels.

Getting There & Away

There are a variety of options for getting to the Stone Forest. Your fastest option might be a minibus from the Camellia Hotel in Kunming: one group of travellers made it there nonstop in two hair-raising hours. In most cases the trip takes around three hours one way – it's much longer going there if you sign on with a tour bus. If you are feeling adventurous, you could a try a bus/train/hitchhiking combination.

It's best to take an overnight stop in the forest for further exploration, although if you're just looking at the forest itself then a day trip will do.

Bus Head down to the long-distance bus station in Kunming and buy a one way ticket for Y18.50. There are buses leaving at 7.30 and 8.40 am.

The Kunming Hotel and Three Leaves Hotel – and others – sell tickets for tour buses to Shilin for Y20 (Y10 in low periods), but if you take this option you'll be stuck with a tour that takes in at least three caves en route (complete with special foreigner entry fees); once you've pigged out on the obligatory lunch, you'll be lucky to have had two hours wandering around the forest. It's much better to buy the tickets at the long-distance bus station and leave yourself the option of staying over-night or returning the same day, as you please. The street adjacent to the King World (Jinhua) Hotel is lined with Shilin tour buses. They will swear on their ancestors' graves that they don't stop at any caves. Take these claims with large grains of salt. These buses also cost Y20 one way, although they may be flexible in low tourist periods.

The Camellia Hotel runs a minibus that goes straight to the Stone Forest. The bus leaves at 8 am and costs Y40 for a return trip, but the catch is that there must be at least six people, or you pay Y240 regardless of the number. Although you escape the caves, there is a stop at an awful jade market along the way, ostensibly for you to use the bathroom.

Getting back from the Stone Forest to Kunming is fairly simple. There are usually minibuses waiting along the road outside the entrance, and once they're full, they tend to go straight back to Kunming. There are also local buses leaving at 7 am and between 2.30 and 3.30 pm, but these can be cancelled if they don't look like filling up. You could also try hitching back to Kunming from the Stone Forest.

Bus & Train The old French narrow-gauge line that runs all the way from Kunming to Hanoi (Chinese trains now terminate at Hekou near the Vietnamese border) is an interesting alternative way of getting to Shilin. Trains bound for Kaiyuan stop at the town of Yiliang, which is only 45 minutes by bus from Shilin. Stations along the way sport steep roofs and painted shutters in the French style. Unfortunately, no trains are all that convenient. Trains to Hekou get you in around 5 pm; the other alternative, the Kaiyuan train, gets you to Yiliang at midnight. Buses from Yiliang are infrequent (be prepared for a wait of a couple of hours), and often only go as far as Lunan, from where you will have to hitch to Shilin.

LUNAN
(lùnán)

Lunan is a small market town about 10km from the Stone Forest. It's not really worth making a special effort to visit, but if you do go, try and catch a market day (Wednesday or Saturday), when Lunan becomes a colossal jam of donkeys, horse carts and bikes. The streets are packed with produce, poultry and wares, and the Sani women are dressed in their finest.

To get to Lunan from the Stone Forest, head back towards Kunming and turn left at the first major crossroads. Go straight on at the second crossroads, but veering to the right. You'll have to hitch a truck or hire a three wheeler (Y5 to Y10 or some foreign cigarettes for a 20 minute ride). Plenty of trucks head that way on market day, some from the parking lot near the forest.

XIAGUAN
(xiàguān)

Xiaguan lies at the southern tip of Erhai Lake, about 400km west of Kunming. It was once an important staging post on the Burma Road and is still a key centre for transport in north-west Yunnan. Xiaguan is the capital of Dali Prefecture and is also referred to as Dali City *(dàlǐ shì)*. This confuses some travellers, who think they are already in Dali, book into a hotel and head off in pursuit of a banana pancake only to discover they haven't arrived yet. (See the Dali & Erhai Lake Region map later in this chapter.) Nobody stays in Xiaguan unless they have an early bus the next morning.

Upon arriving, turn left out of the long-distance bus station, and at the first intersection make a left. Just up from the corner, diagonally opposite the Dali Hotel, is the station for the No 4 local bus, which runs to the real Dali. Ignore the big sign telling you to wait at the street corner, and walk up to where the buses are. If you want to be sure, ask for *dàlǐ gǔchéng* (Dali Old City). The trip takes 30 minutes and costs Y1.20.

Things to See

Xiaguan has developed into an industrial city specialising in tea processing, cigarette making and the production of textiles and chemicals. There is little to keep you here other than transport connections.

There are good views of the lake and mountains from **Erhai Park** *(ěrhǎi gōng-yuán)*. You can reach the park on foot or by motor-tricycle for around Y3.

Local travel agents around the bus station also sell tickets for day trips up and down Erhai Lake, taking in all the major sights. Prices for the all-day tours range from Y60 to Y80.

Places to Stay
Some travellers end up staying a night in
Xiaguan in order to catch an early-morning
bus from the long-distance bus station. If
this is the case, there are two hotels close
to the bus station, all much the same. Forget
the *Dali Hotel*, near the No 4 bus stop,
which has transformed itself into a three
star monster for outlandish prices. A host
of cheap *zhāodàisuǒs* (guesthouses) surround the bus station which may or may
not accept foreigners.

Right next to the bus station is the *Keyun
Hotel* (☎ 212-5286) *(kèyùn fàndiàn)*. It has
five-bed rooms for Y40, four-bed dorms for
Y52, triples for Y54 and doubles for Y50.
Singles cost Y50. More upmarket singles/
doubles with attached bathroom are available at Y90 and above. These are Chinese
prices which you may or may not get. Some
staff seem amenable to it, others don't.

Almost directly opposite is the *Xiaguan
Hotel* (☎ 212-5579) *(xiàguān bīnguǎn)*, the
most upmarket of the cheap hotels. Basic
triples are available for Y72 per bed and
doubles with bathroom are Y198. These
rooms are all right for the price.

Those seeking luxury need go no further
than across the street and to the right of
the bus station to the *Jinpeng Hotel* (☎ 217-
4933; fax 216-8889) *(jīnpéng dàjiǔdiàn)*,
which offers air-con doubles with direct
dial telephone and satellite TV for Y190,
and triples for Y198. There are plenty of
other upmarket hotels in the vicinity.

Getting There & Away
Air Xiaguan's new airport is 15km from
town. Flights leave daily – some days there
are frequent flights – and the one way fare
from Kunming is Y320. A railway link
with Kunming is also under construction.
Xiaguan should fare well, but it remains
to be seen how the small town of Dali will
cope with the ensuing deluge of visitors.

Bus Xiaguan has two bus stations, which
also throws some travellers. Luckily, they
are both on the same street, and on the same
side of the street, approximately two blocks

apart. You might get dropped off at either
one; the key in any event is to walk *left* after
exiting onto the street. The main bus station
is the one closer to the Dali Hotel on the
corner to the left. Both have departures
throughout the province, so if the main
station doesn't have a good departure time
for you, wander over to the other one.

Unless you're making for one of the
typical traveller's destinations (ie Kunming
or Lijiang), you'll probably have to head
into the Xiaguan long-distance bus station
to organise your onward transport; you can
buy just about any ticket in Dali, but you
have to catch the bus for many destinations
in Xiaguan.

Other bus options include Baoshan for
Y26, Mangshi (Luxi) for Y50, Lijiang for
Y20 and Zhongdian for Y32.

There's also a new sleeper bus direct –
more or less – to Chengdu, leaving at 6 pm
daily and taking two nights and one day;
this fun for Y210. Once the railway line is
completed, this will probably stop running.

For the interesting possibility of buses
from Xiaguan to Xishuangbanna, you can
try getting a 6.10 am bus via Jingdong,
which should put you into Jinghong the following night for a total of some 32 hours.
Roads are very bad along this route, and
travel times have been known to stretch to
three or four days. A sleeper should cost
around Y145.

For Mt Jizu, buses run from the *other*
bus station to Binchuan around 8 am, take
around two hours and cost Y10.

AROUND XIAGUAN
All of Dali Prefecture is open nowadays, so
you shouldn't have any problems with
PSB officials if you wander off the beaten
track. The chief attraction for travellers is
Jizushan, an ancient Buddhist pilgrimage
site.

Jizushan
(jīzú shān)
Jizushan (or to translate its Chinese name,
Chicken-Foot Mountain) is a major attraction for Buddhist pilgrims – both Chinese

and Tibetan. At the time of the Qing Dynasty there were approximately 100 temples on the mountain and somewhere in the vicinity of 5000 resident monks. The Cultural Revolution's anarchic assault on the traditional past did away with much that was of interest on the mountain, although renovation work on the temples has been going on since 1979.

Today, it is estimated that more than 150,000 tourists and pilgrims clamber up the mountain every year to watch the sun rise. Jinding, or the Golden Summit, is at a cool 3240m so you will need some warm clothing.

Sights along the way include the **Zhusheng Temple** *(zhùshèng sì)*, about an hour's walk up from the bus stop at Shazhi. This is the most important temple on the mountain. **Zhongshan Temple** *(zhōngshān sì)*, about halfway up the mountain, is a fairly recent construction and holds little of interest.

Just before the last ascent is the **Huashou Gate** *(huáshǒu mén)*. At the summit is the **Lengyan Pagoda**, a 13 tier Tang Dynasty pagoda that was restored in 1927, and some basic accommodation at the **Jinding Temple** next to the pagoda – a sleeping bag might be a good idea at this altitude.

A popular option for making the ascent is to hire a pony. The ponies were originally used to carry supplies up until a local hit on the idea of hiring them out to the big noses with the bulging wallets. Travellers who have done the trip claim it's a lot of fun. A cable car to the summit is a good way to cheat.

Places to Stay & Eat Accommodation is available at the base of the mountain, about halfway up and on the summit. Prices average Y10 to Y15 per bed. Food gets fairly expensive once you reach the summit so you may want to consider bringing some of your own.

If you wish to stay overnight in Binchuan, there are a few hotels around with dorm beds for as low as Y5.

Getting There & Away To reach Jizushan from Xiaguan you should first take a bus to Binchuan, which is 70km east of Xiaguan. Buses leave at 8 am from the long-distance bus station. From Binchuan take another bus or minibus to the foot of mountain. If you turn up in Binchuan, the locals will probably guess your destination.

Some travellers have hiked from Wase on the east shore of Erhai Lake to Jizushan. It is certainly a possibility, but it isn't recommended, and should only be undertaken by experienced hikers. Locals in Dali claim that it is easy to get lost in the mountainous terrain and in bad weather the hike could turn into a bad experience. Take care, and talk to locals in Dali about your plans before you go.

Weishan
(wēishān)
Weishan is famous for the Taoist temples on nearby Weibaoshan *(wēibǎoshān)*. There are reportedly some fine Taoist murals here. It's 61km due south of Xiaguan, so it could be done as a day trip.

Yongping
(yǒngpíng)
Yongping is 103km south-west of Xiaguan on the old Burma Road. The Jinguang Monastery *(jīnguāng sì)* is the attraction here.

DALI
(dàlǐ)
Dali is a perfect place to tune out for a while and forget about trains, planes and bone-jarring buses. The stunning mountain backdrop, Erhai Lake, the old city, cappuccinos, pizzas and the herbal alternative to cheap Chinese beer (you can pick it yourself) make it, along with Yangshuo, one of the few places in China where you can well and truly take a vacation from travelling.

Dali lies on the western edge of Erhai Lake at an altitude of 1900m, with the imposing Cangshan Mountain range (with an average height of 4000m) behind it. For much of the five centuries in which Yunnan governed its own affairs, Dali was the centre of operations, and the old city still retains a historical atmosphere that is hard to come by in other parts of China. Certainly the area has become a mecca for travellers, but it's easy enough to escape the crowds on the narrow backstreets lined with old stone houses.

The main inhabitants of the region are the Bai, who number about 1.5 million, according to a 1990 census. The Bai people have long-established roots in the Erhai Lake region, being thought to have settled the area some 3000 years ago. In the early 8th century they grouped together and succeeded in defeating the Tang imperial army, establishing the Nanzhao kingdom.

The kingdom exerted considerable influence throughout south-west China and even, to a lesser degree, South-East Asia, since the kingdom controlled upper Burma for much of the 9th century, which later established Dali as an end node on the famed Burma Road. In the mid-13th century it fell before the invincible Mongol hordes of Kublai Khan. It was this event that brought Yunnan back into the imperial Chinese ambit.

Orientation

Dali is a midget-sized city which has preserved some cobbled streets and traditional stone architecture within its old walls. Unless you are in a mad hurry (in which case use a bike), you can get your bearings just by taking a walk for an hour or so. It takes about half an hour to walk from the South Gate across town to the North Gate. Many of the sights around Dali couldn't be considered stunning on their own, but they do provide a destination towards which you can happily dawdle even if you don't arrive. Huguo Lu is the main strip for cafes – locals call it 'foreigner's street' (*yángrén jiē*) – and this is where to turn to for your café latté, burritos, ice-cold beer and other treats.

Maps of Dali and the Erhai Lake area are available at street stalls near the corner of Huguo Lu and Fuxing Lu.

Information

PSB The office is between the No 3 and No 4 Guesthouses on Huguo Lu. Previous goodwill has been overtaxed by some travellers, so this is no longer the place to get a second or third visa extension.

Money The Bank of China is in the centre of town, near the corner of Huguo Lu and Fuxing Lu. The bank generally will only change money Monday to Friday – this is probably one of the few reasons you would want to keep track of what day it is in Dali. The new Industrial and Commercial Bank right on Huguo Lu changes cash and travellers cheques daily and is open until 9 pm.

Post & Communications The post office is at the corner of Fuxing Lu and Huguo Lu. This is the best place to make international calls, as it has direct dial and doesn't levy a service charge. You still can't use an international calling card, however.

Dali Museum
(*dàlǐ bówùguǎn*)

This small collection of archaeological pieces relating to Bai history is nothing to get particularly excited about, but is certainly worth a browse in between coffees or fruit shakes on Huguo Lu. There's an interesting permanent art exhibition at the back of the museum, featuring various artists who have leapt onto the Yunnan school of art bandwagon. The museum is open from 8.30 am to 5 pm and admission is Y1.

Three Pagodas
(*sāntǎsì*)

Standing on the hillside a couple of kilometres north-west of Dali, the pagodas look pretty, particularly when seen reflected in the nearby lake. They are, in fact, among the oldest standing structures in south-western China.

The tallest of the three, Qianxun Pagoda, has 16 tiers that reach a height of 70m. It was originally erected in the mid-9th century by Xi'an engineers. It is flanked by two smaller 10-tiered pagodas, which are each 42m high.

The temple behind the pagodas, **Chongsheng Temple**, is laid out in the traditional Yunnanese style, with three layers of buildings lined up with a sacred peak in the background. The temple has been recently restored and converted into a museum that chronicles the history, construction and renovation of the pagodas. Also on exhibit are marble slabs that have been cut and framed so that the patterns of the marble appear to depict landscapes.

Many travellers find the pagodas more impressive from a distance. Up close there's not all that much to see except for a seemingly endless row of souvenir and trinket stands. Admission is charged.

Organised Tours

Numerous travel agencies near the No 2 Guesthouse have tours to sights around Dali. A newer activity includes horse riding. Some of the cafes also offer trips, mostly in the form of boat outings across Erhai Lake to Wase, which has an open-air market every five days. Private entrepreneurs run cruises around the lake daily if there is enough demand. During festivals, many of the cafes arrange transport, which can spare you the fight to board jam-packed local buses out to festival sites at nearby villages.

Festivals

If you don't mind crowds, probably the best time to be in Dali is during the Third Moon Fair *(sānyuè jiē)*, which begins on the 15th day of the third lunar month (usually April) and ends on the 21st day. The origins of the fair lie in its commemoration of a fabled visit by Guanyin, the Buddhist goddess of mercy, to the Nanzhao kingdom. Today it's more like an extra festive market, with people from all over Yunnan arriving to buy, sell and make merry.

The Three Temples Festival *(ràosān-líng)* is held between the 23rd and 25th days of the fourth lunar month (usually

May). The name of the festival refers to making a tour of three temples and this is basically what the participants do. The first day involves a walk from Dali's South Gate to the Xizhou Shengyuan Temple at the foot of Mt Wutai. Here the walkers stay up until dawn, dancing and singing, before moving on to Jingui Temple at the shore of the Erhai Lake. The final day involves walking back to Dali by way of Majiuyi Temple.

The Torch Festival *(huǒbǎ jié)* is held on the 24th day of the sixth lunar month (normally July). Flaming torches are paraded at night through homes and fields. Other events include fireworks displays and dragon-boat racing.

Places to Stay

The addition of several new, low-budget hotels has greatly improved the accommodation situation in Dali. Even so, places tend to fill up quickly, and those visiting during the peak summer months may find themselves trekking around town in search of that perfect bed on their first day.

Certainly *the* place to see and be seen on the backpacker circuit Dali stop is the *MCA Guesthouse* (☎ 267-3666) south of the south gate. This self-contained little community has spacious dorms with hardwood floors. Beds are Y10. (The only very minor downside is that the OK bathrooms are across the compound; the showers at least have 24 hour hot water.) Spartan doubles without bath are not all that nice for Y50. Good doubles with private bath cost Y100, but also face the popular pool area.

The guesthouse also has book rental, laundry service, poste restante (Y5), bikes for rent, and – one of the few places in south-west China for this – Internet browsing (Y2 per minute) and email service (Y15 per message). Weekends feature a Tibetan brunch.

Dali is known for its numbering system on local guesthouses. The newest and without question the most interesting place to stay is the *No 5 Guesthouse*, known locally as the *(sìjì kèzhàn)* or *Old Dali Four*

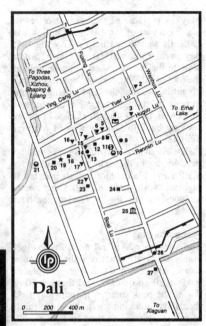

Dali

0   200   400 m

To Xiaguan

Seasons Inn (☎ 267-0382) at No 51 Boai Lu. Opened by a Taiwanese investor with a keen eye for hotels, this one makes use of one of the street's oldest and most distinctive original-style buildings. Two wings of the two storey complex face a flower-laden courtyard, which has a gazebo and lots of greenery. A cafe serves good food. The bathrooms are clean and showers have reliable hot water 18 hours a day. Dorm rooms start at Y10 per hard bed in clean quads; for an extra Y5, you can get the 'luxury dorm', which means a soft bed. Singles/doubles with common bath cost Y40. There are also doubles with private bath for around Y120. Bicycles can be rented here.

Before now, the most popular place was the *No 4 Guesthouse*, also known as the *Yu'an Garden* (☎ 267-2093) *(yú'ān yuán)*, and it still is rated highly by travellers. Perched at the top of Huguo Lu, this idyllic little spot has it all – bamboo pavilions, 24 hour hot water, a lovely Thai-style cafe, washing machines, a score of laundry lines, friendly staff, and dorm beds for Y15, as

DALI   大理

PLACES TO STAY
8   Jinhua Hotel
金花大酒店
12 No 2 Guesthouse
第二招待所
18 No 3 Guesthouse
(Sunny Garden)
第三招待所(桑尼园)
20 No 4 Guesthouse
(Yu'an Garden)
第四招待所(榆安园)
23 Old Dali Four Seasons Inn
(No 5 Guesthouse)
大理四季客栈
24 Dali Hotel
大理宾馆
27 MCA Guesthouse

PLACES TO EAT
2   Apricot Flower Restaurant
李花餐厅

3   Yunnan Cafe
云南咖啡馆
5   Marley's Cafe
马丽咖啡馆
6   Tibetan Cafe
西藏餐厅
7   Old Wooden House
如意饭店
13 Cafe de Jack
樱花阁
15 Sunshine Cafe
16 Happy Cafe
17 Mr China's Son Cafe
22 Jim's Peace Cafe &
Guesthouse
吉母和平饭店和招待

OTHER
1   North Gate
北门
4   Post Office
邮电局

9   Dali Passenger
Service Ticket
Office
大理客运站售票处
10 Buses to Xiaguan
往下关的公共汽车
11 Bank of China
中国银行
14 Dali Passenger
Service Ticket
Office
大理客运站售票处
19 PSB
公安局
21 Local Buses to
Shaping
往沙平的公共汽车
25 Dali Museum
大理博物馆
26 South Gate
南门

well as doubles for Y50 (although these tend to suffer from poor ventilation). Look at a few options, since there's a wide variety. The only problem with the No 4 is that the best rooms always seem to be full.

If you miss out, don't despair, as there are other options, and none of them is terrible. Just down from the No 4 Guesthouse, the friendly *No 3 Guesthouse*, or *Sunny Garden* (☎ 267-0213) *(sāngní yuán)* as it's also called, is obviously modelled along the lines of its successful neighbour. Unfortunately, the hotel is crammed into an area about half the size of the No 4, which gives some travellers a touch of claustrophobia. The staff are friendly and do their best to make it worthwhile. Six or seven bed dorms are Y60 to Y70, triples are Y45, doubles Y40 and singles Y20. A couple of rooms with private bathroom and TV are available for Y50 per person.

Just to confuse things, there's now a rival for the name of No 3. Down on Boai Lu, the relocated *Jim's Peace Cafe (jímǔ hépíng fàndiàn)* is another *No 3 Guesthouse*, and just to make it even more confusing, Jim was planning to change this to *No 6 Guesthouse* at some point. (It's not clear why No 3 was chosen in the first place.) In this brand new guesthouse, Jim offers a triple for Y45, one single room with private bathroom for Y50, and one double for Y140. The latter two have absolutely fantastic bathtubs, brand new and big enough to stretch out in.

Closest to all the action on Huguo Lu, the *No 2 Guesthouse* (☎ 267-0423) *(dì'èr zhāodàisuǒ)* has long been Dali's old stand-by. Though a bit lacking in charm, it's actually not a bad place to stay, especially if you get a room on the 2nd or 3rd floor of the old wing. First floor rooms tend to be damp and dark. Doubles/triples with common washroom are Y30/36. Singles are Y30. There are also doubles with attached bath in the old wing for Y90, but these are mostly on the 1st floor, and not really worth the money. Hot water is available from 8 pm until around midnight, and sometimes, if you're lucky, there may even

be some left over in the morning. The No 2 also has standard doubles, with 24 hour hot water, in the new building for Y180. This is the best place to rent a bicycle. The *Dali Hotel* (☎ 267-0386) *(dàlǐ bīnguǎn)* is a bit further away, on Fuxing Lu, but the exercise of walking the 10 minutes or so to Huguo Lu may give you the illusion of having earned your banana pancake. It has triples with private bath for Y105 – not great value, but an acceptable option if all the other places are booked up. Basic doubles with attached bath start at Y110, with a bit of variety so check a few, while standard doubles with all the mod cons are Y240.

Sticking out like a sore thumb at the corner of Huguo Lu and Fuxing Lu, the newly opened *Jinhua Hotel (jīnhuā dàjiǔdiàn)* probably won't see much in the way of backpacker traffic. Standard doubles with air-con, satellite TV and all the rest start at Y210. Sporting red-capped doormen and a marble staircase, and yet more hostesses with colourful and ill-fitting headgear, the Jinhua definitely seems out of sync with the rest of Dali. But if you're in the mood for luxury, or are toting the kids around, this might be a good choice.

Dali also has its own five star hotel, an enormous luxury monster that is thankfully parked several kilometres south of town. A China-Taiwan joint venture, it stands out clearly against the mountain backdrop when viewed from the lake.

Places to Eat

The top section of Huguo Lu is where most of the travellers' hang-outs are, clustered around the entrance to the No 2 Guesthouse. Most of them are good value for money, and have good food and pleasant staff, all of which is a welcome relief if you've been on the road for a while. Basically, it's a good idea to move around a bit and share your patronage. Most of the cafes have decent food and they all try hard to please.

There are many more than those listed here, but truthfully many restaurants in

YUNNAN

places like Dali (and Yangshuo in Guangxi Province) are nothing more than cookie-cutter tedium – not bad, simply unremarkable. So many restaurants have opened up that some restaurants reported a 10 fold drop in business from one summer to the next.

If you're a misanthropic type and want to avoid the other travellers, you can eat with the locals in any number of Chinese restaurants around town. This may be a good idea anyway – you would be surprised indeed how many little very, very local places way off the main drags have English menus, but you'd never know it without some exploring. So get around and experiment.

It's difficult to make recommendations – as in Yangshuo, restaurants wax and wane in popularity for all kinds of reasons. One place that seems certain to keep drawing a steady crowd is the steady-as-a-rock *Marley's Cafe*, which relocated after 10 years a half-block south into a great new building. The mostly wooden interiors are tastefully decorated with art, and Marley's has a tome of a menu with western and Chinese food; particularly popular is the Sunday Bai food group dinner (make reservations). A new deck on the roof will allow for a great excuse to while away the day and the outdoor seating here is some of the most popular in town. Marley herself is also a great source of local information and she also gets kudos for having one of the few places in town with a bathroom.

Long popular also is the *Tibetan Cafe*, almost next door to Marley's. Across the street, the *Star Cafe* is dark but cosy and has good Japanese food. A little ways west, don't miss the friendliest folks in town at the *Sunshine Cafe* where the smiles never end. They've got a couple of good Tibetan dishes and whip up the best brownies in town. Their couch, placed under a nice skylight, is possibly the most comfortable seat in Dali. Near there, the *Old Wooden House* has good outside seating and its bolognaise is definitely worth trying – a roving Italian gave them the recipe.

The *Yunnan Cafe* is about a five minute walk down Huguo Lu. Formerly called the Coca Cola Restaurant (until the long arm of Coca-Cola Inc sniffed out the use of its name and dispatched warnings to Dali), it serves consistently good food. On the last couple of visits, service was way down in quality if not attitude from previous years, but hopefully that's an aberration. Travellers routinely plant themselves on the rooftop sun deck until the night-time chill or closing time drives them away. The cafe also has an extensive book exchange and rental service (the sale prices are high to discourage people from buying the books and exhausting the library). Xiangxia, who runs the place, is a fluent English speaker and a mine of useful information on Dali.

There's an *MCA Coffeeshop* with computers at the ready on Huguo Lu.

Back up on Boai Lu, the number one choice for hip music and a congenial atmosphere is *Cafe de Jack*, known for its amazing chocolate cake with ice cream; it also has good pizza and another couch seating arrangement worth a mention. For an interesting afternoon of conversation, you can try *Mr China's Son*, a cafe opened by an old gentleman who has penned an English-language account of his trials and tribulations during the Cultural Revolution.

If you're a fan of Japanese food, try the *Happy Cafe* – it serves the Japanese travellers' market and is a good place to meet wandering souls from Tokyo, Osaka and so on. The food is rivalled by that of *Sister's Cafe*. True party-goers should head to *Jim's Peace Cafe* for rock 'n' roll and late-night sessions. Jim is part-Tibetan, a very cool guy, and mixes up some potent concoctions – look out for his No 1 Special.

Things to Buy

Dali is famous for its marble, and while a slab of the stuff in your backpack might slow you down a bit, local entrepreneurs produce everything from ashtrays to model pagodas in small enough chunks to make it feasible to stow one or two away in your pack.

Huguo Lu has become a mini Khao San Rd in its profusion of clothes shops. It won't take you long to decide whether the clothes are for you or not – you could outfit yourself for a time-machine jaunt back to Woodstock here, but bear in mind that the shopkeepers can also make clothes to your specifications, so you're not necessarily just stuck with the ready-made hippie stuff. Prices are very reasonable.

Most of the 'silver' jewellery sold in Dali is really brass. Occasionally it actually is silver, although this will be reflected in the starting price. The only advice worth giving, if you're in the market for this kind of thing, is to bargain hard.

Batik wall hangings also have become popular in Dali. Several places near the No 2 Guesthouse on Huguo Lu have a good collection, but don't believe the proprietors when they tell you they make the stuff themselves and start justifying the extortionate prices they charge by telling how many hours they worked on a piece. Most of the batik, as in Yangshuo, comes from Guizhou where it can be bought for a song. Check with cafe owners and other locals about prices before you set out shopping.

Getting There & Away

The opening of Xiaguan's new airport has brought Dali to within 45 minutes' flying time from Kunming. Flights run daily, and will probably pick up as tourists become aware of the new air route. The one way fare is Y320.

Many travellers will probably still opt for the overnight sleeper bus service from Kunming. Mid-sized buses (Y55) leave five times from 7 to 10.20 am and take around 11 hours; sleepers (Y92) leave at 7.20 and 7.40 pm. You should rarely have to pay this much. Starting at the King World (Jinhua) Hotel in Kunming and working your way south, you should be able to line up a cheaper private sleeper bus, usually just before they leave. Several shrewd travellers have claimed they got a driver, desperate to fill a bus, to knock the price down to Y40 or Y45! Though the

road gets a bit bumpy, this is altogether not a bad ride, and you usually will meet fellow travellers to share any mild misery you may feel.

The long-distance bus station in Kunming also has regular buses (Y41) to Xiaguan leaving from 7 am to 8.20 pm and a couple of sleepers (Y90) between 7 and 8 pm. For those travellers who simply cannot sleep on sleeper buses, there is a new super-luxury bus departing from just east of the Camellia Hotel on the opposite side of the road. The Yunnan Tourist Transport Company runs luxury buses with reclining seats and tons of leg room at 8 am direct to Dali, via Xiaguan. For around Y90 you get a good lunch at the halfway point, the odd trinket or souvenir, and, if you're lucky, an English movie.

Leaving Dali, the best thing to do is *shop around*. Plenty of tour and travel agencies means plenty of options and competitive prices. Most buses for Lijiang and Kunming depart right in Dali; for other destinations, you can buy tickets in Dali, but must return to Xiaguan to get on the bus.

So many buses ply the Kunming to Dali route that in a six month period prices dropped by some 15%. Day buses to Kunming generally leave from next to whatever agency sells the tickets between 6.30 and 9 am, and cost Y40 to Y55. Most of these are middle-sized buses which theoretically should get you there more quickly than large buses. Claims vary wildly – eight to 12 hours – with about 10 being right, depending on traffic. All agencies have big sleeper buses, generally leaving between 6.30 and 7.30 pm and costing Y55 or so.

Buses to Lijiang leave between 7 am and 2.30 pm. Tickets for the five hour trip cost Y20 (Y25 for minibuses) and can be bought from the above ticket office, another one on Fuxing Lu, or any travel agency on Huguo Lu. You can also catch any one of numerous buses to Lijiang that originate in Xiaguan.

To catch buses to other points, such as Baoshan, Ruili or Jinghong, you'll have to go to Xiaguan, although there is rumoured to be a bus to Jinghong originating in Dali, and stopping in Xiaguan on the way.

Tickets for most of these routes can be bought in Dali. The No 4 local bus to Xiaguan starts up early enough – around 6 am – runs every 10 minutes, and there are stops along Boai Lu. The trip takes around 30 minutes and costs Y1.20. If your bus leaves earlier than 6.30 or 7 am, you'll have to overnight in Xiaguan.

Getting Around

A taxi to the airport should take around 45 minutes and cost around Y50.

Bikes are the best way to get around. Prices average Y2 per hour or Y5 per day for clunky Chinese models, Y2 per hour and Y10 for better mountain bikes. The No 2 Guesthouse has the largest selection, although the No 5 and MCA guesthouses also have them and more places are starting to get in on the act too.

AROUND DALI
Goddess of Mercy Temple
(guānyīn táng)

The temple is built over a large boulder said to have been placed there by the goddess of mercy to block the advance of an invading enemy. It is 5km south of Dali.

Erhai Lake
(ěrhǎi hú)

The lake is a 50 minute walk from town or a 10 minute downhill zip on a bike. You can watch the large junks or the smaller boats with their queue of captive cormorants waiting on the edge of the boat for their turn to do the fishing. A ring placed around their necks stops them from guzzling the catch.

From Caicun, the lakeside village east of Dali, there's a ferry at 4.30 pm to Wase on the other side of the lake. You can stay overnight and catch a ferry back at 6 am. Plenty of locals take their bikes over.

Since ferries crisscross the lake at various points, there could be some scope for extended touring. Close to Wase is Putuo Island *(pǔtuó dǎo)* with the Lesser Putuo Temple *(xiǎopǔtuó sì)*. Other ferries run between Longkan and Haidong, and between Xiaguan and Jinsuo Island. Ferries appear to leave early in the morning (for market) and return around 4 pm; timetables are flexible.

Zhonghe Temple
(zhōnghé sì)

Zhonghe is a long, steep hike up the mountainside behind Dali. When you finally get there, you might be received with a cup of tea and a smile. Then again, you might not. Smile or no, it's Y2 per person. Branching out from either side of the temple is a trail that winds along the face of the mountains, taking you in and out of steep lush valleys and past streams and waterfalls.

It's a great day trip with fantastic vistas of Dali and Erhai Lake. You can cheat and take a new chairlift (Y35) up Cangshan, that big hill overlooking Dali. The road leading north to the Three Pagodas crosses the road up to the chairlift and by the time you read this, there should be a sign, hopefully in English.

You could also hike up the hill, a sweaty hour for those in relatively good shape. No one path leads directly up the hill; instead, oodles of local paths wind and switchback through farm fields, local cemeteries, and even one off-limits military area (there is a sign in English here!). Walk about 200m north of the chairlift base to the riverbed (often dry). Follow the left bank for about 50m and you'll see lots of ribbony trails leading up. Basically, all roads lead to Rome from here, just keep the chairlift in sight and when in doubt, bear left. You should eventually come upon a well-worn trail and, following that, some steps near the top.

Gantong Temple
(gāntōng sì)

This temple is not far south of the town of Guanyintang, which is about 6km from Dali in the direction of Xiaguan. From Guanyintang follow the path uphill for 3km. Locals will have to pantomime directions.

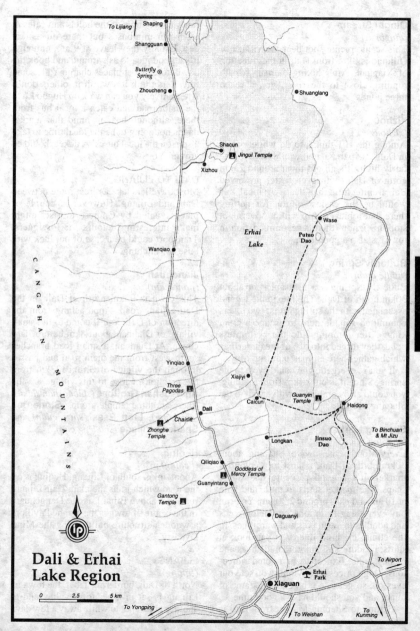

To Lijiang
Shaping
Shangguan
Butterfly
Spring
Zhoucheng
Shuanglang

Shacun
Jingui Temple
Xizhou

Erhai
Lake
Wase
Putuo
Dao
Wanqiao

CANGSHAN

Yinqiao
Xiajiyi
Three
Pagodas
Dali
Caicun
Guanyin
Temple
Haidong
Chairlift
Zhonghe
Temple
Longkan
Jinsuo
Dao
To Binchuan
& Mt Jizu

MOUNTAINS

Qiliqiao
Goddess of
Mercy Temple
Guanyintang
Gantong Temple
Daguanyi

Dali & Erhai
Lake Region
Erhai
Park
Xiaguan
To Airport

0   2.5   5 km
To Yongping
To Weishan
To Kunming

YUNNAN

Qingbi Stream
(qīngbì xī)
This scenic picnic spot near the village of Qiliqiao is 3km from Dali in the direction of Xiaguan. After hiking 4km up a path running close to the river, you'll reach three ponds.

Xizhou
(xǐzhōu)
Among the 101 things to do while you're in Dali, a trip to Xizhou would have to rate fairly high. It's an old town around 25km north of Dali, with even better preserved Bai architecture than Dali. A local bus would be the easiest option for getting there, but a bicycle trip with an overnight stop in Xizhou (there's accommodation in town) is also a good idea.

Butterfly Spring
(húdié quán)
Butterfly Spring is a pleasant spot about 30km north of Dali. The inevitable legend associated with the spring is that two lovers committed suicide here to escape a cruel king. After jumping into the bottomless pond, they turned into two of the butterflies which gather here en masse during May.

If you're energetic you could cycle to the spring. Since it is only 4km from Shaping, you could also combine it with a visit to the Shaping Market.

Shaping Market
(shāpíng gǎnjí)
Every Monday the town of Shaping, about 30km north of Dali, is host to a colourful market. It's a good place to take some snaps. The market starts to rattle and hum at 10 am and ends around 2.30 pm. You can buy everything from tobacco, melon seeds and noodles to meat, pots and wardrobes. In the ethnic clothing line, you can look at shirts, headdresses, embroidered shoes and money belts. Expect to be quoted ridiculously high prices on anything you set your eyes on, so get into a bargaining frame of mind, and you should have a good time.

Getting to Shaping Market from Dali is fairly easy. Some of the hotels and cafes in town run minibuses out there on market day. Usually they leave at 9 am, although it's a good idea to ask around and book the day before. Most places charge Y11; some travellers think it's worth it, others don't. Alternatively you can walk up Huguo Lu to the main road and catch a local bus from there, although bear in mind that market day is not going to be the ideal time to take a spin on the local buses. A ticket should be around Y6.

DALI TO LIJIANG
Most travellers take a direct route between Dali and Lijiang. However, a couple of places visited by Chinese tourists might make interesting detours for foreigners. Transport could be a case of pot luck with buses or hitching.

Jianchuan
(jiànchuān)
This town is 92km north of Dali on the Dali-Lijiang road. Approaching from the direction of Dali, you'll come to the small village of Diannan about 8km before Jianchuan. At Diannan, a small road branches south-west from the main road and passes through the village of **Shaxi** (23km from the junction). Close to this village are the **Shibaoshan Grottoes** *(shíbǎoshān shíkū)*. There are three temple groups: **Stone Bell** *(shízhōng)*, **Lion Pass** *(shīzi guān)* and **Shadeng Village** *(shādēng cūn)*.

Heqing
(hèqìng)
About 46km south of Lijiang, Heqing is on the road which joins the main Dali-Lijiang road just above Erhai Lake at Dengchuan. In the centre of town is the Yunhe Pavilion, a wooden structure built during the Ming Dynasty.

LIJIANG
(lìjiāng)
North of Dali, bordering Tibet, the town of Lijiang is set in a beautiful valley and is another great spot to while away a few days

The Naxi

Lijiang is the base of the Naxi (also spelt Nakhi and Nahi) minority,
278,000 in Yunnan and Sichuan. The Naxi are descended from Tibetan
until recently in matriarchal families, though local rulers were always m
seem to run the show, certainly in the old part of Lijiang.

The Naxi matriarchs maintained their hold over the men with flexible ar   ...ments for
love affairs. The *azhu* (friend) system allowed a couple to become lovers without setting up
joint residence. Both partners would continue to live in their respective homes; the boyfriend
would spend the nights at his girlfriend's house but return to live and work at his mother's
house during the day. Any children born to the couple belonged to the woman, who was
responsible for bringing them up. The father provided support, but once the relationship was
over, so was the support. Children lived with their mothers; no special effort was made to
recognise paternity. Women inherited all property, and disputes were adjudicated by female
elders. The matriarchal system appears to have survived around Yongning, north of Lijiang.

There are strong matriarchal influences in the Naxi language. Nouns enlarge their
meaning when the word for 'female' is added; conversely, the addition of the word for 'male'
will decrease the meaning. For example, 'stone' plus 'female' conveys the idea of a boulder;
'stone' plus 'male' conveys the idea of a pebble.

Naxi women wear blue blouses and trousers covered by blue or black aprons. The T-shaped
traditional cape not only stops the basket always worn on the back from chafing, but also
symbolises the heavens. Day and night are represented by the light and dark halves of the
cape; seven embroidered circles symbolise the stars. Two larger circles, one on each shoulder, are used to depict the eyes of a frog, which until the 15th century was an important
god to the Naxi. With the decline of animist beliefs, the frog eyes fell out of fashion, but the
Naxi still call the cape by its original name: 'frog-eye sheepskin'.

The Naxi created a written language over 1000 years ago using an extraordinary system
of pictographs. The most famous Naxi text is the Dongba classic *The Creation*, and ancient
copies of it and other texts can still be found in Lijiang, as well as in the archives of some
US universities. Dongba were Naxi shamans who were caretakers of the written language
and mediators between the Naxi and the spirit world. The Dongba religion eventually absorbed itself into an amalgam of Lamaist Buddhism, Islam and Taoism. The Tibetan origins
of the Naxi are confirmed by references in Naxi literature to Lake Manasarovar and Mt
Kailas, both in western Tibet. ∎

or weeks. Your initial response when you
pull into the bus station and start the long
trudge through what appears to be another
dusty Chinese city might be 'Get me out of
here!'. It's not until you get into the old
town – a delightful maze of cobbled streets,
rickety old wooden buildings, gushing
canals and the hurly-burly of market life –
that you realise Lijiang is more than a
boring Chinese urban sprawl in the middle
of nowhere.

Lijiang can consider itself lucky. In February 1996 an earthquake measuring over 7
on the Richter scale rocked the Lijiang area,
killing over 100 – including one western
traveller – and injured many times that
number. Damage was estimated at over half
a billion US dollars. The Chinese government took note and today is sinking millions
of yuan into rebuilding most of Lijiang
County with traditional Naxi architecture:
cobblestone and wood will replace cement
on streets and bridges. (Modern necessities
such as sanitation and sewage treatment will
also factor in.) This isn't simply a cynical
attempt to lure tourists – while much of

ver Lijiang was levelled, the old-style architecture was largely unscathed. The UN was so impressed by the survival of Lijiang that it has placed all of Lijiang County on the World Heritage Site list.

There are a number of interesting sights around Lijiang – some of which can be reached by bicycle. You can also use a bike to get out of town to the mountains, where you can hike around. You may need time to acclimatise to the height (2400m).

Yunnan was a hunting ground for famous foreign plant-hunters such as Kingdon Ward and Joseph Rock. Rock, an Austro-American, lived almost continuously in Lijiang between 1922 and 1949. 'Hef', as he was known, is still remembered by some locals. A man of quick and violent temper, he commissioned local carpenters to build special chairs and a desk to accommodate his stocky frame. He burdened his large caravans with a gold dinner service and a collapsible bathtub from Abercrombie & Fitch. He also wrote a definitive guide to Hawaiian flora before devoting the rest of his life to researching Naxi culture and collecting the flora of the region.

The Ancient Nakhi Kingdom of Southwest China is Joseph Rock's definitive work; the two volumes are heavy-duty reading. For a lighter treatment of the man and his work, take a look at *In China's Border Provinces: The Turbulent Career of Joseph Rock, Botanist-Explorer* by JB Sutton.

Another venerable work on Lijiang that's worth reading if you can find it is *The Forgotten Kingdom* by Peter Goulart. Goulart was a White Russian who studied Naxi culture and lived in Lijiang from 1940 to 1949.

Orientation

Lijiang is separated into old and new towns that are as different as day and night. The approximate line of division is Lion Hill, the bump in the middle of town that's topped by a radio mast. Everything west of the hill is the new town, and everything east of the hill is the old town.

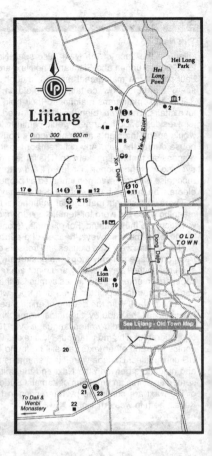

The easiest way into the old town is to head up to the cinema, turn east into a small square that also serves as the town's night market, and head south. The old town is a delightful maze of twists and turns – although it's small, it's easy to get lost in there which, of course, is part of the fun. Enjoy!

Information

It was only a matter of time before Chinese cities got their own website addresses too. Check out Lijiang's (www.lijiang.com).

LIJIANG 丽江

PLACES TO STAY
4 Guluwan Hotel
   古路湾宾馆
8 Red Sun Hotel
   红太阳宾馆
12 Jiamei Hotel
   佳美宾馆
13 Lijiang Hotel
   丽江宾馆
22 Yunshan Hotel
   云杉饭店

PLACES TO EAT
6 Ali Baba's Cafe
   阿里巴巴餐厅

OTHER
1 Dongba Museum & Shop
   东巴博物馆
2 Dongba Research Institute
   东巴研究所
3 Yunling Theatre
   云岭剧场
5 CITS
   中国国际旅行社
7 Mao Square
   毛主席广场
9 Lijiang Bus Passenger Station
   丽江客运站
10 Bank of China
   中国银行
11 Xinhua Bookstore
   新华书店

14 Bank of China
   中国银行
15 PSB
   公安局
16 Hospital
   门诊所
17 CAAC
   民航售票处
18 Post Office
   邮电局
19 Radio Mast
   狮子山
20 Sports Ground
   体育场
21 Long-Distance Bus Station
   长途汽车站
23 CITS/FIT
   中国国际旅行社

Tourist Offices Some travel information can be gleaned from the cafes near Mao Square and in the old town. At the time of writing, CITS (☎ 25999) was opening a Family-Independent Traveller (FIT) Department in Lijiang, across the street from the entrance to the Yunshan Hotel, although the main office, across the street from the Guluwan Hotel, is also worth a visit. The Lijiang staff are generally quite helpful, and should be able to give you ideas for local outings and book plane and even train tickets. Stop by the office to see if this latter dream has become a reality.

PSB The PSB is opposite the Lijiang Hotel. There seems to be no problem extending visas in Lijiang.

Money The Bank of China is on Xin Dajie almost opposite the intersection of the road that leads off to the Lijiang Hotel and the PSB.

There is also a small branch just next to the entrance of the Lijiang Hotel. It is possible to change travellers cheques at both branches.

Post & Communications The Post and Telecommunications office is on Xin Dajie, just south of the turn to get to Old Town. It's open from 8.30 am to around 6 pm. You still can't make reverse charge calls or use a calling card; to do so, use the little phone kiosk up at the corner to the north.

Dangers & Annoyances In May 1997 two solo western women were robbed at knifepoint – in separate incidents – atop Elephant Hill in Hei Long Tan Park. Both attacks occurred in broad daylight in the early afternoon. At least one of the assailants followed his victim for some time before the robbery, so keep your eyes sharp for people lurking behind you. It would obviously be a good idea to pair up with at least one other traveller.

Lijiang also has had some pickpockets appear north of the old town near the square.

Old Town
Criss-crossed by canals and a maze of narrow streets, the old town is not to be missed. Arrive by mid-morning to see the market square full of Naxi women in traditional dress. Parrots and plants adorn the front porches, old women sell griddle cakes in front of teahouses, men walk past with hunting falcons proudly keeping balance on their gloved fists, and more old women

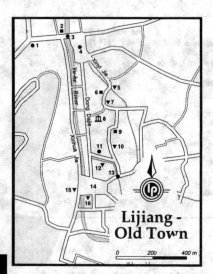

energetically slam down the trumps on a card table in the middle of the street. You can buy embroidery and lengths of striped cloth in shops around the market.

Above the old town is a beautiful park which can be reached on the path leading past the radio antenna. Sit on the slope in the early morning and watch the mist clearing as the old town comes to life.

Now acting as sentinel of sorts for the town is the Wan Gou Lou, a pagoda being raised at a cost of over one million yuan. It's famed for a unique design using dozens of four storey pillars, but unfortunately these were culled from northern Yunnan old-growth forests.

Hei Long Tan Park
(hēilóngtán gōngyuán)
This park (which means Black Dragon Pool) is on the northern edge of town. Apart from strolling around the pool, you can visit the Dongba Research Institute, which is part of a renovated complex on the hillside. There is a small museum here with Dongba scrolls and artefacts on display – admission is Y2.

At the far side of the pond are renovated buildings used for an art exhibition, a pavilion with its own bridge across the water and the Wufeng Temple which dates from the Ming Dynasty.

Trails lead straight up Elephant Hill to a dilapidated gazebo and then across a spiny ridge past a communications centre and back down the other side, making a nice morning hike. Up and down can take as little as 45 minutes if you push it. Entry to the park costs Y8.

Xuan Ke Museum

Mr Xuan Ke, a Naxi scholar who spent 20 years in labour camps following the suppression of the Hundred Flowers movement, has turned his Lijiang family home into a small repository for Naxi and Lijiang cultural items. Besides clothing and musical instruments (including an original Persian lute that has been used in Naxi music for centuries), his home displays Dr Joseph Rock's large, handmade furniture and has a small library of out-of-print books on Lijiang. Dr Rock was a close family friend.

Xuan Ke speaks English and is always willing to discuss his original ideas about world culture (for example, that music and dance originated as rites of exorcism). He has taken an active role in working to preserve traditional Chinese music, which he maintains is in danger of being wiped out by the corrosive influence of popular music and its evil offspring, karaoke.

His home is in the old town, at No 11 Jishan Alley, diagonally opposite the No 40 Restaurant.

Festivals

The 13th day of the third moon (late March or early April) is the traditional day to hold a Fertility Festival. July brings Hub Jie *(huǒbǎ jié)*, the Torch Festival, also celebrated by the Bai in the Dali region. The origin of this festival can be traced back to the intrigues of the Nanzhao kingdom, when the wife of a man burned to death by the king eluded the romantic entreaties of the said monarch by leaping into a fire.

Places to Stay

Lijiang has added two newer guesthouses with traditional Naxi architecture.

Coming south from the square into the old town, the first place you'll stumble across is the *Sanhe Naxi Guesthouse*, a cacophonic place with claustrophobic rooms that don't really capture the spirit of the old building. You also have to deftly side-step all kinds of boisterous traditional dancing and singing to get to your room. Beds were originally available for Y15 but have already jumped to Y40 for a bed in a tr, with clean common bath.

You're better off giving it a miss and continuing south to one of south-west China's best lodging options, the first-rate *First Bend Inn* (☎ 518-1688) *(dìyīkèzhàn)*. One of the old city's most distinctive and well preserved buildings, it features rooms on two levels around an attractive courtyard. Little touches include bicycle rental (planned to be operating by the time you read this), travel information, and even motion-sensor lights for late-night trips to use the facilities. Rooms are comfortable and bathrooms are quite clean; showers have reliable hot water in the evenings *and* mornings (from 8 to 9 am). Doubles/triples/quads are Y80/Y90/Y100; all rooms have common bath. The staff are attentive and friendly and are full of information on local sights.

The first place you're likely to come across when you arrive in town is the *Yunshan Hotel* (☎ 512-1315) *(yúnshān fàndiàn)*, also known as the *No 3 Guesthouse*, next to the new bus station. The Yunshan has fallen victim to rising prices and slipping standards. Given its inconvenient location in a boring part of town, there's not much reason to stay here: even if you're catching an early bus you can usually board at the north bus station. The Yunshan has three bed dorms with TV for Y60, and two bed dorms for Y70. Doubles with attached bathroom are Y170.

North of the old town are the remainder of Lijiang's central options, not all of which are budget. Adjacent to Mao Square, the *Red Sun Hotel* (☎ 512-1018) *(hóngtàiyáng jiǔdiàn)* is the next-cheapest choice for budget travellers. Beds in six to eight bed dorms cost Y20, while those in doubles without bath are Y35. The hotel also has doubles/triples with attached washroom for Y150/180. There are more higher-priced choices.

The Red Sun manages to snare a fair number of travellers due to its prominent location, but has received mixed reports. Some find the place perfectly fine while others, having endured several nights of ear-shattering karaoke, warn to avoid it like the plague. The dorms are large and bright, and the facilities are fine, although a few travellers have reported the smell of petrol in the shower room.

The *Lijiang Hotel* (☎ 512-1911) *(lìjiāng bīnguǎn)*, also known as the *No 1 Hotel (dìyī zhāodàisuǒ)*, is probably Lijiang's leader in terms of friendly service and cheap sleep. The cheapest choice is a bed in a 15 bed room for Y12. A bed in a five bed or seven bed dorm goes for Y17. Clean triples/doubles are Y44/51. In the more luxurious block at the back, nicely furnished doubles/triples with attached bath cost Y200/280. As long as there are no small-scale construction projects on the grounds, the Lijiang Hotel should be the quietest of the town's low-end places to stay.

Just to the east of the Lijiang Hotel, the *Jiamei Hotel* (☎ 512-2046) *(jiāměi bīnguǎn)* offers doubles and triples with attached bath, telephone and 24 hour hot water for Y125. The rooms are nothing special, but are fair value all the same.

For more upmarket accommodation, two options are centrally located. The *Guluwan Hotel* (☎ 512-1446) *(gǔlùwān bīnguǎn)* is north of Mao Square and no longer a budget option. Standard doubles now start at Y220, triples are available for Y280. The Guluwan has a small travel agency on the grounds, as well as an air ticket booking office (check to see how much their commission is – it might be better to try CITS across the street). The hotel is at the end of a driveway.

Hovering ominously at the northern edge of the old town, the *Lijiang Grand Hotel* (☎ 512-8888; fax 512-7878) *(gélán dàjiǔdiàn)* is a hulking luxury monster with facilities and prices (US$90 for a double) that seem completely at odds with the rest of Lijiang. At least you get a breakfast buffet for your money, which you then lose in the 15% service charge. The hotel is a Chinese-Thai joint venture managed in part by several Europeans.

Places to Eat
Like Dali, Lijiang has a legion of small, family-operated restaurants catering to the fantasies of China backpackers. Kitchens are tiny and waits can be long, but the food is usually interesting.

There are always several 'Naxi' items on the menu, including the famous 'Naxi omelette' and 'Naxi sandwich' (goat's cheese, tomato and fried egg between two pieces of local *baba* flatbread). Try locally produced *yinjiu*, a lychee-based wine with a 500 year history – it tastes like a decent semi-sweet sherry.

Mao Square Most people stumble across the restaurants lining Mao Square first. *Peter's*, a former favourite with travellers, has taken a nosedive following the departure of founder Crystal and her American husband Tom The food is acceptable, but the place is now gloomy if not fly-ridden and all traces of personality seem to have been surgically removed.

At the northern edge of the square, *Ali Baba's* is a better bet, with good food and friendly people. It is also a good spot to find out about details on Tiger Leaping Gorge and Lugu Lake.

Old Town There are some great places to eat in the old part of town. Like Dali and Yangshuo, new eateries crop up all the time, so there's never a dearth of choices. As always, sampling different places is a great way to go.

The Old Market Inn is oft-mentioned for its atmosphere. Seats downstairs look out onto the market square, allowing you to take in the market sights and sounds over a cold beer or hot Yunnan coffee.

At the western edge of the square, across the stream and hidden up an alley, is *The Tower Cafe*, which has a wide range of tasty dishes in a courtyard setting: a bit like eating at someone's home. Try their outstanding potato croquettes.

Walking along Xinyi Jie into the old quarter you will come across *Din-Din's* and the *No 40 Restaurant*: two long-time cafes which do a fairly steady trade despite the competition from the market square cafes. The 2nd floor of the No 40 Restaurant gives good views of old town rooftops, good for contemplating over a coffee following a lengthy discourse with Mr Xuan Ke, who lives nearby.

But by far the best new option is the *Well Bistro*, around the corner and down from the First Bend Inn. The exceedingly friendly owners have got a good head for the restaurant business and it shows, from the cosy all-wood interiors and tastefully understated decor down to the superb food. Everything is made from scratch, including the bread and to-die-for desserts, which change daily. The pizza here is tops in south-west China without a doubt. Lots of good vegetarian options are on the menu as well. Hip, eclectic music echoes quietly throughout the day. You'll probably spend lots of time here reading their books and making your collect calls. They speak great English – the owner was in fact reading Dostoyevsky in English on our last visit.

Other Places to Eat Elsewhere around Lijiang and off the travellers' circuit, look out for places serving *baba*, the Lijiang local speciality – thick flatbreads of wheat, served plain or stuffed with meats, vegetable or sweets. Morning is the best time to check out the baba selection.

In the old town, you can buy baba from street vendors. In the southern section of the old town is a string of grubby but charming little hole-in-the-wall eateries so desperate for your business that they've Anglicised their signs to read *Old Town Small Eat* and the like, although they haven't gotten around to translating the menu yet. East of the cinema across the bridge is a night market where you can get a steaming bowl of tasty noodles for Y2, roasted potatoes dipped in chilli powder for Y0.30, and other assorted snacks.

There are several smaller restaurants just before the entrance to the Hei Long Tan Park on Xin Dajie; at the corner where the road bends toward Black Dragon Park is a

restaurant soon to open billing itself as, in a hastily scribbled sign, *Naxi Typical Restaurant* although it looked like any other point-and-choose restaurant. Nearby are restaurants with 'medicinal herb chicken in steampot' and a few pastry shops.

Entertainment

One of the few things you can do in the evening in Lijiang is attend performances of the *Naxi orchestra*. Performances are given every night in a beautiful old building inside the old town, usually from 8 to 10 pm.

What's distinctive about the group is not only that all 20 to 24 members are Naxi, but that they play a type of Taoist temple music that has been lost elsewhere in China. The pieces they perform are supposedly faithful renditions of music from the Han, Song and Tang dynasties, played on original instruments (in most of China such instruments didn't survive the Cultural Revolution: several of this group hid theirs by burying them underground). They also play plenty of Han Chinese music, so don't be surprised.

This is a rare chance to hear Chinese music as it must have sounded in classical China. Xuan Ke usually speaks for the group at performances, explaining each musical piece and describing the instruments. There are taped recordings of the music available: a set of two costs Y30. If you're interested, make sure you buy the tape at the show – tapes on sale at shops around town, and even in Kunming, are pirated copies, from which the orchestra receives no revenue.

You can usually turn up on your own and watch a performance, but you might want to arrive 15 minutes early to ensure a good seat. Tickets are Y20. To get to the performance venue, from the No 40 Restaurant turn left and then right, crossing a small courtyard to enter a narrow alley. At the end of the alley, go past the First Bend Inn and turn left. Going straight past the Well Bistro you'll come to a junction of alleys. A sign should be there with 'Naxi

Music' written on it; the main door is just to the right.

Eyeing the popularity of the Naxi orchestra, CITS and other travel agencies have hopped on the bandwagon, organising various 'minority music concerts'. These are better off skipped; it's better to support the original Naxi orchestra, whose members managed to retain both their skills and their instruments throughout the officially sanctioned insanity of the Cultural Revolution.

Getting There & Away

Air With the opening of a new airport 25km to the east of town, Yunnan Airlines can now fly you from Kunming to Lijiang daily in 45 minutes for Y390. From Kunming, flights leave daily at 7.20 am, and on Tuesdays and Sundays there is an additional afternoon flight. In Lijiang, tickets can be booked at the CAAC ticket office (☎ 512-0289), the Guluwan Hotel (which levies a service charge) and CITS (another service charge). Yunnan Airlines was also planning flights direct to and from Xishuangbanna, without stopping in Kunming first.

Bus The bus situation in Lijiang is complicated by the existence of two bus stations. If you're staying up around the Lijiang Hotel or the No 2 Guesthouse, check to see what's on offer at the north bus station before making the long trek down to the main long-distance bus station. The ticket window is just south of the Red Sun Hotel.

Some, but not all, buses originate from the north station and then stop at the main bus station before heading out, or vice versa. This means departure times from one station are generally 15 minutes ahead of those from the other. In most cases, you won't experience this, but just be sure you know where to get on your bus.

Buses for Xiaguan pass by Dali to the west and leave from the main bus station at 6.45, 7.50 and 10 am on big buses (Y20), and eight times from 9 am to 3.30 pm on small buses (Y35) which at five hours

should be faster than the big buses, which take forever. The north bus station also has buses to Xiaguan passing through Dali five times between 7.30 am and 2 pm. Two of these – 7.30 and 11 am – are large buses which take an hour longer. Tickets are Y21 for the big bus, Y27 for the small buses. Several local bus companies also run buses to Dali: check on Xin Dajie just north of the Bank of China to see what's on offer. Most buses to Dali continue on to Xiaguan.

The other most popular destinations are Kunming and Jinjiang (for rail connections with Chengdu). Sleeper buses for Kunming leave the main bus station at 3.30, 5.30 and 6 pm (Y105 for a top berth, Y115 for the bottom). From the north bus station, sleepers (Y115) leave at 4 and 5.30 pm. Jinjiang buses leave at 6.30 am, noon and 3.30 pm from the north bus station; failing a major breakdown, the early bus will allow you to connect with trains to Chengdu at 5.56 and 8.08 pm. The 6.30 am should stop at the main bus station too at 6.45 am, but check to be sure. Otherwise, the main bus station has departures at 2, 5 and 6 pm for Y45.

During the rainy season (July to September), the Lijiang-Jinjiang road is often washed out and Chengdu-bound travellers have no option but to return to Kunming to catch a train or plane onward. At the time of writing it was still impossible for foreigners to book tickets of any kind for the train here.

Buses to Zhongdian leave from the north bus station at 6.30 and 8 am, and 1.30 pm. Otherwise, the main bus station has departures at 7.10 and 7.50 am, noon and 1 pm. If not full, they may stop at the north station. Tickets cost Y27.

Other buses from Lijiang's north station include: Qiaotou at 2 pm (Y13); Shigu at 2.30 pm (Y7) and Ninglang at 7.10 am (Y29). The main bus station has a minibus (Y30) to Ninglang at 9 am, a better option than the large bus at 7.30 am.

Getting Around

Yunnan Airlines has a bus service to and from the airport for Y5.

The modern part of town is a tedious place to walk around. The old town, however, is best seen on foot. Bike hire is readily available around town at Mao Square and, by the time you read this, the First Bend Inn. Bikes should cost around Y12 for the day.

Lijiang (nicknamed 'Land of Horses') is famous for its easily trained horses, which are usually white or chestnut with distinctive white stripes on the back. It may be possible to arrange an excursion on horseback.

AROUND LIJIANG
Monasteries

Lijiang's monasteries are Tibetan in origin and belong to the Red Hat sect. Most of them were extensively damaged during the Cultural Revolution and there's not much monastic activity to be seen nowadays. Nevertheless, it's worth hopping on a bicycle and heading out of town for a look.

Puji Monastery *(pǔjí sì)* Around 5km north-west of town (on a trail that passes the two ponds to the north of town) are a few monks at the Puji Monastery, who are usually happy to show the occasional stray traveller around.

Fuguo Monastery *(fùguó sì)* Not far from the town of Baisha, this was once the largest of Lijiang's monasteries. Much of it was destroyed during the Cultural Revolution. In the monastery compound look out for the Hufa Hall; the interior walls have some interesting frescoes.

Yufeng Monastery *(yùfēng sì)* This small lamasery is on a hillside about 5km past Baisha. The last 3km of the track requires a steep climb. If you decide to leave your bike at the foot of the hill, don't leave it too close to the village below – the local kids have been known to let the air out of the tyres!

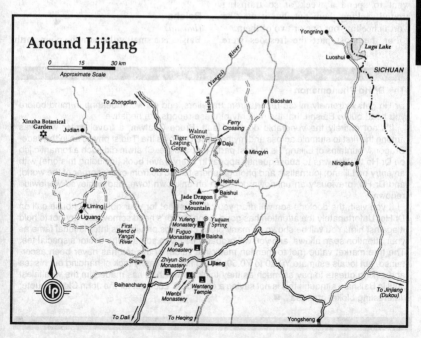

The monastery sits at the foot of Yulong-xueshan and was established in 1756. The monastery's main attraction nowadays is the Camellia Tree of 10,000 Blossoms *(wànduǒ shānchá)*. Ten thousand might be something of an exaggeration, but locals claim that the tree produces at least 4000 between February and April. A monk on the grounds risked his life to keep the tree secretly watered during the years of the Cultural Revolution.

Wenbi Monastery *(wénbǐ sì)* The Wenbi Monastery involves a fairly steep uphill ride to the south-west of Lijiang. The monastery itself is not that interesting, but there are some good views and pleasant walks in the near vicinity.

Frescoes

Lijiang is famed for its temple frescoes. Most travellers are probably not going to want to spend a week or so traipsing around seeking them out, but it may be worth checking out one or two of them.

For the most part the frescoes were carried out during the 15th and 16th centuries by Tibetan, Naxi, Bai and Han artists. Many of them were subsequently restored during the Qing Dynasty. They depict variously Taoist plus Chinese and Tibetan Buddhist themes and can be found on the interior walls of temples in the area. The best example is said by experts to be the fresco in Baisha's Dabaoji Hall. Again, the Red Guards came through here slashing and gouging during the Cultural Revolution, but there's still a lot left to see.

In Baisha ask around for the **Dabaoji Hall** *(dàbǎojī gōng)*, the **Liuli Temple** *(liúlí diàn)* or the **Dading Pavilion** *(dàdìng gé)*. Check the little shop for reasonably priced Naxi scrolls and paintings.

In the nearby village of Longquan *(lóngquán)*, frescoes can also be found on the interior walls of the **Dajue Temple** *(dàjué gōng)*. See the earlier Fuguo Monastery entry in this section for other frescoes.

Baisha
(báishā)
Baisha is a small village on the plain north

The Dr Ho Phenomenon

Dr Ho gets extremely mixed reports from travellers, and it's worth bearing in mind before you head out to Baisha that the majority of these reports are negative.

It's not entirely the venerable doctor's fault. Bruce Chatwin, a travel writer who was among the first to stumble across and mythologise Dr Ho as the 'Taoist physician in the Jade-Dragon Mountains of Lijiang', is at least partly responsible. Chatwin did such a romantic job on Dr Ho that he was to subsequently appear in every travel book (including this one) with an entry on Lijiang; journalists and photographers turned up from every corner of the world; and Dr Ho, previously an unknown doctor in an unknown town, had achieved worldwide renown.

If you visit, the doctor's son will drag you off the street for your obligatory house call on Dr Ho. Unfortunately the attention has gone to the doctor's head somewhat – try not to hold it against him. You will be shown as many press clippings proving his international fame as your attention span allows, and you will probably be given some of the doctor's special tea. The true market value (not to mention medicinal value) of this tea has never been ascertained, but locals estimate Y0.20 to Y0.50. Dr Ho has the canny trick of handing out his tea and asking guests to pay as much as they think it's worth. It has made him the wealthiest soul in Baisha – although this is not saying a great deal. Look out for the John Cleese quote: 'Interesting bloke; crap tea'. ∎

of Lijiang in the vicinity of several old temples (see the earlier Frescoes section). Before Kublai Khan made it part of his Yuan Empire (1271-1368), it was the capital of the Naxi kingdom. It's hardly changed since then and though at first sight it seems nothing more than a desultory collection of dirt roads and stone houses, it offers a close-up glimpse of Naxi culture for those willing to spend some time nosing around.

The star attraction of Baisha will probably hail you in the street. Dr Ho (or He) looks like the stereotype of a Taoist physician and there's a sign outside his door: 'The Clinic of Chinese Herbs in Jade Dragon Mountains of Lijiang'.

Jade Dragon Snow Mountain
(yùlóng xuěshān)
Soaring 5500m above Lijiang is Mt Satseto, also known as Yulongxue Shan (Jade Dragon Snow Mountain). Thirty-five kilometres north of Lijiang, the peak was climbed for the first time in 1963 by a research team from Beijing.

A chairlift has recently opened which brings you about halfway up a nearby slope, from where you can rent horses which will take you to a large meadow. There, if the weather is clear, you will be greeted by a stunning view of Yulongxue Shan, and probably groups of Naxi women dancing and singing. The latter is clearly aimed at garnering tourist yuan, but it's still pleasant. This trek, aimed mainly at Chinese tourists, is an expensive one. Getting out to the mountain from Lijiang will either require hitching, hiring your own van for around Y130, or catching a ride on one of the private buses to Daju. (Getting this same bus back could be tricky.) You could also try getting there on one of the buses to Daju from Ali Baba's, but again, it's getting back that would be tricky, since buses don't go directly to the mountain.

Local tour operators in Lijiang have prohibitively priced tours taking in the mountain; a couple are located on Mao Square. Once there, the chairlift ride will

cost you Y50, and the horse rental another Y20.

Alternatively, you can reach the snow line on one of the adjoining peaks if you continue along the base of the hillside near Baisha but ignore the track to Yufeng Monastery. On the other side of the next obvious valley, a well-worn path leads uphill to a lake. It might be a good idea to ask locals about conditions in this area before setting out.

Shigu & First Bend of the Yangzi
(shígǔ/chángjiāng dìyīwān)
The small town of Shigu sits on the first bend of China's greatest river. Shigu means Stone Drum in Chinese, and the stone drum itself is a marble plaque shaped like a drum that commemorates a 16th century Naxi victory over a Tibetan army. The other plaque on the river's edge celebrates the People's Army crossing of the river here in 1936 in the Great March to the north.

Buses to Shigu leave at 2.30 pm from Lijiang's north bus station, and take three hours. This would probably require an overnight stay. At the time of writing, the morning bus service had been suspended, but it's probably worth checking to see if it has resumed. Alternatively, try buses bound for Judian or get a bus as far as Baihanchang and hitch from this point.

Tiger Leaping Gorge
(hǔtiào xiá)
After making its first turn at Shigu the mighty Yangzi River (at this point known as the Jinsha River) surges between the Haba Mountains and the Jade Dragon Snow Mountain, through what is one of the deepest gorges in the world. The entire gorge measures 16km, and from the waters of the Yangzi to the mountaintops is a giddy 3900m.

Within five years the hike through the gorge went from obscure to the can't-miss experience of northern Yunnan, although you'll probably only encounter several other travellers on the trail. All up, plan on spending three or four days away from

YUNNAN

Lijiang doing the hike. Ideally you can do the walk in two days, although some travellers, enchanted with Walnut Grove, have lengthened it to over a week.

One American hiked through the gorge in one day, but if you didn't bring your superhero suit you'll have to stay overnight at Walnut Grove. It's worth spending an extra day in Daju. It is a good town featuring the Tiger Leaping Gorge Hotel – a great place to stay.

Dangers & Annoyances The gorge trek is not to be taken lightly. A half-dozen people – including a few foreign travellers – have died in the gorge. Most perished because they wandered off the trail, got lost and/or were unable to return to the trail, or fell. One hiker was buried while trying to scramble over a landslide. Two solo travellers have also reported being assaulted on the trail by locals, although this couldn't (or wouldn't) be officially confirmed.

The newest danger is just as serious: dynamite. A new highway is literally being blasted along the lower route. If you choose this path, you should note the very real danger you could be blown to bits.

On a less severe note, several travellers have reported becoming ill after eating in Qiaotou or from drinking water along the trek.

Gorge Trek The first thing to do is to check with Ali Baba's, Ma Ma Fu's, the First Bend Inn or the Well Bistro in Lijiang for the latest gossip on the mini-trek, particularly the weather and its possibly lethal effects on the trail.

Transport is easier than it once was, but this also can still be where problems arise. It's difficult to recommend which end of the gorge to start at (Qiaotou or Daju), but we will say this: while finishing at Qiaotou has the advantage of easier transport links back to Lijiang, you should consider the fact that, even if you have to wait a day for a bus to Lijiang from Daju, there are much worse places to hang around for a couple of days.

If you have to overnight in Qiaotou, avoid the place with the English sign that says 'stay/put up'. The second half is a good description of what you have to do with all the shrieking karaoke from the uninterested staff. Instead, head for the *Valley Village Hotel*, also known as the *Gorge Village Hotel*. It's fronted by a small shop, and presently the nice woman who owns the place has clean doubles for Y10 with no TV, Y12 with TV. Bathrooms are OK and there is an elaborate system for evening hot water. The family is currently working to open a bigger hotel next door. South of this hotel, the *Jade Dragon Hotel* has dorm beds from Y15; hot water here is solar, so you might not get any. In this block there are also a couple of more upmarket options. Across from the bridge in Qiaotou is the nerve-centre of trail information, the *Backpacker Cafe*, with an English menu, passable English spoken, and backpack storage.

There is a new admission fee of Y20 at the gorge, which many people have avoided simply by walking through at 5 am. The following description starts at Qiaotou.

There are now two trails – the higher (the older route, known as the 24 bend path, although it's more like 30), and the lower (easier but more dangerous while the road is being built). One traveller aptly points out, 'The low road is more dangerous, but the high road leaves less time for drinking beer in Walnut Grove'. You could do one going and one returning the next day, as many have discovered, avoiding Daju altogether, or even combine the two roads in an extremely ambitious and hair-raising day trip. It is also possible to rent a taxi to go as far as is drivable on the new road and then start from there, taking shortcuts up to the high road. Obviously, don't go without asking around on that one. There are now yellow arrows – a godsend – pointing you along the upper path. To get to the high road, after crossing through the gate, cross a small stream and go 150m. Take a left fork, go through the schoolyard, and from there follow the yellow arrows. Pay attention – many travellers miss the *info out of date now (sept. 2002).*

high road and get mired in the TNT-laden low road. Via the upper path, it's a strenuous eight to ten hours; via the new path it'll be seven hours, but you should be prepared to flee the blasting and scramble up and over landslides. Along the high road is a new 'halfway lodge' in Ben Di Wan village, but it's tiny and almost always full.

Both roads can be hair-raising during the rainy months of July and August – or any time it rains really – when landslides and swollen waterfalls can place themselves in your path. Ask locals in Lijiang or at the *Backpacker Cafe* about conditions.

Walnut Grove is the approximate halfway point, and there are two hotels nestled among the walnut trees. The *Spring Guesthouse*, which incorporates *Sean's Cafe*, is the spot for more lively evenings and socialising. *Chateau de Woody*, the other option, is considered the quiet alternative. Both places have dorm beds for Y7 (perhaps less in low season), some doubles for Y10 per person, 24 hour hot water, and both have won praise from travellers. Food and beer are also available here. Supplies of bottled water can be chancy; it's probably best to bring your own. Be aware that in peak times – particularly late summer – up to 100 people a day can make the trek in *each direction*, and at those times bed space is short. Both hotels are planning to expand, but be prepared to sleep in a back room somewhere. (A good rule of thumb is: the more travellers in Lijiang, the more trekkers will be here.)

The next day's walk is slightly shorter at four to six hours. Note too that this path has changed from years past because of landslides. Walk 1½ hours from the Grove to the river – Woody's or Sean's will have guides – and take the ferry across. It's a flat fee of Y10 to cross ... ridiculous, but what can you do? From here it's an additional two hours, or less. The *Tiger Leaping Gorge Hotel*, Daju's premier vacationer's residence, costs Y8 a bed and is on the left-hand side as you walk southward out of town; it's about 600m from the department store. It has good food and is a good place

to hang out for at least a day. Nearby, the *Snowflake Hotel* also has beds in fairly clean rooms for similar prices.

If you're doing the walk the other way round and heading for Qiaotou, walk north through Daju, aiming for the white pagoda at the foot of the mountains.

Getting There & Away Buses run to Zhongdian via Qiaotou daily from the main long-distance bus station in Lijiang from 7.10 am onward for Y11. Buses to Daju (Y30, five hours) leave from near Ali Baba's restaurant at 8.30 am and, sometimes, 1.30 pm. These return to Lijiang, although don't count on that second one being there. In either case be prepared to get out and push. There is also sometimes a bus from the Yunchuan Hotel on Mao Square. The new highway being blasted along the bottom of the gorge will eventually link Qiaotou, Walnut Grove, Daju and then bend north to link up with Baishuitai and probably allow travellers to get to Zhongdian from there.

Returning to Lijiang from Qiaotou, buses start running through from Zhongdian around 7 am, though 8 am is more like it; just plop yourself on a chair in front of the Backpacker Cafe and stick your arm out. It'll cost you around Y11, though Y15 isn't unheard of. The last one headed toward Lijiang should be around 4.30 pm. When demand is sufficient, a local bus originates in Qiaotou, opposite the market at the car park. If running, it leaves at 7 am and returns from Lijiang at 2 pm from the main bus station.

Lugu Lake
(lúgū hú)
This remote lake overlaps the Yunnan-Sichuan border and is a centre for several Tibetan, Yi and Mosu (a Naxi subgroup) villages. The Mosu still practise matriarchy, and many of the Naxi customs now lost in Lijiang are still in evidence here. The lake itself is fairly high at 2685m and is usually snowbound over the winter months. The best times to visit the lake are April to May and September to October,

YUNNAN

when the weather is dry and mild. The Chinese government is busily preparing to invest more millions of yuan into a new road here north, which will eventually reduce travel time from nine hours to half that. No doubt this will increase the swells of tour groups and the flutter of shutters already apparent.

Things to See In addition to just admiring the gorgeous scenery, you can visit several islands on the lake via large dugout canoes, which the Mosu call 'pig troughs' (*zhūcáo*). The canoes, which are rowed by Mosu who also serve as guides, generally take you out to Liwubi Island (*lǐwùbǐ dǎo*), the lake's largest. From here you can practically wade across to a spit of land in Sichuan province, or throw a stone, or both. Out to the island and back is around Y15 per person, Y30 if you want to be rowed around the island as well. (These price hikes brought to you courtesy of Chinese tour group saturation turning it into a seller's market.) The canoes can hold around seven people, but the price should be the same regardless of how many of you there are. At those prices you should stretch it into a whole day of picnicking. Canoes leave from near the Mosu Yuan Hotel.

Twelve kilometres west of the lake is **Yongning Monastery** (*yǒngníng sì*), a lamasery with at least 20 lamas in residence. There is also a hot spring (*wēnquán*) up around here; a private bus costs Y15 a head for the half-hour ride and entry is 1Y. A bus passes through Luoshui to Yongning for Y5; you could opt to walk the 12 or so miles through nice scenery.

Places to Stay & Eat Visitors to Lugu Lake arrive at the lakeside village of Luoshui (*luòshuǐcūn*), where you can stay in Mosu homes for around Y10 per bed. Most of the homes are equipped to take guests, so you won't be short of options. There are no showers. Food is cooked up for you by the Mosu: little fish, potatoes and barbecued hard-boiled eggs are the order of the day. Average prices are Y5 to

Y10, depending on how well you want to eat. The *Peace Garden* (*móānyuán*) is good and far away from the clutter for Y15.

There are also three guesthouses in Luoshui, all very similar – only triples and quads are available, for Y45 and Y40 respectively. There is no running water: you can wash up from a cistern in the courtyard. Of the three, the *Mosu Yuan* (*mósuōyuàn*) seems to be the centre of action: occasional Mosu song-and-dance performances are held here, and morning buses to Ninglang leave from in front of the hotel.

Finally, there are also several guesthouses in Yongning, which make a good base from which to hike out to the nearby hot spring. Beds average around Y20.

If you have to stay overnight in Ninglang, the changeover point between Lijiang and Lugu Lake, probably most convenient is the *Bus Station Guesthouse* (*kèyùn zhāodàisuǒ*), with doubles for Y10. Then there's the recently opened *Lugu Hotel* (*lǔgú fànzhuāng*), which has beds in doubles/triples for Y8/10, as well as standard doubles for Y150. It's right in the centre of town, about a three minute walk from the bus station, and near lots of shops and restaurants. Travellers used to frequent the *Government Guesthouse* (*zhèngfǔ zhāodàisuǒ*),which has dorms beds for Y8 to Y15 and standard doubles for Y140. The problem here is that the hotel is about 1km from the bus station up a fairly steep hill: transport links are not convenient and there's not much in the way of places to eat nearby. Also, tour groups tend to book this place solid, so getting a room can sometimes be a hassle.

Getting There & Away From Lijiang it's a nine hour bus trip to Ninglang, the Lugu County seat. From Ninglang it's another four or five hours by bus to Lugu Lake. Sometimes minibuses meet buses coming in from Lijiang to take travellers onward to Lugu Lake, but there's still a chance you'll have to overnight there. If you take the 7.10 am bus from Lijiang's north station (Y29), you should have no problem hooking up with a minibus immediately. The three hour ride bound for Yongning costs Y20. All told, you'll get to Luoshui by around 7.30 pm. Back to Lijiang, a bus (Y40) leaves at 7.10 am and gets into Lijiang around 4 pm.

If you don't get a minibus meeting you in Ninglang, the town has two bus stations on the main street quite close to one another. Check in both for the next bus to Lugu. There is also an English-language speaker in the Government Guesthouse who is usually happy to provide information. Coming back from Lugu Lake, buses (Y20) to Ninglang leave in the morning from in front of the Mosu Yuan Hotel or along the main road. The first one usually leaves around 9 am. Going this way you will probably have to overnight in Ninglang as there is no afternoon connection to Lijiang.

Some travellers have tried hiking from Yongning on to Muli in Sichuan Province, from where there is bus transport to Xichang on the Kunming-Chengdu line. But be warned: it's a dangerous route with no accommodation. You'll need to bring a tent, a warm sleeping bag and all your own provisions. There's also no reason to expect the Tibetan tribespeople (all armed) you come across en route to be friendly either. One Canadian traveller we met had a frightening experience with locals while hiking this route and headed back to Yongning. Most travellers head back to Lijiang the same way they came.

ZHONGDIAN
(zhōngdiàn)
Zhongdian, 198km north-west of Lijiang, used to be the last stop in Yunnan for more hardy travellers looking at a rough five or six day journey to Chengdu via the Tibetan townships and rugged Ming Dynasty terrain of western Sichuan (at least before the PSB choked off this route in 1997, so be warned).

It is also a jumping-off point for those looking to slip into Tibet by the back door. There are rumours that the Yunnan route into Tibet will open up in coming years, but it is extremely unlikely. The route is considered quite dangerous and the PSB is still keeping a vigilant eye out for errant backpackers nearing the provincial border.

Whether Zhongdian merits a trip in itself is a difficult question. If you don't have time to make it into Tibet, Zhongdian, a principally Tibetan town with a heavy Han overlay and a sprinkling of Hui (Muslim), Bai and Naxi, is worth a look. It's perhaps worth visiting in combination with the Tiger Leaping Gorge trek. Start at Daju and then take a bus from Qiaotou at the end of the trek to Zhongdian. The bus journey from Qiaotou takes only three or four hours. One thing you'll definitely notice is that Zhongdian has become perhaps the supreme example of a Chinese construction zone. At the time of writing, Zhongdian appeared to be a bombed out shell of a city. With all this construction, by the time you read this, there should be all kinds of new stuff around. Not to worry – Zhongdian still had an interesting old section of town.

In mid-June Zhongdian plays host to a horse racing festival that sees several days of dancing, singing, eating and of course, horse racing. The horses are actually more akin to ponies, and the races don't exactly proceed at thoroughbred speed. But travellers who have witnessed the event have raved about it. Accommodation can be a bit tight around this time, so you may want to arrive a day or two early. If you are in Lijiang, you can probably ask CITS to help you book a room.

Zhongdian is at 3200m and very close to the Tibetan border. About an hour's walk north of town is **Songzanlin Monastery** *(sōngzànlín sì)*, a 300-year-old Tibetan monastery complex with several hundred monks. (You can get blessed for Y5.) It sits upon a hill surrounded by mountains, and is without question worth a trip to Zhongdian.

Much closer to the centre of things, overlooking the old town district is another monastery with exceedingly friendly monks.

Places to Stay & Eat

Almost all budget travellers head to the *Tibet Hotel* (☎ 822-3263) *(yǒngshēng fàndiàn)*, a clean and friendly spot. Dorm beds here cost Y16, and there are doubles for Y42; all come with satellite television. The hotel also has money exchange, international calls, and laundry service, all of which are available on a hit-or-miss basis. Getting there is easy: exit the bus station and look way up. Atop the building across the way is a sign pointing you to the right. Keep going all the way until the first major intersection. Turn left and keep walking two giant blocks.

That's about your only option for clean, cosy budget options. Next to the bus station, the *Bus Station Guesthouse* is no longer accepting foreigners. Across the street and left five minutes or so is a small friendly *zhāodàisuǒ* on the corner with Y20 beds in very large four-bed rooms. The only problem is that the bathrooms are outside and putrid. To the right of the bus station on the other side of the street a hundred metres or so is the *Kangba Hotel* (☎ 822-4488) *(kāngbā jiǔdiàn)*, a new place with dorm beds for Y25. Doubles and triples with private bathroom are Y210/180 and up.

Up in the north of town are some Sichuan-style restaurants and a little place cranking out pretty good dumplings. One giant block from the bus station in the direction of the Tibet Hotel, the *AAA Cafe* has obviously set itself up to be *the* travellers' hang-out. Reports on the food have been mixed – the food's good, but the wait's not – but it's a good place to go for info. The owner is the same one who previously ran the legendary Zhongdian hangout, the *Lhasa Cafe*, and later, the *Chocolate Cafe*. The apple pie and mashed potatoes come highly recommended.

A new place was supposed to open by the time this edition comes out. Ten minutes to the left out of the AAA Cafe should be the *Tibetan Art Cafe and Coffee Shop*, run by a Tibetan woman who speaks good English. There are also a few Tibetan and Naxi restaurants south of the bus station.

Getting There & Away

Buses for Zhongdian (Y27) leave daily from Lijiang's north bus station at 7.30 and 8 am and 1.30 pm and take anywhere from four to six hours. From the main bus station, buses leave at 7.10 and 7.50 am, noon and 1 pm. The 7.10 and 7.50 am buses should stop at the north station, but check to be sure. Buses to Zhongdian pass through Qiaotou, at the southern end of the Tiger Leaping Gorge trek. Returning to Lijiang, buses leave officially at 7 am and 1.30 pm (Y20 to Y26) but there are independent operators leaving from in front of the station at other times.

Sleepers back to Kunming leave at 6.30 am (two buses) and cost Y75 to Y98. Buses to Xiaguan leave at 6.20 or 7.10 am for Y41.

Onward travel from Zhongdian offers some interesting possibilities. The long-awaited destination from Zhongdian is Tibet and, who knows, by the time you have this book in your hands the miraculous may have occurred and this route may be open – don't count on it, though. For more information see the Road Routes section of the Tibet chapter.

The one that is now very much back to illegal is the arduous bus-hopping trek to Chengdu, in Sichuan. If you're up for this you're looking at a minimum of five to six days' travel at some very high altitudes – you'll need warm clothes. The first stage of the trip is Zhongdian to Xiangcheng *(xiāngchéng)* in Sichuan, a journey of around 12 hours. You could break this up with a stop in Dêrong *(déróng)* just over the Sichuan border and only about seven hours from Zhongdian. From Xiangcheng, head to Litang *(lǐtáng)* (10 hours); however, if roads are bad you may be forced to stay overnight in Daocheng *(dàochéng)*. From Litang it's 12 hours to Kangding *(kāngdìng)* and another 12 hours on to Chengdu. Accommodation on the way is rough and your fellow passengers are likely to be chain-smoking phlegm removalists whose idea of fun is leaving the windows open and letting the sub-zero mountain breezes ruffle their hair. Have fun!

Warning The route to Litang via Xiangcheng was definitely closed at the time of writing. Not only was the Zhongdian bus station denying tickets to foreigners, but those few who did make it were finding themselves shelling out fines arbitrarily priced, but usually around Y300! For the record, the Zhongdian bus station has a bus leaving at 7.30 daily for Xiangcheng; the rattletrap costs Y29.10.

One way to thumb your nose at the PSB would be to try and get a ticket to Dehrong, just over the border with Yunnan, which has a bus departing to it every other day at 8 am. Otherwise, many people have arrived, discovered the route closed, and been stuck since they've already seen Dali, Lijiang, and Kunming.

Your best bet from Zhongdian would be to take the 10.30 am sleeper bus (Y80) directly to Jinjiang, via Lijiang, which should allow you to hook up with a train that day.

AROUND ZHONGDIAN

There are numerous as yet unexplored possibilities for trips out of Zhongdian. At present the two most popular options are **Baishuitai** *(báishuǐ tái)* and **Meilixueshan** *(méilǐ xuěshān)*. The former is a limestone deposit plateau 108km to the south-east of Zhongdian with some breathtaking scenery and Tibetan villages en route. The terraces are resplendent in sunlight, but can be tough to access if rainfall has made trails slick. Mt Meilixue straddles the Yunnan-Tibet border and, at 6740m, rates as Yunnan's highest peak. Getting to the mountain can be a problem in the winter months. If you are planning to head to Mt Meilixue, try and combine it with a visit to Dêqên *(déqīn)*, the last major town before the mountain. There is an important Tibetan monastery here.

One very intriguing idea floated by locals is to trek all the way from Baishuitai to Tiger Leaping Gorge using foot power or even ponies. From Baishuitai on the first day it should be a six hour or so walk to a Haba village, then another day to Daju and enter the gorge. Clearly you'll need locals with local expertise to suss out the details of this one. The helpful staff at the Tibet Hotel are can't help with details, but they know people who can help.

Getting There & Away

Transport to sights around Zhongdian is still pretty touch and go. If it is possible to rustle up a group of travellers with similar interests, there are jeeps and minibuses for hire for Y250 to Y350 per day. There are also Chinese day tours of area sights which you should be able to join.

At the time of writing there was a bus to the limestone terraces leaving every other day at 7 am for Y15. Don't count on this always departing, however.

JINJIANG

(jīnjiāng)

Jinjiang is the tiny railhead for the large town of Panzhihua, just over the border in Sichuan Province.

Accommodation in this jolly little hamlet is provided courtesy of various fleapits, the most convenient being the *Railway Hotel (tiělù lǚxíngshè)*. It's directly opposite the railway station; dorm beds cost between Y12 and Y30. Make an effort to get on a train before you book in anywhere – a stay in Jinjiang is not recommended.

For travellers Jinjiang is an important junction for the Lijiang-Chengdu route. To reach Jinjiang from Chengdu, two trains are best. The No 165 leaves Chengdu at 3.25 pm and arrives in Jinjiang at 6 am. The No 117 leaves Chengdu at 10.15 pm and arrives at noon. This should give you time to get to Lijiang without having to stay overnight in Jinjiang, though arriving at noon might make it tough. A hardsleeper for this trip costs Y120. At Jinjiang station the minibus drivers are likely to assault you in droves for the trip to Lijiang.

Travelling in the other direction, from Lijiang to Chengdu, you can forget about getting train tickets of any kind before you get to Jinjiang. The bus station in Lijiang won't sell them to you and there doesn't seem to be a black market for them either.

To make matters worse this is a busy line and even the hard-seat tickets get booked out from time to time. This situation may improve if the FIT Department of the Lijiang CITS comes through on its pledge to help foreigners book train tickets, but you'll have to check for yourself.

Leaving Lijiang on the morning bus may allow you to connect with the No 206/203 to Chengdu departing at 5.56 pm. If you miss that, you can try for the No 208, which leaves at 8.08 pm. After that your last chance is the No 166, which leaves at 12.30 am. If you want anything other than a hard seat, look for the entrance to the toilet to the right of the inquiries booth, turn left into the door just in front of the toilet (remember, this is China), and to the back of the courtyard on the right-hand side is an office selling hard and soft-sleeper tickets.

Xishuangbanna Region

The region of Xishuangbanna (xīshuāng-bǎnnà, or usually, just bǎnnà) is in the deep south of Yunnan Province, next to the Myanmar and Lao borders. The name Xishuangbanna is a Chinese approximation of the original Thai name, Sip Sawng Panna (12 Rice-growing Districts). The place has a laid-back South-East Asian feel to it and it's easy to watch the weeks slip by as you make your way around small villages, tropical forests and the occasional stupa.

In recent years Xishuangbanna has become China's own mini-Thailand, and Chinese tourists have been heading down in droves for the sunshine, Dai minority dancing, water-splashing festivals (held daily nowadays), as well as the ubiquitous tour group lures, such as the 'forest of one tree', the 'king of tea trees' and other trees that suggest something less prosaic than a mere tree. But it's easy to get away from the crowds by jumping on a public bus to some small town, and making it your base for exploring the surrounding countryside and villages.

Xishuangbanna Dai Autonomous Prefecture, as it is known officially, is subdivided into the three counties of Jinghong, Menghai and Mengla. Mengla County is still not on the lists of officially permitted places, and permits seem to be a bit hit or miss, although they can be applied for at the PSB office in Jinghong. You can easily buy a ticket to Mengla in Jinghong, and may make it there and back without running afoul of the PSB, but be ready for fines and a swift ejection all the same. However, if you're headed to the border crossing with Laos, south of Mengla, and have a Lao visa stamped in your passport, then you should have no trouble. No travellers reported any troubles with the PSB despite not having a permit.

Xishuangbanna has wet and dry seasons. The wet season is between June and August, when it rains ferociously almost every day. From September to February there is less rainfall, but thick fog descends during the late evening and doesn't lift until 10 am or even later at the height of winter. Between May and August there are frequent and spectacular thunderstorms.

Between November and March temperatures average about 19°C (66.2°F). The hottest months of the year are from April to September, when you can expect an average of 25°C (77°F).

Like Hainan Island, Xishuangbanna is home to many unique species of plant and animal life. Unfortunately, recent scientific studies have demonstrated the devastating effect of previous government policies on land use; the tropical rainforest areas of Hainan and Xishuangbanna are now as acutely endangered as similar rainforest areas elsewhere on the planet. Studies have indicated that since 1960 the average temperature of Xishuangbanna has risen 1°C, and rainfall has dropped off 10% to 20%.

The jungle areas that remain still contain dwindling numbers of wild tigers, leopards,

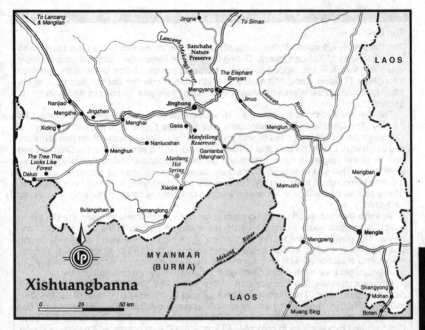

Xishuangbanna

0   25   50 km

elephants and golden-haired monkeys, although sadly the only elephants you're likely to see are the ones chained by the foot to the trees under the tourist lodges built into the triple (now double) thick canopies.

The Tropical Plant Research Institute in Jinghong has gardens with a limited selection of plants that gives you an idea of the spectacular range of flora that once covered the land.

About one-third of the 800,000-strong population of this region are Dai; another third or so are Han Chinese and the rest are a hotchpotch of minorities which include the Miao, Zhuang, Yao and lesser known hill tribes such as the Aini, Jinuo, Bulang, Lahu and Wa.

FESTIVALS

Dai festivals attract hordes of foreigners and Chinese alike. The Water-Splashing Festival held around mid-April (usually 13 to 15 April) washes away the dirt, sorrow and demons of the old year and brings in the happiness of the new. The first day of the festival is devoted to a giant market. The second day features dragon-boat racing, swimming races and rocket launching. The third day features the water-splashing freakout – be prepared to get drenched all day, and remember, the wetter you get, the more luck you'll receive. In the evenings there's dancing, launching of hot-air paper balloons and game playing.

During the Tanpa Festival in February, young boys are sent to the local temple for initiation as novice monks. At approximately the same time (between February and March), Tan Jing Festival participants honour Buddhist texts housed in local temples.

The Tan Ta Festival is held during the last 10 day period of October or November,

The Dai

The Dai people are concentrated in this pocket of Yunnan and exercise a clear upper hand in the economy of Xishuangbanna. During the Cultural Revolution many Dai people simply voted with their feet and slipped across the border to join their fellow Dai who are sprinkled throughout Thailand, Laos, Myanmar and Vietnam. Not only the Dai but also most of the other minorities in these areas display a nonchalant disregard for borders and authority in general.

The Dai are Buddhists who were driven southwards by the Mongol invasion of the 13th century. The Dai state of Xishuangbanna was annexed by the Mongols and then by the Chinese, and a Chinese governor was installed in the regional capital of Jinglan (present-day Jinghong). Countless Buddhist temples were built in the early days of the Dai state and now lie in the jungles in ruins. During the Cultural Revolution, Xishuangbanna's temples were desecrated and destroyed. Some were saved by being used as granaries, but many are now being rebuilt from scratch. Temples are also recovering their role, with or without official blessing, as village schools where young children are accepted for religious training as monks.

To keep themselves off the damp earth in the tropical rainforest weather, the Dai live in spacious wooden houses raised on stilts in the classic style, with the pigs and chickens below. The common dress for Dai women is a straw hat or towel-wrap headdress; a tight, short blouse in a bright colour; and a printed sarong with a belt of silver links. Some Dai men tattoo their bodies with animal designs. Betel-nut chewing is popular and many Dai youngsters get their teeth capped with gold; otherwise they are considered ugly.

Ethnolinguistically, the Dai are part of the very large Thai family that includes the Siamese, Lao, Shan, Thai Dam and Ahom peoples found scattered throughout the river valleys of Thailand, Myanmar, Laos, northern Vietnam and Assam. The Xishuangbanna Dai are broken into four subgroups, the Shui Dai, Han Dai, Huayai Dai and Kemu Dai, each distinguished by variations in costume. All speak the Dai language, which is quite similar to Lao and northern Thai dialects. In fact, Thai is as useful as Chinese once you get off the beaten track a little, and you might have fun with a Thai phrasebook. The written language of the Dais employs a script which looks like a cross between Lao and Burmese. ■

---

with temple ceremonies, rocket launches from special towers and hot-air balloons. The rockets, which often contain lucky amulets, blast off with a curious droning sound like mini-space shuttles before exploding high above; those who find the amulets are assured of good luck.

The farming season (from July to October) is the time for the Closed-Door Festival, when marriages or festivals are banned. Traditionally, this is also the time of year that men aged 20 or older ordain as monks for a period of time. The season ends with the Open-Door Festival, when everyone lets their hair down again to celebrate the harvest.

During festivals, booking airline tickets to Jinghong can be extremely difficult. You can try getting a flight into Simao, 162km to the north, or take the bus. Hotels in Jinghong town are booked solid, but you could stay in a nearby Dai village and commute. Festivities take place all over Xishuangbanna, so you might be lucky further away from Jinghong.

SIMAO

(sīmáo)

Simao, an uninteresting little town, used to be Xishuangbanna's air link with the outside world. Nowadays Jinghong has its own airport and very few travellers stop here. True, the occasional traveller flies from Kunming to Simao and does the final leg to Jinghong by bus, but it's doubtful whether it's worth the effort unless you absolutely can't get a flight to Jinghong. The scenery between Simao and Jinghong is not exactly a Sumatran jungle, and if you're travelling further afield from Jinghong you'll get to see plenty of Xishuangbanna scenery anyway.

Getting There & Away
Air The CAAC office (☎ 223-234) is just off the main street at the northern corner of Hongqi Square. There are four flights weekly (Monday, Wednesday, Friday, Saturday) between Kunming and Simao and the one way fare is Y360.

Bus Not too many travellers head for Simao by bus, although most pass through briefly on the way from Kunming to Jinghong or vice versa. There are buses from Simao to Baoshan and Xiaguan, but most of these originate in Jinghong anyway.

JINGHONG
(jǐnghóng)
Jinghong, the capital of Xishuangbanna Prefecture, lies beside the Lancang River (Mekong River). It's a sleepy town with streets lined with palms, which help mask the Chinese-built concrete boxes until they merge with the stilt-houses in the surrounding villages. It doesn't have much to keep you longer than a couple of days. It's more a base for operations than a place to hang out, although it's not without a certain laid-back charm that somehow endures despite the steady flood of tourist traffic. Given its slow but steady sprawling growth, eventually it will be as neon-laden as any other Chinese regional big town; the karaoke shriekers have taken over a few tourist streets, and the discos can't be far behind.

Information
Tourist Offices CITS (☎ 213-3271/0460) has two offices: one a few doors down from the Mei Mei Cafe and the other across

from the entrance to the Xishuangbanna Guesthouse. The staff are friendly, and can help answer questions about sights and accommodation in the region. CITS also offers several one day tours from Y50 to Y100 per person that generally take in one to two towns and sights en route. These may suit travellers who are on a rushed itinerary and don't want to waste time mucking about with public transport, or who are in the mood to rub shoulders with their Chinese counterparts.

PSB This is opposite Peacock Park in the centre of town. Staff there are polite enough, but clueless nonetheless. Regarding Mengla, the situation seems fluid, to say the least. The office at last check handed out a list of open cities, which did not include Mengla. When asked if travellers could go to Mengla without a permit, they said, 'Sure, why not?.' If you're headed for Laos with a visa stamped in your passport, worry not. If you don't have a visa and don't even plan to visit Laos, you shouldn't have to worry too much – no one reported being hassled in Mengla. The office is open from 8.30 to 11.30 am and from 2.30 to 5 pm.

Money The Bank of China is on Jinghong Nanlu, next door to the Banna Mansion Hotel. It's open Monday through Saturday from 8 to 11.30 am and from 3 to 6 pm. Another branch is south of the Mei Mei Cafe and then down a lane to the right which doubles as a garbage dump. Changing money is possible, but is more problematic here than at the main branch. It's open weekdays from 8 am to 6 pm, with some possible Saturday hours.

Post & Communications The post office is in the centre of town at the intersection of Jinghong west and south roads (Xilu and Nanlu). Phone lines in Xishuangbanna have improved dramatically, and staff are only slightly flustered if you announce plans to place an international call. You can also direct dial from most of the hotels, but as usual their rates are noticeably higher. Postal service is available from 8 am to 8.30 pm, with telecommunication services slightly longer.

Chunhuan Park
(chūnhuān gōngyuán)
Chunhuan Park, in the south of Jinghong down past the Dai restaurants, is a fairly poor excuse for an outing. The park has a couple of replica stupas, Dai dancing girls (you'll probably get to see a water-splashing festival now held daily by popular demand if you hang around) and a pitiful elephant in chains. All this for just Y12. Just before you get to the park entrance is the **Manting Temple** *(màntīng fósì)*. It's claimed to date back 1100 years. Across from the park is the 'Peacock Minority Customs Tourist Village' where you can watch Chinese tour groups gather for daily water-splashing festivals, courtesy of your local travel agent.

Tropical Plant Research Institute
(rèdài zuòwù yánjiùsuǒ)
A short bicycle ride out of town, and a nice walk if not at noon, the institute is one of Jinghong's better attractions. A modest entry fee of Y5 gets you into the institute's inner sanctum, only recently opened to the public, where you can view over 1000 different types of plant life. Unless you're a botanist, telling them all apart could be tricky – of the scant few signs around, more than half are in Chinese only, and the rest carry only the scientific names in English. Still, it's easy to get a feel for the impressive variety of plants that make up Yunnan's tropical forests, and the grounds makes for a pleasant stroll. The Y5 admission also gets you into the **Zhou Enlai Memorial**, a 2001-like sculpture commemorating a 1961 visit by China's best loved premier. (It sounds better than it is.) There may or may not be a shop selling agricultural products grown on the premises, including tea, Chinese medicine and ground coffee – it was closed up and contained scant few items on last check.

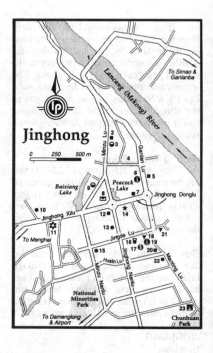

A little way back towards town and on the opposite side of the road is the **Medicinal Botanical Gardens in Xishuangbanna**. Staff at the gate might try to deter you from entering by telling you it's boring. It's not a trick to keep you out ... they're telling the truth. If it wasn't for the Y4 entrance fee, it might actually be a good stroll to kill a half-hour.

Peacock Lake Park
(kǒngquèhú gōngyuán)
This artificial lake in the centre of town isn't much, but the small park next to it is pleasant. There's also a zoo, but as usual the total lack of effort to reproduce even traces of the animals' original habitat tend to leave you feeling as depressed as the animals look to be. The English Language Corner takes place here every Sunday evening, so this is your chance to exchange views or practise your English with the locals.

JINGHONG 景洪

PLACES TO STAY

2 Communications
Hotel
交通饭店

5 Xishuangbanna
Guesthouse
版纳宾馆

7 Jingyong Hotel
景咏宾馆

12 Banna Mansion Hotel;
Bank of China
版纳大厦、中国银行

20 Wanli Dai Hotel &
Restaurant
婉丽傣味楼

22 Dai Building Hotel
傣家花苑小楼

PLACES TO EAT

18 Mei Mei Cafe
美美咖啡厅

21 Forest Cafe
森林咖啡厅

OTHER

1 Bridge Over the Mekong
大桥

3 Long-Distance Bus Station
长途汽车站

4 Market
市场

6 CITS
中国国际旅行社

8 Post Office
邮电大楼

9 No 2 Bus Station
第二客运站

10 Tropical Plant Research
Institute
热带所

11 Medicinal Botanical
Gardens
药用植物园

13 Workers' Cultural Palace
工人文化宫

14 PSB
公安局

15 CAAC
民航售票处

16 Yahu Beer Hall
雅壶啤酒店

17 Bank of China
中国银行

19 CITS
中国国际旅行社

23 Manting Temple
曼听佛寺

National Minorities Park
(mínzú fēngqíng yuán)

If you come in to Jinghong by plane, you'll pass this place on the way into town. It's not that far south of the CAAC booking office. On the map of Jinghong provided by the Banna Hotel bicycle hire service it's mysteriously referred to as the 'Minority Flirtation Expression'. Intrigued? If so, head down on Friday or Saturday when, from 7 to 11 pm, there are minority dances and so on.

Bridge Over the Mekong
(mǐgòng qiáo)

The bridge is no technical wonder, and the views of the river from it are not even that good, but it's there and it is a bridge over the Mekong after all. If rumour is correct, there was an attempt some years ago by a member of a disaffected minority to blow up the bridge. Jinghong is such a splendidly torpid town, it's hard to imagine the excitement. Apparently the hills above the town on the other side make for some OK walks.

Places to Stay

Jinghong definitely does not suffer a lack of hotel space, although most places have little to set them apart from their rivals. But there are a few which stand out from the crowd.

The *Xishuangbanna Guesthouse* (☎ 212-3679/3559) (*xīshuāngbǎnnà bīnguǎn*), in the centre of town (known as the *bǎnnà bīnguǎn*), used to be one of those exceedingly rare Chinese hotels that travellers reminisced about after they had left. It's not quite that idyllic any more – if you want to gaze out over the Mekong you'll have to pay at least Y150 – but you can still lounge in the shade of the surrounding palms, and there are some reasonably priced rooms. The staff are generally very attentive and friendly, even to the cheapskate travellers, and this is the best place to rent a bike in town. It's also got hot water 24 hours a day. Doubles with balcony, bathroom and TV in building Nos 6, 7 and 9 are not a bad deal at Y80: similar triples are Y90. Doubles and triples in the Bamboo House are more basic, but cost the same. After that it's Y150 to Y240 for standard doubles in the Riverview Buildings which already seem to be falling apart. If you get a dorm room on the ground floor, you may want to leave any valuables with

YUNNAN

the front desk, as some travellers have had possessions stolen here.

If you're in the market for basic accommodation with a Dai flavour, head down to Manting Lu. It's a long walk from the bus station (around 25 minutes), in the south of town. There are a couple of places to choose from, most of which charge Y10 per bed. The first and oldest is the *Wanli Dai Restaurant (wǎnlì dǎiwèilóu cāntīng)*. This used to be the 'in spot' with backpackers, but it seems to have fallen on hard times, perhaps because of the indifferent service of the staff, preoccupied as they are with the restaurant. They no longer have dorm rooms.

A bit further south, on the same side of the street, the newly opened *Dai Building Hotel (dǎijiā huāyuán xiǎolóu)* is an up-and-coming backpacker hang-out – one of the first signs you see upon entering the courtyard is for 'Cold Beer'. All accommodation is in separate bamboo bungalows on stilts. Doubles and triples with fan are Y50/75. The bathrooms are exceedingly clean and a new solar-heated hot shower has been installed. The owner, John, speaks good English as he was once an assistant manager of a Holiday Inn in Beijing. When he came to Jinghong to open this hotel, he contracted only Dai designers and workers.

Another place on the opposite side of the street bills itself as *Dai's Bamboo House*. Don't believe it. Nice enough people they are, but the only bamboo is that which has been glued onto the cement building underneath it. For the record, doubles go for Y40 here, and the bathrooms barely pass muster.

For the cheapest lodging on Manting Lu, just south of Dai Building Hotel is a decidedly non-Dai style *guesthouse*. It's hard to spot, so look for the yellow and green tiling around a sign (the front of which has barely recognisable English saying 'guesthouse'). A hard bed in a spartan triple costs Y10. The toilets are passable, but make sure you wear those shower sandals. The shower has very passive solar-heated water.

Right next to the long-distance bus station, the *Communications Hotel (jiāotōng fàndiàn)* is best given a miss. Seemingly falling in on itself, it has no more dorm beds. Its cheapest rooms are doubles with bathroom, fan and TV for Y100. More upmarket standard doubles are Y180.

A more centrally located place with dormitory accommodation is the *Jingyong Hotel (jǐngyǒng bīnguǎn)*, on Jinghong Donglu. It's Y45 for a triple. Clean doubles with fan and attached bath are available for Y70. If it's air-conditioning you're after, it will cost you Y160 for a double. This hotel is one of the few in China which freely mixes Chinese and foreigners in dorm rooms.

Finally, right in the heart of town, the *Banna Mansion Hotel (bǎnnà dàshà)* is Jinghong's luxury option, with air-con doubles for Y238, and triples for Y316. Smiling doormen and the lobby bathroom attendants are complimentary.

Places to Eat

As with accommodation, Manting Lu is the place for Dai-style food. The road is lined with restaurants, most of which are pretty similar. One drawback (or bonus, depending on how you view it) is that the majority of these restaurants dish up Dai dance performances along with their culinary specialities. This explains why the words 'singing and dancing hall' are tacked on to a lot of restaurant names. These places have bored-looking Dai women thumping drums at the entrance and are filled nearly every night with Chinese tourists whooping it up, hollering, playing drinking games and generally being festive. Once is worth a try, but you might not want to sit through the show every evening.

One place that serves Dai food, but *usually* spares diners the dancers, is the *Wanli Dai Restaurant (wǎnlì dǎiwèilóu cāntīng)*, which also has cheap accommodation. Try the roast fish, eel or beef cooked with lemon grass or served with peanut-and-tomato sauce. Vegetarians can order roast bamboo shoot prepared in the same fashion. Other mouth-watering specialities include fried river moss (sounds rather un-appetising but is excellent with beer) and spicy bamboo-shoot soup. Don't forget to try the black glutinous rice. The upstairs balcony is a pleasant place to sit with a beer in the winter and read about the sub-zero temperatures in Beijing. To be sure, some travellers have reported either icy service, high prices, or unremarkable food, but this still probably the best chance you'll have to sample local fare.

Elsewhere around town is pretty much standard Chinese fare. Walk up from Manting Lu and turn left in the direction of the CAAC booking office and you will find a host of tiny Chinese restaurants; most of them are pretty good for lunch. Next to the bus station there are also some good restaurants – look out for the place specialising in dumplings.

Street markets sell coconuts, bananas, papayas, pomelos (a type of grapefruit) and pineapples. The pineapples, served peeled on a stick, are probably the best in China. The covered market near the Banna Guesthouse is at its busiest in the morning.

For good food, strong coffee, really cold beer and (you guessed it) banana pancakes, stop by the *Mei Mei Cafe* on Manting Lu, a pleasant little Akha hole in the wall just down from the intersection with Jingde Lu. You'll be greeted with a smile, and usually find fellow travellers with whom to swap tall tales. Mei Mei was the first cafe to cater to foreigners and is still the most popular. Azhu, the owner, and her staff are delightful and great fun to while away an evening with.

The intersection on which Mei Mei sits has clones in either direction and, like Dali or Yangshuo, feel free to sample any or all. One definitely meriting your attention is found by turning right (east) at the corner of Jingde Lu, following it for some 50 to 100m, then taking the first right. Here you'll find the *Forest Cafe* with I daresay food equal to the Mei Mei Cafe. And the Forest Cafe has unquestionably the greatest hamburger found in China, along with home-baked speciality breads, good juices,

the hippest music, and more books than anywhere else.

Around the corner in the other direction and up a block is the open air *Yahu Beer Hall (yǎhú píjiǔdiàn)*, which brews its own. You can get a pitcher for around Y38. It's also a restaurant specialising in mediocre hotpot.

Getting There & Away

Air More flights and bigger planes (737s) mean that it's a lot easier to fly to Jinghong from Kunming than it used to be. It's usually even possible to book the day before. If one airline or travel agent in Kunming says the flights are all full, check with another place: travel agencies tend to snap up large blocks of seats ahead of time, and often fail to fill them all. In April (Water-Splashing Festival), however, you may need to allow for several days' advance booking, as this is a very popular time for Chinese to visit. And always be careful if you want to change your flight date on or around a weekend. There are normally several flights daily to Jinghong (Banna); at peak seasons up to 17 per day. The flight takes 50 minutes and the one way fare is Y520. Flights back are also daily and can be booked at the CAAC booking office (☎ 212-4774) in Jinghong.

Bus There are daily buses from Kunming to Jinghong (see the Kunming Getting There & Away section for details).

Buses back to Kunming are available from various travel services around town, the long-distance bus station, and bus station No 2. From the main bus station, several sleepers leave each day and cost Y150. Sleepers depart the No 2 bus station from 7 am to 5.30 pm for similar prices. Private companies have buses costing anywhere from Y110 to Y180, depending on the creature comforts offered on board.

If you're torn between the bus and the plane, don't let other travellers give you any crap about missing the scenery on the flight. There are some good views from the bus window, but nothing that won't stop you nodding off to sleep and certainly nothing much that will make you sit up and decide that the 24 hours of inhaling second-hand smoke and bouncing up and down in lieu of sleep were worth it.

The Jinghong long-distance bus station also has buses running to Xiaguan, Baoshan and Ruili. With more than 80 counties and cities now open in Yunnan, the PSB has decided to stop discouraging travellers from making this arduous journey (though they may still think you're crazy to do so, since you must have enough money to fly). The trips to Xiaguan, Ruili and Baoshan shouldn't require any overnighting if on a sleeper, but don't count on it. If so, the bus to Xiaguan will overnight in Zhenyuan, while en route to Baoshan the town of Lincang plays midway host to frazzled passengers. Sleepers to Xiaguan leave at 6 am and cost Y145, ordinary buses Y80. The trip usually takes 32 non-stop hours (outside of meal breaks).

The marathon to Ruili costs Y214. Serious thought should be given to breaking this trip up in Baoshan, if for no other reason than to preserve at least traces of pink in your lungs. Roads are quite poor on these routes, and the buses, even the new sleepers, not much better. If you choose this option, don't do it to save time – many travellers have found their two day trip stretch to three and even four days due to landslides, floods and bus breakdowns.

The Jinghong long-distance bus station has buses running to towns around Xishuangbanna, but it is mainly useful for more distant destinations. The best place to get out of Jinghong and explore other parts of Xishuangbanna is the No 2 bus station, which has frequent buses, minibuses and minivans from 7 am to around 5 pm. Timetables are flexible to say the least. See the Around Jinghong section for details on these buses.

Getting Around

The airport is 5km south of the city; CAAC buses leave from next to the booking office about an hour before scheduled departures.

Jinghong is small enough that you can walk to most destinations, but a bike makes life easier. The Xishuangbanna Guesthouse hires out bikes for Y8 a day, Y18 for mountain bikes.

AROUND JINGHONG

The possibilities for day trips and longer excursions out of Jinghong are endless. Some travellers have hiked and hitched from Menghai to Damenglong, some have cycled up to Menghai and Mengzhe on mountain bikes (it's almost impossible on bikes without gears), and one French photographer hitched up with a local medicine man and spent seven days doing house calls in the jungle.

Obviously, it's the longer trips that allow you to escape the hordes of tourists and get a feel for what Xishuangbanna is about. But even with limited time there are some interesting possibilities. Probably the best is an overnight (or several nights) stay in Ganlanba (also known as Menghan). It's only around 27km from Jinghong, and not that hard to cycle to, even on a local bike. The trip takes two to three hours.

Most other destinations in Xishuangbanna are only two or three hours away by bus, but generally they are not much in themselves – you need to get out and about. Travellers have also raved about a long two day trek to Bulangshan through an Akha village; you have to start out in Damenglong taking a bus to Mengsong. Note that to get to many villages, you'll often first have to bus to a primary village and overnight, since only one bus a day – if that – travels to the tinier villages.

If you're a serious collector of local market experiences, there are plenty to be found in the region. Like anything else, markets are a subjective thing, but most people seem to prefer the Thursday market in Xiding, then Menghun, followed up by Menghai. Take note that Xiding has no accommodation.

The best advice is to get yourself a bike or some sturdy hiking boots, pick up a map, put down this book, and get out of town.

Nearby Villages

Before heading further afield, there are numerous villages in the vicinity of Jinghong that can be reached by bicycle. Most of them are the kinds of places you happen upon by chance, and it's difficult to make recommendations.

On the other side of the Mekong are some small villages, and a popular jaunt involves heading off down Manting Lu – if you go far enough you'll hit a ferry crossing point on the Mekong. There are also villages in this area, and many travellers have been invited into Dai homes for tea and snacks.

Sanchahe Nature Preserve

Sanchahe (*sānchàhé*), north of Jinghong, is one of four enormous forest preserves in southern Yunnan, this one totalling nearly 1.5 million hectares. Whether or not it deserves your attention depends on how pristine you wish to see a forest preserve. It is possible to strike off into dense jungle, usually following the river, and rough it. (Take a local who knows his or her way around.) However, most travellers won't have time to get past the dumb part of the preserve – overexpensive canopy treehouse rooms (Y180 per night), and pitiful elephants chained to trees or giving 'wild' elephant performances for throngs of shutterbug tourists.

Just about any bus travelling north will pass the preserve, or you can inquire at one of the local cafes on minibus departures from the No 2 station. Minibuses should cost Y10.

Mengyang

(*měngyǎng*)

Mengyang is 34km north-east of Jinghong on the road to Simao. It's a centre for the Hani, Lahu and Floral-Belt Dai. Chinese tourists stop here to see a banyan tree shaped like an elephant.

From Mengyang it's another 19km to Jinuo, which is home base for the Jinuo minority. Travellers have reported that the Jinuo are unfriendly, so you'll probably have to stay in Mengyang. Some minorities dislike tourists, and if this is the case with the Jinuo they should be left alone.

Ganlanba (Menghan)

(*gǎnlǎnbà*)

Ganlanba, or Menghan as it's sometimes referred to, lies on the Mekong south-east of Jinghong. In the past the main attraction of Ganlanba was the boat journey down the Mekong from Jinghong. Unfortunately, improved roads sank the popular boat trip (locals prefer to spend an hour on a bus to three hours on the boat), and the only way to travel down the river now is to charter a boat at special tourist prices that most tourists can't afford.

However, Ganlanba remains a wonderful

YUNNAN

The Jinuo People

The Jinuo, sometimes known as the Youle, were officially 'discovered' as a minority in 1979. The women wear a white cowl, a cotton tunic with bright horizontal stripes and a tubular black skirt. Ear-lobe decoration is an elaborate custom – the larger the hole and the more flowers it can contain the better. The teeth are sometimes painted black with the sap of the lacquer tree, which serves the dual dental purpose of beautifying the mouth and preventing tooth decay and halitosis.

Previously, the Jinuo lived in long houses with as many as 27 families occupying rooms on either side of the central corridor. Each family had its own hearth, but the oldest man owned the largest hearth, which was the first at the door. Long houses are rarely used now and it looks like the Jinuo are quickly losing their distinctive way of life. ∎

retreat from hectic Jinghong. The town itself is fairly forgettable, but if you come on a bike (it is also possible to hire one in Ganlanba) there is plenty of scope for exploration in the neighbourhood.

Check the visitors' book in the Dai Bamboo House or the Sarlar Restaurant for some ideas.

Places to Stay The family-run *Dai Bamboo House* is a house on stilts with a dorm for Y12 per bed and small doubles for Y30; all beds are on the floor in the traditional Dai style. The friendly family serves Dai food on tiny lacquered tables: just give them notice several hours before dinner. It costs Y25, so be warned. Search out the visitors' books, which have several helpful maps of the area drawn by previous guests. You can also rent bikes here for Y8. Recent reports have been extremely mixed. The house is sort of under new management – the previous owner's son took it over. The Bamboo House is on the right-hand side of the main road that runs through town (heading away from Jinghong).

Alternatively, check out their new competition, the friendly *Sarlar Restaurant*, which has received nothing but praise from travellers. The capacious restaurant has a handful of small but cosy rooms (Y15) off to one side, with mats on the floor in the traditional Dai style. The bathrooms and shower room are super clean and the food is also excellent. High-quality mountain bikes can be rented here for Y10 per day. To get here, continue past the Dai Bamboo House until just before the road begins to bend to the right. Carved dragons grace the entrance.

Getting There & Away Minivans leave from behind the Jinghong No 2 bus station as they fill up; you purchase your ticket in front of the station at a small desk. The ride costs Y6 to Y8 and takes around 45 minutes. Vans from Ganlanba depart a small bus station found by walking on the main road in the direction of Jinghong, and then turning right at the last intersection of any

size and walking one block. It's possible to cycle the distance in a brisk two hours or a leisurely three hours, and it's a pleasant enough ride.

Getting Around The only way to do this is by bicycle or hiking. If you didn't bring your own bike, you can rent one at the Sarlar Restaurant or Dai Bamboo House. If they're all out, walk back toward town to where a main alley branches off to the left (you can't miss it) through the market. On the left is a place where you can hire bicycles for around Y8 a day.

Around Ganlanba

The stately **Wat Ban Suan Men**, southwest of town, is said to be 730 years old and is one of the best surviving examples of Dai temple architecture in Yunnan. Follow the road closest to the river southwards out of town and then take a path that follows the river. Check at the Dai Bamboo House for information before you leave.

There are numerous temples and villages in the area that are worth exploring. There's an old decaying temple on the road into town from Jinghong, and to the south of this, overlooking the Mekong, is a white stupa.

Most travellers who have spent any time here recommend striking off aimlessly on day trips and seeing what turns up.

Menglun
(měnglún)

Menglun is the next major port of call east of Ganlanba. The major attraction for Chinese visitors is the **Tropical Plant Gardens** *(rèdài zhíwùyuán)*. It's a pleasant enough place, although concrete pathways and guides toting bullhorns dash any hopes of communing with nature. But the gardens are nicely laid out, and the tour groups give it a somewhat festive atmosphere.

After going about two-thirds of the way into town, you'll come to a road leading downhill on the right-hand side. Follow this until you reach a footbridge across the Mekong. The ticket booth is just in front of the bridge. The entry fee is Y20 (foreigners' price).

Reportedly, authorities are planning to open another forest reserve, the **Green Stone Forest** to outside tourists, although no timetable has been set.

Places to Stay For dirt-cheap (although not dirt-free) accommodation you can try the *Friendship Hotel (yǒuyì lǚshè)* on the right side of the road leading to the Tropical Plant Gardens. Beds there are around Y5. There is also budget accommodation within the gardens. After crossing the bridge, follow the main path for about 15 minutes until you arrive at a group of buildings and a fork in the road. Take the right fork and you will find a Dai-style hostel with dorm beds for around Y15. For a more upmarket stay, take the left fork, go over the hill and to the left of the pond, where there is a damp but clean Chinese hotel that has doubles with attached bath for Y88.

Getting There & Away From Jinghong's No 2 bus station there are buses to Menglun (Y13) approximately every 45 minutes between 6.30 am and 3 pm, most between 10 am and 1 pm. The long-distance station has a minivan leaving at 4 pm for Y13. The buses pass through Ganlanba. Minivans occasionally leave from the main street of Ganlanba to Menglun, and also charge Y10.

Some travellers have also cycled here from Ganlanba. Cycling onwards to Mengla could be more difficult because of the PSB. A permit for Mengla might make a difference, but it's hard to say.

Mengla

Mengla may not be a very inspiring town, but it is likely to see an increasing number of travellers passing through en route to Laos via the border crossing at Mohan. As the bus journey from Jinghong, or even Menglun, will take the better part of the day, you will probably have to overnight here.

A couple of the cheap places here have unisex showers. Downhill from the bus station, the *Binya Hotel (bīnyà bīnguǎn)* has hard dorm beds for Y15. Nearby, the *Nanjiang Hotel (nánjiāng bīnguǎn)* offers a more upmarket alternative, with doubles with attached bath for Y60.

CITS has an office with at least one or two English-speaking staff at the *Mengla Hotel (měnglà bīnguǎn)*, which is about 2km uphill from the bus station. The Mengla has dorm beds for around Y20, and doubles with bath and TV for Y60. The location is inconvenient, but a pedicab should get you there for Y3 to Y4.

A day trip from Mengla might include a stop at the Wangtianshu Reserve *(wàngtiānshù zǒuláng)*, a 45 minute bus ride. It has canopy walks but unfortunately sparse facilities. It also costs Y30 to enter.

Getting There & Away There are four or five direct buses a day between Jinghong's No 2 station and Mengla, leaving between 6.30 am and 5 pm. The long-distance bus station also has departures five times a day between 6.40 am and 5.30 pm. The 200km ride takes anywhere from five to seven hours and the fare is Y20 to Y25, depending on the size of the bus. If you scout around the vicinity of Kunming's long-distance bus station, you can find sleepers which go directly to Mengla. Mengla has two bus stations. The first one on the left coming from Jinghong is the short-distance station.

Laos Border Crossing

This crossing sees a fair amount of traffic. From Mengla, there are buses to Mohan (Y8). Once your passport is stamped and you've waved goodbye to the border guards, you can jump on a tractor or truck to take you into Laos for around Y2. If you can't find a bus to Mohan, get on one to Shangyong, from where it should be relatively easy to arrange another ride. Whatever you do, go early. Things wrap up for good around noon on the Laos side (and don't forget they're an hour ahead) and you won't find a truck if you go later. Guesthouses are on the Chinese side only.

Damenglong
(dà měnglóng)

Damenglong (written just 'Menglong' on buses) is about 70km south of Jinghong and a few kilometres from the Myanmar border. It's another sleepy village that serves well enough as a base for hikes around the surrounding hills. The village itself is not much (it rouses itself somewhat for the Sunday market), but the surrounding countryside, peppered with decaying stupas and little villages, is worth a couple of days' exploration. A few hardy travellers have raved about a multi-day trek from Mengsong (often written 'Mengson'), a bus ride south of Menglong, through Akha villages to Bulangshan. You'll have to ask around cafes in Jinghong for specifics, as the trail is very tricky. You can hire bikes at the Damenglong Hotel for Y5 a day.

The town's laid-back feel may change in the next few years, however. The border crossing point with Myanmar (poetically named 2-4-0) has been designated as the entry point for a planned highway linking Thailand, Myanmar and China. The road is due to open by 1999, although at last check things were certainly far from complete on the Chinese side. If and when it does, things should definitely pick up in Damenglong. Just before we last visited, a group of Hong Kong investors was apparently sniffing around for a spot to build a tourist hotel.

Manfeilong Pagoda *(mànfēilóng tǎ)* This pagoda, built in 1204, is Damenglong's premier attraction. According to legend, the temple was built on the spot of a hallowed footprint left by Sakyamuni, who once visited Xishuangbanna – if you're interested in ancient footprints you can look for it in a niche below one of the nine stupas. Unfortunately, in recent years a 'beautification' job has been done on the temple with a couple of cans of silver paint – it probably sounded like a good idea at the time, but now that the paint has started to flake off it creates a very tacky effect. (It's also more white now than silver.)

If you're in Xishuangbanna in late October or early November, check the precise dates of the Tan Ta Festival. At this time Manfeilong Pagoda is host to hundreds of locals whose celebrations include dancing, rockets, paper balloons and so on.

Manfeilong is easy to get to: just walk back along the main road towards Jinghong for 2km until you reach a small village with a temple on your left. From here there's a path up the hill; it's about a 20 minute walk. Some travellers have been charged a Y5 entrance fee, while others haven't since generally no one's around anyway.

Black Pagoda *(hēitǎ)* Just above the centre of town is a Dai monastery with a steep path beside it leading up to the Black Pagoda – one thing you can't help but notice when entering Damenglong. The pagoda itself is not black at all – it's covered in cheap gold paint. Take a stroll up, but bear in mind that the real reason for the climb is for the superb views of Damenglong and the surrounding countryside. An English-speaking Malaysian monk is said to spend most of his time around here, although we didn't run into him.

Places to Stay & Eat The officially sanctioned foreigners' residence is the low-key *Damenglong Guesthouse (dàměnglóng zhàodàisuǒ)*. To get there, walk uphill from the traffic circle (although the road was torn up at last visit) to the end of the road, where the local government building sits. The hotel is in the grounds to the left, just past some ornamental frogs. Basic dorm beds are Y10. Bathrooms are fragrant but passable. Bicycles can be rented here for Y3 per hour, Y15 per day.

A new bus station guesthouse is just on the left as you enter town from Jinghong. It had just opened at the time of writing, and staff were equivocal as to whether foreigners could stay. If you can, clean five-bed rooms are available.

The food situation in Damenglong is OK. Down from the bus station, near the steps leading up to the Black Pagoda are a couple of decent restaurants. The Chinese signs proclaim them to be Dai restaurants, but it's the old story of going out the back, pointing to your vegies and getting them five minutes later in a little pool of oil.

There is also a cold drinks cafe at the traffic circle, where you can get a Coke with ice for Y5. The ice cubes tend to be a little brown, but the staff insist the water has been well boiled, and we suffered no ill effects.

Getting There & Away There are buses to Damenglong (Y10, 2½ hours) every half hour (or less) between 7 am and 5 pm (occasionally until 7 pm) from the No 2 bus station in Jinghong. Purchase your tickets on the bus – just walk through the station and across the parking lot to the far left corner, where they congregate. Remember that the 'Da' character won't be painted on the bus window. Buses for the return trip are on a similar schedule, although the last bus tends to leave a bit earlier.

Around Damenglong
The village of **Xiaojie**, about 15km before Damenglong, is surrounded by Bulang, Lahu and Hani villages. Lahu women shave their heads; apparently the younger ones aren't happy about this any more and hide their heads beneath caps. The Bulang are possibly descended from the Lolo in northern Yunnan. The women wear black turbans with silver decorations; many of the designs are of shells, fish and marine life.

There's plenty of room for exploration in this area, although you're not allowed over the border.

Menghai
(měnghǎi)
This uninspiring place serves as a centre for trips into the surrounding area. The Sunday market attracts members of the hill tribes and the best way to find it is to follow the early-morning crowds.

There are a couple of drab hotels. One near the old bus station at the centre of

town has beds for Y5. About 1km further down the street, near the smaller but more active bus station, the *Liangyuan Hotel (liángyuán bīnguǎn)* has doubles/triples for Y60.

Buses and minibuses (seven small, eight large) run from the No 2 bus station in Jinghong to Menghai approximately every half hour between 7.30 am and 5.20 pm. The fare is Y7 and the trip takes about 90 minutes. Minibuses to Jinghong, Menghun and Jingzhen leave from a smaller bus station, at the western end of Menghai.

Menghun
(měnghùn)
This tiny village is about 26km south-west of Menghai. Some prefer the Sunday market here to that of Menghai. It all begins buzzing around 7 am and lingers on through to noon. The swirl of hill tribes and women sporting fancy leggings, head-dresses, earrings and bracelets alone makes the trip worthwhile. Although the market seems to be the main attraction, a temple and footpaths that wind through the lush hills behind the White Tower Hotel are also worth an extra day or two.

Places to Stay & Eat Right at the centre of town where the buses let you off, the *Yun Chuan Restaurant/Hotel (yúnchuān fàndiàn)* is nothing to get excited about, but the rooms are (barely) acceptable, if you don't mind the occasional brown water spurting from the spigot. It has rooms for around Y8. Further down on the right side of the street, the *Phoenix Hotel (fènghuáng fàndiàn)* is cheaper (Y5 a bed), but very noisy and better off given a miss.

The more secluded *White Tower Hotel* is roomier, quieter and looks out over a lily pond. Beds in doubles here cost Y10, but you can probably talk the price down. From the main intersection, take the road uphill, walk through the archway, then bear left along a small path heading downhill. Even these directions are only approximate; everyone has trouble finding the place, so you'll probably have to ask locals.

There are several good Dai restaurants along the main street, some of which have English menus.

Getting There & Away Buses from Jinghong to Daluo pass through Menghun, and leave the Jinghong No 2 bus station every half hour between 7.30 am and 5 pm. The fare to Menghun is Y12 to Y14. Going back you just have to wait on the side of the road until a bus passes by. Normally you shouldn't have to wait too long.

Unless you have a very good bike with gears, cycling to Menghai and Menghun is not a real option. The road up to Menghai is so steep that you'll end up pushing the bike most of the way.

Intrepid travellers have hitched and hiked all the way from here to Damenglong. This should be no problem, providing you don't inadvertently stray over the Myanmar border at some point. A mountain bike would be the best way to do it. Hitching and walking should take a leisurely seven days.

Jingzhen
(jǐngzhēn)
In the village of Jingzhen, about 14km north-west of Menghai, is the **Octagonal Pavilion** *(bājiǎo tíng)*, first built in 1701. The original structure was severely damaged during the Cultural Revolution, so the present renovated building isn't all that thrilling. Take a close look at the new paintings on the wall of the temple. There are some interesting scenes which appear to depict People's Liberation Army (PLA) soldiers causing death and destruction during the Cultural Revolution; adjoining scenes depict Buddha vanquishing PLA soldiers, one of whom is waving goodbye as he drowns in a pond.

Jingzhen is a pleasant rural spot for walks along the river or the fish ponds be-hind the village. Frequent minibuses from the minibus centre in Menghai go via Jingzhen.

Nanluoshan
(nánlúoshān)
Nanluoshan lies south of the road between Jinghong and Menghai (17km from Menghai). It's best done as a day trip from Menghai, providing you start early and return to the main road before dusk. The bus will drop you off close to a bridge; cross the bridge and follow the dirt track about 6km uphill until you join a newly constructed main road.

About 1km before the junction, you'll round a bend in the road and see a fence with a stile and stone benches beyond. This is the turn-off for the steps down to the overrated **King of Tea Trees** *(cháwáng)* – the name says it all! According to the Hani, their ancestors have been growing tea for 55 generations and this tree was the first one planted. The tree is definitely not worth descending hundreds of steps to see; it is half dead and covered with moss, graffiti

---

The Hani (Akha) People

The Hani (also known in adjacent countries as the Akha) are of Tibetan origin, but according to folklore they are descended from frogs' eyes. They stick to the hills, cultivating rice, corn and the occasional poppy. Trading takes place at weekly markets where the Dai obviously dominate the Hani, who seem only too keen to scamper back to their mountain retreats.

Hani women wear headdresses of beads, feathers, coins and silver rings. At one remote market the women were very nervous and it was only when their backs were turned that I could inspect their headdresses, which were made with French (Vietnamese), Burmese and Indian coins from the turn of the century. ■

and signs forbidding graffiti. A crumbling concrete pavilion daubed with red paint completes the picture. You can get to the tree for Y4 by motorcycle taxi, and an admission of Y2 is charged.

The highway has been bulldozed out of the mountain for the comfort of tourists who can now visit the hill tribes further up the mountain. Repeated exposure to tour buses is certain to cause changes among the Hani and Lahu villagers there. If you leave the main road, there's some pleasant hiking in the area, but don't expect villagers to automatically give you a bed for the night. A Hani villager did invite us into his stilt house for an excellent meal and some firewater that left us wobbling downhill.

Baoshan Region

Travellers who pass through the Baoshan (bǎoshān dìqū) area tend to do so quickly, generally staying overnight in Baoshan city on the way to Ruili and Wanding, but the area is worth a bit more time than that. There are some worthwhile historical sights, the old quarters of Tengchong and Baoshan make for some good browsing, distinctive minority groups are in abundance (as in other parts of southern Yunnan), and the Tengchong area is rich in volcanic activity, with hot springs and volcanic peaks.

As early as the 4th and 5th centuries BC (two centuries before the northern routes through central Asia were established), the Baoshan area was an important stage on the southern Silk Road – the Sichuan-India route. The area did not really come under Chinese control until the time of the Han Dynasty when, in 69 AD, it was named the Yongchang Administrative District.

BAOSHAN
(bǎoshān)
Baoshan is a small city that's easily explored on foot. There are pockets of traditional wooden architecture still standing in the city area and some good walks on the

outskirts of town. It has innumerable speciality products that range from excellent coffee to leather boots and pepper and silk. Tea aficionados might like to try the Reclining Buddha Baoshan Tea, a brand of national repute.

Information
Baoshan is not exactly geared up for a large-scale invasion of foreign visitors, and little in the way of information is available. Shops in the long-distance bus station sell maps of Baoshan Prefecture which include Baoshan city and Tengchong as well as regional sights, with some explanations in English. Otherwise you're pretty much on your own. The Bank of China is next to the Yindou Hotel, and the post office is not far away.

Things to See
Baoshan is an interesting city to wander aimlessly in. The streets are lively and, in many areas, lined with old traditional homes. The major sight within easy walk-ing distance of the centre of town is **Taibao Park** (tàibǎo gōngyuán). It's flanked to the south by the **Wenbi Pagoda** (wénbǐ tǎ) and to the east by the **Yuhuang Pavilion** (yùhuáng gé). All three are worth a look. The Yuhuang Pavilion dates back to the Ming Dynasty and has a small museum next door to it. The small viewing pagodas in the park provide good views of Baoshan, the Wenbi Pagoda and Yiluo Pond.

There are paths in the park striking off to the north, west and south. The northern path doubles back to the south and eventually takes you past a very mediocre zoo (keep walking). Continuing to the south you will reach **Yiluo Pond** (yìluó chí), also known as the Dragon Spring Pond (lóngquán chí). The best thing about the latter are the views of the 13 tiered Wenbi Pagoda. An entrance fee of Y4 is charged to Yiluo Pond.

Places to Stay
There are plenty of inexpensive places to stay in Baoshan. It's service with a snarl right next to the long-distance bus station at

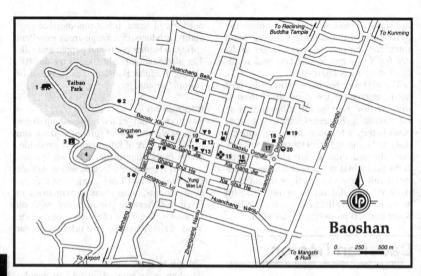

BAOSHAN 保山

PLACES TO STAY
10 Lanhua Hotel
兰苑大酒家
11 Baoshan Guesthouse
保山宾馆
12 Yongchang Hotel
永昌宾馆
14 Yindou Hotel;
Bank of China
银都大酒店、
中国银行
18 Keyun Hotel
客运住宿部
19 Hua Cheng Hotel
花城酒家

PLACES TO EAT
9 Coffee Shop
咖啡冷饮
13 Across-the-Bridge Noodle
Restaurant
过桥园

OTHER
1 Zoo
动物园
2 Yuhuang Pavilion
玉皇阁
3 Wenbi Pagoda
文笔塔
4 Yiluo Pond
易罗池

5 CAAC
中国民航售票处
6 PSB
公安局
7 Workers' Cultural Palace
工人文化宫
8 Youth Palace
青少年宫
15 Department Store
百货大楼
16 Post Office
邮电局
17 Long-Distance Bus Station
汽车总站
20 City Bus Station
市车站

the surly *Keyun Hotel (kèyùn zhùsùbù)*, which hearkens back to the bad old days of China travel and is best avoided, though it has beds in a four-bed dorm for Y12. Really good value is the *Hua Cheng Hotel (huāchéng jiǔjiā)* which used to be known as the *Lanyuan Hotel (lányuàn dàjiǔjiā)*, two or three minutes north of the bus station on the other side of the road. A

friendly army of workers was slapping paint on and changing signs at our last visit. Doubles/triples cost Y40/45 with common bath. But the best deal may be the doubles with attached bathroom for Y50. Rooms are clean, bright and airy and, depending on who your neighbours are for the night, quiet. Deals for stays of three or more nights are available.

Along Baoxiu Xilu are a few sprawling Chinese-style hotels with little to separate them. They all take foreigners and most seem fairly friendly even though they're probably uninspiring places to stay. The first is the *Yongchang Hotel* (☎ 212-2802) *(yǒngchāng bīnguǎn)*, which has dorm beds for Y10. A laundry list of other rooms are available: singles from Y40 to Y120 and doubles from Y30 to Y100: Triples with bath are Y90. Don't expect anything more than a bed in the cheaper rooms. Not far up the road is the *Lanhua Hotel* (☎ 212-2803) *(lánhuā bīnguǎn)*, which has three-bed dorms for Y24. Doubles/triples with attached bathroom start at Y60 and deluxe singles at Y120.

Baoshan's premier accommodation is nearby, brought to you by the Bank of China. The *Yindou Hotel* (☎ 212-0948) *(yíndū dàjiǔdiàn)* is a money-making venture set up by the bank. It offers doubles with international telephone, 24 hour hot water, air-con and satellite TV for Y140. It's probably not a bad deal if you're looking for comfort. But if you're en route to Tengchong, hold out a bit longer: you can get a comparable room there for half the price.

A block south, the pleasant *Baoshan Guesthouse* (☎ 212-2804) *(bǎoshān bīnguǎn)* is where the pedicab drivers will probably take you if you stumble off the bus looking dazed and confused. It has basic doubles with common bath for Y100; from there it goes to slightly upmarket doubles for Y120 (bathroom attached). No multi-bed rooms are available.

Places to Eat
Baoxiu Lu and the road to the south running parallel to it are good places to seek out cheap *restaurants*. Look for the place selling dumplings and noodles down the road from the Yindou Hotel towards the bus station. Next door to the Baoshan Guesthouse is an across-the-bridge *noodle restaurant* that is worth checking out, although it closes quite early. Near the intersection of Baoxiu Xilu and Minhang Lu is

Qingzhen Jie, with a handful of *Muslim restaurants*.

As in Kunming there are plenty of *roadside snacks* available. There's a tiny coffee shop across from the Yongchang Hotel. While its coffee is very sweet and very instant, it's only Y3 per cup, and the place offers you a chance to rest your feet for a few moments. Cold drinks are also served. *A Splendid Tea House* in the long-distance bus compound is notable as a place to avoid. It has terrible coffee, and the owner has a penchant for serenading her guests on a clapped-out karaoke machine at 100 decibels. It is also the entrance for one of the worst discos in China.

Getting There & Away
You can fly in and out of Baoshan, although very few western travellers do. The Baoshan CAAC office (☎ 216-1747) is rather inconveniently located at the intersection of Longquan Lu and Minhang Lu. Look for a large yellow-tiled building. The only English you'll see is on the vertical sign, which says 'Civil Aviation Hotel' at the very bottom. The ticket office is on the 1st floor, facing Longquan Lu. There are three flights weekly (Tuesday, Thursday, Saturday) to Kunming, and tickets cost Y370. The airport is around 9km south of town.

The Baoshan long-distance bus station is a huge new construction, and there are buses running from here to a host of destinations around Yunnan. There are numerous late-afternoon sleeper buses from 3 to 7 pm making the 18 hour haul to Kunming. Fares are Y120 for sleepers.

Buses for the five to six hour ride to Xiaguan (Dali) leave three times between 6.50 and 11 am and cost Y21 to Y27. Buses to Tengchong leave daily at 6.50, 9.30 and 11 am. The 167km ride usually takes at least six hours, and road improvements have taken a lot of the pain out of this once hellish ride. The experience will cost you Y22. Buses on to Yingjiang, past Tengchong, leave at 7.30 am and take pretty much forever. There are several buses to

YUNNAN

Ruili between 6.50 and 10.30 am. The ride takes seven to eight hours, some of it over a newly finished roadway, and costs Y35. Buses to Ruili pass through Mangshi and Wanding. Other buses at 6.50 and 9.30 am go just to Mangshi. There is also the odd bus to Jinghong in Xishuangbanna, although most travellers opt to take the direct Dali-Jinghong bus now. If you take it from Baoshan, it's still a two day travail, with a likely overnight in Lincang.

Across the street at the city bus station you can catch a bus to most of the same destinations as from the long-distance station. A sleeper bus to Tengchong and Yingjiang departs at 8.30 am. To Ruili via Mangshi the first bus departs at 8 am. Kunming sleepers depart from 4.30 pm. Note that the schedule on the wall of this station is woefully out of date.

Getting Around
Baoshan can comfortably be explored on foot, which is probably why there is no evidence of bicycle-hire stands around town. This is a pity because a bicycle would be the ideal way to get to some of the sights around Baoshan. With any luck, an enterprising local may fill this gap as increasing numbers of foreigners pass through the area.

AROUND BAOSHAN
Just 17km north of town, the **Reclining Buddha Temple** *(wòfó sì)* is one of the most important historical sights in the vicinity of Baoshan. The temple dates back to the Tang Dynasty, having a history of some 1200 years. The reclining buddha itself, in a cave to the rear of the temple area, was severely damaged during the Cultural Revolution and has only recently been restored.

The only problem is getting to the temple. There are no local buses or minibuses. A motorcycle with sidecar can take two people there and back for Y40. Taxis ask around Y70 to Y80. It would be a fairly comfortable bicycle trip if you could get hold of a bike.

TENGCHONG
(téngchōng)
Not many travellers get to this town on the other side of the Gaoligong Mountain range, but it's an interesting place. There are some 20 volcanoes in the vicinity and lively geothermal activity – lots of hot springs. It's also prime earthquake territory, having experienced 71 earthquakes measuring over five on the Richter scale since 1500 AD.

The town itself has preserved, on a larger scale, the kind of traditional wooden architecture that has survived only in pockets in Kunming and Baoshan. It's not exactly Dali, but there's a definite charm to some of the narrow backstreets. The town is at an altitude of 1650m and can get quite crisp in the evenings during the winter months.

Information
Tengchong has a small travel office at the front gate of the Teng Chong Guesthouse. The staff don't speak much English, but can provide you with maps of the county, and maybe some assistance. Maps are also sold at the shop in the hotel courtyard.

The post office is on Fengshan Lu. The Bank of China dominates the town's main intersection. The bank won't change travellers cheques, so you'll have to come to Tengchong armed with enough cash to get you through your visit.

Things to See
There's not exactly a wealth of sights in town, but it's worth taking a look at the **Frontier Trade Bazaar of Tengchong** – yes, that's the English sign at the head of the market. It's not as lively as the markets in Ruili, but there's plenty of colour and activity in the mornings.

The best street for old buildings is Yingjiang Lu – both the east and west sections. The backstreets running off the western section of Yingjiang Lu make for some good exploring and photographs.

About 2km south-west of town is the **Laifeng Temple** *(láifēng sì)*. The temple is

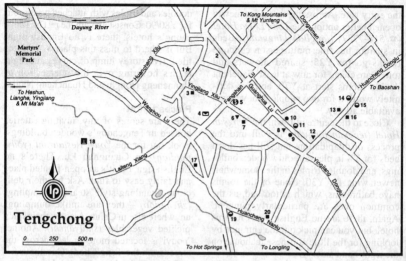

TENGCHONG 腾冲

PLACES TO STAY
3 Hongyan (Swan Goose)
  Hotel
  鸿雁族社
7 Tengyun Hotel
  腾云宾馆
13 Gonglu Hotel
  公路招待所
16 Tong Li Da Hotel
  通利达宾馆
17 Teng Chong Guesthouse
  腾冲宾馆
20 Taian Hotel
  泰安宾馆

PLACES TO EAT
6 Burmese Cafe
  缅甸咖啡厅
8 Youyi Restaurant
  友谊饭店
12 Chunhua Huishiguan
  春华回族食馆

OTHER
1 PSB
  公安局
2 Frontier Trade Bazaar of
  Tengchong
  腾冲边境货物商场
4 Post Office
  邮电局

5 Bank of China
  中国银行
9 Workers' Cultural Palace
  工人文化宫
10 Bicycle Rental
  自行车出租
11 Minibus to Baoshan
  往保山的中巴车
14 Long-Distance Bus Station
  长途汽车站
15 Bus Passenger Station
  客运站
18 Laifeng Temple
  来凤寺
19 Minibuses
  中巴车站

nothing to get excited about, especially as
foreigners are charged Y5 to get in, as
opposed to Y0.5 for locals. But the walk up
to and around the temple takes you through
lush pine forests. The temple also borders
the Fengshan Forest Reserve, which offers
further hiking possibilities and also gives
an idea of what this part of China may have
been like before the trees gave way to
farms.

Places to Stay

Tengchong's accommodation options are
fairly spread out. South of the bus station,
the *Gonglu Hotel (gōnglù zhāodàisuǒ)* has
beds for Y10 in a triple and other options
starting at Y15. It's a noisy place, and the
rooms are nothing special, but it's the
closest place to the bus station. The hotel
has no English sign – look for the ubiquitous bus steering wheel logo at the top of

the entry gate. Across the street is a newly opened better option, the *Tong Li Da Hotel* (☎ 518-7787) *(tōnglìdá bīngguǎn)*. Beds in spartan but fine multi-person concrete rooms go for Y25; shared showers and toilets are clean, for now at least. Excellent double rooms start at Y70, and are definitely worth it for two people. Hot water is available all day.

Close to the centre of town, the *Tengyun Hotel (téngyún bīngguǎn)* is well into the process of dilapidation, but still has dorm beds for Y8 in pleasant old wooden buildings, and doubles/triples in the (somewhat) newer wing for Y30. None of the rooms have bathrooms, which is too bad, as the common ones are particularly pungent. Again, there are no English signs for this hotel, but you can pick out the entrance by looking for the little Burmese teahouse on the right-hand side.

Up on Yingjiang Xilu is the wonderful *Hongyan Hotel* (Swan Goose Hotel) *(hóngyàn lǚshè)*, which had for a long time been the favourite place for budget travellers to stay, set as it was around a lovely courtyard. Unfortunately, the powers that be at the PSB came calling and outlawed foreign guests. Perhaps with enough pestering, the doors can be reopened.

The sprawling *Teng Chong Guesthouse (téngchōng bīngguǎn)* is in a quiet location and, though far from the bus station, is probably worth the walk. Beds in clean, spacious dorms range from Y15 to Y20, and there are singles/doubles with attached bath for Y50. The Teng Chong may be the place to live it up for one night. Very comfortable doubles with attached bathroom and TV cost only Y70, and if you're solo, the reception staff *may* allow you to pay for only one bed: this is one of the few hotels that doesn't seem to mind putting Chinese and foreigners together. It's not exactly the Hilton – the lights in the entire hotel dim when anyone uses the only elevator – but for the money it's great value.

Lastly, the *Taian Hotel* (☎ 518-3385) *(tàiān bīngguǎn)*, a Sino-Burmese joint venture, has what appear to be fairly decent doubles and triples with attached washroom for Y80/90. Consistent with the rest of Tengchong's hotels, there is no English sign. But it's hard to miss this place – a white-tiled, five storey lump of curves and right angles hovering over the intersection of Huancheng Donglu and Huancheng Nanlu.

Places to Eat

There are scores of tiny, inviting eateries housed in Tengchong's wooden buildings. Look out for the *Youyi Restaurant (yǒuyì fàndiàn)* on Guanghua Lu. There's no English sign, but it's an open-fronted place and fairly easy to find. Ask for their delicious Shandong-style steamed dumplings *(zhēngjiǎo)* – they are unlike dumplings anywhere else in China. Also try their spicy pickled vegetables *(shuǐyāncài)*. Another Youyi is located more or less across the street from the Teng Chong Guesthouse.

Towards the long-distance bus station, near the corner of Huancheng Donglu and Guanghua Lu, is the *Chunhua Huishiguan (chūnhuá huíshíguǎn)*, a Muslim place that seems to be worth checking out. It has a green and white sign and light-green doors. Even closer to the long-distance bus station on the opposite side of the road is a hotpot restaurant specialising in lamb – be careful, since dog is also on the menu.

For sweet coffee, excellent samosas, Mekong whisky, and the likely chance of chatting with some of Tengchong's itinerant Burmese jewellery peddlers, stop by the *Burmese Teahouse & Cafe* at the entrance to the Tengyun Hotel. There is an English sign out the front, and usually at least one English speaker within.

Getting There & Away

Tengchong's long-distance bus station must be the only bus station in the whole of the south-west that has a board with English information about bus times and prices. Ignore it – it's completely out of date, although it's a nice thought.

From the long-distance bus station to Baoshan, buses leave at 7.30, 9 and 11 am, and again at noon. The price is Y22. The journey should take around six hours, although it often takes longer, and will leave your bones vibrating well into the night. Directly to Xiaguan (Dali) there is a bus leaving at 7 am for Y55, but it would make sense to overnight in Baoshan.

Buses to Ruili run via Yingjiang and Zhangfeng twice a day, cost Y27 and take eight to 10 hours. Alternatively, if you have time on your hands, travel to Yingjiang (stopping to have a browse in Lianghe on the way), stay overnight there and travel on to Ruili by bus the next day. Buses for the three to four hour ride to Yingjiang leave four times between 7 am and noon. There are also buses to Mangshi at 7.30 am (five hours, Y17) and sleepers to Kunming at 9.30 and 10 am and 1 pm, costing Y170. The ride should take around 24 hours.

Another bus station is located a short way south, on the opposite side of the street. It has a less complicated schedule, but you may find something to your liking if your bus from the long-distance station has just left without you.

Along Guanghua Lu you'll notice a splashy sign advertising a private minibus departing daily for Baoshan. Problem is – they're a bit over-optimistic on the daily part. If it does leave, it's usually around 7 am, or whenever they feel like it, and it costs Y25. The bus will be in much better shape than anything leaving the long-distance bus station. To find out, you have to enter the Tengchong County Transportation Administration guesthouse gate to the right of the sign, turn right immediately, go up the stairs and start poking around until somebody finds you.

You should also be able to get a minibus to Yingjiang at the intersection of Fengshan Lu and Huancheng Nanlu, near the Teng Chong Guesthouse. Buses run from 8 am to around 4 pm, leaving as they fill up. Of late there have been fewer and fewer of these lurking about. You may also be able to hire vans here to take you to the Kong Mountain volcanoes, Mt Yunfeng and other sights in the area, although most of these leave from south of the Teng Chong

Hotel. (See the following Around Tengchong section.)

Getting Around

Tengchong is small enough to walk around, but a bicycle would be useful for getting to some of the closer sights outside town – the surrounding scenery alone justifies a ride. If you're interested, there is a bicycle shop on Guanghua Lu that rents bikes for Y1 per hour, with a deposit of Y200. There's a sign in fractured English out the front, but just look for a mass of bicycles parked in front of a yellow wooden building.

AROUND TENGCHONG

There's a lot to see around Tengchong but, as in Baoshan, the area has only recently opened and getting out to the sights is a bit tricky. Catching buses part of the way and hiking up to the sights is one possibility, while some of the closer sights can be reached by bicycle. Your other option is a hired van, which may be affordable if there are several of you. The Five Continent Travel Service (wǔzhōu lǚxíngshè) within the Teng Chong Guesthouse compound cannot arrange such transport, but they do have nice maps. You can head down to the minibus stand further south, near the Fu Lin Restaurant, where van drivers often sit around puffing cigarettes and waiting for some business to walk their way.

Heshun Village
(héshùn xiāng)
If you come into Tengchong from Ruili and Yingjiang, just 4km before pulling into town you pass through the village of Heshun. It's worth hiking or cycling back to take a closer look at the village. It has been set aside as a kind of retirement village for Overseas Chinese, but for the average western visitor it's likely to be of more interest as a quiet, traditional Chinese village with cobbled streets. There are some great old buildings in the village, providing lots of photo opportunities. You may also get a chance to meet some older English-speaking Chinese.

YUNNAN

Yunfengshan
(yúnfēng shān)

Yunfengshan is a Taoist mountain dotted with temples and monastic retreats, 47km to the north of Tengchong. The temples were built in the early 17th century, and the best example is said to be the Yunfeng Temple at the summit.

Getting there is not so easy. The only budget option is to take a bus to Ruidian *(ruìdiàn)*. Three buses leave the long-distance bus station daily between 7.30 am and 4 pm and cost Y10. After passing through the town of **Gudong** *(gúdōng)*, you will come to a turn-off for the mountain. After getting off here you will have to either walk or hitch the remaining 9km to 10km to reach the base of the mountain. Hiring a vehicle to take you there and back will cost around Y300.

Volcanoes
(huǒshānqún)

Tengchong County is renowned for its volcanoes, and although they have been behaving themselves for many centuries the seismic and geothermal activity in the area probably indicates that they won't always continue to do so. The closest one to town is Ma'anshan *(mǎān shān)*, around 5km to the north-west. It's just south of the main road that runs to Yingjiang.

Around 22km to the north of town, near the village of **Mazhan** *(mǎzhàn)* is a cluster of volcanoes: the Kong Mountains *(kōngshān huǒshānqún)*. Buses to Gudong run past Mazhan. From Mazhan you can either walk or take a motor-tricycle (Y5) to the volcano area. Alternatively, hire a van to take you there and back for around Y150.

Hot Springs

The 'Sea of Heat' *(rèhǎi)*, as the Chinese poetically refer to it, is a cluster of hot springs, geysers and streams around 12km south-west of Tengchong. In addition to the usual indoor baths, there is an outdoor hot spring as well as a warm-water pool, sitting just above a river.

Two hotels at the entrance to the springs have simple doubles for Y30 to Y50, and restaurants serving up local specialities, so it's easy to make this a relaxing overnight trip. However, in summer a fairly active mosquito community can wreak havoc with sleep – you may wish to opt for just a day's sojourn if the weather is hot.

No travel agencies in Tengchong have scheduled charters, so you'll have to head for the Huancheng Nanlu turn-off to the hot springs, next to the Fu Lin Restaurant, to line something up. Minibuses generally leave anytime from 8 am, with the last returning around 8 pm (don't count on this however). Depending on your bargaining skills, you can generally line up a van to the hot springs for around Y5 per person or Y25 for a whole van. This is hard enough if you're in a group of four or five – they'll probably accuse you of robbery if you pay less than Y100 each – but decidedly more difficult if you're a solo traveller trying to hitch up with a Chinese group.

Dehong Region

Dehong Prefecture *(déhóng zhōu)*, like Xishuangbanna, borders Myanmar and is heavily populated by distinctive minority groups, but for some reason it doesn't seem to have captured travellers' imaginations to the extent that Xishuangbanna has. It's in the far west of Yunnan and is definitely more off the beaten track than Xishuangbanna – you're unlikely to see the busloads of Chinese tourists who have overrun Xishuangbanna in recent years.

Most Chinese in Dehong are there for the Myanmar trade that comes through the towns of Ruili and Wanding. Burmese jade is a commodity that many Chinese have grown rich on in recent years, but there are countless other items being spirited over the border that separates China and Myanmar, some of them illicit.

Many minority groups are represented in Dehong, but among the most obvious are the Burmese, Dai and Jingpo (known in

Myanmar as the Kachin, a minority long engaged in armed struggle against the Myanmar government).

In Dehong it is possible to see signs sporting numerous languages: Chinese, Burmese, Dai and English. This is a border region getting rich on trade – in the markets you can see Indian men selling jewellery, tinned fruits from Thailand, Burmese papier-mâché furniture, young bloods with wads of foreign currency, and Chinese plain-clothes police trying not to look too obvious.

YINGJIANG
(yíngjiāng)

Yingjiang is a possible stopover if you're heading to Ruili from Tengchong. It's not really worth a special effort, but the locals are friendly and, even though there's not a damn thing to do, it's a good place to break up the bus ride.

Things to See

There's nothing much really. Take a mini-bus out to **Jiucheng** *(jiùchéng,* literally, old town) to see an old Chinese town. It's only a 20 minute ride, and it's fairly picturesque. Back on the road to Ruili, a couple of kilometres out of town, is an old stupa: **Laomian Pagoda** *(lǎomiǎn tǎ).* The name means Old Burmese Stupa, which is a fairly accurate description. Locals claim it's a nice place to visit in the evenings 'with someone you care about' – see if you can find the local PSB and invite one of the boys in green along.

Places to Stay & Eat

In the vicinity of the long-distance bus station there's a number of low-rent joints. Opposite the long-distance bus station is the drab *State Guesthouse (guóyíng lǚshè).* Locals claim it's a den of iniquity, but unfortunately we didn't come across anything particularly iniquitous. It's Y4 for a bed in a three or five-bed dorm, Y16 for a double and Y10 for a single. None of the rooms have showers. You also need to take a bit of a hike if you want to use the toilet.

Better still, give the State Den of Iniquity a miss and walk towards town (turn right after you exit the bus station) for the *Yingqing Hotel (yíngqīng lǚshé).* It's on the right hand side of the road, on the corner of the first large intersection. This clean and friendly place has singles/doubles for Y15/20 and singles with bathroom and TV for Y40. The hot water is solar heated and doesn't warm up until mid-afternoon.

Yingjiang's answer to the Hilton is the *Great Wall Hotel (chángchéng bīnguǎn),* where the cheapest rooms cost Y60 (no carpet!) and the most expensive are Y600. All rooms have their own TVs and bathrooms. To get there, keep walking from the Yingqing Hotel and turn right at the first major intersection; the Great Wall is on the corner of the next intersection. Turning left at that second intersection brings you to the *Bright Pearl Hotel (míngzhū dàjiǔdiàn),* which has similar standards and rates. It's got a clean and popular restaurant with good food and service, despite the fact that it served up a nasty bug on a last visit.

Otherwise, Yingjiang is not a gastronomical experience that merits a postcard to mum and dad, but the cheap noodle stores over near the bus station will keep you alive for another day.

Getting There & Away

To Yingjiang from Ruili, buses leave daily at 9.30 am and 12.30 and 2 pm, and cost Y16 for the up-down-and-around five hour trip. Buses to Ruili leave at 7, 9 and 10.30 am, and 12.30 and 2 pm, with tickets costing Y16. Buses at 8 and 9.30 am go to Mangshi via Ruili; tickets cost Y35.

From Tengchong, buses leave four times daily for Yingjiang, with tickets costing Y14. Unless you're taking the early bus from Tengchong, you will probably have to stay overnight in Yingjiang as most outbound buses stop around noon. Up to around 4 pm you may be able to catch a minibus across from the bus station to Zhangfeng, where you can connect with buses to Ruili. The whole journey should cost Y25 and take around five hours.

YUNNAN

Going the other way, there are four buses to Tengchong between 7 am and 2 pm. The trip takes three to four hours and costs Y14 to Y20. Baoshan connections are spotty, and you'll probably have to go through Tengchong. You can even get a sleeper bus from here to Kunming, departing daily at 7 am. The 29 hour odyssey costs Y185.

RUILI
(ruìlì)

Ruili is without a doubt one of the more interesting towns in south-western China. It's just a few kilometres from Myanmar and has a real border-town feel about it. There's a great mix of Han Chinese, minorities and ubiquitous Burmese traders hawking jade, and travellers tend to linger longer than they intended just for the atmosphere. At first sight it doesn't seem like much, and the place is getting dustier with all the new construction, but it's worth giving it a couple of days.

Compared with the rest of China, Ruili seems unrestricted, as though people get away with a lot more here. That this atmosphere is generated by proximity to Myanmar and it's repressive military junta makes Ruili all the more interesting. There are some interesting minority villages nearby; the stupas are in much better condition than those in Xishuangbanna, and it's worth travelling onwards to Wanding and Mangshi, either as day trips or as overnight stops.

Hopefully, in the future Myanmar will lighten up on border-crossing travel restrictions for foreigners. By 1999 new highways laid to facilitate border trade should stretch all the way from Jiegao, on the border, to Mandalay, making much more sane what had been a hellish five day journey. One day travellers may be able to recreate the 'Southern Silk Route', of which Ruili and Mandalay were a part.

Information
Tourist Offices The shop next to the reception area of the Ruili Guesthouse has

maps and a few brochures on Ruili, but there's very little else in the way of information available. First stop for all foreigners ought to be the Ruili Dream Coffee Bar where the owner Sun Zhi Gang can point you in the right direction if not take you there himself. He also provides the cheapest maps in town.

PSB The PSB is just up the road from the guesthouse.

Money The Bank of China is not far from the long-distance bus station. In case you're headed to Myanmar, the bank will let you cash travellers cheques for US dollars, which would come in handy if you could get across the border. This Bank of China branch also garners kudos for speed and efficiency.

Post & Communications Heading down the road you'll find the telecommunications building, from where you can make direct-dial international calls.

Dangers & Annoyances You'll hear incessantly of Ruili's image problems, for which there is some empirical evidence. The town's pubs and discos – lots simply fronts for an enormous prostitution industry – have always had a rough reputation. And though most of the populace are simple traders, a significant share of the local commerce is of the poppy-derived variety, Ruili being an entry point for Burmese opium headed to Hong Kong. This has resulted in a serious IV drug use problem in the Dehong region, along with its pernicious sibling – HIV. Purportedly, since 1990 virtually all of China's new HIV cases were reported in Ruili and its vicinity, and by 1995 70% of the nation's cases were in Yunnan, most in Ruili.

Myanmar Border Crossing More rumours fly about regarding the Ruili border crossing than anything in the Dehong or Baoshan regions. Everyone had hoped that with Myanmar's admission into ASEAN in 1997, it would have to crack its borders a bit. Not even close. At present absolutely *nobody* gets into Myanmar's border town of Muse, not even on a day trip. (Japanese or Koreans might be able to sneak across as locals, but definitely not westerners.) The friendly enough Chinese border guards will wince if you approach – so many foreigners have arrived and pleaded for a day pass

that the commander and some of his underlings are planning to study English!

The Chinese government is perfectly willing to OK transit, but the Myanmar government doesn't really have a handle on corruption and lawlessness in the region and claims it doesn't want foreign tourists wandering through that lethal cocktail. The Chinese have actually even tried to facilitate border crossings. Whatever the case, this is a rapidly expanding area and, who knows, by the time you have this book in your hand, things may have done an about face and hordes of tourists will be piling over the border.

Things to See

There is really not a lot to see in Ruili itself, although it's a great town to wander around, and is small enough that you can cover most of it in an hour or so. The market street in the west of town is the most colourful by day, especially in the morning, while by night the market street just around the corner from the Ruili Guesthouse is the liveliest place to hang out. Most of Ruili's sights are outside town, and you'll need a bicycle to get out and see them.

Nobody really comes to Ruili for the *day*life, though. Ruili doesn't even crack a somnolent eye until 10 pm, at which point

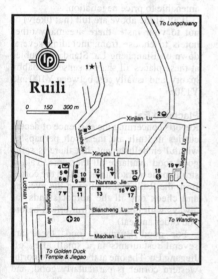

RUILI 瑞丽	12 Jue Jue Cold Drinks Shop 觉觉冷饮店	4 Post Office 邮电大楼
PLACES TO STAY	14 Noodle Shops 面条店	5 Xinhua Bookstore 新华书店
3 Ruili Guesthouse 瑞丽宾馆	16 Ruili Dream Coffee Bar	6 Cinema 电影院
8 Yongchang Hotel 永昌大酒家	瑞丽梦幻咖啡酒吧	9 Yunnan Airlines 云南航空公司
10 Mingrui Hotel 明瑞宾馆	19 Burmese Restaurants 缅甸餐厅	15 Minibus Stand 小型车站
11 Limin Hotel 利民宾馆	**OTHER**	17 Long-Distance Bus Station 长途汽车站
13 Nanyang Hotel 南洋宾馆	1 PSB 公安局	18 Bank of China 中国银行
PLACES TO EAT	2 Buses to Zhangfeng 往章凤的汽车	20 Hospital 医院
7 Burmese Restaurants 缅甸餐厅		

YUNNAN

it transforms itself into an entirely different city altogether. The candlelight power from the neon and flashing lights could probably be viewed from the space station Mir, literally hundreds of sidewalk restaurants spring open, tourists get taken everywhere you look on cheap jade while their friends scream into karaoke microphones. Others take potshots at the ever-present electronic rifle ranges. The population of Ruili seriously seems to triple. All this fun madness is lasting until later and later; it still isn't a city that never sleeps, but it's getting there.

Places to Stay

While everywhere else in Baoshan and Dehong has rock-bottom prices for accommodation, Ruili is the exception to the rule. However, a slew of new hotels has made for stiff competition, and some prices have actually come down in recent years, albeit slightly.

Probably the best deal in town is the *Mingrui Hotel (míngruì bīnguǎn)*, where a triple with bathroom will cost you only Y60. Doubles are Y50, and some singles for Y50 are available. If the hotel is not very full, you'll probably get a room to yourself and if you hang around for a spell, you can talk them into discounts. Rooms are airy and clean, and you can use the hotel's scenic rooftop washing machine – hang your socks while gazing at the Burmese hills.

Across the street, the well-run *Limin Hotel (lìmín bīnguǎn)* has triples with common washroom for Y60. Similar doubles are Y50, while standard doubles with attached bath are Y120. One other place that takes foreigners and has dormitory accommodation is the *Ruili Guesthouse (ruìlì bīnguǎn)*. Being a bit further away from the main strip, it offers refuge from the blaring discos and evil roadside karaoke stands. Beds in basic quads and doubles are Y20 each. Bathrooms and showers are on the 1st floor. There are also doubles for Y160 – not good value for money.

The *Yongchang Hotel (yǒngchāng dàjiǔdiàn)* attracts fewer travellers (possibly because of its location), but is also a comfortable and clean place to stay. Standard singles/doubles here are Y80/Y160, while triples are Y120. There is also one four-bed room for Y160. Back on the main strip, the *Nanyang Hotel (nányáng bīnguǎn)* has doubles for Y70. Though this place doesn't look like much at first, some of the rooms aren't that bad at all, and it has the pluses of 24 hour hot water and a management amenable to price negotiation.

If all of the above are full (not likely) or not to your taste, there are many other hotels to choose from, including several down on Biancheng Lu. Standard doubles at these places all share a sense of shabby luxury, and usually cost between Y100 and Y130.

Places to Eat

Reports concerning the existence of decent curries in Ruili are the result perhaps of wishful embellishment, but there is some good food available all the same. Take a stroll up the market street around the corner from the Ruili Guesthouse in the evening and check out all the hotpot stands (as always with hotpot, confirm prices before you order and eat).

For good Burmese food, there are several restaurants in a small alley off Jiegang Lu. The one at the top of the north-western corner is particularly good, and sees a lot of Burmese patrons. This is also the spot to go for Thai Mekong whisky, served Thai style with soda water and ice. More Burmese places, with outdoor seating in the evenings, can be found just south of the cinema on Renmin Jie. The noodle stalls on the street off Nanmao Jie just west of the bus station are also very good.

For nice iced coffee and fruit juice drinks, or something stronger, try the *Jue Jue Cold Drinks Shop (juéjué léngyǐndiàn)*. There's no English sign, but the shop is at the corner of the side street just east of the Mingrui Hotel, and shouldn't be too hard to find. A proliferation of other 'beer/coffee/tea/ice cream/juice' places – many seriously incorporate all those in their names – have

Jamming

'Don't go to the Yufeng Disco', the locals warned me. 'It's full of Burmese who'll mug you and steal all your money.' Having never been mugged in China, I wandered into the gloomy surroundings of the disco around 9 pm. Within minutes I had met all the Burmese in the bar, including the band members, who invited me up for a number *(all* westerners eat hamburgers and play guitar like ringin' a bell, right?).

After much conferring we came up with 'Get Back' and 'Get Off My Cloud', the former sung in Burmese because I could only remember the chorus and something about JoJo leaving his home somewhere in Alabama. We cranked up the amps and ripped through our numbers, much to the bewilderment of the audience, and to the annoyance of two PSB men (who seemed to sense that this was cultural pollution of the highest order). I left the stage to find that my bar tab had been paid by a Burmese business person.

Thomas Huhti

cropped up along the main drag, including the *1997*, an all-wood joint just east of the Mingrui Hotel.

Take the opportunity to try a freshly squeezed lime juice from one of the numerous stands dotting the town. At Y5 a glass it's a bit more than your average drink, but the taste is superb.

Along Biancheng Lu, one block south of the main drag, is an open-front place that has draught beer, decent coffee, some snacks, and even movies in English. Go early – it turns into yet another karaoke monster around sunset.

Head directly to the long-distance bus station. There you'll find the *Ruili Dream Coffee Bar*, a godsend for travellers braving the wilds of Ruili. This open air bar and restaurant is run by Sun Zhi Gang, a fluent English speaker transplanted from northeastern China. Before you do anything in town, or especially pay for anything, consult Sun. A wealth of information, Sun sells maps at cost, rents bikes, will help you line up onward transport, and if he has time, often heads off on bike tours with travellers.

The Ruili Dream is also a good spot to eat; his employees are all Burmese and the cooks can whip up a mean Burmese meal for you. There's also cold draught beer. More than one traveller has wound up spending two weeks in Ruili because of this oasis.

Entertainment

Ruili may only be a small town, but by Chinese standards it packs a lot of punch on the entertainment level. For the Chinese, Ruili has a reputation as one of *the* happening places in Yunnan, and young people with money head down here just for a few nights out. But where discos used to be the venue of choice, now massage parlours have taken over. Prostitution is rampant in Ruili, and it's difficult to find a sleaze-free bar or dance hall. This is, of course, still China, and things are much more tame than Bangkok or Manila. Everything closes down around 1 to 2 am, and you needn't worry about being flagged down in the street by pimps. Still, be aware if you get adventurous and duck into a dark bar for a drink.

The discos are still in action, although they tend to slow down even earlier, around midnight on a slow night. The *Mingrui Hotel* has a disco on the 2nd floor that seems to do fairly well. There is also a dance hall opposite the Burmese restaurants on Renmin Jie that has a live band playing most nights. There is usually an entrance fee of Y20 or so, depending on where you go, but it's worth it for an insight into China's jiving nightspots.

YUNNAN

Getting There & Away

Ruili has flight connections to Kunming via Mangshi. Flights leave daily, take 50 minutes and cost Y530. Yunnan Airlines (☎ 212-1492 in Mangshi, 414-8275 in Ruili) has an office south of the Yongchang Hotel. You can also use the ticket office to book and reconfirm return flights.

As always, the Chinese government is supposedly hard at work 'improving' roads between Dehong region and Kunming. Although things are much improved these days, it's still a long, long haul. Sleeper buses for the 24 to 28 hour ride (god willing) to Kunming leave from the long-distance bus station 11 times daily from 6.20 am to 4 pm. They cost Y171.

Sleeper buses to Xiaguan (Dali) take 14 hours, leave at 7 pm and cost Y90; the 6.20 am ordinary bus had been cancelled at last check.

Baoshan is seven to eight hours away; there are six buses between 7.20 am and noon for Y35. This ride should become shorter as work progresses on a new primary-grade road linking Ruili and Baoshan.

Two buses for Tengchong leave at 7 am (one small and one large, Y25); the trip takes anywhere between five and seven hours. There are three buses for Yingjiang (Y16): at 9.30 am, 12.30 and 2 pm. On a good day, the ride takes four to five hours, but there are few good days on this rainy route.

Buses leave for Mangshi frequently between 8 am and 3 pm from a driveway just east of the long-distance bus station. The two-hour ride costs Y15 to Y20. Finally, if you're really in the mood to rough it, private sleeper buses leave for Jinghong in Xishuangbanna at 6.30 am and arrive sometime in the afternoon of the third day. Private entrepreneurs advertise lots of destinations from just a few steps to the west of the bus station's ticket window, so check the signs for more convenient departures or prices.

Minibuses and vans leave for more local destinations from opposite the long-distance bus station.

Getting Around

To/From the Airport Minibuses leave daily for the two hour trip to the airport; check that day's flight schedule to see what time they leave.

Other Transport Ruili itself is easily explored on foot, but all the most interesting day trips require a bicycle. Like accommodation, in Ruili bicycles don't come cheap, or at least the deposit doesn't. The only reliable place renting bicycles at present is the Ruili Dream Coffee Bar, which charges Y10 to Y12 per day, with a low deposit of around Y100. The Mingrui Hotel may still have some of their clunkers – they were charging Y15 per day, with a hefty Y300 deposit, if not a passport as well.

At the time of writing, concrete was being poured for a new taxi station adjacent to the long-distance bus station. A flat rate for a route inside the city should be Y5.

AROUND RUILI

Most of the sights around Ruili can be explored easily by bicycle. It's worth making frequent detours down the narrow paths that lead off the main roads to visit minority villages. The people are friendly, and there are lots of photo opportunities. The shortest ride is to take a left at the corner north of the post office and keep going out of the town proper into a little village. There are some half a dozen Shan temples scattered about, and it's a great trip finding them first of all, and then getting a look inside the unique interiors.

Nongan Golden Duck Temple

(nóng'ān jīnyā tǎ)

A short ride to the south-west of town, the Golden Duck Temple is an attractive stupa in a courtyard. It is said to have been established to mark the arrival of a pair of golden ducks that brought good fortune to what was previously an uninhabited marshy area.

Jiegao Border Checkpoint

Continue straight ahead from the Golden Duck Temple, cross the Myanmar bridge over the Ruili River and you will come to Jiegao, a little thumb of land jutting into Myanmar that serves as the main checkpoint for a steady stream of cross-border traffic (see the Myanmar Border Crossing section earlier for more details). There's not a lot to see. But you can still marvel at how laid-back everything seems on both sides of the – quite literally – bamboo curtain and indulge the perennial fascination with illicit borders. Wildly popular casinos and other sordid dens of iniquity line the streets of both sides of the border, and in one case apparently right on the border.

Jiegao is about 7km from the Ruili long-distance bus station. Locals pay Y4 for a ride before 10 pm, and Y5 after that, but you'll likely have to pay Y5 anyway. If there are four or five of you, bargain them down to Y3.

Temples

Just after the Golden Duck Temple is a crossroads. The road to the right leads to the villages of Jiexiang and Nongdao, and on the way are a number of small temples, villages and stupas worth a look. Most of them are not particularly noteworthy and the village life nearby is more interesting – there are often small market areas near the temples.

The first major temple is the **Hansha Temple** *(hánshāzhuāng sì)*, a fine wooden structure with a few resident monks. It's set a little off the road, but is easy to find.

Another 15 minutes or so down the road, look out for a white stupa on the hillside to the right. This is **Leizhuangxiang** *(léizhuāngxiāng)*, Ruili's oldest stupa, dating back to the middle of the Tang Dynasty. There's a nunnery in the grounds of the stupa and fantastic views of the Ruili area. Once the stupa comes into view, take the next path to the right that cuts through the fields. There are signs in Chinese and Dai pointing the way, which leads through a couple of Dai villages. You'll need to get off your bicycle and push for the last ascent up to the stupa.

A couple of kilometres past the town of Jiexiang is **Denghannong Temple** *(děnghánnóngzhuāng sì)*, a wooden Dai temple with pleasant surroundings. Like the other temples in the area, the effect is spoiled somewhat by the corrugated tin roof.

Nongdao

(nóngdǎo)

Around 29km south-west of Ruili, the small town of Nongdao is worth an overnight trip. The locals (mainly Burmese and Dai) don't get all that many foreign visitors and are a friendly lot. There's a solitary hotel in town (you can't miss it) that has cheap doubles. It would be possible to cycle here, stopping off at some of the temple sights along the way, or take a minibus from Ruili – they leave fairly frequently through the day.

Jiele Golden Pagoda

(jiělè jīntǎ)

A few kilometres to the east of Ruili on the road to Wanding is the Jiele Golden Pagoda, a fine structure that dates back 200 years.

WANDING

(wǎndīng)

Many travellers don't make it to Wanding, or do it only as a day trip. It's not as interesting as Ruili, but there's cheaper accommodation here and it's a nice laid-back place to spend a day or so. Part of the attraction is that the town is on the Myanmar border – the Wanding Guesthouse and the Yufeng Hotel both provide good views of the hills, small township and occasional stupa over on the Myanmar side.

Information

The Wanding Travel Bureau can provide you with some information on the area as well as arrange boat trips and other excursions. There's a branch of the Bank of China on the main road that comes in from Ruili. The post office, where you can make international phone calls, is next door to the Xinhua Bookstore on the same road.

Staff at the foreign affairs office of the PSB, just across from the Chinese border

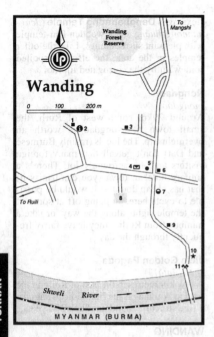

WANDING 畹町

1 Wanding Guesthouse
  畹町宾馆
2 Wanding Travel Bureau
  畹町旅游局
3 Business Hotel
  商业饭店
4 Post Office
  邮局
5 Xinhua Bookstore
  新华书局
6 Yufeng Hotel
  裕丰大楼
7 Minivans to Ruili &
  Mangshi
  芒市
  瑞丽小型汽车站
8 Cooperative Border
  Market
  中缅友谊市场
9 Zhongyin Hotel
  中银宾馆
10 PSB
  公安局
11 Myanmar Border
  Checkpoint
  缅甸边界

checkpoint, seem quite easy-going and, despite the fact they won't help you sneak into Myanmar, they are otherwise quite accommodating.

Things to See & Do

The new **Cooperative Border Market** is a vast multi-storey affair complete with atrium and skylights, and hundreds of stalls for would-be border traders. At the time of writing, occupants numbered only several dozen, and the empty, echoing hallways seemed to be waiting for a vast surge of business that was still nowhere in sight. You might want to stop by to see if things have picked up.

A two minute walk down from the Yufeng Hotel will see you in Myanmar. The only giveaway is the dilapidated Customs office. Apparently a Belgian couple did a day trip into Myanmar for US$20 several years ago (the proceeds were shared by

those who failed to notice them crossing the bridge), but the guards were not interested in allowing a repeat performance when we were in town.

It's worth climbing up to the north of town to take a look at the **Wanding Forest Reserve** (wǎndìng sēnlín gōngyuán). There's a Y2 entry charge and some pleasant walks. Avoid the absolutely pathetic zoo, home to three psychotic monkeys, a couple of peacocks and an unidentifiable ball of fur that was either fast asleep or dead.

The Wanding Travel Bureau can organise river trips which include a barbecue lunch in a minority village. Prices vary depending on the number of participants, but you should be able to do it for around Y50 per person.

Places to Stay & Eat

The cheapest place to stay is the slightly decayed *Yufeng Hotel* (yùfēng dàlóu). If you can get them, dorm beds here are Y15. They'll likely as not push you into basic doubles for Y60.

The better kept and friendly *Wanding Guesthouse (wǎndīng bīnguǎn)* is in a rambling building up on the hill with good views of Myanmar. Beds in quads can be found for Y20, less if business is slow enough for them to bargain. Comfortable doubles with attached bathroom and satellite TV are Y80. Triples are also available for Y90. Look for the alabaster statue of a frolicking maiden holding what looks to be a miniature UFO in her hand at the front entrance.

Up a alleyway off the road to Mangshi, the *Business Hotel (shāngyè fàndiàn)* is quite laid-back despite its name and has basic doubles from Y40. But note that this place had begun 'remaking' itself, so who knows if it will last.

Just up the street from the border, the *Zhongyin Hotel (zhōngyín bīnguǎn)* is the most upmarket choice in Wanding, with singles/doubles from Y60/70.

A brand new hulking thing – the *Traffic Hotel (jiāotōng fàndiàn)* – has opened on the west side of town. Give this pseudo-upmarket thing a miss, unless you have the cash to shell out needlessly.

The area around the Yufeng Hotel is best for *cheap restaurants*. Most of them are of the pick-and-choose variety, and all are much the same. In the mornings try the *dumpling stands* opposite the turn-off for the Wanding Guesthouse.

Getting There & Away

Minibuses run to Ruili for Y15 and to Mangshi for Y30, both prices on the high end of the bargaining scale. They leave throughout the day whenever they are full.

YUNNAN

Guess Who's Coming to Dinner

I was poking around outside the bamboo hut, just checking to make sure it actually *was* still a restaurant (it didn't look like it). The woman cooking, colourfully garbed, gaped wide-eyed at me. I asked about the food, she responded in absolutely unintelligible Mandarin. And then, He appeared.

The appearance of Them – the boys in green, aka the PSB – generally incites the flutter of arrhythmia. He had the look of your worst cop-nightmare – dark-socketed eyes rummy with drink, shirt wide open, rubbing a distended belly, picking dentally with a toothpick. 'Come with me', he motioned. I froze and momentarily wondered whether or not to divulge any linguistic prowess. Generally the last thing you want to do, I spoke Chinese, figuring this guy had the look of long-term hassle to him, requiring cajoling, not dumb-ass gesticulating. I followed him into a poorly lit side room, ducking in and stumbling on the aging woven floor. And panicked.

Around a table sat eight silent, staring PSB officers, with a dangling bulb above them. And an empty chair directly opposite me. A pregnant pause. Finally, he motioned me to sit. 'Come on, sit down', he said. I couldn't move. Eventually, one baby-faced officer looked around and said to uproarious laughter (I couldn't get the words but got the gist) – 'He thinks he's under arrest!'.

The evening thus began as eight of Mangshi's finest treated me to a copious Dai dinner. A couple of them clearly thought this was far beyond the boundaries of proper behaviour, but were overruled by the garrulous commandante. The highlight of the evening came when they all introduced themselves and then, without prompting, the minority group to which most of them belonged. They insisted on footing the bill, and I realised later they had stuck the bill to taxpayers (after padding the charges).

Thomas Huhti

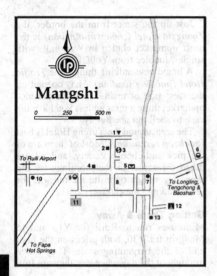

MANGSHI 芒市

1 Dai Restaurants
傣味餐厅
2 Pengcheng Hotel
鹏程酒家
3 Bank of China
中国银行
4 Nanjiang Hotel
南疆饭店
5 Post Office
邮局
6 Long-Distance Bus
Station
客运中心
7 Bicycle Rental
自行党堂
8 Market
市场
9 South Bus Station
汽车南站
10 CAAC
中国民航
11 Mangshi Nationalities
Palace
民族文化宫
12 Temples
寺庙
13 Dehong State Mangshi
Guesthouse
德宏宾馆

You shouldn't have to wait more than 15 minutes for a bus to Ruili; buses to Mangshi are less frequent.

MANGSHI (LUXI)
(mángshì)

Mangshi is Dehong's air link with the outside world. If you fly in from Kunming there are minibuses running direct from the airport to Ruili and most people take this option. But Mangshi has a casual southeast Asian feel to it, and there are a few sights in and around the town that make dallying here a day or so worthwhile if you have the time.

Things to See
Mangshi is not a particularly big place, and it's interesting just to take a wander round. There are a couple of markets in town and a number of **temples** in the vicinity of the Dehong Guesthouse. Around 7km to 8km south of town are the **Fapa Hot Springs** *(fǎpà wēnquán)*; they get good reports from travellers who have cycled out to them.

Near the long-distance bus station is the **Mangshi Nationalities Palace** *(mínzú*

wénhuà gōng), which is more like a large park/plaza full of elderly Chinese practising their *taijiquan*; it has small exhibits on nationalities. It recently relocated here, so perhaps more will be added. A Y3 main gate entrance fee can be circumvented if you get there early enough in the morning.

Places to Stay & Eat
The most popular place to stay is the peaceful, friendly and very well-run *Dehong State Mangshi Guesthouse (déhóng zhōu mángshì bīnguǎn)*. Doubles/triples with bath, TV and fan are Y90/Y105, an excellent deal. Upmarket doubles range from Y120 to Y180.

On the main road, the *Nanjiang Hotel (nánjiāng fàndiàn)* has dorm beds from Y10. Standard doubles/triples go for Y80/90. The place is nothing to rave about, but it's conveniently situated if you're catching an early bus or booking plane tickets. North of the street market, the *Pengcheng Hotel (péngchéng jiǔjiā)* has quads/triples without bathroom for Y40/45 and doubles for Y20. Rooms are clean, but this place is exceedingly no-frills – it has all the feel of a dilapidated truck stop to it.

The *food markets* south of the Pengcheng Hotel have good noodle dishes and there are also numerous pick-and-choose *restaurants* around town

North of the Pengcheng Hotel is a string of attractive thatched-roof restaurants on stilts serving Dai food. These are definitely worth a visit, as much for the food as for the atmosphere and views of the fields and foothills beyond.

Getting There & Away

There are daily flights (737s) between Mangshi and Kunming for Y530; the flight takes around 50 minutes.

Minibuses connect Mangshi proper with Wanding for Y15 to Y20 depending on your bargaining skills. Most of the minibuses to Wanding troll the main road back and forth until full; be prepared for a half hour of circling. The long-distance bus station has scheduled daily buses for the two hour ride to Ruili from 7 am to 1 pm, which costs Y20 to Y25.

Unless demand calls for more, there are buses to Baoshan every other day between 7 am and noon. The five hour ride costs Y25. Buses to Tengchong leave at 6.30 and 9.30 am, take five hours and cost Y13. The Nanjiang Hotel reportedly also runs a minibus there.

There is one sleeper bus daily to Xiaguan at 8 am (12 hours, Y120) and sleeper buses to Kunming at 9.30 am and 6.30 pm (22 hours, Y160).

Getting Around

Buses leave from the airport to Mangshi for Y2 after the second Kunming flight arrives. Buses depart the Mangshi CAAC office for the airport around an hour before flight departures. It is possible to book or reconfirm flights here, or you could wait until you get to Ruili, which most travellers do. A fleet of minibuses to Ruili (Y30) awaits incoming flights.

Sichuan 四川

Sichuan Facts & Highlights

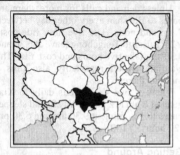

Area: 488,000 sq km

Population: 84.3 million

Capital: Chengdu

Highlights

- Chengdu, with its charming backstreets and great places to eat.
- Jiuzhaigou, a national reserve featuring gorgeous alpine scenery that is being preserved in pristine condition.
- Western Sichuan, with soaring snow-capped peaks, grasslands, glaciers and a heavy Tibetan influence.
- Grand Buddha, which sits in splendour across from the city of Leshan.
- Emeishan, one of China's four Buddhist sacred mountains, great for hiking and monastery-hopping.
- Yangzi River cruises – see the famous Sanxia (Three Gorges) before they are submerged.

Sichuan *(sìchuān)* is one of the largest provinces in China, and the most heavily populated. In the eastern region of Sichuan, the great Chuanxi plain supports one of the densest rural populations in the world, while the regions to the west are mountainous and sparsely populated – principally by Tibetans. Roughly the size of France, give or take Luxembourg, Sichuan has rich natural resources.

Wild mountainous terrain and fast rivers kept it relatively isolated until the present era, and much of the western fringe is still remote. This inaccessibility has made it the site of a number of breakaway kingdoms throughout Chinese history, and it was here that the beleaguered Kuomintang Party spent its final days before being vanquished and fleeing to Taiwan.

The capital is Chengdu, but the largest city is Chongqing, which is also the stepping stone for the ferry ride down the Yangzi River.

The Chinese often refer to Sichuan as *tiānfŭ zhī guó*, the 'Heavenly Kingdom', a reference to its resources and rich cultural heritage. The name Sichuan means 'four rivers' and refers to four of the 80-plus mighty rivers that tumble through the province.

Sichuan became famous during the Warring States Period when engineer Li Bing somehow corralled the River Du on the Chuanxi plain with his weir system, allowing Sichuan some 2200 continuous years of irrigation and prosperity.

The province continues to get rich, having played an active role in China's labouring economic reforms over the last 18 years.

Zhao Ziyang soared from the post of First Party Secretary of Sichuan to General Secretary of the Communist Party before his fall from grace in the wake of the Tiananmen massacre. His reputation was made by instituting pioneering agricultural reforms in the province. Under the so-called 're-sponsibility system', plots of land were let out to farmers for individual use on the condition that a portion of the crops be sold back to the government. By 1984 the reforms had spread throughout China and were later applied to the industrial sector.

A less fortunate result of these reforms is

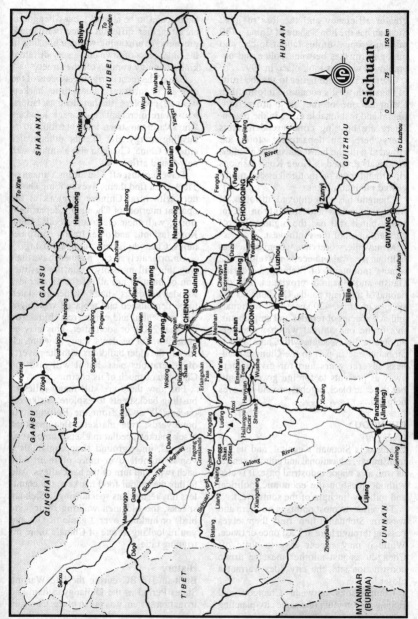

greater efficiency and the loss of jobs; Sichuan has the lion's share of China's 130 million-strong 'surplus labour force', and minor skirmishes between police and unemployed workers took place in 1997.

There is nowhere better to see the fruits of the south-west's economic reforms than Chengdu, one of the most prosperous, liberal and fashionable cities in the region. There are bustling commercial markets everywhere, the department stores are crowded with the latest consumer goodies, and locals dressed in Hong Kong fashions zip around town on motorbikes and multi-geared mountain bikes.

Chengdu has also enjoyed an influx of foreign investors and students in recent years, but it still has the highest 'hello!' quotient in all of the south-west.

Meanwhile, worlds away from the scenes of urban renewal and economic reform, the remote mountains of Sichuan, bordering Gansu and Shaanxi provinces, are the habitat of the giant panda. Of China's 1174 species of birds, 420 species of mammals and 500 species of reptiles and amphibians, this is the one animal which westerners automatically associate with China. This is probably due in part to the Chinese fondness several years ago for giving them away as presents to foreign governments, but the cute black patches around the eyes help too.

CHENGDU
(chéngdū)

Chengdu is Sichuan's capital, and its administrative, educational and cultural centre, as well as a major industrial base. It is also without question the economic, political and military linchpin of the south-west.

Travellers to most points in northern and western Sichuan often find themselves passing through here at least once or twice. While it may appear easy to write off Chengdu as just another massive urban construction site, the city does warrant a closer look.

Comparisons between Chengdu and Beijing are tempting (the same city-planning hand seems to be at work), but Chengdu is an altogether different place, with more greenery, overhanging wooden housing in the older parts of town and a very different kind of energy coming off the streets.

One of the most intriguing aspects of the city is its artisans: small-time basket-weavers, cobblers, itinerant dentists, tailors, houseware merchants and snack hawkers who swarm the streets and contribute to its bustling energy. But like the other major cities of China, Chengdu also abounds with new-found affluence.

Travellers just off a bus from Yunnan or Tibet often find themselves rubbing shoulders with rural Chinese to gawk at the opulent interiors of Chengdu's department stores, with their electronic goods, Hong Kong fashions and other trendy consumer items. Chengdu is bent on modernising.

Unfortunately, if city planners have their way this will probably mean the destruction of most, if not all, of the city's older wooden buildings – half of which are slated to be demolished and replaced with high-rise residential and commercial blocks by the year 2000, or soon after. This may be good news for residents, many of whom associate the older buildings with the poverty of generations past, but it will also rob Chengdu of much of its charm.

For now there are still many miles of bustling backstreets to explore. Strike off on a walk away from the Beijing-style boulevards; free markets, flea markets, black markets, pedlar markets, commercial districts, underground shopping malls – you'll stumble over more of them with each twist and turn of the back alleys. Add to this the indoor food markets, the countless tiny restaurants specialising in Sichuan snacks, the old men walking their song birds or huddled over a game of Go, and you're looking at one of China's more intriguing cities.

History

Built in 316 BC during the late Warring States Period as the Dujiangyan dam and irrigation system was put in place, Chengdu boasts a 2300 year history. Linked closely with the arts and crafts trades, during the Eastern Han Dynasty (25-220 AD) the city was often referred to as Jincheng (Brocade City), due to its thriving silk brocade industry. It would later also be called the Lotus City; a localism for the city still heard today is a synonym for 'lotus'.

By the Tang Dynasty (618-907 AD) it was – along with Handan, Fangzhan, and Changan – considered a cornerstone of Chinese society. Like other major Chinese cities, the place has had its share of turmoil. First it was devastated by the Mongols in retaliation for the fierce fighting put up by the Sichuanese. From 1644 to 1647 it was presided over by rebel Zhang Xiangzhong, who set up an independent state in Sichuan, ruling by terror and mass executions.

Three centuries later the city was set up as one of the last strongholds of the Kuomintang. The name 'Chengdu' means Perfect Metropolis – and today around three million people inhabit the perfect city proper, or three times that if you count the surrounding metropolitan area.

The original city was walled with a moat, gates at the compass points and the Viceroy's Palace (14th century) at its heart. The latter was the imperial quarter. The remains of the city walls were demolished in the early 1960s, and the Viceroy's Palace was blown to smithereens at the height of the Cultural Revolution. In its place was erected the Russian-style Exhibition Centre.

Outside, a massive Mao statue waves merrily down Renmin Lu. The Great Helmsman's gaze also used to take in four enormous portraits of Marx, Engels, Lenin and Stalin, but Chengdu suffers from chronic ad-itis and the forefathers of Communism have been removed in favour of larger-than-life advertisements for cognac and imported watches.

Orientation

Chengdu has echoes of boulevard-sweeping Beijing in its grand scale, except that here flowering shrubs and foliage line many of the expanses. As in Beijing there are ring roads right around the outer city, although Chengdu has only two to Beijing's four: the first ring road (*yīhuánlù*) and the second (*èrhuánlù*). These are divided into numbered segments (*duàn*). The main boulevard that sweeps through the centre of everything is Renmin Lu – in its north (*běi*), central (*zhōng*) and south (*nán*) manifestations.

The nucleus of the city is the square that interrupts the progress of Renmin Lu, with administrative buildings, the Sichuan Exhibition Centre, a sports stadium and, at its southern extent, a colossal Mao presiding over a city long since oblivious to his presence.

The area where Renmin Nanlu crosses the Jin River, near the Jinjiang and Traffic hotels, has become the city's tourist ghetto. This is where you'll find most of the restaurants and arts and crafts shops catering for foreigners, and even nowadays a couple of pubs.

Finally, Chengdu is a true Asian city in its nonchalant disregard of systematic street numbering and naming. It's not unusual, when following street numbers in one direction, to meet another set coming the other way, often leaving the poor family in the middle with five sets of numbers over their doorway. Street names, also, seem to change every 100m or so, with very little apparent logic involved. Bear this in mind when you're looking for somewhere in particular, and rely more on nearby landmarks and relative locations on maps than on street numbers and names.

Maps City bus maps can be found at railway and bus stations, the Traffic Hotel and Xinhua Bookstores. Three different maps in Chinese provide excellent detail of Sichuan Province, Chengdu city or its surrounding areas, and one also has a fair amount of English street and place names. Even the best ones cannot hope to fully capture the insanity that is Chengdu's street naming.

Information

Tourist Offices Unless you're interested in joining a tour group, there's no real point in bothering the people at CITS. Staff in the main office (☎ 667-5578) on Renmin Nanlu opposite the Jinjiang Hotel are friendly, but can't book train tickets and have been trained to say 'Tibet is closed'. If you want to avail yourself of their services, the office is open daily from 8.30 am to 5 pm.

For the kind of help that individual travellers need, try the small outfits in and around the Traffic Hotel.

Consulates The US consulate (☎ 558-3992) is in a small fortress at 4 Lingshiguan Lu, just off Renmin Nanlu between the first and second ring roads.

PSB The main office is on the part of Xinhua Donglu named Wenwu Lu, east of the intersection with Renmin Zhonglu. However, whether you're seeking permits to visit 'closed' areas in Sichuan, visa extensions or even reporting a theft, you'll probably do better at the Foreign Affairs section (☎ 630-1454) – a single-storey building at 40 Wenmiaohou Jie, which is off Nan Dajie to the west of the Jinjiang Hotel.

To get there from the Traffic Hotel, walk up Renmin Lu to Hongzhao Bijie and turn left. Follow it as it bears south-west for a long block or so until it meets up with a road. Turn right and it'll be on the right-hand side. Some members of the staff speak excellent English. This office is open Monday to Friday from 8 to 11 am and from 2.30 to 5 pm, and on Sunday from 8.30 to 11 am. Saturday hours are hit and miss; some travellers have managed to badger guards into tracking down somebody official.

Money Many hotels, including the Traffic and Jinjiang, have foreign-exchange counters. There is a Bank of China branch on Renmin Nanlu in front of the Jinjiang Hotel (the new Bank of China across the road

from this does *not* have foreign-exchange service).

The main branch of the Bank of China is in a huge yellow building up on Renmin Donglu. This is the place for credit card withdrawals and the like. Bank of China hours are 8.30 to 11.30 am and 2.30 to 5 pm.

Post & Communications The main post office is housed in what looks like a converted church on the corner of Huaxingzheng Jie and Shuwa Beijie, close to the Cultural Palace in the centre of town. It's open from 8.30 am to 6 pm daily.

Numerous other little post offices are scattered throughout the central part of town. The ageing main PO is no longer the place to pick up poste restante mail. For that, you need to go to the post office (the EMS building) on Shawan Rd, near the intersection of Bei Yihuan Lu. To get there, take bus No 48 to the second-to-last stop. Walk east along the ring road until you see a statue, and turn right. It'll be ahead on the left.

More convenient might be the poste-restante service at the Traffic Hotel, which holds letters and parcels for 15 days at the luggage storage counter. Items should be mailed care of the Traffic Hotel, 77 Linjiang Road, Xinnanmen, Chengdu 610041.

The best place in town for making collect calls is in the telecommunications centre, east of the Sichuan Exhibition Centre. You can also make direct-dial overseas calls and faxes from here. Public phones which take home-country calling cards are along a wall to the left after entering. The telecommunications service is posted as 24 hours, but you might find it closed very early or very late.

Dangers & Annoyances There have been several reports of foreigners becoming targets for rip-offs and theft in Chengdu. In particular there have been a couple of incidents (one foreigner was stabbed) on the riverside pathway between the Jinjiang and Traffic hotels. Take care late at night – it's best not to walk alone.

To avoid getting ripped off by taxi and pedicab drivers and restaurants, always get the price at the start of proceedings. Pickpockets are common around bus and railway stations and post offices, and watch out for gangs who use razors to slit your bags on buses. If you want to play it safe with train tickets, make a note of the ticket numbers. If the tickets are stolen you'll be given replacements, providing you can supply the numbers of the old ones.

Should things get out of hand, ring the Foreign Affairs section of the PSB. English is spoken and the staff usually do their best.

Wenshu Monastery
(wénshū yuàn)

Wenshu Monastery, which dates back to the Tang Dynasty, is Chengdu's largest and best preserved Buddhist place of worship. Originally known as Xinxiang Temple, it was renamed after a Buddhist monk who lived there in the late 17th century. It is believed that his presence literally illuminated the monastery. Many of the buildings in the complex are decorated with exquisite relief carvings.

Perhaps the best thing about the monastery is the bustling crowds of worshippers who flock to the place. It's a fairly active place of worship and as such is well worth the trip.

The alley off Renmin Zhonglu, on which Wenshu is located, is a curiosity in itself, with joss-stick vendors, foot-callus removers, beggars, blind fortune-tellers with bamboo spills, and flower and fireworks sellers. In the monastery area, check out the teahouse and vegetarian restaurant. The teahouse is one of the largest you'll see, with what seems like acres of tables, and is always full. The monastery is open daily from 6 am to 8.30 pm, and there's an entry charge of Y1. Some travellers have reported not being able to enter until 8 am.

Tomb of Wang Jian
(wángjiàn mù)

In the north-west of town, the Tomb of Wang Jian was until 1942 thought to be

Zhuge Liang's music pavilion (see Wuhou Temple, in the following Temple Parks section). The tomb in the central building is surrounded by statues of 24 musicians all playing different instruments, and is considered to be the best surviving record of a Tang Dynasty musical troupe.

Wang Jian (847-918 AD) was a Tang general who established the Former Shu kingdom in the aftermath of the collapse of the Tang in 907. Also featured are relics taken from the tomb itself, including a jade belt, mourning books and imperial seals. The tomb is open daily from 8.30 am to 5.30 pm.

Temple Parks

There are a couple of worthwhile temple parks in the city area, all within cycling distance of the Jinjiang and Traffic hotels, and all open seven days a week.

Due west of Mao on the western section of the circular road is **Wenhua Park** (wénhuà gōngyuán), home to **Qingyang Palace** (qīngyáng gōng). It is the oldest and most extensive Taoist temple in the Chengdu area.

The story goes that Laotzu, the high priest of Taoism, asked a friend to meet him there. When the friend arrived he saw only a boy leading two goats on a leash ... and, in a fabulous leap of lateral thinking, realised the boy was Laotzu. The goats are represented in bronze in the rear building on the temple grounds.

If the one with only one horn looks slightly ungoat-like, it is because it combines features of all the Chinese zodiac animals: a mouse's ears, a cow's nose, a horse's mouth, the back of a rabbit, a snake's tail, neck of a monkey, and a pig's bum. The solitary horn was borrowed from a dragon. And if you're wondering whether the goat has any goatish qualities at all, take a look at the beard. The other goat can vanquish life's troubles and pains if you stroke its flank. The park is open from 6 am to 8 pm and costs Y1.50 to enter. The palace costs Y2.

Qingyang Palace can be combined with

a visit to **Du Fu Cottage** *(dùfǔ cǎotáng)* nearby, erstwhile home of the celebrated Tang Dynasty poet. Something of a rover, Du Fu (712-70 AD) was born in Henan and left his home province to see China at the tender age of 20. He was an official in Chang'an (the ancient capital on the site of modern-day Xi'an) for 10 years, and was later captured by rebels after an uprising and fled to Chengdu, where he stayed for four years. He built himself a humble cottage and penned more than 200 poems on simple themes around the lives of the people who lived and worked nearby.

The present grounds – 20 hectares of leafy bamboo and luxuriant vegetation – are a much enlarged version of Du Fu's original poetic retreat. It's also the centre of the Chengdu Du Fu Study Society, and several display halls house examples of the poet's work.

Du Fu's statue is accompanied by statues of two lesser poets: Li You and Huang Tingjian. From the time of his death in exile (in Hunan), Du Fu acquired a cult status, and his poems have been a major source of inspiration for many Chinese artists. Du Fu Cottage is open from 7 am to 11 pm. The entry fee is a whopping Y30 for foreigners, as opposed to Y3 for Chinese, but is supposed to include the Y10 admission required to enter the cottage area proper.

To the west of the Jinjiang Hotel and next to Nanjiao Park is **Wuhou Temple** *(wǔhóu cí)*. Wuhou might be translated as 'Minister of War', and was the title given to Zhuge Liang, a famous military strategist of the Three Kingdoms Period (220-80 AD) immortalised in one of the classics of Chinese literature, *The Tale of the Three Kingdoms*. Curiously, Zhuge Liang is not the main attraction of the temple. The front shrine instead is dedicated to Liu Bei, Zhuge Liang's emperor. Liu's temple, the Hanzhaolie Temple, was moved here and rebuilt during the Ming Dynasty, but the Wuhou Temple name stuck all the same.

Liu is a common Chinese surname and many Overseas Chinese with the surname make a point of visiting the temple while they are in Chengdu on the glorious off-chance that the emperor is a distant ancestor. One sour note here is the admission; a mere Y0.5 for Chinese, but Y15 for foreign guests!

In the south-east of town, near Sichuan University, is **River Viewing Pavilion Park** *(wàngjiāng lóu)*. The pavilion itself is a four storey Qing wooden structure overlooking the Jin River. The park is famous for its lush forests of bamboo, and boasts over 150 varieties of bamboo from China, Japan and South-East Asia. They range from bonsai-sized potted plants to towering giants, creating a shady retreat in the heat of summer (and a cold, damp retreat in winter).

The pavilion was built to the memory of Xue Tao, a female Tang Dynasty poet with a great love for bamboo. Nearby is a well, said to be the place where she drew water to dye her writing paper. The park is open from 6 am to 9 pm and the entry fee is Y1.

Renmin Park
(rénmín gōngyuán)

This is one Chinese park well worth recommending. It's to the south-west of the city centre. The teahouse here is excellent (see the Places to Eat section later in this entry) and it's a perfect perch for people-watching and whiling away a lazy afternoon.

The park also holds a bonsai rockery, a kids' playground, a few swimming pools, and the Monument to the Martyrs of the Railway Protection Movement (1911). This obelisk, decorated with shunting manoeuvres and railway tracks, marks an uprising of the people against officers who pocketed cash raised for the construction of the Chengdu-Chongqing line. Since Renmin Park was also at the time a private officer's garden, it was a fitting place to erect the structure.

Across the lake from the teahouse is the entry to an underground museum/funhouse that must count as one of the weirder experiences in Chengdu. An entry fee of

Y10 buys you a tour through a converted air-raid shelter that houses among other things: models of New York, Sydney, Rome and the Taj Mahal (the latter two each having a copy of Moscow's St Basil's Cathedral thrown in for good measure), a life-size statue of Saddam Hussein, and a miniature subway that takes you through 'outer space', 'the rain forest', 'undersea', 'hell' and several other choice locales. The point of all this is anyone's guess, but it makes for an entertaining visit.

Renmin Park opens at 6.30 am and stays open until 2 am to allow free access to patrons of a disco dance hall located on the park grounds. Admission is Y2.

Sichuan Museum
(*sìchuānshěng bówùguǎn*)

The Sichuan Museum is the largest provincial museum in China's south-west, with more than 150,000 items on display. For historians, the displays of tiled murals and frescoes taken from tombs are of great interest in their depiction of ancient daily activities, from agriculture to dance.

The museum is open on weekdays from 9 am to 5 pm, and on weekends from 10 am to 5 pm. Admission is Y20 and was definitely not worth it at the time of writing, since only two exhibition halls were open and free of messy renovation. It's down Renmin Nanlu in the direction of the south railway station, but is still within cycling distance of the Jinjiang Hotel.

Sichuan University Museum
(*sìdà bówùguǎn*)

Founded in 1914 by US scholar DS Dye, this museum underwent several closings and name changes before reopening under its current name in 1984. The four exhibition rooms display more than 40,000 items on a rotating basis. The collection is particularly strong in the fields of ethnology, folklore and traditional arts.

The ethnology room exhibits artefacts from the Yi, Qiang, Miao, Jingpo, Naxi and Tibetan cultures. The Chinese painting and calligraphy room displays works from the Tang, Song, Yuan, Ming and Qing dynasties. Some exhibits have English labels.

The museum is open Monday to Friday, from 8.30 to 11.30 am and from 2.40 to 5 pm. The university grounds are within easy walking distance of Jiuyanqiao bus station in the south-east of the city, next to the Nine-Arch Bridge. From the bus station, cross the bridge and walk south on Wangjiang Lu for 10 minutes until you reach the university's main gate. Enter and go straight until the road ends at a 'T' intersection. The museum is the first building on the right.

Zoo
(*dòngwùyuán*)

Chinese zoos are always depressing experiences, and it's difficult not to compare the lush expansive grounds that the humans get to stroll around with the concrete bunkers allocated to the exhibits.

Although now upstaged by the nearby Giant Panda Breeding Research Base, the Chengdu Zoo still has a respectable collection of six pandas; however, during the hottest summer months they're not very active.

The zoo is about 6km from Chengdu city centre, and is open from 7.30 am to 8 pm daily. Admission is Y2.5. The best way to get there is by bicycle (around half an hour from the Traffic Hotel). There are also minibuses running directly to the zoo from the north railway station.

Zhaojue Temple
(*zhàojué sì*)

Next door to the zoo, Zhaojue Temple is a Tang Dynasty building dating from the 7th century. It underwent extensive reconstruction under the supervision of Po Shan, a famous Buddhist monk, during the early Qing, with waterways and groves of trees being established around the temple. The temple itself has served as a model for many Japanese and South-East Asian Buddhist temples.

Naturally enough, it went through hard times during the Cultural Revolution and

SICHUAN

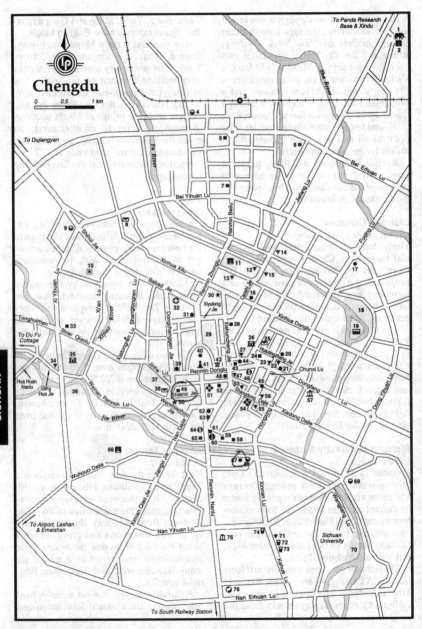

Chengdu

0   0.5   1 km

To Panda Research
Base & Xindu

To Dujiangyan

To Du Fu
Cottage

To Airport, Leshan
& Emeishan

To South Railway Station

Sichuan
University

CHENGDU 城都

PLACES TO STAY

5 Chengdu Grand Hotel
成都大酒店
6 Jingrong Hotel
京蓉宾馆
7 Tibet Hotel
西藏饭店
16 Jindi Hotel
金地饭店
24 Holiday Inn Crowne Plaza
总府皇冠假日酒店
28 Zhufeng Hotel
珠峰宾馆
33 Chengdu College of
Traditional Medicine
成都中医药大学
49 Rongcheng Hotel
蓉成饭店
58 Black Coffee Hotel
黑咖啡饭店
59 Binjiang Hotel
滨江饭店
61 Minshan Hotel
岷山饭店
65 Jinjiang Hotel
锦江宾馆
67 Traffic Hotel
交通饭店

PLACES TO EAT

12 Longyan Baozi
Dumpling Restaurant
龙眼包子
13 Restaurants
餐厅
14 Chen Mapo Doufu
Restaurant
陈麻婆豆腐
15 Guo Soup Balls
Restaurant
郭汤元
22 Shimeixuan Restaurant
市美轩餐厅
23 KFC
肯德鸡
27 Dan Dan Noodle
Restaurant
担担面
34 Chen Mapo Doufu
Restaurant
陈麻婆豆
47 KFC
肯德鸡
53 Chengdu Restaurant
成都餐厅
55 Yaohua Restaurant
耀华餐厅

56 Long Chao Shou Special
Restaurant
龙抄手餐厅
71 Red Brick Cafe Pub
红砖西餐厅

OTHER

1 Chengdu Zoo
动物园
2 Zhaojue Temple
照觉寺
3 North Railway Station
火车北站
4 North Bus Station
城北汽车客运中心
8 General Post Office/EMS
市邮电局
9 Ximen Bus Station
西门汽车站
10 Tomb of Wang Jian
王建墓
11 Wenshu Monastery
文殊院
17 Advance Rail Booking
Office
火车站售票处
18 Recreation Park
市游乐
19 Mengzhuiwan Swimming
Pool
猛追湾游泳池
20 Jinjiang Theatre
锦江剧场
21 Sichuan Foreign
Languages Bookstore
省外文书店
25 Main Post Office
市电信局
26 Cultural Palace
文化宫
29 Municipal Sports Stadium
市体育场
30 PSB
公安局
31 Tape and CD Shop
音像书店
32 No 3 Hospital
三医院
35 Qingyang Palace
青羊宫
36 Baihuatan Park
百华潭公园
37 Renmin Park
人民公园
38 Post Office
邮电局
39 Sichuan Fine Arts
Exhibition Hall
四川美术展览馆

40 Sichuan Exhibition Centre
省展览馆
41 Mao Statue
毛主席像
42 Telecommunications
Centre
电话电报大楼
43 PICC Office
中国人民保险公司
44 Hongqi Market
红旗商场
45 Chunxi Commercial
District
春熙路商业区
46 Bank of China
银行大厦
48 People's Market
人民商场
50 PSB
省公安局外事科
51 Chengdu Department
Store
成都百货大楼
52 Advance Rail Booking
Office
火车站售票处
54 Friendship Store
友谊商店
57 Municipal Museum
市博物馆
60 CITS; CAAC
中国国际旅行社;
中国民航
62 Sichuan Airlines
四川航空公司
63 China Southwest Airlines
中国西南航空公司
64 Bank of China
中国银行
66 Wuhou Temple; Nanjiao
Park
武候祠、南郊公园
68 Xinnanmen Bus Station
新南门汽车站
69 Jiuyanqiao Bus Station
九眼桥汽车站
70 River Viewing Pavilion
Park
望江楼公园
72 Bronx Two Pub
73 Pabst Blue Ribbon
Beertown
蓝带啤酒城
74 Legends of the Fall Pub
75 Sichuan Museum
省博物馆
76 US Consulate
美国领事馆

SICHUAN

TRAFFIC HOTEL

has only been restored in the last 10 years. There's a vegie restaurant on the grounds that serves lunch from 11 am to 2 pm, and a teahouse adjacent. The temple is open from 7 am to 7 pm, and admission is Y1.

Giant Panda Breeding Research Base

About 6km north of the zoo, this research station and breeding ground for both giant and lesser pandas has been in operation since 1990, but was opened to the public only in early 1995.

About 10 to 12 pandas currently reside at the base in quarters considerably more humane than those at the zoo. There is also a breeding area where China's animal ambassadors will eventually be allowed to freely roam and, it is hoped, procreate. Just past the entrance gate, the base museum has detailed exhibits on panda evolution, habits (including rather graphic displays on the, um, more private physiology and reproductive aspects of the bears), habitats and conservation efforts, all with English captions.

The base now covers about 36 hectares, but the breeding ground area is projected to grow to more than 230 hectares sometime early in the next century.

Staff at the base say the best time to visit is between 8.30 and 10 am, when the pandas are feeding; soon thereafter they return to their predominant pastime, sleeping. The entry fee of Y30 is a bit steep, but at least some of the money goes to a good cause, and you are guaranteed a look at these elusive animals – something often denied those who make the long trip up to Wolong Nature Reserve. The base is open daily from 8 am to 6 pm.

Cycling may be your best option to get there. Follow the road north past the zoo for about 2.5km, keeping an eye out for an overhead road sign with a panda on it. At the sign, turn right onto Panda Avenue (Xiongmao Dadao) and keep going for another 3km.

The base is not served by any bus routes, so your other options are to take a taxi all the way there, or to bicycle to the zoo

and from there take a taxi or motor-tricycle (the one way fare should be Y10). Travel outfits at the Traffic Hotel also offer tours for Y80 per person, and since a taxi would be Y85 anyway it'd make sense to take this option.

Places to Stay – budget

The Chengdu PSB has in recent years with great verve gone about closing down most of the cheap Chinese hotels frequented by backpackers. If you search out rooms in old backpacker stand-by hotels you'll be met by staff holding up signs saying, 'Sorry, but the PSB says ...'

One place that just recently opened to foreign friends is the *Chengdu College of Traditional Medicine* (☎ 774-0072) (*chéngdū zhongyīyaò dàxué*), a great find since it's quite cheap, very clean, and the staff is friendly and reasonably used to foreigners. It also fills a need for cheap lodging near the Ximen bus station. Beds in triples with private bath are all of Y20 and the most expensive single is Y85. Each room has a small tiled balcony and fan. On the premises is a tour company whose owner speaks good English. Be careful – there's another guesthouse on the college grounds, and it charges US$22 a night. To get there from Ximen bus station, cross the street and continue south for about 15 or 20 minutes, until you pass a gate with a big statue inside. Continue to the street corner (it should be Shier Qiaolu) and turn left into the gate. Walk straight ahead and look up to your right for a red and white sign (no English) pointing you in the right direction.

The *Traffic Hotel* (☎ 555-1017; fax 558-2777) (*jiāotōng fàndiàn*), next to Xinnanmen bus station, has for a long time been the main hang-out for backpackers. Prices have been on the rise over recent years, but you get your money's worth and with the competition above, the Traffic may reconsider its rates since it's no longer the only game in town. This oasis is clean, comfortable, fairly quiet and close to a number of good dining spots. A bed in a triple with satellite TV and fan is Y50, with immaculate showers and toilet down the hall. Doubles and triples with satellite TV and private bathroom cost Y180 and Y210 respectively. All prices include a decidedly uninspiring although filling breakfast; go for the Chinese version. The staff are mostly friendly and there's a notice board just outside the foyer with travel information. Another useful service here is the baggage room where you can leave a heavy backpacks for a few days while you head off to Emeishan, Jiuzhaigou or wherever (Y1 per day). To get here from the north railway station, take the No 16 bus to across the bridge just south of the Jinjiang Hotel and walk east along the south bank of the river to the hotel.

The *Rongcheng Hotel* (☎ 663-2687) (*róngchéng fàndiàn*) is a slightly chaotic kind of place up an alley west of Renmin Nanlu. It used to be dirt cheap, but has endured a laughable renovation and now charges Y40 for a bed in a triple. Doubles with bathroom go for Y120. There are also 'superior doubles' that start at Y240. Use this as a last resort, since the service is cold, the rooms mediocre and a few travellers recently reported nocturnal visitations by Mr Rat. — *rats !*

For nearly a decade the *Black Coffee Hotel* (*hēi kāfēi fàndiàn*) has offered one of China's unique hotel options. Basically a bomb shelter converted into an underground hotel, karaoke parlour and bar, this somewhat sleazy landmark was closed and still scheduled for an 'upgrade' when we last visited. It's hard to imagine renovating the place with anything other than a wrecking ball, but it still might be worth looking into – you may find yourself in China's first three star bomb shelter.

Places to Stay – middle

Chengdu is pretty short of mid-range accommodation and the best choice is still probably the Traffic Hotel (see the budget section above).

The *Binjiang Hotel*, not far from the Traffic, used to be a popular mid-range

option, but it has gone for a major face-lift, jacked up its prices and for all that still looks not quite worth its Y200 doubles, Y300 triples or the 'foreign friend special' Y280 doubles.

Another option might be the *Jindi Hotel* (674-1339; fax 662-7778) (*jīndì fàndiàn*), at 89 Deshen Jie off Xinhua Lu, which has standard singles/doubles for US$23/28. It is in a good location for visiting sights in northern Chengdu.

Up north by the railway station, the *Jingrong Hotel* (☎ 333-7878) (*jīngróng bīnguǎn*) has doubles with all mod cons for Y298. Another option is the *Zhufeng Hotel*, not far from the Cultural Palace.

Places to Stay – top end

The *Jinjiang Hotel* (☎ 558-2222; fax 558-1849) (*jǐnjiāng bīnguǎn*) at 180 Renmin Nanlu was once the headquarters for all travellers who made it to Chengdu. Now it has become a four star giant with standard doubles starting at Y1000. There are good views to be had from the rooftop Chinese restaurant here, but at a high price: beer and soft drinks are around Y30 each.

Opposite the Jinjiang on Renmin Nanlu is the newer, 21 storey *Minshan Hotel* (☎ 558-3333; fax 558-2154) (*mínshān fàndiàn*) which does a brisk tour-group business. Modern doubles start at Y950 and suites are Y1980, while another building has older rooms from Y700. The Minshan has a couple of bars, a coffee shop and five restaurants.

Opposite the north railway station is the *Chengdu Grand Hotel* (☎ 317-3888) (*chéngdū dàjiǔdiàn*), a plush place designed to attract the roving business account. Prices vary according to demand (they will double when conferences are held in town), but you can reckon on a minimum of Y330 for a standard double.

Just east of the Sichuan Exhibition Centre, the *Holiday Inn Crowne Plaza* (☎ 678-6666; fax 678-6599) (*zǒngfǔ huángguàn rì jiǔdiàn*) is a new top-end place with all the trappings of a Holiday Inn. In addition to the numerous restaurants, it has a

SICHUAN

laundry list of amenities, including one of the few exercise facilities you'll find in China. You can pick up a copy of the *International Herald Tribune* here as well. All this for a mere Y1390 base rate, although they'll likely trim it by 30% since it's never full. You could also try the *Tibet Hotel* north of the city centre near Renmin Beilu.

Places to Eat

For a full discussion of Sichuan's regional food, see the special colour section on Chinese cuisine in the Facts for the Visitor chapter.

Famous Restaurants The *Chengdu Restaurant (chéngdū cāntīng)* at 134 Shangdong Dajie is one of Chengdu's most famous and authentic Sichuan restaurants – it's a favourite with travellers. It has a good atmosphere, decent food and reasonable prices. Downstairs serves set courses of Sichuan appetisers, while full meals can be had upstairs. Try to assemble a party of vagabonds from the hotel before sallying forth; tables are large and you get to sample more with a bigger group. It's about a 20 minute walk along a side alley opposite the Jinjiang Hotel. Arrive early: the place starts shutting down around 8.30 pm.

For guoba roupian, you can't beat the *Shimeixuan Restaurant (shìměixuān cāntīng)* opposite the Jinjiang Theatre on Huaxingzheng Jie. A large plate of the crispy rice in pork and lychee sauce costs around Y10, which is plenty for two. The restaurant has lots of other great dishes, and the proprietors don't seem to mind if you walk through the kitchen and point out what you want. Large, clean dining rooms with wooden tables and ceiling fans make eating here even more enjoyable.

Another main-course restaurant in the heart of the city is the *Yaohua Restaurant* (☎ 672-9518) *(yàohuá fàndiàn)* at the corner of Chunxi Lu and Changsha Dongdajie. A visit by Mao himself in 1958 clinched the restaurant's reputation; today they're as likely to have a Cindy Crawford

photo on the walls. Among Chinese, the restaurant is also renowned for its western food and some of the dishes are not bad at all. You can get a set meal for around Y15.

Riverside Restaurants The southern side of the Jin River between the Jinjiang and Traffic hotels used to be home to a string of small restaurants and teahouses with outdoor tables.

At the time of writing, most buildings in this area had been torn down, and all those up to the Traffic Hotel were slated for demolition. A riverside park is being planned for the area. Whether restaurants will again sprout up here is uncertain.

Vegetarian Restaurants A special treat for ailing vegetarians is to head out to the Wenshu Monastery, where there's an excellent vegetarian restaurant with an English menu. The Zhaojue Temple also serves up vegie dishes for lunch, but the menu is only in Chinese. If you're really keen, you might ride out to the *Monastery of Divine Light* in Xindu, 18km north of Chengdu, in time for lunch (11 am to noon). For details of the bus service, see the Around Chengdu section later in this chapter.

Snack Bars Many of Chengdu's specialities originated as *xiǎo chī*, or 'little eats'. The snack bars are great fun and will cost you next to nothing. In fact, the offerings can be outdone in no other Chinese city – and if you line up several of these places you will get yourself a banquet in stages.

Unfortunately, many of Chengdu's best known snack places are falling prey to the massive reconstruction work that is tearing down neighbourhoods. This is particularly true of the Dongfeng Lu area, although a few places are still hanging in there. We can't promise that all the places marked on the map and mentioned here will still be there by the time you set out in search of them. Take a look anyway – it's worth the effort.

Pock-marked Grandma Chen's Bean Curd (chén mápō dòufu) serves mapo doufu with a vengeance. Soft bean curd is served up with a fiery meat sauce (laced with garlic, minced beef, salted soybean, chilli oil and nasty little peppercorns). The story goes that the madame with the pock-marked face set up shop here (reputed to be the same shop as today's) a century ago, providing food and lodging for itinerant peddlers. The bean curd is made on the premises and costs around Y3 a bowl. Beer is served to cool the fires. Don't worry about the grotty decor – those spices should kill any lurking bugs. Also served are spicy chicken and duck, and plates of tripe.

Situated along Jiefang Lu north of the Fu River, the shop has a vertical sign out front, the outside edge of which has the name in pinyin. Be sure to sit downstairs: the 2nd floor has been redone to look like a typical Chinese banquet hall and carries a Y5 'seating charge'. This place is no longer an unknown cubbyhole – the original is spiffier than it is greasy and it appears to have franchised, with another one across from Wenhua Park.

Another place that is still going strong is *Long Chao Shou Special Restaurant (lóngchāoshǒu cāntīng)*. The beauty of this little restaurant is that it has sampler courses that allow you to dip into the whole gamut of the Chengdu snack experience. The Y5 course gives you a range of sweet and savoury items, while the Y10 and Y15 courses are basically the same deal on a grander and more filling scale. It's on the north-eastern corner of Chunxi Lu and Dong Dajie.

Hotpot Although it is said to have origi-nated in Chongqing, *huǒguō*, or hotpot, is very popular in Chengdu. You'll see lots of sidewalk hotpot operations in the older section of town near the Chunxi Lu market, as well as along the river.

Big woks full of hot, spiced oil (not to be confused with the mild Mongolian version, which employs simmering soup broth) invite passers-by to sit down, pick out skewers of raw ingredients and make a do-it-yourself fondue. You pay by the

skewer – it's best to ask the price of a skewer before you place it in the oil.

During the winter months the skewered items on offer tend to be meat or 'heavy' vegetables like potatoes. In the summer months lighter, mostly vegetarian fare is the norm. This stuff is *very* hot, and many non-Sichuanese can't take it. If this is the case, try asking for *báiwèi*, the hotpot for wimps. Chinese (and some travellers) will turn their noses up at this, claiming that it's not the real thing – just ignore them.

Teahouses The *Renmin Teahouse (rénmín cháguǎn)* in Renmin Park is a leisurely tangle of bamboo armchairs, sooty kettles and ceramics, with a great outdoor location by a lake. It's a family-type teahouse and is crowded on weekends. In the late after-noon workers roll up to soothe factory-shattered nerves, and some just doze off in their armchairs. You can do the same. A most pleasant afternoon can be spent here in relative anonymity over a bottomless cup of stone-flower tea at a cost so ridicu-lous it's not worth quoting. When enough tea freaks appear on the terrace, the stray earpicker, with Q-tips at the ready, roves through, and paper-profile cutters with deft scissors also make the rounds.

A charming indoor family-type teahouse is also to be found in *Wenshu Monastery*, with an amazingly crowded and steamy ambience.

Another place definitely worth checking out is in the *Jinjiang Theatre*, not far from the post office. This place also has perfor-mances of Sichuan opera.

Western Food You'll no doubt happen upon one of Chengdu's five (at last count) *KFC* franchises, China's favourite Ameri-can contribution to its cuisine. Two KFCs are found east of the Mao statue on Renmin Donglu and Dongfeng Lu; another is across from the entrance to Renmin Park. Chinese knock-offs are also found near the two former. There's rumoured to be a Pizza Hut clone opening somewhere in the vicinity of the Mao statue in the near future.

Chengdu's Multipurpose Teahouses

The teahouse, or *chádiàn*, has always been the equivalent in China of the French cafe or the British pub – or at least prior to 1949. Activities you might have encountered ranged from haggling over a bride's dowry to fierce political debate (and sometimes drinking tea). The latter was especially true of Sichuan, which historically has been one of the first areas to rebel and one of the last to come to heel.

Chengdu's teahouses are thus somewhat special. As in other Chinese cities, they were closed down during the Cultural Revolution because they were thought to be dangerous assembly places for 'counter-revolutionaries'. With factional battles raging in Sichuan as late as 1975, re-emergence of this part of daily life has been slow – but you can't keep an old tea addict down! Teahouses sprawl over Chengdu pavements (in back-alley sections) with bamboo armchairs that permit ventilation of one's back.

In the past, Chengdu teahouses also functioned as venues for Sichuan opera – the plain-clothes variety, performed by amateurs or retired workers. However, the advent of VCRs and karaoke has dealt a blow to such live performances; a local may be able to direct to you any that are still ongoing.

Other kinds of entertainment include storytelling and musical performances, while some teahouses seem given over entirely to chess. Most Chinese teahouses cater for the menfolk, young and old (mostly old) who come to meet, stoke their pipes or thump cards on the table. But the women are increasing their presence and can often be found piling up winnings at the mahjong table. ∎

For much better western food head south of the Xinnanmen bus station along Xinnan Lu. Cross Nan Yihuan Lu and continue for five minutes along Kehua Lu. On the left-hand side is the *Red Brick Cafe Pub (hóng zhuān xīcāntīng)* which isn't really a pub and unfortunately doesn't have any English on the sign outside. Look for the sandwich board on the walkway out the front advertising daily specials. The proprietor, who speaks English, and staff, who mostly don't, are a friendly lot. The offerings include two set meals daily (Y38). Otherwise, the food includes moderately priced appetisers, decent burgers and fries, excellent pastas and chicken dishes, and even some pan-Asian and African dishes. Alas, no pizza – yet. All in all, a comfortable, reliable place.

Kehua Lu, incidentally, is chock-full on both sides with glitzy higher-priced seafood restaurants, some with set menus. Most of it is overpriced, but a few places have good seafood hotpot. This area is also known for

having the nickname 'Catfish' on some alleys and streets. The name comes from Qiuxi River catfish *(lián yú)*, a speciality of the Chengdu-Chongqing corridor. Qiuxi town has literally hundreds of catfish and silver carp restaurants, and many chefs relocate to the bright lights of Chengdu.

The healthfulness of eating river fish is debatable, but if you're brave you can find little restaurants specialising in a hot-fired wok stew with hot pepper, ginger, garlic and fresh chopped fish, sprinkled with green onion and parsley.

Entertainment

There is some entertainment to be had in Chengdu, but you will have to hunt. If you don't speak Chinese, ask around among the English-speaking staff at the Traffic Hotel or the travel outfits nearby.

If something strikes your fancy, get it written down in Chinese, and get a good map location – these places are often hard to find, especially at night. If you have more time, try and get advance tickets. Offerings include teahouse entertainment, acrobatics, cinema, Sichuan opera, Beijing opera, drama, traditional music, shadow plays, art exhibits and storytelling, among other things.

Chengdu is the home of Sichuan opera, which has a 200 year tradition and features slapstick dress-ups, men dressed as women, eyeglass-shattering songs and occasional gymnastics. There are several opera houses scattered throughout the older sections of town. As attendances continue to fall, most have cut back performances to only once or twice per week.

One of the easier Sichuan opera venues to find is the *Jinjiang Theatre (jǐnjiāng jùyuàn)* on Huaxingzheng Jie, which is a combination of teahouse, opera theatre and cinema. Sichuan opera performances here are given every Sunday afternoon and are of a high standard.

Lots of local English-speaking tour guides touting their stuff around the Traffic Hotel will organise tours, and most travellers have found the experience well worth it.

Chengdu College of Traditional Chinese Medicine also offers a tour.

Pubs Most of Chengdu's boozing options are of the karaoke variety. These places tend to be expensive and of limited interest to most westerners. However, the area around the Traffic Hotel has the first forays into serious western-style pubs.

Among the first was the *Reggae Lounge*, which does a brisk trade, and although it doesn't play much reggae, the club's dance floor is packed from around 9 pm onwards. To get there, cross the Renmin Nanlu bridge walking north. Just past the Minshan Hotel take a hard right and walk ahead 100m or so. The Reggae is on the right.

A whole slew of pubs has recently sprouted south of the Traffic Hotel on Kehua Lu. (Walk south of the Xinnanmen bus station on Xinan Lu to Nan Yihuan Lu. Cross the road and start the pub run.) A half-dozen pubs include entries with names

such as *Legends of the Fall* (you can guess the decor), *Jurassic Park* (also a disco), *The Bronx Two*, *Noble Bowling* (you really can bowl) and, a personal favourite, *Pabst Blue Ribbon Beertown* – one place which can't decide whether it's a sports pub or a karaoke complex. It also brews its own rather interesting-tasting beer.

Most of these places have draught beer for around Y20, the cheaper ones have jugs *(zhāzā píjiǔ)* for around Y50. Open until the wee hours – from 7 pm to 7 am usually – these spots can make for an entertaining evening, but can also play havoc with early-morning travel plans (did I say I was catching the 7 am bus to Leshan?).

Things to Buy

Chengdu is home to a host of commercial and shopping districts: the Qingyang Palace Commercial Street; the Shudu Boulevard Commercial Street; the Cheng-huang Miao Electronic Market; the Chunxi Lu Commercial Street; and even, as one locally produced English map indicates, 'Electronic Brain Street – No 1 Ring Road' (electronic brain is the translation of the Chinese word for 'computer').

Let's assume, however, that you don't want to spend the rest of your life conspicuously consuming in Chengdu's commercial streets; if this is the case, the pick of the bunch for a stroll and a few purchases is Chunxi Lu. It's the main shopping artery, lined with department stores, art dealers, second-hand bookshops, stationers, spectacle shops and photo stores. At No 10 is the Arts & Crafts Service Department Store *(chéngdū měishùpǐn fúwùbù)*, dealing in most of the Sichuan specialities (lacquerware, silverwork, bamboo products).

The best advice for Chunxi Lu is just to stroll around and dive into any shop that looks interesting. You are almost bound to come up with something you couldn't possibly do without. Look out for the Derentang Chemist, the oldest and largest of all Chengdu's Chinese pharmacies, at the bottom end (south) of the road on the left.

The Sichuan Antique Store that used to be on the northern end of Chunxi Lu has now moved to a huge new building opposite the Sichuan Fine Arts Exhibition Hall on Renmin Donghu. It's worth a visit and, while a lot of the stuff is quite overpriced, there are usually still a few bargains to be had.

For other antiques along with lots of scrollwork and other 'traditional' Chinese forms of souvenir-buying, go north past the Minshan Hotel and take the first right, then the first left. A whole string of shops lines both sides of the street. People's Market (rénmín shìchǎng) is a maze of daily necessity stuff – worth poking your nose into, but not of great interest for purchases.

Getting There & Away

The transport connections in Chengdu are more comprehensive than in other parts of the south-west. Transport between Chongqing and Chengdu is much improved with the completion of the high-speed expressway; plans are also under way to link Leshan with Chengdu via another expressway by 1999, cutting travel time to perhaps two hours. (This will be followed by another highway from Leshan to Chongqing, forming a high-speed triangle.)

Air Shuangliu airport is 18km west of the city. Tickets are available from CAAC (☎ 665-0888 or 665-0999), directly opposite the Jinjiang Hotel. It has a friendly staff and usually one nominal English-speaker on hand.

Major destinations (most flights are daily) include Beijing (Y1560), Chongqing (Y350), Guangzhou (Y1290), Guilin (Y930), Guiyang (Y540), Kunming (Y700), Lhasa (Y1800, but you have to go through a travel agency), Nanjing (Y1450), Ürümqi (Y1870) and Shanghai (Y1630). Several flights a week also go to Hong Kong (Y2510). This list is by no means comprehensive. Chengdu's airport has great dim sum, if you have to leave too early for the Traffic Hotel's breakfast, but give the coffee a miss.

China Southwest Airlines (☎ 666-5911) is diagonally opposite the Jinjiang Hotel, and is a good place to purchase tickets for destinations all across China. The smaller Sichuan Provincial Airlines (☎ 664-7196) also has an office nearby; once a frightening airline, it's recently upgraded its fleet with quite a few Airbuses.

The most frequently asked question in Chengdu must be 'Can I fly to Lhasa?'. If you're on your own, the official answer is 'No'. To get around this, travel agents can sign you on to a 'tour', which usually includes a one way ticket to Lhasa, the two hour transfer from Gonggar airport to Lhasa and your first night's accommodation there. The fact that members of the tour group have never seen each other prior to the flight, and split up immediately after, is overlooked by the authorities. These packages cost as much as Y2200, although at last check had dipped as low as Y1800. You can always try picking up a ticket from one of the airlines yourself; some travellers occasionally get lucky. Just make sure you have the cash on hand to snatch up the ticket before they change their mind. Another trick is to ask for a 1st class ticket.

Bus The main bus station, Xinnanmen bus station sells tickets to most destinations around Sichuan, but not to the north. For northern destinations you will need to head over to the Ximen bus station in the northwest of the city. A third bus station is near the north railway station.

For Emeishan, the best option is the 8.30 am bus that runs direct to Baoguo Monastery (Y19); other departures leave at 10 am and 1.30 pm. Be aware that although your ticket says Baoguo, you might get dropped off in Emei town anyway, in which case you must take a minibus the rest of the way.

There are buses from 6.30 am to 5.30 pm to Leshan (Y19), and four departures from 7 to 10 am to Dujiangyan (Y6.50). Other destinations include Chongqing (Y52 to Y95), Dazu and Kangding (via Luding).

Day buses to Kangding and Luding may

attempt to cross the notoriously dangerous Erlangshan pass, which is often subject to landslides that stretch the 10 hour trip to 18 or 20 hours. Some don't, and the road's often closed, so ask first. All-night sleeper buses now skirt Erlangshan by taking a southern route via Ya'an and Shimian. It's longer at 18 hours (on a good day), but is more likely to get you there on time.

Travelling to Kangding has become more problematic since western Sichuan now requires travellers to purchase insurance, jacking prices up about Y40 to Y50. You're *supposed* to be able to buy it at the station with your ticket, but at last check all one received was a stone-face, followed by a dismissive wave of hands; thus, a trudge up to the PICC office.

An easier alternative is to go to Mr Chen's Travel (☎ 557-3085) adjoining the bus station towards the Traffic Hotel. A Kangding ticket and insurance will cost around Y150, which is close to what you'd pay anyway.

The Ximen bus station is for travellers heading up to Jiuzhaigou or taking the overland route to Xiahe in Gansu Province by way of northern Sichuan. This place also has special foreigners' prices (a surcharge of 70%) for northern routes and they're quite insistent.

There are buses to Songpan (Y64), Jiuzhaigou, Nanping and Maoxian. For tickets to Songpan, it's easier to go to Mr Chen's Travel. You can get a voucher there and exchange it for the bus ticket the following morning. It costs an additional Y10 to Y15, but you'll spend more than that in time or taxi fare getting to Ximen anyway.

Other buses from Ximen (not requiring insurance) include Dujiangyan, Qingcheng Shan, Leshan, (Y19 to Y24), Baoguo Monastery (Y20) and Chongqing (Y65 to Y85).

The north bus station is west of the railway station and has buses to Dujiangyan (Y6.20), Baoguo Monastery (Y15) and Leshan (Y17.50).

Train Getting train tickets out of Chengdu is no easy feat, though it's far easier today than in years past. Many travellers simply give up on the idea and get locals around the Traffic Hotel to fix tickets up for them. This is fine if you don't mind paying extra for their services.

You'll usually need to arrange tickets one and a half days in advance. Don't bother with CITS, although the CAAC office has been known to do advance work. Do give the advance-booking office a try first, as it has been easier and easier to reserve tickets, although most certainly never on the same day for hard-sleeper tickets to Kunming or Xi'an, where everyone and their sister are trying to go.

For those wanting to travel to Lijiang and Dali, there are four trains a day to Panzhihua (also known as Jinjiang) on the Chengdu-Kunming route (Y120).

You can use any of the trains headed for Kunming or Panzhihua to get to Emeishan. Express trains take just under two hours, while fast trains take around three hours. A hard seat should cost Y7. Trains to Kunming take either 23 hours or 26 hours, depending on whether they are express or fast, and the cost is around Y220 for a hard sleeper.

There are four trains daily to Chongqing and same-day tickets are possible, or at least much more so than to Kunming or Xi'an. If you're headed to Dazu, your best bets are the No 203 or 537 trains, which leave around 9 am and arrive at Youtingpu at 4 pm, where you can catch a minibus to Dazu, 30km to the north.

Other rail options include Beijing, Guangzhou, Guiyang, Hefei, Lanzhou, Shanghai, Taiyuan, Ürümqi and Xi'an, which is easily the most popular destination after Kunming. You'll definitely need to hang out in Chengdu for a day and a half waiting for a ticket, although at least you can get one yourself. Hard sleepers cost Y120.

Getting Around

To/From the Airport CAAC runs a bus every half-hour between the ticket office on Renmin Nanlu and Shuangliu airport.

SICHUAN

The fare is Y10. A taxi should cost around Y40 on the meter.

At times the CAAC bus won't run since not enough passengers are there; in that case, you'll be put four to a Speed Racer taxi and the fare should still be Y10.

Bus The most useful bus is No 16, which runs from Chengdu north railway station to the south railway station along Renmin Nanlu. Regular buses cost Y0.60, while the double-deckers cost Y1.

Bus maps carry colour-coding for electric and ordinary buses – bus Nos 2, 4 and 5 can also be electric buses bearing the same number. Electric bus No 5 runs from the north railway station to Xinnanmen station and the Jiuyanqiao bus station. Ordinary bus No 4 runs from the Ximen bus station (north-western end of town) to the south-eastern sector, and continues services until 1 am (most others cease around 9.30 to 10.30 pm).

Minibuses also carry numbers, but the routes differ from those of the big buses. Minibus No 12 circles the city along the first ring road (Yihuan Lu), starting and ending at the north railway station.

Bicycle Many of Chengdu's old bicycle-hire shops have disappeared, and most travellers hire their bikes these days from the Traffic Hotel, which does a fairly good job of bicycle maintenance.

You might try scouting around for other places, but if you're staying in or nearby the Traffic this is the easiest option. The only problem with the Traffic is if you're going to cycle to see the pandas – the shop opens rather late and if you want to espy the pandas before they retire you have to pedal like mad.

The usual rules apply – check your bike before you cycle off; some of them are death traps. Also make an effort to park your bike in a designated parking area. Bicycle theft is a problem here as in most Chinese cities.

Taxi Chengdu takes the cake for the Chinese obsession with mobile phones; as of 1997 even taxis had them. For Y1 per minute you too can show off. By the time you read this, you should be able to make domestic and even international calls.

From the Traffic Hotel to the Ximen bus station, the straight route is around Y14, although most will take the left fork and thus the tourist route for up to Y20.

AROUND CHENGDU
Monastery of Divine Light
(bǎoguāng sì)
This monastery in the north of Xindu County is an active Buddhist temple. It comprises five halls and 16 courtyards, surrounded by bamboo. Pilgrims, monks and tourists head for Xindu, which makes for lively proceedings and attracts a fine line-up of hawkers.

Founded in the 9th century, the temple was subsequently destroyed, before being reconstructed in the 17th century. Among the monastery treasures are a white jade buddha from Myanmar (Burma), Ming and Qing paintings and calligraphy, a stone tablet engraved with 1000 Buddhist figures (540 AD) and ceremonial musical instruments. Unfortunately, most of the more valuable items are locked away and require special permission to view them – you may be able to get this if you can find whoever's in charge around here.

The Arhat Hall, built in the 19th century, contains 500 2m-high clay figurines representing Buddhist saints and disciples. Well, not all of them: among this spaced-out lot are two earthlings – emperors Kangxi and Qianlong. They're distinguishable by their royal costumes, beards, boots and capes. One of the impostors, Kangxi, is shown with a pockmarked face, perhaps a whim of the sculptor.

About 1km from the monastery is **Osmanthus Lake** and its bamboo groves, lotuses and osmanthus trees. In the middle of the lake is a small **memorial hall** for the Ming scholar Yang Shengan.

The temple has an excellent vegetarian restaurant where a huge array of dishes is prepared by monastic chefs. The restaurant's opening hours are from 10 am to 3 pm, although it is best to be here around lunch time, when there is more available. The monastery itself is open daily between 8 am and 5.30 pm.

Getting There & Away Xindu is 18km north of Chengdu; a round trip on a bicycle would be 40km, or at least four hours cycling time on a Chinese bike. Alternatively, buses to Xindu run from in front of the north railway station and from the north bus station from around 6 am to 6 pm. The trip takes just under an hour.

Qingcheng Shan
(qīngchéng shān)
For those with limited time, Qingcheng Shan, a holy Taoist mountain some 65km west of Chengdu, is a good alternative to the more rigorous climb at Emeishan. The peak is 1600m high.

There are numerous Taoist temples en route to the summit. The **Jianfu Temple** *(jiànfú gōng)*, at the entrance to the mountain area, is probably the best preserved. Of the 500 or so Taoist monks in residence on the mountain prior to Liberation, there are now thought to be around 100 left.

There's accommodation and food available at three spots on the mountain: at the base at Jianfu Temple, about halfway up at **Tianshi Cave** *(tiānshī dòng)* and at the summit at **Shangqing Temple** *(shàngqīng gōng)*. Reckon on around Y10 to Y15 per person, or Y20 to Y30 if you want your own bathroom. Unfortunately, most temples now sport freshly painted English signs whose prices don't happen to jibe with the Chinese. You'll be politely pressured to go for Y50/75/100 doubles which certainly aren't worth the price. There are also some smaller privately run hostels along the way, but many of these seem reluctant to take foreigners.

Most people ascend by way of Tianshi Cave and descend via Siwang Pavilion and Banshan Pavilion.

The climb to the top is a four hour hike,

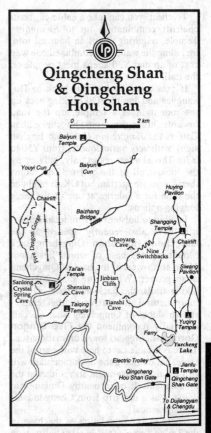

making Qingcheng Shan a pleasant (although fairly long) day trip from Chengdu. Be careful, because there are numerous slick spots, the stairs seem designed for baby feet, and the whole system is poorly marked.

It might be more relaxing to set off around midday, stay overnight at Shangqing Temple and hike up to the summit for the sunrise. This leaves time to walk down and head over to Dujiangyan for the afternoon. There's a Y25 entry charge for the mountain area.

To cheat, you can take a cable-car/boat/chairlift combination up to Shangqing Temple, requiring about an hour all told, including the walk. The combined one way cost of around Y30 keeps most people on the trail.

If you miss the last bus back to Dujiangyan and don't feel like hiking back up the mountain to a temple, up the road towards Dujiangyan from Qingcheng Shan Gate is the *Jianfuguan Hotel* (no English sign), with very basic doubles from Y50 to Y70. This is a last resort only, judging by the look/smell of the toilets. The rooms themselves are spartan, but OK. It might be the time for a splurge at one of the nicer lodging options.

In a bid to bolster tourism, local authorities have also recently opened up the **Qingcheng Hou Shan** (Qingcheng Back Mountain), the base of which lies about 15km north-west of the base of Qingcheng Shan proper. With more than 20km of hiking trails, the back mountain offers a more natural alternative to the temple-strewn slopes of Qingcheng Shan. Locals especially recommend the **Five Dragon Gorge** *(wǔlónggōu)* for its dramatic vistas. There is a cable car to help with part of the route, but climbing the back mountain will still require an overnight stay, either at the mountain itself or in nearby Dujiangyan; doing it as a day trip from Chengdu isn't really practical.

There's accommodation at the base in the Tai'an Temple *(tài'ān sì)* or halfway up at Youyi Village *(yòuyī cūn)*, again at around Y10 to Y15 for a dorm bed.

Getting There & Away There are minibuses to Qingcheng Shan (and Qingcheng Hoshan, so be sure you know which one) leaving from the Chengdu north bus station every half-hour between 7 am and 5 pm. The Ximen bus station has five to six buses to both sides of Qingcheng Shan between 7.10 and 9.50 am. The fare direct to the mountain from both stations is around Y10, Y6.5 to Dujiangyan. From Dujiangyan you can catch a minibus at the city bus station:

they leave as soon as they fill up. The fare is Y3.

From the entrance to the mountain there are buses running back to Chengdu and also to Dujiangyan. The last bus for Chengdu leaves around 5 pm, although you *might* get lucky until as late as 7 pm.

Dujiangyan
(dūjiāngyàn)
The Dujiangyan irrigation project, some 60km north-west of Chengdu, was undertaken in the 3rd century BC by the famed prefect and engineer Li Bing to divert the fast-flowing Min River and re-channel it into irrigation canals.

The Min was subject to flooding at this point, yet when it subsided droughts could ensue. A weir system was built to split the force of the river, and a trunk canal was cut through a mountain to irrigate the Chengdu plain.

Li Bing's brilliant idea was to devise an annual maintenance plan to remove silt build-up. Thus the mighty Min was tamed, and a temple was erected to commemorate the occasion in 168 AD. **Fulong Temple** *(fúlóng guàn)* can still be seen in Lidui Park *(lǐduī gōngyuán)*. A smallish, pleasant place, it has a tame gallery of prideful propaganda photographs showing, among many others, Jimmy Carter visiting the site. Admission to the park itself is Y4.

The project is ongoing. It originally irrigated more than a million hectares of land, and since Liberation this has expanded to three million hectares. Most of the present dams, reservoirs, pumping stations, hydroelectric works, bridgework and features are modern; a good overall view of the outlay can be gained from **Two Kings Temple** *(èrwáng miào)*, which dates from 494 AD. The two kings are Li Bing and his son, Er Lang.

Inside is a shockingly lifelike statue of Li Bing, and in the rear hall is a standing figure of his son holding a dam tool. There's also a Qing Dynasty project map, and behind the temple there is a terrace saying, in effect, 'Mao was here' (1958).

A cable car runs from Lidui Park to Two Kings Temple and also to Yulei Hill Park, but at Y16 to Y25 *per segment* it puts off most travellers.

Dujiangyan receives mixed reports from travellers. Some people love the place, others find the whole idea of visiting a mocha-coloured massive irrigation project boring. There's not a great deal of local flavour, although there are small teahouses lining the river around the funky **South Bridge** *(nánqiáo)*, near the Lidui Park entrance, and visiting the nearby temples is not a bad way to while away an afternoon. The streets lined with canopies of trees make for some nice walks as well. You could also get lost for weeks in Yulei Hill Park (open from 8 am to 6 pm).

Places to Stay Dujiangyan is easy to do as a day trip. Should you decide to stay overnight, perhaps to tackle Qingcheng Shan the next day, the *Dujiangyan Hotel (dūjiāngyàn bīnguǎn)*, about 15 minutes' walk from the city bus station, has beds in triples for as low as Y40, and air-con doubles for Y120. If you're solo, you can usually bargain a bed for around Y60, but not much less.

Don't bother with the *China Travel Service Hotel*, a shabby-looking two star nearby. The management labours under the illusion that some wayward foreigner will consider shelling out US$33 for a mouldy double.

Getting There & Away Buses to Dujiangyan run between 7.10 and 9.50 am from Ximen bus station in Chengdu. There are also hourly buses leaving the Chengdu north bus station from 7.30 am to 5.30 pm. Both cost around Y6.50, and the trip takes 1½ hours.

From the Dujiangyan city bus station it's not a bad idea to catch another bus on to the Two Kings Temple and work your way back. It's also possible to hook up with buses here going to Qingcheng Shan. Returning to Chengdu, there are frequent minibuses departing from along Taiping

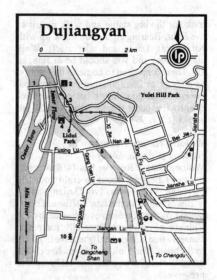

DUJIANGYAN　都江堰

1　Anlan Cable Bridge
　　安澜索桥
2　Two Kings Temple
　　二王庙
3　Chairlift
　　索道
4　Fulong Temple
　　伏龙观
5　South Bridge
　　南桥
6　Dujiangyan Hotel
　　都江堰宾馆
7　City Bus Station
　　市客运站
8　County Bus Station
　　县客运站
9　Post Office
　　邮电大楼
10　Kuiguang Pagoda
　　奎光塔

Jie, in the area of the city bus station. The last one leaves at around 8 pm.

Be aware that a monstrous new bus station has been erected south of town, off the map. If you get dropped off here, just look for the big statue and walk past it to the right. Bearing right, you hook up with Kuangfeng Loulu and take a left. Walk about 300m and you should be at Jiangan Lu. There's no need to come to this station to go back to Chengdu, but for the record, buses to Chengdu's north station leave frequently from here from 6.30 am to 6.30 pm and cost Y7.

Wolong Nature Reserve
(wòlóng zìrán bǎohùqū)
Wolong Nature Reserve lies 140km northwest of Chengdu, about an eight hour trip on rough roads by bus (via Dujiangyan).

It was set up in the late 1970s and is the largest of the 16 reserves set aside by the Chinese government especially for panda conservation. Of these 16 reserves, 11 are in Sichuan. The United Nations has designated Wolong as an international biosphere preserve.

Before setting out for Wolong be forewarned: there is very little chance of seeing a panda in the wild. Dr George Schaller, invited by China to help with panda research and conservation efforts, spent two months trekking in the mountains before he saw one.

To see a live panda in something resembling its natural habitat, your best bet is the Giant Panda Breeding Research Base in Chengdu (see the earlier entry under Chengdu). If you're just out to commune with nature, Wolong is nice, but your time may be better spent making the trip up to Songpan and Jiuzhaigou.

The opening of the research base and improved access to the northern areas of Sichuan Province has dampened demand for tours of the Wolong reserve. Although most travel outfits at the Traffic Hotel have dropped this tour, one or two still offer packages that include transportation, entry to the reserve and one night's accommodation in Wolong town for Y400 per person, with a four person minimum.

Your other option is to catch a bus to Dujiangyan, where there is a bus to Wolong leaving at 1.30 pm from the county bus

station. The latter trip takes about four hours and costs Y14.Entry to the nature reserve is Y50.

In Wolong, the *Wolong Hostel (wòlóng zhāodàisuǒ)* has doubles for around Y100.

EMEISHAN
(éméishān)
Emeishan (Mt Emei), locked in a medieval time warp, receives a steady stream of happy pilgrims with their straw hats, makeshift baggage, walking canes and fans. The monasteries feature sombre Buddhist monks, the tinkle of bells, clouds of incense, and firewood and coal lumped in the courtyards for the winter months.

It is more or less a straight mountain climb, with your attention directed to the luxuriant scenery and, as in *The Canterbury Tales*, to fellow pilgrims. Admirable are the hardened affiliates of Grannies Alpine Club, who slog it up there with the best of them, walking sticks at the ready lest a brazen monkey dare think them easy prey for a food-mugging. They make the pilgrimage annually for the assault, and burn paper money as a Buddhist offering for longevity (no doubt the regular climb contributes to their longevity.

For the traveller itching to do something, the Emei climb is a good opportunity to air the respiratory organs, as well as to observe post-1976 religious freedoms in action, since you are obliged to stay in the rickety monasteries along the route.

One of the Middle Kingdom's four famous Buddhist mountains (the others are Putuo, Wutai and Jiuhua), Emeishan has little of its original temple-work left. The glittering Jinding (Golden Summit) Temple, with its brass tiling engraved with Tibetan script, was completely gutted by fire. A similar fate befell numerous other temples and monasteries on the mount – war with the Japanese and Red Guard looting have taken their toll.

The original temple structures date back as far as the advent of Buddhism itself in China; by the 14th century, the estimated 100 holy structures were home to several

Pandas & Conservation

Estimates place the total number of giant pandas at a round figure of 1000, separated into 30 isolated groups, most of which are distributed in 28 counties of north and north-western Sichuan (with further ranges in Gansu and Shaanxi). Other animals protected here are the golden monkey, golden langur, musk deer and snow leopard. The Wolong reserve is estimated to have some 3000 kinds of plants and covers an area of 200,000 hectares. To the north-west is Siguniangshan (6240m) and to the east the reserve drops as low as 155m. Pandas like to dine in the zone from 2300m to 3200m, but range lower in winter.

The earliest known remains of the panda date back 600,000 years. It's stoutly built, rather clumsy, and has a thick pelt of fine hair, a short tail and a round white face with eyes set in black-rimmed sockets. Although it staggers when it walks, the panda is a good climber, and lives mostly on a vegetarian diet of bamboo and sugar-cane leaves. Mating season has proved a great disappointment to observers at the Wolong reserve, since pandas are rather particular. Related to the bear and the raccoon, pandas can be vicious in self-defence. In captivity they establish remarkable ties with their keepers after a period of time, and can be trained to do a repertoire of tricks.

Chinese literature has references to pandas going back more than 3000 years. It wasn't until 1869 that the west found out about the panda, when a French missionary brought a pelt back with him to Paris. Now, in the 20th century, the giant panda is headed for extinction. Part of the problem is the gradual diminution of their food supply; in the mid-70s more than 130 pandas starved to death when one of the bamboo species on which they feed flowered and withered in the Minshan mountains of Sichuan. Pandas consume enormous amounts of bamboo, although their digestive tracts get little value from the plant (consumption is up to 20kg of bamboo a day in captivity). They are carnivorous, but they're slow to catch animals. Other problems are genetic defects, internal parasites and a slow reproductive rate (artificial insemination has been used at Beijing Zoo).

In a rare move, the Chinese invited the World Wide Fund for Nature (whose emblem is the lovable panda) to assist in research. In 1978 the research centre was set up at Wolong. Eminent animal behaviourist Dr George Schaller has paid several visits to the area to work with Chinese biologist Professor Hu Jinchu.

One of Schaller's research tasks was to fit wild pandas with radio-monitoring devices. In early 1983, the People's Daily reported that Hanhan, one of the very few pandas tagged, was caught in a steel wire trap by a Wolong local. The man strangled the panda, cut off its monitoring ring, skinned it, took it home and ate it. The meal earned the man two years in jail. Since then penalties have increased in severity; in 1990 two Sichuan men who were found with four panda skins were publicly executed.

On a brighter note, laws are now in place strictly forbidding locals to hunt, fell trees or make charcoal in the mountainous habitats of the panda. Peasants in the areas are being offered rewards equivalent to double their annual salary if they save a starving panda. And despite a constant battle with budget deficits, China's central government has established the Giant Panda Breeding Research Base in Chengdu, which is looking at ways to preserve pandas and their habitats. ∎

thousand monks. At present there's 20 active temples, following a Cultural Revolution hiatus, and they bear only traces of their original splendour. Since 1976 the remnants have been renovated, access to the mountain has been improved, hiking paths widened, lodgings added and tourists permitted to climb to the sacred summit.

With all the other tourists, pilgrims and hawkers lining the pathways, there's not much chance for solitude on Emeishan. For all that, the hike offers its share of beautiful views. Fir trees, pines and cedars clothe the slopes; lofty crags, cloud-kissing precipices, butterflies and azaleas together form a nature reserve of sorts.

The major scenic goal of Chinese hikers is to witness a sunrise or sunset over the sea of clouds at the summit. On the rare afternoon there is a phenomenon known as Buddha's Aureole – rainbow rings, produced by refraction of water particles, attach themselves to a person's shadow in a cloud bank below the summit. Devout Buddhists, thinking this was a call from yonder, used to jump off the Cliff of Self-Sacrifice in ecstasy, so during the Ming and Qing dynasties officials set up iron poles and chain railings to prevent suicides. These days your head can be stuck in a cardboard cutout on the site, and you can be photographed in that same act of attaining nirvana.

Climate

The best season to visit is from May to October. Winter is not impossible, but will present some trekking problems – iron soles with spikes can be hired to deal with encrusted ice and snow on the trails.

At the height of summer, which is scorching elsewhere in Sichuan, Emei presents cool majesty. Temperate zones start at 1000m. Cloud cover and mist are prevalent, and will most likely interfere with the sunrise. If (very) lucky, you'll see Gonggashan to the west; if not, you'll have to settle for the telecom tower 'temple' and the meteorological station. Some monthly average temperatures in degrees Celcius are:

	Jan	Apr	Jul	Oct
Emei Town	7	21	26	17
Summit	-6	3	12	-1

What to Bring

Emei is a tall one at 3099m, so the weather is uncertain and you'd be best advised to prepare for sudden changes without weigh-

ing yourself down with a huge pack (steps can be steep).

There is no heating or insulation in the monasteries, but blankets are provided (a couple of places have electric blankets nowadays), and you can hire heavy overcoats at the top. Heavy rain can be a problem, calling for a good pair of rough-soled shoes or boots, so you don't go head over heels on the smooth stone steps further up. Flimsy plastic macs are sold by enterprising vendors on the slopes – these will last about 10 minutes before you get wet. A fixed-length umbrella would be most useful – for the rain, and as a walking stick (scare the hell out of those monkeys by pressing auto-release!). These kinds of umbrellas cost from around Y30 to Y45 in China. If you want to look more authentic you can get yourself a handcrafted walking stick (very cheap) and while you're at it, get a fan and a straw hat too. A torch would be handy. Food supplies are not necessary, but a pocket of munchies wouldn't hurt. Bring toilet paper with you.

More than one traveller has reported coming down with a serious case of conjunctivitis from something in the rooms in guesthouses. About the only way to avoid this is by covering pillows with towels (and then washing them come morning). Some travellers have become sick from contaminated water supplies on the mountain, so you might consider carrying bottled water.

Ascending the Heights

You can dump your bags for a modest charge at the Chuanlin (Lin Ye) Hotel or the Hongzhushan Hotel, both of which are near the Baoguo Monastery. Even better is the nearby, friendly Teddy Bear Cafe. (It also may be possible to dump them at the Baoguo Monastery, the Qinggong Hotel, the Museum Guesthouse or the Emei town railway station.) Most travellers come from Chengdu and leave them there at the Traffic Hotel.

Most people start their ascent of the mountain at Wannian Temple (wànnián sì) and come down through Qingyin Pavilion.

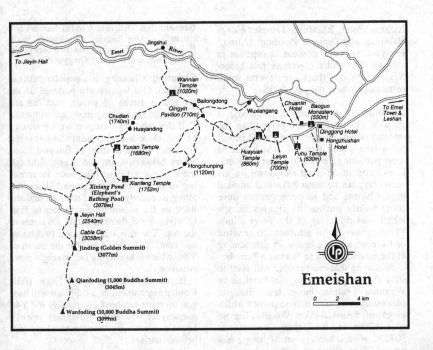

Emeishan

0   2   4 km

From Baoguo Monastery there are mini-buses running close to Wannian Temple and to Qingyin Pavilion between 7 am and 3 pm. Buses leave as soon as they fill up, so it's better to go in the early morning, when there are more passengers about.

Fares range between Y5 and Y10, depending on the driver and your ability to bargain. Buses to Wannian Temple are more frequent. Coming back from Wannian, buses start running around 8 am and stop at 4 pm.

The bus depot near Qingyin Pavilion also has connections back to Emei town and to Leshan, but there are more running from Baoguo Monastery, even more to Leshan from Emei town itself. If you're stuck for connections you may be able to hitch back to Baoguo, otherwise it's a 15km hike.

For a 'softer' combination, take a mini-bus to Qingyin Pavilion and then walk

along the more scenic route via Hongchun-ping and Yuxian up to Jieyin Hall, from where you can catch a chairlift (Y40; Y70 round trip) up to the Golden Summit. From there you can descend the 6km back to Jieyin and take a bus back down. If you want to 'cheat' in earnest, see the Cheating section below.

One thing to watch out for: Emeishan levies a Y50 entry fee for foreigners, good for one entry only. So if, for instance, you catch a bus at Jieyin Hall, and take it down to Wannian Temple, you will be required to buy another entry ticket. Take this unpleasant little fact into account when planning your route. If you're hiking the entire way, this won't be a problem.

Routes Most people ascend Emeishan via Wannian Temple, Chu Temple, Huayan Summit, Xixiang Pond and on to the summit, and descend from the summit via

Xixiang Pond, Xianfeng Temple, Hong-chunping and Qingyin Pavilion. (Almost everyone says the descent is superior in sights.) The paths converge just below Xixiang Pond – there are several small restaurants where the path forks.

Duration Two to three days on site is enough. You usually need one day up and one day down. Enough time should be left for a slow-paced descent, which can be more punishing for the old trotters. A hardy Frenchman made it up and down on the same day, but he must have had unusual legs. Chinese and western sources have some wildly misleading figures on the length and difficulty of the Emei climb. These figures can be attributed to geriatric or Chinese walking times, or discounting of the buses running to Wannian Temple.

Assuming that most people will want to start climbing from Qingyin Pavilion or Wannian Temple, buses from Baoguo Monastery run close to these points, which knocks off the initial 15km. Wannian Temple is at 1020m, and the Golden Summit is at 3077m. With a healthy set of lungs, at a rate of 200m elevation gain per hour, the trip up from Wannian Temple could be done in 10 hours if foul weather does not develop.

Starting off early in the morning from Wannian Temple, you should be able to get to a point below the Golden Summit by nightfall, then continue to the Golden and Ten Thousand Buddha summits the next day, before descending to Baoguo Monastery. Some people prefer to spend two days up and two days down, spending more time exploring along the way. If you have time to spare, you could meander over the slopes to villages hugging the mountain-sides.

On the main routes described above, in climbing time you'd be looking at:

Ascent Qingyin Pavilion (one hour), Wannian Temple (four hours), Xixiang Pond (three hours), Jieyin Hall (one hour), Golden Summit (one hour), Ten Thousand Buddha Summit

Descent Ten Thousand Buddha Summit (45 minutes), Golden Summit (45 minutes), Jieyin Hall (2½ hours), Xixiang Pond (two hours), Xianfeng Temple (3½ hours), Qingyin Pavilion

Cheating 'Cheating' is a popular pastime on Emei. Old women are portered up on the sturdy backs of young men (as are healthy-looking young men and women!).

If this mode of transport isn't your cup of tea, there are also minibuses leaving from the square in front of Baoguo Monastery between 8 am and 5 pm, although the wait can get quite long once the morning rush of tourists has passed. They run along a recently surfaced road around the back of the mountain up to Jieyin Hall (2540m). From there, it's only 1½ hours to the top. The ride takes around two hours and costs Y15. Don't fall for the claim of Y80, which is becoming increasingly more common.

If you don't feel up to the Jieyin Hall-Golden Summit climb, a cable car will haul you up there in about 20 minutes for Y40 one way, or Y70 return (foreigners' prices). Lines can get very long, particularly just before sunrise.

If for some reason you wish to do the whole mountain in one day, most hotels can book you on a bus leaving at 3.30 am. This is *supposed* to get you to the summit in time to see the sunrise, and is a popular option with Chinese tourists. There's a huge 'but' involved – so many buses make this early-morning run now that there is usually an immense traffic jam at the entrance gate (up to a 45 minute wait) and then the clog of tourists up the mountain-side slows to a snail's crawl, and the result is that very, very few people make it to the Golden Summit for a proper sunrise. There's also only one good vantage point for photographs about half an hour below the summit, and it's generally crowded with other shutterbugs.)

The buses head down from Jieyin Hall around mid-morning, stopping at various temples along the way and finally bringing you back to Baoguo at around 5 pm. The round trip costs about Y40 and will probably leave your head spinning. It's best to just do it in segments – buy your ticket up (Y15) at the Teddy Bear Cafe the day before, so once you're up there you can decide if, when and how you return.

Places to Stay & Eat The old monasteries offer food, shelter and sights all rolled into one, and, while spartan, are a delightful change from the regular tourist hotels. They have maybe as much as 1000 years of character.

You may well be asked to pay some ridiculous prices, so be prepared to bargain. Prices range from Y3 in a very large dormitory (10 beds or more) to Y40 per person in a single, double or triple room. It's very difficult to get into the dorms – the staff usually let in only the Chinese. In between are other options like a four bed room at Y10 to Y25 per person – again, the Chinese get preference for these. Plumbing and electricity are primitive; candles are supplied. Rats can be a nuisance, particularly if you leave food lying around your room.

There are eight *monastery guesthouses* – at Baoguo Monastery, Qingyin Pavilion, Wannian Temple, Xixiang Pond, Xianfeng Temple, Hongchunping, Fuhu Temple and Leiyin Temple. There's also a host of smaller lodgings – at Chu Temple, Jieyin Hall, Yuxian, Bailongdong, the Golden Summit and Huayuan, for instance.

The smaller places will accept you if the main monasteries are overloaded. Failing those, you can kip out virtually anywhere – a teahouse, a wayside restaurant – if night is descending.

Be prepared to backtrack or advance under cover of darkness, as key points are often full of pilgrims – old women two to a bed, camped down the corridors, or camping out in the hallowed temple itself, on the floor. Monasteries usually have halfway hygienic restaurants with monk-chefs serving up the vegetarian fare; Y5 to Y10 should cover a meal. There is often a small retail outlet selling peanuts, biscuits, beer and canned fruit within the monastery precincts.

Hotel prices get steep once you reach the summit, except for the Golden Summit Temple (see later in this section). There are some cheap spots, but many may refuse to accept foreigners. Expect to pay a minimum of Y25 for a bed (Y20 for a bed in a quad is average) and the places will have rank facilities.

A good rule of thumb here is to avoid any hotel which has several different time-zone clocks in the lobby unless you are prepared to pay more than Y100 for a double. Another is – the earlier the better. If you are in the mood for (relative) luxury, the Woyun Hotel, located just under the cable-car station, is the summit's only hotel that can boast 24 hour hot water. Standard doubles are Y180.

Along the route are small *restaurants* and *food stalls* where you can replenish the guts and the tea mug. Food gets more expensive and less varied the higher you mount, due to cartage surcharges and difficulties. Be wary of teahouses or restaurants serving 'divine water' *(shénshuǐ)*, or any type of tea or food said to possess mystical healing qualities. While you're very unlikely to witness a miracle, you'll definitely end up being charged Y10 for a cup of tea.

Some notes on the monasteries follow. Most of the ones mentioned are located at key walking junctions and tend to be packed out. If you don't get in, do check out the restaurant and its patrons.

Baoguo Monastery *(bàoguó sì)* This was built in the 16th century, enlarged in the 17th century by Emperor Kangxi and has been recently renovated. Its 3.5m porcelain buddha, made in 1415, is housed near the Sutra Library. To the left of the gate is a rockery for potted miniature trees and rare plants. There's also a nice teahouse and vegetarian restaurant with solid wooden tables. Admission is Y4. Prices range from Y3 for a bed in a seven person dorm to Y25 per bed in a 'fancy' triple. (If you can get in either; they deny the existence of the dorm.)

SICHUAN

Sadly, one unsettling sight at Baoguo is the horde of wranglers who whack and cane their shrieking, chained golden monkeys so they'll cooperate for photo-ops with chuckling tourists.

A museum is diagonally opposite the monastery. Give it and its meagre desiccated taxidermy displays, not to mention chickens running around the place, a miss – it's a waste of Y4.

Fuhu Temple *(fúhǔ sì)* 'Crouching Tiger Monastery' – as it is known in Chinese – is sunk in the forest. Inside is a 7m-high copper pagoda inscribed with Buddhist images and texts.

The monastery has been completely renovated, with the addition of bedding for 400 and restaurant seating for 200. At Y30 to Y40 for a bed in a double, a stay here costs a bit more than at the average Emeishan monastery, but is well worth it if you can get in.

Wannian Temple *(wànnián sì)* The Temple of 10,000 Years is the oldest surviving Emei monastery (reconstructed in the 9th century). It's dedicated to the man on the white elephant, the Bodhisattva Puxian, who is the protector of the mountain. This statue – 8.5m high, cast in copper and bronze, and weighing an estimated 62,000kg – is found in Brick Hall, a domed building with small stupas on it. The statue was made in 980 AD.

Accommodation in the Wannian Temple area is Y20 to Y30 per person, with good vegetarian food. If it's full, go back towards Qingyin Pavilion to *Bailongdong*, a small guesthouse.

Qingyin Pavilion *(qīngyīn gé)* Named the Pure Sound Pavilion because of the sound effects produced by rapid waters coursing around rock formations in the area, the temple itself is built on an outcrop in the middle of a fast-flowing stream.

There are small pavilions from which to observe the waterworks and appreciate the natural music. Swimming is possible here.

Xixiang Pond *(xǐxiàng chí)* According to legend, the Elephant Bathing Pool is the spot where Puxian flew his elephant in for a big scrub, but there's not much of a pool to speak of today.

Being almost at the crossroads of both major trails, this is something of a hang-out and beds are scarce, unless you get here in the early afternoon. New extensions to the accommodation haven't completely solved the problem of pilgrim overload, so be prepared to move on.

Golden Summit Temple *(jīndǐng sì)* To paraphrase a Chinese sage: Expect nothing. At 3077m, the magnificent Golden Summit Temple is as far as most hikers make it. It has been entirely rebuilt since being gutted by a fire several years ago. Covered with glazed tiles and surrounded by white marble balustrades, it now occupies 1695 square metres. The original temple had a bronze-coated roof, which is how it came by the name Jinding (which means 'Gold Top' as well as 'Golden Summit'). However, it's overrun with tourists, pilgrims and monks, and expect to be bumped and jostled. The sun will rarely force its way through the mists, and your photos will have a TV tower in them. Such is the top of China's most popular mountain.

This is one of the noisiest places to stay on the summit, but also one of the cheapest. A bed in a large seven to 10 bed dorm is Y10, if you can get it. Otherwise there are beds in five person dorms for Y20 and quads/doubles for Y30/50.

Coming from the trail leading up to the summit, the rooms are located in a big building just before you reach the temple itself. A short walk down from the temple are a handful of smaller guesthouses with rates from Y25 to Y100, many with heating and hot water.

Xianfeng Temple *(xiānfēng sì)* The surroundings are wonderful, backed onto rugged cliffs, and the Magic Peak Monastery has loads of character. Try and get a room at the rear, where the floors give

Monkey Etiquette

The monkeys have got it all figured out – Xixiang Pond is the place to be. If you come across a monkey 'tollgate', the standard procedure is to thrust open palms towards the outlaw to show you have no food. The Chinese find the monkeys an integral part of the Emei trip, and like to tease them.

As an aside, monkeys form an important part of Chinese mythology – and there is a saying in Chinese, 'With one monkey in the way, not even 10,000 men can pass' – which may be deeper than you think!

Some of them are big buggers, and staying cool when they look like they might make a leap at you is easier said than done. There is much debate as to whether it's better to give them something to eat or to fight them off.

One thing is certain, if you do throw them something, don't do it in too much moderation. They get annoyed very quickly if they think they are being undersold. ∎

pleasant views. It's off the main track so it's not crowded. Nearby is Jiulao Cave, inhabited by big bats.

Around the Base There is also accommodation at the foot of Emeishan, in addition to the Baoguo Monastery. A five minutes walk west of Baoguo is the *Chuanlin Hotel (chuānlín bīnguǎn)* (the signs say 'Lin Ye' and it's known as both), a sleepy place where a bed in a basic quad will cost you Y20, and in a triple Y30. Doubles with attached bath are available for Y80 and Y120. Some travellers have had success in bargaining this down a bit. This place gets mixed reports and some travellers have complained of overcharging; even locals mention the poor service the place is famous for.

Better is the nearby *Museum Guesthouse (bówùguǎn zhāodàisuǒ)*. It's tricky to find. Facing away from the entrance to the Baoguo Monastery, walk towards the large park and museum on the rise ahead of you. Follow the base around to the right and keep going until you – seriously – have to brush through some foliage. You should come out onto a narrow unpaved road. Go left and you'll see a structure built partially onto supports. Walk under that structure and you'll see the sign (no English) for the guesthouse.

If coming from Emei town, just before the turn into the Baoguo Monastery parking area is that unpaved road; take a right and it leads to the guesthouse. Rooms inside are small but comfortable and all have nice verandas off the back – wonderfully tranquil in the evenings. A bed in a double costs Y30, and rooms with private bath start at Y150. Bathrooms are passable and there's evening hot water.

East of the monastery, located at an intersection, is the *Qinggong Hotel (qīnggōng bīnguǎn)* with standard singles/doubles for Y70 per bed (you can split the cost) and triples for Y120. With air-con, TV and evening hot water, it's not bad.

Past the Qinggong, the *Hongzhushan Hotel (hóngzhūshān bīnguǎn)* also lacks cheap accommodation. The cheapest rooms are the Y198 'villa-style' rooms (at least that is what they'll tell you).

Along the trim, landscaped road leading to Emei town are scattered a number of hotels, a few of which may accept foreigners depending on their mood. Prices are generally high, but you may be able to scare up some dorm rooms if the Chuanlin Hotel isn't to your liking. This area also has a slew of small restaurants lining both sides of the street.

One spot on the north side of the street, the *Teddy Bear Cafe*, caters to travellers, and has an English menu and some tasty fare. If you go there in the evening, you may bump into Zhang Guangyui, a local English teacher who seems happy to give advice on places to stay and hike around. The whole staff is extremely friendly and helpful. You can dump your bags here, buy your bus tickets up the mountain, get free information, and they even do laundry now too.

There's a newer place on the same side of the street back towards the monastery. The *Healthy Restaurant* also has an English menu and a vocal, sociable owner. There are a few local specialities on the menu, which you'll surely be told about.

Getting There & Away

The hubs of the transport links to Emeishan are Baoguo village and Emei town. Emei town itself is best skipped, although it does have markets, some cheap hotels, restaurants and a long-distance bus station.

Emei town lies 3.5km from the railway station. Baoguo is another 6.5km from Emei town. At Emei railway station, buses will be waiting for train arrivals – the short trip to Baoguo is Y2 to Y5 in a minibus, depending on the mood of the driver, and Y1 in a local bus.

From Baoguo there are frequent minibuses throughout the day to Emei town and on to Leshan, from where there are good bus connections to Chengdu. The ride to Leshan (Y3 to Y4) takes around one hour. See Leshan for more information. There are also occasional direct buses between Emei and Qingyin Pavilion.

Direct minibuses also run from Baoguo to Chengdu. Again, these depart as they fill up – there is no set timetable. The fare is around Y20 and the trip takes four to five hours.

Emei railway station is on the Chengdu-Kunming railway line and the three hour journey to Chengdu costs Y9 (hard seat, Chinese price). The train from Emei town is more comfortable than the bus, but does not offer the convenience of leaving from Baoguo.

Trains bound for Chengdu depart from Emei station at 4.36 am (No 612), 6.14 am (No 203/206), 12.39 pm (No 166) and 7.34 pm (No 118). To Panzhihua (Jinjiang), there are five departures a day: 12.30 am and 1.20, 5.44, 9.01 and 10.30 pm. The 1.20 pm train is the fastest and newest, but still gets you there in the middle of the night. The 9.01 pm train is probably the easiest to get tickets for since it has an extra sleeper carriage. The trip takes 12 hours. Avoid the glacially slow 10.30 pm local train.

LESHAN
(lèshān)

Once a sleepy counterpart to Emeishan, Leshan has taken off as China's newly affluent tourists flock to see the city's claim to fame, the towering Grand Buddha.

Old brick and plaster homes are increasingly giving way to apartment towers, and the city centre is rife with neon signs for imported electronics, Coca-Cola and stock brokerages. For all that, Leshan is still on a scale you can be comfortable with. The hotel situation is pretty good, decent food can be unearthed and it's a good resting spot for those Emei-weary legs.

Things to See

The **Grand Buddha** *(dàfó)* is 71m high, carved into a cliff face overlooking the confluence of the Dadu and Min rivers. It qualifies as the largest buddha in the world, with the one at Bamian, Afghanistan, as runner-up (besides, the Leshan model is sitting down!). Dafo's ears are 7m long, insteps 8.5m broad, and a picnic could be conducted on the nail of his big toe, which is 1.5m long – the toe itself is 8.5m long.

This lunatic project was begun in the year 713 AD, engineered by a Buddhist monk called Haitong who organised fundraising and hired workers; it was completed 90 years later. Below the buddha was a hollow where boatmen used to vanish – Haitong hoped that the buddha's presence would subdue the swift currents and protect the boatmen, and Dafo did do a lot of good, as the surplus rocks from the sculpting filled the river hollow.

Haitong gouged out his own eyes in an effort to protect funding from disappearing into the hands of officials, but he died before the completion of his life's work. A building once sheltered the giant statue, but it was destroyed during a Ming Dynasty war.

Inside the body, hidden from view, is a water-drainage system to prevent weathering, although the stone statue has seen its fair share. Dafo is so old that foliage is trying to reclaim him – flowers growing on the giant hands, a bushy chest, ferns in his topknots, and weeds winding out of his ear-holes. He gazes down, perhaps in alarm, at the drifting pollutants in the river that presumably come from the paper mill at the industrial end of town (which started large-scale operation in 1979).

Officials are worried about the possibility of a collapse due to soil erosion; one suggestion that has not met with an enthusiastic response is to cover the buddha with a huge transparent shell.

It's worth making several passes at big Buddha, as there are all kinds of angles on him. You can go to the top, opposite the head, and then descend a short stairway to the feet for a Lilliputian perspective. Tour boats pass by for a frontal view, which reveals two guardians in the cliff side that are not visible from land.

To make a round tour that encompasses these possibilities, take a tour boat from the Leshan pier, across from the Taoyuan Hotel. Boats leave approximately every 30 minutes from 7 am to 5 pm and cost Y10; sit on the upper deck facing the dock, since the boat turns around when leaving. To return, there are local ferries departing from jetties north along Lingyun Lu; the service is sporadic and the last rúns are awfully early – around mid-afternoon sometimes. The cost is Y1.

On the way over, you pass in close by the Grand Buddha and the first stop is the **Wuyou Temple** (*wūyōu sì*). The monastery dates, like the Grand Buddha, from the

Tang Dynasty with Ming and Qing renovations – it's a museum piece containing calligraphy, painting and artefacts, and commands panoramic views.

Wuyou also has a hall of 1000 arhats, terracotta monks displaying an incredible variety of postures and facial expressions – no two are alike. The temple's vegie restaurant is famed for its imitation meats dishes: spare ribs and beef strips that look like the real thing. The taste, however, is another matter, and you'll probably be better off with straight vegetables.

If you want you can get off the boat here, go cross-country over the top of Wuyou Hill, and down to a small bridge linking it to Lingyun Hill. Here you will find the entrance to the **Oriental Buddha Park** (*dōngfāng fódū*), a newly assembled collection of 3000 buddha statutes and figurines from all around Asia.

The centrepiece is a 170m-long reclining buddha, said to be the world's longest. Although touted by local tourist authorities as a major attraction, the park seems more a hasty effort to cash in on buddha-mania – the Hong Kong and Chinese sculptors raced to knock off the reclining buddha in a mere two years. Still it makes for an interesting walk, albeit a pricey one at Y30 (foreigners' price).

Nearby is the **Mahaoya Tomb Museum** (*máhàoyámù bówùguǎn*) which has a modest collection of tombs and burial artefacts dating from the Eastern Han Dynasty (25-220 AD).

Continuing past the Buddha Park and up Lingyun Hill brings you to the semi-active **Grand Buddha Temple** (*dàfó sì*), which sits near Dafo's head. From here you can catch views of his head, have a picture taken of you sticking your finger in his ear and walk down a narrow staircase to reach his feet. To get back to Leshan walk west to the small ferry going direct across the Min River.

This whole exercise can be done in less than 1½ hours from the Leshan dock; however, it's worth making a day of it. If you want to avoid the crowds, ÿou should consider doing this route in reverse, that is, starting with the Grand Buddha Temple and Grand Buddha in the morning and on to Wuyou Monastery in the afternoon.

It would be a mistake to think of Leshan as one big buddha, for the area is steeped in history. North of Leshan, 2.5km west of the railway station at Jiajiang, are the **Thousand-Buddha Cliffs** *(jiājiāng qiān-fóyán)*. For once, the name is not an exaggeration: more than 2400 buddhas dot the cliffs, dating back as far as the Eastern Han Dynasty. The statues are said to be in fairly good shape, despite the ravages of time and the Cultural Revolution.

There are some pleasant walks to be had in Leshan itself. By the remains of the town ramparts is an older section of town where you can still find some cobbled streets and green, blue and red-shuttered buildings. The area around the ferry docks and the old town buzzes with market activity. In season, the markets yield a surprising array of fresh fruit and vegetables, so you can do more than look at them.

Further out, by the Jiazhou Hotel, are teahouses with bamboo chairs spilling onto the street. Leshan used to be known for its Grand Buddha Cableway spanning the river. Many advertisements still use it and the structures still stand; unfortunately it has been shut down and probably won't operate again.

There are fantastic day trips to villages outside Leshan, including Luocheng, famed for its old 'boathouse' architecture, and Wutongqiao. The best way to do this is head for the Yangs' restaurant (see Places to Stay & Eat below) and enlist the aid of Mr Yang.

Entry Fees The Grand Buddha park used to pester travellers to death with a surcharge every 50 feet or so. Officials finally tired of complaints and just lumped everything together into a Y40 entrance fee. There are still one or two extra fees lurking out there, and temples still charge around Y2 to get in. Some travellers get very irate about all these hidden costs, but rules is rules!

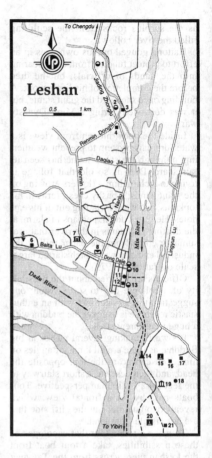

Leshan

It is possible to surreptitiously enter the Grand Buddha by going into Oriental Park first, but since the park costs Y30 it's really not worth the risk for a mere Y10.

Places to Stay & Eat

Around the corner from the bus station, the *Leshan Education Hotel* (☎ 213-4257) *(lèshān jiàoyù yánjiūsuǒ)* at 156 Liren Jie is probably the best value place for backpackers. Beds in passably clean doubles/triples with common bath are Y40/30. Somewhat damp and shabby doubles with

LESHAN 乐山

1 Long-Distance Bus Station
长途汽车站
2 Lianyun Bus Company
联运汽车站
3 Leshan Education Hotel
乐山教育宾馆
4 Jiading Hotel
嘉定饭店
5 The Yangs' Restaurant
杨家餐厅
6 Jiazhou Hotel
嘉州宾馆
7 Workers' Cultural Palace
劳动人民文化宫

8 Post Office
邮电局
9 Central Bus Company
省汽车客运中心站
10 Ferries to Chongqing,
Yibin
长途码头
11 Ferry Ticket Office
渡轮售票处
12 Taoyuan Hotel
桃源宾馆
13 Tour Boat Dock (Leshan
Pier)
途途码头
14 Grand Buddha
大佛

15 Grand Buddha Temple
大佛寺
16 Nanlou Guesthouse
南楼宾馆
17 Jiurifeng Hotel
就日峰宾馆
18 Oriental Buddha Park
东方佛都
19 Mahaoya Tomb
Museum
麻浩崖博物馆
20 Wuyou Temple
乌尤寺
21 Xiandao Hotel
仙岛宾馆

bath attached are considerably more expensive at Y200: definitely not good value. Take a look at more than one room, since consistency is not a virtue around here.

Just south of the Education Hotel, at the corner of Jiading Zhonglu and Renmin Donglu, stands the *Jiading Hotel* (☎ 213-4680) *(jiādìng fàndiàn)*, which is decidedly more proletarian, but still better than the Educational Hotel in most respects. Beds in doubles/triples without bath cost Y25/15 (the washrooms are nothing to write home about, but will do), while standard doubles start at Y80, with some possibility of shaving a few yuan off this. The No 8 bus, which links Leshan pier with the Leshan long-distance bus station, passes near both hotels.

The *Taoyuan Hotel* (☎ 212-7758; fax 212-9904) *(táoyuán bīnguǎn)* is in a much better location down by the Leshan pier and offers excellent views of the Grand Buddha. Unfortunately it's let itself slip recently and the rooms are no longer good value. The staff – mostly students – tries really hard to make things work, but a change of management has effectively killed the place. Common doubles/triples cost Y50 per bed; with a private bathroom, doubles/triples start at Y120. A whole range of rooms is available, up to a Y360 deluxe suite. Rooms at Y120 and up include a breakfast. The hotel offers a fax

service, laundry, international dialling, and a sauna.

Over on the Buddha's side of the Min River are a couple of pricey but pleasant places to stay. Close to the Wuyou Temple is the friendly *Xiandao Hotel* *(xiāndǎo bīnguǎn)* (☎ 213-3268) which has upmarket doubles for Y218. Triples are a bit more affordable at Y188. There appear to be several good restaurants here, and the hotel even has a sauna.

There are two hotels in the area above the head of the Grand Buddha, *Nanlou Guesthouse (nánlóu bīnguǎn)* and *Jiurifeng Hotel (jiùrìfēng bīnguǎn)*. Perhaps due to the buddha's drainage system, the cliff around here is wet, and the dampness can extend to the rooms. The Nanlou, set right next to the Grand Buddha Temple, is definitely out of budget range, only offering standard doubles for around Y450.

The Jiurifeng is only slightly cheaper and not quite as nice, so the former may be the better choice if you're in the mood to spend. If you do stay at the Jiurifeng, go for rooms in the upper building, with commanding views from its heights. A standard double costs Y290.

Top-of-the-line is the three star *Jiazhou Hotel* (☎ 213-9888; fax 213-3233) *(jiāzhōu bīnguǎn)* which has become rather expensive. Doubles and triples start at Y360 and suites at Y600; both include breakfast. The hotel is in a pleasant area; to get there take the No 1 bus from the corner of Jiading Nanlu and Dong Dajie to the end of the line.

The area between the Jiazhou Hotel and the pier is good for small *restaurants* and *street stalls*. For a home-style meal and good conversation, wander over to another of those oases of English menu and Chinese prices – *The Yangs' Restaurant*, a wooden hole-in-the-wall at 49 Baita Jie. The engaging owner, Mr Yang, speaks English and has an exceedingly interesting history. Travellers have raved about his ad hoc tours to small villages around Leshan, and he's also willing to lend a hand in making travel arrangements.

Back towards the centre of town and across from – but not affiliated with – the Jiazhou Hotel is the *Newcastle Arms Pub*, a branch of a Chengdu pub.

Getting There & Away

Construction is underway on an expressway between Chengdu and Leshan, which should shave travel time down to two hours. (And no doubt swell the numbers of tourists on already crowded Emeishan.) No date has been set for completion.

Following that road's completion, Leshan and Chongqing are set to be linked with a similar expressway. The result will be a triangular transportation conduit second to none in south-west China.

Plans are also being finalised for an enormous new airport 20km outside Leshan; when finished (no exact date for this yet) it will be larger than Chengdu's.

Bus There are three bus stations in Leshan, which is understandably confusing for many travellers. The main one for travellers is the Leshan long-distance bus station, somewhat inconveniently located in the northern reaches of the city. And it may get worse – city officials want to relocate all buses far, far out on the northern side of town, beyond the first bridge, although at the time of writing there was no timetable to do this.

Minibuses to Chengdu leave every 10 minutes from 6 am to 6 pm and cost Y15 to Y17. Large buses leave four times a day for Y19 and take pretty much forever to get to Chengdu. (The trip should take four hours.)

One thing to watch out for is the bus's Chengdu destination. Most of the buses run to the Xinnanmen bus station next to the Traffic Hotel, but several run to the north bus station or railway station, which are inconvenient for Chengdu's budget accommodation.

If you're headed to Chengdu, consider treating yourself to one of the nicest bus rides in China. The main bus station offers direct *nonstop* service to Chengdu's Xinnanmen bus station using new South Korean buses that make the trip in just over three hours. They have air-conditioning, the seats recline, you get a bad Hong Kong movie and, best of all, the bus never stops en route to pull in more passengers! For Y29.70 it's a great deal and a welcome break from the standard timetables-be-damned service you're used to. Buses leave up to five times a day between 7 am and 3 pm; you definitely need to book these as far in advance as possible.

From Emeishan to Leshan is 30km; minibuses run every 10 to 15 minutes to Emei town between 6.20 am and 6 pm. The ride is one hour and costs Y3. The buses up the street from the Taoyuan Hotel seem more convenient, but these make tons of stops, including a lengthy one outside of town. Instead, head to the north (long distance) bus station and those that leave from Gate No 15; these are comfy buses and go directly to Emei with few – if any stops – for the same Y3.

Once in Emei, you have to walk left out of the bus station to the intersection where trucks lurk; they'll insist on Y5 and no doubt try to lock you into a room, but locals only pay Y1.

Regular buses (Y54 to Y90) to Chongqing leave daily at 7 and 7.40 am and 5 pm; you may get a luxury air-con bus on this run, so book in advance if you can. Ditto with the sleepers (Y97), which leave at 6, 6.20 and 6.40 pm. The trip takes up to eight hours, but bear in mind the sleeper buses (and the 5 pm regular bus) put you in Chongqing at around 2 am.

The other bus stations around town are the Central Bus Company *(shěng qìchē kèyuǎn zhōngxīn zhàn)* and the Lianyun *(liányùn chēzhàn)*. Both have numerous daily departures for Chengdu, Baoguo and Emei. The former is close to the long-distance ferry dock and the latter is about 30 minutes' walk to the north of the ferry dock, near the Education Hotel.

Boat At one time there was regular boat service between Leshan and Yibin, with further service to Chongqing. River fluctuations and bad management doomed it and it's sporadic at best now, often only running in the summer. (Yibin to Chongqing is more consistent.)

Plans are under way to manipulate water levels and allow a more stable service. When running – now June-August only – tickets cost Y29 to Yibin, from where you can either get another boat to Chongqing or take the train. Better today is the high-speed boat to Yibin, departing Leshan daily at 2.30 pm; tickets cost Y80 and the trip takes 2½ hours. Tickets can be bought at the ticket office across the street from Leshan pier.

Getting Around

The Nos 1 and 4 buses run the length of Jiading Lu and connect the pier area with the long-distance bus station, and the Jiading and Education hotels. Buses runs from 6 am to 6 pm, at roughly 20 minute intervals.

On foot, it's about an hour's walk from one end of town to the other. A pedicab from the bus station to the Taoyuan Hotel should cost Y5; to the Jiading Hotel it's Y2. You can bargain a ride from the Grand Buddha all the way back to the Taoyuan for as little as Y10, although this takes some effort. Also pedicab operators in Leshan all split up the fare, so don't be paranoid

when one of them stops halfway and tells you to get on his buddy's pedicab. Just pay him half (or whatever) and pay the remainder when you arrive. Unfortunately, there doesn't seem to be any bicycle hire.

MEISHAN
(méishān)

Meishan, 90km south-west of Chengdu by road or rail (it's on the Kunming-Chengdu railway line), is largely of interest to those with an interest in Chinese language, literature and calligraphy.

It was the residence of Su Xun and his two sons, Su Shi and Su Zhe, the three noted literati of the Northern Song Dynasty (960-1126). Their residence was converted into a temple in the early Ming Dynasty, with renovations under the Qing emperor Hongwu (1875-1909).

The mansion and pavilions now operate as a museum for the study of the writings of the Northern Song period. Historical documents, relics of the Su family, writings, calligraphy – some 4500 items all told – are on display at the Sansu (Three Sus) shrine.

CHONGQING
(chóngqìng)

Perched on steep hills overlooking the confluence of two rivers, Chongqing is one of China's more unusual cities. Dusty grey tenements and shining office towers cling to the precipitous hillsides that make up much of the city centre.

Another unique aspect is the absence of bicycles. There's barely a cyclist to be found, as the hill climbs make it coronary country for any would-be rider. More shocking: in 1997 the city *banned* outright the use of car horns to improve noise pollution on the congested peninsula.

Chongqing is quite pleasant to stroll around, and even if it's not exactly brimming with 'sights' there's nevertheless a certain picturesque quality to this grey city. For Chinese tourists the 'sights' are usually connected with the Communist Revolution, most being linked to the city's role as the wartime capital of the Kuomintang from 1938 to 1945.

Though it plays second fiddle to Chengdu, Chongqing is hardly a backwater. It is rated as the chief industrial city of southwestern China, with its production amounting to a fifth of Sichuan's total industrial output. The total metropolitan area has a population of some 14 million; of these around three million live in the city proper.

With all this, the city long lobbied for a special status akin to that of Shanghai. In 1997 what it got was not quite province status, but the 30-odd million residents of the three county area (now the largest in China by most statistical methods) separated from Sichuan and became a 'special' municipality directly under the control of the central government, like Beijing, Tianjin and Shanghai.

China's economic boom has infected Chongqing with a severe case of skyscraper fever: at every turn there seems to be either a tower going up or a vast hole in the ground awaiting a foundation. In 10 years the city centre may look a bit like Hong Kong with its sparkling skyscrapers and mountain backdrop.

Within China, Chongqing is famous for its searing summers, when temperatures can exceed 40°C (104°F). This pleasant climate has earned the city a place among the country's 'three furnaces' – the other two being Wuhan and Nanjing.

History

Chongqing (known in pre-pinyin China as 'Chungking') was opened as a treaty port in 1890, but not many foreigners made it up the river to this isolated outpost, and those who did had little impact.

A programme of industrialisation was begun in 1928, but it was in the wake of the Japanese invasion that Chongqing really took off as a major centre, after the Kuomintang retreated to set up its wartime capital here. Refugees from all over China flooded in, swelling the population to more than two million.

The irony of this overpopulated, overstrained city with its bomb-shattered houses is that the name means something like 'double jubilation' or 'repeated good luck'. Emperor Zhao Dun of the Song Dynasty ascended to the throne in 1190, having previously been made the prince of

---

SICHUAN

Edgar Snow

In 1939, Edgar Snow arrived in Chongqing to find a city living in fear of Japanese raids. It was, he said:

... a place of moist heat, dirt and wide confusion, into which, between air raids, the imported central government ... made an effort to introduce some technique of order and construction. Acres of buildings had been destroyed in the barbaric raids of May and June.

The Japanese preferred moonlit nights for their calls, when from their base in Hankow they could follow the silver banner of the Yangzi up to its confluence with the Jialing, which identified the capital in a way no blackout could obscure.

The city had no defending air force and only a few anti-aircraft guns ... Spacious public shelters were being dug, but it was estimated that a third of the population still had no protection. Government officials, given advance warning, sped outside the city in their motor cars – cabinet ministers first, then vice-ministers, then minor bureaucrats.

The populace soon caught on; when they saw a string of official cars racing to the west, they dropped everything and ran. A mad scramble of rickshaws, carts, animals and humanity blew up the main streets like a great wind, carrying all before it. ■

the city of Gongzhou; as a celebration of these two happy events, he renamed Gongzhou as Chongqing.

In more modern times, in the shadow of strutting Kuomintang military leaders, representatives of the CCP (including Zhou Enlai) acted as 'liaisons' between Chongqing and the Communists' headquarters at Yan'an, in Shaanxi Province.

Repeated efforts to bring the sides together in a unified front against the Japanese largely failed due to mutual distrust and Chiang Kaishek's obsession with wiping out the Communists, even at the cost of yielding Chinese territory to an invading army.

The wartime offices and living quarters of the Communist officials form the bulk of Chongqing's tourist attractions, along with museums depicting atrocities committed by the Kuomintang and its US backers.

Orientation

The heart of Chongqing spreads across a hilly peninsula of land wedged between the Jialing River to the north and the Yangzi River to the south. They meet at the tip of the peninsula at the eastern end of the city.

The central focus of this congested peninsula of winding streets for most visitors is the now neon-shrouded Liberation Monument, which is walking distance from most of Chongqing's accommodation.

Getting there from the railway station is a matter of taking one of the frequent minibuses that run between the station, Liberation Monument and the Chaotianmen dock area for Y1. Bus No 102 also runs between the railway station and Chaotianmen. If you're headed for the western part of town, around the Renmin Hotel, you can walk up to Zhongshan Lu; there is a tram, but it's under renovation and will be for some years to come.

Chongqing is a good city to explore on foot. The distances are manageable, and there's always an interesting alley to duck into. Between the Liberation Monument and Chaotianmen are a number of steep, laddered alleyways, usually lined with little

shops. Also of interest, and within walking distance of the Liberation Monument, are the two cable cars over the Jialing and Yangzi rivers.

Maps Good maps in Chinese and less detailed ones in English are available from street vendors (the ones who sell newspapers) around the Liberation Monument area.

Information

Tourist Office CITS (☎ 385-0589) has its office in a building opposite the Renmin Hotel compound. They're friendly enough, but are still oriented towards large tour groups. They're open from 8.30 am to noon and from 2 to 5.30 pm.

PSB The office (☎ 383-1830) is on Linjiang Lu. Bus No 103 from the front of the Renmin Hotel will take you there. If it's permits for the wilds of northern or western Sichuan that you are after, wait until you get to Chengdu, where they are more used to dealing with this kind of thing.

Money The main Chongqing branch of Bank of China is on Minzu Lu, up the road from the Huixianlou Hotel. The branch right next door to the Huixianlou also has a window for changing money on the 2nd floor. Most hotels have foreign-exchange counters.

Post & Communications There's a branch post office on Minzu Lu, which is within walking distance of the Chung King and Huixianlou hotels. It purports to have 24 hour services. Most of the top-end hotels offer limited postal services.

Luohan Temple
(luóhàn sì)

'Luohan' is the Chinese rendering of the Sanskrit 'arhat', which is a Buddhist term referring to people who have released themselves from the psychological bond-age of greed, hate and delusion.

Built about 1000 years ago, the Luohan

Temple has a long entrance-way flanked by rock carvings, a hall of painted terracotta arhat sculptures (the usual 500) and a hall containing a large gold buddha figure. Behind the buddha altar is an Indian-style jataka mural depicting Prince Siddhartha in the process of cutting his hair to renounce the world.

At its peak, Luohan Temple was home to some 70 monks; these days there's around

18 in residence. The temple is popular with local worshippers who burn tonnes of fragrant incense. Try and make an effort to call into this temple, even just to take a quick look at the incredibly lifelike arhats.

The vegetarian restaurant here is excellent and very cheap, but it's only open for lunch (approximately 11.30 am to 1.30 pm). The temple itself is open from 8 am to 5 pm and admission is Y2.

Red Cliff Village
(*hóngyán cūn*)
During the tenuous Kuomintang-Communist alliance against the Japanese during WWII, Red Cliff Village outside Chongqing was used as the offices and living quarters of the Communist representatives to the Kuomintang.

Among others, Ye Jianying, Zhou Enlai and Zhou's wife Deng Yingchao lived here. After the Japanese surrender in 1945, it was also to Chongqing that Mao Zedong – at the instigation of US ambassador Patrick Hurley – came in August of that year to join in the peace negotiations with the Kuomintang. The talks lasted 42 days and resulted in a formal agreement which Mao described as 'words on paper'. One of China's better revolutionary history museums now stands at the site, and has a large collection of photos, although none of the captions is in English.

CHONGQING 重庆

PLACES TO STAY
2 Chongqing Shipin Mansion
食品大厦
3 Chung King Hotel
重庆饭店
8 Huixianlou Hotel
会仙楼宾馆
12 Chongqing Guesthouse
重庆宾馆
17 Yudu Hotel
渝都宾馆

PLACES TO EAT
6 Lamb Restaurant
羊肉馆

7 Lao Sichuan
老四川
9 California Beef Noodles
加州牛肉面
11 Yizhishi Restaurant
颐之时大酒店
14 Little Frog Pub &
Cafe
19 Happy Princess Cafe &
Bar
快乐公主咖啡厅

OTHER
1 Chaotianmen Dock
(Booking Hall)
朝天门码头（售票处）

4 Luohan Temple
罗汉寺
5 Bank of China
中国银行
10 PSB
公安局外事科
13 Xinhua Bookstore
新华书店
15 Liberation Monument
解放碑
16 Post Office
邮电局
18 Foreign Languages
Bookstore
外文书店

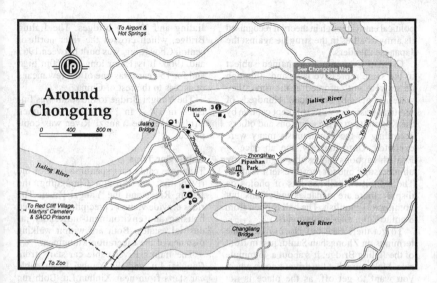

AROUND CHONGQING 重庆地区

1 Buses to SACO Prisons
  至中美合作所汽车站
2 CAAC
  中国民航
3 CITS
  中国国际旅行社
4 Renmin Hotel
  人民宾馆
5 Chongqing Museum
  博物馆
6 Shancheng Hotel
  山城饭店
7 Railway Station
  火车站
8 Long-Distance Bus Station
  长途汽车站

A short walk from the museum is the building which housed the South Bureau of the Communist Party's Central Committee and the office of the representatives of the Eighth Route Army – although there's little to see except a few sparse furnishings and photographs.

To get to Red Cliff Village, you can take bus No 104 from its terminal on Beiqu Lu just north of the Liberation Monument. However, locals insist the best one to take is the No 215, although it's untried as yet.

Most Chinese tour buses from the Chaotianmen dock and the railway station for some reason no longer include Red Cliff on their itinerary. Red Cliff Village is open daily from 8 am to 5.30 pm and admission is Y6.

US-Chiang Kaishek Criminal Acts Exhibition Hall & SACO Prisons
(zhōngměi hézuòsuǒ jízhōngyíng jiùzhǐ)
In 1941, the USA and Chiang Kaishek signed a secret agreement to set up the Sino-American Cooperation Organisation (SACO), under which the USA helped to train and dispatch secret agents for the Kuomintang government.

The chief of SACO was Tai Li, the notorious head of the Kuomintang military secret service; its deputy chief was a US Navy officer, Commodore ME Miles. The SACO prisons were set up outside Chongqing during WWII. The Kuomintang never recognised the Communist Party as a legal

SICHUAN

political entity, though in theory it recognised its army as allies in the struggle against the Japanese invaders.

Civilian Communists remained subject to the same repressive laws and, although these were not enforced at the time, they were not actually rescinded. Hundreds of political prisoners were still kept captive by the Kuomintang in these prisons and others; according to the Communists many were executed. Unfortunately, the absence of English captions makes this sight a fairly uninteresting one for most western visitors. The exhibition hall has lots of photos on display; there are manacles and chains, but nothing too ghoulish. The hall is open from 8 am to 7 pm and admission is Y2.

To get there take bus No 217 from the terminus on Zhongshan Sanlu, just in front of the Jialing Bridge. It's about a 45 minute ride. Make sure that the driver knows where you want to get off, as the place is not obvious. The prisons are a long hour's walk from the hall.

Alternatively, if you are really keen to see these sights, there are Chinese tour buses leaving from the Chaotianmen dock and railway station areas, for a pricey Y60 for four hours and it should include everything. They take in both the hall and the prisons and throw in some other revolutionary sights as well.

Temple Parks

Chongqing's two temple parks get neglected by many visitors, but they are a pleasant enough way to while away an afternoon. **Pipashan Park** *(pípáshān gōngyuán)* at 345m marks the highest point on the Chongqing peninsula. The Hongxing Pavilion at the top of the park provides good views of Chongqing. The park is open from 6 am to 10 pm.

The **Eling Park** *(élíng gōngyuán)* at the neck of the peninsula is more of a hike and not really worth a special trip. You can find the Liangjiang Pavilion here.

Bridges

Worth checking out are the enormous Jialing and Yangzi bridges. The Jialing Bridge, which crosses the river north of central Chongqing, was built between 1963 and 1966. It is 150m long and 60m high and for 15 years was one of the few means of access to the rest of China.

The Yangzi Bridge to the south was finished in 1981. In 1989 the new Shimen Bridge over the Yangzi River was completed.

Cable-Car Trips

There are cable cars spanning both of the rivers that cut through Chongqing: the Jialing River and the Yangzi River. The rides provide views of precipitously stacked housing and environment-unfriendly industrial estates. Both are within walking distance of the Liberation Monument.

The Jialing River cable car starts from Cangbai Lu, and the Yangzi River cable car starts from near Xinhua Lu. Both run from 6.30 am to 9.30 pm and cost Y1.

Chongqing Museum
(chóngqìng bówùguǎn)
If you are really stuck for something to do you might wander over to the museum. The dinosaur skeletons on display were unearthed at Zigong, Yangchuan and elsewhere in Sichuan Province between 1974 and 1977. It's open from 9 am to 5 pm. The museum is at the foot of Pipashan Park in the southern part of town.

Northern Hot Springs
(běi wēnquán gōngyuán)
Fifty-five kilometres north-east of the city, overlooking the Jialing River, the Northern Hot Springs are in a large park which is the site of a 5th century Buddhist temple.

The springs have an Olympic-size swimming pool where you can bathe to an audience. There are also private rooms with hot baths – big tubs where the water comes up to your neck if you sit and up to your waist if you stand. Water temperature averages around 32°C (89.6°F). Swimsuits can be hired here – they're coloured red, symbolising happiness. There's another group of springs 20km south of Chongqing with hotter waters, but the northern group is said to be better.

To get to the springs, hop on bus No 306 at the Liberation Monument.

Places to Stay – budget & middle

Chongqing has a serious shortage of budget accommodation, which means that most travellers get out of town as quickly as possible.

You will be doubtlessly be met by touts at the bus/railway station. They will certainly insist that foreign friends can stay at their cheap hotel (figure Y40 for the cheapest). But remember that these folks only get paid to bring you there; they're pretty clueless on the rules. You may find yourself being refused anyway. Besides that, on the last trip the few guesthouses checked were fairly grotty and a security risk even if they could be cajoled into accepting foreigners.

The only dorms in the central part of the city are the seven bed rooms at the *Huixianlou Hotel* (☎ 384-5101) *(huìxiānlóu bīnguǎn)*, close to the Liberation Monument, where a bed will set you back Y70. It's expensive, but at least this place is well located and the remodelled, air-conditioned dorms are quite nice. From the railway station, walk up to Zhongshan Lu and take bus No 405 to the Liberation Monument *(jiěfàng bēi)*.

A more pleasant option is *Chongqing Shipin Mansion* (☎ 384-7300) *(chóngqìng shípǐn dàshà)* at 72 Shaanxi Lu, near the Chaotianmen dock. This place recently received approval to take foreigners, and has pleasant, clean doubles with bath and air-con for Y150 and triples for Y170. The rate card mentions that foreigners should be charged an extra 50%, but the manager doesn't like the dual-pricing system, which means you pay what the Chinese pay. The hotel also has doubles and triples with common bath for Y60/90, but you probably won't have much luck getting in. They'll also help you book boat and rail tickets here.

Places to Stay – top end

Basically, most hotels in Chongqing charge ridiculous amounts of money. It's probably something to do with the limited room for expansion on the crowded peninsula.

If you don't mind an expensive stay, the *Renmin Hotel* (☎ 385-1421) *(rénmín bīnguǎn)* is one of the most incredible hotels in China, and if you don't stay here you have to at least visit the place. It's quite literally a palace, with a design that seems inspired by the Temple of Heaven and the Forbidden City in Beijing. The hotel comprises three wings (north, south and east), and these are separated by an enormous circular concert hall that is 65m high and seats 4000 people. The hotel was constructed in 1953. Singles are priced at US$48, while doubles range between US$48 and US$60. There's also a presidential suite that commands a cool US$460 a night: it no doubt resembles a scene from *The Last Emperor*.

As this book was being updated, the hotel was closed and had literally hundreds of workers hanging about, giving the place a face-lift. If the previous prices hold, it'll be the deal of the trip. From the railway station, the best way to get to the hotel is to head up to Zhongshan Lu and catch bus No 401 or 405 to the traffic circle and walk east down Renmin Lu. Alternatively, if you are spending this kind of money for a room, catch a taxi for Y15.

The *Chung King Hotel* (☎ 384-9301; fax 384-3085) *(chóngqìng fàndiàn)*, a three star joint-venture operation on Xinhua Lu near the Chaotianmen dock area, has singles for Y380 and doubles for Y580. Facilities include a small gift shop (with a few English titles), currency exchange, post and telecommunications, taxi and clinic. The hotel also has its own shuttle bus to and from the railway station and the airport.

The *Chongqing Guesthouse* (☎ 384-5888) *(chóngqìng bīnguǎn)* on Minsheng Lu has transformed itself into a four star Chinese-style luxury hotel. Doubles in the old wing are Y270, while singles/doubles in the new

VIP wing start at Y540/660, which includes breakfast.

Close to the Liberation Monument, the *Yudu Hotel (yúdū jiǔdiàn)* boasts a good location, and the rooms cost Y220/270/420 for a single/double/triple.

Finally, a fair trudge from all the action, on the southern side of the Yangzi is the *Yangtze Chongqing Holiday Inn* (☎ 280-3380) *(yángzǐjiāng jiàrì jiǔdiàn)*, with all the services that you would expect of a Holiday Inn Group hotel. Room rates start at US$115, although discounts are possible when the hotel isn't flooded with tour groups.

Places to Eat

The central business district in the eastern section of the city near the docks abounds with small *restaurants* and *street vendors*. For tasty noodles and *baozi*, check out Xinhua Lu and Shaanxi Lu towards Chaotianmen dock. There are some good *night markets* behind the Huixianlou Hotel, in the vicinity of Luohan Temple and near the Yudu Hotel.

Chongqing's number one speciality is *huǒguō*, or hotpot. Skewers of pre-sliced meat and vegetables are placed in boiling hot, spiced oil. Hotpot is usually priced by the skewer and, while it's usually cheap, it's a good idea to check prices as you go along.

Although hotpot can be found wherever there are street vendors or small restaurants, Wuyi Lu has the greatest variety and is locally known as *huǒguō jiē*, or 'hotpot street'. Wuyi Lu runs off Minzu Lu, parallel to Xinhua Lu, a couple of blocks away from the Huixianlou and Chung King hotels. Bayi Lu is also a great street for snack hunting.

Zourong Lu is a good street for larger, sit-down restaurants when you have a group and feel like feasting on Sichuanese main courses. Among them is the well known *Yizhishi Restaurant, (yízhīshí cāntīng)*, which serves Sichuan-style pastries in the morning and local specialities like tea-smoked duck and dry-stewed fish at lunch and dinner. The 2nd floor has full-course meals; go up to the 3rd floor and Y25 will buy you a sampler course of famous Chongqing snacks. Draught beer and special 'eight-treasure tea' *(bābǎochá)* do a fine job of washing it all down.

The area around Huixianlou Hotel, where many travellers stay, is teeming with restaurants. Carnivores can try the *Lamb Restaurant (yángròu guǎn)* just up the road from the hotel. All the lamb dishes here are *hot*, but the kebabs aren't too punishing on the taste buds.

Also not far away is the *Lao Sichuan Restaurant (lǎo sìchuān)*, which is going on 80 years old and is considered Chongqing's most famous Sichuan eatery. Prices are reasonable, but get there early: it closes at 9 pm.

Around the corner from the Huixianlou Hotel on Wusi (5-4) Lu is *California Beef Noodles*, one of seemingly dozens of Chinese restaurants employing the name 'California' for no apparent reason. It's pretty good and there may be rough English menu translations by the time you read this.

Of the hotel restaurants, *Chung King Hotel* has the best food. It's expensive by Chinese standards, but moderately priced for most foreigners. Opened shortly after Liberation, this place is another favourite with locals, who just call it 'the old restaurant'. The dishes are nicely presented and accompanied by live Chinese music at night. The hotel's coffee shop serves western breakfasts.

A couple of entertainment options have sprouted up in the Huixianlou Hotel area. Near the Liberation Monument, the *Happy Princess (kuàilè gōngzhǔ kāfēi yuán)* is a 24 hour coffee shop which also has rather pricey beer and local folkies playing their music. It's a great place and the owner, an ex-tour guide, speaks good English. The big 'but' is that the beer is rather expensive – around Y20 for an import; then again, what isn't pricey in Chongqing? There's no English sign for this place, so keep an eye out for the '24 hour coffee' sign, which leads you up to the 2nd floor.

Just south-west of the Huixianlou Hotel is the *Little Frog*, a cafe/bar that has a much more raucous atmosphere, and similar beer prices.

Getting There & Away

Transportation from Chongqing to Chengdu is much easier with the completion of the new expressway.

Plans are also under way to link Leshan with both Chongqing and Chengdu with another high-speed thoroughfare, creating a commerce-friendly triangle of transportation. The Leshan-Chongqing road is second in importance to Leshan-Chengdu at the moment.

Air Chongqing's new Jiangbei airport is 25km north of the city. You can buy tickets at the CAAC office (☎ 386-2970) near the corner of Zhongshan Sanlu and Renmin Lu, which can be accessed from either street. You can also book flights at the Chung King Hotel, and there are numerous ticket offices around the Liberation Monument.

Chongqing has daily flights to Beijing (Y1510), Guangzhou (Y1110), Shanghai (Y1420), Kunming (Y670) and Xi'an (Y630). Other destinations include Chengdu (Y350), Ürümqi (Y2310) and Hong Kong (Y2270).

Bus Bus travel in and out of Chongqing has become much more convenient with the opening of a new multi-storey long-distance bus terminal next to the railway station. With two ticket halls, two waiting halls and dozens of gates, the station can process 800 to 1000 buses daily, or so the management claims.

To Chengdu, there are official buses running from 5.45 am to 9.45 pm virtually all the time. Regular buses take seven hours and cost Y52; express buses – much more comfy – take up to four hours and cost Y95.

In addition to these buses, there are about a zillion hawks out the front who'll be grabbing your arm trying to lead you to a private Chengdu-bound bus. Most take three to four hours and range in cost between Y60 and Y95; shop around, this is a buyer's market.

Most buses are of the micro variety and they'll really pack them full. They depart from 6 am to 8 pm, with six between 8.15 am and 4.15 pm. The trip takes up to four hours and costs Y25.

Train From Chongqing there are direct trains to Shanghai, Xi'an, Guiyang, Nanning, Chengdu, Zhengzhou, Guangzhou, Beijing and Kunming.

For trains to Dazu, there are at least three trains from Chongqing between 7.38 am and 12.45 pm. The 7.45 am train (No 204) gets in to Dazu (it's actually Youtingpu, although schedules say Dazu) at around 11.30 am. Almost no other trains between Chongqing and Chengdu actually stop in Dazu.

Trains to Nanning go via Guiyang and Liuzhou (five or six hours by bus from Guilin) and take around 32 hours; a hard sleeper should cost Y166. Trains to Guiyang take around 12 hours and cost Y89 for a hard sleeper.

Trains to Shanghai also take in Guiyang, before making a long haul through the sticks to Hangzhou and on to the final destination. The journey takes around 50 hours and costs Y291 for a hard sleeper, or Y157 if you're desperate enough to hard seat it.

To Chengdu, it takes around 11 hours and costs Y87 for a hard sleeper, or Y49 for a hard seat. Trains to Kunming and Panzhihua (for Lijiang and Dali) go via Chengdu, and it makes a lot of sense to break your trip at this point.

If you want to get to Guilin in a hurry you will have to fly; travelling by train requires that you change in Guiyang. Alternatively, you might consider travelling to Liuzhou by train (Y145 for a hard sleeper) and go on direct to Yangshuo or Guilin by bus.

Chongqing Getting There & Away section continued on page 948

SICHUAN

Downriver on the Yangzi – Chongqing to Shanghai

The dramatic scenery and rushing waters of China's greatest river may have been inspirational to many of China's painters and poets, but there was very little in the way of inspiration for those charged with the task of negotiating the twists and turns of this dangerous stretch of water.

There was also sheer hard work. A large boat pushing upstream often needed hundreds of coolies (trackers) who lined the riverbanks and hauled the boat with long ropes against the surging waters. Even today smaller boats can still be seen being pulled up the river by their crews.

The Yangzi is China's longest river and the third longest in the world at 6300km, emanating from the snow-covered Tang-gulashan mountains in south-west Qinghai and cutting its way through Tibet and seven Chinese provinces before emptying into the East China Sea just north of Shanghai. Between the towns of Fengjie in Sichuan and Yichang in Hubei lie three great gorges, regarded as one of the great scenic attractions of China.

The steamer ride from Chongqing to Wuhan is a popular tourist trip and the scenery is pleasant, but don't expect to be dwarfed by

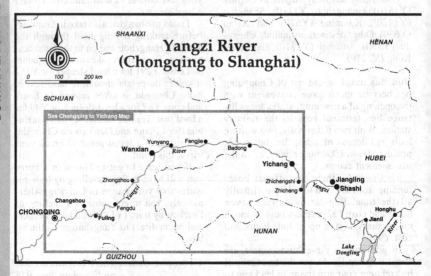

mile-high cliffs! A lot of people find the trip quite boring, possibly because of over-anticipation. There are also a few boats that go beyond Wuhan, including one all the way to Shanghai, which is 2400km downriver – a week's journey.

Tickets

It's good to book two or three days ahead of your intended date of departure, although a rapid expansion in the number of Yangzi cruise operators means tickets are more readily available. CITS adds a service charge of Y15 to the price of the tickets. Budget travellers take note: if you book tickets with CITS, make sure you're not being put on one of the luxury liners reserved solely for foreigners – the price could inflict mortal damage on your cash reserves.

Once you've boarded, a steward will exchange your ticket for a numbered, colour-coded tag that denotes your bed assignment. Hang on to the tag, since it must be exchanged for your ticket at the end of the voyage – without it they may not let you off the boat.

Classes

In a sign of the changing times in what was once egalitarian China, some boats now boast 1st class cabins. These come with two beds, private bathrooms, television and air-con.

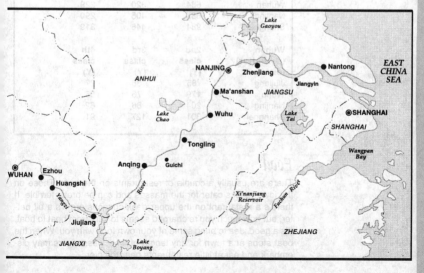

Second class cabins have two to four berths, with soft beds, a small desk and chair, and a washbasin. Third class usually has from six to 12 beds depending on what boat you're on. Fourth class usually has eight to 12, but on older vessels can have over 20 beds. Fifth class can be anything from 15 beds to deck-space. Toilets and showers are communal, although you should be able to use the toilets and showers in 2nd class.

In addition to the above tour boats, there are also several 'foreigner only' vessels. These are mostly reserved for large tour groups who can afford the hundreds of US dollars that these trips cost. CITS and some of the independent booking agents around the Chaotianmen dock area can arrange tickets for these luxury liners.

Fares

The following prices are for foreigners' tickets as posted at the Chaotianmen booking office in Chongqing. Prices will be higher if you book through CITS or one of the independent operators.

Note that there are also 1st and 5th classes – the former most travellers won't go for, with their 100% price mark-up over 2nd class, and the latter is dirt-cheap but not always easy to get.

Chongqing (downriver) to:	2nd class (Y)	3rd class (Y)	4th class (Y)
Yichang	589	259	187
Wuhan	684	320	229
Nanjing	887	405	290
Shanghai	984	446	319
Wuhan (downriver) to:	2nd class (Y)	3rd class (Y)	4th class (Y)
Jiujiang	85	36	27
Wuhu	179	76	55
Nanjing	204	86	62
Shanghai	301	127	91

Food

There are usually a couple of restaurants on the boat. Those on the lower decks cater for the masses and can be pretty terrible. If there's a restaurant on the upper deck chances are it's a bit better, but how much you're charged seems to vary from boat to boat. It's a good idea to bring some of your own food with you. When the boat stops at a town for any length of time, passengers may disembark and eat at little restaurants near the pier.

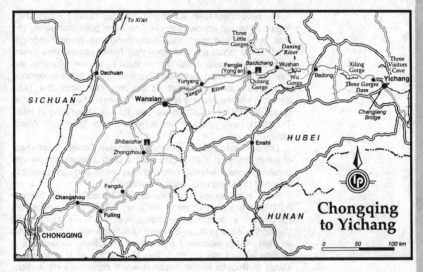

The Route

Boats stop frequently during the cruise to visit cities, towns and a slew of tourist sights. What you will see during daylight hours depends on what time your boat sets sail from Chongqing. Most boats stop between the first and second gorge for six hours for tours of the 'Little Three Gorges' (see the Wanxian to Yichang section below). For travellers who want to avoid this, there are some boats that pass directly through, but you'll have to ask around.

Chongqing to Wanxian

For the first few hours the river is lined with factories, although this gives way to some pretty, green terraced countryside with the occasional small town.

One of the first stops is usually the town of **Fuling**. It overlooks the mouth of the Wu River, which runs southwards into Guizhou; it controls the river traffic between Guizhou and eastern Sichuan.

Near Fuling in the middle of the Yangzi River is a huge rock called Baihe Ridge. On one side of the rock are three carvings known as 'stone fish' which date back to ancient times and are thought to have served as watermarks – the rock can be seen only when the river is at its very lowest.

The next major town is **Fengdu** *(fēngdū)*. Nearby Pingdushan is said to be the abode of devils. The story goes that during the Han Dynasty two men, Yin Changsheng and Wang Fangping, lived on the mountain, and when their family names were joined together they were mistakenly thought to be the Yinwang, the King of Hell. Numerous temples containing sculptures of demons and devils have been built on the mountain since the Tang Dynasty, with heartening names like 'Between the Living and the Dead', 'Bridge of Helplessness' and 'Palace of the King of Hell'. Travellers have given mixed reviews to this little 'Hell World' exhibit.

The boat then passes through **Zhongxian County**. North-east of the county seat of Zhongzhou is the **Qian Jinggou** site, where primitive stone artefacts, including axes, hoes and stone weights attached to fishing nets, were unearthed.

Soon after comes the **Shibaozhai** (Stone Treasure Stronghold) on the northern bank of the river. Shibaozhai is a 30m-high rock which is supposed to look something like a stone seal. During the early years of Emperor Qianlong's reign (1736-97) an impressive red wooden temple, the Lanruodian, shaped like a pagoda and 11 storeys high, was built on the rock. It houses a statue of Buddha and inscriptions which commemorate its construction.

Next is the large town of **Wanxian**, where most morning boats tie up for the night. It's a neat, hilly town and a great place to wander around for a few hours while the boat is in port.

Wanxian to Yichang

Boats overnighting at Wanxian generally depart before dawn. Before entering the gorges the boat passes by (and may stop at) the town of **Fengjie** (Yong'an). This ancient town was the capital of the state of Kui during the Spring and Autumn and Warring States periods from 722 to 221 BC.

The town overlooks the Qutang Gorge, the first of the three Yangzi gorges. Just east of Fengjie is a 1km-long shoal where the remains of stone piles could be seen when the water level was low. These piles were erected in the Stone and Bronze ages, possibly for commemorative and sacrificial purposes, but their remains were removed in 1964 since they were considered a danger to navigation.

Another set of similar structures can be found 7.5km east of Fengjie outside **Baidicheng**. At the entrance to the Qutang Gorge, Baidicheng, or White King Town, is on the river's northern bank. The story goes that a high official proclaimed himself king during the Western Han Dynasty, and moved his capital to this town. A well was discovered which emitted a fragrant white vapour; this struck him as such an auspicious omen that he renamed himself the White King and his capital 'White King Town'.

The spectacular **Sanxia** (Three Gorges), Qutang, Wu and Xiling, start just after Fengjie and end near Yichang, a stretch of about 200km. The gorges vary from 300m at their widest to less than 100m at their narrowest. The seasonal difference in water level can be as much as 50m.

Qutang Gorge *(qútáng xiá)* is the smallest and shortest gorge (only 8km long), although the water flows most rapidly here. High on the northern bank, at a place called Fengxiang (Bellows) Gorge, are a series of crevices. There is said to have been an ancient tribe in this area whose custom was to place the coffins of their dead in high mountain caves. Nine coffins were discovered in these crevices, some containing bronze swords, armour and other artefacts, but they are believed to date back only as far as the Warring States Period.

In past days, the sheer walls, sharp rocks and turbulent waters of the Three Gorges made it one of the most difficult and dangerous stretches of water in China. The Sanxia dam will put paid to all that, submerging the gorges beneath more than 100m of water as part of an artificial lake stretching 550km back from the dam wall at Sandouping.

Wu Gorge *(wū xiá)* is about 40km in length and the cliffs on either side rise to just over 900m. The gorge is noted for the Kong Ming tablet, a large slab of rock at the foot of the Peak of the Immortals. Kong Ming was prime minister of the state of Shu during the period of the Three Kingdoms (220-80 AD). On the tablet is a description of his stance upholding the alliance between the states of Shu and Wu against the state of Wei. **Badong** is a town on the southern bank of the river within the gorge. The town is a communications centre from which roads span out into western Hubei Province.

In between the Qutang and Wu gorges, most boats will stop for five to six hours so passengers can shift to smaller boats for tours of the **Little Three Gorges**. Flanking the Daning River, these gorges are much narrower than their larger counterparts and, some travellers say, more dramatic. The tour usually costs Y50 to Y60, with a foreigners' surcharge of 25% to 50% often tacked on as well. Though some travellers have complained of the cost, many enjoy the chance to get out and view the rock formations up close.

On the way to the Little Three Gorges the boats usually stop at several gratuitous tourist traps, most of which are not worth the entry fee. For example, one stop promises views of a mysterious mountain cave coffin on high, which turns out to mean a brief look through a pair of binoculars.

Xiling Gorge (xīlíng xiá) is the longest of the three gorges at 80km. At the end of the gorge everyone crowds out onto the deck to watch the boat pass through the locks of the huge Gezhou Dam.

The next stop is the industrial town of **Yichang**, which is regarded as the gateway to the upper Yangzi and was once a walled city dating back at least as far as the Sui Dynasty. Near the Yichang railway station you can take bus No 10 to **White Horse Cave** (báimǎ dòng), where for a fee you can boat and walk through caverns with impressive stalactites and stalag-mites. Five minutes' walk from the other end is an equally impressive place – **Three Visitors Cave** (sānyóu dòng), along with a cliff trail that overlooks the Yangzi River.

Yichang to Wuhan

After leaving Yichang, the boat passes under the immense **Changjiang Bridge** at the town of **Zhicheng**. The bridge is 1700m in length and supports a double-track railway with roads for trucks and cars on either side. It commenced operation in 1971.

The next major town is **Shashi**, a light-industrial town. As early as the Tang Dynasty, Shashi was a trading centre of some importance, enjoying great prosperity during the Taiping Rebellion when trade lower down the Yangzi was largely at a standstill. About 7.5km from Shashi is the ancient town of **Jingzhou**, to which you can catch a bus.

After Shashi there's not much to look at: you're out on the flat plains of central China, the river widens immensely and you can see little of the shore. The boat continues down the river to pass by (and possibly stop at) the town of **Chenglingji**, which lies at the confluence of Dongting Lake and the Yangzi River.

East of Dongting Lake is the town of **Yueyang**. Another nine hours will bring you to Wuhan, at which point most travellers are quite ready to part ways with their boat.

Wuhan to Shanghai

Wuhan more or less marks the halfway point in the long navigable stretch of the Yangzi River from Chongqing down to Shanghai. The journey to the sea is far more mundane than the trip upriver to Chongqing; the Yangzi broadens and most of the towns and cities are industrial in character.

Heading downriver on leaving Wuhan, you pass through **Huangshi** in eastern Hubei Province. This town lies on the southern bank of the river and is being developed as a centre for heavy industry. Nearby is an ancient mining tunnel dating back to the Spring and Autumn Period; it contained numerous mining tools, including bronze axes.

Near the border with Jiangxi on the northern bank is the town of **Wuxue**, noted for the production of bamboo goods.

The first major town you come to in Jiangxi is **Jiujiang**, the jumping-off point for nearby Lushan. The mouth of Lake Boyang is situated on the Yangzi River and at this point on the southern bank of the river is Stone Bell Mountain, noted for its numerous Tang Dynasty stone carvings. This was also the place where Taiping troops were garrisoned for five years defending Jinling, their capital.

The first major town you approach in Anhui Province is **Anqing**, on the northern bank, in the foothills of the Dabie mountains. Next comes the town of **Guichi**, from which you can get a bus to Jiuhuashan and the spectacular Huangshan (Yellow mountains).

The town of **Tongling** lies in a mountainous area in central Anhui on the southern bank, west of Tongguanshan. Tongling has been a copper-mining centre for 2000 years and is a source of copper for the minting of coins. Still in Anhui Province, and at the confluence of the Yangzi and Qingyi rivers, is **Wuhu**, also a jumping-off point for Huangshan. Just before Anhui Province ends is the city of **Manshan**, the site of a large iron and steel complex.

In Jiangsu Province the first large city you pass is **Nanjing**, followed by **Zhenjiang**, then the port of **Nantong** at the confluence of the Tongyang and Tonglu canals. The ferry then proceeds along the Yangzi and turns down the Huangpu River to **Shanghai**. The Yangzi empties into the East China Sea.

*Chongqing Getting There & Away section
continued from page 939*

Boat It certainly seems that zillions and
zillions of boats make the run from Chongqing down the Yangzi River to Wuhan.
The ride is a popular tourist trip, a good
way of getting away from the trains, and an
excellent way to get to Wuhan. Consider
doing it before the Chinese government
finishes its massive dam project and floods
the Three Gorges. For details, see the
special section on Yangzi River cruises
earlier in this chapter.

Another boat option, and one that very
few travellers use, is the service to Leshan.
Sorting out just when the boats leave is a bit
of a hassle. Due to river level fluctuations
in recent years, service has been sporadic.

When boats are running, it's much,
much easier to do the float downstream
from Leshan, since most return trips are for
freight only. It's for hard-core river rats
only, unless you don't mind the bother.
Boats leave from the dock. Third class
tickets are around Y131.

Getting Around

To/From the Airport CAAC runs shuttle
buses between the airport and the ticket
office, timed to coincide with flights. Buses
to the airport leave 2½ hours before scheduled flight times. The fare is Y15.

Bus Buses in Chongqing can be tediously
slow, and since there are no bicycles
they're even more crowded than in other
Chinese cities. Useful routes include: No
401, which runs between the Chaotianmen
dock and the CAAC office at the intersection of Renmin Lu and Zhongshan Sanlu;
No 405, running the length of Zhongshan
Lu up to the Liberation Monument; and No
102, which connects the railway station
and Chaotianmen dock.

There are also minibuses running between
the dock and the railway station for Y1.

Taxi Nowadays, as in most other Chinese
cities, flagging down a taxi is no problem.

Flag fall ranges between Y9 and Y12, depending on the size of the car, if you can
get them to use the meter. Otherwise,
expect to pay a minimum of Y15 for all
runs on the peninsula.

DAZU COUNTY
(dàzú)

The grotto art found in Dazu County, 160km
north-west of Chongqing, is rated alongside
China's other great Buddhist cave sculptures at Dunhuang, Luoyang and Datong.
Historical records for Dazu are sketchy.
The cliff carvings and statues (with Buddhist, Taoist and Confucian influences)
amount to thousands of pieces, large and
small, scattered over the county in some
40-odd places.

The main groupings are at Beishan (North
Hill) and the more interesting Baoding.
They date from the Tang Dynasty (9th
century) to the Song (13th century).

The town of Dazu is a small, unhurried
and languid place. Although not hilly,
there's a conspicuous absence of bicycles.
It's one community which definitely makes
use of piped-in social propaganda from
every corner. It's also relatively unvisited
by westerners – though this is gradually
changing – and the surrounding countryside is superb. The only problem is the
low-end accommodation: there isn't any.

Beishan
(běi shān)

Beishan is about a 30 minute hike from
Dazu town – aim straight for the pagoda
visible from the bus station. There are good
overall views from the top of the hill. The
dark niches hold small statues, many in
poor condition; only one or two really
stand out.

Niche No 136 depicts Puxian, the patron
saint (male) of Emeishan, riding a white
elephant. The same niche has the androgy-
nous Sun and Moon Guanyin. Niche 155
holds a bit more talent, the Peacock King.
According to inscriptions, the Beishan site
was once a military camp, with the earliest
carvings commissioned by a general.

At Beishan there's a Y5 entry fee for the park area and a further Y20 entry fee for the sculptures. The park is open from 8 am to 5 pm.

Baoding
(bǎodǐng shān)

About 15km north-east of Dazu town, the Baoding sculptures are definitely more interesting than those at Beishan (although anyone who's seen Datong's grottoes may be slightly underwhelmed).

The founding work is attributed to Zhao Zhifeng, a monk from an obscure Yoga sect of Tantric Buddhism. A monastery with nice woodwork and throngs of pilgrims sits atop a hill; on the lower section of the hill is a horseshoe-shaped cliff sculptured with coloured figures, some of them up to 8m high.

The centrepiece is a 31m-long, 5m-high reclining buddha, depicted in the state of entering nirvana, the torso sunk into the cliff face – most peaceful.

Statues around the rest of the 125m horseshoe vary considerably: Buddhist sages and preachers, historical figures, realistic scenes (on the rear of a postcard one is described as 'Pastureland – Cowboy at Rest') and delicate sculptures a few centimetres in height. Some of them have been eroded by wind and rain, and some have lost layers of paint, but generally there is a remarkable survival rate (some fanatical Red Guards did descend on the Dazu area bent on defacing the sculptures, but were stopped – so the story goes – by an urgent order from Zhou Enlai). You'll note, however, that the ones in the best condition are not to be photographed – gotta keep that postcard business humming ...

Baoding differs from other grottoes in that it was based on a preconceived plan which incorporated some of the area's natural features – a sculpture next to the reclining buddha, for example, makes use of an underground spring.

Completion of the sculptures is believed to have taken 70 years, between 1179 and 1249 AD. It's easy to spend a few hours wandering around this area. The showpieces are the enormous reclining buddha and, inside a small temple on the carved cliff, the goddess of mercy with a spectacular gilt forest of fingers (1007 hands if you care to check). Each hand has an eye, the symbol of wisdom. Besides the major attractions there are countless minor details that will capture your attention.

Minibuses to Baoding leave the Dazu bus station every 30 minutes or so (or as soon as they fill up) throughout the day, although they start to thin out by about 4 pm. The fare is Y1.50, but the locals will charge you Y5. The trip takes anywhere from 30 to 45 minutes.

For a splurge (and a much quicker ride) it's a pretty, winding journey on the back of a motorcycle taxi, which you can bargain down to Y15. The last bus departs Baoding for Dazu at around 6 pm. The sites are open from 8 am to 5 pm, and there's a Y45 foreigners' price entry charge. As you pass by in the bus, keep an eye on the cliff faces for solo sculptures that may occasionally pop up.

Places to Stay & Eat

The local PSB appears to have done a good job of cowing most hotels into refusing foreigners, leaving you with only two options in Dazu, neither of which are cheap.

The *Beishan Hotel (běishān bīnguǎn)* (☎ 22657), near the base of Beishan, is a pleasant though somewhat unkempt place aimed at the less affluent tour-group traveller. Standard doubles cost Y300, but they also have doubles with attached bath for Y150 that are perfectly fine, and triples for Y150. (Some have succeeded in getting doubles for Y100.) They won't volunteer this information, and you will have to do some persuading to get these prices, especially if the hotel is crowded.

To get there, turn left out of the bus station, cross the bridge and proceed past the roundabout straight up the main road through town. After about 500m the road ends in a three way intersection. Turn right; the hotel is on the left-hand side of the

SICHUAN

street. One good point about the Beishan is that it's close to the Beishan stone carvings. Facing the hotel, the road up to the statues is on the left, just next to the indoor sports arena.

The *Dazu Guesthouse (dàzú bīnguǎn)*, like so many other hotels in Chinese tourist towns, has been reborn as a three star hotel which means you won't be able to get a room for under US$50. Should the urge for luxury grab you, turn left out of the bus station, cross over the bridge and bear right at the roundabout. The hotel is about 500m up the road on the left.

Finding a bite to eat in Dazu is no problem. At night the main road, from the bus station all the way to the Beishan Hotel, comes alive with dozens of *street stalls* serving noodles, dumplings, hotpot and wok-fried dishes.

There are also a few point-and-choose *restaurants* along the way, although the selection at these is decidedly more meagre than in other places. You might try wandering down the first street on the right up from the roundabout. You have to walk around 500m before the restaurants start appearing, but along the way are street vendors selling everything from raw handmade noodles to fresh spices to black lace lingerie. The restaurant at the Beishan Hotel is best left to its own devices.

Getting There & Away
Bus There are several options by bus. The first is the direct bus to Dazu from Chongqing's new long-distance bus station. Buses run to Dazu from 6 am to 8 pm, although most run from 8.15 am to 4.15 pm, more or less hourly.

The first leg of the journey follows the Chongqing-Chengdu Expressway, but the trip still can take up to four hours – the second half is still under excruciating construction. Tickets cost Y25.

Buses from Chengdu to Dazu leave from the Xinnanmen bus station next to the Traffic Hotel at 7 and 9 am, and 2.30, 3.30 and 7.55 pm. The trip costs from Y29 to Y45 depending on the bus and should take

only five hours, although be prepared for more, depending on traffic and construction.

From Dazu there are onward buses to Chongqing and Chengdu. Buses to Chongqing from the bus station leave every hour between 6 am to 6 pm and cost Y25. The trip takes three to four hours. For Chengdu there are three buses between 7.30 and 9.30 am using the expressway; at the time of writing there was also one morning bus and one afternoon bus using backroads, although these will likely be phased out when the main highway to the expressway is finished.

Train To get to Dazu by train, you should get off the Chengdu-Chongqing railway line at Youtingpu town (five hours from Chongqing, seven hours from Chengdu), which is the nearest stop to Dazu.

Despite the fact that the town is around 30km from Dazu, train timetables refer to it as Dazu station. See the Chongqing and Chengdu Getting There & Away sections for more information on trains to Dazu. There are frequent minibuses running from the railway station to Dazu.

Western Sichuan & the Road to Tibet

Literally the next best thing to Tibet is the Sichuan mountains to the north and west of Chengdu – heaps of whipped cream that rise above 5000m, with deep valleys and rapid rivers.

Tibetans and Tibetan-related peoples (Qiang) live by herding yaks, sheep and goats on the high-altitude Kangba Plateau Grasslands to the far north-west. Another zone, the Zöigê Grassland (north of Chengdu, towards the Gansu border) is more than 3000m above sea level.

Closer to Chengdu, the Tibetans have been assimilated, speak Chinese and are less bound by tradition, although they're regarded as a separate minority and are exempt from birth control quotas. Further out, Tibetan customs and clothing are much more in evidence.

Towns on the Kangba Plateau experience cold temperatures, with up to 200 freezing days per year; summers are blistering by day and the high altitude invites particularly bad sunburn. Lightning storms are frequent from May to October; cloud cover can shroud the scenic peaks. On a more pleasant note, there appear to be sufficient hot springs in these areas to have a solid bath along the route.

Ancient Chinese poetry has it that the road to Sichuan is harder to travel than the road to heaven. In the present era, with the province more accessible by road, we can shift the poetry to Tibet and the highway connecting it with western Sichuan. The Sichuan-Tibet Highway, begun in 1950 and finished in 1954, is one of the world's highest, roughest, most dangerous and most beautiful roads. The highway has been split into northern and southern routes; it forks 70km west of Kangding.

The northern route (2412km) runs via Kangding, Ganzi and Dêgê before crossing the boundary into Tibet. The southern route (2140km) runs via Kangding, Litang and Batang before entering Tibet (see the Ganzi and Litang sections later in this chapter).

Whether you are able to actually enter Tibet is an open question. The land route between Chengdu and Lhasa is still to all intents and purposes closed to foreigners for reasons of safety and political security. Some palefaces have succeeded and arrived intact in Lhasa, usually by hitching rides on trucks. The PSB has cracked down on this now, however, and it's reportedly getting harder to find rides.

It is possible to do the trip by local buses, but foreigners will definitely encounter problems near the Tibetan border, and may even have trouble buying tickets for Batang or Dêgê. A few travellers have reportedly managed to bribe their way across, but at a cost that makes flying from Chengdu to Lhasa more economical.

Years ago there was a legendary crate, the Chengdu-Lhasa bus, which suffered countless breakdowns and took weeks to arrive. In 1985 a monumental mudslip on the southern route took out the road for dozens of kilometres and the service was discontinued.

Trucks are the only transport consistently long hauls on this highway. The major truck depots are in Chengdu, Chamdo and Lhasa. Trucks usually run from Lhasa or from Chengdu only as far as Chamdo, where you have to find another lift. However, police keep an eye out for truckers giving lifts to foreigners and it's not likely you'll slip past the checkpoints at Dêgê or Batang. If drivers are caught, they could lose their licences or receive massive fines. Foreigners caught arriving from Chengdu are sometimes fined and always sent back. However, if you're arriving from Tibet nobody gives a damn.

Incessant rumours persist that the Chinese government will 'improve' highways to Tibet, probably to facilitate transport of goods, if not tourists. Don't believe it. Instead, in 1997 the Chinese government decided to disregard the advice of international consultants and will attempt to sink 500 million yuan into a project worthy of Sisyphus – tunnelling highways westward all the way to Tibet, part of the way through solid ice. Whether or not it's possible is debatable, but if it is, it's a *long* way off. And if so, they still may not permit foreigners in anyway.

In sum, the odds are stacked much higher against you when travelling into, rather than out of, Tibet. Whatever you do, bear in mind the risk and equip yourself properly with food and warm clothing. And remember, accidents can happen. Some years back a group of Americans and Australians were on the back of a truck which overturned close to Dêgê; one member of the group lost half an arm and another member sustained multiple injuries to her back. It took several days for medical help to be sent and even longer before the injured could be brought back to Chengdu.

SICHUAN

Land Speed Record

We had already been denied entry on one bus (the usual insurance beef) leaving us in that village yet another miserable day. At 6 am, bleary-eyed, we were *going to get on that bus* north. We noticed the minibus appeared to be not too shabby. Before the driver could open his mouth, I said, 'We already bought the damn insurance'. And he said nothing, though one fat guy in the back started grousing about foreigners always getting the front seats.

Then, we descended into that level of Dante's hell reserved for Chinese transportation. The infuriating, but obligatory, two-blocks-and-then-stop-for-gas manoeuvre was followed up 2km later by the first wheezing stop. Off went all the bags, the driver lifted the engine cowling, and the ticket guy grabbed a dishpan and wandered off across the desolate borderland Tibet steppes. 'Where's he going?' I asked a seatmate. 'To get water for the radiator in a river', comes the reply. He didn't return for an hour, and when he did a Tibetan herdsman was giving him a ride. More than half the water had splashed out. A kilometre later the fusebox popped and started a fire.

Only 12 hours to go. Which should have taken five. Every 4 or 5km the driver had to reattach the fan belt, and we had to scrounge water (once using my canteen). Of course no actual road existed, and much of the time we spent racing down hillsides to hydroplane over epic expanses of mud, not always successfully. Push-pull-push-pull-push. Once we got stuck, and buses and trucks coming the other way were stopped for miles, awaiting our extrication. The fat guy yelled at the foreigners to get off and push. He didn't. We destroyed one other guy's axle and two chains before we were pulled out. I fell face-first into the muck.

The worst came as we neared the breaking point of endurance. A shriek from beneath the truck was followed by a very terminal-sounding 'chunk' and a very acrid smell. I swear to God the driver shimmied up a tree to cut a length of bark and tie something rusted to something worn beneath the bus. We nearly walked. The driver convinced us that this time it would be fixed for good. It took hours, and when we finally started up, we rounded the next bend, and we saw our destination ahead – 100m away.

Thomas Huhti

Bus services on the Sichuan-Tibet Highway will take you all the way to the border, and at the time of writing it was not difficult to buy tickets to Batang, Ganzi and Dêgê and other towns in the Ganzi (Garzê) Autonomous Prefecture. Having said that, the Exit-Entry Administration Office of Chengdu's PSB was definitely not keen to give out permits to these places, so clampdowns are always a possibility.

The PSB in Chengdu was actually backtracking all over itself at last check. Xiangcheng, on the backdoor route to Yunnan, was *definitely* closed. All other towns west of Kangding either *were* or *were not* open – numerous trips to find out elicited an equal number of contradictory answers from different official lackeys.

For information on Tibet and Qinghai see the separate chapters in this book.

KANGDING (DARDO)

(kāngdìng)

Kangding (2560m) is a fairly large town nestled in a steep river valley. Swift currents from the rapids of the Zhepuo River provide Kangding with hydroelectric power, the source of heating and electricity for the town.

The town itself is nothing special, but you must stop here en route to anywhere in western Sichuan. The surrounding scenery is beautiful, and there are a few sights worth walking to in the area. Chinese know the town from a popular Chinese love song inspired by the local scenery.

Towering above Kangding is the mighty peak of Gonggashan (7556m) – 'to behold it is worth 10 years of meditation', says an inscription in a ruined monastery by the base. The mountain is apparently often covered with cloud so patience is required for the beholding. It sits in a mountain range, with a sister peak just below it towering to 5200m. Pilgrims used to circle the two for several hundred kilometres to pay homage. Gonggashan is on the open list for foreign mountaineers – in 1981 it buried eight Japanese climbers in an avalanche. Known conquests of this awesome 'goddess' include those by two Americans in 1939, and by six Chinese in 1957.

Things to See
There are several lamaseries in and around Kangding. About half a kilometre from the bus station, the **Anjue Monastery** *(ānjuésì)* is fairly quiet, with several monks and a few prayer wheels. To get there, walk to the right from the bus station along the main road to where the town is divided by the Zhepuo River. Cross the third bridge: the monastery is on the right.

With some 70 to 80 lamas, the **Nanwu Monastery** *(nánwù sì)* is the most active lamasery in the area. Set in the western part of the town on the northern bank of the river, it affords good views of Kangding and the valley. Walk along the main road and follow its bend to the left for 2km, cross the bridge at the end of town and go another 300m. Next to a walled Han Chinese cemetery you will find a dirt path leading uphill along a stream which leads to the lamasery.

For spectacular views of Kangding and (if the weather obliges) nearby snow-capped mountains, try the 500m hike to the top of **Paomashan** *(pǎomǎshān)*. The ascent takes you past oodles of prayer flags, several Buddhist temples and up to a white stupa and another temple (with cows munching grass all over).

From there, if you're lucky, you may even catch a glimpse of Gonggashan. Bear left at the fork in the road just up from the bus station and walk for about 10 minutes until you reach a concrete stairway on the left side of the road. If you miss this one, keep your eyes open for a temple about 50m above the road; a stairway also leads up the hill from here. Either way it's another 30 to 40 minutes to the top.

Places to Stay & Eat
The first option to confront you is the *Bus Station Hotel (chēzhàn jiāotōng lǚshè)*. The place is a noisy, filthy dump, but it is convenient. Beds start from Y20 at foreigner prices.

Next to the Anjue Monastery the *Gonggashan Hostel (gònggàshān lǚshè)* is much better with doubles/triples for Y20/15 per bed. It's quieter, cleaner and a hell of a lot more pleasant. There's no English sign: look for the balcony that looks out over the river. Ask the nice folks at the stand beneath a public phone sign.

Immediately behind this, the chaotic *Kangding Guesthouse* (☎ 282-3153) *(kāngdìng bīnguǎn)* was once the best in town, but no longer. Weary-looking rooms start at Y32 per bed in a triple for foreigners; with a student card it's only Y20. Solo travellers have to bargain them down to around Y50 or Y60 for a room. At least there's hot water at nights which comes on simultaneous to the rousing karaoke sessions.

For more upmarket rooms, just up the street is the *Paoma Guesthouse (pǎomǎ bīnguǎn)*. Their cheapest option is a bed in a triple with attached bath for Y80. Doubles are Y200, which is amazingly expensive for this part of the world.

For a rousing cup of yak butter tea, try the *teahouse* adjacent to the Gongga Shan Hostel. Their noodles are also quite tasty. Otherwise, there are numerous point-and-choose *restaurants* along Kangding's main drag along with a few *shuǐjiǎo* (dumpling) places. Food can't compare to Chengdu in most cases, but you should get by without too much problem.

SICHUAN

Getting There & Away

Kangding is a long haul from anywhere, so be prepared. If you're not particularly gung ho for long rough journeys, it might make some sense to leave from Chengdu or even Leshan and stop for a night in Ya'an.

There's no particular reason to see Ya'an other than rest your bones, but there are connections to Kangding and Leshan. If you wish to break up the journey here, do not take the afternoon sleepers from Kangding or Chengdu, as either one gets you in around 2 or 3 am.

There are daily buses to Kangding departing Chengdu's Xinnanmen bus station at 6.30 (and sometimes 7.30) am and 4 pm. This route is problematic, due to the pesky Sichuan insurance hassle and landslides, and is covered in detail in Chengdu's Getting There & Away section.

Back to Chengdu, there are sleepers at 7.30 am and 2 pm; these should cost Y94, but you likely won't get to pay these Chinese prices. Other regular buses leave sporadically from 7 am onwards, but these are intermittent and are for hard-core riders.

Buses to Luding are scheduled to leave at 7 am and 2, 3.30, 4.30 and 5.30 pm, and cost Y8. There are more unofficial departures than this. Just walk past the ticket window in the bus station and bear right. Down the stairs in the parking lot minibuses and vans sit, waiting to fill up. You can usually get out within 20 minutes.

There was one bus daily to Moxi (Y16) at 6 am, but it wasn't running at last check. If you're headed to Hailuogou Glacier, this bus will save you having to mess around or spend the night in Luding (if it's running). It takes five hours and is always crowded so get there early. And don't always trust the timetable on the wall; ask the clerks. If it isn't running, just get an early bus to Luding and line something up from there.

Going west from Kangding, there are buses daily to Litang (6.40 am, Y54, 12 hours), Batang (7 am, Y95 to Y180, two days) and Ganzi (Y80, 14 hours). Kangding (not Luding) has a bus to Dêgê departing every third day, starting on the third day of each month, although this isn't set in stone around here; if it does go, it leaves at around 7 am and costs Y95.

There is also a bus to Xiangcheng (Y98), which departs at 6.40 am on odd days of the month, and overnights in Litang en route. Be forewarned that although getting a ticket was easy at last check, Xiangcheng was definitely closed and travellers were getting fined up to Y400 upon arrival. The same held for Batang, although fines were less severe.

For more information see the Northern and Southern Route sections later in this chapter.

AROUND KANGDING

About 110km north-west of Kangding lies the **Tagong Grasslands** (tǎgōng cǎoyuán), a vast expanse of green meadow surrounded by snow-capped peaks, and dotted with Tibetan herdsmen and tents. Nearby is the Tagong Lamasery, which blends Han Chinese and Tibetan styles and dates back to the Qing Dynasty. Both areas are being promoted by local tourism authorities, but are still said to be largely unspoiled despite the increase in visitors.

There are daily buses from Kangding at 6 and 7 am, which return in the afternoon. Locals will assure you there are up to six buses a day, but this is only around festival time.

There are also several mountain lakes and hot springs in the vicinity of Kangding. Lying 21km to the north of town, **Mugecuo Lake** (mùgécuò) is one of the highest lakes in north-west Sichuan at 3700m. Locals also boast it's one of the most beautiful, although there are likely to be many such spots in this superb part of China. Be careful not to stray too far off the paths – there are wolves and other wild beasts in these parts. Besides, the meaning of the name in Tibetan is 'Wild Men's Lake' and locals say it isn't hyperbole.

There is no bus service to Mugecuo, so you pretty much have to hire a vehicle. About 300m uphill from the bus station is a small tourism office (note the large map of the region above the shop) that can help you arrange a van and also suggest other wilderness outings. Idle van drivers seem to while away their hours in front of the shop as well, so hiring a vehicle shouldn't be too difficult. Getting to Mugecuo and back should cost around Y150 to Y200.

MOXI
(móxī)
Nestled in the mountains around 50km south-west of Luding, this peaceful one-street town is the gateway to the Hailuogou Glacier Park (see the following section for details).

There's a reception office for Hailuogou Glacier Park several doors up the road from the Catholic church (you can't miss it – it has a steeple with a cross on the top). This place has ponies and guides for hire at around Y30 to Y35 per day, and sells tickets for the glacier. The entrance fee for foreigners is now Y57 which includes a guidebook and map (the former in Chinese).

As for the church, its principal claim to fame is that Mao slept in it during the Long March.

Places to Stay
There are several very basic hotels, two of which flank the main bus stop. To the left, bearing an English sign which says 'Reception Center' is the *Luyou Hotel (lǚyóu fàndiàn)* which has beds in quiet, all-wood rooms for Y10.

To the right is a hotel which, despite lacking any sort of sign, has beds for Y5, although the rooms are a bit grimy and face the main street.

About 500m up the road, near the entrance to Hailuogou, is the *Hailin Guesthouse (hǎilín bīnguǎn)*, a grey concrete hulk that, in addition to marring the scenery, offers beds in a double with attached bath for Y40.

There are more upmarket rooms at the Hailuogou Guesthouse *(hǎiluógōu bīnguǎn)* which has beds from Y35 in nice doubles. It's on the right side along the road to the park off the main road.

Getting There & Away
There should be one bus daily from Kangding to Moxi which leaves at 6 am and costs Y16. It wasn't running at last check, so you may have to go to Luding first. If it is running get there very early, since this crate is always crowded.

From Luding there are three to four buses daily between 7.30 am and 2.30 pm. The 54km trip takes nearly three hours and costs Y8. It should also get your pulse racing: there are several cliffside sections where the road seems to disappear from under your bus, which will almost certainly be bulging with passengers, just to add to the excitement.

From Moxi there are usually several buses back to Luding from 6 am to noon. One goes on to Kangding. The early-morning bus is usually jam-packed with locals heading down to Luding, so if you want a seat you should walk up to where the bus starts, near the Hailin Guesthouse, at around 5.45 or 6.45 am.

Many travellers who come to visit Hailuogou set out by way of Kangding, and return via Luding, which has direct regular buses to Chengdu at 6 and 7 am, and 3 pm. No sleepers depart from Luding; you'll have to flag down a bus from Kangding.

Another option is to continue south and loop around to Emeishan and Leshan. Take the 7 am bus to Luding, but tell the driver to let you off at Maoziping *(māozǐpíng)*. Cross the suspension bridge to the other side of the river and the main road linking Luding with Shimian. From here you can flag down a bus to Wusihe, which is on the Chengdu-Kunming railway line. For more details, see the Luding-Wusihe-Leshan section on page 958.

HAILUOGOU GLACIER PARK
(hǎiluógōu bīngchuān gōngyuán)
Magnificent Hailuogou Glacier Park is part of Gonggashan and is the lowest glacier in Asia. The main glacier (No 1 Glacier) is 14km in length and covers an area of 16 sq km. It's relatively young as glaciers go: around 1600 years.

SICHUAN

956 Western Sichuan – Hailuogou Glacier Park

Guides from the town of Moxi lead inexpensive three to seven day pony treks along glacier trails. The top of Hailuogou can offer incredible vistas of Gonggashan, but how much you actually see is entirely up to Mother Nature.

If you are after spectacular views it will probably pay to build a couple of extra days into your schedule. The rainy season for this area spans July and August, and some travellers have found heavy cloud cover and drizzle take a lot of fun out of the trip. Locals say the best time to visit is during late September and October, when skies are generally clear.

The trek has become much more accessible over recent years, but it's still a good idea to come prepared. Bring warm clothing and good sunglasses with you as a minimum. There is food and drink available en route, but it's still worth bringing some high-calorie food with you. Camping is great – you'll probably be invited to sit with other local trekkers around a roaring bonfire, while listening to workers sing Tibetan songs.

If you are on a pony you can do the entire trip through to the No 3 Camp in around seven to eight hours. On foot you would be better off doing the trip over two days, although it's probably possible to make it to the No 3 Camp in one day if you keep up a brisk pace.

The guides are likely to push you toward the three day, two night trek. This usually consists of spending the first night at No 1 Camp, riding up to No 3 Camp the next day for lunch and glacier viewing, and then heading back down to spend the second night at the No 2 Camp. Pony rental is Y30 to Y35 per day.

If you opt to hike, you can also rent a pack horse for Y30 per day which can carry up to three bags. You can even rent ponies for just the ride up (Y15 to No 1 Camp, Y35 to No 3), and then walk back on your own. Maps with English are available at the park reception office in Moxi.

From Moxi the path follows the Yanzigou River (it's marked in English). Just

after Moxi you'll be stopped at the park gate, where you will be charged a Y57 entry fee, which includes a guidebook and map (both in Chinese). From here it's a straightforward walk or ride (if you are on a pony) around 11km to the **No 1 Camp** *(yīhào yíngdì)*, which is at 1940m. En route you'll cross a rickety bridge over the river. The distance to the next camp is around 6km.

At the **No 2 Camp** *(èrhào yíngdì)* (2620m) the path leaves the river valley and passes through lush rainforest for around 5km. No 2 Camp has the best hot springs. At the **No 3 Camp** *(sānhào yíngdì)* (2940m) there is a sign notifying visitors that you should take a guide to the glacier itself. Pony guides from Moxi do not qualify, but the hire of a glacier guide is included in the park entry fee, so you shouldn't have to pay any extra.

From the No 3 Camp the first stop is the **Glacier Viewing Platform** *(bīngchuān guānjǐngtái)* at 3000m. From here you can see the **Glacier Tongue** to the left and to the right the **No 2 Glacier**.

From the platform it is possible to continue for 2.5km on a path that runs alongside the glacier to the **Glacier Waterfall Viewing Platform** *(bīngchuān pùbù guānjǐngtái)*. There is also an ice cave another half-hour's walk beyond that. Just how far you get from the No 3 Camp will depend entirely on weather conditions.

Places to Stay & Eat

Accommodation in damp and dirty lodges is around Y20 per bed at each of the camps en route to the glacier, and service can be glacial as well. On the brighter side, both the No 1 and No 2 camps have hot springs – those at No 2 are particularly nice – if you are in need of a soak.

Some people do the walk slowly (three or four hours a day), overnighting at each of the camps. But it is possible to head straight up to the No 3 Camp, where there is chalet-style accommodation, albeit a bit run down.

The park authorities appear to frown on

camping, and there isn't a great deal in the way of flat ground on the way up in any case. Naturally you can't expect any showering facilities up here – save your dirt for the hot springs lower down.

The camps all sell some food and drinks. Mineral water, soft drinks and beer are all usually available. Food is uniformly miserable – a steady diet of cabbage soup and green peppers fried with pork fat. You'd better bring some of your own munchies along.

Getting There & Away

Hailuogou is accessible via the town of Moxi, which in turn can be reached by bus from Kangding and Luding. There's a travel agency at the Yagudu Hotel in Luding which organises trips in peak tourist seasons. See the following entry on Luding for details.

LUDING

(lúdìng)

Luding is around halfway between Kangding and Moxi, and is possibly worth a brief stop en route to either destination, or if you're heading back to Chengdu.

Luding is famous throughout China as the site of what is commonly regarded as the most glorious moment of the Long March. The key element in this is the Luding Bridge, a chain suspension affair high over the Dadu River.

In May 1935 the Communist troops were approaching the Luding Bridge, only to discover that Kuomintang troops had beat them to it, removed the planks from the bridge and had it covered with firepower. In response, 20 Communist troops crossed the bridge hand over hand armed with grenades and then proceeded to overcome the Kuomintang troops on the other side. This action allowed the Long March to continue before the main body of the Kuomintang forces could catch up with them.

The **Luding Bridge** *(lúdìng qiáo)* is in the south of town. The original bridge was first constructed in 1705 and was an important link in the Sichuan-Tibet road. On the main street in town you might want to look out for the **Luding Bridge Revolutionary Artefacts Museum** *(lúdìng qiáo gémìng wénwù chénlièguǎn)*, which houses a collection of some 150 items left behind by members of the Long March.

You can also get a gander at some of Mao's calligraphy on a shelter near the **Buddhist Temple** on the hillside above town.

Places to Stay

There are a few hotels in Luding. Off the main road down south of the bus station, the *Luding County Government Guesthouse (xiàn zhāodàisuǒ)* has beds in triples for Y20, and beds in acceptable doubles with bath for Y50. Confusingly, the guesthouse is also referred to as the *Luding Hotel (lúdìng bīnguǎn)* – there's English vertically on the (broken) sign, but you can't see it from the main road.

The *Bus Station Hotel (chēzhàn lǚguǎn)*, near the southern bus station, has beds in triples for Y12, but you won't get them to give you a bed for less than Y22, so walk out, turn right and go about 40m and look for the *Lu He Guesthouse* – there are three Chinese signs and one in English which says 'State Operated Hotel' in small letters. Friendly owners operate this place and there are decent rooms for Y20, with TV and facilities as clean as anything in these parts.

The best rooms in town come south of the Luding Bridge along the main road at the *Yagudu Hotel*. Good doubles cost Y50 and rooms include TV, private bath and evening hot water. There is a tiny English sign which says 'Check in'.

Getting There & Away

For some strange reason, Luding has two bus stations. The local bus station is on the main road from Kangding, at the northern edge of town. It's near a basketball court, just near where the road bends. Don't trust the schedule on the wall and be prepared for a blood-from-stone ordeal getting the clerks to offer up departure times.

From here you can get buses to Moxi (Y8), Kangding (Y8) and even direct to Chengdu (Y55). Buses to Chengdu – no sleepers – leave at 6 and 7 am and take 12 to 18 hours barring landslides and depending on whether they try to brave Erlangshan Pass or skirt it via Shimian.

Buses to Kangding run more or less hourly between 6 am and 4 pm. There are only a couple of buses to Moxi, at 6 and 8.30 am. In peak seasons you can also organise trips to the Hailuogou Glacier Park from the travel agency in the Yagudu Hotel. Several buses each morning depart for Shimian, where you can switch to a bus bound for Wusihe, which is on the Chengdu-Kunming railway line.

At the southern part of town, one street uphill from the main road, is the southern bus station. From here you can also get buses to Chengdu, Kangding (Y8), Ya'an (Y37) and Shimian (Y17). This station has no sleepers, even though the schedule says it does; the 3 pm departure is a regular rattletrap bus which should make for an excruciatingly bouncy evening. All of this fun costs Y55 (Chinese price) and they were selling them to foreigners at last check.

Luding-Wusihe-Leshan If you're headed to Leshan, Emeishan or Kunming, and don't feel like doubling back to Chengdu, you can try heading down to the railhead at Wusihe. There are usually one or two buses daily from Luding to Wusihe, but if you miss these, just jump on a bus to Shimian, where there are frequent onward buses.

Buses from Shimian to Wusihe stop for an hour or so at Hanyuan for some bizarre reason, one of many such halts you're likely to encounter en route. Altogether the 210km journey requires most of the day, but it does take you through some impressive gorge and river scenery.

Trains from Wusihe to Emei and Leshan leave at 1.50 and 5.10 pm, so you should be able to make one without overnighting in Wusihe. There are several hotels clustered around the railway station, all with beds for

Y7 to Y10. The one just off the road that leads into the station is not bad.

There is a 12.26 am train to Leshan, which arrives at 3.47 am, but locals don't recommend it. A hard-seat ticket to either Emei or Leshan should cost around Y8. The ride is about 3½ hours on most trains.

If you're headed south to Panzhihua (where you connect with buses to Lijiang in Yunnan) or Kunming, be advised that you can only buy hard-seat tickets at the Wusihe railway station. You also have a poor option for trains out: 3.01 am. Most trains don't stop in Wusihe.

SICHUAN-TIBET HIGHWAY – NORTHERN ROUTE

Of the two routes, this is the less heavily travelled, probably because it's nearly 300km longer than the southern route.

One added advantage for travellers is that if you are turned back at the Tibet border, you may be able to work your way up to Qinghai Province via Sêrxu *(shíqú)*. However, even getting this far could be a problem; at the time of writing the PSB was doing a good job of closing this route off to foreigners, and the Kangding bus station wouldn't even sell tickets to Ganzi.

If you do make it up here, remember that bus service is sparse and erratic: this is no place to be if you're in a hurry.

Ganzi
(gānzī)

Ganzi, the capital of the Ganzi (Garzê) Autonomous Prefecture sits at 3800m in Cholashan mountain valley 385km north-west of Kangding, and is populated by mostly Tibetans and Khampas.

Very few westerners have sojourned here, in part because the PSB, suspecting you are Tibet-bound, will do their best to stop you from doing so. As the Xining-Chengdu route between Qinghai and Sichuan becomes more popular it may yet get its due, and it's easier to get here if you're headed toward Chengdu.

For now it's little more than an intermediate stop between Sêrxu and Kangding for travellers in a hurry to reach 'civilisation' after the rigours of the Xining-Sêrxu road.

The **Ganzi Lamasery** *(gānzī sì)* just north of the town's Tibetan quarter is worth a visit for its views of the Ganzi valley, although it's not a particularly spectacular structure.

The *Ganzixian Hotel (gānzīxiàn zhāodàisuǒ)* has beds for Y10 to Y20, a decent dining room, friendly staff and plenty of hot water.

For details on the trip north to Xining via Sêrxu, see the Xining section in the Qinghai chapter.

Getting There & Away Buses to Ganzi leave Kangding daily at 6 am, take 14 hours and cost Y80. From Ganzi, there should also be one bus daily to Kangding, leaving around daybreak.

There are buses every third day to Dêgê which originate in Kangding, stay over night in Luhuo and pass through Ganzi at around 10 am.

Under ideal conditions the 200km ride from Ganzi to Dêgê takes eight hours. Similarly, buses to Sêrxu originate in Kangding every third day or so, overnight in Daofu and stop over in Ganzi around 1 pm before resuming their drive.

Dêgê
(dégé)

This is the last town on the northern route before it enters Tibet proper. As such, it's reportedly well patrolled and it may be difficult to slip past the checkpoint. Guards are said to keep a sharp lookout for foreigners trying to sneak through on the backs of trucks, and a fair number of travellers have been turned back at this point. Apparently the best option is to find a postal truck – they're not checked as often – and stay hidden in the back until Qamdo.

Dêgê is home to the 250-year-old **Bakong Scripture Printing Lamasery**, housing an extensive collection of Tibetan scriptures of the five Lamaist sects which are revered by followers the world over. Built in the Qing Dynasty by the 42nd prefect of Dêgê, along with others in Xigaze and Lhasa, it was one of the three most important. Under the direction of the abbot are some 300 workers; housed within the monastery are more than 215,000 hardwood printing plates. Texts include ancient works on astronomy, geography, music, medicine and Buddhist classics, including two of the most important Tibetan sutras. A history of Indian Buddhism, comprising 555 woodblock plates, is the only surviving copy in the world (written in Hindi, Sanskrit and Tibetan).

Half of the interior is taken up by block collections; you can also examine storage chambers, paper-cutting and binding rooms, block-cleaning platforms, and a statue hall. Protecting the monastery from fire and earthquake is a guardian goddess, a green Avalokitesvara.

Accommodation in Dêgê is very basic: no showers and hard wooden beds at the *bus station hotel* for Y5 to Y10.

Getting There & Away There is a direct bus to Dêgê from Kangding. At the time of writing departures were every three days starting on the third of the month (3, 6, 9 etc.) but this schedule is 'flexible' to say the least. Often there won't be a bus for a week.

The bus leaves Kangding around 7 or 7.30 am, overnights in Luhuo, passes through Ganzi around 10 am and arrives in Dêgê that same evening, barring any inevitable delays. All this fun for Y95.

Buses to Ganzi and on to Kangding leave Dêgê every third day starting on the second of the month (2, 5, 8 etc).

SICHUAN-TIBET HIGHWAY – SOUTHERN ROUTE

This route has considerably more traveller traffic – mostly because the Kangding-Litang-Xiangcheng-Zhongdian route into Yunnan used to be a great way to get a Tibet fix without actually making it into Tibet.

Sadly, at the time writing, Xiangcheng was definitely closed, and all foreigners stepping off the bus were facing fines of up to Y400; however, the PSB in Chengdu was inconsistent with other towns. Batang has always been off limits, but some people have been told that Litang is also now closed. If so, nobody's getting hassled there. At least for now.

Between Kangding and the border town of Batang lies more than 500km of dirt roads, 4000m mountain passes, stunning scenery and occasional landslides. A few travellers have made it out to Batang recently, only to be politely turned around.

Litang
(lǐtáng)
The PSB in Chengdu was clueless as to whether Litang was open or not. Three officials gave three answers. If it's closed, at least nobody was being bothered at the time of writing.

At over 4000m Litang is one of the highest towns in China, and even a short hike around here may have you wondering where the oxygen went. The town rests at the edge of a vast grassland and is the watering hole for neighbouring Tibetan herdsmen, who can be seen kicking up a trail of dust through town at dusk.

Some travellers have found great bargains here on yak skin boots, cloaks and other Tibetan clothing. A trading fair and festival lasting 10 days is held here annually beginning on the 13th day of the sixth lunar month; it's sponsored by the Panchen Lama.

Litang also has a lamasery that is said to have been built by the Third Dalai Lama and contains a buddha statue that locals claim was brought over from Lhasa by foot. Friendly monks are apparently happy to pull in any wandering foreigners for extensive tours of the lamasery.

Places to Stay The *hotel* at the bus station, in the southern part of town, has dorm beds for Y8. Like so many of these charming places, you share the bathroom with any and all bus passengers.

Up the road about 150m on the right-hand side is a small *guesthouse* with cleaner,

quieter dorm beds for Y11. Neither place has showers, but around 15 minutes' walk from the bus station is a public bath where you can get all the hot water your heart desires for Y4. The people at the bus station can point you in the right direction.

Getting There & Away There is one bus daily from Kangding to Litang, leaving at 6.40 am. The fare is Y54 and the 284km journey, which crosses several high passes, takes at least 12 hours. Even in summer months it would be best to have some warm clothing to fend off the arctic blasts that live above 4000m.

From Litang, there are buses to Kangding at 6.30 am, although if the bus that day originates from Batang, then you may not leave until later in the morning. There is a mad scramble for seats, so get there early (or before the bus arrives) if you don't wish to stand for 12 hours of bone-jarring dirt-road travel.

Buses for Batang leave daily in the morning; how early depends on whether the bus, which originates in Kangding, overnights in Litang itself or in Yajiang, 136km east of Litang. There are also buses from here to Xiangcheng, leaving around 10 am on even days of the month, but (once again) Xiangcheng was *definitely* a den of hassle for foreign travellers at the time of writing.

Batang
(bātáng)
Lying 32km from the Tibet border, Batang is not much more than a glorified truck park and bus station. But this one-street town is reportedly quite friendly and populated almost completely by Tibetans.

Most of the activity centres around the steady stream of truck traffic heading into Tibet. Several Tibetan truckers separately offered one traveller here a ride to Lhasa for Y500, so it may be possible to sneak across here. Just don't pay in advance, in case you are dragged out of your hiding place at the border crossing and sent back to Chengdu.

CHRIS TAYLOR

DIANA MAYFIELD

JULIET COOMBE/LA BELLE AURORE

DIANA MAYFIELD

The South-West
Top Left: An example of the extraordinary grotto art of Dazu County (Sichuan Province).
Top Right: A Buddhist monastery stands out in a Xishuangbanna village (Yunnan Province).
Bottom Left: A well-worn trekking path along the popular Tiger Leaping Gorge (Yunnan Province).
Bottom Right: Grinding chillies on Small Patou Island in Lake Erhai near Dali (Yunnan Province).

THOMAS HUHTI

THOMAS HUHTI

The South-West
Top: Burning incense in a Guiyang temple (Guizhou Province).
Bottom: Traditional medicinal herbs for sale in an Anshun market (Guizhou Province).

Most travellers who have made it to Batang have been fined and asked to turn back within 24 hours. One traveller reports:

I heard a knock on my door, and opened it to find two PSB officers there. They were really quite polite, and said they were sorry, but I was not supposed to be here, and could I please leave the next day. They then reluctantly fined me Y130, but when I showed them a student card, they gave me a discount of Y95!

Places to Stay Coming from Litang, the *bus station hotel* is halfway into town on the right-hand side and has beds for Y5. Coming out of the bus station, about 50m up the street to the right is a small, two storey white building with yellow trim. There's no sign or reception area, but the place is a hotel all the same, with friendly staff and beds in fairly clean, quiet rooms for Y8.

Getting There & Away There is one bus leaving Batang for Litang daily in the early morning. The trip takes 12 to 14 hours and crosses the 4675m Haizishan Pass.

From Kangding you can get a bus at 7.20 am, but this stops off in Litang anyway. For more details on getting to Batang, see the Litang Getting There & Away section above.

LITANG TO ZHONGDIAN: THE BACK DOOR TO YUNNAN

Formerly the favourite route for travellers with time on their hands and Tibet on the brain, this route was cut off by the killjoys at the PSB in May 1997.

The 400km trip takes you over several breathtaking passes and past fields of Tibetan nomads, semi-submerged Tibetan cabins and endless mountain vistas.

Like the rest of western Sichuan, bus service is limited to one run daily at most, and in many cases buses only leave every other day. But if you're taking this route this shouldn't matter too much: it's a fascinating region that deserves a closer look. And if you can't get to Tibet, this is undoubtedly the next best thing.

Buses leave Litang for Xiangcheng in the morning on even days of the month. The exact departure time varies, as the bus originates in Kangding and may have overnighted in Yajiang. The ride is 200km of rough gravel, single-lane track, takes 10 hours and costs Y36.

If you're headed in the opposite direction, north to Litang, buses leave Xiangcheng on odd days of the month at 6.30 am.

Xiangcheng is a pretty riverside village of square stone houses with wooden roofs, Tibetan monasteries and the occasional nomad passing through. Monks at the monasteries have welcomed foreign visitors and given them guided tours of the premises. The *bus station hotel* has beds in quads for Y5. There's a chance that the local PSB will only let you stay one or two nights here, depending on which day your bus is leaving.

Heading to Zhongdian, buses leave daily at 6 am. The vehicles used are reportedly some of the most haggard in China, so don't expect much. The ride takes 12 hours and costs Y36.

Coming the other way, buses leave Zhongdian for Xiangcheng daily at 7.30 am. For details on Zhongdian, see the Yunnan chapter.

Northern Sichuan

The Aba (Tibet & Qiang) Autonomous Prefecture of northern Sichuan is one of the most Tibetan areas of the province and doesn't require any special permits from the Chengdu PSB, at least for now.

With its dense alpine forests and wide grasslands, it is also a great place to get out and commune with nature. Pony treks around Songpan and hiking in the nature preserve of Jiuzhaigou have made this area increasingly popular with travellers, many of whom pass through here on their way up to Langmusi, Xiahe and other destinations in Gansu Province.

Most of northern Sichuan lies between

2000m and 3000m in altitude, so make sure you take warm clothing: even in summer temperatures can drop to 15°C (59°F) at night. The rainy season lasts from June to August. While you're getting prepared, also bear in mind that there are few places to change money in this region, so bring sufficient cash.

Roads in the region are dangerous so don't expect more than minimum standards of vehicle, driver or road maintenance. Roads are particularly hazardous in summer when heavy rains prompt frequent landslides, and you might want to consider planning this trip for the spring or autumn, when the weather is better anyway.

Several foreigners were killed in the summer of 1995 when their bus was caught in a landslip and plunged into a river. Because of the hazards, travellers are required to purchase insurance – Chinese insurance only – for travel in the north. This is simple enough to do if coming from Chengdu, since it's built into the cost of a bus ticket.

Once you're in the wilds of northern Sichuan, however, you may run into the old Catch-22 of not getting on an onward bus without insurance, but since there's no insurance office in town ...

Many towns have two bus stations, of which one is an officially designated tourist ticket dispenser. Even if the local station has a bus leaving today, and the tourist station tomorrow, they still probably won't let you on the local bus.

SONGPAN
(sōngpān)

Although largely viewed as a stopover point on the road to Jiuzhaigou, this bustling, friendly town merits a visit of its own. A good number of its old wooden buildings are still intact, as are the ancient gates that date from when Songpan was a walled city.

Farmers and Tibetan cattle herders clop down the cobblestone streets on horseback, street artisans peddle their wares in the market area, and several kilometres out of

town there's idyllic mountain forests and emerald-green lakes.

Those great thick Tibetan overcoats are a bit cheaper here than other places. And, whatever you do, take a torch (flashlight). Songpan goes a week at a stretch without electricity.

Horse Treks

Although Songpan is nice, the surrounding mountain scenery is better still. One of the best ways to experience it is by joining up with a horse trek.

Guides take you out for anywhere from two to seven days, bringing you through valleys and forests so pristine and peaceful that you may not believe you're still in China. And don't worry – the horses are tame enough for anyone. Too tame, some people say.

There are several horse trek operators in Songpan. The operator with the longest presence in town is Shun Jiang Horse Treks *(shùnjiāng lǚyóu mǎduì)*, run out of a little office down the road from the bus station. Another company also uses the name 'Shun Jiang' and is run by ex-guides of the former. To be fair, the second company also has a decent reputation and travellers have reported nothing but good experiences. The problem is that there's serious competition brewing and you'll likely be pressured to join their internecine turf battles by coercing other foreigners just getting off the buses. Don't feel obliged; be firm and say no if you don't want to.

You will probably be met by young operators from the newer company while you're still on the bus, and those of the original once you exit. You can tell the original: look for the 'good guy with one bad eye' – you'll know him. Although facing a sales pitch is not the perfect way to cap off the hellish 14 hour ride up from Chengdu, try not to be put off. What they're selling is well worth it. And don't be pressured by either side. Tell them to take a hike for a day while you make up your mind.

For Y60 per day, you get a horse, three meals a day, tents, bedding and even warm jackets in case you get chilly. The guides take care of everything – you won't touch a tent pole or a cooking pot unless you want to. They speak no English unless you count 'yak' and 'potato', but communicate admirably nonetheless. It's not necessary to tip them, but they work their tails off for you, so occasional beer or *bai jiu* (local moonshine) might be a nice idea. Alternatively, take their picture and offer to send them a copy.

The basic three day trip takes you to a series of mountain lakes and a hot spring at Erdao Hai, and then on the next day to the Zhaga Waterfall. They will, however, tailor a trip to your wishes. There are entry fees of Y33 at both areas: the money goes directly to park maintenance.

Food consists mainly of potatoes, some green vegetables and bread (someone told the owner that foreigners love potatoes). Bring some extra snacks along if you want more variety. If you want beer, you'll have to supply that too. If you've been itching to really get out and enjoy China's beautiful scenery, this is a great opportunity to view it up close.

Places to Stay

Many travellers report a hot water dodge from local hotels. They promise evening hot water before you check in, but *voila*, come 8 pm, suddenly there's no hot water. Or the next night, or the next. (This is particularly vexing if you're coming in from three days on a trek.) If it is a local conspiracy, it's a complicated one, since every lodging is in on it.

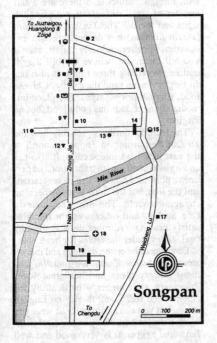

To Jiuzhaigou, Huanglong & Zöigê

Min River

Songpan

0   100   200 m

To Chengdu

SICHUAN

SONGPAN 松潘	PLACES TO EAT	8 Post Office 邮局
PLACES TO STAY	6 Xin Xin Restaurant 忻忻饭店	11 Cinema 电影院
3 Lin Ye Hotel 林业宾馆	9 Yu Lan Restaurant 玉兰饭店	13 National Store of Xue Yu 雪域民族商店
5 Songzhou Hotel 松州宾馆	12 Muslim Restaurant 穆斯林餐厅	14 East Gate 东门
7 Songpan County Government Hostel 县政府招待所	**OTHER** 1 Main Bus Station 汽车北站	15 East Bus Station 汽车东站
10 Huanglong Hotel 屏嚣	2 Shun Jiang Horse Treks 顺江旅游马队	16 Covered Bridge 古城桥
17 Songpan Hotel 松潘宾馆	4 North Gate 北门	18 Hospital 医院
		19 South Gate 南门

Actually, the problem is that the town constantly loses electricity and – supposedly – the water pumps can't operate. Whatever the case, be prepared to stay grimy. In addition to the lodging listed below, there are numerous flyspeck-sized 'guesthouses' that are good as last resorts only, many of them grungy even by bus station hotel standards.

On the main street, the *Songpan County Government Guesthouse (xiànzhèngfǔ zhāodàisuǒ)* has a well earned reputation as a place to avoid. Dorm beds in filthy rooms are outrageously priced at Y20, and triples go from Y120. The bathrooms are disgusting and the service frigid. The staff know it's bad – they're bargaining the price down immediately you've set your eyes on the room.

Across the street, the *Songzhou Hotel (sōngzhōu bīnguǎn)* has similar prices, with beds from Y25, but is considerably more pleasant. They even have rooms with attached bath, although the Y180 price tag is a bit steep.

A bit further down the street, the *Huanglong Hotel (huánglóng bīnguǎn)* is really rundown and was reportedly on the verge of closing, but had dorm beds for Y12 and singles/doubles with common washroom for Y50/80.

Another option is the *Lin Ye Hotel (línyè bīnguǎn)* which is relatively clean and quiet, and sits next to the Min River. Dorm beds are Y30, and doubles are Y100 and up. This place gets mixed reports, but at last check the rooms were adequate and the staff seemed relatively on top of things.

The top spot in town is probably the *Songpan Hotel (sōngpān bīnguǎn)*, which has newly finished standard doubles/triples for Y260/360. Its main drawback is the price – not worth it when there's often no electricity or hot water – and another is location, as it's about 15 minutes' walk from the town centre.

Places to Eat

In the morning, check out the little stalls with dumplings lining the main street. Lots of places sell the local breakfast speciality, dense bread patties heated atop metal drums – they'll stick to your ribs all day and can't be beaten on cold mornings.

Songpan is gradually coming to grips with foreign visitors, and there are a fair number of small restaurants with English signs and menus. The *Xin Xin Restaurant (xīnxīn fàndiàn)* has decent fare and endeavours to be scrupulously honest; even if you tell them you believe the bill they'll outline everything three times. It also has an English menu (and the catchy 'Chinese food, English prices' sign). The place immediately next door has good food, but no English.

The local favourite is probably now the *Yu Lan Restaurant* on Zhong Jie north of the east gate road intersection. It also has an English menu – with translations of pertinent phrases such as 'I'm a vegetarian' and the like, but the draw is its owners, an engaging couple. The menu has muesli, cafe au lait, and other western items to satisfy cravings. Another draw is the tiny coal stoves under the tables for heat.

Down near the covered bridge and market area, the *Muslim Restaurant (mùsīlín fàndiàn)* is very clean and has great food. Prices are a bit higher – particularly for chicken and fish – and there's no English menu, but you can easily pick out what you want in the kitchen. The *yúxiāng qiézi* (fish-flavoured eggplant) is very good and well worth sampling.

Getting There & Away

Although it's a fairly small town, Songpan has two bus stations. The one near the north gate is the only one which will sell tickets to foreigners and includes the cost of insurance in your ticket.

Two buses leave Chengdu's Ximen bus station each day at 6.20 and 7 am for Songpan. They usually end up at the north bus station, but you may be dropped off at the east bus station.

Going back to Chengdu, the north gate station has a bus leaving daily at 6 am; you could also try to flag down one of the two buses en route from Nanping (at around 7 am), although one of these will theoretically be Chinese-only and there's no guarantee you'll get a ticket. To Chengdu costs Y75 on a rattletrap.

The 335km Chengdu-Songpan route includes some of the worst roads in Sichuan Province, so be prepared for 12 to 14 hours of heavy-duty shock absorption. The first 190km from Chengdu are great, but immediately after the lunch stop you'll be side-swiping leviathan lumber trucks or literally be driving atop the river, and sometimes in the riverbed itself. The road is slated for improvement so that tourists can be whisked to Jiuzhaigou in one day, but completion looks to be far, far off.

From Songpan, there are buses to Jiuzhaigou at 6 am which continue to Nanping. For Y35 you can experience a trip of between six and 10 hours and there are times where there literally isn't even a road. At least the scenery is gorgeous.

Buses to Zöigê leave the main station on even-numbered days at 6.30 am, although check this as it's flexible at best. The ride takes six to seven hours and costs Y45 (foreigners' price).

HUANGLONG
(huánglóng)
This valley, studded with terraced, coloured ponds (blue, yellow, white and green) and waterfalls, is about 56km from Songpan, on the main road to Jiuzhaigou.

The **Yellow Dragon Temple** *(huánglóng sì)* and the surrounding area were designated a national park in 1983. The most spectacular terraced ponds are behind the temple, about a two hour walk from the main road.

An annual Miao Hui (Temple Fair) is held here around the middle of the sixth lunar month (roughly mid-August); it attracts large numbers of traders from the Qiang minority.

Huanglong is almost always included on the itinerary for one of the seven day Jiuzhaigou tours run out of Chengdu, but some people find it disappointing and prefer an extra day at Jiuzhaigou.

In the national park there's several small guesthouses with beds for Y5 to Y10 or less – no frills, just hard beds and maybe a coal burner in the winter. The *Huanglong Hotel (huánglóng zhāodàisuǒ)* has slightly more upmarket accommodation, with beds

SICHUAN

Warning

Travellers may be required to purchase insurance from the People's Insurance Company of China (PICC) for bus travel in Sichuan and Gansu provinces. The ticket office at the Ximen bus station in Chengdu used to require that foreigners present a PICC card, but now say they factor insurance into the cost of foreigners' double-priced bus tickets (isn't that nice of them?).

However, travellers in Zöigê and towns in Gansu have been sent to PICC branch offices to pick up insurance cards before being allowed to board their bus, which often leaves without them anyway. Don't bother telling the staff you have travel insurance already: non-PICC coverage is not recognised. This policy apparently follows from a lawsuit brought upon the Chinese government by the family of a Japanese tourist who was killed in a bus crash in the Jiuzhaigou area.

If you're just headed to Jiuzhaigou and back you probably won't have a problem, but for travel further north it may be wise to pick up a card in Chengdu.

The card costs Y30 for one month's cover and is available from the PICC office *(zhōngguó rénmín bǎoxiǎn gōngsī)* on Shudu Dadao (Renmin Donglu), just down the road from the Hongqi Market in Chengdu. ∎

in triples with attached bath for Y30, and standard doubles for Y80. It's down at the entrance to the park. There is a hefty admission fee of Y140 now, which makes up many travellers' minds for them.

There is no public bus service to Huanglong, and it will be difficult to get here unless you've signed up with a tour. You might be able to jump on a tour bus setting out from either Songpan or Jiuzhaigou early in the morning, but drivers are often reluctant to take foreigners, citing the risk of insurance liability.

JIUZHAIGOU
(jiǔzhàigōu)

In northern Sichuan, close to the Gansu border, is Jiuzhaigou (literally: Nine Stockade Gully), which was 'discovered' in the 1970s and is now being groomed for an annual influx of 300,000 visitors.

In 1984 Zhao Ziyang made the famous comment which all Sichuanese tourism officials love to quote: 'Guilin's scenery ranks top in the world, but Jiuzhaigou's scenery even tops Guilin's'.

Jiuzhaigou, which has several Tibetan settlements, offers a number of dazzling features – it is a nature reserve area (with some panda conservation zones) with North American-type alpine scenes (peaks, hundreds of clear lakes, forests). Scattered throughout the region are Tibetan prayer wheels and *chortens*, Tibetan stupas.

The remoteness of the region and the chaotic transport connections have kept it clean and relatively untouristed. Despite the good intentions of the authorities, all this looks certain to change fast. A helicopter landing pad is under construction even though the mountain ranges between Chengdu and Jiuzhaigou are not ideal terrain for helicopters. And Chinese resort-style hotels, though as yet largely empty, line the road leading to the park entrance.

You should calculate between a week and 10 days for the round trip by road. It takes from two to three days to get there and you can easily spend three or four days – or even weeks – doing superb hikes along trails which cross a spectacular scenery of waterfalls, ponds, lakes and forests – it's just the place to rejuvenate polluted urban senses.

In a bid to prevent the forest from being trampled by hordes of tourists, park authorities have stationed locals on some of the off-road trails to turn back wandering hikers. If you run into one, it's best to be friendly and head back to the road. You'll even get the chance to nose around the Tibetan Zaru Temple just inside the entrance; the monks are a friendly lot and seem pleased to see foreign tourists.

The entrance to **Jiuzhaigou National Park** is close to the Yangdong Hotel, where the bus will likely drop you off. Here lies probably the most painful part of the trip: a park entry fee of Y219. This is exceedingly high for China (even locals must pay Y85), and there's no real way around it. Student cards don't work, unless you can back them up with a legitimate residence or work certificate. At least the money goes toward a national park, rather than into the pockets of some shady hotel or tour operator. The entry fee includes one night's stay at one of the three lodging areas – Heye Village, Shuzheng Stockade or Zechachwa Stockade.

From the park entrance to the first hotels within the park it's about 5km along a surfaced road, and 14km to the bifurcation of the road. You can arrange rides from local drivers hanging around the entrance gate. Up to Nuorilang should cost Y10 to Y20 per person, although they'll likely try to charge more. Bargain hard with these guys.

With the low level of traffic – just the occasional blitzkrieg tour bus – it's actually a lovely walk, if you're looking for exercise. An ambitious itinerary: each day walk to the next settlement, with gorgeous scenery along the whole way, and spend the day exploring the immediate area. The fourth day hike/hitch towards Swan Lake and back (though traffic is sparse). Save the ride for the last day.

If you're crunched for time, your group can get a van driver to take you everywhere;

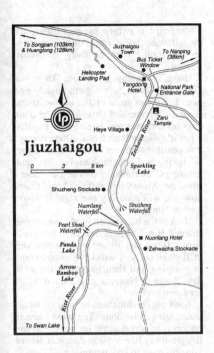

To Songpan (103km) & Huanglong (128km)
Jiuzhaigou Town
To Nanping (38km)
Bus Ticket Window
Helicopter Landing Pad
Yangdong Hotel
National Park Entrance Gate
Zaru Temple
Heye Village
Jiuzhaigou
Zechawa River
0   3   6 km
Sparkling Lake
Shuzheng Stockade
Nuorilang Waterfall
Shuzheng Waterfall
Pearl Shoal Waterfall
Panda Lake
Nuorilang Hotel
Zehwacha Stockade
Arrow Bamboo Lake
Rize River
To Swan Lake

bargaining starts at Y300 or whatever they think you'll stomach for the one day trip.

At the ratty old Nuorilang Hotel the road splits: branch right for Swan Lake, and left for Long Lake. Nuorilang to Long Lake is 18km, Nuorilang to Rize is 9km and Rize to Swan Lake is 8km. Long Lake generally has fewer tourists, as there is no surfaced road leading to it, although at the time of writing, road crews were slowly inching their way towards it.

Places to Stay & Eat

Unless you're catching an early bus the next day, you're better off staying inside the park. Lodging is found in three places – Heye Village, Shuzheng Stockade and Zehwacha Stockade. All feature a choice between funky wooden Tibetan-style rooms with the smell of pine still lingering or concrete-block 'guesthouse' rooms.

The Tibetan-style rooms obviously ooze more character and the owners of some of these are quite friendly, although this may mean sitting through cups of yak butter tea – definitely an acquired taste.

Zehwacha Stockade has a few more up-market rooms. All three areas are set up a bit oddly – you have to locate the 'central service desk', which will be located somewhere in the middle of the village; your first night you'll be issued a voucher, and after that you're left to your own devices. Some places try to tack on an extra foreign-friend surcharge, but a few places don't, so check out a few places if you have time. You can often negotiate a deal on multinight stays. Facilities are primitive, and don't even ask about showers.

Just above Nuorilang Falls, Zehwacha is the hardest one to suss out. You'll likely as not wander about trying to find out where the hell anyone is. There are three lodging places. The first one – the erstwhile Nuorilang Hotel – comes right at the junction of roads. Forget about that dilapidated place and head 200m or so uphill to the left to another. This hotel has great three-bed wooden rooms with common bath for Y22, although they may get you for Y35 for being a foreigner. They also have quite nice doubles with evening hot water and TV for Y90 per room. Further uphill are more forgettable guesthouse options along with the only *restaurant* in this village.

Heye Village is the place where most travellers *don't* stay, since it's the furthest from the local sights (but closest to the park entrance). If you do, rates for standard spartan rooms are around Y30 per person.

Just past Sparkling Lake, *Shuzheng* has rooms with what may be the best view in the country, overlooking spectacular turquoise pools, white baby cascades and dense verdancy. Simple rooms are Y22; go for the wooden ones if they're available, since the buildings are the newest. There are no longer any hotels along the road to Swan Lake – local authorities ordered them closed to preserve the natural environment.

Just outside the park entrance, the *Yangdong Hotel* (*yángdóng bīnguǎn*) offers a more upmarket stay, with standard doubles with attached bath and TV for Y120. It's barely worth it. There are also modest triples on the roof for Y35 per bed; they're not bad, but it's a long trek to the bathrooms and showers.

Cheaper Tibetan-style hotels can be found in Jiuzhaigou town, about 1km west along the road to Songpan and past the capacious tourist trap resort hotels lining the road. There are a couple such places, with beds in comfortable wooden rooms for around Y15.

A good *bīnguǎn* is the *Jin So Hotel* (look for the yellowish building) – a very modest hotel with friendly staff and doubles for Y80, although they seem amenable to negotiation.

The local *làmiàn* is particularly good. Two small *noodle shops* in Zehwacha serve up this outstanding vegie noodle soup with hand-rolled noodles for Y5. One is just uphill from where the road splits, on the right side. The other is next door to the middle hotel. Otherwise, dining options are limited, so it would be wise to bring some of your own food. Chengdu would be a good place to stock up.

Shuzheng and Zehwacha stockades have the only two *eating halls* resembling anything like a restaurant. Prices are about 15% higher than you're used to paying for similar dishes – not to mention the fact that they lack many items – but you don't have much choice if you haven't packed in sustenance.

Neither place seems to mind you wandering through the kitchen to indicate your choice; there are plenty of local 'specialities' they'll point out. Heye Village is limited to snack vendors and Pepsi.

Getting There & Away

Until local authorities get desperate, level a mountain or two and build an airport, the local bus remains the best means of transport. It can be taken in one dose or as part of a bus/train combination.

The most direct route is to catch the bus from Chengdu to Songpan, and then catch a Nanping bus (which passes Jiuzhaigou) the following day at 6 am. For more details, see the Getting There & Away section for Songpan.

If you're coming down from Gansu via Zöigê, you'll also have to go through Songpan. From Songpan to Jiuzhaigou takes around six hours and costs Y35. The road goes up and over and is gorgeous in parts – but it's also hell on a bus. Alternatively, it is possible to travel direct to Jiuzhaigou by taking a Chengdu-Nanping bus and getting off at Jiuzhaigou. The bus leaves from the Ximen bus station. Most times now you will probably overnight in Maowen or Songpan.

Next to the bus station in Maowen is the Renmin Hotel, with inexpensive three bed dorms. If you nod off and miss the entrance to Jiuzhaigou, you will have to overnight in Nanping and then backtrack the next day. Buses to Nanping cost around Y100 for foreigners.

Bus/train combinations are more troublesome, but can be done. The most popular option is to travel north on the Chengdu-Baoji railway line as far as Zhaohua, where you will have to stay overnight.

From Zhaohua there are usually tour buses to both Jiuzhaigou and Huanglong in the height of the tourist season, but if this isn't the case you can either bus to Nanping and overnight there before doing the final 41km the next morning or take a Chengdu-bound bus to Jiuzhaigou.

Buses for Chengdu go via Nanping and Jiuzhaigou (check to be certain). It's a good idea to book your onward bus ticket as soon as you get into Zhaohua. The road between Zhaohua and Nanping is notoriously dangerous – this is not a trip for those with no stomach for adventurous travel.

Another train/bus option is to take a train or bus to either Mianyang or Jiangyou, both north of Chengdu. Then take a bus to Pingwu, where you can change for a bus to Jiuzhaigou. This road is reportedly superior to the one between Zhaohua and Nanping.

Between October and April snow often cuts off access to Jiuzhaigou for weeks on end. Even at the best of times, transport is not plentiful. To maximise your chances of a seat on a bus out of Jiuzhaigou, it's best to try and book your ticket in advance at the entrance to the reserve. There are two buses daily from the park to Chéngdu that cost around Y100. They can be purchased at the ticket office on the opposite side of the main road from the park entrance.

Hitching with tour buses has reportedly happened, but it's a rare occurrence indeed. To guarantee a seat, pick up the bus where it begins in Nanping (see the Nanping section below); you can pick up a handful of buses headed towards Nanping from the main road at the park entrance. You can get onto a small bus or van for Y15 to Y20 per person. It takes an hour and the road is actually paved, although rife with landslides.

Tours

During summer, a number of companies in Chengdu operate tours to Jiuzhaigou. Some include side trips in the general region. These tours take a lot of the hassle out of travelling in a region where roads and transport links are quite poor. Of course, they also dictate your schedule, which could be a problem if you decide you want to spend some more time in Jiuzhaigou or Songpan, for example.

Most of the trips are advertised for a certain day, but the bus will only go if full. If you are unlucky you may spend days waiting. Find out exactly how many days the trip lasts and which places are to be visited. If you're not sure about the tour company, avoid paying in advance. If there's a booking list, have a look and see how many people have registered. You can register first and pay before departure.

A standard tour includes Huanglong and Jiuzhaigou, lasts seven days and costs a minimum of Y250 to Y300 per person. Hotels, food and entry fees are not included. There are longer tours which include visits to the Tibetan grassland areas of Barkam and Zöigê. Prices vary according to the colour of your skin and the scruples of the companies involved.

Chengdu travel agencies in the Traffic Hotel, the Ximen bus station, the Jinjiang Hotel and CITS all offer tours. The latter two are the most expensive. Check around and compare prices. A word of warning: several tour operators in Chengdu have been blacklisted by travellers for lousy service, rip-offs and rudeness. Ask around among travellers to pinpoint a reliable agency.

NANPING

Nanping has little of interest for travellers unless you like the surreal experience of hearing booming Alanis Morissette being followed by social propaganda echoing through speakers throughout town.

Some people head here either to guarantee a seat on a Chengdu-bound bus, or to take the more scenic side routes via Zhaohua and Jiangyou. Buses will drop you off right in the town centre.

Places to Stay & Eat

The *Yin Yuan Hotel* (☎ 232-2799) *(yínyuán bīnguǎn)* is the best you'll find in town. It's also the only one willing to negotiate on the ridiculous local practice of charging foreigners an 80% mark-up on room rates. You can get a triple for Y150, with some arm-twisting. Other places are a few yuan cheaper, but are not as clean – one or two at least have 24 hour hot water. There is nothing to mention, food-wise.

Getting There & Away

The bus station is a bit complicated. There are two of them, both on the same road, and both far from the centre of town. One is for locals, one is for you. To get there from the Yin Yuan Hotel, bear left after exiting the hotel until you cross a small bridge (there's likely to be no water). Take a right and walk along the opposite embankment – remember, this is China – for approximately 100m until it becomes a small road. Follow this uphill until it finished. Turn right and walk *past* the first station, and continue to the second. Here you can get a ticket for Chengdu (6 am, Y91) after filling out a

SICHUAN

registration form – you may have to lie and say you also have your own insurance.

Trying to get to Jiangyou or Zhaohua is more problematic – the roads, already in horrid shape, wash out with an alarming regularity, so you may be stuck for a spell. Both of these buses also leave at 6 am.

CHENGDU TO XIAHE

This journey has emerged as a popular backdoor route into Gansu Province for many travellers. Those who have done this route in the winter months don't recommend it. The roads often become impassable and temperatures plummet way past the tolerance levels of most mere mortals.

Even in good weather, you need to give yourself at least five days to do the trip, more if you want to poke around some monasteries or make a side trip to Jiuzhaigou.

The first leg is from Chengdu to Songpan (see Getting There & Away in the Songpan section earlier in this chapter). Most travellers take a side trip from Songpan to Jiuzhaigou at this point. From Songpan you can travel 168km north-west to your next overnight stop in Zöigê (ruòèrgài), a dusty little town surrounded by sweeping grasslands. There is some confusion as to the status of Zöigê for individual travellers. There is a 'Foreigners' Registration Office' near the main bus station. Some travellers have successfully ignored it, while others have had to pay for a travel permit. Don't worry about it too much – the PSB will find you if they think it's important.

From the cinema in town it is possible to walk up the hills and visit a couple of monasteries. There are superb views from up here.

There are a couple of hotels in Zöigê which take foreigners. The *Grain Bureau Guest House (liángjú bīnguǎn)* is probably the best choice, with beds in very clean triples for Y11 (Y22 with TV); doubles are Y46. There are common showers and toilets on each floor. To get there, turn right out of the main bus station, and take the first left. You'll come to a three way intersection. Turn right: the hotel is on the left-hand side of the street.

Further down the street, also on the left, the *Zöigê County Government Hostel (ruòèrgài xiànzhèngfǔ zhāodàisuǒ)* is a little bit cheaper at Y10 per bed in a triple, but the rooms are filthy and the toilets putrid. Doubles at the back of the building for Y30 are a bit cleaner.

There are a few *restaurants* and lots of cheap *noodle places* near the Grain Bureau Guest House. You can also get public showers in town (Y3).

Getting There & Away

Zöigê has two bus stations (one at either end of town) with buses back to Songpan and on to Langmusi and Hezuo on alternating days. If you can't get an onward ticket for the next day at one bus station, try the other. Buses to Langmusi leave at 6.40 am, take from two to 3½ hours and cost Y24 for foreigners. Direct buses to Hezuo leave at 6.20 am. The eight hour ride costs Y43.

Langmusi is probably worth a stopover. It's an attractive Tibetan village nestled in the mountains, and travellers have had great visits with the monks at the local lamasery.

From Langmusi it's easy to catch a bus to Hezuo. Hezuo is by all accounts a dump, but is only a few hours from Xiahe, so you may not have to overnight there. From Xiahe you have the option of travelling on to Lanzhou or taking the more unusual option of travelling on to Xining in Qinghai Province via Tongren.

Xinjiang 新疆

Xinjiang *(xīnjiāng)* is the largest province in China, comprising 16% of the country's land surface. Remote and desolate, Xinjiang still retains an air of mystery despite substantial development. Vast deserts and arid plains stretch for thousands of kilometres before ending abruptly at the foot of towering mountain ranges, with most of the population sheltered in the oases scattered along the ancient Silk Road.

Xinjiang is inhabited by at least 13 of China's official 56 national minorities. The Turkic-speaking Muslim Uighurs *(wéiwúěr)* are the most numerous in this interesting population of ethnic groups.

To the west of Ürümqi, where the Tianshan Range divides in two, is the Ili Valley. The population in the valley consists of Kyrgyz, Kazakhs and Han Chinese, and even includes a colony of Sibo (the descendants of the Manchu garrison that was stationed here after the conquests of the 18th century). At the western end of the province near Kashgar live the Kyrgyz, Uzbeks and Tajiks, along with the Uighurs and a relatively small proportion of Han Chinese.

In 1955 the province was renamed the Xinjiang Uighur Autonomous Region. At that time more than 90% of the population was non-Chinese. With the building of the railway from Lanzhou to Ürümqi and the development of industry in the region, there was a large influx of Han Chinese who now form a majority in the northern area while the Uighurs continue to predominate in the south.

Xinjiang's population now exceeds 15 million with the Han making up slightly more than half the total. The Uighur population was recently estimated at 7.2 million.

A dominant feature of Xinjiang is the Tarim Basin, a huge, barely inhabited depression whose centre is the sands of the Taklamakan Desert. Streams flowing into the basin lose themselves and evaporate, never reaching the sea.

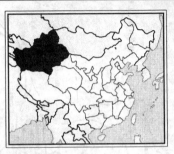

Xinjiang Facts & Highlights

Area: 1,600,000 sq km

Population: 16.9 million

Capital: Ürümqi

Highlights

- Tianchi, a chink of alpine scenery that looks like a Swiss postcard.
- Kashgar, the fabled oasis of the ancient silk road that still retains its exotic eastern feel.
- Travelling the Sino-Pakistani Karakoram Highway, one of the most beautiful road journeys in the world.
- Turpan, a desert oasis, the lowest and hottest spot in China, graced with grape vines, mosques and abandoned ancient cities.

To the east is the remote salt lake of Lop Nur where the Chinese have been testing nuclear bombs since 1964. The western border of the province is defined by the impressive Karakoram mountain range. Near Ürümqi, at Tianchi, and further north near Altai, one can enjoy lush alpine scenery.

Xinjiang is several time zones removed from Beijing, which prefers to ignore the fact. Officially, Beijing time applies; in practice, Xinjiang time is used haphazardly for meal times in hotels, bus departures etc.

XINJIANG

Xinjiang

0 150 300 km

The external boundaries of India on
this map have not been authenticated
and may not be correct.

Xinjiang time is two hours behind Beijing time. Try and straighten out any confusion by asking whether the stated time is Beijing time *(běijīng shíjiān)* or Xinjiang time *(xīnjiāng shíjiān)*. To cater to the time difference, government offices (including the post office and CITS) generally operate from 10 am to 1.30 pm and from 4 to 8 pm. Banking hours are generally 10 am to 7.30 pm, although most outside Ürümqi usually shut the doors for several hours during lunchtime.

History

Xinjiang's history has largely been one of continuing wars and conflicts between the native populations, coupled with repeated Chinese invasions and subjugations.

The first Chinese conquest of Xinjiang was between 73 and 97 AD. With the demise of the Han Dynasty in the 3rd century, the Chinese lost control of the region until the Tang expeditions reconquered it. With the fall of the Tang, the region was once again lost to the Chinese; it was not recovered until the Qing Dynasty (1644-1911).

With the fall of the Qing in 1911, Xin-jiang came under the rule of a succession of warlords, over whom the Kuomintang had very little control. The first of these warlord-rulers was Yang Zhengxin, who ruled from 1911 until his assassination in 1928 at a banquet in Ürümqi (the death rate at Xinjiang banquets was rather appalling).

Yang was followed by a second tyrannical overlord who, after being forced to flee in 1933, was replaced by a still more oppressive leader named Sheng Shicai. The latter remained in power almost until the end of WWII, when he too was forced out.

The only real attempt to establish an independent state was in the 1940s, when a Kazakh named Osman led a rebellion of Uighurs, Kazakhs and Mongols. He took control of south-western Xinjiang and established an independent eastern Turkestan Republic in January 1945.

The Kuomintang convinced the Muslims to abolish their new republic in return for a pledge of real autonomy. This promise wasn't kept, but Chiang Kaishek's preoccupation with the civil war left him with little time to re-establish control over the region.

The Kuomintang eventually appointed a

Foreign Devils on the Silk Road

Adventurers on the road to Xinjiang might like to reflect on an earlier group of European adventurers who descended on Chinese Turkestan, as Xinjiang was then known, and carted off early Buddhist art treasures by the tonne at the turn of the century.

The British first began to take an interest in the Central Asian region from their imperial base in India. They heard from oasis dwellers in the Taklamakan Desert of legendary ancient cities buried beneath the sands of the desert. In 1864 William Johnson was the first British official to sneak into the region, visiting one of these fabled lost cities in its tomb of sand close to Hotan. He was soon followed by Sir Douglas Forsyth, who made a report on his exploits: *On the Buried Cities in the Shifting Sands of the Great Desert of Gobi.* Not long afterwards, the race to unearth the treasures beneath the desert's 'shifting sands' was on.

By 1914, expeditions by Swedes, Hungarians, Germans, Russians, Japanese and French had all taken their share of the region's archaeological treasures. While these explorers were feted and lionised by adoring publics at home, the Chinese today commonly see them as robbers who stripped the region of its past. Defenders point to the wide-scale destruction that took place during the Cultural Revolution and to the defacing of Buddhist artworks by Muslims who stumbled across them. Whatever the case, today most of Central Asia's finest archaeological finds are scattered across the museums of Europe. ∎

XINJIANG

The Beginning or the End?

Uighurs have, with good reason, always viewed Han Chinese as invaders, and relations between the two nationalities have never been good. However, ties have become far more strained since the early 1950s, when Communist China began its policy of bolstering the Xinjiang population with Han settlers.

Although China has actually invested a fair amount of money in developing Xinjiang's economy and infrastructure, Uighurs frequently argue that all the good jobs and business opportunities are dominated by Han Chinese. The more vehement believe that the Chinese regard Uighurs as little more than 'animals, suitable only for hard labour and mindless jobs'. For their part, some Han Chinese have been heard to remark that the Uighurs are 'not a very bright race'. A look through Xinjiang's towns and cities shows little integration between the two nationalities, although there seems to be more Han-Uighur interaction in the capital, Ürümqi. Even there, however, it's possible to detect the underlying tension.

This long simmering Uighur resentment boiled over in February 1997 when Muslim separatists in the northern city of Yining started riots that led to a swift crackdown by Chinese security forces. At least nine people died and nearly 200 were injured, making the protest the most violent to date, according to Chinese media.

Some 30 Muslim residents were arrested for their roles in the riots: three were executed on the day of their trial, the rest were given life sentences. These arrests sparked several deadly responses. In late February separatists blew up three buses in Ürümqi, killing at least nine passengers and wounding many others.

The violence returned to Yining in April, when a mob attacked prison vehicles transporting some of the convicted February rioters. Again, several people were killed or wounded. Uighurs in exile have vowed to continue the campaign of violent protest until Xinjiang gains its freedom from Beijing. At the same time, Beijing has clamped down heavily on separatist activities and is keeping a close watch on all of Xinjiang's Muslims. The question now is: were the February riots the start of a long march towards secession or the last gasp of a hopeless cause? ■

Muslim named Burhan as governor of the region in 1948, unaware that he was actually a Communist supporter.

A Muslim league opposed to Chinese rule was formed in Xinjiang, but in August 1949 a number of its most prominent leaders died in a mysterious plane crash on their way to Beijing to hold talks with the new Communist leaders. Muslim opposition to Chinese rule collapsed, although the Kazakh Osman continued to fight until he was captured and executed by the Chinese Communists in early 1951.

Since 1949, Beijing's main goal has been to keep a lid on minority separatism while flooding the region with Han settlers. Xinjiang's minorities, notably the Uighurs, make little secret of their dislike of China's policies and have staged sporadic protests over the past few decades, some of them violent.

ÜRÜMQI

(wūlǔmùqí)

The capital of Xinjiang, Ürümqi has little to distinguish itself other than the claim to being the furthest city in the world from the ocean. About 1.5 million people live here, 80% of them Han Chinese.

The drab concrete-block architecture has been imported lock, stock and barrel from socialist eastern China, and Ürümqi essentially looks little different from the smoke-stack cities 2000km east. There are few 'sights' as such, but it's an important crossroad and is interesting for all the various nationalities you see on the streets: Uighurs, Kazakhs, Pakistanis, Russians, Uzbeks (and of course Han Chinese and foreign tourists).

Orientation

One of the difficulties of finding your way around is that the streets have a notorious habit of changing names every few blocks. Most of the sights, tourist facilities and hotels are scattered across the city, although they're all easily reached on local buses.

The railway and long-distance bus stations are in the south-western corner of the city. The 'city centre' revolves around the intersection of Minzhu Lu and Jianshe Lu. Here you'll find most of the government offices, fancier hotels and upmarket department stores.

Information

Tourist Offices The Lüyou Hotel (just behind the Holiday Inn) is home to several tourist and travel agencies. Up on the 5th floor is the Xinjiang Overseas Tourist Corporation (☎ 281-4490; fax 282-1445) – a friendly place that can book air tickets, hotels and hire vans.

CITS (☎ 282-6719; fax 281-0689) can be found on the ground floor of the same building, though this branch doesn't seem particularly useful.

CYTS (☎ 281-6018, ext 130; fax 281-7078) seems relatively efficient and cheap for organising tickets and tours. CITS also has an office here that is a bit more helpful than the one in the Lüyou Hotel.

Consulates Kazakhstan has a consulate (☎ 382-1203) in the northern section of the city, several blocks east of Beijing Lu. You can get 10 day transit visas for around US$20 (the cost varies depending on your nationality). There's often a three day wait, although it may take less time if you have an onward visa or if you purchase an airline ticket to Almaty from Kazakhstan Airlines, which has an office in the building (for details see Getting There & Away later in this section).

Tourist visas are also possible to arrange, but only after obtaining a government-authorised invitation from Kazakhstan, a process that can take up to two weeks. The visa section is only open Monday to Thursday from 10 am to 1.30 pm.

To get to the consulate, take bus No 2 up Beijing Lu, get off at the Jingguan Xueyuan (*jīngguǎn xuéyuàn*) stop, and walk north along the road for about 300m until you see a sign for Kazakhstan Airlines. Taking the road to the right from here will bring you to the Huojū Dasha, an enormous maroon and glass hotel/office/commercial complex. The consulate is located one block further east, in a small, white, two storey building.

PSB The main PSB building sits at the north-eastern corner of Minzhu Lu and Jiefang Beilu. Most foreigners, however, will need to continue east along Minzhu Lu. You'll first see an English sign, 'The Administrative Section of Aliens and Exit-Entry of the Municipal Public Security Bureau'. Despite what it says, ignore it and continue around the corner to the left until you reach the 'Aliens Reception Room' (☎ 281-0452, ext 3646) – this is where you'll need to come for visa extensions and travel permits.

Money The Bank of China is at 343 Jiefang Nanlu, close to Renmin Square. There is another Bank of China opposite the main post office.

There are also money-changing facilities inside the Xinjiang Airlines booking office, Lüyou Hotel and Holiday Inn. The latter will only change travellers cheques if you're staying at the hotel.

Post & Communications The main post office is a large Corinthian-colonnaded building directly across the traffic circle from the Hongshan department store. The foreign section is fairly efficient and has a packing service that sells a good variety of boxes and even provides tape that actually sticks to the box, a rarity in China.

XINJIANG

Travel Agencies John's Information Service & Cafe (☎ 231-0191), not far from the Renmin Hotel on Minzhu Lu, is a good source of travel info, and offers competitive rates for vehicle hire and personalised tours around Xinjiang. Staff can also help book air, bus and plane tickets and make hotel reservations.

In addition to the Ürümqi shop, John's has three other branches along the old Silk Road, in Kashgar, Turpan and Dunhuang, which makes them quite reliable for putting together long-distance itineraries. Owner John Hu speaks English and is very helpful, although you usually won't find him in Ürümqi, as he calls Kashgar home.

Xinjiang Autonomous Region Museum

(xīnjiāng wéiwúěr zìzhìqū bówùguǎn)

This museum contains some interesting exhibitions relating to Xinjiang minority groups and is worth a look. Notable among the exhibits are the Daur hats (made from animal heads) with large fur rims – there are about 103,000 Daur people spread across Xinjiang, Inner Mongolia and Heilongjiang.

The Tajik exhibition features silver and coral beads supporting silver pendants – the people number about 29,000 and are found only in Xinjiang. There are about one million Kazakhs living in Xinjiang and their exhibition in the museum features a heavily furnished yurt, complete with a group of stuffed yak, sheep and goats for added realism.

The Mongol exhibit includes particularly ornate silver bridles and saddles studded with semiprecious stones, stringed musical instruments and decorated riding boots.

Another wing of the museum has a fascinating section devoted to history. Prime exhibits are the preserved bodies of nearly a dozen men, women and babies discovered in tombs in Xinjiang: it can get a bit creepy if you're there alone.

The distinctive Soviet-style building with a green dome is on Xibei Lu, about 20 minutes' walk from the Kunlun Guesthouse.

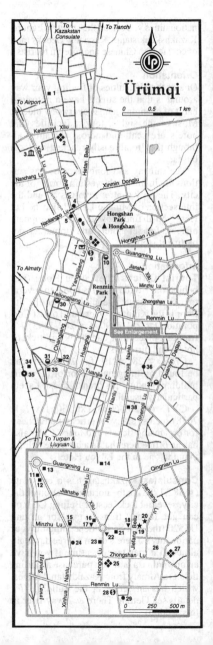

ÜRÜMQI 乌鲁木齐

PLACES TO STAY
1 Kunlun Guesthouse
   昆仑宾馆
11 Holiday Inn
   假日大酒店
12 Lüyou Hotel; CITS
   旅游宾馆
   中国国际旅行社
13 Hongshan Hotel
   红山宾馆
14 Bogda Hotel
   博格达宾馆
16 Renmin Hotel
   人民饭店
21 Xinjiang Electric Power
   Hotel
   新疆电力宾馆
23 City Hotel
   城市大酒店
32 Xinjiang Hotel
   新疆饭店
33 Urumqi Hotel
   乌鲁木齐宾馆
34 Ya'ou Hotel
   亚欧宾馆
38 Overseas Chinese Hotel
   华侨宾馆

PLACES TO EAT
17 John's Information Service
   & Cafe
   约翰咖啡厅

18 Hongchunyuan Restaurant
   鸿春园饭店
22 Dong Nan Wei
   东南味

OTHER
2 Youhao Department
   Store
   友好商场
3 Xinjiang Autonomous
   Region Museum
   新疆维吾尔自治区
   博物馆
4 Xinhua Bookstore
   新华书店
5 China Southern Airlines
   Booking Office
   中国南方航空公司
   售票处
6 Xinjiang Airlines Booking
   Office
   中国新疆航空公司
   售票处
7 Main Post Office
   总邮局
8 Hongshan Department
   Store
   红山商场
9 Bank of China
   中国银行
10 Buses to Tianchi &
   Baiyanggou
   往天池和白杨沟汽车

15 Gleckes Beer Garden
   格力森啤酒庄园
19 PSB Aliens Reception
   Room
   公安局外国人接待室
20 PSB
   公安局
24 Foreign Languages
   Bookstore
   外文书店
25 Dejing Department Store
   德井百货公司
26 Renmin Square
   人民广场
27 Tianbai Department Store
   天百商场
28 Bank of China
   中国银行
29 Xinhua Bookstore
   新华书店
30 Long-Distance Bus
   Station
   长途汽车站
31 Kashgar Bus Station
   喀什办事处
35 Railway Station
   火车站
36 Erdaoqiao Market
   二道桥
37 Buses to Turpan
   (Hengyuan Hotel)
   吐鲁番汽车站
   (恒源饭店)

Opening hours are 9.30 am to 5.30 pm daily and admission is Y25. From Hongshan department store take bus No 7 for four stops and ask to get off at the museum (*bówùguǎn*).

Renmin Park
(*rénmín gōngyuán*)
This scenic, tree-shaded park is about 1km in length and can be entered from either the northern or southern gates. The best time to visit is early in the morning when the Chinese are out here doing their exercises. There are plenty of birds in the park, a few pavilions and a lake where you can hire rowing boats. The park is open from 7.30 am to 10 pm and admission is Y5.

Hongshan Park & Pagoda
(*hóngshān gōngyuán*)
This is Xinjiang's premier amusement park, complete with a ferris wheel, bumper cars and those swinging gondolas designed to bring up your lunch. Other attractions include an eight storey pagoda and sweeping views of the city. It's perhaps an interesting diversion if you've time to spare, but not really worth the Y20 foreigners' entry fee, which doesn't include admission to any of the rides.

Places to Stay – budget
The *Hongshan Hotel* (☎ 281-6018) (*hóngshān bīnguǎn*) is a good base in the centre of town and is not a bad spot for budget travellers. Dorm beds cost Y40 in a three

XINJIANG

bed room without private bath. For Y150 there are cramped and somewhat grubby doubles with private bath; not great value for money.

The Hongshan often becomes full in summer, and some overflow traffic goes to the two star *Bogda Hotel* (☎ 282-3910) *(bógédá bīnguǎn)*. Three-bed dormitories come in at Y47 per person. Double rooms cost Y300, although you can probably bargain them down a bit.

In the vicinity of the railway station, the cheapest option for budget travellers is the *Xinjiang Hotel* (☎ 585-2511) *(xīnjiāng fàndiàn)* at 107 Changjiang Lu. Dorm beds cost Y25 to Y60, and doubles with attached bath are available from Y100.

Another good choice in this area is the *Ya'ou Hotel* (☎ 585-6699) *(yǎ'ōu bīnguǎn)* which is actually adjacent to the railway station. The hotel itself is fine, although the surroundings aren't all that appealing. Dorm beds start at Y20 in a four person room with shared bath. Beds in triples/quads with attached bath are Y58/45, and doubles start at Y158. There is a 50% 'foreigners' surcharge' on these prices, but a bit of bargaining may help. The other plus with this place is that staying here allows you to buy train tickets through the hotel, which is owned by the Ministry of Railways (and thus usually has a good supply of those hard-to-get sleeper tickets).

For relatively cheap doubles, there's the *Overseas Chinese Hotel* (☎ 286-0793) *(huáqiáo bīnguǎn)*, which charges Y140 for rooms in the older, Russian-style building and Y180 in the newer wing.

The *Lüyou Hotel* (☎ 282-1788) *(lǚyóu bīnguǎn)* at 51 Xinhua Beilu is an 11 storey building behind the Holiday Inn. Double rooms are not a bad deal at Y200; they're nothing special, but seem clean enough.

Places to Stay – middle
Ürümqi is overflowing with places that charge between Y300 and Y500 for standard doubles. Most of the better places are located in the city centre, around Minzhu Lu.

In the city centre, the *Xinjiang Electric Power Hotel* (☎ 282-2911) *(xīnjiāng diànlì bīnguǎn)* is actually a pretty good place, despite the silly name. Comfortable doubles range from Y350 to Y480. Nearby, on Hongqi Lu, the newly opened *City Hotel* (☎ 230-9911) *(chéngshì dàjiǔdiàn)* is the fanciest of the mid-range hotels, with well-appointed rooms from Y420, plus a 15% service charge.

Down by the railway station, the *Urumqi Hotel* (☎ 582-2888) *(wūlǔmùqí bīnguǎn)* is also fairly new, and has nice doubles for Y297. Less plush but comfortable triples are pretty good value at Y225.

The *Kunlun Guesthouse* (☎ 484-0411) *(kūnlún bīnguǎn)* at 38 Youhao Beilu is Ürümqi's 'cadre' hotel – a large Russian-style behemoth with overstuffed furniture, a cavernous lobby and Mao-era luxury doubles starting at Y484.

Places to Stay – top end
So far there really is only one place in Ürümqi that can really claim the top-end moniker. The *Holiday Inn Urumqi* (☎ 281-8788; fax 281-7422) *(xīnjiāng jiàrì dàjiǔdiàn)* is the city's sole four star hotel, and its service and facilities still outpace the local competition. Even if you can't afford to stay here, they have great coffee and an excellent breakfast/lunch buffet – all the western food you can eat for Y88. Standard rooms range from Y739 to Y823 depending on the season, while superior rooms are Y924 to Y1050, plus a 15% service charge and 3% tax.

Places to Eat
Ürümqi is not a bad spot to try Uighur foods, such as shish kebab *(kǎoròu)* with flat-bread *(náng)*. Another local speciality is noodles *(lāmiàn)* with spicy vegetables, beef or lamb. There is a row of *restaurants* on Jianshe Lu where you can sample both of these dishes as well as Han Chinese food.

Honqi Lu, in the city centre, is another good street to go restaurant hunting, with lots of noodle and dumpling shops and other small eateries. One place that some locals speak highly of is *Dong Nan Wei (dōng nán wèi)*. It's little more than a hole in the wall, but has a good reputation for its fish *(huángyú)* and spare rib *(páigǔ)* dishes. There's no English to be found anywhere; if you can find a Chinese friend to take you it would help, though you can always resort to pointing at meals on other people's tables.

To soak in the atmosphere of the traditional state-run banquet-style restaurant, you can try the *Hongchunyuan (hóngchūnyuán fàndiàn)*, near the PSB. Here you get the black lacquer tables, gaudy decorations, diffident service and semi-elaborate dishes that foreign tourists used to routinely confront in the late 70s and early 80s. A full meal with drinks will probably cost around Y30 to Y40 per person.

The *Hongshan Hotel Restaurant*, in the southern section of the hotel facing the street, is another good place for reasonably priced Han Chinese dishes. Try their homestyle bean curd *(jiācháng dòufǔ)*, which you can get with a bowl of rice and a beer for Y13.

John's Information Service & Cafe, on Minzhu Lu near the Renmin Hotel, has good Chinese food as well as some reasonably priced western fare, and is a good place to meet up with other travellers and down a few beers.

If you've a craving for western food, the all-you-can-eat breakfast and lunch buffets at the *Holiday Inn* may do the trick. Breakfast is a bit pricey at Y106, but lunch is better value at Y88.

At night the sidewalk area in front of the Renmin Hotel becomes a bustling *night market* with fresh handmade noodle dishes, shish kebab skewers and a whole range of point-and-choose fried dishes. It's definitely worth a look around.

During the summer, the markets are packed with delicious fruit, both fresh and dried. The best is the *Erdaoqiao Market (èrdàoqiáo shìchǎng)* in the southern end of the city, not too far from the Turpan bus station.

Entertainment
One of Ürümqi's more unusual nightlife options has to be *Gleckes Beer Garden*, a combination micro-brewery/discotheque located across from the Lüyou Hotel.

The sister shop of a pub in Beijing, this place is loaded with pseudo-German decor, right down to the frilly blue-and-white striped aprons worn by the waitresses. It's also where the city's rich and famous come to drink and dance. They have to be fairly wealthy, since a pint of beer is around Y35, and a jug Y84! Sadly the beer, made on the premises, is not very good. The entrance to Gleckes is marked by a large beer barrel and some incomprehensible English signs; the bar is located below in the basement.

Getting There & Away
Air China Xinjiang Airlines has flights to Almaty (Kazakhstan), Hong Kong, Islamabad (Pakistan), Novosibirsk (Russia), Tashkent (Uzbekistan) and Moscow. These flights don't always run; for instance the Hong Kong-Ürümqi flight operates only during the peak June-September tourist season.

Siberia Airlines has a booking office (☎ 286-4373) in the Overseas Chinese Hotel and offers twice-weekly flights to Moscow (via Novosibirsk) for US$310, which at the time of writing was less than half the Xinjiang Airlines official price of Y5760. Siberia Airlines also offers flights to Frankfurt via Novosibirsk.

Kazakhstan Airlines (☎ 382-1207) has an office in the Kazakhstan consulate, and offers flights to Almaty for US$141, which again, when we last checked, was cheaper than the Xinjiang Airlines price.

Domestic flights connect Ürümqi with Beijing, Changchun, Changsha, Chengdu, Chongqing, Dalian, Guangzhou, Guilin, Haikou, Hangzhou, Harbin, Kunming, Lanzhou, Qingdao, Shanghai, Shenyang, Shenzhen, Tianjin, Wuhan, Xiamen, Xi'an, Xining and Zhengzhou.

There are also flights from Ürümqi to these towns in Xinjiang: Aksu (Akesu), Altai (Aletai), Fuyun, Hotan (Hetian),

Karamai (Kelamayi), Kashgar (Kashi), Korla (Kuerle), Jumo (Qiemo), Tacheng and Yining. Information on some of these flights can be found in the Getting There & Away sections of the relevant destinations.

The Xinjiang Airlines booking office (☎ 452-0840) is on Youhao Lu, just up the road from the post office; it's open from 10 am to 1.30 pm and from 4 to 8 pm. Bus Nos 1 and 2 go past the office. If this place is crowded, try the China Southern Airlines office just across the street; many of the airline offices in the city are interlinked by computer and can all offer the same tickets.

Bus The long-distance bus station is on Heilongjiang Lu. The departure time given on your ticket is normally Beijing time; check if you're not sure.

There are buses for most cities in Xinjiang, the notable exception being Turpan. Often a 100% foreigners' surcharge is added to the price of tickets, which is a complete scam – you'll still be sitting on the same crowded, ramshackle contraption as the locals. It's also supposedly illegal. You may be able to pay less by showing a student card, but unfortunately this double-pricing rip-off extends to most cities in Xinjiang. There is a tourist complaint hotline (☎ 283-1902) which you can call, although whether this will actually help you get a fair price is questionable.

The most popular destinations within Xinjiang are Turpan and Kashgar. While you can get buses to Kashgar from the main bus station, for both Turpan and Kashgar there are alternative bus stations.

Large public buses and more comfortable minibuses to Turpan run from near the Hengyuan Hotel on Quanyin Dadao, in the southern part of the city. The best way to get there is to hop in a taxi: just tell the driver you want to go to the *tŭlŭfān qìchē zhàn*. The ride shouldn't cost more than Y10 to Y15 from anywhere within the city.

If you're heading to Kashgar, you can get a sleeper bus from either the main station or the Kashgar bus station, which is just east of the railway station. Departure

times and fares are listed in the Getting There & Away sections for the relevant destinations, but always remember that bus schedules in China change like the weather, so try to build some flexibility into your itinerary.

An interesting option is the Almaty *(ālāmùtú)* bus service. The 1052km trip takes 30 hours straight through with three stops for meals, and costs US$50. Getting a visa from the Kazakhstan consulate in Ürümqi might be difficult, as they seem to prefer you take the plane or train.

At the time of writing buses to Almaty were leaving the long-distance bus station once daily at 11 am; check at window No 8 for the latest on this service. The Chinese government might require that you get an exit permit, although when we checked with the Ürümqi PSB, they referred us to the PSB office at the border checkpoint (helpful, eh?). Getting out shouldn't really be a problem, but you should prepare yourself for possible bureaucratic delays.

Train From Ürümqi there are eastbound express trains six times daily. All of these trains run on the same line until Lanzhou, after which they take different routes to their various destinations.

Destination	Train	Departs
Beijing	70	11.14 pm
Chengdu	314	10.33 am
Lanzhou	508	11.50 pm
Shanghai	54	8.47 pm
Xi'an	344	1.47 pm
Zhengzhou	198	1.26 pm

Getting tickets can still be a hassle; hard sleepers on special express trains to places like Beijing and Shanghai sell out quickly, so it's good to book as far in advance as possible.

You might also try going to the station at more irregular hours, such as after 8 pm Beijing time; it's far less crowded and you *may* have luck getting a ticket, although maybe not for the exact departure time you want.

Otherwise try one of the travel agencies

(most charge a Y50 service fee per ticket) or book a room at the Ya'ou Hotel and see if you can buy a ticket through them.

There is a rail link between Ürümqi and Korla via Daheyan (Turpan railway station). The journey lasts about 16 hours and takes you through some interesting desert scenery. This route is served by hard-sleeper trains, making a comfortable journey possible. Apart from the vistas there is not much reason to take these trains, since you end up in Korla (see the Korla section later in this chapter for details).

There are trains running Monday and Saturday from Ürümqi to Almaty, Kazakhstan, which return the following day. The journey takes around 24 hours, and the fare is Y580. At the Ürümqi railway station there's a special ticket window for these trains, inside the large waiting room in the main building. It's only open Monday and Thursday to Saturday, from 10 am to 1 pm and 3 to 7 pm. You will, of course, need a visa for Kazakhstan.

Getting Around

To/From the Airport Minibuses depart from the Xinjiang Airlines office about two hours before flight time and cost Y6. Minibuses also greet all incoming flights and cost Y6.

The airport is 20km from the CAAC office. A taxi should cost between Y40 and Y60, depending on the driver and your bargaining skills.

Bus Ürümqi's public buses are packed to the roof and beyond. It's better to spend a big Y1 for a minibus. If you resort to the public buses, be warned that there have been numerous reports of pickpocketing and bag slashing.

Some of the more useful bus routes include No 7, which runs up Xinhua Lu to Youhao Lu, linking the city centre with the Xinjiang Airlines office and the main post office; and No 2, which runs from the railway station, past the main post office and way up along Beijing Lu, past the Kazakhstan consulate.

AROUND ÜRÜMQI
Tianchi
(tiānchí)
Halfway up a mountain in the middle of a desert, Tianchi (Lake of Heaven) looks like a chunk of Switzerland or Canada that's been exiled to western China.

The small, deep-blue lake is surrounded by hills covered with fir trees and grazed by horses. Scattered around are the yurts of the Kazakh people who inhabit the mountains; in the distance are the snow-covered peaks of the Tianshan Range, and you can climb the hills right up to the snow line. It's a heavily touristed spot, especially in the peak summer season, but is beautiful nonetheless.

The lake is 115km east of Ürümqi at an elevation of 1980m. Nearby is the 5445m-high Bogda Feng, the Peak of God – it can be climbed by well-equipped mountaineers with permits (ask CITS). The lake freezes over in Xinjiang's bitter winter and the roads up here are open only in the summer months.

There are boat cruises on the lake (Y10 per person), although these can be safely skipped. A better way to spend your time is to hike around the lake and even up into the hills. The surrounding countryside is quite beautiful. Follow the track skirting the lake for about 4km to the far end and walk up the valley. During the summer, Kazakhs set up yurts in this area for tourist accommodation at Y40 per person, with three meals. This is not a bad option; during the day the area can get quite cramped with day-trippers, but you'll pretty much have the place to yourself after 4 pm and in the morning. Some people have also brought their owns tents and camped up here.

Horses are also offered (at around Y100 per day) for a trek to the snow line. The return trek takes 10 hours.

The *Xinjiang Tianchi Guesthouse (xījiāng tiānchí bīnguǎn)* on the banks of the lake doesn't do a great job of fitting in with the surroundings, but does have dorm beds for as low as Y15. The food at the restaurant is best avoided.

Buses to Tianchi leave Ürümqi from 9 to

9.30 am from the north gate of Renmin Park. Buy your tickets from a red building to the left of the park entrance: there's a small sign saying 'Regular bus to Tianchi'. Buy your ticket about 30 minutes ahead of time to ensure getting a seat, although more buses are added in summer months to accommodate the crowds.

The return fare is Y25 for large buses, which take three hours one way, or Y50 for the minibuses, which can get there as quickly as two hours. There are also usually private buses leaving from in front of the Hongshan Hotel, and return fares from here can be as little as Y30. Buses back to Ürümqi leave between 4 and 4.30 pm.

Baiyanggou
(báiyánggōu)

Baiyanggou, also known as the Southern Mountains *(nánshān)*, is a vast expanse of grazing land set in a valley surrounded by snow-capped peaks. The valley is 2100m above sea level and 75km south of Ürümqi.

The land is inhabited by Kazakh herdsmen who graze sheep, cattle and horses here during the summer months. Although not quite as stunning as Tianchi, it's nevertheless a beautiful place. The upper end of the valley is most impressive – surrounded by spruce trees is a waterfall with a drop of 40m.

It's a 1½ to 2½ hour ride from Ürümqi, depending on whether you take a minibus or a large bus. The directions for getting a bus are the same as for Tianchi – at the northern and southern gates of Renmin Park in Ürümqi there are buses departing at approximately 9 am from where the sign says 'Regular Bus Service'. However, buses only run from around June to September. Return fares are Y20 to Y25 for the large buses, and Y40 to Y50 for the minibuses.

As at Tianchi, it's possible to stay in the pasturelands at some of the Kazakh yurts.

DAHEYAN
(dàhéyàn)

The jumping-off point for Turpan is a place on the railway line signposted 'Turpan Zhan'

(tǔlǔfān zhàn). In fact, you are actually in Daheyan, and the Turpan oasis is a 58km drive south across the desert. Daheyan is not a place you'll want to hang around, so spare a thought for the locals, who have to eke out a sane living here.

The bus station is a five minute walk from the railway station. Walk up the road leading from the railway station and turn right at the first main intersection; the bus station is a few minutes' walk ahead on the left-hand side of the road.

Minibuses run from here to Turpan about once every 30 minutes throughout the day. The fare is Y6 for the trip, which takes 1½ hours.

Although Daheyan railway station is rarely crowded, buying a ticket to anywhere can be a slow process here, and it can be difficult to get hard-sleeper tickets, as most of these will have already been sold from Ürümqi.

Most travellers are interested in the trains heading east, since people going westwards from Turpan usually opt for the bus to Ürümqi, which is much faster than trekking up here to catch a train. All express trains heading east go as far as Lanzhou, from where they then diverge to other destinations in China.

The schedule of eastbound trains from Daheyan is as follows:

Destination	Train	Departs
Beijing	70	1.40 am
Chengdu	314	1.08 pm
Lanzhou	508	2.23 am
Shanghai	54	11.13 pm
Xi'an	344	4.22 pm
Zhengzhou	198	3.54 pm

Trains from Daheyan to Ürümqi take 2½ hours. It takes 12 hours to get to Liuyuan, 17 hours to Jiayuguan, and 33 hours to Lanzhou (though the special express trains are a bit quicker).

You can also get trains from Daheyan to Korla, although there really is no pressing reason to go there. But for the record, the trip takes 10 to 11 hours. For details see the Korla section later in the chapter.

TURPAN
(tŭlŭfān)

East of Ürümqi the Taishan mountains split into a southern and a northern range; and between the two lie the Hami and Turpan basins. Both are below sea level and receive practically no rain; summers are searingly hot.

Part of the Turpan Basin is 154m below sea level – it's the lowest spot in China and the second lowest depression in the world (after the Dead Sea).

Turpan County is inhabited by about 170,000 people – about 120,000 are Uighurs and the rest mostly Chinese. The centre of the county is the Turpan oasis, a small city set in a vast tract of grain fields. Despite the concrete-block architecture of the city centre, it's a pleasant, relaxing place. Many of the smaller streets have pavements covered with grapevine trellises, which are a godsend in the fierce heat of summer.

Moving further out of town, the narrow streets are lined with mud-brick walls enclosing thatch-plaster houses. Open channels with flowing water run down the sides of the streets; the inhabitants draw water from these and use them to wash their clothes, dishes and themselves.

Some of Turpan's hotels provide good spots to sit underneath the vine trellises and contemplate the moon and stars. The living is relatively cheap, the food is good, the people friendly, and there are numerous interesting sights scattered around to keep you occupied.

Turpan holds a special place in Uighur history, since nearby Gaochang was once the capital of the Uighurs. It was an important staging post on the Silk Road and was a centre of Buddhism before being converted to Islam in the 8th century. During the Chinese occupation it served as a garrison town.

Turpan is also the hottest spot in China – the highest recorded temperature here was 49.6°C (121.3°F). Fortunately, the humidity is low – so low that your laundry is practically dry by the time you hang it out!

Orientation

The centre of the Turpan oasis is called 'Old City' *(lăochéng)* and the western part is called 'New City' *(xīnchéng)*. The Old City is where you'll find the tourist hotels, shops, market, long-distance bus station and restaurants – all within easy walking distance of each other. Most of the sights are scattered on the outskirts of the oasis or in the surrounding desert.

Information

CITS (☎ 521-352) has a branch on the grounds of the Oasis Hotel, and can help book train and aeroplane tickets, as well as arrange tours of local sights, although these tend to be fairly expensive.

The PSB is on Gaochang Lu, north of the Gaochang Hotel.

The Bank of China has a branch near the bus station. You can also change money at the Oasis and Turpan hotels.

The post office is right near the bus station and the bazaar. There is also a post office inside the Oasis Hotel that handles parcels.

Bazaar
(shì màoyī shìchăng)

While this market is fun to poke around, it's nothing like its more exotic counterpart in Kashgar. At the front you'll find a few stalls selling brightly decorated knives, Muslim clothing and some other interesting items, but as you move towards the back it's mainly household goods and synthetic fabrics.

City Mosque
(qīngzhēn sì)

There are several mosques in town. The City Mosque, the most active of them, is on the western outskirts about 3km from the town centre. Take care not to disturb the worshippers. You can get here by bicycle.

Emin Minaret
(émĭn tă)

Also known as Sugongta, this tower and adjoining mosque is just 3km from Turpan on the eastern edge of town. It's designed in a simple Afghani style and was built in 1777 by the local ruler, Emin Hoja.

Rumour has it that the mosque was originally Emin's home, and that he was only able to build the elaborate structure after Qing Dynasty Emperor Qianlong gave him a cash reward for helping to suppress local Muslim rebels. However, there is no historical evidence to support this theory.

The minaret is circular, 44m high and tapers towards the top. The temple is bare inside, but services are held every Friday and on holidays. The surrounding scenery is nice, and from the roof of the mosque you can get a good view of the Turpan oasis. You can't climb the minaret: it was closed off to tourists in 1989 to help preserve the structure.

You can walk or bicycle here, although many people stop here on a minibus tour. The mosque is open during daylight hours and entry is Y12.

Places to Stay

Right next to the busy bus station, the *Jiaotong Hotel* (☎ 523-238) *(jiāotōng bīnguǎn)* is pretty noisy, but is among the cheapest spots in town. It has three, four and five person dorms with fan for Y36/24/16 per person. Doubles with attached bath and aircon cost Y60 or Y80.

A far better deal (and more pleasant environment) can be had at the *Oasis Hotel* (☎ 522-478) *(lǜzhōu bīnguǎn)*. Beds in a four person room with air-con and shared bath cost Y22. Doubles are more expensive,

Turpan

To Ūrūmqi & Daheyan

0   300   600 m
Approximate Scale

Old City

To New City & City Mosque

To Emin Minaret

TURPAN 吐鲁番	PLACES TO EAT	2 Bank of China
		中国银行
PLACES TO STAY	5 Muslim Dumpling Shop	3 Turpan Museum
4 Gaochang Hotel	饺子馆	吐鲁番博物馆
高昌宾馆	7 Silk Road Restaurant	6 Gaochang Park
8 Oasis Hotel;	丝路酒家	高昌公园
CITS	10 Fresh Food Market	16 Department
绿洲宾馆	鲜食市场	Store
中国国际旅行社	11 Small Restaurants	吐鲁番百货大楼
9 Turpan Hotel	小餐厅	18 Long-Distance
(Fandian)	14 Small Restaurants	Bus Station
吐鲁番饭店	小餐厅	长途汽车站
12 Yiyuan Hotel	15 Lanxin Restaurant	19 Post Office
颐园宾馆	兰新餐厅	邮局
13 Grain Trade Hotel	22 John's Information & Cafe	20 Bazaar
粮贸宾馆	约翰中西餐厅	吐鲁番市贸易市场
17 Jiaotong Hotel		21 Bank of China
交通宾馆	**OTHER**	中国银行
23 Turpan Hotel (Binguan)	1 PSB	
吐鲁番宾馆	公安局	

XINJIANG

starting at Y200, and these prices tend to rise during the peak summer season. The hotel enjoys a quiet location and has a fairly nice courtyard with grapevine trellises and tree-lined walkways.

Down from the Oasis is the *Yiyuan Hotel* (☎ 522-170) *(yíyuán bīn-guǎn)*, a small, friendly place which has doubles with attached bath for Y50 per person for older rooms, and Y80 for newer ones.

Just to make things more confusing for non-Chinese speakers, Turpan has two places called the 'Turpan Hotel' (although the Chinese names are different). The more inviting of the two is the *Turpan Hotel (Binguan)* (☎ 522-301) *(tǔlǔfān bīnguǎn)*, which is also sometimes referred to as the Turpan Guesthouse. This place has a nice vine-trellised courtyard, quiet rooms and even a swimming pool, although the water can get a bit slimy. Doubles are Y120 for the older, shabbier rooms, and Y280 for newer rooms in the rather odd-looking 'Uighur-style' wing at the rear of the complex. Neither option is a great bargain, but the location is nice.

The *Turpan Hotel (Fandian)* (☎ 522-170) *(tǔlǔfān fàndiàn)* is large and not terribly attractive, but it is cheaper. Dorm beds cost Y20 in a windowless basement 'cell', Y32 in a triple with fan and Y46/56 in doubles/triples with air-con. Doubles are Y180 to Y280. The entrance to the hotel is via a driveway on the northern side of the building facing the main road: look for the sign that says 'Housekeeping Department'.

Nearby, the *Gaochang Hotel* (☎ 525-134) *(gāochāng bīnguǎn)* is not a bad deal, especially for the triples with attached bath and air-con at Y60 per person. Doubles are Y80 to Y100 per person.

The *Grain Trade Hotel* (☎ 522-448) *(liángmào bīnguǎn)* is another large rambling place that has dorm beds from Y30 and doubles for Y180, although it should be easy to bargain down to a lower price.

Places to Eat
There is a string of small *restaurants* along Laocheng Lu, between Gaochang Lu and Qingnian Lu. Quite a few have English menus, and the food is generally good and reasonably priced. Most of the places serve Sichuan and other Han-style dishes, but you can also get Uighur food on request. There are similar groups of *restaurants* on Qingnian Zhonglu, both north and south of the Yiyuan Hotel.

There are also a few small *Uighur places* between the Gaochang and Turpan hotels on Gaochang Lu. Notable among these is a tiny dumpling *(jiǎozi)* place that serves great mutton boiled dumplings for Y0.5 apiece, surely one of the best bargains in town.

Opposite the Turpan Hotel (Binguan) is *John's Information Service & Cafe* (☎ 524-237). This is the only place in town that does good western food, but there are Chinese meals available too. The menu is in English, prices are reasonable and you can even get cold drinks with ice (much appreciated in Turpan's heat!).

Opposite the Oasis Hotel, the *Silk Road Restaurant* is more of a tourist trap, with fairly pricey Chinese food and the occasional Muslim dish thrown in for good measure.

Entertainment
A traditional Uighur music, song and dance show is staged in the courtyard of the *Turpan Hotel* (Binguan) under the trellises almost nightly in the tourist season (summer). In the off season performances take place on the 2nd floor of the hotel restaurant building. Most of the singers and dancers are women, but there is usually at least one man.

During the summer, the shows are held almost every night from around 10 pm. They're fun nights that usually end up with the front row of the audience being dragged out to dance with the performers. Admission is Y20.

Getting There & Away
Bus The bus station is near the bazaar. Try and get there early, as there is often a long queue for tickets.

There are 10 to 12 buses to Ürümqi that leave between 8 am and 6 pm. The journey should cost Y15, although foreigners are often charged double. It's nice scenery along the way – immense grey sand dunes, and snow-capped mountains visible in the distance. The 180km trip takes four hours. A new highway between the two cities, slated to open in 1999, should cut travel time in half.

Minibuses to Daheyan run approximately once every 30 minutes between 8 am and 6 pm, take 1½ hours for the trip and cost Y6. There is one bus daily to Korla leaving around 8.30 am, but the road is quite poor and locals don't recommend the trip, which takes anywhere from seven to 10 hours. Taking the train from Daheyan is a better option (see the Korla section for details).

Train The nearest railway station is at Daheyan, 58km north of Turpan. There are trains going east and west, but most travellers will only want to use the eastbound ones since direct buses to Ürümqi are faster and more convenient than the train. See the previous Daheyan section for the train schedule.

Getting Around
Public transport around Turpan is by minibus, bicycle or donkey cart. Bicycles are most convenient for the town itself. John's Cafe has a few for rent at Y5 per hour or Y25 for the day. The Turpan Hotel (Binguan) also has bicycle rental, but only during the summer. Minibus drivers usually hang around the hotel gates – negotiate the fare in advance. Donkey carts can be found around the market, but this mode of transport is gradually fading.

AROUND TURPAN
There are many sights in the countryside around Turpan, and it requires at least a day to see everything of importance.

The only way to see the sights is to hire a minibus for a full day (about 10 hours). You won't have to look for them – the drivers will come looking for you. It's easy

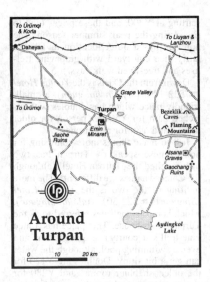

to find other travellers to share the expense. Figure on paying between Y300 and Y500 (depending on your bargaining skill) for the whole group. The minibuses normally hold six passengers; any more than eight would be uncomfortable.

Make sure it's clearly understood which places you want to see. A trip might include Atsana Graves, Gaochang Ruins, Bezeklik Caves, Grape Valley, Emin Minaret, the Karez underground irrigation channels and Jiaohe Ruins (usually in that order). Practically no drivers speak English, but many speak fluent Japanese, a testament to the popularity of Turpan with Japanese tourists.

Don't underestimate the weather. The desert sun is hot – damn hot – and it can bake your brain in less time than it takes to make fried rice. Essential survival gear includes a water bottle, sunglasses and a straw hat. Some sunscreen and vaseline (or chapstick) for your lips will prove useful.

Atsana Graves
(āsītǎnà gǔmùqū)
These graves, where the dead of Gaochang are buried, lie north-west of the ancient city.

Only three of the tombs are open to tourists, and each of these is approached by a short flight of steps which leads down to the burial chamber about 6m below ground level.

One tomb contains portraits of the deceased painted on the walls, while another has paintings of birds. The third tomb holds two well-preserved corpses (one mummy from the original trio seems to have been removed to Turpan's museum) like those in the museums at Ürümqi and Hangzhou.

Some of the artefacts date back as far as the Jin Dynasty, from the 3rd to 5th centuries AD. The finds include silks, brocades, embroideries and many funerary objects, such as shoes, hats and sashes made of recycled paper. The last turned out to be quite special for archaeologists, since the paper included deeds, records of slave purchases, orders for silk and other everyday transactions. Admission is Y15.

Gaochang Ruins
(gāochāng gùchéng)
About 46km east of Turpan are the ruins of Gaochang, the capital of the Uighurs when they moved into the Xinjiang region from Mongolia in the 9th century.

The town was founded in the 7th century during the Tang Dynasty and became a major staging post on the Silk Road. The walls of the city are clearly visible. They stood as much as 12m thick, formed a rough square with a perimeter of 6km, and were surrounded by a moat. Gaochang was divided into an outer city, an inner city within the walls, and a palace and government compound.

A large monastery in the south-western part of the city is in reasonable condition, with some of its rooms, corridors and doorways still preserved. The entry fee is Y20.

Flaming Mountains
(huǒyànshān)
North of Gaochang lie the aptly named Flaming Mountains – they look like they're on fire in the midday sun. Purplish-brown in colour, they are 100km long and 10km wide. The minibus tours don't usually include a stop here, but they drive through on the way to Bezeklik Caves.

The Flaming Mountains were made famous in Chinese literature by the classic novel *Journey to the West*. The story is about the monk Xuan Zang and his followers who travelled west in search of the Buddhist sutra. The mountains were a formidable barrier which they had to cross.

Bezeklik Thousand Buddha Caves
(bózīkèlǐ qiānfó dòng)
On the north-western side of the Flaming Mountains, on a cliff face fronting a river valley, are the remains of these Buddhist cave temples. All the caves are in dreadful condition, most having been devastated by Muslims or robbed by all and sundry.

The large statues which stood at the back of each cave have been destroyed or stolen, and the faces of the buddhas ornamenting the walls have either been scrapped or completely gouged out. Particularly active in the export of murals was a German, Albert von Le Coq, who removed whole frescoes from the stone walls and transported them back to the Berlin Museum – where Allied bombing wiped most of them out during WWII.

Today the caves reveal little more than a hint of what these works of art were like in their heyday. Photography is forbidden inside the caves, but there isn't much reason to bother. Fortunately, the scenery just outside the caves is fine. Admission is Y20.

Grape Valley
(pútáo gōu)
In this small paradise – a thick maze of vines and grape trellises – stark desert surrounds you. Most of the minibus tours stop here for lunch; the food isn't bad, and there are plenty of grapes in season (early September is best).

There is a winery *(guǒjiǔchǎng)* near the valley and lots of well-ventilated brick buildings for drying grapes – wine and raisins are major exports of Turpan. CITS runs an annual 'grape festival' in August, featuring dancing singing, wine-tasting and, of course, a lot of grape eating.

Tempting as it might be, don't pick the grapes here or anywhere else in Turpan. There is a Y15 fine if you do. Considerable effort goes into raising these grapes and the farmers don't appreciate tourists eating their profits. There's a Y10 entry fee for the Grape Valley.

Karez Underground Irrigation Channels
(kǎn ěr jǐng)

These underground channels rate as one of ancient China's greatest public works projects. The word 'karez' means wells. The wells are sunk at various points to the north of Turpan to collect ground water, which comes from melting snow in the Bogdashan mountains. The ground water then passes through underground channels to irrigate farms in the valley below.

The city of Turpan owes its existence to these vital wells and channels, some of which were constructed over 2000 years ago. Part of the channel system is on the surface, but putting them underground greatly reduces water loss from evaporation. They are fed entirely by gravity, thus eliminating the need for pumps.

There are over a thousand wells, and the total length of the channels exceeds 3000km. It's remarkable to think that this extensive irrigation system was all constructed by hand and without modern machinery or building materials.

There are a number of places to view the channels, but most of the minibus tours stop at one particular spot on the western side of Turpan. Admission to this site is Y8.

Jiaohe Ruins
(jiāohé gǔchéng)

During the Han Dynasty, Jiaohe was established by the Chinese as a garrison town to defend the borderlands. The city was decimated by Genghis Khan's 'travelling road show' and there's little left to see.

The buildings are rather more obvious than the ruins of Gaochang though, and you can walk through the old streets and along the roads. A main road cuts through

the city, and at the end is a large monastery with figures of Buddha still visible.

The ruins are around 7km to 8km west of Turpan and stand on an island bound by two small rivers – thus the name Jiaohe, which means 'confluence of two rivers'. During the cooler months you can cycle out here without any problem. Getting in to see them will cost you Y20.

Sand Therapy Clinic
(shā liáo zhàn)

More than 5000 people a year – mostly Kazakhs – come to Turpan to get buried up to their necks in the sand. It is believed that the hot sand can greatly relieve the aches of rheumatism.

The Sand Therapy Clinic is pretty much an outdoor sandbox, and it only operates from June to August. There's not much to see here and the minibuses usually don't include this as part of your tour except by special request.

Aydingkol Lake
(àidīng hú)

At the very bottom of the Turpan depression is Aydingkol Lake, 154m below sea level. The 'lake' usually has little water – it's a huge, muddy evaporating pond with a surface of crystallised salt, but technically it's the second lowest lake in the world, surpassed only by the Dead Sea in Israel and Jordan.

Most of the tours do not stop here. If you want to see Aydingkol Lake, tell your driver and expect to pay extra for the additional distance. And be forewarned that it's a pretty rough ride.

KORLA
(kùěrlè)

Korla was an important junction on the old Silk Road. The famous travelling monk Xuan Zang paid an obligatory visit in the 7th century. However, visits certainly aren't mandatory these days.

There's nothing to see in Korla, and the surrounding sites are of mild interest at best. However, if you're of a mind to travel the traditional northern Silk Road (as opposed to taking the sleeper bus direct from Ürümqi to Kashgar), you'll likely have to stop here.

The town of Yanqi, 52km north of Korla (accessible by rail or bus), has some nearby Buddhist caves. However, the prime attraction is Bosten Lake (*bósīténg hú*), the largest lake in Xinjiang. From Yanqi to the lakeside centre of Bohu is about 12km. Access to the lake from Bohu could involve a mud-wading expedition, but the fishing villages can be worth visiting.

There are two buses daily to Bohu from the Korla bus station. The 64km journey costs Y14. You can also hire a vehicle to take you there and back for around Y300.

Places to Stay
Last we checked there were no cheap places for foreigners to stay in Korla. The *Bosten Hotel* (☎ 202-4103) (*bósīténg bīnguǎn*) is the least expensive, with doubles from Y210.

The *Loulan Hotel* (☎ 202-2999) (*lóulán bīnguǎn*) tore out its dorms when it remodelled, and now only has doubles and triples for Y300.

The top stop in town is the *Bayinguoleng Hotel* (☎ 202-2248) (*bāyīnguólèng bīnguǎn*) where doubles start at Y420. All the hotels are several kilometres from both the bus and railway stations, so you'll probably have to get a taxi to reach them.

Getting There & Away
Air There are one to three flights weekly between Ürümqi and Korla, depending on the season. The one way fare is Y400 and flight time is 1¾ hours.

Bus Korla is 470km from Ürümqi and the bus ride takes 12 hours. There are five buses daily, several of which are sleepers. The Chinese fare is Y33 for the regular bus and Y72 for the sleeper, although the bus stations at either end will probably try and charge you double these prices.

Buses to Kuqa leave when full between 8 am and 5 pm. The ride is a bumpy six to seven hours, and costs Y20 for Chinese,

and Y40 for foreigners. There are also sleeper buses to Kashgar in the morning and evening, although these are sometimes cancelled if there aren't enough passengers. Foreigners are generally charged Y290 for the 36 hour ride.

Going the other direction, there are several buses daily to Turpan, but at the time of writing the road was plagued by frequent landslides, and locals strongly discouraged travellers taking this route.

Train A rail line links Korla with Ürümqi via Daheyan (Turpan railway station). Train No 756 leaves Ürümqi at 3.34 pm, stops at Daheyan at 6.08 pm, and arrives in Korla at 7.18 am.

Train No 202 is a 'tourist' train, which means it only makes a few stops. It leaves Ürümqi at 10.02 pm, departs Daheyan at 12.14 am and arrives in Korla at 9.58 am. Of course with this latter train you miss all the scenery. There is also the No 367 which runs to Xi'an via Daheyan; heading to Korla you can pick it up from Daheyan at 10.34 am. All trains have hard-sleeper cars.

The railway station is about 4km south of the town centre, so you'll need to take a bus or taxi to get to either the hotels or the bus station. Buses heading from the railway station to the north railway station (*běizhàn*) – a freight depot – pass by the bus station.

KUQA
(*kùchē*)
This oasis town was another key stop on the ancient Silk Road. Scattered around the area are at least seven Thousand Buddha Caves (*qiānfó dòng*) which rival those of Dunhuang, Datong and Luoyang. There are also at least four ancient ruined cities in the area.

The Buddhist cave paintings and ruined cities in the area are remains of a pre-Islamic Buddhist civilisation. When the 7th century Chinese monk Xuan Zang passed through Kuqa he recorded that the city's western gate was flanked by two enormous 30m-high buddha statues, and that there was a number of monasteries in the area decorated with beautiful Buddhist frescoes; 1200 years later, the German archaeologist-adventurers Grünwedel and Le Coq removed many of these paintings and sculptures and took them to Berlin.

Although not nearly as drab as Korla, modern-day Kuqa retains little, if any, of its former glory. There is still some traditional architecture remaining, and traffic jams of donkey-cart taxis add some appeal. But for most people, it's the sights outside the town that would justify a stop here.

Molana Eshding Tomb
(mòlánà éshídīng mázā)

Tucked away on a little road north of the Qiuci Hotel is the tomb of Eshding, who is credited with being the first Islamic missionary from the Middle East to visit Kuqa. This place is also known as the Molana Hoja Tomb: 'Molana' means 'the sage's descendants'.

Eshding died in Kuqa from unknown causes, and his tomb is a fairly nice work of art. The four large Chinese characters on the tomb mean 'the Arabian sages'. Supposedly there's an admission fee of Y10, but if you go early in the morning there may not be anyone awake to charge you. To get there, take the dirt path leading back along the eastern side of the Qiuci Hotel.

Qiuci Ancient City Ruins
(qiūcī gǔchéng)

These ruins are all that is left of the ancient capital of Qiuci. Qiuci was one of several ancient feudal states in what was once loosely called the Western Region of China.

Qiuci has had several name changes. During the Han Dynasty it was named Yancheng, but in the Tang era (when Xuan Zang dropped in) it was called Yiluolu. The ruins are along the main road, about a 10 minute walk west of the Qiuci Hotel.

Bazaar & Great Mosque
(lǎochéng bāzā, qīngzhēn dàsì)

Every Friday a large bazaar is held about 2.5km west of town next to a bridge on

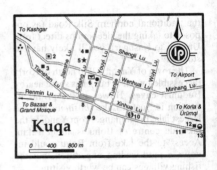

KUQA 库车

1 Qiuci Ancient City Ruins
龟兹古城
2 Molana Eshding Tomb
默拉纳额什丁麻扎
3 Qiuci Hotel
龟兹宾馆
4 Kuqa Hotel
库车宾馆
5 PSB
公安局
6 Post & Telephone Office
邮电局
7 Xinhua Bookstore
新华书店
8 Night Market
夜市
9 Farmers' Market
农贸市场
10 Bank of China
中国银行
11 Tongda Hotel; CITS
通达大饭店
中国国际旅行社
12 Jiaotong Hotel
交通宾馆
13 Bus Station
客运站

Renmin Lu. Traders come in from around the countryside to ply their crafts, wares and foodstuffs. While the local tourism offices are trying to make it a sightseeing draw, the bazaar is thus far largely a local affair, and is worth a visit.

Another kilometre west from the bazaar is the Great Mosque, Kuqa's main centre for Muslim worship. Though large in size, the mosque is a fairly modest affair, but some of the carvings around the main gateway are quite elaborate.

Places to Stay

The cheapest spot in town, without question, is the *Jiaotong Hotel* (☎ 712-2682) *(jiāotōng bīnguǎn)*. Dorm beds in quads/doubles with shared bath are Y10/20, while doubles with attached bath are Y60. Staff claim there's always hot water, but this does seem a bit optimistic.

The *Kuqa Hotel* (☎ 712-2901) *(kùchē bīnguǎn)* offers nicer surroundings and facilities, and has dorm beds for Y22. Fairly clean doubles are Y124.

When you get off the bus, people may try and take you to the *Qiuci Hotel* (☎ 712-2005) *(qiūcī bīnguǎn)*, the main tourist lodgings in town. Unless you're really not concerned with how you spend your money, you should give this place a miss. For Y280 you get a mouldy, grubby double – definitely not worth it. The hotel is also a good 1.5km from the town centre, although it is close to the Molana Eshding Tomb and the Qiuci Ancient City ruins.

Getting There & Away

Air There are flights from Ürümqi (via Korla) once or twice a week, but these only materialise in the summer peak travel months. The one way fare is Y640, and total flight time is 3¼ hours.

It is not possible to fly onwards from Kuqa to Kashgar, so you'll have to backtrack to Ürümqi for this.

Bus The best way to visit Kuqa is probably to come from Kashgar. Of course getting there from Ürümqi is no problem, but getting buses onwards to Kashgar can be a hassle, as you'll probably have to spend half the day at the bus station waiting for an Ürümqi-Kashgar bus to pull in, and only then will you know if a seat or berth is available.

These buses stop in Kuqa some time between 11 am and 4 pm, depending on your progress en route. From Kuqa to Kashgar takes around 15 hours, barring breakdowns and bad weather.

Buses from Ürümqi take about 24 hours to reach Kuqa. From the main bus station in Ürümqi there are two to three buses daily, at least one of which will be a sleeper. Regular buses cost Y52, sleepers Y114 (Chinese price).

From Kuqa there are three to four buses to Ürümqi daily, including one sleeper. The Chinese price is Y122, and for foreigners it's Y244. There are also two buses daily to Daheyan (no sleepers however). The trip takes around 20 hours and costs Y47 for Chinese, and Y94 for foreigners.

The bus station is about 1.5km from the centre of town, so you may want to take a donkey cart or taxi if you're staying at the Kuqa or Qiuci hotels.

Getting Around

To/From the Airport A taxi to the Kuqa airport should cost around Y15 to Y20.

Car Kuqa's sights are scattered around the surrounding countryside, and the only way to get to see them is to hire a vehicle. CITS (☎ 712-2524) has a branch on the 3rd floor of a concrete block in a small courtyard that also houses the Tongda Hotel. They can arrange jeep or car hire for the day.

Taxi drivers will usually offer a better rate, although CITS may be a bit more reliable.

Taxi Within town, taxi rides are a standard Y10 per trip, while horse or donkey carts are generally Y2 to Y3, depending on the distance. Unfortunately at the time of writing there was no bicycle hire in Kuqa.

AROUND KUQA
Kizil Thousand Buddha Caves
(kèzīěr qiānfó dòng)
There are quite a lot of Thousand Buddha Caves around Kuqa, but the most important site is this one, around 70km to the west of Kuqa in Baicheng County. The caves date back to the 3rd century AD.

Although there are more than 230 caves here, only around 10 are generally open to the public unless you pay heavily for the privilege of seeing the others. The basic entry fee is Y45, and access to additional caves can cost up to Y150 per cave! A no-photography rule is in force.

Other Buddhist cave sites around Kuqa include **Kumtura** and **Kizilgaha**. At Kizilgaha, many travellers also like to visit the Beacon Tower (*fēnghuǒtái*), a watchtower where the defenders burned animal dung to signal the approach of the enemy. Other beacon towers passed the message along in the same fashion, thus forming an ancient version of the information superhighway. The tower is 15m high and made out of mud, clay bricks and wood.

Kumtura is only partially opened, and some travellers have told of being charged Y500 for the privilege of viewing the caves here. Considering that it takes most of the day to get there and back, most travellers opt to forgo this particular trip.

The only way to get to these sites is to hire a vehicle. CITS charges Y300 for the return trip, while private taxi drivers offer rates of around Y200. The one way journey to Kizil and Kazilgaha takes one to two hours, that to Kumtura closer to four.

Ancient City Ruins
(*gǔchéng*)
Aside from Qiuci (in Kuqa itself), there are several other ruined cities in the region. Around 23km to the north-east of Kuqa is the ancient city of Subashi. About 20km to the south of Kuqa is the ancient city of Wushkat.

About 60km south-west of Kuqa is Tonggusibashi, one of the largest and best preserved of the ruined cities. Again you'll have to hire a vehicle to get to these spots; rates are similar to those for the Kizil Caves.

KASHGAR
(*kāshí*)
Even as the 20th century draws to a close, the name Kashgar still sparks images of a remote desert oasis, the sole outpost of civilisation separating the vast deserts of Xinjiang from the sheer peaks of the Karakoram Range. Desert nomads, exotic bazaars, dramatic costumes and colourful silks: some or all of these come to mind at the mention of modern China's westernmost city.

Well, it's no longer that remote, and modernisation has certainly made its mark. Kashgar is only 1½ hours by plane from Ürümqi, or less than two days by bus. Modern hotels and even a few office towers signal the start of what will perhaps become the city's 'skyline'. But even so, Kashgar retains an air of the exotic, due mainly to its fascinating ethnic mix of Uighurs (who comprise the majority of the population), Tajiks, Kyrgyz, Uzbeks and a relatively small number of Han Chinese.

Traders from Kazakhstan, Kyrgyzstan, Pakistan and even Russia steadily flow in and out of town, along with travellers from around the globe.

Kashgar's traditional ways of life also continue. An hour's walk through town will reveal Uighur craftsmen with decades of history on their weather-worn faces; markets with rows of shimmering silks, knives and jewellery and narrow backstreets lined with old plaster-thatch homes. With all the trading activity, one couldn't call Kashgar 'laid-back', but it has a great atmosphere and is a fine place to settle back for a week or so. There are also some worthwhile sights outside the city, notably the gorgeous mountain scenery on the way up the Karakoram Highway to Pakistan.

Kashgar experiences blistering hot summers, although at 1290m above sea level it's cooler than Turpan, Kuqa and other stops along the Xinjiang section of the Silk Road.

Some foreign women walking the streets alone have been sexually harassed, by both locals and visiting Pakistanis. The Muslim Uighur women here dress in skirts and stockings like the Uighur women in Ürümqi and Turpan, but here one sees more female faces hidden behind veils of brown gauze. It's probably wise for women travellers to dress as would be appropriate in any Muslim country.

The North & North-West
Top: Camels for hire at the dunes near Baotou (Inner Mongolia Province).
Middle Left: Snowcaps and sand dunes along the Karakoram Highway (Xinjiang Province).
Middle Right: Horse racing at the annual Naadam festival in Hohhot (Inner Mongolia Province).
Bottom: A nomad dwelling on the grasslands near Xiahe (Gansu Province).

CHRIS TAYLOR

ALEXANDER ENGLISH

ALEXANDER ENGLISH

CHRIS TAYLOR

Tibet & Qinghai
Top Left: Once a fortress and now a monastery, the Yumbulagang dominates Yarlung Valley (Tibet).
Top Right: Rapeseed in flower near the Samye Monastery in Yarlung Valley (Tibet)
Bottom Left: A shuttered window at Ta'er Monastery, south of Xining (Qinghai Province).
Bottom Right: A pilgrim with prayer wheel at the Jokhang in Lhasa (Tibet)

History

A large oasis, Kashgar was a key centre on the ancient Silk Road, and saw a steady stream of traders from the Middle East and Central Asia. In the late 1800s it became something of a political pawn in the 'Great Game' – the competition between Britain and Russia for control of Central Asia.

In 1890 the British sent a trade agent to Kashgar to represent their interests, and in 1908 established a consulate. As with Tibet in the 1890s, the rumours soon spread that the Russians were on the verge of gobbling up Xinjiang, and Communist agents did indeed establish a presence in the city.

Peter Fleming, who spent six months making his way to Kashgar by donkey and camel from Beijing, described the Kashgar of 1935 as being 'in effect run by the secret police, the Russian advisers, and the Soviet consulate, and most of the high officials were only figureheads'.

Order was swiftly enforced once the Chinese Communists came to power in 1949: the city walls were ripped down and a huge, glistening white statue of Chairman Mao was erected on the main street. The statue stands today, hand outstretched to the sky above and the lands beyond, a constant reminder to the local populace of the alien regime that controls the city.

Information

Tourist Offices CITS (☎ 282-5390) has an office on the 2nd floor of a small building opposite the Qiniwake Hotel, but they are not geared towards helping individual travellers.

A better place to try is John's Information & Cafe, opposite the Seman Hotel. Owner John Hu was one of the first private entrepreneurs in Xinjiang's tourism sector, and he and his staff know the area well.

PSB The PSB (☎ 282-2030) has its foreign affairs office in the main building on Yunmulakexia Lu. Office hours are 9.30 am to 1.30 pm and 4 to 8 pm. Those same hours hold true for most government offices in Kashgar.

Money You can change cash and travellers cheques, and maybe even arrange a credit card cash advance, at the main branch of the Bank of China. The Seman and Qiniwake hotels are more convenient for changing money, although they tend to be more choosy about which brands of travellers cheques they'll cash (American Express is the brand of choice).

Sunday Market

(xīngqīrì shìchǎng)

You should not miss the bumper market that takes place each Sunday on the eastern fringe of town. Hundreds of donkey carts, horse riders, pedestrians and assorted animals thunder into town for a bargaining extravaganza.

The market is centred on the 'Kashgar International Trade Market of Central and Western Asia', a large concrete structure trying to masquerade as Muslim architecture. The building itself houses numerous stalls, and most of the rug sellers can be found here. However, the real action is out front on Aizilaiti Lu (Izlati Rd), which is jammed with merchants selling all types of food, handicrafts, housewares, clothing etc.

Be especially careful of pickpockets and bag slashers here. Many travellers have lost passports and travellers cheques here to razor-blade artists.

The market is about 2km from the centre of town. A taxi here should cost Y10. In the summer, John's Information & Cafe runs a free minibus service out to the market.

Bazaar

(nóngmào shìchǎng)

Sundays excepted, the bazaar is the focus of activity in Kashgar. The main market street can be reached from the lanes opposite the Id Kah Square which run off the main north-south road.

Kashgar is noted for the ornate knives sold in the bazaar and by hawkers in the streets. It's also a hat-making centre, and certain sections of streets are devoted entirely to stalls selling embroidered caps and

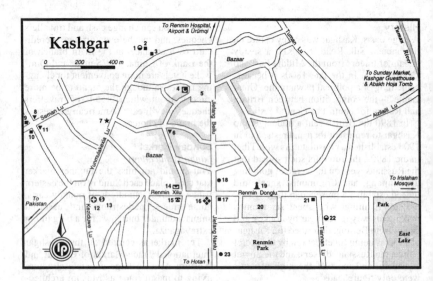

KASHGAR 喀什

PLACES TO STAY
2 Qiniwake Hotel; CITS
其尼瓦克宾馆
中国国际旅 猩
3 Kashgar Gilgit
International
友谊宾馆
9 Overseas Chinese Hotel
喀什华侨宾馆
10 Seman Hotel
色满宾馆
17 People's Hotel
人民饭店
21 Tiannan Hotel
天南饭店

PLACES TO EAT
6 Muslim Restaurant
清真餐厅

8 Small Restaurants
小吃部
11 John's Information
& Cafe
约翰中西餐厅

OTHER
1 Buses to Pakistan
去巴基斯坦的班车
4 Id Kah Mosque
艾提尕清真寺
5 Id Kah Square
艾提尕广场
7 PSB
公安局
12 Nongsanshi Hospital
农三师医院
13 Bank of China
中国银行

14 Post Office
邮局
15 Telephone Office
电信局
16 Department Store
百货大楼
18 Xinhua Bookstore
新华书店
19 Mao Statue
毛泽东塑像
20 Renmin Square
人民广场
22 Long-Distance
Bus Station
长途汽车站
23 Xinjiang Airlines Booking
Office
中国新疆航空公司
售票处

fur-lined headgear. Blacksmiths pound away on anvils, colourful painted wooden saddles are on sale, and you can pick your dinner from a choice line-up of goats' heads and hoofs.

The streets west of Jiefang Beilu have

more in the way of Uighur and Kyrgyz crafts, while those on the eastern side are devoted mainly to household goods and hardware. This is where you can see the tinsmiths, coppersmiths and other craftsmen in action.

Id Kah Mosque
(ài tí gǎ ér qīngzhēn sì)
The Id Kah Mosque is a stark contrast to
the Chinese-style mosques in eastern cities
like Xi'an. It looks like it's been lifted out
of Pakistan or Afghanistan, and has the
central dome and flanking minarets which
westerners usually associate with a mosque.
Prayer time is around 10 pm, although that
may vary throughout the year.

During the festival of Korban Bairam,
usually held in September and October, pilgrims gather in front of the mosque and
gradually twirl themselves into a frenzy of
dancing driven by wailing music from a
small band perched on the mosque's portal.

Abakh Hoja Tomb
(xiāngfēi mù)
This strange construction is in the eastern
part of the oasis. It looks something like a
stubby, multicoloured miniature of the Taj
Mahal, with green tiles on the walls and
dome. To one side of the mosque is a large
cemetery, with a rectangular base sur-
mounted by fat, conical mud structures.
The tomb is the burial place of Hidajetulla
Hoja, a Muslim missionary and saint, and
his 72 descendants.

The Chinese call this place the Fragrant
Concubine's Tomb *(xiāngfēi mù)* in honour
of one daughter of the Hoja clan who was
married to the emperor Qianlong. However, her body was later moved to Hebei
Province and is not actually entombed
here. It's said that she was forced to com-
mit suicide in 1761 by Qianlong's mother,
the empress dowager.

It would be a long walk out to Abakh
Hoja, but it's easily reached on bicycle.
From the Sunday market area, ride about
2km further along Aizilaiti Lu (Izlati Rd).
Look for a sign on the left-hand side, turn
down the dirt road and after about 500m
make a right turn. Admission is Y7.

East Lake Park
(dōnghú gōngyuán)
This pleasant park is centred around a surprisingly large man-made lake. There are
plenty of shade trees and, of course, rowing
boats for hire. It's not a bad place to while
away a few hours if you have time on your
hands. Admission is Y1.

Irislahan Mosque
(aīěrsīlánhǎn qīngzhēnsì)
This is a tranquil little mosque on the
eastern outskirts of town, and makes for a
nice bike-ride destination. It's tucked down
a small dirt path leading west from Aiersilanhan Lu (Irislahan Rd).

Further south along the road is an interesting Muslim cemetery that's worth a
peek. If you're hungry or thirsty, another
500m south will bring you to a traffic circle
with a wide variety of food and drink stalls.
Aiersilanhan Lu intersects with Renmin
Donglu about 1km east of East Lake Park.
Turn right at the intersection to get to the
mosque.

Places to Stay
In terms of value for money, the best place
in town is probably the *Qiniwake Hotel*
(☎ 282-2103) *(qíníwāké bīnguǎn)*. Dorm
beds in spacious, well-appointed quads and
triples cost Y25/30, and many travellers
have managed to knock the price down a
bit. Doubles are also good value at Y135,
and there are fancier rooms for Y220.

The hotel has a nice courtyard and a
bevy of bars and restaurants. The only
drawback is that it can get quite noisy in
the summer months when it fills up with
Pakistani traders. For this reason also, it
may not be the best choice for single
female travellers; some western women
have been sexually harassed by Pakistani
guests here. The Qiniwake is also referred
to as the Chini Bagh Hotel, probably the
result of different translations by the hotel
and CITS, which has numerous advertisements throughout Kashgar pointing out its
location at the 'Chini Bagh'.

Although not as new as the Qiniwake,
the *Seman Hotel* (☎ 282-2129) *(sèmǎn
bīnguǎn)* is another good place to base
yourself in Kashgar. It's in the former
Soviet consulate on the western edge of

town. Dorm beds in doubles with shared bath cost Y30, and beds in larger rooms (normally open only in summer) are Y15. A double with bath costs Y100, a suite Y280.

The *People's Hotel* (☎ 282-3373) *(rénmín fàndiàn)* has a central location, but not a whole lot of charm. Dorm beds are Y24, and it's Y55 for a bed in a triple with attached bath. Doubles are Y180.

The other place in backpacker class is the *Tiannan Hotel* (☎ 282-2211) *(tiānnán fàndiàn)* near the long-distance bus station. It's a bit of a dive, but it has bicycle hire, a laundry service and reasonably priced rooms. Dorms cost from Y16 to Y30 per bed. Doubles and triples with private bath start from Y120 and Y150 respectively.

Just opposite the Seman Hotel is the *Overseas Chinese Hotel* (☎ 283-3255) *(kāshí huáqiáo bīnguǎn)*. It's nothing special, and only has doubles for Y150, but rates are negotiable, and the staff seem fairly friendly. If you're just shaking off the effects of a 36 hour bus ride from Ürümqi and find the Seman and Qiniwake booked up, at least this place offers a nearby option.

The *Kashgar Guesthouse* (☎ 282-2367) *(kāshí gě'ěr bīnguǎn)* is the city's traditional tour-group hotel. Although a bit rundown, it's a pleasant, rambling place with buildings spread throughout a large, quiet yard. The only problem is that it's too far from the town centre. However, you can get into town on the No 10 bus, which will take you as far as Renmin Square, or take a taxi for Y10. Doubles are Y250, and suites are Y400.

In the same complex as the Qiniwake Hotel is the *Kashgar Gilgit International* (☎ 283-3235) *(yǒuyì bīnguǎn)*. It used to be the top-end component of the Qiniwake, but the two operations have since parted ways. Doubles seem fairly comfortable, but are a bit steep at Y280.

Places to Eat
Opposite the Seman Hotel is *John's Information & Cafe* (☎ 282-4186; fax 282-2861), a fine place to eat and to get the lowdown on travelling around Kashgar and on to Pakistan. There are plenty of other small *restaurants* around the Seman Hotel area – quality varies, but some of the places opposite the Overseas Chinese Hotel have some tasty fare.

For a wide variety of Uighur foods, pop into the *food market* close to the Id Kah Mosque. There you can try shish kebab, rice with mutton, fried fish, samosa and fruit. Down one of the little bazaar side streets, the *Muslim Restaurant* has a 2nd floor teahouse with a balcony above the bustling crowds. The tea is quite nice, and cheap at Y1, but eat here at your own risk: hygiene conditions are dodgy, to put it nicely.

Things to Buy
Kashgar is the best place in Xinjiang to buy Uighur handicrafts – check out the bazaar for knives, hats, rugs, woven bags and clothing and other local products. See the preceding sections on the Sunday Market and the Bazaar for more information.

Getting There & Away
Air There are daily flights from Kashgar to Ürümqi, but competition for seats can be keen. It seems more difficult to get a flight out of Kashgar than to get one from Ürümqi to Kashgar. Try and book your ticket at least two to three days in advance. If you can't get a ticket, a travel agent may be able to help, although this will cost you an additional Y50 per ticket. The flight takes 1½ hours and costs a steep Y1270.

The Xinjiang Airlines office (☎ 282-2113) is on Jiefang Nanlu south of the People's Hotel, and is open from 10 am to 1.30 pm and from 4.30 to 8 pm.

Bus Buses link Kashgar with Aksu, Hotan, Kuqa, Tashkurgan, Toksun and Ürümqi. The Kashgar long-distance bus station, like its counterpart in Ürümqi, charges a 100% surcharge for foreigners' tickets. As in Ürümqi, this is technically illegal – you may be able to get around the double-pricing, but be prepared for a vicious battle.

There are up to seven buses a day to Ürümqi, via Aksu, Kuqa, Korla and Toksun.

At least three should be sleepers, although, like departure times, the number of sleepers on any given day varies. The trip takes 36 hours barring any mishaps. The bus seat costs Y200 for foreigners, or Y443 for the more comfortable sleeper. There are also usually a few sleeper buses daily to Kuqa: these take 14 to 16 hours and cost Y218 for foreigners.

Buses to Hotan leave twice a day and take around 20 hours. At the time of writing the sleeper service had been cancelled due to a lack of passengers. It may be reinstated, but if not, a fairly hard seat is your sole option – a painful proposition considering that the ticket costs around Y150. To get to Turpan you'll need to take a bus to Toksun (Y393 sleeper, 30 hours), then change to a bus for Turpan.

There are one to two buses each day between Kashgar and Tashkurgan, the last town of any size before the Karakoram Highway heads into Pakistan. The 291km ride takes six to eight hours, and costs Y60. Buses from Kashgar to Sust, Pakistan, also stop in Tashkurgan. For more details, see the Karakoram Highway section below.

The road between Xinjiang and Tibet, one of the roughest in the world, passes through the disputed territory of Aksai Chin. This route is not officially open to foreigners; some have hitched unofficially from Lhasa to Kashgar in as little as 16 days, but others have taken months. Plenty of foreigners have been fined travelling towards Lhasa from Kashgar, and the PSB's worries about safety are understandable in this instance. At least two foreigners have died on this 'road': one was thrown from the back of a truck when it hit a pothole; the other died of a combination of hypothermia and altitude sickness, also while riding on the back of a truck.

Getting Around

To/From the Airport A Xinjiang Airlines bus meets incoming flights. Going to the airport, buses leave from in front of the Xinjiang Airlines booking office two hours before flight departures. The fare is Y6.

Taxis charge Y30 to Y40 for the 11km trip between the airport and city centre.

Other Transport Except for the No 10 bus, which links the Kashgar Guesthouse with the city centre, city buses aren't of much use for most travellers. The most convenient mode of transport is bicycle. John's Information & Cafe rents bikes for Y2 per hour, or Y15 for the whole day. The Tiannan Hotel outdoes this with a flat rate of Y6 per day, whether it be one hour or eight.

For jeep and minibus hire, the best place to inquire is John's Information & Cafe.

AROUND KASHGAR
Three Immortals Buddhist Caves
(sānxiān dòng)
These Buddhist caves are on a sheer cliff on the southern bank of the Qiakmakh River about 20km north of Kashgar. There are three caves – one with frescoes which are still discernible. Going to the caves makes a pleasant excursion, but it's not worth it just for the art. Hiring a jeep to take you there and back will cost around Y300.

Tomb of Mahmud Kashgari
(máhàmǔdé kāshígělǐ mázā)
About 40km west of Kashgar along the start of the Karakoram Highway lies the tomb of this 11th century Uighur scholar. The son of a court official, Mahmud left Kashgar when royal intrigues resulted in the death of his father. He set off on a 15 year odyssey through Central Asia, ending up in Baghdad, where he finished compiling a Turkic language dictionary and encyclopedia of Central Asian language, customs and culture.

The tomb is a fairly modest structure, but has fared well during its 900 years of existence. It consists of a large entrance gate, and an inner courtyard with a prayer hall that also holds Kashgari's stone casket. What adds to the place's appeal is the surrounding scenery: narrow trails leading through groves of shade trees, a Muslim cemetery, Uighur music in the background,

XINJIANG

and the fantastic backdrop of the Karako-ram mountain range.

Hiring a jeep to get here will cost around Y300. If you've hired a vehicle to go further up the highway, say to Karakuri Lake, you can ask the driver to make a stop here on the way there or back.

KARAKORAM HIGHWAY
(zhōngbā gōnglù)
This highway over the Khunjerab Pass (4800m) is the gateway to Pakistan. For centuries this route was used by caravans plodding down the Silk Road. Khunjerab means 'valley of blood', a reference to local bandits who took advantage of the terrain to plunder caravans and slaughter the merchants.

Nearly 20 years were required to plan, push, blast and level the present road between Islamabad and Kashgar; more than 400 road-builders died. Facilities en route are being steadily improved, but take warm clothing, food and drink on board with you – once stowed on the roof of the bus your baggage will not be easily accessible.

Even if you don't wish to go to Pakistan, it's worth doing the trip up to Tashkurgan from Kashgar – there's plenty to see. From Kashgar, you first cross the Pamir Plateau (3000m), passing the foothills of Kongur-shan *(gōnggé'ér shān)*, which is 7719m high, and nearby Muztag-Atashan *(mùshìtǎgé shān)* at 7546m. In between the two lies Karakuri Lake, one of the most scenic spots on the Chinese side of the highway.

The journey continues through stunning scenery – high mountain pastures with grazing camels and yaks tended by Tajiks who live in yurts. The last major town on the Chinese side is Tashkurgan at 3600m. If you don't continue to Pakistan, you can spend the night here.

Officially, the border opens 15 April and closes 31 October. However, the border can open late or close early depending on conditions at Khunjerab Pass. Travel formalities are performed at Sust, on the Pakistan border; the Chinese border post is at Tash-kurgan. There are also two police checkpoints between Tashkurgan and Kashgar.

Some travellers have managed to get 10 day Pakistan transit visas at the border, though it wouldn't be wise to plan your trip around the possibility of this happening. If you're coming in from Pakistan, make sure you have enough cash on hand – the bank in Tashkurgan doesn't change travellers cheques.

Karakuri Lake
(kǎlākùlì hú)
Sitting at 3800m, this lake is dwarfed on either side by Kongurshan and Muztag-Atashan. When the weather is clear, it's a sight to take your breath away. There's numerous hiking trails around the area, and you can stay in yurts by the lake for Y40 per person. Bring warm clothing even in summer, and maybe your own food – the meals served at the lake's sole restaurant are pretty good, but very pricey.

John's Information & Cafe in Kashgar can supply information about four and five-day treks starting from the lake that skirt the bases of both 7500m-plus peaks.

Tashkurgan
(tǎshíkù'ěrgān)
This predominantly Tajik town can be used as a base to explore the nearby ruined fort, local cemeteries and the surrounding high country.

Most travellers stay at the *Ice Mountain Hotel (bīngshān bīnguǎn)* which has dorm beds for Y20, no hot water and fairly inconsistent food. However, the main street is filled with little *restaurants* offering better fare at lower prices. The *Pamir Hotel (pāmǐ'ěr bīnguǎn)* is a little more upmarket, and has doubles with attached bath for Y120, though prices seem open to negotiation.

Getting There & Away
There are one to two buses daily between Kashgar and Tashkurgan. The full journey takes up to eight hours, and tickets cost Y60. This is a viable way to get to Karakuri Lake, but not so reliable for getting back; many travellers have waited by the side of the road for hours, only to have the bus

blast right past them, despite frantic waves for it to stop.

You can also take the bus to Pakistan and get off at Tashkurgan: the fare is Y61. For more information on this bus service, see the Getting There & Away chapter at the front of this book.

In Kashgar, you can rent jeeps to take you to Tashkurgan or Karakuri Lake and bring you back the following day. John's Information & Cafe in Kashgar charges Y1000 for a Beijing jeep (uncomfortable and unreliable) that can carry four passengers, or Y1600 for hardier (and much more comfortable) Toyota Land Cruisers that can carry five passengers. CITS also rents jeeps, but at twice the price.

HOTAN
(hétián)
About 1980km south-west of Ürümqi by road, Hotan is one of the most remote parts of Xinjiang, sitting at the southern boundary of the Taklamakan Desert.

Like Kuqa, the sights are spread around the surrounding countryside and are of the ruined city variety. Ten kilometres to the west of town are the **Yurturgan Ruins** *(yuètègān yízhǐ)*, the ancient capital of a pre-Islamic kingdom dating from the 3rd to 8th centuries AD.

The **Malikurwatur Ruins** *(málìkèwǎtè gùchéng)* are 12km south of town, and there are some temples and pagoda-like buildings a further 10km to the south. Visiting any of these places will require hiring a vehicle, which can be arranged at the hotels or with the various touts who will no doubt come looking for your business.

Hotan is renowned for its precious stones. Hotan jade is considered the finest in China. You can even see deposits of white jade along the **Jade Dragon Kashgar River** *(yùlóng kāshì hé)*, which runs close to town. You can check out the local selection at the rows of stores and stalls along the town's main street. Other local products include walnuts, silk and carpets.

Jiyaxiang *(jíyǎxiāng)*, a small town 11km north-east of Hotan, still produces hand-woven carpets using looms. Most of the houses in town are tiny, family-run factories. In town itself, on the eastern bank of the Jade Dragon Kashgar River just north of the road to Qiemo, is a carpet factory.

For those setting off on the infrequently explored southern Silk Road (via Qiemo, Ruoqiang and on to Golmud), this is the last place to take care of important errands like changing money, stocking up on supplies or extending your visa.

Places to Stay & Eat
The cheapest reliable accommodation for foreigners is the *Hotan Yinbinguan (guesthouse)* (☎ 202-2203) *(hétián yínbīnguǎn)*. Dorm beds in quads/triples with shared bath cost Y16/21, basic doubles Y90, and more upmarket rooms Y180.

The *Hotan Hotel* (☎ 202-3568) *(hétián dìqū wài bīnguǎn)* is somewhat fancier, with doubles for Y120 and triples for Y160. This place is widely referred to in town as the *lǎobīnguǎn* (old guesthouse). The airline office is here too.

The other option is the *Hotan Guesthouse (hétián bīnguǎn)*, which is newer and probably more expensive than the Hotan Yinbinguan. The *Jiaotong Hotel (jiāotōng bīnguǎn)*, right next to the bus station, sometimes takes foreigners and sometimes doesn't. If you can get in, very basic dorm beds from Y10 await you.

Getting There & Away
There are two flights weekly between Hotan and Ürümqi (Y1250, 1¾ hours).

Buses from Ürümqi to Hotan now travel along the recently opened Cross-Desert Highway, which spans 500km of almost completely deserted land between Luntai and Minfeng. The roadway is actually built on a raised roadbed to help prevent sand storms from building up dunes on the tarmac. Sleeper buses generally leave once a day. The entire trip takes more than 40 hours, and the Chinese ticket price is Y270.

There are two daily buses between Hotan and Kashgar – one in the morning and one in the evening. The 530km trip takes 16 to 20 hours and seats cost Y72, or Y116 for a 'luxury' bus. At the time of writing, sleeper bus service had been discontinued due to insufficient demand.

From Hotan you can catch an early-morning bus to Qiemo (Cherchen), 580km to the east. The trip generally takes two days and costs Y45 (Chinese price). From Qiemo buses continue another 320km east to Ruoqiang (Charklik). The trip takes anywhere from 13 to 16 hours under good conditions, and Chinese-price tickets are Y29.

From Ruoqiang you may be able to get a bus to Golmud, although some travellers have had to resort to private jeep services (Y60, nine hours) that take you to the border with Qinghai. From there you can reportedly take a series of buses on to Dachaidan in Qinghai Province, and from there connect with buses to Golmud. This route requires a few over-night stops, and roads in this area are plagued by washouts and landslides, so don't try this route if you're in a hurry.

YINING

(yīníng)

Also known as Gulja, Yining lies close to the Kazakhstan border, about 700km west of Ürümqi. It is the centre of the Ili Kazakh Autonomous Prefecture.

The Ili Valley has in times past been an easy access point for invaders, as well as for the northern route of the Silk Road. Yining was occupied by Russian troops in 1876 during Yakub Beg's independent rule of Kashgaria. Five years later, the Chinese cracked down on Yakub Beg and Yining was handed back by the Russians. In 1962 there were major Sino-Soviet clashes along the Ili River. In late 1986 the Chinese claimed to have shot six Soviet infiltrators.

More recently, Yining was the scene of violent riots started by Uighur separatists, resulting in a number of deaths. Although the riots were swiftly put down, tension continues. Chinese appear uneasy here and warn against staying out after dark, although the Kazakhs and Uzbeks are generally friendlier toward foreigners than the Han Chinese.

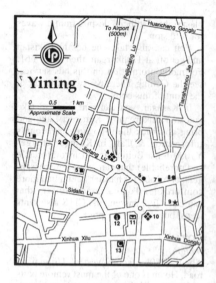

YINING 伊宁

1 Huacheng Hotel
   花城宾馆
2 Bus Station
   长途汽车站
3 Bank of China
   中国银行
4 Department Store
   民贸商场
5 Friendship Hotel
   友谊宾馆
6 Xinjiang Airlines Booking
   Office
   中国新疆航空公司售票处
7 Ili Hotel
   伊犁宾馆
8 Horse Carriages
   马车
9 PSB
   公安局外事科
10 Yining Department Store
   伊宁商场
11 Post Office
   邮局
12 CITS
   中国国际旅行社
13 Mosque
   清真寺

Now that there are direct bus and train services linking Ürümqi and Almaty, there is no overpowering reason to visit Yining itself. It's a grubby place that has a few faded remnants of Russian architecture, but overall there's not much to the town itself.

The Uighur Market near the Huacheng Hotel is mildly interesting, as are some of the back alleys, which pass the occasional Russian-style house with carved window-frames, painted shutters and plaster peeling from ornate designs.

Information

The PSB is two blocks from the Ili Hotel, near a big radio tower. The Bank of China is one block south of the Ili Hotel and the post office is right on the big traffic circle in the centre of town.

Places to Stay

Budget travellers can try the *Friendship Hotel* (☎ 802-3901) *(yǒuyì bīnguǎn)*, which has dorm beds in quads/triples for Y25/32, and you can probably talk them down a bit. Doubles start at Y90. It's located several streets south of the bus station, but isn't that easy to find – it's down an obscure side street and the only sign pointing the way is in Chinese.

The only other budget option open to foreigners at the time of writing was the *Huacheng Hotel* (☎ 812-5050) *(huāchéng bīnguǎn)*, which has dorm beds from Y15 and doubles from Y150. The drawback to both these budget spots is that, although relatively close to the bus station, they're fairly far out from the town centre.

Closer to all the action (such as it is), but far more expensive, is the *Ili Hotel* (☎ 802-3126) *(yìlí bīnguǎn)* where doubles cost Y280 and three-person 'suites' are Y500. The hotel does have very pleasant tree-shaded grounds, but this doesn't exactly justify the room rates.

Getting There & Away

Air Flights between Ürümqi and Yining supposedly leave daily, but in reality there's no set schedule, or at least there wasn't when we last checked. Cancelled and delayed flights are common. Tickets can be hard to get, especially from Yining back to Ürümqi.

The one way fare is Y560 and the flight takes 50 minutes by Boeing 737, or 2¼ hours by De Havilland 6, a twin-engined propeller plane.

The Xinjiang Airlines office is one block west of the Ili Hotel. A airline bus runs between the office and is timed to coincide with incoming and departing flights.

Bus Buses leave fairly frequently from Ürümqi between 9 am and 5 pm. The 691km ride takes 16 to 20 hours. Departures from Yining start at around 8 am. The Chinese price is Y50 for regular buses and Y105 for sleepers.

It is possible to travel by bus from Yining to Almaty in Kazakhstan, although with the advent of the direct Ürümqi-Almaty bus service, few travellers now take this route. Unless you have arranged an overland entry visa for Kazakhstan, you won't have much luck getting across the border. For more information, see the Getting There & Away chapter towards the beginning of this book.

AROUND YINING
Ili Valley
(yīlí gǔ)

About 6km south of the town centre is a bridge over the Ili River. The Ili Valley is pretty – the roads are lined with tall birch trees and there are farms everywhere.

The best way to get out and see the countryside is to take a horse carriage *(mǎ chē)*. These cost about Y50 for a 1½ hour tour. Most of the carriage drivers congregate in an area about one block east of the Ili Hotel.

Sayram Lake
(sàilǐmù hú)

The large and beautiful Sayram Lake is to the north of Yining, and offers some nice hiking opportunities.

If you want to spend some time exploring this alpine lake area, you can get dorm

XINJIANG

beds at the *Sayram Hostel (sàilǐmù zhāodàisǔo)* for Y15. There is food up here, but the selection is limited and prices expensive, so bring what you need.

It is possible to hire horses at the lake and go riding with Kazakh shepherds. Chinese tourists pay Y5 to Y10 per hour, or Y50 for the whole day, so be sure to bargain.

Buses from Yining to Sayram Lake take slightly more than three hours. Buses between Ürümqi and Yining also pass by the lake.

ALTAI
(ā'lètài)

Near the northernmost tip of Xinjiang is Altai, 922m above sea level. It's in a much colder region than Ürümqi – even summer can be chilly. The population is a mere 170,000 – 63% of whom are Han Chinese and the rest mostly Kazakhs.

Altai is close to the border with three nations – Kazakhstan, Russia and Mongolia. For this reason, the Chinese are paranoid about the place and a hard-to-obtain permit is needed if you wish to visit the region to the north of town, although Altai itself is open.

The problem is that you'll need to get to Altai to find out if you can even get a permit. The PSB office in Ürümqi isn't much use in this regard: 'Go to Altai and ask there' was their less-than-helpful response last time we checked in with them.

One way to get around this might be to hire a vehicle and tour guide in Ürümqi, and let the travel agency sort out the permit mess, although this would be a costly option, probably around Y4000 for the round trip. At that rate it's cheaper to fly to Altai and try your luck.

Places to Stay

The only place for foreigners is the *Altai Hotel* (☎ 212-3804) *(ā'lètài dìqū bīguǎn)*. Per-person rates start at Y25, while doubles cost Y150, although you may be able to manage a discount. The hotel is located on the far side of the river, just opposite the town centre.

Getting There & Away

Until the permit situation eases up, there may be little point in visiting Altai unless you have both the time and money to take a chance. If so, Xinjiang Airlines flies there two or three times each week (Y470, two hours).

Buses from Ürümqi leave in the evening and take around 15 hours to get to Altai – road, weather and mechanical conditions permitting. Seats on a regular rattletrap bus cost Y50, while a berth on a sleeper is Y108 (both Chinese prices).

AROUND ALTAI

The area north of Altai is positively stunning, a land of thick evergreen forests, rushing rivers and lakes. The Ertrix River, which drains the area, is the only river in China to flow into the Arctic Ocean. This area is officially labelled the Hanas Nature Reserve and you will need a permit to visit.

Hanas Lake
(kānàsī hú)

The most splendid sight in the Altai region is Hanas Lake, an alpine lagoon surrounded by pines, boulders and mountains. In the autumn, the aspen and maple trees provide a scenic backdrop of riotous colour.

There's an A-frame style hotel here that looks like a ski lodge in the Swiss Alps. However, it probably doesn't see too much business – obtaining the coveted travel permit is usually quite difficult. Access is also impeded by bad roads – the lake is a 100km bone-jarring journey from Altai and you'll need to hire a jeep.

Friendship Peak
(yǒuyì fēng)

At 4374m, this is the highest summit in this mountainous area. Standing on the glacier-covered summit allows you to be in three nations at once. Presumably you won't need a visa for each one, but you will need a climbing permit, a guide, an ice axe, crampons and other mountaineering paraphernalia.

XINJIANG

Gansu 甘肃

A rugged, barren province consisting mostly of mountains and deserts, Gansu *(gānsù)* has long been a poor and forgotten backwater only loosely controlled by Beijing. Nonetheless it has played an important role in Chinese history. The famed Silk Road, the ancient highway along which camel caravans carried goods in and out of China, threaded its way through Gansu.

Travellers and merchants from as far as the Roman Empire entered the Middle Kingdom via this route, using a string of oasis towns as stepping-stones through the barren wastes. Buddhism was also carried into China along the Silk Road, and the Buddhist cave temples found all the way from Xinjiang through Gansu and up through northern China are reminders of the influx of ideas the road made possible. The Great Wall also ends here not far past the town of Jiayuguan.

Traditionally the towns of Gansu have been established in the oases along the major caravan route where agriculture is possible. With the coming of modern transport, some industrial development and mining has taken place. The 1892km Lanzhou-Ürümqi railway line, completed in 1963, was one of the greatest achievements of the early Communist regime – it has done much to relieve the isolation and backwardness of this region. Tourism is now an important cash cow, especially in Lanzhou, Dunhuang and Jiayuguan.

Twenty-three million people now inhabit Gansu. The province is home to a considerable variety of minority peoples, including the Hui, Mongols, Tibetans and Kazakhs, although the Han Chinese are now in the vast majority.

LANZHOU
(lánzhōu)

The capital of Gansu, Lanzhou has been an important garrison town and transport centre since ancient times. Its development as an

Gansu Facts & Highlights

Area: 450,000 sq km

Population: 24.7 million

Capital: Lanzhou

Highlights

- Bingling Si, Buddhist grottoes carved into a splendid area of cliffs towering over a branch of the Yellow River.
- Dunhuang, home of the stunning Mogao Caves, set amid towering sand dunes.
- The Tibetan monastery town of Xiahe, a magnet for pilgrims and a tranquil break from the rigours of the road.

industrial centre began after the Communist victory and the city's subsequent integration into China's expanding national rail network. The city's population increased more than tenfold within little more than a generation. China's economic reform policies have spurred further growth, and office towers and new housing blocks are sprouting up throughout the city.

Although Lanzhou is not a major tourist drawcard in itself, there are some interesting sights in the surrounding area. Lanzhou's strategic location also makes it an important transport hub for travellers heading into the vastness of western China.

GANSU

1003

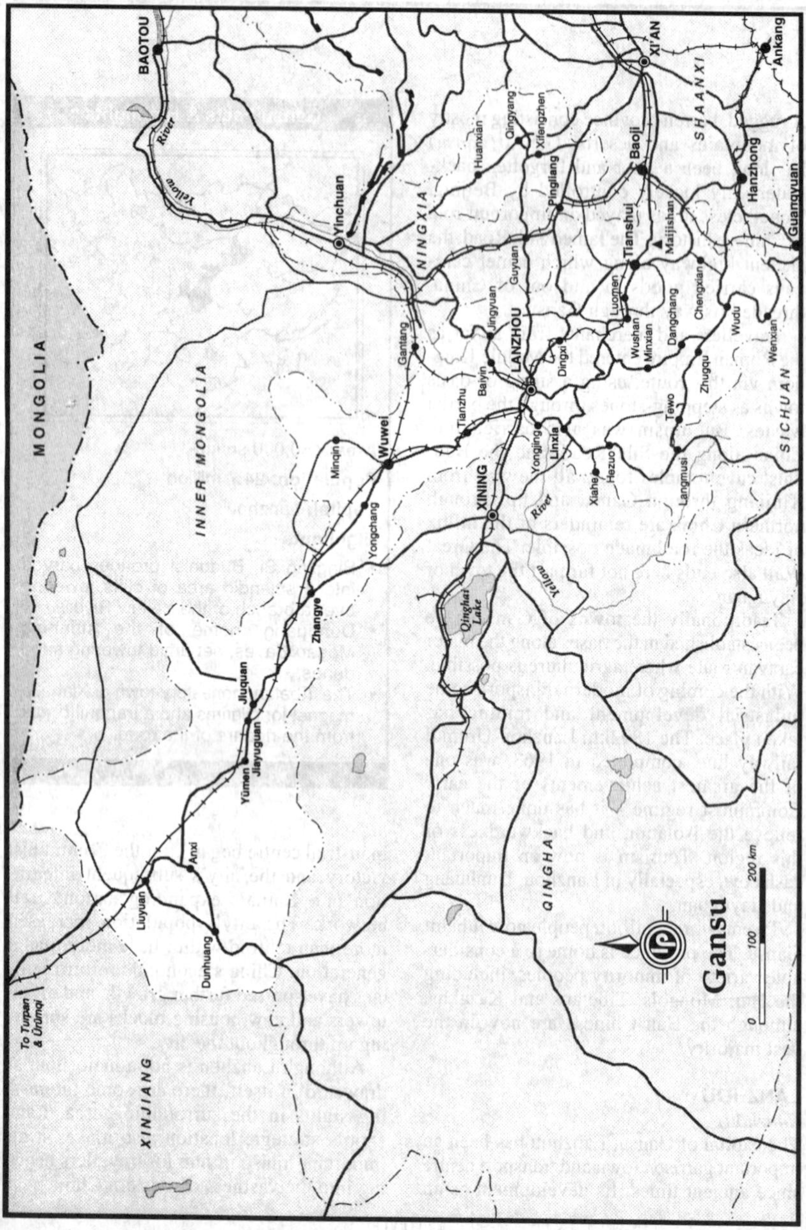

Gansu

MONGOLIA

INNER MONGOLIA

NINGXIA

SHAANXI

SICHUAN

QINGHAI

XINJIANG

To Turpan
& Ürümqi

BAOTOU

Yellow River

Yinchuan

XI'AN

Ankang

Huanxian

Qingyang

Xifangzhen

Pingliang

Baoji

Hanzhong

Guangyuan

Tianshui

Maijishan

Guyuan

Jingyuan

Luomen

Wushan

Minxian

Dangchang

Chengxian

Wudu

Wenxian

Zhugqu

Gangu

LANZHOU

Baiyin

Dingxi

Tianzhu

Yongjing

Linxia

Xiahe

Hezuo

Tewo

Langmusi

WUWEI

XINING

Qinghai Lake

Minqin

Yongchang

Zhangye

Jiuquan

Jiayuguan

Yumen

Anxi

Dunhuang

Liuyuan

Yellow River

Tatung River

0   100   200 km

Orientation

Geography has conspired to make Lanzhou a city of awkward design. At 1600m above sea level, the city is crammed into a narrow valley walled in by steep mountains, forcing it to develop westwards in a long urban corridor that extends for more than 20km along the southern banks of the Yellow River.

The valley is a perfect trap for exhaust fumes from motor vehicles and chimneys, burying Lanzhou in a perpetual haze of pollution. Nevertheless, the rugged topography does give the city a certain unique charm, which is augmented by the general friendliness of the locals.

Information

Tourist Office CITS (☎ 881-3222) is on Nongmin Xiang, the lane running behind the Lanzhou Hotel.

PSB You can obtain visa extensions and permits at the PSB provincial office (☎ 882-7961, ext 8820) at 38 Qingyang Lu near Dongfanghong Square. From the main green-and-white-tiled old building at the front, walk left to a separate wing; the office is on the 3rd floor, left of the stairs. Hours are 8 am to 12 pm and 2.30 pm to 6 pm Monday to Friday, but it's best to go around 9 am to catch the right official.

Money The Bank of China's main branch is in a brand new tower next to the Dongfang Hotel. Bank hours are 9 am to 12 pm and 2.30 to 5 pm Monday to Friday, and 10 am to 4 pm on Saturday.

Post & Communications There are post offices across from Lanzhou (main) railway station and at the west bus station. The main post and telephone office is on the corner of Minzhu Lu and Pingliang Lu and is open daily from 8 am to 7 pm. Parcel packing service is available.

A good place to make international calls is the telephone and telegram office on Qingyang Lu. It's open 24 hours and has fax, telegram and Internet services.

Travel Agencies Heaps of travel agencies cater to the foreign market, offering one day and overnight tours to scenic spots in the Lanzhou vicinity.

One place definitely worth checking out is the reliable Western Travel Service (☎ 841-6321, ext 8638; fax 841-8608) in the west wing of the Lanzhou Hotel. They readily give out information regardless of whether you bring them business, and their prices for tours and ticket bookings are competitive.

There's a string of little travel agents along Nongmin Xiang, the lane running behind the Lanzhou Hotel.

Gansu Provincial Museum

(gānsù shěng bówùguǎn)

If you're a museum type, you should quite enjoy this one, located directly across the street from the Friendship Hotel.

The exhibition *Cultural Relics of the Silk Road* features Neolithic painted pottery taken from a site 300km south-east of here at Dadiwan. The Dadiwan culture existed at least 7000 years ago and is thought by some archaeologists to predate the better known Yangshuo culture.

Exhibits from the Han Dynasty include inscribed wooden tablets used to relay messages along the Silk Road and an outstanding 1.5m-high Tang Dynasty warrior made from glaze-coloured earthenware. Also interesting is a 2nd century BC gilded silver plate depicting Bacchus, the Greek god of wine, from the Eastern Roman Empire. It was unearthed at Jingyuan, 120km north-east of Lanzhou, in 1989 and is evidence of significant contact between the two ancient civilisations.

The museum is open from 9 am to 12 pm and from 2.30 to 5 pm; it's closed on Sunday. Admission is a rather steep Y25.

Lanshan Park

(lánshān gōngyuán)

Lanshan mountain range rises steeply to the south of Lanzhou, reaching 2100m. The temperature on top is normally a good 5°C cooler than in the valley, so it's a good retreat in summer.

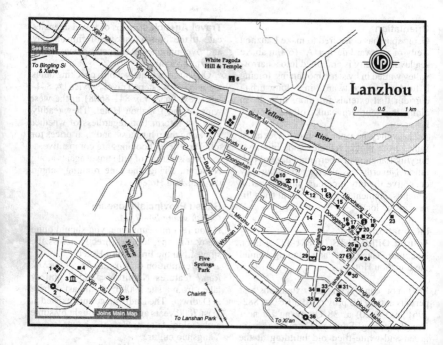

The quickest and easiest way up is by chairlift from behind the Five Springs Park (qǔquán gōngyuán). The chairlift takes about 20 minutes to make the diagonal climb to the upper terminal. On the summit you'll find the Santai Pavilion, refreshment stands and a fun park. A paved trail zigzags its way back down to Five Springs Park, although it's a long walk.

Getting here takes some effort. From the railway station you can take electric bus Nos 31 or 34 four stops to Wuquan Shan (wǔquán shān), get off and walk west until you reach Wuquan Lu. Turn left here and walk about 750m to the Five Springs Park ticket office. You can access the chairlift by going through the park (Y2). The park and chairlift are open from 9 am to 9 pm. Admission to the park is Y2. For foreigners, the chairlift costs Y20 for the ride up and Y16 for the ride back down. Not cheap perhaps, but it's quite a nice ride. Getting

to the park, enjoying it and returning will require most of the afternoon.

White Pagoda Hill
(báitǎ shān)
This pleasant, well-managed park is on the northern bank of the Yellow River near the old Zhongshan Bridge. The steep slopes are terraced, with small walkways leading through the forest to pavilions, teahouses and a plant nursery on a secluded hillside.

On top of the hill is the White Pagoda Temple, originally built during the Yuan Dynasty, from where you get a good view across the city. There are several mosques on the park periphery. In summer it's open from 6.30 am to 10 pm. Admission is Y2. Minibus No 101 goes to the park from Tianshui Lu, in front of the railway station.

Places to Stay
Lanzhou is unfortunately not a great place

LANZHOU 兰州

PLACES TO STAY
4 Friendship Hotel
友谊宾馆
19 Jincheng Hotel; Charter
Flights Booking Office
金城饭店
22 Lanzhou Hotel; Western
Travel Service
兰州饭店、西部旅行
23 Ningwozhuang
Guesthouse
宁卧庄宾馆
25 Lanzhou Legend Hotel
贾莘商斋岳频
26 Dongfang Hotel
东方宾馆
31 Heping Hotel
和平饭店
33 Yingbin Hotel
迎宾饭店
34 Nongken Hotel
农垦宾馆
35 Lanzhou Mansions
兰州大厦

PLACES TO EAT
15 Nongmin Xiang (Street
Food Stalls)
农民巷

20 Fengsheng Restaurant
丰盛饭庄
21 King of Beef Noodles
牛肉面大王

OTHER
1 Huangjin Shopping Centre
黄金大厦
2 West Railway Station
火车西站
3 Gansu Provincial Museum
甘肃省博物馆
5 West Bus Station
汽车西站
6 White Pagoda Temple
白塔
7 Jinda Shopping Centre
金达商厦
8 Asia-Europe Shopping
Centre
亚欧商厦
9 Foreign Languages
Bookstore
外文书店
10 PICC Office
中国人民保险公司
11 Telephone & Telegram
Office
电信大楼

12 PSB Provincial Office
省公安厅
13 Bank of China
中国银行
14 Dongfanghong Square
东方红广场
16 Railway Booking Office;
CAAC Office
火车站售票处
17 China Northwest Airlines
Booking Office
中国西北航空公司
售票处
18 CITS
中国国际旅行社
24 Lanzhou University
兰州大学
27 Bank of China (Main
Branch)
中国银行（兰州支行）
28 East Bus Station
汽车东站
29 Post & Telephone Office
邮电局
30 Lanzhou University
Bookstore
兰州大学书店
32 Dingxi Nanlu Day Market
定西南路市场
36 Main Railway Station
火车总站

for budget accommodation, which is a pity as it's a relatively pleasant city.

The cheapest place you're likely to find is the fairly depressing *Heping Hotel* (☎ 861-1874) *(hépíng fàndiàn)*, an old place that's showing its age. While staff would prefer you take a double with attached bath for Y82, they also have dorm beds from Y15 to Y26.

A few rungs higher on the budget ladder is the enormous *Nongken Hotel* (☎ 841-7878) *(nóngkěn bīnguǎn)*, which has beds in five person dorms with shared bath for Y34, and beds in triples for Y40. Doubles, triples and quads with private bath go for Y180, Y210 and Y240 respectively. All these prices are double what Chinese pay, so you're not getting much for your money. *Lanzhou Mansions* (☎ 841-2210) *(lánzhōu dàshà)*, opposite the railway station, charges Y50 for beds in a double with

shared bath, and Y35 for a triple, if you can get them to rent it to you. Doubles with private bath are Y180; they're a bit nicer than those at the Nongken Hotel, but are still not a great deal. Still, both places are okay if you're just spending one night and want to be near the railway station.

The *Yingbin Hotel* (☎ 888-6552) *(yíng-bīn fàndiàn)* on Tianshui Lu is a bit nicer, and has doubles for Y80 and Y120. There are also triples with shared bath for Y72, but as a rule they don't let foreigners rent these, although if there are three of you, they may make an exception.

Given these prices and conditions, the best deal in town is at the *Lanzhou Hotel* (☎ 841-6321) *(lánzhōu fàndiàn)*. Built back in the 1950s, this Sino-Stalinist edifice has been fully remodelled and is a pleasant place to stay. Best of all, it offers clean, comfortable triples with attached bath for

GANSU

Y50 per bed – this is at the higher end of the budget range, but is decidedly worth it. Doubles range from Y180 to Y230 in the older wings (also a good price for Lanzhou), and cost Y330 in the main building. The hotel is a 20 minute walk from the main railway station or you can take bus No 1 or No 7 for two stops.

Nearby, the *Jincheng Hotel* (☎ 841-6638) *(jīnchéng fàndiàn)* is a three star place that has a well founded reputation for its frosty service. There are concrete-floored doubles and triples for Y102 and Y128 in the dingy south building of the hotel, but front desk staff are reluctant to tell you about them, preferring you take one of the standard doubles for Y298 to Y358.

Opposite the Lanzhou Hotel, but on the same traffic circle, is the four star *Lanzhou Legend Hotel* (☎ 888-2876; fax 888-7876) *(lánzhōu fēitiān dà jiǔdiàn)*. This is the most upmarket place in town. Rates for doubles range from Y869 to Y960, plus a 15% service charge. You may be able to negotiate down to Y700, but that's about it. Next door is the *Dongfang Hotel (dōngfāng bīnguǎn)*, another luxury hotel which was still under construction at the time of writing.

The spacious and sleepily quiet *Ningwozhuang Guesthouse* (☎ 841-6221) *(níngwòzhuāng bīnguǎn)* has basic doubles for Y428, or others in its new four star wing for Y680. Once an exclusive residence for visiting cadres, this place features some amazingly well-kept gardens.

The *Friendship Hotel* (☎ 233-3051) *(yǒuyì bīnguǎn)* is a fairly upmarket place on the western side of town. It's useful if you're catching the west bus station or visiting the early-morning bus to Xiahe from the west bus station or visiting the Provincial Museum, but is convenient for little else. Dorm beds in the old building range from Y30 to Y38, and doubles in the new building start from Y180.

Places to Eat

One of the best spots for street food is Nongmin Xiang, the lane running behind the Lanzhou Hotel. The street is lined with small *restaurants* and *food stalls*. At the east end, across from the travel agencies, are a few good places that have English menus. An excellent spot is the *Fengsheng Restaurant (fēngshèng fànzhuāng)*, opposite the CITS office. With neither English sign nor menu, finding it and then ordering can be difficult, but you'll be rewarded with tasty, inexpensive dishes.

Dingxi Beilu, just south of Lanzhou University, also has rows of *restaurants* and *street stalls*. Prices here are a bit cheaper, to cater to the student clientele. Several typical Lanzhou specialities are sold on the streets. One is called *ròujiābǐng*, which is lamb or pork fried with onion, capsicum and a dash of paprika, served inside a 'pocket' of flatbread.

Lanzhou is famous for its beef noodles served in spicy soup *(niúròu miàn)* – if you don't want the chillies, say '*búyào làjiāo*'. A fine place to try this and other dishes is *King of Beef Noodles (niúròu miàn dàwáng)* on Donggang Xilu, very close to the Lanzhou Hotel. There's an English menu out the front, and bowls of beef noodles with two appetisers and a boiled egg start at Y4.50 – a true bargain.

Getting There & Away

Air China Northwest Airlines has a booking office (☎ 882-1964) on Donggang Xilu, a five minute walk north-west of the Lanzhou Hotel. It's open from 8 am to 9 pm. There's also a CAAC office another 50m west along Donggang Xilu.

There are charter flights usually departing once weekly for Hong Kong. To get tickets you'll need to go to the booking office (☎ 841-6737) in the Jincheng Hotel.

There are daily flights to Beijing (Y1260), Chengdu (Y900), Guangzhou (Y1890) and Xi'an (Y560). Other destinations include Kunming, Shanghai, Shenzhen, Fuzhou, Hangzhou, Nanjing, Qingdao, Shenyang, Ürümqi, Xiamen and Wuhan.

Bus The west bus station *(qìchē xīzhàn)* handles departures to Yongjing (near Bingling Si), Linxia, Xiahe, Hezuo, Zhangye and Dunhuang. Foreigners are charged double for all bus fares unless they can produce a student or resident identity card.

For details on service to Linxia and Xiahe see the relevant destination sections. There are two buses daily to Hezuo (Y40, eight hours) leaving at 7 and 9.30 am.

A daily sleeper bus leaves in the afternoon for Dunhuang that passes through Zhangye and Jiayuguan. Given the double prices, you're better off taking the train.

The east bus station on Pingliang Lu has departures mainly for eastern destinations. Unlike their west station counterparts, staff here aren't as quick to double-charge foreigners. There is one nightly sleeper to Xi'an (Y105, 15 hours), and morning and evening buses for Yinchuan (Y36 regular, Y75 sleeper, 11 hours) and Tianshui (Y27 regular, Y54 sleeper, nine hours). There is one daily bus to Guyuan (in Ningxia) leaving at 6.30 am.

Travel Insurance A regulation requires that foreigners who travel by public bus in Gansu must be insured with the People's Insurance Company of China (PICC), regardless of whether they have taken out their own travel insurance or not.

Some long-distance bus stations may refuse to sell you a ticket unless you can show them your PICC insurance, or else they will charge you an 'insurance fee' on the spot (no receipt issued though).

The requirement is currently being enforced mainly on routes in and out of Lanzhou and in eastern Gansu. Ironically, you couldn't actually collect anything from this insurance policy if you were involved some sort of accident – it is there to insure the government bus company against lawsuits.

In Lanzhou you can buy insurance at the PICC office (☎ 841-6422, ext 114) at 222 Qingyang Lu, as well as at the CITS office, other travel agencies and most of the tourist hotels. It costs Y30 for 14 days; after that you'll need to renew it. CITS and some of the hotels charge an additional Y5 to Y10 commission.

Train Trains run to Ürümqi, to Beijing via Hohhot and Datong, to Golmud via Xining, to Shanghai via Xi'an and Zhengzhou, and to Beijing via Xi'an and Zhengzhou. You can also go south to Chengdu. Heading west, it takes 15 hours to reach Jiayuguan, 20 hours to Liuyuan, 32 hours to Turpan, and 35 hours to Ürümqi.

You can buy tickets at the main railway station, although sleepers are usually only available the day of departure.

There is also a railway booking office (☎ 881-1664) on Donggang Xilu, just next door to the CAAC office (look for the railway track symbol) where you can buy tickets one or two days in advance, including sleeper tickets for some destinations. It's open from 8.30 am to 5 pm daily.

Getting Around

To/From the Airport The airport is at Zhongchuan, almost 90km north of the city. Airport buses leave from the CAAC office three hours before scheduled flight departures. The fare is Y20 for large buses, and Y25 for minibuses. Buses do fill up, so buy your ticket as soon as you've decided on a departure time. Upmarket hotels also run buses out to the airport. CAAC operates several airport hotels for people catching early-morning flights. Most run along the lines of the *Zhongchuan Hotel* (☎ 696-8531) *(zhōngchuān shānzhuāng)* which charges Y230 for a standard double.

Bus The most useful bus routes are No 1 and electric bus No 31 running from the main railway station to the west bus station and the Friendship Hotel. Bus Nos 7 and 10 run from the railway station up the length of Tianshui Lu before heading west and east respectively. Public buses cost Y0.30.

AROUND LANZHOU
Bingling Si
(bǐnglíng sì)

Located 75km south-west of Lanzhou, this set of Buddhist grottoes carved into the cliffs of a 60m-high gorge is one of the more unusual sights in Gansu. Isolated by the waters of the Liujiaxia Reservoir on the Yellow River, the grottoes were spared the vandalism of the Cultural Revolution.

The reservoir itself at one time actually threatened to inundate the caves, but a levy now protects the area from flooding during high-water periods.

Bingling Si is also called the Thousand Buddha Caves *(qiān fódòng)*, although in fact the total number of caves is only 183. The setting is spectacular, with soaring cliffs composed of eroded and porous rock with numerous natural cavities. The creators of these grottoes dangled from ropes while carving their masterpieces into the face of the cliffs – one has to wonder how many artisans fell to their deaths.

The oldest caves have been repaired and added to on numerous occasions since they were built during the Western Qin Dynasty. They contain 694 statues, 82 clay sculptures and a number of frescoes. Cave 169, containing a buddha and two bodhisattvas, is one of the oldest (420 AD) and best preserved in China. Most of the other caves were completed during the prosperous Tang period. The star of the caves is the 27m-high seated statue of Maitreya, the future buddha (cave 172).

Depending on which caves you want to see, entry costs Y12 to Y200. The cheaper tickets are for the unlocked caves, while the Y200 ticket gives you a complete guided tour including the magnificent caves 169 and 172.

Places to Stay In Yongjing you can stay at the *Liudian Hotel* (☎ (0930) 883-2066) *(liúdiàn bīnguǎn)* in a decent double with attached bath for Y50 per person.

Getting There & Away From Lanzhou to the caves is a 12 hour round trip – half of that time on a bus and half on a boat. The caves are inaccessible in winter because the water level in the river is too low and ice may also block the boats.

Western Travel Service (in the Lanzhou Hotel), CITS and Tianma Travel all run tours to the caves whenever they have enough people (the minimum is six unless you're prepared to pay more); the usual tour price is Y170 (including the basic entry ticket), which is reasonable. For a group of four Western Travel Service charges about Y200 per person. Hiring a taxi on your own will cost around Y400 to Y450. Unless you take a tour or charter a vehicle, it's not easy to get to the Bingling Si and back in one day. If you organise the trip yourself, you may have to stay overnight in Yongjing.

Minibuses do hang around the Liujiaxia dock until around 6 pm, but if there aren't enough people, they wait until the next day to head back to Lanzhou. There is one bus from Lanzhou to Yongjing scheduled to leave the west bus station at 7.30 am (Y10, two hours). It often arrives just in time for you to catch one of the boats to Bingling Si. The railway line to Yongjing does not carry passenger services.

All boats depart from Liujiaxia, a tiny port half an hour's walk uphill from Yongjing. The trip costs Y70 for foreigners (no student discounts) and takes three hours each way; boats only stay at the caves for one hour, so don't mess about! There are also speed boats which get there in one hour; these carry eight and usually cost Y800 to charter.

If you're going on to Linxia or Xiahe, you can avoid backtracking to Lanzhou by hopping on the Xining-Linxia bus, which rolls through the main street of Yongjing in the afternoon; the exact time is wildly variable. The trip from Yongjing to Linxia takes about 4½ hours, via an interesting high route east of the Yellow River through areas settled by the Dongxiang ethnic minority.

Xinglongshan
(xīnglóngshān)

The name means Flourishing Mountain, although it's more romantically known as Xiyunshan (Perch Cloud Mountain). The peak nudges 2400m and is decorated by more than 40 temples and pavilions which date back to the Han Dynasty.

The history of this scenic spot extends

back some 2000 years, although it has only recently made it on to the international tourist circuit.

The mountain is 60km east of Lanzhou in Yuzhong county. Buses from Lanzhou's east bus station offer the cheapest transport for individual travellers. Hiring a taxi to take you there and back in one day will cost around Y450, including the driver's waiting time.

MAIJISHAN & TIANSHUI
(màijīshān/tiānshuǐ)
Maijishan, a small mountain south of Tian-

shui town in south-eastern Gansu province, is the site of some fairly impressive Buddhist cave art.

The mountain bears some resemblance to a haystack, hence the name Maijishan (Haystack Mountain). The scenery is also quite nice: a lush valley dotted with fields and surrounded by green hills that offer some nice hiking opportunities.

Orientation
Tianshui has two sections – the railhead, known as Beidao, and the main city area 16km to the east, known as Qincheng. Minibuses run frequently between the two districts (Y1, 40 minutes each way); public bus No 1 also follows the same route. However, unless you have some business with CITS or need to catch a long-distance bus, there's no compelling reason to go to Qincheng.

Maijishan is about 35km south of Beidao. There are no direct public buses to Maijishan, but minibuses leave when full from in front of the railway station. The trip takes about 1½ hours and costs Y5.

Information
CITS (☎ 821-4463) has its main office in Qincheng on the 4th floor of the Xiebin Hotel, which is at 1 Huancheng Donglu.

In Beidao you can change both cash and travellers cheques at the Bank of China branch on Bu Nanlu, about 500m south of the intersection with Weibin Nanlu.

There's also a branch in Qincheng near

TIANSHUI 天水

1 Long-Distance Bus Station
  长途汽车站
2 Post & Telephone Office
  邮电大楼
3 Xiebin Hotel; CITS
  中国国际旅行社
4 Bank of China
  中国银行
5 Tianshui Hotel
  天水宾馆
6 Railway Station
  火车站
7 Post & Telephone Office
  邮电局
8 Government Hostel
  政府招待所
9 Bank of China
  中国银行
10 Asia Pacific Hotel
  亚太大酒店

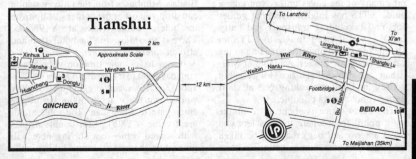

GANSU

the Tianshui Hotel. Hours are 8.30 am to 12 pm and 2.30 to 5.30 pm.

Maijishan Grottoes
(màijīshān shíkū)

The Maijishan grottoes are one of China's four largest temple groups; the others are at Datong, Luoyang and Dunhuang. The caves date back to the Northern Wei and Song dynasties and contain clay figures and wall paintings.

It's not certain just how the artists managed to clamber so high; one theory is that they piled up blocks of wood to the top of the mountain before moving down, gradually removing blocks of wood as they descended. Stone sculptures were evidently brought in from elsewhere, since the local rock is too soft for carving, as at Dunhuang.

Earthquakes have demolished many of the caves in the central section, while murals have tended to drop off due to damp or rain. Fire has also destroyed a large number of the wooden structures. Parts of the rock wall have now been stabilised with sprayed-on liquid cement.

Catwalks and steep spiral stairs have been built across the cliff face, so while the art is not as amazing as that at Dunhuang, getting to it is more fun. Most of the remaining 194 caves can only be seen through wire netting or barred doors – bring a torch (flashlight).

Apart from the Qifo Pavilion and the huge buddha statues which are easily accessible, it's hard to get a rewarding peek into many of the caves unless you take a guide. CITS has English speaking guides for Y80 (excluding transport and entry fees) – you'll need to go to CITS in Qincheng before heading to the caves. There are guides available at Maijishan (ask at the ticket office) for a fee, but getting an English-speaking one at short notice is not always possible.

The ticket office is about a 15 minute walk uphill from where the bus lets you off. Cameras and bags may not be taken into the caves area – the ticket office has a left-luggage section (Y2 per item) for this purpose. The caves are open from 9 am to 5 pm and admission costs Y25. You may also get charged a Y5 'area fee' if the minibus stops at the outermost gateway.

The area behind Maijishan has been turned into a botanical garden, and offers nice hiking opportunities, including access to the high ridge behind Maijishan, which offers fine views of the grottoes. To get to the park, take the stairs off to the right just as the road turns sharply left toward the Maijishan ticket office and upper parking lot.

Places to Stay & Eat
The *Government Hostel* (☎ 273-6246) *(zhèngfǔ zhāodàisuǒ)*, in the green-tiled building near the railway station, accepts foreigners and is friendly and cheap. Dorm beds range from Y8 to Y14, and doubles/triples with attached bath cost Y52/72.

Across the river and east of the railway station is the brand new *Asia Pacific Hotel* (☎ 272-7340), which is vying for the top spot among Tianshui's hotels. Prices seem quite reasonable, given the standard of the rooms: Y120 for a double, Y300 for a suite. Dorm beds are more pricey, ranging from Y25 to Y40, but the rooms should be fairly nice.

The *Tianshui Hotel* (☎ 821-2410) *(tiānshuǐ bīnguǎn)* at 5 Yingbin Lu is where foreigners are often directed when they stay in Qincheng. Its location is inconvenient, since nearly all transport to Maijishan leaves from the railway station in Beidao. Minibuses from the railway station can drop you off at the corner just up from the hotel. Doubles/triples are Y198/195. There is a *restaurant* in the hotel itself and also an *eatery* next door.

If you have some time on your hands, you may want to try the *Maiji Hotel* (☎ 281-1268) *(màijī shānzhuāng)*, a quiet, slightly worn-down place about 500m before the entry gate to Maijishan. The rates aren't great value – Y80/120 for doubles/triples with shared bath – but staying here will give you a chance to do some hiking in the area. The hotel has a small *restaurant*, and there are also *food stalls* and one or two cheap *restaurants* closer to Maijishan.

Getting There & Away

Bus From the long-distance bus station in Qincheng, there are two daily buses to Lanzhou: a regular bus at 6.30 am (Y27, eight hours) and a sleeper at 6.30 pm (Y54). There are also buses to Lanzhou that depart at similar times from in front of the railway station at Beidao.

Other long-distance destinations from the Qincheng bus station include a 6.30 am bus to Linxia (Y29, 13 hours), and a 5.40 am bus to Yinchuan in Ningxia province (Y45, 15 hours). There is also a daily bus to Guyuan (Ningxia) at 7 am (Y21, seven hours).

Train Tianshui is on the Xi'an-Lanzhou railway line; there are dozens of daily trains in either direction, all of which stop here. If you arrive early you can visit Maijishan as a day trip, avoiding the need to stay overnight in Tianshui.

During the day, westbound departures are concentrated between 11.30 am and 1 pm, but at night there are trains approximately hourly from 7 pm to 7 am. Heading east, trains leave about once an hour between 12.45 pm and 7 pm and again from 11 pm to 7 am. From Tianshui it's about seven hours to either Lanzhou or Xi'an.

LUOMEN

(luòmén)

In the Wushan Ranges outside Luomen, a small town 250km south-east of Lanzhou, are the **Buddhist Lashao Caves** and **Water Curtain Temple**. Carved onto a rock face is a remarkable 31m-high figure of Sakyamuni, made during the Northern Wei period.

The temple is a quaint old building nestled in a shallow cave on the nearby forested mountainside. Also nearby is the **Ten Thousand Buddha Cave** which, sadly, is in a state of poor repair.

The Water Curtain Temple and caves are in a remote and spectacular gorge, which is accessible only in good weather via a 17km makeshift road up the dry river bed. You can charter a minibus from Luomen and back for around Y100. The *Government Hostel (zhèngfǔ zhāodàisuǒ)* in Luomen has dorm beds from Y10 and doubles from Y50.

Luomen is on the Lanzhou-Xi'an railway line, but it's a small station and only a few trains stop here. Heading west to Lanzhou, train No 446 departs at 3.40 pm and No 503 leaves at 1.49 pm. Heading east, No 448 (bound for Chengdu via Baoji) leaves at 2.53 pm, and No 504 (to Zhengzhou) departs at 5.44 pm.

You can also get a bus to Luomen from Tianshui; buses leave from in front of the railway station (Beidao) at 2 pm, take four hours and cost Y8.

LINXIA

(línxià)

Linxia was once an important stop on the Silk Road between Lanzhou and Yangguan. The town has a decidedly Muslim Hui character, with a large mosque in the centre of town and old men with long stringy beards and white caps shuffling about the streets.

In the markets you'll see carved gourds, daggers, saddlery, carpets, wrought iron goods and a thriving trade in spectacles made with ground crystal lenses and metal frames.

Linxia is also a regional centre for the Dongxiang minority. The Dongxiang minority speak their own Altaic language and are believed to be descendants of 13th century immigrants from central Asia who were moved forcibly to China after Kublai Khan's conquest of the Middle East. Some have greenish-blue eyes, high cheekbones and large noses.

Places to Stay

The friendly *Shuiquan Hotel* (☎ (0930) 621-4968) *(shuǐquán bīnguǎn)* is 50m along on your right as you leave the south long-distance bus station. It offers beds in three person dorms for Y10, and doubles with bathroom for Y40 and Y80.

Just a few minutes' walk to the left from the bus station is the *Linxia Hotel* (☎ (0930) 621-1321) *(línxià bīnguǎn)*, which is a bit better furnished and has dorms from Y20 and doubles with private bath for Y80.

Getting There & Away
Buses to Linxia (Y22, four hours) leave Lanzhou's west bus station every 30 minutes between 7 am and 2 pm. Private mini-buses also make the trip frequently and run until 6 pm.

In the opposite direction, buses leave Linxia for Lanzhou every 20 minutes or so from 6.30 am to 5 pm. The ride back should only cost Y12, as this bus station doesn't levy a foreigners' surcharge.

From Linxia, buses to Xiahe (three hours, Y10) leave approximately every 40 minutes between 6.30 am and 4.40 pm. Buses to Hezuo (Y10, 3½ hours) leave about every 30 minutes from 6.30 am to 5 pm. There is one daily bus to Xining (Y23, 11 hours) at 6 am, which runs via Yongjing.

There are two long-distance bus stations in Linxia, but you should only need to go to the larger south bus station: the old north bus station is more for local services.

XIAHE
(xiàhé)
Set in a beautiful mountain valley, Xiahe is most definitely worth a visit, especially if you can't get to Tibet. Outside of Lhasa, it's the leading Tibetan monastery town and many Tibetans come here on pilgrimage dressed in their finest, most colourful clothing. Outside of town there are hiking opportunities in nearby grasslands and the surrounding mountains.

Religious activity centres on the Labrang Monastery, one of the six major Tibetan monasteries of the Gelukpa (Yellow Hat sect of Tibetan Buddhism). The others are Ganden, Sera and Drepung monasteries in the Lhasa area; Tashilhunpo Monastery in Shigatse; and Ta'er (Kumbum) Monastery in Huangzhong, Qinghai Province.

Walking through the warrens and alleys of this huge monastery, side by side with pilgrims and monks, feels like you've entered another world.

Xiahe is a microcosm of south-western Gansu, with the area's three principal ethnic groups represented. In rough terms, Xiahe's population is 45% Tibetan, 45% Han and 10% Hui.

Orientation
At 2920m above sea level, Xiahe stretches for several kilometres east-to-west along the valley of the Daxia River. The Labrang Monastery is roughly halfway along, and marks the division between Xiahe's mainly Han and Hui Chinese eastern quarter and the overwhelmingly Tibetan village to the west.

A 3km pilgrims' way, with long rows of prayer wheels (1174 of them!) and Buddhist shrines, encircles the monastery. There are some 40 smaller monasteries affiliated with Labrang in the surrounding mountains (as well as many others scattered across Tibet and China) and the area is a great place for hiking in clean, peaceful surroundings. Take warm clothing and rain gear.

You can follow the river up to Sangke or head up into the surrounding valleys, but carry a stick or a pocket full of rocks, as wild dogs can be a problem.

Information
PSB The PSB is just opposite the Friendship Hotel.

Money There are several banks in Xiahe, but no Bank of China, and it is difficult to change travellers cheques here. However, some of the small antique shops along the main street will give you a reasonable rate for US dollars (cash).

Other Information If you need to buy insurance for bus travel, there is a PICC office in a compound just across the first bridge. You can rent bikes at restaurants or guesthouses for about Y15 a day.

Labrang Monastery
(lābǔlèng sì)
The monastery was built in 1709 by E'ang-zongzhe, the first-generation Jiamuyang (living buddha), who came from the nearby town of Ganjia. It is home to six institutes (Institute of Esoteric Buddhism, Higher & Lower Institutes of Theology, Institute of Medicine, Institute of Astrology and Institute of Law). There are also numerous temple halls, 'living buddha' residences and living quarters for the monks.

At its peak the monastery housed nearly 4000 monks, but their ranks were decimated during the Cultural Revolution, when monks and buildings took a heavy beating. The numbers are gradually recovering, and there are about 1200 monks today, drawn from Qinghai, Gansu, Sichuan and Inner Mongolia.

In April 1985 the main Prayer Hall of the Institute of Esoteric Buddhism was razed in a fire caused by faulty electrical wiring. The fire is said to have burnt for a week and destroyed some priceless relics. The hall's reconstruction was completed at great cost in mid-1990, but the monks remain reluctant to allow the use of electricity in most parts of the monastery.

Entry to the main temple is by tour only (no student discounts). One of the monks (some speak English well) will show you around. Tours generally include the Institute of Medicine, the Ser Kung Golden Temple, the Prayer Hall and the museum. The ticket office and souvenir shop are on the right-hand side of the monastery car park. The office opens from 9.30 am to 12 pm and from 2.30 pm to 5 pm. Admission is Y21.50.

XIAHE & LABRANG MONASTERY
夏河、拉卜楞寺

1 Labrang Hotel; CITS
拉卜楞宾馆
中国国际旅行社
2 Monastery Ticket Office
售票处
3 The Restaurant of Labrang Monastery
拉卜楞寺饭店
4 Labrang Monastery Guesthouse
拉卜楞寺招待所
5 Snowland Restaurant
雪域餐厅
6 Tara Guesthouse
卓玛旅社
7 Mosque
清真寺
8 Daxia Hotel
大厦宾馆
9 White Conch Hotel
白海螺宾馆
10 PSB
公安局
11 Bus Station
汽车站
12 Post & Telephone Office
邮电局
13 Friendship Hotel
友谊宾馆
14 PICC
中国人民保险公司

Access to the rest of the monastery area is free, and you can easily spend several hours just walking around and taking in the atmosphere. Try to make friends with a monk or two: they'll probably be happy to invite you into their living quarters, which always makes for an interesting house call.

Festivals

These are important not only for the monks, but also for the nomads who stream into town from the grasslands in multi-coloured splendour. Since the Tibetans use a lunar calendar, dates for individual festivals vary from year to year.

The Monlam (Great Prayer) Festival starts three days after the Tibetan New Year, which is usually in February or early March. On the 13th, 14th, 15th and 16th days of this month there are some spectacular ceremonies.

On the morning of the 13th a *thangka* (sacred painting on cloth) of Buddha measuring over 30m by 20m is unfurled on the other side of the Daxia River from the hillside facing the monastery. This event is accompanied by processions and prayer assemblies.

On the 14th there is an all-day session of Cham dances performed by 35 masked dancers, with Yama, the lord of death, playing the leading role. On the 15th there is an evening display of butter lanterns and sculptures. On the 16th the Maitreya statue is paraded around the monastery all day.

During the second month (usually starting in March or early April) there are several interesting festivals, especially those held on the seventh and eighth days. Scriptural debates, lighting of butter lamps, collective prayers and blessings take place at other times during the year to commemorate Sakyamuni, Tsong Khapa or individual generations of the 'living buddhas'.

Places to Stay

The best place in town, without a doubt, is *Tara Guesthouse* (☎ 712-1274) (*zhuōmǎ lǚ'shè*) which straddles the border between the Tibetan and Han parts of town. All the rooms are Tibetan style and are very clean and comfortable. Beds in cosy four-bed dorms are Y15 and doubles with shared bath are Y40. There are no showers, but there's a public bathhouse right next door. The owner, Tsering Dolma, speaks fluent English, is a fine host and is quite knowledgeable about the area.

The next best choice in the budget category is probably the *Labrang Monastery Guesthouse* (*lābǔlèng sì zhāodàisuǒ*), a quiet place nestled inside a small courtyard with beds from Y12. It doesn't have showers, but there's always plenty of hot water from the boiler.

Another nice option is the *Labrang Hotel* (☎ 712-1849) (*lābǔlèng bīnguǎn*) by the river a few kilometres up the valley from the village. It's a friendly, tranquil place, and one of the few hotels in China where you can wake to the gentle sound of a rushing stream. The only minus is the 'hot' water, which seems to only get lukewarm at best. In the rear building, beds in triples with private bath are Y35, and doubles are Y100 – both fairly good value for the money. More expensive doubles in the main building (Y240) and in Tibetan style concrete 'tents' (Y320) are not such a good deal, however. You can get there by motor-tricycle for about Y5, or walk there in 45 minutes. The hotel rents bicycles for Y5 per hour or Y15 a day.

In the Chinese quarter are a few standard Chinese-style hotels which offer cheap rooms, but very little in the way of personality. The *Daxia Hotel* (☎ 712-1546) (*dàxià bīnguǎn*) is a fairly grimy place with dorms from Y16 and doubles with bathroom for Y52.

Near the bus station, the *Friendship Hotel* (☎ 712-1498) (*yǒuyì bīnguǎn*) offers dorm beds in quads/triples for Y15/20 and decent doubles for Y80.

The *White Conch Hotel* (☎ 712-2486) (*báihǎiluó bīnguǎn*) is a fairly new place aimed mostly at tour groups. For the record, doubles cost Y200 (not a great deal) and beds in a triple are Y50.

Places to Eat

For Tibetan food, locals say the two best places in town are the *Restaurant of the Labrang Monastery (lābŭlèngsì fàndiàn)* and the *Snowland Restaurant (xuĕyù cāntīng)*. Both are just west of Tara Guesthouse, and have authentic Tibetan dishes such as yak-milk yoghurt and tsampa: a mixture of yak butter, cheese, barley and sugar mixed into a dough with the fingers and eaten uncooked. A bit bland, but worth trying at least once. The Restaurant of the Labrang Monastery also has a rear courtyard where tables are set up during the summer months, allowing you to enjoy your meals outside.

There is a row of small Sichuan and other Chinese style places east of Tara Guesthouse along the main road. One place best avoided is the *Little Tibetan Restaurant*. Not only is it not Tibetan (it's run by Hui Chinese), but the prices are ridiculously high – how about Y21 for fried eggs and tomato and a cup of tea? The only Tibetan item on the menu is yoghurt.

Things to Buy

You can pick up some Tibetan handicrafts in the shops along the main street, including yak-butter pots, daggers, fur-lined boots, colourful Tibetan shawls, tiny silver teapots and Tibetan *laba* trumpets. However, be advised that some items are imported from Nepal or India. Prices in the tourist shops are negotiable, but the Tibetan household goods shops have set prices: don't annoy them by trying to bargain.

Getting There & Away

Xiahe is accessible only by bus. Some travellers arrive from Lanzhou, while others come from Sichuan province to the south.

From Lanzhou, there is only one direct daily bus departing from the west bus station at 7.30 am (Y40). It's an eight to nine-hour ride, including a stop for lunch near Linxia. If you can't get a direct ticket from Lanzhou to Xiahe, then take a morning bus to Linxia and change there (see the Linxia section for more details).

The roads along this route are pretty good and the scenery helps the trip pass more quickly.

From Xiahe the direct bus to Lanzhou leaves at 7.20 am; turn up a bit earlier to get a good seat and store your luggage on the roof. The fare should only be Y20, as the Xiahe bus station wasn't charging foreigners double at the time of writing.

Buses to Linxia (Y10, three hours) run once or twice an hour between 6.30 am and 4 pm. The schedule is similar for buses to Hezuo (Y6.50, 2½ hours).

There is also one daily bus to Tongren, in Qinghai province (Y24, 5 hours), but due to poor road conditions, buses coming from Tongren don't always arrive on time, which usually means the next day's departure from Xiahe is cancelled. From Tongren you can get a connecting bus to Xining.

AROUND XIAHE
Sangke & Ganjia Grasslands
(sāngkē, gānjiā cǎoyuán)

Around and beyond the village of **Sangke**, 14km up the valley from Xiahe, is a small lake surrounded by large expanses of open grassland where the Tibetans graze their yak herds. In summer these rolling pastures are at their greenest and have numerous wildflowers. It's a lovely place for walking.

The Labrang Hotel has some nomad-style tents on the grasslands where you can stay overnight for around Y40 per bed. The road from Xiahe rises gradually and you can bicycle up in about one hour. You can also get there by taking a bus from Xiahe to Sangke village *(sāngkē gōngshè)* or hire a motor-tricycle for about Y20 return.

Around 34km outside of Xiahe, the **Ganjia Grasslands** feature rolling hills and even nicer views than those of Sangke. Buses also run to here: ask to go to *gānjiā gōngshè*. There is a certain gentleman in Xiahe who has made healthy profit by telling foreigners that Ganjia is a closed area and the only way to get there is by taking his van for Y150 per person. Don't believe it: Ganjia is open and you can get there and back on public transport for less than Y10.

HEZUO

(hézuò)

This town is mainly used as a transit point for travellers plying the route between Gansu and Sichuan provinces. It's not too exciting, but certainly has some character – traders walk around with fur pelts slung over their shoulders, Tibetan monks make their way through narrow backstreets and white-capped Chinese Hui Muslims are busy running shops, restaurants and other small businesses.

About 1.8km from the bus station along the main road in the direction of Xiahe is the **Ando Hezuo Mila Riba Palace** *(mǐlāerbā fógé)*. Built in 1777, this 14 storey temple was razed by Red Guards during the Cultural Revolution, and was rebuilt in 1988. The inside furnishings are quite elaborate, and a climb to the top rewards you with views of the beautiful grasslands surrounding Hezuo. Admission is Y5.

Places to Stay & Eat

Travellers often end up having to spend the night in Hezuo, especially those heading south, as buses heading in that direction leave in the morning, far too early for any connecting bus coming from Lanzhou or Xiahe.

The two places that most foreigners wind up staying in are both named *Gannan Hotel* in English, although the Chinese names differ. However, it's not hard to tell them apart. The *Gannan Hotel* (☎ 821-3186) *(gānnán bīnguǎn)* is to the left as you exit the bus station, across the street: look for gold characters on a blue background. Dorm beds in this humble spot range from Y15 in a triple with shared bath to Y25 in doubles/triples with bath attached. Hot water is available from 9 pm to 10 pm.

The other *Gannan Hotel* (☎ 821-3611) *(gānnán fàndiàn)* is 1km from the bus station along the main road in the direction of Sichuan province. It's slightly nicer than its namesake, but its location is inconvenient. Dorm beds cost Y11 to Y21 and doubles are Y82. A motor-tricycle from the bus station to here should cost Y2.

Getting There & Away

Hezuo is the place where buses from Zöige (Sichuan province) and Xiahe meet. There are fairly frequent buses to Xiahe (Y6.5, 2½ hours) from 7.30 am to 4 pm.

Going south is a different story. There is only one bus a day to Zoigê, leaving at 7.30 am (Y27, nine hours). Buses to Langmusi leave at 6.30 am and 8 am (Y14, six hours). At the time of writing a sleeper bus connecting Hezuo with Chengdu was supposed to begin operation, so this may offer an alternative way to get to Zoigê or Songpan.

LANGMUSI

(lǎngmùsì)

This attractive little village has two large Tibetan Buddhist monasteries, each with around 600 monks. There's mountainous scenery on all sides and the local people get around on the back of yaks. It's one of the most Tibetan places outside of Tibet, and a relaxing place to while away a few days.

Accommodation in Langmusi is pretty basic. The *Langmusi Hotel (làngmùsì fàndiàn)* has comfortable dorm beds in triple rooms for Y15. There are no showers, but the washroom does have hot water.

A more grotty alternative is the *Dachang Langmusi Chi Shi Yuan Hotel (dàchāng làngmùsì chīshí yuàn)*. Beds here are only Y10, but rooms are dirtier, have no locks, and some women travellers have reported being hassled by the truck-driving clientele who frequent the place.

There are several small restaurants in town, including two with English signs and menus, the *Langmusi Restaurant* and *The Little Restaurant*. The Little Restaurant is reportedly the better of the two because of its overall larger portions and excellent meat and vegie dumplings.

Unless you take a direct bus to Langmusi from Hezuo, you'll probably get there on one of the Hezuo-Zoigê buses, which drop you off at an intersection about 4km from the village. Motor-tricycles are usually waiting there, and will take you into town for Y1 or Y2 (although they'll no doubt start by charging you a higher price).

To get to Zoigê you'll need to catch one of the buses from Hezuo, which means catching a motor-tricycle out to the intersection with the main road to Sichuan. Buses to Zoigê generally pass by between noon and 3 pm. There is also a daily bus direct to Hezuo departing at 6.30 am (Y14, six hours).

GANSU-SICHUAN ROUTE

This scenic route goes via rough dirt roads along the eastern edge of the Tibetan mountains and is usually done in several stages, stopping at Linxia, Xiahe, Hezuo, Langmusi or Zoigê, and Songpan – a trip taking at least four days.

For travel through this area you'll almost certainly need to have PICC insurance. See the preceding sections on Linxia, Xiahe, Hezuo and Langmusi for accommodation and transport information for these places.

On a highland plateau two hours further south in Sichuan is Zoigê *(ruòěrgài)*, from where it's possible to make a side trip to Jiuzhaigou National Park. Road conditions worsen noticeably once you cross from Gansu into Sichuan, and from Langmusi it's a bumpy four hours to Zoigê.

From Zoigê it's a full day's journey by bus south to Chengdu, although many opt to break up the journey with a stay in Songpan. For more information on these areas, see the Sichuan chapter.

ZHANGYE

(zhāngyè)

Zhangye was once an important garrison town and a stop on the Silk Road (Marco Polo supposedly spent a year here). Photographs taken at the turn of the century show a largely intact old city with high defensive walls, but little remains of the original Zhangye today.

The only real attraction is the Giant Buddha Temple *(dàfó sì)*, which houses an impressive 34m-long sleeping buddha. This clay statue is the largest indoor reclining buddha in China and was built during the Western Xia period. The temple is open from 7.30 am to 6.30 pm and admission is Y22 for foreigners.

Zhangye

ZHANGYE 张掖

1 Post & Telephone Office
邮电大楼
2 Xinhua Bookstore
新华书店
3 Drum Tower
鼓楼
4 Bank of China
中国银行
5 Ganzhou Hotel
甘州宾馆
6 Hexi Hotel
河西宾馆
7 East Bus Station
汽车东站
8 Night Market
夜市
9 PSB
公安局
10 Muta Temple
木塔寺
11 Zhangye Hotel; CITS
张掖宾馆
中国国际旅行社
12 Giant Buddha Temple
大佛寺
13 South Bus Station
汽车南站

Sixty-eight kilometres south of Zhangye in the foothills of Qilianshan, **Mati** *(mǎtí)* was until recently a beautiful Tibetan village centred on the Horse's Hoof Temple *(mǎtí sì)*, which is built within a high cliff face and accessible only via an amazing passageway through the caves. However, CITS and other travel agencies have gotten their hooks into it and the area has lost nearly all its original character. The surrounding scenery is still nice, but it's hard to get away from the fact that this place is now mainly a tourist trap.

Places to Stay

The *Ganzhou Hotel* (☎ 821-2402) *(gānzhōu bīnguǎn)* on Da Nanjie charges Y164 for basic doubles and has beds in concrete floored dorms from Y13.

The *Zhangye Hotel* (☎ 821-2601) *(zhāngyè bīnguǎn)* at 65 Xianfu Nanjie has two sections. In the old wing beds in small dorms are Y25 to Y30 and grungy doubles go for Y124. The newer, two star wing in the back has doubles for Y260 – it's not great value, although they're considerably nicer than those in the old wing. The hotel complex also has a CITS office (☎ 821-3505, ext 394).

The one other hotel taking foreigners when we last visited was the friendly *Hexi Hotel* (☎ 822-4270) *(héxī bīnguǎn)*, which offers clean standard doubles for Y80 per person. If you're looking for a room with attached bath, this is the best choice.

Getting There & Away

All trains running between Lanzhou and Ürümqi stop at Zhangye. From Zhangye it's 3¾ hours to Jiayuguan and nine hours to Liuyuan. Going east it takes 11 hours to reach Lanzhou. The railway station is 10km from the city centre: minibuses make the trip for Y2, taxis Y10.

Zhangye has several bus stations: The east bus station, near the Hexi Hotel, has three buses each morning to Jiayuguan (Y18.50, five hours) and up to eight buses in the evening to Lanzhou, three to four of which are sleepers.

Regular buses cost Y38, sleepers Y85, and the trip takes around 11 hours. The south bus station also has morning departures to Jiayuguan and early-evening departures to Lanzhou. Buses to Mati leave from the south bus station at 3 pm Monday to Friday. The 1¾ hour journey costs Y6, and buses depart from Mati the following morning at 7 am. On the weekend special tourist buses (Y12) leave Zhangye at 8 am, and then head back from Mati at 4 pm the same day.

JIAYUGUAN

(jiāyùguān)

Jiayuguan (Jiayu Pass) is an ancient Han Chinese outpost. The Great Wall once extended beyond here, but in 1372, during the first few years of the Ming Dynasty, a fortress was built. From then on Jiayuguan was considered both the western tip of the wall and the western boundary of the empire.

The city itself lacks soul. Any personality it may have once had was scraped away to make room for the endless rows of socialist public housing blocks that ring the city centre. However, it's not an unfriendly place, and the snow-capped mountains provide a dramatic backdrop when the weather is clear.

Although a mandatory stop for tour groups, Jiayuguan and its surrounding sights are not so amazing as to merit a special visit. However, if you're moving east or west through Gansu at a leisurely pace, a stop here should prove interesting enough.

Information

Tourist Offices Xiongguan Travel Service (☎ 622-6258), in the Jiayuguan Hotel, is allied with CITS. The Chang Cheng Travel Service at the Chang Cheng Hotel is a similar operation. Both are mainly directed at tour groups and can't do much to help individual travellers.

PSB The PSB office is in the south of the city, but has a roving foreign affairs officer who visits the hotels. If you need a visa

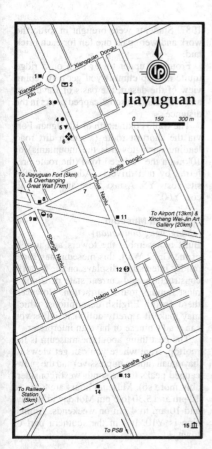

Jiayuguan 嘉峪关

1 Jiayuguan Hotel;
  Xiongguan Travel Service
  嘉峪关宾馆、雄关旅行社
2 Post & Telephone Office
  邮电局
3 CAAC
  民航售票处
4 Xinhua Bookstore
  新华书店
5 Yinguang Restaurant
  银光餐厅
6 Renmin Department Store
  人民商城
7 Night Market
  夜市
8 Yingbin Hotel;
  Linyuan Restaurant
  迎宾大厦、林苑酒家
9 Wumao Hotel
  物贸宾馆
10 Bus Station
  长途汽车站
11 Xiongguan Hotel
  雄关宾馆
12 Bank of China
  中国银行
13 Youth Hotel
  青年宾馆
14 Changcheng Hotel;
  Changcheng Travel Service
  长城宾馆、长城旅行社
15 Great Wall Museum
  长城博物馆

extension, contact the front desk of your hotel and they'll arrange for him or her to come by.

Money The Bank of China is on Xinhua Nanlu and is open from 9.30 am 5.30 pm Monday to Friday and 10 am to 4 pm on Saturday.

Post & Communications The post and telephone office is diagonally opposite the Jiayuguan Hotel, has a parcel service, and is open from 8.30 am to 7 pm.

Jiayuguan Fort
(*jiāyùguān chénglóu*)
This is Jiayuguan's main tourist drawcard, and has taken on a sort of carnival atmosphere. The fort guards the pass which lies between snow-capped Qilianshan peaks and Black Mountain (*hēishān*) of the Mazong Range. During the Ming Dynasty this was considered the terminus of the Great Wall, although crumbling fragments can be seen to the west.

Built in 1372, the fort was dubbed the 'Impregnable Defile Under Heaven'. Although the Chinese often controlled territory far beyond Jiayuguan, this was the last major stronghold of the empire to the west. At the eastern end of the fort is the Gate

GANSU

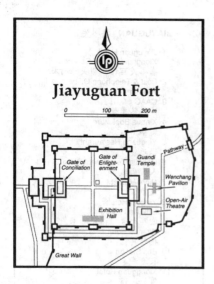

Jiayuguan Fort

Gate of Conciliation

Gate of Enlightenment

Guandi Temple

Pathway

Wenchang Pavilion

Open-Air Theatre

Exhibition Hall

Great Wall

of Enlightenment *(guānghuà mén)* and in the west is the Gate of Conciliation *(róuyuǎn mén)*. Over each gate stand 17m-high towers with upturned flying eaves. On the inside of each gate are horse lanes leading up to the top of the wall. However, the entire complex has been renovated, which makes it a bit hard to get a feel for its history.

The fort is 5km west of Jiayuguan. You can cycle out there in about half an hour, or take a taxi for Y30 return, not including waiting time. The fort is open from 8.30 am to 6 pm, and entry costs Y20, plus another Y3 to go up to the main viewing tower. Video cameras are prohibited inside the fort.

Overhanging Great Wall
(xuánbì chángchéng)
The Overhanging Great Wall is 7km northwest of Jiayuguan and in some respects more interesting than the fort.

Linking Jiayuguan with Black Mountain, the wall is believed to have been constructed in 1540. It had since pretty much crumbled to dust, but was reconstructed in 1987. Students were brought in to do the work and were paid one fen for each brick laid.

From the upper tower high on a ridge (quite a steep climb!) you get a sweeping view of the desert, the oasis of Jiayuguan and the glittering snow-capped peaks in the distance.

The wall is 6km north of Jiayuguan Fort via the shortest route (a rough dirt road leading north towards the mountains) or 10km on the surfaced road (the route preferred by taxi drivers). Admission to the site costs Y5. A taxi there and back will cost Y60.

Great Wall Museum
(chángchéng bówùguǎn)
Built to resemble the towers and turrets of the Great Wall, this museum has some mildly interesting displays on the history, construction, and current state of China's most famous tourist attraction. However, there are no English descriptions, which may make it a pretty dull visit unless you can read Chinese or have an interpreter.

The best thing about the museum is the rooftop, from where you can get views of Jiayuguan (not so impressive) and the snow-capped peaks to the south-west (considerably more so). Museum hours are 8 am to 12 pm and 3.30 to 6 pm Monday to Friday, and 10 am to 4 pm on weekends. Admission is Y10. It's in the southern part of town.

Xincheng Wei-Jin Art Gallery
(xīnchéng wèijìn mù)
This is not really an art gallery, but ancient tombs with original wall paintings. There are literally thousands of tombs in the desert 20km east of Jiayuguan, but only one is currently open to visitors. The tombs date from approximately 220 to 420 AD (the Wei and Jin periods).

Fairly few tourists come here, and there are no regular buses. A taxi costs around Y80 return.

The gallery is open each day from 8 am to 7 pm and admission is Y31.

July 1st Glacier
(qīyī bīngchuān)
The glacier lies at 4300m, high up in the Qilianshan mountains. Hikers can walk a 5km trail alongside the glacier, but at that elevation it gets cold even in summer, so come prepared.

The glacier is about 120km south-west of Jiayuguan and is reached via a rotten road. To charter a small minibus or taxi to the glacier will cost about Y600 return (Xiongguan asks Y200 per person for a minimum of seven people).

Organised Tours
Xiongguan and Changcheng travel agencies usually charge around Y240 per person for day tours to the surrounding sights, and this only if you have a minimum of four people. If you can fill a minibus, the cost will be lower.

Places to Stay
Among the best budget options is the *Yingbin Hotel* (☎ 628-3145) *(yíngbīn dàshà)* which is in a good location by the bus station and a group of restaurants. Dorm beds in fairly new triples with shared bath are priced at Y18. Doubles with attached bath are Y36 per person, while 'luxury' doubles (none too luxurious) cost Y90 per person.

Across the intersection the *Wumao Hotel* (☎ 622-7514) *(wùmào bīnguǎn)* is OK, but not as good value as the Yingbin. Beds in two and three person dorms are Y30 each, while doubles and triples with private bath are Y150.

The *Xiongguan Hotel* (☎ 622-5115) *(xióngguān bīnguǎn)* on Xinhua Nanlu is also not a bad deal. Dorm beds range from Y12 to Y16, and doubles with private bath are Y80 and Y100. The desk staff are friendly, but may try to tack on a foreigner's surcharge; be polite but firm and they may back down.

The *Youth Hotel* (☎ 622-4671) *(qīngnián bīnguǎn)* is built in an incongruous European 'castle style' complete with flags and turrets, but inside it's a fairly standard, depressing Chinese hotel. Dorms in basic concrete rooms costs Y31, and a standard double with private bath Y120 (the latter is not a good deal). The hotel is on Jianshe Xilu, at the southern end of town.

Across Shengli Nanlu is the three star *Changcheng Hotel* (☎ 622-0306) *(chángchéng bīnguǎn)*. Fairly plush doubles are priced at Y398, although you may be able to get them down to Y300 if the hotel isn't filled with tour groups. There are also some lesser appointed triples for Y270, which are better value.

On the traffic circle at the centre of town is the other upmarket option, the *Jiayuguan Hotel* (☎ 622-6983 *(jiāyùguān bīnguǎn)*. Doubles in the new wing are Y320, and in the old wing are Y250; fairly reasonable given the facilities and service. There are also dorms in the old wing, ranging from Y25 per bed in a quad to Y45 in a double with shared bath.

The *Railway Guesthouse (tiědào bīnguǎn)* is next to the railway station, 5km south of central Jiayuguan. Beds in rather grimy rooms range from Y15 to Y30, and doubles with bath attached are Y80. It's not the best spot in town, but convenient if you're catching an early train.

Places to Eat
Restaurants are few and far between in Jiayuguan and tend to close early – around 10 pm. Just opposite the bus station is a collection of competing restaurants. One of the most popular is the *Linyuan Restaurant (línyuàn jiǔjiā)*, which does spicy Sichuan food. It has a sign in English that says 'Linyuan Jiujia' and one or two of the staff speak a little English.

Another good place is the *Yinguang Restaurant (yínguāng cāntīng)* which serves huge portions at reasonable prices. With neither English sign nor menus, it may be a bit tricky to find and then order food. Go to the right-hand side of the Renmin Department Store and look for an covered entrance with a silver gate: the restaurant is inside, on the opposite edge of the inner courtyard.

For cheaper eats try the *night market* or the area in front of the Renmin Department Store, which is crammed with stalls selling grilled beef and chicken skewers, fried dumplings, spicy cold noodles *(liáng miàn)*, and plenty of draft beer, which unfortunately tends to be rather flat.

Getting There & Away
Air There are flights to Dunhuang (Y370, daily in summer), Lanzhou (Y750, three a week) and Xi'an (Y1180, three a week). The flight schedule tends to expand in summer and shrink in winter.

The CAAC booking office (☎ 622-6237) is on Xinhua Nanlu, just to the south of the Jiayuguan Hotel.

Bus There are five direct daily buses between Dunhuang and Jiayuguan – the 380km trip takes nine hours. There are also one to two sleeper coaches daily to Lanzhou (Y180, 16 hours).

There are numerous buses to Zhangye, but only three go directly – at the time of writing they left at 8, 9.30 and 11 am. The 250km trip takes nearly five hours, and costs Y70 for foreigners. The indirect buses take about twice as long.

Train Jiayuguan lies on the Lanzhou-Ürümqi railway line. From here it's five hours to Liuyuan, less than four hours to Zhangye, and 15 hours to Lanzhou. Train No 206 will get you to Lanzhou, but the returning No 205 only goes as far as Yümen, the next major town west of Jiayuguan.

The railway station is 5km south of the town centre. A taxi there should cost no more than Y10. Minibuses run down Xinhua Nanlu to the station and charge Y1. There are regular trains to Beijing, Chengdu, Korla, Lanzhou, Shanghai, Ürümqi, Xi'an and Zhengzhou.

Getting Around
To/From the Airport The airport is 13km north-east of the city and taxis there cost Y40. An airport bus from the CAAC office meets all flights.

Taxi Taxis, motorbikes and minibuses congregate outside the Jiayuguan and Changcheng hotels and around the bus station. As a general rule, taxi drivers charge Y12 for every hour they have to wait for you at a sight, although some will give you the first 30 minutes or hour free. Others may be willing to bargain a single rate that includes waiting time. Hiring a taxi to take in most of the sights will cost around Y400.

Bicycle The Jiayuguan, Changcheng and Youth hotels all rent bicycles for Y2 to Y3 per hour. Bikes are excellent for getting around town, to the fort and (if you don't mind the occasional gulp of dust) to the Overhanging Great Wall too. However, you'll need motorised transport for the other sights.

LIUYUAN
(liǔyuán)
Liuyuan, a forlorn little town on the Lanzhou-Ürümqi railway line, is the jumping off point for Dunhuang, 130km and 2½ hours south by bus.

Unless you're catching an early morning train, there should be no need to stay here. But if you must, the only place that takes foreigners when we last visited was the *Liuyuan Hotel* (☎ 557-2340) *(liǔyuán bīnguǎn*, which has doubles for Y160 and triples for Y150. Across the street there's another *Liuyuan Hotel* (the Chinese name is different), which would be a lot cheaper if you can convince them to let you stay there.

There are six trains daily in each direction. Going east, it takes five hours to reach Jiayuguan and 20 hours to Lanzhou. To the west, it's 12 hours to Turpan and 15 hours to Ürümqi. There are also regular trains to Beijing, Chengdu, Korla, Shanghai, Xi'an and Zhengzhou.

Minibuses for Dunhuang depart from in front of the railway station when trains arrive. If there are enough passengers you will leave immediately; if not be prepared to wait until the bus fills up. The one way fare is Y10, and Y5 for each bag placed on the roof.

If you're coming back from Dunhuang to catch a train, check the weather: if sand storms are blowing, the ride could take as long as four hours. Taxis also make the trip for Y200, and get there in half the time.

DUNHUANG
(dūnhuáng)

After travelling for hours towards Dunhuang, the flat, barren desert landscape suddenly gives way to lush green cultivated fields with mountainous rolling sand dunes as a backdrop. The area has a certain haunting beauty, especially at night under a star-studded sky. It's not so much the desert dunes and romantic nights that attract so many tourists to Dunhuang, but the superb Buddhist art at the nearby Mogao Caves.

During the Han and Tang dynasties, Dunhuang was a major point of interchange between China and the outside world – a stopping-off post for both incoming and outgoing trading caravans. Despite a surge in tourism development, the town still has a fairly relaxed feel to it, and it's easy to kick back here for a few days. There are several sights worth visiting in the surrounding area, and the town is just lively enough to keep you entertained, but not overwhelmed.

Information

Tourist Offices The main CITS office is in the International Hotel and there's also a branch inside the Dunhuang Hotel (Binguan). There are other travel agents scattered about town, sequestered in various hotels. Most can book train and air tickets, as well as tours to remote sights such as Yumen Pass.

PSB The PSB foreign affairs office is in the main PSB building on Xi Dajie, near the Bank of China. It's open Monday to Friday from 8 am to 12 pm and again from 3 to 6.30 pm.

Money The Bank of China keeps the same hours as the PSB.

Post & Communications The post and telephone office is on the north-western side of the main traffic circle and is open between 8.30 am and 7 pm.

Dunhuang County Museum
(dūnhuáng xiàn bówùguǎn)

The museum is on Yangguan Donglu, east of the main traffic circle, and makes for a pleasant browse.

Exhibits include some of the Tibetan and Chinese scriptures unearthed from Cave No 17 at Mogao, sacrificial objects from the Han to Tang dynasties, and relics such as silks, brocades, and reed torches for the beacons from the Yangguan and Yumen passes. For the curious, the incongruously placed MiG-15 fighter jet in the front courtyard was originally destined for the town park, but before it could be moved the museum built a main gate. Today there's no moving the thing unless the wings are shorn off.

Museum hours are 8 am to 12 pm and 3 to 6.30 pm. Admission is Y15.

Places to Stay

Most hotels in Dunhuang vary the rates by season. Basically, the tourist season is from June to September, and hotel rates rise about 30% or more at that time. The rates quoted in this section are for the off season.

Dunhuang has literally dozens of hotels. The following select list represents some of the better choices in terms of value for money (as well as a few that should probably be skipped).

Almost directly opposite the bus station, the two star *Feitian Hotel* (☎ 882-2726) *(fēitiān bīnguǎn)* offers reasonable rates and a good location. Clean, multi-bed dorms start at Y10, and spacious doubles are Y100. Nearby, the *Western Region Hotel* (☎ 882-3017) *(xīyù bīnguǎn)* is another popular choice with budget travellers. Dorms with shared bath cost Y15 to Y25 per person. Doubles with private bath are Y100, though you can also rent these by the bed and pay half.

Opposite the Feitian Hotel, the relatively

new *Five Circles (Olympic) Hotel* (☎ 882-2620) *(wǔhuán zhāodàisuǒ)* may have an awkward name, but it's quite clean and staff are eager to please. Dorm beds in quads/triples with shared bath are Y25/30, and doubles are Y100 and Y120.

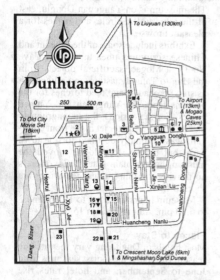

The *Nation Guesthouse* (☎ 882-2690) *(mínzú bīnguǎn)* is a bit more run down, although they give you a cheerful reception when you check in. Beds in basic dorms with shared bath are Y15 to Y20, or Y40 to Y60 per bed in doubles with private bath.

The *Mingshan Hotel* (☎ 882-2130) *(míngshān bīnguǎn)* is an old-style place, but for the money it's not a bad deal and it's conveniently located. Hard, solid dorm beds cost Y12 in a quad, Y15 in a triple, or Y25 in a double. Doubles with private bath are Y45 per person.

There are two places in town calling themselves the 'Dunhuang Hotel' in English, but they have different Chinese names. The budget alternative is the *Dunhuang Hotel (Fandian)* (☎ 882-2413) *(dūnhuáng fàndiàn)* near the bus station. Rates are cheap, but rooms can be grotty. Beds in quads/triples with shared bath are Y20/30. Doubles with attached bath are Y140, but for this kind of room you'd do better at the Feitian or Five Circles hotels.

On the eastern side of town, the larger *Dunhuang Hotel (Binguan)* (☎ 822-2415) *(dūnhuáng bīnguǎn)* is a completely different animal. A three star place aimed at tour groups and visiting cadres, it charges Y580

DUNHUANG 敦煌

PLACES TO STAY
4 Grand Sun Hotel
   太阳能宾馆、
   太阳大酒店
8 Dunhuang Hotel
   (Binguan)
   敦煌宾馆
9 Silk Road Hotel
   丝路宾馆
11 Mingshan Hotel
   鸣山宾馆
14 Dunhuang Hotel (Fandian)
   敦煌饭店
18 Five Circles (Olympic)
   Hotel
   五环招待所
20 Feitian Hotel; John's
   Information & Cafe
   飞天宾馆

21 International Hotel;
   CITS
   国际大酒店
   中国国际旅行社
22 Western Region Hotel
   西域宾馆
23 Nation Guesthouse
   民族宾馆

PLACES TO EAT
10 Night Market
   敦煌夜市
15 Charlie Johng's Cafe
   风味餐馆
16 Muslim Youyi
   Restaurant
   清真友谊饭店
17 Shirley's Cafe
   风味餐馆

OTHER
1 PSB
   公安局
2 Bank of China
   中国银行
3 Post & Telephone Office
   邮电局
5 Dunhuang County
   Museum
   敦煌县博物馆
6 Xinhua Bookstore
   新华书店
7 CAAC Booking Office
   民航售票处
12 Day Market
   农副市场
13 Minibus Stop
   小公共汽车站
19 Long-Distance Bus Station
   长途汽车站

GANSU

for a double. Although rates are negotiable, it still isn't really worth the money.

A better option nearby is the *Silk Road Hotel* (☎ 882-3807) *(sīlù bīnguǎn)*. It's newer and just about as plush as its three star neighbour, but rates are reasonable, and the staff super-courteous. A comfortable triple room with shared bath is Y120 (although Y100 is possible), and doubles with private bath are Y230 to Y280. The clerks at the front desk serve tea and present you with a damp cloth to wipe your face while you're checking in.

If you want to go a bit more upmarket, the *International Hotel* (☎ 882-8678) *(guójì dà jiǔdiàn)* seems to be the best run luxury place in town. Rooms have all the amenities. Doubles start at Y358, and suites at Y498. This is good value, although the prices may rise once the hotel get its official three star rating from the government.

Four kilometres to the south of town, near the great sand dunes of Mingshashan, is the *Silk Road Dunhuang Hotel* (☎ (9473) 25388) *(dùnhuáng shānzhuāng)*, a Chinese-Hong Kong joint venture. Standing out from the desert like a modern-day fortress, this place is definitely the most luxurious in the area, as reflected by the prices. Doubles start at US$100, and suites at US$150. There are dorms, but even these are pretty pricey – US$5 per person in the 'student hostel'. A 15% service charge is added to all rates. Although expensive, it is a tastefully designed place and, being only 1km from the sand dunes, enjoys great sunrise and sunset views.

Places to Eat

Charlie Johng's Cafe, just north of the Feitian Hotel, has excellent western and Chinese food at cheap prices, plus an English menu and nice background music (you can bring your own tapes if you wish). Across the street Charlie's sister operates *Shirley's Cafe*, which is also pretty good.

On the same street, next to the Feitian Hotel, is the Dunhuang branch of *John's Information & Cafe* (☎ 882-7000). Though not as well equipped as the branches in Xinjiang, it has a nice outdoor location (for those evening beers), and friendly staff who can also help with travel arrangements and information.

On this same block there are numerous Chinese restaurants – most have English menus, reasonable prices and are worth trying. One of the few that doesn't have an English sign or menu is the *Muslim Youyi Restaurant (qīngzhēnyǒuyì fànguǎn)*. It's about four shops north of Shirley's Cafe; look for the green sign and white Muslim crescent. Their specialty is *(dàpánjī)*, a whole chicken cut up and stir-fried with potatoes, herbs and vegetables and served on a bed of noodles. It costs Y50, but you'll need three people at the very least to finish the thing, so it's not that pricey and certainly worth a try.

Dunhuang's *night market* is an extremely lively scene, and worth a visit. Mostly contained within a large courtyard off Yangguan Donglu, it houses scores of restaurants and small tables surrounded by lawn chairs. The tables are rented out by entrepreneurs, who charge fairly steep prices for beer, soft drinks and tea. You can either sit here and have them bring you food from the restaurants nearby, or head inside the restaurants themselves, although the atmosphere isn't as interesting.

Among locals, the night market has a reputation for being rowdy. It's a popular drinking spot and by 11 pm the number of drunks starts to rise rapidly – not a bad time to make your exit.

Getting There & Away

Air In the summer peak season there are daily flights to Lanzhou (Y990) and Xi'an (Y1400) and less frequent air services to Beijing (Y2300). At the time of writing, flights to Jiayuguan (Y370) were expected to operate daily during summer. Flight frequency is cut during the winter months. Seats can be booked at the CAAC office (☎ 882-2389) on Dong Dajie, which is open from 8.30 to 11.30 am and 3 to 6 pm. There is also a booking office next to the Grand Sun Hotel on Shazhou Beilu.

GANSU

Bus Minibuses to Liuyuan (130km) depart when full from the bus station. The last bus usually leaves around 8 to 9 pm. The fare is Y10, plus Y5 for each bag that needs to be placed on the roof. The trip takes 2½ hours, but up to four hours if there's a sand storm blowing.

There are four to five buses to Jiayuguan leaving between 6.30 am and 1 pm. There are also two night buses at 9 and 10.30 pm. Foreigners must pay Y48, Y20 of which is 'insurance'. The 383km ride takes up to nine hours, although this should improve once major roadworks are completed.

Departures to Lanzhou are at 8.30 and 10.30 am each day. The latter is a sleeper bus, and costs Y190. Regular buses cost Y102. The 1148km trip takes at least 24 hours.

There's also a daily bus service to Golmud. This is where you begin to see the iron grip that CITS has on travel to Tibet. Foreigners must buy their tickets at a special office to the right-hand side of the main ticket hall – the sign says 'Go through the formalities of Tibet'. 'Insurance' and 'notification' fees plus the bus ticket add up to Y406 for foreigners, compared to the Y48 paid by Chinese for the 524km ride.

Although you ride the same crap bus as everyone else, your extra money does get you a reception committee in Golmud (ie a CITS representative to shuffle you into the Golmud Hotel, your sole accommodation option in that city). Possibly the worst thing about all this is that Golmud is an open city – we found that out from the Dunhuang PSB, who assured us no permit was necessary to go there. The CITS operation is a scam, pure and simple, but most travellers have had little luck getting around it.

The bus to Golmud leaves at 7.30 am, and takes 13 hours via a rugged but scenic route that crosses the snow-capped Altunshan. Arrive early enough to store your luggage on the roof. It's chilly up in the mountains, so keep some warm clothing handy regardless of how hot it may be in Dunhuang itself.

There is a left-luggage room in the bus station (Y1 per bag per day).

Train The closest station is at Liuyuan, on the Lanzhou-Ürümqi railway line (see the Liuyuan section for the train schedule).

Getting Around
To/From the Airport Dunhuang's airport is 13km east of town. In addition to the CAAC bus (Y5), you can hire a minibus for about Y30.

Taxi & Minivan Dunhuang is small enough that you can easily cover it on foot, but taxis and minivans can be chartered for trips to sights outside town. The minibus stop near the Dunhuang Hotel (Fandian) is the place to go to start the negotiations.

Bicycle The Feitian Hotel has modern and well-maintained bikes, and charges a reasonable Y2 per hour. Doing a bit of exploratory pedalling around the oasis is fine, and getting to some outlying sights is also possible, although maybe not such a great idea during the height of summer.

AROUND DUNHUANG
Crescent Moon Lake
(yuèyáquán)
The lake is 6km south of the centre of Dunhuang at the Singing Sand Mountains (míngshāshān), where the oasis meets the desert. Spring water trickles up into a depression between huge sand dunes, forming a small, crescent-shaped pond (not to be confused with the concrete storage pool nearby).

The climb to the top of the dunes is sweaty work, but the dramatic view back across the rolling desert sands towards the oasis makes the effort worthwhile.

Out here the recreational activities include the predictable camel rides, the more novel 'dune surfing' (sand sliding) and paragliding (jumping off the top of high dunes with a chute on your back). There is also a tow-gliding operation closer to the entry gate: continue past it if you want to jump off a dune.

Official foreigner rates for camel rides are Y30 to the spring and Y50 to the top of the sand dunes. If you really are interested

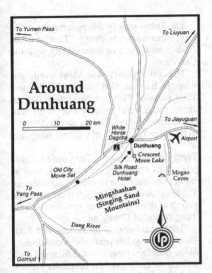

Around
Dunhuang

To Yumen Pass
To Liuyuan
0 10 20 km
White Horse Dagoba
To Jiayuguan
Dunhuang
Airport
Crescent Moon Lake
Old City Movie Set
Silk Road Dunhuang Hotel
Mogao Caves
To Yang Pass
Mingshashan (Singing Sand Mountains)
Dang River
To Golmud

in this, bargain hard. Rental of sand sleds should cost Y5 or Y10, not the Y20 that will be demanded of you. Paragliding should be Y20 a go, although foreigners are routinely asked to pay Y50.

The foreigner's admission fee to the lake and dunes area is Y20. If you cycle here, don't buy your ticket until you get to the large main gateway; there's a small ticket stand about 300m earlier selling tickets to the Dunhuang Folk Arts Museum (Y8), which can definitely be skipped.

Most people head out to the dunes in the evening around 5 pm when the weather starts to cool down. You can ride a bike out there in around 20 minutes. Minibuses cost Y3 and make the run whenever full. Taxis cost Y15 one way, motorised pedicabs Y10.

Old City Movie Set
(fǎngsòng gǔchéng)
This reconstructed Song Dynasty town, complete with 5m-high city walls, was built in 1987 as a movie set for a Sino-Japanese co-production titled *Dunhuang*.

Standing isolated out in the desert some 16km to the south-west of Dunhuang, from a distance the Old City has a dramatic and strikingly realistic appearance. Close up, though, the place is starting to look a bit shabby; the mud-brick walls are crumbling and the bare yards behind the makeshift facades are scattered with rubbish. Nevertheless, it's a reasonably interesting place for a short visit.

You can get there by joining one of the Chinese day tours which take in most of the area sights, or hire a van yourself for Y80. You can also ride a bicycle and arrive fit and thirsty. Entry costs Y20.

Mogao Caves
(mògāo kū)
The Mogao Caves are set into desert cliffs above a river valley about 25km south-east of Dunhuang. The area is highly exposed to the elements and the erosion of wind and water have severely damaged quite a few of the caves.

Today, 492 grottoes are still standing, and are now well protected by a series of stone walls and sealed doors. The grottoes honeycomb the 1600m-long cliff face which sits on a north-south axis. Altogether they contain more than 2000 statues and 45,000 separate murals. Cave 17 is where Wang Yuan discovered the hoard of manuscripts and artwork.

Most of the Dunhuang art dates from the Northern and Western Wei, Northern Zhou, Sui and Tang dynasties, although examples from the Five Dynasties, Northern Song, Western Xia and Yuan can also be found. The Northern Wei, Western Wei, Northern Zhou and Tang caves are in the best state of preservation.

The caves are generally rectangular or square with recessed, decorated ceilings. The focal point of each is a group of brightly painted statues representing Buddha and the Bodhisattvas, or Buddha's disciples.

The smaller statues are composed of terracotta coated with a kind of plaster surface so that intricate details could be etched into the surface.

The walls and ceilings were also plastered with layers of cement and clay and then painted with watercolour. Large sections of the murals are made up of decorative patterns using motifs from nature, architecture, or textiles.

Northern Wei, Western Wei & Northern Zhou Caves The Turkic-speaking Tobas, who invaded and conquered the country in the 4th century, inhabited the region north of China and founded the Northern Wei Dynasty around 386 AD.

Friction between groups who wanted to maintain the traditional Toba lifestyle and those who wanted to assimilate with the Chinese eventually split the Toba empire in the middle of the 6th century.

The eastern part adopted the Chinese way of life and the rulers took the dynasty name of Northern Qi. The western part took the dynasty name of Northern Zhou and tried in vain to revert to Toba customs. By 567 AD, however, they had managed to defeat the Qi to take control of all of northern China.

The fall of the Han Dynasty in 220 AD sent Confucianism into decline. This, plus the turmoil of the Toba invasions, made Buddhism's teachings of nirvana and personal salvation highly appealing to many. Under the patronage of the new rulers, the religion spread rapidly and made a new and decisive impact on Chinese art which can be seen in the Buddhist statues at Mogao.

The art of this period is characterised by its attempt to depict the spirituality of those who had achieved enlightenment and transcended the material world through their asceticism. The Wei statues are slim, ethereal figures with finely chiselled features and comparatively large heads, and clearly show the influence of Indian Buddhist art and teachings.

Sui Caves The Sui Dynasty began when a general of Chinese or mixed Chinese-Toba origin usurped the throne of the Northern Zhou Dynasty. Prudently putting to death all the sons of the former emperor, he embarked on a series of wars which by 589 AD had reunited northern and southern China for the first time in 360 years.

The Tobas simply disappeared from history, either mixing with other Turkish tribes from central Asia or assimilating with the Chinese.

The Sui Dynasty was short-lived, and very much a transition between the Wei and Tang periods. This can be seen in the Sui caves: the graceful Indian curves in the buddha and bodhisattvas figures start to give way to the more rigid style of Chinese sculpture.

Tang Caves During the Tang period, China pushed its borders forcefully westward as far as Lake Balkhash in today's Kazakhstan. Trade expanded and foreign merchants and people of diverse religions streamed into the Tang capital of Chang'an.

Buddhism became prominent and Buddhist art reached its peak; the proud bearing of the Buddhist figures in the Mogao Caves reflects the feelings of the times, the prevailing image of the brave Tang warrior, and the strength and steadfastness of the empire.

This was also the high point of the cave art at Mogao. Some 230 caves were carved, including two impressive grottoes containing enormous seated buddha figures. The statue residing in cave 96 is a towering 34.5m tall – a slightly shorter (26m) counterpart in cave 130 is no less impressive.

The portraits of Tang nobles are considerably larger than those of the Wei and Sui dynasties, and the figures tend to occupy important positions within the murals. In some cases the patrons are portrayed in the same scene as the Buddha.

Later Caves The Tang period marked the ultimate development of the cave paintings. During later dynasties, the economy around Dunhuang went into decline and the luxury and vigour typical of Tang painting began to be replaced by simpler drawing techniques and flatter figures. However, there were some masterpieces in the post-Tang era, notably the 16m-long reclining buddha (cave 158), attended by rows of disciples, all bearing different expressions that show you how close they are to achieving the state of nirvana.

Admission While Chinese have a choice of buying a Y15 ticket that gives access to 10 caves or a Y58 ticket for 30 caves, foreigners have only one option: a 30 cave ticket that costs a steep Y80.

The price includes an English-speaking guide. It doesn't matter if you want one or not – the guide has the keys to doors protecting many of the caves you'll be seeing. If you get a good guide however, it can enhance the visit. It's a pity that foreigners aren't given the 10 cave option, since it can easily take a full day to tramp through 30 caves. Some, like Cave 465, contain Tantric art whose explicit sexual portrayals have been deemed too corrupting for the public to view. (However, you can check it out if you ask special permission and pay a usurious 'additional fee' of Y240!)

The grottoes are theoretically open from 8.30 am to 5 pm, but guides are generally only available between 8.30 and 10 am and again at 2.30 pm. If you come at any other time you may well have to wait several hours before a guide is available and, no matter how you plead, the guards won't let you in to the caves without one.

Photography is strictly prohibited everywhere within the fenced-off caves area, although photos are sometimes permitted after payment of an appropriately large sum of money. Cameras and hand luggage must be deposited at an office near the entrance gate (for a fee of Y2).

Most caves are lit only by indirect sunlight from outside, often making it hard to see detail, particularly in the niches. Heavy but low-powered torches (flashlights) can be hired outside the gate (Y3); if you have your own, bring it.

Despite the high fee and the inconvenience of the guide system, don't be discouraged – entering your first cave will make it all seem worthwhile. And it helps to know that at least some of the money sustains the excellent preservation efforts here.

Places to Stay The entrance complex includes the *Mogao Hotel* (*mògāo shān-zhuāng*), which has doubles for Y180 and dorm beds for a ridiculous Y50, although you should be able to knock this price down a bit.

Getting There & Away The Mogao Caves are 25km and 30 minutes by bus from Dunhuang. Minibuses leave at around 8 am from the Dunhuang Hotel (Fandian) and also across the street from the Feitian Hotel. The one way fare is Y10.

At other times you can hire a minibus for around Y60 to Y80 return, depending on your bargaining skills. If you go in the afternoon, don't bother heading out before 2 pm, as you won't be able to get in to see the caves until at least 2.30 pm.

Some people ride out to the caves on a bicycle, but be warned that half the ride is through total desert – hot work in summer.

Yang & Yumen Passes
(*yángguān, yùménguān*)
Some 76km south-west of Dunhuang is the Yang (South) Pass. Here, Han Dynasty beacon towers marked the caravan route westwards and warned of advancing invaders, but what remains has now largely disappeared under the shifting sands.

Nearby are the ruins of the ancient Han town of **Shouchang**. The Yumen (Jade Gate) Pass, 98km north-west of Dunhuang, is also known for its ancient ruins.

Caravans heading out of China would travel up the Gansu corridor to Dunhuang; the Yumen Pass was the starting point of the road which ran across the north of what is now Xinjiang Province, and the Yang Pass was the start of the route which cut through the south of the region.

The return trip out to Yang Pass takes about two to three hours, and hiring a minibus will cost around Y150. The road to Yumen Pass is little more than a trail in the sand: the trip there and back takes the entire day, and vehicle hire costs around Y500. It's a pretty long journey to see what little remains of the tower, although the trip itself might prove interesting to some.

GANSU

Ningxia 宁夏

Ningxia Facts & Highlights

Area: 66,400 sq km

Population: 5.2 million

Capital: Yinchuan

Highlights

- Yinchuan, the pleasant capital city of this remote province, and jumping off point for trips to Helanshan and the Gobi desert.
- Zhongwei, where the eerie beauty of the sand dunes meets the greenbelt surrounding the Yellow River.

Ningxia *(níngxià)* was carved out as a separate administrative region in 1928 and remained a province until 1954, when it was absorbed into Gansu Province. In 1958 Ningxia re-emerged, this time as an autonomous region with a large Hui population. The boundaries of the region have ebbed and flowed since then – Inner Mongolia was included at one time, but the borders are now reduced.

Part of the arid north-west of China, much of Ningxia suffers a harsh climate. Winters are hard, with plummeting temperatures; blistering summers make irrigation a necessity. In fact, the province would be virtually uninhabitable if it were not for the Yellow River, Ningxia's lifeline. Most of the population lives near the river or the irrigation channels which run off it. These channels were created in the Han Dynasty, when the area was first settled by the Han Chinese in the 1st century BC.

About a third of Ningxia's people are Hui, living mostly in the south of the province. The rest are Han Chinese. The Hui minority are descended from Arab and Iranian traders who travelled to China during the Tang Dynasty. Immigrants from Central Asia increased their numbers during the Yuan Dynasty. Apart from their continued adherence to Islam, the Hui have been assimilated into Han culture.

The completion of the Baotou-Lanzhou railway in 1958 helped to relieve the area's isolation and develop some industry in this otherwise almost exclusively agricultural region. A newly completed line linking Zhongwei with Baoji (Shaanxi Province) should help boost the economy of Ningxia's southern section.

YINCHUAN
(yínchuān)

Sheltered from the deserts of Mongolia by the high ranges of the Helanshan to its west and abundantly supplied with water from the nearby Yellow River, Yinchuan occupies a favoured geographical position in otherwise harsh surroundings.

This city was once the capital of the Western Xia, a mysterious kingdom founded during the 11th century. Today it's one of China's more pleasant, relaxed provincial capitals, with a few interesting sights and a lively market atmosphere.

Orientation

Yinchuan is divided into two parts. The new industrialised section is close to the railway station and is simply called 'New City' *(xīn chéng)*. The 'Old City' *(lǎo chéng)* is about 8km to the west and has most of the town's

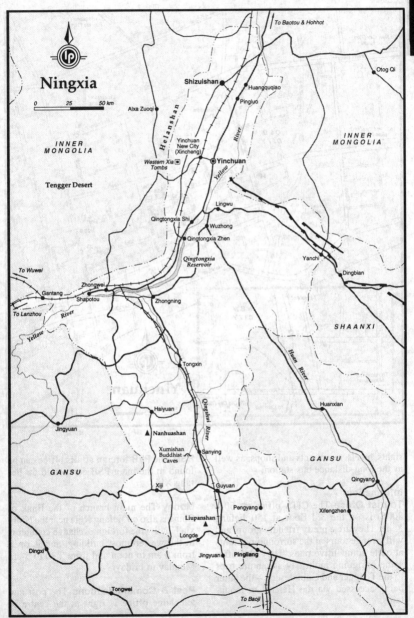

Ningxia

0   25   50 km

INNER MONGOLIA

Tengger Desert

Shizuishan

Aixa Zuoqi

Huangquqiao

Pingluo

Helanshan

Yinchuan New City (Xincheng)

Western Xia Tombs

Yinchuan

To Baotou & Hohhot

River

Yellow

INNER MONGOLIA

Otog Qi

Lingwu

Qingtongxia Shi

Wuzhong

Qingtongxia Zhen

Qingtongxia Reservoir

Yanchi

Dingbian

To Wuwei

Gantang

Shapotou

Zhongwei

Zhongning

River

To Lanzhou

Yellow

Tongxin

SHAANXI

Huan River

Jingyuan

Haiyuan

Nanhuashan

Xumishan Buddhist Caves

Qingshui River

Sanying

Huanxian

GANSU

Xiji

Guyuan

Pengyang

Qingyang

Xifengzhen

Dingxi

Liupanshan

Longde

Jingyuan

Pingliang

Tongwei

To Baoji

GANSU

Yinchuan

sights, hotels, restaurants and shops, as well as the long-distance bus station.

Information

Tourist Office The CITS office (☎ 504-8006) is on the 3rd floor at 150 Jiefang Xijie. They are a pretty friendly group, and will arrange tours of the surrounding sights at quite competitive rates. They also offer some intriguing multi-day adventure trips to the Tengger and Gobi deserts – the latter being accessed via the Helanshan mountains.

PSB The PSB foreign affairs office can be found in the main PSB compound on Jiefang Xijie.

Money The main branch of the Bank of China is also on Jiefang Xijie near the Ningxia Hotel – the foreign exchange counter is in the westernmost building, and is open from 8 am to noon and from 2.30 to 5 pm Monday to Friday.

Post & Communications The post and telephone office is right in the centre of

YINCHUAN 银川	OTHER	20 Drum Tower 鼓楼
PLACES TO STAY	2 Railway Station 火车站	21 Yuhuang Pavilion 玉皇阁
1 Railway Hotel 银川铁路宾馆	6 CITS 中国国际旅行社	22 China Merchants International Travel 招商国际旅游公司
3 Taoyuan Hotel 桃园宾馆	7 Railway City Booking Office 银川火车站售票处	23 Night Market 夜市
4 International Hotel 国际饭店	8 Xinhua Bookstore 新华书店	24 Ningxia Museum; Chengtian Monastery Pagoda 宁夏博物馆、承天寺塔
10 Ningxia Hotel 宁夏宾馆	9 Bank of China 中国银行	
11 Yindu Hotel 银都大酒店	12 PSB 公安局	
14 Yinchuan Hotel 银川饭店	13 Foreign Languages Bookstore 外文书店	25 Indoor/Outdoor Market 商城
19 Ningfeng Hotel 宁丰宾馆	16 Post & Telephone Office 邮电大楼	26 South Gate 南门楼
PLACES TO EAT	17 CAAC Booking Office 民航售票处	27 Long-Distance Bus Station 银川汽车站
5 Muslim Lixin Noodle Restaurant 清真立新面馆	18 Yinchuan Department Store 银川百货大楼	28 Nanguan Mosque 南关清真寺
15 Yingbinlou Islamic Restaurant 迎宾楼清真饭庄		

town on the corner of Minzu Beijie and Jiefang Xijie. Hours are 8 am to 6 pm daily.

Haibao Pagoda
(hǎibǎo tǎ)

Haibao Pagoda, also called North Pagoda *(běi tǎ)*, stands out prominently in the north of the city. Records of the structure date from the 5th century. In 1739 an earthquake toppled the lot, but it was rebuilt in 1771 in the original style.

It's part of a working monastery, but you can still climb up the pagoda, although you may have to ask the gatekeeper to unlock the stairwell door. The structure is some nine storeys high, and offers fine views of the Helanshan mountains to the west and the Yellow River to the east. It's open daily from 9 am to 6 pm and entry is Y5. You may be charged an additional Y3 to ascend the pagoda: don't worry, it's worth it. Behind the pagoda are several interesting temples, including one housing a hefty reclining buddha.

There is no public transport out here, so you'll either have to bicycle or take a taxi. It's a little over 3.5km from the Yinchuan Hotel. It's a nice ride, as the city quickly gives way to farm fields and more rural housing, although this may not last for many more years.

Ningxia Museum
(níngxià bówùguǎn)

The museum is on Jinning Jie, three blocks south of Jiefang Xijie, in the old Chengtian Monastery. Its collection includes Western Xia and Northern Zhou historical relics, as well as material covering the Hui culture.

Within the leafy courtyard is the Chengtian Monastery Pagoda, also known as the West Pagoda *(xī tǎ)*, which you can climb via 13 tiers of rather steep stairs. The museum is open from 8 am to noon and 3 to 6 pm. Admission is (unfortunately) Y20 for foreigners, as opposed to Y2.5 for Chinese.

Yuhuang Pavilion
(yùhuáng gé)

This restored 400-year-old building is on

Jiefang Dongjie, one block to the east of the Drum Tower. The pavilion used to have a museum, but this appears to have been given over to office space, another victim of China's economic reforms. Still, it's worth climbing up for a peek.

Nanguan Mosque
(nánguān qīngzhēn sì)
The mosque is a modern Middle Eastern-style structure showing little Chinese architectural influence, with Islamic arches and dome roofs covered in green tiles. This is Yinchuan's main mosque and is an active place of worship, so be considerate when strolling around. Entry costs Y2 and it's open daily from 8 am to 7 pm.

Places to Stay
Old City The best bet for budget backpackers is the *Yinchuan Hotel* (☎ 602-3053) *(yínchuān fàndiàn)* on Jiefang Xijie. Beds in dorms with shared bath range from Y20 in a triple to Y38 in a single. Doubles/triples with bath and air-con are Y108/120. It's in a good, central location and also has bicycles for rent. There's a brass plaque which reads, 'Foreign Nationals Hotel'.

The only other semi-budget option for foreigners is the north wing of the *Ningxia Hotel* (☎ 504-5131) *(níngxià bīnguǎn)* where concrete-floored doubles with private bath cost Y50 per bed (not a great deal). The main section of the hotel, at 3 Gongyuan Jie near Zhongshan Park, was closed for extensive renovation at the time of writing: expect it to reopen as a classy three star hotel with prices starting at around Y280 for a standard double.

Nearby, the *Yindu Hotel* (☎ 503-1888) *(yíndū dà jiǔdiàn)* on Jiefang Xijie, is a popular spot and offers well appointed doubles for Y146 and Y160, and singles for Y88. The Oasis Hotel next door used to be a good budget spot, but was closed to foreigners when we last checked.

The *Ningfeng Hotel* (☎ 602-8898) *(níngfēng bīnguǎn)*, diagonally opposite the post office, is another good mid-range option, with comfortable doubles for Y174.

At the upper end of the Yinchuan hotel scene is the *International Hotel* (☎ 602-8688) *(guójì fàndiàn)* where doubles start from Y280. The location, up on Beihuan Donglu, is not too convenient, but it's easily the nicest hotel in town.

New City The most convenient place for making a quick getaway is the *Yinchuan Railway Hotel* (☎ 306-9119) *(yínchuān tiělù bīnguǎn)*, just a short walk from the station. It's not cheap though. Beds in triples/quads with shared bath cost a ridiculous Y50, while doubles/triples with private bath are Y200/210.

East of the railway station and accessible by bus No 1 is the *Taoyuan Hotel* (☎ 306-6485) *(táoyuán bīnguǎn)*, which is basic, but much more reasonably priced. Doubles cost Y86, triples Y76.

Places to Eat
Good for street food are the *stalls* in the backstreets around the long-distance bus station or the *night market* nearby on Xinhua Dongjie.

The *Yingbinlou Islamic Restaurant* *(yíngbīnlóu qīngzhēn fànzhuāng)*, next to the Yinchuan Hotel, is a raucous, popular spot with some great dishes. Try potatoes and braised beef *(tǔdòu shāōnïuròu)* (Y11) or spicy eggplant *(jiāchāng qiézǐ)* (Y8). Big, frosty draft beers (Y4) are another plus.

If you're heading back from the Haibao Pagoda and feeling a bit peckish after climbing all those steps, the *Muslim Lixin Noodle Restaurant (qīngzhēn lìxīn miàn-guǎn)* on Minzu Beijie has great noodles and mutton dumplings. There's no English sign or menu, so keep an eye out for the green sign and crescent.

Getting There & Away
Air The main CAAC ticket office (☎ 602-2085) is at 14 Minzu Beijie. There are flights connecting Yinchuan with Beijing (Y1040), Chengdu (Y1130), Guangzhou (Y1900), Shanghai (Y1830) and Xi'an (Y570). A new international airport should

have opened by the time you read this, so more destinations may be available.

Bus The long-distance bus station is in the south-eastern part of town on the square near the South Gate. There are four buses to Zhongwei (four hours, Y13) leaving between 7 and 11.30 am. Privately run buses to Zhongwei can also be found on Yuhuangge Jie just north of the Nanguan Mosque.

Buses to Guyuan (seven hours, Y25) leave every 30 minutes from 6 am to 1 pm.

There are four daily buses leaving in the afternoon for the 17 hour trip to Xi'an – at least one of which is a sleeper (Y85). There is one bus to Lanzhou at 7 am, and several more in the late afternoon, including one sleeper at 6.30 pm (11 hours, Y60). There are two buses a day to Yan'an (Shaanxi Province) at 6 am and 6 pm; the latter is a sleeper. The trip takes at least 12 hours and costs Y38 for the regular bus, and Y70 for the sleeper.

Train Yinchuan is on the Lanzhou-Beijing railway line, which also runs via Baotou, Hohhot and Datong. Express trains from Yinchuan take nine hours to Lanzhou, 11 hours to Hohhot, 17 hours to Xi'an and 22 hours to Beijing. The railway station is in the New City, about 13km from the Old City centre.

There's a railway booking office in the Old City on Jiefang Xijie; there's no English sign. The office is on the ground floor at the eastern end of a five storey building, next door to a flashy red and white hotpot restaurant. It's open daily from 9.30 am to noon and 2 to 5 pm.

Getting Around
To/From the Airport Yinchuan's new airport is 18km east of the city. A CAAC bus meets incoming and departing flights; the bus departure time will be printed on your ticket. Buses to the airport leave from in front of the office on Minzu Beijie and cost Y4. A taxi to the airport will cost around Y40.

Bus Bus No 1 runs from the bus station in the Old City, along Jiefang Jie and then on to the railway station in the New City. The fare is just Y0.70. Minibuses cover the same route faster, but charge Y3.

Taxi Taxis are fairly cheap, with flag fall at Y5 to Y6 depending on the vehicle. A taxi between the railway station and the Old City will cost around Y25.

Bicycle By far the best way to get around town is to cycle. The Yinchuan Hotel rents out good bikes for Y3 for four hours, or Y10 per day.

AROUND YINCHUAN
Helanshan
(hèlánshān)
The mountains of the Helanshan Range are clearly visible from Yinchuan. The range forms an important natural barrier against desert winds and invaders alike, with the highest peak reaching 3556m. Along the foothills of the Helanshan lie some interesting sights.

About 54km north-west of Yinchuan (New City) is the historic pass village of **Gunzhongkou**, where there are walking trails up into the surrounding hills. There are no buses here, so the only way is by taxi, or hiring a vehicle through CITS or another travel agency.

North of Gunzhongkou are the **Twin Pagodas of Baisikou** *(báisìkǒu shuāngtǎ)*, which are 13 and 14 storeys high and decorated with buddha statuettes. These are accessible only by jeep, bicycle or on foot, so don't expect taxis to be able to get you here.

South of Gunzhongkou lie the **Western Xia Tombs** *(xīxià wánglíng)*, the main tourist destination in this area. According to legend, the founder of the Western Xia kingdom, Li Yuanhao, built 72 tombs. One was for himself, others held relatives or were left empty. The Western Xia kingdom lasted for 190 years and 10 successive emperors, and had its own written-language and a strong military.

The Wrath of Khan

The tale goes that Genghis Khan saw the Xia kingdom as a potential vassal/ally, but the Xia baulked at the thought of bowing to another ruler.

Genghis Khan mounted six separate campaigns against the Xia, all of which failed. During the sixth campaign, Xia archers sneaked down to Khan's war camp, near present-day Guyuan, and fatally wounded the military leader with poison-tipped arrows.

Enraged even at death's door, Genghis Khan gave his final order: the total annihilation of the Western Xia kingdom. Looking at the site today, one must conclude that Khan's subordinates carried out his command with a vengeance. ■

Again, you'll need to cycle or hire a vehicle to get here. CITS will give you a jeep and English-speaking guide for Y760 to visit all three destinations. China Merchants International Travel (☎ 607-1854) should be able to offer a similar deal.

Hiring a taxi for the day should cost a flat Y200, although this won't allow you to get to the pagodas.

ZHONGWEI
(zhōngwèi)

Zhongwei lies 167km south-west of Yinchuan on the Lanzhou-Baotou railway line, sandwiched between the sand dunes of the Tengger Desert to the north and the Yellow River to the south. In addition to its unusual setting, Zhongwei has a fairly relaxed pace – a nice change from the rush of most Chinese cities.

Information

Zhongwei Travel Service (☎ 701-2620) can arrange some interesting trips to the sights outside the town (see the following Around Zhongwei section). The office is on the 4th floor of the County Government office building on Xi Dajie. Across the drum tower roundabout is the Bank of China's main branch, which changes cash and travellers cheques from 8 am to noon and 2.30 to 6 pm Monday to Friday.

Gao Temple
(gāo miào)

The main attraction in town is the Gao Temple, an eclectic, multipurpose temple which serves Buddhism, Confucianism and Taoism. Built during the 15th century and flattened by an earthquake during the 18th century, it was later rebuilt and expanded several times until being virtually razed again by fire in 1942.

The present wooden structure's dozens of towers and pavilions look like parts of a jagged wedding cake. The temple includes a hotchpotch of statues from all three religions, so you can see Gautama Buddha, bodhisattvas, the Jade Emperor and the Holy Mother under one roof. It's open daily from 8 am to 6 pm and admission is Y2.

Places to Stay & Eat

The *Railway Hotel* (☎ 701-1441) *(tiělù bīnguǎn)*, directly opposite the station, has beds in doubles/triples with private bath for Y33/22 and singles for Y66. The rooms are fairly comfortable, so this is not a bad deal.

There are two places called the 'Zhongwei Hotel' in English, although the Chinese names differ. The *Zhongwei Hotel (Binguan)* (☎ 701-2609) *(zhōngwèi bīnguǎn)* has long been Zhongwei's main tourist hotel. Decent doubles cost Y110, while 'luxury' rooms are Y180. The reception is to the left as you walk through the main gate.

On Bei Dajie, the other *Zhongwei Hotel (Fandian)* (☎ 710-2219) *(zhōngwèi fàndiàn)* is a more flimsy affair, with beds in dusty doubles/triples with attached bath for Y26/36.

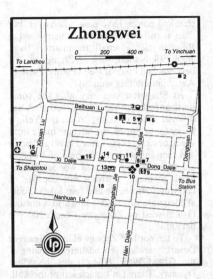

Zhongwei

0   200   400 m

To Yinchuan

To Lanzhou

To Shapotou

To Bus Station

Due to open soon after the time of writing, the *Yi Xing Hotel (yìxīng dàjiǔdiàn)* promises to be the most upmarket place in town, even boasting twin elevators! Management are aiming for the three star rating, so expect prices to be at least Y180 to Y200 for a double.

There's a nice guesthouse at Shapotou (20km from Zhongwei) that's worth considering as an alternative to staying in town (see the Around Zhingwei section below for details).

In Zhongwei there's lots of small restaurants along Bei Dajie. One place worth checking out is the *Hongmei Restaurant (hóngmèi fànzhuāng)*, opposite the Zhongwei Hotel (Fandian). Look for the white sign with red characters. They serve great noodles and *shāguō* (mini-hotpot) for Y5 – cheap and filling.

Another good spot for cheap eats is the night market off Zhongshan Jie; it's a happening spot with all different types of local specialities. The adjacent billiard tables, dance halls and karaoke parlours make for a noisy but very lively atmosphere.

Getting There & Away

Bus The long-distance bus station is about 1km east of the drum tower, on the southern side of Dong Dajie. Buses to Yinchuan (four hours, Y13) leave every 30 minutes from 6.30 am to 4.30 pm. Buses to Lanzhou (eight hours, Y30) leave on even days of the month at 2 pm. There's also a sleeper bus (Y40) that leaves on the same dates at 10.30 pm.

Train From Zhongwei you can catch trains heading north, south, west and south-east. By express it's three hours to Yinchuan, six hours to Lanzhou, 13 hours to Xi'an and 23 hours to Ürümqi. Avoid train No 772, a westbound local that takes a full seven hours to reach Wuwei in Gansu Province. Train No 312 makes the trip in 4½ hours and continues direct to Ürümqi. Other destinations include Beijing, Chengdu and Hohhot.

AROUND ZHONGWEI

The best thing about exploring this area is seeing the abrupt convergence of desert sand dunes and lush farm fields.

Shapotou (*shāpōtóu*), 20km west of Zhongwei, lies on the fringe of the Tengger Desert. It's based around the Shapotou Desert Research Centre (*shāpōtóu shāmò yánjiùsuǒ*), which was founded in 1956 to find a way to keep drifting sand dunes from covering the railway line.

Since 1962, the researchers have been using the 'chequerboard method' for sand blockage and fixation introduced in the 1950s by a Soviet adviser. Plants are protected inside small chequerboards composed of straw bales which are replaced every five years. Even with this protection, plants still require 15 years for full growth. Several thousand hectares of land have now been reclaimed to create an impressive ribbon of greenery beside the railway.

The research centre is not open to the public, although Zhongwei Travel Service may be able to arrange a tour. On the main highway from Zhongwei, just beyond the turn-off for the research centre and the Shapo Guesthouse, is a small viewing platform where you can check out the mix of sand dunes, rice and wheat fields, and the Yellow River. This is where taxis are likely to take you if you ask for Shapotou. It's interesting, but not really worth the Y10 admission fee.

However, if you're looking for a unique entrance to the guesthouse, you can rent a sand sled and skid the sand dunes almost all the way to the front gate.

Water wheels (*shuǐ chē*) used to be a common sight in Ningxia Province. Mechanical pumps have now taken over, but there is still one operational water wheel at Beichangtai, a small mountain village some 50km south-west of Zhongwei. It's best reached by boat (see Getting There & Away later in this section).

At Shapotou you may also see some **leather rafts** (*yángpí fázi*) in action. A traditional mode of transport on the Yellow River for centuries, the rafts are made from sheep or cattle skins soaked in oil and brine and then inflated. An average of 14 hides are tied together under a wooden framework to make a strong raft capable of carrying four people and four bikes. Touts at Shapotou offer rides down to Yingshui (10km west of Zhongwei) for Y100 per person.

To the north of Zhongwei in the Tengger Desert, there's a few scattered remains of the **Great Wall** dating from the Ming Dynasty. There isn't much left of the wall, but getting there is quite interesting.

Organised Tours

Zhongwei Travel Service offers several interesting river and desert trips. Examples include a two day journey into the Tengger Desert that includes a visit to the Great Wall and camping in the dunes. Transport (including camels), guide and accommodation cost around Y150 per person per day, as long as there are at least three of you. Desert trips of up to seven days are available.

Another option is a one day leather raft trip down the Yellow River, starting at Shapotou and ending at Zhongwei. Again with three people this should cost around Y150, including transport to Shapotou from Zhongwei. A more challenging (and expensive) trip is a speedboat up to the water wheel at Beichangtai, followed by a raft trip back to Zhongwei. The section between Beichangtai and Shapotou has some fairly frothy rapids, which may appeal only to more adventurous travellers. This trip costs around Y450 per person: speedboats aren't cheap in China. Two and three-day raft trips are also possible.

Places to Stay

A pleasant, although somewhat pricey, option would be a night or two at the *Shapo Guesthouse* (☎ 768-1481) *(shāpō shānzhuāng)*, built around a garden courtyard on the banks of the Yellow River. They want a steep Y100 per person for doubles/triples with attached bath, but you should be able to talk them down – it doesn't look like a busy spot. There's a small bar/restaurant on the premises.

Getting There & Away

Bus From Zhongwei there are occasional minibuses to Shapotou (one hour, Y5). The frequency increases during the peak tourist months of May, July and August, when buses run as often as every 30 minutes. At other times you may have to wait several hours.

In Zhongwei minibuses leave from in front of the long-distance bus station, stop first at the intersection of Bei Dajie and Beihuan Lu, pause again at the corner of Xi Dajie and Xihuan Lu, and then head off to Shapotou.

From the bus station there is also one large bus direct to Shapotou (one hour, Y3) which leaves at 8.30 am daily.

You can also hire a motor-tricycle to take you there for Y30 one way, or Y40 return.

GUYUAN

(gùyuán)

Guyuan is in the south of Ningxia Province, about 460km from Yinchuan. There is a fine set of Buddhist grottoes at Xumishan *(xūmíshān shíkū)* about 50km north-west of Guyuan. Xumi is the Chinese version of the Sanskrit word *sumeru*, which means 'treasure mountain'.

Cut into five adjacent peaks are 132 caves containing more than 300 Buddhist statues dating back 1400 years, from the

Northern Wei to the Sui and Tang dynasties. The finest statues are in caves 14, 45, 46, 51, 67 and 70. Cave 5 contains the most famous statue on Xumishan: a colossal Maitreya buddha, 19m high. It remains remarkably well preserved even though the protective tower has long since collapsed and left it exposed to the elements.

There is no regular transport to the caves. To get there you'll have to charter a vehicle (minibus or motor-tricycle), either directly from Guyuan or from Sanying *(sānyíng)*. Sanying is on the main road 40km north of Guyuan near the Xumishan turn-off.

Places to Stay

The *Jiaotong Hotel* (☎ 203-2358) *(jiāotōng fàndiàn)*, upstairs in the enormous long-distance bus station, has dorm beds in clean triples for Y12 each. Beds in doubles/triples with private bath are Y23/20.

The *Guyuan Guesthouse* (☎ 203-2479) *(gùyuán bīnguǎn),* on Zhengfu Jie south-east of the bus station, has nicer doubles for Y98, as well as beds in triples with attached bath for Y28.

Getting There & Away

Guyuan is on the newly opened Zhongwei-Baoji railway line. At the time there were only two trains running this route – No 595 (northbound) and No 597 (southbound).

The arrival/departure times in either direction were between 2 am and 3 am – not too convenient. Additional services should be added, hopefully by the time you're reading this.

Buses to Guyuan leave every 30 minutes between 6 am and 1 pm from the Yinchuan long-distance bus station. The ride takes around seven hours and costs Y25. There are buses running once daily from Lanzhou (11 hours, Y27) and Tianshui (seven hours, Y20), which are both in Gansu Province.

Inner Mongolia 内蒙古

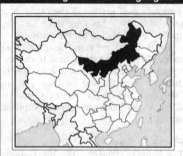
For most foreigners, the big attraction of Inner Mongolia is the chance to view the grasslands, perhaps ride horses and see the Mongolian way of life. But just how much of the Mongolian way of life you can see in China is debatable.

As for horses, the grasslands are indeed perfect horse country, and horse-drawn carts seem to be a common form of transport on the communes (a Hohhot tourist leaflet shows foreigners riding in a decorated camel cart with suspension and truck tyres). However, the small Mongolian horse is being phased out – herders can now purchase motorcycles (preferred over bicycles because of substantial wind force), and on

some of the large state-run farms, helicopters and light aircraft are used to round up steers and spot grazing herds.

It's important to distinguish between Inner Mongolia (the Chinese province) and Mongolia, the independent country to the north, formerly called Outer Mongolia. For more information on the country of Mongolia, see Lonely Planet's *Mongolia* guide.

HISTORY

The nomadic tribes to the north of China have always been a problem for China's rulers. The first emperor of the Qin Dynasty, Qin Shihuang, started building the Great Wall simply to keep them out.

Inner Mongolia *(nèi ménggǔ)* is only one part of what was originally the Mongol homeland, a vast area that also encompasses all of Outer Mongolia and a large slice of Siberia. In the grasslands beyond the Great Wall and the Gobi Desert, the Mongols endured a rough life as shepherds and horse-breeders.

They moved with the seasons in search of pastures for their animals, living in tents known as *yurts* (a Russian word) or *gers* (the Mongolian word). The yurts were made of animal hide usually supported by wooden rods, and could be taken apart quickly to pack onto wagons.

At the mercy of their environment, the Mongols based their religion on the forces of nature: moon, sun and stars were all revered, as were the rivers. The gods were virtually infinite in number, signifying a universal supernatural presence. Mongol priests could speak to the gods and communicate their orders to the tribal chief, the Khan.

The story goes that Genghis Khan overcame the power of the priests by allowing one to be killed for alleging the disloyalty of the Khan's brother – a calculated act of sacrilege which proclaimed the Khan's absolute power.

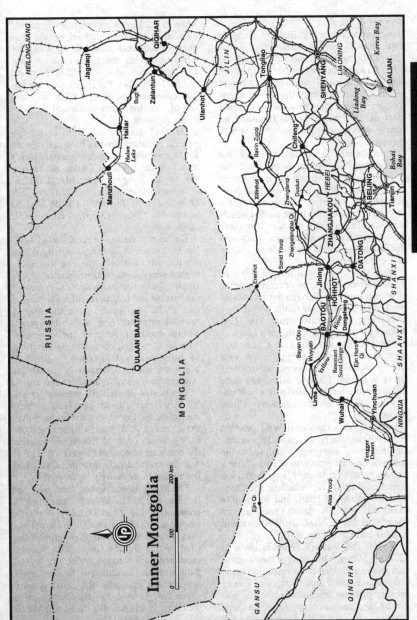

Inner Mongolia

RUSSIA

MONGOLIA

ULAAN BAATAR

HEILONGJIANG

JILIN

LIAONING

HEBEI

SHANXI

SHAANXI

NINGXIA

GANSU

QINGHAI

QIQIHAR

Jagdaqi

Zalantun

Bugt

Hailar

Manzhouli

Hulun Lake

Ulanhot

Tongliao

SHENYANG

DALIAN

Liaodong Bay

Korea Bay

Bairin Zuqi

Chifeng

BEIJING

Tianjin

Bohai Bay

Xilinhot

Zhenglanqi

Duolun

ZHANGJIAKOU

Zhengxiangbai Qi

Sonid Youqi

Erenhot

DATONG

Jining

HOHHOT

BAOTOU

Dongsheng

Bayan Obo

Wuyuan

Yellow River

Linhe

Resonant Sand Gorge

Ejin Horo Qi

Wuhai

Yinchuan

Tengger Desert

Ejin Qi

Alxa Youqi

0   100   200 km

Mongol Empire

The Mongols were united by Genghis Khan after 20 years of warfare; by the year 1206 all opposition to his rule among the tribes had surrendered or been wiped out and the Mongol armies stood ready to invade China. Not only did the Mongols conquer China, they went on to conquer most of the known world, founding an empire which stretched from Vietnam to Hungary.

It was an empire won on horseback; the entire Mongol army was cavalry and this allowed rapid movement and deployment of the armies. The Mongols were highly organised and expert at planning complex strategies and tactics. They excelled in military science and were quick to adopt and improve on Persian and Chinese weaponry. But the cultural and scientific legacy of the Mongols was meagre.

Once they abandoned their policies of terror and destruction, they became patrons of science and art, although not practitioners. Under the influence of the people they had conquered, they also adopted the local religions – mainly Buddhism and Islam.

The Mongol conquest of China was slow, delayed by campaigns in the west and by internal strife. Secure behind their Great Wall, the Chinese rulers had little inkling of the fury the Mongols would unleash in 1211, when the invasion of China began.

For two years the Great Wall deterred them, but the Mongols eventually penetrated through a 27km gorge which led to the northern Chinese plains. In 1215 a Chinese general went over to the Mongols and led them into Beijing. Nevertheless, the Chinese stubbornly held out, and the war in China was placed under the command of one of Genghis' generals so the Khan could turn his attention to the west.

Despite the death of Genghis Khan in 1227, the Mongols lost none of their vigour. Genghis had divided the empire into separate domains, each domain ruled by one of his sons or other descendants. Ogadai was given China and was also elected the Great Khan in 1229 by an assemblage of princes. Northern China was subdued, but the conquest of the south was delayed while the Khan turned his attention to the invasion and subjugation of Russia. With the death of Ogadai in 1241, the invasion of Europe was cancelled and Mangu Khan, a grandson of Genghis Khan, continued the conquest of China.

He sent his brother Kublai and the general Subotai (who had been responsible for Mongol successes in Europe and Russia) to attack the south of China, which was ruled by the Song emperors. Mangu died of dysentery while fighting in China in 1259. Once again, the death of the Khan brought an end to a Mongol campaign on the brink of success.

Kublai was elected Great Khan in China, but his brother Arik-Boko challenged him for the title. Between the two there was a profound ideological difference. Arik-Boko led a faction of Mongols who wanted to preserve the traditional Mongol way of life, extracting wealth from the empire without intermingling with other races. Kublai, however, realised that an empire won on horseback could not be governed on horseback and intended to establish a government in China with permanent power concentrated in the cities and towns.

The deaths of Kublai's enemies in the 'Golden Horde' (the Mongol faction which controlled the far west of the empire) plus the defeat of Arik-Boko's forces by Kublai's generals enabled Kublai to complete the conquest of southern China by 1279. It was the first and only time that China had been ruled in its entirety by foreigners.

The Mongols established their capital at Beijing, and Kublai Khan became the first emperor of the Yuan Dynasty. Kublai's empire was the largest nation the world has ever known. The Mongols improved the road system linking China with Russia, promoted trade throughout the empire and with Europe, instituted a famine relief scheme and expanded the canal system, which brought food from the countryside to the cities. It was into this China that Marco

Polo wandered, and his book *Description of the World* revealed the secrets of Asia to an amazed Europe.

The Mongols' conquest of China was also to lead to their demise. They alienated the Chinese by staffing the government bureaucracy with Mongols, Muslims and other foreigners. The Chinese were excluded from government and relegated to the level of 2nd class citizens in their own country. Landowners and wealthy traders were favoured, taxation was high and the prosperity of the empire did little to improve the lot of the peasant. Even though the Mongols did not mix with their Chinese subjects, they did succumb to Chinese civilisation: the warriors grew soft.

Kublai died in 1294, the last Khan to rule over a united Mongol Empire. He was followed by a series of weak and incompetent rulers who were unable to contain the revolts that spread all over China. In 1368 Chinese rebels converged on Beijing and the Mongols were driven out by an army led by Zhu Yuanzhang, who then founded the Ming Dynasty.

The entire Mongol Empire had disintegrated by the end of the 14th century, and the Mongol homeland returned to the way of life it knew before Genghis Khan.

Once again the Mongols became a loose collection of disorganised roaming tribes, warring among themselves and occasionally raiding China, until the Qing emperors finally gained control over them in the 18th century.

Divided Mongolia

The eastern expansion of the Russian Empire placed the Mongols in the middle of the border struggles between the Russians and the Chinese, and the Russian Empire set up a 'protectorate' over the northern part of Mongolia.

The rest of Mongolia was governed by the Chinese until 1911, when the Qing fell. For eight years Mongolia remained an independent state until the Chinese returned. Then, in 1924 during the Soviet civil war, the Soviet Communist Army pursued the

White Russian leaders to Urga (now Ulaan Baatar), where they helped create the Mongolian People's Republic by ousting the lama priesthood and the Mongol princes. The new republic remained very much under Soviet domination.

During the war between China and Japan in the 1930s and 40s, parts of what is now Inner Mongolia were occupied by the Japanese, and Communist guerrillas also operated there. In 1936 Mao Zedong told Edgar Snow in Yan'an:

As for Inner Mongolia, which is populated by both Chinese and Mongolians, we will struggle to drive Japan from there and help Inner Mongolia to establish an autonomous state ... when the people's revolution has been victorious in China, the Outer Mongolian republic will automatically become part of the Chinese federation, at its own will.

That was not to be. In 1945 Stalin extracted full recognition of the independence of Outer Mongolia from Chiang Kaishek when the two signed an anti-Japanese Sino-Soviet alliance.

Two years later, with the resumption of the civil war in China, the Chinese Communists designated what was left to China of the Mongol territories as the Inner Mongolia Autonomous Region.

With the Communist victory in 1949, Outer Mongolia did not join the People's Republic as Mao had said it would. The region remained firmly under Soviet control, although it was relatively benign until the 1960s when China and the USSR suddenly became enemies. Mongolia found itself the meat in the sandwich – more than 100,000 Soviet soldiers poured into Mongolia, effectively turning it into one huge military base.

It was not until 1962 that the border with Outer Mongolia was finally settled, although parts of the far north-east were disputed by the Soviet Union. Then in 1969 the Chinese carved up Inner Mongolia and donated bits of it to other provinces – they were reinstated in 1979.

The Chinese seem sufficiently confident

about the assimilation of the Mongols to officially talk about historical absurdities like 'Genghis Khan's Chinese armies' or the 'minority assistance in building the Great Wall'.

Mongolia Today

The Mongolians only make up about 15% of the total population of Inner Mongolia – the other 85% are basically Han Chinese. However, there are a smattering of minority Huis, Manchus, Daurs and Ewenkis.

Since 1949 the Chinese have done their best to assimilate the Mongols, but to be fair the Mongolians have been permitted to keep their written and spoken language. Tibetan Buddhism, the traditional religion of the Mongols, has not fared so well.

The Mongolians are scattered throughout China's north-eastern provinces, as well as through Qinghai and Xinjiang. In total, there are some 3.5 million Mongolians living in China, and another half a million in Russia.

Today, the 'Inner Mongolia Autonomous Region' enjoys little or no autonomy at all. Since the break-up of the Soviet Union in 1991, Outer Mongolia has been free of Soviet control and is reasserting its nationalism. This has the Chinese worried – nationalistic movements like those in Tibet and Xinjiang do not exactly please Beijing. As a result, the PSB keeps a tight lid on potential real or imagined independence activists.

Much of the Inner Mongolia region comprises vast areas of natural grazing land. However, the far north is forested – the Greater Hinggan range makes up about one-sixth of the country's forests and is an important source of timber and paper pulp. Inner Mongolia is also rich in minerals such as coal and iron ore, as you will clearly see if you visit Baotou.

The Mongolian climate tends towards extremes. Siberian blizzards and cold currents rake the plains in winter (from December to March) – forget it! In winter you'll even witness the phenomenon of snow on the desert sand dunes. Summer (from June to August) brings pleasant temperatures, but it can get scorchingly hot during the day in the western areas.

Visiting from May to September is recommended, but pack warm clothing for the Inner Mongolian spring or autumn.

HOHHOT

(hūhéhàotè)

Hohhot became the capital of Inner Mongolia in 1952, when it served as the administrative and educational centre. It was founded in the 16th century and, like the other towns, grew around its temples and lamaseries, which are now in ruins.

Hide and wool industries are the mainstay, backed up by machine-building, a sugar refinery, fertiliser plants, a diesel-engine factory and iron and steel production. The population is just under one million if the outlying areas are included.

Hohhot means Blue City in Mongolian, although many Chinese-speaking locals mistakenly claim it means 'green city'. Perhaps the name refers to the crisp blue skies – this is one of the sunniest parts of China outside of the western deserts.

Hohhot is basically a Chinese city, but it serves as a main entrance point for tours of the grasslands. Both CITS and CTS turn on the culture in Hohhot, from the grasslands tour to the equestrian displays at the horseracing ground. Horse racing, polo and stunt riding are put on for large tour groups, if you latch onto one somehow; otherwise, they take place only on rare festive occasions. It's the same with song and dance soirees.

Information

Tourist Offices CITS (☎ 696-4233, ext 8935) has a small office to the right in the corridor at the back of the lobby of the Inner Mongolia Hotel. CTS (☎ 695-0323) has a counter beside the reception of the Inner Mongolia Hotel, and we've found them to be more knowledgeable.

Another outfit that grabs a lot of budget travellers is the CYTS (☎ 629-6139), on the 4th floor of the Tongda Hotel.

INNER MONGOLIA

PSB The PSB for visa extensions and other inquiries is at 39 Zhongshan Xilu, on the northern side of the street near the corner of Zhongshan Lu and Xilin Guole Lu. There's an English plaque just inside the gate. There is a large new building across the street that is also the PSB, but it was not handling foreigners at the time of writing.

Money The most convenient places to change money are the Bank of China branches inside the Inner Mongolia and Zhaojun hotels. The main branch is on Xinhua Dajie.

Post & Communications The main post office is on the left-hand side of the square as you exit the railway station. The entrance closest to the station is the place to make long-distance phone calls. There's another post office near the PSB on Zhongshan Lu.

Inner Mongolia Museum
(nèi měnggǔ bówùguǎn)
Well presented and definitely worth a visit, this is the biggest attraction in town. The museum collection includes a large mammoth skeleton dug out of a coal mine near Manzhouli, dinosaur exhibits, a yurt (circular tent) and a fantastic array of Mongolian costumery, artefacts, archery equipment and saddles. The top floors of the museum are sometimes closed. The flying horse on top of the building is meant to symbolise the forward spirit of the Mongolian people.

The museum is on the western side of Hulunbei'er Lu at the intersections of Xinhua Dajie and Zhongshan Lu. Entry is Y3 for Chinese and Y8 for foreigners.

Five Pagoda Temple
(wǔtǎ sì)
This miniaturised structure dating back to 1740 is now bereft of its temple, leaving the Five Pagodas standing on a rectangular block. The pagodas are built with glazed bricks and are inscribed in Mongolian, Sanskrit and Tibetan. Cut into niches are small Buddhist figures; around the back is a screen wall with an astronomical chart inscribed in Mongolian.

The Five Pagodas are on Wutasi Houjie off Gongyuan Xilu south of Renmin Park on the bus No 1 route. Entry is Y2.

Dazhao Temple
(dàzhào)
The old part of town south-west of Renmin Park has some interesting sights. Down some alleys off a main street is the Dazhao Temple. The temple is incidental; the main action is on the streets. Around the area of the Dazhao Temple are some fascinating adobe houses, low and squat with decorated glass windows. Entry costs Y4.

Xiletuzhao Temple
(xílètúzhào)
Not far from the Dazhao Temple is the Xiletuzhao Temple. It's the stomping ground of the 11th Grand Living Buddha, who dresses in civvies and is apparently active. There's nothing special to see though. The original temple burned down and the present one was built in the 19th century; the Chinese-style building has a few Tibetan touches. The reverse swastika symbols on the exterior have long been used in Persian, Indian, Greek and Jewish cultures – they symbolise truth and eternity (and have no relation to their mirror image, the Nazi swastika). Entry is Y3.

Great Mosque
(qīngzhēn dà sì)
North of Xiletuzhao on Tongdao Jie is the Great Mosque. Built in Chinese style, with the addition of a minaret, it dates from the Qing Dynasty (with later expansions). It is an active place of worship for the Hohhot Muslim community, holding prayers five times a day. You can wander around, as long you don't enter the prayer area. There is no entrance fee.

Wang Zhaojun Tomb
(zhāojūn mù)
The tomb of this Han Dynasty concubine to

Emperor Yuandi (1st century BC) is a bit of a bore, although it does permit some countryside viewing at the edge of town. It basically consists of a large mound of earth and a park below with statues of the couple on horseback. Entry is Y5.

The tomb is 9km from the city at the terminus of the bus No 14 route, which starts from the intersection of Shiyangqiao Xilu and Nanchafang Jie.

Naadam
(nàdámù)

The summer festival known as Naadam features traditional Mongolian sports such as competition archery, wrestling, horse racing and camel racing. Prizes vary from a goat to a fully equipped horse. The fair has its origins in the ancient Obo-Worshipping Festival (an *obo* is a pile of stones with a hollow space for offerings – a kind of shaman shrine).

The Mongolian clans make a beeline for the fairs on any form of transport they can muster, and create an impromptu yurt city. For foreigners, Hohhot is a good place to see the Naadam festivities. Horse racing, camel racing, wrestling and archery takes place at the horse racing grounds *(sài-măchăng)* in the northern part of the city on bus route No 13.

The exact date of Naadam varies in China, but is usually around mid-August. It's worth knowing that Naadam is celebrated at a different time in Outer Mongolia – always from 11 to 13 July, which corresponds to the date of Mongolia's 1921 revolution.

Places to Stay

The *Tongda Hotel* (☎ 696-8731) *(tōngdá fàndiàn)*, at 28 Chezhan Dongjie, is opposite the railway station. Most of the budget travellers seem to end up here because it's the cheapest in Hohhot and it's convenient to the bus and railway stations. They have twins for Y62, Y72 and Y88 that come with attached shower. They also have triples and quads for Y63 and Y76. CYTS has an office on the 4th floor.

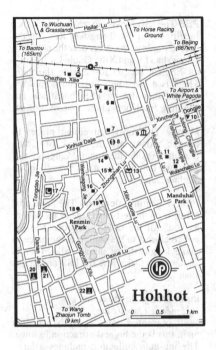

Hohhot

The *Hohhot Hotel* (☎ 696-2858; fax 696-3335) *(hūhéhàotè bīnguăn)* is within walking distance of the railway station and has rooms for Y400 and Y200 in it's north building.

The *Xincheng Hotel* (☎ 629-2288; fax 693-1141) *(xīnchéng bīnguăn)* is in spacious grounds and is rather like living in a park. It's 2km from the railway station. There's no bus from the railway station to the hotel. Bus No 20 stops near the hotel, but to catch this bus you must turn left as you exit the railway station and walk a long block to Hulunbei'er Lu. Otherwise, take a taxi.

Twins in the old wing are Y200, while the new dazzling white building has rooms for Y600 and up, plus a 10% service charge. Bicycle rentals are available outside the main gate on Hulunbei'er Lu to your right as you exit.

The *Inner Mongolia Hotel* (☎ 696-4233;

HOHHOT 呼和浩特

PLACES TO STAY
1 Wangfu Hotel
   王府饭店
5 Tongda Hotel;
   CYTS
   通达饭店、
   中国青年旅行社
6 Hohhot Hotel
   呼和浩特宾馆
7 Zhaojun Hotel
   昭君大酒店
11 Xincheng Hotel
   新城宾馆
12 Inner Mongolia Hotel;
   CITS; CTS
   内蒙古饭店、
   中国国际旅行社、
   中国旅行社

16 Yunzhong Hotel; Minzu
   Department Store
   云中大酒店、
   民族商场

PLACES TO EAT
4 Taiwan Beef Noodle
   台湾牛肉面馆
10 Malaqin Restaurant
   马拉沁饭店
19 Golden Skillet Fried
   Chicken; Dairy Queen
   国际快餐城

OTHER
2 Long-Distance
   Bus Station
   长途汽车站
3 Railway Station
   火车站

8 Bank of China
   中国银行
9 Inner Mongolia Museum
   内蒙古博物馆
13 Post Office
   邮局
14 CAAC
   中国民航
15 PSB
   公安局外事科
17 Great Mosque
   清真大寺
18 Advance Booking Office
   (Train Tickets)
   火车预售票处
20 Dazhao Temple
   大召寺
21 Xiletuzhao Temple
   席勒图召
22 Five Pagoda Temple
   五塔寺

fax 696-1479) *(nèi ménggǔ fàndiàn)* is around the corner from the Xincheng Hotel. A 14 storey high-rise on Wulanchabu Xilu, this is the home of CITS and CTS, and although the standard is three star, the plumbing isn't the greatest. Standard twins range from Y310 to Y580.

The *Yunzhong Hotel* (☎ 696-8822; fax 696-2236) *(yúnzhōng dàjiǔdiàn)* is on Bei'er Lu Nangang off Zhongshan Lu, hidden behind the Minzu Department Store. The hotel has buildings on both sides of the street and the entrance has a traditional Chinese-style roof. Singles are Y80, while twins cost Y120 and Y180, but foreigners have to pay 100% more.

There's a new hotel next to the bus station on Chezhan Xijie that not only looks like the Wangfu (Palace) Hotel in Beijing, but also has the same name. Unfortunately, Hohhot's *Wangfu Hotel* (☎ 696-4531; fax 696-6600) *(wángfǔ fàndiàn)* lacks the sophistication of its namesake. Standard twins are Y160, but foreigners have to pay double that. They also have twins and triples without bath for Y72/90, but expect a surcharge for these as well.

The *Zhaojun Hotel* (☎ 696-2211; fax 696-8825) *(zhāojūn dàjiǔdiàn)* on 11 Xin-

hua Dajie diagonally across from Xinhua Square, is a fancy Hong Kong joint venture. The price for a standard twin is Y400, but foreigners have to pay a Y200 surcharge.

Places to Eat

Budget cuisine is – as always – available from restaurants around the railway station. Food vendors also set up tables on summer nights at the corner in front of the Zhaojun Hotel.

Many travellers inevitably end up at the *Taiwan Beef Noodle (táiwān niúròu miàn-guǎn),* opposite the railway station on the south-eastern corner of Chezhan Dongjie and Xilin Guole Lu. A bowl of noodles is Y6 and they have cold drinks, including beer.

The *Inner Mongolia Hotel* has an English menu for its Chinese restaurant, and it also has a reasonable western-style coffee shop on the ground floor.

The *Xincheng Hotel* has a fancy new western restaurant on its mezzanine floor, and the *Zhaojun Hotel* has a western-style restaurant with somewhat claustrophobic decor on the second floor.

The *Malaqin Restaurant* (malaqin means 'horseman') is recommended for Chinese and Mongolian food, though the buffet is less appetising than the dishes from the menu. Try the Mongolian hotpot, roasted lamb and kebab. Prices are moderate even though this place caters to foreign tour groups, and the friendly staff speak some English.

If you can't get out to the grasslands, but want to have dinner in a yurt, try the *Menggu Yingmei Shicheng (ménggǔ yíngmeǐ shíchěng)* which provides just that. It is located near the horse racing stadium on the eastern side of Hulunbei'er Beilu. Try the traditional stewed leg of mutton dish, *shǒubāròu*.

Finally, if it's western-style fast food you crave, there's a combined *Golden Skillet Fried Chicken* and *Dairy Queen* outlet in the glass building opposite the Minzu Department store. In addition to its french fries, hot dogs, ice-cream sundaes and beef rice dishes, you can also get pints of draught beer for Y10.

Entertainment

Unfortunately, there's not very much available in terms of Mongolian cultural activities going on, unless you happen to be in Hohhot during Naadam. You might try asking CITS or CTS about any upcoming performances. Otherwise there's always bowling at the Zhaojun Hotel.

Things to Buy

The Minority Handicraft Factory is on the southern side of Shiyangqiao Xilu, near the intersection with Nanchafang Jie. It's in the southern section of town on the bus No 1 route and has a retail outlet for tourists. There only carry a limited selection of stock, but wares include inlaid knife and chopstick sets, saddles, daggers, boots, embroidered shoes, costumes, brassware, blankets and curios.

You'll actually find a better selection and lower prices on the second floor of the Minzu Department Store *(mínzú shāngchǎng)*. It's on Zhongshan Lu where the pedestrian bridge crosses the road. Another very good buy in this section of the store is

silver jewellery where earrings, necklaces and bracelets are very cheap.

Many of the souvenir shops have selections of jewellery as well, and the small shop beside the Inner Mongolia Museum has some nice items.

On Xinhua Dajie, across from the Zhaojun Hotel, the Cashmere Products Marketing Centre *(yángróng fúzhuāng fúshì zhíxiāo zhōngxīn)* has cashmere sweaters at cheaper prices than you'll ever find in Beijing and Shanghai.

Getting There & Away

Air CAAC's office (☎ 696-4103) is on Xilin Guole Lu. There are regular flights connecting Hohhot with Beijing, Chifeng, Guangzhou, Hailar, Shanghai, Shenzhen, Shijiazhuang, Tongliao, Ulanhot, Wuhan and Xilinhot.

There are also twice weekly flights to Ulaan Baatar in Outer Mongolia with Mongolian Airlines (☎ 495-2026) which costs US$79 one way.

Bus There are bus connections between Hohhot and Datong (seven hours). Buses to Baotou (three hours) leave about every half hour and there are five buses to Dongsheng (five hours) throughout the day (the first one leaving at 7.40 am).

Train Hohhot is on the Beijing-Lanzhou railway line that cuts a long loop through Inner Mongolia; about 2½ hours out of Beijing you'll pass the crumbled remains of the Great Wall (it looks like little more than a dirt embankment).

On the fastest trains, Beijing to Hohhot is a 12 hour trip, Datong to Hohhot takes five hours, Baotou to Hohhot takes 2½ hours, and Yinchuan to Hohhot takes 10 hours.

Trains are most frequent between Hohhot and Beijing, less so between Yinchuan and Hohhot, and run only twice a day between Lanzhou and Hohhot. There are connections three times a day between Taiyuan and Datong, where a connection to Hohhot can be made. There is also a train to Hailar (48 hours) that passes through Beijing.

You can book sleepers at the advance booking office on Zhongshan Xilu, diagonally opposite the entrance to Renmin Park. CITS, CTS and CYTS can book train tickets for a service fee of around Y40.

Getting Around

To/From the Airport Hohhot airport is about 15km east of the city. The airport bus leaves from the CAAC booking office 1½ hours before flight departure. Tickets are Y4. Taxi drivers ask around Y60 for the journey.

Bus You can get a detailed bus map (in Chinese only), which includes surrounding regions, from hotel gift shops and bookstalls around town. Check with hotel staff for your proposed route. Bus No 1 runs from the railway station to the old part of the city in the south-western corner.

Taxi These are available from the hotels and railway station area. The taxis have meters, but you still have to bargain. It costs around Y15 to go between the railway station and the Inner Mongolia Hotel.

Bicycle Hohhot is reasonably small and, weather permitting, you can go a long way on a pair of self-propelled wheels.

Bikes can be hired at the Xincheng and Inner Mongolia hotels and there's a bike rental place in the small rectangular building to the left as you exit the railway station. It's ridiculously cheap, about Y3 for the whole day.

AROUND HOHHOT

About 20km west of Hohhot, the Sino-Tibetan monastery **Wusutuzhao** is hardly worth looking at, but the surrounding arid landscape is impressive. A mini-van taxi will cost about Y40 to take you there from the railway station.

About 15km east of Hohhot, just past the airport, is the **White Pagoda** (báită), a

seven storey octagonal tower. The pagoda can be reached by a 20 minute suburban train ride that leaves at 8.25 am. Buy your tickets on the train.

You'll probably have to get a taxi back though, because the train only makes the return journey in the evening.

THE GRASSLANDS
(căoyuán)

This is what most travellers come to see in Inner Mongolia, but if you are after a more authentic experience of the grasslands, consider a trip to Hailar or Manzhouli (or better still, the nation of Mongolia).

Organised Tours

Cashing in on the magic draw of 'Mongolia' is the name of the game here. As for visions of the descendants of the mighty Khan riding the endless plains, the herds of wild horses and the remnants of Xanadu, remember that this is China and most of the population is now Han Chinese. Nevertheless, CTS and CITS are only too happy to organise tours to give you a glimpse of the traditional Mongolian lifestyle, which now seems to be an anachronism in Inner Mongolia.

The real country for seeing Mongolians in their own environment is Outer Mongolia, but getting there is both expensive and difficult. Grasslands and yurt dwellings can be seen in other parts of China, such as Xinjiang. Remember that grass is only green in summer – the verdant pasturelands can turn a shrivelled shade of frost-coated brown from November to April. Take warm, windproof clothing – there's a considerable wind-chill factor even in the middle of summer.

There are three grasslands areas targeted for CITS and CTS tours: **Xilamuren** (80km from Hohhot), **Gegentala** (170km away in Siziwang Qi) and **Huitengxile** (120km from Hohhot), which is the most beautiful, but least visited.

There are some fledgling private travel agents who try to solicit business in the lobbies of the tourist hotels – you can talk

Grasslands Tour Prices

To Xilamuren

No of People	Cost per person (Y)		
	1 Day	2 Days	3 Days
1	540	720	950
2-4	440	560	690
5-10	380	465	550
11-15	250	340	450
16-20	200	350	400
over 21	188	268	300

To Gegentala

No of People	Cost per person (Y)		
	1 Day	2 Days	3 Days
1	–	880	1185
2-4	–	585	680
5-10	–	525	630
11-15	–	495	570
16-20	–	460	500
over 21	–	310	400

To Huitengxile

No of People	Cost per person (Y)		
	1 Day	2 Days	3 Days
1	–	820	1140
2-4	–	595	695
5-10	–	480	560
11-15	–	425	520
16-20	–	380	410
over 21	–	246	320

to them and discuss prices. There are also taxi drivers around the railway station who do self-styled grasslands tours for around Y300 per person (extra if you stay overnight). The trip may consist of staying in a yurt belonging to the driver's family.

The name of the game is 'bargain'. Be aware that these unofficial tours get very mixed reviews. One traveller was served a wretched meal in a yurt – cooked over a cow-dung fire – and got food poisoning. As you'll discover if you explore the Mongolian hinterland, sanitation is not a strong point, so watch what you eat and drink. Others have reported that the so-called 'Mongolians' are just Hans dressed up in Mongolian costume. But if you still feel like going on a tour, the table above has prices for tours quoted by CTS.

BAOTOU
(bāotóu)

The largest city in Inner Mongolia, Baotou lies on the bleak northernmost reaches of the Yellow River, to the west of Hohhot. The name means 'land with deer' in Mongolian, and although there is still a deer farm outside of Baotou, you are only likely to encounter these creatures on the dinner plate in some of the upmarket restaurants around town.

Previously set in an area of undeveloped semi-desert inhabited by Mongol herders, Baotou underwent a radical change when the Communists came to power in 1949. Over the next decade, a 1923 railway line linking the town with Beijing was extended south-east to Yinchuan, and roads were constructed to facilitate access to the region's iron, coal and other mineral deposits.

Today, Baotou is an industrial community of about one million people; despite the showcase street signs in Mongolian, nearly the entire population is Han Chinese. While West Baotou has undergone a major facelift, East Baotou must be one of the ugliest urban areas in China, and that's no small accomplishment. Baotou is definitely a city of specialised interests – a couple of nearby monasteries, a steel mill, a steam locomotive museum, quite small sand dunes and a mausoleum dedicated to Genghis Khan. Most of these sights are not in the city itself, but a couple of hours outside town.

Overall, Baotou is a useful transit point and you can keep yourself amused here for a day or so, but if you miss it, don't lose any sleep. The best thing we can say for the place is that the people are friendly.

Orientation

Baotou is a huge town – 20km of urban sprawl separate the eastern and western parts of the city. It's the eastern area that most travellers visit because it's useful as a transit hub – the western area has the steel mill and locomotive museum.

The station for the western area is Baotou railway station *(bāotóu zhàn)*; for

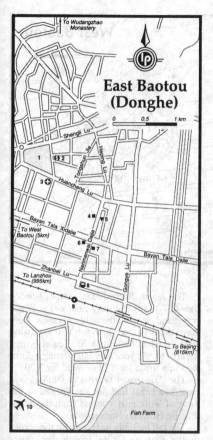

East Baotou (Donghe)

0   0.5   1 km

To Wudangzhao Monastery

To West Baotou (5km)

To Lanzhou (995km)

To Beijing (816km)

Fish Farm

EAST BAOTOU (DONGHE)
包头东河区

1 Renmin Park
   人民公园
2 Bank of China
   中国银行
3 No 2 Hospital
   第二医院
4 Donghe Hotel; CAAC
   东河宾馆、中国民航
5 Prince's Building Hot Pot City
   太子楼肉粥火锅城
6 North Pacific Hotel
   北洋饭店
7 Asia Hotel
   亚细亚大酒店
8 Long-Distance Bus Station
   长途汽车站
9 Baotou East Railway Station
   包头东站
10 Airport
   飞机场

PSB The PSB is at 59 Gangtie Dajie, near the Baotou Department Store.

Money Except for the Tianwaitian Hotel in West Baotou, none of the other hotels has a moneychanging desk, but there are three branches of the Bank of China which handle foreign exchange. In western Baotou, one is on Gangtie Dajie near the TV tower and another is on Wenhua Lu and Xinfu Lu.

In eastern Baotou, the only Bank of China that does currency exchange is near the entrance to Renmin Park.

Baotou Iron & Steel Company
(*bāotóu gāngtiě gōngsī*)
A purple cloud hangs over the western horizon of the city. The source of these colourful sunsets is the Baotou Iron & Steel Company, which was supervised by the Soviets until their abrupt exit in 1960.

The original plan foresaw use of ore from Bayan Obo (about 140km further north). Unfortunately, the local ore couldn't make the grade and the company now imports the stuff. Foreigners can only get inside the steelworks via a CITS or CYTS

the eastern area it's Baotou East railway station (*bāotóu dōng zhàn*). The eastern district is called Donghe; the western area is subdivided into two adjacent districts – Qingshan and Kundulun.

Information
Travel Offices CITS (☎ 515-4615) is at 9 Qingnian Lu north of the Baotou Guesthouse. The offices are on the 2nd floor. There is also a CYTS (☎ 511-0920) on the 3rd floor of the west building in the Baotou Guesthouse.

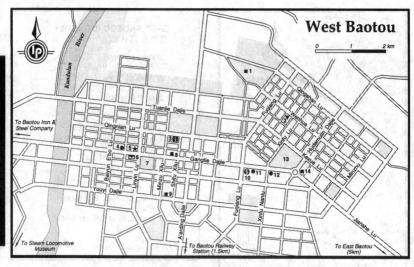

West Baotou

tour. Besides the cost of your guide, there is a Y30 per person admission fee. It's cheaper if you hire your own taxi, as the expense in these tours comes from using the travel agency vehicles, which are about Y300 for half a day.

Steam Locomotive Museum
(zhēngqì huǒchē bówùguǎn)
The museum is fairly small and it is necessary to go through CITS or CYTS. The latter is a bit cheaper and will do the tour for Y50, not including car hire or the entrance fee of Y30.

Keep in mind that steam trains offer a more dramatic spectacle in the wintertime, which is when most people visit the museum and it might be easier to hook up with a tour.

Places to Stay
East Baotou The *Donghe Hotel* (☎ 417-2266; fax 417-2541) (dōnghé bīnguǎn), at 14 Nanmenwai Dajie, is about 15 minutes' walk (or take bus No 5) from the East Baotou railway station. Twins with an attached bath range from Y80 to Y120.

The *North Pacific Hotel* (☎ 417-5656; fax 417-1440) (běiyáng fàndiàn) is better value and closer to the railway station. They have twins without bath for Y70 and twins with attached bath for Y90. You also may be able to talk your way into getting a dorm bed in a triple for Y22 or quad for Y20.

The *Asia Hotel* (yàsīyà dàjiǔdiàn) is a new hotel that had not yet opened at the time of writing. It's across from the North Pacific Hotel on Nanmenwai.

The tall building next door on the corner is the *Phoenix Grand* (fènghuáng dàjiǔdiàn) which was also closed at the time of writing, but may have been resurrected by now. Expect mid to high-range prices for these hotels.

West Baotou Unfortunately, none of the hotels near the railway station will take foreigners. The best option for budget accommodation is the *Friendship Hotel* (☎ 515-4624) (yǒuyì bīnguǎn) on Youyi Dajie, to the north of the railway station. Twins with attached bath are Y89 and triples without bath are Y75.

On Gangtie Dajie, in the Kundulun district,

WEST BAOTOU 包头西部

1 Qingshan Guesthouse
  青山宾馆
2 Dafulin Restaurant
  大福林饭庄
3 CITS
  中国国际旅行社
4 Xinhua Bookstore
  新华书店
5 PSB
  公安局
6 Post Office
  邮局
7 Bayi Park
  八一公园
8 Baotou Guesthouse
  包头宾馆
9 Friendship Hotel
  友谊宾馆
10 Bank of China
   中国银行
11 CAAC
   中国民航
12 TV Tower
   电视塔
13 Laodong Park
   劳动公园
14 Tianwaitian Hotel
   天 馓斋缶频

the *Baotou Guesthouse* (☎ 515-6655; fax 515-4641) *(bāotóu bīnguǎn)*, has a range of rooms in three buildings, from Y83 for doubles without bath in the west building, to Y328 for twins in the luxurious new highrise (plus a 50% surcharge). If arriving by train, get off at Baotou railway station. The station is 8km from the hotel – take bus No 1, a taxi or a motor-tricycle. If arriving by bus from Hohhot, you can ask the driver to drop you off right in front of the hotel.

Qingshan Guesthouse (☎ 313-1199; fax 515-6001) *(qīngshān bīnguǎn)* is a secluded and somewhat unfriendly place. Foreigners are charged Y346 for a twin room while the same room is given to Chinese for Y238. There is no public transport, although bus No 10 runs within 1km of the hotel. Access is usually by taxi.

The *Tianwaitian Hotel* (☎ 313-7766; fax 313-1771) is new, and is the best hotel in Baotou. The only thing that isn't very welcoming is the price. Foreigners are charged 100% more for a standard twin for which Chinese pay Y335.

Places to Eat

A good restaurant in East Batou, the *Prince's Building Hot Pot City (tàizǐlóu ròuzhōu huǒguōchéng)*, is across from the Donghe Hotel and has reasonable prices. It doesn't just serve hotpots, and there's good draught beer on tap for Y6 a pint. If you're looking for a change from the constant meat menu, try their *jiācháng dòufu*, a tasty home-style tofu dish, or *sùmiàn*, noodles with vegetables. There is no English name (or menu for that matter) on the restaurant; look for the red awning at the entrance. Or you can walk down to the Baotou East railway station, where there are the usual *foodstalls*.

If you're visiting in the summer, tables and foodstalls are set up for a lively *night market* just to the north of the Donghe Hotel, at the intersection of Huancheng Lu and Nanmenwai.

Over in the western part of town, the big famous place is the *Dafulin Restaurant (dàfúlín fànzhuāng)* at 90 Wenhua Lu, about 1km from the Qingshan Guesthouse. It has Mongolian and Chinese dishes. Mongolian hotpot with sliced mutton *(shuàn-yángròu)* will set you back about Y50.

Both the *Tianwaitian Hotel* and the new building of the *Baotou Guesthouse* have restaurants that serve something vaguely resembling western-style food.

Things to Buy

The hotel gift shops offer a small selection of tourist-oriented minority handicrafts, but Hohhot is a better place to buy this stuff. As China's mineral capital, Baotou would be a good place to find bargains on iron ore, cobalt and lignite, in case you need to stock up.

Getting There & Away

Air CAAC (☎ 513-5492) has a main ticket office at 26 Gangtie Dajie beside the Bank of China. There's a ticket office at the Baotou Guesthouse; you can also book tickets at the Donghe Hotel and pick them up at the airport. There are flights connecting Baotou with Guangzhou, Wuhan, Shanghai and Xi'an.

Bus Buses go from in front of the long-distance bus station to Hohhot for Y14 and the trip takes three hours. Buy your ticket on the bus.

From West Baotou, buses leave from the intersection of Tuanjie Dajie and Baiyun E'bo Lu, where a long-distance bus station is currently under construction. Tickets are Y16. The new Baotou-Hohhot freeway is nearly completed and should shorten the journey by about an hour.

Train There are frequent trains to and from Hohhot to Baotou which stop in both the eastern and western sections. The journey takes just under two hours on the fast trains.

There are also trains to Beijing (13½ hours), Yinchuan (eight hours), Taiyuan (14½ hours) and other major cities to the south. CITS can book sleepers for a Y50 service charge. It's not easy to get them at the railway stations.

Getting Around
To/From the Airport The airport is 2km south of Baotou East railway station. In spite of the short distance, taxis ask around Y25 for the one way journey. If you are coming from West Baotou, an airport bus leaves from the CAAC ticket office; tickets are Y10.

Bus Bus Nos 5 and 10 stop close to the Baotou Guesthouse and shuttle between the western and eastern sections of Baotou in 45 minutes. The double-decker buses are the most comfortable.

There are also minibuses (zhōngbā), which cost Y2.5 – you board these at the regular bus stops.

Taxi Metered taxis and mini-van taxis, as well as motor-tricycles, congregate at the

railway stations and tourist hotels. Taxi meters start at Y8, but sometimes you still have to bargain (such as when going to the airport.

Bicycle While East Baotou is easy to get around on foot and by bus, West Baotou is a sprawling expanse of long boulevards. The cheapest way to get around is by bicycle, which you can rent from a place to the left of the entrance to the west building of the Baotou Guesthouse.

AROUND BAOTOU
Wudangzhao Monastery
(wǔdāngzhào)
The main tourist attraction near Baotou is the large Wudangzhao Monastery, about 2½ hours from the city by bus.

This monastery of the Gelukpa (Yellow Hat sect of Tibetan Buddhism) was built around 1749 in typical Tibetan style with flat-roofed buildings. It once housed 1200 monks. The ashes of seven reincarnations of the monastery's 'living buddha' are kept in a special hall and there is a collection of Buddhist wall paintings dating from the Qing Dynasty. Today all religious activity is restricted to a handful of pilgrims and doorkeeper-monks who collect the admission fee.

The crowds of day-tripping, camera-clicking tourists make this is no place for religion. Try to walk into the hills away from the pandemonium; the site has a peculiar strength in its secretive, brooding atmosphere.

There's a basic dorm next to the monastery that has beds for Y10 and Y15, but no running water. CITS also organises tours, but you can easily manage on your own. The lighting is a bit dim so you might want to take a torch if you want to see anything inside the monastery. Entry is Y20 (foreign price).

Getting There & Away The monastery is 65km north-east of Baotou. A direct minibus to Wudangzhao leaves from the parking lot in front of the East Baotou bus station at 11 am and leaves the monastery at 3 pm, although keep in mind these departure times are not etched in stone. The journey costs Y10.

Otherwise, bus No 7, at the far left of the parking lot as you exit the long-distance bus station, goes to Shiguai, 40km northwest of Baotou. From Shiguai there are infrequent buses that can do the second leg of the journey. If your time is limited, you'd be better off hiring a taxi from Shiguai to the monastery and back for about Y60, although you will have to add extra for the driver to wait.

Meidaizhao Monastery
(měidàizhào)
This monastery is much smaller than Wudangzhao and consequently little visited, although it's more accessible. Meidaizhao is halfway between Baotou and Hohhot, less than half a kilometre north of the main highway (a 10 minute walk). As long as they take the old highway and not the freeway, buses on the Baotou-Hohhot route can drop you off here. Like Wudangzhao, the monastery is devoted to the Gelukpa. Entry is Y10 for foreigners and Y5 for Chinese.

Resonant Sand Gorge
(yīméng xiǎng shāwān)
The Gobi Desert starts just to the south of Baotou. Some 60km south of Baotou and a few kilometres west of the Baotou-Dongsheng highway is a gorge filled to the brim with sand dunes.

Although the gorge has long been known to locals as a barren place to be avoided (no grass for the sheep), it has recently been turned into a money-spinner by CITS. Japanese tour groups in particular come here to frolic in the sand. To spice up the romance of such frolicking, the area has been named Resonant Sand Gorge, a reference to the swooshing sound made by loose sand when you step on it.

The highest dunes are about 90m above their own base. But you can find much more spectacular sand dunes in other parts of China – in particular, check out Dunhuang in Gansu Province. This is not to say you shouldn't visit Baotou's Resonant Sand Gorge, but getting to the gorge might be problematic unless you are on a tour or charter a taxi. The latter will cost from Y100 to Y150 return to Baotou or Dongsheng.

The Baotou to Dongsheng bus passes by the turn-off, but it's another 8km to the site and it may be difficult to get a ride. The cheapest way to get there is to take a bus to the town Daqi, just north of the turn off, and hire a taxi for about Y50 return.

Entry to the sands is Y10 and you can ride camels (Y10) or try parasailing (Y20) if sliding around in the sand isn't enough for you.

DONGSHENG
(dōngshèng)
Dongsheng lies south-west of Baotou and serves as a staging post for the site of Genghis Khan's Mausoleum. Dongsheng itself is not blessed with scenic attractions, though it's smaller and more attractive than Baotou.

A plan to dress up the town for tourism gave birth to the **Jinyuan Ancient City** *(jīnyuán chéng)* – the 'ancient city' consists of a single street of reconstructed buildings which looks much like a movie set, but happily the local merchants and consumers have turned it into a lively market. Also interesting is the **Minsheng Indoor Market** *(mínshēng shìchǎng)*, where you can buy practical things such as clothing (not Mongolian style).

If you get an early start, it's possible to reach Dongsheng in the morning, visit Genghis Khan's Mausoleum, then return to Dongsheng to spend the night, or possibly travel all the way back to Baotou the same day (this would be exhausting though).

Actually, Dongsheng is not a bad place to spend the night – accommodation is cheap and of good standard. Furthermore, the locals are extremely friendly, and it's certainly a nicer place to hang out than Baotou.

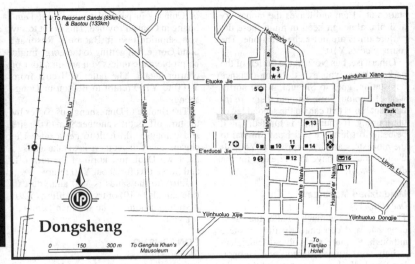

Dongsheng

To Resonant Sands (65km) & Baotou (133km)

Hangkong Lu

Etuoke Jie

Manduhai Xiang

Dongsheng Park

Tianjiao Lu

Jiaoqing Lu

Wenduer Lu

Hangjin Lu

E'erduosi Jie

Dala'te Nanlu

Huaige'er Nanlu

Linyin Lu

Yijinhuoluo Xijie

Yijinhuoluo Dongjie

To Genghis Khan's Mausoleum

To Tianjiao Hotel

0   150   300 m

Information
The CITS and CTS office (☎ 834-1075) is inside the gate of Jinyuan Ancient City, on the second floor a blue tile Islamic-looking building on the right. There's a CITS sign out front.

Places to Stay
No matter where you stay, take your evening shower early. Dongsheng is plagued by water shortages and the water is often turned off by midnight, sometimes earlier. It usually comes on again at 6 am, but that is not guaranteed.

The *Ih Ju League Hotel* (☎ 832-1567; fax 832-7885) *(yīkè zhāoméng bīnguǎn)*, usually just called the *Yimeng Binguan*, is a very popular place with travellers and it's probably the best value in Dongsheng; basic twins without bath are Y54. Other rooms are rather expensive at Y200 and Y300 for twins and triples with attached bath (plus a 30% surcgarge). The hotel is on E'erduosi Jie at the corner of Dala'te Lu.

The *Dongsheng Hotel* (☎ 832-7333; fax 832-3142) *(dōngshèng dà jiǔdiàn)* is also good value, with twin rooms with attached

bath for Y92/104. Triple rooms are Y126 and, if you're with a group, there are four-person rooms for Y88. You can also rent bicycles here, which is the best way to get around (not that there is much to see).

Just opposite the Dongsheng is the *Minzu Hotel* (☎ 832-3629) *(mínzú fàndiàn)*. Singles and twins with bathroom are Y58/66. The place is a bit tattered, but you can't beat the price for a suite at Y93.

The *Continental Grand Hotel* (☎ 832-1532) *(wǔzhōu jiǔdiàn)* is best avoided. They have twins without bath for Y50, but charge 100% more for foreigners. They also have twins for Y90 and Y150.

The most upmarket place in town, which caters to the Japanese crowd, is the *Tianjiao Hotel* (☎ 833-3888; fax 832-4348) *(tiānjiāo dàjiǔdiàn)* at the southern end Dala'te Nanlu. A standard room is only Y280, but foreigners are charged Y400. To get there take minibus No 2 from the bus station and go all the way to the stop past the roundabout.

Places to Eat
There's not a lot available in Dongsheng,

DONGSHENG 东胜

1 Railway Station
  火车站
2 Jinyuan Ancient City
  金元城
3 CITS
  中国国际旅行社
4 PSB
  公安局
5 Bus Station
  长途汽车站
6 Minsheng Indoor Market
  民生市场
7 Meng Hospital
  盟医院
8 Dongsheng Hotel
  东胜大酒店
9 Bank of China
  中国银行
10 Minzu Hotel
  民族饭店
11 Xin Xin Restaurant
  鑫鑫大快活
12 Continental Grand Hotel
  五洲酒店
13 Xinhua Bookstore
  新华书店
14 Ih Ju League Hotel
  伊克昭盟宾馆
15 Dongsheng Department Store
  东胜市百货大楼
16 Post & Telephone Office
  邮电大楼
17 Museum
  博物馆

but a lively restaurant popular with the locals is on E'erduosi Jie just up from the Ih Ju League Hotel. The *Xin Xin Restaurant (xīnxīn àkuàihuo)* doesn't have an English sign or menu, but just point to what other diners are eating. The friendly staff will help you out. For dessert, try *mǐhuā*, a sweet pancake that would go great with maple syrup if you happen to have brought some along. Draught beer is Y8 and the beef noodles are very good, at Y3 a bowl.

The *Tianjiao Hotel* has a restaurant designed in Japanese style (except for tatami) and features a hybrid of Mongolian barbecue and teppanyaki meals that are cooked at your table. The hotel also has a small supermarket in the lobby.

Getting There & Away

Bus Most travellers take the bus directly from Hohhot. It departs at 7.40 am, takes five hours and costs Y25. Sit on the right-hand side of the bus for mountain views along the way (or the left on the way back). The bus goes via Baotou, but doesn't stop there. Just to the south of Baotou, the bus crosses the Yellow River.

There are three buses daily departing Dongsheng for Hohhot, the last one leaving at 12.30 pm.

Another route is to go from Baotou. Catch a bus to Dongsheng from the long-distance bus station (eastern Baotou). Buses run every 20 minutes from 6.20 am. The journey from Baotou to Dongsheng takes about 2½ hours. There is also a bus to Xi'an (16 hours) from Dongsheng, departing in the early afternoon and arriving the next morning.

AROUND DONGSHENG
Genghis Khan's Mausoleum
(chéngjí sīhán língyuán)

The mausoleum is a bus trip away from Dongsheng, in the middle of nowhere. In 1954, what are said to be the ashes of the Khan were brought back from Qinghai (where they had been taken to prevent them from falling into the hands of the Japanese) and a large Mongolian-style mausoleum was built near Ejin Horo Qi.

As for why the Japanese should want the Khan's ashes, it had to do with Japan's attempted invasion of Mongolia – Japanese propagandists, citing legends that Genghis Khan came from across the sea, claimed that the Mongolian people originated in Japan. This was to assure the Mongolians that reuniting with the Japanese motherland was just like getting together with family.

As it turned out, a joint Russian-Mongolian (mostly Russian) force overwhelmingly defeated the Japanese attack on Outer Mongolia in 1939, although the Japanese successfully occupied Inner Mongolia and held it until the war's end in 1945.

The Cultural Revolution did enough damage to the mausoleum to keep the renovators busy for eight years and the result looks new. Since the collapse of Soviet domination in 1991, Mongolia has been whipping itself into a nationalistic fervour and Genghis Khan has been elevated to god-like status. As a result, holy pilgrimages to the mausoleum have become the sacred duty of both Inner and Outer Mongolians. If you would like to meet any true Mongolians, this is probably one of the best places in China to do it.

Ceremonies are held four times a year at the mausoleum to honour his memory. Butter lamps are lit, *khatas* (ritual scarves) presented and whole cooked sheep piled high before the Khan's stone statue while chanting is performed by Mongolian monks and specially chosen elders from the Daur nationality. On the embankment beside the entrance there is an obo festooned with prayer flags in commemoration of Genghis Khan.

Inside are displays of Genghis Khan's martial gear and a statue. Various yurts contain the biers of Genghis and his close relatives. The huge frescoes around the walls are rendered in cartoon style to depict important stages in the Khan's rise – all that's missing is bubble captions with 'pow' or 'zap'.

Buy your ticket at the booth to the right of the parking lot as you enter before you head up the steps to the mausoleum entrance, otherwise they'll send you down again to buy a ticket. Entry is Y25.

After you've taken a look at the mausoleum you can visit the temporary residence of the Khan on the same ticket. It's 1km down the dirt road to the right of the parking lot (when facing the mausoleum).

Nearby is a compound (open only in summer) with nice grasslands, horses, cows, sheep and goats, plus some interesting buildings with traditional clothing, warrior outfits and riding equipment inside – all ready for the Naadam tourist carnival.

Places to Stay & Eat There is a tourist yurt camping ground, the *Ghenghis Khan Hotel (chéngjísīhán bīn-guǎn)*, with yurts *(ménggūbāo)* to stay in at the right of the parking lot as you enter. The cost is Y18 per person. Each yurt holds five people.

There's another place on the side of the road called the *Ghenghis Khan Hostel (chéngjí sīhán líng zhāodàisuǒ)*, but it looks pretty bleak. Most visitors elect to stay in Dongsheng and commute to the mausoleum for a day trip.

There's a couple of restaurants near the parking lot and the *Ghenghis Khan Hotel* also has a restaurant.

Getting There & Away Four buses depart Dongsheng each day heading towards the mausoleum; the first one leaves at 6.20 am and the last one at 12.30 pm. Tickets cost Y7. The driver will let you off, but you won't be able to miss the blue-tiled dome of the museum as it comes into view. It's about a two hour ride.

Another strategy is to take a bus from Dongsheng to Ejin Horo Qi *(yījīn huòluò qí)*, which is 25km from the mausoleum, and then switch to a minibus which takes 30 minutes to complete the journey.

HAILAR
(hǎilāěr)
The northernmost major town in Inner Mongolia, Hailar has very little to offer visitors beyond being a useful transit point. Nearby Manzhouli (see the following entry on that town) does not yet have an airport – when it gets one, there will be little need to visit Hailar.

You can visit the surrounding Hulunbei'er Grasslands from here though, and both CITS and CTS in Hailar offer tours, but they are more geared towards larger tour groups and largely consist of tourist 'yurt camps' rather than places where Mongolians actually live.

Information
CITS (☎ 822-1728) is on the 2nd floor of the post office building *(jiànfā dàshà)* on

Shengli Jie in the eastern section (called *hédōng*, or 'east of the river') of the town. The PSB is directly opposite at 10 Shengli Jie.

The main Bank of China branch is also in Hedong at 5 Shengli Sanlu which runs north off Shengli Jie at the roundabout. There's also a Bank of China beside the Bei'er Hotel, but it only changes cash.

Places to Stay

The rather dilapidated and very sleazy *Minzu Hotel* (☎ 833-2211) *(mínzú fàndiàn)* has a central location at Qiaotou Dajie and Caoshi Jie. Beds cost Y30 each in a twin room with attached bath. The rooms are very dirty, however, and the signs on every floor saying in Russian and Chinese 'No deal-making; violators will be fined' make the place a bit dubious. But then, what do you expect from a hotel that has nothing else but packages of underwear for sale at the reception counter?

The *Friendship Hotel* (☎ 833-1040) *(yǒuyì dà jiǔdiàn)* on Qiaotou Dajie is a good place to stay for mid-range prices. Twins/triples with attached bathrooms cost Y140/180 and include a free breakfast. The reception desk is hidden on the 2nd floor.

The *Bei'er Hotel* (☎ 833-2511) *(bèi'ěr jiǔdiàn)* on Zhongyang Dajie offers very large and comfortable twins for Y160 and Y220. Across the street the *Xisi Hotel* (☎ 833-2911) *(xīsì fàndiàn)* has beds in quads for Y26 and twins with attached bath for Y36, but the beds in rooms for Y42 are more comfortable.

Further north on Zhongyang Dajie, the *Laodong Hotel* (☎ 833-8111) *(láodòng dàshà)* is a luxurious place with friendly staff where you can get beds in nice twins with attached bath for Y65. They also have rooms ranging from Y140 to Y180, and suites for Y388 (that you can probably get cheaper if you bargain). The hotel also provides a free Chinese-style breakfast.

The *Meng Hotel* (☎ 822-2212; fax 822-1123) *(měng bīnguǎn)* consists of two wings – one a Stalin-era building that has twins for Y222 on the first floor and Y266

on the second floor. It's interesting if you'd like to experience Soviet retro. Next door the new building is a typical reform-era marble and chrome sort of place, with twins for Y156 and Y222.

Places to Eat

Most of the hotels have decent *restaurants* and there's a *night food market* in front of the Friendship Hotel. You could also try the *restaurants* on Beixie Jie, which runs alongside the department store, diagonally across from the Friendship Hotel.

Getting There & Away

Air The CAAC office (☎ 833-1010) is on Qiaotou Dajie beside the bridge and diagonally opposite the Minzu Hotel. There are direct flights between Hailar and Beijing five times a week, and also twice a week to Hohhot.

Train You can also reach Hailar by train from Harbin (12 hours), Qiqihar (8½ hours) and Hohhot via Beijing (48 hours). There are also three trains a day to Manzhouli (three hours). There's an advance booking office for sleepers in a little cubicle on the ground floor in the Friendship Store beside the Friendship Hotel on Qiaotou Lu. The station is in the north-western part of town. If you arrive in Hailar by train, it's better to cross the railway tracks using the footbridge to the left of the station as you exit and get a taxi or motor-tricycle from there.

Bus The long-distance bus station is on Chezhan Jie, south-east of the railway station. There is a daily bus to Manzhouli (3 hours) but it's easier to take the train.

Getting Around

To/From the Airport The airport bus leaves from the booking office; tickets are Y3. A taxi costs about Y20.

Other Transport Motor-tricycles are Y5 for most trips in town and taxis are abundant, but you can get around the town easily on foot if you're not in a hurry.

MANZHOULI
(mǎnzhōulǐ)

The border town where the Trans-Siberian Railway crosses from China to Russia, Manzhouli was established in 1901 as a stop for the railway, although the area has long been inhabited by Mongolians and other nomads. There are huge coal deposits in the vicinity, including the open pit mine in nearby Zalainou'er that was first developed by the Russians early in the 20th century. The Russians have played a major role in Manzhouli's history; you can see it in the old buildings and log houses with their filigree windows dotting the town. More recently, they've returned, crossing the border by bus and private car from Siberia to buy Chinese goods. The place feels more Russian than Chinese and there's a special kind of laissez-faire bordertown ambience that can make for some interesting encounters.

Manzhouli also has some of the greenest grasslands in China and is another option for pursuing the topic of the disappearing Mongols. It's possible to arrange taxi or jeep excursions to the grasslands with overnight stops in yurts, tea-tasting and campfires. Should you strike a Mongol living traditionally, you might get a cup of their milk tea. It's made of horse's milk and salt, and tastes revolting; it's also most impolite to refuse.

The main attraction outside Manzhouli is **Hulun Lake** *(hūlún hú)*, also known as Dalai Lake *(dálài hú)*. One of the largest lakes in China, it unexpectedly pops out of the Mongolian grasslands like an enormous inland sea. It's a prime venue for fishing and bird-watching. Slightly further south is Beier Lake *(bèiěr hú)*, which straddles the border with Outer Mongolia.

The other big feature is for train buffs – the steam locomotive storage and repair yards in Zalianuo'er are some of the more impressive in China, as is the mine that still uses steam engines to haul out the coal.

Information
CITS (☎ 622-2982) is at 121 Erdao Jie.

You're better off going to the office on the 5th floor because the downstairs office is pre-occupied with all the Russians. The PSB is also in this building.

You can get maps at the Xinhua Bookstore, which is above a fur shop at the corner of Xinhua Lu and Sidao Jie. The Bank of China is at 16 Erdao Jie.

Things to See & Do
The vast grasslands are the main feature of Manzhouli (if you don't include the Russians) and they surround the town in green splendour. If you're looking for big sky country, this is the place to come to. Except for the fierce wind that blows across the prairie, this would be an excellent place to explore on a mountain bike. CITS can arrange a stay in a yurt with a Mongolian family which can include horse-back riding and a Mongolian banquet. If you're with a group of two or more, it should cost about Y400 to Y500 per person. Expect to leave a tip for the family as well.

Unfortunately, to visit the steam train repair yards and open pit mine at Zalainou'er you'll also need to go through CITS, but it's cheaper to hire your own taxi than use their transport.

The easiest way to get to Dalai Lake is to hire a taxi or try to hitch a ride with one of the Russian or Chinese tour buses that are often parked on Xinhu Jie or in the parking lot by the CITS building. A return trip by taxi will cost about Y80.

If you're visiting in the summer, don't forget your bathing suit; the beach is a bit littered with garbage from tourists, but while the water is muddy around the shore area, it is not polluted.

Places to Stay
One of the cheapest places to stay is the Dianli Hotel (☎ 622-2599) *(diànlì bīnguǎn)*. Beds in twins with attached bath are Y42.50. It's at the intersection of Sandao Jie and Shulin Lu in the eastern part of town. Most of the Russians stay at the *Mingzhu Hotel* (☎ 622-7418; fax 622-3261) *(míngzhū fàndiàn)* which makes it a

lively place. Comfortable twins are Y140. It's on the corner of Xinhua Lu and Xidao Jie. For entertainment you can't beat sitting in the lobby and watching the world go by.

The *International Hotel* (☎ 622-2225; fax 622-2976) *(guójì fàndiàn)* is more expensive, but the rooms, at Y338 and up, are no better than the Mingzhu's. It's beside the CITS building on Erdao Jie. East of the Mingzhu Hotel on Xidao Jie, the *Friendship Hotel* (☎ 622-3056; fax 622-3828) *(yǒuyì bīnguǎn)* has nicer twin rooms for Y228 and up.

Places to Eat

There are many Russian restaurants around town, but by far the best place to eat is the private restaurant inside the *Mingzhu Hotel* (not the Chinese restaurant, which is mediocre). There's a Russian name in lights above the entrance, but no English sign or English menu. They have great breakfasts with Russian tea and pancakes *(nǎibǐng)* with cream and jam.

There's a good *Chinese restaurant* at the Friendship Hotel, and many restaurants in town also have Mongolian food. There's a good place for snacks and delicious bread on the ground floor of the CITS building.

Getting There & Away

The best way to reach Manzhouli is to fly to Hailar or take the train directly from Harbin (15 hours) or Qiqihar (11 hours), or better yet, get off the Trans-Siberian.

At the time of writing, the train between Moscow and Beijing was only stopping once a week and if you want to make a stopover, confirm it when you buy your ticket in Beijing or Moscow.

CITS can book sleepers for other destinations in China for a Y20 service charge. You can also book sleepers yourself at the window to your left as you enter the station. A daily bus leaves in the morning for Hailar (three hours) from the long-distance bus station on Xidao Jie, three blocks west of the Mingzhu Hotel.

XANADU

(yuánshàngdū)

About 320km north of Beijing, tucked away near Duolun in Inner Mongolia, are the remains of Xanadu, the great Kublai Khan's palace of legendary splendour. In the 19th century, Samuel Taylor Coleridge (who never went near the place) stoked his imagination with some opium and composed *Kubla Khan,* a glowing poem about Xanadu that has been on the set menu for students of English literature ever since. It famously begins:

In Xanadu did Kubla Khan
A stately pleasure-dome decree:
Where Alph, the sacred river, ran
Through caverns measureless to man
　Down to a sunless sea.

Over the centuries the deserted palace has crumbled back to dust and the site has been visited by very few foreigners. Hardly anything remains of Xanadu.

Getting There & Away

Unfortunately, foreigners can only visit Xanadu legally by going on a very expensive CITS tour, but perhaps this might change in the future. Check with the PSB (☎ 696-8148) in Hohhot.

The best way to get there would be to bus directly to Duolun or Zhenglanqi and proceed to Xanadu from there, but these are closed areas and at present. The Hohhot CITS will only arrange tours of groups of 10 people or more.

If you want to go, first you have to travel to Xilinhohot and arrange it through the CITS office (☎ 822-4448), which is on the 3rd floor of the Baima Hotel *(báimǎ fàndiàn).*

Tibet 西藏

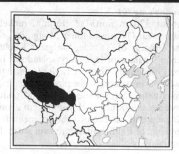

Tibet Facts & Highlights

Area: 1, 220,000 sq km

Population: 2.4 million

Capital: Lhasa

Highlights

- Lhasa, home of Potala Palace, Jokhang Temple and the Barkhor.
- Shigatse, Tibet's second city and site of Tashihunpo Monastery, the traditional home of the Panchen Lama.
- Mt Kailash, a trekker's delight and source of the Ganges River.

Locked away in its mountain fortress of the Himalaya, Tibet *(xīzàng)* has long exercised a unique hold on the imagination of the west: 'Shangri-La', 'the Land of Snows', 'the Rooftop of the World'. Tibet is mysterious in a way few other places are.

Until recently, few outsiders had laid eyes on the holy city of Lhasa and the other secrets of Tibet. It is more the pity that when Tibet finally opened to tourism in the mid-1980s, it was no longer the magical Buddhist kingdom that had so intoxicated early western travellers.

Tibetans have never had it easy. Their environment is harsh, and human habitation has always been a precarious proposition.

By necessity, Tibetans have become a tough and resilient people. Yet despite what appears to be a continuous grim struggle against nature and misfortune, Tibetans have not only survived, but have managed to retain a remarkably cheerful outlook on life.

Most of Tibet is too arid and cold to support human life and the place is still very thinly populated. With a geographical area more than twice that of France, Tibet still manages only a total population of 2.3 million. There are, however, estimated to be some four million more Tibetans spread out over Tibet, Qinghai, Sichuan, Gansu and Yunnan.

Most of Tibet is made up of an immense plateau which lies at an altitude of 4000m to 5000m. The Qamdo region in the east is a somewhat lower section of plateau, drained by the headwaters of the Salween, Mekong and Upper Yangzi rivers. It's an area of considerably greater rainfall than the rest of Tibet and the climate is less extreme. Most of the Tibetan population lives in the valleys of this area. On the uplands surrounding these valleys, the inhabitants are mainly pastoralists who raise sheep, yaks and horses.

Since full-scale treatment of Tibetan regions would take a whole book, Lonely Planet has published a separate *Tibet* guide.

HISTORY

Recorded Tibetan history begins in the 7th century AD when the Tibetan armies were considered as great a scourge to their neighbours as the Huns were to Europe. Under King Songtsen Gampo, the Tibetans occupied Nepal and collected tribute from parts of Yunnan Province.

Shortly after the death of Gampo, the armies moved north and took control of the Silk Road, including the great city of Kashgar. Opposed by Chinese troops, who occupied all of Xinjiang under the Tang

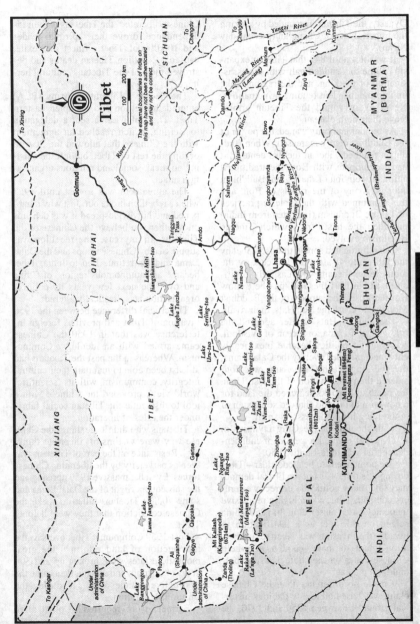

Tibet

0 100 200 km

The external boundaries of India on
this map have not been authenticated
and may not be correct.

Dynasty, the Tibetans responded by sacking the imperial city of Chang'an (present-day Xi'an).

It was not until 842 that Tibetan expansion came to a sudden halt with the assassination of the king, and the region broke up into independent feuding principalities. Never again would the Tibetan armies leave their high plateau.

As secular authority waned, the power of the Buddhist clergy increased. When Buddhism reached Tibet in the 3rd century, it had to compete with Bon, the traditional animistic religion of the region. Buddhism adopted many of the rituals of Bon, and this, combined with the esoteric practices of Tantric Buddhism (imported from India) provided the basis from which Tibetan Buddhism evolved.

The religion had spread through Tibet by the 7th century; after the 9th century the monasteries became increasingly politicised, and in 1641 the Gelukpa (the Yellow Hat sect) used the support of the Buddhist Mongols to crush the Red Hats, their rivals.

The Yellow Hats' leader adopted the title of Dalai Lama, or Ocean of Wisdom; religion and politics became inextricably entwined, presided over by the Dalai Lama, the god-king. Each Dalai Lama was considered the reincarnation of the last. Upon his death, the monks searched the land for a newborn child who showed some sign of embodying his predecessor's spirit.

With the fall of the Qing Dynasty in 1911, Tibet entered a period of independence that was to last until 1950.

One point needs to be made clear – Tibet during this time was not the liberal democracy that many politically correct westerners contend. Tibet was a highly repressive theocracy based on serfdom. In 1950 China seized on this fact as a justification to invade (the invasion was labelled a 'liberation') and to make good a long-held Chinese claim on the strategically important high plateau.

It made no difference that the Chinese claim was based on highly dubious historical grounds: between 1950 and 1970, the

Chinese 'liberated' the Tibetans of their independence, drove their spiritual leader and 100,000 of Tibet's finest into exile, caused 1.2 million Tibetan deaths and destroyed most of the Tibetans' cultural heritage.

The People's Liberation Army (PLA) entered the region and occupied eastern Tibet. The Dalai Lama sent a delegation to Beijing, which reached an agreement with the Chinese that allowed the PLA to occupy the rest of Tibet, but left the existing political, social and religious organisation intact.

The agreement was to last until 1959 when a rebellion broke out. Just why it happened and how widespread it was depends on whether you believe the Chinese or the Tibetans. In any case, the rebellion was suppressed by Chinese troops and the Dalai Lama and his retinue fled to India. Tibet became an 'autonomous region' of China and over the next few years its political organisation was drastically altered.

The crucial difference between the 1950 invasion of Tibet and previous foreign interference was that in 1950 the Chinese came armed with an ideology: Communism. Whereas in the past the Tibetans had at least been able to maintain their cultural integrity, communism, with its 'scientific' world view, provided the Chinese with a tool to dismantle the Tibetan social fabric under the rules of liberation.

Tibetans who didn't see things the Chinese way were victims of 'incorrect thinking'. Resistance on the part of Tibetans was seen as perversity by the liberating Chinese forces. Even the massive 1959 uprising and the subsequent flight of the Dalai Lama and some 80,000 Tibetans failed to shake the Chinese conviction that they were helping Tibet.

Post-1959 Communist Tibet oversaw the introduction of land reform – the great monastic estates were broken up and 300 years of serfdom ended – but then came the destructive policies enforced during the Cultural Revolution.

Farmers were required to plant alien

lowland crops, such as wheat instead of the usual barley, in keeping with Chairman Mao's instruction to 'make grain the key link'.

Strict limits were placed on the number of cattle that peasants could raise privately. Grain production slumped and the animal population declined. Then the Red Guards flooded in, wreaking their own havoc and breaking the power of the monasteries. In 1959 there were at least 1600 monasteries operating in Tibet; by 1979 there were just 10. Most monasteries were used for artillery practice, and monks were either executed or sent to work in fields and labour camps.

The Chinese basically made a mess of Tibet's economy. Of course, it wasn't just Tibet; the Cultural Revolution was a disaster for all of China. Grudgingly, the Chinese have admitted to making 'mistakes' in Tibet.

The Maoist Communist Party chief in Tibet, General Ren Rong, was sacked in 1979. Most of the rural communes were disbanded and the land was returned to private farmers who were allowed to grow or graze whatever they wanted and to sell their produce in free markets. Taxes were reduced and state subsidies to the region increased.

Some of the monasteries have reopened, and the Chinese are wooing the Dalai Lama in the hope that he will return to Tibet. But as his status in the outside world continues to improve, it is becoming increasingly unlikely that he will return to accept what would almost certainly be an office job in Beijing and a tacit acceptance of Chinese rule.

In 1985 the 'celebrations' marking the 20th anniversary of the Tibetan Autonomous Region (TAR) went off like a damp squib. Apart from banning the western press from the event, the Chinese provided Lhasa with a tight military blanket, including sharpshooters on the roof of the Potala Palace. The general picture looked more like a nervous show of strength than anything else.

Despite Chinese efforts to paint a rosy picture of life on the roof of the world, the general picture is of a country under occupation. The Dalai Lama continues to be worshipped by his people, and his acceptance in late 1989 of the Nobel Peace Prize marked a greater sympathy on the part of the western world for the plight of the Tibetan people.

The Dalai Lama himself has referred to China's policies as 'cultural genocide' for the Tibetan people. Unfortunately, China's great potential as a trading nation and as a market for western goods makes many world leaders wary of raising the Tibet issue with China. Those who believe that pressure from western governments will eventually force China to grant Tibet independence or true autonomy are probably being unduly optimistic.

For their part, the Chinese can't understand the ingratitude of the Tibetans. As they see it, China has built roads, schools, hospitals, an airport, factories and a budding tourist industry. The Chinese honestly believe that they saved the Tibetans from feudalism and that their continued occupation is a mission of mercy.

The Tibetans, who cannot forgive the destruction of their monasteries and attacks on their religion and culture, see it differently. Nor do the Tibetans get much joy from the continuous heavy-handed presence of the Chinese police and military. Certainly the Chinese are not winning any friends in Tibet with their policy of stealthy resettlement: a massive influx of Han settlers from surrounding provinces threatens to make Tibetans a minority in their own 'autonomous region' and to swamp Tibetan culture with that of the Han Chinese.

Nevertheless, the Chinese had grown so confident in their ability to control Tibet that they decided to open the area to foreign tourism in late 1984. The situation changed quite dramatically in 1987 when Tibetans in Lhasa gave vent to their rage about the Chinese and their policies. A series of demonstrations virtually became an uprising. Chinese security forces reportedly

TIBET

TIBETAN

Tibetan belongs to the Tibeto-Burman family of languages. It differs in many ways from Chinese, having a different written language, a different grammar and being nontonal. Lhasa dialect, which is the standard form of Tibetan, does employ a system of rising and falling tones, but the differences are subtle and meaning is made clear by context. Beginners need not worry about it.

Pronunciation

Like all foreign languages Tibetan has its fair share of tricky pronunciations. There are quite a few consonant clusters, and Tibetan is a language (like Korean and Thai) that makes an important distinction between aspirated and nonaspirated consonants.

Naturally, the best way to approach these difficulties is to work through a phrasebook with a native speaker or with a tape. Lonely Planet's *Tibetan phrasebook* would be useful if you plan on learning the language in greater depth.

Vowels

The following pronunciation guide is based on standard British pronunciation (North Americans beware).

a	as in 'father'		o	as in 'go'
ay	as in 'play'		oo	as in 'soon''
e	as in 'met'		ö	as the 'ur' in 'fur'
ee	as in 'meet'		ü	as in 'flute'
i	as in 'big'			

Consonants

With the exception of the ones listed below, Tibetan consonants should be pronounced as in English. Where consonants are followed by an 'h', it means that the consonant is aspirated (accompanied by a puff of air).

An English example might be 'kettle', where the 'k' is aspirated and the 'tt' is nonaspirated. The distinction is fairly important, but in simple Tibetan the context should make it clear what you are talking about even if you get the sounds muddled up a bit.

ky	as the 'kie' in 'Kiev'		r	produced with a slight trill
ng	as the 'ng' in 'sing'		ts	as the 'ts' in 'bits'

Pronouns

I	*nga*		we	*nga-tso*
you	*kerang*		you all	*kerang-tso*
he, she	*khong*		they	*khong-tso*

Useful Phrases

Hello.	*tashi dele*		Thank you.	*thoo jaychay*
Goodbye.	*kale phe*		Yes, OK.	*la ong*
(to person leaving)			I'm sorry.	*gonda*
Goodbye.	*kale shoo*		(forgive me)	
(by person leaving)			I want ...	*nga la ... go*

TIBET

Do you speak English?	*injeeke shing gi yö pe?*	How much per day?	*nyima chik la katsö ray?*
Do you understand?	*ha ko song-ngey?*	Where is the ...?	*... kaba yo ray?*
I understand.	*ha ko song*	I'm lost.	*nga lam khag lag song*
I don't understand.	*ha ko ma song*		
How much?	*ka tsö ray?*		
It's expensive.	*gonzg chenpo ray*	right	*yeba*
What's your name?	*kerang gi ming la karey zer gi yö?*	left	*yönba*
		straight ahead	*shar gya*
My name is ...	*ngai ... ming la*	north/south	*chang/lo*
... and you?	*... a ni kerang zer gi yö?*	east/west	*shar/noop*
		porter	*dopo khur khen*
Do you speak English?	*injeeke shing gi yö pe?*	pack animal	*skel semchen*
Where are you from?	*kerang ka-ne ray?*		

Geographical Terms

cave	*trapoo*
hot spring	*chuzay*
lake	*tso*
mountain	*ree*
river	*tsangpo*
road/trail	*lam*
valley	*loong shon*
waterfall	*papchu*

Time

What's the time?	*chutsö katsö ray?*
hour/minute	*chutsö/karma*
When?	*kadü?*
now	*thanda*
today	*thiring*
tomorrow	*sangnyi*
yesterday	*kesa*
morning	*shogay*
afternoon	*nying gung gyab la*
evening/night	*gonta*

Medical

I'm sick.	*nga bedo mindu*
Please call a doctor.	*amjee ke tangronang*
altitude sickness	*lâdu na*
diarrhoea	*troko she*
fever	*tsawa*
hospital	*menkang*

Accommodation

hotel	*dhönkhang*
Do you have a room?	*kang mi yöpe?*
How much is it for one night?	*tsen chik la katsö ray?*
I'd like to stay with a Tibetan family.	*nga phöbe mitsang nyemdo dendö yö*

Numbers

Note: the word in brackets is added before *chik*, 'one' etc to make the compound numbers.

1	*chik*	20	*nyi shu (tsa)*
2	*nyi*	30	*sum shu (so)*
3	*sum*	40	*shi chu (zhe) chig*
4	*shi*	50	*nga chu (nga)*
5	*nga*	60	*troo chu ray*
6	*troo*	70	*dun chu don*
7	*dün*	80	*gye chu gya*
8	*gye*	90	*gu chu go*
9	*gu*	100	*chik gya*
10	*chu*	1000	*chik tong*

Getting Around

I want to go to ...	*nga ... la drondö yö*
I'm getting off.	*nga phap gi yin*
What time do we leave?	*ngatso chutsö katsö la dro gi yin?*
What time do we arrive?	*ngatso chutsö katsö la lep gi yin?*
Where can I get a bicycle?	*kanggari kaba ragi ray?*
airport	*namdrutang*
bicycle	*kanggari*
bus	*lamkhor*

TIBET

opened fire on the demonstrators, many of whom were monks from the monasteries around Lhasa. Both sides suffered casualties and at least one police station was reduced to a smoking pile of rubble.

The response of the Chinese authorities was swift; Lhasa was swamped with plain-clothes police and uniformed security, who put an abrupt end to the uprising. The embarrassment of foreign press coverage was neatly solved when all members of the foreign media covering events in Lhasa were unceremoniously booted out. Within a few weeks, it was the turn of individual travellers to be similarly ejected.

Tibet remained closed to individual travellers for five years – the only way to get in was with a carefully controlled tour group. In 1992, the authorities surprised everyone by reopening Tibet to individuals, although with some ludicrous permit requirements.

The present Chinese policy on individual tourism in Tibet seems to be one of extorting as much cash as possible from foreigners, but not so much as to scare them off completely.

TREKKING

Trekking is not officially approved in Tibet; the local PSB officials will tell you that it is only possible with an approved tour group.

Independent trekking is feasible for the experienced walker, providing you are prepared to be self-sufficient in food, fuel and shelter. There are now supplies available in Lhasa of most trekking goods, but it is still recommended to bring equipment suitable for subzero temperatures, such as a high-quality down sleeping bag, thermal underwear, ground mat, four-season tent, stove and fuel.

TRAVEL RESTRICTIONS

The current regulations (which could change tomorrow) say that all foreigners wanting to visit Tibet must be part of a 'tour group'. This so-called tour group usually breaks up before anyone even knew

that they were part of a group. The cost of the tour group is added to the price of your ticket to Tibet, and this procedure costs anything from Y200 to Y900.

Once in Tibet, there are some places that actually require you to procure a travel permit (the Everest Base Camp, Samye and Mt Kailash etc). The cost of the permit varies, but expect to pay between Y50 and Y100. Getting the permits yourself is a nonstarter – the PSB insists you go through an authorised travel agency and that you be a member of a tour group.

Not surprisingly, Lhasa has a large number of travel agencies catering to this market, organising 'groups' which quickly disband after the permits are issued. At the time of writing, permits were being strictly enforced and travel agencies were only issuing permits for members of valid groups.

Despite all the regulations and paperwork, some travellers have successfully slipped past road blocks and avoided the PSB.

Travellers have reasonable freedom of movement within Tibet, but this doesn't mean they are not watched. If you just go about your business of visiting monasteries and buying jars of yoghurt at the market, there should be no problems.

Visitors who go in with a political agenda are another matter. It's worth bearing in mind that Tibet (much more than the rest of China) is effectively a police state, and political discussions with local Tibetans can have serious consequences. Incidentally, many of the secret police are ethnic Tibetans.

WHAT TO BRING

Figuring out what type of clothing to bring is tricky, due to the extremes of the climate. Department stores in Xining, Golmud and Lhasa have a wide selection of warm clothing. The PLA military overcoats are a cheap alternative to down jackets. You can also keep the cold at bay with a woollen sweater, long underwear, woollen socks, gloves and a woolly hat. Protect yourself against the sun with lip salve, sunscreen, sunglasses and something to cover your head.

Food is no problem in Lhasa, but remote areas offer little to eat beyond lichen, dust and rocks. If you are considering a long journey, like Mt Kailash, then it would be wise to stock up before heading off.

There are several medications which are particularly useful in Tibet, and you should bring them from abroad rather than rely on local supplies. Drugs to consider carrying include Diomox, Tiniba and Flagyl. For more information see the Health section in the Facts for the Visitor chapter at the beginning of the book.

DANGERS & ANNOYANCES
Health Risks
The greatest dangers to travellers' health are Acute Mountain Sickness (AMS) and giardiasis. For a full discussion of prevention and treatment, see the Health section in the Facts for the Visitor chapter at the beginning of the book.

Not Shangri-La
Tibetans are among the friendliest, most hospitable people in the world. At the same time, however, there is little point in pretending that visiting the Land of Snows is a Disneyland holiday.

Most Tibetans are only too happy to have foreign visitors in their country, but do not expect smiles all the way. Travellers who have poked their noses into Tibetan funerals and other personal matters have quite rightly received a very hostile reception.

Stories abound of surly monks, of aggressive Tibetans at checkpoints and of rip-offs. Tibetan tour operators can be just as rapacious as their Chinese counterparts. Some foreigners have had a few bad experiences and come away disillusioned.

Dogs
Tibetan dogs are even more xenophobic than the PSB. They (the dogs) roam in packs around monasteries and towns, and seem to have a particular antipathy to foreigners who look and smell different from the

locals. Keep your distance during the day, and watch your step in the dark.

GETTING AROUND
Transport can be a major hurdle if you want to explore the backwaters. The four main types of vehicle are bus, minibus, truck and 4WD.

On some routes there are modern Japanese buses; other routes are covered by battered wrecks which gasp over each high pass as if it's their last. Trucks are often more comfortable, more fun and faster than the bus. Land Cruisers are pricey, but not impossible for non-budget travellers willing to split the cost among several people.

Bus prices for foreigners are double the local price in Tibet, unless you have a Chinese student card. In such a case you pay the local price. Trucks tend to charge the same as buses, but be aware that hitching is not officially sanctioned.

In Tibet, 'road safety' is just a slogan. Potential hazards include bad roads, vehicle breakdowns, icy weather and reckless drivers (not necessarily your driver, but the other maniacs on the road). Road accidents are frequent and foreigners have been injured or killed in the past. Tibetans take their minds off these variables by praying, and you'd be wise to follow their example unless you want to end up a gibbering bag of nerves.

Be prepared for the cold, which can easily go below zero at night even during summer. All buses have heaters, although these are sometimes broken. More seriously, a mechanical breakdown could have fatal consequences if you have no warm clothing.

As for bicycling – it is possible, but is not without its hazards. Aside from hassles with the PSB, cyclists in Tibet have died from road accidents, hypothermia and pulmonary oedema (pneumonia). Tibet is not the place to learn the ins and outs of long-distance cycling – do your training elsewhere.

Despite the odds, a number of experienced cyclists have individually travelled around Tibet without too many problems.

LHASA
(lāsà)

Lhasa is the heart and soul of Tibet, abode of the Dalai Lamas and an object of devout pilgrimage. Despite the large-scale encroachments of Chinese influence, it is still a city of wonders.

As you enter the Kyi Chu Valley, either on the long haul from Golmud or from Gonggar airport, your first hint that Lhasa is close at hand is the sight of the Potala, a vast white and ochre fortress soaring over one of the world's highest cities. It is a sight that has heralded the marvels of the holy city to travellers for three centuries.

The Potala dominates the Lhasa skyline. The site of the tombs of previous Dalai Lamas, it was once the seat of Tibetan government and the winter residence of the Dalai Lama. While the Potala serves as a symbolic focus for Tibetan hopes for self-government, it is the Jokhang, some 2km to the east of the Potala, that is the spiritual heart of the city.

The Jokhang, a curious mix of sombre darkness, wafting incense and prostrating pilgrims, is the most sacred and active of Tibet's temples. Encircling it is the Barkhor, the holiest of Lhasa's devotional circumambulation circuits. It is here that most visitors first fall in love with Tibet. The medieval push and shove of crowds, the street performers, the stalls hawking everything from prayer flags to jewel-encrusted yak skulls, and the devout tapping their foreheads to the ground at every step is an exotic brew that few newcomers can resist.

Modern Lhasa divides clearly into a Chinese section in the west and a Tibetan section in the east. For travellers who have arrived from other parts of China, the Chinese part of town harbours few surprises. Nestled at the foot of the Potala and extending a couple of kilometres westward is an uninspired muddle of restaurants, karaoke bars, administrative blocks and department stores.

The Tibetan part of town, which begins west of the Jokhang, is altogether more colourful and the better area to be based in.

Information

The best place for the latest on Tibetan individual travel these days is one of the popular Tibetan hotels, or a table in Tashi's Restaurant.

Consulate The Nepalese consulate (☎ 682-2881; fax 683-6890) is on a side street just south of the Lhasa Holiday Inn and north of the Norbu Lingka. It's open for visa applications Monday to Saturday from 9.30 am to 12.30 pm. Visas are issued the following day.

At the time of writing, the visa fee was US$15 for a 15 day visa and US$25 for a 30 day visa. It is possible to pay in RMB and you should remember to bring along one visa photo. It is also possible to obtain visas for the same cost at Kodari, the Nepalese border town, although it would be sensible to check that this has not been changed.

PSB There are two PSB offices in Lhasa, although it's doubtful that either will prove to be of much use. The one on the eastern end of Beijing Donglu issues travel permits, but they are unwilling to issue these to individual travellers and will instead refer you to a travel agency.

The other PSB office on Linkuo Beilu has been more helpful with information and is granting seven day visa extensions.

Money The most convenient place for travellers is a branch of the Bank of China located between the Banak Shol and the Kirey hotels. The main Bank of China is behind the Potala – turn at the yak statues and look for it on the left. Its opening hours are 9 am to 6 pm weekdays and 10.30 am to 2 pm on weekends.

The best bank in town is inside the CAAC office on Niangre Lu. It is open every day from 9 am to 9 pm and can change cash and travellers cheques.

Post & Communications The main post office is opposite the Potala on Beijing Donglu. It is open from 9 am to 8 pm and from 10 am to 6 pm on Sunday. Opening hours are reduced in spring and winter.

The telecommunications office next door is open 24 hours. International calls are available. There is another post and telecommunications centre in the east of Lhasa on the corner of Linkuo Donglu and Linkuo Beilu.

Travel Agencies If you want to do any official trekking or visit remote areas, you need to visit a travel agency in order to secure a permit, motorised transport (usually a jeep) and (possibly) a guide.

Inside the Banak Shol Hotel, you can make contact with Potala Folk Travel Service (☎ 632-3829), although their main office (☎ 633-7027; fax 633-1357) is at 26 Beijing Donglu.

An office calling itself CITS Shigatse (☎ 683-4966; fax 683-6787) is inside the Tibet Hotel and offers better service, but their prices are still high. It is by no means certain that the foregoing travel agencies are the cheapest or best in town; you need to talk to other travellers and shop around. There has been a recent proliferation of travel services in Lhasa; proceed with caution.

Medical Services Several hospitals in Lhasa treat foreigners. The People's Hospital *(rénmín yīyúan)* and the Tibetan Traditional Hospital *(zāng yīyúan)* have been recommended.

There are also a number of clinics along Beijing Donglu that will provide medication for minor ailments. Take a Tibetan or Chinese phrasebook along.

Jokhang Temple
(dàzhāo sì)
The golden-roofed Jokhang is 1300 years old and one of Tibet's holiest shrines. It was built to commemorate the marriage of the Tang princess Wen Cheng to King Songtsen Gampo, and houses a pure gold statue of the Buddha Sakyamuni brought to Tibet by the princess.

Here, too, hundreds of pilgrims prostrate themselves in front of the temple entrance before continuing on their circuit.

Follow the pilgrims through a labyrinth of shrines, halls and galleries containing some of the finest and oldest treasures of Tibetan art. Some originals were destroyed during the Cultural Revolution and have been replaced with duplicates.

The Jokhang is best visited early in the morning; you may not be allowed to enter after 11 am.

Barkhor
(bākuò)
The Barkhor is essentially a pilgrim circuit which is followed clockwise round the periphery of the Jokhang. It is also a hive of market activity, an astounding jamboree, and a Tibetan-style stock exchange.

All around the circuit are shops stalls, teahouses and hawkers. There's a wide variety of items to gladden a Tibetan heart – prayer flags, block prints of the holy scriptures, earrings, Tibetan boots, Nepalese biscuits, puffed rice, yak butter and incense. Whether you buy from a shop or a hawker, many of the Tibetan goods on sale have been imported from Nepal and many of the 'antiques' are not genuine. Be prepared to bargain hard.

People who roll up from remote parts of Tibet include Khambas from eastern Tibet, who braid their hair with red yarn and stride around with ornate swords or daggers, and Goloks (Tibetan nomads) from the north, who wear ragged sheepskins. Golok women display incredibly ornate hairbands down their backs.

Norbu Lingka
(luóbù línkǎ)
About 3km west of the Potala is the Norbu Lingka, which used to be the summer residence of the Dalai Lama. The pleasant park contains small palaces, chapels and a zoo. Admission is Y30, with a student card Y15, and Y1 for monks. The park is open from 9.30 am to 12.30 pm, and 3.30 to 6 pm. The No 2 bus will take you there for Y2.

TIBET

Potala Palace

The most imposing attraction of Lhasa is the Potala Palace *(bùdálāgōng)*, once the centre of the Tibetan government and winter residence of the Dalai Lama. Each day a stream of chanting pilgrims files through this religious maze to offer *khata* (ceremonial scarves) or yak butter at one of the innumerable chapels and shrines.

One of the architectural wonders of the world, this immense construction is 13 storeys tall and contains thousands of rooms, shrines and statues. Construction of the present structure began during the reign of the fifth Dalai Lama in 1645 and took more than 50 years to complete. The first recorded use of the site dates from the 7th century, when King Songtsen Gampo built a palace here. The Potala somehow survived the destruction of the Cultural Revolution, apparently on the direct orders of Zhou Enlai.

The general layout of the Potala includes the White Palace (the main part of the building) for the living quarters of the Dalai Lama and the Red Palace (the central building rising above) for religious

functions. The Red Palace contains many halls and chapels – the most stunning chapels house the jewel-bedecked tombs of the 5th to 13th Dalai Lamas (although the 6th apparently died out of Tibet and is said to be buried in Qinghai). The apartments of the 13th and 14th Dalai Lamas in the White Palace offer an insight into the high life.

In the Red Palace, the principal shrines are the Lokeshvara Chapel and the Practice Chamber of the Dharma King. Both are original to the palace and are major focus points for pilgrims. Don't miss the Chapel of the Dalai Lamas' Tombs either; it contains the three storey golden chorten of the 5th Dalai Lama, made from 3700kg of gold.

The roof offers marvellous views of Lhasa and the region – don't forget your camera (although be prepared for a hefty Y50 charge to bring it into the palace). The Potala is open every day from 9 am to 1 pm only. Foreigners pay Y45 admission or Y22 for students. Avoid the weekends, as the entrance charge goes up to Y85. The long climb to the entrance is not recommended on your first day in town; instead do something relaxing until you acclimatise.

The Potala Palace, captured here in a Thomas Allom etching dating from the early 19th century, has long dominated the skyline of Lhasa.

POTALA PALACE

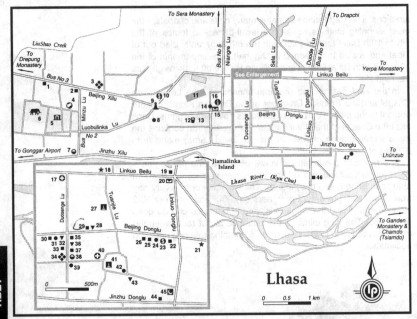

Lhasa

Places to Stay – budget

During the last few years most budget hotels have provided showers and also included a mid-range option with the construction of new rooms. These rooms are often better value than the more expensive hotels.

The *Banak Shol Hotel* (☎ 632-3829) *(bālángxuě lǚguǎn)* at 43 Beijing Donglu has become the most popular abode in Lhasa with a charming Tibetan-style courtyard, a free laundry service, bicycles for hire and a very good information board. Dorms cost from Y25 to Y30 per bed, and a double with attached bathroom costs Y160.

The *Kirey Hotel (jírì lǚguǎn)*, close to the Banak Shol, is a quieter place that charges from Y25 to Y30 for dorm beds in a double room. There are also comfortable doubles for Y110 per room. It has reliable hot showers, a free laundry service and super-friendly staff.

Snowlands Hotel (☎ 632-3687) *(xuěyù lǚguǎn)*, close to the Jokhang Temple, is a friendly place with rooms arranged around a courtyard. Simple dorm beds cost from Y25 to Y30. Doubles/triples with bath cost Y250/Y350. Bike hire and luggage storage are available.

Pentoc Guesthouse (☎ 632-6686; fax 633-0700; email: 101517.1657@compuserve.com) is across the road from Snowlands and is friendly, clean and stylish. Dorm beds are Y35, single rooms Y80, doubles are from Y120 to Y140 and an extra bed costs Y20. They have 24 hour showers and hiking gear for rent.

The *Yak Hotel* (☎ 632-3496) *(yǎkè lǚshè)* on Beijing Donglu has dorm beds from Y25 to Y35. At the time of writing, new expensive doubles with bathroom, TV, and air-con were under construction with a price tag of more than Y300.

Eight Auspicious Hotel (Tashi Tagel

LHASA 拉萨

PLACES TO STAY
1 Tibet Hotel; CITS
Shigatse
西藏宾馆
2 Lhasa Holiday Inn
拉萨假日酒店
(拉萨饭店)
19 Yingqiao Hotel
银桥饭店
22 Banak Shol Hotel;
Kailash Restaurant
八郎学旅馆
25 Gangjian Hotel
刚坚饭店
26 Kirey Hotel; Tashi's II
Restaurant
吉日旅馆
29 Yak Hotel
亚客旅社
30 Kechu Hotel
拉萨吉曲饭店
33 Pentoc Guesthouse
35 Eight Auspicious Hotel
(Tashi Tagel Hotel)
八宝饭店
37 Snowlands Hotel
雪域旅社
44 Khada Hotel
哈达旅馆
46 Himalaya Hotel
喜玛拉亚宾馆

PLACES TO EAT
28 Crazy Yak Restaurant
32 Tashi's Restaurant
咖啡馆

36 Snowlands Restaurant
雪域饭馆
43 Makye Ame Restaurant
情人饭店

OTHER
3 Department Store
百货商店
4 Nepalese Consulate
尼泊尔领使馆
5 Norbu Lingka
罗布林卡
6 Zoo
动物园
7 Bus Station
汽车站
8 Transmitter Mast
电视台
9 Yak Statues
牦牛像
10 Bank of China (Main
Branch)
中国银行
11 Potala Palace
布达拉宫
12 JJ's Disco
劳动人民文化宫
13 Potala Square
布达拉广场
14 Market
市场
15 Main Post Office;
Telecommunications
Office
邮电局
16 CAAC; Bank of China;
Airport Bus Departures
中国民航, 中国银行
机场班车发车处

17 Tibetan Autonomous
Region People's Hospital
西藏自治区人民医院
18 PSB (Visa Extensions)
公安局外事科
20 Post &
Telecommunications
Office
邮电局
21 PSB (Travel Permits)
公安局总部
23 Bank of China
中国银行
24 Cinema
电影院
27 Ramoche Temple
小昭寺
31 Mount Green Trekking
Shop
34 Department Store;
Rollerskating
百货商店
38 Minibus Stand
小型车站
39 Cinema
电影院
40 Tibetan Hospital
藏医院
41 Jokhang Temple; Barkhor
Square
大昭寺
42 Ganden Bus Tickets
汽车售票处
45 Main Mosque
清真寺
47 Tibet University
西藏大学

TIBET

Hotel) (☎ 632-5804; fax 632-3271) is a Chinese-style hotel next to the Snowlands Hotel offering dorm beds for Y25 and double rooms for Y50 (or Y100 with a basin).

The *Khada Hotel* (☎ 632-3008) *(hādá lǚguǎn)* on Jinzhu Donglu is a little out of the way, but offers the cheapest dorm beds in town for Y15. There are also doubles with shared bath for Y120.

Places to Stay – middle

Most of Lhasa's mid-range places are con-structed in the Chinese style that you may be familiar with from elsewhere on your trip. If the Tibetan-style hotels are full, a mid-range Chinese hotel might be worth considering.

Hotel Kechu (☎ 633-8824; fax 632-0234) *(lāsàjìqǔ fàndiàn)* is a new Tibetan-style hotel that is conveniently located at 149 Beijing Donglu. Singles/doubles are Y180/Y280, and it's Y350 for the suite.

The *Gangjian Hotel* (☎ 632-3824) *(gāngjiān fàndiàn)* is between the Kirey and the Banak Shol hotels at 19 Beijing

Xilu. A Chinese-style hotel that lacks atmosphere, it has clean rooms and some dorms for Y40 (no common showers). The double rooms are Y180 and the suite Y380.

One of the older Chinese-style places is the one star *Himalaya Hotel* (☎ 633-1430; fax 633-2675) *(xīmǎlāyǎ fàndiàn)* near the Lhasa River. Doubles with attached bath cost Y275. By mid-98, they hope to have completed a three star hotel next door.

The *Yingqiao Hotel* (☎ 633-6244; fax 633-6246) *(yínqiáo fàndiàn)* is a two star Chinese hotel on Linkuo Beilu. Clean double rooms cost Y240 to Y300.

Places to Stay – top end

The *Lhasa Holiday Inn* (☎ 683-2221; fax 683-5796) *(lāsà fàndiàn)* is just north of the Norbu Lingka at 1 Minzu Lu – or at least it was at the time of writing. Late reports suggest it has closed down and the entire Holiday Inn chain has withdrawn from its partnership with the Chinese government. If it's still operational, prices range from Y660 (economy) to Y1090 (superior). Suites and beautiful Tibetan-style rooms are also available.

The *Tibet Hotel* (☎ 683-4966; fax 683-6787) *(xīzàng bīnguǎn)* is at 221 Beijing Xilu, a few hundred metres up the road from the Lhasa Holiday Inn. Built in mock-Tibetan style, it offers comfortable, if pricey, rooms. Standard doubles cost Y460 and the suites are Y1200.

Places to Eat

Food can be mighty scarce out on the high plateau, but Lhasa offers Chinese, western, Tibetan and even some Nepalese and Indian cuisine.

The staple diet in Tibet is tsampa (roasted barley meal) and butter tea. Momo (dumplings filled with vegetables or meat) and thukpa (noodles with meat) are usually available at small restaurants. Tibetans consume large quantities of chang, a tangy alcoholic drink derived from fermented barley.

Snowlands Restaurant is next door to the hotel of the same name and serves up a good variety of tasty food. The vegie burger (Y12), yak steak (Y35) and chicken butter masala (Y35) are all good fare. If you have a few extra yuan, this is the place to eat.

Tashi's Restaurant on the same street is a cheaper option and serves good food with a smile. *Tashi's II* in the Kirey Hotel has the same menu and the same friendly service. Special praise should be reserved for the bobis (chapatti-like unleavened bread), which most people order with seasoned cream cheese and fried vegetables (Y8) or meat. Tashi's apple momos and cheesecakes are also a hit.

Probably the most popular place in town, the *Kailash Restaurant* is on the 2nd floor of the Banak Shol Hotel.

On the south-eastern corner of the Barkhor circuit is the popular *Makye Ame*. An especially tasty dish is the pasta pesto (Y15). The pot of coffee (Y12) is a good investment.

Another place worth recommending is the *Crazy Yak Restaurant* (next to the Yak Hotel), and for the truly famished and financially solvent, there's a smorgasbord of gastronomical delights at the *Holiday Inn*'s restaurant.

Entertainment

For many Tibetans a night on the town usually involves a visit to a friend's house for some serious consumption of chang and lots of laughter. Alternatively, many Tibetan restaurants around town entertain their customers with karaoke or video shows, and you would be more than welcome to venture in and pull up a pew.

If karaoke isn't your idea of entertainment, then there is a *disco* on the Potala Square in the Workers' Cultural Palace *(láodòng rénmín wénhuā gōng)*. The *Makye Ame*, *Kailash*, *Crazy Yak* and *Tashi* restaurants sometimes have impromptu parties where travellers guzzle beers and share tales of their exploits.

There are also two *cinemas* in town. The main one is opposite the minibus stand and the other is located between the Kirey and Banak Shol hotels.

Things to Buy
Whether it is prayer wheels, daggers, rings or muesli, then you shouldn't have a problem finding it in Lhasa. The Barkhor circuit is especially good for buying souvenirs to fill up your pack.

Mount Green Trekking Shop has a wide selection of trekking equipment available at reasonable prices. It is on Beijing Donglu just east of the Kechu Hotel. The Holiday Inn has a lot of hard-to-find goodies at hard-to-understand prices, like Y120 for slide film and Y120 for camera batteries. Cheaper prices for the same products can be found around Barkhor Square. Tampons are unavailable, and it is advisable to bring in any special medications that you may need.

Getting There & Away
Air Chengdu is Lhasa's window on the world. Flights to Lhasa depart Chengdu twice daily and cost Y1200. There are three flights a week between Lhasa and Beijing – on Monday and Thursday via Xi'an, and on Sunday via Chengdu. From Beijing a ticket costs Y1940 and from Xi'an Y1320.

The only other domestic flight is the twice-weekly (Wednesday and Sunday) Lhasa-Chongqing run (Y1300). Lhasa-Kathmandu flights operate on Tuesday, Thursday and Saturday, departing Lhasa at 10.20 am and leaving Kathmandu at 12.30 pm. No matter whether you fly in from Chengdu, Beijing, Xi'an, Chongqing or Kathmandu, all tickets to Lhasa have to be purchased through a travel agency.

Leaving Lhasa is a lot simpler, as tickets can be purchased from the CAAC office at 88 Niangre Lu. Getting flights at short notice is usually no problem. CAAC is open every day from 9 am until 9 pm.

Bus The bus station is a deserted monstrosity 3km from the main post office, near the Norbu Lingka.

A daily bus leaves for Golmud at 7.30 am. Prices are Y566 for a sleeper, Y283 for a hard seat or Y157 if you have a student card. In Golmud, foreigners pay anywhere

between Y1200 and Y1600 for a ticket to Lhasa on the Chinese bus – the justification is that you are paying for the three day Lhasa tour.

There is also a daily bus (4.30 pm) to Xining for Y395 (hard seat) and Y780 (sleeper). There are daily departures to Shigatse at 9 am (Y70), and to Tsetang at 9, 10 and 11 am. Since the completion of the new Lhasa-Shigatse highway there has been no public transport direct to Gyantse. It is necessary to travel to Shigatse first and then change to a private minibus or a public bus.

Car Although there are five major road routes to Lhasa, foreigners are officially allowed to use only the Nepal and Qinghai routes.

Nepal Route The road connecting Lhasa with Nepal is officially called the Friendship Highway and runs from Lhasa to Zhangmu (the Chinese border post) via Shigatse. It's a spectacular trip over high passes and across the plateau, the highest point being La Lungla Pass (5200m).

If the weather's good, you'll get a fine view of Mt Everest from the Tibetan village of Tingri. Accommodation en route is generally basic with fairly reasonable prices (Y15 to Y25), and there's no great hardship involved, as long as you don't mind doing without luxuries (such as a shower) for the duration of your trip. The food situation has also improved greatly in recent years.

By far the most popular option for the trip is renting a 4WD through a hotel or travel agency, and sorting out a private itinerary with the driver. A direct run to the Nepalese border costs from Y200 to Y400 per person, depending on the numbers and the type of vehicle. The trip normally takes two days to Zhangmu.

When travelling from Nepal to Lhasa, foreigners must arrange transport through tour agencies. If you already have a Chinese visa, you could try turning up at the border. The occasional traveller slips through (even a couple on bicycles). At Zhangmu you can hunt around for buses, minibuses, 4WDs or trucks heading towards Lhasa.

Qinghai Route An asphalt road connects Xining with Lhasa via Golmud; it crosses the desolate, barren and virtually uninhabited Tibetan Plateau. The highest point is Tanggula Pass (5180m), but despite the altitude the scenery is not really very interesting.

Theoretically, local Chinese buses and decidedly more comfortable 'Japanese' buses (made in China) do the run. However, the 'Japanese' buses are often not available, so you get to ride budget class at five star prices.

Reckon on about 35 hours from Golmud to Lhasa by bus and remember to take warm clothing, food and water on the bus, since baggage is not accessible during the trip.

Other Routes Between Lhasa and Sichuan, Yunnan or Xinjiang provinces are some of the wildest, highest and most dangerous routes in the world; these are not officially open to foreigners.

The lack of public transport on these routes makes it necessary to hitch, but that is also prohibited. At the time of writing there were a few travellers hitching into Tibet from Kashgar without any hassles. However, the authorities have come down very heavily on truck drivers giving lifts to foreigners, particularly on the Yunnan and Sichuan routes in or out of Tibet.

Rental Rented vehicles have emerged as the most popular way to get away from Lhasa in recent years. The most popular route is a leisurely and slightly circuitous journey down to Zhangmu on the Tibetan-Nepalese border, taking in Yamdrok-tso lake, Gyantse, Shigatse, Sakya, Tingri and Everest Base Camp on the way.

A six to seven day trip of this sort in a 4WD costs around Y6000, including all necessary permits, driver, guide and car.

Other popular trips include Mt Kailash (Kangrinpoche 6714m), Nam-tso lake and eastern Tibet.

Getting Around
To/From the Airport
Gonggar airport is 90km (1½ hours by bus) from Lhasa. Buses leave from the car park behind the CAAC office every hour from 6 am and cost Y30. Tickets are sold on the bus, so show up early to guarantee yourself a seat. If you need to get to the airport more quickly, you could hire a taxi for about Y150.

CAAC buses greet incoming flights, so getting into town is no problem.

Minibus Privately run minibuses are frequent on and around Beijing Lu. There is a flat Y2 charge. This is a quick and convenient way to get across town. From the minibus terminal near Barkhor Square there are jeeps and minibuses running up to the Drepung and Sera monasteries.

Pedicab There is no shortage of pedicabs plying the streets of Lhasa. A trip between the Banak Shol Hotel and the main post office, for example, costs around Y5 (after much haggling). The best option would be to hire a bike and peddle around yourself.

AROUND LHASA
Monasteries
Prior to 1959, Lhasa had three monasteries which functioned as 'pillars of the Tibetan state' – Drepung, Sera and Ganden. As part of a concerted effort to smash the influence of these, the Cultural Revolution wiped out the monastic population, which once numbered thousands. The buildings of Ganden Monastery were shelled and demolished.

Today, buildings are being reconstructed and, even if Chinese motives in all this are centred more on the tourist dollar than on any notions of religious freedom and making amends for past wrongs, it is still gratifying to see that the monasteries are starting to come to life again, although nowhere near the scale on which they once operated.

Drepung *(zhébàng sì)* Drepung dates back to the early 15th century and lies about 7km west of Lhasa. In its time it was the largest of Tibet's monastic towns and, some maintain, the largest monastery in the world.

Today, the number of monks in residence here has dwindled from 7000 to around 700 (including nearby Namcheng). Around 40% of the monastery's structures have been destroyed.

The monastery is open daily from early morning until 4 pm. Admission is Y30, or Y15 with a student card. Try and catch the lunch break when all the hungry monks eagerly await their tsampa and yak butter tea. Wander into the kitchen and check out the incredible wood-fired stoves and massive pots.

Drepung is easily reached by bike, although most people take the No 3 minibus for Y2 from the minibus stand near Barkhor Square.

Sera *(sèlā sì)* About 4km north of Lhasa, this monastery was founded in 1419 by a disciple of Tsong Khapa.

About 550 monks are now in residence, well down from an original population of around 5000. Debating takes place from 3 pm in a garden next to the central assembly hall (Jepa Duchen) in the centre of the monastery. Sera is open daily from 9 am to 4 pm, and admission is Y30 (Y15 with a student card). An hour's walk will get you up to the monastery, or catch minibus No 5 for Y2.

At the base of a mountain just east of the monastery is a Tibetan 'sky burial' site, where the deceased are chopped up and then served to vultures. Tourism has reduced this admittedly grisly event to an almost daily confrontation between *domden* (undertakers) and scores of photo-hungry visitors. The reactions of the domden have become very violent. Our advice is to leave the place alone.

Ganden *(gāndān sì)* About 45km east of Lhasa, this monastery was founded in 1409 by Tsong Khapa. During the Cultural Revolution the monastery was subjected to intense shelling, and monks were made to dismantle the remains.

Some 400 monks have returned now, but the reconstruction work awaiting them is huge. For all this, the monastery is still well worth visiting and remains an important pilgrimage site.

Pilgrim buses leave for Ganden at 6.30 am and tickets can be bought the day before or on the bus. The ticket office is on the Barkhor circuit, 100m to the right of the main entrance to the Jokhang Temple. Look out for the tin shed. Tickets are sold from 2.30 to 7 pm. The cost is Y16 for a return ticket. If you decide to buy the ticket on the bus, try to arrive in Barkhor Square by 6 am.

Nam-tso Lake
(nàmùcuò)
An overnight stay at Nam-tso, 195km north of Lhasa, has become a popular trip in recent years. The sacred lake is surrounded by mountains with peaks of over 7000m. Coupled with the turquoise-blue lake, the scenery is breathtaking.

Accommodation is available at Tashi Dor Monastery (4700m), which is on the edge of the lake, or you can camp nearby. It costs Y15 to enter the area and another Y15 a night for the bed. The closest public transport to Nam-tso takes you to Damxung, a small town with a couple of Sichuanese restaurants and a military base, but the lake is still another 40km or more. The best option would be to organise a 4WD in Lhasa, which should cost between Y1100 and Y1500 for a two day trip.

Permits and guides are not necessary for the area; however, do not underestimate the rapid ascent of 1100m.

It would be preferable to be in Lhasa at least a week before heading up to Nam-tso.

YARLUNG VALLEY
(yǎlǔ liúyù)
About 170km south-east of Lhasa, this valley is considered to be the birthplace of Tibetan culture. Near the town of Tsetang,

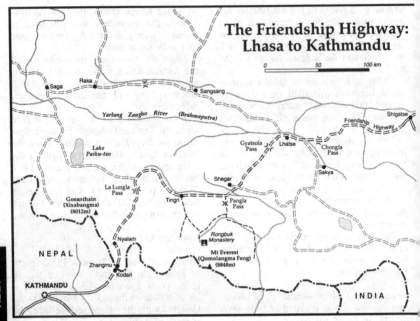

The Friendship Highway: Lhasa to Kathmandu

0   50   100 km

Saga
Raka
Sangsang
Shigatse
Yarlung Zangbo River (Brahmaputra)
Friendship Highway
Gyatsola Pass
Lhatse
Chongla Pass
Lake Paiku-tso
Shegar
Sakya
La Lungla Pass
Gosanthain (Xixabangma) (8012m) ▲
Tingri
Pangla Pass
Nyalam
Rongbuk Monastery ■
Mt Everest (Qomolangma Feng) (8848m) ▲
NEPAL
Zhangmu
Kodari
KATHMANDU
INDIA

which forms the administrative centre of the region, are several sites of religious importance.

Samye Monastery
(sāngyī sì)

This lies about 30km west of Tsetang, on the opposite bank of the Yarlung Zangbo (Brahmaputra) River. It was founded in 775 AD by King Trisong Detsen and was the first monastery in Tibet. Getting there is quite complicated, but it commands a beautiful, secluded position.

To reach Samye, catch one of the morning buses from Lhasa's main bus terminal to Tsetang. At the time of writing the minibuses that depart from the small bus station south of Barkhor Square were unavailable for foreigners. There was also a police check at the ferry crossing for valid permits. So, before you leave Lhasa, ask around about the current situation.

The bus will drop you at the ferry, which will take you across the river whenever it's full. From there, a lift in the back of a truck will carry you the 5km to Samye. The ferry crossing is Y10 and then it's another Y10 for the bumpy truck ride.

Simple accommodation is available next to the monastery for Y20 and there is a new guesthouse being built next door that looks like it will be more comfortable and more expensive. *Snowlands Restaurant* serves up some tasty Amdo momos for Y8.

Yumbulagang
(yōngbùlākǎng)

About 12km south-west of Tsetang on a dirt road, Yumbulagang is the legendary first building in Tibet. Although small in scale, it soars in recently renovated splendour above the valley. Get there by hiring a bike or 4WD in Tsetang, or hitch on a

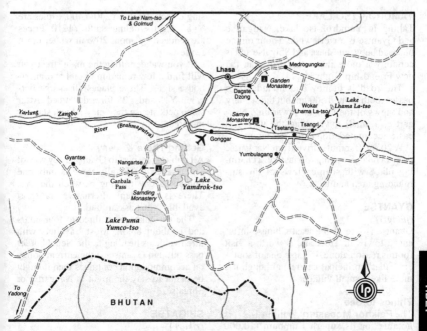

tractor. The roof provides wonderful views of the surrounding valley.

Tombs of the Kings
(zàngwángmù)
At Chongye, about 26km west of Tsetang, these tombs are less of a visual treat than Yumbulagang; their importance is essentially historical. To get there, hire a 4WD or spend half the day pedalling there and back on a bike.

Tsetang
(zédāng)
This rather uninteresting town is 200km from Lhasa and 90km east of Gonggar airport. You may have to spend the night here or organise a permit for the surrounding area. The latter can be done at the PSB, which is on the eastern side of Naidong Lu.

Places to Stay On Naidong Lu, about a five minute walk south from the traffic circle, the *Friendship Hotel* (☎ 782-0816; fax 782-1128) *(yǒuyì fàndiàn)* has dorm beds for Y60. A standard double with bath is Y180.

A little further down Naidong Lu is the *Guesthouse Hotel* (☎ 782-1486) *(kèfángbù)*. Beds are Y40 in a double with bath. Showers are available in the evening.

Tsetang Hotel (☎ 782-1668; fax 782-1490) *(zédāng fàndiàn)* on Naidong Lu is another three star hotel that is deserted most of the year. Standard doubles are Y490 and the Tibetan-style rooms are Y588.

Getting There & Away Buses for Tsetang leave Lhasa three times a day. The first leaves at 9 am from the Lhasa bus station.

Buses heading back to Lhasa depart from the traffic circle in Tsetang every morning.

YAMDROK-TSO LAKE

Taking in Yamdrok-tso lake, Nangartse and Gyantse is a worthwhile detour on the old road between Lhasa and Shigatse and is certainly a more interesting trip than the new Friendship Highway.

The road is bumpy and includes two passes, both around 5000m, but the scenery and views of the lake are rewarding. Nangartse, a small town along the way, has basic accommodation and a restaurant.

A 20 to 30 minute drive from Nangartse brings you to Samding Monastery, a charming place with scenic views of the surrounding area and lake.

GYANTSE

(jiāngzī)

Gyantse is one of the least Chinese-influenced towns in Tibet and is worth a visit for this reason alone. It's also one of southern Tibet's principal centres, although it's more like a small village.

Things to See

The **Palkhor Monastery**, built in 1427, is notable for its superb Kumbum (10,000 images) stupa, which has nine tiers and, according to the Buddhist tradition, 108 chapels. The monks may not allow you to complete the pilgrim circuit to the top, but the lower tiers contain excellent murals. Take a torch (flashlight).

The **Dzong** (old fort), which towers above Gyantse, offers a fine view over the valley. The entrance is usually locked, but you can pick up the key (for a small fee) from a little house at the foot of the steps leading up the hill; it's close to the tiny bridge on the main road.

Places to Stay & Eat

The *Gyantse Hotel* (☎ 817-2222; fax 817-2366) *(jiāngzī fàndiàn)* on Yingxiong Nanlu is officially the only hotel open to foreigners in town. All the guesthouses were closed to foreigners in May 1997 by the PSB, probably due to slow business at the Gyantse Hotel. Avoid the place on principle, but if you want a bit of comfort the singles/doubles are Y240/Y400, triples are Y486 and the deluxe suite Y1210. Prices are reduced by about 20% in winter or on request.

If you wander along the main street you will find a few remaining hotel and guesthouse signs. These places all charge between Y15 and Y25 for a dorm bed. After some persistence they may let you stay for the night.

Getting There & Away

All public transport to Gyantse is by way of Shigatse, and officially there is only one minibus a day running between the two. There is abundant alternative transport available – just ask around.

The trip takes from three to four hours and is about 85km. Most travellers with hired vehicles heading to the Nepal border pass through Gyantse. If the current policy on accommodation continues then it might be better to stay the night in Nangartse or Shigatse.

SHIGATSE

(rìkāzé)

The second largest urban centre in Tibet is Shigatse. This is the seat of the Panchen Lama, a reincarnation of Amitabha (Buddha of Infinite Light), who ranks close to the Dalai Lama. The 10th Panchen Lama, who died in 1989, was taken to Beijing during the 60s and lived largely a puppet existence there, visiting Tibet only occasionally.

The search for his successor has led to verbal conflict between the Dalai Lama and the Chinese government, as the Dalai Lama got in first and nominated a new Panchen Lama. The Chinese subsequently placed the Dalai Lama's nominee, Gedhun Choekyi Nyima, under house arrest in Beijing and nominated their own candidate.

Once the sun goes down packs of dogs take over the streets and it is advisable to avoid a late evening stroll.

Information

Travel Office CITS (☎ 882-2516) in Shigatse is the main travel agency in town and offers expensive tours throughout Tibet. You will find it just south of the Bank of China and it's open from 9 am to 12.30 pm and then from 3.30 to 6.30 pm.

PSB If you want to travel without the cost of a tour and 4WD then ask for a permit at the Shigatse PSB. This PSB has probably

the most useful officials in Tibet. At the time of writing this was the only place where you could get a travel permit without being part of an organised tour. If you are hitching or cycling it would pay to be vague about your means of transportation. The cost of a permit is Y50 per person.

Post & Communications The post office is open from 9 am to 6.30 pm, but international services are closed between 1 and 4 pm for lunch. On Saturday and Sunday the hours are 10.30 am to 2 pm.

Tashilhunpo Monastery
(zhāshílúnbù sì)
The main attraction in Shigatse is the seat of the Panchen Lama – Tashilhunpo Monastery. Built in 1447 by a nephew of Tsong Khapa, the monastery once housed over 4000 monks, but now there are only 600.

Apart from a giant statue of the Maitreya Buddha (nearly 27m high) in the Temple of the Maitreya, the monastery is also famed for its Grand Hall with the opulent tomb (containing 85kg of gold and masses of jewels) of the fourth Panchen Lama. The monastery is open from 9 am to 5 pm and is closed for two hours from noon for lunch. Admission costs the standard Y30 or Y15 with a Chinese student card.

SHIGATSE 日喀则

PLACES TO STAY
8 Sanzhuzi Hotel
 三珠子旅馆
10 Tenzin Hotel;
 Tianfu Restaurant
 天新旅馆、天富餐厅
13 Orchard Hotel
 果园旅馆
17 Hostel (Zhaodaisuo)
 招待所
18 Hostel (Zhaodaisuo)
 招待所
21 Shigatse Hotel
 日喀则宾馆

PLACES TO EAT
6 Yuanfu Restaurant
 远富餐厅
7 Tashi's Restaurant

OTHER
1 Shak Rak Stupa
2 Shigatse Dzong (Fortress)
 日喀则宗
3 Department Store
 商场
4 Market
 农贸市场
5 Department Store
 商场
9 PSB
 公安局外事科
11 Tashilhunpo Monastery
 扎十伦布寺
12 Monastery Entrance
 扎十伦布寺入口
14 People's Hospital
 人民医院
15 Bookshop
 新华书店
16 Department Store
 商场
19 Post Office
 邮局
20 Bus Station
 汽车站
22 Bank of China
 中国银行
23 CITS
 中国国际旅行社

Shigatse Fortress
(rìkāzé zōng)
Very little remains of the old Shigatse Fortress, but the ruins on the skyline are imposing all the same. It's possible to hike up to the fortress from the pilgrim circuit for good views of the town.

Places to Stay & Eat
In the middle of town is the *Tenzin Hotel* (☎ 882-2018) *(tiānxīn lǚguǎn)*, a friendly and busy place. Dorm beds are Y20 or Y30, and double rooms are Y120 or Y180 with bath. Hot water is on and off 24 hours a day. Wear ear muffs if you don't like listening to the dogs who howl all night long.

The *Orchard Hotel (guǒyuán lǚguǎn)* is just across the road from the main entrance to the Tashilhunpo. It's a simple Chinese-style hotel with cheap dorm beds (Y15 or Y20 with TV). Doubles are also available. The hot water is solar and unreliable. Give the hotel's Y15 breakfast a miss.

The *Shigatse Hotel* (☎ 882-2525; fax 882-1900) *(rìkāzé fàndiàn)* is a three star palace in the south of town. Singles/doubles are Y430/Y460. If you stay here, the Tibetan-style rooms for Y460 are the best option. If you want to feel important for the night, the presidential suite is Y1540.

The *Sanzhuzi Hotel* (☎ 882-2280) *(sānzhūzi lǚguǎn)* was being renovated at the time of writing and planned to have standard doubles with bath for about Y160.

The most convenient place to eat if you are staying at the Tenzin Hotel is the *Tianfu Restaurant*, which is on the ground floor of the hotel. It has a wide range of food, including a number of vegetarian options. Just around the corner is the *Yuanfu Restaurant*. The house speciality is the fish-tasting eggplant.

Tashi's Restaurant on the same street has some tasty food and the owner is very helpful for local information.

Getting There & Away
Two buses a day leave for Shigatse from Lhasa's main bus station, at 7 and 9 am for Y38. Going the other way a bus leaves daily at 8.30 am and costs Y72, or Y36 with a student card.

There is a daily bus to Gyantse for Y52 and Y25 (student card) and every two days to Sakya for Y52 and Y32 respectively.

Those heading out to the Nepal border or Tingri have very few options. Hitching is one possibility, or you could inquire at the Shigatse Hotel for minibuses or landcruisers heading out to the border to pick up your tour groups. The cost for hooking up with one of these varies and the service is unreliable.

SAKYA
(sàjiā)
Sakya is 152km west of Shigatse and about 25km south of the main road. The huge, brooding monastery at Sakya was Tibet's most powerful 700 years ago, and was once the centre for the Sakyapa sect founded in the 11th century.

The monastery probably contains the finest collection of Tibetan religious relics remaining in Tibet, although the monks may restrict you to viewing only a couple of halls.

Places to Stay & Eat
If you come into Sakya by bus or rented transport, you may be dropped off at the *Sakya County Guesthouse (sàjiāxiàng zhāodàisuǒ)*, an unexciting Chinese-style hotel notable for its sneering staff. Dorm beds are Y15.

Just down the road towards the monastery is the friendlier *Tibetan Hotel*. At the time of writing it was being rebuilt, but should be open by the time you read this. Tibetan-style rooms will cost Y15 to Y25.

Getting There & Away
Sakya is the last stop for foreigners using public transport. The bus leaves Shigatse every two days and is a slow journey. Buy your ticket the day before.

Most people arrange to see Sakya as an overnight stop when they hire a 4WD to the border or to the Everest Base Camp. It's also possible to hitch, as there is enough transport on the road to Sakya.

RONGBUK MONASTERY & EVEREST BASE CAMP

Before heading down to the border, many travellers doing the Lhasa-Kodari trip take in Rongbuk and the Everest Base Camp (also known as Mt Qomolangma Base Camp).

The road to Rongbuk is a bumpy one to say the least and it takes at least four hours from the Chay checkpoint. It is here that all vehicles pay a Y400 entrance fee and every passenger Y60.

Most 4WD drivers are not keen on driving all the way to the base camp. If you want to go all the way make sure that you mention it in your itinerary.

The walk from Rongbuk to the base camp takes about two or three hours, or 20 minutes in the 4WD. If you are hiking up to the base camp from Rongbuk, you'll know you've reached your destination when you come across a toilet block.

There is dorm accommodation at *Rongbuk Monastery* for Y25 a bed and there is a small *restaurant* with simple supplies nearby.

TINGRI
(dìngrì)

There are in fact two Tingris: new Tingri (Shegar) and old Tingri (Tingri). New Tingri has a checkpoint and a tourist hotel, and not much else. Old Tingri is a Tibetan town. There's not much to do here except look for Everest on the skyline, but most travellers use Tingri as a final stopover before heading on to Zhangmu on the Nepalese border.

There are currently three hotels in town, the *Everest View Hotel*, the *Himalaya* and the *Amdo Hotel*. All have beds for Y20. The kitchen in the Everest View has a big potbelly stove that is an ideal place to eat dinner or just sit back and have a beer.

From Tingri it's four or five spectacular hours to the border – up, up, up and then down, down, down.

ZHANGMU
(zhāngmù)

The last Chinese town you'll see before hitting Nepal is a typical border town that has plenty of places to stay and eat.

Chinese, Tibetan and Nepalese food and goodies are available at most of the restaurants and shops along the main road for reasonable prices.

At the time of writing there was only one hotel available for foreigners, the *Zhangmu Guesthouse*, right down in the south of town next to customs. It's expensive and apathetically run.

If they change the absurd policy of restricting foreigners to a single place to stay, then a good little hotel up the road south of the bank and near a small stupa is the *Himalaya Lodge*. Comfortable doubles here cost Y20 per bed.

ZHANGMU TO KODARI

Access to Nepal is via the Friendship Bridge and Kodari, around 8km below Zhangmu. It is possible to change Chinese yuan and Nepalese rupees before going through Chinese Customs – very good rates can be found, but be careful not to get ripped off.

There is a bus service between the two customs for Y50. Otherwise, you can hitch on one of the many trucks plying the route. If you decide to walk, it will take you a couple of hours to get down to the bridge. Walking may be safer, but it is certainly not easy.

For those looking at continuing straight on to Kathmandu, there are a couple of buses a day from Kodari that leave whenever they are full. If you arrive in Kodari after 2.30 pm then you may have to spend the night somewhere along the way. The local bus costs R100 to Kathmandu and takes about seven hours. The other option is to hire a vehicle. There are touts for vehicles to Kathmandu at Nepalese Customs. The cost is around R1500 to R2000.

TIBET

Qinghai 青海

Qinghai Facts & Highlights

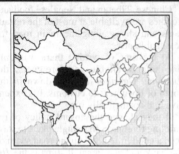

Area: 720,000 sq km

Population: 4.9 million

Capital: Xining

Highlights

- Ta'er Monastery, one of the six great monasteries of the Yellow Hat sect of Tibetan Buddhism.
- Qinghai Lake, China's largest lake, renowned for its breathtaking scenery and abundant wildlife.
- The rough but stunning overland trip into Tibet via Golmud.

Qinghai *(qīnghǎi)* lies on the north-eastern border of Tibet and is one of the great cartographic constructions of our time.

For centuries this was part of the Tibetan world; these days it's separated from the Tibetan Autonomous Region by nothing more than the colours on a Chinese-made map.

With the exception of the eastern area around the provincial capital Xining, Qinghai (formerly known as Amdo) was not incorporated into the Chinese Empire until the early 18th century. And since 1949, the province has served as a sort of Chinese Siberia where common criminals, as well as political prisoners, have been incarcerated. These prisoners have included former Kuomintang army and police officers, 'rightists' arrested during the late 1950s harvesting of the Hundred Flowers, victims of the Cultural Revolution, former Red Guards arrested for their activities during the Cultural Revolution, supporters of the Gang of Four, and opponents of the present regime.

Eastern Qinghai is a high grassy plateau rising between 2500m and 3000m above sea level, and is slashed by a series of mountain ranges with peaks rising up to 5000m. It's also the source of the Yellow River.

Most of the agricultural regions are concentrated in the east around the Xining area, but the surrounding uplands and the regions west of Qinghai Lake have good pasturelands for sheep, horses and cattle.

North-western Qinghai is a great basin consisting mainly of barren desert, surrounded by mountains. It's littered with salt marshes and saline lakes and afflicted by harsh, cold winters.

Southern Qinghai is a high plateau sitting 3500m above sea level. It's separated from Tibet by the Tanggulashan Range, which has peaks rising to more than 6500m; the Yangzi and the Mekong rivers have their source here. Most of the region is grassland and the population is composed almost entirely of semi-nomadic Tibetan herders rearing goats, sheep and yaks.

The population of Qinghai is a mixture of minorities, including the Kazaks, Mongols and Hui. Tibetans are found throughout the province and the Han settlers are concentrated around the area of Xining.

Although a railway line stretching as far as Golmud has helped improve Qinghai's economy, it still remains one of China's poorest provinces. Unemployment is high, and those rural residents that have jobs often earn as little as Y300 per month.

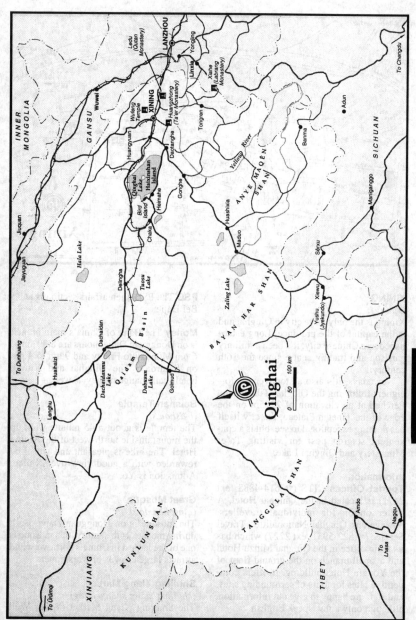

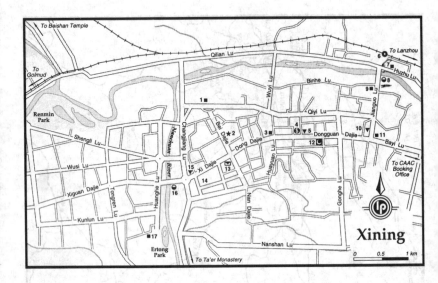

To Beishan Temple

Qilian Lu

To Lanzhou

To Golmud

Huzhu Lu

Binhe Lu

Wuyi Lu

1 ■

Renmin Park

Qiyi Lu

Shengli Lu

Bei Dajie

★ 2

3 ■

4

▼ 5

Dongguan Dajie

10 ▽

■ 11

Changjiang Lu

Nanchuan River

Dong Dajie

12 ◖

Bayi Lu

Wusi Lu

15

Xi Dajie

13

To CAAC Booking Office

Xiguan Dajie

Tongren Lu

Huayuan Lu

14

Gonghe Lu

Huangha

Nan Dajie

Kunlun Lu

16

Xining

■ 17

Ertong Park

Nanshan Lu

0   0.5   1 km

To Ta'er Monastery

XINING
(xīníng)
Xining is the only large city in Qinghai and is the capital of the province. Long established as a Chinese city, it's been a military garrison and trading centre since the 16th century.

Nowadays, it's also a stopover for foreigners following the Qinghai-Tibet route. Perched at an elevation of 2275m on the edge of the Tibetan Plateau, the city itself has nothing exceptional to see, but is a convenient staging post for visiting Ta'er Monastery and Qinghai Lake.

Information
Tourist Offices CITS (☎ 614-4888, ext 2471) is located in the Qinghai Hotel. A better option for individual travellers, however, is Qinghai Nationalities Travel Service (☎ 822-5951, ext 2227) which has its main office in the Qinghai Minzu Hotel and a small branch on the ground floor of the Yongfu Hotel building. It offers competitive rates for tours of surrounding sites, and staff are happy to give out information, although only a few speak English.

PSB The PSB alien affairs section is at 35 Bei Dajie.

Money The Bank of China's main branch is on Dongguan Dajie: hours are 8.30 am to 6 pm Monday to Friday and 9 am to 4 pm on Saturday. The Qinghai and Xining hotels can change money as well.

Beishan Temple
(běishàn sì)
The temple is about a 45 minute walk up the mountainside north-west of the Xining Hotel. The hike is pleasant and you'll be rewarded with a good view over Xining. Admission is Y6.

Great Mosque
(qīngzhēn dà sì)
The mosque is on Dongguan Dajie. Built during the late 14th century, this mosque is one of the largest in China's north-west and attracts large crowds of worshippers.

Shuijing Xiang Market
(shuǐjǐng xiàng shāngchǎng)
The Shuijing Xiang Market (Water Well

QINGHAI

XINING 西宁

PLACES TO STAY
1 Xining Hotel
西宁宾馆
3 Qinghai Minzu Hotel;
Qinghai Nationalities
Travel Service
青海民族宾馆;
青海民族旅行社
7 Youzheng Gongyu Hotel
邮政公寓宾馆
9 Yongfu Hotel
永富宾馆
11 Xining Mansion
西宁大厦
17 Qinghai Hotel; CITS
青海宾馆;
中国国际旅行社

PLACES TO EAT
5 Xiaoyuanmen Restaurant
小园门食府
10 Food Tents
帐蓬食摊
15 Xiaoximen Dumpling
Restaurant
小西门饺子馆

OTHER
2 PSB
公安局
4 Bank of China
中国银行
6 Railway Station
火车站
8 Long-Distance Bus
Station
长途汽车站
12 Great Mosque
东关清真大寺
13 Post Office
邮政大楼
14 Shuijing Xiang Market
水井巷商场
16 Buses to Huangzhong;
Ta'er Monastery
去湟中、塔尔寺中巴

Places to Stay

The best budget bargain in town lies only a few minutes' walk east of the railway station at the *Youzheng Gongyu Hotel* (☎ 814-0711) *(yóuzhèng gōngyù bīnguǎn)* at 138 Huzhu Lu. It's a friendly, fairly clean place with dorm beds from Y16 and Y18 and doubles with private bath for Y38.

Another inexpensive place that takes foreigners is the *Qinghai Minzu Hotel* (☎ 822-5951) *(qīnghǎi mínzú bīnguǎn)*. Beds in triples with shared bath are Y20, while those in triples with bath attached range from Y35 to Y48. Doubles are Y90 or Y108, although these don't look to be such good value. The hotel usually charges foreigners double, but book your room through the Qinghai Nationalities Travel Service and you'll get the Chinese price. The hotel is convenient for exploring the city as it's fairly close to the main shopping and business district, as well as the post office and Bank of China.

Xining Mansion (☎ 814-9995) *(xīníng dàshà)* is a two star hotel, but it does have doubles with an attached bath in the rear building ranging from Y50 to Y80, and doubles in the refurbished front building for Y100 to Y180; the cheaper ones are a pretty good deal. A 30% surcharge is levied on foreigners, and it seems hard to get around it. From the railway station it's a 10 minute walk to the hotel, or take bus No 1 and get off at the second stop.

Although not in a convenient location, the *Xining Hotel* (☎ 823-8701) *(xīníng bīnguǎn)* is a peaceful place with some nice gardens. It's a typical Chinese three star operation, with doubles ranging from Y166 to Y349. There are a few triples with attached bath available for Y48 per bed. The reception is in the building at the rear, behind the Qinghai Qingtai Trust & Investment Corp building. Take bus No 9 from opposite the railway station and get off at the seventh stop *(bīnguǎn)*.

The *Qinghai Hotel* (☎ 614-4888) *(qīnghǎi bīnguǎn)*, a towering pink monolith in the western part of town, is Xining's most upmarket hotel. This is reflected in the rates

Alley) is the most colourful market in town, although even the wells have long since gone dry. Stock up on munchies here, especially if you're heading to Golmud, Qinghai Lake or over the mountains to Chengdu. The market is near the West Gate *(xīmén)*.

which start at Y389 for a double (plus a 15% service charge). This is the only place in town where you can get a refrigerator in your room! Staying here is probably not worth the money, although staff try to do their best.

The *Yongfu Hotel* (☎ 814-9672) *(yǒngfù bīnguǎn)*, a former backpacker stand-by, was closed at the time of writing. A privately run operation, it apparently ran afoul of the local bureaucrats. Staff weren't sure if or when it would reopen. There was a rumour that the Minzu Hotel had plans to buy it and convert it into 'Tibetan-style' lodgings.

Places to Eat

The area around Xining Mansion has a good selection of *food tents* in the evening; check out the kebab stalls and the places selling *shā guō* – a mini-hotpot of beef, mutton, vegetables, tofu and noodles. It's very filling and costs only Y5, including a bowl of rice.

The restaurant at the *Qinghai Minzu Hotel* has a good reputation with locals, as does the *Xiaoyuanmen Restaurant (xiǎoyuánmén shífǔ)*, a Muslim place on Dongguan Dajie. The only English signage is the word 'Qingzhen', a transliteration of the Chinese word for Muslim. Otherwise, look out for the circular entranceway.

Out near the Shuijing Xiang Market is a number of fine places. If you're a fan of dumplings, try the *Dumpling Restaurant (jiǎozi guǎn)*.

Getting There & Away

Air Xining has flights to Beijing (thrice weekly, Y1630), Chengdu (twice weekly, Y1060), Guangzhou (twice weekly, Y1950), and one flight a week to Shanghai (Y1970), Ürümqi (Y1400) and Xi'an (Y710). At the time of writing there was also a weekly flight to Golmud on Sunday (Y640).

The CAAC booking office (☎ 817-4616) is on the eastern edge of town at 34 Bayi Xilu, and is open daily from 8.30 am to noon and 2 to 5.30 pm. To get there take the eastbound No 9 bus from near Xining

Mansion, get off at the second stop and walk east another 50m. You can also book tickets through almost any travel agency or hotel.

Bus The main bus station serves all destinations except Ta'er Monastery. Sleeper buses to Golmud leave daily at 4.30 pm, take 14 hours and cost Y71.5. Buses to Lanzhou (five hours, Y17.5) leave fairly frequently from 7.30 am to 4 pm. There is also a sleeper bus to Dunhuang (Gansu Province) that leaves on odd-numbered days at 10.15 am, and takes 20 hours or more. The price is Y158.

Between 7.30 am and 2 pm there are buses every 30 minutes to Tongren (seven hours, Y16). From Tongren it is possible to take onward buses to Xiahe in Gansu Province. There are also several morning buses to Heimahe, near Qinghai Lake (see the Qinghai Lake entry below).

Some travellers looking for an off-beat Tibetan experience have made the journey from Xining to Chengdu (Sichuan) by bus. The scenery is stunning and very Tibetan, but it's a rough trip that takes nearly a week. The route to Chengdu is as follows: Xining to Maduo *(mǎduō)*; Maduo to Xiewu *(xiēwǔ)*; Xiewu to Sêrxu *(shíqú)*; Sêrxu to Kangding *(kāngdìng)*; and Kangding to Chengdu.

All along the way there are cheap places to stay – the bus company will either put you up at its own hostels or direct you to another hotel. Another option would be to take a bus to Banma (two days), where you could then get a bus to Zōige (one day), then to Songpan (eight hours) and on to Chengdu (14 hours).

From Xining, buses to Maduo leave daily at noon, but those to Banma depart only on the 4th, 10th, 14th, 20th, 24th and 30th of each month.

Train Xining has frequent rail connections to Lanzhou (4½ hours). A special tourist train, No 202, offers soft seats (Y42) and does the trip in a rapid 3½ hours. It leaves Xining daily at 8 am. Other train connections include Beijing, Shanghai, Qingdao, Xi'an and Golmud.

There are two trains to Golmud and the trip takes more than 16 hours (see the Golmud section later in this chapter for the schedule).

Getting Around

To/From the Airport The airport is 16km outside the city, and a taxi fare there should be around Y20.

AROUND XINING
Ta'er Monastery
(tǎ'ěr sì)

One of the six great monasteries of the Yellow Hat sect of Tibetan Buddhism, Ta'er Monastery (or Kumbum in Tibetan) is found in the town of Huangzhong, a mere 26km south of Xining. It was built in 1577 on sacred ground – the birthplace of Tsong Khapa, founder of the Yellow Hat sect.

The monastery is noted for its extraordinary sculptures of human figures, animals and landscapes carved out of yak butter. The art of butter sculpture probably dates back 1300 years in Tibet and was taken up by the Ta'er Monastery in the last years of the 16th century.

It's a pretty place and very popular with local tourists. An earthquake in 1990 and subsequent heavy snows threatened to destroy many of the buildings, and the Chinese government actually forked out Y70 million for a major restoration project. But the place still maintains its historical atmosphere.

Go hiking in the surrounding area or follow the pilgrims clockwise on a scenic circuit round the monastery. Six temples are open; admission tickets (Y21) are sold at the building diagonally opposite the row of stupas. Photography is prohibited inside the temples.

Places to Stay & Eat Just behind the row of stupas is a sign saying 'Kumbun Motel', but when we last visited, the monastery was not taking guests. But they may in future, so it's worth checking.

The other option is the *Ta'er Hotel* (☎ 232-452) *(tǎ'ěr sì bīnguǎn)*, outside the monastery wall about 100m east of the ticket office. Beds in a triple with attached bath are Y55 (Y40 from November to April) and doubles are Y180 (Y120 in the off season) – pretty pricey for what you get. There's a small *restaurant* in the courtyard next to the 'Kumbun Motel' that has a few Tibetan dishes and reasonably priced Chinese food.

For some variety, take a stroll down the hill towards town and try some noodles in a *Muslim restaurant*.

Getting There & Away Some travellers visit the monastery as a stopover on the way to or from Qinghai Lake. This can easily be arranged if you've booked a tour (see the following Qinghai Lake section for details).

Minibuses and taxis to Huangzhong leave from next to the Xining Sports Arena *(xīníng tǐyùguǎn)*. Minibuses leave when full (read packed to the gills) which can take a while. The trip takes around 45 minutes and costs Y2. A minivan taxi costs Y30, not a bad option if there are several of you.

Buses first stop at the Huangzhong bus station, but most will continue on to the town square; from there walk up the road another 500m to the monastery.

Catch your return bus or minibus to Xining from the square in Huangzhong. The last buses leave around 6 pm. To get to the Xining Sports Arena from the railway station, take bus No 1 for seven stops to Ximen Shangchang *(xīmén shāngchǎng)*. From the bus stop, head south, cross over to the south-western corner of the intersection and walk towards the arena. You'll soon see the buses and taxis lined up in a small driveway to the left-hand side.

QINGHAI LAKE
(qīnghǎi hú)

Qinghai Lake (Koko Nor), known as the Western Sea in ancient times, is a somewhat surreal-looking saline lake to the west of Xining. It's the largest lake in China and contains huge numbers of fish.

The main attraction is Bird Island *(niǎo dǎo)* on the western side of the lake, about 300km from Xining. It's a breeding ground for thousands of wild geese, gulls, cormorants, sandpipers, extremely rare black-necked cranes and many other bird species. Perhaps most interesting of them are the bar-headed geese. These hardy birds migrate high over the Himalaya to spend winter on the Indian plains, and have been spotted flying at altitudes of 10,000m. You will see birds in quantity only during the breeding season – between March and early June.

Despite its name, Bird Island is not an island, but used to be before the lake shore receded and made it part of the mainland. There is one small island, Haixinshan, and for Y45 you can take a boat trip from Bird Island around the lake that takes in this and other sights.

It gets chilly at night so bring warm clothing. The lake water is too salty to drink, so be sure to carry a sufficient supply if you intend to do any hiking. There are nomads around the lake – most are friendly and may invite you in for a cup of tea in their tents. There is a Y52 entry fee to the Bird Island area.

Organised Tours

Probably the best deals going are the tours offered by Qinghai Nationalities Travel Service – Y100 for a one day tour in a minibus with a minimum of 10 people. Don't worry about getting enough travellers together. The travel agencies pool their clients, so from May to early September tour buses run almost daily. Hiring a vehicle yourself, on the other hand, will cost Y800 to Y1000.

There are two day tours as well, which overnight at Bird Island, for Y180. Prices don't include accommodation, food or entry fees. These tours often include trips to Ta'er Monastery and a brief stop at Sun Moon Mountain Pass *(rìyuè shānkǒu)* for some photo opportunities. CITS runs similar tours, and offers hire minivans or jeeps for around Y1600.

Places to Stay & Eat

If you're not content with a day trip, you can stay overnight at the *Bird Island Hotel (niǎo dǎo bīnguǎn)*, which offers dorm beds for Y25, and doubles priced from Y120. The restaurant in the hotel is surprisingly good.

Getting There & Away

Bus There are no public buses to Bird Island. The closest you can get to is the small settlement of Heimahe *(hēimǎhé)*, 50km from Bird Island. From Xining there are three departures to Heimahe (near Qinghai Lake) between 7.30 and 9 am.

The trip takes nearly five hours and costs Y18.5. The return schedule from Heimahe is similar. Getting from Heimahe to Bird Island will probably cost you another Y50 for a taxi.

Train The northern shore of the lake is readily accessible by train. Unfortunately, this is not the part of the lake that has many birds and you might be disappointed if this is all you get to see. Ha'ergai railway station is the jumping-off point.

There are a few hostels here with basic accommodation, and occasionally buses run from here to Bird Island along a dirt road. Train No 759 from Xining to Golmud reaches Ha'ergai at 4.50 pm, meaning you almost certainly need to spend at least one night here.

GOLMUD
(géěrmù)

For travellers, the only reason to visit this forlorn outpost in the oblivion end of China is to continue into Tibet. While not a terrible place, you probably wouldn't want to stay around Golmud more than a day or two, and few visitors do. The town owes its existence to mining and oil drilling. It's inhabited mostly by Chinese, but there are a few Tibetans around.

The eerie moonscape of the Tibetan Plateau can be an inhospitable place – come prepared! At 2800m elevation, summer days can be very warm, but the nights are

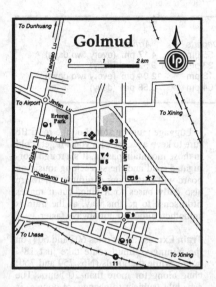

Golmud

To Dunhuang

0   1   2 km

To Airport

To Xining

To Xining

To Lhasa

1 Tibet Bus Station
   西藏汽车站
2 Nongken No 1
   Department Store
   农垦一商场
3 Market
   格尔木集贸市场
4 Xining Peace Restaurant
   西宁和平酒家
5 Golmud Hotel; CITS
   格尔木宾馆
   中国国际旅行社
6 Post Office
   邮局
7 PSB
   公安局
8 Bank of China
   中国银行
9 Potash Company Office
   青海钾肥厂总工办
10 Bus Station
   长途汽车站
11 Railway Station
   火车站

always cool. The daytime sun is incredibly bright – sunglasses and sunblock lotion are *de rigueur*. Winters are brutally cold.

Information

CITS (☎ 412-764; fax 413-003) has an office in the Golmud Hotel. Staff here are usually friendly, but are charged with a harsh mission – carrying out one of the biggest official rip-offs of foreign tourists in China (see the section on Getting to Tibet later in this chapter). If you're planning to go to Lhasa, you'll almost certainly have to visit this office.

You can buy simple (and dated) maps of the city at the Golmud Hotel, although CITS may give you one free of charge. The PSB is on Chaidamu Lu, east of the post office. The Bank of China is on the corner of Kunlun Lu and Chaidamu Lu.

Qinghai Potash Plant
(qīnghǎi jiáfěichǎng)

This is the town's No 1 employer. The plant is 60km from Golmud, but the mining company operates a number of businesses and employee apartment blocks in town.

The potash plant is not exactly a scenic area, but it's different. Only three such plants exist in the world – the others are at Salt Lake City in the USA and Israel's Dead Sea. China's plant was built with US technical assistance. Potash is harvested from three reservoirs 6m deep and three sq km in area.

Tours of the plant are free. To arrange a visit, drop in at the potash company office – the tall, modern building with a steeple, near the railway station – in Golmud. Inside the building, the place you need to find is called the General Engineering Office *(zǒnggōngbàn)*. As you approach the plant, the scenery becomes incredibly desolate – not a blade of grass grows in this salty soil.

Places to Stay

There's only one place accepting foreigners, the *Golmud Hotel* (☎ 412-061) *(géěrmù bīnguǎn)* at 160 Kunlun Lu. The place is divided into two sections – the upmarket

QINGHAI

Xining-Golmud Train Timetable				
Train	From	To	Departs	Arrives
603	Xining	Golmud	9.55 pm	4.17 pm (every two days)
759	Xining	Golmud	12.23 pm	9.52 am (daily)
604	Golmud	Xining	6.18 pm	12.04 pm (every two days)
760	Golmud	Xining	8.04 pm	5.58 pm (daily)

hotel *(bīnguǎn)* and the hostel *(zhāodàisuǒ)*. Beds in a six person room with shared bath in the hostel cost Y27, and those in a triple are Y33. Hot water is only available from 9 to 11 pm, and travellers have reported long waits. Beds in triples and doubles with an attached bath are Y80 or Y150. Doubles in the new building are a steep Y260.

Staff can be surly, but this is probably because they have to constantly deal with cranky foreigners who've just paid for their bus tickets to Lhasa. Minibuses meet all arriving trains and can take you to the hotel for Y3. Walking takes about 35 minutes.

Places to Eat
The *Xining Peace Restaurant (xīníng hépíng jiǔjiā)* has won the thumbs up from travellers for its tasty noodles, dumplings, cheap beer and English menu. There is also a string of cheap eateries alongside the market, and some good places across from the Golmud Hotel.

Getting There & Away
Air At the time of writing there was one return flight a week from Xining to Golmud, on Sunday. The one way fare is Y640. The CAAC office (☎ 414-446) is in the Golmud Hotel, and only opens for a few days during the week.

Bus The Golmud bus station is just opposite the railway station. The journey from Golmud to Dunhuang is 524km (13 hours) and the bus departs at 6.30 am. Foreigners are charged double (Y88) and usually have to pay an additional Y30 for a 'travel permit'. Still, this is better than the Y406 that CITS charges you if you're coming in the opposite direction.

Luggage must be stored on the roof. Be sure to keep a jacket with you – it gets cold in those mountain passes. It's a rough, corrugated road and the screeching music on board will batter your eardrums. There are also daily buses to Xining, but it makes little sense to go this way, as the train is smoother, although not always faster.

Train Express trains (Nos 603 and 604) on the Xining-Golmud route take just 18¼ hours, while the locals (Nos 759 and 760) chug along for more than 20 hours. The schedule (subject to change, of course) is described in the table above.

An attempt to build a railway from Golmud to Lhasa was abandoned after it was discovered that it would be necessary to bore a tunnel through an ice-filled mountain. The Chinese consulted the Swiss (the world's best tunnel builders), who concluded that it was impossible.

Getting Around
To/From the Airport CAAC (☎ 414-446) runs a bus from the hotel to the airport several hours before departures and arrivals. This service has been suspended in the past due to a lack of passengers, so check ahead in Xining if possible.

GETTING TO TIBET
CITS has an iron grip on foreign bus tickets from Golmud to Lhasa – all travellers must buy their tickets through the travel agency, and they pay dearly for it.

The scam runs like this: CITS says it will provide you with a ticket, 'insurance' and a tour guide for three days to escort you to the sights around Lhasa. However, once in Lhasa you will find that the 'tour' does not include transport, entry fees, meals or accommodation! For this extra 'service' you get to pay Y1180 for a seat on a regular rattling bus, or Y1600 for a sleeper. This is nearly eight times what locals pay. (Coming back from Lhasa is a different story: sleepers costs around Y320, or less if you have a student identity card).

Of course travellers try to get around this by going directly to the Tibet bus station to purchase a ticket to Lhasa – the staff at the station politely tell them to go to CITS. Others try to hitch rides on trucks, but the local PSB are wise to this, and drivers have been cowed by the threat of a heavy fine if caught.

One group of travellers spent nearly a week trying to find a way around the CITS monopoly; they ended up being followed everywhere by the PSB and finally fined Y300 for their efforts. In the end you'll probably have to fork out the cash. Hopefully this scheme will eventually by

dropped, for it's something that both CITS and the Chinese government should be ashamed of.

Buses for Lhasa leave from the Tibet bus station on Xizang Lu at around 5 pm. Foreigners are usually rounded up in the Golmud Hotel and taken by CITS to the station. The road to Lhasa has been vastly improved in recent years, and the trip now takes around 26 hours, including stops en route, but barring breakdowns or traffic holdups (always a possibility).

It would be wise to stock up on a few necessities for the trip. Toasty-warm PLA overcoats are available for around Y200 from the department stores – consider getting one even if you wind up giving it away in Lhasa. It can easily get down to minus 10°C or lower in those mountain passes at night; although the buses are heated, you could be in serious trouble if you are unequipped and there is a breakdown.

QINGHAI

Glossary

apsaras – Buddhist celestial beings, similar to angels

bei – north

bīnguǎn – tourist hotel

Boxer Rebellion – A fanatical anti-foreign and anti-Christian movement that emerged from Shandong in 1898

CAAC – The Civil Aviation Administration of China; also the official flag carrier of the PRC (as Air China)

CCP – Chinese Communist Party, founded in Shanghai in 1921

chang – a Tibetan brew made from fermented barley

Chiang Kaishek – Kuomintang leader and avowed opponent of the communists

chops – see name chops

CITS – The China International Travel Service (CITS); deals with China's foreign tourists

Cixi, Empress Dowager – concubine who became ruler of the Qing Dynasty

Confucius (551-479 BC) – Legendary scholar who developed the philosophy of Confucianism which defines codes of conduct and patterns of obedience in society

CTS – The China Travel Service; originally set up to handle tourists from Hong Kong, Macau, Taiwan and Overseas Chinese

Cultural Revolution – a brutal and devastating purge of the arts, religion and the intelligentsia by Mao's Red Guards and later the PLA from 1966-70

CYTS – China Youth Travel Service

Deng Xiaoping – an early protege of Mao's; later he was the architect of economic reform

dong – east

fàndiàn – a hotel or restaurant

fengshui – geomancy, literally 'wind and water', the art of using ancient principles to maximise the flow of 'qi', or universal energy

Gang of Four – members of a clique, headed by Mao's wife Jiang Qing, who were blamed for the disastrous Cultural Revolution

Genghis Khan – uniter of the roaming Mongol tribes, his armies took Beijing in 1215

Great Leap Forward – a failed economic program that resulted in a devastating famine in the early 1960s

guānxì – advantageous social or business connections

hai – sea

Hong Xiuquan – leader of the Taiping Rebellion, from Guangdong

Hundred Flowers – short-lived campaign of Mao's to allow 'freedom' in the arts and sciences

hutong – a narrow alleyway

jiang – river

Jiang Qing – Mao's wife and leader of the Gang of Four, she was blamed for the Cultural Revolution

Jiang Zemin – current state president and Communist Party general secretary

jie – street

kinju – a regional form of classical opera developed in the cities of Suzhou, Hangzhou and Nanjing

Kublai Khan – Grandson of Mongol Genghis Khan and founder of the Yuan Dynasty (1271-1368), the world's largest empire

Kuomintang – Chiang Kaishek's Nationalist Party, the dominant political force after the fall of the Qing Dynasty. Now Taiwan's major party

lama – a Buddhist priest of the Tantric or Lamaist school

Laotzu – a philosopher whose beliefs, inscribed in the slim volume the *Tao Te Ching* (The Way & Its Power), inspired the birth of Taoism as a religion

Long March – the 9500km march in 1934 from Jiangxi to Shaanxi by Communist armies besieged in the south

Mandate of Heaven – a political concept where heaven gives wise leaders a mandate to rule and removes power from those who are evil or corrupt

Mao Zedong – military leader of the early Communist forces, he founded the PRC and was Party Chairman until his death in 1976

Marco Polo – Italian merchant who (supposedly) visited China and the Far East in the 13th century

Mencius – a scholar who raised Confucian ideals into the national consciousness (372-289 BC)

motor-tricycle – an enclosed three-wheeled vehicle with a driver at the front, a small motorbike engine below and seats for two passengers in the back

name chop – a carved name seal that acts as a signature

nan – south

obo – a pile of stones with a hollow space for offerings, a kind of shaman shrine (Inner Mongolia)

pedicab – pedal-powered tricycle with a seat to carry passengers

pinyin – the official system to transliterate Chinese script into roman characters

PLA – People's Liberation Army

Politburo – the 25-member supreme policy-making authority of the CCP

PRC – People's Republic of China

PSB – (Public Security Bureau) the arm of the national police force set up to deal with foreigners

qi – vital energy or cosmic currents manipulated in acupuncture and massage

Red Guards – a pro-Mao faction which persecuted rightists during the Cultural Revolution

shan – mountain

sampan – a motorised launch which can accommodate only a few people and is too small to go on the open sea (Hong Kong)

special municipality – the name given to centrally-administered regions such as Beijing, Tianjin, Chongqing and Shanghai

stele – a stone slab or column decorated with figures or inscriptions

Sun Yatsen – first President of the Republic of China. A revolutionary loved by republicans and communists alike

Taiping Rebellion – A 1.1 million-strong rebellion which attempted to overthrow the Qing from 1850-64

Tiananmen Incident – a 1976 protest sparked by anger against Jiang Zemin and sorrow over the death of Zhou Enlai. Police broke up the protest on the orders of Mao and the politburo

Tiananmen Massacre – the slaughter of pro-democracy demonstrators in Tiananmen Square by government troops in 1989, echoing the Tiananmen Incident of 13 years before

triads – secret societies thought to be involved in criminal activity

Wuchang Uprising – A joint 1911 rebellion by disaffected Chinese troops and Sun Yatsen's republican movement that ended dynastic rule in China

xi – west

yuan – the Chinese unit of currency; also referred to as RMB

yurt – a circular tent made with animal skin or felt (Inner Mongolia)

zhong – middle

Zhou Enlai – an early comrade of Mao's, Zhou exercised the most influence in the day-to-day governing of China following the Cultural Revolution. His death triggered the 1976 Tiananmen Incident

Zhu De – a Communist army leader who, together with Mao and Zhou Enlai, led the 1927 Nanchang uprising and the Long March

Index

TEXT

Thanks

Thanks to the many travellers who wrote in with helpful hints, useful advice and interesting and funny stories about China.

Wal Adamson, Helen Agg, Raya Agmon, Florence Akst, Carol Alderson, Ruth Angove, Thomas Apfel, John Arant, Alessandro Arduino, Ellen Arnberg, Lambert Arno, Constantin Arnocouros, K Askham, Alexander Atepolikhin, Robyn Atkins, David Atwill, Jorg Ausfelt.

Susan Baboomian, Kirsty Bailey, S Baird, Harry Baker, Paul Bakker, Sue Bale, Sue Barnard, Gina Barnes, Buck Barnes, Paul Barrett, Andrew Bartram, Richard Beal, Andrew Beale, Roger Beaud, Bruce Beck, Jos Beelen, Eugenio Bellini, H Ben-Bassat, Diana Bene-detto, Udi & Ronit Berber, David Bercovich, Patrice Berman, Bill Bernhardt, Mary Berry, Jan Beukemas, Leila Susan Binder, Alon Binyamini, N Blasco, Brandon Booth, Geoffrey Bowman, Terry Boyd, Jason Boyd, Kevin Brackley, Ute Braml, John Bratton, Dan Breiner, Claudine Brenner, Joel Bresler, M Breuer, Saskia Brinks, Joe Brock, David & Gaye Bromwich, Kerry Brown, Rita Bryan, Anita & Stefan Burckhardt, Iain Burgess, Lorie Burnett.

Diana Caldwell, Michelle & David Candy, Richard Cann, Juan Carlos Merino, Simona Carobene, Bernard Caron, Peter Carroll, Par Cassel, Lisa Caywood, Penny Chang, Craig Chapin, Charles Chase, J E Chase, Esther Chen, Wing Cheong Chan, Tim Chevassut, Joe Chew, Melinda Choy, Sebastian Christians, Debbie & Frank Chua, May Chua, Kay Clarke, Helen Clarke, Rod Clarke & Family, M Cleave, Robert Clements, RG & ME Cobden, Sara Coes, E Cohen-Cole, Alan Cole, David & Jean Cole, Paul Collins, Jane Colstrom, J Connor, Avril Cooke, Doug Cooper, Lisa Cooper, Adrian Cotter, Alison Coutts, Lizzie Cowan, Elisabeth Cox, Steven Coxhead, Anna Cumming, Don Cuomo, John Currie, R S Curtis.

Ake Dahllof, Hans & Mirjam Damen, Colin Day, Jennifer De Bruyn, Christine Dee, Letizia del Bubba, Marco Del Corona, Tom & Charlotte Dibble, Xin Dinkang, Harreld Dinkins, Jan Dixon, Laura Dobbins, C Docherty, K Donnelly, Gudrun Droop, M Duffy, Anne Dugenetay, Jackie Dumpis. Ebihara Eiko, Keith Eldridge, Mark Elfman, Tim Elliott, Sheila Elsdon, David Erskine, Matthijs Erwich, Jonathon Evans, J Everall.

Michael Fackler, Shane Fairlie, Rebecca Faulkner, Melanie Fenson, Madalena Ferreira, Hedwig Feucht, Gerald Fimberger, Brian Flaherty, Michelles Foo Li Mei, Carol Forsett, H & S Forster, Paul Francis, Robert Francis, Michael Friedman, Tanya Frymersum, John Fuller.

Dennis Gadel, Adrian Gan, Derek Garrison, Adam Gault, Bernd Gaummerl, J Geddes, Alison Gee, Angela Gels, Fotini Georgakopoulou, Charlotte Germundson, Ablimit Ghopor, Massimo Giannini, Lucy Gibbs, A Gibert, Tim Gibson, Maureen Gillard, Jane Gindin, F Gingras, Sabine Gisbert, L Glover, James God-win, R Goldberg, Paul Goodwin, Doreen Gordon-Kirby, Wolf Gotthilf, John Grace, Simon Granger, Glenn Grossman, Kai Grothe, Tony Guilfoyle, Colin Gunther, Sergei Gusarov, Randy Guthrie, Sarah Guthrie.

Mr & Mrs H Kuwada, Paul Hague, Sun Hai Zi, Liz Halsey, Ralf Hamester, Judith Hankke, R Hanley, Chen Hanxiang, Geoff Harman, Victoria Harns, Kieren Haskell, Kamal Hassan, Simon Heeps, S Heidrich, Roland Hellmann, M Helmbrecht, Jane Henderson, Shirley Henderson, Tom Hendrix, Klaus Henke, Jill Henry, Jeanne Hey, Paul Hider, Hanne H-Larsen, Meiling Ho, Don Hoard, Jane Hobson, Teck Hock Toh, Brigitte Hoffmann, Paul Hollis, Guo Hongxing, Vanessa Hoppe, S Horn, Bernard Horowitz, Jim Hoyle, Sue Hucknall, Johannes Humburger, Mark Hunnebell, Nicola Hunt, Charles Hunter, Mikael Huss.

Greg Imazu, Gavin Imhof, V Ingemann, Bjornar Ivarsen, I Jacquemin, Iseult Jacquemin, Bridgett James, Lisa Jensen, Yang Jing, Carol Johnson, Dean Jones, Nena Joy, Elaine & Robert Juhre, Richard Juterbock, Andrzej Kalisz, Simon Kay, Laurence Kaye, Sam Kebby, Thomas Kellermann, Kate Kelly, Nikki Kempton, Emma Kendall, Laura Kennedy, Katherine Keynes, Geoff Kingsmill, Mathias Kirschner, Toni Klein, Simone Klose, Susanne Kob, Cynthia Koens, Markus Kohstall, Frederick Koppl, Arik Korman, Peter Kornberg, G F Kortschak, Michael Koss, Wim Kranendonk, Douglas Kremer, Harald Kuhl, Barak Kushner, Stefan Kuzay.

Paule Lamarque, Suzanne Lamb, Eric Langhammer, Dean Lapthorne, S & K Larsen, Terence Lau, Jean Laurent, Walter Laureys, Bill Lawler, D Le Poidevin, Toby & Esther Leach, Alan Leahy, Sophie Leddet, Marcus Lee, J Leelamanothum, Robert Leibrock, Jean Pierre LeLagadec, F & B Leplingard Cressida Lennox, Anne Leung, Bill Levin, Moran Levy, Andrew

Levy, Sarah Lewis, He Li Yi, Liberty Lidz, Erik Ling, Wallace Lo, Adrienne Lo, Steve Locke, Peter Lockwood, Deanne Lowe, Keith Lyons.

Margie Ma, Ian MacGregor, H Mailander, Don Mainfort, Charlene Makley, Stuart Malcolm, Maureen Maloney, Carol Mansfield, E Marchetti, L Marconi, Joan Marsh, Nina Martins, William & Susan Martorano, Ken Mathers, Cecilia Mau, Shiela Mavinang, Adrienne McAdory, Lisa & Pat McCarthy, Diana McCracken, Justin McDaniel, Dudley McFadden, J B McFie, Leah McKeand, John McKnna, John McKimmy, Stephen McNamara, F & C Mcnicol, Ian McVittie, Michael Meaney, Robert Mehring, Jorgen Mejer, Andrew Mellett, Jean-Paul Messerli, Mark Micallef, A Middlebrook, Nick Midgley, Riikka Miettinen, Burkhard Militzer, Ann. Millen, Phillip Miller, Marti Morthorst, David Mountain, Bryan Murphy, B J Murphy.

Monique Nadal, Jim Needell, R S Needham, Steven Ng, E Niero, Britta Nilgen, Stephen Nojek, Brian Nomi, Maria Noren, Jane Norris, Steve Oades, David Oakley, Roderick O'Brien, Jonathan O'Hara, Sven-Olof Ohlsson, Brent Ohlund, K Oliver, Ivar Olstad, Rudi Ongena, Andrew Oppenheim, C A Osborne, Sandrine & Richard Owen, C Owen, Pam Oxley, R G Palim, Keith Palling, Dimitris Pantelidis, Rod Pantony, M Parikh, Helen Park-Weir, Nancy Patterson, G M Paule, Harry Pearman, Grant Pearse, Jern Pedersen, E Pere, Marsha Pereira, Corina Philip, Roger Phillips, Terese Piccoli, Mark Pickens, Shai Pinto, Dan Pool, Adrian Pootles, Morgan Power, Russ Preston, Marc Proksch, Harald Prytz, Cynthia Pyle.

Beatrice Quevedo, Talya & Rick Rabern, John Raine, Simon Read, M Reddington, Sanya Reid Smith, R Reiderath, Caroline Renter, Mark Ribbands, Sabine Ritter, G Roberts, F Rochat, N Roderick, Ralph Rogers, Bertram Rosen, Charles Roy, Sally Royal, R F Rudderham, Marie Ruggieri, Jose Ruiz, R Russell, Patrick Ryden, Stefan Samuelsson, Umut Sarpel, Maurice Savage, Stefan Scheel, Tim Scheur, Matthias Schluter, Laura Schmuleweitz, Andy Schone-baum, Natalie Schubert, Ben Schwarten, Emma Scott, Joann Scurlock, Stephen Seaunight, Paul Seaver, J Segell, John Sehn, Nicole Shellback, Mike Shen, James Shenfield, Jennifer Shortall, Susan Simerly, Al Sing Yuen, Ho SiokMoi, V Skiauteris, MrsP Skinn, Chris Slade, Geoff Smith, Andrea Smith, Ashley Smith, Sharon Smith, Susan & John Soar, Kim Sonnack, Erika Spencer, Mr & Mrs A Spilman, D Stamboulis, Jane Stannard, Larissa Steiner, Diana Stent, Tia Stephens, Jim Stewart, Lea Stogdale, Gregg Streabog, Meredith Strong, Charlie Stuart-King, Frank Stubbs, Donald Stumpf, H Sumita, Yuming Sun, Peter Swainger, Shannon Sweeney, Hal Swindall, Sophia Szeto.

Danko Taborosi, Gerhard Tanew, Claire Tasker, Miriam Taylor, Guy Taylor, David Taylor, Mary Temignani, Henry Tenby, Marianna Teske, Trinh Thai, Frank Theissen, M Thomas, Dr Axel Thomas, Michel Thomas, Bernard Thompson, Peter Tipping, Jim Tomlinson, Mary Toms, Martin Trueman, Bob Tuaine, Stella-Margareta Tuft, Leonard Turnball, Colin Turner, Jack Turner, Joe Twinn, Victoria Tyson, Heinrich-M Umbach, J Ustes, Christopher Vadot, Jennifer Vardy, W Verschueren, G Versteegh, Nikos Ververidis, Amanda Vincent, Ernst Vogel, Matej Vrenk.

Amir Wachs, Stefanie Wachter, Sylvia Wagner, EO Wagner, Ann Walgraeve, Adam Walter, Jesper Wanberg, Dana Wang, Sarah Ward, LJ Warren, Amy Wayland, Jerrine & Bill Weigand, Robert Weins, I Weissmann-Zeh, Jonathan Wells, Robert Werner, Joel Wester-berg, Hilke Wiese, Madine Wilburn, John Wilkins, Julia Williams, N Williams, Leanne Wilson, Widjaja Winardi, Jean-Philippe Wispelaere, Steve Wood, Ann Wood, Simon Woolrych, Stephen Wrage, Stephen Wrage, Sara Wramner, Christina Wu, Cynthia Wuu, Dan Yao, Emilt Yeh, Dr Yehuda Zeiri, Wang Ying, Elizabeth Ying, Jason Yoshioka, Ling Yu Fong, Daniel Yuen, Prof Marco Zaider, H Zeh, Merrilee Zekner, He Zhanting, Monica Ziezulewicz, Marco Zoli, Arian Zwegers.

LONELY PLANET

Phrasebooks

Lonely Planet phrasebooks are packed with essential words and phrases to help travellers communicate with the locals. With colour tabs for quick reference, an extensive vocabulary and use of script, these handy pocket-sized language guides cover day-to-day travel situations.

- handy pocket-sized books
- easy to understand Pronunciation chapter
- clear & comprehensive Grammar chapter
- romanisation alongside script to allow ease of pronunciation
- script throughout so users can point to phrases for every situation
- full of cultural information and tips for the traveller

'...vital for a real DIY spirit and attitude in language learning'
— *Backpacker*

'the phrasebooks have good cultural backgrounders and offer solid advice for challenging situations in remote locations'
— *San Francisco Examiner*

Arabic (Egyptian) • Arabic (Moroccan) • Australian *(Australian English, Aboriginal and Torres Strait languages)* • Baltic States *(Estonian, Latvian, Lithuanian)* • Bengali • Brazilian • British • Burmese • Cantonese • Central Asia • Central Europe *(Czech, French, German, Hungarian, Italian, Slovak)* • Eastern Europe *(Bulgarian, Czech, Hungarian, Polish, Romanian, Slovak)* • Ethiopian (Amharic) • Fijian • French • German • Greek • Hill Tribes • Hindi/Urdu • Indonesian • Italian • Japanese • Korean • Lao • Latin American Spanish • Malay • Mandarin • Mediterranean Europe *(Albanian, Croatian, Greek, Italian, Macedonian, Maltese, Serbian, Slovene)* • Mongolian • Nepali • Papua New Guinea • Pilipino (Tagalog) • Quechua • Russian • Scandinavian Europe *(Danish, Finnish, Icelandic, Norwegian, Swedish)* • South-East Asia *(Burmese, Indonesian, Khmer, Lao, Malay, Tagalog Pilipino, Thai, Vietnamese)* • South Pacific Languages • Spanish (Castilian) *(also includes Catalan, Galician and Basque)* • Sri Lanka • Swahili • Thai • Tibetan • Turkish • Ukrainian • USA *(US English, Vernacular, Native American languages, Hawaiian)* • Vietnamese • Western Europe *(Basque, Catalan, Dutch, French, German, Greek, Irish)*

LONELY PLANET

Lonely Planet Journeys

OURNEYS is a unique collection of travel writing – published by the company that understands travel better than anyone else. It is a series for anyone who has ever experienced – or dreamed of – the magical moment when they encountered a strange culture or saw a place for the first time. They are tales to read while you're planning a trip, while you're on the road or while you're in an armchair in front of a fire.

These outstanding titles explore our planet through the eyes of a diverse group of international writers. JOURNEYS books catch the spirit of a place, illuminate a culture, recount a crazy adventure or introduce a fascinating way of life. They always entertain, and always enrich the experience of travel.

LOST JAPAN
Alex Kerr

Lost Japan draws on the author's personal experiences of Japan over thirty years. Alex Kerr takes his readers on a backstage tour, exploring different facets of his involvement with the country: friendships with Kabuki actors, buying and selling art, studying calligraphy, and exploring rarely visited temples and shrines.

'one of the finest books about Japan written in decades' – *Insight Japan*

BRIEF ENCOUNTERS
Stories of Love, Sex & Travel
edited by Michelle de Kretser

Love affairs on the road, passionate holiday flings, disastrous pick-ups, erotic encounters … In this seductive collection of stories, 22 authors from around the world write about travel romances. Combining fiction and reportage, *Brief Encounters* is must-have reading – for everyone who has dreamt of escape with that perfect stranger.

Includes stories by Pico Iyer, Mary Morris, Emily Perkins, Mona Simpson, Lisa St Aubin de Terán, Paul Theroux and Sara Wheeler.

Lonely Planet Travel Atlases

L onely Planet has long been famous for the number and quality of its guidebook maps. Now we've gone one step further and produced a handy companion series: Lonely Planet travel atlases – maps of a country produced in book form.

Unlike other maps, which look good but lead travellers astray, our travel atlases have been researched on the road by Lonely Planet's experienced team of writers. All details are carefully checked to ensure the atlas corresponds with the equivalent Lonely Planet guidebook.

- full-colour throughout
- maps researched and checked by Lonely Planet authors
- place names correspond with Lonely Planet guidebooks
- no confusing spelling differences
- legend and travelling information in English, French, German, Japanese and Spanish
- size: 230 x 160 mm

Available now: Chile & Easter Island ● Egypt ● India & Bangladesh ● Israel & the Palestinian Territories ● Jordan, Syria & Lebanon ● Kenya ● Laos ● Portugal ● South Africa, Lesotho & Swaziland ● Thailand ● Turkey ● Vietnam ● Zimbabwe, Botswana & Namibia

Lonely Planet TV Series & Videos

L onely Planet travel guides have been brought to life on television screens around the world. Like our guides, the programs are based on the joy of independent travel, and look honestly at some of the most exciting, picturesque and frustrating places in the world. Each show is presented by one of three travellers from Australia, England or the USA and combines an innovative mixture of video, Super-8 film, atmospheric soundscapes and original music.

Videos of each episode – containing additional footage not shown on television – are available from good book and video shops, but the availability of individual videos varies with regional screening schedules.

Video destinations include: Alaska ● American Rockies ● Australia – The South-East ● Baja California & the Copper Canyon ● Brazil ● Central Asia ● Chile & Easter Island ● Corsica, Sicily & Sardinia – The Mediterranean Islands ● East Africa (Tanzania & Zanzibar) ● Ecuador & the Galapagos Islands ● Greenland & Iceland ● Indonesia ● Israel & the Sinai Desert ● Jamaica ● Japan ● La Ruta Maya ● Morocco ● New York ● North India ● Pacific Islands (Fiji, Solomon Islands & Vanuatu) ● South India ● South West China ● Turkey ● Vietnam ● West Africa ● Zimbabwe, Botswana & Namibia

The Lonely Planet TV series is produced by: Pilot Productions
The Old Studio
18 Middle Row
London W10 5AT, UK

LONELY PLANET

FREE Lonely Planet Newsletters

We love hearing from you and think you'd like to hear from us.

Planet Talk

Our FREE quarterly printed newsletter is full of tips from travellers and anecdotes from Lonely Planet guidebook authors. Every issue is packed with up-to-date travel news and advice, and includes:

- a postcard from Lonely Planet co-founder Tony Wheeler
- a swag of mail from travellers
- a look at life on the road through the eyes of a Lonely Planet author
- topical health advice
- prizes for the best travel yarn
- news about forthcoming Lonely Planet events
- a complete list of Lonely Planet books and other titles

To join our mailing list, residents of the UK, Europe and Africa can email us at go@lonelyplanet.co.uk; residents of North and South America can email us at info@lonelyplanet.com; the rest of the world can email us at talk2us@lonelyplanet.com.au, or contact any Lonely Planet office.

Comet

Our FREE monthly email newsletter brings you all the latest travel news, features, interviews, competitions, destination ideas, travellers' tips & tales, Q&As, raging debates and related links. Find out what's new on the Lonely Planet Web site and which books are about to hit the shelves.

Subscribe from your desktop: www.lonelyplanet.com/comet

LONELY PLANET

Guides by Region

L onely Planet is known worldwide for publishing practical, reliable and no-nonsense travel information in our guides and on our Web site. The Lonely Planet list covers just about every accessible part of the world. Currently there are nine series: travel guides, shoestring guides, walking guides, city guides, phrasebooks, audio packs, travel atlases, diving and snorkeling guides and travel literature.

AFRICA Africa – the South • Africa on a shoestring • Arabic (Egyptian) phrasebook • Arabic (Moroccan) phrasebook • Cairo • Cape Town • Central Africa • East Africa • Egypt • Egypt travel atlas • Ethiopian (Amharic) phrasebook • The Gambia & Senegal • Healthy Travel Africa • Kenya • Kenya travel atlas • Malawi, Mozambique & Zambia • Morocco • North Africa • South Africa, Lesotho & Swaziland • South Africa, Lesotho & Swaziland travel atlas • Swahili phrasebook • Tanzania, Zanzibar & Pemba • Trekking in East Africa • Tunisia • West Africa • Zimbabwe, Botswana & Namibia • Zimbabwe, Botswana & Namibia travel atlas
Travel Literature: The Rainbird: A Central African Journey • Songs to an African Sunset: A Zimbabwean Story • Mali Blues: Traveling to an African Beat

AUSTRALIA & THE PACIFIC Australia • Australian phrasebook • Bushwalking in Australia • Bushwalking in Papua New Guinea • Fiji • Fijian phrasebook • Islands of Australia's Great Barrier Reef • Melbourne • Micronesia • New Caledonia • New South Wales & the ACT • New Zealand • Northern Territory • Outback Australia • Papua New Guinea • Papua New Guinea (Pidgin) phrasebook • Queensland • Rarotonga & the Cook Islands • Samoa • Solomon Islands • South Australia • South Pacific Languages phrasebook • Sydney • Tahiti & French Polynesia • Tasmania • Tonga • Tramping in New Zealand • Vanuatu • Victoria • Western Australia
Travel Literature: Islands in the Clouds • Kiwi Tracks • Sean & David's Long Drive

CENTRAL AMERICA & THE CARIBBEAN Bahamas and Turks & Caicos • Barcelona • Bermuda • Central America on a shoestring • Costa Rica • Cuba • Dominican Republic & Haiti • Eastern Caribbean • Guatemala, Belize & Yucatán: La Ruta Maya • Jamaica • Mexico • Mexico City • Panama
Travel Literature: Green Dreams: Travels in Central America

EUROPE Amsterdam • Andalucía • Austria • Baltic States phrasebook • Barcelona • Berlin • Britain • British phrasebook • Brussels, Bruges & Antwerp • Canary Islands • Central Europe • Central Europe phrasebook • Corsica • Croatia • Czech & Slovak Republics • Denmark • Dublin • Eastern Europe • Eastern Europe phrasebook • Edinburgh • Estonia, Latvia & Lithuania • Europe • Finland • France • French phrasebook • Germany • German phrasebook • Greece • Greek phrasebook • Hungary • Iceland, Greenland & the Faroe Islands • Ireland • Italian phrasebook • Italy • Lisbon • London • Mediterranean Europe • Mediterranean Europe phrasebook • Norway • Paris • Poland • Portugal • Portugal travel atlas • Prague • Provence & the Côte d'Azur • Romania & Moldova • Rome • Russia, Ukraine & Belarus • Russian phrasebook • Scandinavian & Baltic Europe • Scandinavian Europe phrasebook • Scotland • Slovenia • Spain • Spanish phrasebook • St Petersburg • Switzerland • Trekking in Spain • Ukrainian phrasebook • Vienna • Walking in Britain • Walking in Italy • Walking in Ireland • Walking in Switzerland • Western Europe • Western Europe phrasebook
Travel Literature: The Olive Grove: Travels in Greece

INDIAN SUBCONTINENT Bangladesh • Bengali phrasebook • Bhutan • Delhi • Goa • Hindi/Urdu phrasebook • India • India & Bangladesh travel atlas • Indian Himalaya • Karakoram Highway • Mumbai • Nepal • Nepali phrasebook • Pakistan • Rajasthan • South India • Sri Lanka • Sri Lanka phrasebook • Trekking in the Indian Himalaya • Trekking in the Karakoram & Hindukush • Trekking in the Nepal Himalaya
Travel Literature: In Rajasthan • Shopping for Buddhas

The Lonely Planet Story

Lonely Planet published its first book in 1973 in response to the numerous 'How did you do it?' questions Maureen and Tony Wheeler were asked after driving, bussing, hitching, sailing and railing their way from England to Australia.

Written at a kitchen table and hand collated, trimmed and stapled, *Across Asia on the Cheap* became an instant local bestseller, inspiring thoughts of another book.

Eighteen months in South-East Asia resulted in their second guide, *South-East Asia on a shoestring*, which they put together in a backstreet Chinese hotel in Singapore in 1975. The 'yellow bible', as it quickly became known to backpackers around the world, soon became *the* guide to the region. It has sold well over half a million copies and is now in its 9th edition, still retaining its familiar yellow cover.

Today there are over 350 titles, including travel guides, walking guides, language kits & phrasebooks, travel atlases, diving guides and travel literature. The company is the largest independent travel publisher in the world. Although Lonely Planet initially specialised in guides to Asia, today there are few corners of the globe that have not been covered.

The emphasis continues to be on travel for independent travellers. Tony and Maureen still travel for several months of each year and play an active part in the writing, updating and quality control of Lonely Planet's guides.

They have been joined by over 120 authors and 280 staff at our offices in Melbourne (Australia), Oakland (USA), London (UK) and Paris (France). Travellers themselves also make a valuable contribution to the guides through the feedback we receive in thousands of letters each year and on our web site.

The people at Lonely Planet strongly believe that travellers can make a positive contribution to the countries they visit, both through their appreciation of the countries' culture, wildlife and natural features, and through the money they spend. In addition, the company makes a direct contribution to the countries and regions it covers. Since 1986 a percentage of the income from each book has been donated to ventures such as famine relief in Africa; aid projects in India; agricultural projects in Central America; Greenpeace's efforts to halt French nuclear testing in the Pacific; and Amnesty International.

LONELY PLANET OFFICES

Australia
PO Box 617, Hawthorn, Victoria 3122
☎ 03 9819 1877 fax 03 9819 6459
email: talk2us@lonelyplanet.com.au

USA
150 Linden St, Oakland, CA 94607
☎ 510 893 8555 TOLL FREE: 800 275 5555
fax 510 893 8572
email: info@lonelyplanet.com

UK
10a Spring Place, London NW5 3BH
☎ 020 7428 4800 fax 020 7428 4828
email: go@lonelyplanet.co.uk

France
1 rue du Dahomey, 75011 Paris
☎ 01 55 25 33 00 fax 01 55 25 33 01
email: bip@lonelyplanet.fr
minitel: 3615 lonelyplanet *(1.29 F TTC/min)*

World Wide Web: www.lonelyplanet.com *or* AOL keyword: lp
Lonely Planet Images: lpi@lonelyplanet.com.au